Komm mit!®

Your
passport to
proficiency

Dein Pass zur Welt!

Plan your itinerary for

What's your **Destination?**

Communication!

Komm mit! takes your classroom there.

It's even possible that **"What's next?"** becomes your students' favorite question!

Communication
and culture in context

The clear structure of each chapter makes it easy to present, practice, and apply language skills—all in the context of the location where the chapter takes place!

Grammar support
and practice in every lesson

Komm mit! builds a proven communicative approach on a solid foundation of grammar and vocabulary so students become proficient readers, writers, and speakers of German. With the Grammatikheft, Grammar Tutor, and CD-ROM Tutor, students can practice the way they learn best.

Technology that takes you there

Bring the world into your classroom with integrated audio, video, CD-ROM, and Internet resources that immerse students in authentic language and culture.

Assessment for state and national standards

Every chapter features a variety of writing activities, including process writing strategies. To help you incorporate standardized test practice, the Lies mit mir! Reader and Reading Strategies and Skills Handbook offer additional reading practice and reading skills development.

Easy lesson planning for all learning styles

Planning lessons has never been easier with a Lesson Planner with Substitute Teacher Lesson Plans, an editable One-Stop Planner® CD-ROM, and a Student Make-Up Assignments with Alternative Quizzes resource.

Travel a balanced program that's easy to navigate.

Die Welt erwartet dich!

Komm mit!

Program components

Texts
- Pupil's Edition
- Teacher's Edition

Middle School Resources
- Exploratory Guide
- TPR Storytelling Book

Planning and Presenting
- One-Stop Planner CD-ROM with Test Generator
- Lesson Planner with Substitute Teacher Lesson Plans
- Student Make-Up Assignments with Alternative Quizzes
- Teaching Transparencies

Grammar
- Grammatikheft
- Grammar Tutor for Students of German

Reading and Writing
- Reading Strategies and Skills Handbook
- Lies mit mir! Reader
- Übungsheft

Listening and Speaking
- Audio CD Program
- Listening Activities
- Activities for Communication
- TPR Storytelling Book (Levels 1 and 2)

Assessment
- Testing Program
- Alternative Assessment Guide
- Student Make-Up Assignments with Alternative Quizzes

Technology
- One-Stop Planner CD-ROM with Test Generator
- Audio CD Program
- Interactive CD-ROM Tutor (Levels 1 and 2)
- Video Program
- Video Guide

Internet
- go.hrw.com
- www.hrw.com
- www.hrw.com/passport

Komm mit!®

HOLT GERMAN

LEVEL **3**

220780

HOLT, RINEHART AND WINSTON

A Harcourt Classroom Education Company

Austin · New York · Orlando · Atlanta · San Francisco · Boston · Dallas · Toronto · London

FL-G
H475
2003
8
t.s.

For permission to reprint copyrighted material in the Teacher's Edition, grateful acknowledgment is made to the following sources:
National Standards in Foreign Language Education Project: "National Standards Report" from **Standards for Foreign Language Learning:** Preparing for the 21st Century. Copyright © 1996 by National Standards in Foreign Language Education Project.

For permission to reprint copyrighted material in the Pupil's Edition and the Teacher's Edition, grateful acknowledgment is made to the following sources:
Alibaba Verlag GmbH, Frankfurt am Main: "Sabines Eltern" by Mustafa S. From *Wir leben hier!* edited by Ulrike Holler and Anne Teuter. Copyright © 1992 by Alibaba Verlag GmbH.
Baars Marketing GmbH: Advertisement, "Leerdammer Light: Das haben Sie jetzt davon," from Stern, no. 27, June 25, 1992.
Bauconcept: Advertisement, "Die Oase in der City!," from Südwest Presse: Schwäbisches Tagblatt, Tübingen, July 14, 1990.

ACKNOWLEDGMENTS

Cover Credits
Front cover (bkgd), Morton Beebe/Corbis
Front cover (teens), Steve Ewert/HRW Photo
Back cover (c) Hans Wolf/The Image Bank, ©2003 Image Farm, Inc.
Title page (teens), Steve Ewert/HRW Photo

All photos by George Winkler/Holt, Rinehart and Winston, Inc. except:

Master element icons: Community Link: HBJ Photo; CD-Rom tutor: Courtesy Neel Heisel; Internet Connection computers: Digital imagery® © 2003 PhotoDisc, Inc.; Jupiter page: Digital imagery® © 2003 PhotoDisc, Inc.; Chess piece: Digital imagery® © 2003 PhotoDisc, Inc.; Clock: Digital imagery® © 2003 PhotoDisc, Inc.; Globes: Mountain High Maps® Copyright © 1997 Digital Wisdom, Inc.; Euros: © European Communities; Recipe border fabric: Victoria Smith/HRW Photo; All Teacher to Teacher photos supplied by the teachers themselves.

Front Matter: (sunflowers, mill, clock tower), Image Copyright (©)2003 Photodisc, Inc., (boy on bike), (c) Digital Vision; (band, girl with textbook, group of girls), HRW Photo; (girl writing, statue at sunset), Creatas; (tulips, man with globe), Corbis Images; T9 (I), Victoria Smith/HRW Photo.
Chapter One: 3D (tr-porcelain), Courtesy of Staatliche Porzellan-Manufaktur Meissen; 3H (br), Sam Dudgeon/HRW Photo. Chapter Two: 31P (br), Scott Van Osdol/HRW Photo; 31U (cr), Scott Van Osdol/ HRW Photo; 31W (br), Scott Van Osdol/HRW Photo. Chapter Three: 59D (rice pudding), Sam Dudgeon/ HRW Photo, (red liquid), Victoria Smith/HRW Photo, (bl), Victoria Smith/HRW Photo; 59U (bl), Scott Van Osdol/HRW Photo. Chapter Four: 91D (br), Victoria Smith/HRW Photo; *(continued on page R100)*

Art Credits
All art, unless otherwise noted, by Holt, Rinehart & Winston.

Chapter One: Page 3V, Antonia Enthoven. Chapter Three: Page 59C, Eduard Böhm. Chapter Four: Page 91C, Giorgio Mizzi. Chapter Six: Page 147C, Jon Sayer; 147X, Jon Sayer. Chapter Seven: Page 179C, Jon Sayer. Chapter Ten: Page 263B, MapQuest.com.

ACKNOWLEDGMENTS continued on page R98, which is an extension of the copyright page.

Komm mit! Level 3
Teacher's Edition

CONTRIBUTING WRITERS

Ulrike Puryear
Austin, TX
Mrs. Puryear wrote background information, activities, and teacher suggestions for all chapters of the *Teacher's Edition.*

Phyllis Manning
Vancouver, WA
Dr. Manning wrote teacher suggestions for the **Zum Lesen** pages.

CONSULTANTS

The consultants conferred on a regular basis with the editorial staff and reviewed all the chapters of the Level 3 *Teacher's Edition.*

Dorothea Bruschke, retired
Parkway School District
Chesterfield, MO

Diane E. Laumer
San Marcos High School
San Marcos, TX

REVIEWERS

The following educators reviewed one or more chapters of the *Teacher's Edition.*

Nancy Butt
Washington and Lee High School
Arlington, VA

Kathleen Cooper
Burnsville High School
Burnsville, MN

Susan DeBoard
Conway High School
Conway, AR

Frank Dietz
The University of Texas at Austin
Austin, TX

Connie Frank
John F. Kennedy High School
Sacramento, CA

Rolf M. Schwägermann
Stuyvesant High School
New York, NY

Jim Witt
Grand Junction High School
Grand Junction, CO

FIELD TEST PARTICIPANTS

We express our appreciation to the teachers and students who participated in the field test. Their comments were instrumental in the development of the entire **Komm mit!** program.

Eva-Marie Adolphi
Indian Hills Middle School
Sandy, UT

Connie Allison
MacArthur High School
Lawton, OK

Linda Brummett
Redmond High School
Redmond, WA

M. Beatrice Brusstar
Lincoln Northeast High School
Lincoln, NE

Jane Bungartz
Southwest High School
Fort Worth, TX

Devora D. Diller
Lovejoy High School
Lovejoy, GA

Margaret Draheim
Wilson Middle School
Appleton, WI

Kay DuBois
Kennewick High School
Kennewick, WA

Elfriede A. Gabbert
Capital High School
Boise, ID

Petra A. Hansen
Redmond High School
Redmond, WA

Christa Hary
Brien McMahon High School
Norwalk, CT

Ingrid S. Kinner
Weaver Education Center
Greensboro, NC

Diane E. Laumer
San Marcos High School
San Marcos, TX

J. Lewinsohn
Redmond High School
Redmond, WA

Judith A. Lidicker
Central High School
West Allis, WI

Linnea Maulding
Fife High School
Tacoma, WA

Jane Reinkordt
Lincoln Southeast High School
Lincoln, NE

Elizabeth A. Smith
Plano Senior High School
Plano, TX

Elizabeth L. Webb
Sandy Creek High School
Tyrone, GA

PROFESSIONAL ESSAYS

Bringing Standards into the Classroom
Paul Sandrock
Foreign Language Education
Department of Public Instruction
Madison, WI

Reading Strategies and Skills
Nancy A. Humbach
Miami University
Oxford, OH

Technology in the Language Classroom
Cindy A. Kendall
Williamston High School
Williamston, MI

Using Portfolios in the Language Classroom
Jo Anne S. Wilson
J. Wilson Associates
Glen Arbor, MI

Teaching Culture
Nancy A. Humbach
Miami University
Oxford, OH

Dorothea Bruschke, retired
Parkway School District
Chesterfield, MO

Multi-Level Classrooms
Joan H. Manley
University of Texas at El Paso, TX

Learning Styles and Multi-Modality Teaching
Mary B. McGehee
Louisiana State University
Laboratory School
Baton Rouge, LA

To the Teacher

Principles and Practices

As nations become increasingly interdependent, the need for effective communication and sensitivity to other cultures becomes more important. Today's youth must be culturally and linguistically prepared to participate in a global society. At Holt, Rinehart and Winston, we believe that proficiency in more than one language is essential to meeting this need.

The primary goal of the Holt, Rinehart and Winston World Languages programs is to help students develop linguistic proficiency and cultural sensitivity. By interweaving language and culture, our programs seek to broaden students' communication skills while at the same time deepening their appreciation of other cultures.

We believe that all students can benefit from foreign language instruction. We recognize that not everyone learns at the same rate or in the same way; nevertheless, we believe that all students should have the opportunity to acquire language proficiency to a degree commensurate with their individual abilities.

Holt, Rinehart and Winston's World Languages programs are designed to accommodate all students by appealing to a variety of learning styles.

We believe that effective language programs should motivate students. Students deserve an answer to the question they often ask: "Why are we doing this?" They need to have goals that are interesting, practical, clearly stated, and attainable.

Holt, Rinehart and Winston's World Languages programs promote success. They present relevant content in manageable increments that encourage students to attain achievable functional objectives.

We believe that proficiency in another language is best nurtured by programs that encourage students to think critically and to take risks when expressing themselves in the language. We also recognize that students should strive for accuracy in communication. While it is imperative that students have a knowledge of the basic structures of the language, it is also important that they go beyond the simple manipulation of forms.

Holt, Rinehart and Winston's World Languages programs reflect a careful progression of activities that guide students from comprehensible input of authentic language through structured practice to creative, personalized expression. This progression, accompanied by consistent re-entry and spiraling of functions, vocabulary, and structures, provides students with the tools and the confidence to express themselves in their new language.

Finally, we believe that a complete program of language instruction should take into account the needs of teachers in today's increasingly demanding classrooms.

At Holt, Rinehart and Winston, we have designed programs that offer practical teacher support and provide resources to meet individual learning and teaching styles.

TEACHER'S EDITION
Contents

Pacing and Planning

Traditional Schedule

Days of instruction: 180

Location Opener	2 days per Location Opener x 6 Location Openers	12 days
Chapter	13 days per chapter x 12 chapters	156 days
		168 days

If you are teaching on a traditional schedule, we suggest following the plan above and spending 13 days per chapter. A complete set of lesson plans in the interleaf provides detailed suggestions for each chapter. For more suggestions, see the **Lesson Planner with Substitute Teacher Lesson Plans.**

Block Schedule

Blocks of instruction: 90

Location Opener	1/2 block per Location Opener x 6 Location Openers	3 blocks
Chapter	7 blocks per chapter x 12 chapters	84 blocks
		87 blocks

If you are teaching on a block schedule, we suggest following the plan above and spending seven blocks per chapter. A complete set of lesson plans in the interleaf provides detailed suggestions for each chapter. For more suggestions, see the **Lesson Planner with Substitute Teacher Lesson Plans.**

One-Stop Planner CD-ROM

Use the **One-Stop Planner CD-ROM with Test Generator** to aid in lesson planning and pacing.

- Editable lesson plans with direct links to teaching resources
- Printable worksheets from resource books
- Direct launches to the HRW Internet activities
- Video and audio segments
- Test Generator
- Clip Art for vocabulary items

Pacing Tips

At the beginning of each chapter, you will find a Pacing Tip to help you plan your lessons.

Articulation Across Levels

The following chart shows how topics are repeated across levels in *Komm mit!* from the end of Level 1 to the beginning of Level 3.

- In each level, the last chapter is a review chapter.
- In Levels 2 and 3, the first two chapters review the previous level.

LEVEL 1

CHAPTER 12
Review of Level 1

- The **möchte**-forms; **noch ein** and **kein**
- Nominative and accusative pronouns; definite and indefinite articles
- Possessive pronouns
- The verb **können; für;** accusative pronouns; **du**-commands
- The verb **wissen;** word order; formal commands
- The verbs **wollen** and **müssen;** word order
- Asking where something is and giving directions

LEVEL 2

CHAPTER 1
Review of Level 1

- **Haben** and **sein**
- **Mein, dein, sein,** and **ihr**
- The **möchte**-forms and **wollen**
- The nominative and accusative forms of indefinite and definite articles
- Regular and stem-changing verbs
- Third person pronouns
- Asking for and giving information
- Describing people
- Expressing likes and dislikes
- Giving and responding to compliments; expressing wishes

CHAPTER 2

- Clauses with **weil** and **denn**
- Dative case of **mein, dein, sein,** and **ihr**
- **Du**-commands
- The interrogative **warum**
- **Kein**
- **Müssen, können, sollen,** and **mögen**
- **Noch ein**
- Personal pronouns
- Possessives
- Past tense of **sein**
- Asking and telling what to do
- Discussing gift ideas
- Expressing obligations

CHAPTER 12
Review of Level 2

- Adjective endings
- Command forms of strong verbs
- Comparative forms of adjectives
- The past tense
- Prepositions
- Questions and statements
- **Sollen; würde** forms
- Asking for and giving advice
- Asking for, making, and responding to suggestions
- Expressing hearsay; regret

LEVEL 3

CHAPTER 1
Review of Level 2

- Dative-case forms
- **Dieser** and **welcher**
- Past tense
- Prepositions followed by dative-case forms
- Reflexive and object pronouns
- Asking and telling what you may or may not do
- Asking for information
- Asking how someone liked something; expressing enthusiasm, disappointment
- Expressing hope
- Inquiring about someone's health

CHAPTER 2

- Reporting past events
- Adjective endings
- Two-way prepositions
- The verb **hatte**
- Word order in **dass-** and **ob**-clauses
- Asking for and making suggestions
- Asking for, making, and responding to suggestions
- Expressing doubt, conviction, and resignation
- Expressing hearsay
- Expressing preference and giving a reason
- Expressing wishes

CHAPTER 12
Review of Level 3

- Direct and indirect object pronouns
- Infinitive forms of verbs
- The narrative past (imperfect)
- Subjunctive
- The **würde**-forms
- Reporting past events
- Agreeing; agreeing with reservations
- Expressing determination or indecision
- Expressing surprise and disappointment
- Giving advice; reasons
- Hypothesizing

Komm mit! German Level 1
Scope and Sequence

FUNCTIONS	GRAMMAR	VOCABULARY	CULTURE	RE-ENTRY

VORSCHAU, Pages 1–11

FUNCTIONS	GRAMMAR	VOCABULARY	CULTURE	RE-ENTRY
		• Das Alphabet • Wie heißt du? • Im Klassenzimmer • Die Zahlen von 0 bis 20		

KAPITEL 1   Wer bist du?, Pages 16–41

FUNCTIONS	GRAMMAR	VOCABULARY	CULTURE	RE-ENTRY
• Saying hello and goodbye • Asking someone's name and giving yours • Asking who someone is • Asking someone's age and giving yours • Talking about places of origin • Talking about getting to school	• Forming questions • Definite articles **der, die, das** • Subject pronouns and **sein**	• Numbers 0-20 • Words to describe how students get to school	• Greetings • Using **der** and **die** in front of people's names • Map of German states and capitals • **Wie kommst du zur Schule?**	• Asking someone's name • Numbers 0–20 • Geography of German-speaking countries

KAPITEL 2   Spiel und Spaß, Pages 42–67

FUNCTIONS	GRAMMAR	VOCABULARY	CULTURE	RE-ENTRY
• Talking about interests • Expressing likes and dislikes • Saying when you do various activities • Asking for an opinion and expressing yours • Agreeing and disagreeing	• The singular subject pronouns and present tense verb endings • The plural subject pronouns and verb endings • Present tense of verbs • Word order • Verbs with stems ending in **d**, **t**, or **n**	• Sports, instruments, and games you play • Leisure activities and hobbies • Seasons of the year	• Formal and informal address • **Was machst du gern?** • German weekly planner	• Question formation • Greetings • Expressions **stimmt/ stimmt nicht** used in a new context

KAPITEL 3   Komm mit nach Hause!, Pages 68–95

FUNCTIONS	GRAMMAR	VOCABULARY	CULTURE	RE-ENTRY
• Talking about where you and others live • Offering something to eat and drink and responding to an offer • Saying please, thank you, you're welcome • Describing a room • Describing the family • Describing people	• The **möchte**-forms • Indefinite articles **ein, eine** • The pronouns er, sie, es, and sie • The possessive adjectives **mein, dein, sein,** and **ihr**	• Words to describe where you live • Food and drink items • Words to describe a room • Members of the family	• The German preference for **Mineralwasser** • **Wo wohnst du?**	• Definite articles **der, die, das** • Asking someone's name and age • Asking who someone is • Talking about interests

Brandenburg

KAPITEL 4 Alles für die Schule!, *Pages 100–127*

FUNCTIONS	GRAMMAR	VOCABULARY	CULTURE	RE-ENTRY
• Talking about class schedules • Using a schedule to talk about time • Sequencing events • Expressing likes, dislikes, and favorites • Responding to good news and bad news • Talking about prices • Pointing things out	• The verb **haben** • Using **Lieblings-** • Noun plurals	• Classes at school • School supplies	• The German school day • 24-hour time system • The German grading system • **Was sind deine Lieblingsfächer?** • German currency	• Numbers • Likes and dislikes: **gern** • Degrees of enthusiasm • The pronouns **er, sie, es,** and **sie** (pl)

KAPITEL 5 Klamotten kaufen, *Pages 128–155*

FUNCTIONS	GRAMMAR	VOCABULARY	CULTURE	RE-ENTRY
• Expressing wishes when shopping • Commenting on and describing clothes • Giving compliments and responding to them • Talking about trying on clothes	• Definite and indefinite articles in the accusative case • The verb **gefallen** • Direct object pronouns • Separable-prefix verbs • Stem-changing verbs **nehmen** and **aussehen**	• Clothing items • Colors • Words to describe clothing	• Exchange rates • German store hours • German clothing sizes • **Welche Klamotten sind „in"?**	• Numbers and prices • Colors • Pointing things out • Expressing likes and dislikes • Asking for and expressing opinions • The verb **aussehen**

KAPITEL 6 Pläne machen, *Pages 156–183*

FUNCTIONS	GRAMMAR	VOCABULARY	CULTURE	RE-ENTRY
• Starting a conversation • Telling time and talking about when you do things • Making plans • Ordering food and beverages • Talking about how something tastes • Paying the check	• The verb **wollen** • The stem-changing verb **essen**	• Telling time • Words used to make plans • Food and drink items in a café	• Clocks on public buildings • **Was machst du in deiner Freizeit?** • Tipping in Germany	• Expressing time when referring to schedules • Vocabulary: School and free-time activities • Inversion of time elements • Sequencing events • Accusative case • The verb **nehmen** • Using **möchte** to order food

Schleswig-Holstein

KAPITEL 7 Zu Hause helfen, *Pages 188–215*

FUNCTIONS	GRAMMAR	VOCABULARY	CULTURE	RE-ENTRY
• Extending and responding to an invitation • Expressing obligations • Talking about how often you do things • Offering help and explaining what to do • Talking about the weather	• The modals **müssen** and **können** • The separable-prefix verb **aufräumen** • The accusative pronouns • Using present tense to refer to the future	• Household chores • Words describing how often you have to do things • Words to describe the weather • Months	• **Was tust du für die Umwelt?** • German weather map and weather report • Weather in German-speaking countries	• Separable-prefix verbs • The verb **wollen** • Time expressions • Vocabulary: Free-time activities • Vocabulary: School supplies • Using numbers in a new context, temperature

KAPITEL 8 Einkaufen gehen, *Pages 216–243*

FUNCTIONS	GRAMMAR	VOCABULARY	CULTURE	RE-ENTRY
• Asking what you should do • Telling someone what to do • Talking about quantities • Saying you want something else • Giving reasons • Saying where you were and what you bought	• The modal **sollen** • The du- and ihr-commands • The conjunctions **weil** and **denn** • The past tense of **sein**	• Groceries • Weights • Time expressions	• Specialty shops and markets • **Was machst du für andere Leute?** • Weights and measures • German advertisements	• The **möchte**-forms and **können** • Numbers used in a new context, weights and measures • Expressing wishes when shopping • Responding to invitations • Vocabulary: Activities • Vocabulary: Household chores • Sequencing words • Vocabulary: Clothing

KAPITEL 9 Amerikaner in München, *Pages 244–271*

FUNCTIONS	GRAMMAR	VOCABULARY	CULTURE	RE-ENTRY
• Talking about where something is located • Asking for and giving directions • Talking about what there is to eat and drink • Saying you do/don't want more • Expressing opinions	• The verb **wissen** • The verb **fahren** • The formal commands with **Sie** • The phrase **es gibt** • Using **kein** • The conjunction **dass**	• Places in a city • Words used to give directions • Food and appetite	• The German **Innenstadt** • **Was isst du gern?** • Map of a German neighborhood • **Imbissstube** menu • **Leberkäs**	• Vocabulary: Stores and food items • **Du**-commands, **möchte**, and **zu** • Saying you want something else • Indefinite articles: accusative case • Expressing opinions • Subordinate-clause word order

München

KAPITEL 10 Kino und Konzerte, *Pages 276–303*

FUNCTIONS	GRAMMAR	VOCABULARY	CULTURE	RE-ENTRY
• Expressing likes and dislikes • Expressing familiarity • Expressing preferences and favorites • Talking about what you did in your free time	• **Mögen, kennen, sehen, lesen** • **Sprechen** and **sprechen über** • **Lieber, am liebsten, gern**	• Film genres • Words describing how much you do or don't like something • Entertainers and forms of entertainment • Words used to describe films • Book genres	• The German movie rating system • German movie ads • A German pop chart • **Welche kulturellen Veranstaltungen besuchst du?** • German upcoming events poster • German best-seller lists • German video hits list • Popular German novels	• Expressing likes and dislikes • Expressing opinions; giving reasons • Describing people • **Aussehen, nehmen, wissen, essen, können** • Vocabulary: Activities • Talking about when and how often you do things

KAPITEL 11 Der Geburtstag, *Pages 304–331*

FUNCTIONS	GRAMMAR	VOCABULARY	CULTURE	RE-ENTRY
• Using the telephone in Germany • Inviting someone to a party • Talking about birthdays and expressing good wishes • Discussing gift ideas	• Introduction to the dative case • Word order in the dative case	• Telephone vocabulary • Dates of the year • Holidays and holiday greetings • Gift ideas	• Using the telephone • Saints' days • German good luck symbols • **Was schenkst du zum Geburtstag?** • German gift ideas	• Numbers 0–20 • Time and days of the week • Months • Accusative case • Vocabulary: Family members

KAPITEL 12 Die Fete, *Pages 332–383*   *Review Chapter*

FUNCTIONS	GRAMMAR	VOCABULARY	CULTURE	RE-ENTRY
• Offering help and explaining what to do • Asking where something is located and giving directions • Making plans and inviting someone to come along • Talking about clothing • Discussing gift ideas • Describing people and places • Saying what you would like and whether you do or don't want more • Talking about what you did	• The verb **können**; the preposition **für**; accusative pronouns; **du**-commands • The verb **wissen** and word order following **wissen**; formal commands • The verbs **wollen** and **müssen**; word order • Nominative and accusative pronouns; definite and indefinite articles • The nominative pronouns **er, sie, es,** and **sie** (pl); possessive pronouns • The **möchte**-forms; **noch ein** and **kein**	• Ingredients • Freetime activities • Words used to describe clothing • Furniture and appliances	• **Spätzle** and **Apfelküchle** • **Musst du zu Hause helfen?** • German gift ideas • Photos from furniture ads • Menu from an **Imbissstube**	• Chapter 12 is a global review of Chapters 1–11, Level 1.

Baden-Württemberg

Komm mit! German Level 2
Scope and Sequence

FUNCTIONS	GRAMMAR	VOCABULARY	CULTURE	RE-ENTRY

KAPITEL 1   Bei den Baumanns, *Pages 4–31*   *Review Chapter*

FUNCTIONS	GRAMMAR	VOCABULARY	CULTURE	RE-ENTRY
• Asking for and giving information about yourself and others; describing yourself and others; expressing likes and dislikes • Identifying people and places • Giving and responding to compliments; expressing wishes when buying things • Making plans; ordering food; talking about how something tastes	• Present tense forms of **haben** and **sein** • **Mein, dein, sein,** and **ihr** (nom.) • The nominative and accusative forms of the definite and indefinite articles • The third person pronouns • Regular and stem-changing verbs • The **möchte**-forms and **wollen**	• Personal characteristics • Sports and hobbies • Clothing accessories	• Questionnaire: **Was für eine Person bist du?** • Article: **Sebastian über seine Familie** • Article: **Popstars machen Mode** • **Und was hast du am liebsten?** • Advertisements	• Chapters 1 and 2 are a global review of *Komm mit!*, Level 1.

KAPITEL 2   Bastis Plan, *Pages 32–59*   *Review Chapter*

FUNCTIONS	GRAMMAR	VOCABULARY	CULTURE	RE-ENTRY
• Expressing obligations; extending and responding to an invitation; offering help and telling what to do • Asking and telling what to do; telling that you need something else; telling where you were and what you bought • Discussing gift ideas; expressing likes and dislikes; expressing likes, preferences, and favorites; saying you do or don't want more	• **Müssen, können, sollen,** and **mögen** • **Warum** • **Weil** and **denn** • Personal pronouns (acc.) • The possessives **mein, dein, sein, ihr** (acc.) • The **du**-commands • **Sein**: past tense • The dative case of **mein, dein, sein, ihr** • **Noch ein** (nom./acc.) • **Kein** (nom./acc.)	• Words useful for traveling • Things to take on a picnic	• **Was nimmst du mit, wenn du irgendwo eingeladen bist?** • Grocery advertisements • German gift ideas	• Chapters 1 and 2 are a global review of *Komm mit!*, Level 1.

KAPITEL 3   Wo warst du in den Ferien?, *Pages 60–89*

FUNCTIONS	GRAMMAR	VOCABULARY	CULTURE	RE-ENTRY
• Reporting past events, talking about activities • Reporting past events, talking about places • Asking how someone liked something; expressing enthusiasm or disappointment; responding enthusiastically or sympathetically	• Conversational past • Past tense of **haben** and **sein** • **An** and **in** with dative-case forms to express location • The definite article, dative plural • Personal pronouns, dative case • The dative-case forms of **ein**	• Film media • Places in Frankfurt a.M. • Time expressions • Places to eat or spend the night	• Information on Dresden and **Frankfurt am Main** • **Was hast du in den letzten Ferien gemacht?**	• Expressions of time/ frequency • **Weil**-clauses • Expressing likes and dislikes (For additional Re-entry, see Ch. 3, p. 59A.)

Bayern

KAPITEL 4 Gesund leben, *Pages 94–121*

FUNCTIONS	GRAMMAR	VOCABULARY	CULTURE	RE-ENTRY
• Expressing approval and disapproval • Asking for information and responding emphatically or agreeing, with reservations • Asking and telling what you may or may not do	• The verb **schlafen (schläft)** • **Für** + accusative • Reflexive verbs (accusative) • **Jeder, jede, jedes** (nominative) • The accusative forms of **kein** • The verb **dürfen**	• Words describing healthy habits • Words for how you feel where • Fruits, vegetables, fish, meat	• Interviews of German teenagers • **Was tust du, um gesund zu leben?** • Survey on health habits • **Bioläden** and **Reformhäuser**	• **Essen, sollen** and **müssen** • **Dass**-clauses; **für; kein** • Conjunctions **weil** and **denn** • Expressions of place, time, frequency, and quantity • Giving reasons • Responding to an invitation (For additional Re-entry, see Ch. 4, p. 93A.)

KAPITEL 5 Gesund essen, *Pages 122–149*

FUNCTIONS	GRAMMAR	VOCABULARY	CULTURE	RE-ENTRY
• Expressing regret and downplaying; expressing skepticism and making certain • Calling someone's attention to something and responding • Expressing preference and strong preference	• **Dieser, diese, dieses** • The possessives (Summary) • Verbs used with dative case • **Welcher, welche, welches; zu**	• **Schulpause** foods • Things to put on bread • Foods from the supermarket	• **Was isst du, was nicht?** • Nutritious snacks for **Gymnasiasten** • German meals	• Talking about quantities • The possessives • Talking about how food tastes • Comparatives and superlatives • Saying you want more • The interrogative **was für** (For additional Re-entry, see Ch. 5, p. 121A.)

KAPITEL 6 Gute Besserung!, *Pages 150–177*

FUNCTIONS	GRAMMAR	VOCABULARY	CULTURE	RE-ENTRY
• Inquiring about someone's health and responding; making suggestions • Asking about and expressing pain • Asking for and giving advice; expressing hope	• Reflexive pronouns in dative • The inclusive command • Verbs used with dative case • The verbs **brechen, waschen, messen,** and **wehtun** • The dative case to express the idea of something too expensive, too large, too small for you	• Aches and pains • Body parts and injuries • Healthy habits • Toiletries	• **Was machst du, wenn dir nicht gut ist?** • **Apotheke** and **Drogerie** • Article about sun exposure	• The verb **sich fühlen** • The accusative reflexive pronouns • Expressing obligations • The conversational past • **Dass**-clauses (For additional Re-entry, see Ch. 6, p. 149A.)

Hamburg

KAPITEL 7 Stadt oder Land?, *Pages 182–209*

FUNCTIONS	GRAMMAR	VOCABULARY	CULTURE	RE-ENTRY
• Expressing preference and giving a reason • Expressing wishes • Agreeing, with reservations; justifying your answers	• Comparative forms of adjectives • The verb **sich wünschen** • Adjective endings following **ein**-words • Adjective endings of comparatives	• Places to live • Advantages and disadvantages of city and country life • Parts of a house • Wishes for the future • Noisy things	• **Wo wohnst du lieber? Auf dem Land? In der Stadt?** • **Schule im Garten** • Letter from a German pen pal	• Talking about where something is located • Reflexive dative verbs • Expressing opinions • Dative verb **gefallen** (For additional Re-entry, see Ch. 7, p. 181A.)

KAPITEL 8 Mode? Ja oder nein?, *Pages 210–237*

FUNCTIONS	GRAMMAR	VOCABULARY	CULTURE	RE-ENTRY
• Describing clothes • Expressing interest, disinterest, and indifference; making and accepting compliments • Persuading and dissuading	• Adjective endings following **der** and **dieser**-words • **Passen (zu), stehen, tragen,** and **sich interessieren** • The conjunction **wenn** • **Kaufen** with dative	• Clothing • Words to describe clothing • Fabrics	• **Was trägst du am liebsten?** • Clothes typically worn by German-speaking youths • Interviews about fashion	• Talking about what you bought • Accusative reflexive verbs • **Für** + accusative • Giving reasons • Word order with subordinate conjunctions (For additional Re-entry, see Ch. 8, p. 209A.)

KAPITEL 9 Wohin in die Ferien?, *Pages 238–265*

FUNCTIONS	GRAMMAR	VOCABULARY	CULTURE	RE-ENTRY
• Expressing indecision; asking for and making suggestions • Expressing doubt, conviction, and resignation • Asking for and giving directions	• Articles/names for mountains • **Nach, in, an,** and **auf; ob**-clauses • Expressing direction and location (Summary) • Prepositions followed by dative • **Durch, um, vor, neben,** and **zwischen**	• Means of transportation • Vacation activities • Words for giving directions in a city	• **Wohin fährst du in den nächsten Ferien?** • **Urlaub in letzter Minute** • Statistics on transportation • Students talk about vacations • **Stadtrundgang durch Bietigheim**	• Inclusive commands • **Können, fahren,** and **wissen** • Giving directions • Inviting someone and responding to an invitation (For additional Re-entry, see Ch. 9, p. 237A.)

Stuttgart

KAPITEL 10 Viele Interessen!, *Pages 270–297*

FUNCTIONS	GRAMMAR	VOCABULARY	CULTURE	RE-ENTRY
• Asking about and expressing interest • Asking for and giving permission; asking for information and expressing an assumption • Expressing surprise, agreement, and disagreement; talking about plans	• Verbs with prepositions • **Wo**-compounds and **da**-compounds • The verbs **lassen** and **laufen** • The use of **kein** to negate a noun • The future tense with **werden**	• TV programs • TV accessories • Standard and optional car equipment	• Television channels • **Was machst du, um zu relaxen?** • Statistics on television programs • Getting a driver's license in Germany • Statistics on cars	• **Weil** and **dass,** and **was für** • Word order with modals • Time expressions • Expressing future events with present tense • Making plans • Expressing interest • **Können, dürfen,** and **sich freuen** (For additional Re-entry, see Ch. 10, p. 269A.)

KAPITEL 11 Mit Oma ins Restaurant, *Pages 298–325*

FUNCTIONS	GRAMMAR	VOCABULARY	CULTURE	RE-ENTRY
• Asking for, making, and responding to suggestions • Expressing hearsay • Ordering in a restaurant; expressing good wishes	• The **würde**-forms • Unpreceded adjectives • The **hätte**-forms	• Cultural activities • Cuisine of Germany and other countries • Words to describe food • Things to order in a restaurant	• **Für welche kulturellen Veranstaltungen interessierst du dich?** • State-supported art in Germany • International cuisine • Menu	• Cultural activities and sights • The impersonal pronoun **man** • Talking about favorites • The modal **sollen** • Saying what's available • Ordering and asking for the bill (For additional Re-entry, see Ch. 11, p. 297A.)

KAPITEL 12 Die Reinickendorfer Clique, *Pages 326–353*   *Review Chapter*

FUNCTIONS	GRAMMAR	VOCABULARY	CULTURE	RE-ENTRY
• Reporting past events; asking for, making, and responding to suggestions • Ordering food; expressing hearsay and regret; persuading and dissuading • Asking for and giving advice; expressing preference, interest, disinterest, and indifference	• The past tense • **Sollen** and the **würde**-forms • Questions and statements • Prepositions • The command forms of strong verbs • Adjective endings • Comparative forms of adjectives	• Places near water • Sport sites • International cuisine • Clothing	• **Welche ausländische Küche hast du gern?** • Article on travel habits • Etiquette in German restaurants • Franziska van Almsick	• Chapter 12 is a global review of Chapters 1–11, Level 2.

Berlin

Komm mit! German Level 3
Scope and Sequence

FUNCTIONS	GRAMMAR	VOCABULARY	CULTURE	RE-ENTRY

Die neuen Bundesländer

KAPITEL 1   Das Land am Meer, *Pages 4–31* — *Review Chapter*

FUNCTIONS	GRAMMAR	VOCABULARY	CULTURE	RE-ENTRY
• Reporting past events • Asking how someone liked something; expressing enthusiasm, disappointment, and sympathy • Asking and telling what you may or may not do • Asking for information • Inquiring about someone's health and responding; expressing pain • Expressing hope	• Prepositions followed by dative-case forms • Past tense • Dative-case forms • Forms of **dieser** and **welcher** • Reflexive and object pronouns	• Time expressions • Errands • Produce and cuts of meat • Things to put on bread • Body parts and injuries	• **Insel Rügen** • **Fit ohne Fleisch** • **Währungen und Geld wechseln**	• Chapters 1 and 2 are a global review of *Komm mit!*, Levels 1 and 2.

KAPITEL 2   Auf in die Jugendherberge!, *Pages 32–59* — *Review Chapter*

FUNCTIONS	GRAMMAR	VOCABULARY	CULTURE	RE-ENTRY
• Asking for and making suggestions • Expressing preference and giving a reason • Expressing wishes • Expressing doubt, conviction, resignation • Asking for information, expressing assumptions • Expressing hearsay • Asking for, making, and responding to suggestions • Expressing wishes when shopping	• Two-way prepositions • Word order in **dass-** and **ob-**clauses • Adjective endings • The verb **hätte**	• Words useful for traveling • Things to take on a picnic	• **Jugendherbergen** • **Einkaufsliste** • **Programm für eine 6-Tage-Reise nach Weimar** • **Weimar im Blickpunkt** • Poems	• Chapters 1 and 2 are a global review of *Komm mit!*, Levels 1 and 2.

KAPITEL 3   Aussehen: wichtig oder nicht?, *Pages 60–87*

FUNCTIONS	GRAMMAR	VOCABULARY	CULTURE	RE-ENTRY
• Asking for and expressing opinions; expressing sympathy and resignation • Giving advice; giving a reason • Admitting something and expressing regret	• **Da** and **wo-** compounds (Summary) • Infinitive clauses	• Words teens use in conversation • Phrases used to express sympathy, resignation, and to give advice	• **Die deutsche Subkultur** • Teenagers talking about what they do to feel better	• Expressing interest • Sequencing events • Expressing opinions • Verbs requiring prepositional phrases • Hobby and clothing vocabulary • **Wo-** and **da-** compounds • Responding sympathetically • Asking for and giving advice • Making suggestions • Giving reasons • Infinitives • **Weil-**clauses

KAPITEL 4 Verhältnis zu anderen, *Pages 92–119*

FUNCTIONS	GRAMMAR	VOCABULARY	CULTURE	RE-ENTRY
• Agreeing; giving advice • Introducing another point of view; hypothesizing	• Ordinal numbers • Relative clauses • **Hätte** and **wäre** • The genitive case	• Words used for describing relationships • Words used for getting along with others	• Importance of **Cliquen** • **Die verschiedenen Bildungswege in Deutschland**	• Agreeing • **Wenn-, weil-,** and **dass**-clauses • Cardinal numbers • Pronouns (nom., acc., and dat.) • Giving advice • **Wenn**-phrases • Subjunctive (**würde-, hätte-, wäre**-forms) • The preposition **von** + dative

KAPITEL 5 Rechte und Pflichten, *Pages 120–147*

FUNCTIONS	GRAMMAR	VOCABULARY	CULTURE	RE-ENTRY
• Talking about what is possible • Saying what you would have liked to do • Saying that something is going on right now • Reporting past events • Expressing surprise, relief, and resignation	• The **könnte**-forms • Further uses of **wäre** and **hätte** • Verbs used as neuter nouns • The past tense of modals (the imperfect)	• Words to describe rights and responsibilities • Military terms • Time expressions	• **Artikel 38/2. Absatz des Grundgesetzes** • **Artikel 12a des Grundgesetzes** • Cartoon • **Gleichberechtigung im deutschen Militär?** • **Wehrpflicht**	• **Hätte**-forms and **wäre**-forms • **Weil**-clauses • Giving reasons • The modals **können, wollen,** and **müssen** • Reporting past events • Expressing surprise • Expressing resignation • Expressing hearsay

KAPITEL 6 Medien: stets gut informiert?, *Pages 148–175*

FUNCTIONS	GRAMMAR	VOCABULARY	CULTURE	RE-ENTRY
• Asking someone to take a position; asking for reasons; expressing opinions • Reporting past events • Agreeing or disagreeing; changing the subject; interrupting • Expressing surprise or annoyance	• Narrative past (imperfect) • Superlative forms of adjectives	• Terms used in discussions • Words related to media • Words of quantity	• **Die TV-Kids** • **Die Schülerzeitung** • **Leserbriefe an die Redaktion der Pepo**	• Talking about favorites • Leisure-time activities • Expressing opinions • The conversational past • Agreeing and disagreeing • Television vocabulary • Expressing surprise • The comparative forms of adjectives • Time expressions • Words of quantity

Würzburg

Frankfurt

KAPITEL 7 Ohne Reklame geht es nicht!, *Pages 180–207*

FUNCTIONS	GRAMMAR	VOCABULARY	CULTURE	RE-ENTRY
• Expressing annoyance • Comparing • Eliciting agreement and agreeing • Expressing conviction, uncertainty, and what seems to be true	• **Derselbe, der gleiche** • Adjective endings following determiners of quantity • Introducing relative clauses with **was** and **wo** • **Irgendein** and **irgendwelche**	• Words used in advertising • Words preceded by **irgend**	• **Werbung—pro und contra** • **Warum so wenig Unterbrecherwerbung?** • Excerpt from *Frankfurter Allgemeine* • Cartoon	• Expressing annoyance • The conjunctions **wenn** and **dass** • Comparative and superlative • Adjective endings • Agreeing • Relative pronouns • Word order in dependent clauses • Expressing conviction • Expressing uncertainty

KAPITEL 8 Weg mit den Vorurteilen!, *Pages 208–235*

FUNCTIONS	GRAMMAR	VOCABULARY	CULTURE	RE-ENTRY
• Expressing surprise, disappointment, and annoyance • Expressing an assumption • Making suggestions and recommendations • Giving advice	• The conjunction **als** • Coordinating conjunctions (Summary) • Verbs with prefixes (Summary)	• Words used to express prejudices and clichés • Personal characteristics	• Cartoon • **Verständnis für Ausländer?** • **Der sympathische Deutsche**	• Expressing surprise • Expressing disappointment • **Dass**-clauses • Narrative past • Conversational past • Coordinating conjunctions • Expressing an assumption • Prepositions followed by dative • Separable-prefix verbs • Making suggestions • Giving advice

KAPITEL 9 Aktiv für die Umwelt!, *Pages 236–263*

FUNCTIONS	GRAMMAR	VOCABULARY	CULTURE	RE-ENTRY
• Expressing concern • Making accusations • Offering solutions • Making polite requests • Saying what is being done about a problem • Hypothesizing	• Subjunctive forms of **können, müssen, dürfen, sollen,** and **sein** • The passive voice, present tense • Use of a conjugated modal verb in the passive • Conditional sentences	• Words describing pollution and the environment	• Environmental concerns • **Ein umweltfreundlicher Einkauf**	• Adjective endings • **Dass-, wenn-** and **weil**-clauses • **Hätte-, würde-,** and **könnte**-forms • **Werden** and **sollen** • Environment vocabulary • Subjunctive forms

KAPITEL 10   Die Kunst zu leben, *Pages 268–295*

FUNCTIONS	GRAMMAR	VOCABULARY	CULTURE	RE-ENTRY
• Expressing preference, given certain possibilities • Expressing envy and admiration • Expressing happiness and sadness • Saying that something is or was being done	• Prepositions with genitive • The passive voice (Summary)	• Words used in the arts and in theaters	• Film critiques • **Aphorismen** • **Kultur findet man überall!**	• Expressing preference • **Würde**-forms • Genitive case forms • Prepositions • **Da-** and **wo-** compounds • Past participles • Subjunctive forms of modals • **Von** + dative case

KAPITEL 11   Deine Welt ist deine Sache!, *Pages 296–323*

FUNCTIONS	GRAMMAR	VOCABULARY	CULTURE	RE-ENTRY
• Expressing determination or indecision • Talking about whether something is important or not important • Expressing wishes • Expressing certainty and refusing or accepting with certainty • Talking about goals for the future • Expressing relief	• The use of **wo-** compounds to ask questions • Two ways of expressing the future tense • The perfect infinitive with modals and **werden**	• Careers and occupations • Words used to talk about the future	• German universities • **Wie findet man eine Arbeitsstelle in Deutschland?** • **Umfragen und Tests**	• Reflexive verbs • Expressing indecision • Conversational past and conditional • **Ob-** and **dass**-clauses • **Um ... zu** • **Wo**-compounds • Expressing wishes • **Wäre** • Determiners of quantity • Negation with **kein** • Future tense formation

KAPITEL 12   Die Zukunft liegt in deiner Hand!, *Pages 324–351*   *Review Chapter*

FUNCTIONS	GRAMMAR	VOCABULARY	CULTURE	RE-ENTRY
• Reporting past events • Expressing surprise and disappointment • Agreeing; agreeing, with reservations • Giving advice; giving reasons • Expressing determination or indecision • Talking about what is important or not important • Hypothesizing	• The narrative past (imperfect) • The **würde**-forms • Infinitive forms of verbs • Direct and indirect object pronouns • Subjunctive	• Careers and occupations • Words used to talk about the future	• **Kummerkasten** • **Pauken allein reicht nicht** • **Claudias Pläne für die Zukunft** • **Textbilder**	• Chapter 12 is a global review of Chapters 1–11, Level 3.

Dresden

Pupil's Edition

Proficiency is the goal of language instruction in Komm mit! *Every chapter begins with authentic interviews or discussions that model communicative needs common among young people. Through these texts students learn the functions, vocabulary, and grammar that support natural expression. They also become interested, involved, and responsive— in short, they answer the invitation to* Komm mit! *and to communicate.*

Komm mit! Level 3

The **Komm mit!** *Pupil's Edition* opens with a two-chapter review of the functions, vocabulary, and grammar learned in Levels 1 and 2. Following this comprehensive review, Chapters 3–11 provide a carefully sequenced program of balanced skills instruction in the four areas of listening, speaking, reading, and writing. The **Mehr Grammatikübungen** include various activities that strengthen students' understanding of the grammar points presented in each chapter. These activities can also be used for review and reinforcement. In addition, every chapter is rich in authentic culture and language.

Chapter 12 is a review of the third year's study of German. It provides an opportunity to reinforce skills and remediate deficiencies before the end of the school year. This opportunity to pause and reflect on what has been learned provides closure and gives students a sense of accomplishment and renewed purpose.

At the end of the *Pupil's Edition,* a Reference Section summarizes functions and grammar rules for quick reference. It also provides a list of Additional Vocabulary as well as German>English and English>German glossaries. Throughout the year, students are encouraged to consult the Reference Section to review, expand their choices, and further practice functional expressions, vocabulary, and structures.

Activity-Based Instruction

In **Komm mit!,** language acquisition is an active process. From the first day, students are using German. Within each lesson, a progression of activities moves students from discrete point use of language to completely open-ended activities that promote personalized expression and meaningful communication. This sequence allows students to practice receptive skills before moving on to language production. It is this carefully articulated sequence that ensures success.

A Guided Tour

On the next several pages, you will find a guided tour of **Komm mit!** On these pages, we have identified for you the essential elements of the textbook and the various resources available. If, as you are using **Komm mit!,** you encounter any particular problems, please contact your regional office for information or assistance.

Starting Out…

Location Opener In *Komm mit!* chapters are arranged in groups of three, with each group set in a different German-speaking location. Each new location is introduced by four pages of colorful photos and information of the city or region presented. · · · · · · · · · · ·

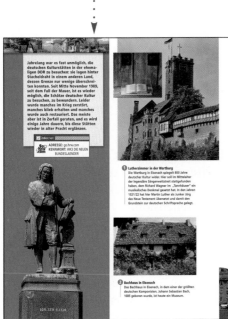

Chapter Opener These pages are a visual introduction to the theme of the chapter and include a list of objectives students will be expected to achieve.

Setting The Scene...

Los geht's! and **Weiter geht's!**
After students have been introduced to the location, situation, and functional outcomes of the chapter, the next step is to provide authentic cultural and linguistic input. This input at Level 3 takes the form of interviews or discussions that focus on the chapter theme and introduce students to language that they will practice as they go through the chapter.

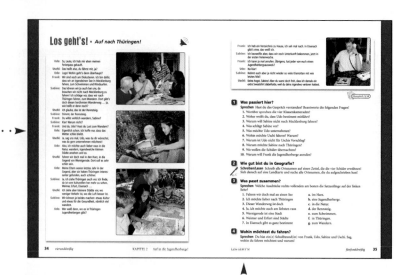

Following **Los geht's!** and **Weiter geht's!** is a series of activities to check comprehension.

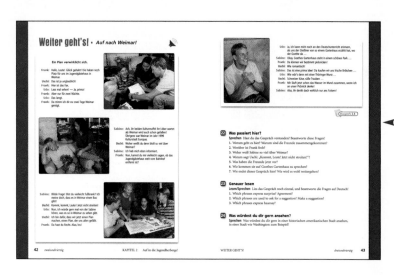

Building Proficiency Step By Step...

Erste and **Zweite Stufe** are the core instructional sections where language acquisition will take place. The communicative goals in each chapter center on the functional expressions presented in **So sagt man das!** boxes. These expressions are supported by material in the **Wortschatz, Grammatik,** and **Ein wenig Grammatik** sections. Activities following the above features are designed to practice recognition or to provide closed-ended practice. Activities then progress from controlled to open-ended practice where students are able to express themselves in meaningful communication.

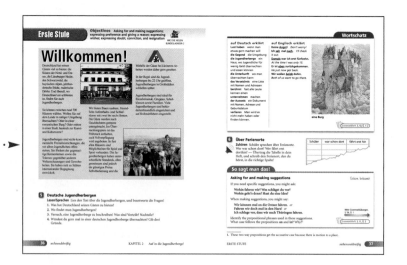

Discovering the People and the Culture...

There are two major cultural features to help students develop an appreciation and understanding of the cultures of German-speaking countries.

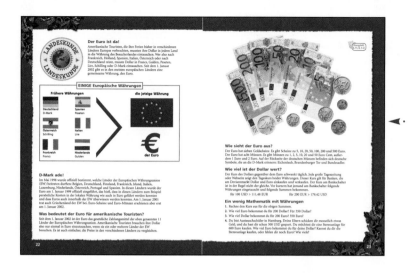

Landeskunde presents interviews conducted throughout Germany on a topic related to the chapter theme. The interviews may be presented on video or done as a reading supplemented by the Audio CD recording. Culminating activities on this page verify comprehension and encourage students to think critically about the target culture as well as their own.

Ein wenig Landeskunde helps students gain knowledge and understanding of the other culture and can be used to enrich and enliven activities and presentations at various places throughout each chapter.

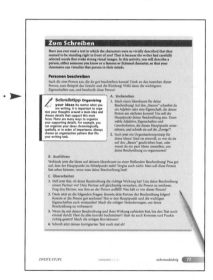

Understanding Authentic Documents...

Zum Lesen presents reading strategies that help students understand authentic German documents and literature presented in each chapter. The reading selections vary from advertisements to letters to short stories or poems in order to accommodate different interests and familiarize the students with different styles and formats. The accompanying prereading, reading, and postreading activities develop students' overall reading skills and challenge their critical thinking abilities. A **Lesestrategie** provides effective ways to enhance students' reading comprehension.

Zum Schreiben helps students develop their writing skills by focusing on the writing process. Each **Zum Schreiben** gives students a topic related to the theme and functions of the chapter.

Wrapping It All Up...

Mehr Grammatikübungen provide additional practice on the grammar concepts presented in the chapter. These activities are divided by **Stufe** and may be assigned as homework or as a review for quizzes and tests. · · · · · · · · · · ▶

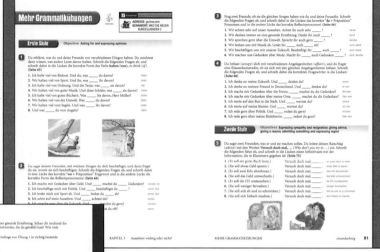

Anwendung gives students the opportunity to review what they have learned and to apply their skills in new communicative contexts. Focusing on all four language skills as well as cultural awareness, the **Anwendung** can help you determine whether students are ready for the Chapter Test.

Kann ich's wirklich? is a checklist that students can use on their own to see if they have achieved the goals stated on the Chapter Opener page. Each communicative function is paired with one or more activities for students to use as a self-check. · · · · · · · · · ▶

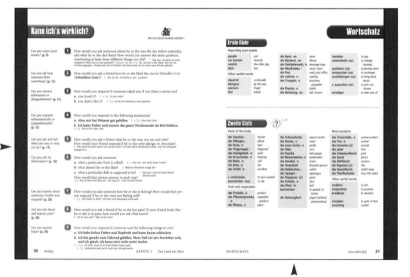

Wortschatz presents the chapter vocabulary grouped by **Stufe** and arranged according to function or theme. · · · · · · · · · · · · · · · · · · ·

Technology Resources

The Video Program

The *Video Program* provides the following video support:

• **Location Opener** documentaries

• **Videoclips** which present authentic footage from target cultures

The **Level 3 video** has a different structure and serves a somewhat different purpose than the Level 1 and Level 2 video programs.

• A narrated Location Opener introduces students to each of the four regions explored in the *Pupil's Edition.* This guided tour of the area in which the subsequent three chapters take place expands students' knowledge of the geography, culture, and people of that area. The on-the-street interviews that are the core of the Level 3 Video Program cover questions and issues that reflect the challenges all Germans, both in the east and the west, are facing in the aftermath of reunification. These issues touch almost every facet of life in the unified Germany: unemployment, housing, pollution, education, confusing new choices for consumers, and the pain of facing the realities and consequences of the past. The interviews serve as a springboard for student discussions in German.

• A special **Videoclips** section provides authentic television commercials related to the chapter theme.

• The *Video Guide* contains background information, suggestions for presentation, and activities for all portions of the *Video Program.*

Internet Connection

Keywords in the *Pupil's Edition* provide access to two types of online activities:

• **Interaktive Spiele** are directly correlated to the instructional material in the textbook. They can be used as homework, extra practice, or assessment.

• **Internet Aktivitäten** provide students with selected Web sites in German-speaking countries and activities related to the chapter theme. A printable worksheet in PDF format includes pre-surfing, surfing, and post-surfing activities that guide students through their research.

For easy access, see the keywords provided in the *Pupil's* and *Teacher's Editions.* For chapter-specific information, see the F page of the chapter interleaf.

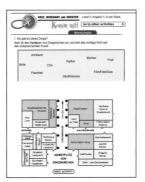 

One-Stop Planner CD-ROM with Test Generator

The *One-Stop Planner CD-ROM* is a convenient tool to aid in lesson planning and pacing.

Easy navigation through menus or through lesson plans allows for a quick overview of available resources. For each chapter the *One-Stop Planner* includes:

• Editable lesson plans with direct links to teaching resources

• Printable worksheets from resource books

• Direct launches to the HRW Internet activities

• Video and audio segments

• Test Generator

• Clip Art for vocabulary items

Ancillaries

The *Komm mit!* German program offers a comprehensive ancillary package that addresses the concerns of today's teachers and is relevant to students' lives.

Lesson Planning

One-Stop Planner with Test Generator

- editable lesson plans
- printable worksheets from resource books
- direct link to HRW Internet activities
- entire video and audio programs
- Test Generator
- Clip Art

Lesson Planner with Substitute Teacher Lesson Plans
- complete lesson plans for every chapter
- block scheduling suggestions
- correlations to Standards for Foreign Language Learning
- a homework calendar
- chapter by chapter lesson plans for substitute teachers
- lesson plan forms for customizing lesson plans

Student Make-Up Assignments
- diagnostic information for students who are behind in their work
- copying masters for make-up assignments

Listening and Speaking

Listening Activities
- print material associated with the *Audio Program*
- Student Response Forms for all *Pupil's Edition* listening activities
- Additonal Listening Activities
- scripts, answers
- lyrics to each chapter's song

Audio Compact Discs
Listening activities for the *Pupil's Edition*, the Additional Listening Activities, and the *Testing Program*

Activities for Communication
- Communicative Activities for partner work based on an information gap
- Situation Cards to practice interviews and role-plays
- Realia: reproductions of authentic documents

Grammar

Grammatikheft
- re-presentations of major grammar points
- additional focused practice
- *Teacher's Edition* with overprinted answers

Grammar Tutor for Students of German
- presentations of grammar concepts in English
- re-presentations of German grammar concepts
- discovery and application activities

Assessment

Testing Program
- Grammar and Vocabulary quizzes
- **Stufe** quizzes that test the skills
- Chapter Tests
- Speaking Tests
- Midterm and Final Exams
- Score sheets, scripts, answers

Alternative Assessment Guide
- Suggestions for oral and written Portfolio Assessment
- Performance Assessment
- rubrics, portfolio checklists, and evaluation forms

Student Make-Up Assignments
Alternative Grammar and Vocabulary quizzes for students who missed class and have to make up the quiz

Reading and Writing

Reading Strategies and Skills Handbook
- explanations of reading strategies
- copying masters for application of strategies

Lies mit mir!
- readings on familiar topics
- cultural information
- additional vocabulary
- interesting and engaging activities

Übungsheft
- activities for practice
- *Teacher's Edition* with overprinted answers

Teaching Transparencies
Colorful transparencies that help present and practice vocabulary, grammar, culture, and a variety of communicative functions

- Mehr Grammatikübungen
- Grammatikheft

Teacher's Edition

Using the Chapter Interleaf

Each chapter of the **Komm mit!** *Teacher's Edition* includes the following interleaf pages to help you plan, teach, and expand your lessons.

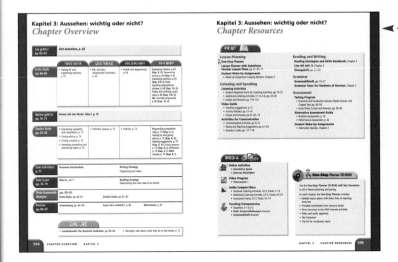

Chapter Overview

The Chapter Overview chart outlines at a glance the functions, grammar, vocabulary, re-entry, and culture featured in the chapter. You will also find a list of corresponding print and audiovisual resources organized by listening, speaking, reading, and writing skills, grammar, and assessment.

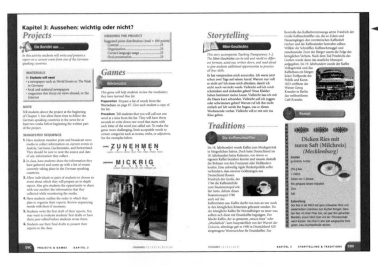

Projects/Games/Storytelling/Traditions

Projects allow students to personalize and expand on the information from the chapter. Games reinforce the chapter content. In the Storytelling feature, you will find a story related to a *Teaching Transparency*. The Traditions feature concentrates on a unique aspect of the culture of the region. A recipe typical for the region accompanies this feature.

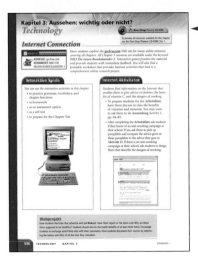

Technology

This page assists you in integrating technology into your lesson plans. The Technology page provides Internet resources and activities for your lesson. You will also find an Internet research project in each chapter.

· ·

Textbook Listening Activities Scripts

Textbook Listening Activities Scripts provide the scripts of the chapter listening activities for reference or for use in class.

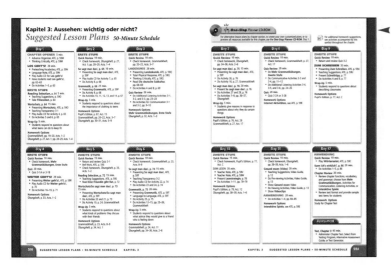

◀ · · · · · · · ·

Suggested Lesson Plans—50-Minute Schedule

This lesson plan is used for classes with 50-minute schedules. Each lesson plan provides a logical sequence of instruction along with homework suggestions.

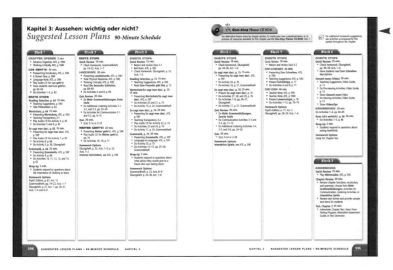

◀ · · · · · · · ·

Suggested Lesson Plans—90-Minute Schedule

This lesson plan is used for classes with 90-minute schedules. Each lesson plan provides a logical sequence of instruction along with homework suggestions.

The Teacher's Edition
Using the Interleaf Teacher Text

Connections and Comparisons

Under this head you will find connections and comparisons with other languages, cultures, and disciplines.

Resource Boxes provide a quick list of all the resources you can use for each chapter section.

Cultures and Communities

Under this head you will find helpful cultural information and suggestions that relate the content to students' families and communities.

ERSTE STUFE

Teaching Resources
pp. 124–127

PRINT
▸ Lesson Planner, p. 32
▸ Listening Activities, pp. 35–36, 39–40
▸ Video Guide, pp. 21–23
▸ Activities for Communication, pp. 17–18, 72, 74, 121–122
▸ Grammatikheft, pp. 37–40
▸ Grammar Tutor for Students of German, Chapter 5
▸ Übungsheft, pp. 54–57
▸ Testing Program, pp. 89–92
▸ Alternative Assessment Guide, p. 34
▸ Student Make-Up Assignments, Chapter 5

MEDIA
▸ One-Stop Planner
▸ Audio Compact Discs, CD5, Trs. 7–8, 13, 18–20
▸ Video Program
  Videocassette 1, 42:02–44:37
▸ Teaching Transparencies
  Situation 5-1
  Vocabulary 5A
  Mehr Grammatikübungen Answers
  Grammatikheft Answers

ERSTE STUFE

PAGE 124

Bell Work
Ask students to imagine the day that they reach legal adulthood. How would they like that day to unfold? (Wie stellst du dir den Tag vor, an dem du volljährig wirst?)

Cultures and Communities

The German **Grundgesetz** (basic law or constitu- ... on May 23, 1949.

the Video

... 42:02–44:37
... *In einer Fahrschule,*
...ducation class talk about
...*Video Guide,* p. 22, for

KAPITEL 5

Connections and Comparisons

Thinking Critically
Comparing and Contrasting Go over the list of changes that occur as a result of reaching legal adulthood (18) in Germany (See "Was bedeutet das?"). Then ask students to compare the required age in the United States for each of the nine points listed.

PRESENTING: Wortschatz
After introducing the new vocabulary to the class, assign each word or phrase to individual students. Give them a few moments to come up with a brief scenario in which the word or phrase could be used. Have several students share their word or phrase with the class. Example: Ich schwänze heute.
  Prüfung: Ich glaube, ich schwänze heute lieber nicht, denn wir haben eine wichtige Matheprüfung.

PAGE 125

Communication for All Students

A Slower Pace
3 Before listening to the recording on compact disc, go over Pictures a through e and ask students to describe each picture briefly in German.

Challenge
3 After students have listened to the five narra- tions and completed the matching exercise, ask them to listen again, this time noting two or three things about each person and thus telling more about the situation pictured. (Example: for Picture c: Jutta ist froh, dass sie jetzt wählen darf. Sie ist politisch sehr aktiv, ist Mitglied einer Partei. Sie arbeitet für eine politische Zeitung. Sie sieht sich täglich die Nachrichten an und …)

PRESENTING: So sagt man das!
• Write the following sentence on the board: "Du könntest dich wirklich ein bisschen für Politik interessieren!" Why would someone say this, and what does it indicate about the other person's interest in politics? Can students think of alternate ways to state this sentence?
Examples:
Es ist wichtig, sich für Politik zu interessieren.
Du solltest mehr Interesse an Politik haben!
• Go over the explanation in So sagt man das! with students.

STANDARDS: 1.2, 4.2

Erste Stufe

Objectives Talking about what is possible; saying what you would have liked to do

Artikel 38/2. Absatz des Grundgesetzes: „Wahlberechtigt ist, wer das achtzehnte Lebensjahr vollendet hat; wählbar ist, wer das Alter erreicht hat, mit dem die Volljährigkeit eintritt."

Seit 1975 sind Jugendliche in der Bundesrepublik Deutschland mit dem vollendeten achtzehnten Lebensjahr volljährig.

Was bedeutet das?
1. Man kann selbst bestimmen, wo man wohnen will.
2. Man kann nach Hause kommen, wann man will.
3. Man kann Ausbildungs- und Arbeitsverträge selbst unterschreiben.
4. Man kann Entschuldigungen für die Schule selbst schreiben.
5. Man kann Verträge über Käufe, Kredite, Mieten, usw. selbst abschließen.
6. Man kann heiraten.
7. Man kann selbst wählen und gewählt werden.
8. Man kann den Führerschein machen.
9. Man kann im Lokal alkoholische Getränke bestellen.

Wortschatz

auf Deutsch erklärt
der Unterricht das Lernen eines Schulfaches, zum Beispiel Deutsch (der Deutschunterricht)
die Prüfung der Test
schwänzen nicht in die Schule gehen, weil man keine Lust hat
fehlen nicht da sein
Ich kann es mir nicht erlauben. Ich darf es nicht.
Du irrst dich. Du denkst falsch.
Das dauert lange. Das braucht eine lange Zeit.
wählen man sagt einem politischen Kandidaten offiziell ja
sich politisch engagieren politisch aktiv sein
kurzfristig nach wenig Zeit, schnell

auf Englisch erklärt
Er ist Mitglied unseres Vereins. *He is a member of our club.*
Ich will von meinen Eltern unabhängig sein. *I want to be independent from my parents.*
Wir werden im Juni heiraten. *We're going to get married in June.*
Es scheint, du willst nicht. *It seems you don't want to.*
Das wäre zu schade ums Geld. *It wouldn't be worth the money.*
Unterschreiben Sie den Vertrag! *Sign the contract!*
In dieser Hinsicht ist es umgekehrt. *In this respect it's the other way around.*
Es ist schwer, sich zu ändern. *It's difficult to change yourself.*

Übungsheft, S. 54–55, Ü. 1–3
Grammatikheft, S. 37–38, Ü. 1–4

124 *hundertvierundzwanzig*   KAPITEL 5   Rechte und Pflichten

---

Presenting Features offer useful sugges- tions for presenting new material.

Correlations to the Standards for Foreign Language Learning are provided for your reference.

T34

Teaching Suggestion

4 Replay the recording on compact disc several times and have students list all the plans that the three German students talk about.

Communication for All Students

Challenge

4 Have students listen for the reasons the three German teenagers give for their choices. They should tell why they want to do certain things and not others.

PRESENTING: Ein wenig Grammatik

Könnte-forms After introducing the könnte-forms, ask pairs of students to scan the two Location Openers (**die neuen Bundesländer** and **Würzburg**) for things they could do if they were to visit these places. Also, what would they suggest that others go and see during a visit?
Example:
Wir könnten uns das Bachhaus in Eisenach anschauen, denn das ist heute ein Museum.

PAGE 126

Communication for All Students

A Slower Pace

6 Do the following activity in class before beginning Activity 6. Ask for suggestions and have students take notes. If students have trouble coming up with ideas, ask questions.
Examples:
Kannst du jetzt …
   jeden Tag arbeiten gehen?
   mit Freunden in den Ferien wegfahren?
   ein Auto haben?
After the discussion, have students write their own lists with reasons why they were not able or not allowed to do these various things.

PAGE 127

Teaching Suggestion

10 To give students time to think about these questions, you may want to assign them for homework.

Connections and Comparisons

Multicultural Connection
Ask students to interview foreign exchange students, other foreign language teachers, or anybody else they know from a different country about how reaching legal adulthood is important to a young person of that country. What is the legal age in that country and in which way does it change a young person's status? Discuss students' findings in class.

Speaking Assessment

10 After some practice in class, you may want to use these questions for oral evaluation. Have students come to your desk and answer three or four questions for assessment using the following rubric.

Speaking Rubric	Points			
	4	3	2	1
Content (Complete – Incomplete)				
Comprehension (Total – Little)				
Comprehensibility (Comprehensible – Incomprehensible)				
Accuracy (Accurate – Seldom accurate)				
Fluency (Fluent – Not fluent)				

18–20: A   16–17: B   14–15: C   12–13: D   Under 12: F

Assess

▶ Testing Program, pp. 89–92
  Quiz 5-1A, Quiz 5-1B
  Audio CD5, Tr. 13

▶ Student Make-Up Assignments
  Chapter 5, Alternative Quiz

▶ Alternative Assessment Guide, p. 34

ERSTE STUFE

Sidebar

Communication for All Students
Under this head you will find helpful suggestions for students with different learning styles and abilities.

Teaching Suggestions
offer helpful suggestions and information at point-of-use. You will also find references to other ancillaries.

Assessment
At the end of every **Stufe** and again at the end of the chapter, you will find references to assessment material available for that section of the chapter.

T35

Inset Page (127)

8 Grammatik im Kontext

Sprechen Setzt euch in kleinen Gruppen zusammen und erzählt, was ihr gern getan hättet! Ihr könnt die letzte Übung zu Hilfe nehmen. Gebt auch einen Grund dafür an!
DU   Ich hätte gern …
PARTNER   Und warum hast du das nicht getan?
DU   Ja, weil …
PARTNER   Schade!   oder   Ja, wirklich!   oder   Zu dumm!

Warum nicht?

zu viel Geld kosten
Eltern nicht erlauben
keine Zeit haben
krank sein
gar keine Lust dazu haben
nicht wissen, wie

9 Für mein Notizbuch

Schreiben Denk an drei Dinge, die du in letzter Zeit gern getan hättest! Gib Gründe an, warum sie nicht getan hast!

BEISPIEL   Gestern Abend hätte ich gern ferngesehen, aber leider war unser Fernseher kaputt, und ich hatte keine Lust, zu meiner Klassenkameradin zu gehen.

10 Was hältst du davon?

Schreiben/Sprechen Denk über folgende Fragen nach, und schreib die Antworten in Stichworten auf! Diskutiere darüber mit deinen Klassenkameraden!
1. Wie ist die Schule für dich? Leicht? Stressig? Warum?
2. Würdest du den Unterricht schwänzen, wenn du könntest?
3. Hast du schon einmal die Schule geschwänzt? Warum?
4. Was wird sich bei dir ändern, wenn du achtzehn wirst?
5. Was hat sich geändert, als du sechzehn geworden bist?
6. Freust du dich darauf, dass du mit achtzehn wählen darfst? Wen oder welche Partei würdest du wählen? Warum?
7. Bist du politisch aktiv oder wenigstens gut informiert? Kennst du Schüler, die sich politisch engagieren?
8. Wie wichtig ist für dich der Führerschein? Hast du schon den Führerschein? Wenn ja, was hast du alles machen müssen, um ihn zu bekommen?

11 Für mein Notizbuch

Schreiben Wähle eins der beiden Themen unten, und schreib einen Kurzbericht darüber!
1. Der Führerschein auf Probe ist eine gute Idee.
2. Jeder Schüler sollte sich ein wenig politisch engagieren.

ERSTE STUFE   STANDARDS: 1.3   *hundertsiebenundzwanzig*   **127**

Bringing Standards into the Classroom

by Paul Sandrock, Foreign Language Consultant, Wisconsin Department of Public Education

The core question that guided the development of the National Standards and their accompanying goals was simply: what matters in instruction?

Each proposed standard was evaluated. Did the standard target material that will have application beyond the classroom? Was the standard too specific or not specific enough? Teachers should be able to teach the standard and assess it in multiple ways. A standard needs to provide a target for instruction and learning throughout a student's K–12 education.

In the development of standards, foreign languages faced other unique challenges. The writers could not assume a K–12 sequence available to all students. In fact, unlike other disciplines, they could not guarantee that all students would experience even any common sequence.

From this context, the National Standards in Foreign Language Education Project's task force generated the five C's, five goals for learning languages: communication, cultures, connections, comparisons, and communities. First presented in 1995, the standards quickly became familiar to foreign language educators across the US, representing our professional consensus and capturing a broad view of the purposes for learning another language.

To implement the standards, however, requires a shift from emphasizing the means to focusing on the ends. It isn't a matter of grammar versus communication, but rather how much grammar is needed to communicate. Instead of teaching to a grammatical sequence, teaching decisions become based on what students need to know to achieve the communicative goal.

The Focus on Communication

The first standard redefined communication, making its purpose **interpersonal, interpretive,** and **presentational** communication. Teaching to the purpose of interpersonal communication takes us away from memorized dialogues to spontaneous, interactive conversation, where the message is most important and where meaning needs to be negotiated between the speakers. Interpretive communication is not an exercise in translation, but asks beginners to tell the gist of an authentic selection that is heard, read, or viewed, while increasingly advanced learners tell deeper and deeper levels of detail and can interpret based on their knowledge of the target culture. In the presentational mode of communication, the emphasis is on the audience, requiring the speaker or writer to adapt language to fit the situation and to allow for comprehension without any interactive negotiation of the meaning.

Standards challenge us to refocus many of the things we've been doing all along. The requirements of speaking and our expectation of how well students need to speak change when speaking is for a different purpose. This focus on the purpose of the communication changes the way we teach and test the skills of listening, speaking, reading, and writing.

Standards help us think about how to help students put the pieces of language to work in meaningful ways. Our

Standards for Foreign Language Learning

Communication Communicate in Languages Other than English	**Standard 1.1** Students engage in conversations, provide and obtain information, express feelings and emotions, and exchange opinions. **Standard 1.2** Students understand and interpret written and spoken language on a variety of topics. **Standard 1.3** Students present information, concepts, and ideas to an audience of listeners or readers on a variety of topics.
Cultures Gain Knowledge and Understanding of Other Cultures	**Standard 2.1** Students demonstrate an understanding of the relationship between the practices and perspectives of the culture studied. **Standard 2.2** Students demonstrate an understanding of the relationship between the products and perspectives of the culture studied.
Connections Connect with Other Disciplines and Acquire Information	**Standard 3.1** Students reinforce and further their knowledge of other disciplines through the foreign language. **Standard 3.2** Students acquire information and recognize the distinctive viewpoints that are only available through the foreign language and its cultures.
Comparisons Develop Insight into the Nature of Language and Culture	**Standard 4.1** Students demonstrate understanding of the nature of language through comparisons of the language studied and their own. **Standard 4.2** Students demonstrate understanding of the concept of culture through comparisons of the cultures studied and their own.
Communities Participate in Multilingual Communities at Home and Around the World	**Standard 5.1** Students use the language both within and beyond the school setting. **Standard 5.2** Students show evidence of becoming life-long learners by using the language for personal enjoyment and enrichment.

standards answer *why* we are teaching various components of language, and we select *what* we teach in order to achieve those very standards.

The 5 C's

Originally the five C's were presented as five equal circles. During the years since the national standards were printed, teachers implementing and using the standards to write curriculum, texts, and lesson plans have come to see that communication is at the core, surrounded by four C's that influence the context for teaching and assessing.

The four C's surrounding our core goal of **Communication** change our classrooms by bringing in real-life applications for the language learned:

- **Cultures:** Beyond art and literature, learning occurs in the context of the way of life, patterns of behavior, and contributions of the people speaking the language being taught.

- **Connections:** Beyond content limited to the culture of the people speaking the target language, teachers go out to other disciplines to find topics and ideas to form the context for language learning.

- **Comparisons:** Foreign language study is a great way for students to learn more about native language and universal principles of language and culture by comparing and contrasting their own to the target language and culture.

- **Communities:** This goal of the standards adds a broader motivation to the context for language learning. The teacher makes sure students use their new language beyond the class hour, seeking ways to experience the target culture.

Implementation at the Classroom Level: Assessment and Instruction

After the publication of the standards, states developed more specific performance standards that would provide evidence of the application of the national content standards. Standards provide the organizing principle for teaching and assessing. The standards-oriented teacher, when asked what she's teaching, cites the standard "students will sustain a conversation." With that clear goal in mind, she creates lessons to teach various strategies to ask for clarification and to practice asking follow-up questions that explore a topic in more depth.

Textbook writers and materials providers are responding to this shift. Standards provide our goals; the useful textbooks and materials give us an organization and a context. Standards provide the ends; textbooks and materials can help us practice the means. Textbooks can bring authentic materials into the classroom, real cultural examples that avoid stereotypes, and a broader exposure to the variety of people who speak the language being studied. Textbooks can model the kind of instruction that will lead students to successful demonstration of the knowledge and skill described in the standards.

To really know that standards are the focus, look at the assessment. If standards are the target, assessment won't consist only of evaluation of the means (grammatical structures and vocabulary) in isolation. If standards are the focus, teachers will assess students' use of the second language in context. The summative assessment of our target needs to go beyond the specific and include open-ended, personalized tasks. Regardless of how the students show what they can do, the teacher will be able to gauge each student's progress toward the goal.

Assessment is like a jigsaw puzzle. If we test students only on the means, we just keep collecting random puzzle pieces. We have to test, and students have to practice, putting the pieces together in meaningful and purposeful ways. In order to learn vocabulary that will help students "describe themselves," for example, students may have a quiz on Friday with an expectation of close to 100% accuracy. But if that is all we ever do with those ten words, they will quickly be gone from students' memory, and we will only have collected a puzzle piece from each student. It is absolutely essential to have students use those puzzle pieces to complete the puzzle to provide evidence of what they "can do" with the language.

During this period of implementing our standards, we've learned that the standards provide a global picture, the essence of our goals. But they are not curriculum, nor are they lesson plans. The standards influence how we teach, but do not dictate one content nor one methodology. How can we implement the standards in our classrooms? Think about the targets; think about how students will show achievement of those targets through our evaluation measures; then think about what we need to teach and how that will occur in our classrooms. Make it happen in your classroom to get the results we've always wanted: students who can communicate in a language other than English.

Reading Strategies and Skills

by Nancy Humbach, Miami University, Oxford, Ohio

Reading is the most enduring of the language skills. Long after a student ceases to study the language, the ability to read will continue to provide a springboard to the renewal of the other skills. We must consider all the ways in which our students will read and address the skills needed for those tasks.

How can we accomplish this goal? How can we, as teachers, present materials, encourage students to read, and at the same time foster understanding and build the student's confidence and interest in reading?

Selection of Materials

Reading material in the foreign language classroom should be relevant to students' backgrounds and at an accessible level of difficulty, i.e., at a level of difficulty only slightly above the reading ability of the student.

Authentic materials are generally a good choice. They provide cultural context and linguistic authenticity seldom found in materials created for students, and the authentic nature of the language provides a window on a new world. The problem inherent in the selection of authentic materials at early levels is obvious: the level of difficulty is frequently beyond the skill of the student. At the same time, however, readers are inspired by the fact that they can understand materials designed to be read by native speakers.

Presenting a Selection/ Reading Strategies

We assume that students of a second language already have a reading knowledge in their first language and that many of the skills they learned in their "reading readiness" days will serve them well. Too often, however, students have forgotten such skills as activating background knowledge, skimming, scanning, and guessing content based on context clues. Helping student to reactivate these skills is part of helping them become better readers.

Teachers should not assume their students' ability to transfer a knowledge set from one reading to another. Students use these skills on a regular basis, but often do not even realize they are doing so. To help students become aware of these processes, they need to be given strategies for reading. These strategies offer students a framework for the higher level skills they need to apply when reading. Strategies also address learners of different learning styles and needs.

Advance Organizers

One way to activate the student's background knowledge is through advance organizers. They also serve to address the student's initial frustrations at encountering an unfamiliar text.

Advance organizers call up pertinent background knowledge, feelings, and experiences that can serve to focus the attention of the entire group on a given topic. In addition, they provide for a sharing of information among the students. Background information that includes cultural references and cultural information can reactivate in students skills that will help them with a text and provide for them clues to the meaning of the material.

A good advance organizer will provide some information and guide students to think about the scenarios being presented. An advance organizer might include photographs, drawings, quotations, maps, or information about the area where the story takes place. It might also be posed as a question, for example, "What would you do if you found yourself in….?" Having students brainstorm in advance, either as a whole class or in small groups, allows them to construct a scenario which they can verify as they read.

Prereading Activities

Prereading activities remind students of how much they really know and can prepare students in a number of ways to experience the language with less frustration. While we know that we must choose a reading selection that is not far beyond students' experience and skill level, we also know that no group of students reads at the same level. In the interest of assisting students to become better language learners, we can provide them with opportunities to work with unfamiliar structures and vocabulary ahead of time.

Preparing students for a reading selection can include a number of strategies that may anticipate but not dwell on potential problems to be encountered by students. Various aspects of grammar, such as differences in the past tenses and the meanings conveyed, can also cause problems. Alerting students to some of the aspects of the language allows them to struggle less, understand more quickly, and enjoy a reading selection to a greater degree.

Grouping vocabulary by category or simply choosing a short list of critical words for a section of reading is helpful. Providing an entire list of vocabulary items at one time can be overwhelming. With a bit of organization, the task becomes manageable to the point where students begin to master words they will find repeated throughout the selection.

Teaching students to skim for a particular piece of information or to scan for words, phrases, indicators of place, time, name, and then asking them to write a sentence or two about the gist of a paragraph or story, allows them to gain a sense of independence and success before they begin to read.

Getting into the Assignment

Teachers can recount the times they have assigned a piece of reading for homework, only to find that few students even attempted the work. Therefore, many teachers choose to complete the reading in class. Homework assignments should then be structured to have the student return to the selection and complete a assignment that requires critical thinking and imagination.

During class, several techniques assist students in maintaining interest and attention to the task. By varying these techniques, the teacher can provide for a lively class, during which students realize they *are* able to read. Partners can read passages to each other or students can take turns reading in small groups. The teacher might pose a question to be answered during that reading. Groups might also begin to act out short scenes, reading only the dialogue. Student might read a description of a setting and then draw what they imagine it to be. Of course, some selections might be silent reading with a specific amount of time announced for completion.

Reading aloud for comprehension and reading aloud for pronunciation practice are two entirely unrelated tasks. We can all recount classes where someone read aloud to us from weary lecture notes. Active engagement of the readers, on the other hand, forces them to work for comprehension, for the development of thought processes, and for improvement of language skills.

Postreading Activities

It is important to provide students with an opportunity to expand the knowledge they have gained from the reading selection. Students should apply what they have learned to their own personal experiences. How we structure activities can provide students more opportunities to reflect on their reading and learn how much they have understood. We often consider a written test the best way to ensure comprehension; however, many other strategies allow students to keep oral skills active. These might include acting out impromptu scenes from the story and creating dialogues that do not exist in a story, but might be imagined, based on other information. Consider the possibility of debates, interviews, TV talk show formats, telephone dialogues, or a monologue in which the audience hears only one side of the conversation.

Written assignments are also valid assessment tools, allowing students to incorporate the vocabulary and structures they have learned in the reading. Students might be encouraged to write journal entries for a character, create a new ending, or retell the story from another point of view. Newspaper articles, advertisements, and other creations can also be a means of following up. Comparisons with other readings require students to keep active vocabulary and structures they have studied previously. Encourage students to read their creations aloud to a partner, to a group, or to the class.

Conclusion

Reading can be exciting. The combination of a good selection that is relevant and rates high on the interest scale, along with good preparation, guidance, and post-reading activities that demonstrate to the students the level of success attained, can encourage them to continue to read. These assignments also allow for the incorporation of other aspects of language learning, and incorporate the Five C's of the National Standards. Communication and culture are obvious links, but so are connections (advance organizers, settings, and so on), comparisons (with other works in the heritage or target language), and communities (learning why a type of writing is important in a culture).

Komm mit!

offers reading practice and develops reading skills and strategies in the following ways:

THE PUPIL'S EDITION

▸ Provides an extensive reading section in each chapter called **Zum Lesen**. Each **Zum Lesen** section offers a strategy students apply to an authentic text, as well as activities to guide understanding and exploration of the text.

THE TEACHER'S EDITION

▸ Provides teachers with additional activities and information in every **Zum Lesen** section. Additional suggestions are provided for Pre-reading, Reading, and Postreading activities.

THE ANCILLARY PROGRAM

▸ *Lies mit mir!* This component offers reading selections of various formats and difficulty levels. Each chapter has a prereading feature, a reading selection with comprehension questions, and two pages of activities.

▸ The *Reading Skills and Strategies Handbook* offers useful strategies that can be applied to reading selections in the *Pupil's Edition*, *Lies mit mir!*, or a selection of your choosing.

▸ The *Übungsheft* contains a reading selection, tied to the chapter theme, and reading activities for each chapter in *Komm mit!*

Using Portfolios in the Language Classroom

by JoAnne S. Wilson, J. Wilson Associates

Portfolios offer a more realistic and accurate way to assess the process of language teaching and learning.

The communicative, whole-language approach of today's language instruction requires assessment methods that parallel the teaching and learning strategies in the proficiency-oriented classroom. We know that language acquisition is a process. Portfolios are designed to assess the steps in that process.

What Is a Portfolio?

A portfolio is a purposeful, systematic collection of a student's work. A useful tool in developing a student profile, the portfolio shows the student's efforts, progress, and achievements for a given period of time. It may be used for periodic evaluation, as the basis for overall evaluation, or for placement. It may also be used to enhance or provide alternatives to traditional assessment measures, such as formal tests, quizzes, class participation, and homework.

Why Use Portfolios?

Portfolios benefit both students and teachers because they:

- **Are ongoing and systematic.** A portfolio reflects the real-world process of production, assessment, revision, and reassessment. It parallels the natural rhythm of learning.

- **Offer an incentive to learn.** Students have a vested interest in creating the portfolios, through which they can showcase their ongoing efforts and tangible achievements. Students select the works to be included and have a chance to revise, improve, evaluate, and explain the contents.

- **Are sensitive to individual needs.** Language learners bring varied abilities to the classroom and do not acquire skills in a uniformly neat and orderly fashion. The personalized, individualized assessment offered by portfolios responds to this diversity.

- **Provide documentation of language development.** The material in a portfolio is evidence of student progress in the language learning process. The contents of the portfolio make it easier to discuss their progress with the students as well as with parents and others.

- **Offer multiple sources of information.** A portfolio presents a way to collect and analyze information from multiple sources that reflects a student's efforts, progress, and achievements in the language.

Portfolio Components

The language portfolio should include both oral and written work, student self-evaluation, and teacher observation, usually in the form of brief, nonevaluative comments about various aspects of the student's performance.

The Oral Component

The oral component of a portfolio might be an audio- or videocassette. It may contain both rehearsed and extemporaneous monologues and conversations. For a rehearsed speaking activity, give a specific communicative task that students can personalize according to their individual interests (for example, ordering a favorite meal in a restaurant). If the speaking activity is extemporaneous, first acquaint students with possible topics for discussion or even the specific task they will be expected to perform. (For example, tell them they will be asked to discuss a picture showing a sports activity or a restaurant scene.)

The Written Component

Portfolios are excellent tools for incorporating process writing strategies into the language classroom. Documentation of various stages of the writing process—brainstorming, multiple drafts, and peer comments—may be included with the finished product.

Involve students in selecting writing tasks for the portfolio. At the beginning levels, the tasks might include some structured writing, such as labeling or listing. As students become more proficient, journals, letters, and other more complicated writing tasks are valuable ways for them to monitor their progress in using the written language.

Student Self-Evaluation

Students should be actively involved in critiquing and evaluating their portfolios and monitoring their own progress.

The process and procedure for student self-evaluation should be considered in planning the contents of the portfolio. Students should work with you and their peers to design the exact format. Self-evaluation encourages them to think about what they are learning (content), how they learn (process), why they are learning (purpose), and where they are going in their learning (goals).

Teacher Observation

Systematic, regular, and ongoing observations should be placed in the portfolio after they have been discussed with the student. These observations provide feedback on the student's progress in the language learning process.

Teacher observations should be based on an established set of criteria that has been developed earlier with input from the student. Observation techniques may include the following:

- Jotting notes in a journal to be discussed with the student and then placed in the portfolio

- Using a checklist of observable behaviors, such as the willingness to take risks when using the target language or staying on task during the lesson

- Making observations on adhesive notes that can be placed in folders

- Recording anecdotal comments, during or after class, using a cassette recorder.

Knowledge of the criteria you use in your observations gives students a framework for their performance.

Electronic Portfolios

Technology can provide help with managing student portfolios. Digital or computer-based portfolios offer a means of saving portfolios in an electronic format. Students can save text, drawings, photographs, graphics, audio or video recordings, or any combination of multimedia information. Teachers can create their own portfolio templates or consult one of the many commercial software programs available to create digital portfolios. Portfolios saved on videotapes or compact discs provide a convenient way to access and store students' work. By employing technology, this means of alternative assessment addresses the learning styles and abilities of individual students. Additionally, electronic portfolios can be shared among teachers, and parents have the ability to easily see the students' progress.

Logistically, the hypermedia equipment and software available for students' use determine what types of entries will be included in the portfolios. The teacher or a team of teachers and students may provide the computer support.

How Are Portfolios Evaluated?

The portfolio should reflect the process of student learning over a specific period of time. At the beginning of that time period, determine the criteria by which you will assess the final product and convey them to the students. Make this evaluation a collaborative effort by seeking students' input as you formulate these criteria and your instructional goals.

Students need to understand that evaluation based on a predetermined standard is but one phase of the assessment process; demonstrated effort and growth are just as important. As you consider correctness and accuracy in both oral and written work, also consider the organization, creativity, and improvement revealed by the student's portfolio over the time period. The portfolio provides a way to monitor the growth of a student's knowledge, skills, and attitudes and shows the student's efforts, progress, and achievements.

How to Implement Portfolios

Teacher-teacher collaboration is as important to the implementation of portfolios as teacher-student collaboration. Confer with your colleagues to determine, for example, what kinds of information you want to see in the student portfolio, how the information will be presented, the purpose of the portfolio, the intended purposes (grading, placement, or a combination of the two), and criteria for evaluating the portfolio. Conferring among colleagues helps foster a departmental cohesiveness and consistency that will ultimately benefit the students.

The Promise of Portfolios

The high degree of student involvement in developing portfolios and deciding how they will be used generally results in renewed student enthusiasm for learning and improved achievement. As students compare portfolio pieces done early in the year with work produced later, they can take pride in their progress as well as reassess their motivation and work habits.

Komm mit!

supports the use of portfolios in the following ways:

THE PUPIL'S EDITION

▸ Includes numerous oral and written activities that can be easily adapted for student portfolios, such as **Notizbuch, Zum Schreiben,** and **Rollenspiel.**

THE TEACHER'S EDITION

▸ Suggests activities in the Portfolio Assessment feature that may serve as portfolio items.

THE ANCILLARY PROGRAM

▸ Includes criteria in the *Alternative Assessment Guide* for evaluating portfolios.

▸ Provides Speaking Tests in the *Testing Program* for each chapter that can be adapted for use as portfolio assessment items.

Multi-Level Classrooms

by Joan H. Manley, University of Texas at El Paso

There are positive ways, both psychological and pedagogical, to make this situation work for you and your students.

So you have just heard that your third-period class is going to include both Levels 2 and 3! While this is never the best news for a foreign language teacher, there are positive ways, both psychological and pedagogical, to make the multi-level classroom work for you and your students.

Relieving student anxieties

Initially, in a multi-level class environment, it is important to relieve students' anxiety by orienting them to their new situation. From the outset, let all students know that just because they "did" things the previous year, such as learn how to conjugate certain verbs, they may not yet be able to use them in a meaningful way. Students should not feel that it is demeaning or a waste of time to recycle activities or to share knowledge and skills with fellow students. Second-year students need to know they are not second-class citizens and that they can benefit from their classmates' greater experience with the language. Third-year students may achieve a great deal of satisfaction and become more confident in their own language skills when they have opportunities to help or teach their second-year classmates. It is important to reassure third-year students that you will devote time to them and challenge them with different assignments.

Easing your own apprehension

When you are faced with both Levels 2 and 3 in your classroom, remind yourself that you teach students of different levels in the same classroom every year, although not officially. After one year of classroom instruction, your Level 2 class will never be a truly homogeneous group. Despite being made up of students with the same amount of "seat time," the class comprises multiple layers of language skills, knowledge, motivation, and ability. Therefore, you are constantly called upon to make a positive experience out of a potentially negative one. Your apprehension will gradually diminish to the extent that you are able to …

- make students less dependent on you for the successful completion of their activities.
- place more responsibility for learning on the students.
- implement creative group, pair, and individual activities.

How can you do this? Good organization will help. Lessons will need to be especially well-planned for the multi-level class. The following lesson plan is an example of how to treat the same topic with students of two different levels.

Teaching a lesson in a multi-level classroom

Lesson objectives:
Relate an incident in the past that you regret.

- Level 2: Express surprise and sympathy.
- Level 3: Offer encouragement and make suggestions.

Lesson plan

1. **Review and/or teach the past tense.**
   Present the formation of the past tense. Model its use for the entire class or call upon Level 3 students to give examples.

2. **Practice the past tense.**
   Have Level 3 students who have mastered the past tense teach it to Level 2 students in pairs or small groups. Provide the Level 3 student instructors with several drill and practice activities they may use for this purpose.

3. **Relate your own regrettable past experience.**
   Recount a personal regrettable incident—real or imaginary—to the entire class as a model. For example, you may have left your automobile lights on, and when you came out of school, the battery was dead and you couldn't start your car. Or you may have scolded a student for not doing the homework and later discovered the student had a legitimate reason for not completing the assignment.

4. **Prepare and practice written and oral narratives.**

   Have Level 2 students pair off with Level 3 students. Each individual writes about his or her experience, the Level 3 partner serving as a resource for the Level 2 student. Partners then edit each other's work and listen to each other's oral delivery. You might choose to have students record their oral narratives.

5. **Present communicative functions.**

   A. Ask for a volunteer to recount his or her own regrettable incident for the entire class.

   B. Model reactions to the volunteer's narrative.
   (1) Express surprise and sympathy (for Level 2): "Really! That's too bad!"
   (2) Offer encouragement and make suggestions (for Level 3): "Don't worry!" "You can still…."

6. **Read narratives and practice communicative functions.**

   Have Level 2 students work together in one group or in small groups, listening to classmates' stories and reacting with the prescribed communicative function. Have Level 3 students do the same among themselves. Circulate among the groups, listening, helping, and assessing.

7. **Assess progress.**

   Repeat your personal account for the entire class and elicit reactions from students according to their level. Challenge students to respond with communicative functions expected of the other level if they can.

Every part of the above lesson plan is important. Both levels have been accommodated. The teacher has not dominated the lesson. Students have worked together in pairs and small groups, while Level 3 students have helped their Level 2 classmates. Individual groups still feel accountable, both within their level and across levels.

Any lesson can be adapted in this way. It takes time and effort, but the result is a student-centered classroom where students share and grow, and the teacher is the facilitator.

Komm mit!

addresses the *multi-level classroom* in the following ways:

THE PUPIL'S EDITION

▸ Provides creative activities for pair and group work that allow students at different levels to work together and learn form one another.

THE TEACHER'S EDITION

▸ Offers practical suggestions for *Projects* and *Cooperative Learning* that engage students of different levels.

▸ Provides a clear, comprehensive outline of the functions, vocabulary, and grammar that are recycled in each chapter. The *Chapter Overview* of each chapter is especially helpful to the teacher who is planning integrated or varied lessons in the multi-level classroom.

THE ANCILLARY PROGRAM

▸ Provides a variety of materials and activities to accommodate different levels in a multi-level classroom.

Teaching Culture

by Nancy A. Humbach, Miami University, and Dorothea Bruschke, Parkway School District

We must integrate culture and language in a way that encourages curiosity, stimulates analysis, and teaches students to hypothesize.

The teaching of culture has undergone some important and welcome changes in recent years. Instead of teaching the standard notions of cultures, language and regions, we now stress the teaching of analysis and the critical thinking skills required to evaluate a culture, not by comparing it to one's own, but within its own setting. The setting includes the geography, climate, history, and influences of peoples who have interacted within that cultural group.

The National Standards for the Teaching of Foreign Languages suggests organizing the teaching of culture into three categories: products, practices, and perspectives. Through the presentation of these aspects of culture, students should gain the skill to analyze the culture, evaluate it within its context, compare it to their culture and develop the ability to function comfortably in that culture.

Skill and practice in the analysis of cultural phenomena equip students to enter a cultural situation, assess it, create strategies for dealing with it and accepting it as a natural part of the people. The ultimate goal of this philosophy is to reduce the "we vs. they" approach to culture. If students are encouraged to accept and appreciate the diversity of other cultures, they will be more willing and better able to develop the risk-taking strategies necessary to learn a language and to interact with people of different cultures.

There are many ways to help students become culturally knowledgeable and to assist them in developing an awareness of differences and similarities between the target culture and their own. Two of these approaches involve critical thinking, that is, trying to find reasons for a certain behavior through observation and analysis, and putting individual observations into larger cultural patterns. We must integrate culture and language in a way that encourages curiosity, stimulates analysis, and teaches students to hypothesize.

First Approach: Questioning

The first approach involves *questioning* as the key strategy. At the earliest stages of language learning, students learn ways to greet peers, elders, strangers, as well as the use of **du, ihr,** and **Sie.** Students need to consider questions such as: How do German-speaking people greet each other? Are there different levels of formality? Who initiates a handshake? What's considered a good handshake? Each of these questions leads students to think about the values that are expressed through words and gestures. They start to "feel" the other culture, and at the same time, understand how much of their own behavior is rooted in their cultural background.

Magazines, newspapers, advertisements, and television commercials are all excellent sources of cultural material. For example, browsing through a German magazine, one finds an extraordinary number of advertisements for health-related products. Could this indicate a great interest in staying healthy? To learn about customs involving health, reading advertisements can be followed up with viewing videos and films, or by interviewing native speakers or people who have lived in German-speaking countries. Students might want to find answers to questions such as: "How do Germans treat a cold? What is their attitude toward fresh air? Toward exercise?" This type of questioning might lead students to discover that some of the popular leisure-time activities, such as **einen Spaziergang machen** or **eine Wanderung machen,** are related to health consciousness.

An advertisement for a refrigerator or a picture of a German kitchen can provide an insight into practices of shopping for food. Students first need to think about the refrigerator at home, take an inventory of what is kept in it, and consider when and where their family shops. Next, students should look closely at a German refrigerator. What is its size? What could that mean? (Smaller refrigerators might mean that shopping takes place more often, stores are within walking distance, and people eat more fresh foods.)

Food wrappers and containers also provide cultural insight. For example, in German-speaking countries, bottled water is preferred to tap water even though tap water is safe to drink in most places. Why, then, is the rather expensive bottled water still preferred? Is it a tradition stemming from a time when tap water was not pure? Does it relate to the Germans' fondness of "taking the waters," i.e., drinking fresh spring water at a spa?

Second Approach: Associating Words with Images

The second approach for developing cultural understanding involves *forming associations of words with the cultural images they suggest.* Language and culture are so closely related that one might actually say that language is culture. Most words, especially nouns, carry a cultural connotation. Knowing the literal equivalent of a word in another language is of little use to students in understanding this connotation. For example, **Freund** cannot be translated simply as *friend,* **Brot** as *bread,* or **Straße** as *street.* The German word **Straße,** for instance, carries with it such images as people walking, sitting in a sidewalk café, riding bicycles, or shopping in specialty stores, and cars parked partly over the curb amid dense traffic. There is also the image of **Fußgängerzone,** a street for pedestrians only.

When students have acquired some sense of the cultural connotation of words—not only through explanations but, more importantly, through observation of visual images—they start to discover the larger underlying cultural themes, or what is often called deep culture.

These larger cultural themes serve as organizing categories into which individual cultural phenomena fit to form a pattern. Students might discover, for example, that Germans, because they live in much more crowded conditions, have a great need for privacy (cultural theme), as reflected in such phenomena as closed doors, fences or walls around property, and shutters on windows. Students might also discover that love of nature and the outdoors is an important cultural theme as indicated by such phenomena as flower boxes and planters in public places, well-kept public parks in every town, and people going for a walk or hiking.

As we teach culture, students learn to recognize elements not only of the target culture but also of their American cultural heritage. They see how elements of culture reflect larger themes or patterns. Learning what makes us Americans and how that information relates to other people throughout the world can be an exciting discovery for a young person.

As language teachers, we are able to facilitate this discovery of our similarities with others as well as our differences. We do not encourage value judgments about others and their culture, nor do we recommend adopting other ways. We simply say to students, "Other ways exist. They exist, just as our ways exist, due to our history, geography, and what our ancestors have passed on to us through traditions and values."

Komm mit!

develops *cultural understanding and cultural awareness* in the following ways:

THE PUPIL'S EDITION

▸ Informs students about daily life in German-speaking countries through culture notes.

▸ Provides deeper insight into cultural phenomena through personal interviews in the **Landeskunde** section.

▸ Helps students associate language and its cultural connotations through authentic art and photos.

THE TEACHER'S EDITION

▸ Provides additional cultural and language notes and background information.

▸ Suggests critical thinking strategies that encourage students to hypothesize, analyze, and discover larger underlying cultural themes.

THE ANCILLARY PROGRAM

▸ Includes realia to develop cultural insight by serving as catalyst for questioning and discovery.

▸ Offers activities that require students to compare and contrast cultures.

▸ Provides songs, short readings, and poems, as well as many opportunities for students to experience regional variation and idioms in the accompanying reader **Lies mit mir! 3** as well as in the video and audio programs. The use of German Web sites in the **Internet Aktivitäten** provides an additional source for cultural understanding.

Learning Styles and Multi-Modality Teaching

by Mary B. McGehee, Louisiana State University

Incorporating a greater variety of activities to accommodate the learning styles of all students can make the difference between struggle and pleasure in the foreign language classroom.

The larger and broader population of students who are enrolling in foreign language classes brings a new challenge to foreign language educators, calling forth an evolution in teaching methods to enhance learning for all our students. Educational experts now recognize that every student has a preferred sense for learning and retrieving information: visual, auditory, or kinesthetic. Incorporating a greater variety of activities to accommodate the learning styles of all students can make the difference between struggle and pleasure in the foreign language classroom.

Accommodating Different Learning Styles

A modified arrangement of the classroom is one way to provide more effective and enjoyable learning for all students. Rows of chairs and desks must give way at times to circles, semicircles, or small clusters. Students may be grouped in fours or in pairs for cooperative work or peer teaching. It is important to find a balance of arrangements, thereby providing the most comfort in varied situations.

Since visual, auditory, and kinesthetic learners will be in the class, and because every student's learning will be enhanced by a multi-sensory approach, lessons must be directed toward all three learning styles. Any language lesson content may be presented visually, aurally, or kinesthetically.

Visual presentations and practice may include the chalkboard, charts, posters, television, overhead projectors, books, magazines, picture diagrams, flash cards, bulletin boards, films, slides, or videos. Visual learners need to see what they are to learn. Lest the teacher think he or she will never have the time to prepare all those visuals, Dickel and Slak (1983) found that visual aids generated by students are more effective than ready-made ones.

Auditory presentations and practice may include stating aloud the requirements of the lesson, oral questions and answers, paired or group work on a progression of oral exercises from repetition to communication, tapes, CDs, dialogues, and role-playing. Jingles, catchy stories, and memory devices using songs and rhymes are good learning aids. Having students record themselves and then listen as they play back the cassette allows them to practice in the auditory mode.

Kinesthetic presentations entail the students' use of manipulatives, chart materials, gestures, signals, typing, songs, games, and role-playing. These lead the students to associate sentence constructions with meaningful movements.

A Sample Lesson Using Multi-Modality Teaching

A multi-sensory presentation on greetings might proceed as follows:

For Visual Learners

As the teacher begins oral presentation of greetings and introductions, he or she simultaneously shows the written forms on transparencies, with the formal expressions marked with an adult's hat, and the informal expressions marked with a baseball cap.

The teacher then distributes cards with the hat and cap symbols representing the formal and informal expressions. As the students hear taped mini-dialogues, they hold up the appropriate card to indicate whether the dialogues are formal or informal. On the next listening, the students repeat the sentences they hear.

For Auditory Learners

A longer taped dialogue follows, allowing the students to hear the new expressions a number of times. They write from dictation several sentences containing the new expressions. They may work in pairs, correcting each other's work as they "test" their own understanding of the lesson at hand. Finally, students respond to simple questions using the appropriate formal and informal responses cued by the cards they hold.

For Kinesthetic Learners

For additional kinesthetic input, members of the class come to the front of the room, each holding a hat or cap symbol. As the teacher calls out situations, the students play the roles, using gestures and props appropriate to the age group they are portraying. Non-cued, communicative role-playing with props further enables the students to "feel" the differences between formal and informal expressions.

Helping Students Learn How to Use Their Preferred Mode

Since we require all students to perform in all language skills, part of the assistance we must render is to help them develop strategies within their preferred learning modes to carry out an assignment in another mode. For example, visual students hear the teacher assign an oral exercise and visualize what they must do. They must see themselves carrying out the assignment, in effect watching themselves as if there were a movie going on in their heads. Only then can they also hear themselves saying the right things. Thus, this assignment will be much easier for the visual learners who have been taught this process, if they have not already figured it out for themselves. Likewise, true auditory students, confronted with a reading/writing assignment, must talk themselves through it, converting the entire process into sound as they plan and prepare their work. Kinesthetic students presented with a visual or auditory task must first break the assignment into tasks and then work their way through them.

Students who experience difficulty because of a strong preference for one mode of learning are often unaware of the degree of preference. In working with these students, I prefer the simple and direct assessment of learning styles offered by Richard Bandler and John Grinder in their book *Frogs into Princes*, which allows the teacher and student to quickly determine how the student learns. In an interview with the student, I follow the assessment with certain specific recommendations of techniques to make the student's study time more effective.

It is important to note here that teaching students to maximize their study does not require that the teacher give each student an individualized assignment. It does require that each student who needs it be taught how to prepare the assignment using his or her own talents and strengths. This communication between teacher and student, combined with teaching techniques that reinforce learning in all modes, can only maximize pleasure and success in learning a foreign language.

References

Dickel, M.J. and S. Slak. "Imaging Vividness and Memory for Verbal Material." *Journal of Mental Imagery* 7, i (1983):121–126.

Bandler, Richard, and John Grinder. *Frogs into Princes.* Real People Press, Moab, UT. 1978.

Komm mit!

accommodates different learning styles in the following ways:

THE PUPIL'S EDITION

▸ Presents basic material in audio, video, print, and online formats.

▸ Includes role-playing activities and a variety of multi-modal activities, including an extensive listening strand and many art-based activities.

THE TEACHER'S EDITION

▸ Provides suggested activities for visual, auditory, and kinesthetic learners as well as suggestions for slower-paced learning and challenge activities.

▸ Includes Total Physical Response activities.

THE ANCILLARY PROGRAM

▸ Provides additional reinforcement activities for a variety of learning styles.

▸ Presents a rich blend of audiovisual input through the video program, audio program, transparencies, blackline masters and Internet activities.

Professional References

The Professional References section provides you with information about many resources that can enrich your German class. Included are addresses of German government and tourist offices, pen pal organizations, subscription agencies, and many others. Since addresses change frequently, you may want to verify them before you send your requests.

PEN PAL ORGANIZATIONS

The Student Letter Exchange will arrange pen pals for your students. For the names of other pen pal groups, contact your local chapter of AATG. There are fees involved, so be sure to write for information.

Student Letter Exchange (League of Friendship)
211 Broadway, Suite 201
Lynbrook, NY 11563
(516) 887-8628

EMBASSIES AND CONSULATES

Embassy of the Federal Republic of Germany
4645 Reservoir Rd. N.W.
Washington, D.C. 20007-1998
(202) 298-4000

Consulate General of the Federal Republic of Germany
460 Park Avenue
New York, NY 10022-1971
(212) 308-8700
(also in Atlanta, Boston, Chicago, Detroit, Houston, Los Angeles, San Francisco, Seattle)

Embassy of Austria
3524 International Court N.W.
Washington, D.C. 20008
(202) 895-6700

Austrian Consulate General
31 East 69th Street
New York, NY 10021
(212) 737-6400
(also in Los Angeles and Chicago)

Embassy of Switzerland
2900 Cathedral Ave. NW
Washington, DC 20008
(202) 745-7900

Consulate General of Switzerland
665 5th Av. 8th Floor
New York, NY 10022
(212) 758-2560
(also in San Francisco, Los Angeles, Atlanta, Houston, Chicago)

CULTURAL AGENCIES

For historic and tourist information and audiovisual materials relating to Austria, contact:

Austrian Cultural Institute
950 Third Avenue
New York, NY 10022
(212) 759-5165

Material on political matters is available from **Bundeszentrale für politische Bildung,** a German federal agency.

Bundeszentrale für politische Bildung
Berliner Freiheit 7
53111 Bonn, GERMANY
(0228) 5150

For free political, cultural, and statistical information, films, and videos, contact:

German Information Center
871 United Nations Plaza
New York, NY 10017
(212) 610-9800

For various materials and information about special events your classes might attend, contact the **Goethe Institut** nearest you. For regional locations, contact:

Goethe Haus, German Cultural Center
1014 Fifth Avenue
New York, NY 10028
(212) 439-8700

The **Institut für Auslandsbeziehungen** provides cultural information to foreigners. The institute offers books and periodicals on a limited basis as well as a variety of two- and three-week professional seminars which allow educators to learn about the people, education, history, and culture of German-speaking countries.

Institut für Auslandsbeziehungen
Charlottenplatz 17
70173 Stuttgart, GERMANY
(0711) 2225-147

Inter Nationes, a nonprofit German organization for promoting international relations, supplies material on all aspects of life in Germany (literature, posters, magazines, press releases, films, slides, audio and video tapes) to educational institutions and organizations abroad.

Inter Nationes
Kennedyallee 91-103
53175 Bonn, GERMANY
(0228) 8800

TOURIST BUREAUS

Write to the following tourist offices for travel information and brochures.

German National Tourist Office
122 East 42nd St. 52nd Floor
New York, NY 10168
(212) 661-7200
(also in Chicago and San Francisco)

Deutsche Zentrale für Tourismus e.V.
Beethovenstraße 69
60325 Frankfurt GERMANY
(609) 974840

Switzerland Tourism
608 Fifth Avenue
New York, NY 10020
(212) 757-5944

PROFESSIONAL ORGANIZATIONS

The two major organizations for German teachers at the secondary school level are:

American Council on the Teaching of Foreign Languages (ACTFL)
6 Executive Plaza
Yonkers, NY 10701
(914) 963-8830

American Association of Teachers of German (AATG)
112 Haddontowne Court
Suite 104
Cherry Hill, NJ 08034
(609) 795-5553

PERIODICALS

Following are some periodicals published in German. For the names of other German magazines and periodicals contact a subscription agency.

Deutschland Nachrichten, a weekly newsletter available in both German and English, is published by the German Information Center *(see address under Cultural Agencies).*

Goethe Haus *(see address under Cultural Agencies)* publishes **Treffpunkt Deutsch,** a magazine of information, bibliographies, and ideas for teachers.

Bundeszentrale für politische Bildung *(see address under Cultural Agencies)* publishes **Politische Zeitung (PZ),** a quarterly magazine covering issues of social interest.

The Austrian Press and Information Service publishes a monthly newsletter. Write to:

Austrian Information
3524 International Court N.W.
Washington, D.C. 20008

Juma classroom magazine is a free publication to which you can subscribe. You can order multiple copies by writing to:

Redaktion Juma
Frankfurter Straße 40
51065 Köln, GERMANY
(0221) 962513-0

SUBSCRIPTION SERVICES

German magazines can be obtained through subscription agencies in the United States. The following companies are among the many which can provide you with subscriptions:

EBSCO Subscription Services
P.O. Box 1943
Birmingham, AL 35201-1943
(205) 991-6600

Continental Book Company
8000 Cooper Ave. Bldg. 29
Glendale, NY 11385
(718) 326-0572

EXCHANGE PROGRAMS

German American Partnership Program (GAPP)
c/o Goethe-Institut New York
1014 Fifth Avenue
New York, NY 10028
(212) 439-8715

Experiment in International Living
World Learning
Kipling Road, P.O. Box 676
Brattleboro, VT 05302-0676
(802) 257-7751 or
(800) 345-2929

MISCELLANEOUS

(ADAC) Allgemeiner Deutscher Automobil Club
Am Westpark 8
81373 München, GERMANY
(089) 76760

For students who want to find a summer job in Germany, write to:

Zentralstelle für Arbeitsvermittlung (ZAV)
Dienststelle 08100
Postfach 170545
60079 Frankfurt, GERMANY
(069) 71110
(Applicants must have a good knowledge of German.)

For international student passes and other student services contact:

CIEE Student Travel Services
205 E. 42nd Street
New York, NY 10017-5706
(212) 822-2700
(has branch offices in several other large cities)

A Bibliography for the German Teacher

This bibliography is a compilation of several resources available for professional enrichment.

SELECTED AND ANNOTATED LIST OF READINGS

I. Methods and Approaches

Cohen, A. (1994). *Assessing language ability in the classroom* **(2nd ed.). Boston: Heinle and Heinle.**

- An introduction to assessing students' foreign language ability. Discussions of various assessment techniques including role-playing activities, portfolios, and oral interviews provide instructors with alternatives to more traditional testing techniques. Computer-based testing is also examined.

Lafayette, R. (Ed.). (1996). *National standards: A catalyst for reform.* **Lincolnwood, IL: National Textbook Co.**

- Provides an outline of the National Standards movement and its implications for the modern foreign language classroom. Issues such as technology, teacher training, materials development, and the changing learning environment are each addressed in terms of the national standards.

Lee, J., & VanPatten, B. (1995). *Making communicative language teaching happen.* **New York: McGraw-Hill.**

- Discussion of communicative language teaching centered on a task-based approach to second language education. The authors provide both a theoretical and a practical framework for teaching the four skills (reading, writing, listening, speaking). The book includes some two hundred activities as well as test sections to help instructors encourage communicative interaction in their classrooms.

Omaggio Hadley, A. (1993). *Teaching language in context* **(2nd ed.). Boston: Heinle and Heinle Publishers.**

- Overview of the proficiency movement as well as a survey of past foreign language teaching methods and approaches. The author briefly presents the theory and history of the proficiency movement and then applies these concepts to each of the five skills in foreign language education. Includes sample activities, teaching suggestions, summaries, and references for further reading.

II. Second-Language Theory

Brown, H. D. (1994). *Principles of language learning and teaching* **(3rd ed.). Englewood Cliffs, NJ: Prentice Hall Regents**

- Addresses the cognitive, psychological, and sociocultural factors influencing the language learning process. Also includes theories of learning, styles and strategies, motivation, and culture; as well as an introduction to assessment, error analysis, communicative competence, and theories of acquisition along with practical vignettes describing classroom applications.

Ellis, R. (1994). *The study of second language acquisition.* **Oxford: Oxford University Press.**

- Provides an overview of second language acquisition: error analysis, acquisition orders, social factors, affective variables, individual differences, and the advantages and disadvantages of classroom instruction.

Krashen, S. (1987). *Principles and practice in second language acquisition.* **New York: Prentice-Hall.**

- Summary and discussion of Krashen's Monitor Model and its implications for foreign language instruction. Krashen discusses each of his five hypotheses regarding second language acquisition and their implications for the foreign language classroom.

III. Technology Enhanced Language Learning

Bush, M., & Terry, R. (Eds.). (1997). *Technology enhanced language learning.* **Lincolnwood, IL: National Textbook Co.**

Muyskens, J. (Ed.). (1997). *New ways of learning and teaching: Focus on technology and foreign language education.* **Boston: Heinle and Heinle.**

- Both works include articles on application of technology in the modern foreign language classroom. Topics include: multimedia, electronic discussions and computer-mediated communication, the WWW, videos, hypermedia, and the Internet. The authors describe techniques for applying these tools to all aspects of foreign language learning including reading, writing, listening, speaking, and culture. Questions of implementation, teacher training, and language laboratories are also discussed.

IV. Professional Journals

Calico
(Published by the Computer Assisted Language Instruction Consortium)

- Emphasizes applications of technology to foreign language learning. Articles include research on computer assisted language learning, videos and television in the classroom, and the use of the Internet and the WWW for learning and instruction.

Foreign Language Annals
(Published by the American Council on the Teaching of Foreign Languages)

- Publishes both research-based and practical articles on foreign language instruction and learning. In addition to learning and teaching strategies and methods, the journal also features articles on curriculum development and recent trends in foreign language pedagogy.

The IALL Journal of Language Learning Technologies
(Published by the International Association for Learning Laboratories)

- Practical and theoretical articles on technology and language instruction with emphasis on the effective use of media centers for language teaching, learning, and research.

The Modern Language Journal

- Features articles on the most recent research in the fields of language learning and second language acquisition.

Die Unterrichtspraxis
(Published by the American Association of Teachers of German)

- Emphasizes practical reports of successful pedagogical methods and strategies. Ideas for the German language classroom can be found in every issue along with reports on the current state of German studies in the United States.

Komm mit! ®

HOLT GERMAN

LEVEL **3**

HOLT, RINEHART AND WINSTON

A Harcourt Classroom Education Company

Austin • New York • Orlando • Atlanta • San Francisco • Boston • Dallas • Toronto • London

EXECUTIVE EDITOR
George Winkler

SENIOR EDITOR
Konstanze Alex Brown

MANAGING EDITOR
Chris Hiltenbrand

EDITORIAL STAFF
Sara Anbari
Sunday Ballew
Mark Eells,
  Editorial Coordinator
Augustine Agwuele,
  Department Intern

EDITORIAL PERMISSIONS
Janet Harrington,
  Permissions Editor

ART, DESIGN, & PHOTO
BOOK DESIGN
Richard Metzger,
  Design Director
Marta L. Kimball,
  Design Manager
Virginia Hassell
Andrew Lankes
Alicia Sullivan
Ruth Limon

IMAGE SERVICES
Joe London, *Director*
Tim Taylor, *Photo Research*
  Supervisor
Stephanie Friedman
Michelle Rumpf, *Art Buyer*
  Supervisor
Coco Weir

DESIGN NEW MEDIA
Susan Michael, *Design Director*
Amy Shank, *Design Manager*
Kimberly Cammerata,
  Design Manager
Czeslaw Sornat,
  Senior Designer
Grant Davidson

MEDIA DESIGN
Curtis Riker, *Design Director*
Richard Chavez

GRAPHIC SERVICES
Kristen Darby, *Manager*
Linda Wilbourn
Jane Dixon
Dean Hsieh

COVER DESIGN
Richard Metzger,
  Design Director
Candace Moore,
  Senior Designer

PRODUCTION
Amber McCormick,
  Production Supervisor
Diana Rodriguez,
  Production Coordinator

MANUFACTURING
Shirley Cantrell, *Supervisor,*
  Inventory & Manufacturing
Deborah Wisdom, *Senior*
  Inventory Analyst

NEW MEDIA
Jessica Bega, *Senior Project*
  Manager
Lydia Doty, *Senior Project*
  Manager
Elizabeth Kline, *Senior Project*
  Manager

VIDEO PRODUCTION
Video materials produced by
Edge Productions, Inc.,
Aiken, S.C.

ACKNOWLEDGMENTS
Front cover: (bkgd), Morton Beebe/Corbis; (c), Steve Ewert/HRW Photo

Back cover: (c), Hans Wolf/The Image Bank; (c), © 2003 Image Farm, Inc.

Title page: (c), Steve Ewert/HRW Photo.

For permission to reprint copyrighted material, grateful acknowledgment is made to the following sources:

Alibaba Verlag GmbH, Frankfurt am Main: "Sabines Eltern" by Mustafa S. From *Wir leben hier!* edited by Ulrike Holler and Anne Teuter. Copyright © 1992 by Alibaba Verlag GmbH.

Baars Kaas Marketing GmbH: Advertisement, "Da haben wir den Salat…kein Leerdammer im Haus," from freundin, 14/94, June 6, 1994, p. 149.

Acknowledgments continued on page 446, which is an extension of the copyright page

AUTHOR
George Winkler
Austin, TX

Mr. Winkler developed the scope and sequence and framework for the chapters, created the basic material, selected realia, and wrote activities.

CONTRIBUTING WRITERS
Margrit Meinel Diehl
Syracuse, NY

Mrs. Diehl wrote activities to practice basic material, functions, grammar, and vocabulary.

Patricia Casey Sutcliffe
Austin, TX

Mrs. Sutcliffe wrote the process writing activities for the **Zum Schreiben** feature.

Carolyn Roberts Thompson
Abilene Christian University
Abilene, TX

Mrs. Thompson was responsible for the selection of readings and for developing reading activities.

CONSULTANTS
The consultants conferred on a regular basis with the editorial staff and reviewed all the chapters of the Level 3 textbook.

Dorothea Bruschke, retired
Parkway School District
Chesterfield, MO

Diane E. Laumer
San Marcos High School
San Marcos, TX

Phyllis Manning
Vancouver, WA

Ingeborg H. McCoy
Southwest Texas State University
San Marcos, TX

REVIEWERS
The following educators reviewed one or more chapters of the Pupil's Edition.

Nancy Butt
Washington and Lee High School
Arlington, VA

Susan DeBoard
Conway High School
Conway, AR

Joan Gosenheimer
Franklin High School
Franklin, WI

Jacqueline Hastay
Lyndon Baines Johnson High School
Austin, TX

Jan L. Haverty
Blue Valley North High School
Leawood, KS

Carol Masters
Edison High School
Tulsa, OK

Linnea Maulding
Fife High School
Tacoma, WA

Amy McMahon
Parkway Central High School
Chesterfield, MO

David A. Miller
Parkway South High School
Manchester, MO

Linda Miller
Craig High School
Janesville, WI

Mike Miller
Cheyenne Mountain Junior High
Colorado Springs, CO

Doug Mills
Greensburg Central Catholic
High School
Greensburg, PA

Rolf Schwägermann
Stuyvesant High School
New York, NY

Mary Ann Verkamp
Hamilton Southeastern High School
Fisher, IN

Linda Wiencken
The Austin Waldorf School
Austin, TX

Scott Williams
Language Acquisition Center
University of Texas, Arlington

Jim Witt
Grand Junction High School
Grand Junction, CO

FIELD TEST PARTICIPANTS
We express our appreciation to the teachers and students who participated in the field test. Their comments were instrumental in the development of the entire **Komm mit!** program.

Eva-Maria Adolphi
Indian Hills Middle School
Sandy, UT

Connie Allison
MacArthur High School
Lawton, OK

Linda Brummett
Redmond High School
Redmond, WA

Beatrice Brusstar
Lincoln Northeast High School
Lincoln, NE

Jane Bungartz
Southwest High School
Forth Worth, TX

Devora D. Diller
Lovejoy High School
Lovejoy, GA

Margaret Draheim
Wilson Middle School
Appleton, WI

Kay DuBois
Kennewick High School
Kennewick, WA

Elfriede A. Gabbert
Capital High School
Boise, ID

Petra A. Hansen
Redmond High School
Redmond, WA

Christa Hary
Brien McMahon High School
Norwalk, CT

Ingrid S. Kinner
Weaver Education Center
Greensboro, NC

Diane E. Laumer
San Marcos High School
San Marcos, TX

J. Lewinsohn
Redmond High School
Redmond, WA

Judith A. Lidicker
Central High School
West Allis, WI

Linnea Maulding
Fife High School
Tacoma, WA

Jane Reinkordt
Lincoln Southeast High School
Lincoln, NE

Elizabeth A. Smith
Plano Senior High School
Plano, TX

Elizabeth L. Webb
Sandy Creek High School
Tyrone, GA

TO THE STUDENT

Some people have the opportunity to learn a new language by living in another country. Most of us, however, begin learning another language and getting acquainted with a foreign culture in a classroom with the help of a teacher, classmates, and a textbook. To use your book effectively, you need to know how it works.

Komm mit! (*Come along*) is organized to help you learn German and become familiar with the culture of the people who speak German. Each chapter presents basic concepts in German and strategies for learning a new language. This book has four Location Openers and twelve chapters.

Location Opener You'll find four four-page photo essays called Location Openers which introduce different states or cities in Germany. You can see these locations on video.

Chapter Opener The Chapter Opener pages tell you the chapter theme and goals, and outline what you learn to do in each section of the chapter.

Los geht's! (*Getting started*) and **Weiter geht's** (*Keep going!*) These illustrated stories show you German-speaking people in real-life situations, using the language you'll learn in the chapter.

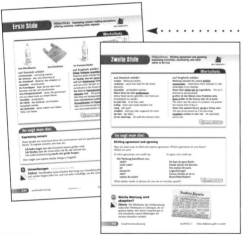

Erste and **Zweite Stufe** (*First* and *Second Step*) The chapter is divided into two sections called **Stufen**. At the beginning of each **Stufe**, there is a reminder of the goals for this part of the chapter. Within the **Stufe** are **So sagt man das!** (*Here's how you say it!*) boxes that contain the German expressions you'll need to communicate and **Wortschatz** and **Grammatik / Ein wenig Grammatik** boxes that give you the German words and grammar structures you'll need to know. Activities in each **Stufe** enable you to practice the new expressions, vocabulary, and structures and thereby develop your skills in listening, speaking, reading, and writing.

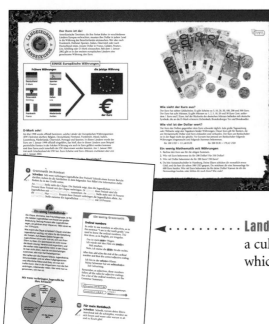

Ein wenig Landeskunde (*Culture Note*) In many chapters, there are notes with more information about the culture in German-speaking countries. These notes tell you interesting facts, describe common customs, or offer other information that will help you learn more about these countries.

Landeskunde (*Culture*) On this page you find brief essays dealing with a cultural aspect of the chapter. Following, there are some activities which let you further explore the topic.

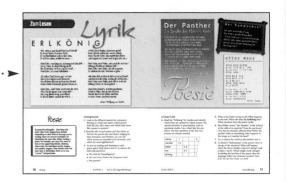

Zum Lesen (*For reading*) The reading section follows the two **Stufen**. The selections are related to the chapter themes and will help you develop your reading skills in German. The **Lesetrick** boxes in these sections are strategies to help you improve your reading comprehension.

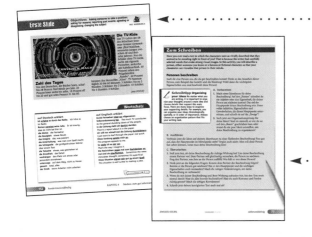

Wortschatz (*Vocabulary*) May be presented visually, or the word or phrase may be rephrased in German — **auf Deutsch erklärt** — or an English translation may be given — **auf English erklärt.**

Zum Schreiben (*Let's write!*) will develop the writing skills. Each chapter will guide you to write a composition related to the themes of the chapter. The **Schreibtip** box will help you develop a specific writing strategy.

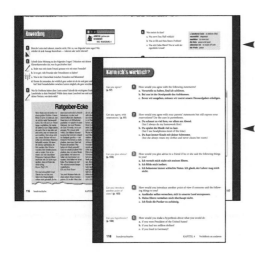

Anwendung (*Review*) The activities on these pages practice what you've learned in the chapter and help you improve your listening, reading, and communication skills. You'll also review what you've learned about culture.

Kann ich's wirklich? (*Can I really do it?*) This page at the end of each chapter contains a series of questions and short activities to help you see if you've achieved the chapter goals. Page numbers beside each section will tell you where to go for help if needed.

Wortschatz (*Vocabulary*) On the German-English vocabulary list on the last page of the chapter, the words are grouped by **Stufe**. These words and expressions will appear on quizzes and tests.

You'll also find German-English and English-German vocabulary lists at the end of the textbook. The words you'll need to know for the quizzes and tests are in boldface type.

At the end of your textbook, you'll find more helpful material, such as:
- a summary of the expressions you'll learn in the **So sagt man das!** boxes
- a summary of the grammar you'll study
- a section of additional activities to practice the grammar you'll learn
- additional vocabulary words that you might want to use
- a grammar index to help you find where grammar is presented

Komm mit! Come along on an exciting trip to a new culture and a new language!

Gute Reise!

Explanation of Icons in *Komm mit!*

*Throughout **Komm mit!** you'll see these symbols, or icons, next to activities.*
They'll tell you what you'll probably do with that activity.
Here's a key to help you understand the icons.

 Video Whenever this icon appears, you'll know there is a related segment in the *Komm mit! Video Program.*

 Listening Activities This icon indicates a listening activity.

  Pair Work/Group Work Activities

 Writing Activities

 CD-ROM Activities Whenever this icon appears, you'll know there is a related activity on the *Komm mit! Interactive CD-ROM Tutor.*

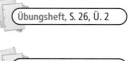

Übungsheft, S. 26, Ü. 2

Grammatikheft, S. 8, Ü. 1

 **Practice Activities** These icons tell you which activities from the *Übungsheft* and the *Grammatikheft* practice the material presented.

Mehr Grammatikübungen S. 88, Ü. 1 →

Mehr Grammatikübungen This reference tells you where you can find related additional grammar practice in the review section of the chapter.

 Internet Activities This icon provides the keyword you'll need to access related online activities at **go.hrw.com**.

Komm mit! Contents

Come along—
to a world of new experiences!

Komm mit! *offers you the opportunity to learn the language spoken by millions of people in several European countries and around the world. Let's find out about these people and their culture.*

die neuen Bundesländer!

KAPITEL 1

WIEDERHOLUNGSKAPITEL

Das Land am Meer 4

KAPITEL 2

WIEDERHOLUNGSKAPITEL

Auf in die Jugendherberge! 32

Aussehen: wichtig oder nicht? 60

Würzburg!

KAPITEL 4

Verhältnis zu anderen 92

KAPITEL 5

Rechte und Pflichten.....120

KAPITEL 6

Medien: stets gut informiert? 148

KOMM MIT NACH
Frankfurt!

LOCATION • KAPITEL 7, 8, 9 176

LOCATION OPENER 175A–175A

KAPITEL 7

Ohne Reklame geht es nicht!.....180

KAPITEL 8
Weg mit den Vorurteilen!.....208

KAPITEL 9

Aktiv für die Umwelt! 236

Dresden!

Die Kunst zu leben 268

KAPITEL 11

Deine Welt ist deine Sache! 296

KAPITEL 12

WIEDERHOLUNGSKAPITEL
Die Zukunft liegt in deiner Hand! 324

Cultural References

Page numbers referring to material in the Pupil's Edition *appear in regular type.*
When the material referenced is located in the Teacher's Edition, *page numbers*
appear in boldface type.

POINTS OF INTEREST

see also Castles and Fortresses, Churches,
Museums, and Statues and Monuments

POLITICAL PARTIES

PROVERBS

Map of the Federal Republic of Germany

DÄNEMARK

Ostsee

Nordsee

0 50 100 Kilometer
0 50 100 Meilen

N

Kiel

SCHLESWIG-HOLSTEIN

Rostock

Lübeck

MECKLENBURG-VORPOMMERN

HAMBURG

Schwerin

Neubrandenburg

Elbe

Havel

POLEN

BREMEN

NIEDERSACHSEN

BUNDESREPUBLIK

BRANDENBURG

Oder

BERLIN

NIEDERLANDE

Ems

Weser

Teutoburger Wald

Hannover

Braunschweig

Magdeburg

Potsdam

Frankfurt a.d. Oder

Oder

Rhein

Münster

SACHSEN-ANHALT

Spree

Neiße

NORDRHEIN-WESTFALEN

Harz

Elbe

Cottbus

Essen Dortmund

Ruhrgebiet

DEUTSCHLAND

Halle

Leipzig

Neuss Düsseldorf

Kassel

Saale

SACHSEN

Dresden

Köln

Erfurt

Chemnitz

Erzgebirge

Aachen

HESSEN

Thüringer Wald

Gera

Bonn

THÜRINGEN

BELGIEN

Eifel

Westerwald

Rhein

Suhl

Koblenz

Taunus

Oberpfälzer Wald

TSCHECHISCHE REPUBLIK

RHEINLAND-PFALZ

Wiesbaden

Frankfurt a. M.

Böhmerwald

Mosel

Mainz

Main

LUX.

Würzburg

Mannheim

Nürnberg

Bayerischer Wald

SAARLAND

Heidelberg

Saarbrücken

BADEN-WÜRTTEMBERG

BAYERN

Regensburg

Karlsruhe

Donau

Rhein

Stuttgart

Schwäbische Alb

Isar

Neckar

Ulm

Augsburg

FRANKREICH

Schwarzwald

München

Freiburg

Salzburger Alpen

Rhein

Bodensee

Bayerische Alpen

Zugspitze

SCHWEIZ

ÖSTERREICH

Map of Liechtenstein, Switzerland, and Austria

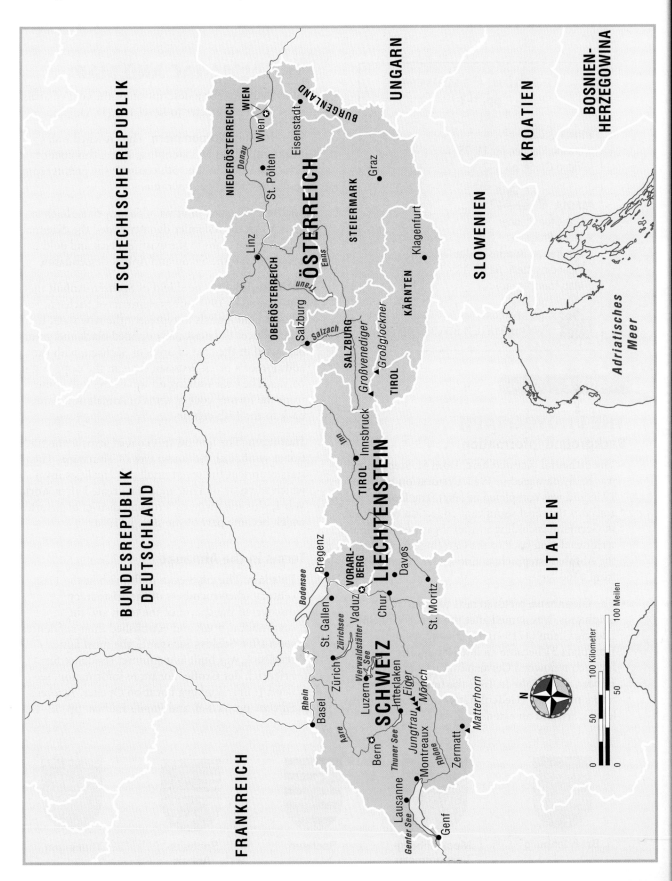

TSCHECHISCHE REPUBLIK

BUNDESREPUBLIK
DEUTSCHLAND

FRANKREICH

NIEDERÖSTERREICH

WIEN

Wien

BURGENLAND

UNGARN

KROATIEN

BOSNIEN-
HERZEGOWINA

St. Pölten

Eisenstadt

ÖSTERREICH

Donau

Linz

OBERÖSTERREICH

STEIERMARK

Graz

Enns

Traun

Salzburg

Salzach

SALZBURG

KÄRNTEN

Klagenfurt

SLOWENIEN

Großvenediger

Großglockner

TIROL

Innsbruck

Inn

TIROL

Adriatisches
Meer

LIECHTENSTEIN

VORARL-
BERG

Bregenz

Davos

Vaduz

Chur

St. Moritz

ITALIEN

Bodensee

St. Gallen

Zürichsee

Zürich

Rhein

Basel

Aare

Luzern

Vierwaldstätter
See

SCHWEIZ

Interlaken

Eiger

Jungfrau

Mönch

Thuner See

Bern

Montreaux

Rhône

Zermatt

Matterhorn

Lausanne

Genfer See

Genf

N

0   50   100 Meilen

0   50   100 Kilometer

Die neuen Bundesländer

Teaching Resources
pp. 1–3

PRINT
▸ Lesson Planner, pp. 11, 75
▸ Video Guide, pp. 1–2

MEDIA
▸ One-Stop Planner
▸ Video Program
Die neuen Bundesländer
Videocassette 1, 02:02–13:42
▸ Map Transparency

 go.hrw.com
WK3 DIE NEUEN BUNDESLAENDER

PAGE 1

THE PHOTOGRAPH
Background Information

• The cathedral pictured here, **Dom St. Stephanus,** was badly damaged in 1945. Restoration began in 1946 and was completed in 1960. The **Domschatz** contains the most significant collection of its kind in Germany, including medieval garments, original writings dating back to the Carolingian period, and the **Abrahamsteppich,** a nine-meter long tapestry from 1160.

• The **Gleimhaus,** pictured next to **Dom St. Stephanus,** was named after the writer Wilhelm Ludwig Gleim (1719–1803). His home at **Domplatz 31** became an intellectual meeting place for such renowned German literaries as Klopstock, Herder, and Jacobi. In 1862 the house was made into a memorial (**Gedenkstätte**) and now contains letters, art, and an extensive library.

THE ALMANAC AND MAP

Brandenburg For a description of the coat of arms of Brandenburg, refer to Level 1 (p. 11A).

Mecklenburg-Vorpommern The crowned bull's head symbolizes Mecklenburg, where this coat of arms appeared in the 13th century; the griffin represents the rulers of Pomerania.

Sachsen The coat of arms of Saxony dates back to 1261 when the **Askanier** dynasty added the diagonal row of green clubs to the existing black and gold bars. It symbolized the Saxon and Anhalt descendants.

Sachsen-Anhalt The shield of **Sachsen-Anhalt** that was created in 1991 unites elements of **Sachsen, Prussia,** and **Anhalt** to represent the new state. It reintroduces the diagonally divided black and gold bars used in the coat of arms of **Sachsen,** with the addition of a black Prussian eagle in the upper right corner. The bear walking on top of the wall comes from the former coat of arms of **Anhalt** and dates back to the 15th century.

Thüringen The lion on this coat of arms is the traditional symbol of the landgraves of Thuringia. The stars represent the seven small principalities from which the state of Thuringia was created after World War I, plus the formerly Prussian district of Erfurt which became part of the state in 1944.

Terms in the Almanac

• Potsdam: The city began to flourish in the 17th century when members of the aristocracy discovered the charm of the town and the surrounding areas and established their residences soon after. **Schloss Sanssouci,** the most famous residence, was built as a summer residence for **Friedrich der Große.** For more information, see Level 1: Brandenburg Location Opener, *Teacher's Edition,* pp. 11A-B, and *Pupil's Edition,* pp. 12–15.

Brandenburg

Mecklenburg-Vorpommern

Sachsen

Sachsen-Anhalt

Thüringen

- **Schwerin:** This city's history can be traced back as far as the 8th or 9th century. Schwerin was officially founded in 1160 by Duke Henry the Lion (**Heinrich der Löwe**) and later became home to the Dukes of Mecklenburg.

- **Dresden:** This city was introduced to students in Level 2 (p. 69). For more information, see Level 3, *Teacher's Edition,* pp. 263A-B and *Pupil's Edition,* pp. 264–265.

- **Meißen:** This town's history dates back to 929 when King Henry I built the castle Misni on the **Burgberg.** Meißen is also home to Europe's oldest porcelain factory, known for its famous **Meissener Porzellan.** For more information, see p. 3D.

- **Magdeburg:** Located on the river Elbe, Magdeburg has a history dating back a thousand years. The name Magdeburg first appeared in official records in 805. Magdeburg was badly damaged during the Thirty Years' War and was almost destroyed during World War II. It was was rebuilt after 1945 under the communist regime.

- **Wittenberg:** Also referred to as **Lutherstadt Wittenberg,** this city became famous after Martin Luther posted his "95 Theses" on the door of the castle church.

- **Erfurt:** First mention of this city dates back to 729. As early as the 9th century, under **Karl der Große** (*Charlemagne*), Erfurt flourished as a trading center. Its first university was founded in 1379 and closed in 1816; Martin Luther taught there from 1501 to 1505. Today this state capital has a population of 220,000 making it **Thüringen's** largest city. The city is described as **turmreich** because of its large number of churches and monasteries (80 churches and 36 monasteries) dating back to the Middle Ages, many of which are still standing today.

Map Activities

Have students identify the country or countries that share borders with Mecklenburg-Vorpommern (**Polen**), Brandenburg (**Polen**), and Sachsen (**Polen** and **Tschechische Republik**). You may also want to use *Map Transparency* 1.

THE PHOTO ESSAY

1 The Wartburg was built in 1067 by **Ludwig der Springer** and later became the seat of the Thuringian landgraves. (See Level 1, *Teacher's Edition,* p. T78 for further information.)

2 Johann Sebastian Bach (1685–1750), one of the greatest composers of all times, wrote more than two hundred church cantatas, including the *Weihnachtsoratorium* and the *Johannes- und Matthäuspassion,* as well as many secular works such as the six *Brandenburger Konzerte* and four *Orchesterzüge.* In 1723 he became cantor of the **Thomaskirche** in Leipzig.

3 Some of the first demonstrations leading to the fall of the Berlin Wall were held in Leipzig. Banners with slogans such as **"Wir sind das Volk. Wir sind ein Volk! Mauer ins Museum!,"** and **"Nie wieder selbsternannte Diktatur!"** were some early public signs of dissatisfaction that ultimately led to the downfall of the communist regime.

4 Aside from being an important cultural city, Weimar has also played a significant role in history. In 1919, the German National Assembly met in Weimar to adopt a new constitution for the short-lived Weimar Republic (**Weimarer Republik**).

5 The **Dom St. Maria** was built in several stages beginning in the early 13th century and continuing until the late 15th century. The interior reflects the changing styles of art from the two centuries during which it was built.

5 Born in Wedel, Ernst Barlach (1870–1938) was an expressionistic sculptor and writer whose works were simple yet revealed great depth. At the Ernst Barlach Memorial in Güstrow, located in the house the artist built in 1930, visitors can view over 100 sculptures, drawings, and several of his original manuscripts.

Komm mit in die neuen Bundesländer!

	Brandenburg	Mecklenburg-Vorpommern	Sachsen	Sachsen-Anhalt	Thüringen
Einwohner	2,7 Mio.	1,85 Mio.	4,6 Mio.	2,8 Mio.	2,5 Mio.
Fläche (qkm)	29 000	23 200	18 300	20 400	16 250
Hauptstadt	Potsdam	Schwerin	Dresden	Magdeburg	Erfurt
Sehenswerte Städte	Brandenburg Chorin	Stralsund Rostock	Meißen	Halberstadt Halle Wittenberg	Weimar Eisenach
Berühmte Leute	Fontane Kleist	Barlach Otto Lilienthal C.D. Friedrich	Lessing Karl May Schumann	Klopstock Luther Händel Nietzsche	Bach

go.hrw.com

WK3 DIE NEUEN BUNDESLAENDER

VIDEO

STANDARDS: 2.2, 3.1

Map of Germany

Der Dom St. Stephanus in Halberstadt, ▶ **eine dreischiffige, gotische Basilika, 1235 begonnen und 1491 eingeweiht**

DÄNEMARK Ostsee

Nordsee

Kiel

Mecklenburg-Vorpommern

Hamburg

NIEDER-LANDE

Berlin

POLEN

Brandenburg

Sachsen-Anhalt

Sachsen

BEL.

Thüringen

Frankfurt

TSCHECHIEN

LUX.

München

FRANK-REICH

ÖSTERREICH

SCHWEIZ

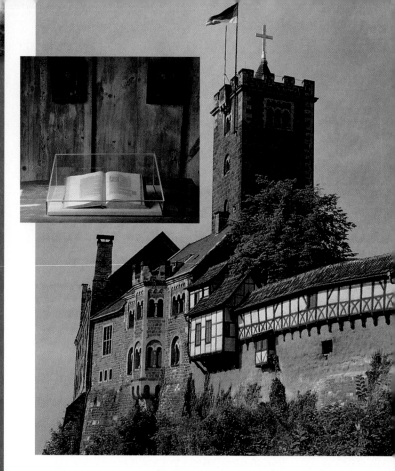

Jahrelang war es fast unmöglich, die deutschen Kulturstätten in der ehemaligen DDR zu besuchen: sie lagen hinter Stacheldraht in einem anderen Land, dessen Grenze nur wenige überschreiten konnten. Seit Mitte November 1989, seit dem Fall der Mauer, ist es wieder möglich, die Schätze deutscher Kultur zu besuchen, zu bewundern. Leider wurde manches im Krieg zerstört, manches blieb erhalten und manches wurde auch restauriert. Das meiste aber ist in Zerfall geraten, und es wird einige Jahre dauern, bis diese Stätten wieder in alter Pracht erglänzen.

🖅 internet

go.hrw.com **ADRESSE:** go.hrw.com
KENNWORT: WK3 DIE NEUEN BUNDESLAENDER

IOH.SEB.BACH.

① Lutherzimmer in der Wartburg
Die Wartburg in Eisenach spiegelt 800 Jahre deutscher Kultur wider. Hier soll im Mittelalter der legendäre Sängerwettstreit stattgefunden haben, dem Richard Wagner im „Tannhäuser" ein musikalisches Denkmal gesetzt hat. In den Jahren 1521/22 hat hier Martin Luther als Junker Jörg das Neue Testament übersetzt und damit den Grundstein zur deutschen Schriftsprache gelegt.

② Bachhaus in Eisenach
Das Bachhaus in Eisenach, in dem einer der größten deutschen Komponisten, Johann Sebastian Bach, 1685 geboren wurde, ist heute ein Museum.

❸ Thomaskirche in Leipzig

Die berühmte Stadt Leipzig, einst
Zentrum des deutschen Buchhandels,
war und ist eine deutsche Musikstadt:
das Gewandhausorchester, der
Thomaschor und die Hochschule für
Musik sind hier zu Hause. In der
berühmten Thomaskirche war J.S. Bach
von 1723 bis zu seinem Tod
1750 Kantor der Kirche. Hier
schrieb Bach die meisten
seiner Werke. Seit 1950
ist die Thomaskirche auch
Bachs Ruhestätte.

❹ Stadtschloss in Weimar

Weimar ist als „Stadt der deutschen
Klassik" weltweit bekannt. Luther, Cranach
und Bach wirkten hier. Im 18. Jahrhundert
begann mit den großen deutschen Dichtern
Wieland, Goethe, Herder und Schiller die
bedeutendste Epoche Weimars. Im
Stadtschloss befindet sich eine ständige
Kunstausstellung, insbesondere die
Cranach-Galerie mit 28 Bildern von
Lucas Cranach d. Ä., sowie Gemälden
von Dürer, Veronese, Tiepolo,
Tintoretto, u.a.

❺ Im Dom von Güstrow

Im Dom (1226-1335) von Güstrow
befindet sich Barlachs Bronzeskulptur
„Der Schwebende" (1927), die vielleicht
bedeutendste Skulptur des Bildhauers,
Grafikers und Dichters Ernst Barlach
(1870-1938), der 1910 Güstrow zu seiner
Heimat wählte.

Los geht's! pp. 6–7	*Zwei Freunde treffen sich, p. 6*			

	FUNCTIONS	**GRAMMAR**	**VOCABULARY**	**RE-ENTRY**
Erste Stufe pp. 8–12	• Reporting past events, p. 9 • Asking how someone liked something; expressing enthusiasm or disappointment; responding enthusiastically or sympathetically, p. 12	• Prepositions followed by dative case forms, p. 9 • Past tense, p. 10 • Dative case forms, p. 12	• Time expressions, p. 9 • Errands, p. 10	• Chapters 1 and 2 are a global review of *Komm mit!* Levels 1 and 2

Weiter geht's! pp. 14–15	*Gregor besucht Johannes, p. 14*			

Zweite Stufe pp. 16–23	• Asking and telling what you may or may not do, p. 17 • Asking for information, p. 18 • Inquiring about someone's health and responding; asking about and expressing pain, p. 20 • Expressing hope, p. 20	• Forms of **dieser** and **welcher**, p. 18 • Reflexive pronouns, p. 20	• Produce and meats, p. 17 • Things to eat on or with sandwiches, p. 18 • Injuries and body parts, p. 19	• Chapters 1 and 2 are a global review of *Komm mit!* Levels 1 and 2

Zum Schreiben p. 13	Was ich in den Ferien gemacht habe.	**Writing Strategy** Brainstorming and freewriting
Zum Lesen pp. 24–25	Moderne Literatur	**Reading Strategy** Using time lines for comprehension
Mehr Grammatik-übungen	**pp. 26–29** Erste Stufe, pp. 26–27 Zweite Stufe, pp. 27–29	
Review pp. 30–31	Kann ich's wirklich?, p. 30 Wortschatz, p. 31	

CULTURE

- Insel Rügen, p. 8
- Fit ohne Fleisch, p. 16
- Landeskunde: Der Euro ist da!, pp. 22–23

Kapitel 1: Das Land am Meer

Chapter Resources

 **PRINT**

Lesson Planning

One-Stop Planner

Lesson Planner with Substitute Teacher Lesson Plans, pp. 11–15, 75

Student Make-Up Assignments
- Make-Up Assignment Copying Masters, Chapter 1

Listening and Speaking

Listening Activities
- Student Response Forms for Listening Activities, pp. 3–6
- Additional Listening Activities 1-1 to 1-6, pp. 7–10
- Scripts and Answers, pp. 100–107

Video Guide
- Teaching Suggestions, p. 4
- Activity Masters, pp. 5–6
- Scripts and Answers, pp. 59, 74

Activities for Communication
- Communicative Activities, pp. 1–4
- Realia and Teaching Suggestions, pp. 51–55
- Situation Cards, pp. 113–114

Reading and Writing

Reading Strategies and Skills Handbook, Chapter 1

Lies mit mir! 3, Chapter 1

Übungsheft, pp. 1–13

Grammar

Grammatikheft, pp. 1–9

Grammar Tutor for Students of German, Chapter 1

Assessment

Testing Program
- Grammar and Vocabulary Quizzes, **Stufe** Quizzes, and Chapter Test, pp. 1–14
- Score Sheet, Scripts and Answers, pp. 15–21

Alternative Assessment Guide
- Portfolio Assessment, p. 16
- Performance Assessment, p. 30

Student Make-Up Assignments
- Alternative Quizzes, Chapter 1

 **MEDIA**

 Online Activities
- Interaktive Spiele
- Internet Aktivitäten

 Video Program
- Videocassette 1

 Audio Compact Discs
- Textbook Listening Activities, CD 1, Tracks 1–9
- Additional Listening Activities, CD 1, Tracks 14–19
- Assessment Items, CD 1, Tracks 10–13

 Teaching Transparencies
- Situations 1-1 to 1-2
- **Mehr Grammatikübungen** Answers
- **Grammatikheft** Answers

 **One-Stop Planner CD-ROM**

Use the **One-Stop Planner CD-ROM with Test Generator** to aid in lesson planning and pacing.

For each chapter, the **One-Stop Planner** includes:
- Editable lesson plans with direct links to teaching resources
- Printable worksheets from resource books
- Direct launches to the HRW Internet activities
- Video and audio segments
- Test Generator
- Clip Art for vocabulary items

Kapitel 1: Das Land am Meer

Projects ·····················

Die Bewerbung

*Students will compose a letter to a company in a German-speaking country as if they were applying for a summer internship. Begin this project after students have worked through the **Zum Schreiben** section on page 13 and are comfortable with the writing elements taught there. This project is intended to review vocabulary and grammatical structures from Level 2 and incorporate the writing skills introduced in **Zum Schreiben**.*

MATERIALS

✂ **Students will need**
- paper
- pens
- a small photograph of themselves

SUGGESTED SEQUENCE

1. Students brainstorm as to what kind of information they could include in their letter. For what internship are they applying? Why? When would they like to begin? Why should they get the position? What information about themselves would help them be selected?

2. Students organize their notes and make an outline of their letter.

3. Students write their first draft and share it with classmates for peer input. At this point, you may also want to check students' drafts and make suggestions if necessary.

4. Students evaluate what they wrote, make changes as necessary, and rewrite the letter, attaching a small photo of themselves to the final copy.

GRADING THE PROJECT

Suggested point distribution (**total = 100 points**)
Content	50
Organization	25
Accuracy	25

TEACHER NOTE

When giving assignments that entail the disclosure of personal information, keep in mind that some students and their families may consider these matters private. In some cases, you may want to give an alternate assignment in which students may substitute fictitious information.

Games ·····················

Das ist ja die Frage!

This game will help students review questions and vocabulary in a variety of categories.

Preparation Make a game grid on the board or on a transparency. The grid should have several columns, each labeled with a category, and five boxes below it containing the point values 100, 200, 300, 400, and 500. The example game grid shown below can be used for this chapter or modified for others. The words in parentheses should not be written on the grid that students see, but are given as potential answers.

Rügen		Tierprodukte		Körperteile		Pflanzenprodukte		Hauptstädte	
(Badeort)	100	(Schweine-fleisch)	100	(die Ferse)	100	(Zwiebeln)	100	(Potsdam)	100
(Hansestadt)	200	(Leber)	200	(die Zehe)	200	(Mais)	200	(Dresden)	200
(Caspar David Friedrich)	300	(Speck)	300	(das Handgelenk)	300	(Spargel)	300	(Erfurt)	300
(Rügendamm)	400	(Hasenfleisch)	400	(die Wade)	400	(Paprika)	400	(Magdeburg)	400
(926 km²)	500	(Rippchen)	500	(die Kniescheibe)	500	(Rosenkohl)	500	(Schwerin)	500

Procedure Divide the class into two or three teams. After deciding the order of play, have one player from the first team choose a category and a numerical value. Then, make a statement appropriate to the category. For example, if a student chooses the category **Hauptstädte** for 100 points, you might say **"Diese Stadt ist die Hauptstadt von Brandenburg."** The player must then respond in question form, **"Was ist Potsdam?"** If the player responds correctly, the answer is written in the box and the team receives the appropriate number of points. If the player responds incorrectly or is unable to respond accurately in question form, a player from the other team has the opportunity to answer the same question for the same number of points. You might want to have one student keep score and write the answers in the boxes, and another student act as an impartial judge in cases where an answer is close, pronounced incorrectly, or not given in appropriate question form. For example, **"Wer ist Potsdam?"** would not be an acceptable response.

Storytelling

This story accompanies Teaching Transparency 1-1. The **Mini-Geschichte** *can be told and retold in different formats, acted out, written down, and read aloud to give students additional opportunities to practice all four skills.*

„Sag mal, Horst, wo warst du denn in den Ferien?" „Ich war mit meiner Clique beim Zelten in Kanada. Es hat fast dauernd geregnet, aber wir hatten trotzdem viel Spaß." „Was habt ihr denn alles gemacht?" „Wir sind viel in den Bergen gewandert. Wir sind in Bergseen und Flüssen geschwommen. Brrr! … Das Wasser war vielleicht kalt! Ich habe auch viel fotografiert, vor allem Tiere." „Habt ihr auch Grizzlybären gesehen?" „Ja, viele. Ich hab sogar einen fotografiert, als er gerade einen riesigen Lachs aus dem Fluss holt."

Unter dem Zeichen der blauen Schwerter werden bis heute Gebrauchsgegenstände und Kunstwerke für die ganze Welt produziert. Eine eigene Ausbildungsstätte in der Manufaktur sichert seit dem 18. Jahrhundert die exakte Überlieferung der Manufakturtechniken.

Traditions

Meissener Porzellan

Im 17. und beginnenden 18. Jahrhundert sammelte der europäische Adel mit Leidenschaft Porzellan aus Japan und China. Da die Beschaffung und der Transport sehr kostspielig waren, gab es aber nur wenig Porzellan in Europa. Das sollte sich im Jahre 1708 mit der Entdeckung des europäischen Porzellans ändern.

August der Starke

Am Hofe des sächsischen Kurfürsten und polnischen Königs „August des Starken" (1670–1733) in Dresden war der Chemiker Johann Friedrich Böttger (1682–1719) damit beauftragt, Gold zu produzieren. Allerdings entdeckte der Chemiker nicht Gold, sondern die Rohmaterialien für das weiße europäische Hartporzellan, das so genannte „weiße Gold". Um die Rezeptur geheim zu halten, wurde die Manufaktur von Dresden auf die sichere Albrechtsburg in die tausendjährige Stadt Meißen verlegt.

Von 1861 bis 1864 wurde die Meissener Manufaktur in ihre heutige Betriebsstätte in Meißen-Triebischtal verlegt.

Rezept

Arme Ritter
(Thüringen)
Für 3–4 Personen

Zutaten
g=Gramm

500 g Kartoffelbrei	Muskatnuss
3 Eier	Salz
Mehl	Fett

Zubereitung

Die Eier in den abgekühlten Kartoffelbrei einrühren. Durch ein Sieb so viel Mehl zugegeben, bis ein geschmeidiger Teig entsteht. Den Teig mit einer Muskatnuss und Salz abschmecken. In einer Pfanne Fett erhitzen und den Teig in ca. 1 cm starke Scheiben drücken. Die Scheiben dann im heißen Fett goldgelb ausbacken.

Kapitel 1: Das Land am Meer
Technology

One-Stop Planner CD-ROM

To preview all resources available for this chapter, use the **One-Stop Planner CD-ROM**, Disc 1.

Internet Connection

ADRESSE: go.hrw.com
KENNWORT: WK3 DIE NEUEN BUNDESLAENDER-1

*Have students explore the **go.hrw.com** Web site for many online resources covering all chapters. All Chapter 1 resources are available under the keyword **WK3 Die neuen Bundeslaender-1**. Interactive games practice the material and provide students with immediate feedback. You will also find a printable worksheet that provides Internet activities that lead to a comprehensive online research project.*

Interaktive Spiele

Use the interactive activities in this chapter

- to practice grammar, vocabulary, and chapter functions
- as homework
- as an assessment option
- as a self-test
- to prepare for the Chapter Test

Internet Aktivitäten

Students will read descriptions of sights and determine which German cities are home to these sights. They will also choose a city in Thuringia and describe its history and sights.

- To prepare students for the **Arbeitsblatt,** have them study the map and read the descriptions of Stralsund and Sassnitz on p. 8. You may also have them do Activity 4.

- After completing the **Arbeitsblatt,** ask students to pick up brochures of their hometown at the chamber of commerce. Have students use the information provided on the brochures to design and write in German a one-page pamphlet (or website) describing their hometown.

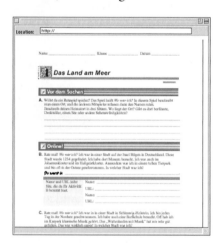

Webprojekt

Have students go online grocery shopping in Germany. They should buy a weekly supply of groceries for a family of four. Have them report on the kind and amount of food items they bought and the money they spent. Encourage students to exchange useful Web sites with their classmates. Have students document their sources by referencing the names and URLs of all the sites they consulted.

The following scripts are for the listening activities found in the *Pupil's Edition.* For Student Response Forms, see *Listening Activities,* pages 3–6. To provide students with additional listening practice, see *Listening Activities,* pages 7–10.

Erste Stufe

5   p. 9

RÜDIGER   Hallo, Heike! Na, bist du endlich aus dem Urlaub zurück?

HEIKE   Hallo, Rüdiger! Hallo, Antje! Ja, wir sind gestern Abend erst zurückgekommen, meine Eltern und ich. War echt toll. Wir waren fast drei Wochen lang weg. Wir sind schon in der ersten Augustwoche abgereist.

ANTJE   Wo habt ihr denn dieses Jahr Urlaub gemacht?

HEIKE   Dieses Jahr haben wir was ganz Neues ausprobiert. Wir waren auf Sylt, du weißt schon, an der Nordsee. Meine Mutter wollte schon immer mal auf diese Insel fahren, und dieses Jahr hat sie meinen Vater tatsächlich dazu überredet. Mir hat es dort wahnsinnig gut gefallen.

RÜDIGER   Na, da hast du ja Glück gehabt. Wir waren auch in Urlaub, aber schon letzten Monat. Leider waren wir nur eine Woche lang weg. Wir sind nach Österreich in die Berge gefahren. War echt langweilig dort. Sogar meine Eltern waren von diesem Urlaub enttäuscht.

HEIKE   Und warum seid ihr denn in die Berge gefahren, wenn es dir dort nicht gefallen hat?

RÜDIGER   Na ja, das war so. Meine Großeltern sind dieses Jahr mitgefahren, und sie wollten auf jeden Fall in die Berge. Es hat aber fast jeden Tag geregnet, und wir haben die meiste Zeit im Hotel rumgesessen. Einfach scheußlich, sage ich euch.

ANTJE   Und fahrt ihr nächstes Jahr wieder in die Berge oder nicht?

RÜDIGER   Hoffentlich nicht! Ich möchte auch mal nach Amerika. Mensch du, Florida oder Kalifornien, da möchte ich gern mal hin.

HEIKE   Und du, Antje? Seid ihr dieses Jahr in Urlaub gefahren?

ANTJE   Nein, diesmal waren wir nicht weg. Aber letztes Jahr waren wir auf Ibiza. Das war echt toll dort. Ich war mit meiner Schwester dort, weil sie unbedingt ihre Spanischkenntnisse ausprobieren wollte. Bestimmt fahre ich nächstes Jahr wieder mit ihr in die Ferien.

Answers to Activity 5
Heike: erste Augustwoche; Sylt; Mutter wollte schon immer dorthin
Rüdiger: letzten Monat; Österreich; Großeltern wollten in die Berge
Antje: letztes Jahr; Ibiza; Schwester wollte Spanischkenntnisse ausprobieren

10   p. 10

VOLKER   Hallo, Britta, wie geht's? Du siehst heute aber fesch aus!

BRITTA   Danke! Ich war vorhin beim Friseur, weil ich mir die Haare schneiden lassen wollte. Danach bin ich noch schnell beim Juwelier Werner vorbeigegangen, weil ich ein neues Armband und eine Batterie für meine Uhr brauchte. Meine Uhr funktioniert jetzt wieder, nur leider gab es kein Armband, das mir gefallen hat. Aber dafür habe ich mir diese Ohrringe hier gekauft. Schau mal! Toll, nicht? Und was hast du heute in der Stadt zu erledigen, Volker?

VOLKER   Ach, ich habe gerade ein paar Flaschen zum Getränkemarkt zurückgebracht, und dann war ich noch im Obstladen. Meine Mutter macht heute Nachmittag nämlich Obstkuchen, und sie braucht halt Erdbeeren dazu. Jetzt war ich gerade im Reisebüro, weil mein Freund Uli da arbeitet und ich ihn fragen wollte, ob er heute Abend ins Kino gehen will. Was hast du denn da in der Tasche?

BRITTA   Ach, ich war heute Morgen in der Bücherei. Ich habe mir mehrere Bücher über Amerika ausgeliehen, weil wir diesen Sommer in Urlaub dorthin fahren wollen. Du, schau mal, da ist der Thomas! He, Thomas!

THOMAS   Hallo, Britta! Hallo, Volker! Puh, habt ihr heute auch so viel zu erledigen wie ich?

VOLKER   Wieso, was musst du denn heute alles machen?

THOMAS   Na ja, ich hab halt heute ein volles Programm! Das meiste hab ich aber schon erledigt. Also zuerst war ich beim Lambert und habe die Fotos von unserem Urlaub in der Türkei abgeholt. Dann bin ich beim Musikladen vorbeigegangen und habe mir die neue CD von Sting und zwei Kassetten gekauft. Jetzt komme ich gerade aus der Bank. Ich musste noch das restliche Geld von unserem Urlaub wechseln.

BRITTA   Also, da hast du heute schon eine ganze Menge zu tun gehabt.

THOMAS   Ach übrigens, ich will gleich ins Schwimmbad gehen. Wollt ihr mitkommen?

BRITTA   Nein, danke. Diese Bücher hier sind echt schwer und ich muss nach Hause, um meinen Eltern im Garten zu helfen.

THOMAS   Und du, Volker? Kommst du mit?

VOLKER   Ja, gerne. Also, tschüs dann, Britta!

BRITTA   Tschüs ihr zwei!

Answers to Activity 10
Britta: Friseur / hat sich die Haare schneiden lassen; Juwelier/ hat Batterie für Uhr und Ohrringe gekauft; Bücherei/ hat Bücher ausgeliehen
Volker: Getränkemarkt / hat Flaschen zurückgebracht; Obstladen / hat Erdbeeren gekauft; Reisebüro / hat Freund gefragt, ob er mit ins Kino will
Thomas: Fotogeschäft / Urlaubsfotos abgeholt; Musikladen / CD und Kassetten gekauft; Bank / Geld umgetauscht

14 p. 12

ULI	Hallo, Sabine! Endlich treffen wir uns ja mal wieder!
SABINE	Ach, hallo, Uli! Ja, seit du nicht mehr im Schwimmverein bist, sieht man dich ja kaum noch! Ach, übrigens, ich war gestern zum ersten Mal in dem neuen Freibad in Kreuzing.
ULI	Wie war's denn? Ich habe gehört, das Freibad soll echt toll sein.
SABINE	Also, mir hat es dort echt super gefallen, weil es ganz modern und funkelnagelneu ist. Ich war mit dem Tobias und der Valerie da. Wir sind den ganzen Vormittag geschwommen und haben uns so richtig schön fit gefühlt. Mittags haben wir dann im Stadtpark ein tolles Picknick gemacht. Es hat mir echt gut gefallen, weil ich gerne draußen an der frischen Luft bin.
ULI	Also, ich gehe nächstes Wochenende auch mal ins neue Freibad. Du hast auf jeden Fall mehr Spaß gehabt als ich gestern.
SABINE	Wieso? Was hast du denn gestern gemacht?
ULI	Na ja, wir sind gestern gleich nach dem Frühstück in die Stadt gefahren. Im Deutschen Museum gab es eine neue Ausstellung, die mein Vater unbedingt sehen wollte.
SABINE	Und, wie hat dir die Ausstellung gefallen?
ULI	Sie war fürchterlich langweilig. Es war eine Sammlung von alten römischen Münzen und diese Ausstellung hat mich überhaupt nicht interessiert.
SABINE	Das ist aber schade! Ich finde solche Sachen eigentlich sehr interessant.
ULI	Ich aber nicht. Wir waren drei Stunden lang im Museum. Und dann am Nachmittag musste ich zu Hause bleiben, um für eine Mathearbeit zu lernen. War ebenfalls langweilig, weil ich die meisten Aufgaben gar nicht verstanden habe. Aber am Abend war ich dann mit Heiko im Kino. Wir haben uns einen Thriller mit Steven Seagal angeschaut.
SABINE	Und, wie hat dir der Film gefallen?
ULI	War echt toll! Spannende Thriller sind meine Lieblingsfilme.
SABINE	Ja, ich glaube, ich gehe mir den Film nächstes Wochenende anschauen.
MANUELA	Bernd, da bist du ja! Wir haben gestern versucht, dich anzurufen, aber du warst nicht zu Hause. Wo hast du denn nur gesteckt?
BERND	Ach, hallo Manuela! Du, der Jörg und ich, wir haben gestern eine Fahrradtour nach Ising gemacht. Stell dir mal vor, wir haben über sechzig Kilometer zurückgelegt! Wir sind schon ganz früh morgens losgefahren. Es war echt super!
MANUELA	Ach, ich wusste gar nicht, dass du so sportlich bist! Machst du gerne solche langen Radtouren?
BERND	Und wie! Ich mache Sport überhaupt sehr gerne, aber Radeln ist mir immer noch am liebsten. Wir sind übrigens bei der Stefanie vorbeigefahren und haben sie besucht. Sie wohnt doch jetzt in Ising.
MANUELA	Wirklich? Und, hat sie sich über euren Besuch gefreut?
BERND	Ja, ich glaub schon. Es war echt nett, weil wir uns schon länger nicht gesehen haben. Ach übrigens, sie lässt dir schöne Grüße ausrichten. Wieso habt ihr denn eigentlich gestern versucht, mich anzurufen?
MANUELA	Der Thomas und ich wollten dich zum Volleyballspielen auf dem Sportplatz einladen. Ich spiele

doch so gerne Volleyball. Das hat echt Spaß gemacht. Nachher haben wir dann bei mir zu Hause das Fußballspiel angeschaut.

BERND	Und, wie hat es euch gefallen? Muss doch echt aufregend gewesen sein.
MANUELA	Nein, im Gegenteil! Es ist null zu null ausgegangen. Mir hat es eigentlich nicht so gut gefallen. Es war ein ziemlich langweiliges Spiel.
BERND	Schade! Aber da habe ich ja nicht viel verpasst. Na, vielleicht können wir uns ja heute Abend treffen und Volleyball spielen!
MANUELA	Ja, gerne! Ich ruf nachher mal den Thomas an und sag ihm, er soll noch ein paar Leute mitbringen.
BERND	Super! Bis heute Abend dann!
MANUELA	Tschüs!

Answers to Activity 14

Sabine: im Freibad / ist geschwommen / ihr hat es gut gefallen / weil das Freibad modern und neu ist; im Stadtpark / hat Picknick gemacht / ihr hat es gut gefallen / weil sie gern draußen an der frischen Luft ist
Uli: in der Stadt / hat ein Museum besucht / es hat ihm nicht gefallen / weil er sich nicht für die Ausstellung interessiert; zu Hause / hat für eine Mathearbeit gelernt / es hat ihm nicht gefallen / weil er die Aufgaben nicht verstanden hat; im Kino / hat sich einen Thriller angeschaut / es hat ihm gut gefallen / weil spannende Thriller seine Lieblingsfilme sind
Bernd: in Ising / hat eine Fahrradtour gemacht / es hat ihm gut gefallen / weil er gern Sport macht und am liebsten radelt; in Ising / hat Stefanie besucht / es hat ihm gut gefallen / weil sie sich schon länger nicht gesehen haben
Manuela: auf dem Sportplatz / hat Volleyball gespielt / es hat ihr gut gefallen / weil sie gern Volleyball spielt; zu Hause / hat sich das Fußballspiel angeschaut / es hat ihr nicht gefallen / weil es ein langweiliges Spiel war

Zweite Stufe

21 p. 17

JULIA	He, Franziska! Willst du heute Abend mitkommen? Wir gehen ins argentinische Steakhaus. Die haben diese leckeren Rippchen da! Ich kann's kaum abwarten! Ich freu mich schon so auf diese leckere gemischte Fleischplatte für mehrere Personen.
FRANZISKA	Ach, ich weiß nicht so recht, Julia! Mir schmeckt argentinisches Essen echt gut, aber ich esse überhaupt kein Fleisch mehr.
JULIA	Wie, du isst kein Fleisch mehr? Wieso denn nicht? Fleisch schmeckt doch fabelhaft!
FRANZISKA	Also, ich habe vor einigen Monaten beschlossen, nur noch vegetarisch zu essen. Ich finde, das ist viel gesünder. Und außerdem fühle ich mich auch schon viel fitter, seit ich kein Fleisch mehr esse! Ich esse jetzt am liebsten Nudeln oder Reis mit viel Gemüse. Rosenkohl und Spargel mag ich besonders gern.
JULIA	Ich bin gegen Spargel allergisch. Den darf ich nicht essen. Außerdem mag ich Gemüse überhaupt nicht gern. Aber dafür schmeckt mir Obst ganz gut, besonders Wassermelone. Aber am liebsten esse ich Fleisch und Wurst. Einmal in der Woche gibt es bei uns Innereien und ab und zu sogar mal Reh. Leber mag ich übrigens wahnsinnig gern.
FRANZISKA	Igitt! Also, Leber, nein danke! Du, schau mal, da drüben ist der Mehmet. Der geht sicher gerne mit ins argentinische Restaurant.

JULIA Ja bestimmt! Komm, fragen wir ihn doch! He, Mehmet! Willst du heute Abend mit uns essen gehen? Ich versuche gerade, Franziska dazu zu überreden, mitzukommen.

MEHMET Ja, ich komme gerne mit! Hauptsache, wir gehen irgendwohin, wo es nicht nur Schweinefleisch gibt. Das darf ich nämlich nicht essen.

JULIA Wieso denn nicht? Bist du etwa allergisch dagegen?

MEHMET Nein, das ist es nicht. Ich esse kein Schweinefleisch, weil ich Moslem bin.

JULIA Ach ja, das hatte ich ganz vergessen! Ich bin sicher, dass es im argentinischen Steakhaus etwas gibt, was ihr beiden essen dürft. Wie wär's mit einem Salat oder einer Gemüseplatte?

MEHMET Also, Salat mag ich eigentlich nicht so gerne, aber hoffentlich gibt es dort auch Lammfleisch mit grünen Bohnen. Das mag ich gerne.

FRANZISKA Also gut! Dann treffen wir uns heute Abend dort. So gegen sieben?

JULIA Super! Tschüs!

MEHMET Bis heute Abend!

Answers to Activity 21
Franziska: mag argentinisches Essen, Nudeln, Reis, Gemüse (Rosenkohl, Spargel); mag kein Fleisch und keine Leber; isst nur vegetarisch.
Julia: mag Wurst, Fleisch (Rippchen, Innereien, Leber, Reh) und Obst (Wassermelone); mag kein Gemüse; darf keinen Spargel essen; sie ist allergisch gegen Spargel.
Mehmet: mag Lamm und grüne Bohnen; mag keinen Salat; darf kein Schweinefleisch essen; er ist Moslem.

24 p. 19

MARKUS Du, Jens, was hast du da auf deinem Pausenbrot?

JENS Ach, das ist Quark mit Schnittlauch. Das esse ich am liebsten auf meinem Brot. Manchmal habe ich auch Tomaten und ein Blatt Salat drauf.

MARKUS Na also, so was schmeckt mir nicht besonders gut. Quark esse ich zwar auch gern, aber nicht auf 'ner Scheibe Brot, sondern nur als Nachspeise mit Früchten. Ich habe lieber eine gute Portion Wurst oder Käse auf meinem Pausenbrot. Salami ist am besten, aber Schinken schmeckt auch nicht schlecht.

JENS Nee, Markus! So was schmeckt mir eigentlich nicht so gut. Sag mal, Antje, was isst du denn am liebsten auf deinem Pausenbrot?

ANTJE Also, heute habe ich Erdnussbutter auf meinem Brot, aber sonst esse ich auch gerne Quark oder Naturjoghurt auf meinem Brot. Ab und zu schmeckt mir Leberwurst auch ganz gut. Und du Heike, was isst du denn immer auf deinem Pausenbrot?

HEIKE Mir ist Abwechslung am wichtigsten. Ich mag nicht immer nur das Gleiche auf meinem Pausenbrot essen. Also, ich mag am liebsten Käse und Radieschen auf meinem Brot oder aber auch Leberwurst oder gekochten Schinken mit etwas Senf. Und ich esse außerdem auch gerne Honig auf meinem Pausenbrot.

Answers to Activity 24
Markus isst viel Fleisch und Wurst; Jens isst vegetarisch; Markus, Antje und Heike essen sowohl Tierprodukte als auch Pflanzenprodukte.

26 p. 20

ANNABELLA He, Jungs! Darf ich euch für die Schülerzeitung interviewen? Also, das war ja diesmal wieder ein tolles Sportfest! Herzlichen Glückwunsch zu eurem Sieg! Das Fußballspiel war wirklich spitzen-

One-Stop Planner CD-ROM

For resource information, see the **One-Stop Planner CD-ROM**, Disc 1.

mäßig! Aber mir scheint, dass ihr eine ganze Menge Verletzungen davongetragen habt! Fangen wir mal mit dir an, Jürgen! Was hast du dir alles verletzt?

JÜRGEN Ja, also, als ich auf dem nassen Gras ausgerutscht bin, habe ich mir meinen rechten Arm und auch mein linkes Knie verletzt. Aber es tut eigentlich nicht so sehr weh. Am wichtigsten ist für mich, dass wir das Spiel gewonnen haben. Aber leider habe ich noch ein bisschen Kopfschmerzen und sogar eine Beule am Kopf.

ANNABELLA Ja, aber dafür hast du doch das phänomenale Tor mit diesem Kopfball geschossen! Alle Achtung! Und Markus, wie sieht's bei dir aus mit den Verletzungen?

MARKUS Tja, ich glaube, dass ich heute ziemlich viel Glück hatte. Meine Verletzung hält sich in Grenzen. Als ich mit dem Uli zusammengestoßen bin, habe ich mir nur ganz leicht die Stirn verletzt, sonst nichts. Aber ich glaube, den Uli hat's schlimmer erwischt!

ANNABELLA Dann fragen wir doch direkt mal den Uli! Uli, was ist dir beim Zusammenprall mit dem Markus passiert?

ULI Also, wie du sehen kannst, habe ich ein Pflaster auf der Nase. Sofort nach dem Zusammenprall hat sie angefangen, fürchterlich zu bluten. Zuerst habe ich gedacht, sie ist gebrochen, aber zum Glück ist sie nur blau und grün. Sie tut aber doch ganz schön weh.

ANNABELLA Das tut mir wirklich Leid für dich! Kim, was hast du dir denn verletzt?

KIM Ja, also mich hat es am linken Ellbogen erwischt. Er ist ein bisschen verstaucht. Aber sonst geht es mir gut.

ANNABELLA Ja, also ich glaube, dass alle eure Fans sich freuen, dass ihr trotz den Verletzungen so gute Laune habt. Vielen Dank für das Interview. Ihr seid ein tolles Team.

Answers to Activity 26
Jürgen ist Nummer 7; Markus ist Nummer 1; Uli ist Nummer 3; Kim ist Nummer 2.

Kapitel 1: Das Land am Meer

Suggested Lesson Plans *50-Minute Schedule*

Day 1

LOCATION OPENER 15 min.
- Present Location Opener, pp. 1–3
- The Almanac and Map, ATE, p. T78
- Show **Die neuen Bundesländer** Video
- Do Pre-viewing and Viewing Activities, Video Guide, p. 2

CHAPTER OPENER 10 min.
- Building Context, ATE, p. 3M
- Teaching Suggestions, ATE, p. 3M

LOS GEHT'S! 20 min.
- Preteaching Vocabulary, ATE, p. 3N
- Culture Note, ATE, p. 3N
- Play Audio CD for **Los geht's!**
- Have students read **Los geht's!**, pp. 6–7
- Do Activities 1-3, p. 7

Wrap-Up 5 min.
- Students respond to questions about what they did on their summer vacation

Homework Options
Übungsheft, p. 1, Acts. 1–2

Day 2

ERSTE STUFE
Quick Review 10 min.
- Bell Work, ATE, p. 3O
- Check homework, Übungsheft, p. 1, Acts. 1–2

Reading Selection, p. 8 20 min.
- Review: Reading Strategies, ATE, p. 3O
- Read **Rügen**, p. 8
- Do Activity 4, p. 8

So sagt man das!/Ein wenig Grammatik/Wortschatz, p. 9 15 min.
- Presenting **So sagt man das!** and **Ein Wenig Grammatik**, ATE, p. 3O
- Present **Wortschatz**, p. 9
- Teaching Transparency 1-1
- Play Audio CD for Activity 5, p. 9
- Do Activities 6 and 7, p. 9

Wrap-Up 5 min.
- Students respond to questions about where they have gone on vacation with their parents

Homework Options
Grammatikheft, pp. 1–2, Acts. 1–4
Übungsheft, p. 2, Act. 1

Day 3

ERSTE STUFE
Quick Review 10 min.
- Check homework, Grammatikheft, pp. 1–2, Acts. 1–4

Wortschatz/Ein wenig Grammatik, p. 10 35 min.
- Presenting **Ein wenig Grammatik/Wortschatz**, ATE, p. 3P
- Teaching Transparency 1-1
- Do Activities 8 and 9, p. 10
- Play Audio CD for Activity 10, p. 10
- Do Activities 11, 12, and 13, p. 11

Wrap-Up 5 min.
- Students respond to questions about where they were and what they did last weekend

Homework Options
Grammatikheft, p. 3, Acts. 5–6
Übungsheft, p. 2, Act. 2

Day 4

ERSTE STUFE
Quick Review 10 min.
- Check homework, Grammatikheft, p. 3, Acts. 5–6

So sagt man das!/Ein wenig Grammatik, p. 12 20 min.
- Presenting **So sagt man das!**, ATE, p. 3P
- Present **Ein wenig Grammatik**, p. 12
- Play Audio CD for Activity 14, p. 12
- Do Activities 15 and 16, p. 12

ZUM SCHREIBEN 15 min.
- Teacher Notes, ATE, p. 3Q
- Present **Schreibtipp**, p. 13
- Do Activity A, p. 13

Wrap-Up 5 min.
- Students respond to questions about what they liked and didn't like about their last vacation

Homework Options
Grammatikheft, p. 4, Acts. 7–8
Übungsheft, pp. 3–5, Acts. 3–9

Day 5

ERSTE STUFE
Quick Review 10 min.
- Check homework, Übungsheft, pp. 3–5, Acts. 3–9

Quiz Review 20 min.
- Do **Mehr Grammatikübungen, Erste Stufe**
- Do Additional Listening Activities 1-1, 1-2, and 1-3, pp. 7–8
- Do Communicative Activities 1-1 and 1-2, pp. 1–2

Quiz 20 min.
- Quiz 1-1A or 1-1B

Homework Options
Pupil's Edition, p. 13, Acts. B and C

Day 6

WEITER GEHT'S! 15 min.
- Preteaching Vocabulary, ATE, p. 3S
- Play Audio CD for **Weiter geht's!**, pp. 14–15
- Do Activities 17, 18, and 19, p. 15

ZWEITE STUFE
Quick Review 15 min.
- Return and review Quiz 1-1
- Bell Work, ATE, p. 3S
- Check homework, Pupil's Edition, p. 13, Acts. B and C

Reading Selection, p. 16 15 min.
- Thinking Critically, ATE, p. 3S
- Read **Fit ohne Fleisch**
- Do Activity 20, p. 16

Wrap-Up 5 min.
- Students respond to questions about eating healthy foods

Homework Options
Übungsheft, p. 6, Act. 1

One-Stop Planner CD-ROM

For alternative lesson plans by chapter section, to create your own customized plans, or to preview all resources available for this chapter, use the **One-Stop Planner CD-ROM**, Disc 1.

 For additional homework suggestions, see activities accompanied by this symbol throughout the chapter.

Day 7

ZWEITE STUFE

Quick Review 10 min.
- Check homework, Übungsheft, p. 6, Act. 1

Wortschatz, p. 17 10 min.
- Presenting **Wortschatz**, ATE, p. 3T
- Play Audio CD for Activity 21, p. 17

So sagt man das!, p. 17 10 min.
- Presenting **So sagt man das!**, ATE, p. 3T
- Do Activity 22, p. 18

So sagt man das!/Ein wenig Grammatik, p. 18 15 min.
- Presenting **So sagt man das!/Ein wenig Grammatik**, ATE, p. 3T
- Do Activity 23, p. 18

Wrap-Up 5 min.
- Students respond to questions about what they eat on sandwiches

Homework Options
Grammatikheft, pp. 5–6, Acts. 9–11
Übungsheft, p. 7, Act. 1
Internet Aktivitäten, see ATE, p. 3E

Day 8

ZWEITE STUFE

Quick Review 10 min.
- Check homework, Grammatikheft, pp. 5–6, Acts. 9–11

Wortschatz, p. 18 10 min.
- Presenting **Wortschatz**, ATE, p. 3T
- Teaching Transparency 1-2
- Play Audio CD for Activity 24, p. 19
- Do Activity 25, p. 19

Wortschatz/So sagt man das!, pp. 19–20 15 min.
- Presenting **Wortschatz/So sagt man das!**, ATE, p. 3U
- Play Audio CD for Activity 26, p. 20

So sagt man das!/Ein wenig Grammatik, p. 20 10 min.
- Presenting **So sagt man das!**, ATE, p. 3U
- Present **Ein wenig Grammatik**, p. 20
- Do Activity 27, p. 20
- Do Activities 28, 29, and 30, p. 21

Wrap-Up 5 min.
- Students respond to questions about how they have injured themselves

Homework Options
Grammatikheft, pp. 6–9, Acts. 12–20

Day 9

ZWEITE STUFE

Quick Review 10 min.
- Check homework, Grammatikheft, pp. 6–9, Acts. 12–20

LANDESKUNDE 20 min.
- Presenting **Landeskunde**, ATE, p. 3U
- Read **Der Euro ist da!**, pp. 22–23
- Do Activities 1 and 2, p. 23

Junge Sportler (Video) 15 min.
- Teaching Suggestions, Video Guide, p. 4
- Show **Junge Sportler** Video

Wrap-Up 5 min.
- Students respond to questions about the currency of countries in Europe

Homework Options
Übungsheft, pp. 7–10, Acts. 2–9; p. 11, Acts. 1–3

Day 10

ZWEITE STUFE

Quick Review 10 min.
- Check homework, Übungsheft, p. 11, Acts. 1–3

Quiz Review 20 min.
- Do Communicative Activities 1-3 and 1-4, pp. 3–4
- Do Additional Listening Activities 1-4, 1-5, and 1-6, pp. 9–10

Quiz 20 min.
- Quiz 1-2A or 1-2B

Homework Options
Realia 1-3, p. 53, practice the **Deutsches Buchstabieralphabet**

Day 11

ZWEITE STUFE

Quick Review 15 min.
- Return and review Quiz 1-2
- Check homework, Realia 1-3

ZUM LESEN 30 min.
- Background Information, ATE, p. 3V
- Teaching Suggestions, ATE, p. 3W
- Thinking Critically, ATE, p. 3W
- Present **Lesestrategie**, p. 24
- Do Activities 1-8 and 10, pp. 24–25

Wrap-Up 5 min.
- Students respond to questions relating their experiences to the story

Homework Options
Pupil's Edition, p. 25, Act. 9
Übungsheft, pp. 12–13, Acts. 1–4
Interaktive Spiele, see ATE, p. 3E

Day 12

REVIEW

Quick Review 10 min.
- Check homework, Übungsheft, pp. 12–13, Acts. 1–4

Kann ich's wirklich?, p. 30 20 min.
- Do Activities 1-9, p. 30

Chapter Review 20 min.
- Review chapter functions, vocabulary, and grammar; choose from **Mehr Grammatikübungen**, Activities for Communication, Listening Activities, or **Interaktive Spiele**
- Review test format and provide sample test items for students

Homework Options
Study for Chapter Test

Assessment

Test, Chapter 1 45 min.
- Administer Chapter Tests. Select from Testing Program, Alternative Assessment Guide or Test Generator.

Kapitel 1: Das Land am Meer

Suggested Lesson Plans *90-Minute Schedule*

Block 1

LOCATION OPENER 15 min.
- Present Location Opener, pp. 1–3
- The Almanac and Map, ATE, p. T78
- Show **Die neuen Bundesländer** Video
- Do Pre-viewing and Viewing Activities, Video Guide, p. 2

CHAPTER OPENER 10 min.
- Building Context, ATE, p. 3M
- Teaching Suggestions, ATE, p. 3M

LOS GEHT'S! 20 min.
- Preteaching Vocabulary, ATE, p. 3N
- Culture Note, ATE, p. 3N
- Play Audio CD for **Los geht's!**
- Have students read **Los geht's!**, pp. 6–7
- Do Activities 1-3, p. 7

ERSTE STUFE
Reading Selection, p. 8 20 min.
- Read **Rügen**, p. 8
- Do Activity 4, p. 8

So sagt man das!/Ein wenig Grammatik/Wortschatz, p. 9 20 min.
- Presenting **So sagt man das!, Ein Wenig Grammatik**, ATE, p. 3O
- Present **Wortschatz**, p. 9
- Teaching Transparency 1-1
- Play Audio CD for Activity 5, p. 9
- Do Activities 6 and 7, p. 9

Wrap-Up 5 min.
- Students respond to questions about where they have gone on vacation with their parents

Homework Options
Grammatikheft, pp. 1–2, Acts. 1–4
Übungsheft, p. 1, Acts. 1–2; p. 2, Act. 1

Block 2

ERSTE STUFE
Quick Review 10 min.
- Check homework, Grammatikheft, pp. 1–2, Acts. 1–4

Wortschatz/Ein wenig Grammatik, p. 10 35 min.
- Presenting **Ein wenig Grammatik/Wortschatz**, ATE, p. 3P
- Teaching Transparency 1-1
- Do Activities 8 and 9, p. 10
- Play Audio CD for Activity 10, p. 10
- Do Activities 11, 12, and 13, p. 11

So sagt man das!/Ein wenig Grammatik, p. 12 25 min.
- Presenting **So sagt man das!**, ATE, p. 3P
- Present **Ein wenig Grammatik**, p. 12
- Play Audio CD for Activity 14, p. 12
- Do Activities 15 and 16, p. 12

ZUM SCHREIBEN 15 min.
- Teacher Notes, ATE, p. 3Q
- Present **Schreibtipp**, p. 13
- Do Activity A, p. 13

Wrap-Up 5 min.
- Students respond to questions about what they liked and didn't like about their last vacation

Homework Options
Pupil's Edition, p. 13, Acts. B and C
Grammatikheft, pp. 3–4, Acts. 5–8
Übungsheft, pp. 2–5, Acts. 2–9

Block 3

ERSTE STUFE
Quick Review 10 min.
- Check homework, Übungsheft, pp. 2–5, Acts. 2–9

Quiz Review 20 min.
- Do **Mehr Grammatikübungen, Erste Stufe**
- Do Additional Listening Activities 1-1, 1-2, and 1-3, pp. 7–8
- Do Communicative Activities 1-1 and 1-2, pp. 1–2

Quiz 20 min.
- Quiz 1-1A or 1-1B

WEITER GEHT'S! 20 min.
- Presenting **Weiter geht's!**, ATE, p. 3R
- Play Audio CD for **Weiter geht's!**, pp. 14–15
- Do Activities 17, 18, and 19, p. 15

ZWEITE STUFE
Reading Selection, p. 16 15 min.
- Thinking Critically, ATE, p. 3S
- Read **Fit ohne Fleisch**
- Do Activity 20, p. 16

Wrap-Up 5 min.
- Students respond to questions about eating healthy foods

Homework Options
Übungsheft, p. 6, Act. 1
Internet Aktivitäten, see ATE, p. 3E

One-Stop Planner CD-ROM

For alternative lesson plans by chapter section, to create your own customized plans, or to preview all resources available for this chapter, use the **One-Stop Planner CD-ROM**, Disc 1.

For additional homework suggestions, see activities accompanied by this **H** symbol throughout the chapter.

Block 4

ZWEITE STUFE

Quick Review 10 min.
- Check homework, Übungsheft, p. 6, Act. 1

Wortschatz, p. 17 15 min.
- Presenting **Wortschatz**, ATE, p. 3T
- Play Audio CD for Activity 21, p. 17
- Do Activity 1, p. 7, Übungsheft

So sagt man das!, p. 17 10 min.
- Presenting **So sagt man das!**, ATE, p. 3T
- Do Activity 22, p. 18

So sagt man das!/Ein wenig Grammatik, p. 18 15 min.
- Presenting **So sagt man das!/Ein wenig Grammatik**, ATE, p. 3T
- Do Activity 23, p. 18

Wortschatz, p. 18 10 min.
- Presenting **Wortschatz**, ATE, p. 3T
- Teaching Transparency 1-2
- Play Audio CD for Activity 24, p. 19
- Do Activity 25, p. 19

Wortschatz/So sagt man das!, pp. 19–20 25 min.
- Presenting **Wortschatz/So sagt man das!**, ATE, p. 3U
- Play Audio CD for Activity 26, p. 20
- Do Activities 13–15, p. 7, Grammatikheft
- Do Situation 1-2, pp. 113–114, Activities for Communication

Wrap-Up 5 min.
- Students respond to questions about how they have injured themselves

Homework Options
Grammatikheft, pp. 5–6, Acts. 9–12; p. 8, Acts. 16–17
Übungsheft, pp. 7–9, Acts. 2–6

Block 5

ZWEITE STUFE

Quick Review 10 min.
- Check homework, Grammatikheft, pp. 5–6, Acts. 9–12; p. 8, Acts. 16–17

So sagt man das!/Ein wenig Grammatik, p. 20 15 min.
- Presenting **So sagt man das!**, ATE, p. 3U
- Present **Ein wenig Grammatik**, p. 20
- Do Activity 27, p. 20
- Do Activities 28, 29, and 30, p. 21
- Do Activity 18, p. 8, Grammatikheft

LANDESKUNDE 20 min.
- Presenting **Landeskunde**, ATE, p. 3U
- Read **Der Euro ist da!**, pp. 22–23
- Do Activities 1 and 2, p. 23

Junge Sportler (Video) 20 min.
- Teaching Suggestions, Video Guide, p. 4
- Show **Junge Sportler** Video
- Do Pre-viewing, Viewing, and Post-viewing activities, Video Guide, p. 5

Quiz Review 20 min.
- Do Communicative Activities 1-3 and 1-4, pp. 3–4
- Do Additional Listening Activities 1-4, 1-5, and 1-6, pp. 9–10

Wrap-Up 5 min.
- Students respond to questions about the currency of countries in Europe

Homework Options
Grammatikheft, p. 9, Acts. 19–20
Übungsheft, p. 10, Acts. 7–9; p. 11, Acts. 1–3

Block 6

ZWEITE STUFE

Quick Review 15 min.
- Check homework, Übungsheft, p. 10, Acts. 7–9; p. 11, Acts. 1–3

Quiz 20 min.
- Quiz 1-2A or 1-2B

ZUM LESEN 35 min.
- Background Information, ATE, p. 3V
- Teaching Suggestions, ATE, 3W
- Thinking Critically, ATE, p. 3W
- Present **Lesestrategie**, p. 24
- Do Activities 1-10, pp. 24–25

Kann ich's wirklich?, p. 30 15 min.
- Do Activities 1-9, p. 30

Wrap-Up 5 min.
- Students respond to questions relating their experiences to the story

Homework Options
Übungsheft, pp. 12–13, Acts. 1–4
Interaktive Spiele, see ATE, p. 3E

Block 7

REVIEW

Quick Review 15 min.
- Return and review Quiz 1-2
- Check homework, Übungsheft, pp. 12–13, Acts. 1–4

Chapter Review 30 min.
- Review chapter functions, vocabulary, and grammar; choose from **Mehr Grammatikübungen,** Activities for Communication, Listening Activities, or **Interaktive Spiele**
- Review test format and provide sample test items for students

Test, Chapter 1 45 min.
- Administer Chapter 1 Test. Select from Testing Program, Alternative Assessment Guide or Test Generator.

Teaching Suggestions, pages 4–31

Teacher Notes

- Chapter 1 is a review chapter that reintroduces functions, grammar, and vocabulary from *Komm mit!* Levels 1 and 2.

- As an additional way to quickly review Levels 1 and 2, you may want to use the *Komm mit! Interactive CD-ROM Tutor.*

- Some activities suggested in the *Teacher's Edition* ask students to contact various people, businesses, and organizations in the community. Before assigning these activities, it is advisable to request permission from parents and contactees.

- In *Komm mit!* Level 3, most pieces that reflect the traditional spelling are **Zum Lesen** selections and pieces of realia. These are permissioned documents that cannot be altered.

PAGES 4–5

CHAPTER OPENER

Pacing Tips

Chapter 1 is a review chapter. In the **Erste Stufe,** students review the functions of 'reporting past events' and 'asking how someone liked something; expressing enthusiasm or disappointment; responding enthusiastically or sympathetically.' Many other functions from previous levels are reviewed in the **Zweite Stufe.** The **Wortschatz** centers around food, injuries, and body parts. Because this is a review chapter, you should spend more time on whichever **Stufe** your students need to review most. For Lesson Plans and timing suggestions, see pages 3I–3L.

Meeting the Standards

Communication

- Reporting past events, p. 9
- Asking how someone liked something; expressing enthusiasm or disappointment; responding enthusiastically or sympathetically, p. 12
- Asking and telling what you may or may not do, p. 17
- Asking for information, p.18
- Inquiring about someone's health and responding; asking about and expressing pain, p. 20

Cultures

- Landeskunde, pp. 22–23
- Culture Note, p. 3N
- Culture Note, p. 3U

One-Stop Planner CD-ROM

For resource information, see the **One-Stop Planner CD-ROM,** Disc 1.

- Background Information, p. 3V
- Teacher Note, p. 3W

Connections
- Language-to-Language, p. 3P
- Thinking Critically, p. 3W

Comparisons
- Thinking Critically, p. 3U

Communities
- Career Path, p. 3P

Building Context

Ask students about a place or places they visited during the summer. Write the places on the board. Then ask the class what a visitor or tourist might find to do at some of the places listed. (**Was könnten Besucher oder Touristen in … unternehmen?**)

Teaching Suggestions

To reacquaint students with one another as well as to introduce new students, have them ask a partner the following questions:

1. Was hast du in den Ferien gemacht?
2. Ist etwas Interessantes oder Besonderes passiert?
3. Was hat dir im Sommer am besten gefallen?
4. Was war weniger schön?

After students have asked each other these questions, have them summarize the information they got from their partner. Then call on several students to tell about their partner's summer activities.

Chapter Sequence

CHAPTER OPENER

LOS GEHT'S!

Teaching Resources
pp. 6–7

PRINT
▸ Lesson Planner, p. 11
▸ Übungsheft, p. 1

MEDIA
▸ One-Stop Planner
▸ Audio Compact Discs, CD1, Tr. 1

PAGES 6–7

Los geht's! Summary

In *Zwei Freunde treffen sich,* Johannes and Gregor meet for the first time after their summer vacation. The following learning outcomes listed on p. 5 are modeled in the conversation: reporting past events, asking how someone liked something, expressing enthusiasm or disappointment, and responding enthusiastically or sympathetically.

Preteaching Vocabulary

Activating Prior Knowledge

Tell students that Johannes and Gregor are seeing each other while running errands after the **Sommerferien.** Then have students read each sentence and identify which sentences are in the present tense and which ones are in the past tense. Make a list of the past participles with their auxiliaries (**haben** or **sein**) and meanings on the board or on a transparency. Remind students to be on the lookout for separable-prefix past participles. Which past participles are familiar to the students? Which ones are new to them? Have students guess what the new past participles mean.

Advance Organizer

Ask students to discuss the chores and errands that must be taken care of when the family returns home after a vacation. (**Was müsst ihr alles zu Hause machen, wenn ihr aus den Ferien zurückkommt?**)

Using the Audio CD

Have students read along as they listen to the audio recording of *Zwei Freunde treffen sich* at least two times. Ask students to make note of any words or expressions they don't know. Afterwards, they can use the context and other clues to help each other define or explain unfamiliar words and phrases.

Cultures and Communities

Culture Note

On p. 6, Gregor mentions his grandmother's frugality (**Sie ist immer sehr sparsam**). His grandmother most likely grew up during World War II when staples were often scarce or rationed. This required people to develop thrifty habits that have remained with many of them ever since.

Thinking Critically

Comparing and Contrasting Ask students if they can think of a time period in U.S. history that required similar habits. (Example: the Great Depression beginning in 1929)

Comprehension Check

A Slower Pace

1 Ask students to work with a partner as they answer the eight questions in writing. As students refer back to the text, ask them to make note of where in the text they find each answer and what led them to the answer. When students have completed the activity, call on eight different students to share their answers with the rest of the class.

Building on Previous Skills

3 Before doing this activity, ask students what conjunctions they should use to introduce the clause that gives the reason. (**weil** or **denn**) Remind students of the differing word order when using **denn** and **weil.** Help students also with the prepositions and prepositional phrases they will need for expressing location for the places listed.

Teaching Suggestion

Ask pairs of students to come up with a scenario depicting what could happen next. Give students five minutes to write down some notes and a rough summary of what they predict as a continuation of the conversation between the two friends. (**Wie stellt ihr euch eine Fortsetzung dieser Unterhaltung vor? Macht euch einige Stichwörter, und schreibt eine kurze Zusammenfassung darüber.**)

LOS GEHT'S!

Teaching Resources
pp. 8–12

PRINT
▶ Lesson Planner, p. 12
▶ Listening Activities, pp. 3–5, 7–8
▶ Activities for Communication, pp. 1–2, 51, 54, 113–114
▶ Grammatikheft, pp. 1–4
▶ Grammar Tutor for Students of German, Chapter 1
▶ Übungsheft, pp. 2–5
▶ Testing Program, pp. 1–4
▶ Alternative Assessment Guide, p. 30
▶ Student Make-Up Assignments, Chapter 1

MEDIA
▶ One-Stop Planner
▶ Audio Compact Discs, CD1, Trs. 2–4, 10, 14–16
▶ Teaching Transparencies
   Situation 1-1
Mehr Grammatikübungen Answers
Grammatikheft Answers

> **PAGE 8**

Bell Work

Ask students what kind of information is typically included in travel and guide books. Using their own city or town as an example, what information can students come up with that could or should be given to visitors in a short description? Have them list ideas first. Then combine ideas on a transparency or on the chalkboard.

Preteaching Vocabulary

Here is some additional vocabulary you may want to introduce prior to reading the text with the class:
trutzig: mächtig, stark
künden: von etwas berichten
Hiddensee-Goldschmuck: *Viking gold jewelry from about 950 A.D., found between 1872 and 1874 on the isle of Hiddensee close to Rügen*
die Mole: *pier*
die Schlucht: *ravine, gorge*

Review: Reading Strategies

You may want to review reading strategies from Level 2, such as *analyzing different types of texts, using grammatical and lexical clues to derive meaning,* and *predicting the context of a text* to help students read this article about Rügen. Another reading strategy that will be helpful is *finding the main clause* before reading the many subordinate clauses used for describing places in this piece.

Communication for All Students

Visual Learners

Ask students to read the text quietly to themselves while you prepare two columns on a transparency or on the board like the ones below.

Was wissen wir über …?	
Stralsund	Sassnitz

Now ask students to scan the text again, extracting facts and information that will help them complete the chart. List their answers under the appropriate heading.

> **PAGE 9**

PRESENTING: So sagt man das!

Have students scan the **Los geht's!** conversation on pages 6–7 to identify the various verbs that are used to report past events. Then ask them to separate the verb forms into the following categories: conversational past formed with **haben,** conversational past formed with **sein,** and narrative past.

PRESENTING: Ein wenig Grammatik

Prepositions and case The three prepositions **an, auf,** and **in** indicate location and are therefore used with the dative case. Ask students when these same prepositions must be used with the accusative case. (when indicating direction) Ask students to come up with sample sentences using these prepositions with the accusative case.

Portfolio Assessment

6 You might want to suggest this activity as an oral portfolio item for your students. See *Alternative Assessment Guide,* p. 16.

STANDARDS: 1.2

Cultures and Communities

Career Path

Have students imagine they are authors writing a travel guide about the new **Bundesländer.** The guide they are writing specializes in accommodations, restaurants, and interesting sites to visit. Ask them to brainstorm places where they would need to speak German in order to obtain information for their travel guide. (Suggestion: Imagine visiting the city tourism office to get information about museum hours.)

PRESENTING: Ein wenig Grammatik

The past tense Using the brief descriptions given in the **Wortschatz** as a starting point, ask students to tell what they did last time they were at the six places mentioned.
Example:
Ich war auf der Post. Dort habe ich Briefmarken gekauft und einen Brief nach Österreich geschickt.
Next have students ask each other: **Wo warst du denn?** and give their own answers.

PRESENTING: Wortschatz

Use props to present the new vocabulary. For example, you could use foreign money to pantomime the exchanging of money, use a phone and bring an old bill for the next expressions, and so on. Tell students what you did at the different places. Then ask: **Wo war ich, und was habe ich da gemacht?**

Teaching Suggestions

10 Preview the map of **Dingskirchen** on p. 11 with students before they listen to the recording. Make sure they are familiar with all the places in town.

10 When students report back on the activities of Britta, Volker, and Thomas, encourage them to tell you several things in sequence using appropriate sequencing words.

10 You may want to use the script for this activity (p. 3F) to prepare a **Lückentext.** For example, you could leave out all of the place names and ask students to fill them in as they listen to the conversation.

Communication for All Students

Challenge

11 If you would like students to go beyond listing the things that one can do, ask them to incorporate their ideas into an ad-like skit. One student is the store owner who tries to interview the other student for a part-time position and is telling him or her about all the jobs that are involved. The owner gets interrupted several times by the third student, who plays the role of a customer asking for service.

PRESENTING: So sagt man das!

After reviewing the expressions in **So sagt man das!,** have students respond to a number of questions and statements.
Examples:
Im Sommer habe ich mir das linke Bein gebrochen.
Wie hat euch das Konzert von … gefallen?
Mike, wie war dein Fußballcamp diesen Sommer?
Ich war am … beim …spiel. Mir hat es gut gefallen.

Teaching Suggestion

14 Since the exchanges between Sabine and Uli and Bernd and Manuela are quite long, it might be best to play one scene at a time and repeat it if necessary. Check after each set of exchanges how much students understood and entered in the different columns.

Connections and Comparisons

Language-to-Language

Students might be interested to know that, like German, Spanish often uses a construction in which a verb in the third person singular requires an object pronoun.
Examples:
German: **Es gefällt mir.**
Spanish: **Me gusta.**
German: **Was fehlt dir?**
Spanish: **¿Qué te pasa?**

Ask students if they can think of other examples of this construction. (Examples: **Es schmeckt mir; Es tut mir weh; Es geht mir gut; Mir ist schlecht.**)

ERSTE STUFE

Teacher Note

16 In Levels 1 and 2, **Für mein Notizbuch** pages were provided for the students in the *Übungsheft*. Since students are expected to do more extensive writing in Level 3, you may want to ask them to keep a folder or a spiral notebook in which to write their *Notizbuch* entries.

PRESENTING: Ein wenig Grammatik

Verbs and dative case After you have reviewed the list of verbs in the Grammar Summary, help students organize the different types of verbs used with the dative case into the following categories. Some of the verbs could fall into more than one category.
a) verbs that involve physical discomfort or comfort (Example: **Mir tut der Kopf weh.**)
b) verbs whose objects refer to people (Examples: **gefallen, glauben, gehören**)
c) verbs that express personal opinion and are used with the impersonal **es** (Examples: **Es schmeckt mir gut. Es tut mir Leid.**)
Students may want to keep this list in their notebooks and add to it as they learn similar words.

Teaching Suggestion

Put the following topic on the board and ask students to discuss it: **Warum ich keine Postkarten aus den Ferien geschickt habe.** Have students write down their ideas, and then call on students to find out how they responded to the question. Ask them to give reasons for their opinion. (**Begründe deine Aussage.**)

> ### Assess
> ▶ Testing Program, pp. 1–4
>   Quiz 1-1A, Quiz 1-1B
>   Audio CD1, Tr. 10
>
> ▶ Student Make-Up Assignments
>   Chapter 1, Alternative Quiz
>
> ▶ Alternative Assessment Guide, p. 30

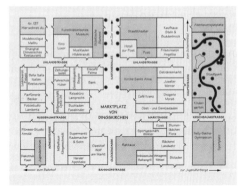

ZUM SCHREIBEN

> ### Teaching Resources
> #### p. 13
>
> **PRINT**
> ▶ Lesson Planner, p. 15
> ▶ Alternative Assessment Guide, p. 16
>
> **MEDIA**
> ▶ One-Stop Planner
> ▶ Test Generator, Chapter 1

Teacher Notes

• Encourage the process aspect of the **Zum Schreiben** activities by making sure students always do the entire writing assignment. Students need to work through all the steps of the assignments to become better writers. Some assignments may have to be started in class and completed as homework.

• You might want to consider selecting a few samples of students' final products from each of these major writing tasks with which to compile a class publication at the end of the term.

• You may want to use the portfolio evaluation forms found in the *Alternative Assessment Guide* to help you evaluate students' final products.

• Remember to consider the **Zum Schreiben** activities as you and your students determine what they will include in their portfolios.

> ### Writing Strategy
>
> The targeted strategy in this writing activity is *brainstorming and freewriting.* Students should learn about this strategy before beginning the assignment.

Prewriting
Building Context

Ask students if they document their holidays and vacations. If so, how do they do it? Does the family buy postcards or souvenirs, take pictures, or make videos? Does anybody keep a travel journal to record the daily activities?

Communication for All Students

Visual Learners

A Tell students to bring pictures, souvenirs, postcards, or maps from recent trips that will provide them with ideas for this activity.

Auditory Learners

A1 Allow students to record their ideas on audiocassette. When students have finished, have them play back their ideas and transcribe them.

Teaching Suggestion

A3 After students have collected their ideas, remind them to think about the order in which they plan to present them. Organizing events in chronological order is one way students should already be familiar with. Review sequencing words if necessary.

Writing
Teaching Suggestion

Turn students' desks to face away from each other so they can concentrate as they write. You may want to play Mozart or other classical music while they are writing.

Post-Writing
Cooperative Learning

C After students have finished Activity C1, ask them to sit together with two other classmates. Students in each group exchange papers and proceed with Activities C2 and C3 as a cooperative learning activity. Peer evaluation should focus on content and organization as well as spelling and grammar. Peers should point out strengths and weaknesses and make specific suggestions to help the writer improve his or her text.

Teaching Suggestion

You may want to have students put their journal entries in a folder or a notebook, which will become their writing journal for the term. This journal can be used for completing prewriting activities throughout the school year, and students may want to keep final versions of their writing in it as well.

Writing Assessment

You may choose to evaluate students' written work of **Was ich in den Ferien gemacht habe** using the writing rubric below.

Writing Rubric	Points			
	4	3	2	1
Content (Complete – Incomplete)				
Comprehensibility (Comprehensible – Seldom comprehensible)				
Accuracy (Accurate – Seldom accurate)				
Organization (Well-organized – Poorly organized)				
Effort (Excellent – Minimal)				

18–20: A   16–17: B   14–15: C   12–13: D   Under 12: F

WEITER GEHT'S!

Teaching Resources
pp. 14–15

PRINT
▸ Lesson Planner, p. 13
▸ Übungsheft, p. 6

MEDIA
▸ One-Stop Planner
▸ Audio Compact Discs, CD1, Tr. 5

PAGES 14–15

Weiter geht's! Summary

In *Gregor besucht Johannes,* Gregor stops by to visit Johannes and his family. The following learning outcomes listed on p. 5 are modeled in the scene: asking and telling what you may and may not do, asking for information, inquiring about someone's health and responding, asking about and expressing pain, and expressing hope.

Preteaching Vocabulary

Activating Prior Knowledge

Have students use their prior knowledge to locate different foods in the text. Some of the foods they might mention are **Kaffee, Kuchen, Erdbeeren, Fisch, Fleisch, Obst, Gemüse, Huhn.** Then have students use context to guess what **Teigwaren** is. Finally, have students reread Gregor's first line: **Ich hab's dir doch versprochen, und versprochen ist versprochen!** Can they guess what the sentence means? What form of the verb is **versprochen?**

Advance Organizer

Ask students about their most recent visit to a friend's home. When did they go, whom did they visit, and why? What were some of the things they did? What did they eat? (**Berichte der Klasse über deinen letzten Besuch bei einem Freund oder einer Freundin. Wann war das und bei wem? Warum warst du dort, und was habt ihr so gemacht? Was hast du gegessen?**)

Communication for All Students

Challenge

17 Have students use the answers to the nine questions to help them write a summary of *Gregor besucht Johannes.* (**Benutzt die Antworten zu den neun Fragen, um eine Zusammenfassung vom Inhalt dieser Unterhaltung zu schreiben!**) Tell students not to get lost in detail but to concentrate on the main points and major information.

Thinking Critically

Ask students what type of questions Johannes' parents might ask Gregor when he shares his **Rügen-Prospekte** with them. (**Was für Fragen könnten Johannes' Eltern dem Gregor stellen, wenn er ihnen seine Rügen-Prospekte zeigt?**)

ZWEITE STUFE

Teaching Resources
pp. 16–23

PRINT
▶ Lesson Planner, p. 14
▶ Listening Activities, pp. 5–6, 9–10
▶ Video Guide, pp. 3–5
▶ Activities for Communication, pp. 3–4, 52–53, 54–55, 113–114
▶ Grammatikheft, pp. 5–9
▶ Grammar Tutor for Students of German, Chapter 1
▶ Übungsheft, pp. 7–11
▶ Testing Program, pp. 5–8
▶ Alternative Assessment Guide, p. 30
▶ Student Make-Up Assignments, Chapter 1

MEDIA
▶ One-Stop Planner
▶ Audio Compact Discs, CD1, Trs. 6–8, 11, 17–19
▶ Video Program
Junge Sportler
Videocassette 1, 13:58–18:13
▶ Teaching Transparencies
Situation 1-2
Mehr Grammatikübungen Answers
Grammatikheft Answers

> **PAGE 16**

Bell Work

Ask students if they or people they know follow a vegetarian diet. If so, why? In pairs, have them discuss the pros and cons of vegetarianism. (**Bist du Vegetarier? Kennst du Leute, die Vegetarier sind? Warum bist du/sind diese Leute Vegetarier? Was sind die Vorteile und die Nachteile?**)

Thinking Critically

20 Drawing Inferences Ask students to scan the reading to identify what type of text it is. Then ask students if they generally read the Letters to the Editor section of magazines or newspapers. Can students think of the function that this section provides? (It is a forum for readers to voice their opinions.) (**Liest du gewöhnlich die Leserbriefe in Zeitschriften oder Zeitungen? Wozu dient dieser Teil einer Zeitung?**)

PRESENTING: Wortschatz

- Before introducing the new vocabulary, ask students to think of foods they already know that are either **Tierprodukte** or **Pflanzenprodukte** and make a list of them.

- To introduce the new vocabulary, use food props.

- To practice this and previously learned vocabulary, ask students to describe a dish that includes one of the featured products. (**In welchen Gerichten esst ihr diese aufgelisteten Produkte? Könnt ihr diese Gerichte ein wenig beschreiben?**)

Teaching Suggestion

21 Stop the recording intermittently and check students' understanding of key information. When students have finished, have them report back on their findings. Then ask for a summary of the eating habits of each of the three students.

PRESENTING: So sagt man das!

After reviewing the content of **So sagt man das!,** ask students for the meaning of the German modal verb **dürfen.** (expresses the idea of permission: *may, to be allowed to,* and *can* as in *What can't you eat? Can you eat everything?*)

Communication for All Students

Visual Learners

22 Once students have completed this partner activity, gather and record the information about students' eating and drinking habits. Make a simple chart to display the information on a transparency or on the board. Ask students to examine the information in the chart. Then ask them to analyze the data and give a brief summary of the class's eating habits. (**Schaut euch die Informationen an der Tafel näher an. Was sagen sie über die Essgewohnheiten dieser Klasse aus?**)

PRESENTING: So sagt man das!/ Ein wenig Grammatik

Dieser, welcher Review phrases in **So sagt man das!** through question and answer practice. Then place on a table at the front of the classroom various pictures representing items from each of the following categories: **Obst, Gemüse, Fleisch,** and **Getränke.** Mark the items with prices and freshness dates.

TEACHER	Welches Fleisch ist heute frisch?
STUDENT(S)	Dieses Schweinefleisch ist heute frisch.
TEACHER	Welche Getränke trinkst du gern?
STUDENT(S)	Diese hier, Milch, Wasser und Limonade.
TEACHER	Welche Gemüsesorten isst du nicht gern?
STUDENT	Diese hier, Mais, Rosenkohl und Spargel.
TEACHER	Welches Obst ist am teuersten?
STUDENT(S)	Diese Wassermelone ist am teuersten.

You may want to provide students with a model of the above exchange, either on the board or on a transparency. Switch roles occasionally with students so that they can practice with forms of **welcher** as well as with forms of **dieser.**

Communication for All Students

Kinesthetic Learners

23 Ask students to follow the same directions but to role-play a conversation that takes place in the cafeteria line. You may provide some props such as trays and utensils. Students take turns performing their scenes in front of the class.

PRESENTING: Wortschatz

- Prior to introducing the vocabulary, make a list of the items and bring them to class. Arrange them on a table and ask students to gather around as you introduce the foods and prepare a sandwich.

- Ask a couple of volunteers to take over and describe what they are doing as they each prepare a sandwich.

PRESENTING: Wortschatz

- Introduce the first four statements and phrases and provide immediate practice by asking students to take the roles of the people pictured and to respond accordingly when you ask: **Was ist passiert? Hast du dich verletzt?** Then ask students if they have ever suffered from any of these injuries and when, where, and how it happened. (**Ist euch so etwas Ähnliches schon mal passiert? Wann, wo und wie ist das passiert?**)

- To introduce the eight parts of the body, point them out on yourself. You may want to include other previously learned body parts by having students point to the place where it hurts as they answer your questions. (Examples: **Was tut dir weh, das Handgelenk? Was hast du dir verletzt, die Schulter? Hast du dich in den Daumen geschnitten?**)

Using the Video

Videocassette 1, 13:58–18:13
In the video clip *Junge Sportler,* students from Dresden tell how their training program in sports has changed since there reunification of Germany. See *Video Guide,* p. 4, for suggestions.

PRESENTING: So sagt man das!

Ask students to come up with questions a physician might ask a patient who is not feeling well. Make a list of the questions students suggest and then ask them to come up with possible answers for each of the physician's questions.

PRESENTING: So sagt man das!

- Using the four pictures in the top row of the **Wortschatz** on p. 19, have individual students tell what happened to them. Then have another student express hope that something isn't broken or that he or she will soon feel better.

- Ask students to react to you in a caring way when you tell them what happened to you. Students thus get practice with the polite form **Ich hoffe, dass Ihnen …** or **Hoffentlich haben Sie sich nicht ….**

Portfolio Assessment

28 You might want to suggest this activity as a written portfolio item for your students. See *Alternative Assessment Guide,* p. 16.

Von der Schule zum Beruf

30

Encourage students to look at German health Web sites to research specific vocabulary used.

 LANDESKUNDE

Cultures and Communities

Culture Note

The graphic art on euro bills reflects different eras and styles in Europe. The architectural styles shown focus on seven periods of European cultural history: Classical, Romantic, Gothic, Renaissance, Baroque, Rococo, and the architecture of the twentieth century. Architectural elements such as gates, windows, and bridges symbolize the openness and cooperation of the member states. The euro bills were designed by Robert Kalina, an employee of the Austrian Nationalbank, whose designs were chosen from 43 proposed designs.

Thinking Critically

Comparing and Contrasting Have students choose three countries that do not belong to the **Währungsunion.** Then give students the following scenario: An American tourist is travelling to the three countries students just chose. The tourist starts his trip by exchanging $1000 into the currency of the first of the three countries. Seeing that he still has some of the foreign currency left at the end of the first leg of his trip, he exchanges that money into the currency of the second non-**Währungsunion** country on his itinerary. He still has some foreign money left at the end of his stay in the second country, and he exchanges that money into the currency of the third country he's visiting. Have students calculate how much the tourist's original $1000 lost in value through the many foreign currency exchanges. Students should realize that visitors fare better when they don't need to exchange their money more than once.

Teacher Note

Encourage students to research several Euro Web sites and to check out German department store Web sites to see the newly introduced currency in real-life situations.

 Game

Play the game **Der besetzte Stuhl.** Choose one student to start the game. Seat him or her on a chair in front of the class (**der besetzte Stuhl**). The student must answer questions asked by his or her classmates. When the student on **der besetzte Stuhl** has answered three questions correctly, he or she may choose another student to sit in **der besetzte Stuhl.** While asking questions, students should use the function and vocabulary boxes taught in the **Zweite Stufe** as a point of departure, but questions can also be related to any previously learned words and expressions.

Examples:

Nenne mindestens zwei Tierprodukte, die du neu gelernt hast!

Was ist Rote Grütze?

Wie kann man sich in der Küche verletzen?

Assess

▸ Testing Program, pp. 5–8
  Quiz 1-2A, Quiz 1-2B
  Audio CD1, Tr. 11

▸ Student Make-Up Assignments
  Chapter 1, Alternative Quiz

▸ Alternative Assessment Guide, p. 30

ZUM LESEN

Teaching Resources
pp. 24–25

PRINT 📖
▸ Lesson Planner, p. 15
▸ Übungsheft, pp. 12–13
▸ Reading Strategies and Skills, Chapter 1
▸ Lies mit mir! 3, Chapter 1

MEDIA 💿
▸ One-Stop Planner
▸ Audio Compact Discs, CD1, Tr. 9

Prereading
Building Context

Ask students to think about the concept of time. Time, as measured by our watches, is something that we usually think of as "objective"—that is, a kind of universal truth, quite independent of human thought. Do students ever think about how arbitrary our division of time into days, hours, minutes, and seconds truly is? Are five minutes spent talking to a good friend really the same as five minutes spent sleeping or five minutes spent waiting for a bus? Have they ever had the experience of dreaming about a seemingly endless event or series of events, only to wake up and find that only a few minutes have passed and that it's still a long time until morning?

Cultures and Communities

Background Information

Many readers of Kafka have remarked on the "irrational and dreamlike quality" of his prose. Although we tend to think of him as a unique writer, the notion that dreams are a key to the understanding of the individual (or at least his or her repressed emotions) and of the collective unconscious was quite current among European intellectuals of Kafka's time. What is perhaps most unique about Kafka is that he presents such experiences in a very "unemotional" style, pretending to report them more or less objectively, rather than commenting on the intensity of feeling that underlies his writing. The words "repressed emotion" may come to mind when reading his short stories and novels.

Teacher Note

Activity 1 is a prereading activity.

Reading
Teaching Suggestion

The first indirect quote in the text is short and is introduced by the verb **sagen** ("… sagt man ihm, daß B, … gegangen sei …"). Students should be able to at least skim over it without losing the thread of the narrative. However, the second, long indirect quote may cause them to entirely misread that part of the narrative. Tell students that everything between "Zu Hause erfährt er" and "…noch oben in A's Zimmer" is reported speech—from persons unknown. The forms **sei, habe,** and **befinde sich** in these three sentences come from the special pattern used in German to indicate indirect quotations, or reported speech. Another way to write this would have been: **Zu Hause erfährt er, dass B doch schon gleich früh gekommen ist …** Kafka, however, chose to use the more formal, impersonal style of quotation.

Thinking Critically

2 **Analyzing** If students have trouble getting started on the "Why?" portion of this question, you might ask where else they could find this kind of representation of individuals. Are **A, B,** and **H** similar to the X, Y, and Z in math, or to the John/Jane Doe in judicial warrants for unknown persons? Why did Kafka not choose the letters M, R, and W, for instance? How are these names different from the fictional ones used in reports with the disclaimer "Only the names have been changed to protect the innocent"?

Teaching Suggestion

3 You may want to draw students' attention to the indefinite **man** as the "other character or characters" in the story in addition to **A** and **B.** There are actually two settings in the story, the town or village of **H,** and **A's** village and home. Also, students should note the discrepancy between **zehn Minuten** and **zehn Stunden**—this is crucial. Why, for example, did Kafka not make it ten minutes and *three* hours?

Teacher Note

4 The idea of "confusion" should be at the center of the summary statements.

Thinking Critically

8 **Analyzing** Students will need to take into consideration the concept of "human error" as opposed to some kind of cause outside the characters' control. Is **A's** disorientation internally or externally caused? A key question is: what causes **A's** incomprehensible behavior to **B** in the second paragraph? Does **A** later remember this episode? How do we know it happened? Why does Kafka use indirect quotes from an unidentified source? What is **A** planning to explain to **B** as he runs up the stairs?

Teaching Suggestion

9 You may want to point out to students that a **Nacherzählung** is a little different from an abstract or summary—more like a concise abridgement—but not more than half as long as the original.

Cultures and Communities

Teacher Note

The **Selbstporträt** shown on p. 24 is that of Karl Schmidt-Rottluff who co-founded the group of expressionists in Dresden in 1905 called **Die Brücke.** The group was dissolved by 1913 due to quarrels among group members concerning the group's philosophy.

Connections and Comparisons

Thinking Critically

Evaluating Kafka's story is not an "objective" report—for example, a police report or the kinds of facts that the ambulance attendants might string together if called to assist **A** after his accident. The human portrait in the text is also quite obviously not the same as a photograph. But are they "subjective" in the same ways? To get students started on this discussion, ask them to think about some other portraits and some other short stories that everyone in the class is familiar with. (Examples: Mona Lisa, some of Picasso's paintings, one of Poe's "strange" stories, some contemporary science fiction or fantasy literature)

Post-Reading
Teacher Note

Activity 10 is a post-reading task that will show whether students can apply what they have learned.

Class Discussion

Ask students to think about how they would make a short film of this story. How would they depict the characters? What film devices would they use to handle the time elements? Students should discuss their ideas with the class, using everyone's knowledge of the various film techniques currently available.

Zum Lesen Answers

Answers to Activity 1 A common confusion, an ordinary occurrence

Answers to Activity 2 **A** and **B** designate the main characters, and **H** represents a town or a city; answers will vary, possible answer: the letters stress how generic or common the situation is.

Answers to Activity 3 **A** and **B** (two male adults); unnamed town (where **A** resides) and **H**. **A** goes to see **B** in **H** to do business. The next morning he makes the same journey, but arrives too late to speak with **B**. A hurries back home, but arrives too late because it took him ten hours to get to **H**.

Answers to Activity 4 **A** is doing business with **B**, but arrives too late to speak to him in **H**. He hurries home to catch **B** at his office, but falls as he runs up his stairs. **B** does not see him and leaves **A**'s office.

Answers to Activity 5 Time lines will vary. The important thing students should notice is that time is distorted in the story, however they choose to depict it.

Answers to Activity 6 **wichtig:** the business deal; **ermüdet:** A; **ärgerlich:** B; **in Angst:** A; **eilig:** A; **unverständlich:** A's behavior; **glücklich:** A; **ohnmächtig:** A; **unfähig:** A; **winselnd:** A; **undeutlich:** B's distance from A; **wütend:** B

Answers to Activity 7 **Schnelligkeit:** *speed;* **Nebenumstände:** *minor circumstances;* **Ausbleiben:** *absence;* **Augenblick:** *moment*

Answers to Activity 8 **A** arrives too late to meet **B**; it takes him ten hours to get to **H**, instead of ten minutes; **B** is angry about **A** not showing up in **H** and (in the doorway at **A**'s room) for being told by **A** that he has no time to talk; **B** first goes to **A**'s town to see him, and then, after meeting him in the doorway, he decides to wait upstairs in **A**'s room for **A** to return; the conflict is not resolved. When **B** decides to leave **A**'s house and not wait for **A**, **B** does not see **A** lying on the stairs and never finds out what happened. The business deal is left unresolved.

MEHR GRAMMATIKÜBUNGEN

The **Mehr Grammatikübungen** activities are designed as supplemental activities for the grammatical concepts presented in the chapter. You might use them as additional practice, for review, or for assessment.

For more grammar presentations, review, and practice, refer to the following:
• Grammatikheft
• Grammar Tutor for Students of German
• Grammar Summary on pp. R22–R39
• Übungsheft
• Grammar and Vocabulary quizzes
  (Testing Program)
• Test Generator
• Interaktive Spiele at go.hrw.com

KANN ICH'S WIRKLICH?

This page helps students prepare for the test. It is a brief checklist of the major points covered in the chapter. The students should be reminded that it is only a checklist and not necessarily everything that will appear on the test.

For additional self-check options, refer students to the *Grammar Tutor* and the Online self-test for this chapter.

WORTSCHATZ

Review and Assess

Visual Learners
Provide students with an illustration of a body with lines pointing to body parts you wish to review. Ask studens to label the body parts.

Circumlocution
Play **Das treffende Wort suchen** to review food vocabulary. Write words for some popular American snacks and drinks on the board, or use words from the **Zweite Stufe** vocabulary. Ask student volunteers to describe these foods in German to someone who is new to our country and may not have tried these foods. Here are some examples you might use: dill pickle, donut, banana split, frozen yogurt, peanut butter, corn chips, smoothie, hot apple cider. See p. 31C for procedures.

Using the Video
Videocassette 1, 18:18–20:28
At this time, you might want to use the authentic advertising footage from German television. See *Video Guide*, p. 4, for suggestions.

Teacher Note
Give the **Kapitel 1** Chapter Test: *Testing Program*, pp. 9–14 Audio CD 1, Trs. 12–13.

KAPITEL 1   REVIEW   3X

1
Das Land am Meer

Objectives

In this chapter you will review and practice how to

Erste Stufe

- report past events
- ask how someone liked something
- express enthusiasm or disappointment
- respond enthusiastically or sympathetically

Zweite Stufe

- ask and tell what you may or may not do
- ask for information
- inquire about someone's health and respond
- ask about and express pain
- express hope

internet

go.hrw.com
.com
ADRESSE: go.hrw.com
KENNWORT: WK3 DIE NEUEN BUNDESLAENDER-1

◀ **Ferienparadies Insel Rügen**

Los geht's! · *Zwei Freunde treffen sich*

Johannes: Hallo, Gregor!

Gregor: Hallo, Hannes! Schon lange nicht gesehen!

Johannes: Stimmt! <u>Ich find's toll</u>, dass du auch mal wieder im Lande bist!

Gregor: Tja, du freust dich, dass ich wieder da bin, und <u>ich find's schade.</u>

Johannes: Wirklich? Hat es dir auf Rügen so gut gefallen?

Gregor: <u>Es war einsame Spitze!</u> Wirklich Superferien!

Johannes: Na, <u>das freut mich.</u>

Gregor: Was machst du denn jetzt? Du siehst so nach Arbeit aus.

Johannes: Ich war gerade im Getränkemarkt, hab Flaschen zurückgebracht. Bei uns ist heute großer Aufräumetag. Alle sind am Arbeiten. Ich hab heute schon die Garage aufgeräumt, den Müll sortiert und weggebracht — ja, ich muss arbeiten, und du gehst spazieren.

Gregor: Du, bei uns ist Waschtag — wir müssen die ganze Ferienwäsche waschen. Ich war eben in der Bücherei und hab unsere Ferienlektüre zurückgebracht. Und vorher war ich einkaufen. Übrigens, im Supermarkt hab ich die Ulla getroffen. Sie war in Kalifornien; <u>hat ihr echt prima gefallen.</u> Sag, wie war's denn in den Bergen?

Johannes: <u>Nicht besonders!</u> Da hat's dauernd geregnet. Wir sind kaum gewandert, und ich habe die meiste Zeit im Hallenbad verbracht. Na ja. Was kann man machen?

Gregor: Du, ich muss weiter. Ich muss vor zwölf noch was erledigen. Ich muss auf der Bank Geld wechseln für meine Oma. Sie war in Amerika und hat die meisten Dollar wieder zurückgebracht. Das kann auch nur die Oma! Sie ist immer sehr sparsam.

Johannes: Meine aber auch! Ja, also … du, komm doch mal rüber zu uns! Meine Eltern waren noch nie an der Ostsee, und sie würden sich bestimmt für Rügen interessieren. Bring deine Fotos mit!

Gregor: Mach ich. Ich bring auch ein paar Prospekte mit, da können sie sich schon mal etwas aussuchen.

Johannes: Okay! Also, tschüs!

Gregor: Tschüs!

Übungsheft, S. 1

1 Was passiert hier?

Sprechen Hast du das Gespräch verstanden? Dann beantworte die Fragen!

1. Wo, glaubst du, treffen sich Johannes und Holger?
2. Warum findet es Johannes toll, dass Gregor wieder da ist?
3. Wo war Gregor? Mit wem war er weg, und wie hat es ihm gefallen?
4. Wo war Johannes? Was erzählt er über seine Ferien?
5. Warum können die beiden Jungen nicht länger miteinander sprechen?
6. Was erzählt Gregor über seine Oma, und warum erzählt er das überhaupt?
7. Warum soll Gregor Johannes besuchen und Prospekte mitbringen?
8. Was haben die beiden Jungen heute schon alles getan?

1. auf der Straße
2. weil Gregor lange weg war
3. auf Rügen / mit seiner Familie; super
4. in den Bergen / es hat geregnet; sind kaum gewandert; war meistens im Hallenbad
5. Gregor muss noch zur Bank.
6. Sie war in Amerika und hat die meisten Dollar wieder zurückgebracht; weil er die Dollar auf der Bank umtauschen muss
7. weil Johannes' Eltern sich für Rügen interessieren würden
8. Johannes: Flaschen in den Getränkemarkt zurückgebracht; Garage aufgeräumt; Müll sortiert und weggebracht / Gregor: Wäsche gewaschen; Ferienlektüre in die Bücherei zurückgebracht; war einkaufen

2 Genauer lesen

For answers, see underlined words in text on page 6.

Lesen Read the text again, then answer these questions.

1. Which phrases express liking something or not?
2. Which ones express enthusiasm and disappointment?

3 Wer war wo?

Sprechen/Schreiben Sag, wo jede von diesen vier Personen war und warum! Du kannst das auch aufschreiben.

a. Gregor
b. Johannes
c. Ulla
d. Gregors Oma

a. Rügen: hat Ferien gemacht; Bücherei: hat Ferienlektüre zurückgebracht; Supermarkt: war einkaufen
b. in den Bergen: hat Ferien gemacht; Hallenbad: weil es meistens geregnet hat; Getränkemarkt: hat Flaschen zurückgebracht
c. Kalifornien: hat Ferien gemacht
d. Amerika: hat Urlaub gemacht

Amerika   Rügen   Getränkemarkt

Berge   Hallenbad   Kalifornien

Bücherei   Supermarkt

Erste Stufe

Objectives Reporting past events; asking how someone liked something; expressing enthusiasm or disappointment; responding enthusiastically or sympathetically

WK3 DIE NEUEN
BUNDESLAENDER-1

Die über 750 Jahre alte HANSE-STADT STRALSUND liegt, vom Festland kommend, am Anfang und am Ende jeder Rügen-Reise. Der Rügendamm und viele geschichtliche Ereignisse verbinden die 926 km² große Insel mit dem Festland. Eine trutzige Stadtmauer, die prächtigen Giebel jahrhundertealter Kaufmannshäuser, hochhinaufragende Kirchen, das prunkvolle Rathaus am Alten Markt und schöne Klosteranlagen in mittelalterlicher Backsteingotik künden vom einstigen Reichtum der Stadt am Strelasund. Ein Bummel durch die alten Gassen, vorbei an bunten Geschäften der Fußgängerzone, Besuche des Kulturhistorischen Museums, wo der berühmte Hiddensee-Goldschmuck aufbewahrt wird und des Meeresmuseums mit Aquarien sind unvergeßliche Erlebnisse für jung und alt.

SASSNITZ, einst Badeort, später Stadt der Rügenfischer und Fährhafen nach Skandinavien, liegt am Tor zum Nationalpark Jasmund. Entlang der Mole im Fischerhafen riecht's nach Meer, Teer und Fisch. Saßnitz ist Ausgangspunkt für die romantische Tour auf den Spuren Caspar David Friedrichs[1], vorbei an den Wissower Klinken, den Tälern und Schluchten des Stubnitzwaldes bis zum 107m hohen Königsstuhl, dem magischen Anziehungspunkt aller Rügen-Besucher. Jedoch, wer das Auto benutzt, vermag den wahren Reiz dieser Landschaft nur zu ahnen.

Königsstuhl

Stralsunder Rathaus

4 Von Stralsund nach Saßnitz

Lesen Lies diesen Bericht über Rügen, und beantworte die Fragen!

1. Wo liegt Rügen, und wie kommt man auf diese Insel? *1. in der Ostsee / über den Rügendamm*

2. Wie zeigt sich, dass Stralsund im Mittelalter sehr reich war?
2. hat trutzige Stadtmauer, Kaufmannshäuser mit prächtigen Giebeln, prunkvolles Rathaus, schöne gotische Klosteranlagen

3. see answer no. 2, alte Gassen, bunte Geschäfte, Kulturhistorisches Museum, Hiddensee-Goldschmuck, Meeresmuseum

3. Was kann man in Stralsund alles sehen?

4. Was für ein Ort ist Saßnitz?

5. Wofür ist Saßnitz bekannt?

4. früherer Badeort, Stadt der Rügenfischer, Fährhafen nach Skandinavien

5. Wissower Klinken, Stubnitzwald, Königsstuhl

---

1. Caspar David Friedrich wurde 1774 in Greifswald geboren und starb 1840 in Dresden. Er ist der bekannteste Meister der protestantischen-norddeutschen Landschaftsmalerei der Romantik.

So sagt man das!

Reporting past events

Schon bekannt

When asking someone about something in the past, you might ask:

Sag mal, was hast du denn am Sonntag gemacht?

And the response might be:

Du, ich bin mit meiner Fahrradclique in den Bergen gewesen. Wir waren auf dem Wallberg. Dort sind wir gewandert, und ich hab viel fotografiert. Ach ja, am Abend waren wir noch im Kino.

Ein wenig Grammatik

Schon bekannt

You know sentences such as:

**Gregors Familie war an der Ostsee.
Sie waren auf der Insel Rügen.
Johannes war mit den Eltern in den Bergen.
Aber die meiste Zeit war er im Hallenbad.**

Point out the prepositions in these sentences. Which case form follows them? What do these phrases express? For more on this point, see the Grammar Summary.

Grammatikheft, S. 1, Ü. 1

Mehr Grammatikübungen, S. 26, Ü. 1

Und dann noch...

letzte	Woche
letztes	Wochenende
letzten	Monat
letztes	Jahr
gerade	*just*
vor kurzem	*recently*
neulich	*the other day*

What do the different endings of **letzt-** indicate? Which case are these time expressions in?[1] You may also use **dies-** and **nächst-** in the same way.

Übungsheft, S. 2, Ü. 1   Grammatikheft, S. 2, Ü. 2–4

---

5 **Grammatik im Kontext**   Script and answers on p. 3G

CD 1 Tr. 2

Zuhören Schüler erzählen, wann sie Ferien gemacht haben und wo sie waren. Sie sagen auch, warum sie dort Ferien gemacht haben. Schreib ihre Aussagen auf unter den Rubriken (*columns*): Wann? Wo? und Warum?!

6 **Grammatik im Kontext**

a. **Schreiben** Schreib mehrere Ferienorte, die du schon kennst oder von denen du schon gehört hast, auf eine Liste! Dann stell eine kleine Ferienreise zusammen!

b. **Sprechen** Such dir jetzt eine Partnerin! Erzähl ihr, wo du in den letzten Ferien überall warst! Gebrauch dabei die Adverbien: zuerst, dann, danach und zuletzt! Tauscht dann die Rollen aus!

7 **Wo übernachtet und esst ihr gewöhnlich?**

a. **Schreiben** Schreib auf, wo du gewöhnlich übernachtest und isst, wenn du mit deinen Eltern unterwegs bist!

b. **Sprechen** Sprich dann mit deinem Partner darüber! Gib auch Gründe dafür an!

BEISPIEL
DU Wo übernachtet ihr gewöhnlich, wenn ihr unterwegs seid?
PARTNER Wir übernachten gewöhnlich in einem Motel, weil es nicht so teuer ist.

---

1. In German, definite time expressions involving nouns are always in the accusative case.

ERSTE STUFE   STANDARDS: 1.1, 1.2   *neun*   **9**

Ein wenig Grammatik

Schon bekannt

1–1

Read this paragraph:

Zuerst habe ich den Rasen gemäht. Dann habe ich meiner Mutter im Haus geholfen — ich habe für sie die Küchenfenster geputzt. Danach bin ich zum Bäcker gegangen und hab ein paar Brötchen gekauft. Am Nachmittag bin ich noch im Schwimmbad gewesen, und am Abend war ich mit meinen Freunden im Kino.

Which tense is used in this paragraph? Name the verb forms used to express that tense. For more on this point, see the Grammar Summary.

Übungsheft, S. 2, Ü. 2

Mehr Grammatikübungen, S. 26, Ü. 2

8 Grammatik im Kontext

a. Schreiben In der letzten Woche hast du bestimmt zu Hause geholfen. Schreib auf, was du alles getan hast und für wen!

b. Sprechen Frag deinen Partner, was er in der letzten Woche zu Hause für seine Eltern, Geschwister oder andere Verwandte getan hat! Danach sagst du ihm, was du für deine Familie getan hast.

9 Grammatik im Kontext

a. Schreiben Schreib auf, was du in den letzten zwei Tagen alles gemacht hast, um dich körperlich fit zu halten! Schreib mindestens sechs Sätze auf!

b. Sprechen Erzähl einer Partnerin, was du vorgestern alles gemacht hast! Sie erzählt dir dann, was sie gestern getan hat.

Wortschatz

Wo warst du, und was hast du dort erledigt?

Ich war auf der Bank. Ich hab Geld umgewechselt, Dollar in Euro.

Ich war auf der Post. Dort hab ich telefoniert und eine Rechnung bezahlt.

Ich war im Sportgeschäft Winkler. Da hab ich eine Jacke umgetauscht, denn sie war zu klein.

Ich war in der Bücherei. Ich hab Bücher zurückgebracht und einige ausgeliehen.

Ich war im Getränkemarkt. Ich hab leere Flaschen zurückgebracht und vier Flaschen Limo gekauft.

Ich war im Musikladen. Dort hab ich mir eine CD bestellt, eine neue CD von den „Prinzen".

Grammatikheft, S. 3, Ü. 5–6

Mehr Grammatikübungen, S. 27, Ü. 3

10 **Was haben die Schüler in der Stadt gemacht?** Script and answers on p. 3G

CD 1 Tr. 3

Zuhören Schüler erzählen, was sie in der Stadt gemacht haben. Schau beim Zuhören auf den Stadtplan von Dingskirchen auf Seite 11! Schreib für jeden Schüler zuerst auf, wo er war und danach, beim zweiten Zuhören, was er dort gemacht hat! Vergleiche deine Notizen mit denen deines Partners! Habt ihr beiden wirklich alles verstanden und wisst, was diese Schüler alles gemacht haben? Wenn ihr nicht alles verstanden habt, müsst ihr euch die Übung zusammen noch einmal anhören.

11 Was kann man dort tun?

Lesen/Sprechen Bildet drei oder vier kleine Gruppen! Überlegt euch so viele Antworten wie möglich zu folgender Frage: Was kann man alles in den Geschäften und Institutionen tun, die auf dieser Skizze eingezeichnet sind? Ein Schriftführer von jeder Gruppe schreibt die Antworten auf.

BEISPIEL In einem Buchladen kann man: Bücher kaufen, Bücher bestellen …

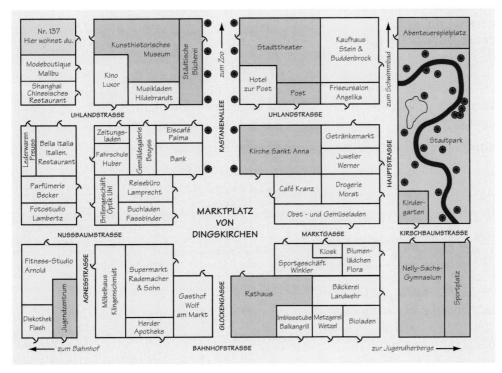

12 Überall in Dingskirchen

Sprechen Frag deinen Partner, wo er etwas gemacht hat! Stellt euch abwechselnd diese Fragen!

BEISPIEL DU **Wo hast du die Äpfel gekauft?**
PARTNER **Im Obst- und Gemüseladen in der Nussbaumstraße.**

T-Shirt kaufen	Geburtstag feiern	Nussbaumstrasse	Bank (auf der)
Limo kaufen	Taschenrechner kaufen	Brillengeschäft	Stadtpark
CD hören	Geld umwechseln	Supermarkt	Metzgerei
Hackfleisch holen	Lehrer treffen (*meet*)	Schul-Shop	Musikladen
Volleyball spielen	Geld abholen	Restaurant	Getränkemarkt
Brille bekommen	telefonieren	Post (auf der)	Sportgeschäft

13 Grammatik im Kontext

a. **Schreiben** Auf dem Weg zur Schule hast du an drei oder vier verschiedenen Geschäften angehalten und dir etwas besorgt. Schreib auf, wo du überall warst und was du dort gekauft hast!

b. **Schreiben** Auf dem Weg von der Schule nach Hause hast du an drei oder vier verschiedenen Stellen gestoppt, um etwas zu erledigen. Schreib auf, wo du warst und was du dort erledigt hast!

c. **Lesen/Sprechen** Lies deinem Partner vor, was du aufgeschrieben hast! Wenn er auch dort war, wo du warst, muss er es dir sagen. Tauscht dann die Rollen aus!

Asking how someone liked something; expressing enthusiasm or disappointment; responding enthusiastically or sympathetically

Schon bekannt

In order to find out how someone liked something or someplace, you might ask:

> **Wie hat dir der Film gefallen?**
> **Hat euch Österreich gefallen?**
> **Na, wie war's denn? Hat es euch gefallen?**

If you liked it, you may say:

> **Er war super!**
> **Mir hat es gefallen.**
> **Also, uns hat's gut gefallen.**

If you didn't like it, you may say:

> **Er hat uns überhaupt nicht gefallen.**
> **Mir hat es nicht gefallen.**

The other person may respond enthusiastically or sympathetically:

> **Das freut mich!**
> **Na, super!**

> **Das tut mir Leid.**
> **Das ist aber schade!**

Übungsheft, S. 3, Ü. 3–4

Script and answers on p. 3G

14 Grammatik im Kontext

CD 1 Tr. 4

Zuhören Vier Schüler erzählen, wo sie gestern gewesen sind, was sie dort gemacht haben, wie es ihnen gefallen hat und warum oder warum nicht. Übertrag die Tabelle rechts in dein Heft, und trag die Information ein, die du hörst!

wer?	wo?	was?	gefallen?	warum?

15 Grammatik im Kontext

a. Sprechen Such dir eine Partnerin! Entscheidet euch für (*decide on*) einen Ort auf dem Stadtplan von Dingskirchen! Überlegt euch, was euch an diesem Platz gefallen oder nicht gefallen hat und warum! Denkt dabei an einen ähnlichen Platz in eurem Heimatort!

b. Schreiben Schreibt eure Gedanken auf einen Zettel! Ordnet eure Gründe nach: was euch (gut, besonders gut) gefallen hat und was euch nicht (gar nicht, überhaupt nicht) gefallen hat!

c. Sprechen Danach erzählt einer von euch der ganzen Klasse, wo ihr wart und was euch dort gefallen oder nicht gefallen hat. Der Rest der Klasse macht entsprechende Bemerkungen wie: Das freut uns! oder: Das tut uns aber Leid!

16 Für mein Notizbuch

Schreiben Schreib in dein Notizbuch, wann und wo du deine letzten Ferien verbracht hast, was du dort alles gemacht hast und wie dir alles gefallen oder nicht gefallen hat! Vergiss nicht, deine Aussagen zu begründen!

Ein wenig Grammatik

Schon bekannt

There are some verbs that are always used with the dative case.

> **Der Urlaub hat meinen Eltern überhaupt nicht gefallen.**
> **Die Ferien haben mir gut gefallen.**

For dative case forms and for verbs that are used with the dative case, see the Grammar Summary.

Übungsheft, S. 4–5, Ü. 5–9

Grammatikheft, S. 4, Ü. 7–8

Mehr Grammatikübungen, S. 27, Ü. 4

Zum Schreiben

Vacationers very often like to keep a record of what they see and do. Some people take pictures or make videos, some buy postcards, and some record their activities in a journal. In this activity, you will choose an experience you had during your last vacation and write about it as though you were writing in your journal.

Was ich in den Ferien gemacht habe.

Mach eine Liste von allen Erlebnissen, die du in den Ferien gehabt hast! Dann wähl ein oder zwei von den interessantesten (oder lustigsten, traurigsten usw.) Erlebnissen aus, und schreib sie in dein Tagebuch!

Schreibtipp

Brainstorming and freewriting Whatever your purpose in writing — whether you are writing an assignment for one of your classes, for the school paper, or for yourself, as in your journal — you will write more effectively if you develop an idea of what you want to write about, then focus on that idea. A good way to develop ideas is to brainstorm and freewrite, writing down everything that comes to mind without worrying about grammar or sequencing. Once you have several ideas, narrow your focus to the one or two ideas that really convey what you want to say.

A. Vorbereiten

1. Schreib eine Liste von allen Dingen, die du in den Ferien gemacht hast! (Was hast du alles gemacht? Bist du zu Hause geblieben, oder bist du verreist? Wohin bist du gereist? Wer war dabei? Was hast du dort gemacht? Was hast du gesehen? Wo hast du gewohnt? usw.)

2. Wähl jetzt eine oder zwei Ideen von der Liste, um dein Thema zu beschränken! Unterstreiche alle anderen Ideen, die auch mit deinem „Hauptthema" zusammenhängen!

3. Schreib jetzt über dieses Erlebnis! Wenn möglich, verwende auch die Ideen, die du unterstrichen hast — aber denk noch nicht an die Grammatik oder die Wortstellung!

B. Ausführen

Verwende jetzt deine Liste und deinen frei geschriebenen Text, um eine geordnete und logische Tagebucheintragung zu schreiben! Vergiss nicht, das Datum zu notieren!

C. Überarbeiten

1. Lies deine Eintragung durch, und vergleiche sie mit dem frei geschriebenen Text und mit der Liste! Hast du alles geschrieben, was du schreiben wolltest, oder hast du etwas in der endgültigen Version ausgelassen? Wenn ja, trag diese Ideen jetzt ein!

2. Wie sieht dein Text jetzt aus? Hast du die Ideen logisch geordnet? Hast du dein Erlebnis ausführlich beschrieben, oder hast du nur eine Liste von Erlebnissen gemacht?

3. Lies die Eintragung noch einmal durch, und denk diesmal auch an Grammatik und Wortstellung! Hast du alles richtig geschrieben? Hast du die Zeitformen beachtet? Hast du die richtigen Fälle (Akkusativ oder Dativ) mit den richtigen Präpositionen verwendet?

4. Schreib jetzt den korrigierten Text noch einmal in dein Tagebuch ab!

Weiter geht's! • *Gregor besucht Johannes*

CD 1 Tr. 5

Johannes: Hallo, Gregor! Prima, dass du uns besuchen kommst!

Gregor: Ich hab's dir doch versprochen, und versprochen ist versprochen!

Johannes: Komm rein und setz dich! Meine Eltern kommen auch bald, und dann gibt's Kaffee und Kuchen. Sag, magst du etwas trinken? Oder möchtest du Obst? Du, wir haben ganz süße Erdbeeren aus unserem Schrebergarten — mit Sahne, ja? Lecker!

Gregor: Kann schon sein, aber ich darf das nicht essen. Ich bin nämlich allergisch gegen Erdbeeren.

Johannes: Wirklich? Das hab ich nicht gewusst. Tut mir Leid.

Gregor: Du kannst wohl alles essen, ja?

Johannes: Sicher! Ich hab keine Allergien. Nur mag ich eben vieles nicht; ich mag zum Beispiel keinen Fisch.

Gregor: Und warum nicht?

Johannes: Schmeckt mir einfach nicht.

Gregor: Dann isst du wohl viel Fleisch, ja?

Johannes: Nicht unbedingt. Wir essen viel Obst und Gemüse, Teigwaren, ja und, wie gesagt, auch Fleisch, Huhn und so.

Gregor: Weil du grad Teigwaren erwähnst: was ich gern mag, ist ein Gericht … na ja, wie heißt es denn schnell … hat was mit Salzburg zu tun.

Johannes: Ach ja! Du meinst Salzburger Nockerln, ja?

Gregor: Genau! Ess ich unwahrscheinlich gern.

Johannes: Hab ich auch ein paarmal in den Ferien gegessen. Wir waren ja gar nicht weit von Salzburg entfernt.

Salzburger Nockerln: A plural form for a "singular" dish. This dessert soufflé was served in the 16th century and is still popular today.

Gregor: Ja, erzähl doch mal was über deine Ferien!

Johannes: Du, da gibt's nicht viel zu erzählen. Ich hab dir ja schon gesagt, es hat fast nur geregnet. Wir sind kaum gewandert, und trotzdem hab ich mir auf so einer kleinen Wanderung den Knöchel verstaucht.

Gregor: So ein Pech! Geht's dem Knöchel wieder besser?

Johannes: Klar, es geht wieder. Ich muss nur noch ein bisschen vorsichtig sein.

Gregor: Übrigens, hier hab ich ein paar Rügen-Prospekte für deine Eltern.

Johannes: Prima! Sie werden sich bestimmt darüber freuen. — Ja, da kommen sie auch schon. Ich höre unser Auto!

Übungsheft, S. 6

17 Was passiert hier?

Sprechen Hast du das Gespräch verstanden? Beantworte die folgenden Fragen!

1. Warum besucht Gregor den Johannes?
2. Was bietet Johannes seinem Freund an? Warum wohl?
3. Wie reagiert Gregor darauf? Was sagt er?
4. Was mag Johannes nicht essen? Was isst er meistens?
5. Was für ein Gericht erwähnt Gregor, und warum erwähnt er es?
6. Kennt Johannes das Gericht? Woher?
7. Wie waren Johannes' Ferien? Was sagt er darüber?
8. Was ist dem Johannes passiert? Wie geht's ihm jetzt?
9. Was hat Gregor mitgebracht? Warum?

1. weil er es dem Johannes versprochen hat; weil er die Rügen Prospekte Johannes' Eltern zeigen will
2. Erdbeeren mit Schlagsahne / weil sie frisch aus dem eigenen Garten sind
3. Gregor sagt nein. / dass er gegen Erdbeeren allergisch ist
4. Fisch. / Obst, Gemüse, Teigwaren, Fleisch, Huhn
5. Salzburger Nockerln; weil er das Gericht gern mag
6. Ja. / Er hat es in den Ferien gegessen.
7. Nicht besonders. / Er sagt, dass es nicht viel zu erzählen gibt; dass es fast nur geregnet hat; dass sie kaum gewandert sind
8. Er hat sich den Knöchel verstaucht. / besser
9. Rügen-Prospekte / um sie Johannes' Eltern zu zeigen

18 Genauer lesen

Lesen/Sprechen Lies das Gespräch noch einmal, und beantworte diese Fragen auf Deutsch!

1. Which phrases are used to ask and tell what you may or may not do?
2. Which phrases express concern about someone's health or are responses to such concern? For answers, see underlined words in text on pages 14 and 15.

19 Wie steht's mit dir?

Sprechen Beantworte diese Fragen!

1. Welche Gerichte magst du und welche nicht?
2. Was darfst du nicht essen? Warum nicht?
3. Was hast du dir schon einmal verletzt, und wie ist es passiert?

Zweite Stufe

Objectives Asking and telling what you may or may not do; asking for information; inquiring about someone's health and responding; expressing pain; expressing hope

go.hrw.com

WK3 DIE NEUEN
BUNDESLAENDER-1

20 **Gesund essen? Gesund leben?**

Lesen/Sprechen Lies die Leserbriefe an die Jugendzeitschrift „Girl!", und beantworte danach die folgenden Fragen!

1. Welche Schüler sind für Tierprodukte oder für Pflanzenprodukte?
2. Welche Tierprodukte und welche Pflanzenprodukte erwähnen die Mädchen?
3. Mit welchem Satz drückt jedes Mädchen ihre Meinung am besten aus?
4. Mit welcher Schülerin kannst du dich identifizieren? Warum?

1. **für Tierprodukte: Susi, Simone, Michaela; für Pflanzenprodukte: Vanessa, Melanie** 2. **Fleisch, Käse, Honig** (acc. to biological science), **Schweinefleisch; Anti-Fleisch-Burger, Vollkornbrötchen, Naturjoghurt, Salatblätter, Gurken, Tomaten, Zwiebelringe, Paprika, Möhren, Gemüse, Honig** (acc. to nutritional science), **Tee, Brot** 3. Answers will vary. 4. Answers will vary.

Fit ohne Fleisch

Im Urlaub in Italien habe ich gemerkt, dass es auch ohne Fleisch geht. Seit einigen Wochen lebe ich nun schon vegetarisch. Am Anfang hatte ich noch unangenehme Hungergefühle, doch die habe ich mit der Zeit besiegt. Übrigens: Kennt Ihr schon den Anti-Fleisch-Burger? Das Rezept: Ein Vollkornbrötchen aufschneiden, beide Hälften mit Naturjoghurt bestreichen, dazwischen Salatblätter, eine Scheibe Käse, Gurken, Tomaten, Zwiebelringe, Paprika und Möhren packen. Ich sage Euch: ein Genuss!

Vanessa, Bielefeld

Wer weiß denn eigentlich genau, ob Vegetarier wirklich so viel gesünder leben als Fleischesser? Was, bitte schön, ist denn alles an Pflanzenschutzmitteln in unserem Gemüse drin? Oder denkt doch mal an den jüngsten Skandal mit den Tees, wo Unmengen von Schwermetallen und Pflanzenschutzmitteln drin gefunden wurden. An alle Vegetarier: Macht mal halblang!

Susi, München

An alle Veganer: Ihr könnt ruhig Honig essen, da er kein Tierprodukt ist. Die Bienen nehmen bei seiner Herstellung keinen Schaden, es ist sogar ihre Lebensaufgabe. Brot ist ja auch kein Menschenprodukt, nur weil ein Bäcker es herstellt, sondern ein Pflanzenprodukt.

Melanie, Dielheim-Balzfeld

Wir sind der Meinung, dass Nahrung, sorgfältig ausgesucht (nur ein- bis zweimal die Woche Schweinefleisch), die vernünftigste Form ist, sich zu ernähren. Als Voll-Vegetarier zu leben, würde für uns eine Einschränkung des alltäglichen Lebens bedeuten. Davon haben wir eigentlich schon genug (Eltern, Schule, Gesetze etc.). Wenn man alles zu negativ sieht, vermiest man sich das Leben. Da kann man ja gleich Schluss machen.

Simone und Michaela, Eisenberg

Was für Produkte essen wir?

Note that **der Paprika** is a spice; **die Paprika** is short for **die Paprikaschote** (bell pepper).

p. 3X

Pflanzenprodukte

Zwiebeln

Paprika

Rosenkohl

Mais

Spargel

Wassermelone

Tierprodukte

Rippchen

Speck

Schweinefleisch

Innereien

Leber

Reh- und Hasenfleisch

Welche anderen Pflanzenprodukte kennst du? Welche anderen Tierprodukte? Welche Produkte isst du gern oder überhaupt nicht gern? Warum?

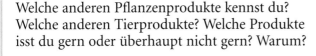

Übungsheft, S. 7, Ü. 1   Grammatikheft, S. 5, Ü. 9

---

21   ### Was mögen die Schüler essen?   Script and answers on p. 3H

Zuhören Drei Schüler sprechen über ihre Essgewohnheiten. Was mag jeder und was nicht? Wer darf etwas überhaupt nicht essen und warum nicht? Mach eine Tabelle mit diesen Kategorien: Wer? Mag was? Mag was nicht? Darf das nicht essen! Warum nicht? Schreib in die Tabelle die Information, die du hörst!

CD 1 Tr. 6

So sagt man das!

Asking and telling what you may or may not do

Schon bekannt

When asking someone what he or she may or may not do, you might ask:

> **Was darfst du essen und trinken?**
> **Darfst du alles essen?**
> **Was darfst du nicht essen?**
> **Was darfst du nicht tun?**

When inquiring about the reason, you might ask:

> **Warum darfst du keine Rosinen essen?**
> **Warum darfst du nicht joggen?**

And the answer may be:

> **Gemüse, Obst … und so.**
> **Na klar!**
> **Ich darf keine Rosinen essen.**
> **Joggen darf ich jetzt nicht und auch nicht Tennis spielen.**

And the answer might be:

> **Weil ich allergisch gegen Rosinen bin.**
> **Weil ich mir den Knöchel verstaucht habe.**

Mehr Grammatikübungen, S. 27, Ü. 5

Grammatikheft, S. 5, Ü. 10

---

22 Was darfst du essen und was nicht?

Sprechen Such dir einen Partner! Frag ihn, was er nicht gern isst oder trinkt, und ob es etwas gibt, was er nicht essen oder trinken darf! Warum oder warum nicht? Tauscht dann die Rollen aus!

So sagt man das!

Asking for information

Schon bekannt

You know many different ways to ask for information. For instance:

Sag mal, wie heißt dieses Gemüse?
Welche Suppe magst du?
Welchen Salat isst du gern?

And you know many different ways to respond. You might answer:

Das ist doch Spinat!
Ich mag Nudelsuppe.
Thunfischsalat.

23 Grammatik im Kontext

Sprechen Frag den Jens, deinen deutschen Gastbruder, welches von zwei Gerichten er mag! Er weiß es noch nicht und fragt dich, was du nimmst. Du sagst es ihm und auch, warum du dieses Gericht nimmst. Such dir einen Partner für die Rolle von Jens!

Nudelsuppe	Gemüsesuppe
Hähnchen	Fisch
Speck	Leber
Bratkartoffeln	Salzkartoffeln
Nudeln	Reis
Rosenkohl	Mais
Tomatensalat	Gurkensalat
Äpfel	Trauben

> ### Ein wenig Grammatik
>
> *Schon bekannt*
> For the forms of **dieser** and **welcher**, see the Grammar Summary.
>
> Grammatikheft, S. 6, Ü. 11 → Mehr Grammatikübungen, S. 28, Ü. 6–7

BEISPIEL

DU Nun, Jens, magst du diese(n) … oder diese(n) …?
JENS Ich weiß nicht. Welche Suppe nimmst du?
DU Also, ich nehme diese …

Wortschatz

Was hast du alles auf dem Brot?

 p. 3X   1–2

Ich habe es zuerst mit Naturjoghurt bestrichen.

oder isst du vielleicht lieber …

Darauf kommt ein Blatt Salat

oder

Radieschen

und dann eine Scheibe Tomate

oder

Erdnussbutter

saure Gurken

Thunfischsalat

Übungsheft, S. 7–8, Ü. 2–4   Grammatikheft, S. 6, Ü. 12

24 **Was haben die Schüler auf ihrem Brot?** Script and answers on p. 3I

Zuhören Vier Schüler erzählen, was sie auf ihrem Brot haben. Wer von diesen vier isst viel Fleisch und Wurst? Wer ist wohl Vegetarier? Wer isst sowohl Tierprodukte als auch Pflanzenprodukte?

CD 1 Tr. 7

25 **Was für ein tolles belegtes Brot!**

Sprechen Bildet Gruppen zu sechs oder acht Schülern! Einer fängt an und sagt, was er auf seinem Brot hat. Der nächste wiederholt das und gibt etwas anderes dazu, bis alle etwas gesagt haben und euer belegtes Brot fertig ist. (Kann und will man das auch wirklich essen?)

Wortschatz

Was ist passiert? Hast du dir wehgetan?

Übungsheft, S. 9, Ü. 5–6   Grammatikheft, S. 7, Ü. 13–15

Ich hab mich verletzt, bin vom Rad gefallen.

Ich bin ausgerutscht und hingefallen. Ich hab mich aber nicht verletzt.

Ich hab mich verbrannt, hab mir die Hand verbrannt.

Ich hatte einen Unfall, einen kleinen Autounfall.

Was hast du dir verletzt? — Ich hab mir ... verletzt.

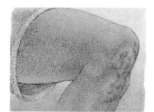

die Kniescheibe

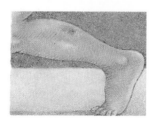

die Wade

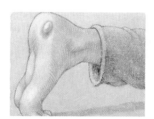

die Ferse

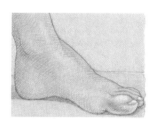

die Zehe

den Ellbogen

das Handgelenk

den Daumen

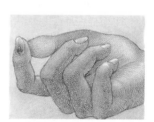

den Fingernagel

Was für andere Körperteile kann man sich verletzen? Wann hast du dir das letzte Mal wehgetan? Was ist passiert? Wobei hast du dich verletzt?

beim Fußballspielen?   beim Radfahren?

beim Tennisspielen?   beim Joggen?

Und dann noch...

Was hast du dir schon mal gebrochen?

den Kiefer   das Schlüsselbein

das Schulterblatt   eine Rippe

So sagt man das!

Inquiring about someone's health and responding; asking about and expressing pain

Schon bekannt

To inquire about someone's health, you might ask:

> **Wie fühlst du dich?**
> **Was fehlt dir?**

To inquire about pain someone may be suffering, you might ask:

> **Tut dir etwas weh?**
> **Was tut dir weh?**

And the response might be:

> **Ich fühl mich überhaupt nicht wohl.**
> **Mir fehlt nichts.**

The response might be:

> **Ja, der Arm tut mir weh.**
> **Mir tut der Hals weh.**

Mehr Grammatikübungen, S. 29, Ü. 8

Grammatikheft, S. 8, Ü. 16–17

---

26 **Grammatik im Kontext**

Script and answers on p. 3I

CD 1 Tr. 8

Zuhören Es war ein ganz tolles Fußball-spiel. Aber das Spiel war hart, und viele Spieler haben sich dabei verletzt. — Hör zu, wie jeder Spieler über seine Verletzung spricht, und identifiziere jeden Spieler an seiner Verletzung!

So sagt man das!

Expressing hope   *Schon bekannt*

To express hope, you might say:

> **Ich hoffe, dass** es dir bald wieder besser geht.
> **Hoffentlich** hast du dir nicht den Fuß gebrochen.

Grammatikheft, S. 8, Ü. 18

---

27 **Grammatik im Kontext**

Jeder von euch denkt sich eine Verletzung aus. Drückt diese Verletzung durch Gestik (*gestures*) und Mimik (*mime*) aus! — Fragt euch dann gegenseitig, was ihr euch verletzt habt, was passiert ist und wie, und ob es wehtut! Am Ende muss jeder die Hoffnung ausdrücken, dass es dem verletzten Schüler oder der verletzten Schülerin bald wieder besser geht.

Ein wenig Grammatik

Schon bekannt
Look at the following sentences:

> **Ich hab mich verletzt. Ich hab mir die Hand verletzt.**

How are the object pronouns different, and why? For the reflexive pronouns, see the Grammar Summary.

Übungsheft, S. 10, Ü. 7–9

Grammatikheft, S. 9, Ü. 19–20

Mehr Grammatikübungen, S. 29, Ü. 9–10

28 Eine Entschuldigung schreiben

Schreiben Du bist Gastschüler an einem deutschen Gymnasium. Du hast dich am Wochenende verletzt und konntest deshalb am Montag nicht in die Schule gehen. Schreib eine Entschuldigung! Schreib, was du dir verletzt hast und wie es passiert ist! Deine Gasteltern unterschreiben die Entschuldigung, und du gibst sie in der Schule ab.

29 Was ist mit dir?

a. Schreiben Such dir eine Partnerin! Sucht euch zwei von diesen Illustrationen aus, und erfindet ein Gespräch, das zwischen den zwei Leuten in beiden Bildern stattfindet!

b. Sprechen Führt anschließend das Gespräch der Klasse vor! Eure Mitschüler müssen raten (*guess*), welche Illustrationen ihr vorführt.

a.

b.

c.

d.

e.

f.

g.

h.

30

Von der Schule zum Beruf

You are a nurse at a hospital. A patient has arrived with a mysterious, severe flu-like illness that the doctor can't identify. Ask the patient what he has eaten in the past 48 hours, where he has been in the last 48 hours, and also if he has traveled out of town in the last 6 months. Be sure to ask if he is allergic to anything. Type the information in a report to be sent to the doctor, the lab, and the Health Department.

31 Rollenspiel

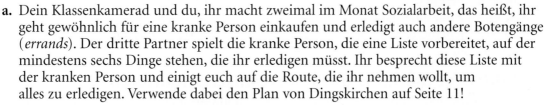

Bereite eins von diesen beiden Rollenspielen mit zwei anderen Schülern vor!

a. Dein Klassenkamerad und du, ihr macht zweimal im Monat Sozialarbeit, das heißt, ihr geht gewöhnlich für eine kranke Person einkaufen und erledigt auch andere Botengänge (*errands*). Der dritte Partner spielt die kranke Person, die eine Liste vorbereitet, auf der mindestens sechs Dinge stehen, die ihr erledigen müsst. Ihr besprecht diese Liste mit der kranken Person und einigt euch auf die Route, die ihr nehmen wollt, um alles zu erledigen. Verwende dabei den Plan von Dingskirchen auf Seite 11!

b. Uli, der am Wochenende eine Bergtour machen wollte, ist am Montag nicht in die Schule gekommen. Am Nachmittag gehst du ihn mit einem Klassenkameraden besuchen. Er sieht schlecht aus und scheint sogar Schmerzen zu haben. Ihr fragt ihn, wie die Bergtour war. Uli erzählt euch dann, was passiert ist und was ihm fehlt.

Der Euro ist da!

Amerikanische Touristen, die ihre Ferien bisher in verschiedenen Ländern Europas verbrachten, mussten ihre Dollar in jedem Land in die Währung des Besucherlandes eintauschen. Wer also nach Frankreich, Holland, Spanien, Italien, Österreich oder nach Deutschland reiste, musste Dollar in Francs, Gulden, Peseten, Lire, Schilling oder D-Mark eintauschen. Seit dem 1. Januar 2002 gibt es in den meisten europäischen Ländern eine gemeinsame Währung, den Euro.

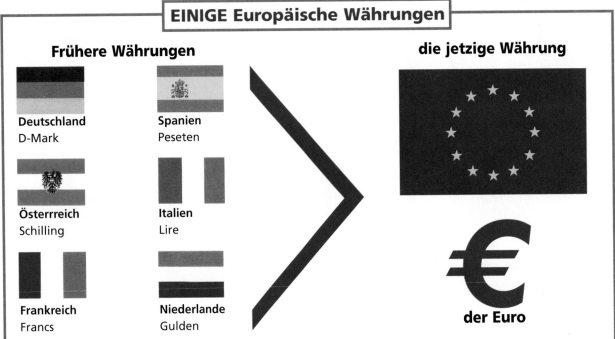

EINIGE Europäische Währungen

Frühere Währungen

Deutschland
D-Mark

Spanien
Peseten

Österrreich
Schilling

Italien
Lire

Frankreich
Francs

Niederlande
Gulden

die jetzige Währung

der Euro

D-Mark ade!

Im Mai 1998 wurde offiziell bestimmt, welche Länder der Europäischen Währungsunion (EW) beitreten durften: Belgien, Deutschland, Finnland, Frankreich, Irland, Italien, Luxemburg, Niederlande, Österreich, Portugal und Spanien. In diesen Ländern wurde der Euro am 1. Januar 1999 offiziell eingeführt, das hieß, dass in diesen Ländern zum Beispiel persönliche Konten in der lokalen Währung wie auch in Euro geführt werden konnten und dass Euros auch innerhalb der EW überwiesen werden konnten. Am 1. Januar 2001 trat auch Griechenland der EW bei. Euro-Scheine und Euro-Münzen erschienen aber erst am 1. Januar 2002.

Was bedeutet der Euro für amerikanische Touristen?

Seit dem 1. Januar 2002 ist der Euro das gesetzliche Zahlungsmittel der oben genannten 11 Länder der Europäischen Währungsunion. Amerikanische Touristen brauchen ihre Dollar also nur einmal in Euro einzutauschen, wenn sie ein oder mehrere Länder der EW besuchen. Es ist auch einfacher, die Preise in den verschiedenen Ländern zu vergleichen.

Übungsheft, S. 11, Ü. 1–3

Wie sieht der Euro aus?

Der Euro hat sieben Geldscheine. Es gibt Scheine zu 5, 10, 20, 50, 100, 200 und 500 Euro. Der Euro hat acht Münzen. Es gibt Münzen zu 1, 2, 5, 10, 20 und 50 Euro Cent, außerdem 1 Euro und 2 Euro. Auf der Rückseite der deutschen Münzen befinden sich deutsche Symbole, die an die D-Mark erinnern: Eichenlaub, Brandenburger Tor und Bundesadler.

Wie viel ist der Dollar wert?

Der Kurs des Dollars gegenüber dem Euro schwankt täglich. Jede große Tageszeitung oder Webseite zeigt den Tageskurs beider Währungen. Dieser Kurs gilt für Banken, die am Devisenmarkt Dollar und Euro einkaufen und verkaufen. Der Kurs am Bankschalter ist in der Regel nicht der gleiche. Vor kurzem hat jemand am Bankschalter folgende Währungen eingetauscht und folgende Summen bekommen.

für 100 USD > 111,48 EUR   für 200 EUR > 179,42 USD

Ein wenig Mathematik mit Währungen   There are many **Umrechnungstabellen** on the Web.

1. Rechne den Kurs aus für die obigen Summen.   0.897
2. Wie viel Euro bekommst du für 200 Dollar? Für 350 Dollar?   € 222,97 / € 390,18
3. Wie viel Dollar bekommst du für 200 Euro? 350 Euro? $ 179,12 / $ 313,99
4. Du bist Austauschschüler in Hamburg. Deine Eltern schicken dir monatlich etwas Geld, und du hast dir schon 300 USD gespart. Du möchtest dir eine Stereoanlage für 600 Euro kaufen. Wie viel Euro bekommst du für deine Dollar? Kannst du dir die Stereoanlage kaufen, oder fehlen dir noch Euro? Wie viele?   € 333,44 / yes / € 265,56

CD1 Tr. 9

Eine alltägliche Verwirrung von Franz Kafka

„Selbstporträt" von Karl Schmidt-Rottluff

Moderne Literatur

Lesestrategie Using time lines for comprehension You don't need to know the exact meaning of every word to figure out what a story is about. By first taking a moment to discover how a story is organized, you can make up for not knowing every word. Try to organize a text around a single guiding principle. For example, a narrative usually contains many words that indicate the sequence of events. You can use those words to construct a time line and better understand the flow of the story.

Many *Zum Lesen* selections are permissioned documents that cannot be altered. They therefore do not reflect the changes enacted by the **Rechtschreibreform.**

Getting Started For answers, see p. 3X

1. Read the title of this selection. If **Alltag** means *everyday life* or *routine*, what kind of confusion is Kafka writing about?

2. Skim the story once. Scan for occurrences of the letters **A**, **B**, and **H**. Using context, try to determine what each letter represents. Why do you think the writer uses letters?

3. Read the first paragraph again. Who are the main characters? What is the setting? What happens in this paragraph? Why?

4. Reread the first paragraph and continue reading to the end of the story. Try to summarize the story in two or three sentences.

A Closer Look

5. Together with your partner, scan the story for any words that establish the sequence of

Ein alltäglicher Vorfall: sein Ertragen eine alltägliche Verwirrung. A hat mit B aus H ein wichtiges Geschäft abzuschließen. Er geht zur Vorbesprechung nach H, legt den Hin- und Herweg in je zehn Minuten zurück und rühmt sich zu Hause dieser besonderen Schnelligkeit. Am nächsten Tag geht er wieder nach H, diesmal zum endgültigen Geschäftsabschluß. Da dieser voraussichtlich mehrere Stunden erfordern wird, geht A sehr früh morgens fort. Obwohl aber alle Nebenumstände, wenigstens nach A's Meinung, völlig die gleichen sind wie am Vortag, braucht er diesmal zum Weg nach H zehn Stunden. Als er dort ermüdet abends ankommt, sagt man ihm, daß B, ärgerlich wegen A's Ausbleiben, vor einer halben Stunde zu A in sein Dorf gegangen sei und sie sich eigentlich unterwegs hätten treffen müssen. Man rät A zu warten. A aber, in Angst wegen des Geschäftes, macht sich sofort auf und eilt nach Hause.

Diesmal legt er den Weg, ohne besonders darauf zu achten, geradezu in einem Augenblick zurück. Zu Hause erfährt er, B sei doch schon gleich früh gekommen — gleich nach dem Weggang A's; ja, er habe A im Haustor getroffen, ihn an das Geschäft erinnert, aber A habe gesagt, er hätte jetzt keine Zeit, er müsse jetzt eilig fort.

Trotz diesem unverständlichen Verhalten A's sei aber B doch hier geblieben, um auf A zu warten. Er habe zwar schon oft gefragt, ob A nicht schon wieder zurück sei, befinde sich aber noch oben in A's Zimmer. Glücklich darüber, B jetzt noch zu sprechen und ihm alles erklären zu können, läuft A die Treppe hinauf. Schon ist er fast oben, da stolpert er, erleidet eine Sehnenzerrung und fast ohnmächtig vor Schmerz, unfähig sogar zu schreien, nur winselnd im Dunkel hört er, wie B — undeutlich ob in großer Ferne oder knapp neben ihm — wütend die Treppe hinunterstampft und endgültig verschwindet.

events. Draw a time line of events that indicates time and place for both characters **A** and **B**. Discuss any problems you notice with the rest of the class.

The endings **-lich** and **-ig** in German signal that a word is an adverb or adjective. When reading fiction, you can often use these words as clues to how people or things are.

---

6. Read the story again to find out how the characters act or react. Decide who or what is characterized by each of the following adverbs and adjectives:

wichtig	**in Angst**
ermüdet	**eilig**
ärgerlich	**unverständlich**
glücklich	**undeutlich**
ohnmächtig	**wütend**
unfähig	**winselnd**

7. Find the following words in the passage and, using context and familiar elements of compound words, try to derive their meanings: **Schnelligkeit**, **Nebenumstände**, **Ausbleiben**, and **Augenblick**.

8. What is **A**'s problem? What is the cause? What is **B**'s reaction? What does he do? How is the conflict resolved? Or is it?

9. Using the time line you created in Activity 5, reconstruct the story (in writing) using complete sentences. Your **Nacherzählung** should be one to two paragraphs.

10. Kafka's story depicts some rather bizarre events, yet the title seems to suggest the opposite — that the situation is commonplace. How can you reconcile or explain the apparent contradiction?

Übungsheft, S. 12-13, Ü. 1-4

Mehr Grammatikübungen

Answers

Erste Stufe

Objectives Reporting past events; asking how someone liked something; expressing enthusiasm or disappointment; responding enthusiastically or sympathetically

1 Ein Schüler berichtet über seine Ferien. Schreib den folgenden Bericht ab, und setz dabei die Vergangenheitsform des Verbs **sein** ein! (**Seite 9**)

Gregor: „Letzte Woche _____ ich mit meinen Eltern auf der Insel

Rügen. Das Wetter _____ super, und wir alle _____ fast jeden Tag am

Strand. Mein Bruder, der Stefan, _____ schon einmal an der Ostsee;

das _____ vor zwei Jahren, als er mit den Pfadfindern dort _____ .

Stefan sagt, es _____ dieses Jahr schöner am Strand, weil das Wasser

wärmer _____ . Nun, _____ du schon einmal an der Ostsee?"

war

war; waren

war

war; war

war

war; warst

2 Einige Schüler berichten über ihre Ferien. Schreib die folgenden drei Berichte ab, und setz dabei die richtigen Verbformen ein, eine Form des Verbs **haben** oder **sein** und die Partizipform eines passenden Verbs! (**Seite 10**)

1. Andreas: „Vor kurzem _____ ich eine Woche in den Alpen _____ . Ich _____ mit meinen Eltern in einer wirklich netten Pension _____ . Jeden Tag _____ wir in den wunderschönen Bergen _____ , und am Nachmittag _____ wir gewöhnlich in einem kühlen Bergsee _____ . Der war kalt! Am Abend _____ wir gewöhnlich in einen netten Gasthof _____ , wo wir viele tolle Speisen _____ _____ . Ich muss sagen, dass uns das Essen immer ganz prima _____ _____ ."

habe; verbracht; habe
gewohnt; sind
gewandert; sind
geschwommen; sind
gegangen; gegessen; haben
geschmeckt; hat

2. Sabine: „Letzten Samstag _____ ich mit meinen Eltern nach Berlin _____ . Wir _____ nur drei Tage in Berlin _____ , aber ich muss sagen, dass ich in den drei Tagen sehr viel _____ _____ . In Berlin ist wirklich viel los! Gleich am Samstag _____ wir in eine Oper _____ , und am Sonntag _____ wir ein Symphonieorchester _____ . Mit einem kleinen Ausflugsschiff _____ wir auf der Spree durch die Stadt _____ . Das war super! Wir _____ auch das Pergamonmuseum _____ , und in diesem Museum _____ wir den berühmten Pergamonaltar _____ ."

bin; gefahren; sind
geblieben
gesehen; habe; sind
gegangen; haben; gehört
sind; gefahren
haben; besucht
haben; gesehen

3. Monika: „Ich _____ heute Morgen mit der Mutti auf der Bank _____ . Mutti _____ Euro in Dollar _____ , denn nächste Woche fliegen wir in die USA. Wir _____ drei Reisebücher in die Bücherei _____ , und in einem Buchladen _____ wir uns eine Karte von den USA _____ . Dann waren wir bei Sport-Müller. Mutti _____ eine Windjacke _____ , weil sie ihr zu klein ist. Und danach _____ wir die Flugtickets _____ ; das war im Reisebüro Lamprecht."

bin; gewesen; hat
umgetauscht; haben
zurückgebracht; haben
gekauft; hat
umgetauscht; haben
abgeholt

3 Sieh dir die Illustrationen an und schreib in die ersten zwei Lücken, wo du warst, und in die anderen Lücken, was du dort gemacht hast. (**Seite 10**)

1. Ich _____ in der _____ . Ich _____ Bücher _____ und einige neue Bücher _____ .   war; Bücherei; habe; zurückgebracht; ausgeliehen

2. Ich _____ auf der _____ . Ich habe Geld _____ , Dollar in Euro.   war; Bank; umgewechselt

3. Bernd _____ im _____ . Er _____ leere Flaschen _____ und 6 Flaschen Limo _____ .   war; Getränkeladen; hat; zurückgebracht; gekauft

4. Wir _____ auf der _____ . Dort _____ wir _____ und eine Rechnung _____ .   waren; Post; haben; telefoniert; bezahlt

5. Vati _____ im _____ . Seine CD war nicht da. Da hat er eine andere CD _____ .   war; Musikladen; bestellt

4 Wie hat es verschiedenen Familienmitgliedern in den Ferien gefallen? Schreib die folgenden Sätze ab, und schreib dabei in zwei Lücken das Perfekt des Verbs **gefallen,** *to like*, und in die anderen Lücken die Endungen, die du gebrauchen musst, wenn du das Verb **gefallen** benutzt! (**Seite 12**)

1. Die Stadt Stralsund _____ mein_____ Eltern sehr gut _____ .   hat; en; gefallen
2. Die Insel Rügen _____ mein_____ Vater auch gut _____ .   hat; em; gefallen
3. Der weiße Sandstrand _____ mein_____ Geschwister_____ echt toll _____ .   hat; en; n; gefallen
4. Der Golfplatz _____ mein_____ Mutter besonders _____ .   hat; er; gefallen
5. Mein_____ klein_____ Schwestern _____ der Swimmingpool _____ .   en; en; hat; gefallen
6. Ich muss sagen, dass _____ der Volleyballcourt am besten _____ _____ .   mir; gefallen; hat

---

Zweite Stufe   **Objectives** Asking/telling what you may or may not do; asking for information; inquiring about someone's health and responding; expressing pain; expressing hope

5 Es gibt viele Leute, die gewisse Lebensmittel nicht essen können, weil sie bestimmte Allergien haben. Schreib die folgenden Sätze ab, und schreib dabei in eine Lücke eine Form von **dürfen** und in die andere eine Form von **kein!** (**Seite 17**)

Viele Leute sind allergisch gegen etwas.

1. Mein Vater _____ _____ Pilze essen; er ist allergisch gegen Pilze.   darf; keine
2. Meine Großeltern _____ _____ Tomaten essen.   dürfen; keine
3. Ich _____ _____ Milch trinken; ich bin allergisch gegen Milch.   darf; keine
4. Gregor und Stefan, warum _____ ihr _____ Mais essen?   dürft; keinen
5. Wir _____ _____ Mais essen und auch _____ Spargel.   dürfen; keinen; keinen
6. Und du _____ doch _____ Erdnussbutter essen, Uli, nicht wahr?   darfst; keine
7. Stimmt! Ich _____ _____ Erdnussbutter essen und auch _____ Eis.   darf; keine; kein
8. Ich habe einen Freund, der _____ Schweinefleisch essen _____ .   kein; darf

6 Du schreibst, dass dir diese illustrierten Lebensmittel gut schmecken. Schreib die korrekte Form von **dieser** in die erste Lücke, und was dir schmeckt (was abgebildet ist) in die zweite Lücke. (**Seite 18**)

1. _____ _____ schmecken gut. Sie sind so mild.   Diese; Radieschen

2. _____ _____ ist ausgezeichnet!   Dieser; Thunfischsalat

3. _____ _____ ist so gut und so gesund.   Diese; Erdnussbutter

4. _____ _____ schmecken gar nicht sauer.   Diese; sauren Gurken

5. _____ _____ schmeckt so gut und so süß.   Dieser; Mais

6. _____ _____ schmeckt einfach ganz toll!   Diese; Wassermelone

7 Du fragst einen Freund, welche Speisen er möchte oder am liebsten isst. Schreib die folgenden Fragen ab, und schreib dabei in die erste Lücke die korrekte Form von **welcher** und in die zweite Lücke die korrekte Form von **dieser**! (**Seite 18**)

1. _____ Suppe möchtest du? Möchtest du _____ Gemüsesuppe?   Welche; diese
2. _____ Salat nimmst du? Isst du lieber _____ Fischsalat?   Welchen; diesen
3. _____ Eis magst du am liebsten? Magst du _____ Vanilleeis?   Welches; dieses
4. _____ Fisch isst du am liebsten? Magst du _____ Thunfisch?   Welchen; diesen
5. _____ Gemüse magst du am liebsten? Magst du _____ Rosenkohl?   Welches; diesen
6. _____ Kartoffeln magst du? Magst du _____ Bratkartoffeln?   Welche; diese
7. _____ Nachspeise willst du? Willst du _____ Stück Kuchen?   Welche; dieses
8. _____ Fleisch möchtest du? Magst du vielleicht _____ Schweinefleisch?   Welches; dieses

8 Du fragst verschiedene Leute, wie es ihnen gesundheitlich geht, und sie antworten dir. Schreib die folgenden Fragen und Antworten ab, und schreib dabei die korrekte Form des Reflexivpronomens in die Lücken! (**Seite 20**)

1. Hallo, Gregor! Wie fühlst du _____ heute? Tut _____ der Arm noch weh?   dich; dir
2. Du, ich fühle _____ wieder wohl, und der Arm tut _____ nicht mehr weh.   mich; mir
3. Hallo, Jungs! Wie fühlt ihr _____ ? Tun _____ noch immer die Beine weh?   euch; euch
4. Wir fühlen _____ wohl, und _____ tut nichts mehr weh.   uns; uns
5. Wie fühlen Sie _____ , Herr Meier? Tut _____ noch immer die Schulter weh?   sich; Ihnen
6. Nein, die Schulter tut _____ nicht mehr weh. Ich fühl _____ wieder wohl.   mir; mich
7. Was hast du, Meike? Was fehlt _____ ? Tut _____ etwas weh?   dir; dir
8. Du, _____ fehlt nichts, und _____ tut überhaupt nichts mehr weh.   mir; mir

9 Du fragst verschiedene Leute, wie sie sich gesundheitlich fühlen. Schreib die folgenden Fragen und Antworten ab, und schreib dabei die korrekte Form des Reflexivpronomens in die Lücken! (**Seite 20**)

(Du fragst einen Freund.)

1. Sag, hast du _____ verletzt? Hast du _____ vielleicht die Hand gebrochen?   dich; dir
2. Sag, hast du _____ wehgetan? Hast du _____ verbrannt?   dir; dich
3. Sag, hast du _____ den Knöchel verstaucht? Was tut _____ denn weh?   dir; dir

(Du fragst zwei Klassenkameraden.)

4. Habt ihr _____ verletzt? Was tut _____ denn weh?   euch; euch
5. Was fehlt _____ denn? Fühlt ihr _____ nicht wohl?   euch; euch
6. Tun _____ die Beine weh? Wo habt ihr _____ denn verletzt?   euch; euch

(Du fragst deinen Lehrer.)

7. Frau Becker, ist _____ nicht gut? Fühlen Sie _____ nicht wohl?   Ihnen; sich
8. Haben Sie _____ verletzt, Frau Becker? Tut _____ etwas weh?   sich; Ihnen
9. Tut _____ der Hals weh, Frau Becker? Wie fühlen Sie _____ sonst?   Ihnen; sich

10 Du hoffst, dass deine Freunde sich nicht ernsthaft verletzt haben. Schreib die folgenden Sätze ab, und schreib dabei in die erste Lücke die korrekte Form des Reflexivpronomens und in die zweite das Perfekt des Verbs, das in der Klammer steht! (**Seite 20**)

1. (Fuß brechen)   Gregor, ich hoffe, dass du _____ nicht _____ .   dir; den Fuß gebrochen hast
2. (verletzen)   Astrid, ich hoffe, dass du _____ nicht _____ .   dich; verletzt hast
3. (Hand verletzen) Mark, hoffentlich hast du _____ nicht _____ .   dir; die Hand verletzt
4. (Arm brechen)   Anna, hoffentlich hast du _____ nicht _____ .   dir; den Arm gebrochen
5. (Wade verletzen) Paul, ich hoffe, dass du _____ nicht _____ .   dir; die Wade verletzt hast
6. (Auge verletzen) Sabine, ich hoffe, dass du _____ nicht _____ .   dir; das Auge verletzt hast

Kann ich's wirklich?

Can you report past events? (p. 9)

1 How would you ask someone where he or she was the day before yesterday, and what he or she did there? How would you answer the same question, mentioning at least three different things you did? 1. Sag mal, wo warst du denn vorgestern? Was hast du dort gemacht? / Answers will vary. E.g.: Du, ich war in der Stadt. Dort bin ich ins Kino gegangen. Danach war ich im Eiscafé. Und dann habe ich mir noch neue Schuhe gekauft.

Can you ask how someone liked something? (p. 12)

2 How would you ask a friend how he or she liked the movie *Schindler's List* (**Schindlers Liste**)? 2. Wie hat dir „Schindlers Liste" gefallen?

Can you express enthusiasm or disappointment? (p. 12)

3 How would you respond if someone asked you if you liked a movie and
a. you loved it? 3. a. E.g.: Es war super!
b. you didn't like it? b. E.g.: Es hat mir überhaupt nicht gefallen.

Can you respond enthusiastically or sympathetically? (p. 12)

4 How would you respond to the following statements?
a. Also, mir hat Weimar gut gefallen. 4. a. E.g.: Das freut mich!
b. Ich hatte Fieber und musste das ganze Wochenende im Bett bleiben.
b. E.g.: Das tut mir aber Leid.

Can you ask and tell what you may or may not do? (p. 17)

5 How would you ask a friend what he or she may not eat and why? How would your friend respond if he or she were allergic to chocolate?
5. Was darfst du nicht essen und warum nicht? / Ich darf keine Schokolade essen, weil ich allergisch dagegen bin.

Can you ask for information? (p. 18)

6 How would you ask someone
a. what a particular fruit is called? 6. a. Sag mal, wie heißt diese Frucht?
b. what dessert he or she likes? b. Welchen Nachtisch magst du?
c. what a particular dish is supposed to be? c. Sag mal, was soll denn dieses Gericht sein?
How would that person answer in each case?
E.g.: Das ist doch eine Banane! / Ich mag Eis. / Das ist doch Paella!

Can you inquire about someone's health and respond? (p. 20)

7 How would you ask someone how he or she is feeling? How would that person respond if he or she were not feeling well?
7. E.g.: Wie fühlst du dich? / Ich fühl mich überhaupt nicht wohl.

Can you ask about and express pain? (p. 20)

8 How would you ask a friend if he or she has pain? If your friend looks like he or she is in pain, how would you ask what hurts?
8. Tut dir was weh? / Was tut dir weh?

Can you express hope? (p. 20)

9 How would you respond if someone said the following things to you?
a. Ich habe hohes Fieber und Kopfweh und kann kaum schlucken.
b. Ich bin gerade vom Fahrrad gefallen. Mein Fuß tut mir furchtbar weh, und ich glaub, ich kann jetzt nicht mehr laufen.
9. a. E.g.: Ich hoffe, dass es dir bald wieder besser geht.
b. E.g.: Hoffentlich hast du dir nicht den Fuß gebrochen.

Erste Stufe

Reporting past events

gerade	*just*
vor kurzem	*recently*
neulich	*the other day*
letzt-	*last*

Other useful words

dauernd	*continually*
übrigens	*by the way*
sparsam	*frugal*
leer	*empty*

die Bank, -en	*bank*
die Bücherei, -en	*library*
der Getränkemarkt, ⁻e	*beverage shop*
der Musikladen, ⁻	*music store*
die Post	*mail; post office*
die Lektüre, -n	*reading*
der Prospekt, -e	*brochure, pamphlet*
die Flasche, -n	*bottle*
die Rechnung, -en	*bill, invoice*

bezahlen	*to pay*
umwechseln (sep)	*to change (money)*
ausleihen (sep)	*to borrow, lend*
umtauschen (sep)	*to exchange*
zurückbringen (sep)	*to bring back, return*
s. aussuchen (sep)	*to pick out, choose*
erledigen	*to take care of*

Zweite Stufe

p. 3X

Parts of the body

der Daumen, -	*thumb*
der Ellbogen, -	*elbow*
die Ferse, -n	*heel*
der Fingernagel, ⁻	*fingernail*
das Handgelenk, -e	*wrist*
die Kniescheibe, -n	*kneecap*
die Wade, -n	*calf*
die Zehe, -n	*toe*
der Unfall, ⁻e	*accident*
s. verbrennen	*to burn oneself*
ausrutschen (sep)	*to slip*

Fruit and vegetables

das Produkt, -e	*product*
das Pflanzenprodukt, -e	*vegetable produce*
die Pflanze, -n	*plant*

die Erdnussbutter	*peanut butter*
die Rosine, -n	*raisin*
die saure Gurke, -n	*pickle*
der Mais	*corn*
die Paprika	*bell pepper*
die Wassermelone, -n	*watermelon*
die Zwiebel, -n	*onion*
der Rosenkohl	*Brussels sprouts*
das Radieschen, -	*radish*
der Spargel, -	*asparagus*
die Teigwaren (pl)	*pasta*
die Scheibe, -n	*slice*
das Blatt, ⁻er	*leaf*
bestreichen	*to spread, to butter*
der Naturjoghurt	*yogurt (without preservatives)*

Meat products

das Tierprodukt, -e	*animal product*
das Tier, -e	*animal*
die Innereien (pl)	*innards*
die Leber	*liver*
das Schweinefleisch	*pork*
der Speck	*bacon*
das Rehfleisch	*venison*
die Rippchen (pl)	*ribs*
das Hasenfleisch	*rabbit meat*
der Thunfischsalat	*tuna fish salad*

Other useful words

erzählen	*to tell*
versprechen	*to promise*
erwähnen	*to mention*
trotzdem	*in spite of that*
vorsichtig	*careful*

Kapitel 2: Auf in die Jugendherberge! *Review Chapter*
Chapter Overview

Los geht's! pp. 34–35	*Auf nach Thüringen!, p. 34*

	FUNCTIONS	**GRAMMAR**	**VOCABULARY**	**RE-ENTRY**
Erste Stufe pp. 36–41	• Asking for and making suggestions, p. 37 • Expressing preference and giving a reason, p. 39 • Expressing wishes, p. 40 • Expressing doubt, conviction, and resignation, p. 40	• Two-way prepositions (**So sagt man das!**), p. 37 • Word order in **dass** and **ob**-clauses (**So sagt man das!**), p. 40	• Words useful for traveling, p. 37	• Chapters 1 and 2 are a global review of *Komm mit!* Levels 1 and 2

Weiter geht's! pp. 42–43	*Auf nach Weimar!, p. 42*

	FUNCTIONS	**GRAMMAR**	**VOCABULARY**	**RE-ENTRY**
Zweite Stufe pp. 44–49	• Asking for information and expressing an assumption, p. 45 • Expressing hearsay, p. 46 • Asking for, making, and responding to suggestions, p. 46 • Expressing wishes when shopping, p. 48	• Adjective endings, p. 48 • The verb **hätte** (**So sagt man das!**), p. 48	• Words useful on vacation, p. 45 • Picnic items, p. 47	• Chapters 1 and 2 are a global review of *Komm mit!* Levels 1 and 2

Zum Lesen pp. 50–52	Poesie	**Reading Strategy** Deriving the main idea from supporting details

Zum Schreiben p. 53	… ist eine Reise wert!	**Writing Strategy** Selecting information

Mehr Grammatik-übungen	**pp. 54–57**
	Erste Stufe, pp. 54–55 Zweite Stufe, pp. 55–57

Review pp. 58–59	**Kann ich's wirklich?**, p. 58 Wortschatz, p. 59

CULTURE

- Explanation of **Jugendherbergen**, p. 36
- **Einkaufsliste**, p. 39
- **Programm für eine 6-Tage-Reise nach Weimar**, p. 44
- **Landeskunde: Weimar im Blickpunkt**, p. 49

Kapitel 2: Auf in die Jugendherberge! *Review Chapter*
Chapter Resources

Lesson Planning

One-Stop Planner

Lesson Planner with Substitute Teacher Lesson Plans, pp. 16–20, 76

Student Make-Up Assignments
- Make-Up Assignment Copying Masters, Chapter 2

Listening and Speaking

Listening Activities
- Student Response Forms for Listening Activities, pp. 11–14
- Additional Listening Activities 2-1 to 2-6, pp. 15–18
- Scripts and Answers, pp. 108–115

Video Guide
- Teaching Suggestions, p. 8
- Activity Masters, pp. 9–10
- Scripts and Answers, pp. 60–61, 74

Activities for Communication
- Communicative Activities, pp. 5–8
- Realia and Teaching Suggestions, pp. 56–60
- Situation Cards, pp. 115–116

Reading and Writing

Reading Strategies and Skills Handbook, Chapter 2

Lies mit mir! 3, Chapter 2

Übungsheft, pp. 14–26

Grammar

Grammatikheft, pp. 10–18

Grammar Tutor for Students of German, Chapter 2

Assessment

Testing Program
- Grammar and Vocabulary Quizzes, **Stufe** Quizzes, and Chapter Test, pp. 23–36
- Score Sheet, Scripts and Answers, pp. 37–43

Alternative Assessment Guide
- Portfolio Assessment, p. 17
- Performance Assessment, p. 31

Student Make-Up Assignments
- Alternative Quizzes, Chapter 2

 Online Activities
- Interaktive Spiele
- Internet Aktivitäten

 Video Program
- Videocassette 1

 Audio Compact Discs
- Textbook Listening Activities, CD 2, Tracks 1–14
- Additional Listening Activities, CD 2, Tracks 19–24
- Assessment Items, CD 2, Tracks 15–18

 Teaching Transparencies
- Situations 2-1 to 2-2
- **Mehr Grammatikübungen** Answers
- **Grammatikheft** Answers

Use the **One-Stop Planner CD-ROM with Test Generator** to aid in lesson planning and pacing.

For each chapter, the **One-Stop Planner** includes:
- Editable lesson plans with direct links to teaching resources
- Printable worksheets from resource books
- Direct launches to the HRW Internet activities
- Video and audio segments
- Test Generator
- Clip Art for vocabulary items

Kapitel 2: Auf in die Jugendherberge! *Review Chapter*

Projects

Auf in die Jugendherberge

*In this activity students will write a letter requesting information about **Jugendherbergen.***

MATERIALS

✂ **Students may need**

addresses for tourist information centers, travel agencies, and youth hostels, as well as writing paper, envelopes, and airmail stamps. Here are some addresses that might be helpful:

Deutsches Jugendherbergswerk, Hauptverband e.V., 32754 Detmold, Germany (Fax: 011-49-5231-993666; e-mail: e-mail@djh.de)

Österreichischer Jugendherbergsverband, Schottenring 28, A-1010 Wien, Austria (Fax: 011-43-1-5350861; e-mail: Backpacker-Austria@oejhv.or.at)

Schweizer Jugendherbergen, Schaffhauserstr. 14, Postfach, 8042 Zürich, Switzerland (Fax: 011-41-1-3601460; e-mail: bookingoffice@youthhostel.ch)

SUGGESTED SEQUENCE

1. Have students brainstorm together what they would need to include in a letter to a **Jugendherberge.** (Examples: name of town, city, or general area to be visited, time of year of trip, age of those traveling, return address)

2. Have pairs of students decide what place they would like to visit.

3. Pairs outline their letters, including all important information.

4. Pairs write their letters in letter format with appropriate greetings and closings. You may want to remind students to use formal address and to date their letter using the German style.

5. Students exchange their letters with another pair for comments and corrections.

6. Pairs revise their letters and mail them to the appropriate agency.

GRADING THE PROJECT

Suggested point distribution (**total = 100 points**)
Content (clear and to the point) 50
Format and Style 25
Grammar and Usage 25

Games

Das treffende Wort suchen

This game will help your students develop the skill of circumlocution.

Preparation Create a list of words in English related to the vocabulary presented in the chapter/**Stufe.** Write each vocabulary word from the list you created on an index card. Arrange four desks at the front of the room in such a way so that two partners from each team can face each other. Place the cards face down where they can easily be reached by the players from any of the desks. On the board or on a transparency, write the following key phrases:

Aussehen:

Es ist ein Ding / eine Person … Das Ding ist aus Metall / Glas / Papier. Es ist … klein / groß / alt / neu. Es sieht aus wie …

Funktion:

Man benutzt das Ding für … Das Gegenteil ist … Man kann es … essen, trinken …

Ort:

Man kann dort … Man findet es …

Procedure Divide the class into two teams. Have two players from each team sit at the four desks. A player from Team A selects a card and shows it to one of the players from Team B. Using circumlocution phrases, the Team A player attempts to describe the vocabulary word to his or her partner without saying the word itself. (For example, one could say about an elephant: **Das ist ein Tier. Es ist groß und grau.**) If the partner in Team A guesses the word, Team A receives five points. If not, the Team B player in turn gives a clue to his or her partner. If the partner guesses correctly, Team B receives four points.

Alternate turns between the two teams, with the points earned dropping by one each time someone guesses incorrectly. If a player is unable to give a clue within thirty seconds, his or her team loses its turn and the opposing team gives another clue. If no team scores a point after five clues, any student on Team A may make a guess. If the guess is correct, Team A receives one point. If not, any student from Team B is given the same opportunity. If this guess is also incorrect, announce the correct answer.

Storytelling

Mini-Geschichte

*This story accompanies Teaching Transparency 2-2. The **Mini-Geschichte** can be told and retold in different formats, acted out, written down, and read aloud, to give students additional opportunities to practice all four skills.*

„Du, Uwe, schau mal aus dem Fenster! Unsere Jugendherge liegt direkt am Strand! Wir haben einen herrlichen Blick aufs Meer!" „Einfach toll! Ich habe gelesen, dass die Jugendherberge in einer Bucht liegt, an einem schneeweißen 13 km langen Sandstrand. Ich weiß auch, dass wir hier einen Kaminraum und eine Großschachanlage haben." „Uwe, was meinst du, wollen wir morgen ein Picknick am Strand machen?" „Gute Idee! Hoffentlich regnet es nicht. Lass uns vorsichtshalber *(as a precaution)* mit dem Einkaufen bis morgen abwarten."

Traditions

Der Rennsteig

Der 168 km lange Rennsteig, der auf dem Kamm des Thüringerwaldes von der Werra bis zur Saale verläuft, ist der älteste und berühmteste Höhenfernwanderweg Deutschlands. Er ist auch deshalb so bekannt, weil er früher eine der wichtigsten kulturellen und politischen Grenzen Deutschlands darstellte. Entlang des Rennsteigs stehen mehr als 1300 Grenzsteine, die ältesten aus dem 16. Jahrhundert. Der Rennsteig war auch eine schnelle Gebirgsroute für Eilboten und Kuriere. Nach Öffnung der innerdeutschen Grenze 1990 ist der Rennsteig nach 45jähriger Unterbrechung wieder durchgehend wanderbar.

Der Rennsteig hat eine lange Geschichte: Im 9. Jahrhundert wird er zum ersten Mal erwähnt. 1530 überquerte ihn Martin Luther auf einer seiner Predigerreisen. 1806 zogen Napoleons Truppen über den Rennsteig zu den entscheidenden Schlachten von Jena und Auerstedt. Ende des 19. Jahrhunderts wurde die Rennsteigwanderung zum Erlebnis für jedermann. Es entstanden sogar Sprach- und Wandergebräuche. Zum Beispiel begrüßten sich Rennsteigwanderer mit „Gut Runst!" (Gute Rennsteig-Wanderung!) und 1951 erklang zum ersten Mal das Rennsteiglied.

Rennsteiglied

1. Strophe
Ich wand're ja so gerne
Am Rennsteig durch das Land.
Den Beutel auf dem Rücken
Die Klampfe (Gitarre) in der Hand.
Ich bin ein lust'ger Wandersmann,
So völlig unbeschwert,
Mein Lied erklingt durch Busch und Tann,
Das jeder gerne hört.
Refrain:
Diesen Weg auf den Höh'n
Bin ich oft gegangen.
Vöglein sangen Lieder.
Bin ich weit in der Welt
Habe ich Verlangen
Thüringer Wald nur nach dir.

Rezept

Forellen in Apfelsoße (Sachsen)

Zutaten für 2 Personen

2 Forellen	Essig
4 Äpfel	Zitronenschale
1/4 Liter süßer Weißwein	Muskat
Zucker	Butter
Zimt	Salz

Zubereitung
Die Forellen in Salzwasser mit etwas Essig abkochen, herausnehmen und abtropfen lassen. Unterdessen die Äpfel schälen, schneiden und in dem Wein mit etwas Zucker und Zimt weichkochen, durch ein Sieb schlagen und mit Zitronenschale und Muskat würzen. Apfelsoße über die Forellen gießen und mit einem Stückchen Butter aufkochen.

Beilage Petersilienkartoffeln

Technology

⊙ ☝ **One-Stop** Planner CD-ROM

To preview all resources available for this chapter,
use the **One-Stop Planner CD-ROM**, Disc 1.

Internet Connection

🔊 internet

**go.
hrw
.com**
ADRESSE: go.hrw.com
KENNWORT: WK3 DIE
NEUEN BUNDESLAENDER-2

*Have students explore the **go.hrw.com** Web site for many online resources
covering all chapters. All Chapter 2 resources are available under the keyword
WK3 Die neuen Bundeslaender-2. Interactive games practice the material
and provide students with immediate feedback. You will also find a printable
worksheet that provides Internet activities that lead to a comprehensive
online research project.*

Interaktive Spiele

You can use the interactive activities in this chapter

- to practice grammar, vocabulary, and
  chapter functions
- as homework
- as an assessment option
- as a self-test
- to prepare for the Chapter Test

Internet Aktivitäten

*Students read about the length, location, and
history of the Thuringian Rennsteig and find a
youth hostel in a city located on the Rennsteig.
They read **Wanderlieder** and write a poem
about hiking.*

- To prepare students for the **Arbeitsblatt,**
  ask students to find information about
  hiking clubs or hiking trails in their
  hometown. Have them present their
  findings to the class.

Webprojekt

Have students find a youth hostel on the island of Rügen. They should report on its location, accommodations,
amenities, prices, and other pertinent information. Encourage students to exchange useful Web sites with
their classmates. Have students document their sources by referencing the names and URLs of all the sites
they consulted.

The following scripts are for the listening activities found in the *Pupil's Edition*. For Student Response Forms, see *Listening Activities*, pages 11–14. To provide students with additional listening practice, see *Listening Activities*, pages 15–18.

Erste Stufe

6 p. 37

USCHI Na, Herbert! Was machst du denn hier? Ich dachte, du bist die ganzen Sommerferien lang im Bayerischen Wald bei deiner Oma.

HERBERT Ach hallo, Uschi! Nein, doch nicht die ganzen sechs Wochen! Ich war nur in den ersten drei Wochen dort. Ich bin gestern erst zurückgekommen.

USCHI Erzähl mal! Wie war's denn?

HERBERT Ach, es gefällt mir immer unheimlich gut bei meiner Oma. Sie kocht ganz tolle Sachen und ist immer guter Laune. Außerdem treffe ich dort immer den Martin. Er wohnt im Haus neben meiner Oma, und wir haben schon als Kinder zusammen gespielt, jedesmal wenn wir zu Besuch bei meiner Oma waren. Diesmal haben wir auch eine Menge zusammen unternommen. Martin ist echt ein super Kumpel. Er ist mit mir in der ganzen Gegend rumgefahren. Ich glaub, ich kenn den Bayerischen Wald jetzt besser als unsere Gegend!

USCHI Meine Schwester war auch schon mal im Bayerischen Wald. Ihr hat es dort auch gut gefallen.

HERBERT Und du? Warst du denn schon weg?

USCHI Nein! Wir fahren erst am Samstag früh.

HERBERT Und wohin geht's diesmal?

USCHI Wir fahren nach Südfrankreich, nach Nizza, um genau zu sein!

HERBERT Nizza! Super! Warst du schon mal dort?

USCHI Nein, aber ich freu mich schon wahnsinnig drauf! Dort soll es einen tollen Sandstrand geben und viele gute Restaurants, die frische Meeresfrüchte anbieten.

HERBERT Schau mal, da drüben kommt der Frank! He, Frank, komm, setz dich zu uns!

FRANK Hallo, ihr beiden!

USCHI Wir unterhalten uns gerade über unsere Ferien! Wie sieht's bei dir aus? Warst du schon weg?

FRANK Nein, leider noch nicht! Ich hab die ersten drei Wochen der Sommerferien bei meinen Eltern im Supermarkt geholfen. Jetzt habe ich genug Taschengeld gespart, um mit dem Thorsten nach Thüringen zu fahren.

HERBERT Thüringen! Hört sich super an. Was wollt ihr denn da alles machen?

FRANK Ach, wir wollen verschiedene Orte besuchen und so eine Art Rundreise machen. Wir fangen in Eisenach an und weiter nach Gotha, über Erfurt bis nach Weimar. Dort bleiben wir dann eine Weile. Da gibt es kulturell 'ne Menge zu sehen. Ach, da ist Moni! Ich hab mich hier mit ihr verabredet. Sie ist gestern aus den Ferien zurückgekommen und will mir erzählen, wie es war!

MONI Hallo, alle zusammen!

FRANK Hallo, Moni! Du bist ja richtig braun geworden! Wie war's auf Mallorca?

MONI Spitze! Sonne, Sand und Meer! Einfach sagenhaft! Ich wär so gern noch länger dort geblieben.

Answers to Activity 6
Herbert: Bayern/war schon dort
Uschi: Nizza/fährt erst hin
Frank: Thüringen/fährt erst hin
Moni: Mallorca/war schon dort

9 p. 38

THOMAS Hallo, Uta. Warum hast du es denn so eilig?

UTA Ja, weißt du, ich fahre morgen früh mit meiner Klasse in den Harz. Ich komme gerade vom Fotostudio Lambertz, weil ich ein paar Filme für meine Kamera kaufen musste. Dann muss ich noch in den Supermarkt, um Reiseverpflegung zu besorgen. Und was machst du hier, Thomas?

THOMAS Also, ich war vorhin im Getränkemarkt und hab ein paar Flaschen zurückgebracht. Und jetzt gerade war ich im Sportgeschäft Winkler und habe mir meine neue Skiausrüstung für diesen Winter ausgesucht. Echt toll, sage ich dir.

UTA Du, schau mal, da drüben ist der Jürgen, der fährt auch morgen mit in den Harz. He, Jürgen!

JÜRGEN Hallo, Thomas! Hallo, Uta! Na, hast du schon alles für unsere Reise eingekauft?

UTA So ziemlich. Und du?

JÜRGEN Ich weiß nicht. Ich muss noch in den Obstladen, um mir ein bisschen Verpflegung für unterwegs einzukaufen. Vorhin war ich gerade bei Stein & Buddenbrock. Ich konnte meine Badehose nicht mehr finden, also habe ich mir noch schnell eine neue gekauft.

THOMAS Da drüben läuft meine Schwester. He, Angelika! Jürgen, Uta, kennt ihr meine Schwester Angelika?

UTA Also, ich habe sie noch nicht kennen gelernt. Hallo!

ANGELIKA Hallo, Uta! Grüß dich Jürgen!

THOMAS Sag mal, Angelika, was machst du denn in der Stadt?

ANGELIKA Ich war gerade in der Parfümerie Becker und habe ein Parfüm für Oma gekauft. Sie hat doch morgen Geburtstag. Jetzt gehe ich ins Fitness-Studio. Ich mach dort einen Aerobic-Kurs.

THOMAS Ach so, ja. Mensch, ich muss noch schnell was für Oma besorgen. Ich glaub, ich hol ihr ein neues

Brillenetui. Ich lauf mal schnell zu Optik Uhl. Tschüs!

UTA   Tschüs, Thomas! Viel Spaß im Fitness-Studio, Angelika!

ANGELIKA   Danke! Tschüs!

Answers to Activity 9
Uta: geht zuletzt in den Supermarkt
Thomas: geht zuletzt zu Optik Uhl
Jürgen: geht zuletzt in den Obstladen
Angelika: geht zuletzt ins Fitness-Studio

13   p. 39

CHRISTOPH   Na, was meint ihr? Was sollen wir in den Ferien machen? Ich war noch nie an der Nordsee. Ich würde wahnsinnig gern dorthin fahren und ein bisschen segeln gehen. Und ihr? Wozu habt ihr denn Lust? Was meinst du, Annette?

ANNETTE   Also, ich weiß nicht so recht. Ich war vor zwei Jahren in Bremerhaven, und ich fand es dort nicht so toll. Die Nordsee war ziemlich schmutzig, und es war kalt und sehr windig. Wenn wir schon an den Strand wollen, sollten wir lieber an die Ostsee fahren. Dort waren wir noch nie, und außerdem sind da nicht so viele Touristen. Was sagst du dazu, Isabella?

ISABELLA   Wieso wollt ihr denn immer nur an den Strand? Also, ich war noch nie in Berlin. Das wäre doch toll, was meint ihr? Ich interessiere mich sehr für Kultur, und Berlin hat eben einfach alles: Denkmäler, Museen … das ist eine richtig internationale Stadt. Jörg, du warst doch auch noch nie in Berlin. Was hältst du von der Idee?

JÖRG   Ich weiß nicht so recht. So eine Großstadt ist mir einfach zu hektisch und voll. Ich habe keine Lust, dort meine Ferien zu verbringen. Außerdem hat mir meine Schwester erzählt, dass die Jugendherbergen dort meistens ausgebucht sind. Es wird schwierig sein, so kurzfristig zu reservieren. Ich finde, wir sollten irgendwohin fahren, wo wir wandern und schwimmen können. Was haltet ihr vom Schwarzwald?

ANNETTE   Ja, das hört sich gut an, Jörg. Vielleicht können wir ja auch unsere Fahrräder mitnehmen.

ISABELLA   Unbedingt! Dort können wir radeln, wandern und schwimmen, und Jugendherbergen gibt es dort sicherlich auch. Was hältst du davon, Christoph?

CHRISTOPH   Das ist keine schlechte Idee. Im Schwarzwald war ich auch noch nie. Schau mal im Verzeichnis nach, Isabella, ob wir eine gute Jugendherberge finden!

ISABELLA   Ja, in Freiburg ist bestimmt eine. Also, ich freu mich schon auf den Schwarzwald.

Answers to Activity 13
Christoph: möchte an die Nordsee — war noch nie dort, möchte segeln gehen
Annette: möchte nicht an die Nordsee — war schon dort, fand es nicht toll, Nordsee ist schmutzig, es war kalt und windig; möchte an die Ostsee — war noch nie dort, es gibt dort nicht viele Touristen
Isabella: möchte nach Berlin — interessiert sich für Kultur
Jörg: möchte nicht nach Berlin — Großstadt ist zu hektisch und voll, Jugendherbergen sind meistens ausgebucht; möchte in den Schwarzwald — will wandern und schwimmen

18   p. 41

1. ASSAM   Du, Werner, ich bin noch nicht sicher, ob ich dieses Wochenende mitkomme. Ich sollte eigentlich zu Hause bleiben und für die Biologiearbeit am Montag lernen.

WERNER   Ach was, Assam! Du kannst mir glauben, der Bio-Test wird total einfach sein. Der Hoffmann macht nie schwierige Prüfungen. Du musst einfach mitkommen. Die Radtour wird ein Riesenspaß.

2. ANJA   Elke, ich bezweifle, dass wir in Thüringen in der Jugendherberge noch Unterkunft bekommen. Da ist doch sicherlich alles voll.

ELKE   Mach dir nur keine Sorgen, Anja! Ich bin sicher, dass sie noch was freihaben. Die Jugendherberge dort ist ziemlich groß. Das dauert lange, bis da mal alle Betten voll sind.

3. MARION   Du musst einfach mit ins Rockkonzert kommen, Eva. Das gefällt dir ganz bestimmt, da bin ich mir sicher.

EVA   Ich weiß nicht, ob mir die Musik so liegt, Marion. Ich höre eigentlich lieber ruhige Musik.

2. FRANK   Meinst du, dass Mutter das Geschenk gefallen wird, Claudia? Ich weiß nicht so recht. Ich bin mir nicht sicher, ob sie Blau gern hat.

CLAUDIA   Mach dir nur keine Sorgen, Frank! Du kannst mir glauben, dass ihr das gefallen wird. Sie mag Blau echt gern.

Answers to Activity 18
1. Assam bezweifelt etwas; Werner ist sicher.
2. Anja bezweifelt etwas; Elke ist sicher.
3. Eva bezweifelt etwas; Marion ist sicher.
4. Frank bezweifelt etwas; Claudia ist sicher.

Zweite Stufe

26   p. 45

1. BRITTA   Was meinst du, Gerhard? Sollen wir in den Ferien lieber in einer Jugendherberge oder bei Verwandten und Bekannten bleiben?

GERHARD   Also, Britta, ich habe gehört, die Jugendherbergen sollen ganz toll sein. Der Werner hat gesagt, die Verpflegung soll hervorragend sein, und die Unterkünfte sollen sehr sauber und günstig sein.

BRITTA   Also, ich weiß nicht so recht. Jugendherbergen sind zwar billig und meistens auch in einer schönen Gegend, aber ich kann nicht gut schlafen, wenn zu viele Leute in einem Zimmer sind.

GERHARD   Also, Britta, ich finde Jugendherbergen einfach toll.

BRITTA   Na ja, vielleicht sollten wir es mal ausprobieren.

2. KLAUS   Du, Bruno, wenn wir nach Weimar fahren, sollten wir unbedingt in der Jugendherberge übernachten. Was meinst du?

BRUNO   Von mir aus. Warst du denn schon mal dort in der Jugendherberge?

KLAUS Ja, wir sind letztes Jahr ganz kurz dort gewesen, nur ein Wochenende lang. Ich wär gern noch länger geblieben, aber wir wollten ja weiter bis nach Dresden, und deshalb hab ich nicht viel von Weimar gesehen. Aber ich erinnere mich, dass die Jugendherberge ein ganz tolles Programm angeboten hat.

BRUNO Tatsächlich? Was denn, zum Beispiel?

KLAUS Ja, also, es laufen dort Dia-Vorträge über Weimar, man kann eine Stadtführung machen oder Kulturdenkmäler besichtigen. Und stell dir vor, alles ist von der Jugendherberge aus organisiert!

BRUNO Super! Was wird sonst noch dort angeboten?

KLAUS Es gibt dort auch eine Diskothek und Grillabende und …

BRUNO Phantastisch! Du, wenn in Weimar in der Jugendherberge so viel los ist, dann bin ich echt dafür, dass wir uns dort einquartieren!

Answers to Activity 26
1. Britta und Gerhard sprechen über Jugendherbergen im Allgemeinen.
2. Klaus und Bruno sprechen über Jugendherbergen in Weimar.

30 p. 46

CLAUDIA Na, was sollen wir dieses Wochenende machen? Meine Kusine aus Düsseldorf kommt doch zu Besuch, und sie hat mich am Telefon gefragt, ob wir mal eine Radtour um den Chiemsee mit ihr machen würden. Ich finde die Idee toll! Und wie sieht's mit euch aus? Habt ihr auch Lust dazu? Was meinst du, Holger?

HOLGER Also, ich weiß nicht so recht, Claudia! Ich war erst letzte Woche mit meinen Eltern am Chiemsee. Ich würde lieber was anderes machen.

CLAUDIA Was schlägst du denn vor?

HOLGER Lasst uns doch ins Freibad gehen! Ich hab Lust, mal wieder ein paar Sprünge vom Drei-Meter-Turm zu machen. Du nicht auch, Jens?

JENS Also, ich finde Claudias Vorschlag gut. Am Chiemsee gibt es ausgezeichnete Radwege, und ich würde gern mal wieder 'ne lange Radtour machen.

CLAUDIA Genau! Wir können uns doch was zu essen mitnehmen und den ganzen Tag am Chiemsee bleiben.

JENS Wie wär's mit einem Picknick? Ute, kannst du wieder deinen tollen Kartoffelsalat machen? Ich mach dann die Frikadellen dazu.

UTE Ja also, eigentlich habe ich keine Lust, schon wieder eine Radtour zu machen. Ich fahr halt jeden Tag mit dem Rad zur Schule, und würd am Wochenende lieber mal das Rad im Keller lassen. Können wir nicht alle einfach nur so zum Bummeln in die Stadt gehen? Vielleicht läuft ja ein toller Film im Kino, und danach könnten wir doch ins Eiscafé gehen.

CLAUDIA Ach nein, das ist mir zu langweilig. Ich mache auf jeden Fall die Radtour um den Chiemsee mit meiner Kusine. Du kommst also mit, Jens?

JENS Ja, klar! Ich freu mich schon.

For resource information, see the **One-Stop Planner CD-ROM**, Disc 1.

Answers to Activity 30
Holger: ist nicht einverstanden; war erst letzte Woche am Chiemsee
Jens: ist einverstanden; Chiemsee hat ausgezeichnete Radwege
Ute: ist nicht einverstanden; fährt jeden Tag mit dem Rad zur Schule

33 p. 47

MARKUS Also, die belegten Brote sind fertig. Jetzt müssen wir nur noch die restlichen Sachen einpacken. Sag mal, Andreas, wo ist eigentlich unsere Kühlbox? Da müssen die ganzen Getränke rein.

ANDREAS Ist schon erledigt, Markus! Silvia hat gerade die Kühlbox und den Picknickkorb aus dem Keller geholt. Also, was kommt alles in den Korb? Ein Schneidebrett, drei Becher zum Trinken, drei Teller und drei Gabeln.

SILVIA Wieso nur Gabeln? Wir brauchen auch Messer und Löffel. Und vergiss nicht, dein Taschenmesser mit dem Flaschenöffner einzupacken, damit wir die Limoflaschen aufmachen können.

ANDREAS Gut. Also, das Besteck habe ich. Dann brauchen wir noch Servietten. Das wäre alles!

MARKUS Denkst du! Wir brauchen außerdem noch einen Salz- und einen Pfefferstreuer. Ich hab doch auch Tomaten fürs Picknick gekauft. Silvia, hast du schon eine Abfalltüte für unseren Müll eingepackt?

SILVIA Ja, sie liegt ganz unten im Picknickkorb. Hier ist die Thermosflasche mit dem heißen Tee. Andreas, hast du schon den Erdbeerjoghurt in die Kühlbox getan?

ANDREAS Ja, klar! Ich hab auch schon die Bananen dort reingelegt. Du, Markus, kannst du bitte die karierte Decke aus dem Schrank holen? Die nehmen wir natürlich auch noch mit.

MARKUS Okay, hier ist sie. Brauchen wir sonst noch was?

SILVIA Ich glaube, wir haben alles. Los geht's!

Answers to Activity 33
belegte Brote, Kühlbox, Getränke (Limo), Picknickkorb, Schneidebrett, Becher, Teller, Besteck (Gabeln, Messer, Löffel), Messer mit Flaschenöffner, Salz- und Pfefferstreuer, Tomaten, Abfalltüte, Thermosflasche mit heißem Tee, Erdbeerjoghurt, Bananen, karierte Decke

Kapitel 2: Auf in die Jugendherberge! *Review Chapter*
Suggested Lesson Plans 50-Minute Schedule

Day 1

CHAPTER OPENER 5 min.
- Building Context, ATE, p. 31M
- Building on Previous Skills, ATE, p. 31M

LOS GEHT'S! 20 min.
- Preteaching Vocabulary, ATE, p. 31N
- Background Information, ATE, p. 31N
- Teaching Suggestions, ATE, p. 31N
- Play Audio CD for **Los geht's!**
- Have students read **Los geht's!**, pp. 34–35
- Do Activities 1–4, p. 35

ERSTE STUFE
Reading Selection, p. 36 20 min.
- Teaching Suggestion, p. 31O
- Culture Note, ATE, p. 31O
- Read **Willkommen**, p. 36
- Do Activity 5, p. 36

Wrap-Up 5 min.
- Students respond to questions about where they want to go on their next vacation

Homework Options
Übungsheft, p. 14, Act. 1

Day 2

ERSTE STUFE
Quick Review 10 min.
- Check homework, Übungsheft, p. 14, Act. 1

Wortschatz, p. 37 15 min.
- Presenting **Wortschatz**, ATE, p. 31O
- Play Audio CD for Activity 6, p. 37

So sagt man das!, p. 37 20 min.
- Presenting **So sagt man das!**, ATE, p. 31P
- Teaching Transparency 2-1
- Do Activities 7 and 8, p. 38
- Play Audio CD for Activity 9, p. 38
- Do Activity 10, p. 38
- Do Activities 11 and 12, p. 39
- Play Audio CD for Activity 13, p. 39

Wrap-Up 5 min.
- Students respond to questions about how to get places in Dingskirchen

Homework Options
Pupil's Edition, p. 39, Act. 12
Grammatikheft, pp. 10–11, Acts. 1–3

Day 3

ERSTE STUFE
Quick Review 10 min.
- Check homework, Grammatikheft, pp. 10–11, Acts. 1–3

So sagt man das!, p. 39 10 min.
- Presenting **So sagt man das!**, ATE, p. 31P
- Do Activity 14, p. 39
- Do Activity 15, p. 40

So sagt man das!, p. 40 10 min.
- Presenting **So sagt man das!**, ATE, p. 31P
- Do Activities 16 and 17, p. 40

So sagt man das!, p. 40 15 min.
- Presenting **So sagt man das!**, ATE, p. 31P
- Play Audio CD for Activity 18, p. 41
- Do Activities 19, 20, and 21, p. 41

Wrap-Up 5 min.
- Students respond to questions about where they wish to go and what they would like to do on their next vacation

Homework Options
Grammatikheft, pp. 12–13, Acts. 4–7
Übungsheft, pp. 15–18, Act. 1–9

Day 4

ERSTE STUFE
Quick Review 10 min.
- Check homework, Grammatikheft, pp. 12–13, Acts. 4–7

Quiz Review 20 min.
- Do Additional Listening Activities 2-1, 2-2, and 2-3, pp. 15–16
- Do **Mehr Grammatikübungen, Zweite Stufe**

Quiz 20 min.
- Quiz 2-1A or 2-1B

Homework Options
Activities for Communication, pp. 5–6, prepare Communicative Activities 2-1 and 2-2

Day 5

ERSTE STUFE
Quick Review 10 min.
- Do Communicative Activities 2-1 and 2-2, pp. 5–6

WEITER GEHT'S! 20 min.
- Preteaching Vocabulary, ATE, p. 31Q
- Building Context, ATE, p. 31Q
- Thinking Critically, ATE, p. 31Q
- Play Audio CD for **Weiter geht's!**, pp. 42–43
- Do Activities 22, 23, and 24, p. 43

ZWEITE STUFE
Reading Selection, p. 44 15 min.
- Teaching Suggestion, ATE, p. 31R
- Teacher Note, ATE, p. 31R
- Read **Jugendgästehaus Weimar**

Wrap-Up 5 min.
- Students respond to questions about activities possible at a **Jugendherberge**

Homework Options
Pupil's Edition, p. 44, Act. 25
Übungsheft, p. 19, Acts. 1–2
Internet Aktivitäten, see ATE, p. 31E

Day 6

ZWEITE STUFE
Quick Review 10 min.
- Return and review Quiz 2-1
- Check homework, Pupil's Edition, p. 44, Act. 25

Wortschatz, p. 45 10 min.
- Presenting **Wortschatz**, ATE, p. 31S
- Play Audio CD for Activity 26, p. 45

So sagt man das!, p. 45 10 min.
- Presenting **So sagt man das!**, ATE, p. 31S
- Do Activity 27, p. 45

So sagt man das!, p. 46 15 min.
- Presenting **So sagt man das!**, ATE, p. 31S
- Do Activities 28 and 29, p. 46

Wrap-Up 5 min.
- Students respond to questions about the location of **Jugendherbergen**

Homework Options
Grammatikheft, pp. 14–15, Acts. 8–11
Übungsheft, pp. 20–21, Acts. 1–5

One-Stop Planner CD-ROM

For alternative lesson plans by chapter section, to create your own customized plans, or to preview all resources available for this chapter, use the **One-Stop Planner CD-ROM**, Disc 1.

 For additional homework suggestions, see activities accompanied by this symbol throughout the chapter.

Day 7

ZWEITE STUFE
Quick Review 10 min.
- Check homework, Grammatikheft, pp. 14–15, Acts. 8–11

So sagt man das!, p. 46 15 min.
- Presenting **So sagt man das!**, ATE, p. 31T
- Play Audio CD for Activity 30, p. 46
- Do Activities 31 and 32, pp. 46–47

Wortschatz, p. 47 10 min.
- Presenting **Wortschatz**, ATE, p. 31T
- Play Audio CD for Activity 33, p. 47
- Do Activity 34, p. 47

Ein wenig Grammatik/So sagt man das!, p. 48 10 min.
- Presenting **Ein wenig Grammatik/So sagt man das!**, ATE, p. 31T
- Do Activity 35, p. 48

Wrap-Up 5 min.
- Students respond to questions about what food and utensils they would take on a picnic

Homework Options
Pupil's Edition, p. 48, Acts. 36 and 37
Grammatikheft, pp. 16–18, Acts. 12–16
Übungsheft, pp. 22–23, Acts. 6–9

Day 8

ZWEITE STUFE
Quick Review 10 min.
- Check homework, Grammatikheft, pp. 16–18, Acts. 12–16

LANDESKUNDE 20 min.
- Background Information, ATE, p. 31T
- Culture Note, ATE, p. 31T
- Read **Weimar im Blickpunkt,** p. 49
- Do Activities 1–4, p. 49

Quiz Review 15 min.
- Do Situation 2-2, pp. 115–116
- Do Communicative Activity 2-3 or 2-4, pp. 7–8
- Do Additional Listening Activities 2-4, 2-5, and 2-6, pp. 16–18

Wrap-Up 5 min.
- Students respond to questions about why they would like to visit Weimar

Homework Options
Übungsheft, p. 24, Acts. 1–3
Activities for Communication, p. 58, Realia 2-3, do the word search
Mehr Grammatikübungen, Zweite Stufe

Day 9

ZWEITE STUFE
Quick Review 10 min.
- Check homework, **Mehr Grammatikübungen, Zweite Stufe**

Quiz 20 min.
- Quiz 2-2A or 2-2B

Ein neues Schulsystem (Video) 15 min.
- Show **Ein neues Schulsystem** and **Werbung** Videos
- Teaching Suggestions, Video Guide, p. 8
- Do Pre-viewing, Viewing, and Post-viewing Activities, Video Guide, p. 9

Wrap-Up 5 min.
- Students respond to questions about freedom of speech at their school

Homework Options
Interaktive Spiele, see ATE, p. 31E

Day 10

ZWEITE STUFE
Quick Review 10 min.
- Return and review Quiz 2-2

ZUM LESEN 35 min.
- Teacher Notes, ATE, p. 31U
- Background Information, ATE, pp. 31U–31V
- Teaching Suggestions, ATE, p. 31V
- Present **Lesestrategie,** p. 50
- Do Activities 1–8, pp. 50–51

Wrap-Up 5 min.
- Students brainstorm topics for poems they want to write

Homework Options
Pupil's Edition, p. 52, Act. 13: write a poem
Übungsheft, pp. 25–26, Acts. 1–7

Day 11

ZWEITE STUFE
Quick Review 15 min.
- Have students present poems

ZUM SCHREIBEN 30 min.
- Writing Strategy ATE, p. 31W
- Present **Schreibtipp**, p. 53
- Do Activities A and B, p. 53

Wrap-Up 5 min.
- Students discuss the layout of their pamphlets

Homework Options
Pupil's Edition, p. 53, Act. C

Day 12

REVIEW
Quick Review 15 min.
- Check homework, Pupil's Edition, p. 53, Act. C

Kann ich's wirklich?, p. 58 20 min.
- Do Activities 1–12, p. 58

Chapter Review 15 min.
- Review chapter functions, vocabulary, and grammar; choose from **Mehr Grammatikübungen**, Activities for Communication, Listening Activities, or **Interaktive Spiele**
- Review test format and provide sample test items for students

Homework Options
Study for Chapter Test

Assessment

Test, Chapter 2 45 min.
- Administer Chapter 2 Test. Select from Testing Program, Alternative Assessment Guide or Test Generator.

Kapitel 2: Auf in die Jugendherberge! *Review Chapter*
Suggested Lesson Plans *90-Minute Schedule*

Block 1

CHAPTER OPENER 5 min.
- Building Context, ATE, p. 31M
- Building on Previous Skills, ATE, p. 31M

LOS GEHT'S! 25 min.
- Preteaching Vocabulary, ATE, p. 31N
- Background Information, ATE, p. 31N
- Teaching Suggestions, ATE, p. 31N
- Play Audio CD for **Los geht's!**
- Have students read **Los geht's!**, pp. 34–35
- Do Activities 1–4, p. 35
- Do Activity 1, p. 14, Übungsheft

ERSTE STUFE
Reading Selection, p. 36 20 min.
- Teaching Suggestion, p. 31O
- Culture Note, ATE, p. 31O
- Read **Willkommen**, p. 36
- Do Activity 5, p. 36

Wortschatz, p. 37 15 min.
- Presenting **Wortschatz**, ATE, p. 31O
- Play Audio CD for Activity 6, p. 37

So sagt man das!, p. 37 20 min.
- Presenting **So sagt man das!**, ATE, p. 31P
- Teaching Transparency 2-1
- Do Activities 7 and 8, p. 38
- Play Audio CD for Activity 9, p. 38
- Do Activity 10, p. 38
- Do Activities 11 and 12, p. 39
- Play Audio CD for Activity 13, p. 39

Wrap-Up 5 min.
- Students respond to questions about how to get places in Dingskirchen

Homework Options
Grammatikheft, pp. 10–11, Acts. 1–3
Internet Aktivitäten, see ATE, p. 31E

Block 2

ERSTE STUFE
Quick Review 10 min.
- Check homework, Grammatikheft, pp. 10–11, Acts. 1–3

So sagt man das!, p. 39 10 min.
- Presenting **So sagt man das!**, ATE, p. 31P
- Do Activity 14, p. 39
- Do Activity 15, p. 40

So sagt man das!, p. 40 10 min.
- Presenting **So sagt man das!**, ATE, p. 31P
- Do Activities 16 and 17, p. 40

So sagt man das!, p. 40 15 min.
- Presenting **So sagt man das!**, ATE, p. 31P
- Play Audio CD for Activity 18, p. 41
- Do Activities 19, 20, and 21, p. 41

Quiz Review 20 min.
- Do Additional Listening Activities 2-1, 2-2, and 2-3, pp. 15–16
- Do Communicative Activities 2-1 and 2-2, pp. 5–6
- Show **Freizeit** Video
- Teaching Suggestions, Video Guide, p. 8
- Do **Mehr Grammatikübungen, Zweite Stufe**

WEITER GEHT'S! 20 min.
- Preteaching Vocabulary, p. 31Q
- Building Context, ATE, p. 31Q
- Thinking Critically, ATE, p. 31Q
- Play Audio CD for **Weiter geht's!**, pp. 42–43
- Do Activities 22, 23, and 24, p. 43

Wrap-Up 5 min.
- Students respond to questions about where they go with friends on vacation

Homework Options
Grammatikheft, pp. 12–13, Acts. 4–7
Übungsheft, pp. 15–18, Acts. 1–9; p. 19, Acts. 1–2

Block 3

ERSTE STUFE
Quick Review 10 min.
- Check homework, Grammatikheft, pp. 12–13, Acts. 4–7

Quiz 20 min.
- Quiz 2-1A or 2-1B

ZWEITE STUFE
Reading Selection, p. 44 15 min.
- Teaching Suggestion, ATE, p. 31R
- Teacher Note, ATE, p. 31R
- Read **Jugendgästehaus Weimar** p. 44
- Do Activity 25, p. 44

Wortschatz, p. 45 10 min.
- Presenting **Wortschatz**, ATE, p. 31S
- Play Audio CD for Activity 26, p. 45

So sagt man das!, p. 45 15 min.
- Presenting **So sagt man das!**, ATE, p. 31S
- Do Activity 27, p. 45
- Do Activity 10, p. 15, Grammatikheft

So sagt man das!, p. 46 15 min.
- Presenting **So sagt man das!**, ATE, p. 31S
- Do Activities 28 and 29, p. 46

Wrap-Up 5 min.
- Students respond to questions about the location of **Jugendherbergen**

Homework Options
Grammatikheft, pp. 14–15, Acts. 8–9 and 11
Übungsheft, pp. 20–21, Acts. 1–5

One-Stop Planner CD-ROM

For alternative lesson plans by chapter section, to create your own customized plans, or to preview all resources available for this chapter, use the **One-Stop Planner CD-ROM**, Disc 1.

 For additional homework suggestions, see activities accompanied by this symbol throughout the chapter.

Block 4

ZWEITE STUFE
Quick Review 10 min.
- Return and review Quiz 2-2, pp. 14–15, Acts. 8–11
- Check homework, Grammatikheft, pp. 14–15, Acts. 8–11

So sagt man das!, p. 46 15 min.
- Presenting **So sagt man das!**, ATE, p. 31T
- Play Audio CD for Activity 30, p. 46
- Do Activity 31, p. 47
- Do Activity 32, p. 47

Wortschatz, p. 47 10 min.
- Presenting **Wortschatz**, ATE, p. 31T
- Play Audio CD for Activity 33, p. 47
- Do Activity 34, p. 47

Ein wenig Grammatik/So sagt man das!, p. 48 10 min.
- Presenting **Ein wenig Grammatik/So sagt man das!**, ATE, p. 31T
- Do Activity 35, p. 48

LANDESKUNDE 25 min.
- Background Information, ATE, p. 31T
- Culture Note, ATE, p. 31T
- Read **Weimar im Blickpunkt,** p. 49
- Do Activities 1–4, p. 49
- Do Activities 1, 2, and 3, p. 24, Übungsheft

Quiz Review 15 min.
- Do Additional Listening Activities 2-4, 2-5, and 2-6, pp. 16–18
- **Mehr Grammatikübungen, Zweite Stufe**

Wrap-Up 5 min.
- Students respond to questions about why they would like to visit Weimar

Homework Options
Pupil's Edition, p. 48, Acts. 36 and 37
Grammatikheft, pp. 16–18, Acts. 12–16
Übungsheft, pp. 22–23, Acts. 6–9

Block 5

ZWEITE STUFE
Quick Review 10 min.
- Check homework, Grammatikheft, pp. 16–18, Acts. 12–16

Ein neues Schulsystem (Video) 20 min.
- Show **Ein neues Schulsystem** and **Werbung** Videos
- Teaching Suggestions, Video Guide, p. 8
- Do Pre-viewing, Viewing, and Post-viewing Activities, Video Guide, p. 9

Quiz 20 min.
- Quiz 2-2A or 2-2B

ZUM LESEN 35 min.
- Teacher Notes, ATE, p. 31U
- Background Information, ATE, pp. 31U–31V
- Teaching Suggestions, ATE, p. 31V
- Present **Lesestrategie,** p. 50
- Do Activities 1–12, pp. 50–51

Wrap-Up 5 min.
- Students brainstorm topics for poems they want to write

Homework Options
Pupil's Edition, p. 52, Act. 13: write a poem
Übungsheft, pp. 25–26, Acts. 1–7

Block 6

ZWEITE STUFE
Quick Review 20 min.
- Return and review Quiz 2-2
- Have students present poems

ZUM SCHREIBEN 45 min.
- Writing Strategy, ATE, p. 31W
- Present **Schreibtipp,** p. 53
- Do Activities A, B, and C, p. 53

REVIEW
Kann ich's wirklich?, p. 58 20 min.
- Do Activities 1–12, p. 58

Wrap-Up 5 min.
- Students discuss the layout of their pamphlets

Homework Options
Interaktive Spiele, see ATE, p. 31E

Block 7

REVIEW
Quick Review 20 min.
- Have students present **Zum Schreiben** flyers

Chapter Review 25 min.
- Review chapter functions, vocabulary, and grammar; choose from **Mehr Grammatikübungen,** Activities for Communication, Listening Activities, or **Interaktive Spiele**
- Review test format and provide sample test items for students

Test, Chapter 2 45 min
- Administer Chapter 2 Test. Select from Testing Program, Alternative Assessment Guide or Test Generator.

Kapitel 2: Auf in die Jugendherberge! *Review Chapter*
Teaching Suggestions, *pages 32–59*

Teacher Note

Chapter 2 is a review chapter that reintroduces functions, grammar, and vocabulary from *Komm mit!* Levels 1 and 2.

Using the Video

Before you begin the chapter, you may want to preview the *Video Program* and consult the *Video Guide.* Suggestions for integrating the video into each chapter are given in the *Video Guide.* Activity masters for video selections can be found in the *Video Guide.*

PAGES 32–33

CHAPTER OPENER

Pacing Tips

Chapter 2 is a review chapter. The **Erste Stufe** centers around the topic of **Jugendherbergen,** with review of several functions from Levels 1 and 2. Many additional functions are reviewed in the **Zweite Stufe.** Because this is a review chapter, you should spend more time on whichever **Stufe** your students need to review most. You might also spend a significant amount of time on **Landeskunde (Weimar)** and **Zum Lesen (Poesie),** which includes Goethe's poem *Erlkönig.* For Lesson Plans and timing suggestions, see pages 31I–31L.

Meeting the Standards

Communication
- Asking for and making suggestions, p. 37
- Expressing preference and giving a reason, p. 39
- Expressing wishes, p. 40
- Expressing doubt, conviction, and resignation, p. 40
- Asking for information and expressing an assumption, p. 45
- Asking for, making, and responding to suggestions, p. 46
- Expressing wishes when shopping, p. 48

Cultures
- Landeskunde, p. 49
- Culture Note, p. 31M
- Culture Note, p. 31O
- Culture Note, p. 31R

For resource information, see the **One-Stop Planner CD-ROM,** Disc 1.

- Background Information, p. 31T
- Background Information, p. 31V

Connections
- Language-to-Language, p. 31O
- Language Notes, p. 31V

Comparisons
- Background Information, p. 31U

Communities
- Teacher Note, p. 31R
- Career Path, p. 31T

Building Context

Ask students if they have gone on short trips with their friends. When did they go, where did they go, how long did they stay, and how did they plan for this trip? (**Bist du schon mal mit Freunden auf einer Kurzreise gewesen? Wann war das? Wohin ging es? Wie lange wart ihr dort? Wie habt ihr diese Reise geplant?**)

Building on Previous Skills

Ask students for names of **öffentliche Verkehrsmittel** that they learned. (Examples: **der Bus, die Straßenbahn, die U-Bahn, die S-Bahn**) In addition, you may ask them which types of public transportation are available in their area. (**Welche öffentlichen Verkehrsmittel gibt es in dieser Stadt? Könnt ihr die aufzählen?**)

Chapter Sequence

LOS GEHT'S!

▶ **PAGES 34–35**

Los geht's! Summary

In *Auf nach Thüringen!*, a group of friends talk about a trip they are planning together. The following learning outcomes listed on p. 33 are modeled in their conversation: asking for and making suggestions; expressing preference and giving a reason; expressing wishes; expressing doubt, conviction, and resignation.

Preteaching Vocabulary

Identifying Keywords

Start by asking students to guess the context of the **Los geht's!** episode (students deciding on a place to vacation). Then have students use the German they know and the context of the situation to identify key words and phrases that tell what is happening. Students should look for words that seem important or that occur several times. Here are a few of the words and phrases they might identify as keywords: **Thüringen, wandern, Rennsteig, Gegend, Jugendherbergen, Ferienwoche.** Which of the words they selected as keywords refer to places?

Advance Organizer

Put students into pairs or small groups and ask them to share with their peers how their family goes about making a decision about where to go on vacation. Put some key questions on the board or on a transparency.
Examples:
Wie entscheidet deine Familie, wohin ihr in den Sommerferien fahrt?
Gibt es verschiedene Meinungen?

Cultures and Communities

Background Information

The **Rennsteig** is a famous German hiking trail. It originates near Eisenach and ends in Bavaria, 15 km (9.3 miles) from the border with the Czech Republic. The first mention of it dates back to the early fourteenth century. The **Rennsteig** was used as a courier line and part of a shortcut to the Danube. The 170 km (105.4 miles) long trail usually takes at least five days to hike.

Culture Note

Erfurt is not only the state capital of **Thüringen**, but also its largest city. Erfurt's history dates back to 729 when it was first mentioned in official records. The city is described as **turmreich** because of its large number of churches and monasteries (80 churches and 36 monasteries) dating back to the Middle Ages, many of which are still standing today.

Comprehension Check

Teaching Suggestion

For teaching purposes, divide the text into three sections. Play the recording of the first part while students follow along in the book. Ask some questions to check for comprehension. Play the compact disc again. Follow the same procedure for parts 2 and 3. Then play the entire conversation and have students read along.

Teaching Suggestion

1 After students have listened to the recording of the conversation and have read it, ask the ten questions to check for comprehension. Allow students to look at the conversation while answering.

Building on Previous Skills

4 For this activity, ask students to look back at the information in the Location Opener on pp. 1–3. The Almanac as well as Photos 1, 2, and 4 provide some additional information on the state of **Thüringen**.

Teaching Suggestion

Ask students to review the conversation among the four students and then decide with whom they most identify based on their interests and statements. What made them decide on that person? (**Lest euch noch mal die Unterhaltung durch! Mit welchen von den vier Schülern identifiziert ihr euch am meisten? Warum?**)

LOS GEHT'S!

Teaching Resources
pp. 36–41

PRINT

▸ Lesson Planner, p. 17
▸ Listening Activities, pp. 11–12, 15–16
▸ Video Guide, pp. 7–9
▸ Activities for Communication, pp. 5–6, 56–57, 59–60, 115–116
▸ Grammatikheft, pp. 10–13
▸ Grammar Tutor for Students of German, Chapter 2
▸ Übungsheft, pp. 15–18
▸ Testing Program, pp. 23–26
▸ Alternative Assessment Guide, p. 31
▸ Student Make-Up Assignments, Chapter 2

MEDIA

▸ One-Stop Planner
▸ Audio Compact Discs, CD2, Trs. 2–5, 15, 19–21
▸ Video Program
  Freizeit
  Videocassette 1, 21:06–24:03
▸ Teaching Transparencies
  Situation 2-1
  Mehr Grammatikübungen Answers
  Grammatikheft Answers

PAGE 36

Bell Work
The game **Stadt, Land, Fluss** was introduced in Level 2 (p. 59C). You may want to play this as a warm-up activity to review German geography as well as vocabulary from this and the previous chapter.

Communication for All Students

Challenge
Read the text aloud as if you were speaking on the radio. After each of the six paragraphs, ask students to summarize what they have just read. Put the numbers 1 through 6 on the board or a transparency and make a list of the six summary statements.

Teaching Suggestion
5 Ask students to use the summary statements from the previous activity to help them answer the four questions in writing. Encourage students to paraphrase

or answer the questions in their own words, rather than simply copying the answers out of the text.

Cultures and Communities

Culture Note

The text mentions that **Jugendherbergen** are for all kinds of groups, including school groups. A **Klassenfahrt** is a yearly occurrence for most German students. The cost of such trips is kept low through inexpensive accommodations such as **Jugendherbergen**.

PAGE 37

PRESENTING: Wortschatz

• After you have gone over the vocabulary with students, ask them to use the various words or phrases in a meaningful context by creating sentences. This can be done orally or in writing. Challenge students to incorporate more than one new word or phrase into a sentence. The sentences can be simple or complex.

• Make up statements or questions that paraphrase a word or phrase from the **Wortschatz**. Students have to guess which one you mean and restate what you said.
Example:
Teacher: **Fast jeder weiß, wer ich bin.**
Student: **Du bist/Sie sind berühmt.**

Connections and Comparisons

Language-to-Language
You may want to tell your students that the German constructions **Hunger/Durst/Angst/Lust haben** are similar to the Spanish **tener hambre/sed/miedo/ganas** and the French **avoir faim/soif/peur/envie**; all use the equivalent of the verb *to have*.

Communication for All Students

A Slower Pace
6 Before students listen to the activity, ask them which time phrases they should be listening for in order to differentiate between **war schon dort** and **fährt erst dorthin**. What verb forms and tenses should they expect to hear? Ask students to give some examples.

PRESENTING: So sagt man das!

Ask students to look back at the **Los geht's!** conversation and make a list of the expressions that are used to ask for and make suggestions. Then discuss the expressions in **So sagt man das!** Ask students to find the key element in each of the choices for making suggestions.

Wir können mal …

… wir doch mal …

Ich schlage vor, dass …

Then ask students for examples using each of the introductory phrases for making suggestions.

▶ PAGE 38

Communication for All Students

A Slower Pace

8 Before students do the partner activity, practice with them the proper use of prepositions and cases for expressing motion toward a place and location at a place. Do this for all the places given in the suggestion box through quick question-answer practice. Examples:

Teacher: **Wohin fährst du?**

Student: **Auf die Insel Rügen.**

Teacher: **Wo warst du?**

Student: **Auf der Insel Rügen.**

A Slower Pace

9 Stop the recording after each exchange and play it again if necessary for students to understand where each of the four characters was last before running into his or her friends. Warn them to pay special attention to Thomas, who seems to have last been at the **Sportgeschäft** but later on in the conversation thinks of something else he needs to do.

▶ PAGE 39

Communication for All Students

Challenge

11A When putting together a shopping route, ask students to disagree with some of their partner's suggestions and propose going to a different shop or doing the shopping in a different order.

A Slower Pace

13 Stop the recording after each report and repeat if necessary. Since the key information is embedded each time in a rather lengthy monologue, students might need time to process each monologue before going on to the next.

PRESENTING: So sagt man das!

To review and practice previously learned vocabulary and functions, encourage students to express preference in different contexts.

Examples:

Was isst du lieber als Fisch? Warum?

Was ziehst du als Urlaubsort vor? Die See oder die Berge? Und warum?

▶ PAGE 40

PRESENTING: So sagt man das!

Have students look back at the **Los geht's!** conversation and make a list of the expressions Uschi and Udo use to express wishes. Ask students to quote these expressions from the conversation and then restate them in different ways.

PRESENTING: So sagt man das!

After reviewing the expressions, remind students that intonation plays a big role in the perception of what is being said. Then give students several statements to which they must react, expressing either doubt, conviction, or resignation.

Examples:

Du kannst mir glauben, es gibt heute Roastbeef in der Schulcafeteria.

Wir können dieses Jahr leider nicht in ein deutsches Restaurant zum Essen gehen.

▶ PAGE 41

Teaching Suggestion

18 Put the pairs of names for each exchange on the chalkboard or a transparency. Names should be in the same sequence in which they are heard on the compact disc.

Using the Video

Videocassette 1, 21:06–24:03

In the video clip *Freizeit*, students of the **Drittes Gymnasium** in Prenzlauer Berg talk about their leisure activities. See *Video Guide*, p. 8, for suggestions.

Challenge

20 Students may want to "leave a telephone message" and make their invitation orally on audiocassette. Let the other group listen to the message and respond on tape as well.

Reteaching: Expressing Preference and Giving Reasons

Present pairs of students with the following situation: You have plans to visit **die neuen Bundesländer** together and have studied brochures and made plans that don't necessarily coincide. Tell each other why you prefer a particular place and give several reasons that you hope will change the other's mind.

Speaking Assessment

21 You may wish to use this activity for assessment using the rubric below. Have groups come to your desk and present the **Rollenspiel**.

Speaking Rubric	Points			
	4	3	2	1
Content (Complete – Incomplete)				
Comprehension (Total – Little)				
Comprehensibility (Comprehensible – Incomprehensible)				
Accuracy (Accurate – Seldom accurate)				
Fluency (Fluent – Not fluent)				

18–20: A   16–17: B   14–15: C   12–13: D   Under 12: F

Assess

▸ Testing Program, pp. 23–26
  Quiz 2-1A, Quiz 2-1B
  Audio CD2, Tr. 15

▸ Student Make-Up Assignments
  Chapter 2, Alternative Quiz

▸ Alternative Assessment Guide, p. 31

WEITER GEHT'S!

PAGES 42–43

Weiter geht's! Summary

In *Auf nach Weimar!*, Frank, Udo, Uschi, and Sabine are making more detailed plans for their trip to Weimar. The following learning outcomes listed on p. 33 are modeled in their conversation: asking for information and expressing an assumption; expressing hearsay; asking for, making, and responding to suggestions; expressing wishes when shopping.

Recognizing Cognates

Los geht's! contains several words that students will be able to recognize as cognates. Some are compound words in which only part of the word is a cognate. Have students identify these words and describe what is happening in the story. Here are some of the compound words they should find: **Jugendgästehaus, Kulturmuffel, fußkrank, Deutschunterricht, Gartenhaus.** In addition, have students use cognates to guess the meanings of these phrases: **Ich hab mich eben informiert. / Bist du vielleicht fußkrank? / Mir läuft jetzt schon das Wasser im Mund zusammen, wenn ich an unser Picknick denke!**

Building Context

Ask students to brainstorm things they need to do when planning a trip. (**Was müsst ihr alles machen, wenn ihr euch auf eine Reise vorbereitet?**)

Thinking Critically

Drawing Inferences Before students begin reading *Auf nach Weimar!*, ask them to predict what might happen next with the vacation plans the four classmates made. Write some of the students' ideas on the board.

Teaching Suggestions

• Ask students to scan the conversation to find out what the German students are talking about. Were their predictions accurate?

• Play the recording of the entire conversation while students follow along in their books. Then play the recording again, this time stopping it at brief intervals to ask some comprehension questions.

Cultures and Communities

 Culture Note
Udo refers to his German teacher as **der Gleißner** instead of **Herr Gleißner.** It is common practice for secondary level and university students to refer to their teachers and professors that way.

Communication for All Students

Challenge
22 Ask students to use their answers to the seven questions to help them compose a written summary of the **Weiter geht's!** conversation. This may be done for homework.

Teaching Suggestion

After students have worked with the text in Activities 23 and 24, put them into groups of four with each student taking one of the four roles from the **Weiter geht's!** conversation. Ask students to enact the conversation by speaking rather than reading their parts aloud, using a lot of expression to bring it alive.

Communication for All Students

Challenge
Ask pairs of students to rewrite the conversation (or part of it) by using synonymous expressions and restatements, or by paraphrasing where they can, without changing the content and the flow of the conversation.

Closure

Ask students to make a list of information they can recall about **Thüringen** from the **Los geht's!** and **Weiter geht's!** conversations.

ZWEITE STUFE

Teaching Resources
pp. 44–49

PRINT
▸ Lesson Planner, p. 19
▸ Listening Activities, pp. 13–14, 16–18
▸ Video Guide, pp. 7–10
▸ Activities for Communication, pp. 7–8, 57–58, 59–60, 115–116
▸ Grammatikheft, pp. 14–18
▸ Grammar Tutor for Students of German, Chapter 2
▸ Übungsheft, pp. 20–24
▸ Testing Program, pp. 27–30
▸ Alternative Assessment Guide, p. 31
▸ Student Make-Up Assignments, Chapter 2

MEDIA
▸ One-Stop Planner
▸ Audio Compact Discs, CD2, Trs. 7–9, 16, 22–24
▸ Video Program
  Ein neues Schulsystem
  Videocassette 1, 24:05–27:34
  Videoclips: Werbung
  Videocassette 1, 27:40–29:16
▸ Teaching Transparencies
  Situation 2-2
  Mehr Grammatikübungen Answers
  Grammatikheft Answers

 **PAGE 44**

 Bell Work
Drawing Inferences Ask students how they could find out about hotel accommodations in a city they plan to visit. (**Wie würdest du dich über die Hotels in einer Stadt, die du besuchen willst, informieren?**)

Teaching Suggestion

Read the prospectus for **Jugendgästehaus Weimar** aloud to the class. Stop as needed to provide definitions for unfamiliar phrases or words, but refrain from using English.

Cultures and Communities

Teacher Note
A **Baudenabend** is an evening of social interaction with refreshments and musical entertainment that usually takes place in a **Hütte** in the forest. **Baude** means **Hütte.**

Cooperative Learning

25 Divide students into groups of three or four and have group members take the role of reader, writer/proofreader, discussion leader (optional), or reporter. Each group tries to answer Questions 1 through 4 within a set amount of time. Call on the reporters to share their group's responses with the class.

Portfolio Assessment

25 You might want to suggest this activity as a written and oral portfolio item for your students. See *Alternative Assessment Guide*, p. 17.

> **PAGE 45**

PRESENTING: Wortschatz

• Go over the words in the **Wortschatz** with students.

• Have students identify the verbs from the **Wortschatz** that correspond to the following nouns:
das Andenken (denken an)
die Erinnerung (sich erinnern)
der Streit (streiten)

• Finally, ask students to give definitions for the nouns based on the definitions for the verbs.

Teaching Suggestion

26 Ask students to listen to the two conversations again, this time listing all the positive things that are being said about youth hostels by any of the speakers.

Using the Video

Videocassette 1, 24:05–27:34
In the video clip *Ein neues Schulsystem*, students in Dresden talk about how school today compares with what it used to be in former East Germany. See *Video Guide*, p. 8, for suggestions.

PRESENTING: So sagt man das!

• To review and practice the phrases in **So sagt man das!**, ask several questions incorporating **ob**-clauses and have students answer them.
Examples:
Michael, kannst du mir sagen, ob es heute Pizza in der Cafeteria zu kaufen gibt?
Weißt du, ob unser Schuldirektor heute in der Schule ist?

• Ask simple yes/no questions that students have to change into questions with **ob**-clauses. Put several introductory clauses on the board or on a transparency.
Examples:
Weißt du,
Wisst ihr,   } ob …
Wissen Sie,
Ich möchte wissen, ob …
Darf ich mal fragen, ob …
Kannst du
Könnt ihr   } mir sagen, ob …
Können Sie
Have other students answer.

Teaching Suggestion

27 Students may refer to the text on p. 40 as they discuss their plans to visit Weimar with their partner. Monitor students' conversations as you walk around the classroom. Be available to answer specific questions about **Jugendherbergen**.

> **PAGE 46**

PRESENTING: So sagt man das!

• Present each of the statements and ask students immediately after each **Weiß ich das oder habe ich das nur so gehört?** to help students understand the idea of hearsay. You may want to add a few hearsay statements on your own.

• Next, present several factual statements that students have to change into hearsay. Use the context of Weimar.
Examples:
Weimar ist eine schöne Stadt.
Es gibt dort einen Stadtpark.

• Ask students to share some news or gossip about an actor, musician, or other celebrity. You may want to begin by sharing your own bit of news.
Example:
Ich habe gehört, dass die David Letterman Sendung heute Abend eine Wiederholung ist.

Communication for All Students

For Additional Practice

28 For further practice, you may want to add other topics such as **Pensionen, Sommercamps, Fahrschulen,** and **Campingplätze.** Students follow the directions for Activity 28 as they discuss the additional topics.

ZWEITE STUFE

PRESENTING: So sagt man das!

Ask students to use the different ways of making suggestions as they discuss the Location Opener on pp. 1–3. Students ask each other for suggestions, make suggestions, and respond to suggestions about what they would like to do and see in **die neuen Bundesländer**.

Teaching Suggestion

31 You may want to give students the option of writing about what they would like to see or do in other locations in order to appeal to all students' interests.

> **PAGE 47**

PRESENTING: Wortschatz

- Bring the utensils and other kitchen items presented in the **Wortschatz** to class. Present the various items to the students and have them repeat.

- Next, ask questions to which one or two of the utensils are the answer.
Example:
Was brauche ich zum Brotschneiden? (ein Messer und ein Schneidebrett)

> **PAGE 48**

PRESENTING: Ein wenig Grammatik

Unpreceded adjectives Remind students that unpreceded adjectives have to assume the role of an article; their endings have to indicate the gender, number, and case of the noun that follows.

PRESENTING: So sagt man das!

- Remind students that the umlauts in **möchte** and **hätte** indicate the subjunctive mood. The subjunctive is used to express wishes or something that someone would like to do.

- Have students practice making requests with the **möchte**-forms and **hätte**-forms using the food vocabulary in the boxes above **So sagt man das!** Students work in pairs and role-play a conversation between vendor and customer at the **Marktplatz**.

Teacher Note

In **So sagt man das!**, **Schweizer** is used as an adjective. Unlike most other adjectives, **Schweizer** is always capitalized and never changes its endings.

Teaching Suggestion

Ask students to practice the adjective endings and food vocabulary as they prepare an order for their favorite sandwich, which they plan to phone in to a nearby deli.

Von der Schule zum Beruf

Have students do the **Webprojekt** on p. 31E, or have them research German hotel and resort Web sites, before beginning this activity.

Cultures and Communities

Career Path

Have students brainstorm reasons why it would be advantageous for an American interested in sports to have a knowledge of German. (Suggestions: Imagine you are an American ski instructor working in the **Tirol** for the season; imagine you have been hired to coach a German basketball team; imagine you are a player or coach on an American-style football team in Germany or Austria.)

> **PAGE 49**

LANDESKUNDE

Cultures and Communities

Background Information

- The Goethe-Schiller memorial is located near the entrance to the **Deutsches Nationaltheater.** It was erected in 1857 by the sculptor Ernst Rietschel, who is also known for his works around **Schloss Charlottenburg** in Berlin.

- **Goethes Gartenhaus** is located in the **Park an der Ilm.** The house was built in the 17th century. Goethe lived there between 1776 and 1782. It contains all the original furnishings and is open to the public.

Culture Note

The Ministers of Culture of the European Community awarded Weimar the title of European City of Culture for 1999. During the year-long celebration, the city honored the achievements of its classical past, recognizing such famous residents as Herder, Schiller, Goethe, Liszt, and Nietzsche. Other celebrations were also linked to Weimar's history.

Teaching Suggestion

Remind students of the reading skills they have learned, such as reading for comprehension. Emphasize that they should try to focus on understanding ideas rather than isolated words. You may want to divide the text into the following five sections to help them:

1) Weimar wurde 1999 Kulturstadt Europas.

2) Wem hat Weimar das zu verdanken?

3) Das alte Weimar

4) Weimar heute

5) Zwei deutsche Städte als „Kulturstädte Europas"

Teacher Note

Mention to your students that the **Landeskunde** will also be included in Quiz 2-2 given at the end of the **Zweite Stufe**.

(TPR) Total Physical Response

Prior to this activity, you may want to gather all the items from the **Wortschatz** on p. 47. Call on students to come to the front of the class. Give them specific instructions on what to do with the various items. Examples:
Stell den Becher rechts neben den Teller!
Leg Messer, Gabel und Löffel auf den Teller!

Using the Video

 Videocassette 1, 27:40–29:16
At this time, you might want to use the authentic advertising footage from German television. See *Video Guide*, p. 8, for suggestions.

Assess

▸ Testing Program, pp. 27–30
  Quiz 2-2A, Quiz 2-2B
  Audio CD2, Tr. 16

▸ Student Make-Up Assignments
  Chapter 2, Alternative Quiz

▸ Alternative Assessment Guide, p. 31

ZUM LESEN

Teaching Resources
pp. 50–52

PRINT
▸ Lesson Planner, p. 20
▸ Übungsheft, pp. 25–26
▸ Reading Strategies and Skills, Chapter 2
▸ Lies mit mir! 3, Chapter 2

MEDIA
▸ One-Stop Planner
▸ Audio Compact Discs, CD2, Trs. 10–14

Teacher Notes

• You may want to remind students that the interpretation of poetry is very subjective; there is no single correct interpretation of the poems featured in this **Zum Lesen** selection.

The following poems are recorded on CD 2, Tracks 10–14: *Erlkönig, Der Panther, Der Radwechsel, ottos mops,* and *Kinderlied.*

Connections and Comparisons

Background Information

Erlkönig: Like the English Romantic poets Wordsworth and Coleridge, many of the late 18th-century and 19th-century poets in Germany tried to revive old folk forms. The first poem students will read derives from that impulse, although Goethe later changed styles and went on, with Schiller, to develop the style known as German classicism.

ZUM LESEN

Prereading

Cultures and Communities

Background Information

- *Der Panther:* Rilke (1875–1926) was born and began writing in Prague, where he was a contemporary of Kafka. Together with the sculptor Rodin, Rilke thought out his notion of the artist as a person who sees things purely and completely and depicts their true nature in precise, concrete form. *Der Panther* is from this genre.

- *Der Radwechsel:* Bertolt Brecht (1898–1956) went through several stages of lyric style during his lifetime, beginning as an expressionist, but later developing a starker, less emotional language.

- *ottos mops:* Ernst Jandl (1925–2000) was born in Vienna. After World War II, he studied English and German and taught at a **Gymnasium.** During the 1950s, Jandl developed a form of poetry he called **Sprechgedichte,** experimental texts characterized by the constant repetition of words and by playful distortions of sound. Jandl himself has become known for his lively recitations of these poems. He died in 2000.

- *menschenskind* and *Apfel:* Reinhard Döhl was born in Wattenscheid in 1934 and now lives in Stuttgart. The two pieces of Döhl's work included here are examples of concrete poetry. Among many other things, concrete poetry is a recognition of, and an attempt to come to poetic terms with, the fact that people no longer recite poetry orally in our culture.

- *Kinderlied:* Günter Grass, born in 1927, was a stonecutter, sculptor, and painter before he began his career as poet, novelist, and playwright. In his novels and plays he purports to deal with man's existential guilt, a guilt that must be individually borne and reckoned with. Grass won the Nobel prize for literature in 1999.

Building Context

Before reading the poems, have students think about some poems they know in English or in English translation, including song lyrics. Which would they call *folk* poetry, and which would they call *artistic* poetry? If students can't think of many examples, you might ask them about some of the following: Homer's *Iliad, Beowulf,* Milton's *Paradise Lost,* Shakespeare's sonnets, and the songs *My Darling Clementine, Sweet Betsy from Pike, Blowing in the Wind,* and Stephen Foster's *Old Folks at Home.*

Teacher Note

Activity 1 is a prereading activity.

Reading
Teaching Suggestions

2 In addition to playing the poem *Erlkönig* on compact disc for the students, you might want to obtain a recorded version of Schubert's **Lied.** The Schubert version will give the students a feeling for the dramatic quality of the poem, even if they don't understand all the words.

- Ask students to describe the stanza form of the ballad *Erlkönig:* how many lines are in a stanza? Which lines rhyme? What is the rhythm? Compared with a genuine folk ballad like *Yankee Doodle,* in which there is usually one narrator or a dialogue between at most two singers, how does Goethe heighten the sense of drama?

9 Before students read *ottos mops,* you might want to point out that poetry isn't always earnest and intense. Ask them if they can think of some verses (including songs) that are just plain fun and some that are both fun and intended to make the listener or reader think. As students read the poem by Jandl, they should try to decide what his purpose was in writing it.

Teacher Note

The poem *menschenskind* is made up of one block of text in four different positions.

Connections and Comparisons

Language Notes

11 Students should note that the only part of **menschenskind** that remains constant throughout the poem is **kind** = *kind.* All the other letters are shifted in various meaningless combinations until the English-German equation is reversed. Note that *kind* does not mean *kindly* in this poem. It is closer, instead, to *child of man,* i.e., *human.*

11 **Mensch!** or **Menschenskind!** is a fairly established colloquial expression that conveys surprise, often tinged with disapproval or dismay. However, it is likely in this poem to convey more of a sense of wonder similar to *gee whiz* or *man alive!*

Post-Reading
Teacher Note

Activity 13 is a post-reading task that will show whether students can apply what they have learned.

Thinking Critically

Evaluating Looking at the poems presented in this chapter, do students feel that poetry is more successful and lasting when it is pure art for art's sake? Or do they feel that a poet has some obligation to entertain the public at the public's level? What about poetry that is primarily intended to teach the reader a particular philosophy or set of ideas? (Examples: Emerson and/or Alexander Pope) To what extent should a poet care about the audience, and to what extent should he or she create simply in order to please himself or herself? Which of the poems from **Zum Lesen** do students think are the most successful, according to students' criteria?

Teaching Suggestion

Have students choose one of the poems to present in a different mode. For example, they could compose a melody to which they sing the poem, or sketch an illustration that fits the mood of the poem and illustrates some important feature of its content. They should each present their work to the class and discuss the various ways in which these presentations support certain interpretations of the poems.

Zum Lesen Answers
Answers to Activity 1
Answers will vary. Students should notice that the *Apfel* and *menschenskind* poems look different from the others, more like pictures or geometric designs.
Answers to Activity 2
dramatic: *Erlkönig, Der Panther, Der Radwechsel, Kinderlied*
Lighthearted: *ottos mops*
Answers to Activity 3
Erlkönig: **Vater, Sohn, Erlkönig;** riding through the fields and forests, night; see Answers to Activity 5. *Der Panther:* **Panther;** in a cage at the zoo in Paris; the panther is walking in circles in his cage. *Der Radwechsel:* ich; at the side of the street; the narrator is looking on as the driver changes a tire. *ottos mops:* Otto, **mops;** Otto is trying to train his dog. *Kinderlied:* no specific characters, time, or setting are mentioned
Answers to Activity 4
The quotes designate the lines spoken by the **Erlkönig,** and the dashes indicate a change of speaker (narrator, father, and son). The chart should help students see that the lines spoken by the narrator form a frame for the poem.

stanza	1	2	3	4	5	6	7	8
narr.	1-4							29-32
father		5, 8		15-16		23-24		
son		6-7		13-14		21-22	27-28	
elf king			9-12		17-20		25-26	

Answers to Activity 5
The father is taking his son somewhere to get help; the son dies at the end of the poem; the **Erlkönig** is trying to take the child away; answers will vary.
Answers to Activity 6
in captivity; the panther is looking through bars; the panther is tired, numb, hopeless, and tense; the image ceases to exist.
Answers to Activity 8
No, the narrator looks on passively as the driver changes the tire; they will continue on their journey; **herkomme>hinfahre;** no, it is a description of what is happening and how the narrator feels about his situation, but stated without any emotion until the last line; answers will vary.
Answers to Activity 9
beginning of direct speech; a dog
Answers to Activity 10
They let the reader know that the first line of each stanza is a question. The reader can assume that lines 2–4 of each stanza are the answers. Actions: laughing, crying, speaking, remaining silent, playing, and dying. Because the idea of reason is central to the poem; it ties the five stanzas together and brings closure to the poem. There's nothing childlike about the idea presented in the poem.
Answers to Activity 11
The poet relies on concrete visual images, as well as words, to convey his meaning.

> **PAGE 53**

ZUM SCHREIBEN

Teaching Resources
p. 53

PRINT
▸ Lesson Planner, p. 20
▸ Alternative Assessment Guide, p. 17

MEDIA
▸ One-Stop Planner
▸ Test Generator, Chapter 2

Writing Strategy

The targeted strategy in this writing activity is *selecting information.* Students should learn about this strategy before beginning the assignment.

Prewriting

Visual Learners

A Tell students to plan carefully each step of the process of gathering, preparing, and organizing their materials. They can do this in the form of a chart, which will help them organize their notes and visuals, as well as help them keep track of individual responsibilities.

Writing
Teaching Suggestions

B You may want to set up research tables with books and pamphlets from travel agencies in the classroom to facilitate students' research.

B Remind students to use vocabulary that will be familiar to the rest of the class, since too many unknown words from the dictionary might confuse readers. Each group should make a list of unfamiliar words and phrases and try to simplify them by paraphrasing or using synonyms.

Post-Writing
Closure

After groups have completed the travel brochures, let students tour through the classroom to see the different brochures that were produced. Display them on a bulletin board. Afterwards, students can discuss in different groups which place they would most like to visit and why.

PAGES 54–57

MEHR GRAMMATIKÜBUNGEN

The **Mehr Grammatikübungen** activities are designed as supplemental activities for the grammatical concepts presented in the chapter. You might use them as additional practice, for review, or for assessment.

For more grammar presentations, review, and practice, refer to the following:
- Grammatikheft
- Grammar Tutor for Students of German
- Grammar Summary on pp. R22–R39
- Übungsheft
- Grammar and Vocabulary quizzes (Testing Program)
- Test Generator
- **Interaktive Spiele** at go.hrw.com

PAGE 58

KANN ICH'S WIRKLICH?

This page helps students prepare for the test. It is a brief checklist of the major points covered in the chapter. The students should be reminded that it is only a checklist and not necessarily everything that will appear on the test.

For additional self-check options, refer students to the *Grammar Tutor* and the Online self-test for this chapter.

PAGE 59

WORTSCHATZ

Kinesthetic Learners

Gather the picnic items listed in the **Wortschatz** and arrange them on a table in the front of the class. Have students set a table for two including all necessary utensils and dishes. Then tell them to set it up for a less formal setting like a picnic. Have students tell what they are doing as they do it.

Teaching Suggestion

Students should have their books closed for this activity. Ask individual students what specific items are used for.
Example:
Wozu braucht man einen Flaschenöffner?

Circumlocution

To review, play **Das treffende Wort suchen** using the **Zweite Stufe** picnic vocabulary. You might want to incorporate a chain idea. The first student says **Ich plane ein Picknick und möchte etwas mitbringen, was so aussieht: Es ist oft aus Papier, weiß und klein, und man wischt sich damit den Mund ab.** The next student says **Ich plane ein Picknick und will Servietten und etwas anderes mitbringen.** The third student must first name the first two items and add a third one and so forth. See p. 31C for procedures.

Teacher Note

Give the **Kapitel 2** Chapter Test:
Testing Program, pp. 31–36
Audio CD 2, Trs. 17–18.

REVIEW

2

Auf in die Jugendherberge!

Objectives

In this chapter you will review and practice how to

Erste Stufe

- ask for and make suggestions
- express preference and give a reason
- express wishes
- express doubt, conviction, and resignation

Zweite Stufe

- ask for information and express an assumption
- express hearsay
- ask for, make, and respond to suggestions
- express wishes when shopping

 internet

go.hrw.com	**ADRESSE:** go.hrw.com **KENNWORT:** WK3 DIE NEUEN BUNDESLAENDER-2

◀ **Fahrt ihr auch nach Konstanz?**

Los geht's! ▪ *Auf nach Thüringen!*

CD 2 Tr. 1

Udo: So, Leute, ich hab mir eben meinen Ferienpass gekauft.

Uschi: Das heißt also, du fährst mit, ja?

Udo: Logo! Wohin geht's denn überhaupt?

Frank: Wir sind noch am Diskutieren. Ich bin dafür, dass wir an irgendeinen See in Mecklenburg fahren, zum Schwimmen und Windsurfen.

Sabine: Das können wir ja auch bei uns, da brauchen wir nicht nach Mecklenburg zu fahren! Ich schlage vor, dass wir nach Thüringen fahren, zum Wandern. Dort gibt's doch diesen berühmten Wanderweg … ja, wie heißt er denn noch?

Uschi: Ich glaube, das ist der Rennsteig.

Sabine: Stimmt, der Rennsteig.

Frank: Du willst wirklich wandern, Sabine?

Sabine: Klar! Warum nicht?

Frank: Und du, Udo? Hast du Lust zum Wandern?

Udo: Eigentlich schon. Ich hoffe nur, dass das Wetter schön bleibt.

Uschi: Ja, sag uns mal, Udo, was du dir wünschst, was du gern unternehmen möchtest!

Udo: Also, ich möchte auch lieber raus in die Natur, wandern, irgendwelche kleinen Städte ansehen und so.

Uschi: Fahren wir doch mal in den Harz, in die Gegend von Wernigerode. Dort soll es sehr schön sein.

Udo: Meine Eltern waren letztes Jahr in der Gegend, aber sie haben Thüringen interessanter gefunden, auch schöner.

Sabine: Ja, ich ziehe Thüringen auch vor. Ich finde, da ist vom Kulturellen her mehr zu sehen, Weimar, Erfurt, Eisenach …

Uschi: Ich ziehe aber kleinere Städte vor, wo weniger Verkehr ist, wo die Luft besser ist.

Sabine: Wir können ja beides machen: etwas Kultur und etwas für die Gesundheit, nämlich viel wandern.

Udo: Wer weiß denn, wo es in Thüringen Jugendherbergen gibt?

Frank: Ich hab ein Verzeichnis zu Hause, ich seh mal nach. In Eisenach gibt's eine, das weiß ich.

Sabine: Ich bezweifle aber, dass wir noch Unterkunft bekommen, jetzt in der ersten Ferienwoche.

Frank: Ich kann ja mal anrufen. Übrigens, hat jeder von euch einen Jugendherbergsausweis?

Udo: Na klar!

Sabine: Nehmt euch aber ja nicht wieder so viele Klamotten mit wie letztes Mal!

Uschi: Keine Angst, Sabine! Aber du warst doch froh, dass ich damals ein extra Sweatshirt dabeihatte, weil du deins irgendwo verloren hattest.

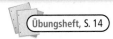

Übungsheft, S. 14

1 Was passiert hier?

Sprechen Hast du das Gespräch verstanden? Beantworte die folgenden Fragen!

1. Worüber sprechen die vier Klassenkameraden?
2. Woher weißt du, dass Udo bestimmt mitfährt?
3. Warum will Sabine nicht nach Mecklenburg fahren?
4. Was schlägt Sabine vor?
5. Was möchte Udo unternehmen?
6. Wohin möchte Uschi fahren? Warum?
7. Warum ist Udo nicht für Uschis Vorschlag?
8. Warum möchte Sabine nach Thüringen?
9. Wo wollen die Schüler übernachten?
10. Warum will Frank die Jugendherberge anrufen?

1. Sie sprechen darüber, wo sie ihre Ferien verbringen.
2. Er hat sich einen Ferienpass gekauft.
3. Sie meint, dass sie auch zu Hause schwimmen und windsurfen können.
4. Sie schlägt vor, zum Wandern nach Thüringen zu fahren.
5. in der Natur wandern; sich Städte ansehen
6. Sie möchte in den Harz, in die Nähe von Wernigerode.
7. Er sagt, dass seine Eltern es in Thüringen interessanter fanden.
8. Sie findet, dort gibt es mehr Kulturelles zu sehen.
9. in der Jugendherberge
10. um zu sehen, ob sie noch Unterkunft bekommen

2 Wie gut bist du in Geografie?

Schreiben/Lesen Schreib alle Ortsnamen auf einen Zettel, die die vier Schüler erwähnen! Sieh danach auf eine Landkarte und suche alle Ortsnamen, die du aufgeschrieben hast!

Mecklenburg, Thüringen, Harz, Wernigerode, Weimar, Erfurt, Eisenach

3 Was passt zusammen?

Sprechen Welche Ausdrücke rechts vollenden am besten die Satzanfänge auf der linken Seite?

1. Fahren wir doch mal an einen See   e   **a.** im Harz.
2. Ich möchte lieber nach Thüringen   g   **b.** eine Jugendherberge.
3. Dieser Wanderweg ist doch   d   **c.** in die Natur.
4. Ja, ich möchte auch am liebsten raus   c   **d.** der Rennsteig.
5. Wernigerode ist eine Stadt   a   **e.** zum Schwimmen.
6. Weimar und Erfurt sind Städte   f   **f.** in Thüringen.
7. In Eisenach gibt es ganz bestimmt   b   **g.** zum Wandern.

4 Wohin möchtest du fahren?

Sprechen Du bist ein(e) Schulfreund(in) von Frank, Udo, Sabine und Uschi. Sag, wohin du fahren möchtest und warum!

Erste Stufe

Objectives Asking for and making suggestions; expressing preference and giving a reason; expressing wishes; expressing doubt, conviction, and resignation

WK3 DIE NEUEN
BUNDESLAENDER-2

Willkommen!

Deutschland hat seinen Gästen viel zu bieten: die Küsten der Nord- und Ostsee, die Lüneburger Heide, den Schwarzwald, die bayrischen Alpen, jahrhundertealte Städte, malerische Dörfer. Und überall, wo Deutschland am schönsten ist, finden Sie auch Jugendherbergen.

Sie können zwischen rund 700 Häusern wählen. Wollen Sie auf dem Lande in ruhiger Umgebung übernachten? Oder in einer romantischen Burg? Oder mitten in einer Stadt, hautnah zur Kunst- und Kulturszene?

Jugendherbergen sind nicht-kommerzielle Freizeiteinrichtungen, die vor allem Jugendlichen offenstehen. Sie fördern das gegenseitige Kennenlernen sowie die Toleranz gegenüber anderen Weltanschauungen und Gewohnheiten. Sie haben sich zu Stätten internationaler Begegnung entwickelt.

Wir bieten Ihnen saubere, freundliche Aufenthalts- und Schlafräume mit zwei bis sechs Betten. Die Gäste werden nach Geschlechtern getrennt untergebracht. Im Übernachtungspreis ist das Frühstück enthalten, auch Vollverpflegung wird angeboten. In fast allen Häusern sind Möglichkeiten für Spiel und Sport vorhanden. Die Jugendherbergen haben unterschiedliche Standards, allen gemeinsam sind jedoch die günstigen Preise. Selbstbedienung und die

Mithilfe der Gäste bei kleineren Arbeiten werden daher gern gesehen.

In der Regel sind die Jugendherbergen bis 22 Uhr geöffnet, Jugendherbergen in Großstädten schließen später.

Jugendherbergen sind ideal für Einzelreisende, Gruppen, Schulklassen sowie Familien. Viele Jugendherbergen sind behindertenfreundlich eingerichtet und auf Rollstuhlfahrer eingestellt.

1. die Küsten der Nord- und Ostsee; die Lüneburger Heide; den Schwarzwald; die bayerischen Alpen; jahrhundertealte Städte; malerische Dörfer 2. Dort, wo es in Deutschland am schönsten ist. 3. Answers will vary. / nicht-kommerzielle Einrichtungen; fördern das gegenseitige Kennenlernen und Toleranz; sind Stätten internationaler Begegnung; günstige Preise usw. / Selbstbedienung; Mithilfe bei kleineren Arbeiten; sind nur bis 22 Uhr geöffnet usw. 4. Answers will vary.

5 Deutsche Jugendherbergen

Lesen/Sprechen Lies den Text über die Jugendherbergen, und beantworte die Fragen!

1. Was hat Deutschland seinen Gästen zu bieten?

2. Wo findet man Jugendherbergen?

3. Versuch, eine Jugendherberge zu beschreiben! Was sind Vorteile? Nachteile?

4. Würdest du gern mal in einer deutschen Jugendherberge übernachten? Gib drei Gründe.

auf Deutsch erklärt

Lust haben wenn man etwas gern machen will
die Gegend die Umgebung
die Jugendherberge ein Haus, wo Jugendliche für wenig Geld übernachten und essen können
die Unterkunft wo man übernachten kann
das Verzeichnis eine Liste mit Namen und Adressen
berühmt fast alle Leute kennen einen
unternehmen machen
der Ausweis ein Dokument mit Namen, Adresse und Geburtsdatum
verlieren Man wird es nicht mehr haben oder finden können.

auf Englisch erklärt

Keine <u>Angst</u>! *Don't worry!*
Ich <u>seh</u> mal <u>nach</u>. *I'll check it out.*
<u>Damals</u> war ich erst fünfzehn. *At the time I was only 15.*
Er ist <u>eben</u> zurückgekommen. *He just now got back.*
Wir wollen *<u>beide</u>* dahin. *Both of us want to go there.*

eine Burg an artistic rendition of **Burg Eltz** near Frankfurt

Grammatikheft, S. 10, Ü. 1–2

---

6 **Über Ferienorte** Script and answers on p. 31G

CD 2 Tr. 2

Zuhören Schüler sprechen über Ferienorte. Wer war schon dort? Wer fährt erst dorthin? — Übertrag die Tabelle in dein Heft, und schreib den Ferienort, den du hörst, in die richtige Spalte!

Schüler	war schon dort	fährt erst hin

So sagt man das!

Asking for and making suggestions

2-1 Schon bekannt

If you need specific suggestions, you might ask:

Wohin fahren wir? Was schlägst du vor?
Wohin geht's denn? Hast du eine Idee?

When making suggestions, you might say:

Wir können mal an die Ostsee fahren. *or*
Fahren wir doch mal in den Harz! *or*
Ich schlage vor, dass wir nach Thüringen fahren.

Identify the prepositional phrases used in these suggestions. What case follows the prepositions **an** and **in**? Why?[1]

Mehr Grammatikübungen, S. 54, Ü. 1

Grammatikheft, S. 11, Ü. 3

---

1. These two-way prepositions get the accusative case because there is motion to a place.

7 Wohin geht's?

a. Schreiben Wie gut kennst du Deutschland schon? Schreib vier Orte oder Gegenden, die du gern besuchen möchtest, auf einen Zettel, und schreib daneben, was du dort gern machen möchtest!

b. Sprechen Such dir eine Partnerin, mit der du gern reisen möchtest! Sie fragt dich nach deinen Vorschlägen. Gib zwei Alternativen, und sag in jedem Fall, warum du dieses Ziel vorschlägst!

8 Nö, da war ich schon!

Sprechen Such dir einen Partner! Lad ihn ein, mit dir wegzufahren! Dein Partner ist aber ein Reisemuffel. Er sagt dir immer, dass er schon dort war, wo du hin willst, und er sagt dir auch, warum er nicht mitfahren will. Im Kasten unten stehen ein paar Ideen. Gebrauche aber auch deine eigenen!

wohin?/wo?

Thüringen	Ostsee	Alpen	Harz
Bodensee	Rhein		Schweiz
Wernigerode		Zugspitze	
Berge	Insel Rügen		Meer

BEISPIEL

DU Du, ich möchte mal nach Thüringen fahren. Willst du mit?

PARTNER Nö. Ich war schon mal in Thüringen. Es hat mir dort nicht gefallen.

9 Was machen die Schüler in Dingskirchen? Script and answers on p. 31G

Zuhören Schüler erzählen, was sie in Dingskirchen machen. Schreib auf, wo jeder zuletzt hingeht oder zuletzt war!
CD 2 Tr. 3

10 In Dingskirchen

Sprechen Kennst du dich in Dingskirchen aus? Ein Tourist stellt dir viele Fragen. Such dir einen Partner, der den Touristen spielt!

BEISPIEL

TOURIST Entschuldigung, wo ist das Restaurant „Bella Italia"?

DU Das ist in der Uhlandstraße, an der Ecke Agnesstraße.

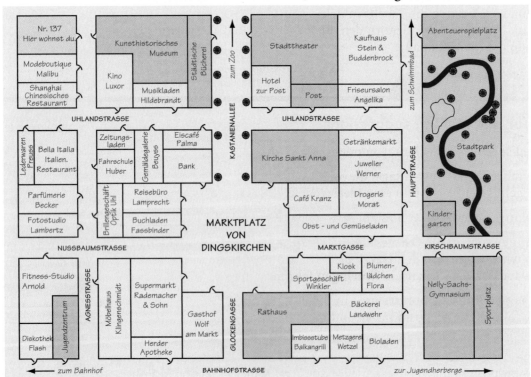

11. a. Answers will vary. E.g.: **Zuerst gehen wir ins Brillengeschäft in der Agnesstraße. Dann gehen wir nach links in die Nussbaumstraße bis zum Marktplatz. Dort gehen wir in den Buchladen usw.**

11 Mein Einkaufsweg

a. Lesen/Sprechen Du wohnst in Dingskirchen in der Agnesstraße 137. Du musst jetzt für deine Mutter einkaufen gehen. Sie hat dir einen Einkaufszettel gegeben. Als du aus dem Haus kommst, triffst du einen Klassenkameraden. Er hat nichts vor und will dir beim Einkaufen helfen. — Such dir einen Partner, und stellt einen guten Einkaufsweg zusammen!

b. Sprechen Zu Hause erzählst du deiner Mutter, wo du überall warst und was du an jedem Ort gemacht hast. — Such dir eine Partnerin für die Rolle der Mutter!

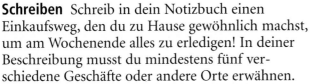

1 l Milch
5 kg Kartoffeln
1/2 kg Tomaten
1 frisches Brot
250 g Leberwurst
die Flaschen
    zurückbringen
CD für Vati
10 Briefmarken
Buch umtauschen
Sonnenbrille

12 Für mein Notizbuch

Schreiben Schreib in dein Notizbuch einen Einkaufsweg, den du zu Hause gewöhnlich machst, um am Wochenende alles zu erledigen! In deiner Beschreibung musst du mindestens fünf verschiedene Geschäfte oder andere Orte erwähnen.

13 Wohin fahren die Schüler nun?

Script and answers on p. 31H

Zuhören Vier Schüler (Christoph, Annette, Jörg und Isabella) unterhalten sich darüber, wo sie am liebsten eine Ferienwoche verbringen würden. Am Anfang möchte jeder woandershin fahren und sagt auch warum. Am Ende einigen sie sich (*they agree*) auf ein Ziel. Schreib die folgende Tabelle ab und trag ein, was du hörst!

CD 2 Tr. 4

	Wohin?	Warum?
Christoph		
Annette		

So sagt man das!

Expressing preference and giving a reason

Schon bekannt

To express preference and give a reason, you may say:

Mir gefällt die Ostsee besser als die Nordsee; die Ostsee ist ruhiger.
Ich finde Weimar schöner als Erfurt, weil Weimar mehr Kulturelles bietet.
Ich ziehe eine kleine Stadt wie Wernigerode vor, weil da die Luft einfach besser ist als in einer größeren Stadt.

(Übungsheft, S. 15–16, Ü. 1–4) (Grammatikheft, S. 12, Ü. 4)

Mehr Grammatikübungen, S. 54, Ü. 2

14 Wann und warum?

a. Schreiben Denk an zwei bekannte Reiseziele, die du gern besuchen möchtest! Schreib auf, welches Reiseziel du lieber hast, und gib einen Grund an, warum du dorthin möchtest!

b. Sprechen Such dir einen Partner! Er fragt dich, wohin du in den Ferien fährst. Du sagst es ihm und begründest deine Antwort. Tauscht danach die Rollen aus!

15 Und in Dingskirchen?

Sprechen Such dir eine Partnerin! Nenne ihr drei Geschäfte, wo du immer einkaufst! Nenne ihr auch Gründe dafür! Gebrauche in deiner Begründung Adjektive oder Komparative! Rechts stehen einige Anregungen.

Fleisch — gut

CDs — billig

Kleidung — schick

Brot — frisch

Answers will vary. E.g.: **Ich kaufe meine Sachen nur in der Modeboutique Malibu.**
Dort gibt es schickere Kleidung als im Kaufhaus.

So sagt man das!

Expressing wishes

Schon bekannt

When asking someone about his or her wishes, you may ask:

And the answer may be:

Mehr Grammatikübungen,
S. 54, Ü. 3

Wohin möchtest du gern mal fahren?
Was wünschst du dir mal?

Ich möchte gern mal in den Harz fahren.
Ich wünsche mir mal einen schönen, langen Urlaub an der Ostsee.

Grammatikheft,
S. 12, Ü. 5

Was hättest du gern?

Ich hätte gern viel Schnee im Winter.

16 Was für Wünsche hast du?

a. Schreiben Schreib vier Dinge auf einen Zettel, die du dir einmal wünschst! Gebrauche die Kategorien Reisen, Schule, Freunde und Kleidung!

b. Sprechen Such dir eine Partnerin, und frag sie nach ihren Wünschen!

17 Also, wohin geht's?

Sprechen Setzt euch in Gruppen zu fünft oder zu sechst zusammen! Das Thema heißt: Wohin sollen wir fahren? Sprecht über eure Wünsche, diskutiert darüber, was euch gefällt, nicht gefällt oder besser gefällt, und macht verschiedene Vorschläge, bis (*until*) ihr euch auf ein gemeinsames Ziel geeinigt habt!

So sagt man das!

Expressing doubt, conviction, and resignation

Schon bekannt

When expressing doubt, you might say:

Ich weiß nicht, ob wir noch eine Unterkunft bekommen.
Ich bezweifle, dass es in der Jugendherberge einen Tennisplatz gibt.
Ich bin nicht sicher, dass wir am Ostseestrand tauchen können.

When expressing conviction, you might say:

Du kannst mir glauben, dort gibt es eine ganz tolle Jugendherberge.
Ich bin sicher, dass dir Thüringen gut gefallen wird.

Mehr Grammatikübungen,
S. 55, Ü. 4–5

What happens to the conjugated verb in **dass-** and **ob-**clauses?[1]

Übungsheft,
S. 17–18, Ü. 5–9

When faced with bad news, you can express resignation. For example, if you hear:

You might respond:

Grammatikheft,
S. 13, Ü. 6–7

Die Jugendherbergen sind überfüllt!
In dem See darf man nicht baden!

Da kann man nichts machen.
Schade. Das ist leider so.

---

1. The conjugated verb is in last position.

18 Sicher oder nicht Script and answers on p. 31H

 Zuhören Du hörst als Kellnerin im Café verschiedene Gesprächsfetzen (*scraps of conversation*). Wer von den Sprechenden bezweifelt etwas, und wer ist sicher?

CD 2 Tr. 5

	bezweifeln	sicher sein
1		
2		

 19 Bist du sicher?

 Sprechen Such dir eine Partnerin! Sie ist sicher, dass es in dem Ferienort, den ihr euch ausgesucht habt, ganz bestimmte Einrichtungen gibt und dass ihr dort ganz bestimmte Sportarten ausüben könnt. Du bezweifelst das und gibst dafür deine Gründe an. Deine Partnerin ist ganz enttäuscht. — Benutzt die Illustrationen als Anregungen! Answers will vary. E.g.: **Ich bezweifle, dass man an der Nordsee segeln kann. Dort ist das Wetter immer sehr stürmisch und es regnet zu oft. / Schade. Da kann man nichts machen.**

 20 Eine Einladung schreiben — und eine Einladung beantworten

 Schreiben Bildet Gruppen zu viert! Jede Gruppe wählt einen Schriftführer, also eine Person, die alles aufschreiben muss. Jede Gruppe schreibt einer anderen Gruppe eine Einladung. Ihr macht zwei oder drei Vorschläge und schreibt, was ihr persönlich vorzieht. — Tauscht dann eure Einladungen aus, und beantwortet sie gegenseitig! Schreibt, dass ihr gern mitfahren wollt, aber dass ihr ganz bestimmte Wünsche habt. Ihr wollt an den vorgeschlagenen Orten bestimmte Dinge tun, bezweifelt aber, dass es dort alle Einrichtungen gibt, die ihr euch wünscht!

21 R o l l e n s p i e l

Bereite eins von diesen beiden Rollenspielen mit drei anderen Schülern vor!

a. Du gehst mit drei Schülern in ein Reisebüro. Ihr sucht euch ein Reiseziel aus, das euch allen gefällt. Einer von euch spielt die Rolle des Angestellten im Reisebüro.

b. Du diskutierst mit deinen drei Freunden über ein Picknick, das du für die ganze Klasse organisieren musst. Besprecht zuerst, was ihr alles braucht, und wer was zum Picknick mitbringen muss! Anschließend kauft ihr Proviant fürs Picknick ein. Einer von euch übernimmt die Rolle des Verkäufers.

Weiter geht's! · *Auf nach Weimar!*

CD 2 Tr. 6

Ein Plan verwirklicht sich.

Frank: Hallo, Leute! Glück gehabt! Die haben noch Platz für uns im Jugendgästehaus in Weimar.

Uschi: Das ist ja unglaublich!

Frank: Hier ist das Fax.

Udo: Lass mal sehen! — Ja, prima!

Frank: Aber nur für zwei Nächte.

Udo: Das langt.

Frank: Da stimm ich dir zu: zwei Tage Weimar genügt.

Sabine: Ach, ihr beiden Kulturmuffel ihr! Aber wartet ab: Weimar wird euch schon gefallen! Übrigens war Weimar im Jahr 1999 Kulturstadt Europas.

Uschi: Woher weißt du denn bloß so viel über Weimar?

Sabine: Ich hab mich eben informiert.

Frank: Nun, kannst du mir vielleicht sagen, ob das Jugendgästehaus weit vom Bahnhof entfernt ist?

Sabine: Blöde Frage! Bist du vielleicht fußkrank? Ich meine doch, dass es in Weimar einen Bus gibt!

Uschi: Kommt, kommt, Leute! Jetzt nicht streiten!

Udo: Nun, ich würde gern mal von der Sabine hören, was es so in Weimar zu sehen gibt.

Uschi: Ich bin dafür, dass wir jetzt einen Plan machen, einen Plan, der uns allen gefällt.

Frank: Da hast du Recht. Also, los!

Udo:	Ja, ich kann mich noch an den Deutschunterricht erinnern, <u>als uns der Gleißner von so einem Gartenhaus erzählt hat, wo der Goethe da …</u>
Sabine:	Okay. Goethes Gartenhaus steht in einem schönen Park …
Frank:	Da können wir bestimmt picknicken!
Uschi:	Wie romantisch!
Sabine:	<u>Das ist eine prima Idee!</u> Da kaufen wir uns frische Brötchen …
Udo:	<u>Wie wär's denn</u> mit einer Thüringer Wurst …
Uschi:	Schweizer Käse, süße Trauben …
Frank:	Mir läuft jetzt schon das Wasser im Mund zusammen, wenn ich an unser Picknick denke!
Sabine:	Also, ihr denkt doch wirklich nur ans Futtern!

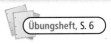

Übungsheft, S. 6

22 ## Was passiert hier?

Sprechen Hast du das Gespräch verstanden? Beantworte diese Fragen!

1. Worum geht es hier? Warum sind die Freunde zusammengekommen?
2. Worüber ist Frank froh?
3. Woher weiß Sabine so viel über Weimar?
4. Warum sagt Uschi: „Kommt, Leute! Jetzt nicht streiten!"?
5. Was haben die Freunde jetzt vor?
6. Wie kommen sie auf Goethes Gartenhaus zu sprechen?
7. Wie endet dieses Gespräch hier? Wie wird es wohl weitergehen?

1. Es geht um die Fahrt nach Weimar. / Sie besprechen, was sie alles in Weimar unternehmen können.

2. Darüber, dass sie noch einen Platz im Jugendgästehaus in Weimar bekommen haben.

3. Sie hat sich informiert.

4. Sabine ärgert sich über Franks Frage, ob das Jugendgästehaus weit vom Bahnhof entfernt ist.

5. Sie wollen einen Plan für ihre Unternehmungen in Weimar machen.

6. Udo erinnert sich daran, dass ihr Deutschlehrer davon gesprochen hat.

7. Es endet mit der Idee, ein Picknick zu machen. / Answers will vary. E.g.: Sie werden besprechen, was sie sonst noch alles in Weimar unternehmen können.

23 ## Genauer lesen
For answers, see underlined words in text on pages 42 and 43.

Lesen/Sprechen Lies das Gespräch noch einmal, und beantworte die Fragen auf Deutsch!

1. Which phrases express surprise? Agreement?
2. Which phrases are used to ask for a suggestion? Make a suggestion?
3. Which phrases express hearsay?

24 ## Was würdest du dir gern ansehen?

Sprechen Was würdest du dir gern in einer historischen amerikanischen Stadt ansehen, in einer Stadt wie Washington zum Beispiel?

Zweite Stufe

Objectives Asking for information and expressing an assumption; expressing hearsay; asking for, making, and responding to suggestions; expressing wishes when shopping

WK3 DIE NEUEN
BUNDESLAENDER-2

JUGENDGÄSTEHAUS WEIMAR

Jugendgästehaus Weimar
Herbergsmutter Danuta Keller
Zum Wilden Graben 12
99425 Weimar
Tel. Weimar / 3471

6-Tage-Reise nach Weimar

Das Programm ist variabel und nicht an bestimmte Tagesabläufe gebunden, so daß die Teilnehmer selbst den Ablauf bestimmen können.

Folgende Leistungen sind im Teilnehmerpreis enthalten:

- Dia-Vortrag „Weimar — eine Perle im Land Thüringen"
- Exkursion mit Stadtführung in Weimar
- Besichtigung interessanter Kulturdenkmäler der Stadt
- Diskothek im hauseigenen Keller
- Im Sommer Grillparty
- Im Winter Kaminabend
- Besichtigung Schloß Belvedere und Bustransfer zur Gedenkstätte Buchenwald

Zusätzlich zum Programm können folgende Leistungen bestellt werden:

- Baudenabend 5 EUR
- Busfahrt nach Erfurt 8 EUR

Busfahrt nach Eisenach, Preis nach Angebot. Die Mitarbeiter des Jugendgästehauses beraten Sie gern und geben zu den einzelnen Leistungen ausführliche Informationen.

Ort und Umgebung

Das Jugendgästehaus liegt im südlichen Teil der Stadt Weimar. Weimar, bekannt als Stadt der Dichter Goethe und Schiller, ist eingebettet zwischen den Höhenzügen des Ettersberges im Norden und den Parkanlagen von Schloß Belvedere im Süden.

Anreise

Auf der Eisenbahnstrecke Frankfurt – Berlin, oder Frankfurt – Leipzig, bis Bahnhof Weimar. Dann mit der Stadtbuslinie 5 oder 8 von der Haltestelle am Bahnhof bis Haltestelle „Zum Wilden Graben".

Lage

Das Jugendgästehaus liegt in einer wunderschönen und sehr ruhigen Villenanlage der Stadt.

Ausstattung

58 Betten in 1- bis 6-Bett-Zimmern. Lehrerzimmer, 2 Aufenthaltsräume, Clubkeller.

Sport und Freizeit

Auf dem Außengelände des Hauses sind vielfältige Möglichkeiten der Freizeitgestaltung gegeben; Volleyball, Großschachanlage, Grillplatz. Im Inneren des Hauses lädt der Kaminraum und der Club im Keller zum gemütlichen Verweilen ein.

---

25 **Das Jugendgästehaus in Weimar**

1. im südlichen Teil Weimars in einer wunderschönen und ruhigen Villenanlage / See paragraph captioned **"Ausstattung."** / See paragraph captioned **"Anreise."**

Lesen/Sprechen Lies das Angebot des Jugendgästehauses, und beantworte danach diese Fragen!

1. Wo liegt das Jugendgästehaus? Wie ist es ausgestattet, und wie kommt man dorthin?
2. Welche Leistungen sind im Preis enthalten? 2. See first seven bullets in text.
3. Für welche Leistungen würdest du dich besonders interessieren? Für welche Freizeitmöglichkeiten? 3. Answers will vary.
4. Welche bekannten Orte gibt es in der Nähe vom Gästehaus? 4. Erfurt u. Eisenach

auf Deutsch erklärt

die Nacht die Zeit zwischen Abend und Morgen
fußkrank sein (ironisch) nicht gern zu Fuß gehen
futtern sehr viel essen
genügen genug sein
es langt das ist genug
streiten argumentieren
verweilen Zeit verbringen
der Kaminraum wo man sich vor ein schönes Feuer hinsetzen kann
die Großschachanlage wo man draußen Schach mit großen Spielfiguren spielen kann

auf Englisch erklärt

Die Jugendherberge ist sicher <u>behinderten-freundlich</u>. *The youth hostel is surely accessible to the physically challenged.*
Sie ist 10 Kilometer <u>entfernt</u>. *It's 10 kilometers away.*
<u>Warte</u> nur <u>ab</u>! *Just wait and see!*
Ich kann <u>mich</u> noch <u>an</u> die Zeit <u>erinnern</u>. *I can still remember that time.*
Das Wasser läuft mir im Mund zusammen, wenn ich <u>an</u> das Picknick <u>denke</u>. *My mouth waters when I think of the picnic.*
Folgende <u>Leistungen</u> sind im Teilnehmerpreis <u>enthalten</u>. *The following services are included in the price for participants.*

Grammatikheft, S. 14, Ü. 8–9

---

26 ### Über Jugendherbergen

Script and answers on p. 31H

CD 2 Tr. 7

Zuhören Schüler unterhalten sich über Jugendherbergen. Sprechen sie über Jugendherbergen im Allgemeinen (*in general*) oder über Jugendherbergen in Weimar? Übertrag die Tabelle und hake ab, was du hörst!

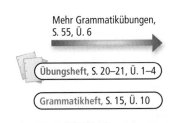

	Jugendherbergen	
	im Allgemeinen	in Weimar
1		
2		

So sagt man das!

Asking for information and expressing an assumption

Schon bekannt

When asking for information, you may ask:

> **Gibt es** in Weimar eine Jugendherberge? *or*
> **Weißt du, ob** es in Weimar eine Jugendherberge gibt? *or*
> **Kannst du mir sagen, ob** die Herberge in der Stadt liegt?

As a response, you may express an assumption by saying:

> **Ich glaube schon, dass** es dort eine Jugendherberge gibt. *or*
> **Ich meine doch, dass** die Herberge in der Stadt liegt.

Mehr Grammatikübungen, S. 55, Ü. 6

Übungsheft, S. 20–21, Ü. 1–4

Grammatikheft, S. 15, Ü. 10

---

27 ### Ich will nach Weimar

Sprechen Weil du eine Reise nach Deutschland und Weimar planst, hast du natürlich viele Fragen über Jugendherbergen in Deutschland im Allgemeinen und ganz bestimmte Fragen über die Jugendherbergen in Weimar. Such dir eine Partnerin, und frag sie, was sie darüber weiß! Du hast bestimmt auch andere Fragen. Deine Partnerin glaubt schon, dass es gibt, wonach du sie fragst. Tauscht dann die Rollen aus!

So sagt man das!

Expressing hearsay

Schon bekannt

Mehr Grammatikübungen,
S. 56, Ü. 7

Übungsheft, S. 21, Ü. 5

Grammatikheft, S. 15, Ü. 11

To express hearsay, you may want to say:

Ich habe gehört, dass es in Weimar zwei Jugendherbergen gibt.
Man hat mir gesagt, dass sie behindertenfreundlich eingerichtet sind.
Die Herbergen **sollen** gutes Essen **haben.**

How would you express these statements in English?

---

28 Weißt du auch etwas über Jugendherbergen?

Sprechen Such dir einen Partner! Was weiß er über Jugendherbergen in deiner Stadt oder in einem Ort, den du kennst? Stell ihm mindestens vier Fragen darüber! In seiner Antwort kann er Folgendes ausdrücken: er weiß es, er glaubt es oder er hat gehört, dass es so ist. Tauscht dann die Rollen aus! Answers will vary. E.g.: **Weißt du, ob die Jugendherberge hier einen Tennisplatz hat? Ich habe gehört, sie soll einen Tennisplatz haben.**

---

29 Warum nach Weimar?

Schreiben Schreib deinem Briefpartner in Deutschland, dass du gern mit ihm die Jugendherberge in Weimar besuchen möchtest, und gib mindestens fünf Gründe dafür an!

So sagt man das!

Asking for, making, and responding to suggestions

Schon bekannt

You could ask for a suggestion by saying:

Wo **sollen** wir denn unser Picknick **machen?**

When making suggestions, you might also say:

Würdest du gern mal in einem
    Hotel übernachten? or
Wie wär's denn mit einem Picknick?

How would you express these sentences in English?

And you could make a suggestion by saying:

Ich bin dafür, dass wir in den Park an der Ilm gehen.

When responding to a suggestion, you might say:

Ja schon, aber ich würde am liebsten mal
    zelten gehen.
Das wär' nicht schlecht!

Mehr Grammatikübungen,
S. 56, Ü. 8

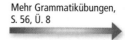

Grammatikheft, S. 16, Ü. 12

---

30 Reaktionen zu Vorschlägen Script and answers on p. 31I

Zuhören Claudia macht ihren Freunden einen Vorschlag. Wie reagieren sie darauf? Sind sie damit einverstanden oder nicht? Warum oder warum nicht?
CD 2 Tr.8

---

31 Für mein Notizbuch

Schreiben Schreib fünf Dinge in dein Notizbuch, die du in Deutschland gern einmal sehen oder machen möchtest! Gib auch jeweils einen Grund dafür an!

Also los! Was wollt ihr?

Sprechen Setzt euch in kleinen Gruppen zusammen, und plant eure Klassenreise nach Deutschland! Jeder muss drei Vorschläge machen und jeweils einen Grund für seinen Vorschlag angeben. Die anderen müssen sagen, ob sie dafür oder dagegen sind und müssen ihre Antworten begründen.

> **BEISPIEL**   **DU**   Also, ich würde gern nach Weimar fahren, weil ich schon so viel über Weimar gelesen und gehört habe. Weimar soll …
>
> **PARTNER**   Ich würde auch am liebsten nach Weimar fahren, denn dort …

Wortschatz

Was man zum Picknick mitnimmt:

p. 31X   2–2

einen Teller   das Besteck   ein Messer   einen Löffel   eine Gabel

einen Becher   ein Schneidebrett   eine Serviette   einen Picknickkorb   eine Kühlbox

eine Thermosflasche   einen Salz- und Pfefferstreuer   ein Messer mit Flaschenöffner   eine Abfalltüte   eine Decke

Was nimmst du alles mit, wenn du picknickst?
Was packst du in die Kühlbox ein?

Übungsheft, S. 22–23, Ü. 6–7   Grammatikheft, S. 17, Ü. 13–14

 Vorbereitungen fürs Picknick   Script and answers on p. 31I

Zuhören Drei Schüler planen ein Picknick. Hör ihrem Gespräch gut zu, und schreib auf, was sie alles mitnehmen wollen!
CD 2 Tr. 9

 Grammatik im Kontext

Sprechen Die Schüler planen ein Picknick im Park an der Ilm in Weimar. Was sollen sie alles mitnehmen? Was sollen sie sich zum Essen und zum Trinken kaufen? — Such dir eine Partnerin und plane das Picknick mit ihr! In den Kästen auf Seite 48 stehen ein paar Ideen für den Proviant.

> **DU**   Also, ich würde dunkles Brot mitnehmen und …
> **PARTNER**   Wie wär's denn mit ein paar saftigen Tomaten und …

Brot	Käse	dunkel	Schweizer
Brötchen	Schafskäse	frisch	bulgarisch
Salami	Tomaten	hart	italienisch
Schinken	Trauben	gekocht	blau
Gurken	Cola	sauer	eiskalt
Kartoffel-	Oliven	würzig	griechisch
salat			

Ein wenig Grammatik

Mehr Grammatikübungen, S. 57, Ü. 9

Schon bekannt

Look at these sentences:

Ich würde gern das dunkle Brot essen.
Ich würde gern dunkles Brot kaufen.

Can you explain why the adjective endings are different? For a table of the adjective endings, see the Grammar Summary.

So sagt man das!

Expressing wishes when shopping

Schon bekannt

When shopping for groceries, the clerk might ask you:

Was möchten Sie? *or* **Was hätten Sie gern?**

You may request the item by saying:

Ich möchte 250 Gramm Schweizer Käse. *or*
Ich hätte gern blaue Trauben. Ein Pfund, **bitte!**

What does the verb **hätte** express in these statements?

Mehr Grammatikübungen, S. 57, Ü. 10

Übungsheft, S. 23, Ü. 8–9

Grammatikheft, S. 18, Ü. 15–16

35 **Fürs Picknick einkaufen**

Sprechen Such dir eine Partnerin und geh mit ihr fürs Picknick einkaufen! — Deine Partnerin spielt die Rolle der Verkäuferin. Tauscht dann die Rollen aus!

36 **Für mein Notizbuch**

Schreiben Schreib in dein Notizbuch die Information, die du brauchst, um irgendwo in einer Jugendherberge zu übernachten und auch in diesem Ort zu picknicken! Schreib jetzt einen Brief an eine Jugendherberge, in dem du deine Fragen stellst und um weitere Informationen bittest!

37 **Von der Schule zum Beruf**

You are a manager at a German company that holds an annual week-long business retreat. Every year the retreat is in a different location at a resort or hotel. You surveyed the other managers in your department and narrowed down this year's choices to three places. Write an e-mail telling your boss about the three places that were suggested and why they should be considered. You should include things you have heard about the locations and any questions you have about the facility. Then add a paragraph saying where you yourself really want to go and why!

Übungsheft, S. 24, Ü. 1–3

Weimar im Blickpunkt: Die deutsche Klassikermetropole war 1999 Kulturstadt Europas

„Die Weimarer Bürger vollführten nach der Entscheidung regelrecht Luftsprünge", schildert Weimars Oberbürgermeister Klaus Büttner die Reaktion auf die gute Nachricht: Weimar wird Europas Kulturstadt 1999! Unter den Bewerberstädten Avignon, Bologna, Istanbul, Graz, Prag und Stockholm war Weimar mit seinen 63 500 Einwohnern die kleinste.

In erster Linie hatte es die thüringische Stadt Johann Wolfgang von Goethe zu verdanken, dass sie das Rennen machte. Denn 1999 jährte sich sein Geburtstag zum 250. Mal. Zwar ist Goethe nicht in Weimar geboren, doch lebte er 57 Jahre lang bis zu seinem Tod in der Stadt. Hier schrieb er seine großen Werke. Er war Minister, Theaterdirektor und trat auch als Stadtplaner auf (er hat — neben einem Gartenhaus für sich selbst — einen großen Park an der Ilm entworfen). Zusammen mit anderen Größen der Geistesgeschichte, besonders mit Friedrich von Schiller, machte er das kleine Fürstentum zur „Hauptstadt des deutschen Geistes", die Dichter und Denker, später auch Musiker und Maler anlockte. Weimar heute steckt voller Sehenswürdigkeiten. Zu besichtigen sind das Goethehaus, Goethes Gartenhaus, das Schillerhaus, in dem der schwäbische Dichter sein Freiheitsdrama „Wilhelm Tell" schrieb, das Liszthaus, in dem Franz Liszt Klavierunterricht gab, und die Zentralbibliothek der Deutschen Klassik mit ihren rund 800 000 Büchern. Nach Berlin, das 1988 den Titel Kulturstadt Europas trug, ist Weimar die zweite deutsche Stadt, die ein Jahr kulturell im Mittelpunkt Europas stand.

Goethe-Schiller Denkmal

Goethes Gartenhaus

1. Wofür ist Weimar berühmt?   1. für die „Klassiker" Goethe und Schiller, die dort gelebt haben
2. Gibt es Städte in Amerika, die ähnliche Angebote haben?
3. Was muss eine Stadt haben, um als Kulturstadt bezeichnet zu werden?   3. kulturelle Sehenswürdigkeiten
4. Was wäre deine Wahl für eine amerikanische Kulturstadt des Jahres? Worauf würdest du die Wahl begründen?

STANDARDS: 2.1, 2.2, 3.2, 4.2

Lyrik

CD2 Tr. 10

ERLKÖNIG

Wer reitet so spät durch Nacht und Wind?
Es ist der Vater mit seinem Kind;
Er hat den Knaben wohl in dem Arm,
Er faßt ihn sicher, er hält ihn warm. —

Mein Sohn, was birgst du so bang dein Gesicht? —
Siehst, Vater, du den Erlkönig nicht?
Den Erlenkönig mit Kron und Schweif? —
Mein Sohn, es ist ein Nebelstreif. —

»Du liebes Kind, komm, geh mit mir!
Gar schöne Spiele spiel ich mit dir;
Manch bunte Blumen sind an dem Strand;
Meine Mutter hat manch gülden Gewand.«

Mein Vater, mein Vater, und hörest du nicht,
Was Erlenkönig mir leise verspricht? —
Sei ruhig, bleibe ruhig, mein Kind!
In dürren Blättern säuselt der Wind. —

»Willst, feiner Knabe, du mit mir gehn?
Meine Töchter sollen dich warten schön;
Meine Töchter führen den nächtlichen Reihn
Und wiegen und tanzen und singen dich ein.«

Mein Vater, mein Vater, und siehst du nicht dort
Erlkönigs Töchter am düstern Ort? —
Mein Sohn, mein Sohn, ich seh es genau;
Es scheinen die alten Weiden so grau. —

»Ich liebe dich, mich reizt deine schöne Gestalt;
Und bist du nicht willig, so brauch ich Gewalt.«
Mein Vater, mein Vater, jetzt faßt er mich an!
Erlkönig hat mir ein Leids getan! —

Dem Vater grauset's, er reitet geschwind,
Er hält in Armen das ächzende Kind,
Erreicht den Hof mit Mühe und Not;
In seinen Armen das Kind war tot.

Johann Wolfgang von Goethe

Poesie

Lesestrategie Deriving the main idea from supporting details
Depending on what kind of passage you're reading, there are several strategies for identifying the main idea. When reading a poem, for example, you may first want to look at the supporting details, thinking about what the individual words, images, and symbols suggest. Then decide what the main idea is. Remember, there is no one "correct" interpretation.

Getting Started

1. Look at the different poems for a moment. Relying on visual cues alone, which poems look like they tell a story, and which look more like a poster or picture?

2. Read the title of each poem and then listen as the first five poems are read aloud. Judging by their intonation and rhythm, can you tell which poems are intended to be dramatic, and which are more lighthearted?

3. As you are reading and listening to each poem again, think about and try to answer the following questions:

   a. Wer sind die Hauptfiguren?

   b. Wo und wann finden die Ereignisse statt?

   c. Was passiert?

For answers, see p. 31W.

Der Panther
Im Jardin des Plantes, Paris

Sein Blick ist vom Vorübergehn der Stäbe
so müd geworden, daß er nichts mehr hält.
Ihm ist, als ob es tausend Stäbe gäbe
und hinter tausend Stäben keine Welt.

Der weiche Gang geschmeidig starker Schritte,
der sich im allerkleinsten Kreise dreht,
ist wie ein Tanz von Kraft um eine Mitte,
in der betäubt ein großer Wille steht.

Nur manchmal schiebt der Vorhang der Pupille
sich lautlos auf —. Dann geht ein Bild hinein,
geht durch der Glieder angespannte Stille —
und hört im Herzen auf zu sein.

Rainer Maria Rilke

Poesie

CD 2, Tr. 11

CD 2, Tr. 12

Der Radwechsel

Ich sitze am Straßenhang.
Der Fahrer wechselt das Rad.
Ich bin nicht gern, wo ich herkomme.
Ich bin nicht gern, wo ich hinfahre.
Warum sehe ich den Radwechsel
Mit Ungeduld?

Bertolt Brecht

ottos mops

ottos mops trotzt
otto: fort mops fort
ottos mops hopst fort
otto: soso

otto holt koks
otto holt obst
otto horcht
otto: mops mops
otto hofft

ottos mops klopft
otto: komm mops komm
ottos mops kommt
ottos mops kotzt
otto: ogottogott

Ernst Jandl

CD 2, Tr. 13

A Closer Look

4. Read the "Erlkönig" by Goethe and identify which lines are spoken by which person. Pay special attention to punctuation, such as quotation marks. Use a chart like the one below. The line numbers of the first two stanzas are already marked.

stanza	1		4
narrator	1-4		
father		5, 8	
son		6-7	
elf king			

5. What is the father trying to do? What happens to the son? What role does the **Erlkönig** play? What emotions does the poem evoke?

6. Read Rilke's poem "Der Panther." Is the animal in the wild or in captivity? How do you know? How has his situation affected him? When the panther looks at something, what happens to the image as it reaches his heart?

7. Try to sketch the world as the panther sees it.

8. In Brecht's "Radwechsel," is the person (Ich) in charge of the situation? What will happen when the driver finishes what he's doing? Look at lines 3 and 4. Which single word changes? Excluding the last line of the poem, does the language reflect any dramatic tension? How does the last line make you feel?

Kinderlied

Wer lacht hier, hat gelacht?
Hier hat sich's ausgelacht.
Wer hier lacht, macht Verdacht,
daß er aus Gründen lacht.

Wer weint hier, hat geweint?
Hier wird nicht mehr geweint.
Wer hier weint, der auch meint,
daß er aus Gründen weint.

Wer spricht hier, spricht und schweigt?
Wer schweigt, wird angezeigt.
Wer hier spricht, hat verschwiegen,
wo seine Gründe liegen.

Wer spielt hier, spielt im Sand?
Wer spielt, muß an die Wand,
hat sich beim Spiel die Hand
gründlich verspielt, verbrannt.

Wer stirbt hier, ist gestorben?
Wer stirbt, ist abgeworben.
Wer hier stirbt, unverdorben
ist ohne Grund verstorben.

Günter Grass

CD 2, Tr. 14

Reinhard Döhl

Reinhard Döhl

9. Read Jandl's poem "ottos mops," paying close attention to the colons. What do they indicate? Listen to the poem several times and add periods where you hear full stops. Can you guess to what the word **Mops** refers? See if your guess helps to explain what is going on in the poem.

10. Read "Kinderlied" by Grass. How do the question marks help you understand the organization of the poem? Which actions are mentioned? Why do you think some form of the word **Grund** is used in the last line of every stanza? What makes the title ironic?

11. Now look at the two selections of concrete poetry. Why do you think this is called concrete poetry? How does the poet convey his message? Through words alone or some other way?

12. Skim the seven poems you've just read again. What do all these poems have in common? In what ways are they different? Do you think all the poets had the same idea about the purpose of poetry? Support your answers, based on the poems.

13. Schreib jetzt dein eigenes Gedicht im Stil der konkreten Poesie. Denk zuerst daran, was diesen Stil von anderen Gedichten unterscheidet! Versuch, diese Eigenschaften in dein Gedicht zu integrieren!

Übungsheft, S. 12-12, Ü. 1-4

STANDARDS: 1.2, 3.1

KAPITEL 2   Auf in die Jugendherberge!

Zum Schreiben

Sometimes a spontaneous vacation can be a lot of fun — but more often, careful planning will reduce stress and make your vacation more enjoyable. Whichever approach you prefer, one important decision you will have to make is where to go; travel brochures are a good resource for ideas. In this activity you will work together with classmates to select a good vacation spot and write a travel brochure about that place.

... ist eine Reise wert!

Wähl zusammen mit einer Gruppe eine Stadt oder ein Land aus, und schreib ein Flugblatt darüber, damit die Leser Lust haben, dahin zu reisen! Jeder in der Gruppe soll ein Thema bearbeiten, zum Beispiel die Sehenswürdigkeiten, das kulturelle Angebot, das Wetter, die Einkaufsmöglichkeiten usw., die der Ort zu bieten hat. Illustriert eure Ideen mit Fotos!

Schreibtipp Selecting information In order to write effectively about an unfamiliar topic, you will have to do some research, then select the appropriate information to include. You also need to be aware of your audience and the kinds of information they want or expect to read. Once you know that, you can focus on that particular information. When writing a travel brochure, for example, you'll want to select information that makes your destination appealing, such as a pleasant climate, fascinating local culture, or shopping and entertainment, while at the same time providing information about expenses and accommodations.

A. Vorbereiten

1. Wähl mit deiner Gruppe einen Ort aus, und mach eine Liste von wichtigen Themen, die ihr erforschen wollt! Teil die Arbeit ein, damit jeder genau weiß, worauf er achten muss!

2. Geh in eine Bücherei oder auch in ein Reisebüro und erforsche dein Thema! Mach dir Notizen von wichtigen Fakten! Denk an Informationen, die den Leser zu einer Reise überzeugen werden! Sammle auch Fotos von zutreffenden Orten und Sehenswürdigkeiten!

3. Vergleicht eure Notizen und Fotos in der Gruppe! Macht zusammen ein Layout des Flugblatts, und wählt die Informationen und Fotos aus, die ihr verwenden wollt!

B. Ausführen

Schreib die ausgewählten Informationen für dein Thema in kurzen, überzeugenden und auch logischen Sätzen auf! Stellt dann alle Teile zusammen, und illustriert sie mit Fotos! Denkt an ein zutreffendes Schlagwort für das Flugblatt!

C. Überarbeiten

1. Vergleich deinen Teil des Flugblatts mit deinen Notizen! Hast du alle wichtigen Fakten mit einbezogen? Passen Text und Fotos zusammen?

2. Lest euer Flugblatt in der Gruppe laut vor, und zeigt die entsprechenden Fotos! Besprecht die ganze Wirkung des Flugblatts! Würdet ihr jetzt „euren Ort" gern besuchen? Verändert die Sprache und den Ton, wenn nötig!

3. Wenn ihr mit dem Flugblatt zufrieden seid, lest es noch einmal durch! Korrigiert die Schreibfehler! Achtet besonders auf die Buchstabierung der komparativen Adjektive! Habt ihr auch die Präpositionen mit den richtigen Dativ- oder Akkusativformen verwendet?

4. Schreibt das korrigierte Flugblatt noch einmal ab, und klebt die Fotos auf das Papier!

Mehr Grammatikübungen

Erste Stufe

Objectives Asking for and making suggestions; expressing preference and giving a reason; expressing wishes; expressing doubt, conviction, and resignation

1 Du schlägst eine Menge Ferienorte vor. Schreib die folgenden Vorschläge ab, und schreib dabei in die Lücken den Ort deines Vorschlags (er steht in Klammern) zusammen mit der richtigen Präposition und dem richtigen Artikel! (**Seite 37**)

1. (Nordsee)　　Wir können mal _____ fahren. Ich war noch nie _____ !　　an die N.; an der N.
2. (Rhein)　　Fahren wir mal _____ ! Ich war noch nie _____ !　　an den R.; am R.
3. (Bayern)　　Wir können _____ fahren. Ich war noch nie _____ .　　nach B.; in B.
4. (Schweiz)　　Fahren wir _____ ! Ich war noch nie _____ .　　in die Sch.; in der Sch.
5. (Schwarzwald)　　Wir können _____ fahren. Ich war noch nie _____ .　　in den Sch.; im Sch.
6. (Bodensee)　　Fahren wir _____ ! Ich war noch nie _____ .　　an den B.; am B.
7. (Meer)　　Wir können auch _____ fahren. Ich war noch nie _____ .　　ans M.; am M.
8. (Berge)　　Fahren wir mal _____ ! Ich war lange nicht _____ !　　in die B.; in den Bergen

2 Du drückst jetzt aus, welchen Ort du vorziehst. Ergänze (*complete*) die folgenden Satzanfänge mit der Information, die in Klammern steht. Verwende dabei die Komparativform des Adjektivs und **als**! (**Seite 39**)

1. (Hamburg; schön; Bremen)　　Ich finde _____ .　　Hamburg schöner als Bremen
2. (Ostsee; gut; Nordsee)　　Mir gefällt _____ .　　die Ostsee besser als die Nordsee
3. (München; gemütlich; Frankfurt)　　Ich finde _____ .　　München gemütlicher als Frankfurt
4. (Frankfurt; groß; Würzburg)　　Ich finde _____ .　　Frankfurt größer als Würzburg
5. (Berlin; sauber; Dresden)　　Ich finde _____ .　　Berlin sauberer als Dresden

3 Du fragst deine Freunde, was sie in den Ferien machen möchten. Schreib die folgenden Antworten ab, und schreib dabei in die Lücken eine entsprechende Verbform und andere Formen, die nötig sind, um die Antworten zu vervollständigen (*complete*)! (**Seite 40**)

1. Wohin möchtest du mal fahren? — Ich _____ gern mal _____ Meer fahren.　　möchte; ans
2. Was wünschst du dir mal? — Ich _____ _____ mal eine Reise _____ Berge.　　wünsche; mir; in die
3. Was hättest du gern mal? — Ich _____ gern mal einen toll_____ Urlaub.　　hätte; en
4. Wohin möchtet ihr mal fahren? — Wir _____ mal _____ Rhein fahren.　　möchten; an den
5. Was wünscht ihr euch mal? — Wir _____ _____ eine Reise _____ Schweiz.　　wünschen; uns; in die
6. Was hättet ihr gern mal? — Wir _____ gern mal eine Reise _____ Ostsee.　　hätten; an die

4 Du bist nicht sicher, dass es in deinem Ferienort all die Dinge gibt, die du gerne machen möchtest. Schreib die folgenden Sätze ab, und verwende dabei die Information, die in Klammern steht! **(Seite 40)**

1. (einen Tennisplatz geben)   Ich bezweifle, dass es im Hotel _____ .   einen Tennisplatz gibt
2. (tauchen können)   Ich weiß nicht, ob du dort _____ .   tauchen kannst
3. (eine Disko haben)   Ich bin nicht sicher, dass das Hotel _____   eine Disko hat
4. (einen Pool geben)   Ich bezweifle, dass es dort _____ .   einen Pool gibt
5. (windsurfen können)   Ich weiß nicht, ob wir dort _____ .   windsurfen können
6. (eine Sauna haben)   Ich bin nicht sicher, dass es _____ .   eine Sauna hat

5 Du bist überzeugt, dass dein Ferienort all die vielen Dinge anbietet, die du gerne möchtest. Schreib die folgenden Sätze ab, und schreib dabei in die Lücken die Information, die in Klammern gegeben ist! **(Seite 40)**

1. (die Gegend schön sein)   Du kannst mir glauben, dass _____ .   die Gegend schön ist
2. (die Hotels überfüllt sein)   Du kannst mir glauben, dass _____ .   die Hotels überfüllt sind
3. (viel unternehmen können)   Ich bin sicher, dass du dort _____ .   viel unternehmen kannst
4. (segeln können)   Ich bin sicher, dass du dort _____ .   segeln kannst
5. (einen Sandstrand geben)   Ich bin sicher, dass es dort _____ .   einen Sandstrand gibt
6. (einen Ausweis brauchen)   Du kannst mir glauben, dass du _____ .   einen Ausweis brauchst

Zweite Stufe   **Objectives** Asking for information and expressing an assumption; expressing hearsay; asking for, making, and responding to suggestions; expressing wishes

6 Du kannst verschiedene Redewendungen benützen, um etwas zu erfragen. Du kannst deine Fragen mit **gibt es,** oder **wissen** oder **sagen können** anfangen. Schreib jetzt je dreimal dieselbe Frage und benütze dabei das Verb, das in Klammern steht und die Information, die jeweils über den Fragen in Klammern steht! **(Seite 45)**

(in Weimar eine Jugendherberge geben)

1. (es gibt)   Du, Udo, _____ ?   gibt es in Weimar eine Jugendherberge
2. (wissen)   Du, Udo, _____ ?   weißt du, ob es in Weimar eine J. gibt
3. (sagen können)   Du, Udo, _____ ?   kannst du mir sagen, ob es in W. eine J. gibt

(am Samstag eine Grillparty geben)

4. (es gibt)   Uschi und Udo, _____ ?   gibt es am Samstag eine Grillparty
5. (wissen)   Uschi und Udo, _____ ?   wisst ihr, ob es am Samstag eine G. gibt
6. (sagen können)   Uschi und Udo, _____ ?   könnt ihr mir sagen, ob es am S. eine G. gibt

(in Weimar ein Kunstmuseum geben)

7. (es gibt)   Frau Wolf, _____ ?   gibt es in Weimar ein Kunstmuseum
8. (wissen)   Frau Wolf, _____ ?   wissen Sie, ob es in Weimar ein K. gibt
9. (sagen können)   Frau Wolf, _____ ?   können Sie mir sagen, ob es in W. ein K. gibt

7 Udo, Uschi und Sabine haben viel über Thüringen gehört, und sie drücken diese Information auf verschiedene Weise aus. Beantworte die folgenden Fragen, und benütze dabei die Information, die in Klammern steht! (**Seite 46**)

(In Thüringen gibt es viel zu sehen.)

1. Was hast du gehört, Udo?   Ich _____ .   habe gehört, dass es in T. viel zu sehen gibt

2. Was hat man dir gesagt?   Man _____ .   hat mir gesagt, dass es in T. viel zu sehen gibt

3. Was soll es in Thüringen geben?   _____ .   In Thüringen soll es viel zu sehen geben.

(Die Jugendherberge ist überfüllt.)

4. Was hast du gehört, Uschi?   Ich _____ .   habe gehört, dass die J. überfüllt ist

5. Was hat man dir gesagt?   Man _____ .   hat mir gesagt, dass die J. überfüllt ist

6. Was soll überfüllt sein?   _____ .   Die Jugendherberge soll überfüllt sein.

(Thüringer Wurst schmeckt gut.)

7. Was hast du gehört, Sabine?   Ich _____ .   habe gehört, dass T. Wurst gut schmeckt

8. Was hat man dir gesagt?   Man _____ .   hat mir gesagt, dass T. Wurst gut schmeckt

9. Was soll gut schmecken?   _____ .   Thüringer Wurst soll gut schmecken.

8 Du machst Pläne für die Ferien. Ein Freund stellt dir verschiedene Fragen, die du ihm beantwortest. Benütze dabei die Information, die in Klammern steht! (**Seite 46**)

(an die Ostsee fahren)

1. Was würdest du gern mal machen?   Ich _____ .   würde gern an die Ostsee fahren

2. Was sollen wir tun? Wofür bist du?   Ich _____ .   bin dafür, dass wir mal an die O. fahren

(in einer Jugendherberge)

3. Wo würdest du gern übernachten?   Ich _____ .   würde gern in einer J. übernachten

4. Wo übernachten wir? Wofür bist du?   Ich _____ .   bin dafür, dass wir in einer J. übernachten

(mit dem Rad fahren)

5. Womit würdest du gern fahren?   Ich _____ .   würde gern mit dem Rad fahren

6. Wie fahren wir dorthin? Wofür bist du?   Ich _____ .   bin dafür, dass wir mit dem R. dorthin fahren

9 Was würdest du gern zum Picknick mitnehmen? Schreib die korrekte **würde**-Form in die erste Lücke und den abgebildeten Gegenstand in die zweite Lücke. (S. 46)

1. Ich _____ gern _____ zum Picknick mitnehmen.
würde; eine Abfalltüte

2. Wir _____ gern _____ mitnehmen.
würden; einen Picknickkorb

3. Mike _____ gern _____ mitnehmen.
würde; eine Decke

4. Du _____ doch gern _____ mitnehmen.
würdest; eine Kühlbox

5. Marta _____ gern _____ mitnehmen.
würde; ein Messer

6. Wir _____ auch gern _____ mitnehmen.
würden; eine Thermosflasche

10 Verschiedene Leute drücken ihre Wünsche aus. Schreib die folgenden Wünsche ab, und schreib dabei in die erste Lücke eine Form von **hätte** und in die zweite Lücke die korrekte Endung des Adjektivs. (**Seite 48**)

1. Was hätten Sie gern? — Ich _____ gern ein Pfund süß_____ Trauben. hätte; e

2. Was hättest du gern? — Ich _____ gern 200 Gramm gekocht_____ Schinken. hätte; en

3. Was hättet ihr gern? — Wir _____ gern ein halbes Pfund Schweiz_____ Käse. hätten; er

4. Was hätten Sie gern? — Ich _____ gern zwei italienisch_____ Tomaten. hätte; e

5. Was hättest du gern? — Ich _____ gern frisch_____ Obst. hätte; es

6. Was hättet ihr gern? — Wir _____ gern bayrisch_____ Senf. hätten; en

Kann ich's wirklich?

Can you ask for and make suggestions? (p. 37)

1 How would you ask a friend to suggest a place where both of you might go on vacation? E.g.: Wohin fahren wir in den Ferien? Was schlägst du vor?

2 How would you respond if a friend asked you **Was schenken wir der Brigitte zum Geburtstag?** E.g.: Ich schlage vor, dass wir ihr eine CD schenken.

Can you express preference and give a reason? (p. 39)

3 How would you respond if someone asked you what American city you prefer and why? E.g.: Ich ziehe eine große Stadt wie New York vor, weil dort mehr los ist.

Can you express wishes? (p. 40)

4 How would a German-speaking genie ask you what your wishes are? How would you then make three wishes to be granted by the genie?
E.g.: Was wünschst du dir mal? / Ich möchte gern mal nach Europa fliegen. Ich wünsche mir Gesundheit. Ich hätte gern ein Motorrad.

Can you express doubt, conviction, and resignation? (p. 40)

5 How would you say to a friend
   a. that you doubt there is a hotel in Dingskirchen? a. E.g.: Ich bezweifle, dass es ein Hotel in Dingskirchen gibt.
   b. that you're sure there is a youth hostel?
   b. E.g.: Ich bin sicher, dass es dort eine Jugendherberge gibt.

6 How would you respond if you were on vacation and someone said to you **Das Wetter soll diese Woche furchtbar sein?** E.g.: Schade. Da kann man nichts machen.

Can you ask for information and express an assumption? (p. 45)

7 How would you ask someone if there is a swimming pool in Dingskirchen?
E.g.: Gibt es in Dingskirchen ein Schwimmbad?

8 How would you say that you assume your town has a youth hostel?
E.g.: Ich glaube schon, dass es hier eine Jugendherberge gibt.

Can you express hearsay? (p. 46)

9 How would you say that a. E.g.: Ich habe gehört, dass die Deutschen sehr gesund leben.
   a. you heard that German-speaking people live very healthfully?
   b. German food is supposed to be very good? b. E.g.: Deutsches Essen soll sehr gut sein.

Can you ask for, make, and respond to suggestions? (p. 46)

10 How would you ask a friend
   a. what you both should study for the test? a. E.g.: Was sollen wir denn für den Test lernen?
   b. if he or she would like to study with you? b. E.g.: Würdest du gern mit mir zusammen lernen?
   How would you say that you are in favor of studying in the park instead of at home? E.g.: Ich würde lieber im Park lernen als zu Hause.

11 How would you respond if a friend asked you **Würdest du gern mal in einer Jugendherberge übernachten?** E.g.: Ja. Das wär' nicht schlecht!

Can you express wishes when shopping? (p. 48)

12 How would a grocery store clerk ask you what you need? How would you respond if you needed a pound of blue grapes?
E.g.: Was möchten Sie? Was hätten Sie gern? / Ich möchte ein Pfund blaue Trauben, bitte.

Erste Stufe

Words useful for traveling

die Natur	nature
die Burg, -en	castle
die Gegend, -en	area
die Jugendherberge, -n	youth hostel
die Unterkunft, ¨e	accommodations
das Verzeichnis, -se	listing
der Ausweis, -e	identification

Other useful words and expressions

also (part)	well, okay
eben (gerade)	just now
damals	at that time
beide	both
berühmt	famous
nämlich	namely

Keine Angst!	Don't worry!
Lust haben	to want to
nachsehen (sep)	to check on
unternehmen	to undertake
verlieren	to lose

p. 31X

Zweite Stufe

Things to take on a picnic

das Picknick, -s	picnic
die Decke, -n	blanket
das Besteck, -e	silverware
die Gabel, -n	fork
der Löffel, -	spoon
das Messer, -	knife
der Teller, -	plate
der Becher, -	mug
der Picknickkorb, ¨e	picnic basket
die Kühlbox, -en	cooler
der Salzstreuer, -	salt shaker
der Pfefferstreuer, -	pepper shaker
der Flaschenöffner, -	bottle opener
das Schneidebrett, -er	cutting board
die Serviette, -n	napkin
die Thermosflasche, -n	thermos bottle
die Abfalltüte, -n	trash bag

Other useful words and expressions

der Mund, ¨er	mouth
die Nacht, ¨e	night
der Plan, ¨e	plan
der Kaminraum, ¨e	room with open fireplace
die Großschachanlage, -n	giant-sized chessboard
die Leistung, -en	service
entfernt	away, at a distance
frisch	fresh
behindertenfreundlich	accessible to the physically challenged
fußkrank sein	(ironic) to be too lazy to walk

abwarten (sep)	to wait and see
futtern	to stuff oneself
s. informieren	to inform oneself
denken an (acc)	to think of or about
s. erinnern an (acc)	to remember
genügen	to be enough
es langt	that's enough
stehen	to stand, to be
streiten	to quarrel
verweilen	to stay
enthalten sein	to be included

Kapitel 3: Aussehen: wichtig oder nicht?
Chapter Overview

Los geht's!
pp. 62–63

Gut aussehen, p. 62

	FUNCTIONS	GRAMMAR	VOCABULARY	RE-ENTRY
Erste Stufe **pp. 64–69**	• Asking for and expressing opinions, p. 65	• Da- and wo-compounds (Summary), p. 66	• Health and appearance, p. 64	Expressing interest, p. 65 **(Kap. 8, II)**; sequencing events, p. 65 **(Kap. 4, I)**; expressing opinions, p. 65 **(Kap. 2/9, I)**; verbs requiring prepositional phrases, p. 66 **(Kap. 10, II)**; hobby and clothing vocabulary, p. 66 **(Kap. 1/8, II)**; **wo-** and **da-**compounds, p. 66 **(Kap. 10, II)**

Weiter geht's!
pp. 70–71

Immer mit der Mode. Oder?, p. 70

Zweite Stufe **pp. 72–76**	• Expressing sympathy and resignation, p. 73 • Giving advice, p. 74 • Giving a reason, p. 75 • Admitting something and expressing regret, p. 76	• Infinitive clauses, p. 75	• Fashion, p. 73	Responding sympathetically, p. 73 **(Kap. 4, I)**; Asking for and giving advice, p. 73 **(Kap. 6, II)**; Making suggestions, p. 74 **(Kap. 6, II)**; Giving reasons, p. 75 **(Kap. 8, I)**; Infinitives, p. 75 **(Kap. 2, I)**; **Weil-**clauses, p. 75 **(Kap. 8, I)**

Zum Schreiben **p. 77**	**Personen beschreiben**	**Writing Strategy** Organizing your ideas
Zum Lesen **pp. 78–79**	**Was ist „in"?**	**Reading Strategy** Determining the main idea of an article
Mehr Grammatik-übungen	**pp. 80–83** Erste Stufe, pp. 80–81	Zweite Stufe, pp. 81–83
Review **pp. 84–87**	**Anwendung,** pp. 84–85	**Kann ich's wirklich?,** p. 86 **Wortschatz,** p. 87

CULTURE

• **Landeskunde: Die deutsche Subkultur,** pp. 68–69   • Teenagers talk about what they do to feel better, p. 72

Kapitel 3: Aussehen: wichtig oder nicht?
Chapter Resources

 **PRINT**

Lesson Planning
One-Stop Planner
Lesson Planner with Substitute Teacher Lesson Plans, pp. 21–25, 77
Student Make-Up Assignments
- Make-Up Assignment Copying Masters, Chapter 3

Listening and Speaking
Listening Activities
- Student Response Forms for Listening Activities, pp. 19–22
- Additional Listening Activities 3-1 to 3-6, pp. 23–26
- Scripts and Answers, pp. 116–123

Video Guide
- Teaching Suggestions, p. 12
- Activity Masters, pp. 13–14
- Scripts and Answers, pp. 61–62, 74

Activities for Communication
- Communicative Activities, pp. 9–12
- Realia and Teaching Suggestions, pp. 61–65
- Situation Cards, pp. 117–118

Reading and Writing
Reading Strategies and Skills Handbook, Chapter 3
Lies mit mir! 3, Chapter 3
Übungsheft, pp. 27–39

Grammar
Grammatikheft, pp. 19–27
Grammar Tutor for Students of German, Chapter 3

Assessment
Testing Program
- Grammar and Vocabulary Quizzes, **Stufe** Quizzes, and Chapter Test, pp. 45–58
- Score Sheet, Scripts and Answers, pp. 59–65

Alternative Assessment Guide
- Portfolio Assessment, p. 18
- Performance Assessment, p. 32

Student Make-Up Assignments
- Alternative Quizzes, Chapter 3

 **MEDIA**

 go.hrw.com
Online Activities
- Interaktive Spiele
- Internet Aktivitäten

 Video Program
- Videocassette 1

 Audio Compact Discs
- Textbook Listening Activities, CD 3, Tracks 1–15
- Additional Listening Activities, CD 3, Tracks 20–25
- Assessment Items, CD 3, Tracks 16–19

 Teaching Transparencies
- Situations 3-1 to 3-2
- **Mehr Grammatikübungen** Answers
- **Grammatikheft** Answers

 **One-Stop Planner CD-ROM**

Use the **One-Stop Planner CD-ROM with Test Generator** to aid in lesson planning and pacing.

For each chapter, the **One-Stop Planner** includes:
- Editable lesson plans with direct links to teaching resources
- Printable worksheets from resource books
- Direct launches to the HRW Internet activities
- Video and audio segments
- Test Generator
- Clip Art for vocabulary items

Kapitel 3: Aussehen: wichtig oder nicht?

Projects

Ein Bericht aus . . .

In this activity students will write and present a report on a current event from one of the German-speaking countries.

MATERIALS

✂ **Students will need**
- a newspaper such as *World Events* or *The Week in Germany*
- local and national newspapers
- magazines that focus on news abroad, or the Internet

NOTE

Tell students about the project at the beginning of Chapter 3, but allow them time to follow the German-speaking countries in the news for at least two weeks before beginning the written part of the project.

SUGGESTED SEQUENCE

1. Have students monitor print and broadcast news media to collect information on current events in Austria, Germany, Liechtenstein, and Switzerland. They should be sure to note the source and date of any information they collect.

2. In class, have students share the information they have gathered and come up with a list of events currently taking place in the German-speaking countries.

3. Allow individuals or pairs of students to choose an event about which they will prepare an in-depth report. Also give students the opportunity to share with one another the information that they collected while monitoring the media.

4. Have students outline the order in which they plan to organize their reports. Review sequencing words with them if necessary.

5. Students write the first draft of their reports. You may want to evaluate students' first drafts or have them peer-edited before students revise them.

6. Students use their final drafts to present their reports to the class.

GRADING THE PROJECT

Suggested point distribution (total = 100 points)
Content 25
Organization 25
Correct language usage 25
Oral presentation........................25

Games

Wörtersalat

This game will help students review the vocabulary they have learned thus far.

Preparation Prepare a list of words from the **Wortschatz** on page 87. Give each student a copy of the list.

Procedure Tell students that you will call out one word at a time from the list. They will have thirty seconds to write down one word that starts with each letter of the word you called out. To make the game more challenging, limit acceptable words to certain categories such as nouns, verbs, or adjectives. See the examples below.

(verbs) **Z U N E H M E N**
zugeben umrühren nehmen essen holen mähen erhalten nennen

(adjectives) **M I C K R I G**
modisch italienisch chic kalt reich intelligent gut

Storytelling

*This story accompanies Teaching Transparency 3-2. The **Mini-Geschichte** can be told and retold in different formats, acted out, written down, and read aloud to give students additional opportunities to practice all four skills.*

Er hat versprochen mich anzurufen. Ich warte jetzt schon zwei Tage auf seinen Anruf. Warum nur ruft er nicht an? Ich muss mich ablenken, damit ich nicht noch verrückt werde. Vielleicht soll ich mich schminken und einkaufen gehen? Neue Kleider heben bestimmt meine Laune. Vielleicht lass ich mir die Haare kurz schneiden. Vielleicht soll ich joggen oder schwimmen gehen? Warum ruf ich ihn nicht einfach an? Ich werde ihn fragen, was er dieses Wochenende vorhat. Vielleicht will er mit mir ins Kino gehen?

Traditions

Die Kaffeeschnüffler

Im 18. Jahrhundert wurde Kaffee zum Modegetränk in bürgerlichen Salons. Doch hatte Deutschland im 18. Jahrhundert keine Kolonien, von denen es eigenen Kaffee beziehen konnte und musste deshalb die Bohnen von den Franzosen oder Holländern kaufen. Eine zeitweilig rigide Boykottpolitik sollte verhindern, dass enorme Geldmengen aus Deutschland flossen. Friedrich der Große, der 1766 die Kaffeeeinfuhr zum Staatsmonopol erklärt hatte, dehnte dieses Staatsmonopol 1780 auch auf das Kaffeerösten aus. Kaffee durfte von nun an nur noch in den königlichen Röstereien gebrannt werden. Da der königliche Kaffee für Normalbürger zu teuer war, sollten sich diese mit Ersatzkaffee begnügen. Der falsche Kaffee, der so genannte „mocca faux" oder „Muckefuck", kam hauptsächlich von der Wurzel der Zichorie. Es gab 1900 in Deutschland 420 eingetragene Warenzeichen für Ersatzkaffee. Zur Kontrolle des Kaffeebrennzwangs hatte Friedrich der Große Kaffeeschnüffler, die an Ecken und Hauseingängen den verräterischen Kaffeeduft riechen und die Kaffeesünder bestrafen sollten. Willkür der Schnüffler, Kaffeeschmuggel und zunehmender Zorn der Bürger waren die Folge des königlichen Verbots. Nach dem Tod Friedrichs des Großen wurde dann das staatliche Monopol aufgegeben. Im 19. Jahrhundert wurde der Kaffee Volksgetränk und das Kaffeehaus ein bürgerlicher Treffpunkt der Politik und Kunst. 1825 eröffnete der Wiener Georg Kranzler in Berlin das weltberühmte Café Kranzler.

Café Kranzler

Rezept

Dicken Ries mit suren Saft (Milchreis) (Mecklenburg)

Zutaten
g=Gramm, l=Liter

250 g Reis

½ l Milch

Schale von ¼ Zitrone

fein gehackte bittere Mandeln

Zimt

Salz

Zubereitung
Den Reis in der Milch bei ganz schwacher Hitze und wiederholtem Umrühren zum Kochen bringen. Dann den Reis mit einer Prise Salz, ein paar fein gehackten Mandeln, einem Stück Zimt und der Zitronenschale weich kochen. Den Brei in eine kalt ausgespülte Form geben. Dazu Fruchtsaftsoße reichen.

Kapitel 3: Aussehen: wichtig oder nicht?
Technology

One-Stop Planner CD-ROM

To preview all resources available for this chapter, use the **One-Stop Planner CD-ROM**, Disc 1.

Internet Connection

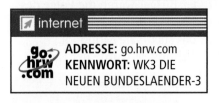

ADRESSE: go.hrw.com
KENNWORT: WK3 DIE NEUEN BUNDESLAENDER-3

*Have students explore the **go.hrw.com** Web site for many online resources covering all chapters. All Chapter 3 resources are available under the keyword **WK3 Die neuen Bundeslaender-3**. Interactive games practice the material and provide students with immediate feedback. You will also find a printable worksheet that provides Internet activities that lead to a comprehensive online research project.*

Interaktive Spiele

You can use the interactive activities in this chapter

- to practice grammar, vocabulary, and chapter functions
- as homework
- as an assessment option
- as a self-test
- to prepare for the Chapter Test

Internet Aktivitäten

Students find information on the Internet that enables them to give advice on fashion, the benefits of vitamin C, and the dangers of smoking.

- To prepare students for the **Arbeitsblatt,** have them discuss in class the benefits of vitamins and minerals. You may want to ask them to do **Anwendung** Activity 1, pp. 84–85.
- After completing the **Arbeitsblatt,** ask students if they know of an anti-smoking campaign at their school. If yes, ask them to pick up pamphlets and compare the advice given in these pamphlets to the advice they gave in **Aktivität D.** If there is no anti-smoking campaign at their school, ask students to design flyers that describe the dangers of smoking.

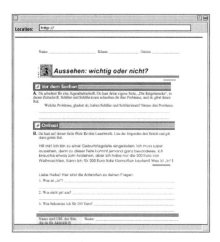

Webprojekt

Have students find sites that advertise and sell **Biokost.** Have them report on the items sold. Why are these items supposed to be healthful? Students should discuss the health benefits of at least three items. Encourage students to exchange useful Web sites with their classmates. Have students document their sources by referencing the names and URLs of all the sites they consulted.

Textbook Listening Activities Scripts

The following scripts are for the listening activities found in the *Pupil's Edition*. For Student Response Forms, see *Listening Activities*, pages 19–22. To provide students with additional listening practice, see *Listening Activities*, pages 23–26.

Erste Stufe

4 p. 65

DR. BEHRENS Guten Tag, alle zusammen. Hier ist wieder Radio Pop-shop mit dem Kummerkasten. Wie immer warte ich, Dr. Uwe Behrens, auf eure Anrufe und freue mich, heute den ersten Zuhörer oder die erste Zuhörerin zu begrüßen. Bitte stell dich kurz vor, wenn du möchtest, und erzähl uns dann von deinem Problem!

KRISTINA Ja, hallo, Dr. Behrens. Also, ich bin die ... ach ... ich möcht lieber nicht sagen, wie ich heiße ... oder ... na ja, eigentlich ist es auch egal. Also, ich bin die Kristina und bin 16 Jahre alt.

DR. BEHRENS Hallo, Kristina. Schön, dass du anrufst. Sag doch einfach, was du auf dem Herzen hast.

KRISTINA Ja, also, ich brauche einen Rat. Es ist nämlich so: Meine beste Freundin ist sauer auf mich. Wir waren verabredet und wollten ins Kino gehen. Und gerade, als ich losgehen wollte, hat mein kleiner Bruder gefragt, ob ich ihm bei seinen Matheaufgaben helfen könnte. Das habe ich natürlich gemacht. Und sofort danach hat ein Mädchen aus meiner Klasse angerufen, um zu fragen, ob ich ihr meine Jeansweste für die Fete am Samstag leihen könnte. Ich kann es selbst nicht glauben, dass ich ja gesagt habe. Ich wollte die Weste nämlich selber anziehen. Na ja, wie auch immer, ich bin zu spät ins Kino gekommen. Meine Freundin war natürlich echt sauer. Ja, und so was passiert mir andauernd.

DR. BEHRENS Also, wenn ich dich recht verstanden habe, dann ist das eigentliche Problem nicht, dass deine Freundin sauer auf dich ist, sondern dass du nicht nein sagen kannst.

KRISTINA Ja, stimmt genau! Ich schaffe es einfach nicht, jemandem zu sagen, dass ich zum Beispiel gerade keine Zeit habe oder keine Lust habe, etwas zu tun. Also, ich mach mir echt Gedanken darüber, wie ich das Problem lösen könnte. Aber ich weiß einfach nicht wie. Ich habe manchmal das Gefühl, alle nutzen mich aus. Was soll ich bloß machen?

DR. BEHRENS Kristina, hast du dir schon mal überlegt, warum es so schwer ist, nein zu sagen? Hast du vielleicht Angst, deine Freunde zu verlieren? Oder vielleicht glaubst du, dass man dich dann nicht mehr so gern mag.

KRISTINA Mhhm ... das kann schon sein.

DR. BEHRENS Also, Kristina, was hältst du davon, einmal auszuprobieren, wie deine Freunde und Geschwister auf ein Nein von dir reagieren? Wahrscheinlich ist es gar nicht so schlimm, wie du meinst. Im ersten Moment sind sie vielleicht enttäuscht oder sogar sauer, aber es ist ziemlich unwahrscheinlich, dass sie aufhören, dich zu mögen. Im Gegenteil, sie werden dich sogar sicher mehr respektieren, wenn du deine ehrliche Meinung sagst.

KRISTINA Wirklich?

DR. BEHRENS Ja, bestimmt! Vielleicht hilft es auch, einen kleinen Streit zu riskieren, damit die anderen wirklich merken, dass dir eine Sache wichtig ist und sie auch mal deine Wünsche akzeptieren müssen.

KRISTINA Ja, also, ich glaube, das ist ein guter Ratschlag. Vielen Dank, Herr Dr. Behrens, und auf Wiederhören!

DR. BEHRENS Viel Glück und auf Wiederhören, Kristina!

Answers to Activity 4
Soll ausprobieren, nein zu sagen; soll einen kleinen Streit riskieren, damit die anderen merken, dass ihr eine Sache wichtig ist.

7 p. 65

VANESSA Schau mal, Martin, da hinten geht die Claudia! Mensch, die sieht ja mal wieder toll aus! Total gestylt! Also, die hat ja echt eine super Figur! Und erst mal die Klamotten! Der letzte Schrei!

MARTIN Ja, stimmt! Sie sieht wirklich klasse aus!

VANESSA Ach, ich muss die Claudia unbedingt zu meiner Fete einladen. Aber guck doch mal, der komische Typ, der neben ihr geht. Ach du meine Güte! Wie sieht der denn aus? Potthässlich! Und mit so einem Typ lässt die sich blicken!

MARTIN Also, hör mal Vanessa! Du tust ja so, als ob alles nur vom Aussehen abhängt! Ich wusste gar nicht, dass du so oberflächlich bist! Was hältst du davon, erst mal jemanden kennen zu lernen, bevor du dir eine Meinung bildest?

VANESSA Ach was! Davon halte ich nichts! Ich kann meistens schon auf den ersten Blick erkennen, ob jemand toll oder langweilig ist. Menschenkenntnis nennt man das!

MARTIN Also, ich finde, du spinnst! Für mich sind zum Beispiel innere Werte und Charakter viel wichtiger als nur das Aussehen.

VANESSA Ja, aber ich hab echt keine Lust, Leute großartig kennen zu lernen, die mir äußerlich überhaupt nicht gefallen. Also, Leute, die sich schlampig anziehen und total hässlich aussehen.

MARTIN	Aber deswegen können es doch trotzdem ganz tolle Menschen sein, die Eigenschaften und Talente haben, von denen man auf den ersten Blick gar nichts bemerkt!
VANESSA	Ja, aber ist es meine Schuld, wenn sie ihre Qualitäten verstecken? Bei gut aussehenden und attraktiven Leuten weiß man wenigstens sofort, woran man ist. Man kann auf den ersten Blick erkennen, dass sie Wert auf ihr Äußeres legen. Ich würde sagen, dass schöne Menschen sogar viel sympathischer sind.
MARTIN	Das würde ich eigentlich nicht sagen! Außerdem, was verstehst du denn unter „schön"?
VANESSA	Also schön ist, wer seine Haut pflegt, seine Haare stylt, einen sportlichen Body hat, Modetrends mitmacht ... im Prinzip kann jeder was aus seinem Aussehen machen!
MARTIN	Ja, klar kann man sein Äußeres mit Make-up, Haarfarbe, Kleidung und von mir aus sogar mit Schönheitsoperationen verändern. Aber ich finde, dass man dadurch seinen Charakter oder seine Persönlichkeit noch lange nicht verbessert. Und wenn man einen tollen Charakter hat, ist es völlig egal, wie man aussieht. Das ist jedenfalls meine Meinung.

Answers to Activity 7
Sie unterhalten sich übers Aussehen; Vanessa hält viel vom Aussehen; Martin hält mehr von inneren Werten.

Zweite Stufe

22 p. 74

1.

BRITTA	Hallo, Susi! Na, hast du wieder mal dein Lieblings-T-Shirt an? Du scheinst es wirklich zu mögen. Jedesmal, wenn ich dich treffe, hast du es an!
SUSI	Ach, hallo Britta! Mein T-Shirt? Ja, da hast du Recht. Ich ziehe es wirklich sehr gerne an, weil es so ein auffälliges Motiv hat. Nur leider kann ich es am Samstag zur Fete nicht schon wieder anziehen. Ich habe es nämlich bereits auf der letzten Fete vom Klaus getragen.
BRITTA	Ja, also ich würde es auch nicht noch mal zur Fete anziehen. Sag mal, warum kaufst du dir nicht mal was Neues? Es ist doch gerade Schlussverkauf. Da findest du bestimmt was. Sollen wir morgen zusammen in die Stadt gehen?
SUSI	Au ja, toll! Das machen wir!

2.

BRITTA	Schau mal, da hinten an der Bushaltestelle steht der Hans-Jörg!
SUSI	Ach ja, und er liest natürlich, wie immer. Es ist schon echt komisch, dass er ständig liest, sei es nun an der Bushaltestelle oder in der Pause. Wenn er wenigstens nur Comics oder Zeitschriften lesen würde, aber stell dir mal vor, er nimmt manchmal sogar das Geschichtsbuch mit in die Pause und lernt daraus!
BRITTA	Ja, das ist eben typisch Hans-Jörg! Also, an seiner Stelle würde ich mich in der Pause mit den anderen unterhalten und mich nicht so von allen absondern.

SUSI	Ja, da hast du Recht. Du, übrigens, ich wollte gerade den Tobias abholen gehen. Wir wollen zusammen eine Radtour machen. Hast du Lust mitzukommen?
BRITTA	Ja, gerne! Also, ich geh dann mal nach Hause und hol mein Rad aus dem Keller.
SUSI	Gut! Wir kommen dich dann abholen! Bis nachher!
BRITTA	Tschüs! Bis nachher!

3. *[Doorbell rings]*

TOBIAS	Hallo, Susi. Ich hab schon auf dich gewartet!
SUSI	Grüß dich, Tobias! Mensch, wie siehst du denn aus? Hast du gerade gepennt? Du siehst noch ganz verschlafen aus. Wir wollten doch heute die Radtour machen!
TOBIAS	Ja, äh, also, ich bin echt müde. Ich glaub, ich bin gestern zu spät ins Bett gegangen. Weißt du, da läuft seit ein paar Tagen nachts so eine unheimlich spannende Krimiserie. Die ersten drei Folgen hab ich schon gesehen, und es kommen noch fünf weitere. Das Blöde ist, ich kann dann am nächsten Morgen kaum wach werden!
SUSI	Also, versuch doch mal, früher ins Bett zu gehen! Du wirst schon sehen, dass du dich dann am nächsten Morgen viel besser fühlst! Die Krimiserie kannst du doch auf Video aufnehmen und tagsüber gucken. Also, was ist nun mit unserer Radtour?
TOBIAS	Äh ... Uaaahh *[Yawning]* ...
SUSI	Komm, hol deine Jacke und schmeiß dich aufs Rad! Wenn wir erst mal 'ne Weile geradelt sind, wirst du schon munter! Die Britta kommt übrigens auch mit. Wir müssen sie nur noch von zu Hause abholen.
TOBIAS	Was? Die Britta Zellmann? Du, der Uwe findet die echt nett, glaub ich! Lass uns doch schnell mal beim Uwe vorbeifahren und ihn abholen!
SUSI	Kannst du ihn nicht einfach anrufen? Vielleicht hat er ja gar keine Lust! So wie ich ihn kenne, sitzt er doch eh' lieber vor der Glotze.
TOBIAS	Nee du, den Uwe, den muss man vor vollendete Tatsachen stellen. Wenn ich da erst anrufe und frage, ob er Lust hat, dann zögert er nur rum und kann sich nicht entscheiden. Aber wenn wir einfach vor der Tür stehen, kann er nicht so leicht nein sagen!
SUSI	Also, gut. Dann mal los!

4. *[Doorbell rings]*

UWE	Hey! Hallo Tobias, hallo Susi! Was macht ihr denn hier?
TOBIAS	Tja, also, wir wollen dich zu 'ner Fahrradtour abholen. Wie sieht's aus? Hast du Lust?
UWE	Äh, also, ich guck mir gerade das Fußballspiel zwischen Fortuna Düsseldorf und Kaiserslautern an ...
SUSI	Das gibt's doch wohl nicht! Soll das etwa heißen, dass du lieber vor dem Fernseher hängst als mit uns was zu unternehmen? Also, ich finde sowieso, du solltest etwas mehr Sport treiben! Na komm schon! Wir müssen uns beeilen. Die Britta wartet!
UWE	Die Britta? ... Äh, also gut ... ich komm ja schon!

Answers to Activity 22
1. c; 2. d.; 3. a; 4. b

Anwendung

1b p. 85

One-Stop Planner CD-ROM

For resource information, see the **One-Stop Planner CD-ROM**, Disc 1.

RUNDFUNKMODERATOR	Und nun, liebe Zuhörer, möchten wir Sie mit den neuesten Erkenntnissen aus der Ernährungswissenschaft bekannt machen. Wir beginnen jeweils mit der Nennung einiger weit verbreiteter Annahmen über den Nährwert verschiedener Lebensmittel und lassen dann unsere Expertin Stellung dazu nehmen. Wir begrüßen heute hier bei uns im Studio die Leiterin des Ernährungswissenschaftlichen Institutes in Bonn, Frau Professor Doktor Lohmann. Herzlich Willkommen!
PROF. DR. LOHMANN	Danke schön!
RUNDFUNKMODERATOR	Erstens: Das beste Brot ist dunkles Brot. Richtig oder falsch, Frau Professor Doktor Lohmann?
PROF. DR. LOHMANN	Falsch! Dunkles Brot ist oft nur mit Zuckerfarbe gefärbtes Brot — aber es wird dunkel, weil es lange gebacken wird. Das beste Brot, weiß oder dunkel, ist das Brot, das aus Vollkorn hergestellt ist.
RUNDFUNKMODERATOR	Zweitens: Braune Eier sind gesünder als weiße Eier. Richtig oder falsch?
PROF. DR. LOHMANN	Ganz eindeutig falsch! Braune Eier haben nur eine dickere Schale als weiße Eier. Ansonsten haben sie den gleichen Nährwert wie weiße Eier.
RUNDFUNKMODERATOR	Drittens: Kartoffeln machen dick. Ja, das hat auch schon immer meine Großmutter gesagt. Was sagt die Ernährungswissenschaft dazu, Frau Professor?
PROF. DR. LOHMANN	Auch diese weit verbreitete Annahme ist falsch! Kartoffeln sind arm an Kalorien und haben viele Vitamine.
RUNDFUNKMODERATOR	Viertens: Fisch hat weniger Nährwert als Fleisch. Richtig oder falsch?
PROF. DR. LOHMANN	Wiederum falsch! Fisch hat im Allgemeinen weniger Fett als Fleisch, aber fast so viele Proteine wie Fleisch. Außerdem ist Fisch reich an Vitamin D.
RUNDFUNKMODERATOR	Fünftens — und hier bin ich selbst neugierig: Öl ist Öl. Es spielt keine Rolle, welches man im Haushalt gebraucht. Frau Professor Doktor Lohmann, richtig oder falsch?
PROF. DR. LOHMANN	Auch diese Annahme ist falsch! Der Gesundheit zuliebe bitte nur Pflanzenöle verwenden, denn Pflanzenöle enthalten kein Cholesterin.
RUNDFUNKMODERATOR	Sechstens: Orangen und Zitronen sind die Vitamin-C-reichsten Früchte. Richtig oder falsch?
PROF. DR. LOHMANN	Falsch! Zitrusfrüchte enthalten pro 100 Gramm Fruchtgewicht nur 50 Milligramm Vitamin C. Kiwis enthalten dreimal so viel Vitamin C, nämlich 150 Milligramm.
RUNDFUNKMODERATOR	Siebtens: Brot macht dick. Wie sieht's hier aus, richtig oder falsch?
PROF. DR. LOHMANN	Falsch! Brot hat weniger Kalorien als Fett oder Zucker. Was auf dem Brot liegt, die Butter, die Wurst, der Käse, das macht dick!
RUNDFUNKMODERATOR	Achtens: Alle Mineralwässer sind gleich. Auch hier wieder die Frage: richtig oder falsch?
PROF. DR. LOHMANN	Falsch! Die Substanzen, die im Wasser sind, können sehr verschieden sein. In vielen Wässern ist sehr viel Salz, und Salz ist sowieso schon in vielen Lebensmitteln. Jeder weiß natürlich, dass zu viel Salz ungesund für den Körper ist.
RUNDFUNKMODERATOR	Neuntens: Wenn es heiß ist, soll man nichts oder nur wenig trinken. Oh, das hört sich sehr falsch an. Was sagt unsere Expertin dazu?
PROF. DR. LOHMANN	In der Tat: sehr falsch! Wenn es heiß ist, soll man besonders viel trinken, weil der Körper in der Hitze viel Flüssigkeit verliert.
RUNDFUNKMODERATOR	Zehntens: Brauner Zucker enthält mehr Vitamine und Mineralien als weißer Zucker. Richtig oder falsch?
PROF. DR. LOHMANN	Auch hier wieder lautet die eindeutige Antwort: falsch! Weder brauner noch weißer Zucker enthalten Vitamine oder Mineralien. Der braune Zucker ist heute meist gefärbt.
RUNDFUNKMODERATOR	Und damit sind wir am Ende der Sendung. Wir bedanken uns ganz herzlich bei Frau Professor Doktor Lohmann und möchten Sie, liebe Zuhörer, bitten, uns weitere Anfragen zuzuschicken, die wir gerne wieder von einem Experten im Studio beantworten lassen.

Answers to Activity 1b
Alle Aussagen in der Umfrage von Übung 1a sind falsch.

Kapitel 3: Aussehen: wichtig oder nicht?
Suggested Lesson Plans *50-Minute Schedule*

Day 1

CHAPTER OPENER 5 min.
- Advance Organizer, ATE, p. 59M
- Thinking Critically, ATE, p. 59M

LOS GEHT'S! 20 min.
- Preteaching Vocabulary, ATE, p. 59N
- Language Note, ATE, p. 59N
- Play Audio CD for **Los geht's!**
- Have students read **Los geht's!**, pp. 62–63
- Do Activities 1–3, p. 63

ERSTE STUFE
Reading Selection, p. 64 5 min.
- Teaching Suggestions, p. 59O
- Take **Fitnesstest**, p. 64

Wortschatz, p. 64 15 min.
- Presenting **Wortschatz,** ATE, p. 59O
- Teaching Transparency 3-1
- Play Audio CD for Activity 4, p. 65
- Do Activities 5 and 6, p. 65

Wrap-Up 5 min.
- Students respond to questions about what teens can do to keep fit

Homework Options
Grammatikheft, pp. 19–20, Acts. 1–2
Übungsheft, p. 27, Act. 1; pp. 28–29, Acts. 1–4

Day 2

ERSTE STUFE
Quick Review 10 min.
- Check homework, Übungsheft, p. 27, Act. 1; pp. 28–29, Acts. 1–4

So sagt man das!, p. 65 10 min.
- Presenting **So sagt man das!**, ATE, p. 59P
- Play Audio CD for Activity 7, p. 65
- Do Activity 8, p. 66

Grammatik, p. 66 25 min.
- Presenting **Grammatik,** ATE, p. 59P
- Do Activity 9, p. 66
- Do Activities 10, 11, 12, 13, and 14, p. 67

Wrap-Up 5 min.
- Students respond to questions about the importance of clothing to teens

Homework Options
Pupil's Edition, p. 67, Act. 15
Grammatikheft, pp. 20–22, Acts. 3–7
Übungsheft, pp. 30–31, Acts. 5–9

Day 3

ERSTE STUFE
Quick Review 10 min.
- Check homework, Grammatikheft, pp. 20–22, Acts. 3–7

LANDESKUNDE 20 min.
- Presenting **Landeskunde,** ATE, p. 59Q
- Total Physical Response, ATE, p. 59Q
- Thinking Critically, ATE, p. 59Q
- Read **Die deutsche Subkultur,** pp. 68–69
- Do Activities A and B, p. 69

Quiz Review 15 min.
- Do Additional Listening Activities 3-1, 3-2, and 3-3, pp. 23–24
- Do Activities for Communication 3-1 and 3-2, pp. 9–10

Wrap-Up 5 min.
- Students respond to questions about the importance of eating healthfully to teens

Homework Options
Mehr Grammatikübungen, Erste Stufe
Übungsheft, p. 32, Acts. 1–3

Day 4

ERSTE STUFE
Quick Review 10 min.
- Check homework, **Mehr Grammatikübungen, Erste Stufe**

Quiz 20 min.
- Quiz 3-1A or 3-1B

WEITER GEHT'S! 20 min.
- Preteaching Vocabulary ATE, p. 59R
- Play Audio CD for **Weiter geht's!**, p. 70
- Do Activities 16–19, p. 71

Wrap-Up 5 min.
- Students respond to questions about the importance of being with the "in" crowd

Homework Options
Übungsheft, p. 33, Acts. 1–2

Day 5

ZWEITE STUFE
Quick Review 15 min.
- Return and review Quiz 3-1
- Bell Work, ATE, p. 59S
- Check homework, Übungsheft, p. 33, Acts. 1–2

Reading Selection, p. 72 15 min.
- Teaching Suggestion, ATE, p. 59S
- Read **Eine Freundin gibt Rat,** p. 72

Wortschatz/So sagt man das!, p. 73 15 min.
- Presenting **Wortschatz/So sagt man das!,** ATE, p. 59T
- Do Activities 20 and 21, p. 73
- Do Activity 10, p. 24, Grammatikheft

Wrap-Up 5 min.
- Students respond to questions about what kinds of problems they discuss with their friends

Homework Options
Grammatikheft, p. 23, Acts. 8–9
Übungsheft, p. 34, Act. 1

Day 6

ZWEITE STUFE
Quick Review 10 min.
- Check homework, Grammatikheft, p. 23, Acts. 8–9

So sagt man das!, p. 74 15 min.
- Presenting **So sagt man das!,** ATE, p. 59T
- Teaching Transparency 3-2
- Play Audio CD for Activity 22, p. 74
- Do Activities 23 and 24, p. 74

Grammatik, p. 75 20 min.
- Presenting **Grammatik,** ATE, p. 59T
- Language-to-Language, ATE, p. 59T
- Do Activity 25, p. 75
- Do Activities 12–15, pp. 25–26, Grammatikheft

Wrap-Up 5 min.
- Students respond to questions about what advice they would give to a friend who is feeling down

Homework Options
Grammatikheft, p. 24, Act. 11
Übungsheft, pp. 34–36, Acts. 2–6

One-Stop Planner CD-ROM

For alternative lesson plans by chapter section, to create your own customized plans, or to preview all resources available for this chapter, use the **One-Stop Planner CD-ROM**, Disc 1.

 For additional homework suggestions, see activities accompanied by this symbol throughout the chapter.

Day 7

ZWEITE STUFE
Quick Review 10 min.
- Check homework, Übungsheft, pp. 34–36, Acts. 2–6

So sagt man das!, p. 75 15 min.
- Presenting **So sagt man das!**, ATE, p. 59T
- Do Activity 26, p. 76
- Do Activity 16, p. 27, Grammatikheft

So sagt man das!, p. 76 20 min.
- Present **So sagt man das!**, p. 76
- Do Activities 27 and 28, p. 76
- Do Activities 7–9, pp. 36–37, Übungsheft

Wrap-Up 5 min.
- Students give reasons in response to questions about why they do certain things

Homework Options
Pupil's Edition, p. 76, Act. 29
Grammatikheft, p. 27, Act. 17

Day 8

ZWEITE STUFE
Quick Review 10 min.
- Check homework, Grammatikheft, p. 27, Act. 17

Quiz Review 20 min.
- Do **Mehr Grammatikübungen, Zweite Stufe**
- Do Communicative Activities 3-3 and 3-4, pp. 11–12
- Do Additional Listening Activities 3-4, 3-5, and 3-6, pp. 24–26

Quiz 20 min.
- Quiz 3-2A or 3-2B

Homework Options
Internet Aktivitäten, see ATE, p. 59E

Day 9

ZWEITE STUFE
Quick Review 10 min.
- Return and review Quiz 3-2

ZUM SCHREIBEN 35 min.
- Presenting **Zum Schreiben**, ATE, p. 59U
- Teaching Suggestions, ATE, p. 59U
- Present **Schreibtipp**, p. 77
- Do Activities A and B, p. 77

Wrap-Up 5 min.
- Students respond to questions about describing classmates

Homework Options
Pupil's Edition, p. 77, Act. C

Day 10

ZWEITE STUFE
Quick Review 15 min.
- Check homework, Pupil's Edition, p. 77, Act. C

ZUM LESEN 30 min.
- Teacher Note, ATE, p. 59V
- Teacher Note, ATE, p. 59W
- Present **Lesestrategie**, p. 78
- Do Activities 1–11, pp. 78–79

Wrap-Up 5 min.
- Students respond to questions about the importance of slang

Homework Options
Pupil's Edition, p. 79, Act. 12
Übungsheft, pp. 38–39, Acts. 1–6

Day 11

ZWEITE STUFE
Quick Review 10 min.
- Check homework, Übungsheft, pp. 38–39, Acts. 1–6

Gesund essen (Video) 20 min.
- Teaching Suggestions, Video Guide, p. 12
- Do Pre-viewing Activities, Video Guide, p. 13
- Show **Gesund essen** Video
- Do Viewing Activities, Video Guide, p. 13
- Show **Videoclips**

ANWENDUNG 15 min.
- Do Activities 1–4, pp. 84–85

Wrap-Up 5 min.
- Students respond to questions about the importance of surveys

Homework Options
Interaktive Spiele, see ATE, p. 59E

Day 12

ANWENDUNG
Quick Review 10 min.
- Play **Wörtersalat**, ATE, p. 59C

Kann ich's wirklich?, p. 86 20 min.
- Do Activities 1–5, p. 86

Chapter Review 20 min.
- Review chapter functions, vocabulary, and grammar; choose from **Mehr Grammatikübungen,** Activities for Communication, Listening Activities, or **Interaktive Spiele**
- Review test format and provide sample test items for students

Homework Options
Study for Chapter Test

Assessment

Test, Chapter 3 45 min.
- Administer Chapter Test. Select from Testing Program, Alternative Assessment Guide, or Test Generator.

Kapitel 3: Aussehen: wichtig oder nicht?
Suggested Lesson Plans *90-Minute Schedule*

Block 1

CHAPTER OPENER 5 min.
- Advance Organizer, ATE, p. 59M
- Thinking Critically, ATE, p. 59M

LOS GEHT'S! 20 min.
- Preteaching Vocabulary, ATE, p. 59N
- Language Note, ATE, p. 59N
- A Slower Pace, p. 59N
- Play Audio CD for Los geht's!
- Have students read Los geht's!, pp. 62–63
- Do Activities 1–3, p. 63

ERSTE STUFE
Reading Selection, p. 64 10 min.
- Teaching Suggestions, p. 59O
- Take Fitnesstest, p. 64

Wortschatz, p. 64 15 min.
- Presenting Wortschatz, ATE, p. 59O
- Teaching Transparency 3-1
- Play Audio CD for Activity 4, p. 65
- Do Activities 5 and 6, p. 65

So sagt man das!, p. 65 10 min.
- Presenting So sagt man das!, ATE, p. 59P
- Play Audio CD for Activity 7, p. 65
- Do Activity 8, p. 66
- Do Activity 5, p. 30, Übungsheft

Grammatik, p. 66 25 min.
- Presenting Grammatik, ATE, p. 59P
- Do Activity 9, p. 66
- Do Activities 10, 11, 12, 13, and 14, p. 67

Wrap-Up 5 min.
- Students respond to questions about the importance of clothing to teens

Homework Options
Pupil's Edition, p. 67, Act. 15
Grammatikheft, pp. 19–22, Acts. 1–7
Übungsheft, p. 27, Act. 1; pp. 28–31, Acts. 1–4 and 6–9

Block 2

ERSTE STUFE
Quick Review 10 min.
- Check homework, Grammatikheft, pp. 19–22, Acts. 1–7

LANDESKUNDE 20 min.
- Presenting Landeskunde, ATE, p. 59Q
- Total Physical Response, ATE, p. 59Q
- Thinking Critically, ATE, p. 59Q
- Read Die deutsche Subkultur, pp. 68–69
- Do Activities A and B, p. 69

Quiz Review 15 min.
- Do Mehr Grammatikübungen, Erste Stufe
- Do Additional Listening Activities 3-1, 3-2, and 3-3, pp. 23–24
- Do Activities for Communication 3-1 and 3-2, pp. 9–10

Quiz 20 min.
- Quiz 3-1A or 3-1B

WEITER GEHT'S! 20 min.
- Presenting Weiter geht's!, ATE, p. 59R
- Play Audio CD for Weiter geht's!, p. 70
- Do Activities 16–19, p. 71

Wrap-Up 5 min.
- Students respond to questions about the importance of eating healthfully to teens

Homework Options
Übungsheft, p. 32, Acts. 1–3; p. 33, Acts. 1–2
Internet Aktivitäten, see ATE, p. 59E

Block 3

ZWEITE STUFE
Quick Review 15 min.
- Return and review Quiz 3-1
- Bell Work, ATE, p. 59S
- Check homework, Übungsheft, p. 33, Acts. 1–2

Reading Selection, p. 72 15 min.
- Teaching Suggestion, ATE, p. 59S
- Read Eine Freundin gibt Rat, p. 72

Wortschatz/So sagt man das!, p. 73 15 min.
- Presenting Wortschatz/So sagt man das!, ATE, p. 59T
- Do Activities 20 and 21, p. 73
- Do Activity 10, p. 24, Grammatikheft

So sagt man das!, p. 74 20 min.
- Presenting So sagt man das!, ATE, p. 59T
- Teaching Transparency 3-2
- Play Audio CD for Activity 22, p. 74
- Do Activities 23 and 24, p. 74
- Do Activity 11, p. 24, Grammatikheft

Grammatik, p. 75 20 min.
- Presenting Grammatik, ATE, p. 59T
- Language-to-Language, ATE, p. 59T
- Do Activity 25, p. 75
- Do Activities 12–15, pp. 25–26, Grammatikheft

Wrap-Up 5 min.
- Students respond to questions about what advice they would give to a friend who was feeling down

Homework Options
Grammatikheft, p. 23, Acts. 8–9
Übungsheft, pp. 34–36, Act. 1–6

One-Stop Planner CD-ROM

For alternative lesson plans by chapter section, to create your own customized plans, or to preview all resources available for this chapter, use the **One-Stop Planner CD-ROM**, Disc 1.

 For additional homework suggestions, see activities accompaned by this symbol throughout the chapter.

Block 4

ZWEITE STUFE

Quick Review 10 min.
- Check homework, Übungsheft, pp. 34–36, Act. 1–6

So sagt man das!, p. 75 15 min.
- Presenting **So sagt man das!**, ATE, p. 59T
- Do Activity 26, p. 76
- Do Activity 16, p. 27, Grammatikheft

So sagt man das!, p. 76 25 min.
- Present **So sagt man das!**, p. 76
- Do Activities 27, 28, and 29, p. 76
- Do Activities 7–9, pp. 36–37, Übungsheft
- Do Activity 17, p. 27, Grammatikheft

Quiz Review 20 min.
- Do **Mehr Grammatikübungen, Zweite Stufe**
- Do Communicative Activities 3-3 and 3-4, pp. 11–12
- Do Additional Listening Activities 3-4, 3-5, and 3-6, pp. 24–26

Quiz 20 min.
- Quiz 3-2A or 3-2B

Homework Options
Interaktive Spiele, see ATE, p. 59E

Block 5

ZWEITE STUFE

Quick Review 10 min.
- Return and review Quiz 3-2

ZUM SCHREIBEN 40 min.
- Presenting **Zum Schreiben**, ATE, p. 59U
- Teaching Suggestions, ATE, p. 59U
- Present **Schreibtipp**, p. 77
- Do Activities A and B, p. 77

ZUM LESEN 35 min.
- Teacher Note, ATE, p. 59V
- Teacher Note, ATE, p. 59W
- Present **Lesestrategie**, p. 78
- Do Activities 1–12, pp. 78–79

Wrap-Up 5 min.
- Students respond to questions about the importance of slang

Homework Options
Pupil's Edition, p. 77, Act. C
Übungsheft, pp. 38–39, Acts. 1–6

Block 6

ZWEITE STUFE

Quick Review 25 min.
- Check homework, Übungsheft, pp. 38–39, Acts. 1–6
- Have students read **Zum Schreiben** descriptions

Gesund essen (Video) 20 min.
- Teaching Suggestions, Video Guide, p. 12
- Do Pre-viewing Activities, Video Guide, p. 13
- Show **Gesund essen** Video
- Do Viewing Activities, Video Guide, p. 13
- Show **Videoclips**

ANWENDUNG 20 min.
- Do Activities 1–4, pp. 84–85

Kann ich's wirklich?, p. 86 20 min.
- Do Activities 1–5, p. 86

Wrap-Up 5 min.
- Students respond to questions about all aspects of healthful living

Homework Options
Study for Chapter Test

Block 7

ANWENDUNG

Quick Review 15 min.
- Play **Wörtersalat**, ATE, p. 59C

Chapter Review 30 min.
- Review chapter functions, vocabulary, and grammar; choose from **Mehr Grammatikübungen**, Activities for Communication, Listening Activities, or **Interaktive Spiele**
- Review test format and provide sample test items for students

Test, Chapter 3 45 min.
- Administer Chapter Test. Select from Testing Program, Alternative Assessment Guide, or Test Generator.

Kapitel 3: Aussehen: wichtig oder nicht?
Teaching Suggestions, *pages 60–87*

Before you begin the chapter, you may want to preview the *Video Program* and consult the *Video Guide.* Suggestions for integrating the video into each chapter are given in the *Video Guide* and in the chapter interleaf of the *Teacher's Edition.* Activity masters for video selections can be found in the *Video Guide.*

One-Stop Planner CD-ROM

For resource information, see the **One-Stop Planner CD-ROM**, Disc 1.

PAGES 60–61

CHAPTER OPENER

Pacing Tips

The **Erste Stufe** centers around fitness, mood, and appearance. A presentation of **da-** and **wo-**compounds occurs on p. 66. Infinitive clauses are introduced in the **Zweite Stufe** alongside the functions of 'expressing sympathy and resignation,' 'giving advice,' giving a reason,' and 'admitting something and expressing regret.' The **Landeskunde** and **Zum Lesen** readings focus on teen cliques and slang expressions. For Lesson Plans and timing suggestions, see pages 31I–31L.

Meeting the Standards
Communication
- Asking for and expressing opinions, p. 65
- Expressing sympathy, p. 73
- Giving advice, p. 74
- Giving a reason, p. 75
- Admitting something and expressing regret, p. 76

Cultures
- Landeskunde, p. 69

Connections
- Language Note, p. 59N
- Language-to-Language, p. 59T

Comparisons
- Language Note, p. 59T

Communities
- Family Link, p. 59Q
- Career Path, p. 59R

Advance Organizer

Here are two sayings related to appearance:
Kleider machen Leute.
Schönheit vergeht, Tugend besteht.

Write these statements on the board and give students a few minutes to think about what they mean. Divide students into two groups and have each group talk about one of the two sayings, discussing what it means and thinking of an example to which it would apply.

Thinking Critically

Comparing and Contrasting Ask students about sayings in English that are related to appearance. (Examples: *Don't judge a book by its cover. Beauty is only skin deep.*) Do any of the English sayings express the same ideas as those discussed in the Advance Organizer?

Communication for All Students

Visual Learners

Ask students to comment in German on the similarities and the differences in hairstyle and clothing of the students pictured. Then have students describe the group as a whole. Write some of the words and expressions brainstormed by students on the chalkboard or on a transparency.

Chapter Sequence

LOS GEHT'S!

Teaching Resources
pp. 62–63

PRINT
▶ Lesson Planner, p. 21
▶ Übungsheft, p. 27

MEDIA
▶ One-Stop Planner
▶ Audio Compact Discs, CD3, Trs. 1–6

> **PAGES 62–63**

Los geht's! Summary

In *Gut aussehen,* four students explain how they feel about appearance and what they do to look their best. The following learning outcome listed on p. 61 is modeled in the episode: asking for and expressing opinions.

Preteaching Vocabulary

Guessing Words from Context

Ask students what functions they would expect in a conversation about looking good (expressing an opinion; giving a reason). Students should scan **Los geht's!** for German phrases that match those functions. Then have students identify adjectives used in expressing an opinion or in giving a reason. Finally, have students use contextual clues to guess the meanings of these words and phrases: **zunehmen, schlampig, abnehmen, vollwertige Sachen, regelmäßiges Krafttraining, mickrig.**

Advance Organizer

Bring pictures of several different people to class. Ask students in German what kind of person each might be, based strictly on their appearance. (**Schaut euch diese Person an. Wie sieht die Person aus? Was meint ihr, was für eine Person das ist?**) Ask students if it is fair to judge people strictly on their appearance. (**Ist es fair oder unfair, eine Person nur nach dem Aussehen zu beurteilen? Warum oder warum nicht?**)

Connections and Comparisons

Language Note

In her last statement on p. 63, Tanja uses the words **mickrig** and **schief gehen** (schief gegangen). You might want to paraphrase these terms for students:

sich mickrig fühlen: sich überhaupt nicht gut fühlen

schief gehen: wenn etwas nicht so geht, wie es geplant war

Comprehension Check

A Slower Pace

1 Ask students to reread the interviews and to make a list of the words and expressions they don't understand. Write them on the chalkboard or on a transparency and ask for volunteers to explain the meaning of the terms in German.

Teaching Suggestions

1 Before students make their lists, remind them of the strategy of note-taking they learned in Level 2 (p. 346). These notes will be helpful when students do Activity 3.

2 Have students write their own narration in paragraph form rather than writing a series of disconnected sentences. Students should respond as if they too had been asked by an interviewer: **Warum ist dir dein Aussehen wichtig, und was tust du dafür?**

3 Ask students to use the notes they took in Activity 1. Students should avoid rereading the interviews and should instead rely on their notes.

ERSTE STUFE

PRINT

▶ Lesson Planner, p. 22
▶ Listening Activities, pp. 19–20, 23–24
▶ Video Guide, pp. 11–13
▶ Activities for Communication, pp. 9–10, 61–62, 64–65, 117–118
▶ Grammatikheft, pp. 19–22
▶ Grammar Tutor for Students of German, Chapter 3
▶ Übungsheft, pp. 28–32
▶ Testing Program, pp. 45–48
▶ Alternative Assessment Guide, p. 32
▶ Student Make-Up Assignments, Chapter 3

MEDIA

▶ One-Stop Planner
▶ Audio Compact Discs, CD3, Trs. 7–8, 16, 20–22
▶ Video Program
   Gesund essen
   Videocassette 1, 29:48–32:17
▶ Teaching Transparencies
   Situation 3-1
   Mehr Grammatikübungen Answers
   Grammatikheft Answers

PAGE 64

Bell Work

Ask students to define physical fitness and well-being. Ask them how they would rate themselves in these two categories. Then ask them about some physical activities in which they participate regularly.

Teaching Suggestions

• The **Fitnesstest** at the top of p. 64 contains new vocabulary items. You might want to introduce them to students by paraphrasing them in question form:

> Allgemeines Wohlbefinden: Wie fühlt ihr euch generell?
> Körperliche Leistungsfähigkeit: Wie fit seid ihr?
> Ausdauer: Wie lange könnt ihr etwas machen?
> Konzentrationsfähigkeit: Wie gut könnt ihr euch konzentrieren?
> Lebensfreude, Spannkraft: Wie viel Spaß macht euch das Leben? Wie vital fühlt ihr euch?

• After finishing the test, students should form pairs and ask their partner about his or her fitness level according to the answers that were given on the test. Students could use the questions from the definitions or make up their own.

PRESENTING: **Wortschatz**

Introduce the new vocabulary to students. Then ask them to work with a partner to write a series of short dialogues between two or more people containing at least one of the new expressions. Tell students that they can vary the expressions according to their needs and interests.
Example:
— Wie entspannst du dich am besten?
— Durch Sport, besonders Jogging. Und du?
— Ich entspanne mich durch Lesen und Musik.

Using the Video

 Videocassette 1, 29:48–32:17
In the video clip **Gesund essen,** the owner of a health food store talks about trends in health food consumption. See *Video Guide,* p. 12, for suggestions.

PAGE 65

Communication for All Students

Challenge

4 After students have listened to the **Höranruf,** ask them what advice they would give the caller. Do students agree or disagree with Dr. Behrens's advice? (Was würdet ihr diesem Mädchen raten? Meint ihr, Dr. Behrens hat das Mädchen gut oder schlecht beraten? Warum?)

For Additional Practice

5 Ask students to assume the role of a popular musician, actor or actress, or any celebrity of their choice. Partners should interview each other using questions similar to the ones in Activity 5.

Teaching Suggestion

6 Ask students to talk about what can make them feel down or unhappy. List their answers on one side of the board or a transparency. Once students have mentioned several things, start from the top of the list and ask the class about things that would make them feel better in each of the instances. Write the solutions in the other column.

PRESENTING: So sagt man das!

Ask students to give you their opinions of the latest fashions, movies, or current events using the expressions they already know.
Example:
— Wie findest du den neuen Harrison Ford Film?
— Den finde ich ganz toll! or
— Ich glaube, dass der Film ein großer Hit wird!
Then introduce the new expressions from **So sagt man das!**

> **PAGE 66**

For Additional Practice

8 Prepare a list of additional topics on a transparency and have students tell you or write their opinions of each of the listed items. (Examples: **Was hältst du von schnellen Wagen? … von Schulklubs? … vom Leben auf dem Land? … von Telekommunikation? … von einem Job nach der Schule? … von Natursendungen?**)

PRESENTING: Grammatik

Da- and wo-compounds Students learned about **da-** and **wo-compounds** in Level 2 (p. 277). To review them briefly, list the following prepositions on the board or on a transparency: **aus, an, auf, bei, mit, nach, von, zu, für, gegen, in, durch,** and **um.** Bring a few props to class such as a comb and a toothbrush. While combing your hair, say **Ich kämme mir die Haare mit einem Kamm.** Put the comb down and ask **Womit kämme ich mir die Haare?** Pointing to the comb, say **mit einem Kamm.** Then ask **Womit?**

Pointing to the comb, say **Damit!** Write the compounds **womit** and **damit** on the board or on a transparency to help visual learners. Give a few additional examples of compounds that do not require the addition of an "r." Next, review the compounds that require the "r." Put a book on your desk and say **Ich lege das Buch auf den Tisch.** Look at the class and ask **Worauf habe ich das Buch gelegt?** Point to the desk and say **auf den Tisch.** Then ask **Worauf?** Point to the desk and say **Darauf!** Write the compounds **worauf** and **darauf,** as well as other compounds that include an "r," on the board or a transparency. See if students can remember in what instances an "r" must be added to form the compound.

Teaching Suggestion

Ask students to find all the **wo-** and **da-compounds** contained in the interviews of the **Los geht's!** section on pp. 62 and 63. Students should also identify the part of the sentence the compound refers to. For example, in the sentence **Und was das Essen angeht, … ich mach mir keine großen Gedanken darüber,** the compound **darüber** refers to **das Essen.**

> **PAGE 67**

Group Work

10 Divide the class into groups of three and assign one discussion topic to each group. Tell students that they should be ready to share their opinions with the rest of the class after the activity and that they will have to support each of their opinions. (Example: **Biokost ist zwar sehr gesund, aber nicht alle Leute sollten unbedingt Biokost essen, denn …**)

Auditory Learners

11 Write the six questions from this activity on as many index cards as there are students in the class. Give each student a card. Ask students to mingle with classmates and ask three different people the question on their index card. Tell students that they will have about five minutes before they must return to their seats. Then call on some students to report the responses they got to their questions.

Teaching Suggestions

12 You may want to record students' conversations. Afterwards, play some of the conversations for the class and ask students to take notes on how students supported their opinions. Students should decide whether the opinions stated were well supported or not. If they think an opinion was not well supported, they should offer an alternative.

13 Tell students to imagine they are writing for a teen magazine and that their piece will be read by German-speaking teenagers eager to find out more about young Americans' attitude toward appearance and fitness.

Writing Assessment

13 You may wish to assess students' written work with the following rubic.

Writing Rubric	Points			
	4	3	2	1
Content (Complete – Incomplete)				
Comprehensibility (Comprehensible – Seldom comprehensible)				
Accuracy (Accurate – Seldom accurate)				
Organization (Well-organized – Poorly organized)				
Effort (Excellent – Minimal)				

18–20: A   16–17: B   14–15: C   12–13: D   Under 12: F

Reteaching: Vocabulary

Prepare a list of questions. Call on individual students to answer your questions. Here are a few examples you might want to use:
Wie entspannst du dich gewöhnlich?
Was hältst du von Biokost an Schulen?
Was hebt die Laune bei dir?
Was ist denn vollwertiges Essen?

PAGES 68–69

LANDESKUNDE

Building Context

Have students think of certain teenage "happenings" in the past or present that elicit "cult"-like behavior.

(Example: the viewing of the *Rocky Horror Picture Show* to which teens flocked week after week in strange outfits and where they exhibited certain group behaviors, such as chanting, clapping, getting up, or throwing things)

 Total Physical Response

Bring the following props to class to introduce the vocabulary of items teenagers take to **Tekkno-Parties:** hard hat, sunglasses, rubber gloves, surgical mask, plastic bag, and whistle. Ask one student to be a **Tekkno-Fan** and have other students tell him or her to put on the different items.

Cooperative Learning

A Divide the class into groups of three students. Assign each of the group members a specific task as reader, recorder, or reporter. Once the groups have completed their assignments, call on the reporters to present their answers. You may also want to collect the papers at the end to verify that the task has been completed by all groups.

FAMILY LINK

Have students interview their parents about expressions or words they used when they were teenagers. What do the expressions mean? Are they still around or are they now obsolete? Encourage students with parents who grew up in other countries to share their expressions with the class as well.

Thinking Critically

Analyzing After students complete the activities in the **Landeskunde** section, write the following statement on the board and ask students how it relates to the **Lexikon** at the end of the **Landeskunde: Sprache ist immer lebendig!** *(Language is a living thing!)*

Teacher Note

Mention to your students that the **Landeskunde** will also be included in Quiz 3-1B given at the end of the **Erste Stufe.**

Communication for All Students

Challenge

Ask students about their opinions of current fashions worn by actors and actresses on TV programs. Do these fashions influence the way students dress? (**Was hältst du von dem Kleidungsstil von … in der Sendung …?** or **Was hältst du von dem Kleidungsstil von Schauspielern im Fernsehen? Meinst du, ihr Stil beeinflusst dich?**)

Cultures and Communities

Career Path

Have students brainstorm situations in which it would be advantageous for Americans with careers in entertainment to know German. (Suggestions: Imagine you are a backup singer with a German rock band; imagine you have been given the opportunity to be part of the work crew for a German rock band, to work on such things as advance publicity and setting up stage.)

Assess

▸ Testing Program, pp. 45–48
  Quiz 3-1A, Quiz 3-1B
  Audio CD3, Tr. 16

▸ Student Make-Up Assignments
  Chapter 3, Alternative Quiz

▸ Alternative Assessment Guide, p. 32

Philipp

WEITER GEHT'S!

Teaching Resources
pp. 70–71

PRINT
▸ Lesson Planner, p. 23
▸ Übungsheft, p. 33

MEDIA
▸ One-Stop Planner
▸ Audio Compact Discs, CD3, Trs. 9–13

▶ **PAGES 70–71**

Weiter geht's! Summary

In *Immer mit der Mode. Oder?,* four students talk about what fashion means to them and how closely they follow trends. The following learning outcomes listed on p. 61 are modeled in the reports: expressing sympathy and resignation, giving advice, giving a reason, admitting something and expressing regret.

Preteaching Vocabulary

Activating Prior Knowledge

Have students use their knowledge of separable-prefix verbs to locate them in the text. Students should pay attention to the different ways that separable-prefix verbs are presented (i.e. present tense, infinitive, past participle). List the verbs they locate on the board. Which verbs occur more than once? Finally, ask students to use context in order to guess the meanings of the listed verbs. Which verb is used to admit something? (**zugeben**)

Advance Organizer

Have students bring pictures from fashion magazines. Ask students what they think of fashion in general and what they think of the styles shown in the pictures. What do students think of designer clothes? How do students choose their clothes? (**Was haltet ihr von der derzeitigen Mode? Was denkt ihr über Designer-Kleidung? Wie entscheidet ihr euch für eure Klamotten? Was beeinflusst eure Wahl?**)

Teaching Suggestion

Have students listen to one report at a time, following along in the book. Then work through the text, asking questions to detect any problems in comprehension caused by new words and phrases. Use synonyms or paraphrasing to explain new words.

Example:

Philipp sagt: „Ich geb zu, dass ich mich von der Mode schon ein wenig beeinflussen lass." Was meint er damit?

Once students have been given some examples showing how to get around new words, they should be able to do this on their own, using context to establish meaning.

Group Work

16 Divide the class into four or more groups and have each group work on one of the reports from p. 70. Ask groups to do tasks a and b. Students might need help with task b, finding the main point of each response. Have students quote the key sentence(s) and then identify the sentences that support each one.

Teaching Suggestion

17 Since matching the fifteen statements with people requires a lot of close reading, encourage students to look first for the most obvious ones, such as number 3 (Sonja) or number 14 (Tanja). After students have completed this activity, ask them which of the fifteen statements would best describe them. (**Welche dieser Aussagen trifft auf dich/euch zu?**)

Closure

Put students in pairs. Each pair should write down as many words as they can to fit the categories that you call out or write on the board or on a transparency. Give students three to four minutes per category. Then ask four or five pairs of students to share their lists with the rest of the class. Here are a few categories and some related words students might come up with:

ausgeflippte Klamotten: zerrissenes T-Shirt, verwaschene Jeans
Bodybuilding: Krafttraining, Anstrengung
Biokost: Tofu, Sojasprossen, gesund, umweltfreundlich
Aussehen: schminken, schön, mickrig
guter Geschmack: gutes Aussehen, gefallen
Diät ohne Fleisch: Vegetarier(in), gesund

To make the activity more challenging, you could ask students to use some of the words they thought of in sentences and then paragraphs. (Example: **Was ich über Biokost denke? Ja, ich glaube, dass Biokost sehr gesund und noch dazu umweltfreundlich ist, weil ...**)

ZWEITE STUFE

Teaching Resources
pp. 72–76

PRINT 📖
▸ Lesson Planner, p. 24
▸ Listening Activities, pp. 21–22, 24–26
▸ Activities for Communication, pp. 11–12, 63, 65, 117–118
▸ Grammatikheft, pp. 23–27
▸ Grammar Tutor for Students of German, Chapter 3
▸ Übungsheft, pp. 34–37
▸ Testing Program, pp. 49–52
▸ Alternative Assessment Guide, p. 32
▸ Student Make-Up Assignments, Chapter 3

MEDIA 📀📹
▸ One-Stop Planner
▸ Audio Compact Discs, CD3, Trs. 14, 17, 23–25
▸ Teaching Transparencies Situation 3-2
  Mehr Grammatikübungen Answers
  Grammatikheft Answers

PAGE 72

Bell Work

Ask students whom they confide in most of the time when they need to talk to someone. (**Wem vertraust du dich an, wenn du Probleme hast? Deiner Freundin? Deinem Freund? Deinen Eltern?**)

Teaching Suggestion

Ask two students to read the conversation between Elke and Tanja aloud in class. Then ask the class to tell you a) the gist of the problem, b) Elke's reaction, and c) the way Tanja tries to help. (**Was ist mit Elke los? Wie reagiert sie? Was rät Tanja ihrer Freundin?**)

PRESENTING: Wortschatz

Introduce the new words and expressions. For each one, ask a question or make a statement to which students have to respond. Then ask students to write two related sentences or a question and a response incorporating at least one of the new vocabulary items.

PRESENTING: So sagt man das!

Ask students to reread the conversation between Elke and Tanja and identify all expressions of sympathy and resignation in the text. Ask students to quote these in the context in which they were used.

Connections and Comparisons

Language Note

You may want to point out to students that **eine Pechsträhne haben** has an equivalent in English: *to have a streak of bad luck.*

Building on Previous Skills

21 In Level 2, p. 167, students learned expressions used to ask for and give advice. Review those expressions with students and ask them to give some advice to their partner responding to their partner's resignation.
Examples:
Geh doch mal früher zu Bett!
Du brauchst unbedingt Nachhilfe in Mathe!

PRESENTING: So sagt man das!

Present the new expressions, then ask students how the words **doch** and **mal** affect the meaning of the statements. What might be an equivalent for these words in English? (There is probably no single "right" translation, but expressions such as *why don't you* as in *Why don't you wear something stylish?* or *go ahead* as in *Go ahead and try wearing fashionable clothes!* or *just* as in *You should just wear something really cool!* might be feasible equivalents.)

Communication for All Students

A Slower Pace

24 Do this activity orally with the class. Have students come up with several different problems or situations, then let the whole class offer advice.

PRESENTING: Grammatik

Infinitive clauses Introduce the **Grammatik**, focusing on one point at a time. Give special attention to each section by giving additional examples. Contrast modals with other verbs to give students practice using infinitives with and without **zu**.
Examples:
Wir wollen ins Kino gehen. ⟶ Wir haben vor, ins Kino zu gehen. or Wir haben uns entschieden, ins Kino zu gehen.
Ich möchte baden gehen. ⟶ Ich werde versuchen, baden zu gehen.

Connections and Comparisons

Language-to-Language

Like German, French has no special present-tense constructions for verb conjugations, such as *I go/ I am going/ I do go.* Nuances in meaning are sometimes expressed with adverbs. You might want to have students give possible contexts (situations) for each of the following examples:

English: *I go home.*
German: **Ich gehe nach Hause.**
French: **Je rentre chez moi.**

English: *I am going home.*
German: **Ich gehe (gerade) nach Hause.**
French: **Je rentre chez moi.**

English: *I do go home.*
German: **Ich gehe (wirklich) nach Hause.**
French: **Je rentre chez moi.**

PRESENTING: So sagt man das!

• When presenting the phrases in **So sagt man das!**, ask students to pay special attention to the connecting words **weil, damit,** and **um ... zu.** They all are used to introduce an explanation or expression of purpose. Their meanings, though, as in English, are slightly different. Can students guess what they mean? If not, put the English equivalents on a transparency or on the board in random order and have students match the meanings. (**weil** *because,* **damit** *so that,* **um ... zu** *in order to*)

• Point out to students that a subordinate clause with the conjugated verb in last position follows the conjunctions **weil** and **damit**. Um ... zu is followed by an infinitive construction.

ZUM SCHREIBEN

Communication for All Students

Challenge

26 Have students initiate some statements with explanations, talking about things they do frequently, referring to school, then job, then friends, then home life. (Examples: **Ich helfe zu Hause, damit ich …; ich arbeite nach der Schule, um … zu …**)

Teacher Note

27 Remind students to use the correct word order in **dass**-clauses and to use reflexive verbs and verbs with separable prefixes properly.

Thinking Critically

Drawing Inferences Discuss with students the saying **Freunde erkennt man in der Not** and determine how it applies to the functions presented in the **Zweite Stufe.**

Von der Schule zum Beruf

29

Encourage students to research German clothing Web sites to find out about the latest trends in fashion.

Assess

▸ Testing Program, pp. 49–52
   Quiz 3-2A, Quiz 3-2B
   Audio CD3, Tr. 17

▸ Student Make-Up Assignments
   Chapter 3, Alternative Quiz

▸ Alternative Assessment Guide, p. 32

Teaching Resources
p. 77

PRINT
▸ Lesson Planner, p. 25
▸ Alternative Assessment Guide, p. 18

MEDIA
▸ One-Stop Planner
▸ Test Generator, Chapter 3

Writing Strategy

The targeted strategy in this reading is *determining the main idea of an article.* Students should learn about this strategy before beginning Question 2.

Prewriting
Building Context

On the board or on a transparency, write the name of a celebrity that students recognize. Give students one to two minutes to write down any physical features or other characteristics they associate with that person. Ask students to share their ideas with the class and write down any descriptive words or phrases they come up with. Ask students how one could group these words or phrases to organize the ideas. Point out that although each student was focusing on the same person, not all of them used the same words to describe that person. Each student had a unique mental image associated with that person.

Teaching Suggestions

• You might want to bring magazine pictures to class and let students choose one of the people depicted in the photos for their written descriptions.

• Students should use the motivating activity as an example and jot down as many descriptive German words as they can to describe their subject before starting their **Ideenbaum.**

Teacher Note

To help students organize their **Ideenbaum**, you might want to show them a sample on the overhead projector:

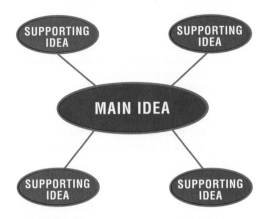

Writing
Teaching Suggestion

Encourage students to use the German vocabulary, expressions, and constructions that they know, rather than trying to *translate* every thought into German. Students should feel free to consult the end-of-book vocabulary lists to reactivate vocabulary they might have forgotten or to spur their creativity, but should avoid relying heavily on a bilingual dictionary. You might want to tell them that the point of the exercise is not to translate their English ideas into German, but to actively communicate using the language they have acquired thus far.

Post-Writing
Closure

Display the final drafts of students' descriptions along with the corresponding drawings in the classroom. This will reinforce student pride and will also serve to show first and second level students the tasks they will be able to carry out once they reach Level 3.

ZUM LESEN

Teaching Resources
pp. 78–79

PRINT
▸ Lesson Planner, p. 25
▸ Übungsheft, pp. 38–39
▸ Reading Strategies and Skills, Chapter 3
▸ Lies mit mir! 3, Chapter 3

MEDIA
▸ One-Stop Planner

Prereading
Building Context

Have students ask an older person to tell them the meanings of some of the following slang expressions: *the bee's knees, fly boy, peachy keen, can you dig it?, square, flower power*. With the class, decide which terms belong to which generation. ("Flapper" generation: *the bee's knees*, meaning *the best*; World War II generation: *fly boy*, meaning *pilot*; *peachy keen*, meaning *really good*; 50s generation: *can you dig it?*, meaning *can you understand or accept it?*; *square*, meaning *old fashioned*; 60s generation: *flower power*, meaning *persuasive power of gentleness and peacefulness*)

Reading
Teacher Note

The word **geil**, as used in the text, means **toll** or **großartig**. It is roughly equivalent to the American teen use of *cool!* or even *hot!*

Teaching Suggestion

In order to complete Activities 4–9, students will first need to go systematically through the many quotes in this article and sort them into three sources: teens, parents, and experts. Within the teens category, they then should distinguish between a) specific teens' quotes and b) terms that have been put into quotes by the writer in order to indicate that they are slang. Students may need help with the quotes-within-a-quote ('Ächz-Stöhn' and 'Kotz-Würg' from a woman's fifteen-year-old) and with determining the source of **Ich geb dir 20 Pfennig ...**, a saying supposedly recommended by psychologists to exasperated parents for use on their complaining offspring. This activity lends itself well to cooperative learning with

ZUM LESEN

students in groups of three or four: one or two researchers, a recorder, and a reporter. Groups could "specialize" in finding the quotes made by teens, parents, and experts.

Teacher Note

You might want to point out to students after they've completed Activity 5 that the adults in this article use some relatively negative language. The 36-year-old mother's **bescheuert** (*stupid*) is a slang term which has somewhat replaced **blöd. Gymnasial-Pädagoge Kutschke** chooses to use **maulfaul** instead of **mund-faul.** And the advice, "… erzähl's der nächsten Parkuhr!" is the way some Germans say *I don't want to hear about it!*

Thinking Critically

Analyzing The author of this article states that teen slang mixes a variety of areas of experience, including borrowings from English, technical German, and comic book language. Can students analyze the examples given in the text in terms of where they might have come from? Is this any different from the sources of the slang currently used by American teens? If so, how?

Teaching Suggestion

9 Presumably, the language expert is trying to reassure parents by saying that teen slang is "only a phase." Students need to know what kind of magazine this article appeared in, and who the intended audience must have been. (**Frauenzeitschrift;** parents)

Post-Reading

Teacher Note

Activity 12 is a post-reading task that will show whether students can apply what they have learned.

Closure

Using the German slang they already know and the terms introduced in this article, pairs of students should try to carry on a conversation using as much slang as possible.

Zum Lesen Answers

Answers to Activity 1
teen language/slang; teenagers and parents

Answers to Activity 2
Teenage slang is just a phase; **Der Sprachforscher … hält die Jugend-Sprüche lediglich für eine „Durchgangsstation".**

Answers to Activity 3
teenagers: Tanja, Uli, Olaf, Lilo; parents: mother of Tanja, mother of 15-year-old boy; experts: psychologists, educator (**Pädagoge**), language expert; a series of interviews in essay form

Answers to Activity 4
pfiff sich 'ne Mafia-Torte rein: hat eine Pizza gegessen; **legte Emaille auf:** hat sich geschminkt; **Kalkleisten:** Leute über 25; **Grufties:** Eltern/Erwachsene; **Lappen:** Geld; **heavy:** schwer
If the writer wants to be understood by her readers, she must make sure they know what the words mean.

Answers to Activity 5
Possible answers: **Die Sprüche klingen blöd. Die Teenager sind einfach faul. Die Eltern können ihre Kinder nicht verstehen. Teenager wollen miteinander über wichtige Sachen nicht reden oder diskutieren.**

Answers to Activity 6
Parents are no better. They only talk about the most essential things (**Die meisten Eltern sprechen zu Hause auch nur das Allernötigste**). They sit in front of the TV and don't say anything (**Die Alten sitzen doch nur stumm wie die Fische vor dem Fernseher**).

Answers to Activity 7
psychologists; Teenagers do talk and think about important issues (**Da sind Sachen dabei, die zeigen, dass die sich auf ihre Art ebenfalls Gedanken machen**). Their language shows they want to make things better (**Sie wollen … etwas Eigenes, Besseres erfinden**).

Answers to Activity 8
Parents should avoid imitating their children (**Nicht nachäffen, nicht mitspielen!**).

Answers to Activity 9
The writer quotes the language expert in the final paragraph to support the idea that teenspeak is just a phase.

Answers to Activity 10
Die Sprache von der Jugend ist nur eine Phase.

Answers to Activity 11
Die Jugendlichen werden wieder normal sprechen, wenn die Clique sich auflöst und die Berufe beginnen. Die heutige Jugend ist wie frühere Generationen: Sie wollen einfach etwas Eigenes erfinden. Ihre Sprüche zeigen, dass sie sich Gedanken machen.

> **PAGES 80–83**

MEHR GRAMMATIKÜBUNGEN

The **Mehr Grammatikübungen** activities are designed as supplemental activities for the grammatical concepts presented in the chapter. You might use them as additional practice, for review, or for assessment.

For more grammar presentations, review, and practice, refer to the following:
- Grammatikheft
- Grammar Tutor for Students of German
- Grammar Summary on pp. R22–R39
- Übungsheft
- Grammar and Vocabulary quizzes (Testing Program)
- Test Generator
- **Interaktive Spiele** at <u>go.hrw.com</u>

ANWENDUNG

Teaching Resources
pp. 84–85

PRINT
▶ Lesson Planner, p. 25
▶ Listening Activities, p. 22
▶ Video Guide, pp. 11–12, 14
▶ Grammer Tutor for Students of German, Chapter 3

MEDIA
▶ One-Stop Planner
▶ Video Program
  Videoclips: Werbung
  Videocassette 1, 32:24–33:18
▶ Audio Compact Discs, CD3, Tr. 15

Apply and Assess

 Using the Video
At this time, you might want to use the authentic advertising footage from German television Videocassette 1, 32:24–33:18. See *Video Guide*, p. 12, for suggestions

Portfolio Assessment
1 You might want to suggest this activity as a written and oral portfolio item for your students. See *Alternative Assessment Guide*, p. 18.

Teaching Suggestion
2 Before starting the activity, brainstorm with students words and expressions that will help them discuss the statements. Write each word or expression on the board or on a transparency. Examples:
Ich glaube, dass …
Ich finde es …, dass …
Ja schon, aber …
Ja, ich stimme da schon zu, aber …
Ich finde das überhaupt nicht richtig, denn …
Ich würde sagen, dass …
Meiner Meinung nach …

Multicultural Connection
Have students present these statements to students from other countries or various cultural backgrounds and report back to the class whether the opinions or reactions of those students differ from their own.

KANN ICH'S WIRKLICH?

This page helps students prepare for the test. It is a brief checklist of the major points covered in the chapter. The students should be reminded that it is only a checklist and not necessarily everything that will appear on the test.

For additional self-check options, refer students to the *Grammar Tutor* and the Online self-test for this chapter.

WORTSCHATZ

Review and Assess

Games
Play the game **Wörtersalat** using the vocabulary from this chapter. See p. 59C for the procedure.

Play the game **Heiße Kartoffel.** See Level 2, p. 269C, for the procedure. Here are some phrases or words you may want to use: **Biokost, Pechsträhne, herumblättern, vorhaben**

Teaching Suggestion
Ask students to complete the following statements:
… ist jemand, der gerade eine Pechsträhne hat.
Ich … und …, um mich zu entspannen.
Ich mache mir oft Gedanken über …
Ich habe vor, …
Ich spare Geld, um … zu …

Circumlocution
To use **Das treffende Wort suchen** as a vocabulary review, tell your students that you will first play the game with adjectives from both **Stufen,** then with verbs, and then with nouns. Verbs such as **zunehmen** and **abnehmen** can be described either verbally or by pantomime, as can many of the adjectives and nouns in this chapter. See p. 31C for procedures.

Teacher Note
Give the **Kapitel 3** Chapter Test: *Testing Program*, pp. 53–58 Audio CD 3, Trs. 18–19.

3

Aussehen: wichtig oder nicht?

Objectives

In this chapter you will review and practice how to

Erste Stufe

• ask for and express opinions

Zweite Stufe

• express sympathy and resignation
• give advice
• give a reason
• admit something and express regret

internet

go.hrw.com

ADRESSE: go.hrw.com
KENNWORT: WK3 DIE
NEUEN BUNDESLAENDER-3

◀ Ich hab meinen eigenen Stil.

Los geht's! · *Gut aussehen*

CD 3 Trs. 1–6

**Vier Gymnasiasten erzählen, warum ihnen ihr Aussehen wichtig ist
und was sie für ihr Aussehen tun.** CD 3 Tr. 1

Philipp: Ich achte schon darauf, wie ich aussehe. Wenn ich mir zum Beispiel etwas zum Anziehen kauf, so achte ich schon darauf, was zusammenpasst. Und man kauft sich halt auch Sachen, die „in" sind: Designer Jeans, Lederjacken, ja und Cowboystiefel, die sind halt jetzt „in". Und was das Essen angeht, na ja … ehrlich gesagt, ich mach mir keine großen Gedanken darüber. Ich ess, was mir schmeckt, und das dann, wenn möglich, in Massen. Ich trink zum Beispiel zu viel Cola, was auch nicht grad gesund ist. Aber es schmeckt halt. CD 3 Tr. 2

Sonja: Bei mir ist's ungefähr genauso. Ich mach auch Sport, hauptsächlich, weil man sich einfach besser fühlt. Und mit dem Essen pass ich schon auf; ich will ja nicht zunehmen. Und ja mit der Kleidung, hm … da trag ich eben, was mir gefällt. Manchmal ist es modisch, manchmal nicht so. Es muss aber immer bequem sein, aber nicht schlampig. CD 3 Tr. 3

Tanja: Ich würd schon sagen, mir ist mein Aussehen wichtig. Ich mach auch ein bisschen Sport, hauptsächlich Volleyball und Tennis. Und mit dem Essen? Ich ess halt weniger rotes Fleisch, mehr Hühnerfleisch, viel Obst und Gemüse. Ich möcht schon ein bisschen darauf achten, was gut für meine Gesundheit ist. CD 3 Tr. 4

Michael: Ich achte schon aufs Aussehen, und zwar … also, ich mach sehr viel Sport, um fit zu bleiben, ich ess vernünftig — viel Gemüse, weniger Fleisch — ich rauch nicht, ja … und wenn ich mal ein paar Pfund abnehmen will, dann mache ich eben mehr Sport. CD 3 Tr. 5

Sonja: Meine Mutter achtet darauf, dass wir vollwertige Sachen essen, Gemüse, Obst und so. Aber Biokost machen wir nicht. Man soll's nicht übertreiben.

Michael: Wenn ich mal down bin, mach ich halt Sport. Ich versuch, mich mit Sport abzulenken. Ich geh schwimmen oder joggen …

Tanja: Das tun, glaub ich, aber viele.

Michael: Ja schon, aber an der Schule gibt's halt einige Leute, die zweimal in der Woche ins Fitness-Center gehen und ein regelmäßiges Krafttraining machen.

Philipp: Ich halt überhaupt nichts von Bodybuilding. Ich fahr lieber Rad, oder ich geh wandern. Das ist gesünder.

Tanja: Wenn ich mich mal mickrig fühl, wenn etwas schief gegangen ist, dann mach ich erstens einmal Ordnung um mich herum. Ich räum mein Zimmer auf. Und zweitens mach ich mich hübsch. Ich zieh mich nett an, ich schminke mich — nicht zu viel, aber wirkungsvoll. Das hebt die gute Laune. Und drittens mach ich irgendetwas, was mir Spaß macht: ich hör gute Musik, ich les ein tolles Buch, oder ich beschäftige mich mit meinem Hobby, mit meinen Briefmarken. Dabei kann ich mich so richtig entspannen. CD 3 Tr. 6

Übungsheft, S. 27

1 Wer macht was?

a. Lesen/Schreiben Was tun die vier Schüler, um gut auszusehen? Mach eine Liste mit verschiedenen Kategorien, zum Beispiel Kleidung, Sport usw.!

	Kleidung	Sport	Essen	Ges
Philipp	kauft Klamotten, die „in" sind			
Sonja				

b. Schreiben Beantworte die folgenden Fragen!

1. Welche Schüler geben Gründe an? Schreib die Gründe auf!
2. Für wen steht Sport oben auf der Liste? Kleidung? Essen?
3. Was machen die Schüler, wenn sie „down" sind?

b. 1. Sonja: macht Sport, weil man sich dann besser fühlt; passt mit dem Essen auf, weil sie nicht zunehmen will. / Tanja: isst vernünftig, weil sie auf ihre Gesundheit achtet. / Michael: macht Sport, um fit zu bleiben.

b. 2. Sport: Michael / Kleidung: Philipp / Essen: Tanja

b. 3. Michael: schwimmt oder joggt. / Tanja: räumt auf; macht sich hübsch; macht, was ihr Spaß macht.

2 Und was machst du?

Schreiben Schreib deinen Namen auf die Liste mit den vier Schülern, und schreib auf, was du alles machst, um gut auszusehen!

3 Was berichten die Schüler?

Schreiben Erzähle jetzt einem Klassenkameraden, was die vier Schüler alles für ihr Aussehen tun! Was ist das Wichtigste aus den Berichten?

BEISPIEL **Michael achtet auf sein Aussehen: Er macht viel Sport, um fit zu bleiben. Er isst auch vernünftig und raucht nicht.**

Ein Fitnesstest

Lesen/Sprechen Machen Sie den Fitnesstest! Beurteilen Sie Ihre gegenwärtige Fitness anhand der nebenstehenden fünf Punkte mit je einer Bewertung von 1 bis 10 (1 = ungenügend, 10 = ideal). Essen Sie während der nächsten 3 Monate täglich frisches Obst. Dann wiederholen Sie die Bewertung und stellen Sie fest, wie sich Ihre Fitness verbessert hat!

Allgemeines Wohlbefinden	1	2	3	4	5	6	7	8	9	10
Körperliche Leistungsfähigkeit	1	2	3	4	5	6	7	8	9	10
Ausdauer	1	2	3	4	5	6	7	8	9	10
Konzentrationsfähigkeit	1	2	3	4	5	6	7	8	9	10
Lebensfreude, Spannkraft	1	2	3	4	5	6	7	8	9	10

Wortschatz

p. 59X   3–1

Tanja schminkt sich ab und zu.

Sie ist schlampig angezogen.

Er fühlt sich mickrig.

Sie macht sich hübsch.

auf Deutsch erklärt

sich entspannen   relaxen

auf das Aussehen achten   das Aussehen ist dir wichtig

mit dem Essen aufpassen   darauf achten, dass man Gutes isst

Was hältst du davon?   Wie findest du das?

die Sache   das Ding

zunehmen   Wenn man zu viel isst, nimmt man zu.

abnehmen   Wenn man eine Diät macht, nimmt man ab.

vollwertig   hat gute Nährstoffe

regelmäßig   immer zur gleichen Zeit

wirkungsvoll   effektiv

übertreiben   schlimmer oder besser machen, als es wirklich ist

schief gehen   nicht gut gehen

auf Englisch erklärt

Er macht sich Gedanken darüber.   *He's thinking about it.*

Sie beschäftigt sich mit Umweltproblemen.   *She is involved in environmental problems.*

Er lenkt sich mit Sport ab.   *Sport is a diversion for him.*

Was das Essen angeht …   *As far as food goes …*

Biokost schmeckt mir gut.   *I like organic food.*

Das hebt die gute Laune.   *That makes one feel better.*

Seine Kleidung passt gut zusammen.   *His clothes go together well.*

Übungsheft, S. 28–29, Ü. 1–4   Grammatikheft, S. 19–20, Ü. 1–2

4 Radio Pop-shop
Script and answers on p. 59G

Zuhören Zweimal in der Woche beantwortet Radio Pop-shop Höreranrufe junger Leute. Jungen und Mädchen können mit dem bekannten Jugend-Psychologen Dr. Uwe Behrens über ihre Probleme sprechen. — Hört euch das Problem eines Jugendlichen an und schreibt auf, was das Problem ist und was Dr. Behrens dem Jugendlichen rät (*advises*)!

CD 3 Tr. 7

5 Wie steht's bei dir?

Sprechen Interessierst du dich dafür, wie deine Klassenkameraden leben? Such dir eine Partnerin und frag sie, wie es bei ihr mit dem Essen, dem Aussehen, der Gesundheit und der Freizeit steht!

richtig? schlampig? wohl? Hobbys

gesund? modisch? krank? Sport

falsch? konservativ? mickrig? Fernsehen

> PARTNER **Wie steht's bei dir mit dem Essen? Wie ernährst du dich?**
>
> DU **Ich ernähr mich falsch. Ich ess zu viel …**

1. Wie steht's mit dem Anziehen? Wie ziehst du dich an?

2. Wie steht's mit deiner Gesundheit? Wie fühlst du dich?

3. Wie steht's mit deiner Freizeit? Womit beschäftigst du dich?

6 Was hebt deine Laune?

Schreiben Schreib alle Dinge auf, die deine Laune heben, wenn du einmal down bist! Erzähl dann der Klasse, was du machst! Sind folgende Dinge auf deiner Liste? Andere Dinge?

> DU **Wenn ich einmal down bin, mache ich zuerst Ordnung. Dann … danach …**

Buch lesen	s. hübsch machen
Musik hören	s. modisch anziehen
Zimmer aufräumen	s. beschäftigen mit …
Sport machen	s. ablenken mit …
spazieren gehen	s. hinlegen
Ordnung machen	s. etwas Nettes
Rad fahren	kaufen
Freund(in) anrufen	

So sagt man das!

Asking for and expressing opinions

To ask for someone's opinion, you might ask:

Was hältst du von Biokost?

Was würdest du dazu sagen?

To give your opinion, you could say:

Ich halte viel/wenig davon.
Ich halte nichts davon.
Ich würde sagen, dass …

Mehr Grammatikübungen, S. 80, Ü. 1

Übungsheft, S. 30, Ü. 5

Grammatikheft, S. 20, Ü. 3

How would you express these phrases in English? What case is used after **von?**[1]

7 Sind die Meinungen positiv oder negativ?

Zuhören Hör zu, wie verschiedene Schüler ihre Meinungen zu bestimmten Themen äußern! Worüber äußern sich die Schüler? Welche Meinung hat jeder Schüler? Ist sie positiv oder negativ? Mach dir Notizen!

CD 3 Tr. 8

Script and answers on p. 59G

---

1. the dative case

8 Und du? Was hältst du davon?

Sprechen Du unterhältst dich mit einem Klassenkameraden. Er will wissen, was du meinst. Was würdest du zu diesen Themen sagen? Was hältst du davon — viel? wenig? nicht viel? nichts? Gib Gründe an!

> PARTNER **Was hältst du von Kleidung, die „in" ist?**
> DU **Ich halte …** Answers will vary. E.g.: **Ich halte viel davon, weil man dann modisch aussieht.**

Kleidung, die „in" ist

Biokost

Bodybuilding

Designer Jeans

einer Diät ohne Fleisch

einem regelmäßigen Training

Grammatik

Da- and wo-compounds (Summary)

Read the following exchange:

> HOLGER **Worüber sprecht ihr?**
> ANTJE **Wir sprechen über die Schule.**
> HOLGER **Wir haben auch gerade darüber gesprochen.**

What would be the English equivalents of **worüber** and **darüber** in the sentences above? To what does **darüber** refer? Why does Holger say **darüber** rather than **über** followed by the pronoun **sie**?

Many verbs you know are paired with particular prepositions:

> Sie **spricht** gern **über** Politik, während sie **auf** den Bus **wartet.**

When you want to replace the nouns in those prepositional phrases with pronouns, you have to watch out for certain things.

1. When the object of the preposition is a person, use an appropriate pronoun to replace it. Always consider the case of the noun:

   > Ich warte **auf Anja/sie. Auf wen** wartest du?
   > Heiko kommt **mit Susi.** Wer kommt noch **mit ihr**? **Mit wem** kommst du?

2. However, when the object of the preposition is a thing, use the appropriate **da-** or **wo-**compound:

   > **Worauf** wartest du? Ich warte **auf den Bus/darauf.**
   > Ich weiß nicht, **worauf** sie warten.
   > Wir reden **über die Hausaufgaben/darüber. Worüber** redet ihr?

3. You should also use a **da-**compound when the object of the preposition is an entire clause, rather than just a noun.

   > **Woran** denkst du? Ich denke **daran, dass ich morgen zum Zahnarzt muss.**

Mehr Grammatikübungen, S. 80–81, Ü. 2–4

Übungsheft, S. 30–31, Ü. 6–9

Grammatikheft, S. 21–22, Ü. 4–7

9 Grammatik im Kontext

Sprechen Was machen deine Freunde? Frag sie mal! Benutze in jeder Frage eine wo-Konstruktion!

> DU **Also, ich beschäftige mich mit meinen Briefmarken. Und du?**
> PARTNER **Ich beschäftige mich …**

1. Ich beschäftige mich mit …
2. Ich interessiere mich nicht für …
3. Ich lenke mich mit … ab.
4. Ich halte nichts von …

Fahrradfahren	Computerspielen
Kleidung	Briefmarken
Mode	gesunde Ernährung
Bodybuilding	Zukunft
Kunst	Beruf
Musik	regelmäßiges
Aussehen	Training

Klassendiskussion

Sprechen Ein Klassenkamerad äußert die folgenden Meinungen. Was meint ihr dazu? Diskutiert darüber!

1. Es ist überhaupt nicht wichtig, wie man aussieht und was man anhat.

2. Alle Leute sollten nur Biokost essen!

3. Wenn man mal down ist, kann man überhaupt nichts machen. Da hilft nichts.

 Was sagst du dazu?

Sprechen Stell deiner Partnerin die folgenden Fragen! Reagiere auf das, was deine Partnerin sagt! Jedes Gespräch soll ein paar Mal hin- und hergehen.

| Ist dir gutes Aussehen wichtig? | Was willst du übers Wochenende machen? | Isst du immer alles, was auf den Tisch kommt? |
| Willst du ab- oder zunehmen, oder so bleiben, wie du bist? | Wie geht's dir denn heute? Warum? | Wie oft machst du Sport? |

 Wichtig oder nicht?

Sprechen Jetzt sprecht ihr über Dinge, die euch wichtig sind! Was sagen deine Klassenkameraden? Was sagst du? Warum ist das so?

PARTNER **Wie wichtig ist dir dein Aussehen?**

DU **Ich würde sagen, mein Aussehen ist mir sehr wichtig.**

PARTNER **Warum? Kannst du mir das erklären?**

DU **(Wenn ich mich zum Beispiel modisch anziehe, fühl ich mich wohl.)**

> deine Hobbys   deine Ernährung   die Schule
> deine Gesundheit   deine Freunde
> Sport   deine Kleidung   dein Aussehen

 Für mein Notizbuch

Schreiben Schreib einen Kurzbericht zum Thema: „Mein Aussehen ist mir (nicht) wichtig". Schreib etwas über deine Ernährung, über Sport und über Kleidung!

 Und deine Meinung über Kleidung?

Sprechen Erzähl einer Partnerin, was du von Kleidung hältst! Wie wichtig sind dir neue Sachen? Was trägst du gern? Was nicht? Muss alles zusammenpassen? Wie finden die Eltern deine Kleidung?

 Was hältst du von Kleidung?

Schreiben Schreib einen Absatz zum Thema Kleidung! Hier sind ein paar Schreibhilfen.

| Sachen tragen, die | halten von | was andere denken, ist | |
| ist/sind mir wichtig | am liebsten tragen | darauf achten, dass | zusammenpassen |

Die deutsche Subkultur

Tekkno-Fieber

Tekkno-Parties locken tausende Jugendliche an. Kids in abenteuerlichen Verkleidungen warten vor den Discos auf Einlaß: Sie tragen Bauhelme, Sonnenbrillen, Gummihandschuhe, Mundschutz oder Plastiksäcke. Einer hat sogar einen Staubsauger auf dem Rücken. Drinnen dröhnt die härteste Musik der Welt: Rhythmus ist alles, Melodie nichts. Die Tekkno-Fans begleiten das Ganze mit Trillerpfeifen.

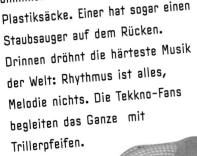

Lisa, 15
Ideologie

Gymnasiastin, 9. Klasse. Mutter Spanisch-Lehrerin an der Volkshochschule. Vater Internist. „Ich bin Punk, weil ich gegen die Ellenbogen-Gesellschaft rebelliere. Ich hab' mal einen Spruch gelesen, der mir sehr gut gefällt: ‚Ich fühle mich einsam, wenn ich eine Hand suche und nur Fäuste finde.'"

Je schlampiger, umso schöner! Zum Grunge-Look gehören strähnige Haare (einfach Haarwachs in die Spitzen kneten), lässig weite Opa-Hemden oder karierte Shirts.

STANDARDS: 1.2, 2.1, 2.2, 3.2, 4.2

68

RaverRaver
GruNgerPuNker
Grunger Punker

Raver (engl. to rave = rasen), die Hippies der 90er — sanft, gegen Gewalt. Sie feiern die längsten Partys (24 Stunden), ihre Musik (Tekkno) zerreißt Eltern das Trommelfell, 220 Baßschläge in der Minute. Ihr Look: Latzhosen, Minikleider mit „adidas"® Streifen, Springer-Stiefel.

Tom, 18
Liebe

„Ich habe gerade eine ewig lange Beziehung beendet. Wir haben uns auseinander entwickelt, weil ich Raver wurde und nicht wie sie Abi machen wollte. Mein Traum wäre es, eine Freundin zu finden, die mir ähnlich ist. Ich finde es schön, wenn es jemanden gibt, dem man vertrauen kann."

Sprache

„Im Raver-Slang bedeutet >>ChillOut<<: sich ausruhen. >>Afterhour<<-Party: die Party nach der Party, morgens ab sechs Uhr bis mittags."

Raver Girls lieben Plüschtier Rucksäcke (z.B. Drache oder Dinosaurier)

LEXIKON

Wörter, die voll im Trend liegen, und was sie bedeuten

DAS IST DURCHAUS
ich stimme total zu

END DIE MEILE
weit entfernt

ENTERGIGANT
mehr als gigant, gigantischer

GESCHMEIDIG DIE LORCHE
prima, stark, optimal

KRASS IN DER BIRNE SEIN
verrückte Ideen haben

PSEUDO
jemand, der so tut, als ob er etwas ist, was er in Wirklichkeit nicht ist

A. 1. Schau die Fotos an, und lies die verschiedenen Texte! Wie viele verschiedene Trends kannst du feststellen? Beschreibe sie! Worauf beziehen sich die Trends hauptsächlich? Auf Mode? Musik? Sprache? Oder Weltanschauung?

2. Welche Trends sind dir schon bekannt? Gibt es ähnliche Trends in den USA? Was für Unterschiede gibt es?

B. Lies den Text links! Worum geht es? Was bedeuten die Ausdrücke? Wie sagt man sie auf Englisch? Wie kann man sie anders auf Deutsch ausdrücken?

A. 1. vier; Answers will vary; **Punk: Weltanschauung / Grunge: Mode / Tekkno: Musik / Rave: Kombination von allem.**
B. **Umgangssprache der Jugend;** (see chart); I agree / very far away / humongous / fantastic / to be crazy / a wannabe; **einverstanden / ganz weit weg / ganz groß / toll; Spitze / komisch sein / ein Möchtegern.**

STANDARDS: 1.2, 2.1, 2.2

Weiter geht's! ▪ *Immer mit der Mode. Oder?*

CD 3 Tr. 9-13

Unsere vier Freunde erzählen, was sie von der Mode halten. CD 3 Tr. 9

Philipp: Ich geb zu, dass ich mich von der Mode schon ein wenig beeinflussen lass. Meine Mutter sagt schon manchmal: „für diese Klamotten zahl ich dir nichts dazu. Die sind mir viel zu ausgefallen. Was hast du denn bloß für einen Geschmack? Du hättest dir das nicht kaufen sollen!" Aber mir gefällt's eben. CD 3 Tr. 10

Tanja: Ich mach auch mit der Mode mit. Das geb ich ohne weiteres zu. Mit der Mode kann man ausdrücken, wie man sich fühlt. Wie ich aussäh, ... das sagt auch etwas über mich aus, wie ich bin und so. Und das ist wichtig für mich. Ich zieh mich also schon modisch an. Es macht Spaß, ja und ... äh ... ich fühle mich wohl. Ich bedaure nur, dass ich oft nicht genug Geld habe, um mir wirklich schicke Sachen kaufen zu können. Manche Sachen näh ich mir auch selbst, um Geld zu sparen. CD 3 Tr. 11

Sonja: Ich kenn Leute, die wollen eben bei anderen immer gut ankommen. Und sie glauben, sie können das mit der Mode machen. Die tun mir Leid, diese Leute, die ... die machen alles nur mit, weil es gerade „in" ist. Ich würde mich nie so ausgeflippt anziehen, wie es manche tun. Ich seh halt, was mir gefällt, und das kauf ich mir halt. Aber ich muss auch zugeben, ich pass mich schon irgendwie meinen Freunden an. Man möchte sich nicht von andern beeinflussen lassen, aber man tut es halt doch. Man möchte auch andere nicht nach der Kleidung beurteilen. Aber leider tut man das auch oft, ohne es zu wollen. Wenn ich jemand seh, der sich ganz verrückt anzieht, na, da denk ich, wie kann man nur so herumlaufen? Haben die Leute denn überhaupt keinen Geschmack? Die müssen ganz schön blöd sein! CD 3 Tr. 12

Michael: Ich finde, man sollte schon ein bisschen mit der Mode gehen, aber nicht unbedingt den letzten Schrei tragen. Vieles sieht echt dumm aus, wenn man da mal in einer Modezeitschrift herumblättert. Ich finde, man sollte seinen eigenen Stil entwickeln. Ich zieh eigentlich nur das an, was mir gefällt. Zu Hause lauf ich meist im Trainingsanzug herum. Ich könnte es den CD 3 Tr. 13 ganzen Tag in Jeans nicht aushalten.

Übungsheft, S. 33

16 Hast du alles verstanden?

a. **Sprechen** Was für ein Text ist das? Ein Bericht? Ein Interview? Eine Erzählung? ein Interview

b. **Lesen/Schreiben** Lies den Text noch einmal, und stell für jeden Schüler fest, was der Hauptpunkt der Aussage ist! Welche Gründe geben die Schüler an, um den Hauptpunkt zu unterstützen? P: lässt sich von der Mode beeinflussen. / T: drückt mit Mode Gefühle aus. / S: interessiert sich nicht für verrückte Mode. / M: findet, dass man seinen eigenen Stil entwickeln sollte.   P: Mode gefällt ihm. / T: Es ist ihr wichtig, dass Mode etwas über sie aussagt; Mode macht ihr Spaß, sie fühlt sich wohl. / S: Es ist nicht ihr Geschmack. / M: findet, dass vieles, was modisch ist, dumm aussieht.

17 Was halten die vier von Mode?

Lesen/Schreiben Lies die Aussagen der vier Schüler über Mode! Dann schreib auf, zu welchem Schüler jede Beschreibung passt!

1. Hat eine Mutter, die die Klamotten von ihrem Kind kritisiert. Philipp
2. Will mit der Mode ausdrücken, wie er oder sie sich fühlt. Tanja
3. Zieht sich nie ausgeflippt an. Sonja
4. Möchte andere Leute nicht nach ihrer Kleidung beurteilen. Sonja
5. Glaubt, dass viele Leute keinen guten Geschmack haben. Sonja
6. Will schick sein, aber muss nicht den letzten Schrei tragen. Michael
7. Kauft sich manchmal sehr ausgefallene Sachen. Philipp
8. Bedauert, dass er oder sie nicht genug Geld für wirklich schicke Sachen hat. Tanja
9. Passt sich mit der Kleidung den Freunden an. Sonja
10. Möchte sich nicht von anderen beeinflussen lassen, aber tut es doch. Sonja
11. Will einen eigenen Stil entwickeln. Michael
12. Kauft sich, was ihm oder ihr gefällt. Philipp; Sonja; Michael
13. Findet, dass vieles in Modezeitschriften dumm aussieht. Michael
14. Näht sich manche Sachen selbst. Tanja
15. Läuft zu Hause immer im Trainingsanzug herum. Michael

18 Jeder wird jetzt Designer

Sprechen Wähl dir eine Schülerin oder einen Schüler in diesen Interviews aus, und zeichne ein tolles Outfit, das diese Person wahrscheinlich tragen würde! Zeig deine Zeichnung deinen Klassenkameraden! Können sie erraten (*guess*), zu wem das Outfit passt?

19 Und du? Was sagst du dazu?

Sprechen Überleg dir folgende Fragen, und stell sie einem Partner! Gib deinem Partner so viel Auskunft, wie du kannst! Tauscht dann die Rollen aus!

1. Machst du mit der Mode mit? Gib ein Beispiel dazu!
2. Was ist für dich wichtig, wenn du an Kleidung denkst?
3. Du möchtest bei deinen Freunden gut ankommen. Was tust du?
4. Würdest du dich ausgeflippt anziehen? Wann? Was würdest du tragen?
5. Wie läufst du gewöhnlich herum? In der Schule? Zu Hause?

Zweite Stufe

Objectives Expressing sympathy and resignation; giving advice; giving a reason; admitting something and expressing regret

WK3 DIE NEUEN BUNDESLAENDER-3

Eine Freundin gibt Rat

TANJA   Ja, Elke. Du bist's? Aber was ist denn los mit dir? Wie siehst du denn bloß aus?

ELKE   Warum, wie seh ich denn aus?

TANJA   Ist alles in Ordnung mit dir? Wie geht's denn? Erzähl mal!

ELKE   Na ja, zur Zeit geht mal alles wieder schief bei mir.

TANJA   <u>Das ist schlimm!</u> Hast du Probleme zu Hause? In der Schule?

ELKE   Überall! In der Schule, zu Hause, mit meinem Freund …

TANJA   <u>Wie schrecklich!</u> Kann ich dir irgendwie helfen?

ELKE   Nö. <u>Ich hab eben jetzt eine Pechsträhne</u>, weißt du, und <u>da kann man nichts machen.</u>

TANJA   Das würd' ich nicht sagen. <u>An deiner Stelle würd' ich</u> erst mal ein wenig positiver denken.

ELKE   Ach, komm! <u>Was kann ich schon tun? Es ist halt so.</u>

TANJA   <u>Versuch doch mal</u>, irgendetwas zu tun, was dir Spaß macht, verstehst du? <u>Du solltest …</u>

ELKE   Du hast gut reden! Du hast …

TANJA   Lass mich mal ausreden! <u>Du solltest</u> mal etwas tun, was deine Laune hebt!

ELKE   Was denn?

TANJA   <u>Warum gehst du</u> nicht mal joggen? <u>Oder spiel doch</u> Volleyball draußen im Park!

ELKE   Ach, Quatsch! Und wer spielt denn schon mit?

TANJA   Du, kein Problem! Ich ruf schnell mal einige Klassenkameraden an, und dann spielen wir! So was hebt meine Laune. Das hilft. Jedenfalls mir.

auf Deutsch erklärt

ausgefallen angezogen interessante Klamotten tragen, die nicht jeder hat

bei anderen gut ankommen wenn dich andere Leute mögen

Ich pass mich meinen Freunden an. Ich möchte so sein, wie meine Freunde, und machen, was sie machen.

Er trägt den letzten Schrei. Er trägt, was gerade Mode ist.

in der Zeitung herumblättern die Zeitung nicht lesen, sondern nur Seite für Seite ansehen

auf Englisch erklärt

Ich lasse mich von der Mode beeinflussen.
I let myself be influenced by fashion.

Aber ich mache nicht mit der Mode mit. *But I don't go along with fashion.*

Man drückt sich durch Kleidung aus. *You can express yourself with clothes.*

Ich gebe schon zu, dass ich einige Menschen nach ihrer Kleidung beurteile. *I admit that I judge some people by their clothes.*

Sagt das etwas über solche Leute aus? *Does that say something about such people?*

p. 59X

Sie näht gern.

Er spart Geld.

Sie zieht sich verrückt an.

Übungsheft, S. 34, Ü. 1

Grammatikheft, S. 23, Ü. 8–9

So sagt man das!

Expressing sympathy and resignation

Grammatikheft, S. 24, Ü. 10

You have already learned some ways of expressing sympathy:

Es tut mir Leid! Wirklich!

Other ways of expressing sympathy are:

Das ist ja schlimm!
Das muss schlimm sein!
Wie schrecklich!
So ein Pech!

And resignation:

Da kann man nichts machen.

To express resignation you could say:

Was kann ich schon tun?
Es ist halt so.
Ich hab eben eine Pechsträhne.

20 **Wo sagen sie das?** For answers, see underlined words in text on page 72.

Lesen/Sprechen Lest euch jetzt das Gespräch zwischen Tanja und Elke noch einmal durch! Sucht zusammen die Stellen heraus, die Mitleid (*sympathy*), Resignation und Rat ausdrücken!

21 **Dein Freund hat Probleme**

Sprechen Dein Partner erzählt dir etwas über seine Probleme. Du drückst dein Mitleid aus, aber dein Freund ist resigniert. Vielleicht kannst du ihm auch einen Rat geben.

FREUND **Ich habe eine Fünf in Geschichte bekommen.**
DU **Das ist ja schlimm!**
FREUND **Was kann ich schon tun? Es ist halt so.**

Answers will vary. E.g.: **Vielleicht solltest du mehr lernen.**

1. Ich bin immer müde.
2. Ich hab mein Taschengeld verloren.
3. Meine Freundin mag mich nicht mehr.
4. In Mathe bin ich eine absolute Niete (*loser*).
5. Meine Eltern schimpfen (*scold*) die ganze Zeit mit mir.

Giving advice

3–2

Here are several ways of making suggestions and giving advice:

Warum machst du dich nicht mal hübsch?
Versuch doch mal, dich fesch anzuziehen!
Du solltest mal etwas Tolles tragen.
An deiner Stelle würde ich versuchen, positiver zu denken.
Lass dir doch die Haare schneiden!

Übungsheft, S. 34–35, Ü. 2–4

Grammatikheft, S. 24, Ü. 11

22 Welche Ratschläge passen? Script and answers on p. 59H

Zuhören Welche Ratschläge passen für wen?

CD 3
Tr. 14

a.

b.

c.

d.

23 Komm, ich geb dir mal einen guten Rat!

Sprechen Dein Partner ist heute etwas down. Rate ihm, was er tun soll! Er reagiert positiv oder negativ.

Du   **Warum liest du nicht mal ein Buch?**
Partner   **Tja, ich habe keine Lust dazu.**   *oder*
    Gute Idee!

Einige Ratschläge

sich mal hübsch machen	sich mit einem Hobby ablenken
ein gutes Buch lesen	sich die Haare schneiden lassen
vernünftig essen	mehr auf das Aussehen achten
Sport machen	sich etwas modisches kaufen
positiver denken	einen Tag zu Hause bleiben
Ordnung schaffen	
sich modisch anziehen	
eine Reise machen	

24 Hast du einen guten Rat?

Schreiben Denk an fünf verschiedene Leute, die du gut kennst! Hast du einen guten Rat für sie? Schreib auf einen Zettel, was du ihnen rätst!

Beispiel   Meine Schwester isst sehr viele Süßigkeiten. Ich rate ihr:
    An deiner Stelle würde ich nicht so viele Süßigkeiten essen!   *oder*
    Warum versuchst du nicht, mehr Obst zu essen!   *oder*
    Du solltest wirklich nicht so viele Süßigkeiten essen!

Infinitive clauses

Compare the following sentences:

> **Ich versuche, dir zu helfen.**   *I am trying to help you.*
> **Ich bin bereit, nach Hause zu gehen.**   *I am ready to go home.*
> **Ich habe vor mitzumachen.**   *I plan to participate.*

Find the verbs in the sentences above. Compare verb positions in English and German. What differences do you see? What do you notice about the verb **mitmachen** in the sentences above?

1. In infinitive clauses, the German infinitive is always preceded by **zu** and is placed at the end of the sentence. With separable-prefix verbs, **zu** is inserted between the prefix and the verb. **Zu** is never added in sentences when the conjugated verb is a modal, **werden** or **würde**!

2. A comma precedes the infinitive clause whenever anything is added to it, for example:

> **Ich versuche zu lernen.**
> **Ich versuche, heute Abend Deutsch zu lernen.**

3. Infinitive clauses can also be introduced by **um** and **ohne**. For example, **um zu** (*in order to*) and **ohne zu** (*without …ing*).

> **Ich näh mir Kleider selbst, um Geld zu sparen.**
> **Man tut das oft, ohne es zu wollen.**

Mehr Grammatikübungen, S. 81–82, Ü. 5–7

(Übungsheft, S. 36, Ü. 5–6)   (Grammatikheft, S. 25–26, Ü. 12–15)

---

25   ### Grammatik im Kontext

Sprechen/Schreiben Was haben deine Klassenkameraden vor? Jeder sagt, was für Vorsätze er oder sie hat.

gesund leben	nicht alles mitmachen
etwas abnehmen	sich nicht beeinflussen
fit bleiben	lassen
sich modisch anziehen	andere nicht nach
sich mit Sport ablenken	der Kleidung beurteilen
etwas zunehmen	seinen eigenen
positiver denken	Stil entwickeln

BEISPIEL   **DU**   Ich habe vor, weniger zu essen. Und du?

       PARTNER   Ich habe vor, mehr Obst und Gemüse zu essen.

So sagt man das!

Giving a reason

Mehr Grammatikübungen, S. 82–83, Ü. 8–9

There are different ways of expressing purpose and giving a reason. If someone asks you, for example: **Wozu machst du so viel Sport?**

You could answer:

> **Ich mache so viel Sport,**   {   **weil ich mich nach dem Sport besser fühle.**
>   **damit ich mich besser fühle.**
>   **um mich besser zu fühlen.**

(Grammatikheft, S. 27, Ü. 16)

26 Grammatik im Kontext

Sprechen Deine Partnerin sagt dir, warum sie verschiedene Sachen macht. Sag ihr, ob du das auch machst und wozu! Wenn du es nicht machst, sag warum!

PARTNER **Ich mach viel Sport, damit ich fit bleibe.**

DU **Bei mir ist das auch so. Ich mach auch viel Sport, um fit zu bleiben.**

1. Ich kauf mir teure Klamotten, damit ich …
2. Ich zieh mich nett an, damit ich …
3. Ich kauf mir Modezeitschriften, damit ich …
4. Ich geh in Bioläden, damit ich …
5. Ich ess keine Süßigkeiten, damit ich …
6. Ich mach eine Diät, damit ich …

So sagt man das!

Admitting something and expressing regret

To admit something, you might say:

Ich geb's zu.
Ich geb's zu, dass ich …
Ich muss zugeben, dass …

To express regret, you have already learned:

Leider!
Ich bedaure, dass …
Ich bedaure es wirklich, dass …

Übungsheft, S. 36–37, Ü. 7–9

Grammatikheft, S. 27, Ü. 17

27 Mensch, gib's doch zu!

Sprechen Du unterhältst dich mit einer Partnerin. Du fragst, ob sie folgende Sachen macht. Deine Partnerin gibt es zu und fragt dich auch. Was sagst du dazu? Bedauerst du das?

DU **Sag mal, machst du mit der Mode mit?**

PARTNERIN **Na ja, ich geb's zu, dass ich mit der Mode mitmache. Und du?**

DU **Ich eigentlich auch. Manchmal bedaure ich es, dass …** *oder* **Nein. Das …**

sich ab und zu ausgeflippt anziehen	zu viel Geld für Kleidung ausgeben
sich manchmal die Haare färben	zu kritisch sein
sich oft neue Klamotten kaufen	Leute nach der Kleidung beurteilen
sich zu sehr seinen Freunden anpassen	zu konservativ sein

28 Das bedaure ich, aber …

Schreiben Denk an die Dinge in deinem Leben, die du bedauerst und schreib sie auf! Wie lang ist deine Liste? Vergleiche deine Liste mit der Liste eines Mitschülers!

BEISPIEL **Ich bedaure, dass ich mich nicht fit halte.**

29

 Von der Schule zum Beruf

You are a summer intern at your uncle's advertising agency in Germany. The boss has asked you to write a report to be used in marketing products to teens. You should include information about how teenagers dress nowadays and their attitudes toward fashion, grooming, nutrition, and personal appearance. Then make suggestions about which products or clothing would be hot sellers, and which would not. *Optional:* You must also present your report to the company bigwigs during a meeting. Have a hand-out, a big chart, and overhead transparencies or PowerPoint slides.

Zum Schreiben

Have you ever read a text in which the characters were so vividly described that they seemed to be standing right in front of you? That is because the writer had carefully selected words that evoke strong visual images. In this activity, you will describe a person, either someone you know or a famous or fictional character, so that your classmates can visualize that person in their minds.

Personen beschreiben

Such dir eine Person aus, die du gut beschreiben kannst! Denk an das Aussehen dieser Person, zum Beispiel das Gesicht und die Kleidung! Wähl dann die wichtigsten Eigenschaften aus, und beschreib diese Person!

> ✏ **Schreibtipp Organizing your ideas** No matter what you are writing, it is important to organize your thoughts around a main idea and choose details that support this main focus. There are many ways to organize your supporting details. For example, you can organize your ideas chronologically, spatially, or in order of importance. Always choose an organization pattern that fits your writing task.

A. Vorbereiten

1. Mach einen Ideenbaum für deine Beschreibung! Auf den „Stamm" schreibst du ein Adjektiv oder eine Eigenschaft, die deiner Person am nächsten kommt! Das soll der Hauptpunkt deiner Beschreibung sein. Dann wähle Adjektive, Eigenschaften und Gewohnheiten, die diesen Hauptpunkt unterstützen, und schreib sie auf die „Zweige"!

2. Such jetzt ein Organisationsprinzip für deine Ideen! Sind sie sinnvoll, so wie du sie auf den „Baum" geschrieben hast, oder musst du ein paar Ideen umstellen, um deine Beschreibung zu organisieren?

B. Ausführen

Verbinde jetzt die Ideen auf deinem Ideenbaum zu einer fließenden Beschreibung! Pass gut auf, dass der Hauptpunkt im Mittelpunkt steht! Vergiss auch nicht: Man soll diese Person fast sehen können, wenn man deine Beschreibung liest!

C. Überarbeiten

1. Stell jetzt fest, ob deine Beschreibung die richtige Wirkung hat! Lies deine Beschreibung einem Partner vor! Dein Partner soll gleichzeitig versuchen, die Person zu zeichnen. Frag den Partner, was ihm an der Person auffällt! Was hält er von dieser Person?

2. Denk jetzt an die folgenden Fragen: Konnte dein Partner der Beschreibung folgen? Konnte er die Person gut zeichnen? Hat er den Hauptpunkt und die wichtigen Eigenschaften auch verstanden? Mach die nötigen Veränderungen, um deine Beschreibung zu verbessern!

3. Wenn du mit deiner Beschreibung und ihrer Wirkung zufrieden bist, lies den Text noch einmal durch! Hast du alles korrekt buchstabiert? Hast du auch Kommas und Punkte richtig gesetzt? Mach die nötigen Korrekturen!

4. Schreib jetzt deinen korrigierten Text noch mal ab!

Zum Lesen

Das Thema, das uns alle angeht...

Das macht viele Erwachsene richtig sprachlos

Unsere heutige Jugend und ihre Sprüche

Es begann harmlos, mit einem gedehnten „Ey, affengeil!" Von da an fing Tanja (16) jeden Satz mit „Ey …" an. „Ey, Mom", „Ey, Dad" — und ihre Schulfreunde hießen alle „Ey, Alter!"

Sie aß keine Pizza mehr, sondern „pfiff sich 'ne Mafia-Torte rein". Wenn Tanja im Bad vor dem Spiegel stand, schminkte sie sich nicht, sondern „legte Emaille" auf.

„Sag mal, was sind denn das für Sprüche?" fragte ihre Mutter. „Reden die in deiner Klasse jetzt alle so?"

In der Tat — sie tun's.

„Die heutige Jugend will sich auf diese Art bewußt von der Sprache der Erwachsenen abheben", stellten Psychologen fest.

„Da kriegt Mama 'n Föhn!"

„Jede Clique hat ihre eigenen Sprüche, auf die sie stolz ist." Und die Begriffe wechseln so schnell, daß die „Kalkleisten" (Leute über 25) kaum mitkommen.

„Wenn ich richtig loslege", sagt Uli (14) lachend zur Reporterin, „dann brennt bei Paps ein Chip durch, und Mama kriegt 'nen Föhn."

Was ist „in"?

Lesestrategie Determining the main idea of an article
When reading magazine or newspaper articles, you can usually determine the main idea by reading the title, captions, and the first paragraph. In the case of a feature article, which is in essay form, you will also need to look carefully at the last paragraph.

For answers, see p. 59W.

Getting Started

1. Read the title, subtitle, and caption. In your opinion, what is this passage about? On what group of people does it focus?

2. Now read the first and last paragraphs. Based on this information, what would you say is the main idea? Support your answer with evidence from the passage.

3. Scan the article to see what types of people the writer quotes. How has the writer organized the article? Is it a story, a report, or something else?

A Closer Look

4. Now read the article once carefully. Find some examples of teenage slang. What do they mean, according to the writer's "translations?" Do you think such translations are needed? Why or why not?

In der neuen Jugendsprache wird alles durcheinandergemischt: Technik, Englisch, Comic-Sprechblasen …

„Sobald mein 15jähriger im Haushalt helfen muß", klagt eine Mutter (36), „ist alles ‚Ächz-Stöhn' oder ‚Kotz-Würg' — das klingt wirklich bescheuert".

Ganz unberechtigt sind die Sorgen vieler Eltern nicht.

Der Marburger Gymnasial-Pädagoge Joachim Kutschke (49) hält die heutige Generation für maulfaul. „Ihr fehlt das Bedürfnis, sinnvoll miteinander zu reden. Wozu lange Diskussionen, Begründungen, Erklärungen. Das stört doch nur."

Die Jugendlichen, mit denen er darüber sprach, sehen das anders. Olaf (17): „Was wollt ihr überhaupt? Die meisten Eltern sprechen zu Hause auch nur das Allernötigste." Und Lilo (16): „Die Alten sitzen doch nur stumm wie die Fische vor dem Fernseher."

Und umgekehrt. „Mein 15jähriger kommt heim, geht wortlos in sein Zimmer und dröhnt sich den ganzen Tag mit Musik voll."

Allerdings sehen viele Psychologen in den neuesten „Sprach-Schöpfungen" der Jugend auch Gutes. „Da sind Sachen dabei, die zeigen, daß sie sich auf ihre Art ebenfalls Gedanken machen."

Über das Waldsterben zum Beispiel. „Sauer macht lustig — der Wald lacht sich krank", geistert zur Zeit durch die Schulen. Sie wollen, wie frühere Generationen auch, die Welt der „Grufties" (Erwachsenen) entlarven, ablehnen und dafür etwas Eigenes, Besseres erfinden.

„Das war schon immer das Bedürfnis der Jugend", geben auch die Pädagogen zu.

… alles schon mal dagewesen

„Und dieses Gefühl finden die Kids dann eben oberaffen-megaturbo-geil. Aber sie sind dabei nicht anders als wir, als wir jung waren."

„Fetenmäßig" muß alles stimmen, „actionmäßig" der Tag in Ordnung sein, also immer was los sein.

Aber das kostet „Lappen" (Geld), und für die braucht man wieder die „Kalkleisten" (Eltern), und die haben da manchmal leider einen „Hörsturz", wenn's zuviel wird …

Echt „heavy" (schwer), das Leben, hohl, gichtig, schlaff, abgefahren. Aber alles schon mal dagewesen.

Der einzige Rat, den Psychologen Eltern geben können, ist: Nicht nachäffen, nicht mitspielen! Wobei natürlich eigene Sprüche erlaubt sind wie „Ich geb' dir 20 Pfennig, erzähl's der nächsten Parkuhr!"

Der Sprachforscher Johannes Schwittalla hält die Jugend-Sprüche lediglich für eine „Durchgangsstation": „Wenn die Clique sich auflöst, der Beruf beginnt, sprechen die alle wieder ganz normal." Logisch, ey?

—*Emily Reuter*

5. Write one to three sentences summarizing adults' complaints about teenage slang.

6. How do the teenagers in the article respond to those complaints?

7. Who comes to the defense of teenagers' language? What do these people have to say about the slang used by teens?

8. What advice do the psychologists give parents?

9. Why does the writer quote the language expert in the final paragraph?

10. Was meinst du jetzt, was der Hauptgedanke von diesem Artikel ist? Schau auf deine Antwort von Frage 2, und ändere deine erste Aussage, wenn nötig! Schreib deine Formulierung auf!

11. Welche Sätze oder Absätze unterstützen den Hauptgedanken des Textes? Schreib drei unterstützende Aussagen unter deine Formulierung des Hauptgedankens!

12. Schreib jetzt eine Zusammenfassung des Textes! Verwende dabei die Informationen von Fragen 10 und 11! Vergiss nicht, auch einen Schlusssatz zu schreiben!

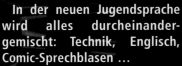
Übungsheft, S. 38-39, Ü. 1-6

Mehr Grammatikübungen

 **ADRESSE:** go.hrw.com
KENNWORT: WK3 DIE NEUEN BUNDESLAENDER-3

Answers

1 Du erklärst, was du und deine Freunde von verschiedenen Dingen halten. Du möchtest dann wissen, was andere Leute davon halten. Schreib die folgenden Fragen ab, und schreib dabei in die Lücken die korrekte Form des Verbs **halten (von)**, *to think (of)*. **(Seite 65)**

1. Ich halte viel von Biokost. Und du, was _____ du davon?   hältst
2. Wir halten viel von Sport. Und ihr, was _____ ihr davon?   haltet
3. Ich halte viel von Ordnung. Und die Tanja, was _____ sie davon?   hält
4. Wir halten viel von guter Musik. Und diese Schüler, was _____ sie davon?   halten
5. Ich halte viel von guten Büchern. Was _____ Sie davon, Herr Müller?   halten
6. Wir halten viel von der Umwelt. Was _____ du davon?   hältst
7. Wir halten viel vom Segeln. Und was _____ ihr davon?   haltet
8. Und was _____ du vom Angeln?   hältst

2 Du sagst deinen Freunden, mit welchen Dingen du dich beschäftigst, und dann fragst du sie, womit sie sich beschäftigen. Schreib die folgenden Fragen ab, und schreib dabei in eine Lücke das korrekte "**wo** + Präposition" Fragewort und in die andere Lücke die korrekte Form des Reflexivpronomens! **(Seite 66)**

1. Ich mache mir Gedanken über Geld. Und _____ machst du _____ Gedanken?   worüber; dir
2. Ich beschäftige mich mit Politik. Und _____ beschäftigst du _____ ?   womit; dich
3. Ich lenke mich mit Sport ab. Und _____ lenkst du _____ ab?   womit; dich
4. Ich achte auf mein Aussehen. Und _____ achtest du?   worauf
5. Ich spreche gern über die Zukunft. Und _____ sprichst du gern?   worüber
6. Ich denke oft an meine Schulzeit. Und _____ denkst du oft?   woran

3 Frag zwei Freunde, ob sie die gleichen Sorgen haben wie du und deine Freundin. Schreib die folgenden Fragen ab, und schreib dabei in die Lücken das korrekte "**da** + Präposition" Pronomen und in die andere Lücke das korrekte Reflexivpronomen! (**Seite 66**)

1. Wir achten sehr auf unser Aussehen. Achtet ihr auch sehr _____ ? darauf
2. Wir denken immer an eine gesunde Ernährung. Denkt ihr auch _____ ? daran
3. Wir sprechen gern über die Umwelt. Sprecht ihr auch gern _____ ? darüber
4. Wir lenken uns mit Musik ab. Lenkt ihr _____ auch _____ ab? euch; damit
5. Wir beschäftigen uns mit unserer Zukunft. Beschäftigt ihr _____ auch _____ ? euch; damit
6. Wir machen uns Gedanken über Mode. Macht ihr _____ auch Gedanken _____ ? euch; darüber

4 Du befasst (*occupy*) dich mit verschiedenen Angelegenheiten (*affairs*), und du fragst eine Klassenkameradin, ob sie sich mit den gleichen Angelegenheiten befasst. Schreib die folgenden Fragen ab, und schreib dabei die korrekten Fragewörter in die Lücken! (**Seite 66**)

1. Ich denke an meine Zukunft. Und _____ denkst du? woran
2. Ich denke an meinen Freund in Deutschland. Und _____ denkst du? an wen
3. Ich mache mir Gedanken über die Ferien. _____ machst du dir Gedanken? Worüber
4. Ich mache mir Gedanken über meine Oma. _____ machst du dir Gedanken? Über wen
5. Ich warte auf den Bus in die Stadt. Und _____ wartest du? worauf
6. Ich warte auf meine Kusine. Und _____ wartest du? auf wen
7. Ich rede gern über Politik. Und _____ redest du gern? worüber
8. Ich rede gern über meine Biolehrerin. _____ redest du gern? Über wen

Zweite Stufe

Objectives Expressing sympathy and resignation; giving advice; giving a reason; admitting something and expressing regret

5 Du sagst zwei Freunden, was er und sie machen sollen. Du leitest deinen Ratschlag (*advice*) mit den Worten **Versuch doch mal, …** (*Why don't you try to …*) ein. Schreib die folgenden Sätze ab, und schreib in die Lücken einen Infinitivsatz mit der Information, die in Klammern gegeben ist! (**Seite 75**)

1. (Er soll ein gutes Buch lesen.) Versuch doch mal, _____ . ein gutes Buch zu lesen
2. (Sie soll etwas Geld sparen.) Versuch doch mal, _____ . etwas Geld zu sparen
3. (Er soll zwei Kilo abnehmen.) Versuch doch mal, _____ . zwei Kilo abzunehmen
4. (Sie soll das Geld umwechseln.) Versuch doch mal, _____ . das Geld umzuwechseln
5. (Er soll die CD umtauschen.) Versuch doch mal, _____ . die CD umzutauschen
6. (Sie soll weniger fernsehen.) Versuch doch mal, _____ . weniger fernzusehen
7. (Sie soll sich ab und zu schminken.) Versuch doch mal, _____ . dich ab und zu zu schminken
8. (Sie soll sich hübsch machen.) Versuch doch mal, _____ . dich hübsch zu machen

6 Du rätst einem Freund, was er machen soll. Schreib die folgenden Ratschläge ab, und schreib dabei in die Lücken einen Infinitivsatz anstatt der gegebenen Befehlsform (*command form*)! (**Seite 75**)

1. Entspann dich mal!   Versuch doch mal, _____ .   dich zu entspannen
2. Zieh dich mal schick an!   Versuch doch mal, _____ .   dich schick anzuziehen
3. Pass dich mal den andern an!   Versuch doch mal, _____ .   dich den andern anzupassen
4. Drück dich mal besser aus!   Versuch doch mal, _____ .   dich besser auszudrücken
5. Erinnere dich mal daran!   Versuch doch mal, _____ .   dich daran zu erinnern
6. Beschäftige dich damit!   Versuch doch mal, _____ .   dich damit zu beschäftigen

7 Du erklärst, warum du verschiedene Dinge tust. Schreib die folgenden Sätze ab, und schreib dabei in die Lücken einen Infinitivsatz, der mit **um** beginnt! Verwende dabei die Information in Klammern! (**Seite 75**)

1. (Ich spare Geld.)   Ich fahre mit dem Rad, _____ .   um Geld zu sparen
2. (Ich sehe gut aus.)   Ich trage schicke Sachen, _____ .   um gut auszusehen
3. (Ich nehme nicht zu.)   Ich esse vernünftig, _____ .   um nicht zuzunehmen
4. (Ich mache mit der Mode mit.) Ich trage den letzten Schrei, _____ .   um mit der M. mitzumachen
5. (Ich passe mich schnell an.)   Ich lerne viel über Bayern, _____ .   um mich schnell anzupassen
6. (Ich mache beim Sport mit.)   Ich rauche nicht, _____ .   um beim Sport mitzumachen

8 Du gibst auf jeweils drei verschiedene Arten einen Grund an. Schreib die folgenden Sätze ab, und drücke dabei den Grund, der in Klammern steht, auf drei verschiedene Arten aus! (**Seite 75**)

(Ich möchte Deutsch lernen.)

1. Ich gehe in den Deutschkurs, weil _____ .   ich Deutsch lernen möchte
2. Ich gehe in den Deutschkurs, um _____ .   Deutsch zu lernen
3. Ich gehe in den Deutschkurs, damit _____ .   ich Deutsch lerne

(Ich möchte zwei Kilo abnehmen.)

4. Ich mache viel Sport, weil _____ .   ich zwei Kilo abnehmen möchte
5. Ich mache viel Sport, um _____ .   zwei Kilo abzunehmen
6. Ich mache viel Sport, damit _____ .   ich zwei Kilo abnehme

(Ich möchte mich umziehen.)

7. Ich gehe gleich nach der Schule nach Hause, weil _____ .   ich mich umziehen möchte
8. Ich gehe gleich nach der Schule nach Hause, um _____ .   mich umzuziehen
9. Ich gehe gleich nach der Schule nach Hause, damit _____ .   ich mich umziehen kann

9 Sieh dir jeweils die Zeichnungen und die Gründe in Klammern an, und schreib dann die folgenden Sätze zu Ende. Du drückst dabei deine Gründe auf drei verschiedene Arten aus. Achte darauf, dass du manchmal das Modalverb weglassen musst und dass du manchmal ein anderes Modalverb hinzufügen musst. **(Seite 75)**

(Du möchtest gesund bleiben.)

1. Ich esse Vitamin-C-reiche Früchte,

    a. um _____ .   gesund zu bleiben

    b. damit _____ .   ich gesund bleibe

    c. weil _____ .   ich gesund bleiben möchte

(Du möchtest Geld sparen.)

2. Ich nähe meine Klamotten selbst,

    a. um _____ .   Geld zu sparen

    b. damit _____ .   ich Geld spare

    c. weil _____ .   ich Geld sparen möchte

(Du möchtest dort tauchen.)

3. Ich fahre auf eine Insel im Karibischen Meer,

    a. um _____ .   dort zu tauchen

    b. damit _____ .   ich dort tauchen kann

    c. weil _____ .   ich dort tauchen möchte

(Du möchtest dort italienische Tomaten kaufen.)

4. Ich gehe zur Gemüsefrau am Markt,

    a. um _____ .   dort italienische Tomaten zu kaufen

    b. damit _____ .   ich dort italienische Tomaten kaufen kann

    c. weil _____ .   ich dort italienische Tomaten kaufen möchte

Anwendung

ADRESSE: go.hrw.com
KENNWORT: WK3 DIE NEUEN BUNDESLAENDER-3

1 **a.** Du möchtest dich mit richtiger Ernährung fit halten. Wie viel weißt du über den Nährwert von Lebensmitteln? Lies die Umfrage! Entscheide dann, ob die Aussagen richtig oder falsch sind!

Umfrage: Nährwert von Lebensmitteln

1. Das beste Brot ist dunkles Brot.

richtig ☐
falsch ☐

2. Braune Eier sind gesünder als weiße Eier.

richtig ☐
falsch ☐

3. Kartoffeln machen dick.

richtig ☐
falsch ☐

4. Fisch hat weniger Nährwert als Fleisch.

richtig ☐
falsch ☐

5. Öl ist Öl. Es spielt keine Rolle, welches man im Haushalt gebraucht.

richtig ☐
falsch ☐

6. Orangen und Zitronen sind die Vitamin-C-reichsten Früchte.

richtig ☐
falsch ☐

7. Brot macht dick.

richtig ☐
falsch ☐

8. Alle Mineralwässer sind gleich.

richtig ☐
falsch ☐

9. Wenn es heiß ist, soll man nichts oder weniger trinken.

richtig ☐
falsch ☐

10. Brauner Zucker enthält mehr Vitamine und Mineralien als weißer Zucker.

richtig ☐
falsch ☐

CD 3 Tr. 15   Script on p. 59I

b. Du hörst im Radio einen Bericht über gesunde Ernährung. Schau dir nochmal die Umfrage von Übung 1 an und die Antworten, die du gewählt hast! Wie viele Antworten hast du richtig?

c. Schreib jetzt die Aussagen aus der Umfrage von Übung 1 in richtig lautende Aussagen um! 1. c. Answers will vary. Encourage students to use the information presented in the listening activity (1. b.).

2 Diskutiert die folgenden Äußerungen!

— Was haltet ihr von diesen Bemerkungen?

— Wie würdet ihr darauf reagieren?

> **Schuluniformen sind eine gute Lösung für Kleiderprobleme in der Schule.**
> Ute

> **Eins ist sicher: gut gekleidete Leute finden eher Freunde als andere.**
> Sven

> **Wenn bei uns in der Klasse jemand etwas Neues anhat, wollen die andern gleich das Etikett mit der Marke sehen. Wer sich keine teuren Klamotten leisten kann, schneidet als erstes das Etikett heraus. Aber das merken die andern auch sofort. Was soll man da tun?**
> Tanja

> **Ich trag gern verrückte Klamotten. Ich trag auch einen Ohrring, und ab und zu färb ich mir auch die Haare. Ich will mit meinem Aussehen provozieren. Und wie die Leute reagieren! Besonders ältere Leute sprechen mit mir über mein Aussehen. Und es ist ein tolles Gefühl, wenn die Leute merken, dass ich gar nicht so negativ bin, wie sie immer glauben.** Uwe

> **Wer nicht perfekt gekleidet ist, bekommt nie einen guten Job. Ich hab neulich eine Einladung zu einer Fete bekommen. Am Ende stand: Festliche Kleidung erwünscht.**
> Michael

3 Schreib eine Antwort zu einer dieser fünf Äußerungen! Lies danach deinen Klassenkameraden vor, was du geschrieben hast!

4

Rollenspiel

Spiel einen Dialog mit einem Partner vor der Klasse! Folgende Anleitungen helfen dir dabei.

1. Du hast dir eine Jacke und eine Hose gekauft, die deinem Vater überhaupt nicht gefallen. Er kritisiert dich. Schreib auf, was er alles sagen kann! Gebrauche diese Stichwörter!

wie aussehen — Hose, eng — Jacke, ausgefallen — Geschmack? — nicht kaufen sollen — nichts dazu zahlen

2. Du verteidigst (*defend*) dich. Schreib auf, was du alles sagen kannst! Gebrauche diese Stichwörter!

Freunde haben auch solche Klamotten — mit der Mode mitmachen — „in" sein — Aussehen wichtig — Sachen waren billig — nicht genug Geld für schicke Sachen

Kann ich's wirklich?

Can you ask for and express opinions? (p. 65)

1 How would you ask for an opinion and give your own opinion of

a. Biokost?　a. E.g.: **Was hältst du von Biokost?; Ich halte viel davon.**

b. eine Ernährung ohne Fleisch?　b. E.g.: **Was hältst du von einer Ernährung ohne Fleisch?; Ich halte nichts davon.**　c. E.g.: **Was würdest du zu Bodybuilding sagen?; Ich würde sagen, dass es Spaß macht.**

c. Bodybuilding?

Can you express sympathy and resignation? (p. 73)

2 How would you express sympathy or resignation in response to these statements?

a. Ich hab jetzt schon die zweite Fünf in Geschichte.　a. E.g.: **Das ist ja schlimm!**

b. Du hast wohl Probleme mit deiner Frisur!　b. E.g.: **Ja, was kann ich schon tun?**

c. Stell dir vor, ich hab meine Kamera verloren!　c. E.g.: **So ein Pech!**

d. Meine beste Freundin hat mich nicht zu ihrer Fete eingeladen.　d. E.g.: **Das tut mir Leid! Wirklich!**

e. Der Peter, der passt sich seinen Freunden überhaupt nicht an.

e. E.g.: **Da kann man nichts machen. Er ist halt so.**

Can you give advice? (p. 74)

3 What advice would you give to a friend who told you the following?

a. Meine Mutter sagt, ich zieh mich zu schlampig an.　a. E.g.: **Warum ziehst du nicht mal was Konservatives an?**　b. E.g.: **Lass dir doch die Haare schneiden!**

b. Sie sagt, meine Haare sind viel zu lang.

c. Sie sagt, mein Zimmer ist nie aufgeräumt.　c. E.g.: **An deiner Stelle würde ich es mal aufräumen.**　d. E.g.: **Versuch doch mal, etwas weniger Fernsehen zu schauen!**

d. Sie sagt, dass ich zu viel fernsehe.

Can you give a reason? (p. 75)

4 How would you complete these statements so that they tell why you do these things?

a. Ich ess eigentlich keine Süßigkeiten, ...　a. E.g.: **weil sie nicht gut für meine Zähne sind.**

b. Mit dem Essen pass ich schon auf, ...　b. E.g.: **damit ich nicht zunehme.**

c. Ich treibe natürlich viel Sport, ...　c. E.g.: **um fit zu bleiben.**

d. Ich beschäftige mich aber auch mit meinen Hobbys, ...　d. E.g.: **weil es mir Spaß macht.**

Can you admit something and express regret? (p. 76)

5 How would you admit and express regret that you

a. paid too much for ...?　a. E.g.: **Ich geb's zu, dass ich zu viel Geld für (diese Jacke) ausgegeben habe. Leider habe ich zu viel Geld für (diese Jacke) ausgegeben.**

b. judge your friends by their clothes?　b. E.g.: **Ich muss zugeben, dass ich meine Freunde nach ihrer Kleidung beurteile. Ich bedaure es wirklich, dass ich meine Freunde nach ihrer Kleidung beurteile.**

c. dress in a ... way (schlampig)?

c. E.g.: **Ich geb's zu, dass ich mich schlampig anziehe. Ich bedaure, dass ich mich schlampig anziehe.**

Erste Stufe

 p. 59X

Giving opinions

Du hältst viel von unserer Lehrerin, oder?	*You think highly of our teacher, don't you?*

Other useful words and phrases

s. Gedanken machen über (acc)	*to think about*
s. entspannen	*to relax*
s. ablenken mit (sep)	*to divert oneself (with)*
s. beschäftigen mit	*to keep busy with*
s. schminken	*to put on makeup*

achten auf (acc)	*to pay attention to*
zunehmen (sep)	*to gain weight*
abnehmen (sep)	*to lose weight*
übertreiben	*to exaggerate*
schief gehen (sep)	*to go wrong*
treffen	*to meet*
zusammenpassen (sep)	*to go together, match*
aufpassen (sep)	*to pay attention*
was (das) angeht	*as far as (that) goes*
heben	*to lift*
hübsch	*pretty, handsome*
mickrig	*lousy*
schlampig	*sloppy*

vollwertig	*nutritious*
regelmäßig	*regularly*
hauptsächlich	*mainly*
wirkungsvoll	*effective*
die Kleidung	*clothing*
die Laune	*mood*
die Sache, -n	*thing*
die Biokost	*organic food*
das Krafttraining	*weight lifting*

Zweite Stufe

Expressing sympathy and resignation

Das muss ja schlimm sein!	*That must be really bad!*
Wie schrecklich!	*How terrible!*
Ich hab eben eine Pechsträhne.	*I'm just having a streak of bad luck.*
Da kann man nichts machen.	*There's nothing you can do.*
Was kann ich schon tun?	*Well, what can I do?*
Es ist halt so.	*That's the way it is.*

Giving advice

Komm, ich geb dir mal einen guten Rat!	*Okay, let me give you some good advice.*
Versuch doch mal, etwas zu machen!	*Why don't you try to do something?*
Du solltest mal ins Kino gehen.	*You should go to the movies.*

An deiner Stelle würde ich mehr lernen.	*If I were you, I'd study more.*
Lass dir doch die Haare schneiden!	*Why don't you get your hair cut?*

Other useful words and phrases

Das sagt etwas über dich aus.	*That says something about you.*
mitmachen mit (sep)	*to go along with*
beurteilen nach (dat)	*to judge according to*
ankommen bei (sep)	*to be accepted by*
s. anpassen (sep, dat)	*to conform to*
beeinflussen	*to influence*
ausdrücken (sep)	*to express*
zugeben (sep)	*to admit*
entwickeln	*to develop*
versuchen	*to attempt, try*
vorhaben (sep)	*to plan*

aushalten (sep)	*to endure, stand something*
nähen	*to sew*
sparen	*to save money*
herumblättern (sep)	*to leaf through (a newspaper)*
der Geschmack	*taste*
das Mitleid	*pity, sympathy*
der letzte Schrei	*the latest fashion*
die Kleider (pl)	*clothes*
ausgefallen	*unusual*
verrückt	*crazy*
ohne	*without*
ohne weiteres	*easily, readily*
ohne ... zu machen	*without doing ...*
um ... zu machen	*in order to do ...*
damit (conj)	*so that, in order to*

Würzburg

Teaching Resources
pp. 88–91

PRINT
▶ Lesson Planner, pp. 26, 78
▶ Video Guide, pp. 15–16

MEDIA
▶ One-Stop Planner
▶ Video Program
  Würzburg
  Videocassette 1, 34:01–37:27
▶ Map Transparency

go.hrw.com
WK3 WUERZBURG

PAGES 88–89

THE PHOTOGRAPH
Background Information

• The history of Würzburg can be traced back as far as the Celtic time (700 B.C.). In A.D. 741, Bonifatius, who soon after became archbishop of Mainz, founded the **Bistum** (*bishopric*) of Würzburg. The city was then ruled for centuries by **Fürstbischöfe** (*prince-bishops*), and the diets of the Holy Roman Empire sometimes met in Würzburg. Secularized in 1802, Würzburg became part of Bavaria in 1815.

• Würzburg is situated at the beginning of the **Romantische Straße,** which follows the Tauber River, a tributary of the Main. The **Romantische Straße** then continues south to Rothenburg ob der Tauber, to Augsburg, and finally ends in Hohenschwangau, near the Neuschwanstein Castle.

• The statue in the foreground of the photograph represents St. Kilian, the apostle of the Franks and patron saint of Würzburg. July 8th is celebrated in his honor in Würzburg.

• The building in the background is the **Festung Marienberg** (*Marienberg fortress.*) It sits 266 meters (872 feet) above the city. The fortress was originally a Celtic **Fliehburg** (*refuge*). In 706, **Herzog Heltan II.** commissioned a church to be built on the

Marienberg. Today, it remains the oldest church building (**Rundkirchenbau**) east of the Rhine. Between 1253 and 1719, it became the residence of the **Fürstbischöfe.** After several fires, Julius Echter transformed it into a Renaissance-style castle. Then, after the new **Residenz** was built in town, the fortress was used for military purposes through much of the 19th century. Today it houses the **Mainfränkisches Museum.**

Thinking Critically

Comparing and Contrasting Ask students if they can think of other German towns or cities that have a castle or a fortress located above the city. (Examples: Heidelberg—**Schloss;** Eisenach—**Wartburg**)

Geography Connection

Ask students to trace the path of the **Romantische Straße** in an atlas. Can students think of reasons why this stretch of road might have received its name? (Examples: beautiful landscape, picturesque towns)

THE ALMANAC AND MAP

 Würzburg's coat of arms shows a tilted red and gold flag on a silver lance before a black background. This coat of arms is related to that of the former duchy of Franconia and has been used since the sixteenth century, when it replaced an older emblem displaying an image of St. Kilian. The colors red and gold are also found in the coat of arms of the modern district **Unterfranken,** whose capital is Würzburg.

Terms in the Almanac

• **Tilman Riemenschneider:** He was the principal wood-carving artist of the German Gothic period. He came to Würzburg in 1483 and created altars, statues, and sculptures that are now found throughout the region. Riemenschneider became a member of the Würzburg city council in 1509 and served as mayor from 1520 to 1521. During the **Bauernkriege,** he supported the farmers who fought against the **Kirchenfürst** (*ecclesiastical prince*) Konrad von Thingen. After the defeat of the farmers at Marienberg, Riemenschneider was taken to prison and tortured for eight weeks. He died a broken man and forgotten artist in 1531. The **Marienkapelle** in Würzburg features 14 **Riemenschneiderfiguren** as well as replicas of his famous carvings of Adam and Eve.

- **Mathias Grünewald:** Grünewald, whose real name was Mathis Gothardt Nithardt, was a major figure in a generation of great German Renaissance painters that also included Albrecht Dürer and Lucas Cranach. He remained relatively unknown until the 20th century. Today only about 13 of his paintings remain. His greatest masterpiece is the **Isenheimer Altar** (*Isenheim Altarpiece*), which is now in the Colmar Museum in Alsace.

- **Julius Echter:** Prince-bishop Julius Echter of Mespel-brunn was responsible for several noteworthy contributions to the city of Würzburg. Following two damaging fires to the Marienberg fortress and residence of the bishops in 1572 and 1600, he was largely responsible for the renovations that gave Marienberg a much more elegant and Renaissance-style look. In 1576, Echter founded the **Juliusspital,** which was built in the baroque style. Finally, in 1582, he founded the University of Würzburg.

- **Weinbau:** October, the month of wine harvesting, is one of the best times to be in Würzburg because of the many festivals. Between the Main and Danube rivers lies the heavily agricultural region of Franconia. *Stein* and *Leisten* are among the finest wines of this area. Their grapes grow in the vineyards on the slopes surrounding the Marienberg fortress.

- **Zwiebelkuchen:** This is a pastry dish in which browned onions are spread over a bread crust. A mixture of egg, cream, and spices is poured on top of the onions and baked. It is served hot with wine or beer.

Geography Connection

Can students think of other regions in Germany that are known for their quality wines? (Examples: the Rhine and Mosel river areas, Baden)

Map Activities

Have students look at the map and infer why the location of Würzburg would be good for trade. (You may also want to use *Map Transparency* 1.) Discuss with students the relationship of the agricultural region, resources, and the navigable Main River to Würzburg's economy. (Examples: good conditions for growing grapes because of mild climate and fertility of land; access to waterways to export goods)

> **PAGES 90–91**

THE PHOTO ESSAY

1 The **Residenz** was built under Balthasar Neumann from 1719 to 1744 and is considered one of the most significant palaces of Europe. This building took the place of Marienberg as residence of the **Fürstbischöfe.** The Baroque building encompasses five large halls, more than 300 rooms, and a church. The cellar was built to hold 1.4 million liters (369,600 gallons) of wine. One of the most impressive features is a unique staircase designed by Balthasar Neumann with vaulted ceilings that were painted by the Italian artist Giovanni Battista Tiepolo.

2 **Das Haus zum Falken** is a former inn famous for its rich stucco work. The building was heavily damaged in 1945 during World War II, but was later rebuilt to its original form. It now houses the tourist office and the public library.

3 The **Alte Mainbrücke mit den Apostelfiguren** is shown in the foreground of this photograph. The **Alte Mainbrücke** was built as the first stone bridge in the 12th century. It was restored from 1473 to 1543 to its present form. In the 18th century, large statues of apostles were added to the bridge's pillars, including the one of St. Kilian.

3 Rising in the background of the photo is **Dom St. Kilian.** Although construction of **Dom St. Kilian** began in 1045, the main building was not dedicated until 100 years later. During the 13th, 16th, and 17th centuries, the church was expanded and renovated. In 1945, it was heavily damaged, and reconstruction was not completed until 1967. Inside are several tombs, a christening font dating back to 1279, a Renaissance-style pulpit from 1609, and a wood carving of Christ and two apostles from 1502–1506.

Komm mit nach Würzburg!

Map of Germany

Bundesland: Bayern

Einwohner: 128 000

Fluss: Main

Sehenswürdigkeiten: Festung Marienberg, Dom, Residenz, Haus zum Falken

Berühmte Künstler: Tilman Riemenschneider (1460-1531), Mathias Grünewald (ca. 1480-1529)

Fürstbischöfe: Rudolf von Scherenberg (1466-1495), Julius Echter (1545-1617), Franz von Schönborn (1674-1746)

Industrie: Weinbau, Textil, Elektronik, Tourismus

Bekannte Gerichte: Bratwürste, Zwiebelkuchen, Zwetschgenkuchen

go.hrw.com
WK3 WUERZBURG

VIDEO

STANDARDS: 2.2, 3.1

Nordsee · DÄNEMARK · Ostsee
NIEDER-LANDE
Berlin
POLEN
BEL.
Würzburg · TSCHECHIEN
LUX.
B A Y E R N
FRANK-REICH
ÖSTERREICH
SCHWEIZ

▶ St. Kilian, Frankenapostel und Schutzheiliger Würzburgs, mit Festung Marienberg, einst Residenz der Fürstbischöfe

Würzburg

Würzburg feierte 1992 seinen 1250. Geburtstag! Die Geschichte dieser Stadt reicht bis in die keltische Zeit zurück. Schon im 8. Jahrhundert erhob St. Bonifatius den damals kleinen Ort zum Bistum. Im 12. Jahrhundert erhob Kaiser Friedrich Barbarossa die Bischöfe von Würzburg zu Herzögen von Franken. Damit begann eine Entwicklung, die in den folgenden Jahrhunderten Würzburg zu einem kulturellen Zentrum Europas machte.

Im Zentrum steht der Dom St. Kilian, im Jahre 1045 begonnen. Der Dom ist die viertgrößte romanische Kirche Deutschlands. Im Innern befinden sich die Grabmäler von Bischöfen, u.a. die Grabmäler von Rudolf von Scherenberg (gest. 1495) und Lorenz von Bibra (gest. 1519), beide von Riemenschneider aus Salzburger Rotmarmor geschaffen.

internet

ADRESSE: go.hrw.com
KENNWORT:
WK3 WUERZBURG

1 Residenz

Die fürstbischöfliche Residenz, der bedeutendste Profanbau des deutschen Barocks, wurde 1719-1744 unter der Leitung von Balthasar Neumann errichtet. Im Innern ist das großartige Treppenhaus mit dem berühmten Freskogemälde von Tiepolo und der einzigartig dekorierte Kaisersaal, in dem jährlich die Konzerte des Mozartfestes stattfinden.

2 Haus zum Falken
Das Haus zum Falken, das heute das Fremdenverkehrsamt beherbergt, hat die schönste Rokokofassade (1751) der Stadt.

3 Mainbrücke und Würzburg
Die Alte Mainbrücke mit den Apostelfiguren führt in die Innenstadt zum Dom.

Kapitel 4: Verhältnis zu anderen
Chapter Overview

Kapitel 4: Verhältnis zu anderen
Chapter Resources

Lesson Planning

One-Stop Planner

Lesson Planner with Substitute Teacher Lesson Plans, pp. 26–30, 78

Student Make-Up Assignments
- Make-Up Assignment Copying Masters, Chapter 4

Listening and Speaking

Listening Activities
- Student Response Forms for Listening Activities, pp. 27–30
- Additional Listening Activities 4-1 to 4-6, pp. 31–34
- Scripts and Answers, pp. 124–132

Video Guide
- Teaching Suggestions, p. 18
- Activity Masters, pp. 19–20
- Scripts and Answers, pp. 62–63, 74

Activities for Communication
- Communicative Activities, pp. 13–16
- Realia and Teaching Suggestions, pp. 66–70
- Situation Cards, pp. 119–120

Reading and Writing

Reading Strategies and Skills Handbook, Chapter 4

Lies mit mir! 3, Chapter 4

Übungsheft, pp. 40–52

Grammar

Grammatikheft, pp. 28–36

Grammar Tutor for Students of German, Chapter 4

Assessment

Testing Program
- Grammar and Vocabulary Quizzes, **Stufe** Quizzes, and Chapter Test, pp. 67–80
- Score Sheet, Scripts and Answers, pp. 81–87

Alternative Assessment Guide
- Portfolio Assessment, p. 19
- Performance Assessment, p. 33

Student Make-Up Assignments
- Alternative Quizzes, Chapter 4

 Online Activities
- **Interaktive Spiele**
- **Internet Aktivitäten**

 Video Program
- Videocassette 1

 Audio Compact Discs
- Textbook Listening Activities, CD 4, Tracks 1–8
- Additional Listening Activities, CD 4, Tracks 13–18
- Assessment Items, CD 4, Tracks 9–12

 Teaching Transparencies
- Situations 4-1 to 4-2
- **Mehr Grammatikübungen** Answers
- **Grammatikheft** Answers

One-Stop Planner CD-ROM

Use the **One-Stop Planner CD-ROM with Test Generator** to aid in lesson planning and pacing.

For each chapter, the **One-Stop Planner** includes:
- Editable lesson plans with direct links to teaching resources
- Printable worksheets from resource books
- Direct launches to the HRW Internet activities
- Video and audio segments
- Test Generator
- Clip Art for vocabulary items

Kapitel 4: Verhältnis zu anderen

Projects

Ein Tisch ist ein Tisch

In this activity, students will recreate the story **Ein Tisch ist ein Tisch** by illustrating it with a captioned collage. Begin this project after students have completed the **Zum Lesen** section. This project is designed for students to do in small groups.

MATERIALS

✂ **Students may need**
- posterboard
- paper
- catalogs
- scissors
- markers
- dictionaries

SUGGESTED SEQUENCE

1. Discuss the project with students and divide the class into small groups.

2. Within their groups, students brainstorm and make an outline of what they feel should be included in their recreation of the story. Notes should include how certain parts can be illustrated and what types of pictures and sources could be useful.

3. Students plan the layout of the collage and begin with the artistic part of the project.

4. Students write a caption for each illustration.

5. Groups present their completed projects to the class.

GRADING THE PROJECT

Suggested point distribution (**total = 100 points**)
Illustration/Creativity............................40
Written information..............................30
Oral presentation................................30

Games

Wort für Wort

Playing this game will help students review the vocabulary of the **Erste Stufe** along with previously learned vocabulary.

Preparation Divide the class into groups of three to four students. Each group assigns one member to be the writer/recorder and another student to be the reporter. Prepare a list of words you plan to review and make sure that each group has a piece of paper and a pen or pencil.

Procedure The use of books is not allowed during this game. Call out a word from the list and signal the groups to begin writing down as many related words as they can within a set amount of time. All members should actively suggest vocabulary, which the writer records. When time is called, the writer transfers his or her group's list to the board. Go over each list, review the meanings, and verify spelling before awarding a point for the vocabulary item. The group with the most related words wins.

Examples:

reden	sprechen
	der Mund
	die Sprache
	diskutieren
angehören	die Clique
	die Familie
	die Gruppe
	der Klub

Culture

Mini-Geschichte

This story accompanies Teaching Transparency 4-1. The **Mini-Geschichte** *can be told and retold in different formats, acted out, written down, and read aloud to give students additional opportunities to practice all four skills.*

Liebe Bettina!

Ich brauche unbedingt Rat. Ich hab nur noch Krach mit meinen Eltern. Vor zwei Wochen hab ich meinen Kumpel mit meinem Auto fahren lassen und er hatte einen Unfall. Meine Eltern meinen, dass mein Freund für die Reparatur *(repair)* bezahlen soll. Ich geb ihnen ja Recht, aber mein Freund hat kein Geld. Jetzt schimpfen meine Eltern nur noch mit mir. Sie schimpfen, wenn ich meine Stereoanlage oder den Fernseher einschalte. Gestern hat mein Vater sogar gesagt, dass er meinen Haarschnitt nicht leiden kann! Was soll ich nur machen?

Traditions

Bayerische Julius-Maximilians-Universität

Universitätsstadt Würzburg

Würzburg gehört zu den ältesten Universitätsstädten im deutschsprachigen Raum. 1402 erhielt der Fürstbischof von Würzburg die Genehmigung von Papst Bonifaz IX. eine Universität in Würzburg zu gründen. Finanzielle Unsicherheiten und unmoralische Ausschreitungen führten jedoch zum Niedergang der ersten Würzburger Universität. Im Jahre 1582 gründete Fürstbischof Julius Echter von Mespelbrunn erneut die Würzburger Universität, die damals einen rein katholischen Charakter hatte. Um die Moral der Universität aufrechtzuerhalten, verbot Julius Echter

Trunkenheit, Würfelspiel, das Mitnehmen von Waffen in die Vorlesung, den Besuch zweifelhafter Wirtshäuser und das Baden im Main.

Seit dem 19. Jahrhundert heißt die Würzburger Universität offiziell Bayerische Julius-Maximilians-Universität. Die Medizinische Fakultät richtete hier die erste Kinderklinik der Welt ein. In den naturwissenschaftlichen Disziplinen wirkten der Botaniker Schwab und der Biologe Boveri. Im Jahre 1895 entdeckte hier der Physiker und erste Nobelpreisträger für Physik, Wilhelm Conrad Röntgen, die nach ihm benannten Röntgen-Strahlen. Heute zählt die Universität mit 20.000 Studenten zu den größten Universitäten Bayerns.

Rezept

Saure Zipfel (Blaue Bratwürste)
Für 4 Personen

Zutaten
l=Liter, TL=Teelöffel, EL=Esslöffel

8	Zwiebeln	10 Wacholderbeeren
1,25 l	Wasser	5 Nelken
0,75 l	Weißweinessig	3 Lorbeerblätter
1 TL	Instant-Brühe	2 EL Öl
2	EL Zucker	8 fränkische Bratwürste
6	Pimentkörner	gemahlener schwarzer Pfeffer

Zubereitung
Die Zwiebeln schälen und in Ringe schneiden. Das Wasser mit dem Essig, den Gewürzen, dem Öl und den Zwiebeln vermengen. Den Sud erhitzen und 10 Minuten kochen lassen. Vom Herd nehmen und abkühlen lassen. Wenn der Sud erkaltet ist, die Bratwürste zugeben und kalt stellen. Die Bratwürste 3 Stunden im Sud ziehen lassen. Den Sud mit den Bratwürsten bis kurz vor dem Siedepunkt erhitzen und 15 Minuten garen lassen.
Achtung: Der Sud darf nicht mehr kochen, da sonst die Bratwürste aufplatzen!

Beilage Schwarzbrot oder dunkles Gewürzbrot

Kapitel 4: Verhältnis zu anderen
Technology

One-Stop Planner CD-ROM

To preview all resources available for this chapter, use the **One-Stop Planner CD-ROM**, Disc 1.

Internet Connection ....

internet
ADRESSE: go.hrw.com
KENNWORT: WK3 WUERZBURG-4

*Have students explore the **go.hrw.com** Web site for many online resources covering all chapters. All Chapter 4 resources are available under the keyword **WK3 Wuerzburg-4**. Interactive games help students practice the material and provide them with immediate feedback. You will also find a printable worksheet that provides Internet activities that lead to a comprehensive online research project.*

Interaktive Spiele

You can use the interactive activities in this chapter

- to practice grammar, vocabulary, and chapter functions
- as homework
- as an assessment option
- as a self-test
- to prepare for the Chapter Test

Internet Aktivitäten

Students evaluate online youth magazines and suggest changes to improve the quality of these magazines. They compare the problems German youths have to those American teens face.

- To prepare students for the **Arbeitsblatt,** have them read the **Ratgeber-Ecke** on p. 116. If students have not done **Anwendung** Activities 3–5, you may want to ask them to do these activities now.
- After completing the **Arbeitsblatt,** ask students to write an article (in English) for their school newspaper that compares the interests and problems of American teens to those of German teens. This could be a class project.

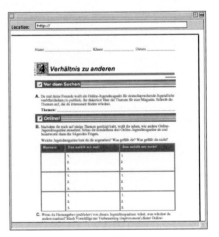

Webprojekt

Have students scan online articles about foreign workers (**Arbeitsemigranten,** or previously **Gastarbeiter**) in a large German city, e.g. Berlin, Hamburg, or Munich. Students should discuss any advantages or disadvantages these minorities may face in Germany. Encourage students to exchange useful Web sites with their classmates. Have students document their sources by referencing the names and URLs of all the sites they consulted.

The following scripts are for the listening activities found in the *Pupil's Edition*. For Student Response Forms, see *Listening Activities*, pages 27–30. To provide students with additional listening practice, see *Listening Activities*, pages 31–34.

Erste Stufe

5 p. 97

1. MARITA Du, Mutti! Ich hab einen ganz tollen Pulli bei Malibu-Moden gesehen. Meinst du, ich kann ihn haben?

MUTTER Ach, Marita! Schon wieder was Neues? Du hast doch schon so viele Sachen.

MARITA Stimmt ja gar nicht! Außerdem habe ich schon lange nichts Neues mehr bekommen!

MUTTER Also, hör mal, hast du denn ganz vergessen, dass ich dir erst vor zwei Wochen das silberfarbene T-Shirt gekauft habe, das du unbedingt für die Fete haben wolltest?

MARITA Ach, Mutti! Das T-Shirt hat doch kurze Ärmel. Das kann ich doch jetzt, wo es wieder kälter wird, nicht mehr anziehen. Aber der Pulli, der ist ganz weich und warm, aus reiner Schurwolle! Das ist genau das Richtige, jetzt für den Herbst!

MUTTER Also Marita, du hast wirklich genug Pullover und Jacken im Schrank! Du brauchst einfach keinen neuen Pulli!

MARITA Mutti, bitte! Er kostet doch nur 39 Euro!

MUTTER Wie bitte? Ich hör wohl nicht richtig! 39 Euro? Das kann ja wohl nicht dein Ernst sein. Also, nein, das ist viel zu teuer! Die Diskussion ist beendet!

2. HERBERT Also, tschüs dann! Frank, sag Mutti und Vati, dass ich so gegen zehn wieder zu Hause bin!

FRANK He, Herbert! Moment mal! Wo willst du denn hin?

HERBERT Ich geh mit der Tina ins Kino. Hast du was dagegen?

FRANK Allerdings! Du bist heute mit dem Geschirrspülen dran. Na los, mach schon, bevor die Mama zurückkommt! Vorher lass ich dich nicht gehen!

HERBERT Was soll das heißen, ich soll das Geschirr spülen?! Heute ist Montag, und montagabends bist du mit dem Geschirrspülen dran, Brüderchen!

FRANK Ja, normalerweise schon! Aber erinnere dich mal daran, wer denn am Samstagabend das Geschirr gespült hat! Du jedenfalls nicht, obwohl du an der Reihe warst!

HERBERT Ach ja, da wollte ich ja unbedingt auf die Fete vom Klaus-Jürgen!

FRANK Genau! Und was war, bevor du losgedüst bist? Du hast mir versprochen, …

HERBERT … dass ich das Geschirr am Montag spüle, wenn du es am Samstag für mich spülst! Mensch, Frank, das hab ich total vergessen! Tut mir echt Leid!

FRANK Ist schon gut! Hauptsache, du machst es überhaupt!

HERBERT Kannst du schnell die Tina anrufen und ihr sagen, dass ich fünf Minuten später komme?

FRANK Klar, mach ich!

3. ANDREAS Du, Vati, ich hab einen Job gefunden, wo ich mir nebenbei etwas Geld verdienen kann. Du weißt doch, dass das Taschengeld für mein Hobby nicht ausreicht.

VATER Na, Andreas, ich weiß nicht, ob das so eine gute Idee ist. Deine Noten in der Schule, das weißt du ja selbst, dürfen nicht schlechter werden. Du hast doch neben den Hausaufgaben gar keine Zeit für einen Job.

ANDREAS Doch! Ich hab mir die Zeit schon genau eingeteilt. Nachmittags von zwei bis vier lerne ich für die Schule, und von halb fünf bis halb sieben gehe ich jobben.

VATER Was? Nur zwei Stunden pro Tag willst du für die Schule lernen?

ANDREAS Ach Vati! Dann mach ich eben am Wochenende mehr für die Schule!

VATER Sag mal, Andreas, was für ein Job soll das denn sein?

ANDREAS Ach, weißt du, auf der Nievenheimer Dorfstraße ist doch dieser neue, große Supermarkt. Dort suchen sie Schüler, die die neuen Waren auspacken und in die Regale einordnen. Ich hab mir gedacht, dass ich das doch ganz locker nebenbei machen könnte. Also, was sagst du dazu?

VATER Hm … also, die Schule …

ANDREAS Ja ja, ich weiß schon, was du sagen willst. Die Schule ist wichtiger. Also, ich versprech dir, mit dem Job sofort aufzuhören, wenn meine Noten schlechter werden. Lass es mich doch probieren, bitte! Einverstanden?

VATER Na gut, mein Sohn!

4. ELKE Also, Papa, ich hau jetzt ab!

VATER Warte mal, Elke! Wohin denn so eilig?

ELKE Zum Tanzen. Das hab ich dir doch schon gesagt!

VATER Hm … hab ich nicht gehört. Du warst doch gestern Abend erst weg. Und Mutti hat gesagt, dass du ganz schön spät nach Hause gekommen bist!

ELKE Ja und?

VATER Also, wenn du heute Abend wieder weg willst, musst du aber früher nach Hause kommen, hörst du?!

ELKE Ach, wie gemein! Immer soll ich nach Hause kommen, wenn es erst richtig anfängt, Spaß zu machen. Kann ich nicht mal so lange wegbleiben, wie ich will?

VATER Na so was! Das kommt überhaupt nicht in Frage! Mit wem gehst du denn heute weg?

ELKE Warum willst du das denn wissen?

VATER Also, hör mal! Als Vater darf ich doch wohl fragen, mit wem meine Tochter ihre Zeit verbringt! Also, mit wem gehst du zum Tanzen?

ELKE Weiß nicht! Da kommen ein paar aus der Klasse. Die Ulrike ist auch dabei.

VATER Soso, die Ulrike … und welche Jungs kommen mit?

ELKE Ach Papa, die kennst du doch sowieso nicht! Aber wenn du's halt unbedingt wissen willst: der Uli, der Thomas und der Matthias. Sonst noch was?

VATER Also, um halb elf bist du wieder zu Hause, hörst du?

ELKE Waaas? Halb elf? Da kann ich ja gleich hier bleiben! Um zehn wird doch erst die Disko richtig voll! Papa, das kannst du mir nicht antun! Da mach ich mich ja lächerlich vor den anderen. Die dürfen alle viel länger bleiben. Kann ich nicht bis zwölf Uhr bleiben?

VATER Ich hab halb elf gesagt, und dabei bleibt's! Verstanden?

ELKE Ach, manno!

Answers to Activity 5

1. Marita will einen neuen Pulli. Der Streit endet schlecht für Marita, sie erreicht nichts.
2. Herbert hat das Geschirr nicht gespült. Der Streit endet gut/produktiv für Frank.
3. Andreas will jobben. Der Streit endet gut/produktiv für Andreas.
4. Elke will länger ausbleiben. Der Streit endet schlecht für Elke, sie erreicht nichts.

7 p. 97

PATRICK Hallo, Claudia! Du siehst heute aber nicht besonders glücklich aus. Was hast du denn?

CLAUDIA Ach, bei uns zu Hause hat es wieder Krach gegeben.

PATRICK Hast du dich wieder mit deinem Vater gestritten?

CLAUDIA	Ja, ja, immer das alte Thema. Nie darf ich weg, wenn ich will! Er behandelt mich wie ein kleines Kind. Dabei werde ich schon bald siebzehn!
PATRICK	Was war denn diesmal los?
CLAUDIA	Ach, er hat mir gesagt, dass ich heute Abend nicht ins Kino gehen darf, bevor ich mein Zimmer aufgeräumt habe. Kannst du das glauben? Ich habe ihn gefragt, wieso er sich plötzlich dafür interessiert, wie es in meinem Zimmer aussieht. Er kommt ja sonst auch nie zu mir ins Zimmer!
PATRICK	Ja, bei mir ist das auch so! So lange man zu Hause rumhängt, ist alles in Ordnung. Aber kaum will man mal weg, fangen die Eltern an zu meckern!
CLAUDIA	Da geb ich dir Recht. Sofort heißt es: „Hast du schon deine Schulaufgaben gemacht? Hast du schon das Geschirr gespült?" Bla bla bla … Ich kann es schon wirklich bald nicht mehr hören!
PATRICK	Ganz meine Meinung!
CLAUDIA	Und stell dir mal vor, ich muss nicht nur mein Zimmer aufräumen, sondern auch noch tausend Fragen beantworten! Mein Vater wollte wissen, mit wem ich weggehe, welchen Kinofilm wir uns anschauen wollen, wann der Film zu Ende ist … und so weiter und so fort! So was Blödes!
PATRICK	Und hast du ihm mal gesagt, dass dich das nervt?
CLAUDIA	Ja, also, er war ganz schön sauer und wollte eigentlich gar nicht mit ihm diskutieren. Aber dann habe ich ihm gesagt, dass ich nicht verstehe, warum er mich so kontrolliert! Ich finde, er hat nicht genug Vertrauen zu mir, wenn er denkt, dass ich schlimme Sachen mache oder was anstelle!
PATRICK	Und was hat er dazu gesagt?
CLAUDIA	Ach, er meint, das hat nichts mit Vertrauen zu tun, sondern mit Verantwortung. Ach, du weißt doch, typisch Eltern!
PATRICK	Ja, ich weiß genau, was du meinst!

Answers to Activity 7
Claudia darf nicht weg, wenn sie will. Sie findet, dass ihr Vater sie wie ein kleines Kind behandelt. Sie muss ihr Zimmer aufräumen, sonst darf sie nicht ins Kino. Sie muss ihrem Vater viele Fragen beantworten. Claudia findet, dass ihr Vater sie kontrolliert und ihr nicht genug vertraut. Answers will vary.

Zweite Stufe

14   p. 102

KALLE	Na, Hannes, hast du schon ein paar Worte mit unseren neuen Klassenkameraden gewechselt?
HANNES	Ja, ich hab gestern nach der Schule im Bus neben dem Thomas gesessen. Weißt du, der große, dunkelhaarige Typ. Er ist vor ein paar Wochen mit seinen Eltern aus Gundersheim nach hier gezogen.
KALLE	Und, was hat er so gesagt? Wofür interessiert er sich?
HANNES	Ach, er hat sich beschwert, dass die Lehrer doof sind, und er meint, dass ihn keiner in der Klasse leiden kann.
KALLE	Also, woher will der das denn wissen? Er kennt uns alle doch noch gar nicht! Und außerdem hat er gestern noch nicht einmal beim Fußballtraining mitgemacht. Er ist einfach nach der Schule abgehauen, obwohl er wusste, dass wir uns noch auf dem Sportplatz treffen wollten.
HANNES	Ja, er ist schon komisch! Auf der Schulfete haben wir uns alle verrückt angezogen, nur er nicht. Ich finde, er sollte mehr mit den anderen mitmachen und sich nicht nur beschweren. Die Silke, zum Beispiel, weißt du, die mit den …
KALLE	Ach, meinst du die kleine Rothaarige?
HANNES	Ja, genau die! Also, die Silke hat uns alle am Samstag zu einer Gartenparty bei ihr zu Hause eingeladen. Das find ich echt toll.
KALLE	Allerdings! Dabei ist sie doch ganz neu und kennt noch niemanden.
HANNES	Mensch, Kalle! Deswegen macht sie doch die Gartenparty! Damit sie die anderen alle kennen lernen kann, kapiert?
KALLE	Ach so, ja klar! Hör mal, da gibt es doch noch eine Neue, Renate heißt die, glaub ich. Die Anne hat mir gestern erzählt, dass diese Renate ganz schön frech ist.

HANNES	Wieso das denn?
KALLE	Ach, die Anne hat diese Neue, also die Renate gefragt, ob sie bei der Umwelt-AG mitmachen will. Und stell dir mal vor, die Renate soll ganz schnippisch gesagt haben, dass sie keine Lust dazu hat, weil sie was Besseres vorhat.
HANNES	Mensch, wenn die immer so ist, dann macht sie sich aber ganz schön schnell unbeliebt.
KALLE	Stimmt! Du, hast du schon mal mit dem Joachim geredet?
HANNES	Ja, aber nur ganz kurz. Er ist von Düsseldorf nach hier gezogen, weil seine Mutter einen Job hier an der Uni in Tübingen bekommen hat. Aber sonst weiß ich nichts über ihn.
KALLE	Also, ich finde, er sondert sich immer von allen ab. In der Pause sitzt er irgendwo in einer stillen Ecke und liest. Er unterhält sich mit keinem und ist auch sonst ziemlich zugeknöpft.
HANNES	Ach, vielleicht vermisst er einfach nur seine Freunde in Düsseldorf.
KALLE	Ja, kann schon sein.

Answers to Activity 14
Thomas passt sich nicht an.
Silke passt sich an.
Renate passt sich nicht an.
Joachim passt sich nicht an.

16   p. 103

PAUL	Na, Ulf, was gibt's? Du siehst heute aber nicht gerade fröhlich aus!
ULF	Ach, Paul, ich hab mich wieder mal mit meinem Bruder gestritten. Manchmal kann ich es gar nicht erwarten, bis der Jens anfängt zu studieren. Dann wohnt er wenigstens nicht mehr zu Hause. Er hilft nie und lässt immer alles rumliegen. Ich muss dann immer seine Sachen wegräumen. Und dazu noch das Geschirr spülen und den Rasen mähen, auch wenn er eigentlich dran ist. Das stinkt mir echt!
PAUL	Mensch, Ulf! Ich würde meinen Eltern sagen, dass dein Bruder seine Arbeit nicht macht. Sie werden sich dann schon darum kümmern.
ULF	Das glaube ich nicht! Du darfst nicht vergessen, dass meine Eltern beide arbeiten gehen. Sie wissen gar nicht, dass er tagsüber fast nie zu Hause ist und alles liegen lässt. Er hängt immer nur mit seiner Clique herum. Außerdem habe ich keine Lust, wie ein kleines Kind zu petzen!
PAUL	Vielleicht kannst du einfach nur deinen Teil der Arbeit machen und den Rest liegen lassen. Dann sehen deine Eltern doch, wie faul er ist.
ULF	Ach Paul, so einfach ist das nicht! Denk doch mal daran, dass meine Eltern abends total gestresst von der Arbeit heimkommen. Wenn meine Mutter sieht, dass alles herumliegt, regt sie sich nur auf und räumt selber auf. Und dann wird sie meistens sauer.
PAUL	Das mag schon sein, aber du kannst ja nichts dafür. Weißt du, ich finde es wichtig, dass du mal vernünftig mit dem Jens redest anstatt nur zu streiten. Vielleicht begreift er dann ja endlich mal, dass sein Verhalten dir gegenüber nicht fair ist.
ULF	Ja, also ich glaube, du hast Recht. Ich werde gleich mal mit ihm reden, wenn er nach Hause kommt. Danke für deinen Rat, Paul.
PAUL	Ach, nicht der Rede wert, Kumpel!

Answers to Activity 16
Ulf hat sich mit seinem Bruder Jens gestritten, weil Jens nie zu Hause hilft und Ulf alles machen muss.
Paul rät Ulf, es seinen Eltern zu erzählen. Ulf will diesem Rat nicht folgen.
Paul rät Ulf, nur seinen Teil zu machen und den Rest liegen zu lassen. Ulf will diesem Rat nicht folgen.
Paul rät Ulf, mal vernünftig mit Jens zu reden anstatt zu streiten. Ulf will diesem Rat folgen.

KERSTIN Puh! Also, ich freue mich schon wahnsinnig auf unsere Reise nach Amerika! Komm, Gertrud, lass uns mal überlegen, was wir uns alles anschauen wollen!

GERTRUD Ja, okay! Du, Kerstin, ich finde deine Idee wirklich prima, mit dem Campingwagen durchs Land zu reisen. Das mit dem Wagen geht doch klar, oder?

KERSTIN Ja, ist schon alles organisiert! Den Campingwagen kriegen wir ganz bestimmt. Meine Verwandten in Kalifornien leihen ihn uns gern. Als Allererstes schauen wir uns San Francisco an. Meine Kusine Cindy kommt ja auch mit auf unsere Tour. Und sie will noch eine Freundin fragen. Dann wären wir zu viert.

GERTRUD Hm, hoffentlich wird das dann nicht zu schwierig, wenn wir uns entscheiden wollen, wohin wir fahren und was wir besichtigen wollen. Du weißt ja, viele Leute, viele verschiedene Interessen! Du, ich möcht aber auf jeden Fall auch nach Los Angeles!

KERSTIN Ich weiß nicht, Gertrud, ich glaube, das liegt nicht auf unserer Tour. Von San Francisco aus fahren wir doch nach Nevada. Ich will unbedingt nach Las Vegas.

GERTRUD Nee, also Kerstin, das mit Las Vegas, das müssen wir aber noch mal besprechen. Da kann man doch nichts anderes tun als Geld verspielen. Dazu hab ich nun wirklich keine Lust! Ich will lieber weiter nach Utah und mir den Bryce Canyon ansehen.

KERSTIN Ach Gertrud, ich würd lieber direkt von Nevada nach Arizona weiterfahren. Bis zum Grand Canyon! Den müssen wir unbedingt sehen!

GERTRUD Ja, davon träum ich schon ewig! Ich kann's kaum glauben, dass wir schon bald dort sein werden. Du, Kerstin, meinst du, wir könnten noch weiter bis nach New Mexico zu den Rocky Mountains fahren?

KERSTIN Ich weiß nicht, Gertrud. Bestimmt hat meine Kusine keine Lust dazu. Sie hat doch in New Mexico gewohnt und kennt dort doch schon die ganze Gegend. Lass uns lieber weiter runter nach Tucson fahren, wenn wir schon mal in Arizona sind.

GERTRUD Na gut! Aber nur, wenn wir dann auf dem Rückweg auch nach San Diego fahren! Okay?

KERSTIN Ja, San Diego liegt auf der Rücktour. Das schauen wir uns ganz bestimmt an.

GERTRUD Hm! Vielleicht schaffen wir es doch, uns auch noch Los Angeles anzuschauen!

KERSTIN Also, ich glaube, dass wir dann wahrscheinlich keine Zeit mehr dazu haben!

GERTRUD Na ja, sehen wir mal!

Answers to Activity 19
Was Kerstin und Gertrud bestimmt machen: mit dem Campingwagen fahren; San Francisco anschauen; in Arizona den Grand Canyon ansehen; nach Tucson, Arizona fahren; nach San Diego fahren
Was spekulativ bleibt: Los Angeles anschauen; nach Las Vegas, Nevada fahren; Bryce Canyon in Utah ansehen; zu den Rocky Mountains nach New Mexico fahren

One-Stop Planner CD-ROM

For resource information, see the **One-Stop Planner CD-ROM**, Disc 1.

Anwendung

1. MARTIN Also dieser Dieter ist schon komisch! Wie der sich anzieht! Und seine Haare sehen auch immer so ungepflegt aus! Typisch Punker! Bin ich froh, dass der nicht in unserer Clique ist!

2. EVA Also, mein Lieblingsfach in der Schule ist Erdkunde. Ich finde andere Kulturen und Völker einfach faszinierend. Ich möchte später mal unbedingt ein Jahr lang nach Afrika ziehen, am liebsten nach Namibia. Ich möchte alles über die Bantu-Völker lernen, sogar ihre Sprache. Sie haben ganz andere Sitten und Gebräuche als wir. Das find ich toll!

3. BRITTA Ich verstehe einfach nicht, wieso die Tina nicht mit uns ins Konzert will! Also, solche Leute, die nur klassische Musik hören und keine Rockmusik mögen, sind einfach komisch! Wie kann sie nur daheim bleiben, wenn sie stattdessen mit uns mitgehen könnte! Na, vielleicht will sie nur nicht mit, weil sie nichts Besonderes zum Anziehen hat! Ich finde die Klamotten von der Tina echt altmodisch!

4. ANDREAS Also, ich verstehe mich ganz gut mit dem Herbert. Er ist in der Schule ziemlich unbeliebt, weil er sich immer von den anderen absondert. Aber er bleibt nun mal lieber allein, weil er sehr schüchtern ist. Außerdem liest er wahnsinnig gern. In der Pause nimmt er sich immer ein Buch mit und liest. Ich habe aber neulich mit ihm gesprochen, und er ist sehr gescheit. Er interessiert sich für Archäologie und war mit seinen Eltern schon auf vielen Reisen im Ausland.

Answers to Activity 1
1. Martin: nicht tolerant
2. Eva: tolerant
3. Britta: nicht tolerant
4. Andreas: tolerant

Kapitel 4: Verhältnis zu anderen
Suggested Lesson Plans 50-Minute Schedule

Day 1

LOCATION OPENER 15 min.
- Present Location Opener, pp. 88–89
- Background Information, ATE, p. 87A
- The Almanac and Map, ATE, p. 87A
- Show **Würzburg** Video
- Do Viewing and Post-viewing Activities, Video Guide, p. 15

CHAPTER OPENER 10 min.
- Advance Organizer, ATE, p. 91M
- Teaching Suggestions, ATE, p. 91M

LOS GEHT'S! 20 min.
- Preteaching Vocabulary, ATE, p. 91N
- Teaching Suggestions, ATE, p. 91N
- Play Audio CD for **Los geht's!**
- Have students read **Los geht's!**, pp. 94–95
- Do Activities 1–3, p. 95

Wrap-Up 5 min.
- Students respond to questions about how well they get along with their parents

Homework Options
Übungsheft, p. 40, Acts. 1–2

Day 2

ERSTE STUFE
Quick Review 10 min.
- Check homework, Übungsheft, p. 40, Acts. 1–2
- Bell Work, p. 91O

Wortschatz, p. 96 20 min.
- Presenting **Wortschatz**, ATE, p. 91O
- Teaching Transparency 4-1
- Do Activity 4, p. 96
- Play Audio CD for Activity 5, p. 97
- Do Activity 6, p. 97

So sagt man das!, p. 97 15 min.
- Presenting **So sagt man das!**, ATE, p. 91O
- Play Audio CD for Activity 7, p. 97
- Do Activity 8, p. 97

Wrap-Up 5 min.
- Students respond to questions about why their parents scold them

Homework Options
Grammatikheft, pp. 28–29, Acts. 1–2
Übungsheft, p. 41, Act. 1

Day 3

ERSTE STUFE
Quick Review 10 min.
- Check homework, Grammatikheft, pp. 28–29, Acts. 1–2

Ein wenig Grammatik, p. 98 10 min.
- Presenting **Ein wenig Grammatik**, ATE, p. 91P
- Do Activity 9, p. 98

Ein wenig Landeskunde, p. 98 10 min.
- Presenting **Ein wenig Landeskunde**, ATE, p. 91P
- Do Activity 10, p. 98

Grammatik, p. 99 15 min.
- Presenting **Grammatik**, ATE, p. 91P
- Do Activity 11, p. 99
- Do Activity 3, p. 42, Übungsheft

Wrap-Up 5 min.
- Students respond to questions about school cliques

Homework Options
Grammatikheft, pp. 29–31, Acts. 3–5
Übungsheft, pp. 41–44, Acts. 2 and 4–8

Day 4

ERSTE STUFE
Quick Review 10 min.
- Check homework, Grammatikheft, pp. 29–31, Acts. 3–5

Im Freizeitzentrum (Video) 15 min.
- Teaching Suggestions, Video Guide, p. 18
- Do Pre-viewing, Viewing and Post-viewing Activities, p. 19, Video Guide
- Show Video, **Im Freizeitzentrum**
- Do Pre-viewing, Viewing and Post-viewing Activities, p. 20, Video Guide
- Show **Videoclips, Werbung**

Quiz Review 25 min.
- Do **Mehr Grammatikübungen, Erste Stufe**
- Do Additional Listening Activities 4-1 and 4-2, p. 31
- Do Activity for Communication 4-1, pp. 13–14

Homework Options
Activities for Communication, pp. 67, 69, Realia 4-2; read article, determine tense and differentiate between essential and non-essential text

Day 5

ERSTE STUFE
Quick Review 5 min.
- Check homework, Realia 4-2

Quiz 20 min.
- Quiz 4-1A or 4-1B

WEITER GEHT'S! 20 min.
- Preteaching Vocabulary, p. 91Q
- Play Audio CD for **Weiter geht's!**, pp. 100–101
- Do Activities 12 and 13, p. 101

Wrap-Up 5 min.
- Students respond to questions about their relationships to other people

Homework Options
Übungsheft, p. 45, Act. 1

Day 6

ZWEITE STUFE
Quick Review 10 min.
- Return and review Quiz 4-1
- Bell Work, ATE, p. 91R
- Check homework, Übungsheft, p. 45, Act. 1

Wortschatz, p. 102 15 min.
- Presenting **Wortschatz**, ATE, p. 91R
- Teaching Transparency 4-2
- Play Audio CD for Activity 14, p. 102
- Do Activity 15, p. 102

So sagt man das!, p. 103 20 min.
- Presenting **So sagt man das!**, ATE, p. 91R
- Play Audio CD for Activity 16, p. 103
- Do Activities 17 and 18, p. 103

Wrap-Up 5 min.
- Students respond to questions about prejudices some students may have

Homework Options
Grammatikheft, pp. 32–33, Acts. 6–7
Übungsheft, p. 46, Act. 1

One-Stop Planner CD-ROM

For alternative lesson plans by chapter section, to create your own customized plans, or to preview all resources available for this chapter, use the **One-Stop Planner CD-ROM**, Disc 1.

 For additional homework suggestions, see activities accompanied by this symbol throughout the chapter.

Day 7

ZWEITE STUFE

Quick Review 10 min.
- Check homework, Grammatikheft, pp. 32–33, Acts. 6–7

So sagt man das!, Ein wenig Grammatik, p. 104 15 min.
- Presenting **So sagt man das!, Ein wenig Grammatik,** ATE, p. 91S
- Play Audio CD for Activity 19, p. 104
- Do Activities 20 and 21, p. 104

Grammatik, p. 105 20 min.
- Presenting **Grammatik,** ATE, p. 91S
- Teacher Note, ATE, p. 91S
- Do Activities 22 and 23, p. 105
- Do Activities 9, 10 and 11, pp. 35–36, Grammatikheft

Wrap-Up 5 min.
- Students respond to questions about why they do different things

Homework Options
Grammatikheft, p. 34, Act. 8
Übungsheft, pp. 46–49, Acts. 2–9

Day 8

ZWEITE STUFE

Quick Review 10 min.
- Check homework, Übungsheft, pp. 46–49, Acts. 2–9

LANDESKUNDE 20 min.
- Preteaching Vocabulary, ATE, p. 91T
- Background Information, ATE, p. 91T
- Read **Die verschiedenen Bildungswege in Deutschland,** p. 106
- Do Activities A and B, p. 106

Quiz Review 20 min.
- Do Realia 4-3, Activities for Communication, pp. 68, 70
- Do Communicative Activities 4-2, pp. 15–16
- Do Additional Listening Activities 4-4, 4-5 or 4-6, pp. 32–34

Homework Options
Mehr Grammatikübungen, Zweite Stufe
Übungsheft, p. 50, Acts. 1–3

Day 9

ZWEITE STUFE

Quick Review 10 min.
- Check homework, **Mehr Grammatikübungen, Zweite Stufe**

Quiz 20 min.
- Quiz 4-2A or 4-2B

ZUM SCHREIBEN 15 min.
- Present Writing Strategy, ATE, p. 91U
- Teaching Suggestions, ATE, p. 91U
- Present **Schreibtipp,** p. 107

Wrap-Up 5 min.
- Students respond to questions about seeking answers to various problems

Homework Options
Pupil's Edition, p. 107, Act. 24
Pupil's Edition, p. 107, Acts. A and B, **Zum Schreiben**

Day 10

ZWEITE STUFE

Quick Review 10 min.
- Return and review Quiz 4-2

ZUM SCHREIBEN 20 min.
- Students complete Act. C, p. 107 and read **Zum Schreiben** letters

ZUM LESEN 15 min.
- Teacher Notes, ATE, p. 91V
- Language-to-Language, ATE, p. 91W
- Present **Lesestrategie,** p. 108
- Do Activities 1 and 2, pp. 108–109

Wrap-Up 5 min.
- Students respond to questions about being an exchange student

Homework Options
Pupil's Edition, p. 109, Acts. 3–5, complete first reading of **Zum Lesen** selection
Übungsheft, pp. 51–52, Acts. 1–5

Day 11

ZWEITE STUFE

Quick Review 5 min.
- Check homework, Übungsheft, pp. 51–52, Acts. 1–5

ZUM LESEN 20 min.
- Do Activities 6–12, pp. 109–111

ANWENDUNG 20 min.
- Do Activities 1–5, pp. 116–117

Wrap-Up 5 min.
- Students respond to questions about what they would say to a friend who has problems with his parents

Homework Options
Internet Aktivitäten, see ATE, p. 91E

Day 12

ANWENDUNG

Quick Review 10 min.
- Play game, **Wort für Wort,** ATE, p. 91C

Kann ich's wirklich?, p. 118 20 min.
- Do orally **Kann ich's wirklich?,** Activities 1–5, p. 118

Chapter Review 20 min.
- Review chapter functions, vocabulary, and grammar; choose from **Mehr Grammatikübungen,** Activities for Communication, Listening Activities, or **Interaktive Spiele**
- Review test format and provide sample test items for students

Homework Options
Study for Chapter Test
Interaktive Spiele, see p. 91E

Assessment

Test, Chapter 4 45 min.
- Administer Chapter 4 Test. Select from Testing Program, Alternative Assessment Guide or Test Generator.

Kapitel 4: Verhältnis zu anderen
Suggested Lesson Plans 90-Minute Schedule

Block 1

LOCATION OPENER 15 min.
- Present Location Opener, pp. 88–89
- Background Information, ATE, p. 87A
- The Almanac and Map, ATE, p. 87A
- Show **Würzburg** Video
- Do Viewing and Post-viewing Activities, Video Guide, p. 15

CHAPTER OPENER 5 min.
- Advance Organizer, ATE, p. 91M
- Teaching Suggestion, ATE, p. 91M

LOS GEHT'S! 20 min.
- Pre-teaching Vocabulary, ATE, p. 91N
- Advance Organizer, ATE, p. 91N
- Teaching Suggestions, ATE, p. 91N
- Play Audio CD for **Los geht's!**
- Have students read **Los geht's!**, pp. 94–95
- Do Activities 1–3, p. 95

ERSTE STUFE

Wortschatz, p. 96 20 min.
- Presenting **Wortschatz**, ATE, p. 91O
- Teaching Transparency 4-1
- Do Activity 4, p. 96
- Play Audio CD for Activity 5, p. 97
- Do Activity 6, p. 97

So sagt man das!, p. 97 15 min.
- Presenting **So sagt man das!**, ATE, p. 91O
- Play Audio CD for Activity 7, p. 97
- Do Activity 8, p. 97

Ein wenig Grammatik, p. 98 10 min.
- Presenting **Ein wenig Grammatik**, ATE, p. 91P
- Do Activity 9, p. 98

Wrap-Up 5 min.
- Students respond to questions about school cliques

Homework Options
Grammatikheft, pp. 28–29, Acts. 1–3
Übungsheft, p. 40, Acts. 1–2; pp. 41–42, Acts. 1, 2 and 4

Block 2

ERSTE STUFE

Quick Review 10 min.
- Check homework, Grammatikheft, pp. 28–29, Acts. 1–3

Ein wenig Landeskunde, p. 98 10 min.
- Presenting **Ein wenig Landeskunde**, ATE, p. 91P
- Do Activity 10, p. 98

Grammatik, p. 99 30 min.
- Presenting **Grammatik**, ATE, p. 91P
- Do Activity 11, p. 99
- Do Activity 3, p. 42, Übungsheft
- Do Activity 4, p. 30, Grammatikheft

Im Freizeitzentrum (Video) 15 min.
- Teaching Suggestions, Video Guide, p. 18
- Do Pre-viewing, Viewing and Post-viewing Activities, p. 19, Video Guide
- Show Video, **Im Freizeitzentrum**
- Do Pre-viewing, Viewing and Post-viewing Activities, p. 20, Video Guide
- Show **Videoclips, Werbung**

Quiz Review 25 min.
- Do **Mehr Grammatikübungen, Erste Stufe**
- Do Additional Listening Activities 4-1 and 4-2, p. 31
- Do Activity for Communication 4-1, pp. 13–14
- Do Realia 4-1, p. 66, Activities for Communication

Homework Options
Grammatikheft, p. 31, Act. 5
Übungsheft, pp. 43–44, Acts. 5–8
Internet Aktivitäten, see ATE, p. 91E

Block 3

ERSTE STUFE

Quick Review 10 min.
- Check homework, Grammatikheft, p. 31, Act. 5

Quiz 20 min.
- Quiz 4-1A or 4-1B

WEITER GEHT'S! 20 min.
- Preteaching Vocabulary, ATE, p. 91Q
- Play Audio CD for **Weiter geht's!**, pp. 100–101
- Do Activities 12 and 13, p. 101

ZWEITE STUFE

Wortschatz, p. 102 15 min.
- Presenting **Wortschatz**, ATE, p. 91R
- Teaching Transparency 4-2
- Play Audio CD for Activity 14, p. 102
- Do Activity 15, p. 102

So sagt man das!, p. 103 20 min.
- Presenting **So sagt man das!**, ATE, p. 91R
- Play Audio CD for Activity 16, p. 103
- Do Activities 17 and 18, p. 103

Wrap-Up 5 min.
- Students respond to questions about prejudices some students may have

Homework Options
Grammatikheft, pp. 32–33, Acts. 6–7
Übungsheft, p. 45, Act. 1; p. 46, Act. 1

One-Stop Planner CD-ROM

For alternative lesson plans by chapter section, to create your own customized plans, or to preview all resources available for this chapter, use the **One-Stop Planner CD-ROM**, Disc 1.

 For additional homework suggestions, see activities accompanied by this symbol throughout the chapter.

Block 4

ZWEITE STUFE
Quick Review 10 min.
- Return and review Quiz 4-1
- Check homework, Grammatikheft, pp. 32–33, Acts. 6–7

So sagt man das!, Ein wenig Grammatik, p. 104 15 min.
- Presenting **So sagt man das!, Ein wenig Grammatik,** ATE, p. 91S
- Play Audio CD for Activity 19, p. 104
- Do Activities 20 and 21, p. 104

Grammatik, p. 105 20 min.
- Presenting **Grammatik,** ATE, p. 91S
- Teacher Note, ATE, p. 91S
- Do Activities 22 and 23, p. 105
- Do Activities 9, 10 and 11, pp. 35–36, Grammatikheft

LANDESKUNDE 20 min.
- Preteaching Vocabulary, ATE, p. 91T
- Background Information, ATE, p. 91T
- Read **Die verschiedenen Bildungswege in Deutschland,** p. 106
- Do Activities A and B, p. 106

Quiz Review 25 min.
- Do **Mehr Grammatikübungen, Zweite Stufe**
- Do Communicative Activities 4-2, pp. 15–16
- Do Additional Listening Activities 4-4, 4-5 and 4-6, pp. 32–34

Homework Options
Pupil's Edition, p. 107, Act. 24
Grammatikheft, p. 34, Act. 8
Übungsheft, pp. 46–49, Acts. 2–9; p. 50, Acts. 1–3

Block 5

ZWEITE STUFE
Quick Review 10 min.
- Check homework, Übungsheft, pp. 46–49, Acts. 2–9; p. 50, Acts. 1–3

Quiz 20 min.
- Quiz 4-2A or 4-2B

ZUM SCHREIBEN 35 min.
- Present Writing Strategy, ATE, p. 91U
- Teaching Suggestions, ATE, p. 91U
- Present **Schreibtipp,** p. 107
- Do Activities A, B, and C, p. 107

ZUM LESEN 20 min.
- Teacher Notes, ATE, p. 91V
- Language-to-Language, ATE, p. 91W
- Present **Lesestrategie,** p. 108
- Do Activities 1, 2 and 3, pp. 108–109

Wrap-Up 5 min.
- Students respond to questions about being an exchange student

Homework Options
Pupil's Edition, p. 109, Acts. 4–5, complete first reading of **Zum Lesen** selection
Übungsheft, pp. 51–52, Acts. 1–5

Block 6

ZWEITE STUFE
Quick Review 15 min.
- Return and review Quiz 4-2
- Check homework, Übungsheft, pp. 51–52, Acts. 1–5

ZUM LESEN 20 min.
- Do Activities 6–12, pp. 109–111

ANWENDUNG 25 min.
- Do Activities 1–6, pp. 116–117

Kann ich's wirklich?, p. 118 20 min.
- Do orally **Kann ich's wirklich?,** Activities 1–5, p. 118

Wrap-Up 10 min.
- Students respond to questions about what they would say to a friend who has problems with his parents

Homework Options
Study for Chapter Test
Interaktive Spiele, p. 91E

Block 7

ANWENDUNG
Quick Review 15 min.
- Play game, **Wort für Wort,** ATE, p. 91C

Chapter Review 30 min.
- Review chapter functions, vocabulary, and grammar; choose from **Mehr Grammatikübungen,** Activities for Communication, Listening Activities, or **Interaktive Spiele**
- Review test format and provide sample test items for students

Test, Chapter 4 45 min.
- Administer Chapter 4 Test. Select from Testing Program, Alternative Assessment Guide or Test Generator.

Kapitel 4: Verhältnis zu anderen
Teaching Suggestions, *pages 92–119*

Using the Video

Before you begin the chapter, you may want to preview the *Video Program* and consult the *Video Guide*. Suggestions for integrating the video into each chapter are given in the *Video Guide*. Activity masters for video selections can be found in the *Video Guide*.

PAGES 92–93

CHAPTER OPENER

Pacing Tips

The **Erste Stufe** centers around the function of 'agreeing.' Ordinal numbers and the concept of relative clauses are introduced. The **Zweite Stufe** focuses on the functions of 'giving advice; introducing another point of view' and 'hypothesizing,' which includes **hätte** and **wäre**. The genitive case is presented on p. 105. The **Landeskunde** section explains the school system in Germany, with a chart showing the types of schools and educational paths. The **Zum Lesen** reading is "**Ein Tisch ist ein Tisch**" by Peter Bichsel. For Lesson Plans and timing suggestions, see pages 91I–91L.

Meeting the Standards
Communication
- Agreeing, p. 97
- Giving advice, p. 103
- Introducing another point of view, p.103
- Hypothesizing, p.104

Cultures
- Ein wenig Landeskunde, p. 98
- Landeskunde, p. 106
- Teacher Note, p. 91T
- Background Information, p. 91T

Connections
- Language Note, p. 91N
- Language Note, p. 91Q
- Music Connection, p. 91S
- Language-to-Language, p. 91S
- Multicultural Connection, p. 91T

Comparisons
- Language-to-Language, p. 91W

Communities
- Journalism Connection, p. 91U

One-Stop Planner CD-ROM

For resource information, see the **One-Stop Planner CD-ROM**, Disc 1.

Advance Organizer

Have students describe their close circle of friends. When and how often do they get together? What do they typically do? (**Beschreib deinen Freundeskreis! Wann und wie oft trefft ihr euch gewöhnlich, und was macht ihr so?**)

Teaching Suggestion

Give students a few moments to think about how they would most like to spend their time outside of school and with whom. (**Wie würdest du deine Freizeit am liebsten verbringen? Wenn nicht allein, mit wem und warum gerade mit dieser Person?**)

Communication for All Students

Challenge
To review vocabulary ask students to write riddles in German for vocabulary items. On one side of an index card write the word for which you want students to create a riddle. Let students write their riddle on the other side. Each gets to read his or her riddle and lets the rest of the class guess the word. Following is a list of words learned in Levels 1 and 2: **Halbbruder, Halbschwester, Clique, Fete, Eltern, Austauschschüler, Nachbar, Jugendzentrum, Mannschaft, Freizeit, Brieffreund(in).**

Chapter Sequence

LOS GEHT'S!

Teaching Resources
pp. 94–95

PRINT
▸ Lesson Planner, p. 26
▸ Übungsheft, p. 40

MEDIA
▸ One-Stop Planner
▸ Audio Compact Discs, CD4, Tr. 1

PAGES 94–95

Los geht's! Summary

In *Verhältnis zu Eltern und Freunden,* an interviewer talks to Sonja, Tanja, Michael, and Philipp about their relationships with their friends and families. The following learning outcome listed on p. 93 is modeled in the interviews: agreeing.

Preteaching Vocabulary

Guessing Words from Context

Have students skim **Los geht's!** for general meaning, and ask them what the teens are discussing (their relationships with parents and friends). Then have students scan for cognates that are new to them. After students have a good idea of what **Los geht's!** is about, have them use contextual clues to guess the meaning of these words and phrases on page 94: **Verhältnis, Wie kommt ihr mit euern Eltern aus?, Streitigkeiten, Alltäglichkeiten, Kumpel, Freundeskreis.** Finally, ask students to find three more unfamiliar words on their own that they can define by using contextual clues.

Advance Organizer

Discuss with students some of the typical things their parents ask of them or comment on. (**Könnt ihr einige typische Beispiele geben von Sachen, die ihr von euren Eltern zu hören bekommt? Worum bitten sie euch? Was sollt ihr zu Hause alles tun?**)

Teaching Suggestion

In Level 2 (Chapter 7) students learned to use grammatical and lexical clues to derive meaning when reading a text. Remind them of this strategy and encourage them to use it to determine the meaning of new phrases and statements in the interview. For example, they might not understand the phrase **ein echter Kumpel.** They should read the preceding and following sentences: "**Ich verstehe mich jetzt mit meinen Eltern so prima.**" and "**Wir gehen zusammen Tennis spielen und so …**" to help them determine the meaning.

Connections and Comparisons

Language Note

Azubi, used by the interviewer in his final question, is an abbreviated form of the word **Auszubildender** *(apprentice)* that has replaced **Lehrling.** The verb **ausbilden** means *to train,* or *to educate.* An **Auszubildender** is someone who is being trained in a profession.

Comprehension Check

A Slower Pace

1 Copy the chart on the chalkboard and write the phrases in as you go along. Have students find corresponding statements in the text and help them rephrase them to focus on main points. For example, they might read **Ich versteh mich jetzt mit meinen Eltern so prima.** Students rephrase it and write alongside Philipp's name, **versteht sich prima mit ihnen.**

Challenge

2 To expand this activity, ask students to use the notes about their relationship with parents and friends to write a short cohesive paragraph for homework.

Career Path

Have students work in small groups to think of reasons why an American student might need a working knowledge of German. (Suggestion: Imagine that you have been selected to be an exchange student and are going to live in Salzburg, Austria, for a year.)

Closure

Have students take a close look at the photos accompanying the **Los geht's!** section. Ask students what impressions they have about the atmosphere and social interaction of the people in the photos based on the main theme of the interview (**Verhältnis zu Eltern und Freunden**). What might the people in each photograph be saying?

Teaching Resources
pp. 96–99

PRINT

▸ Lesson Planner, p. 27
▸ Listening Activities, pp. 27, 31–32
▸ Video Guide, pp. 17–19
▸ Activities for Communication, pp. 13–14, 66–67, 69–70, 119–120
▸ Grammatikheft, pp. 28–31
▸ Grammar Tutor for Students of German, Chapter 4
▸ Übungsheft, pp. 41–44
▸ Testing Program, pp. 67–70
▸ Alternative Assessment Guide, p. 33
▸ Student Make-Up Assignments, Chapter 4

MEDIA

▸ One-Stop Planner
▸ Audio Compact Discs, CD4, Trs. 2–3, 9, 13–15
▸ Video Program
Im Freizeitzentrum
Videocassette 1, 37:45–40:00
▸ Teaching Transparencies
Situation 4-1
Mehr Grammatikübungen Answers
Grammatikheft Answers

▶ PAGE 96

Bell Work
Ask students to name two common situations that cause friction or conflict between them and their parents. (**Nennt zwei Situationen, die bei euch zu Hause gewöhnlich zu Problemen zwischen euch und euren Eltern führen!**)

PRESENTING: Wortschatz

To present the **Wortschatz**, do the following for each word or expression. First, read it to students. Then incorporate the item into statements about yourself and people in your life. Finally, use it in questions directed at individual students.
Examples:
Brett, kommst du gut mit deinen Eltern aus?
Tommy, wie verstehst du dich mit deinen Geschwistern?

Building on Previous Skills

4 After students have matched the phrases with the corresponding illustrations, ask them to come up with a reprimand that a parent would give to the teenager in each picture.

Communication for All Students

Thinking Critically
4 Comparing and Contrasting Discuss the situations with students and find out which ones they can relate to. Have students elaborate on the situation with a sentence or two.

▶ PAGE 97

Teaching Suggestion

5 Play the conversation again and have students determine a reason for each of the four arguments. (**Hört noch einmal diesen vier Gesprächen zu, um herauszufinden, worüber sich die Leute streiten!**)

PRESENTING: So sagt man das!

Before introducing the new expressions on p. 97, review some ways to express agreement that were presented in Level 2.
Examples:
Da stimm ich dir zu!
Da hast du Recht!
Einverstanden!
Then present the new expressions and have students find statements that express agreement in the **Los geht's!** interview.

Communication for All Students

Challenge
8 To provide students with additional written practice, have them choose one of the five statements on which to express their opinion in three to five sentences.

STANDARDS: 1.1

PRESENTING: **Ein wenig Grammatik**

Ordinal numbers Explain to students that if they want to express the ordinals in numerals, the number must be followed by a period, as in **in der 10. Klasse.** Ordinal numerals are often used in dates. (Example: **3. 10. 2002**)

* Prepare a handout for practicing ordinal numbers as adjectives using sentences like the following:
  Wir haben Deutsch in der _____ Stunde.
  Meine Mutter feiert nächstes Jahr ihren _____ Geburtstag.

PRESENTING: **Ein wenig Landeskunde**

Briefly discuss the concept of **Cliquen** in German with your students, including both positive and negative aspects. You may want to direct the discussion with the following questions:
Gibt es in dieser Schule Cliquen?
Woher weißt du das?
Gehörst du einer Clique an?
Wo trefft ihr euch?
Was macht ihr gewöhnlich?

Teacher Note

As students look at the chart entitled **Mit wem verbringen Jugendliche ihre Freizeit?**, remind them to use the title to help them interpret the information.

Using the Video

VIDEO Videocassette 1, 37:45–40:00
In the video clip *Im Freizeitzentrum,* some students from Würzburg talk about their friends and their activities at the youth center. See *Video Guide,* p. 18, for suggestions.

PRESENTING: **Grammatik**

Relative clauses Tell students that one way to increase German writing proficiency is to use more complex sentence structures, such as relative clauses.

* Write several pairs of sentences on the board or a transparency and walk students through the steps involved in combining them into one sentence. Example:
  Ich habe am Samstag Milch gekauft. Sie war schon sauer.
  Ich habe am Samstag Milch gekauft, die schon sauer war.

* Tell students that in German a relative clause is always introduced by a relative pronoun; in English the relative pronoun is often not used. Example:
  Die Milch, die ich am Samstag gekauft habe, war schon sauer.
  The milk (that) I bought on Saturday was already spoiled.
* Point out also that a relative clause is a dependent clause; therefore, the verb must be the last element in the clause.

Reteaching: **Relative clauses**

Tell students to imagine that they are looking through a catalog, and there are a lot of things they would like to have for one reason or another. Have them tell you or a partner what they want and why.

Example: **Da ist die Kette, die ich für die Fete am Samstag haben will.**

 Game

Play the game **Wort für Wort** to review the vocabulary of the **Erste Stufe.** See p. 91C for the procedure.

Assess
▶ Testing Program, pp. 67–70
  Quiz 4-1A, Quiz 4-1B
  Audio CD4, Tr. 9

▶ Student Make-Up Assignments
  Chapter 4, Alternative Quiz

▶ Alternative Assessment Guide, p. 33

ERSTE STUFE

Teaching Resources
pp. 100–101

PRINT
▶ Lesson Planner, p. 28
▶ Übungsheft, p. 45

MEDIA
▶ One-Stop Planner
▶ Audio Compact Discs, CD4, Tr. 4

▶ **PAGES 100–101**

Weiter geht's! Summary

In *Verhältnis zu anderen Leuten,* an interviewer talks with Sonja, Tanja, Michael, and Philipp about their relationships with different types of people. The following learning outcomes listed on p. 93 are modeled in the interview: giving advice, introducing another point of view, and hypothesizing.

Preteaching Vocabulary

Recognizing Cognates

Weiter geht's! contains several words that students will be able to recognize as cognates or borrowed words. Some are compound words in which only part of the word is a cognate. Have students identify these words and describe what is happening in the story. Here are some of the cognates and borrowed words they might find: **Gruppen, Punker, Raver, Gruppe, Grunger, Öko-Freaks, Raver-Musik, Muttersprache, akzeptiert, kulturbedingt, isoliert, Interessen, Kultur, organisieren.** In addition, have students use cognates and context to guess the meanings of these phrases:
Ich find es okay, wenn man zu einer Gruppe gehört. / Was würdest du denn einem ausländischen Schüler raten, der sich isoliert fühlt?

Advance Organizer

Have students take a look at the makeup of their class. How many different nationalities are represented? How many students speak a language other than English at home? Are there any foreign exchange students or other students from different countries living here temporarily?

Teaching Suggestions

• Divide the interview into its two parts and have students read along as they listen to the first segment. Repeat and ask some detailed questions to check comprehension. Work with the new vocabulary by paraphrasing, using synonyms, and asking either/or questions. Follow the same procedure for the second segment of the interview.

• After students have a good understanding of the interview, divide the class into groups of four and have each student assume one of the roles. Give the role of the interviewer (who has only two questions) to the student who plays Sonja. Tell students to practice reading the conversation until it sounds spoken, not read, with typical hesitations, pauses, self-corrections, and repetitions one hears in natural speech.

Connections and Comparisons

Language Note

The abbreviation **AG** is an acronym for **Arbeitsgemeinschaft,** a group of students that meets after school to discuss and work on topics of common interest, similar to an American school club. An **Umwelt-AG,** for example, is a group of students who want to know about and do more for the environment.

Communication for All Students

Visual Learners

13 Divide a transparency into three sections, one for each question. Ask students to scan the interview for all the phrases and statements that answer each question. Help students rephrase the quotes if necessary to get to the key information from the interviews and write that in the corresponding section of the transparency.

Closure

Have students brainstorm other ways than those mentioned in the interview to bridge the cultural differences between Germans and foreigners living in Germany.

ZWEITE STUFE

Teaching Resources
pp. 102–107

PRINT
- Lesson Planner, p. 29
- Listening Activities, pp. 29–30, 32–34
- Activities for Communication, pp. 15–16, 68, 70, 119–120
- Grammatikheft, pp. 32–36
- Grammar Tutor for Students of German, Chapter 4
- Übungsheft, pp. 46–50
- Testing Program, pp. 71–74
- Alternative Assessment Guide, p. 33
- Student Make-Up Assignments, Chapter 4

MEDIA
- One-Stop Planner
- Audio Compact Discs, CD4, Trs. 5–7, 10, 16–18
- Teaching Transparencies Situation 4-2
- **Mehr Grammatikübungen** Answers
- Grammatikheft Answers

PAGE 102

Bell Work

Ask students to whom they usually go for advice. Does anyone ever ask them for advice? (**Wem vertraust du dich gewöhnlich an? Vertrauen sich andere Leute dir an?**)

PRESENTING: Wortschatz

Introduce the new vocabulary to students by using each item in context. Then ask students to respond to a statement or question you make, using the context of the interview in **Weiter geht's!** or the context of your students' lives.
Example:
Wir haben auch ein paar Ausländer an unserer Schule.
Ich finde, die sondern sich nicht von den anderen Schülern ab.

Teaching Suggestion

15 After students have completed their group work, ask for volunteers to report their findings. Put them on a transparency or on the chalkboard and use the ideas to discuss the problem of prejudices. You may want to provide students with the following additional

vocabulary to help them discuss the pictures and answer the questions:
der Rollstuhl *wheelchair*
mit jemandem gehen *to go steady with someone*
der Haarschnitt *haircut*

PAGE 103

PRESENTING: So sagt man das!

After introducing the first function, *giving advice*, ask students to come up with statements on their own in reaction to situations that you set up.
Examples:
Wir haben einen Punker in unserer Klasse. Er sondert sich ganz ab von uns. Sicher findet er uns sehr langweilig und altmodisch.
Ich kann mit meinen Eltern nicht reden. Es gibt nur Streit.
For practicing the second function, *introducing another point of view*, express opinions in different situations, and ask students to react.
Examples:
Ausländer haben es schwer, einen guten Job zu finden.
Wenn man in ein fremdes Land kommt, muss man sich vielen neuen kulturellen Dingen anpassen.

Communication for All Students

Challenge
16 Ask students to list the things that got Ulf into the situation he is in. Which character traits make him susceptible to being used by his brother? (**Wie kommt es, dass Ulf sich von seinem Bruder ausnutzen lässt?**)

A Slower Pace
17b Help students get started by giving them the first line of the conversation.

Challenge
17b Ask students to add comments, reactions, and questions to the eight statements given in order to bring the conversation alive and make it more real.

A Slower Pace
18 Review the different ways of giving advice and introducing another point of view listed in **So sagt man das!** on this page before starting on this activity. Students should use these expressions when playing the role of teacher, Markus, or friend.

PRESENTING: So sagt man das!

To help students understand the concepts of real versus unreal conditions, present several situations in both forms so students see the difference. Let them discover it.

Examples:

Ich bin <u>nicht</u> in Deutschland. Ich bin in Amerika. Aber wenn ich in Deutschland wäre, würde ich aufs Oktoberfest gehen.

Ich habe <u>keine</u> schlechten Noten, nur Einsen und Zweien. Aber wenn ich schlechte Noten hätte, würde ich viel mehr für die Schule lernen.

PRESENTING: Ein wenig Grammatik

- **Hätte = würde + haben** After students have reviewed these subjunctive verb forms, ask them what the expressions all have in common.
- Point out to students that the use of the subjunctive makes questions, requests, and wishes somewhat more polite and more formal. (Examples: **Ich hätte gern …, ich würde gern …, ich wäre lieber …**)
- Ask students how they would express the given examples in English.

Connections and Comparisons

Music Connection

For additional reading, give students a copy of the song *Ich wär so gerne Millionär* by **Die Prinzen,** Level 1 *Video Guide,* p. 104. Ask students to look at the first four lines of the text (the chorus of the song) and to circle the subjunctive forms they find. (**wär**) How would they translate these lyrics? You might also want to play the music video, Level 1 *Video Program* (Videocassette 4), Chapter 10.

Communication for All Students

Challenge

20 After students have correctly completed the activity, ask them to use the given clauses for making speculations on their own. Have them first work with the four conditions, then with the four solutions. Ask students to share their ideas with the class.

PRESENTING: Grammatik

The genitive case

- Point out to students that the genitive case (**das Auto meines Vaters**) often indicates an "of-relationship" denoting possession. That is why it is also referred to as the possessive case. Can students recall another way of expressing the same idea? (**von** + dative as in **das Auto von meinem Vater**)
- Explain to students that in spoken German the genitive case is used less and less frequently. It shows that standard German, like English, is moving to a less formal way of expression.

Connections and Comparisons

Music Connection

For additional reading, refer students to the text *Das Lied der Deutschen,* Level 1 *Listening Activities,* p. 78. Have them underline the genitive forms they find (**des/ dieses Glückes**). You may also want to play the song, Level 1 CD 10, Track 33.

Language-to-Language

You may want to tell your students that the use of phrases with **von** to show possession in German is similar to the way **de** is used in French and **de** in Spanish. For example, "**Das ist das Auto von meiner Mutter.**" is "**C'est la voiture de ma mère.**" in French and "**Es el carro de mi madre.**" in Spanish.

Reteaching: Genitive case

Ask students to use the genitive case to talk about people and things. Following are some examples that you can either do orally as a class activity or in writing:

die Handtasche von der Austauschschülerin
das Problem von der türkischen Bevölkerung
die Eltern von dem Punker

Teacher Note

22 The **Grammatik** states that the genitive case can replace **von** when showing possession. Point out to students that the genitive can also replace relative clauses.

Example:

Die Probleme, die unsere Schüler haben, werden immer schwieriger.

Die Probleme unserer Schüler werden immer schwieriger.

LANDESKUNDE

Building on Previous Skills

In Levels 1 and 2, students were introduced to various aspects of school life in Germany. Before you begin **Landeskunde,** ask students what they remember about the school system. Jot down students' ideas, then discuss some of the differences as well as the similarities between the German and American schools.

Preteaching Vocabulary

You may want to discuss the following vocabulary before students begin to read the text:
Bildungsweg: *schooling; course of instruction*
Kaufhof: *name of a large chain of German department stores*
Berufsschule: *trade school, vocational school*
ausbilden: *to train*
wird ausgebildet: *is being trained*
der Abteilungsleiter: *department supervisor*
der Krankenpfleger: *male nurse*
Bundeswehr: *Federal armed forces*
Zivildienst: *alternate service*

Cultures and Communities

Teacher Note

Schools that provide education to students with special needs are called **Sonderschulen.** They are separate from other public schools and are staffed entirely by teachers with special education certification. For additional information on the German school system, refer to pp. 31R and 181O of the Level 2 *Teacher's Edition.*

Background Information

• School attendance is mandatory in Germany for everyone between the ages of six and eighteen. Students must attend school full-time for the first nine years, in some **Bundesländer** for ten years. Afterwards, part-time attendance is required at vocational schools.

• Men in Germany are expected to serve ten months of basic military service. Exceptions are made when young men, for moral reasons, choose not to enter the service. They then agree to Zivildienst (alternate service).

Communication for All Students

Visual Learners

A Ask students to review each student's educational path. Have them read again what Hassan, Helga, and Klaus are doing. Follow their educational career on the chart. Discuss with students how the three educational paths differ. Who will be the first one to finish training and get a job? Who has the longest training ahead? Which one has chosen a profession that is always in demand?

Connections and Comparisons

Multicultural Connection

B Ask students to interview foreign exchange students or other foreign people to gather information about the school system in their countries. Students should prepare a short explanation of the school systems of those countries. Compare the various systems and discuss unfamiliar aspects.

Teacher Note

Mention to your students that the **Landeskunde** will also be included in Quiz 4-2B given at the end of the **Zweite Stufe** and in the Chapter Test.

Von der Schule zum Beruf

24

Before starting this activity, have students walk around the classroom and ask classmates where they were born and if they have relatives not born in the United States. Have students identify common goals of all classmates interviewed.

Assess

▸ Testing Program, pp. 71–74
Quiz 4-2A, Quiz 4-2B
Audio CD4, Tr. 10

▸ Student Make-Up Assignments
Chapter 4, Alternative Quiz

▸ Alternative Assessment Guide, p. 33

ZWEITE STUFE

ZUM SCHREIBEN

Teaching Resources
p. 107

PRINT
▸ Lesson Planner, p. 30
▸ Alternative Assessment Guide, p. 19

MEDIA
▸ One-Stop Planner
▸ Test Generator, Chapter 4

Writing Strategy

The targeted strategy for this writing activity is *determining the purpose*. Students should learn about this strategy before beginning the assignment.

Prewriting
Building Context

Ask students where one can typically find advice columns. Have students make a list of sources and come up with some problems people might write about in each publication.

Teaching Suggestion

Students should feel free to invent a problem if they choose.

Connections and Comparisons

Journalism Connection

A Ask the journalism teacher to come to your class and talk about the importance of readers' letters to a newspaper or a magazine. What makes letters so interesting and how do they differ, in terms of format and style, from articles?

Writing
Review

B In Level 2 (p. 167) students first learned expressions used to ask for advice. Review those expressions if necessary with students to help them put their ideas into cohesive sentences.

Post-Writing
Teaching Suggestions

C You may want to suggest the following guidelines for students to use as they evaluate each other's composition:

1. Content: Does everything make sense? Is the problem described clearly? Are the supporting details all directly related to the problem?

2. Organization: Is the problem the main idea of the letter? Are the details relevant and easy to follow?

3. Grammar and usage: Are there mistakes in grammar, spelling, or punctuation that need to be corrected?

4. Final thoughts/suggestions: What is your general impression of the text? What can the writer do to improve it?

C4 Have students type or neatly print their letters in columns so that they appear as in a newspaper. Post the best letters on a bulletin board or have students read them to the class.

Writing Assessment

You may want to assess students' completed work with the following rubric.

Writing Rubric	Points			
	4	3	2	1
Content (Complete – Incomplete)				
Comprehensibility (Comprehensible – Seldom comprehensible)				
Accuracy (Accurate – Seldom accurate)				
Organization (Well-organized – Poorly organized)				
Effort (Excellent – Minimal)				

18–20: A   16–17: B   14–15: C   12–13: D   Under 12: F

ZUM LESEN

Teaching Resources
pp. 108–111

PRINT
▶ Lesson Planner, p. 30
▶ Übungsheft, pp. 51–52
▶ Reading Strategies and Skills, Chapter 4
▶ Lies mit mir! 3, Chapter 4

MEDIA
▶ One-Stop Planner

Prereading
Building Context

In the course of their study of German, students might have asked themselves more than once why humans have evolved different natural languages and whether each language isn't purely arbitrary. In order to get students started thinking more critically about language, you might explain that even body language differs from one culture to another. For example, Germans, Americans, and Japanese all use slightly different ways of counting on their fingers; and the Japanese gesture for "come here" (waggling the fingers with the palm facing downward) can look to westerners like it should mean "go away!" or "get out of here!" Have students discuss the basic functions of human languages. Does Latin fulfill any of these functions? How about computer programming languages such as BASIC or FORTRAN? Is the periodic table in chemistry a universal language? What functions does it fulfill?

Reading
Teacher Notes

1e It will probably be clear to students that the story is told in the third person, and that the opening "**Ich will ... erzählen**" is a similar convention to that used in oral storytelling. The two instances of **vielleicht** in the second paragraph might suggest that the narrator is not omniscient. However, this assumption will not stand the test, as we later find the narrator reporting the man's thoughts. Later in the story, when the narrator tells his audience: "**Jetzt könnt ihr die Geschichte selbst weiterschreiben,**" we find confirmation that the narrator is fully in control of and stands above the character. If the students think of this as a children's story or as a fable told for adults, they can easily understand the narrative conventions without much analysis.

4 Perhaps the students know the expression *calling a spade a spade,* meaning using the plain, ordinary name for a plain, ordinary thing. In German, this is **das Ding beim rechten Namen nennen.**

Teaching Suggestion

6 As they do this activity, students should look especially for the instances of the verb **sich ändern** in the central paragraphs of the story.

Teacher Note

The expression **an die Füße frieren** at the top of p. 110, would be **an den Füßen frieren** in modern standard German.

Post-Reading
Teacher Note

Activities 11 and 12 are post-reading tasks that will show whether students can apply what they have learned.

Thinking Critically

Analyzing Tell students a little about Peter Bichsel: He was born (1935) in Lucerne, Switzerland, and was an elementary school teacher before becoming a writer. Does this deepen their understanding of the story in any way? The class should be aware that German Swiss people speak many different local dialects of **Schwyzerdütsch** but have to learn to write the standard version of German in school. Additionally, they are exposed to many influences from the French-Swiss and the Italian-Swiss and are aware of the existence of an almost extinct fourth language, **Romansch.** Would students argue that Bichsel's background would heavily influence what he has to say, or that it would, at most, suggest some choices of topic to him?

Connections and Comparisons

Language-to-Language

Students might find it interesting to know that there are at least a thousand "planned languages." The most successful is probably Bahasa Indonesia, which was developed by a Dutch linguist in the 1920s on the basis of the various languages spoken in Java. It is spoken today by at least 60 million people in the Republic of Indonesia. Other constructed languages students may have heard about are Esperanto, J.R.R. Tolkien's Elvish tongues from *The Lord of the Rings*, and Marc Okrand's tlHingan (Klingon) familiar to *Star Trek*® fans.

You may want to ask your students to find more information on Esperanto, such as who developed the language and when (L. L. Zamenhof of Warsaw, Poland; between 1877–1885); who speaks it (perhaps as many as two million people mostly in central and eastern Europe, mainland China and other areas of East Asia, and certain areas of South America and southwest Asia); and why it is easy to learn (regular and phonetic spelling system, regular and exception-free grammar, and an easy system of forming new words).

Closure

Ask students to think about the following questions: If someone is bored and tired of life, which of the following would be good advice?

get a new hobby; take a class; learn a new skill; change jobs or schools; change hair styles or buy a new wardrobe; join a group and meet people; buy some new video games; get involved in a simulation; take a trip; go to a foreign country; move to a new place and start fresh; do some self-analysis

Which of these might have worked for the man in Bichsel's story?

Zum Lesen Answers
Answers to Activity 1
a. ein alter Mann; b. im obersten Stock eines Hauses in einer kleinen Stadt am Ende der Straße, nahe einer Kreuzung; c.müdes Gesicht, dünner Hals, trägt graue Kleider; d. geht morgens und nachmittags spazieren, spricht mit Nachbarn, sitzt abends am Tisch;
e. limited third person (see first sentence of story)

Answers to Activity 3
There was a special day, and everything was perfect; the weather was just right, people were friendly, the sun was shining, etc.; the man was suddenly happy.
Answers to Activity 4
The old man thinks things will be different, but when he gets home, he finds nothing has changed. His room is still the same, the table is still a table, etc.
Answers to Activity 5
The man gets angry that nothing changes. He begins to rename things and invents his own language. In the end, he can no longer understand people, and they can't understand him. He stops communicating with other people altogether. Answers will vary.
Answers to Activity 6
Answers will vary.
Answers to Activity 7
paragraph 5; **dann** signals to the reader that something in the story is going to change; **jetzt** is used every time the man believes his life is going to change, and **aber** indicates a contrast: in contrast to what the man believes is going to happen, his life does not change.
Answers to Activity 8
He thought that renaming objects would change his life; he thought his new language was funny, and it kept him busy and amused; he could no longer communicate with other people.
Answers to Activity 10
Answers will vary.
Answers to Activity 11
Answers will vary. (possible answers: language is a social tool; at least two or more people have to understand it for it to be a language. Language is by nature communicative.)
Answers to Activity 12
Answers will vary. (possible answers: similarity—both the teens and the old man invent their own language; difference—the teens' language is understood by more than one person (the whole group); consequence—the teens' language brings the group closer together; therefore, it serves as a social tool. However, for the old man it only serves to isolate him because no one else can understand him.

> **PAGES 112–115**

MEHR GRAMMATIKÜBUNGEN

The **Mehr Grammatikübungen** activities are designed as supplemental activities for the grammatical concepts presented in the chapter. You might use them as additional practice, for review, or for assessment.

For more grammar presentations, review, and practice, refer to the following:
• Grammatikheft
• Grammar Tutor for Students of German
• Grammar Summary on pp. R22–R39
• Übungsheft
• Grammar and Vocabulary quizzes (Testing Program)
• Test Generator
• Interaktive Spiele at go.hrw.com

ANWENDUNG

> ### Teaching Resources
> **pp. 116–117**
>
> **PRINT** 📖
> ▶ Lesson Planner, p. 30
> ▶ Listening Activities, p. 30
> ▶ Video Guide, pp. 17–18, 20
>   **Videoclips: Werbung**
> ▶ Grammar Tutor for Students of German, Chapter 4
>
> **MEDIA** 💿 📼
> ▶ One-Stop Planner
> ▶ Video Program
>   Videocassette 1, 40:09–41:20
> ▶ Audio Compact Discs, CD4, Tr. 8

Apply and Assess

 Using the Video
Videocassette 1, 40:09–41:20
At this time, you might want to use the authentic advertising footage from German television. See *Video Guide,* p. 18, for suggestions.

1 Teaching Suggestion
After students have listened to the statements and completed the activity, ask them how they would feel or react in each of the situations. (**Wie würdest du auf … Aussage reagieren?**)

2 Cooperative Learning
Divide the class into four groups, assigning each group one of the questions. Each group then discusses the assigned question in detail, with the recorder taking notes as they go along. After a set amount of time, call on the reporter from each group to a) reread the question to the rest of the class, b) share how the group feels about the question and what its opinion is, and c) pose at least two questions to the rest of the class to elicit some reactions or opinions.

📁 **Portfolio Assessment**
2 You might want to suggest this activity as an oral portfolio item for your students. See *Alternative Assessment Guide,* p. 19.

5 You might want to suggest this activity as a written portfolio item for your students. See *Alternative Assessment Guide,* p. 19.

Apply and Assess

Teaching Suggestion
5 Divide the class into smaller groups of two or three students in order to get more than one response to each of the letters. This also helps the peer writing process, which is easier in a smaller group. Have each group share its response letter with the rest of the class.

KANN ICH'S WIRKLICH?

This page helps students prepare for the test. It is a brief checklist of the major points covered in the chapter. The students should be reminded that it is only a checklist and not necessarily everything that will appear on the test.

For additional self-check options, refer students to the *Grammar Tutor* and the Online self-test for this chapter.

WORTSCHATZ

Review and Assess

Circumlocution
Nouns used to talk about relationships and about getting along with others can be reviewed by using the circumlocution game, **Das treffende Wort suchen.** An **Ausländer** can be described simply as **eine Person, die nicht in diesem Land geboren ist.** Many of the other nouns in this chapter also lend themselves well to circumlocution. See p. 31C for procedures.

Teaching Suggestion
To review and practice the vocabulary, call on several students to answer a question like one of the following:
Was würdest du tun, wenn du in einem fremden Land wärst?
Was findest du gut an deiner besten Freundin?

Teacher Note
 Give the **Kapitel 4** Chapter Test:
Testing Program, pp. 75-80
Audio CD 4, Trs. 11–12.

4
Verhältnis zu anderen

Objectives

In this chapter you will review and practice how to

Erste Stufe

• agree

Zweite Stufe

• give advice
• introduce another point of view
• hypothesize

 internet

go.hrw.com	ADRESSE: go.hrw.com
	KENNWORT: WK3
	WUERZBURG-4

◀ **Wir verstehen uns gut.**

Los geht's! ▪ *Verhältnis zu Eltern und Freunden*

CD 4 Tr. 1

Über ihr Verhältnis zu Eltern und Freunden sprach ein Interviewer mit vier Gymnasiasten. Er unterhielt sich mit Sonja (17), Tanja (18), Michael (17) und Philipp (17).

Interviewer: Wie kommt ihr mit euern Eltern aus?

Michael: Ja, bei mir läuft seit zwei Jahren alles prima.

Interviewer: Was meinst du damit? War's vorher anders?

Michael: Na ja, bis vor zwei Jahren hat's ab und zu Streitigkeiten gegeben.

Interviewer: Kannst du mal ein Beispiel geben?

Michael: Es ist damals meistens um so kleine Alltäglichkeiten gegangen — die Mutter will, dass man schnell noch aufräumt, bevor man weggeht und so weiter.

Tanja: Ja, bei mir ist es auch so: jetzt gibt's keine Streitigkeiten mehr. Das Problem mit dem Weggehen, das früher ein Streitpunkt war, hat sich jetzt erledigt — ich bin ja jetzt achtzehn — und ja, alles andere, darüber kann man ja reden, da braucht man nicht streiten.

Sonja: Da geb ich dir Recht, Tanja. Und ich möchte dazu noch sagen, dass … also, es dauert eben auch eine Zeitlang, bis sich die Eltern daran gewöhnen, dass aus ihren Kindern erwachsene Leute geworden sind.

Philipp: Eben. Ich versteh mich jetzt mit meinen Eltern so prima. Mein Vater ist ein echter Kumpel. Wir gehen zusammen Tennis spielen und so … und ich frag mich oft, warum es früher nicht so gut geklappt hat.

Interviewer: Wer sind eure Freunde? Mit wem seid ihr gewöhnlich zusammen?

Philipp: Unser Freundeskreis? Ja, das sind eigentlich die Leute aus der letzten Klasse. Es ist ja so: in der Kollegstufe gibt es keine festen Klassen, also man ist immer mit anderen Leuten zusammen. Aber im Jahr davor, da waren wir in der 10. Klasse und eben schon seit der 5. Klasse mit den gleichen Leuten zusammen. Und da haben sich gewisse Cliquen gebildet, die eben jetzt was zusammen machen.

Interviewer: Was macht ihr so? Geht ihr tanzen?

Michael: Nee, wirklich nicht!

Sonja: Wir gehen öfters weg, einfach so in ein Café, trinken irgendwas und unterhalten uns, oder wir schauen uns zusammen einen Videofilm an oder …

Michael: Ins Kino gehen wir auch ab und zu zusammen, manchmal sogar auch ins Theater.

Tanja: Besonders, wenn wir Freikarten kriegen.

Philipp: Und wir machen Sport zusammen, wir spielen Tennis, und im Sommer gehen wir halt oft zusammen schwimmen.

Interviewer: Seid ihr auch mit anderen Leuten zusammen, mit denen ihr in der Grundschule wart?

Sonja: Kaum.

Michael: Ich kenn einen, der mit mir im Schwimmverein ist. Ich war mit dem in der Grundschule zusammen und hatte aber keinen Kontakt mehr zu ihm bis eben jetzt … aber wir machen nichts zusammen. Er haut immer gleich ab und fährt zu seiner Clique.

Sonja: Man macht sicher auch etwas mit anderen Leuten, aber ich würd' auch sagen, dass man hauptsächlich mit den eigenen Leuten unterwegs ist. Mit der Zeit merkt man halt, mit was für Leuten man sich versteht, wer die gleichen Interessen hat, ja und demnach richtet man seinen Freundeskreis ein.

Interviewer: Was machen denn die Azubis in ihrer Freizeit?

Michael: Keine Ahnung. Weiß nicht.

Tanja: Ich hab früher in einer Gegend gewohnt — da war ein Freizeitheim, in dem sich meistens Azubis getroffen haben. Aber ich weiß nicht, was die sonst so gemacht haben.

Übungsheft, S. 40

1 Verhältnis zu Eltern und Freunden

Lesen/Schreiben Welche Aussagen (*statements*) machen die vier Schüler zu den Fragen?

a. Wie ist euer Verhältnis zu den Eltern?

b. Wer sind eure Freunde, und was macht ihr mit ihnen?

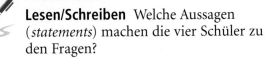

NAME	ELTERN	FREUNDE
Michael	Alles läuft prima.	
Tanja	Es gibt keine Streitigkeiten mehr.	
Philipp		
Sonja		
_____		

2 Und du? Wie steht's mit dir?

Sprechen Trag deinen Namen in die Tabelle ein und berichte kurz, wie dein Verhältnis zu deinen Eltern und Freunden ist!

3 Was erzählt Philipp?

Sprechen Erzähle, was Philipp über sein Verhältnis zu seinen Eltern und Freunden berichtet!

a. Philipp versteht sich mit seinen Eltern prima. Sein Vater …

b. Die Freunde, die er hat, sind Leute aus der 10. Klasse. Er ist mit ihnen …

c. Sie machen …

Wortschatz

auf Deutsch erklärt

Ich <u>komme</u> gut <u>mit</u> ihnen <u>aus</u>.   Wir haben keine
Probleme miteinander.

Wir <u>verstehen</u> <u>uns</u> nicht so gut <u>mit</u> ihnen.
Wir kommen nicht gut mit ihnen aus.

Wir <u>richten</u> <u>uns</u> <u>nach</u> euch.   Wir machen gern,
was ihr machen wollt.

der Kumpel   ein guter Freund

der Freundeskreis   die Gruppe von Freunden

erwachsen sein   kein Kind mehr sein

reden   sprechen

auf Englisch erklärt   p. 91X

Wir haben ein problematisches <u>Verhältnis</u>.
We have a difficult relationship.

Wir haben aber wenig <u>Krach</u> miteinander.
We really don't argue much with one another.

Meine Eltern **schimpfen** immer mit mir!
My parents are always scolding me!

Das <u>kann</u> ich <u>nicht leiden</u>!   *I can't stand that!*

der Streit   *quarrel*

der Streitpunkt   *point of contention*

<u>Worum geht es</u>?   *What's it about?*

Sie <u>gehört</u> einem Volleyballclub <u>an</u>.
She belongs to a volleyball club.

(Übungsheft, S. 41, Ü. 1)   (Grammatikheft, S. 28, Ü. 1)

---

4 ## Gibt es hier Konflikte?   4–1

Schreiben Was können Eltern manchmal nicht leiden? Schau dir die
Zeichnungen an und suche die Satzteile
ganz unten, die zu den Zeichnungen
am besten passen! Schreib dann die
Sätze richtig auf, indem du sie mit den
Konjunktionen verbindest!

Es gibt Krach, …   E.g.: **Es gibt Krach, wenn ich mein Zimmer nicht aufräume.**

Meine Eltern schimpfen, …

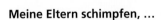  

Sie können es nicht leiden, …

(wenn) ich räume
mein Zimmer nicht auf

(wenn) ich komme zu
spät nach Hause

(wenn) ich sehe zu viel fern

(dass) ich habe mir
die Haare gefärbt

(weil) ich helfe nicht immer

(wie) ich ziehe mich an

(weil) meine Noten
sind schlecht

Mehr Grammatikübungen,
S. 112, Ü. 1

(wenn) ich spiele
die Musik laut

5 Worüber streiten sich die Leute? Scripts and answers on p. 91G

CD 4 Tr. 2

Zuhören Ihr hört jetzt vier Gespräche. Die Leute, die sich unterhalten, streiten sich. Worüber streiten sie? Endet in jedem Fall der Streit gut, also produktiv, oder schlecht, d.h. die Personen erreichen nichts?

6 Die Eltern schimpfen so oft!

Lesen/Sprechen Erzähle deiner Partnerin, wann es bei dir zu Hause Krach gibt, und deine Partnerin erzählt dir dann, wie es bei ihr zu Hause ist!

Du Es gibt Krach, wenn ich … *oder*
Meine Mutter schimpft immer, weil … *oder*
Die Eltern können es nicht leiden, dass …

Zimmer nicht aufräumen
einen Freund/eine Freundin haben
zu viel ausgehen
die Musik zu laut spielen
zu spät nach Hause kommen

schlechte Noten haben
zu viel Geld ausgeben
sich verrückt anziehen
sich die Haare färben
sich zu sehr schminken

So sagt man das!

Agreeing

You have learned a number of ways to express agreement. Here are a few more:
If your friend says:

Du sollst nicht so viel streiten.
Wir müssen unsere Hausaufgaben erledigen.
Bei uns ist der Streitpunkt das Geschirrspülen.

You may answer:

Da geb ich dir Recht.
Ganz meine Meinung.
Bei mir ist es auch so.

Mehr Grammatikübungen,
S. 112, Ü. 2

Grammatikheft,
S. 29, Ü. 2

What are some other ways you have learned to express agreement?[1]

7 Streit mit dem Vater Script and answers on p. 91H

CD 4 Tr. 3

Zuhören Claudia erzählt Patrick, dass sie Streit mit ihrem Vater hatte. Hör gut zu, und mach dir Notizen, worum es geht! Stimmt Patrick Claudias Meinung zu oder nicht? Anhand deiner Notizen spiel dann mit einem Partner die Rollen von Claudia und ihrem Vater!

8 Was sagst du dazu?

Sprechen Diskutier über die folgenden Aussagen mit deinem Partner! Stimmst du diesen Aussagen ganz zu oder nur teilweise? Was kannst du noch dazu sagen?

1. Eltern sollen mehr Vertrauen zu ihren Kindern haben.
2. In unserem Alter braucht man nicht streiten. Über Probleme kann ich mit meinen Eltern immer reden.
3. Die meisten Streitigkeiten gehen nur um Alltäglichkeiten.
4. Eltern können sich nicht daran gewöhnen, dass aus ihren Kindern erwachsene Leute werden.
5. Man sollte ab und zu auch mal mit den Eltern ins Theater oder in ein klassisches Konzert gehen.

---

1. **Da hast du Recht; Ich meine das auch; Stimmt!; Das finde ich auch.**

9 Grammatik im Kontext

Schreiben Mit wem verbringen Jugendliche ihre Freizeit? Schreib einen kurzen Bericht darüber, indem du die Satzlücken in dem folgenden Text füllst! Die Information dafür findest du in der Grafik unten.

An ~~erster~~ Stelle steht die Clique. Die Statistik zeigt, dass die Jugendlichen ~~32~~ Prozent ihrer Freizeit mit der Clique verbringen. 24 ~~Prozent~~ ihrer Freizeit sind die Jugendlichen mit ~~dem Freund/der Freundin~~ zusammen. An ~~dritter~~ Stelle steht mit 18 Prozent die ~~Familie~~. Nur ~~16~~ Prozent ihrer Freizeit verbringen die Jugendlichen allein. An ~~fünfter/letzter~~ Stelle nannten die Jugendlichen ~~sonstige Personen~~ mit 10 Prozent.

Ein wenig Landeskunde

Die Clique, die kleine, lose Freundesgruppe, ist für die meisten Jugendlichen von heute von großer Bedeutung. Sechzig Prozent aller Jugendlichen sagen, sie gehören einer Clique an; 1962 waren es nur 15 Prozent.

Was macht die Clique so beliebt? Cliquen sind den Jugendlichen wichtig, vor allem für die Gestaltung der Freizeit. Auf diesem Gebiet fangen die Jugendlichen schon sehr früh an, sich von ihren Eltern zu lösen. Ein Sportverein ist nicht immer die ideale Lösung: Vereine sind organisiert, und das wollen viele Jugendliche nicht. In der Clique ist man nicht allein, man ist mit Gleichaltrigen zusammen, also man hat Freizeitpartner.

Wo treffen sich die Cliquen? Diskos, Jugendheime, Schwimmbäder und vor allem Fußgängerzonen und öffentliche Plätze sind Orte, wo man sich treffen kann. Hier in der Clique kann man die Zeit verbringen, miteinander reden. Hier wird man so genommen, wie man ist.

Mit wem verbringen Jugendliche ihre Freizeit?

mit sonstigen Personen 10%

allein 16%

mit der Familie 18%

mit dem Freund/ der Freundin 24%

mit der Clique 32%

Ein wenig Grammatik

Ordinal numbers

In order to use numbers as adjectives, as in the sentence "I am in the tenth grade," you need to know the ordinal numbers. The first three, as in English, are irregular.

Das ist mein **erst**er Wagen.
Ich würde mir den Film ein **zweit**es Mal ansehen.
Nein, ich meine die **dritt**e Straße rechts.

After that, add a **t** to the end of the cardinal number and then the correct adjective ending.

Ich bin in der **zehnt**en Klasse.
Meine Schwester hat am **achtzehnt**en Juli Geburtstag.

Remember, as adjectives, these numbers follow all the rules for adjective endings. For a list of the ordinal numbers, see the Grammar Summary.

Übungsheft, S. 41–42, Ü. 2&4

Grammatikheft, S. 29, Ü. 3

Mehr Grammatikübungen, S. 113, Ü. 3

10 Für mein Notizbuch

Schreiben Schreib, warum deine Eltern manchmal mit dir schimpfen, worüber sie sich freuen und wann oder warum es ab und zu Krach gibt!

Relative clauses

1. Sometimes you may want to say more than you can express in a simple sentence. One solution is to create a new sentence.

   Ich kenne einen netten Jungen. Er ist in meinem Schwimmverein.

2. For a more fluid style you can also use a relative clause. A relative clause is introduced by a relative pronoun that refers back to the noun it replaces.

   Ich kenne einen netten Jungen, **der in meinem Schwimmverein ist.**

   Siehst du die Frau, **die da drüben steht?**

3. The gender of a relative pronoun depends on the word it refers back to.

   Der Freundeskreis, der aus sieben Schülern besteht, trifft sich im Café.
   Die Clique, die jedes Wochenende zusammenkommt, spielt gern Tennis.
   Das Problem, das früher ganz groß war, ist jetzt gelöst.
   Die Schüler, die jetzt von der Schule kommen, sind bei mir in der Klasse.

4. The case of the relative pronoun is determined by its *function in the relative clause* as a subject, direct object, indirect object, or object of a preposition.

Die Schüler, **die** sich immer treffen, …	(subject)
Der Freundeskreis, **den** ich gern mag, …	(direct object)
Die Clique, **der** ich angehöre, …	(object of a verb taking the dative)
Die Frau, **über die** wir jetzt reden, …	(object of an accusative preposition)
Die Leute, **mit denen** ich ausgehe, …	(object of a dative preposition)

5. As relative clauses are dependent clauses, the conjugated verb in the relative clause is always in last position.

6. Here are the relative pronouns:

	Masculine	Feminine	Neuter	Plural
Nominative	der	die	das	die
Accusative	den	die	das	die
Dative	dem	der	dem	denen

Übungsheft, S. 42–44, Ü. 3, 5–8   Grammatikheft, S. 30–31, Ü. 4–5

Mehr Grammatikübungen,
S. 113–114, Ü. 4–5

---

11 ## Grammatik im Kontext

Lesen/Schreiben Eine Schülerin erzählt, wie ihr Verhältnis zu Eltern, Freunden und Lehrern ist. Füll die Satzlücken mit den richtigen Relativpronomen!

Mir geht's eigentlich sehr gut. Ich habe Eltern, ⸺die⸺ ganz vernünftig und tolerant sind. Ich habe Freunde, mit ⸺denen⸺ ich mich gut verstehe. Ich habe Lehrer, ⸺die⸺ sehr nett sind. Ein Lehrer, ⸺den⸺ wir alle furchtbar gern haben, trifft sich mit uns nach der Schule. Wir diskutieren über irgendein Problem, ⸺das⸺ einer von uns gerade hat. Meine Freundin Renate, mit ⸺der⸺ ich schon in der Grundschule war, ist auch immer dabei. Nach einer Diskussion, ⸺die⸺ besonders interessant war, sind wir in ein Café gegangen, ⸺das⸺ nicht weit von der Schule ist, und haben uns noch lange darüber unterhalten.

Weiter geht's! · *Verhältnis zu anderen Leuten*

CD 4 Tr. 4

Die deutschen Schulklassen sind längst nicht mehr so homogen wie früher. Heute gibt es nicht nur Randgruppen in den Klassen, sondern auch viele ausländische Schüler. Was sagen unsere vier Gymnasiasten dazu?

Interviewer: Gehört ihr irgendwelchen Gruppen wie Punker, Raver oder so was an? Kennt ihr vielleicht Leute aus solchen Gruppen?

Michael: Bei uns, also an unserer Schule, gibt es ein paar Punker, Grunger, Öko-Freaks und so ..., und die sondern sich schon ab von den andern. Die Punker zum Beispiel sind immer zusammen, aber sie unterhalten sich genauso mit andern Leuten wie untereinander. Und ich versteh mich mit denen auch ganz gut, aber wir machen außerhalb der Schule nie etwas zusammen.

Tanja: Ja, also ich bin in einer Raver-Clique. Wir ziehen uns gern anders an und hören Raver-Musik, aber ich habe auch Freunde, die keine Raver sind.

Philipp: Also, was ich an den Randgruppen gut finde ist, die bringen die Interessen der anderen Schüler an die Lehrer. Manche sind eben doch aufsässig ...

Sonja: Ja, und damit machen sie sich auch manchmal unbeliebt bei vielen Lehrern. Aber so mit den Punkern zum Beispiel gibt's keine Schwierigkeiten. Ich hab da auch keine Vorurteile, und ich find es okay, wenn man zu einer Gruppe gehört.

Interviewer: Wie ist euer Verhältnis zu ausländischen Schülern? Sind da welche an euerm Gymnasium?

Philipp: Ja, wir haben schon einige Ausländer, aber fast alle von ihnen sind in Deutschland geboren und sprechen Deutsch genauso gut wie wir, sogar besser als ihre Muttersprache.

Tanja: Meine Schwester geht auf die Realschule, in die 7. Klasse, und da sind ein paar türkische Schüler mit ihr in der Klasse. Und die Elke, so heißt meine Schwester, sagt, dass sie meistens unter sich bleiben, also in der Pause und auch nach der Schule.

Michael: Die sind selber schuld daran. Sie versuchen oft gar nicht, sich in unserm Land anzupassen.

Philipp: Das stimmt aber so nicht! Auch wenn sie versuchen, sich anzupassen, werden sie oft von uns Deutschen nicht akzeptiert, weil sie Ausländer sind. Aber die Mädchen tun mir echt Leid. Viele müssen sich hier so anziehen wie in der Türkei, ein Kopftuch tragen und so. Ihre Eltern wollen das so.

Tanja: Genau. Meine Schwester sagt zum Beispiel, dass einige Mädchen beim Sport überhaupt nicht mitmachen dürfen. Die Eltern verbieten das einfach.

Sonja: Die haben eben in der Türkei andere Sitten und Gebräuche. Ich finde, wir sollten nicht vergessen, dass sie sich nicht absichtlich absondern, sondern dass es kulturbedingt ist.

Michael: Ja, klar. Aber wenn ich als Gast in einem anderen Land wohne, so muss ich doch versuchen, mich ein wenig anzupassen.

Tanja: Was würdest du denn einem ausländischen Schüler raten, der sich isoliert fühlt?

Michael: Ja, ich würde ihm sagen, du, es ist wichtig, dass du mit uns Sport machst, oder vielleicht kannst du in unserer Umwelt-AG mitmachen …

Tanja: Sicher, aber denk doch mal daran, dass diese Leute oft ganz andere Interessen haben!

Michael: Eine Möglichkeit wäre, mal mit ihnen was zu unternehmen, um ihre Kultur besser kennen zu lernen.

Sonja: Das find ich gut. Das machen aber viel zu wenige Deutsche. Warum organisieren wir nicht mal eine Fete für nächsten Samstag und laden Hassan und seine Clique dazu ein?

Michael: Find ich prima!

Übungsheft, S. 45

12 Stimmt oder stimmt nicht?

Lesen/Schreiben Wenn der Satz nicht stimmt, schreib die richtige Antwort!

1. Die Punker in dieser Schule sprechen nicht mit anderen Leuten.
2. Die Lehrer haben ab und zu Schwierigkeiten mit den Punkern.
3. Alle Ausländer an dieser Schule können nicht sehr gut Deutsch.
4. Einige ausländische Kinder dürfen sich nicht so kleiden wie die Deutschen.
5. Die meisten ausländischen Schüler sind mit anderen Sitten und Gebräuchen aufgewachsen.

1. Stimmt nicht. Die Punker unterhalten sich auch mit anderen Leuten.
2. Stimmt nicht. Mit den Punkern gibt es keine Schwierigkeiten.
3. Stimmt nicht. Die Ausländer an der Schule sprechen gut Deutsch.
4. Stimmt.
5. Stimmt.

13 Was hast du verstanden?

Lesen/Schreiben Beantworte die folgenden Fragen.

1. Wie beschreiben die vier Schüler die Randgruppen an ihrer Schule?
2. Was ist anders bei türkischen Schülern als bei deutschen Schülern?
3. Wie könnten deutsche und ausländische Schüler vielleicht besser zusammenkommen?

Objectives Giving advice; introducing another point of view; hypothesizing

WK3 WUERZBURG-4

Wortschatz

auf Deutsch erklärt

Was <u>an</u> dir <u>gut ist</u>, ist deine Toleranz. Ich finde deine Toleranz gut.

Sie sind <u>anders</u>. Sie sind nicht wie wir.

Wir <u>verbieten</u> es dir. Wir sagen dir, dass du es nicht darfst.

Sie <u>bleiben</u> <u>unter</u> <u>sich</u>. Sie gehen nicht mit anderen aus.

unbeliebt Man mag ihn oder sie nicht.

der Ausländer einer aus einem anderen Land

die Schwierigkeit Problem

auf Englisch erklärt

Sie haben andere <u>Sitten</u> und <u>Gebräuche</u>. *They have different customs and traditions.*

Wir haben nicht die gleiche <u>Muttersprache</u>. *We don't share the same native language.*

Das Mädchen dort <u>sondert</u> <u>sich</u> <u>von</u> den anderen <u>ab</u>. *That girl there keeps to herself.*

Sie macht es nicht <u>absichtlich</u>. *She doesn't do it on purpose.*

Es ist <u>kulturbedingt</u>. *It is for cultural reasons.*

Sie gehören einer <u>Randgruppe</u> an. *They belong to a fringe group.*

Wir <u>sind</u> ja selber <u>schuld</u> dar<u>an</u>! *It's our own fault!*

Aber <u>Vorurteile</u> haben, find ich schlimm. *But I think having prejudices is really bad.*

 p. 91X 4–2  (Übungsheft, S. 46, Ü. 1) (Grammatikheft, S. 32, Ü. 6)

---

14 **Neue Schüler in der Klasse** Script and answers on p. 91H

CD 4 Tr. 5

Zuhören Kalle und Hannes sind in der 10. Klasse. Es ist zu Anfang des Schuljahres, und sie sprechen über die neuen Schüler in der Klasse. Hör ihrem Gespräch gut zu und bestimme, welche von den neuen Schülern sich anpassen und welche nicht!

15 **Hast du Vorurteile?**

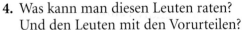

Sprechen Setzt euch in kleinen Gruppen zusammen und seht euch die Illustrationen an! Überlegt euch Folgendes und diskutiert darüber!

1. Was sind Vorurteile? Definiert dieses Wort auf Deutsch!
2. Welche Vorurteile, die ihr kennt, gibt es gegen die Leute in den Illustrationen?
3. Welche Vorurteile gibt es gegen Leute in deiner Stadt? Welche Schwierigkeiten haben sie?
4. Was kann man diesen Leuten raten? Und den Leuten mit den Vorurteilen?

So sagt man das!

Giving advice; introducing another point of view

When giving advice, you could begin your sentence by saying:

Vielleicht kannst du dich anpassen.
Es ist wichtig, dass man frei von Vorurteilen bleibt.
Ich würde mit den anderen Sport machen.

When presenting another point of view, you might begin your sentence with:

Das mag schon sein, aber es ist schwerer, als du meinst.
Es kommt darauf an, ob deine Eltern es dir verbieten.
Aber denk doch mal daran, dass sie aus einer anderen Kultur kommen.
Du darfst nicht vergessen, dass jeder Mensch irgendwo Ausländer ist.

Grammatikheft, S. 33, Ü. 7

---

16 Er hat immer eine Meinung Script and answers on p. 91H

CD 4 Tr. 6

Zuhören Der Paul hat zu allem eine Meinung und gibt gern seinen Freunden Rat. Aber nicht alle akzeptieren blind, was er meint. Hör zu, wie er versucht, einem unglücklichen Kumpel Rat zu geben! Was ist das Problem? Welchem Rat will der Kumpel folgen, welchem nicht?

17 Was sagen die Gruppen?

Zwei verschiedene Gruppen von Schülern machen die Aussagen rechts. Lies mit einer Partnerin die verschiedenen Aussagen und entscheide, wer wahrscheinlich diese Aussagen macht!

a. Sprechen Beschreib diese Personen, wer sie sind, woher sie kommen, was sie machen, usw.!

b. Schreiben Schreibt dann zusammen ein Gespräch, das zwischen den zwei Gruppen stattfindet! Wer gibt Rat? Wer akzeptiert ihn?

Die einen sagen:

Ihr habt andere Sitten und Gebräuche.

Ihr sondert euch ab.

Ihr seid selber schuld daran, weil ihr euch nicht anpasst.

Ihr tut euch schwer.

Die anderen sagen:

Wir haben Schwierigkeiten mit der Sprache.

Wir fühlen uns isoliert.

Ihr habt Vorurteile, weil wir anders sind.

Wir sind hier fremd.

18 Der Markus tut sich schwer in der Schule

Markus' Freunde machen sich Sorgen um (*worry about*) ihn, weil der Lehrer meint, dass Markus Schwierigkeiten in der Schule hat. Markus selber ist natürlich unglücklich darüber. Such dir eine Partnerin! Hört euch Markus' Probleme an! Danach ratet ihm, was er tun soll!

a. Lesen Lest zuerst zusammen die Beobachtungen unten, die Markus' Lehrer gemacht hat! Spielt dann die Rollen von Lehrer und Markus! Der Lehrer sagt Markus, was er macht und nicht macht!

BEISPIEL Markus, du kommst oft sehr spät in die Schule!

b. Sprechen Dann tauscht die Rollen aus! Einer spielt die Rolle eines Freundes von Markus und gibt ihm Rat.

BEISPIEL Markus, es ist wichtig, dass du pünktlich kommst.

ist ziemlich aufsässig

passt sich nicht an

macht sich bei den Lehrern unbeliebt

sondert sich von den andern ab

So sagt man das!

Hypothesizing

People often make hypotheses about how things might or could be. In English, we often use an "if …, then …" statement to make a hypothesis. In German, „wenn …, dann …" statements express the same idea, although **dann** is often omitted.

When hypothesizing, you might say:

> **Wenn** du in einem fremden Land **wärst**, **(dann) würdest** du schon mit den andern **mitmachen**.
> **Wenn** sie Schwierigkeiten mit der Sprache **hätte**, **(dann) würde** sie sich isoliert **fühlen**.

What do you notice about the word order and punctuation in these statements?

---

19 **Grammatik im Kontext**

Script and answers on p. 91l

CD 4 Tr. 7

Zuhören Kerstin und Gertrud sprechen über ihre nächste Reise, die sie in den amerikanischen Westen machen wollen. Hör gut zu, wie sie über ihre Pläne spekulieren! Was werden sie bestimmt machen? Was bleibt spekulativ?

20 **Grammatik im Kontext**

Lesen/Schreiben Füll die Satzlücken mit Formen von **hätte, wäre** und **würde**. Verbinde dann die Sätze, und pass auf die Wortstellung auf!

1. Wenn meine junge Schwester jetzt erwachsen wäre,
2. Wenn wir Krach mit unseren Eltern hätten,
3. Wenn er mein Kumpel wäre,
4. Wenn ich eine schlechte Note in Mathe hätte,

a. wir würden ruhig darüber reden.
b. wir würden zum Fußballspiel gehen.
c. mein Lehrer würde schimpfen.
d. sie würde auch Auto fahren dürfen.

1. d
2. a
3. b
4. c

Ein wenig Grammatik

When making hypotheses, German speakers use two very common verbs to shorten a phrase. As you already know, **hätte** means the same as **würde** plus **haben**.

> **Wenn ich Angst haben würde, (dann) würde ich nicht hingehen.**

or

> **Wenn ich Angst hätte, …**

Another is **wäre**, which is the same as **würde** plus **sein**.

> **Ich würde lieber in München sein.**

or

> **Ich wäre lieber in München.**

The endings for **wäre** are the same as for **hätte** and **würde**.

Übungsheft, S. 46, Ü. 2

Grammatikheft, S. 34, Ü. 8

Mehr Grammatikübungen, S. 114–115, Ü. 6–7

---

21 **Als Austauschschüler in Deutschland**

Sprechen Setzt euch in Gruppen zusammen und sagt, was ihr tun würdet, wenn ihr in einem anderen Land wärt, zum Beispiel als Austauschschüler an einem Gymnasium in Deutschland!

BEISPIEL

DU   Was würdest du tun, wenn du als Austauschschüler an einem deutschen Gymnasium wärst?

PARTNER 1   Also, wenn ich an einem deutschen Gymnasium wäre, würde ich mich mit meinen Klassenkameraden unterhalten. Und du?

PARTNER 2   Wenn ich in Deutschland wäre, …

The genitive case

You have learned to use phrases with **von** to show possession. For example: **Das ist das Auto von meinem Vater.** You can also use the genitive case to show possession: **Das ist das Auto meines Vaters.**

How would you say that in English? Notice also the difference between English and German word order.

Definite and indefinite articles as well as possessives have the following forms in the genitive case:

Das ist das Auto …

	Masculine	Feminine	Neuter
Def. article	**des Jungen**	**der Chefin**	**des Geschäfts**
Indef. article	**eines Freundes**	**einer Frau**	**eines Mädchens**
Possessive	**meines Vaters**	**meiner Mutter**	**meines Kindes**

Definite articles and possessives have the same form in the plural as the feminine singular.

Das sind die Autos der Schüler der dreizehnten Klasse, und hier sind die Mofas meiner jüngeren Schüler.

The following applies to the genitive:

- Most masculine nouns that end in **-e** add **-n.**
- Masculine and neuter nouns of one syllable add **-es.**
- Masculine and neuter nouns with two or more syllables add **-s.**
- Adjectives add **-en** regardless of the gender and number of the noun.

Prepositional phrases with **von** are more common in spoken than in written German. For example, **Das Haus von meinem Onkel …** is more common than **Das Haus meines Onkels …** There are also some fixed expressions with the genitive that you will learn as you become more familiar with the language.

Mehr Grammatikübungen, S. 115, Ü. 8–9

Übungsheft, S. 47–49, Ü. 3–9

Grammatikheft, S. 35–36, Ü. 9–11

 22 **Grammatik im Kontext**

 Schreiben Schreib die folgenden Sätze um, und verwende dabei Genitivformen!

1. Die Schüler vom Einstein-Gymnasium sind sehr gescheit (*clever*).
2. Die Leute von der letzten Klasse sind jetzt unsere Freunde.
3. Die Ziele von diesen Cliquen gefallen mir überhaupt nicht.
4. Die Mitglieder von diesem Schwimmverein treffen sich morgen.
5. Die Interessen, die ein Freund hat, können ganz anders sein.
6. Die Vorurteile, die unsere Schüler haben, sind oft groß.
7. Das Deutsch, das der türkische Schüler spricht, ist sehr gut.
8. Der Lehrer, den meine Schwester hat, ist aus Deutschland.

1. Die Schüler des Einstein-Gymnasiums sind sehr gescheit.
2. Die Leute der letzten Klasse sind jetzt unsere Freunde.
3. Die Ziele dieser Cliquen gefallen mir überhaupt nicht.
4. Die Mitglieder dieses Schwimmvereins treffen sich morgen.
5. Die Interessen eines Freundes können ganz anders sein.
6. Die Vorurteile unserer Schüler sind oft groß.
7. Das Deutsch des türkischen Schülers ist sehr gut.
8. Der Lehrer meiner Schwester ist aus Deutschland.

 23 **Für mein Notizbuch**

 Schreiben Schreib in dein Notizbuch, wie du dich mit deinen Klassenkameraden verstehst! Hast du Vorurteile gegen Schüler, die anders sind als du? Kennst du Schüler, die sich isoliert fühlen? Hast du Kontakte zu ihnen?

LANDESKUNDE · LANDESKUNDE

Die verschiedenen Bildungswege in Deutschland

Übungsheft, S. 50, Ü. 1–3

Helga, Klaus und Hassan sind im gleichen Alter und wohnen in derselben Nachbarschaft. Sie kennen sich schon jahrelang. Als Kinder haben sie dieselbe Grundschule besucht, bis sie 10 Jahre alt waren. Danach hat jeder einen anderen Bildungsweg genommen. Jetzt sind sie 18 Jahre alt und sehen einander selten.

Hassan lernt jetzt für das Abitur. Er muss sehr gute Noten bekommen, weil er Psychologie an einer Universität studieren will.

Helga ist auch sehr fleißig und hat neulich ihre Lehre (*apprenticeship*) im Kaufhof als Verkäuferin begonnen. Sie geht zweimal die Woche in die Berufsschule; an den restlichen drei Tagen wird sie in den verschiedenen Abteilungen des Kaufhauses ausgebildet. Sie hat vor, eines Tages Abteilungsleiterin zu werden.

Klaus besucht jetzt die Fachoberschule und will danach eine Lehre als Krankenpfleger machen. Deshalb möchte er auch nach der Lehre nicht zur Bundeswehr, sondern Zivildienst in einem Krankenhaus machen.

A. 1. Schau dir die Tabelle an!

2. Welche Bildungswege sind Hassan, Klaus und Helga gegangen? Was fällt dir am deutschen Schulsystem auf? Diskutier über die Hauptmerkmale mit einem Klassenkameraden!

3. Wodurch unterscheidet sich das deutsche Schulsystem von dem amerikanischen System? Mach eine ähnliche Tabelle vom amerikanischen System.

B. Vergleiche das deutsche Schulsystem mit dem amerikanischen Schulsystem! Was findest du besser oder schlechter?

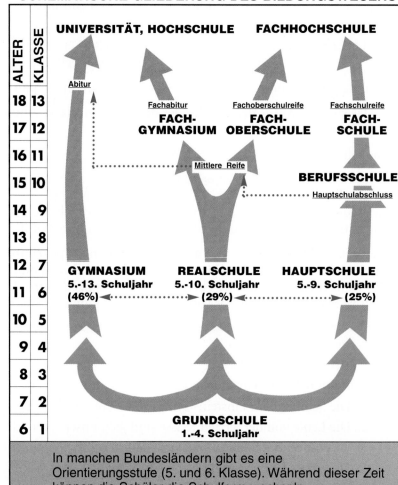

SCHEMATISCHE GLIEDERUNG DES BILDUNGSWESENS

In manchen Bundesländern gibt es eine Orientierungsstufe (5. und 6. Klasse). Während dieser Zeit können die Schüler die Schulform wechseln.

Für Haupt- und Realschüler gibt es die Möglichkeit, auf ein Gymnasium zu gehen, wenn sie beim Schulabschluss überdurchschnittliche Noten haben.

STANDARDS: 2.1, 2.2, 3.2, 4.2

As an Employee Relations specialist at a computer firm in Dresden, you notice that employees of different ethnic and national groups—Germans, Poles, Indians, Pakistanis, Africans, etc.—don't mix during the lunch hour. Develop an educational program that encourages employees to know people of other cultures and to concentrate on personal similarities, not differences. Make handouts or a packet for those attending the program, including an agenda and a detailed explanation of why this program is so important. You could even include a food-tasting menu, a questionnaire, or a get-to-know-you game.

Zum Schreiben

As a teenager you have a lot of difficult decisions to make. Good advice can often help you make these decisions, and one place to get it is from advice columns. In this activity, you will ask for advice in a letter to an advice column.

Lieber Herr Weißalles!

Denk an ein Problem, das du hast oder das vielleicht deutsche Schüler haben! Schreib einen kurzen Brief an eine Zeitung, um Rat für dieses Problem zu holen!

> **Schreibtipp Determining the purpose** Before you begin to write, carefully consider the purpose of what you are writing. You may be writing to express yourself, to entertain, to persuade someone of something, to get or to give information, or for many other reasons. In fact, some writing may have more than one purpose. In a personal letter, for example, you may want to convey information but also entertain a friend. Thinking about the purpose(s) of your writing helps to clarify who your audience is and what tone of language you should choose.

A. Vorbereiten

1. Schreib das Problem auf, wofür du Rat suchst! Dann schreib alle Ideen auf, die mit diesem Problem zusammenhängen!

2. Denk an den Zweck (*purpose*) deines Briefes! Warum schreibst du den Brief? Was willst du damit erreichen? Wähl Ideen von der Liste aus, die diesen Zweck unterstützen und unterstreiche sie!

B. Ausführen

Verwende jetzt die Punkte, die du gewählt hast, und beschreib das Problem in einem kurzen Brief an Herrn Weißalles! Erfinde einen Namen und einen Ort für den Absender (dich)!

C. Überarbeiten

1. Lies deinen Brief einem Partner vor! Hat er dein Problem gut verstanden? Frag deinen Partner, welche Punkte geholfen haben, dein Problem klarzumachen, und streiche unnötige Punkte aus! Besprich die Wirkung der Sprache in deinem Brief!

2. Wenn dein Brief viele kurze Sätze enthält, mach ihn fließender mit Nebensätzen!

3. Wenn du mit dem Brief zufrieden bist, lies ihn noch einmal durch! Hast du alles richtig buchstabiert? Hast du Nebensätze durch Kommas getrennt?

4. Jetzt schreib deinen Brief sehr ordentlich in Spaltenform auf (du kannst auch einen Computer benutzen), damit er aussieht, wie ein Brief in einer Zeitung!

Ein Tisch ist ein Tisch
von Peter Bichsel

Ich will von einem alten Mann erzählen, von einem Mann, der kein Wort mehr sagt, ein müdes Gesicht hat, zu müd zum Lächeln und zu müd, um böse zu sein. Er wohnt in einer kleinen Stadt, am Ende der Straße, nahe der Kreuzung. Es lohnt sich fast nicht, ihn zu beschreiben, kaum etwas unterscheidet ihn von andern. Er trägt einen grauen Hut, graue Hosen, einen grauen Rock und im Winter den langen grauen Mantel, und er hat einen dünnen Hals, dessen Haut trocken und runzelig ist, die weißen Hemdkragen sind ihm viel zu weit.

Im obersten Stock des Hauses hat er sein Zimmer, vielleicht war er verheiratet und hatte Kinder, vielleicht wohnte er früher in einer andern Stadt. Bestimmt war er einmal ein Kind, aber das war zu einer Zeit, wo die Kinder wie Erwachsene angezogen waren. Man sieht sie so im Fotoalbum der Großmutter. In seinem Zimmer sind zwei Stühle, ein Tisch, ein Teppich, ein Bett und ein Schrank. Auf einem kleinen Tisch steht ein Wecker, daneben liegen alte Zeitungen und das Fotoalbum, an der Wand hängen ein Spiegel und ein Bild.

Der alte Mann machte morgens einen Spaziergang und nachmittags einen Spaziergang, sprach ein paar Worte mit seinem Nachbarn, und abends saß er an seinem Tisch.

Das änderte sich nie, auch sonntags war das so. Und wenn der Mann am Tisch saß, hörte er den Wecker ticken, immer den Wecker ticken.

Dann gab es einmal einen besonderen Tag, einen Tag mit Sonne, nicht zu heiß, nicht zu kalt, mit Vogelgezwitscher, mit freundlichen Leuten, mit Kindern, die spielten — und das Besondere war, daß das alles dem Mann plötzlich gefiel.

Er lächelte.

„Jetzt wird sich alles ändern", dachte er. Er öffnete den obersten Hemdknopf, nahm den Hut in die Hand, beschleunigte seinen Gang, wippte sogar beim Gehen ein bißchen in den Knien und freute sich. Er kam in seine Straße, nickte den Kindern zu, ging vor sein Haus, stieg die Treppe hoch, nahm die Schlüssel aus der Tasche, freute sich über ihr Klingeln und schloß sein Zimmer auf.

Aber im Zimmer war alles gleich, ein Tisch, zwei Stühle, ein Bett. Und wie er sich hinsetzte, hörte er wieder das Ticken, und alle Freude war vorbei, denn nichts änderte sich.

Und den Mann überkam eine große Wut.

Eine Kurzgeschichte

Lesestrategie Determining the main idea of a story Focusing on the main idea (or ideas) of a short story, rather than trying to understand every word, is a strategy that will make reading German more manageable and enjoyable. In a short story, the main idea is rarely stated explicitly, but rather illustrated through a series of events. As you read, ask yourself from time to time what point or statement the author is making.

Getting Started

1. Read the title and the first four paragraphs. Answer the following questions using words and phrases from the story.

   a. Wer ist die Hauptfigur?

   b. Wo wohnt er?

   c. Wie sieht er aus?

   d. Was macht der Mann an einem gewöhnlichen Tag?

   e. Wer erzählt die Geschichte? Woher weißt du das?

For answers, see p. 91W.

Er sah im Spiegel sein Gesicht rot anlaufen, sah, wie er die Augen zukniff; dann verkrampfte er seine Hände zu Fäusten, hob sie und schlug mit ihnen auf die Tischplatte, erst nur einen Schlag, dann noch einen, und dann begann er auf den Tisch zu trommeln und schrie dazu immer wieder:

„Es muß sich ändern, es muß sich ändern!"

Und man hörte den Wecker nicht mehr. Und dann begannen seine Hände zu schmerzen, seine Stimme versagte, dann hörte man den Wecker wieder, und nichts änderte sich. »Immer derselbe Tisch", sagte der Mann, »dieselben Stühle, das Bett, das Bild. Und dem Tisch sage ich Tisch, dem Bild sage ich Bild, das Bett heißt Bett, und den Stuhl nennt man Stuhl. Warum denn eigentlich?" Die Franzosen sagen dem Bett »li", dem Tisch »tabl", nennen das Bild »tablo" und den Stuhl „schäs", und sie verstehen sich. Und die Chinesen verstehen sich auch.

„Weshalb heißt das Bett nicht Bild", dachte der Mann und lächelte, dann lachte er, lachte, bis die Nachbarn an die Wand klopften und »Ruhe" riefen.

„Jetzt ändert es sich", rief er, und er sagte von nun an dem Bett »Bild".

„Ich bin müde, ich will ins Bild", sagte er, und morgens blieb er oft lange im Bild liegen und überlegte, wie er nun dem Stuhl sagen wolle, und er nannte den Stuhl »Wecker".

Er stand also auf, zog sich an, setzte sich auf den Wecker und stützte die Arme auf den Tisch. Aber der Tisch hieß jetzt nicht mehr Tisch, er hieß jetzt Teppich. Am Morgen verließ also der Mann das Bild, zog sich an, setzte sich an den Teppich auf den Wecker und überlegte, wem er wie sagen könnte.

Dem **Bett** sagte er Bild.
Dem **Tisch** sagte er Teppich.
Dem **Stuhl** sagte er Wecker.
Der **Zeitung** sagte er Bett.
Dem **Spiegel** sagte er Stuhl.
Dem **Wecker** sagte er Fotoalbum.
Dem **Schrank** sagte er Zeitung.
Dem **Teppich** sagte er Schrank.
Dem **Bild** sagte er Tisch.
Und dem **Fotoalbum** sagte er Spiegel.

2. Versuche jetzt, das Zimmer des alten Mannes zu zeichnen!

3. Read to the end of the sixth paragraph. Explain what happened one day. What was that day like? How was it different from any other day?

4. Read to the end of the eighth paragraph. How does this part of the story explain the title?

5. Continue reading to the end. Outline the plot by listing the main events of the story. In your opinion, what is the main idea?

A Closer Look

6. Read the story again more carefully and, as you read, try to determine the main idea of each paragraph or each group of paragraphs. Based on the main ideas, divide the story into sections and supply a title for each section.

7. Scan to find the first use of **dann** in the story. What purpose does **dann** serve at that point? What does the word signal in the unfolding of the story? What about **jetzt** and **aber**? How do these words help to organize the story?

Also:

Am Morgen blieb der alte Mann lange im Bild liegen, um neun läutete das Fotoalbum, der Mann stand auf und stellte sich auf den Schrank, damit er nicht an die Füße fror, dann nahm er seine Kleider aus der Zeitung, zog sich an, schaute in den Stuhl an der Wand, setzte sich dann auf den Wecker an den Teppich und blätterte den Spiegel durch, bis er den Tisch seiner Mutter fand.

Der Mann fand das lustig, und er übte den ganzen Tag und prägte sich die neuen Wörter ein. Jetzt wurde alles umbenannt. Er war jetzt kein Mann mehr, sondern ein Fuß, und der Fuß war ein Morgen und der Morgen ein Mann.

Jetzt könnt ihr die Geschichte selbst weiterschreiben. Und dann könnt ihr, so wie es der Mann machte, auch die andern Wörter austauschen:

läuten heißt stellen,
frieren heißt schauen,
liegen heißt läuten,
stehen heißt frieren,
stellen heißt blättern

So daß es dann heißt:

Am Mann blieb der alte Fuß lange im Bild läuten, um neun stellte das Fotoalbum, der Fuß fror auf und blätterte sich auf den Schrank, damit er nicht an die Morgen schaute.

Der alte Mann kaufte sich blaue Schulhefte und schrieb sie mit den neuen Wörtern voll, und er hatte viel zu tun damit, und man sah ihn nur noch selten auf der Straße.

Dann lernte er für alle Dinge die neuen Bezeichnungen und vergaß dabei mehr und mehr die richtigen. Er hatte jetzt eine neue Sprache, die ihm ganz allein gehörte.

Hie und da träumte er schon in der neuen Sprache, und dann übersetzte er die Lieder aus seiner Schulzeit in seine Sprache, und er sang sie leise vor sich hin. Aber bald fiel ihm auch das Übersetzen schwer, er hatte seine alte Sprache fast vergessen, und er mußte die richtigen Wörter in seinen blauen Heften suchen. Und es machte ihm Angst, mit den Leuten zu sprechen. Er mußte lange nachdenken, wie die Leute den Dingen sagen.

8. Rarely does an author want just to relate a sequence of events. Usually a more important idea is the cause or the effect of the events. What caused the man to rename everything? What effect did this have in the short run? And in the long run? Which sentences from the story support your answers?

9. Look again at what you wrote about the main idea and revise your statement if necessary.

10. Discuss with your classmates some of the funny parts of the story and some of the sad parts. How do the funny parts actually make the story sad?

Seinem *Bild* sagen die Leute **Bett**.
Seinem *Teppich* sagen die Leute **Tisch**.
Seinem *Wecker* sagen die Leute **Stuhl**.
Seinem *Bett* sagen die Leute **Zeitung**.
Seinem *Stuhl* sagen die Leute **Spiegel**.
Seinem *Fotoalbum* sagen die Leute **Wecker**.
Seiner *Zeitung* sagen die Leute **Schrank**.
Seinem *Schrank* sagen die Leute **Teppich**.
Seinem *Tisch* sagen die Leute **Bild**.
Seinem *Spiegel* sagen die Leute **Fotoalbum**.

Und es kam so weit, daß der Mann lachen mußte, wenn er die Leute reden hörte.

Er mußte lachen, wenn er hörte, wie jemand sagte: »Jetzt regnet es schon zwei Monate lang.« Oder wenn jemand sagte: »Ich habe einen Onkel in Amerika.«

Er mußte lachen, weil er all das nicht verstand.

Aber eine lustige Geschichte ist das nicht. Sie hat traurig angefangen und hört traurig auf.

Der alte Mann im grauen Mantel konnte die Leute nicht mehr verstehen, das war nicht so schlimm.

Viel schlimmer war, sie konnten ihn nicht mehr verstehen.

Und deshalb sagte er nichts mehr.

Er schwieg, sprach nur noch mit sich selbst, grüßte nicht einmal mehr.

11. Think again about the results of the man's actions in the long run. What is the author saying about the nature and purpose of language?

12. Compare and contrast the points made about language in Bichsel's "Ein Tisch ist ein Tisch" with "Unsere heutige Jugend und ihre Sprüche" (pp. 78-79). What similarities or differences do you see between what teenagers do and what the old man does with language, especially in terms of consequences?

Übungsheft, S. 51-52, Ü. 1-5

Mehr Grammatikübungen

Answers

internet

ADRESSE: go.hrw.com
KENNWORT:
WK3 WUERZBURG-4

Erste Stufe   Objective Agreeing

1 Wann schimpfen deine Eltern? Schreib wenn-Sätze mit den Ideen, die in den Zeichnungen abgebildet sind. (**Seite 96**)

1. Meine Eltern schimpfen, _____ .   wenn ich ein schlechtes Zeugnis habe

2. Sie können es nicht leiden, _____ .   wenn ich die Musik zu laut spiele

3. Es gibt Krach, _____ .   wenn ich mein Zimmer nicht aufräume

4. Es gibt Krach, _____ .   wenn ich zu spät nach Hause komme

5. Sie können es nicht leiden, _____ .   wenn ich mir die Haare färbe

2 Verschiedene Leute geben ihre Meinung (*opinion*), und du stimmst zu (*agree with*). Schreib die folgenden Sätze ab, und schreib dabei das passende Pronomen in die Lücken! (**Seite 97**)

1. Jörg: „Fernsehen ist blöd."   Da geb ich _____ Recht.   dir
2. Herr Kohl: „Fremdsprachen sind wichtig."   Da geb ich _____ Recht.   Ihnen
3. Ann und Ina: „Dieser Krach war nicht gut." Da geb ich _____ Recht.   euch
4. Frau Blick: „Toleranz ist wichtig."   Da geb ich _____ Recht.   Ihnen
5. Ann und Ina: „Unser Freundeskreis ist groß." Da geb ich _____ Recht. euch
6. Tanja: „Hier gibt's zu viele Cliquen."   Da geb ich _____ Recht.   dir

3 Du erzählst deinen Freunden etwas über dich selbst, und du stellst ihnen auch verschiedene Fragen. Schreib die folgenden Sätze ab, und schreib dabei die korrekte Ordinalzahl in die Lücken! **(Seite 98)**

1. Das ist mein (1) _____ Auto, aber schon mein (4) _____ Fahrrad.   erstes; viertes

2. Peter war mein (1) _____ Freund, die Ann meine (1) _____ Freundin.   erster; erste

3. Das (1) _____ Buch hat mir gefallen, aber das (2) _____ Buch war blöd.   erste; zweite

4. Das ist mein (7) _____ Tennisspiel und mein (3) _____ Volleyballspiel.   siebtes; drittes

5. Hast du den (1) _____ Film gesehen oder den (2) _____ ?   ersten; zweiten

6. Am (8) _____ Juni arbeite ich nicht; der (8) _____ Juni ist ein Feiertag.   achten; achte

7. Wer hat am (19) _____ Geburtstag? Und wer am (20) _____ ?   neunzehnten; zwanzigsten

8. Am (5) _____ März fahre ich nach Berlin, am (9) _____ nach Köln.   fünften; neunten

4 Schreib jeden Satz, der mit einem Demonstrativpronomen beginnt, als einen Relativsatz. Achte auf die Wortstellung des Verbs. **(Seite 99)**

BEISPIEL   Ich kenne ein nettes Mädchen. Die ist in meinem Tennisverein.
             Ich kenne ein nettes Mädchen, <u>die in meinem Tennisverein ist.</u>

1. Wir haben einen tollen Deutschlehrer. Den mögen wir alle.   den wir alle mögen

2. Das ist unser Biolehrer. Der hat gerade geheiratet.   der gerade geheiratet hat

3. Hier kommt Frau Weiß. Mit der verstehen wir uns gut.   mit der wir uns gut verstehen

4. Das ist mein Freund. Mit dem gehe ich gern weg.   mit dem ich gern weggehe

5. Hier kommen die jungen Schüler. Denen helfen wir oft.   denen wir oft helfen

6. Wie heißt die Schülerin? Die steht dort drüben.   die dort drüben steht

7. Hier ist das Problem. Über das sprechen wir jetzt.   über das wir jetzt sprechen

8. Das ist ein super Film. Den musst du sehen.   den du sehen musst

5 Auch in der gesprochenen Sprache kann man einen Relativsatz nicht immer vermeiden. Man braucht daher ein bisschen Übung, um das korrekte Relativpronomen spontan zur Verfügung zu haben. Schreib die folgenden Relativsätze ab, und schreib dabei das korrekte Relativpronomen in die Lücken! (**Seite 99**)

   1. Die Schüler, _____ ich kenne, fahren mit dem Rad zur Schule.   die

   2. Kennst du den Schüler, _____ mit dem Moped zur Schule kommt?   der

   3. Das ist der Schüler, _____ die Clique nicht leiden kann.   den

   4. Wer ist der Schüler, _____ du mit den Hausaufgaben geholfen hast?   dem

   5. Wer sind die Schüler, mit _____ du ins Kino gehen willst?   denen

   6. Die Clique, _____ ich angehöre, hat vielleicht acht bis zehn Leute.   der

   7. Das ist die Clique, _____ du auch schon kennst.   die

   8. Das Haus, in _____ ich wohne, stammt aus dem 17. Jahrhundert.   dem

   9. Das Fachwerkhaus, _____ am Marktplatz steht, ist auch sehr alt.   das

10. Die CD, _____ ich im Musikladen gekauft habe, ist supertoll!   die

11. Das ist eine CD, _____ du noch nicht gehört hast.   die

12. Ich muss die Bücher, _____ ich mir ausgeliehen habe, wieder zurückbringen.   die

Zweite Stufe

Objectives Giving advice; introducing another point of view; hypothesizing

6 Du machst bestimmte Annahmen (*assumptions*) über dich und über andere. Schreib die folgenden Annahmen ab, und schreib dabei die korrekten Formen von **wäre, hätte,** oder **würde** in die Satzlücken! (**Seite 104**)

   1. Wenn du nicht so arrogant _____ , _____ du dich den anderen anpassen.   wärst; würdest

   2. Wenn Michael nicht so faul _____ , _____ er bestimmt mehr Sport machen.   wäre; würde

   3. Wenn wir im Ausland _____ , _____ wir neue Gebräuche kennen lernen.   wären; würden

   4. Wenn ich mehr Zeit _____ , _____ ich in der Umwelt-AG mitmachen.   hätte; würde

   5. Wenn wir keine Lust _____ , _____ wir nicht in der Theatergruppe mitmachen.   hätten; würden

   6. Wenn ihr mehr Geld _____ , _____ ihr dann mit uns in die Türkei fliegen?   hättet; würdet

7 Schreib die richtigen Verbformen in die Lücken. (**Seite 104**)

hätte	hätten	hättet	hättest	würde	würden	würdet	würdest

1. Du _____ bestimmt ins Kino gehen, wenn du Zeit _____ .   würdest; hättest
2. Ich _____ lieber zu Hause bleiben, wenn ich kein Geld _____ .   würde; hätte
3. Was _____ deine Kusine tun, wenn sie Ferien _____ ?   würde; hätte
4. Wir _____ nach Bayern fahren, wenn wir eine neues Auto _____ .   würden; hätten
5. Was _____ ihr tun, wenn ihr einmal Pech _____ ?   würdet, hättet
6. Die Kinder _____ zu Hause bleiben, wenn sie keine Schule _____ .   würden; hätten

8 Du gibst deinen Freunden Ratschläge. Schreib die folgenden Sätze ab, und schreib dabei den korrekten Artikel in die Lücken, um den Genitiv auszudrücken! (**Seite 105**)

1. Ich würde den Schülern _____ 8. Klasse raten: macht bei der Umwelt-AG mit!   der
2. Es ist wichtig, dass die Kinder _____ Ausländer gutes Deutsch lernen.   der
3. Vielleicht kannst du mal die Größe _____ Sees nachschauen.   des
4. Ich würde nichts Schlechtes über die Schüler _____ Gymnasiums sagen.   des
5. Es ist wichtig, dass du die Eltern _____ Schüler anrufst.   der
6. Ich würde die Vorurteile _____ polnischen Schülers abbauen.   des

9 Schreib die folgenden Sätze um und gebrauche dabei den Genitiv, wie im Beispiel. (**Seite 105**)

BEISPIEL   Das Auto gehört meinem Vater.
<u>Das ist das Auto meines Vaters.</u>

1. Das Fahrrad gehört meiner Schwester.   Das ist das Fahrrad meiner Schwester.
2. Das Haus gehört meinen Eltern.   Das ist das Haus meiner Eltern.
3. Das Buch gehört meinem Bruder.   Das ist das Buch meines Bruders.
4. Der Ring gehört meiner Freundin.   Das ist der Ring meiner Freundin.
5. Die Tasche gehört meiner Großmutter.   Das ist die Tasche meiner Großmutter.
6. Die Blumen gehören meinem Onkel.   Das sind die Blumen meines Onkels.
7. Der Teppich gehört meiner Tante.   Das ist der Teppich meiner Tante.
8. Der Rechner gehört meinem Lehrer.   Das ist der Rechner meines Lehrers.

CD 4 Tr. 8

internet

ADRESSE: go.hrw.com
KENNWORT:
WK3 WUERZBURG-4

1 Manche Leute sind tolerant, manche nicht. Hör zu, was folgende Leute sagen! Wie würdest du jede Aussage bezeichnen — tolerant oder nicht tolerant? Script and answers on p. 91I

2 Schreib deine Meinung zu den folgenden Fragen! Diskutiere mit deinen Klassenkameraden das, was du geschrieben hast!

a. Redet man mit einem Freund genauso wie mit einer Freundin?

b. Ist es gut, viele Freunde oder Freundinnen zu haben?

c. Was ist der Unterschied zwischen Freunden und Bekannten?

d. Kennst du jemanden, der wirklich ganz anders ist als du und ganz andere Interessen hat? Sind Freundschaften zwischen Leuten möglich, die ganz verschieden sind?

3 Was für Probleme haben diese Leute unten? Schreib die wichtigsten Punkte jedes Leserbriefes in dein Notizheft! Wähle dann einen Leserbrief aus und erzähle anhand deiner Notizen, was darin steht!

Ratgeber-Ecke

Mein Mann und ich stehen vor einem großen Problem. Unsere Heike ist jetzt 16 Jahre alt, und sie möchte mehr Taschengeld haben. Sie will auch am Abend länger wegbleiben. Sie meint, die andern in der Clique dürfen das auch. Das ist nun alles gut und schön, und wir freuen uns auch darüber. Aber etwas stört uns: unsere Tochter will weiterhin wie ein kleines Mädchen behandelt werden. Ich muss ihr Zimmer aufräumen, ihr Bett machen, ihre Wäsche waschen, ihre Schuhe putzen, und so weiter. Und sie benimmt sich wie eine kleine Prinzessin. Und mein Mann macht das mit. Er lacht sogar darüber. Aber ich finde das nicht richtig.
Regine Pfaff (38)

Wir sind verzweifelt! Unser Ältester hat vor fast zwei Jahren den Hauptschulabschluss nicht geschafft. Er hat dann doch noch eine Lehrstelle bekommen, ist aber nach einem halben Jahr abgehauen. Dann hat er als Hilfsarbeiter gearbeitet, wir glauben in einer Gärtnerei. Vor zwei Wochen, als Gerd 18 wurde, ist er ausgezogen. Wir wissen nicht wohin. Ein früherer Klassenkamerad hat Gerd jetzt einmal im Stadtpark gesehen — mit Punkern! Wir können es nicht glauben, dass unser Gerd mit Punkern herumläuft. Was haben wir falsch gemacht? Sind wir schuld an allem? Wir glauben, dass wir unser Bestes getan haben: wir haben uns früher mit Gerd immer verstanden. Jetzt haben wir keine Ruhe. Was können wir tun? Wir möchten unsern Jungen wiederhaben.
Elli und Hans Bauer

Vor zwei Monaten habe ich einen netten Jungen kennen gelernt. Er ist drei Jahre älter als ich, und er ist Türke. Er sieht phantastisch aus. Seitdem das meine Eltern wissen, gibt es zu Hause wieder Streitigkeiten, auch um kleine Dinge. Dabei helfe ich zu Hause, halte mein Zimmer in Ordnung, gehe einkaufen. Nun, vor einer Woche bin ich erst um 22 Uhr nach Hause gekommen, und seitdem verbieten mir die Eltern, abends auszugehen. Achmed ist nett, so lustig — besonders wenn er Deutsch spricht und Fehler macht! Ich sollte nächste Woche seine Eltern kennen lernen. Seine Schwester und seine Mutter hab ich schon einmal in der Stadt gesehen: echte Türkinnen, Kleider über den Hosen und mit Kopftuch und so. Ich hatte mich schon auf den Besuch gefreut. Was soll ich tun? Soll ich mit Achmed abbrechen, damit zu Hause wieder Friede wird?
Julia (16)

4 Was meinst du dazu?

a. Was nervt Frau Pfaff wirklich?

b. Was ist Elli und Hans Bauers Problem?

c. Was stört Julias Eltern? Was ist wohl der eigentliche Grund?

s. benehmen (wie)	*to behave (like)*
verzweifelt	*desperate*
ausziehen	*to move out*
die Ruhe	*peace and quiet*
abbrechen mit	*to break off with*
der Friede	*peace*

5 Bildet drei Gruppen! Jede Gruppe hat die Aufgabe, einen der drei Leserbriefe zu beantworten.

a. Überlegt euch zuerst, welche Ratschläge ihr geben wollt! Benutzt dabei die Redemittel, die ihr in dieser Lektion gelernt habt!

b. Formuliert dann eure Antwort! Seid höflich!

c. Wählt dann einen in der Gruppe aus, der eure Antwort den andern vorliest!

d. Wer hat die beste Antwort geschrieben? Diskutiert darüber!

6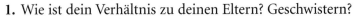

R o l l e n s p i e l

Such dir einen Partner! Zuerst interviewst du deinen Partner, dann interviewt dein Partner dich. Wenn ihr wollt, könnt ihr euer Interview auf eine Tonkassette aufnehmen. Hier sind die Interviewfragen:

1. Wie ist dein Verhältnis zu deinen Eltern? Geschwistern?

2. Mit wem unterhältst du dich am liebsten?

3. Worüber redet ihr am meisten?

4. Wofür interessiert ihr euch gemeinsam?

5. Mit wem verstehst du dich am besten?

6. Zu wem hast du keinen Kontakt? Warum nicht?

Es ist wichtig, dass euer Interview nicht nur aus Fragen und Antworten besteht, sondern dass es ein richtiges, natürliches Interview wird. Gebraucht deshalb zum Beispiel die Ausdrücke, die man benutzt, wenn man etwas nicht ganz versteht oder wenn man mehr Information braucht!

Kann ich's wirklich?

WK3 WUERZBURG-4

Can you agree?
(p. 97)

1 How would you agree with the following statements?
  a. **Vorurteile zu haben, find ich schlimm.** E.g.: Ganz meine Meinung.
  b. **Bei uns ist der Streitpunkt das Aufräumen.** E.g.: Bei mir ist es auch so.
  c. **Bevor wir ausgehen, müssen wir zuerst unsere Hausaufgaben erledigen.**
  E.g.: Da geb ich dir Recht.

Can you agree, with reservations? (p. 97)

2 How would you agree with your parents' statements but still express your reservations? Use the cues in parentheses.
  a. **Du schaust zu viel fern, vor allem am Abend.**
  (but I always do my homework first) Aber erst mache ich immer die Hausaufgaben!
  b. **Du spielst die Musik viel zu laut.**
  (but I use headphones most of the time) Aber meistens benutze ich Kopfhörer!
  c. **Du hast immer Krach mit deiner Schwester.**
  (but she always wears my clothes and never cleans her room)
  Aber sie trägt immer meine Kleider, und sie macht ihr Zimmer nie sauber!

Can you give advice?
(p. 103)

3 How would you give advice to a friend if he or she said the following things to you?
  a. **Ich versteh mich nicht mit meinen Eltern.** E.g.: Vielleicht kannst du mit ihnen darüber reden.
  b. **Ich fühle mich isoliert.** E.g.: Ich würde mit den anderen ausgehen.
  c. **Ich bekomme immer schlechte Noten. Ich glaub, der Lehrer mag mich nicht.** E.g.: Es ist wichtig, dass du mehr für die Schule lernst.

Can you introduce another point of view? (p. 103)

4 How would you introduce another point of view if someone said the following things to you? a. E.g.: Das mag schon sein, aber es ist nicht so einfach.
  a. **Ausländer sollen versuchen, sich in unserm Land anzupassen.**
  b. **Meine Eltern verstehen mich überhaupt nicht.** b. E.g.: Du darfst nicht vergessen, dass sie ganz anders denken als du.
  c. **Ich finde die Punker zu aufsässig.**
  c. E.g.: Es kommt darauf an, was sie machen.

Can you hypothesize?
(p. 104)

5 How would you make a hypothesis about what you would do
  a. if you were President of the United States? a. E.g.: Wenn ich Präsident der Vereinigten Staaten wäre, (dann) würde ich mehr für die Umwelt tun.
  b. if you had ten million dollars?
  c. if you lived in Germany? b. E.g.: Wenn ich zehn Millionen Dollar hätte, (dann) würde ich eine Weltreise machen.
  c. E.g.: Wenn ich in Deutschland leben würde, (dann) würde ich die deutsche Sprache viel schneller lernen.

KAPITEL 4   Verhältnis zu anderen

Erste Stufe

 p. 91X

Words useful for talking about relationships

Wir kommen gut miteinander aus.	We get along well with one another.
Ich verstehe mich super mit ihr.	She and I really get along.
Wir richten uns nach euch.	We'll do whatever you want to do.
Worum geht es?	What's it about?
Das kann ich nicht leiden!	I can't stand that!
der Kumpel, -	buddy

der Freundeskreis, -e	circle of friends
das Verhältnis	relationship
der Krach	quarrel
der Streit	quarrel, argument
die Streitigkeit, -en	quarrel
der Streitpunkt, -e	point of contention
die Toleranz	tolerance
gleich	immediately
reden	to speak
schimpfen	to scold
angehören (sep, dat)	to belong to
erwachsen sein	to be grown up

Agreeing

Da geb ich dir Recht.	I agree with you about that.
Ganz meine Meinung.	I completely agree.
Bei mir ist es auch so.	That's the way it is with me, too.

Ordinal numbers

erst-	first
zweit-	second
dritt-	third

Zweite Stufe

Giving advice

Vielleicht kannst du …	Perhaps you can …
Es ist wichtig, dass …	It's important that …
Ich würde (ihr) sagen, …	I would tell (her) …

Introducing another point of view

Das mag schon sein, aber …	That may well be, but …
Es kommt darauf an, ob …	It depends on whether …
Aber denk doch mal daran, dass …	But just consider that …
Du darfst nicht vergessen, dass …	You mustn't forget that …

Hypothesizing

Wenn du … wärst, dann würdest du …	If you were …, then you would …
Wenn sie … hätte, würde sie …	If she had …, she would …

Getting along with others

Was an dir gut ist, ist deine Freundlichkeit.	What I like about you is your friendliness.
die Sitten und Gebräuche (pl)	customs and habits
das Vorurteil, -e	prejudice
die Schwierigkeit, -en	difficulty
die Randgruppe, -n	fringe group
Ausländer(in), -/nen	foreigner
geboren	born
die Muttersprache, -n	native language
anders	different

aufsässig	rebellious
kulturbedingt	for cultural reasons
unbeliebt	unpopular
untereinander	among one another
unter sich bleiben	to keep to oneselves
s. absondern von (sep)	to separate oneself from
die Fete, -n	party
raten (dat)	to give advice
verbieten	to forbid
schuld sein an etwas (dat)	to be at fault
absichtlich	on purpose
die Möglichkeit, -en	possibility
außerhalb (gen)	outside of
nicht nur … sondern auch	not only … but also

Kapitel 5: Rechte und Pflichten
Chapter Overview

	FUNCTIONS	GRAMMAR	VOCABULARY	RE-ENTRY
Erste Stufe pp. 124–127	• Talking about what is possible, p. 125 • Saying what you would have liked to do, p. 126	• The **könnte**-forms, p. 125 • Further uses of **wäre** and **hätte**, p. 126	• Things to do at 18, p. 124	The modal **können**, p. 125 (**Kap. 7, I**); **hätte**-forms and **wäre**-forms, p. 126 (**Kap. 11, II; 4, III**); **weil**-clauses, p. 127 (**Kap. 8, I**); giving reasons, p. 127 (**Kap. 8, I**)

Zweite Stufe pp. 130–135	• Saying that something is going on right now, p. 131 • Reporting past events, p. 132 • Expressing surprise, relief, and resignation, p. 134	• Use of verbs as neuter nouns, p. 132 • The past tense of modals (the imperfect), p. 133	• The military, p. 131 • Past time expressions, p. 134	The modals **können, wollen,** and **müssen,** p. 132 (**Kap. 6/7, I**); reporting past events, p. 132 (**Kap. 3, II**); expressing surprise, p. 134 (**Kap. 10, II**); expressing resignation, p. 134 (**Kap. 9, II**); expressing hearsay, p. 134 (**Kap. 9, II**)

Zum Lesen pp. 136–138	Nie wieder!	**Reading Strategy** Determining purpose
Zum Schreiben p. 139	Lerne Land und Leute durch ein Interview kennen!	**Writing Strategy** Asking questions to gather ideas

Mehr Grammatik-übungen	**pp. 140–143** **Erste Stufe,** pp. 140–141	**Zweite Stufe,** pp. 142–143	
Review pp. 144–147	Anwendung, pp. 144–145	Kann ich's wirklich?, p. 146	Wortschatz, p. 147

CULTURE

• Artikel 38/2. Absatz des Grundgesetzes, p. 124
• Cartoon, p. 124

• Landeskunde: Gleichberechtigung im deutschen Militär? p. 130
• Ein wenig Landeskunde: Wehrpflicht, p. 132

Kapitel 5: Rechte und Pflichten
Chapter Resources

PRINT

Lesson Planning
One-Stop Planner
**Lesson Planner with Substitute
Teacher Lesson Plans,** pp. 31–35, 79
Student Make-Up Assignments
- Make-Up Assignment Copying Masters, Chapter 5

Listening and Speaking
Listening Activities
- Student Response Forms for Listening Activities, pp. 35–38
- Additional Listening Activities 5-1 to 5-6, pp. 39–42
- Scripts and Answers, pp. 133–141

Video Guide
- Teaching Suggestions, p. 22
- Activity Masters, pp. 23–24
- Scripts and Answers, pp. 63–64, 74–75

Activities for Communication
- Communicative Activities, pp. 17–20
- Realia and Teaching Suggestions, pp. 71–75
- Situation Cards, pp. 121–122

Reading and Writing
Reading Strategies and Skills Handbook, Chapter 5
Lies mit mir! 3, Chapter 5
Übungsheft, pp. 53–65

Grammar
Grammatikheft, pp. 37–45
Grammar Tutor for Students of German, Chapter 5

Assessment
Testing Program
- Grammar and Vocabulary Quizzes, **Stufe** Quizzes, and Chapter Test, pp. 89–102
- Score Sheet, Scripts and Answers, pp. 103–109

Alternative Assessment Guide
- Portfolio Assessment, p. 20
- Performance Assessment, p. 34

Student Make-Up Assignments
- Alternative Quizzes, Chapter 5

MEDIA

Online Activities
- Interaktive Spiele
- Internet Aktivitäten

Video Program
- Videocassette 1

Audio Compact Discs
- Textbook Listening Activities, CD 5, Tracks 1–12
- Additional Listening Activities, CD 5, Tracks 18–23
- Assessment Items, CD 5, Tracks 13–17

Teaching Transparencies
- Situations 5-1 to 5-2
- **Mehr Grammatikübungen** Answers
- **Grammatikheft** Answers

One-Stop Planner CD-ROM

Use the **One-Stop Planner CD-ROM** with Test Generator to aid in lesson planning and pacing.

For each chapter, the **One-Stop Planner** includes:
- Editable lesson plans with direct links to teaching resources
- Printable worksheets from resource books
- Direct launches to the HRW Internet activities
- Video and audio segments
- Test Generator
- Clip Art for vocabulary items

Kapitel 5: Rechte und Pflichten

Projects

Mach mit!

*In this project students will create an illustrated recruitment advertisement for either the **Bundeswehr** or the **Zivildienst**. Students can work individually or with a partner.*

MATERIALS
✂ **Students will need**
- posterboard
- paper
- pens
- subject-related materials such as photos, brochures, or magazine cutouts

SUGGESTED TOPICS

Bundeswehr
Zivildienst

SUGGESTED SEQUENCE

1. Individuals or pairs of students decide on the topic for the recruitment advertisement and make an outline showing how the project will be organized.

2. Students gather resources and prepare a convincing visual presentation. The project should include facts and data from the **Landeskunde** on pp. 130 and 132 of this chapter. Drawings, slogans, photos, or other eye-catching materials should also be incorporated into the poster.

3. Students present their posters and give a brief (1 minute) statement to the rest of the class to convince them to join the service, whether it is the **Bundeswehr** or the **Zivildienst**.

GRADING THE PROJECT

Suggested point distribution (total = 100 points)
Originality and Design...........................40
Language usage.....................................30
Oral presentation / Sales pitch 30

Games

Seeschlacht

This game allows students to review new words and phrases with a competitive and familiar game.

Preparation Prepare a grid on a sheet of paper that you copy for students. Also prepare a list of questions that are based on the **Wortschatz** on p. 147.

	A	B	C	D	E	F	G	H	I	J	K	L	M	N
1														
2														
3							U							
4							U							
5												Z		
6		S	S	S							Z			
7										Z				
8														
9					K									
10					K									
11									F	F	F	F		
12														

Procedure Divide the class into equally sized teams. Each team of students gets a sheet of paper with a grid. Teams then hide the following five ships on the grid: **das Schlachtschiff, der Flugzeugträger, der Kreuzer, der Zerstörer,** and **das U-Boot.** Each ship takes up a specific number of spaces on the grid, which you can change according to the size of the grid. Write the verbs **getroffen, verfehlt,** and **gesunken** on the board for teams to use during the game. Ask a member of the first team a question from the list you prepared ahead of time. If he or she answers correctly, he or she gets to guess a position of an opposing team's ship using German letters and numbers. The first team to knock out all of the other teams' ships wins.

COMMUNITY LINK
Ask students to find out what services the Red Cross provides in their community. (Examples: training, maintaining blood banks, relief services)

Storytelling

Mini-Geschichte

*This story accompanies Teaching Transparency 5-1. The **Mini-Geschichte** can be told and retold in different formats, acted out, written down, and read aloud to give students additional opportunities to practice all four skills.*

Unser Reporter hat einhundert Jugendliche gefragt, was sie sich für die Zukunft wünschen. Über die Hälfte haben geantwortet, dass sie sich einen guten Job wünschen. Fünfundzwanzig freuen sich darauf, den Führerschein zu machen und ein eigenes Auto zu kaufen. Elf Jugendliche, die jetzt politisch sehr engagiert sind, haben geantwortet, dass sie sich freuen, wenn sie mit achtzehn wahlberechtigt sind. Vier der Befragten wollen so bald wie möglich heiraten und zwei wollen eine Weltreise machen. Nur einer hat behauptet, dass er keine Wünsche für die Zukunft hat.

Jugendpost, den 4.10.2002

Traditions

St. Kilian - der Frankenapostel

Der irische Missionsbischof Kilian und seine beiden Gefährten Kolonat und Totnan brachten im Jahre 686 das Christentum nach Franken. Kilian taufte den in Würzburg residierenden thüringischen Herzog Gozbert. Daraufhin traten die meisten Bewohner Frankens zum christlichen Glauben über. Allerdings hatte Gozbert nach alter Sitte die Witwe seines Bruders, Geilana, zur Frau genommen. Dies galt nach dem damaligen christlichen Recht als Blutschande. Kilian bedrängte den Herzog, die Ehe aufzulösen und zog damit den Hass Geilanas auf sich. Geilana veranlasste dann im Jahre 689 die Ermordung Kilians und seiner Gefährten. Im 11. Jahrhundert wurde die Neumünsterkirche über der Grabstätte des heiligen Kilian und seiner Gefährten errichtet. Kilians Namenstag, der 8. Juli, wird heute mit dem Kiliani-Volksfest, dem größten Volksfest Nordbayerns, gefeiert.

Rezept

Zwetschgenkuchen mit Makronen-Gitter

Für 20 Personen

Zutaten

g=Gramm, kg=Kilogramm, l=Liter

Teig		Belag	
375 g	Mehl	2 kg	Zwetschgen
½	Würfel Hefe	4	Eier
75 g	Zucker	250 g	Zucker
⅛ l	Milch	1	Becher Crème fraîche (250 g)
1	Ei	200 g	Kokosraspel
75 g	Butter		
1	Zitrone		
Mehl zum Ausrollen			

Zubereitung

Das Mehl in eine Schüssel geben. In die Mitte eine Mulde drücken. Zerbröckelte Hefe, einen Teelöffel Zucker und fünf Esslöffel lauwarme Milch dazugeben und zu einem Vorteig verrühren. Abgedeckt an einem warmen Ort 20 Minuten gehen lassen. Die restliche lauwarme Milch, den Zucker, ein Ei, die Butter und die abgeriebene Zitronenschale zum Vorteig geben und alles zu einem glatten Teig verkneten. Abgedeckt etwa 20 Minuten gehen lassen. Den Teig auf ein wenig Mehl ausrollen und dann ein Backblech damit auslegen. Nochmals 20 Minuten gehen lassen. Inzwischen die Zwetschen abspülen, halbieren und entsteinen. Das Eigelb und 100 g Zucker dickschaumig schlagen. Die Crème fraîche und die Hälfte der Kokosraspel unterheben und auf den Hefeteig streichen. Die Zwetschen dicht an dicht in den Guss setzen. Den Teig im vorgeheizten Backofen bei 200 Grad Celsius etwa 25 bis 30 Minuten backen. Inzwischen das Eiweiß steif schlagen, den restlichen Zucker dabei einrieseln lassen. Die restlichen Kokosraspel unterrühren und in einen Spritzbeutel mit Sterntülle füllen. Kuchen herausnehmen und die Makronenmasse als Gitter daraufspritzen. Weitere 10 bis 15 Minuten goldbraun überbacken.

Kapitel 5: Rechte und Pflichten
Technology

One-Stop Planner CD-ROM

To preview all resources available for this chapter, use the **One-Stop Planner CD-ROM**, Disc 2.

Internet Connection

internet

go.hrw.com

ADRESSE: go.hrw.com
KENNWORT:
WK3 WUERZBURG-5

*Have students explore the **go.hrw.com** Web site for many online resources covering all chapters. All Chapter 5 resources are available under the keyword **WK3 Wuerzburg-5**. Interactive games practice the material and provide students with immediate feedback. You will also find a printable worksheet that provides Internet activities that lead to a comprehensive online research project.*

Interaktive Spiele

You can use the interactive activities in this chapter

- to practice grammar, vocabulary, and chapter functions
- as homework
- as an assessment option
- as a self-test
- to prepare for the Chapter Test

Internet Aktivitäten

Students read German laws concerning compulsory service for German men and women. They discuss the history and function of the German Federal Defense Force and community service.

- To prepare students for the **Arbeitsblatt,** have them read **Landeskunde,** p. 130, and **Ein wenig Landeskunde,** p. 132. You may also have them study **Wortschatz, Zweite Stufe,** p. 131.

- After completing the **Arbeitsblatt,** ask students to pick up pamphlets at the nearest recruiting office. They should compare the information provided on the pamphlets to the answers they gave in **Aktivität C.**

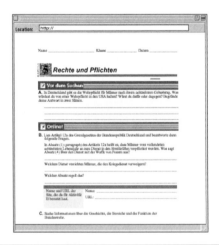

Webprojekt
Have students research the role of women in the German Federal Defense Force. They should report on the numbers of enlisted women. What branches of the armed forces do women prefer and why? Encourage students to exchange useful Web sites with their classmates. Have students document their sources by referencing the names and URLs of all the sites they consulted.

Kapitel 5: Rechte und Pflichten
Textbook Listening Activities Scripts

The following scripts are for the listening activities found in the *Pupil's Edition*. For Student Response Forms, see *Listening Activities*, pages 35–38. To provide students with additional listening practice, see *Listening Activities*, pages 39–42.

Erste Stufe

3 p. 125

1. Also, ich bin wahnsinnig froh, endlich 18 zu sein. Jetzt kann ich nämlich Verträge unterschreiben und bin natürlich auch selbst dafür verantwortlich, sie einzuhalten. Also, den ersten Vertrag, den ich selbst unterschrieben hab, war der Kaufvertrag mit dem Möbelhaus Wellenroth. Ich wollte nämlich unbedingt dieses kleine, schicke, schwarze Ledersofa für mein Zimmer haben. Meine Eltern wollten es mir nicht kaufen, weil sie meinten, ich würde ja bestimmt sowieso bald ausziehen, um in einer anderen Stadt zu studieren, oder so. Ja, und da haben sie gesagt, ich bräuchte in meinem Zimmer kein neues Sofa. Na ja, eigentlich haben sie ja auch Recht. Aber ich fand das Sofa nun mal total scharf, und es hatte auch so einen günstigen Preis. Also habe ich es mir gekauft, und jetzt steht es bei mir im Zimmer. Das heißt, bezahlt habe ich es natürlich noch nicht ganz, weil ich ja so viel Geld auf einmal gar nicht hab! Also, laut Vertrag muss ich jetzt jeden Monat 40 Euro ans Möbelhaus Wellenroth bezahlen, zwölf Monate lang. Tja, und dann gehört das Sofa mir! Und wenn ich mal von zu Hause ausziehe, dann nehm ich's natürlich mit! Das einzig Blöde ist, ich hab jetzt halt nicht mehr so viel von meinem Taschengeld übrig!

2. Ja, also, was sich bei mir auf jeden Fall verändert hat, ist, dass ich am Wochenende länger ausbleibe. Früher musste ich immer um zehn zu Hause sein. Seit ich 18 bin, bleibe ich halt auf den Partys so lange, wie es mir Spaß macht. Gestern bin ich bis kurz vor Mitternacht mit Freunden unterwegs gewesen. Wir waren halt auf 'nem Rockkonzert. Die Stimmung war super! Die Band hat eine Zugabe nach der anderen gespielt, einfach sagenhaft! Tja, da ist es halt fast Mitternacht geworden. Meine Eltern waren ja nicht sehr erfreut, als ich so spät heimkam. Aber was wollen sie machen — ich bin ja jetzt erwachsen. Na ja, ich weiß, dass es auch eine Menge Pflichten gibt, aber warum soll ich nicht auch mal meine Rechte genießen? Ich finde es toll, 18 zu sein.

3. Mir ist es sehr wichtig, dass ich jetzt wählen darf. Ich bin ja schon seit ein paar Jahren politisch aktiv. Ich bin Mitglied in der Jugendabteilung einer Partei seit meinem sechzehnten Lebensjahr. Letzten Monat bin ich zur Vorsitzenden gewählt worden. Außerdem bin ich Mitarbeiterin beim „Politischen Forum". Das ist eine Zeitung für Schüler und Jugendliche, die sich politisch informieren wollen. Tja, und natürlich schaue ich mir täglich die Nachrichten im Fernsehen an und lese die Tageszeitung. Wenn ich im Sommer mein Abi mache, melde ich mich an der Uni in Bochum an, um Politik und Soziologie zu studieren. Tja, also, wie gesagt, ich bin echt stolz darauf, dass ich im Oktober zum ersten Mal einen Stimmzettel ausfüllen darf! Auch wenn man nicht so politisch engagiert ist wie ich, finde ich es doch wichtig, wählen zu gehen. Für mich ist jede politische Wahl Recht und Pflicht zugleich!

4. Peter und ich, wir haben vor kurzem geheiratet. Als meine Eltern von unseren Hochzeitsplänen erfuhren, haben sie zuerst gemeint, wir sollen noch etwas warten. Sie fanden, wir sind noch zu jung. Aber wir sind ja beide volljährig und haben das selbst entschieden. Na ja, wir haben ja auch nicht Hals über Kopf geheiratet, sondern erst mal die Schule fertig gemacht. Peter und ich, wir kennen uns doch schon so lange. Wir sind schon ein Jahr lang, bevor wir geheiratet haben, miteinander ausgegangen. Meine Eltern haben sich auch Sorgen über unsere finanzielle Situation gemacht. Zuerst hatte ich auch große Angst davor, aber eigentlich klappt alles ganz gut. Peter macht zur Zeit Zivildienst in einem Krankenhaus, und ich habe eine Ausbildung als Fotografin angefangen.

5. Ich nehme seit zwei Monaten Fahrstunden bei der Fahrschule Drombusch. Die Fahrstunden und die theoretische Ausbildung sind ja nicht gerade billig, aber man muss diese gründliche Ausbildung auf jeden Fall haben. Die Prüfungen sind nämlich ganz schön streng! Wenn man nicht hundertprozentig aufpasst, lassen manche Prüfer einen glatt durchrasseln! Mein Fahrlehrer ist echt okay. Er sagt immer ganz genau, worauf ich achten muss und lässt mich alles wiederholen, was ich beim Autofahren falsch mache. Für die Theorie muss man halt ziemlich viel büffeln und eine Menge auswendig lernen. Ich habe mich in vier Wochen zur Prüfung angemeldet. Hoffentlich klappt alles. Ich kann's kaum erwarten!

Answers to Activity 3
1. d 2. e 3. c 4. b 5. a

4 p. 125

MARTINA	Du, Tobias, hast du dich schon um einen Studienplatz beworben, oder suchst du dir einen Job, wenn wir mit der Schule fertig sind?
TOBIAS	Ja also, ich hab mich schon vor ein paar Wochen bei der ZVS beworben. Ich möchte am liebsten Anglistik in Göttingen studieren. Weißt du, Martina, wenn ich nach Göttingen ziehe, suche ich mir als Allererstes eine eigene Wohnung.
MARTINA	Wieso das denn? Du könntest dir doch im Studentenwohnheim ein Zimmer nehmen.
TOBIAS	Was? Du machst wohl Witze! Also, ich hab keine Lust, in einem kleinen quadratischen Kasten zu hocken und die Küche und das Badezimmer mit zig Leuten zu teilen!
MARTINA	Ja und? Das ist doch nicht so schlimm! Wenn ich einen Studienplatz in Berlin bekomme, dann will ich auf jeden Fall im Studentenwohnheim wohnen.
TOBIAS	Nee, also das ist nichts für mich. Mensch, Martina, ich versteh gar nicht, dass du so heiß darauf bist.
MARTINA	Überleg doch mal, Tobias! Wenn man im Studentenwohnheim wohnt, lernt man doch am schnellsten neue Leute kennen.
CHRISTA	Ja, die Martina hat Recht! Ich finde es wichtig, mit anderen Studenten zusammen zu sein, besonders, wenn man doch sonst ganz fremd in der Stadt ist.
TOBIAS	Ach Christa! Du hast gut reden. Du ziehst doch gar nicht woanders hin! Du bleibst doch nach der Schule hier in Düsseldorf, oder?
CHRISTA	Ja, stimmt! Ich will auf jeden Fall hier bleiben. Ich werde mich bei der Firma Kallenbroich um einen Ausbildungsplatz zum Industriekaufmann bewerben.

MARTINA Spitze! Dann kannst du ja zu Hause wohnen bleiben und sparst dir das Geld für die Miete!

CHRISTA Ja! Und stellt euch mal vor, an der Straßenbahnhaltestelle vor unserem Haus hält die Linie 5, und die fährt direkt bis vor das Werkstor von Kallenbroichs! Ist das nicht super? Ich brauch noch nicht mal umsteigen.

TOBIAS Mensch! Was heißt hier umsteigen? Ich werde mir bestimmt ein Auto kaufen, wenn ich nach Göttingen ziehe!

MARTINA Ja, aber dafür musst du erst mal Geld verdienen! Studieren und dabei das große Geld machen, das geht ja wohl nicht alles auf einmal!

TOBIAS Wieso nicht? Ich werd mir ganz locker neben meinem Studium Geld verdienen. Jobs für Studenten gibt's doch überall! Du, Christa, du kaufst dir doch bestimmt auch ein eigenes Auto, sobald du Geld verdienst, oder?

CHRISTA Nee, du, ganz bestimmt nicht. Das wäre zu schade ums Geld! Ich komm prima überall mit dem Bus, der Bahn oder dem Rad hin. Ich werd mein Geld für Reisen ausgeben.

MARTINA So? Wohin willst du denn?

CHRISTA Also, wenn ich Urlaub habe, fahr ich mit der Bahn nach Frankreich. Ich will unbedingt mal nach Paris. Das habe ich mir schon immer gewünscht!

Answers to Activity 4
Tobias: Anglistik in Göttingen studieren; sich eine Wohnung suchen; sich ein Auto kaufen; neben dem Studium Geld verdienen
Martina: Studienplatz in Berlin bekommen; im Studentenwohnheim wohnen
Christa: um einen Ausbildungsplatz zum Industriekaufmann bewerben; zu Hause wohnen bleiben; Reise nach Paris machen
Tobias hat am meisten vor.

Zweite Stufe

14 p. 133

— Ja guten Tag, Herr Heckel! Ich hab Sie ja schon lange nicht mehr gesehen. Wie geht's denn heute?

— Ach, guten Tag, Frau Erhard! Ich hab Sie fast gar nicht erkannt! Haben Sie eine neue Frisur?

— Ja. Das ist aber nett, dass Sie das bemerken! Ich komm gerade vom Friseur. Stellen Sie sich vor, die ganze Prozedur hat fast zwei Stunden gedauert. Jetzt ist mir doch fast dadurch der ganze Vormittag verloren gegangen. Und dabei hab ich noch so viel zu erledigen!

— Was haben Sie denn alles noch zu tun?

— Ach, wissen Sie, wir bekommen heute Abend Besuch. Wir haben Freunde aus dem Kegelclub zum Abendessen eingeladen. Na, und ich muss noch alles aus dem Supermarkt besorgen. Mein Mann kocht seine Spezialität, Eisbein mit Sauerkraut und Semmelknödeln! Ach, zum Metzger muss ich ja auch noch, das hätte ich fast vergessen!

— Wenn ich das gewusst hätte! Ich komm gerade vom Metzger. Zu dumm! Da hätte ich Ihnen doch das Fleisch mitbringen können. Und im Supermarkt war ich auch schon.

— Ja, also ich muss mich wirklich beeilen, damit ich alles noch rechtzeitig schaffe. Zum Glück habe ich heute früh schon die Fenster geputzt und Staub gesaugt. Meine Güte, heute ist aber wirklich ein hektischer Tag für mich. Und das dauert wieder mal so lange am Schalter.

— Frau Erhard, ich lasse Sie gern vor! Ich hab's nicht so eilig.

— Danke schön, Herr Heckel! Wie gut, dass Sie schon alles besorgt haben.

— Na ja, alles hab ich auch noch nicht erledigt. Ich muss noch zum Bäcker. Aber das kann warten. Ich wollte für heute Nachmittag Kuchen besorgen. Meine Frau hat Geburtstag.

— Ach, dann richten Sie ihr doch bitte schöne Grüße aus und gratulieren ihr von mir!

— Ja, danke! Mach ich gern.

— Ach! Endlich bin ich an der Reihe. Ich muss doch Geld abheben, weil ich gleich noch den Kindern neue Schuhe kaufen gehe, wenn sie aus der Schule kommen.

Answers to Activity 14
Answers will vary. E.g.: Heute Vormittag habe ich ein Gespräch zwischen zwei Leuten in der Bank mitangehört. Die Frau ist gerade beim Friseur gewesen usw…

17 p. 134

INGO Du, Paul, ich bin eigentlich ganz froh, dass ich am 1. Juli zum Bund gehe.

PAUL Ach, seit wann das denn? Vor ein paar Monaten hast du aber noch ganz anders geredet, Ingo.

INGO Ach weißt du, ich bin ja jetzt bald mit meiner Lehre fertig, und ich hatte überhaupt keine festen Pläne für die Zeit danach.

PAUL Wieso? Kannst du denn nicht nach deiner Lehre dort weiter arbeiten?

INGO Nee, du! Die bauen gerade Personal ab, und keiner von uns Lehrlingen kann bleiben. Aber so schlecht find ich das gar nicht.

PAUL Ach, deswegen willst du erst mal zum Bund.

INGO Ja, genau. Jetzt kann ich mir für 'ne Weile in Ruhe überlegen, was ich nach dem Bund machen will. Außerdem komme ich in eine technische Einheit, da lerne ich bestimmt etwas, was mir später beruflich hilft. Und du, Paul?

PAUL Mensch, Ingo, so froh wie du bin ich ja nicht. Weißt du, vorgestern, aus heiterem Himmel hab ich plötzlich diesen Brief bekommen — „Kreiswehrersatzamt" stand da drauf. Ich war vielleicht überrascht, sag ich dir!

INGO Und, wann musst du zur Musterung?

PAUL Ich hab in zwei Wochen einen Termin. Der Bund will mich haben, ich soll schon am ersten März eingezogen werden.

INGO Was? So früh schon?

PAUL Ja! Ich kann dir sagen, mir passt das überhaupt nicht in den Kram. Ich wollte eigentlich noch jobben, und dann im Herbst mit dem Studium anfangen.

INGO Ja, das ist natürlich jetzt blöd für dich.

PAUL Ja, find ich auch. Irgendwie habe ich gedacht, die ziehen mich erst später ein. Dass es so schnell gehen kann, das ist mir neu. Na, wie steht's bei dir, Alfred?

ALFRED Ich hab auch einen Einberufungsbefehl bekommen. Am ersten Juli muss ich nach Ingolstadt zu einer Panzereinheit. Na ja, was soll's? Ich wollte eigentlich im Herbst Soziologie studieren, aber ich wusste, dass der Bund mir vielleicht dazwischenkommt. Jetzt muss die Uni eben ein paar Semester warten. Da kann man nichts machen. Und du? Was machst du jetzt, Gerd?

GERD Ich habe mich jetzt endgültig entschieden, Zivildienst zu machen und bin wirklich froh, dass das jetzt klar ist. Ich hab auch schon eine Stelle im Städtischen Krankenhaus in Erlangen.

ALFRED Ja, Gerd, du hast dir ja lange hin und her überlegt, ob du zum Bund gehen sollst oder lieber Zivildienst machen sollst.

GERD Ja, stimmt! Ich muss schon sagen, ich habe mir die ganze Sache lange überlegt, aber ich kann einfach nicht mit der Waffe dienen. Dass alles mit der Zivi-Stelle so schnell geklappt hat, ist schon eine Riesenerleichterung.

PAUL   Ich find's super, dass du deinen Zivildienst im Krankenhaus machst. Da kannst du doch bestimmt 'ne Menge lernen. Du willst doch Krankenpfleger werden, oder?

GERD   Ja, auf jeden Fall! Ich glaube, nach dem Zivildienst mache ich auf jeden Fall 'ne Lehre als Krankenpfleger.

Answers to Activity 17
Überraschung: Paul war überrascht, als er einen Brief vom Bund bekommen hat, denn er wollte lieber zuerst studieren. Paul hat gedacht, dass er erst später eingezogen wird.
Resignation: Alfred wollte im Herbst anfangen zu studieren, hat aber gewusst, dass er vielleicht zuerst zum Bund muss.
Erleichterung: Ingo ist froh, dass er zum Bund geht, denn er hat noch keine festen Pläne, wenn er mit der Lehre fertig ist. Ingo meint, dass er beim Bund bestimmt etwas lernt, was ihm beruflich hilft. Gerd macht Zivildienst und ist erleichtert, dass er so schnell eine Stelle bekommen hat.

Anwendung

 p. 144

— Ja, so eine Überraschung! Die Dagmar! Schön, dass du mich wieder mal besuchst.

— Hallo, Opa! Wie geht's? Du, ich will dich für ein Schulprojekt interviewen.

— Was? Mich interviewen? Ja, was willst du denn wissen, Kind?

— Also, wir machen eine Ausstellung mit dem Thema „Unsere Großeltern als Teenager". Jeder sammelt Kommentare von seinen Großeltern, und wir stellen dann Plakate, Collagen und Illustrationen her.

— Und wo macht ihr die Ausstellung, Dagmar?

— Die Ausstellung wird dann am „Tag der offenen Tür" gezeigt. In zwei Wochen ist es so weit.

— Na, da bin ich ja mal gespannt. Also, fang mal ruhig an mit deinen Fragen!

— Also, findest du, dass du es als Teenager leichter oder schwerer hattest, als die Teenager der neunziger Jahre?

— Ja, ich bin überzeugt, dass wir es in vielen Dingen schwerer hatten. Zunächst mal waren wir ja eine große Familie mit sechs Kindern. Da hatten wir nicht viel Geld übrig.

— Woran hast du denn gemerkt, dass das Geld bei euch zu Hause knapp war? Hast du weniger Taschengeld bekommen?

— Taschengeld? Taschengeld haben wir Kinder gar nicht bekommen! Du, damals war das nicht so wie heute, wenn du sagst: „Mutti, ich will die CD haben, oder Papa, gib mir mal Geld, ich will ins Kino!" Von wegen! Geschenke haben wir nur zum Geburtstag und zu Weihnachten bekommen. Und sonst nicht!

— Aber du hast mir doch mal erzählt, dass du so gern als Junge ins Kino gegangen bist. Woher hattest du denn das Geld?

— Tja, das Geld hab ich mir erst verdienen müssen!

— Welche Jobs hast du denn so gemacht?

— Also, bei uns hatte jedes Kind eine Aufgabe zu Hause! Ich habe die Schuhe von der ganzen Familie geputzt. Für jedes Paar Schuhe habe ich von meinem Vater fünf Pfennig bekommen. Dann hab ich morgens vor der Schule Milch und Zeitungen ausgetragen. Na ja, und das Geld hab ich mir dann zusammengespart.

— Wofür hast du dein Geld denn noch ausgegeben?

— Hmm, lass mich mal überlegen. Ja, einmal, da war Tanz im Dorf. Da wollte ich so eine fesche Weste haben, wie sie in der Stadt modern waren. Weißt du, ich wollte doch der Elfriede aus meiner Klasse imponieren. Nun ja, aber die Weste war natürlich

One-Stop Planner CD-ROM

For resource information, see the **One-Stop Planner CD-ROM**, Disc 2.

viel zu teuer. Da hab ich in der Stadt den Stoff gekauft, und die Mutter hat die Weste dann für mich genäht!

— Mensch, Opi, das find ich ja stark! Ich wusste gar nicht, dass du dich für Mode interessierst! Hat deine Mutter auch sonst alle Kleidung für euch genäht?

— Nein, dafür hatte sie gar keine Zeit. Die Ältesten haben, wenn es nötig war, neue Sachen bekommen, aber wir Kleinen mussten immer die Klamotten und Schuhe der größeren Geschwister auftragen.

— Ach übrigens, Opa? Hast du denn mit deiner neuen Weste großen Eindruck auf die Elfriede aus deiner Klasse gemacht? Bist du dann mit ihr ausgegangen?

— [lacht] Was du dir so denkst! Na ja, getanzt habe ich an jenem Abend schon ein paar Mal mit ihr. Aber ausgegangen bin ich nicht mit ihr. Damals musste man sich doch schon gleich mit dem Mädel verloben, wenn man mit ihr gehen wollte. Und dazu war ich ja noch viel zu jung, damals! Ach ja, damals …

— Du, Opa, erzähl mir doch jetzt mal bitte was aus deiner Schulzeit! Hast du manchmal blau gemacht?

— Na, von wegen! So was konnten wir uns damals gar nicht leisten! Die Schule war ja viel strenger als heutzutage. Wir mussten noch viel auswendig lernen — Gedichte, Lieder, historische und geographische Daten. Ich kann dir heute noch alle Nebenflüsse der Donau aufzählen! Und den „Erlkönig" kann ich dir auch auswendig aufsagen!

— Ja ja, Opa. Ich glaub's dir ja! Wie waren denn die Lehrer so? Hattest du manchmal Streit mit denen?

— Ach was, wenn da mal in der Klasse einer von uns aus der Reihe getanzt ist, gab's direkt 'nen Tadel! Und du darfst auch nicht vergessen, damals war es den Lehrern noch erlaubt, die Schüler mit dem Stock auf die Finger zu hauen!

— Ach du meine Güte! Na ja, das gibt es ja heutzutage zum Glück schon lange nicht mehr!

— Ja, und die Lehrer waren auch strenger — der alte Oberlehrer Breitenbach sagte immer, „Eiserne Disziplin ist wichtig!" Weißt du, Dagmar, ich glaube, ihr habt jetzt viel mehr Freiheiten als wir damals.

— Ja, das glaub ich auch. Mensch, danke Opi, für das klasse Interview. Du musst unbedingt zum „Tag der offenen Tür" kommen und dir unsere Ausstellung anschauen.

— Na klar, das ist doch Ehrensache!

Answers to Activity 1
Großvater sagt, dass er es als Teenager schwerer hatte als die Teenager heutzutage; seine Familie hatte sechs Kinder und nicht viel Geld übrig; er hat kein Taschengeld bekommen; er hat Geschenke nur zum Geburtstag und zu Weihnachten bekommen; er ist gern ins Kino gegangen; er hat sein eigenes Geld verdient; hat die Schuhe von der Familie geputzt; er ist zum Tanz ins Dorf gegangen; er konnte sich keine modische Weste leisten, weil sie zu teuer war; er hat von seinem Geld Stoff gekauft; seine Mutter hat die Weste für ihn genäht; nur die älteren Geschwister haben manchmal neue Sachen bekommen; die jüngeren Kinder mussten die Klamotten und Schuhe der älteren auftragen; hatte keine Freundin, weil er zu jung war, um sich zu verloben; die Schule war strenger; er musste vieles auswendig lernen; die Lehrer durften damals die Schüler mit dem Stock auf die Finger hauen.

Kapitel 5: Rechte und Pflichten
Suggested Lesson Plans 50-Minute Schedule

Day 1

CHAPTER OPENER 5 min.
- Teaching Suggestion ATE, p. 119M
- Background Information, ATE, p. 119M

LOS GEHT'S! 20 min.
- Preteaching Vocabulary, ATE, p. 119N
- Cooperative Learning, p. 119N
- Play Audio CD for **Los geht's!**
- Have students read **Los geht's!**, pp. 122–123
- Do Activities 1 and 2, p. 123

ERSTE STUFE
Reading Selection, p. 124 10 min.
- Thinking Critically, p. 119O
- Read **Was bedeutet das?**, p. 124

Wortschatz, p. 124 10 min.
- Presenting **Wortschatz**, ATE, p. 119O
- Play Audio CD for Activity 3, p. 125

Wrap-Up 5 min.
- Students respond to questions about what will change when they reach the age of majority

Homework Options
Grammatikheft, pp. 37–38, Acts. 1–4
Übungsheft, p. 53, Acts. 1–2; pp. 54–55, Acts. 1–3

Day 2

ERSTE STUFE
Quick Review 10 min.
- Check homework, Grammatikheft, pp. 37–38, Acts. 1–4

So sagt man das!, Ein wenig Grammatik, p. 125 20 min.
- Presenting **So sagt man das!, Ein wenig Grammatik,** ATE, pp. 119O–119P
- Teaching Transparency 5-1
- Play Audio CD for Activity 4, p. 125
- Do Activity 5, p. 125
- Do Activity 6, p. 126

Seeschlacht 15 min.
- Play **Seeschlacht,** ATE, p. 119C

Wrap-Up 5 min.
- Students respond to questions about what they could do if they were 18

Homework Options
Grammatikheft, p. 39, Acts. 5–6

Day 3

ERSTE STUFE
Quick Review 10 min.
- Check homework, Grammatikheft, p. 39, Acts. 5–6

So sagt man das!, Grammatik, p. 126 35 min.
- Presenting **So sagt man das! Grammatik,** ATE, p. 119P
- Do Activity 7, p. 126
- Do Activities 8–11, p. 127

Wrap-Up 5 min.
- Students respond to questions about what they would have done and why they hadn't done it

Homework Options
Grammatikheft, p. 40, Acts. 7–8
Übungsheft, pp. 55–57, Acts. 4–9

Day 4

ERSTE STUFE
Quick Review 10 min.
- Check homework, Grammatikheft, p. 40, Acts. 7–8

Reading Selection 15 min.
- Teaching Suggestions, Video Guide, p. 22
- Do Pre-viewing, Viewing and Post-viewing Activities, p. 23, Video Guide
- Show Video, **In einer Fahrschule**
- Do Pre-viewing, Viewing and Post-viewing Activities 8 and 9, p. 24, Video Guide

Quick Review 25 min.
- Do **Mehr Grammatikübungen, Erste Stufe**
- Do Additional Listening Activities 5-1 and 5-2, p. 39
- Do Activities for Communication 5-1 and 5-2, pp. 17–18
- Do Realia 5-2, pp. 72 and 74, Activities for Communication

Homework Options
Internet Aktivitäten, see ATE, p. 119E

Day 5

ERSTE STUFE
Quick Review 5 min.
- Do Additional Listening Activity 5-3, p. 39

Quiz 20 min.
- Quiz 5-1A or 5-1B

LANDESKUNDE 20 min.
- Teaching Suggestion, ATE, p. 119R
- Read **Gleichberechtigung im deutschen Militär?**, p. 130
- Do Activities 1–5, p. 130

Wrap-Up 5 min.
- Students respond to questions about what they would do if they were to win the lottery

Homework Options
Übungsheft, p. 58, Acts. 1–2

Day 6

ERSTE STUFE
Quick Review 10 min.
- Return Quiz 5–1
- Check homework, Übungsheft, p. 58, Acts. 1–2

WEITER GEHT'S! 20 min.
- Preteaching Vocabulary, ATE, p. 119Q
- Play Audio CD for **Weiter geht's!**, pp. 128–129
- Do Activity 12, p. 129

ZWEITE STUFE
Wortschatz, So sagt man das!, p. 131 15 min.
- Presenting **Wortschatz, So sagt man das!,** ATE, p. 119S
- Teaching Transparency 5-2
- Do Activities 1 and 2, p. 60, Übungsheft

Wrap-Up 5 min.
- Students respond to questions about what they are doing right now

Homework Options
Grammatikheft, pp. 41–42, Acts. 9–11
Übungsheft, p. 59, Acts. 1–4

 **One-Stop** Planner CD-ROM

For alternative lesson plans by chapter section, to create your own customized plans, or to preview all resources available for this chapter, use the **One-Stop Planner CD-ROM**, Disc 2.

 For additional homework suggestions, see activities accompanied by this symbol throughout the chapter.

Day 7

ZWEITE STUFE

Quick Review 10 min.
- Check homework, Grammatikheft, pp. 41–42, Acts. 9–11

Ein wenig Grammatik, p. 132 10 min.
- Presenting **Ein wenig Grammatik,** ATE, p. 119S
- Do Activity 13, p. 132

Ein wenig Landeskunde, So sagt man das!, p. 132 10 min.
- Presenting **Ein wenig Landeskunde, So sagt man das!,** ATE, p. 119S
- Play Audio CD for Activity 14, p. 133

Grammatik, p. 133 15 min.
- Presenting **Grammatik,** ATE, p. 119T
- Do Activity 15, p. 133
- Do Activities 13 and 14, pp. 43–44, Grammatikheft

Wrap-Up 5 min.
- Students respond to questions about what they could, should, or had to do in the past

Homework Options
Grammatikheft, p. 43, Act. 12
Übungsheft, pp. 61–62, Acts. 3–6

Day 8

ZWEITE STUFE

Quick Review 10 min.
- Check homework, Übungsheft, pp. 61–62, Acts. 3–6

Wortschatz, So sagt man das!, p. 134 20 min.
- Presenting, **Wortschatz, So sagt man das!,** ATE, p. 119T
- Do Activity 16, p. 134
- Play Audio CD for Activity 17, p. 134
- Do Activity 18, p. 134
- Do Activities 19, 20 and 21, p. 135

Quiz Review 20 min.
- **Mehr Grammatikübungen, Zweite Stufe**
- Do Communicative Activities 5-3 and 5-4, pp. 19–20
- Do Additional Listening Activities 5-4 and 5-5, pp. 40–41

Homework Options
Grammatikheft, p. 45, Acts. 15–16
Übungsheft, pp. 62–63, Acts. 7–10
Pupil's Edition, p. 135, Acts. 22 and 23

Day 9

ZWEITE STUFE

Quick Review 5 min.
- Check homework, Übungsheft, pp. 62–63, Acts. 7–10

Quiz 20 min.
- Quiz 5-2A or 5-2B

ZUM LESEN 20 min.
- Background Information, ATE, pp. 119U, 119V
- Language-to-Language, ATE, p. 119U
- Present **Lesestrategie,** p. 136
- Do Activities 1–4, pp. 136–137

Wrap-Up 5 min.
- Students respond to questions about the advantages and disadvantages of compulsory service

Homework Options
Pupil's Edition, p. 137, Acts. 5–7
Übungsheft, pp. 64–65, Acts. 1–7

Day 10

ZWEITE STUFE

Quick Review 10 min.
- Return Quiz 5–2
- Check homework, Pupil's Edition, p. 137, Acts. 5–7

ZUM LESEN 20 min.
- Do Activities 8–12, pp. 137–138

ZUM SCHREIBEN 20 min.
- Writing Strategy, ATE, p. 119W
- Teaching Suggestions, ATE, p. 119W
- Present **Schreibtipp,** p. 139
- Do Activity A, p. 139

Wrap-Up
- Students respond to questions about the differences in technology between then and now

Homework Options
Pupil's Edition, p. 139, Act. B

Day 11

ZWEITE STUFE

Quick Review 10 min.
- Check homework, Pupil's Edition, p. 139, Act. B

ZUM SCHREIBEN 15 min.
- Do Activity C, p. 139
- Present interviews to class

ANWENDUNG 20 min.
- Do Activities 1–5 and 7–8, pp. 144–145

Wrap-Up 5 min.
- Students respond to questions about what they would do if they had more time

Homework Options
Interaktive Spiele, see ATE, p. 119E
Pupil's Edition, p. 145, Act. 6

Day 12

ANWENDUNG

Quick Review 10 min.
- Check homework, Pupil's Edition, p. 145, Act. 6

Kann ich's wirklich?, p. 146 20 min.
- Do **Kann ich's wirklich?,** Activities 1–5, pp. 144–145

Chapter Review 20 min.
- Review chapter functions, vocabulary, and grammar; choose from **Mehr Grammatikübungen,** Activities for Communication, Listening Activities, or **Interaktive Spiele**
- Review test format and provide sample test items for students

Homework Options
Study for Chapter Test

Assessment

Test, Chapter 5 45 min.
- Administer Chapter 5 Test. Select from Testing Program, Alternative Assessment Guide or Test Generator.

Kapitel 5: Rechte und Pflichten
Suggested Lesson Plans *90-Minute Schedule*

Block 1

CHAPTER OPENER 5 min.
- Teaching Suggestion, ATE, p. 119M
- Background Information, ATE, p. 119M

LOS GEHT'S! 30 min.
- Preteaching Vocabulary, ATE, p. 119N
- Cooperative Learning, p. 119N
- Play Audio CD for **Los geht's!**
- Have students read **Los geht's!**, pp. 122–123
- Do Activities 1 and 2, p. 123
- Do Activities 1 and 2, p. 53, Übungsheft

ERSTE STUFE
Reading Selection, p. 124 10 min.
- Thinking Critically, p. 119O
- Read **Was bedeutet das?**, p. 124

Wortschatz, p. 124 20 min.
- Presenting **Wortschatz**, ATE, p. 119O
- Play Audio CD for Activity 3, p. 125
- Do Activities 1–4, pp. 37–38, Grammatikheft

So sagt man das!, Ein wenig Grammatik, p. 125 20 min.
- Presenting **So sagt man das!, Ein wenig Grammatik**, ATE, p. 119O
- Teaching Transparency 5-1
- Play Audio CD for Activity 4, p. 125
- Do Activity 5, p. 125
- Do Activity 6, p. 126

Wrap-Up 5 min.
- Students respond to questions about what they could do if they were 18

Homework Options
Grammatikheft, p. 39, Acts. 5–6
Übungsheft, pp. 54–55, Acts. 1–3

Block 2

ERSTE STUFE
Quick Review 10 min.
- Check homework, Grammatikheft, p. 39, Acts. 5–6

So sagt man das!/Grammatik, p. 126 35 min.
- Presenting **So sagt man das! Grammatik**, ATE, p. 119P
- Do Activity 7, p. 126
- Do Activities 8–11, p. 127

Reading Selection 15 min.
- Teaching Suggestions, Video Guide, p. 22
- Do Pre-viewing, Viewing and Post-viewing Activities, p. 23, Video Guide
- Show Video, **In einer Fahrschule**
- Do Pre-viewing, Viewing and Post-viewing Activities 8 and 9, p. 24, Video Guide

Quick Review 25 min.
- Do **Mehr Grammatikübungen, Erste Stufe**
- Do Additional Listening Activities 5-1 and 5-2, p. 39
- Do Activities for Communication 5-1 and 5-2, pp. 17–18
- Do Realia 5-2, pp. 72 and 74, Activities for Communication

Wrap-Up 5 min.
- Students respond to questions about what they would have done and why they hadn't done it

Homework Options
Grammatikheft, p. 40, Acts. 7–8
Übungsheft, pp. 55–57, Acts. 4–9

Block 3

ERSTE STUFE
Quick Review 10 min.
- Check homework, Übungsheft, pp. 55–57, Acts. 4–9

Quiz 20 min.
- Quiz 5-1A or 5-1B

LANDESKUNDE 20 min.
- Teaching Suggestion, ATE, p. 119R
- Read **Gleichberechtigung im deutschen Militär?**, p. 130
- Do Activities 1–5, p. 130

WEITER GEHT'S! 20 min.
- Preteaching Vocabulary, p. 119Q
- Play Audio CD for **Weiter geht's!**, pp. 128–129
- Do Activity 12, p. 129

ZWEITE STUFE
Wortschatz, So sagt man das!, p. 131 15 min.
- Presenting **Wortschatz, So sagt man das!**, ATE, p. 119S
- Teaching Transparency 5-2
- Do Activities 1 and 2, p. 60, Übungsheft

Wrap-Up 5 min.
- Students respond to questions about what they are doing right now

Homework Options
Grammatikheft, pp. 41–42, Acts. 9–11
Übungsheft, p. 58, Acts. 1–2; p. 59, Acts. 1–4
Internet Aktivitäten, see ATE, p. 119E

One-Stop Planner CD-ROM

For alternative lesson plans by chapter section, to create your own customized plans, or to preview all resources available for this chapter, use the **One-Stop Planner CD-ROM**, Disc 2.

 For additional homework suggestions, see activities accompanied by this symbol throughout the chapter.

Block 4

ZWEITE STUFE
Quick Review 10 min.
- Check homework, Grammatikheft, pp. 41–42, Acts. 9–11

Ein wenig Grammatik, p. 132 10 min.
- Presenting **Ein wenig Grammatik**, ATE, p. 119S
- Do Activity 13, p. 132

Ein wenig Landeskunde, So sagt man das!, p. 132 10 min.
- Presenting **Ein wenig Landeskunde, So sagt man das!**, ATE, p. 119S
- Play Audio CD for Activity 14, p. 133

Grammatik, p. 133 15 min.
- Presenting Grammatik, ATE, p. 119T
- Do Activity 15, p. 133
- Do Activities 13 and 14, pp. 43–44, Grammatikheft

Wortschatz, So sagt man das!, p. 134 25 min.
- Presenting **Wortschatz, So sagt man das!**, ATE, p. 119T
- Do Activity 15, p. 45, Grammatikheft
- Do Activity 16, p. 134
- Play Audio CD for Activity 17, p. 134
- Do Activity 18, p. 134
- Do Activities 19, 20, and 21, p. 135

Quiz Review 20 min.
- Mehr Grammatikübungen, Zweite Stufe
- Do Communicative Activities 5-3 and 5-4, pp. 19–20
- Do Additional Listening Activities 5-4 and 5-5, pp. 40–41

Homework Options
Grammatikheft, p. 43, Act. 12; p. 45, Act. 16
Übungsheft, pp. 61–63, Acts. 3–10
Pupil's Edition, p. 135, Acts. 22 and 23

Block 5

ZWEITE STUFE
Quick Review 30 min.
- Check homework, Übungsheft, pp. 61–63, Acts. 3–10
- Play **Seeschlacht**, ATE, p. 119C

Quiz 20 min.
- Quiz 5-2A or 5-2B

ZUM LESEN 35 min.
- Background Information, ATE, pp. 119U–119V
- Language-to-Language, ATE, p. 119U
- Present **Lesestrategie**, p. 136
- Do Activities 1–12, pp. 136–138

Wrap-Up 5 min.
- Students respond to questions about the differences in technology between now and then

Homework Options
Interaktive Spiele, see ATE, p. 119E
Übungsheft, pp. 64–65, Acts. 1–7

Block 6

ZWEITE STUFE
Quick Review 20 min.
- Check homework, Übungsheft, pp. 64–65, Acts. 1–7

ZUM SCHREIBEN 20 min.
- Teaching Suggestions, ATE, p. 119W
- Present **Schreibtipp**, p. 139
- Do Activity A, p. 139

ANWENDUNG 25 min.
- Do Activities 1–8, pp. 144–145

Kann ich's wirklich?, p. 146 20 min.
- Do **Kann ich's wirklich?**, Activities 1–5, p. 146

Wrap-Up 5 min.
- Students respond to questions about what they would do if they had more time

Homework Options
Pupil's Edition, p. 139, Acts. B and C
Study for Chapter Test

Block 7

ANWENDUNG
Quick Review 15 min.
- Check homework, Pupil's Edition, p. 139, Acts. B and C

Chapter Review 30 min.
- Review chapter functions, vocabulary, and grammar; choose from **Mehr Grammatikübungen,** Activities for Communication, Listening Activities, or **Interaktive Spiele**
- Review test format and provide sample test items for students

Test, Chapter 5 45 min.
- Administer Chapter 5 Test. Select from Testing Program, Alternative Assessment Guide or Test Generator.

Kapitel 5: Rechte und Pflichten
Teaching Suggestions, pages 120–147

Using the Video

Before you begin the chapter, you may want to preview the *Video Program* and consult the *Video Guide*. Suggestions for integrating the video into each chapter are given in the *Video Guide*. Activity masters for video selections can be found in the *Video Guide*.

PAGES 120–121

CHAPTER OPENER

Pacing Tips

The **Erste Stufe** centers around the topic of things 18-year-olds can do. The functions presented are 'talking about what is possible' and 'saying what you would have liked to do' alongside the **könnte**-forms and further uses of **hätte** and **wäre**. Ordinal numbers and the concept of relative clauses are introduced. The **Zweite Stufe** focuses on **Wehrpflicht** and **Zivildienst.** Students learn the past tense of modals (the imperfect) on p. 133. The **Landeskunde** section discusses the recent change concerning women in the military. You may want to spend a little extra time on the **Zum Lesen** section, which centers around texts from WWII. For Lesson Plans and timing suggestions, see pages 119I–119L.

Meeting the Standards
Communication
- Talking about what is possible, p. 125
- Saying what you would have liked to do, p. 126
- Saying that something is going on right now, p.131
- Reporting past events, p.132
- Expressing surprise, relief, and resignation, p.134

Cultures
- **Landeskunde,** p. 130
- **Ein wenig Landeskunde,** p. 132
- Background Information, p. 119M
- Background Information, p. 119U

Connections
- Multicultural Connection, p. 119P
- Music Connection, p. 119S
- Language-to-Language, p. 119U

Comparisons
- Thinking Critically, p. 119O

For resource information, see the **One-Stop Planner CD-ROM,** Disc 2.

Communities
- Community Link, p. 119C
- Career Path, p. 119S

Advance Organizer
Go around the classroom and ask students how they are involved in their community. Do they take an interest or an active role in local politics, concerns, or interest groups? Are other members of their families involved? What are some of their concerns?

Teaching Suggestion
After students have looked at the photo, ask them where they typically hang out with their friends and what they usually talk about. Make a list of some of the topics. (**Wo trefft ihr euch gewöhnlich mit eurer Clique oder euren Freunden? Über welche Themen diskutiert ihr normalerweise?**)

Cultures and Communities

Background Information
In Germany, men are required to serve ten months of compulsory military service; however, Article 4 of the **Grundgesetz** *(constitution)* states that men can be exempt from the service if it is against their conscience to make use of arms. In such a case the **Kriegsdienstverweigerer** *(conscientious objector)* must perform **Zivildienst** *(alternate service),* e.g., at the Red Cross.

Chapter Sequence

LOS GEHT'S!

Teaching Resources
pp. 122–123

PRINT
- Lesson Planner, p. 31
- Übungsheft, p. 53

MEDIA
- One-Stop Planner
- Audio Compact Discs, CD5, Trs. 1–6

PAGES 122–123

Los geht's! Summary

In *Mit achtzehn darf man alles. Oder?*, Julia, Angie, Stefan, and Martin talk about the rights and obligations that come with being an adult. The following learning outcomes listed on p. 121 are modeled in the interviews: talking about what is possible and saying what you would have liked to do.

Preteaching Vocabulary

Identifying Keywords

Start by asking students to guess the context of Los geht's! (students telling what they may do at 18). Then have students use the German they know and the context of the situation to identify key words and phrases that tell what is happening for each person. Students should look for words that seem important or that occur several times. Here are a few of the words they might identify as keywords: **Geburtstag, Führerschein, unabhängiger, Schuleschwänzen, wählen.** List the keywords on the board or on a transparency and separate them according to whether or not they are cognates.

Building Context

Have students make a list of things that will change for them when they reach legal maturity.

Teaching Suggestion

Play the recording of the interviews and have students follow along in the text. Stop the recording after each response and ask detailed questions to check for understanding. Explain new vocabulary in German by paraphrasing and using synonyms. Be sure to clarify the time frames in which the interviews operate.

Martin: present - past; Angie: present - past - present; Stefan: present - future; Julia: present. Finally, work with the last part of the interview in which all four German teenagers participate. Again, stop after each major point (cost, length of training, and comparison of the two driver education systems) and ask some quick questions to check comprehension.

Comprehension Check

Challenge

Ask students to make up a couple of sentences in German that summarize the main ideas of the first three interviews. (Martin: Mit 18 darf man Auto fahren, aber sonst hat sich nicht viel geändert. Angie: Mit 18 darf man seine eigene Entschuldigung schreiben, aber man sollte die Schule nicht schwänzen. Jeder Tag ist wichtig. Stefan: Mit 18 kann man wählen, aber man sollte sich vorher gut informieren.)

Cooperative Learning

1 Have students work in groups of three to read the responses of Martin, Angie, Stefan, and Julia. Students should take on the role of group writer, proofreader, or reporter as they complete the activity. While students work in groups, go around the classroom to help clarify unfamiliar phrases or answer questions they might have. Upon completion, call on groups to discuss their notes.

Visual Learners

2 Make a chart on the board to compare and contrast the requirements for getting a driver's license in the United States and in Germany for Part 3 of this activity.

Multicultural Connection

2 Have students find out what requirements and fees exist for getting a driver's license in other countries. If possible, obtain samples or copies of foreign licenses to compare. What information do all provide? Which ones differ slightly?

Closure

Ask students to take a moment to think about how they would complete the following statement: **Volljährigkeit wird für mich sehr wichtig sein, denn …**

ERSTE STUFE

Teaching Resources
pp. 124–127

PRINT

- Lesson Planner, p. 32
- Listening Activities, pp. 35–36, 39–40
- Video Guide, pp. 21–23
- Activities for Communication, pp. 17–18, 72, 74, 121–122
- Grammatikheft, pp. 37–40
- Grammar Tutor for Students of German, Chapter 5
- Übungsheft, pp. 54–57
- Testing Program, pp. 89–92
- Alternative Assessment Guide, p. 34
- Student Make-Up Assignments, Chapter 5

MEDIA

- One-Stop Planner
- Audio Compact Discs, CD5, Trs. 7–8, 13, 18–20
- Video Program
  In einer Fahrschule
  Videocassette 1, 42:02–44:37
- Teaching Transparencies
  Situation 5-1
  Vocabulary 5A
  Mehr Grammatikübungen Answers
  Grammatikheft Answers

PAGE 124

Bell Work

Ask students to imagine the day that they reach legal adulthood. How would they like that day to unfold? (**Wie stellst du dir den Tag vor, an dem du volljährig wirst?**)

Cultures and Communities

The German **Grundgesetz** (*basic law or constitution*) came into effect on May 23, 1949.

Using the Video

Videocassette 1, 42:02–44:37
In the video clip *In einer Fahrschule*, trainees in a driver's education class talk about their experiences. *See Video Guide, p. 22, for suggestions.*

Connections and Comparisons

Thinking Critically

Comparing and Contrasting Go over the list of changes that occur as a result of reaching legal adulthood (18) in Germany (See "**Was bedeutet das?**"). Then ask students to compare the required age in the United States for each of the nine points listed.

PRESENTING: Wortschatz

After introducing the new vocabulary to the class, assign each word or phrase to individual students. Give them a few moments to come up with a brief scenario in which the word or phrase could be used. Have several students share their word or phrase with the class. Example: **Ich schwänze heute.**

> **Prüfung: Ich glaube, ich schwänze heute lieber nicht, denn wir haben eine wichtige Matheprüfung.**

PAGE 125

Communication for All Students

A Slower Pace

3 Before listening to the recording on compact disc, go over Pictures a through e and ask students to describe each picture briefly in German.

Challenge

3 After students have listened to the five narrations and completed the matching exercise, ask them to listen again, this time noting two or three things about each person and thus telling more about the situation pictured. (Example: for Picture c: **Jutta ist froh, dass sie jetzt wählen darf. Sie ist politisch sehr aktiv, ist Mitglied einer Partei. Sie arbeitet für eine politische Zeitung. Sie sieht sich täglich die Nachrichten an und …**)

PRESENTING: So sagt man das!

- Write the following sentence on the board: "**Du könntest dich wirklich ein bisschen für Politik interessieren!**" Why would someone say this, and what does it indicate about the other person's interest in politics? Can students think of alternate ways to state this sentence?
  Examples:
  Es ist wichtig, sich für Politik zu interessieren.
  Du solltest mehr Interesse an Politik haben!
- Go over the explanation in **So sagt man das!** with students.

Teaching Suggestion

4 Replay the recording on compact disc several times and have students list all the plans that the three German students talk about.

Communication for All Students

Challenge

4 Have students listen for the reasons the three German teenagers give for their choices. They should tell why they want to do certain things and not others.

PRESENTING: Ein wenig Grammatik

Könnte-forms After introducing the **könnte**-forms, ask pairs of students to scan the two Location Openers (**die neuen Bundesländer** and **Würzburg**) for things they could do if they were to visit these places. Also, what would they suggest that others go and see during a visit?
Example:
Wir könnten uns das Bachhaus in Eisenach anschauen, denn das ist heute ein Museum.

PAGE 126

Communication for All Students

A Slower Pace

6 Do the following activity in class before beginning Activity 6. Ask for suggestions and have students take notes. If students have trouble coming up with ideas, ask questions.
Examples:
Kannst du jetzt …
 jeden Tag arbeiten gehen?
 mit Freunden in den Ferien wegfahren?
 ein Auto haben?
After the discussion, have students write their own lists with reasons why they were not able or not allowed to do these various things.

PRESENTING: So sagt man das!/Grammatik

Wäre und hätte
- Review with students the previously introduced function of hypothesizing in which students used the forms **wäre** and **hätte**.

- Provide students with practice by having them complete the following statements:
Ich wäre letzten Sommer gern …, aber …
Ich hätte gestern Abend …, aber …

Teaching Suggestion

10 To give students time to think about these questions, you may want to assign them for homework.

Connections and Comparisons

Multicultural Connection

Ask students to interview foreign exchange students, other foreign language teachers, or anybody else they know from a different country about how reaching legal adulthood is important to a young person of that country. What is the legal age in that country and in which way does it change a young person's status? Discuss students' findings in class.

Speaking Assessment

10 After some practice in class, you may want to use these questions for oral evaluation. Have students come to your desk and answer three or four questions for assessment using the following rubric.

Speaking Rubric	Points			
	4	3	2	1
Content (Complete – Incomplete)				
Comprehension (Total – Little)				
Comprehensibility (Comprehensible – Incomprehensible)				
Accuracy (Accurate – Seldom accurate)				
Fluency (Fluent – Not fluent)				

18–20: A   16–17: B   14–15: C   12–13: D   Under 12: F

Assess

▸ Testing Program, pp. 89–92
 Quiz 5-1A, Quiz 5-1B
 Audio CD5, Tr. 13

▸ Student Make-Up Assignments
 Chapter 5, Alternative Quiz

▸ Alternative Assessment Guide, p. 34

STANDARDS: 1.1, 3.2, 4.2   **KAPITEL 5   ERSTE STUFE   119P**

WEITER GEHT'S!

Teaching Resources
pp. 128–129

PRINT
▸ Lesson Planner, p. 33
▸ Übungsheft, p. 58

MEDIA
▸ One-Stop Planner
▸ Audio Compact Discs, CD5, Tr. 9

PAGES 128–129

Weiter geht's! Summary

In *Die Wehrpflicht: dafür oder dagegen?*, four young people are asked to talk about their opinions of military service. The following learning outcomes listed on p. 121 are modeled in the interviews: saying that something is going on right now; reporting past events; and expressing surprise, relief, and resignation.

Preteaching Vocabulary

Identifying Keywords

Start by asking students to guess the context of **Weiter geht's!** (students discussing mandatory service for males in Germany). Then have students use the German they know and the context of the situation to identify key words and phrases that tell what is happening for each person. Students should look for words that seem important or that occur several times. Here are a few of the words they might identify as keywords: **Bundeswehr, Wehrdienst, Zivildienst, Diskussion, Bund, Mädchen, freiwillig.** List the keywords on the board or on a transparency and separate them according to whether or not they are cognates.

Advance Organizer

Ask students about their opinions of compulsory military service. Is it a good idea? In the United States military service is voluntary. Does the U.S. system work? What do they think about women fighting in combat? Have students list some advantages and disadvantages to being in the armed forces.

Teaching Suggestion

Divide the interview into three sections. Play the recording for each section as students read along in the text. Then ask questions to check for understanding and explain any unfamiliar terms in German, using synonyms or paraphrasing. Put the key terms on the chalkboard or a transparency to aid comprehension.
Examples:
Wehrpflicht, Wehrdienst, Bundeswehr (Bund), Streitkräfte, vermeiden, einziehen

Comprehension Check

Auditory Learners

12 Prepare a blank chart like the one suggested for this activity and make a copy for each student (see example below). Go over the activity with students, then have them listen to the continuation of the interview at least twice. As students listen, they should take notes and fill in the chart as best they can.

Die Wehrpflicht: dafür oder dagegen?
Was sagen die folgenden Schüler dazu?

Stefan	Martin	Angie	Julia
Wehrdienst soll freiwillig sein.	Bundeswehr ist sinnlos.	Streitkräfte sind nicht mehr wichtig.	ist froh, dass sie als Mädchen nicht wehrpflichtig ist.

Discuss the opinions of the four German teenagers with students.

Closure

Ask students if they know anyone who has served or is still serving in the United States military. Do they know what those people specifically did or do in the service and for how long they served or will serve?

LANDESKUNDE

Teaching Suggestion

You might want to introduce the following vocabulary to help students understand the text:

die Gleichberechtigung: eine Frau darf das Gleiche machen wie ein Mann und hat die gleichen Rechte

der Dienst: die Arbeit

der Bundestagsabgeordnete: ein Politiker

verbieten: etwas nicht erlauben

die Streitkräfte: Truppen, das ganze Militär

die Kaserne: wo die Soldaten wohnen

der Stahlhelm: was Soldaten auf dem Kopf tragen

Ausschluss: Teilnahmeverbot

widersprechen: eine andere Meinung haben

der öffentliche Dienst: ein Beruf, in dem man für die Regierung arbeitet

Aufstiegsmöglichkeit: die Möglichkeit, schnell nach oben zu kommen, eine bessere Position zu bekommen oder beruflich Karriere zu machen

Teaching Suggestions

• After introducing the additional vocabulary, remind students of the reading strategy of scanning a text for specific information. (Level 1, Chapter 2, p. 60)

• Before reading the text, have students preview Questions 1–5 to determine what they should be looking for as they read. If they understand what is being asked, they can identify key information more easily.

Group Work

Divide the class into seven groups and assign each group a question. Ask each group to read the text to determine the answer to their question. For Questions 6 and 7, have the group discuss their opinions and come to a consensus. Call on all seven groups to share their answers or ideas with the rest of the class.

Teacher Note

Mention to your students that the **Landeskunde** will also be included in the Chapter Test.

ZWEITE STUFE

Teaching Resources
pp. 131–135

PRINT
▶ Lesson Planner, p. 34
▶ Listening Activities, pp. 37, 40–42
▶ Video Guide, pp. 21–22, 24
▶ Activities for Communication, pp. 19–20, 71, 73–75, 121–122
▶ Grammatikheft, pp. 41–45
▶ Grammar Tutor for Students of German, Chapter 5
▶ Übungsheft, pp. 59–63
▶ Testing Program, pp. 93–96
▶ Alternative Assessment Guide, p. 34
▶ Student Make-Up Assignments, Chapter 5

MEDIA
▶ One-Stop Planner
▶ Audio Compact Discs, CD5, Trs. 10–11, 14, 21–23
▶ Video Program
   Der Zivildienst
   Videocassette 1, 44:39–47:47
▶ Teaching Transparencies
   Situation 5-2
   Mehr Grammatikübungen Answers
   Grammatikheft Answers

Bell Work

Ask students about their opinions of computer or video games that depict war themes. (Was haltet ihr von Computer- und Videospielen, die mit Krieg zu tun haben? Begründet eure Meinung!)

Teaching Suggestion

Discuss with students any current conflicts around the world that involve military forces. What are the most recent images that they can recall? (Gibt es zur Zeit Krisen, Konflikte oder Kriege in der Welt, an denen Militärstreitkräfte teilnehmen? Welche Bilder kommen dir in den Sinn?)

Cultures and Communities

Career Path

Ask students to brainstorm reasons why American military personnel might need to know German. (Suggestions: Imagine you are an American pilot training German flyers at the American air force base in El Paso, Texas; imagine you are stationed in Germany.)

PRESENTING: Wortschatz

- To introduce the new vocabulary to students you could collect posters and flyers from military recruitment offices or the ROTC. Describe the realia, incorporating as much of the new vocabulary as possible.

- If you want students to produce the new vocabulary, ask either/or questions such as **Ist das ein Laster oder ein Panzer?** as well as open-ended questions such as: **Was machen diese jungen Leute beim Wehrdienst?**

PRESENTING: So sagt man das!

- Have students point out the specific word(s) in each of the three sentences that express the idea of current action.

- Adverbs such as **gerade** or **eben** appear often with the prepositions **an** or **bei** and a nominalized infinitive. (Example: **am** and **beim Diskutieren**) Have students create additional sentences from phrases you give them. (Examples: **Briefe schreiben, das Zimmer aufräumen, das Essen kochen, Geschenke kaufen—Ich bin gerade am Briefeschreiben**)

▶ PAGE 132

Communication for All Students

Kinesthetic Learners

13 As a variation, have students take turns acting out what Martin is doing. Ask the class to describe what is being acted out using the expressions listed in So sagt man das! on p. 131. Have students do the same for additional actions such as **Hausaufgaben machen, den Koffer packen, den Tisch decken, Schuhe putzen, sich anziehen,** and **sich schminken.**

PRESENTING: Ein wenig Grammatik

Verbs as nouns Read aloud several sentences like the following and have students rephrase them, using the verb as a noun. Note that there will be multiple correct ways for students to phrase their answers.
Ich sauge nicht gern Staub. (Das Staubsaugen habe ich nicht gern.)
Sie spielt gerade Fußball. (Sie ist beim Fußballspielen.)
Er findet es schwer zu singen. (Das Singen findet er schwer.)

Connections and Comparisons

Music Connection

For additional reading, refer students to the text of the poem *Das Wandern ist des Müllers Lust,* Level 1 *Listening Activities,* p. 14. What verb is repeatedly used as a noun? (**wandern**) Ask students to give you a rough English translation of the first section of the poem. You may also want to play the song, Level 1 CD 2, Track 33.

PRESENTING: Ein wenig Landeskunde

After students have read the **ein wenig Landeskunde** segment, ask them to work with a partner to come up with at least three questions to check for comprehension of the text. Then have pairs direct their questions to other students.
Examples:
Wie lange dauert die Wehrpflicht in der BRD?
Wie lange dauert der Grundwehrdienst in Österreich?
Woraus bestehen die Streitkräfte der Bundeswehr?

Using the Video

Videocassette 1, 44:39–47:47
In the video clip *Der Zivildienst,* four young men discuss their duties as community service workers. See *Video Guide,* p. 22, for suggestions.

PRESENTING: So sagt man das!

After students have recognized that the past tense is expressed with a simple past tense form of the modal together with an infinitive, refer back to the pictures in Activity 13 and have students restate what Martin had to do. (Example: **Martin musste zu Hause Staub saugen.**) Now have students imagine what he wanted to do but couldn't because he had to do certain chores.
(Example: **Martin <u>wollte</u> Tennis spielen gehen, aber er <u>konnte</u> nicht, denn er <u>musste</u> Staub saugen.**)

PRESENTING: Grammatik

The past tense of modals (the imperfect)

• Have students compare the imperfect modal forms with the forms in the present tense.

• Make a transparency with two columns showing verb forms in the present and past tense. Have students point out the differences between the forms.

Communication for All Students

Challenge

14 After students have completed Activity 14, have them listen to the conversation again, this time focusing on all the chores and errands that the speakers have already completed and those they are still planning to do. Have students make a simple chart to organize their notes.

	hat schon gemacht	muss noch tun
die Frau		
der Mann		

PAGE 134

PRESENTING: Wortschatz

• Use a large calendar to review previously introduced vocabulary, as well as the new phrases. Talk about events in the past, making specific references to them on the calendar.
Example:
Im vergangen Monat, also im Juni, hat die Rockgruppe Rolling Stones in der Konzerthalle gespielt. Wer von euch war denn da und hat sie spielen hören?

• Have students order the words and phrases according to how far they reach into the past. Have them start with **im neunzehnten Jahrhundert** and end with **heute.**

PRESENTING: So sagt man das!

• In Level 2 (pp. 249 and 287), students learned some ways to express resignation and surprise. Review these before beginning **So sagt man das!**

• Remind students that intonation plays a big role in the perception of what is being said.

Teaching Suggestion

17 Divide the conversation into four parts and play one part at a time, repeating, if necessary. Then discuss students' findings immediately afterwards.

PAGE 135

Communication for All Students

Challenge

21 After the discussion, ask each pair to compose a letter to the editorial section of the school paper giving their opinions about one of the two issues.

Visual Learners

Bring to class old photos or magazines that depict life in your area or town several decades ago. Ask students how things must have been different then.

Von der Schule zum Beruf

23  Von der Schule zum Beruf

Have students complete the **Webprojekt** on p. 119E, before assigning this activity.

Assess

▸ Testing Program, pp. 93–96
Quiz 5-2A, Quiz 5-2B
Audio CD5, Tr. 14

▸ Student Make-Up Assignments
Chapter 5, Alternative Quiz

▸ Alternative Assessment Guide, p. 34

ZUM LESEN

Teaching Resources
pp. 136–138

PRINT
▶ Lesson Planner, p. 35
▶ Übungsheft, pp. 64–65
▶ Reading Strategies and Skills, Chapter 5
▶ Lies mit mir! 3, Chapter 5

MEDIA
▶ One-Stop Planner

Prereading
Building Context

Discuss with students the basic rights guaranteed by the U.S. Constitution and ask them to imagine giving up these rights. Then discuss with them the following question:

Which would be preferable: a party that promises to uphold basic rights for every individual—or a party that promises prosperity and national strength at the expense of certain basic rights?

Cultures and Communities

Background Information

The Weimar Constitution (adopted in August, 1919 and officially in effect until March, 1933) was modeled after the U.S. Constitution and British law and included similar human rights provisions. But millions of Germans became unemployed during the time it was in effect, and inflation was rampant. Many Germans lost faith in the ability of a democratic government to provide political and economic solutions to their problems. When the National Socialists promised prosperity and national security, their promises fell on many receptive ears. Eventually, many Germans opted for the promise of prosperity and national strength, only to discover too late that they had lost most of their basic rights along the way.

Teacher Note

Activities 1–3 are prereading activities.

Cultures and Communities

3 The following background information will provide students with a context for the reading selections:

October 1929: Beginning of the Great Depression, which brings widespread unemployment to the United States and Europe.

September 1930: National Socialist Party receives 6.5 million votes in the national election and becomes the second-largest party in the **Reichstag.**

Summer 1932: Approximately 34% of the German work force is unemployed.

July 31, 1932: Nazi Party wins even more seats in the **Reichstag** with the promise that it will create jobs for everyone.

November 1932: In parliamentary elections, Nazis lose several seats, while Communists gain additional seats. This loss of support among German voters convinces Nazi officials to take a more militant and aggressive stance in order to remain in power.

January 30, 1933: Hitler is named Chancellor by President Hindenburg.

February 27, 1933: Fire in the **Reichstag.** Hitler blames the Communists. Four thousand of his opponents are arrested.

March 1, 1933: Emergency decree suspends guarantee of all civil rights.

March 23, 1933: German Parliament votes 441-94 in favor of a law that will enable the executive branch to govern, to make new laws, and to revise the Constitution without consent of the **Reichstag.**

April 1, 1933: First (unsuccessful) boycott of Jewish businesses.

May 10, 1933: Students burn "undesirable" books at several universities.

August 1934: Death of President Hindenburg. Hitler becomes president and chancellor. He gives himself the official title **"der Führer."**

Connections and Comparisons

Language-to-Language

You may want to tell your students that German, like other spoken languages, integrates new vocabulary in order to meet the needs of the time. German vocabulary reflects social, political, economic, and technical upheavals in German history. For example, World War I and World War II led to a dramatic expansion of military vocabulary and gave birth to words such as **Schützengraben, Bunker, Bomber,**

Connections and Comparisons

continued from p. 119U

Luftschutzkeller, Blitzkrieg, Luftwaffe, and **Sirene.** Socioeconomic changes brought about new terms, such as **Aushungerung, durchhalten, hamstern, Ersatz, Schiebung, Schwarzschlachtung,** and **Schlange stehen.**

You may want to ask your students to find 20th-century vocabulary in the excerpts from Hitler's speeches on p. 136. (Examples: **Lebensraum, Gewaltanwendung, Rüstungspotential, Offensive, Wehrmacht, propagandistisch, Rasse, Minderwertigkeitsempfindungen**)

Reading

Cultures and Communities

Background Information

6 To fully understand what Hitler had in mind with these speeches, students need to know what was happening in Germany at the time each speech was given. In 1933, although France and Great Britain had agreed to stop their demands for World War I reparations payments, Germany broke the Versailles Treaty and walked out of the League of Nations. In 1937, when Hitler first proposed the **Lebensraum** policy to the military, Defense Minister von Blomberg, Foreign Minister von Neurath, and **Wehrmacht** General von Fritsch protested. Hitler eventually got rid of all three and put the War Department directly under his own command. Following its 1938 annexation of the border province of Sudetenland and the subsequent occupation of the remainder of Czechoslovakia in 1939, Germany bullied Lithuania into giving up the Memelland on the Baltic Sea coast. Then Hitler made plans to invade and partition Poland with the help of the Soviet Union. In 1940, Nazi troops invaded France, and then in June, 1941, they invaded the Soviet Union itself, with the ultimate goal of subjugating all "non-Aryan" peoples in Europe.

Teaching Suggestion

8 Before students attempt to understand the **Flugblatt,** ask them to hypothesize about the main idea of the text based on what they know about the purpose of the text. Then ask students to read the text to confirm or refute their predictions. Students should apply the reading strategies of *determining the main idea* and *reading to get the gist.* Remind stu-

dents that the main idea of each paragraph is usually stated in the first or second sentence of the paragraph.

Cultures and Communities

Background Information

9 The reference to Hitler as a **Dilettant** *(amateur)* in military strategy was most likely born of frustration at Hitler's disastrous policy on the Eastern Front and of anguish from having experienced the Russian campaign personally, as a number of the Munich White Rose group had done. When the Russian winter of 1941 slowed the troops' advance toward Moscow, Hitler fired several generals and personally took over command of the Eastern Front. It was as a result of his orders to hold Stalingrad at all costs through the winter of 1942/43 that the frozen, starving Sixth Army was encircled and defeated by Stalin's forces. Thus the writers of the **Flugblatt** felt justified in referring to Hitler as a **Dilettant** and in calling for passive resistance against his policies.

11 The article "**Verführt von dummen, mörderischen Sprüchen**" is based on an incident that took place in 1993 in Germany. A group of German young people in Solingen set fire to an apartment building inhabited primarily by Turkish families. Several people were killed in the fire. The exchange here between the judge (**Richter**) and Felix K. (**der Angeklagte** or *defendant*) took place at the trial following that incident.

Post-Reading

Teacher Note

Activity 12 is a post-reading task that will show whether students can apply what they have learned.

Closure

From what students now know, do they think that student protests at that time made a difference? How would they have organized such protests? Was there a period in American history when similar student protests were significant in the outcome of events? (Examples: Vietnam War, civil rights movement of 1960s) What issues do students think could cause student protest today?

Zum Lesen Answers

Answers to Activity 1
excerpts from speeches, political flyer, excerpt of an interview; Hitler, **Geschwister Scholl,** source: *Focus;* 1933-1942, 1943, 1994

Answers to Activity 2
Hans and Sophie, brother and sister, college students during World War II, founder/member of the resistance movement **Weiße Rose**

Answers to Activity 3
See Background Information on p. 119U.

Answers to Activity 4

Hitler: the German people (excerpts 2 and 3 directed to German military), Scholls: fellow students; Hitler: to convince the German population/military to support Hitler and the National Socialist agenda (war and expansionism) and ideology (anti-Semitism), Scholls: to convince others to join the fight against Hitler and the party, both are examples of political propaganda; inform readers of facts

Answers to Activity 5

anerkennen *to acknowledge;* **Gewaltanwendung** *use of force;* **ergreifen** *to take;* **Erkenntnis** *realization;* **vorbereiten** *to prepare for;* **hinwegströmen** *to stream forth;* **fürchten** *to fear*

Answers to Activity 6

victory, conqueror, conquering; the desire to feel superior, to conquer, and to take revenge on others for Germany's troubles

Answers to Activity 7

Die Welt ist gegen Deutschland; Die Regierung kann froh sein, dass die Leute nicht viel denken; Deutschland muss in die Offensive gehen und mehr Lebensraum gewinnen; Sieg ist wichtiger als das Recht; Die Bedeutung von Rasse ist eine unwiderstehliche Idee; Die Deutschen sollen ihre Minderwertigkeitsgefühle aufgegen, und sie sollen über andere Nationen siegen und von anderen gefürchtet sein; speeches evoke images of an embattled Germany, the importance of victory and power; the tone is aggressive and provocative, designed to evoke aggressive feelings in listeners.

Answers to Activity 8

fellow students; other college students; Hitler and his party (**Kampf gegen die Partei**); freedom and honor (**Freiheit und Ehre**)

Answers to Activity 9

amateur: he is an incompetent military leader responsible for the deaths of thousands of young Germans; Hitler and his party

Answers to Activity 11

seduced by dumb and deadly slogans; Felix K., by neo-Nazi slogans; National Socialism is still an ideology among right-wing extremists in Germany today.

PAGE 139

ZUM SCHREIBEN

Teaching Resources
p. 139

PRINT
▶ Lesson Planner, p. 35
▶ Alternative Assessment Guide, p. 20

MEDIA
▶ One-Stop Planner
▶ Test Generator, Chapter 5

Writing Strategy

The targeted strategy in this writing activity is *asking questions to gather ideas.* Students should learn about this strategy before beginning the assignment.

Prewriting
Building Context

Have students imagine that they are going to be interviewed by German students about life in the United States. What kind of questions would they anticipate? What would they like to talk about? What would they want to convey about life in America? What would be easy questions? Difficult ones? Have students brainstorm ideas in pairs or small groups and then share their responses with the class.

Teaching Suggestions

• If students cannot find interviewees who grew up in another country and culture, you could invite several foreign-born guests to class and have group interviews for each person. Some sources might be local or state foreign language organizations, any local or regional agency working with immigrants, area universities or colleges, and civic and religious groups.

A1 Have pairs or small groups of students work together to brainstorm specific interview questions.

A2 In addition to the written statements, students may want to ask the person they plan to interview if they could take a picture of him or her or borrow some photos that would provide visual support for their reports.

Communication for All Students

Visual Learners

A3 You may want to remind students about the **Ideenbäume** they made for the **Zum Schreiben** activity in Chapter 3. Students may find it helpful to organize their report using an outline or **Ideenbaum**.

Writing
Teaching Suggestion

B Remind students to double- or triple-space their first drafts so they have room to make revisions during the **Überarbeiten** stage of the activity.

Post-Writing
Teaching Suggestion

Students could post their reports along with pictures of their interviewees on bulletin boards in the classroom which should be organized according to geographical location.

Closure

After reports have been presented and displayed, have small groups of students discuss how their lives would be different if they lived or had lived in the native country of the interviewees.

STANDARDS: 1.1

PAGES 140–143

MEHR GRAMMATIKÜBUNGEN

The **Mehr Grammatikübungen** activities are designed as supplemental activities for the grammatical concepts presented in the chapter. You might use them as additional practice, for review, or for assessment.

For more grammar presentations, review, and practice, refer to the following:
- Grammatikheft
- Grammar Tutor for Students of German
- Grammar Summary on pp. R22–R39
- Übungsheft
- Grammar and Vocabulary quizzes (Testing Program)
- Test Generator
- **Interaktive Spiele** at <u>go.hrw.com</u>

PAGES 144–145

ANWENDUNG

Teaching Resources
pp. 144–145

PRINT
▶ Lesson Planner, p. 35
▶ Listening Activities, p. 38
▶ Video Guide, pp. 21–22, 24
▶ Grammar Tutor for Students of German, Chapter 5

MEDIA
▶ One-Stop Planner
▶ Video Program
   Videoclips: Werbung
   Videocassette 1, 48:08–48:27
▶ Audio Compact Discs, CD5, Tr. 12

Apply and Assess

 Using the Video
Videocassette 1, 48:08–48:27
At this time you might want to use the authentic advertising footage from German television. See *Video Guide*, p. 22, for suggestions.

 Portfolio Assessment
2 You might want to suggest this activity as a written portfolio item for your students. See *Alternative Assessment Guide*, p. 20

Apply and Assess

History Connection
6 If students are unable to interview an older person, ask them to use an autobiography or biography of a historically significant person as the source for their report.

 Portfolio Assessment
8 You might want to suggest this activity as an oral portfolio item for your students. See *Alternative Assessment Guide*, p. 20.

PAGE 146

KANN ICH'S WIRKLICH?

This page helps students prepare for the test. It is a brief checklist of the major points covered in the chapter. The students should be reminded that it is only a checklist and not necessarily everything that will appear on the test.

For additional self-check options, refer students to the *Grammar Tutor* and the Online self-test for this chapter.

PAGE 147

WORTSCHATZ

Review and Assess

 Games
Play the game **Seeschlacht** to review the Chapter 5 vocabulary. See p. 119C for the procedure.

 Circumlocution
To review military terms, play **Das treffende Wort suchen** with the nouns in the **Zweite Stufe**. To set the scene, tell your students that they have just been "drafted" into the **Bund** and are having a discussion with fellow **Bundeswehrsoldaten** about the function of the **Bund**. Unfortunately, your students don't know German military terms, so each noun will need to be described. For instance, for submarine one could say **Das ist ein Boot, das unter Wasser fährt.** See p. 31C for procedures.

 Teacher Note
Give the **Kapitel 5** Chapter Test:
Testing Program, pp. 97–102
Audio CD 5, Trs. 15–17.

REVIEW

5

Rechte und Pflichten

Objectives

In this chapter you will learn to

Erste Stufe

- talk about what is possible
- say what you would have liked to do

Zweite Stufe

- say that something is going on right now
- report past events
- express surprise, relief, and resignation

 internet

go. hrw .com	**ADRESSE:** go.hrw.com **KENNWORT:** WK3 WUERZBURG-5

◀ **Hier steht es schwarz auf weiß. Schau!**
Was sagt ihr dazu?

Los geht's! · *Mit achtzehn darf man alles. Oder?*

CD 5 Trs. 1–6

Über dieses Thema haben wir mit Julia (17), Angie (18), Stefan (fast 18) und Martin (18) gesprochen. CD 5 Tr. 1

Das Einzige, was sich wirklich mit meinem achtzehnten Geburtstag geändert hat, ist, dass ich mich jetzt im Auto selbst hinters Steuer setzen darf. Wenn man den Führerschein hat, ist man eben unabhängiger. Man kann schnell mal ein paar Freunde besuchen und kurzfristig zusammen wegfahren. Aber sonst hat sich an meinem 18. Geburtstag überhaupt nichts geändert. Ich hatte schon vorher ein gutes Verhältnis zu meinen Eltern, also da hat sich auch in dieser Hinsicht nichts zu ändern brauchen. Für mich war also der 18. Geburtstag ein Geburtstag wie jeder andere.

CD 5 Tr. 2 **Martin, 18**

Jetzt könnte ich die Schule schwänzen und meine eigene Entschuldigung schreiben! Als ich 15 war, war das Schuleschwänzen oft ein großes Problem. Da hätte ich oft gern geschwänzt, weil ich die Hausaufgaben nicht gemacht hatte, weil ich den Unterricht blöd fand, weil ich Angst vor der Prüfung hatte und so weiter und so fort. Und heute? Die Schule ist weiterhin stressig, aber ich weiß, dass jede Schulstunde wichtig ist. Ich kann es mir gar nicht erlauben zu fehlen. Ich muss das Abi schaffen, sonst ist es aus mit dem Studieren.

Angie, 18 CD 5 Tr. 3

Der nächste Punkt ist halt, dass man wählen kann. Ich bin noch nicht achtzehn, und ich wüsste auch heute gar nicht, wen ich wählen sollte. Ich bin politisch überhaupt nicht aktiv. Ich kenn aber einige Schüler, die sich schon sehr politisch engagieren. Die sind noch unter achtzehn und sind schon Mitglied in der Jungen Union.[1] Übrigens, bei meinen Eltern ist es lustig: wenn mein Vater CSU wählt, dann wählt meine Mutter bestimmt SPD, und auch umgekehrt. Vielleicht würd' ich meine Stimme den Grünen[2] geben; die sind für die Umwelt, sagen sie. Aber bevor ich wähle, werde ich mich bestimmt besser informieren.

CD 5 Tr. 4 **Stefan, fast 18**

---

1. Die Junge Union ist die Jugendorganisation der CDU/CSU. 2. Die CDU (Christlich-Demokratische Union) und die SPD (Sozialdemokratische Partei Deutschlands) sind die beiden größten Parteien. In Bayern gibt es die CSU (Christlich-Soziale Union); ihre Ziele stimmen weitgehend mit denen der CDU überein. Ferner gibt es die FDP (Freie Demokratische Partei), die Grünen (die Umweltpartei), die PDS (Partei des Demokratischen Sozialismus), die Nachfolgepartei der früheren SED in der ehemaligen DDR und noch viele andere, kleinere Parteien.

Bei mir ist es halt so, dass ich den Führerschein nicht gezahlt bekomm, und ich ihn also nicht machen kann. Ich würd' ihn zwar gern machen, aber er ist mir zu teuer. Und es ist mir zu schade um mein eigenes Geld.
Julia, 17 CD 5 Tr. 5

Interviewer: Und wie teuer ist der Führerschein? CD 5 Tr. 6

Julia: Im Schnitt 700 Euro. Und wenn ich mich nicht irre, hat meine Schwester über 1000 Euro gezahlt. Es kommt eben darauf an, wie viel Stunden man braucht.[3]

Angie: Es dauert auch sehr lange. Also man kann durchaus ein halbes Jahr daran herummachen; drei Monate dauert's aber bestimmt.

Martin: Ja, da zieh ich das amerikanische System vor. Wir haben hier an der Schule ein paar Leute, die waren ein halbes Jahr oder ein Jahr in den Staaten und haben dort den Führerschein gemacht, und die fahren damit hier herum.

Julia: Mir scheint, drüben ist es einfacher.

Martin: Der Jens hat mir gesagt, er hat nur ein paar Fragen beantworten müssen, ein paar Dollar gezahlt und ist einmal um den Block gefahren. Das war's.

Stefan: Soviel ich weiß, hat er sogar schlecht eingeparkt!

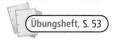
Übungsheft, S. 53

---

3. Seit 1986 gibt es in der Bundesrepublik den **Führerschein auf Probe**. Jeder Fahranfänger muss sich zwei Jahre unter besonderer Aufsicht im Straßenverkehr bewähren, bevor er die endgültige Fahrerlaubnis erhält. Im Jahr 1985 verursachten die 18- bis 24jährigen 39 Prozent aller Unfälle. Der Führerschein auf Probe soll dazu beitragen, die hohen Unfallquoten der jungen Leute zu verringern. 1998 war die Unfallquote dieser Altersgruppe auf 24,3 Prozent gesunken. 1996 lag die Unfallquote nur noch bei 28 Prozent.

1 Der 18. Geburtstag: Was bedeutet er für diese Schüler?

Schreiben/Sprechen Schreib in Stichworten die wichtigsten Dinge auf, die Martin, Angie, Stefan und Julia gesagt haben! Erzähle dann der Klasse, was einer von den vier deutschen Schülern erzählt hat!

Martin	
Angie	
Stefan	

2 Beantworte die Fragen!

Sprechen/Schreiben Beantworte die folgenden Fragen.

1. Warum kann Julia den Führerschein nicht machen?   bekommt ihn nicht gezahlt; ist zu teuer
2. Warum zahlt sie nicht selbst dafür?   Das eigene Geld ist ihr zu schade.
3. Welche Unterschiede gibt es beim Führerscheinmachen zwischen der Bundesrepublik und den Vereinigten Staaten?   E.g.: **Preis; Dauer; Prüfung; Gültigkeit**

Artikel 38/2. Absatz des Grundgesetzes:
„Wahlberechtigt ist, wer das achtzehnte Lebensjahr vollendet hat; wählbar ist, wer das Alter erreicht hat, mit dem die Volljährigkeit eintritt."

Wieso Führerschein? Ich denke, den bekommt man erst mit achtzehn Jahren!

Seit 1975 sind Jugendliche in der Bundesrepublik Deutschland mit dem vollendeten achtzehnten Lebensjahr volljährig.

Was bedeutet das?

1. Man kann selbst bestimmen, wo man wohnen will.
2. Man kann nach Hause kommen, wann man will.
3. Man kann Ausbildungs- und Arbeitsverträge selbst unterschreiben.
4. Man kann Entschuldigungen für die Schule selbst schreiben.
5. Man kann Verträge über Käufe, Kredite, Mieten, usw. selbst abschließen.
6. Man kann heiraten.
7. Man kann selbst wählen und gewählt werden.
8. Man kann den Führerschein machen.
9. Man kann im Lokal alkoholische Getränke bestellen.

Wortschatz

auf Deutsch erklärt

der Unterricht das Lernen eines Schulfaches, zum Beispiel Deutsch (der Deutschunterricht)
die Prüfung der Test
schwänzen nicht in die Schule gehen, weil man keine Lust hat
fehlen nicht da sein
Ich kann es mir nicht erlauben. Ich darf es nicht.
Du irrst dich. Du denkst falsch.
Das dauert lange. Das braucht eine lange Zeit.
wählen man sagt einem politischen Kandidaten offiziell ja
sich politisch engagieren politisch aktiv sein
kurzfristig nach wenig Zeit, schnell

auf Englisch erklärt

Er ist Mitglied unseres Vereins. *He is a member of our club.*
Ich will von meinen Eltern unabhängig sein. *I want to be independent from my parents.*
Wir werden im Juni heiraten. *We're going to get married in June.*
Es scheint, du willst nicht. *It seems you don't want to.*
Das wäre zu schade ums Geld. *It wouldn't be worth the money.*
Unterschreiben Sie den Vertrag! *Sign the contract!*
In dieser Hinsicht ist es umgekehrt. *In this respect it's the other way around.*
Es ist schwer, sich zu ändern. *It's difficult to change yourself.*

Übungsheft, S. 54–55, Ü. 1–3

Grammatikheft, S. 37–38, Ü. 1–4

3 **Was hat sich geändert?** Script and answers on p. 119G

 Zuhören Schüler erzählen, was sich in ihrem Leben mit dem 18. Geburtstag geändert hat. Welche Aussagen passen zu den Illustrationen?
CD 5 Tr. 7

a.   b.   c.   d.   e.

So sagt man das!

Talking about what is possible

If you ask yourself **Was soll ich morgen machen?**, here is a way to say what you could possibly do:

> **Ich könnte die Schule schwänzen, aber ich kann es mir nicht erlauben.**

If your friend tells you **Ich habe Lust, Auto fahren zu lernen,** you can answer by saying:

> **Du könntest den Führerschein machen, weil du jetzt alt genug bist.**

How would you talk about what is possible in English?

4 **Grammatik im Kontext** Script and answers on p. 119G

 Zuhören Drei Freunde sprechen über ihre Pläne. Hör zu und schreib auf, was die drei vorhaben! Wer scheint am meisten vorzuhaben?
CD 5 Tr. 8

5 **Grammatik im Kontext**

Sprechen/Schreiben Stellt euch vor, ihr wohnt in Deutschland und seid schon 18! Sag, was du jetzt alles tun könntest, und sag auch, warum du es nicht tust! Tauscht die Rollen aus!

DU	**Ich könnte jetzt …**
PARTNER	**Ja, und warum tust du 's nicht?**
DU	**Weil ich …**

Ein wenig Grammatik

To express possibility, you need to know the **könnte**-forms. Of what verbs do these forms remind you?

Ich	**könnte**	das Abi schaffen.
Du	**könntest**	ausziehen.
Es	**könnte**	einfacher sein.
Wir	**könnten**	den Meier wählen.
Ihr	**könntet**	euch informieren.
Sie	**könnten**	jetzt heiraten.

Mehr Grammatikübungen, S.140–141, Ü. 1–3

Grammatikheft, S. 39, Ü. 5–6

selbst eine Wohnung mieten

wohnen, wo ich will

die eigene Entschuldigung schreiben, wenn ich die Schule schwänze

nach Hause kommen, wann ich will

heiraten   den Führerschein machen   wählen   von zu Hause ausziehen   allein wegfahren

6 **Ich könnte, aber ich tu's nicht.**

Schreiben Denk an fünf Dinge, die du jetzt tun könntest, aber aus irgendeinem Grund nicht tust und schreib sie auf!

BEISPIEL Ich bin jetzt (16). Ich könnte abends bis elf Uhr wegbleiben, aber ich tu's nicht, weil ich früh aufstehen muss.

So sagt man das!

Saying what you would have liked to do

Sometimes you have intentions that just don't get carried out. When you want to express these intentions, you can say:

Ich hätte gern die Schule **geschwänzt,** aber ich bin doch hingegangen.
Ich wäre gern zu Hause **geblieben,** aber wir hatten heute eine Prüfung.

How would you express these phrases in English?

Grammatik

Further uses of **wäre** and **hätte**

In the **So sagt man das!** box you learned that intentions that don't get carried out are expressed with **hätte** or **wäre.** In that case, **hätte** and **wäre** are auxiliary verbs, and are both used with a past participle.

Sie **hätten** gern **geheiratet,** aber die Eltern wollten es nicht.
Ich **hätte** meine Hausaufgaben **gemacht,** aber ich war krank.

The decision to use **hätte** or **wäre** as the auxiliary verb depends on the past participle. If it normally takes **sein** in the past tense (like **gekommen**), then **wäre** is correct.

Wir **wären** gestern nach Berlin **gefahren,** aber unser Auto ist kaputt.
Ich **wäre** heute schwimmen **gegangen,** aber es hat furchtbar geregnet.

Mehr Grammatikübungen,
S. 141, Ü. 4–5

(Übungsheft, S. 55–57, Ü. 4–9) (Grammatikheft, S. 40, Ü. 7–8) ⟶

7 **Grammatik im Kontext**

Sprechen/Schreiben Leider gehen nicht alle Wünsche in Erfüllung. Sag einer Klassenkameradin, was du alles gern getan hättest! Hier sind einige Wünsche. Hast du andere? Schreib danach sieben Wünsche, die du hast.

hätte	Freunde besuchen	(die CDU) wählen	hätte
hätte	den Führerschein machen	meine Stimme (den Grünen) geben	hätte
hätte	die Schule schwänzen	etwas für die Umwelt tun	hätte
hätte	die Hausaufgaben machen	mit Freunden wegfahren	wäre
hätte	die Fragen beantworten	länger im Urlaub bleiben	wäre
hätte	sich politisch engagieren	sich besser informieren	hätte
wäre	Mitglied im Fußballklub werden	nach (Österreich) fahren	wäre
hätte	eine tolle Sendung sehen	den Vertrag unterzeichnen	hätte
wäre	nach Deutschland fliegen	ins Kino gehen	wäre

8 Grammatik im Kontext

Sprechen Setzt euch in kleinen Gruppen zusammen und erzählt, was ihr gern getan hättet! Ihr könnt die letzte Übung zu Hilfe nehmen. Gebt auch einen Grund dafür an!

DU	**Ich hätte gern …**
PARTNER	**Und warum hast du das nicht getan?**
DU	**Ja, weil …**
PARTNER	**Schade!** *oder* **Ja, wirklich?** *oder* **Zu dumm!**

Warum nicht?

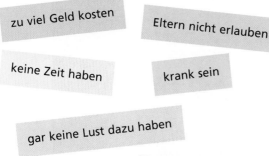

zu viel Geld kosten

Eltern nicht erlauben

keine Zeit haben

krank sein

gar keine Lust dazu haben

nicht wissen, wie

9 Für mein Notizbuch

Schreiben Denk an drei Dinge, die du in letzter Zeit gern getan hättest! Gib Gründe an, warum du sie nicht getan hast!

BEISPIEL **Gestern Abend hätte ich gern ferngesehen, aber leider war unser Fernseher kaputt, und ich hatte keine Lust, zu meiner Klassenkameradin zu gehen.**

10 Was hältst du davon?

Schreiben/Sprechen Denk über folgende Fragen nach, und schreib die Antworten in Stichworten auf! Diskutiere darüber mit deinen Klassenkameraden!

1. Wie ist die Schule für dich? Leicht? Stressig? Warum?

2. Würdest du den Unterricht schwänzen, wenn du könntest?

3. Hast du schon einmal die Schule geschwänzt? Warum?

4. Was wird sich bei dir ändern, wenn du achtzehn wirst?

5. Was hat sich geändert, als du sechzehn geworden bist?

6. Freust du dich darauf, dass du mit achtzehn wählen darfst? Wen oder welche Partei würdest du wählen? Warum?

7. Bist du politisch aktiv oder wenigstens gut informiert? Kennst du Schüler, die sich politisch engagieren?

8. Wie wichtig ist für dich der Führerschein? Hast du schon den Führerschein? Wenn ja, was hast du alles machen müssen, um ihn zu bekommen?

11 Für mein Notizbuch

Schreiben Wähle eins der beiden Themen unten, und schreib einen Kurzbericht darüber!

1. Der Führerschein auf Probe ist eine gute Idee.

2. Jeder Schüler sollte sich ein wenig politisch engagieren.

Weiter geht's! · *Die Wehrpflicht: dafür oder dagegen?*

CD 5 Tr. 9

Das Interview geht weiter. Die vier jungen Leute unterhalten sich über das Thema „Wehrpflicht".

> ***Artikel 12a des Grundgesetzes:***
> „Männer können vom vollendeten achtzehnten Lebensjahr an zum Dienst in den Streitkräften, im Bundesgrenzschutz oder in einem Zivilschutzverband verpflichtet werden."

Stefan: Eine Pflicht, die jeder Achtzehnjährige hat, ist, zur Bundeswehr zu gehen. Und das ist auch nicht gerade angenehm, weil man fast zwei Jahre vom Studium oder von der Arbeit verliert.

Interviewer: Habt ihr euch schon entschieden, ob ihr den Wehrdienst oder den Zivildienst macht?

Martin: Ja, wir sind halt immer noch am Diskutieren. Ich, zum Beispiel …

Stefan: Darf ich dich schnell mal unterbrechen, Martin?

Martin: Bitte.

Stefan: Es ist nämlich so: wir hatten vorigen Monat einen Bundeswehroffizier zu einer Fragestunde eingeladen. Die Diskussion war sehr interessant, und wir konnten uns dabei gut informieren.

Angie: Und was ist dabei herausgekommen?

Martin: Ja, für mich wenig.

Stefan: Für mich auch nicht viel. Aber trotzdem! Ich hab die Diskussion prima gefunden.

Martin: Das ist mir neu, was du da sagst.

Stefan: Ich hab nur gesagt, die Diskussion war prima, interessant. Es hat sich gelohnt, ihn einzuladen. Das kannst du doch nicht abstreiten.

Martin: Tu ich auch nicht. Ich frag mich bloß, ob jemand wirklich seine Meinung nach dieser Diskussion geändert hat.

Stefan: Das glaub ich nicht. Die einen sind eben für die Bundeswehr, die anderen sind dagegen. Daran ändert sich nichts. Jeder muss allein für sich entscheiden, ob er zum Bund geht oder nicht.

Angie: Gehst du zum Bund, Martin?

Martin: Also, ich sag's mal so: wenn ich's vermeiden kann, nicht. Weil ich's heutzutage für sinnlos halte. Und wenn ich muss, geh ich halt hin.

Julia: Ich bin wahnsinnig froh, dass ich so eine Entscheidung nicht machen muss.

Martin: Ja, ihr Mädchen habt's gut. Man sollte euch einziehen, wie in Israel.

Angie: Meinst du das im Ernst?

Martin: Ja, warum denn nicht? Ihr müsst nicht unbedingt ein Gewehr in den Kampf tragen. Es gibt viele Sachen, die Mädchen bei der Bundeswehr machen könnten. Sie sollten aber wenigstens den Zivildienst machen müssen!

Stefan: Das mag sein. Ich find es aber wirklich schlecht, dass man in Deutschland Wehrdienst machen muss.

Angie: Sonst würd's keiner machen.

Martin: Ja, stimmt. Wir müssen aber Streitkräfte haben, auf die wir uns verlassen können!

Angie: Das ist heutzutage nicht mehr so wichtig, wie es noch vor kurzem war.

Stefan: Immerhin — der Wehrdienst sollte freiwillig sein. In England klappt's, in den USA klappt's.

Martin: Wir haben wenigstens noch einen Ersatzdienst.

Stefan: Ja, schon! Aber der Zivildienst kann noch anstrengender sein. Es kommt eben darauf an, was man machen muss.

Angie: Ich hab einen Bekannten, der gerade seinen Zivildienst in einem Altenheim macht. Er sagt, er kann es bald nicht mehr aushalten. Die alten Leute, die er betreuen muss, tun ihm so furchtbar Leid: sie können sich nicht mehr selber helfen. Und das belastet ihn wahnsinnig.

Stefan: Und ich find es ausgesprochen fies, dass es Firmen gibt, die keine Zivildienstleute einstellen.

Martin: Andererseits nutzt dir der Zivildienst mehr als der Wehrdienst, wenn du zum Beispiel Arzt werden willst.

Stefan: Ja, schon. Aber was soll's! Ich nehm's, wie's kommt. Vielleicht mag mich der Bund gar nicht. Mit meinen Kontaktlinsen und meinem schwachen Kreuz werd ich bei der Musterung bestimmt durchfallen.

See page 130 for the latest update.

Übungsheft, S. 58

12 ## Was haben die vier Schüler gesagt?

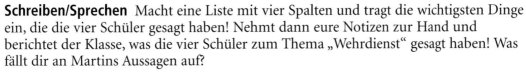

Schreiben/Sprechen Macht eine Liste mit vier Spalten und tragt die wichtigsten Dinge ein, die die vier Schüler gesagt haben! Nehmt dann eure Notizen zur Hand und berichtet der Klasse, was die vier Schüler zum Thema „Wehrdienst" gesagt haben! Was fällt dir an Martins Aussagen auf?

Übungsheft, S. 59, Ü. 1–4

Gleichberechtigung im deutschen Militär?

Der Bundesrat hat am 1. Dezember 2000 mit der notwendigen Zwei-Drittel-Mehrheit das Grundgesetz dahin gehend geändert, dass Frauen in der Bundeswehr der freiwillige Dienst an der Waffe erlaubt ist.

In Artikel 12a des Grundgesetzes heißt es künftig: „Sie (Frauen) dürfen auf keinen Fall zum Dienst mit der Waffe verpflichtet werden". In der bisherigen Formulierung hieß es: „Sie dürfen auf keinen Fall Dienst mit der Waffe leisten".

Das neue Gesetz ist am 1. Januar 2001 in Kraft getreten, und die ersten 244 Frauen haben ihren Dienst als Soldatinnen in der Bundeswehr am 2. Januar 2001 angetreten. 151 Frauen dienen im Heer, 76 in der Luftwaffe, 17 bei der Marine. Fast 2000 weitere Bewerbungen lagen zu dieser Zeit schon vor.

Seit 1975 haben Frauen bei der Bundeswehr hauptsächlich in verwaltungstechnischen Berufen und im Musik- und Pflegedienst gedient, z. B. als Ärztinnen oder Apothekerinnen.

Frauen im Militärdienst sind nichts Neues. Israels Frauen müssen mit 18 Jahren für 20 Monate zur Armee. Sie leisten Wehrdienst wie ihre männlichen Kollegen. Sie werden an allen Waffen ausgebildet – sie sind Pilotinnen und kommandieren Kampfpanzer.

In den USA stellen Soldatinnen heute über zehn Prozent aller Streitkräfte, mehr als in jeder anderen Berufsarmee der Welt. Sie fliegen Transportflugzeuge, reparieren Panzer, fahren Armeelaster, bewachen Kasernen, bilden Rekruten aus und ziehen mit Stahlhelm und Maschinengewehr nicht nur ins Manöver, sondern setzen ihr Leben an der Front aufs Spiel. Frauen sind Offiziere und auch Generäle.

1. von der Gleichberechtigung der Frauen im deutschen Militär
2. Das geänderte Grundgesetz ist am 1. Januar 2001 in Kraft getreten.
3. Deutschland, Israel, USA / Deutschland: seit 1.1. 2001 dürfen Frauen den Dienst mit der Waffe leisten / Israel: Frauen müssen zur Armee / USA: keine Wehrpflicht sondern Berufsarmee; Frauen dienen, wie Männer, in allen Streitkräften

Beantworte die Fragen

1. Wovon handelt der Artikel?
2. Warum können jetzt Frauen überall in der Bundeswehr dienen?
3. Welche Länder werden verglichen? Wie unterscheidet sich das Militär in diesen Ländern?
4. Was konnten Frauen zwischen 1975 und dem 1. Dezember 2000 bei der Bundeswehr tun?
5. Sind Frauen für den Militärdienst geeignet? Was meinst du?

4. Seit 1975 haben Frauen in verwaltungstechnischen Berufen und im Musik- und Pflegedienst gedient.

Zweite Stufe

Objectives Saying that something is going on right now; reporting past events; expressing surprise, relief, and resignation

WK3 WUERZBURG-5

Wortschatz

 p. 119X   5-2

In der Bundeswehr kommandieren Frauen bestimmt einmal ...

einen Panzer   einen Bomber   einen Laster   ein Transportflugzeug   ein U-Boot

Was würdest du gern kommandieren?

auf Deutsch erklärt

die Streitkräfte das ganze Militär
die Bundeswehr die deutsche Armee
der Bund die Bundeswehr
die Wehrpflicht wenn man in die Armee gehen muss, also nicht freiwillig
freiwillig wenn man etwas nicht machen muss, aber machen will
der Frieden wenn es keinen Krieg gibt
sich entscheiden wenn man zwischen zwei Dingen wählt
ausgesprochen ganz besonders

auf Englisch erklärt

Er schießt mit dem Gewehr. *He shoots the gun.*
Ein Panzer ist eine wichtige Waffe. *A tank is an important weapon.*
Der Kampf war hart. *The battle was heavy.*
Muss man bei euch Wehrdienst machen? *Do you have to serve in the military where you're from?*
Wir dürfen auch den Zivildienst wählen. *We can also choose community service.*
Unsere Demokratie hat ein Grundgesetz. *Our democracy has a constitution.*
Gleichberechtigung für alle! *Equality for all!*
Können wir uns auf dich verlassen? *Can we rely on you?*
Aber im Ernst! *But seriously!*

(Grammatikheft, S. 41–42, Ü. 9–10)

So sagt man das!

Saying that something is going on right now

Here are three ways of expressing that something is occurring at this moment:

> **Wir diskutieren gerade darüber.**
> **Wir sind dabei, dieses Thema zu besprechen.**
> **Wir sind am (beim) Überlegen.**

What common English form do these sentences express?

(Übungsheft, S. 60, Ü. 1–2)   (Grammatikheft, S. 42, Ü. 11)   Mehr Grammatikübungen, S. 142, Ü. 6–7 →

13 Grammatik im Kontext

Michael möchte mit Martin Tennis spielen, aber Martin hat vorher noch viel zu tun. Michael ruft Martin an und will wissen, wie weit er ist und ob sie bald spielen können. Spiel die Rollen mit einem Partner!

MICHAEL   **Hallo, Martin! Willst du Tennis spielen?**

MARTIN   **Ich bin gerade beim Fensterputzen. Vielleicht später.**

MICHAEL   **Gut, bis später.**

Was Martin alles machen muss:

Ein wenig Grammatik

Verbs can be used as neuter nouns:

> **Das Lernen** war früher ein Problem.

Verb phrases are written as one word:

> **Zum Rasenmähen** habe ich wenig Lust. Er war **beim Tennisspielen**.

Grammatikheft, S. 43, Ü. 12

Mehr Grammatikübungen, S. 142, Ü. 8

Ein wenig Landeskunde

In der Bundesrepublik besteht seit 1956 die allgemeine Wehrpflicht für Männer. Diese Wehrpflicht kann durch den 9-monatigen Wehrdienst oder den 10-monatigen Zivildienst erfüllt werden. In Österreich dauert der Grundwehrdienst 8 Monate. In der Schweiz gibt es eine Rekrutenausbildung von 15 Wochen und alle zwei Jahre neunzehntägige Wehrübungen bis zum vollendeten 42. Lebensjahr.

Die Streitkräfte der Bundeswehr bestehen aus Armee, Luftwaffe und Marine. Viele junge Männer gehen zur Bundeswehr, weil sie Interesse am Soldatenberuf haben oder weil sie hoffen, später einen sicheren Arbeitsplatz zu finden. Soldaten haben nämlich die Möglichkeit — wenn sie längere Zeit beim Bund bleiben — sich während der Dienstzeit beruflich ausbilden zu lassen. Abiturienten können auch an den Bundeswehruniversitäten in Hamburg und München studieren. Ungefähr 30 Prozent der wehrpflichtigen Männer in Deutschland entscheiden sich für den Zivildienst.

So sagt man das!

Reporting past events

 Übungsheft, S. 61, Ü. 3–4

Here is a more expressive way to report something that happened in the past:

> **Wir haben letzten Monat einen Bundeswehroffizier eingeladen. Die Diskussion war sehr interessant, und wir konnten uns gut informieren. Wir wollten noch mehr hören, aber wir mussten zum Unterricht gehen.**

What verb forms do you recognize? What are the infinitives of those verbs?

Grammatik

The past tense of modals (the imperfect)

1. The modals have these forms in the imperfect:

dürfen	müssen	können	mögen	sollen	wollen
ich durf-**t-e**	musste	konnte	mochte	sollte	wollte
du durf-**t-est**	musstest	konntest	mochtest	solltest	wolltest
er durf-**t-e**	musste	konnte	mochte	sollte	wollte
wir durf-**t-en**	mussten	konnten	mochten	sollten	wollten
ihr durf-**t-et**	musstet	konntet	mochtet	solltet	wolltet
sie durf-**t-en**	mussten	konnten	mochten	sollten	wollten

a. The modals in the imperfect do not carry over the umlaut of the infinitive.

b. All modals are conjugated.

c. The imperfect of **mögen** also has a consonant change.

2. In conversation, the imperfect forms of modals are almost always used rather than the present perfect.

— Was ist bei eurer Diskussion herausgekommen?
— Nichts. Aber wir **konnten** uns gut informieren.
— Und wie hast du die Diskussion gefunden?
— Sie **war** prima! Die Klassenkameraden **wollten** gar nicht nach Hause gehen. Sie **hatten** so viele Fragen.

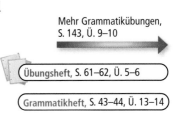

Mehr Grammatikübungen, S. 143, Ü. 9–10

Übungsheft, S. 61–62, Ü. 5–6

Grammatikheft, S. 43–44, Ü. 13–14

14 Grammatik im Kontext
Script and answers on p. 119H

CD 5 Tr. 10

Zuhören Du stehst in einer langen Schlange am Bankschalter. Zwei Leute vor dir sprechen darüber, was sie am Vormittag alles erledigt haben oder noch tun müssen. Hör ihrem Gespräch gut zu, und mach dir Notizen über die Besorgungen (*errands*)! Anhand der Notizen erzähl dann deinem Partner von dem Gespräch, das du mit angehört hast.

15 Grammatik im Kontext

Sprechen/Schreiben Sag einem Partner, wie's früher war und wie's heute ist! Schreib danach, was du gesagt hast.

BEISPIEL **Früher musste ich eine Brille tragen, heute kann ich Kontaktlinsen tragen.**

Schon bekannt

gestern, gestern (Vormittag)
vorgestern, vorgestern (Abend)
letzt-: letzte Woche, letztes Jahr

Neu

vergangen-: vergangenes Jahr   früher
          vergangenen Monat
vorig-:   vorige Woche
          im vorigen Jahrhundert

16 Als ich zwölf war …

Sprechen Denk an sechs Dinge, die du nicht tun konntest oder durftest, als du zwölf warst! Schreib sie auf und vergleiche deine Liste mit der Liste eines Partners!

BEISPIEL   **Als ich zwölf war, musste ich/konnte ich/durfte ich (nicht) …**

So sagt man das!

Expressing surprise, relief, and resignation

If someone said something surprising to you, for example:

    Also, bei uns dürfen die Hunde mit ins Restaurant gehen.

You might answer:

    Das ist mir (völlig) neu!

If you heard reassuring news, for example:

    Gestern ist Mari gesund aus dem Krankenhaus gekommen.

You might express relief by saying:

    Ich bin (sehr) froh, dass es ihr besser geht.

If someone complained to you:

    Ich musste das ganze Wochenende mit dem Matheheft verbringen.

You might express resignation about the plight of students by saying:

    Ach, was soll's! Das ist leider so.

Übungsheft, S. 62–63, Ü. 7–10

Grammatikheft, S. 45, Ü. 16

17 Gehst du zum Bund? Script and answers on p. 119H

Zuhören Hör gut zu, wie einige Schüler darüber diskutieren, ob sie zum Bund gehen oder nicht! Welche Schüler drücken Überraschung aus? Resignation? Erleichterung?
CD 5 Tr. 11

18 Was für eine Reaktion hast du darauf?

Lesen/Sprechen Wie reagierst du auf folgende Aussagen? Lies einer Partnerin eine Aussage vor, und sie wird darauf reagieren! Gebrauch dabei die Ausdrücke, die du gelernt hast!

1. Ich hab gehört, dass wir jetzt das ganze Jahr zur Schule gehen müssen und dass wir keine langen Sommerferien mehr haben.
2. Ich hab gehört, dass junge Männer zwischen 16 und 25 über $1000 im Jahr für ihre Autoversicherung bezahlen müssen.
3. Ich hab gehört, dass es jetzt auch bei uns einen Führerschein auf Probe geben soll.
4. Ich hab gehört, dass Frauen in der amerikanischen Marine jetzt auf U-Booten dienen dürfen.

19 Reaktionen hervorrufen!

a. Schreiben Schreib zuerst ein paar Situationen auf, auf die ein Partner mit Überraschung, Resignation oder Erleichterung reagieren könnte! Hier sind ein paar Anregungen, aber du kannst dir selber etwas ausdenken.

wie eine Sportmannschaft gespielt hat

monatliches Taschengeld von den Eltern

eine Prüfung in einem Schulfach

das kuriose Leben eines Film- oder Popstars

... oder anderes vom Leben!

b. Lesen/Sprechen Lies dann einem Partner die Situationen vor, und er muss jeweils darauf reagieren!

20 Vorteile und Nachteile

Sprechen Der Militärdienst und der Zivildienst haben Vor- und Nachteile. Einige sind hier aufgelistet, andere kannst du dir selbst ausdenken. Du nimmst eine Position ein und ein Klassenkamerad eine andere. Diskutiert darüber!

Vorteile	Militärdienst	Nachteile
ein geregeltes Leben haben etwas lernen neue Leute kennen lernen Kameradschaft haben Karriere machen können		Zeit verlieren nicht viel lernen wenig Freiheit haben ein rauhes Leben haben Familie und Freunde verlassen müssen

Vorteile	Zivildienst	Nachteile
anderen Menschen helfen etwas Gutes tun etwas Nützliches lernen offen gegen Krieg sein können		lange Arbeitszeit haben oft deprimierende Arbeit haben berufliche Nachteile haben können wenig Geld verdienen

21 Was sagst du dazu?

Sprechen Diskutier mit deinen Klassenkameraden über folgende Themen!

a. Die USA haben seit vielen Jahren keine Wehrpflicht mehr. Sollte man die Wehrpflicht wieder einführen — für Männer und für Frauen? Warum oder warum nicht?

b. Manche Schulen in den USA verlangen (*demand*), dass Schüler in ihrer Schulzeit etwas Zivildienst leisten. Wird so was in eurer Schule verlangt? Was sind die Bedingungen (*conditions*)? Bist du dafür oder dagegen und warum oder warum nicht?

22 Für mein Notizbuch

Schreiben Wenn du mit der Schule fertig bist, wirst du dann zum Militär gehen? Warum oder warum nicht? Möchtest du an einer Militärakademie studieren? An welcher? Schreib deine Gedanken dazu auf!

 23  **Von der Schule zum Beruf**

You are a civilian working for the military. Your boss has asked you to write a form letter to be sent to young German women, since women are now allowed to serve in the German armed forces. Explain what the military has to offer women and try to convince them to join.

Zum Lesen

Auszüge aus Hitlers Reden

Die Welt, sie verfolgt uns. Wir wollen den Frieden. Sie wendet sich gegen uns. Sie will nicht unser Recht zum Leben anerkennen. Mein deutsches Volk, wenn so die Welt gegen uns steht, dann müssen wir umso mehr zu einer Einheit werden.

Aus einer Rede Hitlers im Mai 1933

Was für ein Glück für die Regierenden, daß die Menschen nicht denken!

Bemerkungen Hitlers bei einer Geheimkonferenz mit Generälen im Jahre 1937

Deutschland muß zusätzlichen Lebensraum gewinnen—und zwar in Europa. Ohne Gewaltanwendung geht das nicht. Wir können damit auch nicht mehr lange warten. Denn unser Rüstungspotential wird in den Jahren 1943 bis 45 seinen Höhepunkt erreicht haben. Wir müssen die Offensive ergreifen, bevor die übrige Welt unseren Vorsprung einholt.

Geheime Anweisung Hitlers an die Wehrmacht, sich auf einen Krieg mit Polen vorzubereiten. April 1939

Ich werde den propagandistischen Anlaß zur Auslösung des Krieges geben, gleichgültig, ob glaubhaft. Der Sieger wird später nicht danach gefragt, ob er die Wahrheit gesagt hat oder nicht. Bei Beginn und Führung des Krieges kommt es nicht auf das Recht an, sondern auf den Sieg.

Aus einer Rede Hitlers

Über einen humanen Weltbegriff erhebt sich heute die Erkenntnis von der Bedeutung des Blutes und der Rasse! Nichts kann das mehr aus der Welt schaffen. Das ist eine siegende Idee, die heute wie eine Welle über die ganze Erde hinwegströmt …

Noch eine besondere Aufgabe haben wir: die Beseitigung all jener Minderwertigkeitsempfindungen, die in unserem Volk waren, da die früheren Regierungen sie notwendig benötigten und brauchten. Wir sind Todfeinde der sogenannten halben, weil falschen Bescheidenheit, die da sagt, wir wollen uns etwas zurückhalten, wir wollen nicht immer von uns reden und alles übertrumpfen, wir wollen bieder bleiben und nicht übel auffallen, man soll uns mehr lieben, die anderen sollen uns nicht mit schiefen Augen ansehen. Im Gegenteil: wir wollen unser Volk ganz nach vorne führen! Ob sie uns lieben, das ist uns einerlei! Wenn sie uns nur respektieren! Ob sie uns hassen, ist uns einerlei, wenn sie uns nur fürchten …

Adolf Hitler am 18. Januar 1942

NIE WIEDER!

Getting Started · For answers, see p. 119W.

Lesestrategie Determining the purpose Determining the purpose of a text before you read allows you to read more critically. It will also help you guess the meaning of unfamiliar words as you read. Use your prereading strategies (looking at visual clues, titles, captions, and format) to hypothesize about the purpose for which a text was written. You'll also want to use any background knowledge you have about the author and the time in which he or she was writing.

1. Look at the photos and read the titles, captions, and source references for each reading selection. What kinds of texts are these? Who are the authors? When was each written?

2. Read the caption for the Geschwister Scholl again. Who were the Geschwister Scholl and why were they important?

3. Before reading further, find out as much as you can about German history before and during World War II and about Hitler and the resistance movement specifically. Together with your classmates, construct a time line of major events. What was happening at the time Hitler was making his speeches? And at the time Hans and Sophie Scholl were writing?

GESCHWISTER SCHOLL

Hans, geb. 1918, Medizinstudent, Begründer der Widerstandsbewegung „Weiße Rose" im 2. Weltkrieg. Sophie, geb. 1921, Philosophiestudentin, Mitglied der „Weißen Rose". Beide 1943 zum Tode verurteilt und hingerichtet.

WIDERSTAND GEGEN DIE DIKTATUR:
DAS LETZTE FLUGBLATT

Erschüttert steht unser Volk vor dem Untergang der Männer von Stalingrad. Dreihundertdreißigtausend deutsche Männer hat die geniale Strategie des Weltkriegsgefreiten sinn- und verantwortungslos in Tod und Verderben gehetzt. Führer, wir danken dir!

Es gärt im deutschen Volk: Wollen wir weiter einem Dilettanten das Schicksal unserer Armeen anvertrauen? Wollen wir den niederen Machtinstinkten einer Parteiclique den Rest der deutschen Jugend opfern? Nimmermehr! Der Tag der Abrechnung ist gekommen, der Abrechnung der deutschen Jugend mit der verabscheuungswürdigsten Tyrannis, die unser Volk je erduldet hat. Im Namen der deutschen Jugend fordern wir vom Staat Adolf Hitlers die persönliche Freiheit, das kostbarste Gut des Deutschen zurück, um das er uns in der erbärmlichsten Weise betrogen.

---

4. Using what you've learned from questions 1-3, think about the occasions for which Hitler's speeches and **Das letzte Flugblatt** were written. Who was the intended audience in each case? Can you guess what the purpose of each text was? What is the purpose of the magazine interview?

A Closer Look

5. Read the excerpts from Hitler's speeches and try to determine the meaning of the following words using root words, context, and your understanding of the purpose of the text.

anerkennen	to stream forth
Gewaltanwendung	to acknowledge
ergreifen	to fear
Erkenntnis	realization
vorbereiten	to take
hinwegströmen	use of force
fürchten	to prepare for

6. Look for occurrences of the words **Sieg, Sieger,** and **siegend**. In your own words, state what you think Hitler had in mind when he used them. What emotions is he appealing to in his various audiences?

7. In one or two sentences, summarize the main idea of each excerpt from Hitler's speeches. Does the text confirm your hypothesis about the purpose of these speeches? Adjust your original statement, if necessary. What tone and what images does Hitler use to convince his audiences?

8. Read the passage by Hans and Sophie Scholl several times. What do you think **Kommilitonen** and **Kommilitoninnen** mean? Who were the intended readers? What were the Scholls fighting against? What were they fighting for? Support your answer with words and phrases from the passage.

In einem Staat rücksichtsloser Knebelung jeder freien Meinungsäußerung sind wir aufgewachsen. HJ, SA, SS haben uns in den fruchtbarsten Bildungsjahren unseres Lebens zu uniformieren, zu revolutionieren, zu narkotisieren versucht. Weltanschauliche Schulung hieß die verächtliche Methode, das aufkeimende Selbstdenken in einem Nebel leerer Phrasen zu ersticken ...

Es gibt für uns nur eine Parole: Kampf gegen die Partei! ... Es geht uns um wahre Wissenschaft und echte Geistesfreiheit! Kein Drohmittel kann uns schrecken, auch nicht die Schließung unserer Hochschulen. Es gilt den Kampf jedes Einzelnen von uns um unsere

Zukunft, unsere Freiheit und Ehre in einem seiner sittlichen Verantwortung bewußten Staatswesen ...

Freiheit und Ehre! Zehn Jahre lang haben Hitler und seine Genossen die beiden herrlichen deutschen Worte bis zum Ekel ausgequetscht, abgedroschen, verdreht, ... Studentinnen! Studenten! Auf uns sieht das deutsche Volk! Von uns erwartet es, wie 1813 die Brechung des Napoleonischen, so 1943 die Brechung des nationalsozialistischen Terrors aus der Macht des Geistes. Beresina und Stalingrad flammen im Osten auf; die Toten von Stalingrad beschwören uns!

1943

VERFÜHRT VON DUMMEN, MÖRDERISCHEN SPRÜCHEN

ANGEKLAGT:
Felix K., 16

RICHTER:
Wolfgang Steffen

Im Prozeß um den Solinger Brandanschlag gab einer der Angeklagten Auskunft über seine Ideologie:

Richter: Was ist denn für Sie „rechts"?
Felix: Na ja, Störkraft*, dann halt Hitler und so.
Richter: Und weiter?
Felix: Na ja, Ausländer raus.
Richter: Und weiter?
Felix: Juden raus.
Richter: Und weiter?
Felix: Türken raus, und dann noch Sieg heil und Deutschland erwache.
Richter: Und weiter?
Felix: Das war's.

*Musikgruppe mit rechtsradikalen Texten
FOCUS

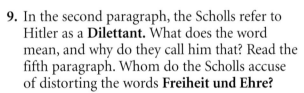

9. In the second paragraph, the Scholls refer to Hitler as a **Dilettant.** What does the word mean, and why do they call him that? Read the fifth paragraph. Whom do the Scholls accuse of distorting the words **Freiheit und Ehre?**

10. Does the passage confirm your hypothesis about the authors' purpose? Explain.

11. Read the interview with Felix K. What does the title mean? Who has been "seduced," and by what? What is the significance of this interview in relation to the other two texts? Is there any connection?

12. Wie würdest du jemanden überzeugen, mit dir gegen eine Ungerechtigkeit zu kämpfen? Schreib jetzt dein eigenes Flugblatt, um für deine Meinung zu einer bestimmten Ungerechtigkeit zu plädieren. Bevor du schreibst, denke daran, wer dein Flugblatt lesen wird, zum Beispiel andere Schüler, Erwachsene usw. Versuche, deine Ideen so überzeugend wie möglich zu machen!

Übungsheft, S. 64-65, Ü. 1-7

Zum Schreiben

In this chapter you have learned how life for German teenagers can be different from that of American teenagers. People who live or have lived in different places do things in a variety of ways that are new to us and sometimes hard for us to understand. In this activity, you will interview a person from another place to find out what life is like in his or her native country. You will write the results of your interview in a report to share with the class.

Lerne Land und Leute durch ein Interview kennen!

Denk an eine Person, die aus einem anderen Land kommt, und interview diese Person! Stell durch das Interview fest, wie das Leben in der Heimat dieser Person ist! Was habt ihr in eurem Leben gemeinsam, und was ist anders? Fass danach das Interview zu einem Bericht zusammen!

 Schreibtipp Asking questions to gather ideas
You have already learned many ways to gather ideas for your writing, including brainstorming and freewriting. Another way is to ask people questions to find out what they know or about their experiences. When asking people questions, try to phrase them in a way that is specific enough to focus in on your topic, but also open-ended enough to allow people the freedom to answer as they please. You should have a plan for your questioning, but allow yourself the flexibility to follow up with unplanned questions as the interview leads in new directions.

A. Vorbereiten

1. Was willst du wissen? Formuliere deine Fragen, und schreib sie auf ein Blatt Papier! Lass zwischen deinen Fragen genug Platz für deine Notizen!

2. Interview deine ausgewählte Person! Das Interview soll ganz zwanglos (*informal*) sein. Wenn dich eine Antwort besonders interessiert, stell weitere Fragen!

3. Benutze deine Notizen, um eine Struktur für deinen Bericht zu schaffen! Welche Ideen tauchen immer wieder auf? Welche Antworten passen gut zusammen? Kannst du jetzt erkennen, welche Aussagen für deinen Bericht brauchbar sind und welche nicht?

B. Ausführen

Wähle die interessantesten Aussagen aus, und schreib einen Bericht über das Leben im anderen Land auf Deutsch! Präsentiere Unterschiede und Gemeinsamkeiten, die zwischen dieser Person und dir bestehen!

C. Überarbeiten

1. Lies deinem Interviewpartner deinen Bericht vor, wenn er oder sie Deutsch spricht! Wenn nicht, erkläre, was du geschrieben hast! Wie findet diese Person deine Darstellung?

2. Hast du alle interessanten und wichtigen Punkte erwähnt? Vergleiche den Bericht mit deinen Notizen!

3. Lies den Bericht noch einmal durch! Hast du alles richtig geschrieben? Achte besonders auf die Modalverben!

4. Schreib den korrigierten Bericht noch einmal ab!

Mehr Grammatikübungen

Answers

▱ internet
ADRESSE: go.hrw.com
KENNWORT:
WK3 WUERZBURG-5

Erste Stufe   **Objectives** Talking about what is possible; saying what you would have liked to do

1 Schreib die Sätze mit den Formen von **könnte** zu Ende und mit der Information, die in den Illustrationen gezeigt wird. Im Kasten findest du Satzteile, die du gebrauchen kannst. (**Seite 125**)

den Führerschein machen	heiraten	wählen	einen Vertrag unterschreiben	später nach Hause kommen

1. Wenn wir 18 wären, _____.   könnten wir einen Vertrag unterschreiben

2. Wenn ihr 18 wärt, _____.   könntet ihr den Führerschein machen

3. Wenn Tammy 18 wäre, _____.   könnte sie heiraten

4. Wenn ich 18 wäre, _____.   könnte ich später nach Hause kommen

5. Wenn du 18 wärst, _____.   könntest du wählen

2 Du und dein Freund, ihr spekuliert darüber nach, was man mit 18 Jahren alles machen könnte. Schreib die folgenden Sätze ab, und schreib dabei die korrekte Form von **können** in die Lücken, um auszudrücken, was möglich wäre! (**Seite 125**)

1. Mit achtzehn _____ ich bestimmen, wo ich wohnen will.   könnte
2. Mit achtzehn _____ wir schon heiraten.   könnten
3. Mit achtzehn _____ ihr den Führerschein machen.   könntet
4. Mit achtzehn _____ der Martin selbst wählen.   könnte
5. Mit achtzehn _____ du Verträge selbst abschließen.   könntest
6. Mit achtzehn _____ die Schüler ihre Entschuldigungen selbst schreiben.   könnten

3 Was könntest du alles tun, wenn du 18 Jahre alt wärst? Schreib Sätze, die mit **Wenn ich achtzehn wäre,** beginnen und im zweiten Teil ausdrücken, was du tun könntest! Verwende die in Klammern gegebenen Ausdrücke! **(Seite 125)**

1. (von zu Hause ausziehen)   Wenn ich achtzehn wäre, könnte ich von zu Hause ausziehen.
2. (sich politisch engagieren)   Wenn ich achtzehn wäre, könnte ich mich politisch engagieren.
3. (Verträge selbst unterschreiben)   Wenn ich achtzehn wäre, könnte ich Verträge selbst unterschreiben.
4. (den Führerschein machen)   Wenn ich achtzehn wäre, könnte ich den Führerschein machen.
5. (die Schule schwänzen)   Wenn ich achtzehn wäre, könnte ich die Schule schwänzen.
6. (heiraten)   Wenn ich achtzehn wäre, könnte ich heiraten.

4 Was hättet ihr gern in den Ferien gemacht? Aber ihr konntet es nicht tun! Schreib Sätze wie im Beispiel. Die Illustrationen zeigen an, was ihr gern gemacht hättet. Die Satzteile im Kasten helfen auch dabei. **(Seite 126)**

am Strand liegen   Golf spielen
in die Sauna gehen
im Kraftraum trainieren   Tennis spielen
in die Disco gehen

BEISPIEL   Wir _____ gern _____.
Wir <u>wären</u> gern <u>im Pool geschwommen.</u>

1. Ich _____.
hätte gern Tennis gespielt

4. Die Mädchen _____.
wären gern in die Sauna gegangen

2. Du _____.
hättest gern Golf gespielt

5. Ihr _____.
hättet gern im Kraftraum trainiert

3. Wir _____.
hätten gern am Strand gelegen

6. Ich _____.
wäre gern in die Disco gegangen

5 Was hättest du und deine Freunde gern getan? Ihr habt es aber nicht getan und aus ganz bestimmten Gründen. Schreib die folgenden Sätze ab, und schreib dabei die korrekte Form von **hätte** oder **wäre** in die Lücken! **(Seite 126)**

1. Ich _____ gern die Schule geschwänzt, aber das Wetter war zu schlecht.   hätte
2. Ich _____ gern zu Hause geblieben, weil ich mich nicht wohl fühlte.   wäre
3. Du _____ bestimmt den Vertrag unterschrieben, wenn du hier gewesen wärst.   hättest
4. Du _____ bestimmt mit dem Rad zur Schule gefahren, aber du hattest wenig Zeit.   wärst
5. Tanja _____ gern den Führerschein gemacht, aber sie hatte zu wenig Geld dazu.   hätte
6. Martin _____ gern in die Staaten geflogen, um dort den Führerschein zu machen.   wäre
7. Ihr _____ doch bestimmt gewählt, aber ihr wart an diesem Tag noch nicht 18.   hättet
8. Ihr _____ doch bestimmt nach Hause gefahren, um in euerm Ort zu wählen.   wärt

Mehr Grammatikübungen

Zweite Stufe

Objectives Saying that something is going on right now; reporting past events; expressing surprise, relief, and resignation

6 Du und deine Freunde, ihr seid gerade dabei, etwas zu tun. Schreib die folgenden Sätze ab, und schreib dabei einen Infinitivsatz in die Lücken mit der Information, die gegeben ist! **(Seite 131)**

1. Wir diskutieren gerade darüber. — Wir sind gerade dabei, _____ .   darüber zu diskutieren
2. Wir entscheiden uns dafür. — Wir sind gerade dabei, _____ .   uns dafür zu entscheiden
3. Wir beschäftigen uns damit. — Wir sind gerade dabei, _____ .   uns damit zu beschäftigen
4. Wir denken darüber nach. — Wir sind gerade dabei, _____ .   darüber nachzudenken
5. Wir wechseln das Geld um. — Wir sind gerade dabei, _____ .   das Geld umzuwechseln
6. Wir tauschen die CD um. — Wir sind gerade dabei, _____ .   die CD umzutauschen

7 Du und deine Freunde, ihr seid gerade dabei, etwas zu tun. Schreib die folgenden Sätze ab, und schreib dabei einen Infinitivsatz in die Lücken mit der Information, die gegeben ist! **(Seite 131)**

1. Wir besprechen den Wehrdienst. — Wir sind gerade dabei, _____ .   den Wehrdienst zu besprechen
2. Wir laden einen Offizier ein. — Wir sind gerade dabei, _____ .   einen Offizier einzuladen
3. Wir machen den Führerschein. — Wir sind gerade dabei, _____ .   den Führerschein zu machen
4. Wir kaufen neue Kontaktlinsen. — Wir sind gerade dabei, _____ .   neue Kontaktlinsen zu kaufen
5. Wir gehen ins Altenheim. — Wir sind gerade dabei, _____ .   ins Altenheim zu gehen
6. Wir ziehen uns jetzt um. — Wir sind gerade dabei, _____ .   uns jetzt umzuziehen

8 Du sagst, was du im Moment tust. Schreib die folgenden Sätze ab, und schreib dabei in die Lücken die Information, die gegeben ist! Gebrauch dabei das Wort **beim**! **(Seite 132)**

1. Wir essen gerade. — Wir sind gerade _____ .   beim Essen
2. Wir spielen gerade Tennis. — Wir sind gerade _____ .   beim Tennisspielen
3. Wir putzen gerade die Fenster. — Wir sind gerade _____ .   beim Fensterputzen
4. Wir mähen gerade den Rasen. — Wir sind gerade _____ .   beim Rasenmähen
5. Wir saugen gerade Staub. — Wir sind gerade _____ .   beim Staubsaugen
6. Wir gießen gerade die Blumen. — Wir sind gerade _____ .   beim Blumengießen

9 Vervollständige die folgenden Sätze und gebrauche dabei die Vergangenheitsform der gegebenen Modalverben und die Information in den Illustrationen und im Kasten. **(Seite 133)**

jede Woche Geld sparen   sich die Kleider selbst nähen   sich verrückt anziehen

nur dunkles Brot essen   nur braune Eier essen   keine Kartoffeln essen

1. (wollen)   Ich _____.   wollte mich verrückt anziehen

2. (können)   Marga _____.   konnte sich die Kleider selbst nähen

3. (müssen)   Mike _____.   musste jede Woche Geld sparen

4. (sollen)   Wir _____.   sollten nur dunkles Brot essen

5. (mögen)   Ich _____.   mochte nur braune Eier essen

6. (dürfen)   Meine Mutter _____.   durfte keine Kartoffeln essen

10 Du berichtest über Dinge, die in der Vergangenheit *(past time)* liegen. Schreib die folgenden Sätze ab, und schreib dabei die Vergangenheitsform der gegebenen Modalverben in die Lücken! **(Seite 133)**

1. (wollen)   Warum _____ du nicht den Wehrdienst machen?   wolltest
2. (müssen)   Mein Freund _____ alte Leute im Altenheim betreuen.   musste
3. (können)   Ich _____ diese Entscheidung nicht alleine machen.   konnte
4. (sollen)   Ihr _____ doch in der Klasse über den Bund sprechen, nicht?   solltet
5. (mögen)   Warum _____ du nicht zur Bundeswehr gehen?   mochtest
6. (können)   _____ du dich nicht besser über den Zivildienst informieren?   Konntest
7. (müssen)   Warum _____ du dich für dieses Thema entscheiden?   musstest
8. (mögen)   Ich _____ diese Clique überhaupt nicht.   mochte

Anwendung

1 Eine Schülerin fragt ihren Großvater, wie das Leben war, als er jung war. Hör gut zu, und schreib in Stichworten auf, was der Großvater über seine Jugendzeit berichtet!

Script and answers on p. 119I
CD 5 Tr. 12

2 Einige Schüler reden darüber, wie es früher war. Sabine erzählt von ihrer Oma. Lies, was sie berichtet!

Meine Oma hat einmal erzählt, wie es war, als sie ein Kind war. Morgens musste sie immer sehr früh aufstehen, um zur Schule zu gehen. Sie musste zu Fuß gehen, über drei Kilometer! Auch am Samstag musste sie zur Schule. In der Klasse mussten die Schüler still sitzen und die Hände auf den Tisch legen. Sie durften keinen Krach machen, nicht miteinander sprechen. Wer etwas sagen wollte, musste die Hand heben. Wenn ein Schüler frech war, durfte ihn der Lehrer schlagen. Die Schüler mussten auch auf ihre Kleidung achten. Alles musste sauber sein, kein Knopf durfte fehlen! Ja, und die Mädchen durften auch keine Hosen tragen, nur Röcke. Nach der Schule musste meine Oma immer gleich die Hausaufgaben machen, bevor sie mit ihren Freundinnen spielen durfte. Wenn ihre Mutter einkaufen gehen wollte, musste meine Oma ihre Geschwister betreuen. Nur einmal im Monat durfte sie ins Kino gehen. Meine Oma meint, heute geht es den Kindern viel besser als früher. Sie müssen zwar mehr lernen, haben aber mehr Freizeit für sich.

3 Schreib auf, was die Schüler zu Omas Zeiten alles tun mussten und was sie nicht tun durften!

sie mussten:	sie durften nicht:
früh aufstehen	Hosen tragen (Mädchen)

4 Beschreibe das Foto auf Seite 144! Was ist in diesem Foto anders als heute?

5 Was hat sich alles von früher geändert? Sag einer Partnerin, wie es früher war und wie es heute ist!

Früher	durften	die Schüler	immer
	konnten	die Mädchen	(fast) nie
	mussten	die Jungen	selten
Heute	können	die Kinder	oft
	dürfen	die Lehrer	manchmal

ihre Meinung frei sagen

auch samstags in die Schule gehen

anziehen, was sie wollen

die Schüler schlagen

politisch aktiv sein

sehr viel auswendig lernen

in der Klasse still sein

selber Vorschläge machen

6 **a.** Interview eine ältere Person, Bekannte oder Verwandte, über das Thema: Wie war das Leben, als du (Sie) sechzehn Jahre alt warst (waren)? Mach dir kurze Notizen!

b. Schreib einen kurzen Bericht über das, was du erfahren hast! Lies deinen Bericht der Klasse vor!

c. Vergleiche das Leben, das in dem Bericht geschildert wird, mit deinem Leben heute!

7 Ein Recht, das junge Leute mit der Volljährigkeit erwerben, ist das Recht, ihren Wohnsitz frei bestimmen zu können. — Stell dir vor, du möchtest jetzt von zu Hause ausziehen, oder du musst ausziehen, weil du in einem anderen Ort zur Universität gehst! Denk über die Vorteile und Nachteile nach und schreib sie auf!

Vorteile:

Ich könnte jetzt …

Nachteile:

Ich müsste (*would have to*) jetzt …

8 **R o l l e n s p i e l**

Es gibt Krach in der Familie!

Du bist gerade achtzehn geworden und willst von zu Hause ausziehen, aber deine Eltern sind leider nicht dafür. Schreib zuerst eine Liste von den Vorteilen und Nachteilen, die beide Perspektiven — Eltern und Kind — berücksichtigt! Dann spielt ein Gespräch zwischen euch vor!

Kann ich's wirklich?

Can you talk about what is possible? (p. 125)

1 How would you respond if a friend said the following things to you?

a. Wen soll ich wählen?   E.g.: Du könntest die (… Partei) wählen.

b. Ich weiß nicht, wem ich meine Stimme geben soll.   b. E.g.: Du könntest deine Stimme der (… Partei) geben.

c. Der Führerschein ist mir zu teuer.
c. E.g.: Du könntest dir das Geld für den Führerschein mit einem Job verdienen.

Can you say what you would have liked to do? (p. 126)

2 How would you say that   Ich hätte gern die Schule geschwänzt, aber ich weiß, dass ich das niemals tun soll.

a. you would have liked to skip class, but you know you should never do that?

b. you would have liked to go to the movies, but you had to help your parents?   Ich wäre gern ins Kino gegangen, aber ich musste meinen Eltern helfen.

Can you say that something is going on right now? (p. 131)

3 How would you respond if your parents asked you when you were going to do the following things, and you were already doing them when they asked?

a. Hast du den Artikel über den Zivildienst schon gelesen?   a. E.g.: Ich bin dabei, diesen Artikel zu lesen.

b. Überlegst du dir, ob du zur Bundeswehr gehst?   b. E.g.: Ich bin am Überlegen.

c. Wann diskutierst du mit deinem Bruder darüber?
c. E.g.: Wir diskutieren gerade darüber.

Can you report past events? (p. 132)

4 How would you say that

a. you wanted to go out last Sunday, but you couldn't because you had too much to do?   Ich wollte letzten Sonntag ausgehen, aber ich hatte zu viel zu tun.

b. your friends couldn't come along and had to stay home?
Meine Freunde konnten nicht mitkommen und mussten zu Hause bleiben.

Can you express surprise, relief, and resignation? (p. 134)

5 How would you respond to the following statements?   a. Das ist mir völlig neu!

a. Leute mit Kontaktlinsen dürfen nicht in der Bundeswehr dienen.

b. In der Bundeswehr hatte ich mir den Fuß gebrochen, aber jetzt ist er wieder in Ordnung.   b. Ich bin froh, dass es dir wieder besser geht.

c. Ich finde es nicht gut, dass wir eine Wehrpflicht in Deutschland haben.
c. Ach was soll's! Das ist leider so.

Erste Stufe

Talking about what is possible

Ich könnte das machen, wenn …	*I could do that, if …*

Saying what you would have liked to do

Ich hätte gern die Sendung gesehen.	*I would have liked to have seen the show.*
Ich wäre gern nach München gereist.	*I would have liked to have traveled to Munich.*

Other useful words

der Unterricht	class, school
die Prüfung, -en	test
das Mitglied, -er	member
der Verein, -e	club
der Vertrag, -̈e	contract
die Pflicht, -en	duty
das Recht, -e	right
in dieser Hinsicht	as far as that goes
bevor (conj)	before
kurzfristig	on short notice
schade sein um	to be a shame/waste
umgekehrt	vice-versa

schwänzen	to cut class
fehlen	to be missing
s. erlauben	to permit oneself
dauern	to last
schaffen	to achieve, make
s. irren	to be wrong
scheinen	to seem
wählen	to vote for
s. engagieren	to be active in
unterschreiben	to sign (your name)
heiraten	to marry
unabhängig sein	to be independent
s. ändern	to change oneself

Zweite Stufe

p. 119X

Saying that something is going on right now

Ich arbeite an dem Projekt.	*I'm working on the project.*
Ich bin dabei, am Projekt zu arbeiten.	*I'm getting started on the project.*
Ich bin am (beim) Arbeiten.	*I'm working.*

Reporting past events

Ich konnte gestern meine Hausaufgaben erledigen.	*I was able to finish my homework yesterday.*

Expressing surprise, relief, and resignation

Das ist mir neu!	*That's news to me!*
Ich bin aber froh, dass …	*I'm sure happy that …*
Ach, was soll's? Das ist leider so.	*Well, what's the use? That's the way it is.*

Other useful words

das Krankenhaus, -̈er	hospital
der Panzer, -	tank
der Laster, -	truck

das Transportflugzeug, -e	transport plane
der Bomber, -	bomber
die Streitkräfte (pl)	armed forces
die Bundeswehr	German Federal Defense Force
der Bund = die Bundeswehr	
das U-Boot, -e	submarine
der Wehrdienst	armed forces
die Wehrpflicht	compulsory service
der Offizier, -e	officer
der Frieden	peace
das Gewehr, -e	gun
die Waffe, -n	weapon
der Kampf, -̈e	struggle, battle
der Zivildienst	community service
die Demokratie, -n	democracy
das Grundgesetz	basic law
die Gleichberechtigung	equality
die Entscheidung, -en	decision
das Studium	university studies
im Ernst	seriously
das Thema, Themen	theme, matter
abstreiten (sep)	to argue against
belasten	to weigh on, burden

betreuen	to care for
einstellen (sep)	to hire
einziehen (sep)	to draft
s. entscheiden für	to decide on
halten für	to consider something as
kommandieren	to command
s. lohnen	to be worth it
schießen	to shoot
unterbrechen	to interrupt
s. unterhalten über (acc)	to discuss
s. verlassen auf (acc)	to count on
angenehm	pleasant
fies	awful
anstrengend	strenuous
sinnlos	senseless
freiwillig	voluntary
vergangen-, vorig-	past last
früher	earlier
ausgesprochen	particularly

Kapitel 6: Medien: stets gut informiert?
Chapter Overview

Los geht's! pp. 150–151	*Die Macht der Medien, p. 150*

	FUNCTIONS	GRAMMAR	VOCABULARY	RE-ENTRY
Erste Stufe pp. 152–157	• Asking someone to take a position, p. 153 • Asking for reasons, p. 153 • Expressing opinions, p. 153 • Reporting past events, p. 154 • Agreeing or disagreeing, p. 156 • Changing the subject, p. 156 • Interrupting, p. 156	• Narrative past (imperfect), pp. 154, 155	• News and entertainment media, p. 152	Talking about favorites, p. 153 (**Kap. 10, I**); leisure-time activities, p. 153 (**Kap. 2/6, I**); expressing opinions, p. 153 (**Kap. 2/9, I**); the conversational past, p. 154 (**Kap. 3, II**); agreeing and disagreeing, p. 156 (**Kap. 10, II**); television vocabulary, p. 156 (**Kap. 10, II**)

Weiter geht's! pp. 158–159	*Unsere eigene Zeitung!, p. 158*

Zweite Stufe pp. 160–163	• Expressing surprise or annoyance, p. 161	• Superlative forms of adjectives, p. 162	• Terms useful for a school newspaper editor, p. 160 • Words of quantity, p. 163	Expressing surprise, p. 161 (**Kap. 10, II**); the comparative forms of adjectives, p. 162 (**Kap. 7, II**); time expressions, p. 163 (**Kap. 6, II**); words of quantity, p. 163 (**Kap. 8, I**)

Zum Lesen pp. 164–166	Ein Märchen	**Reading Strategy** Predicting outcome

Zum Schreiben p. 167	Ich nehme dazu Stellung.	**Writing Strategy** Using an outline

Mehr Grammatik-übungen	**pp. 168–171** Erste Stufe, pp. 168–169	Zweite Stufe, pp. 170–171	

Review pp. 172–175	Anwendung, pp. 172–173	Kann ich's wirklich?, p. 174	Wortschatz, p. 175

CULTURE

• Die TV-Kids, p. 152
• Landeskunde: Die Schülerzeitung, p. 157
• Leserbriefe an die Redaktion der Pepo, p. 160

Kapitel 6: Medien: stets gut informiert?
Chapter Resources

Lesson Planning

One-Stop Planner

Lesson Planner with Substitute Teacher Lesson Plans, pp. 36–40, 80

Student Make-Up Assignments
- Make-Up Assignment Copying Masters, Chapter 6

Listening and Speaking

Listening Activities
- Student Response Forms for Listening Activities, pp. 43–46
- Additional Listening Activities 6-1 to 6-6, pp. 47–50
- Scripts and Answers, pp. 142–149

Video Guide
- Teaching Suggestions, p. 26
- Activity Masters, pp. 27–28
- Scripts and Answers, pp. 64–65, 75

Activities for Communication
- Communicative Activities, pp. 21–24
- Realia and Teaching Suggestions, pp. 76–80
- Situation Cards, pp. 123–124

Reading and Writing

Reading Strategies and Skills Handbook, Chapter 6

Lies mit mir! 3, Chapter 6

Übungsheft, pp. 66–78

Grammar

Grammatikheft, pp. 46–54

Grammar Tutor for Students of German, Chapter 6

Assessment

Testing Program
- Grammar and Vocabulary Quizzes, **Stufe** Quizzes, and Chapter Test, pp. 111–124
- Score Sheet, Scripts and Answers, pp. 125–131

- Midterm Exam, pp. 133–140
- Midterm Exam Score Sheets, Script and Answers, pp. 141–146

Alternative Assessment Guide
- Portfolio Assessment, p. 21
- Performance Assessment, p. 35

Student Make-Up Assignments
- Alternative Quizzes, Chapter 6

 Online Activities
- Interaktive Spiele
- Internet Aktivitäten

 Video Program
- Videocassette 1

 Audio Compact Discs
- Textbook Listening Activities, CD 6, Tracks 1–11
- Additional Listening Activities, CD 6, Tracks 21–26
- Assessment Items, CD 6, Tracks 14–20

 Teaching Transparencies
- Situations 6-1 to 6-2
- **Mehr Grammatikübungen** Answers
- **Grammatikheft** Answers

 One-Stop Planner CD-ROM

Use the **One-Stop Planner CD-ROM with Test Generator** to aid in lesson planning and pacing.

For each chapter, the **One-Stop Planner** includes:
- Editable lesson plans with direct links to teaching resources
- Printable worksheets from resource books
- Direct launches to the HRW Internet activities
- Video and audio segments
- Test Generator
- Clip Art for vocabulary items

Kapitel 6: Medien: stets gut informiert?

Projects ·······························

Unsere Schülerzeitung

In this activity students will design and plan the premiere issue of a German-language newspaper for their school. This project should start after the **Zum Schreiben** *and* **Anwendung** *sections, where students receive many suggestions that will prove helpful for this project.*

MATERIALS
✂ **Students may need**
- paper
- pens
- pencils
- scissors
- glue
- photos

SUGGESTED SEQUENCE

1. Ask students to brainstorm what this German paper should look like. What type of articles and features should be included?

2. Let the class choose a title for the paper.

3. Students divide up the work, and each team works on a specific feature.

4. Students prepare drafts of the features or articles for which they are responsible.

5. Students peer edit each other's work and make necessary changes.

6. Students work together to design a layout and determine what types of illustrations should be included in the final copy. If possible, have students prepare the final layout using a computer.

7. Students evaluate the first proof and correct any errors.

8. The final copy is printed, copied, and distributed to all German students.

GRADING THE PROJECT
Suggested point distribution (**total = 100 points**)
Content 25
Appearance of pages.............................25
Accurate language usage 25
Originality..25

Games ·······························

Eine unmögliche Geschichte aus dem Schuhkarton

This game will help students review the vocabulary from this and previous chapters.

Preparation Write vocabulary words and phrases on small slips of paper and put them all in a shoebox. Here are some suggested vocabulary items:

vermissen	Schüleraustausch
besuchen	allein
erfahren	der Musikladen
die Wahrheit	die Jugendherberge

Procedure The first student takes a piece of paper from the shoebox and begins to tell a story incorporating the vocabulary item he or she has chosen. He or she then passes the box to another student in the class, who draws another slip of paper and continues the story by incorporating the word or phrase on his or her piece of paper. The story must end with the last piece of paper in the box.

NOTE: You may want to record the story on an audiocassette and then play it back to the class.

Storytelling ....

Mini-Geschichte

This story accompanies Teaching Transparency 6-1. The Mini-Geschichte can be told and retold in different formats, acted out, written down, and read aloud to give students additional opportunities to practice all four skills.

Als das Fax kam, las mein Vater gerade die Zeitung, meine Mutter unterhielt sich mit unserer Nachbarin in der Küche, mein kleiner Bruder saß vor der Glotze und mein großer Bruder las ein Buch und hörte Musik. Ich versuchte, meiner Familie das Fax vorzulesen, aber sie ließen mich nicht ausreden. Sie ließen mich nicht einmal richtig zu Wort kommen! Ich druckte das Fax aus, aber niemand wollte es lesen! Als ich das Fax zu Ende gelesen hatte, schrie ich: „Wir sind zur Familie des Jahres gewählt worden. Ist denn niemand daran interessiert?"

Traditions ....

Walter von der Vogelweide

Die Wartburg

Walther von der Vogelweide ist der bedeutendste und erfolgreichste Minnesänger und Spruchdichter des Mittelalters. Seine Elegien zählen zu den bedeutendsten Texten der deutschen Literatur. Es sind 100 Texte von ihm überliefert. Wahrscheinlich wurde er 1170 in Niederösterreich geboren. Er war Minnesänger am Hofe der österreichischen Herzoge in Wien. Eigenen Angaben zufolge lernte er in Österreich „singen und sagen" (d. h. komponieren und dichten). Er wirkte als Minnesänger und Spruchdichter auch an verschiedenen Fürstenhöfen in Thüringen, Bayern, Passau und Meißen, sowie auf der Wartburg.

Die Frage nach dem richtigen Herrscher dominiert in seinen politischen Sprüchen. Seine Dichtung kritisiert vor allem den Einfluss des Papstes. Der Dichter starb wahrscheinlich um 1230 in Würzburg, wo er 1220 von Friedrich II. ein kleines Lehen erhalten hatte. Er ist im Kreuzgang des Neumünster begraben.

Die folgenden Zeilen sind aus einem seiner bekanntesten Gedichte.

Ich saz ûf eime steine
und dahte bein mit beine,
dar ûf satzt ich den ellenbogen;
ich hete in mîne hant gesmogen
daz kinne und ein mîn wange.
dô dâhte ich mir vil ange,
wie man zer welte solte leben.

[Ich saß auf einem Stein, hatte Bein über Bein geschlagen, den Ellbogen drauf gestützt, in die Hand schmiegte ich Kinn und Wange.

Mit allen Gedanken fragte ich mich, wie man auf der Welt leben sollte.]

Rezept

Apfel-Quark-Auflauf
Für 4 Personen

g=Gramm

Zutaten

50 g	Butter	50 g Rosinen
150 g	Zucker	50 g Mandelblätter
4 Eier	Salz	
500 g	Magerquark	abgeriebene Zitronenschale
100 g	Haferflocken	Butterflöckchen
750 g	säuerliche Äpfel	Puderzucker

Zubereitung

Butter, Zucker, Eier, Salz und Zitronenschale zusammen schaumig schlagen. Den Quark und die Haferflocken unterrühren. Die Äpfel schälen, in Spalten schneiden und mit den Rosinen und Mandelblättern vermischt lagenweise im Wechsel mit Quark in eine gefettete Form schichten. Die letzte Schicht soll der Quark sein. Mit Butterflöckchen garnieren und bei etwa 200 Grad Celsius 60 Minuten backen. Dann mit Puderzucker bestreuen.

Technology

One-Stop Planner CD-ROM

To preview all resources available for this chapter, use the **One-Stop Planner CD-ROM**, Disc 2.

Internet Connection ....

internet

ADRESSE: go.hrw.com
KENNWORT:
WK3 WUERZBURG-6

*Have students explore the **go.hrw.com** Web site for many online resources covering all chapters. All Chapter 6 resources are available under the keyword **WK3 Wuerzburg-6**. Interactive games help students practice the material and provide them with immediate feedback. You will also find a printable worksheet that provides Internet activities that lead to a comprehensive online research project.*

Interaktive Spiele

You can use the interactive activities in this chapter

- to practice grammar, vocabulary, and chapter functions
- as homework
- as an assessment option
- as a self-test
- to prepare for the Chapter Test

Internet Aktivitäten

Students visit the sites of German TV stations and discuss programs they like. They will also evaluate the approach of online newspapers to politics, environmental issues, and compulsory service.

- To prepare students for the **Arbeitsblatt,** have them list the pros and cons of TV and newpapers. You may want to allow students to include the opinions given in **Los geht's!,** pp. 150–151.

- After completing the **Arbeitsblatt,** ask students to compile the topics suggested in **Aktivität E.** How many chose the same topic? Are the most-mentioned topics of interest to all students? Are the least-mentioned topics of interest to only particular students?

<u>Webprojekt</u>

Have students find a report about the same current world event in a German and an American online newspaper or newsmagazine. Students should report on the event and compare the two articles. Do the reports present the event from the same political or social perspective? Why or why not? Encourage students to exchange useful Web sites with their classmates. Have students document their sources by referencing the names and URLs of all the sites they consulted.

Kapitel 6: Medien: stets gut informiert?
Textbook Listening Activities Scripts

The following scripts are for the listening activities found in the *Pupil's Edition.* For Student Response Forms, see *Listening Activities*, pages 43–46. To provide students with additional listening practice, see *Listening Activities*, pages 47–50.

Erste Stufe

4 p. 153

Kässi	Sagt mal, habt ihr gestern Abend auch den Bericht über Serbien im Fernsehen gesehen?
Antje	Nee. Du, Holger?
Holger	Nein. Ich hab gestern Radio gehört.
Kässi	Also, der Bericht war wirklich interessant, muss ich sagen. Ich sehe mir sowieso gern die Nachrichten im ZDF an. Du etwa nicht, Antje?
Antje	Nein, nicht so gern. Weißt du, Kässi, meiner Meinung nach sind die Nachrichten im Fernsehen ziemlich oberflächlich.
Kässi	Finde ich aber nicht! Das reicht doch als Information aus.
Antje	Hm! Also, ich brauche schon etwas mehr Information.
Thomas	Was genau meinst du denn? Ich finde, dass man durchs Fernsehen am besten informiert wird.
Antje	Also, pass mal auf, Thomas! Es reicht mir nicht, wenn der Nachrichtensprecher im Fernsehen einfach nur sagt: Es gibt einen Konflikt im Land A und die Völker B und C streiten aus dem Grund D! Ich will mehr über die historischen, politischen und wirtschaftlichen Hintergründe wissen.
Thomas	Ja, aber das geht nun mal nicht in einer Nachrichtensendung, die nur kurze, sachliche Informationen herausbringt!
Antje	Das stimmt! Deswegen lese ich eben lieber Zeitung!
Kässi	Ach Antje! Viele Zeitungen und Magazine bringen doch nur Sensationsnachrichten und keine Tatsachen.
Antje	Ich meine ja auch seriöse Zeitungen, so wie die Frankfurter Allgemeine oder die Süddeutsche Zeitung.
Holger	Also, ich finde, wenn man sich schnell über Neuigkeiten informieren will, schaltet man am besten das Radio an. Dort kommen alle 30 Minuten Kurznachrichten.
Thomas	Dann lies doch einfach nur die Schlagzeilen!
Kässi	Bloß nicht! So kann man sich auf keinen Fall informieren! Die Schlagzeilen sind doch meistens extra ganz provokativ formuliert und spiegeln nicht unbedingt Tatsachen wider!
Antje	Ja, da hast du Recht, Kässi. Deswegen ist es wichtig, den ganzen Artikel zu lesen.

Answers to Activity 4
Kässi: TV; Antje: Zeitung; Holger: Radio; Thomas: TV

5 p. 153

Markus	He, Leute! In der letzten Ausgabe der Frankfurter Allgemeinen Zeitung gibt es einen tollen Artikel über Umweltprobleme. Hat den einer von euch gelesen? Du, Michaela?
Michaela	Nein! Was für ein Artikel war denn das, Markus?
Markus	Ja, also in dem Artikel steht, dass es verboten werden sollte, mit dem Auto zu fahren. Ich finde das auch.
Rüdiger	Kannst du das begründen?
Markus	Mensch, Rüdiger, die Abgase werden doch zu einem immer größeren Problem für die Umwelt!
Michaela	Das stimmt! Wenn wir nicht vorsichtig sind, werden wir bald überhaupt keine saubere Luft und kein sauberes Trinkwasser mehr haben.
Markus	Ja, genau! Ich stimme der Michaela zu. Und deswegen bin ich heute auch gleich mit dem Fahrrad zur Schule gekommen, weil ich bei mir selbst anfangen möchte, die Umwelt zu schonen. Ich finde, du solltest auch nicht mehr mit deinem Moped kommen, Rüdiger.
Rüdiger	Ach, das ist doch völliger Quatsch! Ich fahre weiter mit dem Moped.
Markus	Also, Rüdiger! Wieso ist das Quatsch? Dazu musst du jetzt aber wirklich mal genauer Stellung nehmen.
Rüdiger	Ach, das ist doch ganz einfach! Ich finde, diese Nachrichten, die immer von den Umweltbelastungen reden, sind doch sowieso nur Sensationsmeldungen.
Michaela	Na ja, also meiner Meinung nach sollte man vielleicht nicht ganz aufs Autofahren verzichten.
Cornelia	Wie meinst du das, Michaela?
Michaela	Weißt du, Cornelia, ich finde, dass es okay ist, mit dem Auto zu fahren, wenn man einen Notfall hat. Also, wenn man zum Beispiel schnell ins Krankenhaus muss.
Cornelia	Also, Michaela, meinst du denn wirklich, dass die Leute in Deutschland nur noch in Notfällen mit dem Auto fahren? Das funktioniert niemals. Das kannst du mir glauben.
Markus	Und wieso nicht, Cornelia?
Cornelia	Ich weiß nicht! Das kann ich mir halt einfach nicht vorstellen!

Answers to Activity 5
Grund: Markus, Michaela, Rüdiger; keinen Grund: Cornelia; Answers will vary.

11 p. 156

Wolfgang	Sagt mal, habt ihr gestern den Krimi im RTL gesehen? Der war echt toll! Du, Simone, du musst deine Familie endlich mal dazu überreden, einen Fernseher zu kaufen. Sonst kannst du ja nie mitreden.

SIMONE	Also, weißt du, Wolfgang, wir brauchen keinen Fernseher. Wir unternehmen lieber etwas zusammen als Familie.
DIRK	Wirklich?
SIMONE	Ja! Wir finden nämlich, dass die meisten Familien, die einen Fernseher haben, abends nur vor der Glotze sitzen und kaum miteinander reden. Ist dir das denn noch nie aufgefallen, Dirk?
DIRK	Hm! Da ist schon was dran. Bei uns zu Hause ist das ähnlich. Bei euch doch bestimmt auch, oder, Beate?
BEATE	Quatsch! Das stimmt gar nicht! Bei uns zu Hause wird viel geredet. Wir diskutieren oft über das, was wir im Fernsehen gesehen haben.
WOLFGANG	Richtig! Außerdem kann man sich durchs Fernsehen viel leichter über alle wichtigen Ereignisse in der Welt informieren.
SIMONE	Moment mal, Wolfgang! Das kann man auch wenn man Zeitung liest oder Radio hört. Ich finde außerdem, dass man in seiner Freizeit viel weniger aktiv ist, wenn man zu viel fernsieht.
DIRK	Ja, da hat die Simone Recht. Ich finde auch, dass man sich von anderen Menschen isoliert und nicht so viel unternimmt.
WOLFGANG	Lass mich mal wieder zu Wort kommen, Dirk! Also, für mich ist das Fernsehen wichtig. Außer den Nachrichten oder Fernsehserien kann ich mir nämlich auch Opern, Theaterstücke und Konzerte ansehen.
BEATE	Ja! Finde ich auch, Wolfgang! Erstens ist das nicht so teuer wie Opern- oder Konzertkarten und zweitens kann man schön zu Hause die Aufführung genießen, ohne erst irgendwo hinfahren zu müssen.
WOLFGANG	Eben! Und außerdem kann man eine Sendung aufnehmen. Dann kann man sich später das Video anschauen! Das ist doch total praktisch!
SIMONE	Ach! Das kommt doch alles aufs Gleiche raus! Tatsache ist, dass man vorm Fernseher hockt und nichts unternimmt! 75 Prozent aller Leute, die täglich vier oder mehr Stunden vor dem Fernseher sitzen, essen zu viel! Sie werden häufiger krank, beklagen sich über Müdigkeit und haben keine Energie!
DIRK	Ja! Richtige Gesundheitsmuffel sind das!

Answers to Activity 11
Answers will vary.

Zweite Stufe

16 p. 161

BERNHARD	He, Leute, denkt dran! Wir treffen uns heute Abend bei mir zu Hause, damit wir noch mal das Layout für den Druck besprechen können!
REGINA	Ja, in Ordnung, Bernhard! Ich hab auch schon die Seite mit den Leserbriefen fertig gemacht.
BERNHARD	Spitze, Regina! Du hast bestimmt stundenlang daran gesessen.
REGINA	Ach was! Mir hat es echt Spaß gemacht. Und ich glaub, ich hab die richtige Mischung aus guten und kritischen Leserbriefen zusammengestellt!
BERNHARD	Gut! Wir müssen nur noch die Ergebnisse aus unserer letzten Umfrage in den Computer eintippen, damit wir eine tolle Grafik in der Zeitung abbilden können.
GERD	Schon erledigt! Hab ich gestern Nachmittag gemacht.
REGINA	Super, Gerd! Was gibt es sonst noch zu tun?
BERNHARD	Tina hat ihren Artikel über die Schulfete noch nicht fertig geschrieben.
REGINA	Das ist ja unglaublich! Immer fängt sie alles an und macht das dann nie zu Ende!
BERNHARD	Ja, leider! So ist sie nun mal. Da kann man nichts machen.
GERD	Und wer schreibt ihren Artikel bis heute Abend fertig?
BERNHARD	Keine Panik! Ich schreib den Artikel heute Nachmittag zu Ende.
GERD	Mensch, Bernhard! Auf dich kann man sich wirklich verlassen. Aber fair find ich das nicht! Das ist jetzt schon das dritte Mal, dass du für die Tina einspringst. Stimmt's Regina?
REGINA	Ja, leider, Gerd. Es überrascht mich wirklich, dass Tina so faul ist.
BERNHARD	Ja, das ist echt schade, denn sie schreibt wirklich gute Artikel, wenn sie Lust hat.
REGINA	Also, was müssen wir sonst noch alles bis heute Abend erledigen?
GERD	Wir müssen uns auf das Titelblatt einigen. Regina hat drei Vorschläge ausgearbeitet.
REGINA	Ja, ich glaub, ich hab drei super Ideen. Wir müssen nur noch die Heidi fragen, ob sie für uns die Illustrationen machen kann. Ach, da kommt sie ja! Hallo, Heidi!
HEIDI	Hallo, alle zusammen! Was gibt's?
BERNHARD	Du, Heidi, meinst du, du schaffst es, bis heute Abend drei Illustrationen fürs Titelbild zu machen?
HEIDI	Was? Fürs Titelbild? Heißt das etwa, dass wir noch kein Titelbild haben, obwohl die nächste Ausgabe morgen gedruckt werden soll? Das darf doch wohl nicht wahr sein!
REGINA	Doch, leider! Also, was ist? Können wir mit dir rechnen?
HEIDI	Also, es stört mich wirklich, dass immer alles bis auf die letzte Minute verschoben wird! Fragt doch jemand anders!
BERNHARD	Ach, komm schon, Heidi! Wir sind doch alle unter Stress wegen dem Abi und den Noten und so!
HEIDI	Ja, ja! Schon gut! Ich bring heute Abend die Illustrationen mit, okay?!
REGINA	Klasse, Heidi!

Answers to Activity 16
gern: Bernhard, Regina, Gerd; nicht gern: Heidi, Tina

17 p. 161

ANGELIKA	Also, Leute! Ich habe euch hierher gebeten, damit jeder seine Meinung zu unserer Schülerzeitung sagen kann ...
BODO	Meine Meinung kann ich dir gern sagen, Angelika! Es ist wirklich frustrierend, wenn wir nichts als Kritik über ...
ANGELIKA	Moment mal, Bodo! Lass mich kurz ausreden! Dann kommst du dran. Also, ich will mit euch über unseren nächsten Leitartikel sprechen und die

Aufgaben neu verteilen. Aber als Erstes sollten wir über unsere letzte Ausgabe diskutieren. Also, Bodo?

BODO   Na ja, wie gesagt, ich habe halt echt hart an dem Artikel über die neue Umwelt-AG gearbeitet. Und dann höre ich von den Schülern, dass ihnen alles Mögliche nicht daran gefallen hat, oder dass der Artikel blöd war oder so! Stimmt's, Georg?

GEORG   Da ist schon was dran, Bodo. Mich stört es auch, wenn ich viel Zeit in einen Artikel investiere, und dann nur kritisiert werde.

ANGELIKA   Es überrascht mich, dass ihr so sauer seid! Überlegt doch mal, vielleicht ist es auch unsere eigene Schuld, wenn die Schülerzeitung nur kritisiert wird!

GEORG   Wieso?

ANGELIKA   Ganz einfach! Weil wir offensichtlich nicht das bringen, was den Schülern gefällt! Wir sollten eine Umfrage machen, um herauszufinden, für welche Themen sich die Schüler interessieren.

CLAUDIA   Also, ich bin überrascht, dass du das vorschlägst, Angelika! Wir haben doch erst letzten Monat eine Umfrage gemacht, und kaum jemand hat sich daran beteiligt!

GEORG   Eben! Den meisten Schülern ist es doch egal, was und worüber wir schreiben, stimmt's, Claudia?

CLAUDIA   Ja, leider, Georg! Ich finde es einfach unglaublich, dass die meisten Schüler einfach nicht verstehen, wie viel Arbeit in so einer Schülerzeitung steckt!

BODO   Ja, genau! Mich stört es wirklich, dass keiner Vorschläge macht, wie wir unsere Zeitung besser machen können!

CLAUDIA   Genau! Was Bodo sagt, stimmt! Die letzten Leserbriefe waren voller Kritik! Kein einziger Verbesserungsvorschlag! Es ist wirklich frustrierend!

ANGELIKA   Moment mal, Claudia! Ich würde das alles nicht so pessimistisch sehen. Ich bin der Meinung, dass die Kritik doch gerade das ist, was uns weiter hilft!

CLAUDIA   Wie meinst du das, Angelika?

ANGELIKA   Passt mal auf! Erstens müssen wir die kritischen Kommentare ganz genau durchlesen. Zweitens dürfen wir die Sachen, die kritisiert worden sind, nicht wieder machen. Und drittens fangen wir an, diese Sachen zu verbessern, so dass es jeder merkt.

GEORG   Mensch, Angelika! Das ist ein super Vorschlag! Ich bin überrascht, dass wir nicht schon früher darauf gekommen sind.

CLAUDIA   Ja! Dann hätten wir uns 'ne Menge Frust erspart!

Answers to Activity 17
Bodo: frustriert; Angelika: überrascht; Georg: frustriert und überrascht; Claudia: überrascht und frustriert

Anwendung

2   p. 172

— Also, Axel, hast du schon ein paar gute Ideen für die Artikel in unserer nächsten Ausgabe?

— Na klar, Michaela! Ich hab da ganz verschiedene Vorschläge. Also, Umwelt ist immer ein gutes Thema! Viele Schüler interessieren sich dafür und ...

— Nun sag schon, worüber du berichten willst!

For resource information, see the **One-Stop Planner** CD-ROM, Disc 2.

— Du lässt mich ja nicht ausreden! Also, pass auf! Die Verschmutzung der Mosel ist zur Zeit hier in der Stadt ein heißes Thema!

— Hm. Bist du sicher, dass sich die Schüler dafür interessieren?

— Ganz bestimmt! Ich wollte den Hans-Joachim fragen, ob er Lust hat, darüber zu schreiben. Seine Berichte zum Thema Umwelt kommen immer gut an!

— Da hast du Recht, Axel! Was schlägst du noch vor?

— Wir könnten eine Kritik über den neuen Film mit Arnold Schwarzenegger schreiben.

— Gut! Ich hab auch einen Vorschlag. Die Susanne Krämer aus der Theater-AG hat mir von dem Theaterstück erzählt, das für die Weihnachtsfeier geprobt wird. Wir könnten einen Artikel über die ganzen Vorbereitungen schreiben.

— Das hört sich gut an. Du, Michaela, wie wär's denn außerdem mit einem Artikel über das neue Austauschprogramm mit der Schule in unserer Partnerstadt Austin in Texas?

— Hm. Nicht schlecht! Die Schüler wissen fast gar nichts darüber. Hast du sonst noch eine Idee?

— Klar, und das ist eigentlich mein bester Vorschlag: Ich finde, wir sollten einen Artikel über die ausländischen Schüler an unserer Schule schreiben. Die Raffaela und der Assam haben schon einige Vorschläge zu dem Artikel. Was hältst du davon?

— Klasse Idee! Vielleicht können wir daraus eine Serie machen und in jeder Ausgabe über einen anderen Schüler berichten!

— Spitze! Du, Michaela, ich würd' gern den Artikel über die ausländischen Schüler schreiben. Übernimmst du den Artikel über das amerikanische Austauschprogramm?

— Nee, Axel, keine Zeit! Ich muss noch das Interview mit der neuen Biologielehrerin machen.

— Ach ja, stimmt! Dann fragen wir eben die Steffi, ob sie den Artikel schreiben will.

— Hat Holger schon die Cartoons gezeichnet?

— Glaub ich nicht! Er wollte warten, bis wir die Themen für die Artikel festgelegt haben.

— Logo! Ach übrigens, der Peter Hamacher aus der 12b macht für uns die Fotos auf der Schulfete!

— Spitze! Für die nächste Ausgabe scheint ja alles ziemlich gut organisiert zu sein!

— Ja! Wir müssen uns nur noch ein Thema für die Umfrage ausdenken.

— Vielleicht sollten wir diesmal keine Umfrage machen.

— Doch, doch! Auf jeden Fall! Die Schüler finden es toll, wenn wir sie nach ihrer Meinung fragen und dann das Ergebnis der Umfrage in der Schülerzeitung veröffentlichen.

Answers to Activity 2
Answers will vary.

Kapitel 6: Medien: stets gut informiert?
Suggested Lesson Plans 50-Minute Schedule

Day 1

CHAPTER OPENER 5 min.
- Advance Organizer, ATE, p. 147M
- Thinking Critically, ATE, p. 147M

LOS GEHT'S! 20 min.
- Preteaching Vocabulary, ATE, p. 147N
- Advance Organizer, p. 147N
- Teacher Note, p. 147N
- Play Audio CD for Los geht's!
- Have students read Los geht's!, pp. 150–151
- Do Activities 1 and 2, p. 151

ERSTE STUFE
Reading Selection, p. 152 10 min.
- Thinking Critically, p. 147O
- Read Die TV-Kids p. 152

Wortschatz, p. 152 10 min.
- Presenting Wortschatz, ATE, p. 147O
- Do Activity 3, p. 153
- Play Audio CD for Activity 4, p. 153

Wrap-Up 5 min.
- Students respond to questions about their TV habits

Homework Options
Grammatikheft, p. 46, Acts. 1–2
Übungsheft, p. 66, Acts. 1–2

Day 2

ERSTE STUFE
Quick Review 10 min.
- Check homework, Übungsheft, p. 66, Acts. 1–2

So sagt man das!, p. 153 20 min.
- Presenting So sagt man das!, ATE, p. 147O
- Teaching Transparency 6-1
- Play Audio CD for Activity 5, p. 153
- Do Activity 6, p. 153
- Do Activities 7 and 8, p. 154

Game 15 min.
- Play Eine unmögliche Geschichte aus dem Schuhkarton, ATE, p. 147C

Wrap-Up 5 min.
- Students respond to questions about their opinions on the media

Homework Options
Grammatikheft, p. 47, Act. 3
Übungsheft, p. 67, Acts. 1–2

Day 3

ERSTE STUFE
Quick Review 10 min.
- Check homework, Grammatikheft, p. 47, Act. 3

So sagt man das!, Grammatik, pp. 154–155 20 min.
- Present So sagt man das!, Grammatik, ATE, p. 147P
- Do Activity 9, p. 155
- Do Activity 10, p. 156
- Do Activities 4 and 5, pp. 48–49, Grammatikheft

So sagt man das!, p. 156 15 min.
- Play Audio CD for Activity 11, p. 156
- Play Audio CD for Activity 12, p. 156

Wrap-Up 5 min.
- Students respond to questions about past events

Homework Options
Grammatikheft, p. 50, Act. 6
Übungsheft, pp. 68–70, Acts. 3–9

Day 4

ERSTE STUFE
Quick Review 10 min.
- Check homework, Übungsheft, pp. 68–70, Acts. 3–9

LANDESKUNDE 20 min.
- Building Context, ATE, p. 147Q
- Teaching Suggestion, ATE, p. 147Q
- Read Die Schülerzeitung, p. 157
- Do Activities 1–4, p. 157

Über Kinos und Videos 15 min.
- Teaching Suggestions, Video Guide, p. 26
- Do Pre-viewing, Viewing, and Post-viewing Activities, p. 27, Video Guide
- Show Video, Über Kinos und Videos

Wrap-Up 5 min.
- Students respond to questions about how often and which movies or videos they see

Homework Options
Übungsheft, p. 71, Acts. 1–4
Mehr Grammatikübungen, Erste Stufe

Day 5

ERSTE STUFE
Quick Review 10 min.
- Check homework, Mehr Grammatikübungen

Quiz Review 20 min.
- Do Additional Listening Activities 6-1 and 6-2, pp. 47–48
- Do Activities for Communication 6-1 or 6-2, pp. 21–22
- Do Realia 6-1, pp. 76 and 79–80, Activities for Communication

Quiz 20 min.
- Quiz 6-1A or 6-1B

Homework Options
Activities for Communication, pp. 77 and 79–80, Realia 6-2; list information included on advertisement
Internet Aktivitäten, ATE, p. 147E

Day 6

WEITER GEHT'S!
Quick Review 30 min.
- Return and review Quiz 6-1
- Check homework, Realia 6-2
- Present Weiter geht's!, pp. 158–159
- Play Audio CD for Weiter geht's!, pp. 158–159
- Do Activities 13 and 14, p. 159

ZWEITE STUFE
- Bell Work, ATE, p. 147R 5 min.

Reading Selection, p. 160 10 min.
- Teaching Suggestion, p. 147N
- Read Leserbriefe an die Redaktion der Pepo, p. 160

Wrap-Up 5 min.
- Students respond to questions about what types of articles their school newspaper contains

Homework Options
Übungsheft, p. 72, Acts. 1–3

One-Stop Planner CD-ROM

For alternative lesson plans by chapter section, to create your own customized plans, or to preview all resources available for this chapter, use the **One-Stop Planner CD-ROM**, Disc 2.

 For additional homework suggestions, see activities accompanied by this symbol throughout the chapter.

Day 7

ZWEITE STUFE
Quick Review 10 min.
- Check homework, Übungsheft, p. 72, Acts. 1–3

Wortschatz, p. 160 10 min.
- Presenting **Wortschatz**, ATE, p. 147R
- Do Activity 15, p. 160
- Play Audio CD for Activity 16, p. 161

So sagt man das!, p. 161 10 min.
- Presenting **So sagt man das!**, ATE, p. 147S
- Teaching Transparency 6-2
- Play Audio CD for Activity 17, p. 161
- Do Activity 18, p. 161

Grammatik, p. 162 15 min.
- Presenting **Grammatik**, ATE, p. 147S
- Do Activity 19, p. 162
- Do Activities 20, 21, and 22, p. 163

Wrap-Up 5 min.
- Students respond to questions about being surprised or annoyed

Homework Options
Grammatikheft, pp. 51–54, Acts. 7–13
Übungsheft, pp. 73–75, Acts. 1–5

Day 8

ZWEITE STUFE
Quick Review 15 min.
- Check homework, Grammatikheft, pp. 51–54, Acts. 7–13

Wortschatz, p. 163 10 min.
- Presenting **Wortschatz**, ATE, p. 147S
- Do Activity 23, p. 163

Quiz Review 25 min.
- Mehr Grammatikübungen, Zweite Stufe
- Do Communicative Activities 6-3 and 6-4, pp. 23–24
- Do Additional Listening Activities 6-4 and 6-5, pp. 49–50
- Do Situation 6-2: Role-playing, Activities for Communication, p. 124

Homework Options
Übungsheft, pp. 75–76, Acts. 6–9

Day 9

ZWEITE STUFE
Quick Review 5 min.
- Check homework, Übungsheft, pp. 75–76, Acts. 6–9

Quiz 20 min.
- Quiz 6-2A or 6-2B

ZUM LESEN 20 min.
- Background Information, ATE, p. 147T
- Teacher Notes, ATE, p. 147U
- Present **Lesestrategie**, p. 164
- Do Activities 1–5, pp. 164–165

Wrap-Up 5 min.
- Students answer questions about their favorite fairy tales

Homework Options
Pupil's Edition, p. 165, Acts. 6–7
Übungsheft, pp. 77–78, Acts. 1–7

Day 10

ZWEITE STUFE
Quick Review 10 min.
- Return Quiz 6-2
- Check homework, Pupil's Edition, p. 165, Acts. 6–7

ZUM LESEN 15 min.
- Do Activities 8–10, p. 166

ZUM SCHREIBEN 20 min.
- Writing Strategy, ATE, p. 147V
- Present **Schreibtipp**, p. 167
- Do Activity A, p. 167

Wrap-Up 5 min.
- Students answer questions about the media that are important to them

Homework Options
Pupil's Edition, p. 167, Act. B

Day 11

ZWEITE STUFE
Quick Review
- Check homework, Pupil's Edition, p. 167, Act. B

ZUM SCHREIBEN 30 min.
- Do Activity C, p. 167
- Present compositions to class

ANWENDUNG 15 min.
- Do Activities 1–6 and 8, pp. 172–173

Wrap-Up 5 min.
- Students discuss the features in their school newspapers that they like best

Homework Options
Pupil's Edition, p. 173, Act. 7
Interaktive Spiele, ATE, p. 147E

Day 12

ANWENDUNG
Quick Review 10 min.
- Check homework, Pupil's Edition, p. 173, Act. 7

Kann ich's wirklich?, p. 174 20 min.
- Do **Kann ich's wirklich?**, Activities 1–9, p. 174

Chapter Review 20 min.
- Review chapter functions, vocabulary, and grammar; choose from **Mehr Grammatikübungen,** Activities for Communication, Listening Activities, or **Interaktive Spiele**
- Review test format and provide sample test items for students

Homework Options
Study for Chapter Test

Assessment

Test, Chapter 6 45 min.
- Administer Chapter 6 Test. Select from Testing Program, Alternative Assessment Guide or Test Generator.

Kapitel 6: Medien: stets gut informiert?
Suggested Lesson Plans 90-Minute Schedule

Block 1

CHAPTER OPENER 5 min.
- Advance Organizer, ATE, p. 147M
- Thinking Critically, ATE, p. 147M

LOS GEHT'S! 20 min.
- Preteaching Vocabulary, ATE, p. 147N
- Advance Organizer, p. 147N
- Teacher Note, p. 147N
- Play Audio CD for Los geht's!
- Have students read Los geht's!, pp. 150–151
- Do Activities 1 and 2, p. 151

ERSTE STUFE
Reading Selection, p. 152 10 min.
- Thinking Critically, p. 147O
- Read Die TV-Kids p. 152

Wortschatz, p. 152 10 min.
- Presenting Wortschatz, ATE, p. 147O
- Do Activity 3, p. 153
- Play Audio CD for Activity 4, p. 153

So sagt man das!, p. 153 20 min.
- Presenting So sagt man das!, ATE, p. 147O
- Teaching Transparency 6-1
- Play Audio CD for Activity 5, p. 153
- Do Activity 6, p. 153
- Do Activities 7 and 8, p. 154

So sagt man das!, Grammatik, pp. 154–155 20 min.
- Presenting So sagt man das!, Grammatik, ATE, p. 147P
- Do Activity 9, p. 155
- Do Activity 10, p. 156
- Do Activities 4 and 5, pp. 48–49, Grammatikheft

Wrap-Up 5 min.
- Students respond to questions about past events

Homework Options
Grammatikheft, p. 46–47, Acts. 1–3
Übungsheft, p. 66, Acts. 1–2; pp. 67–69, Acts. 1–6

Block 2

ERSTE STUFE
Quick Review 10 min.
- Check homework, Übungsheft, p. 66, Acts. 1–2; pp. 67–69, Acts. 1–6

So sagt man das!, p. 156 15 min.
- Play Audio CD for Activity 11, p. 156
- Play Audio CD for Activity 12, p. 156

LANDESKUNDE 20 min.
- Building Context, ATE, p. 147Q
- Teaching Suggestion, ATE, p. 147Q
- Read Die Schülerzeitung, p. 157
- Do Activities 1–4, p. 157

Über Kinos und Videos 15 min.
- Teaching Suggestions, Video Guide, p. 26
- Do Pre-viewing, Viewing, and Post-viewing Activities, p. 27, Video Guide
- Show Video, Über Kinos und Videos

Quiz Review 25 min.
- Do Additional Listening Activities 6-1 and 6-2, pp. 47–48
- Do Activities for Communication 6-1 and 6-2, pp. 21–22
- Do Realia 6-1, pp. 76 and 79, Activities for Communication

Wrap-Up 5 min.
- Students respond to questions about how often and which movies or videos they see

Homework Options
Grammatikheft, p. 50, Act. 6
Übungsheft, p. 70, Acts. 7–9; p. 71, Acts. 1–4
Mehr Grammatikübungen, Erste Stufe

Block 3

ERSTE STUFE
Quick Review 10 min.
- Check homework Mehr Grammatikübungen, Erste Stufe

Quiz 20 min.
- Quiz 6-1A or 6-1B

WEITER GEHT'S! 20 min.
- Present Weiter geht's!, pp. 158–159
- Play Audio CD for Weiter geht's!, pp. 158–159
- Do Activities 13 and 14, p. 159

ZWEITE STUFE
- Bell Work, p. 147R

Reading Selection, p. 160 10 min.
- Read Leserbriefe an die Redaktion der Pepo, p. 160

Wortschatz, p. 160 10 min.
- Presenting Wortschatz, ATE, p. 147R
- Do Activity 15, p. 160
- Play Audio CD for Activity 16, p. 161

So sagt man das!, p. 161 15 min.
- Presenting So sagt man das!, ATE, p. 147S
- Teaching Transparency 6-2
- Play Audio CD for Activity 17, p. 161
- Do Activity 18, p. 161
- Do Activity 10, p. 52, Grammatikheft

Wrap-Up 5 min.
- Students respond to questions about being surprised or annoyed

Homework Options
Grammatikheft, p. 51, Acts. 7–9
Übungsheft, p. 72, Acts. 1–3

One-Stop Planner CD-ROM

For alternative lesson plans by chapter section, to create your own customized plans, or to preview all resources available for this chapter, use the **One-Stop Planner CD-ROM**, Disc 2.

 For additional homework suggestions, see activities accompanied by this symbol throughout the chapter.

Block 4

ZWEITE STUFE

Quick Review 10 min.
- Return and review Quiz 6-1
- Check homework, Grammatikheft, p. 51, Acts. 7–9

Grammatik, p. 162 25 min.
- Presenting **Grammatik,** ATE, p. 147S
- Do Activity 19, p. 162
- Do Activities 20, 21, and, 22, p. 163
- Do Activity 5, p. 75, Übungsheft
- Do Activities 11, 12, and 13, pp. 53–54, Grammatikheft

Wortschatz, p. 163 15 min.
- Presenting, **Wortschatz,** ATE, p. 147S
- Do Activity 23, p. 163
- Do Activities 6–9, pp. 75–76, Übungsheft

Quiz Review 20 min.
- **Mehr Grammatikübungen, Zweite Stufe**
- Do Communicative Activities 6-3 and 6-4, pp. 23–24
- Do Additional Listening Activities 6-4 and 6-5, pp. 49–50

Quiz 20 min.
- Quiz 6-2A or 6-2B

Homework Options
Internet Aktivitäten, ATE, p. 147E

Block 5

ZWEITE STUFE

Quick Review 10 min.
- Return and review Quiz 6-2

ZUM LESEN 35 min.
- Background Information, ATE, p. 147P
- Teacher Notes, ATE, p. 147U
- Present **Lesestrategie,** p. 164
- Do Activities 1–10, pp. 164–166

ZUM SCHREIBEN 40 min.
- Writing Strategy, ATE, p. 147V
- Present **Schreibtipp,** p. 167
- Do Activities A, B and C, p. 167

Wrap-Up 5 min.
- Students answer questions about their favorite fairy tales

Homework Options
Activities for Communication, pp. 77 and 79–80, Realia 6-2; list information included on advertisement
Interaktive Spiele, ATE, p. 147E

Block 6

ANWENDUNG

Quick Review 35 min.
- Check homework, Realia 6-2
- Do Activities 1–8, pp. 172–173

Project 50 min.
- Do Newspaper Project, ATE, p. 147C

Wrap-Up 5 min.
- Students answer questions about their favorite media

Homework Options
Pupil's Edition, p. 174, **Kann ich's wirklich?** Activities 1–5, Study for Chapter Test

Block 7

ANWENDUNG

Quick Review 15 min.
- Pupil's Edition, p. 174, Activities 1–5

Chapter Review 30 min.
- Review chapter functions, vocabulary, and grammar; choose from **Mehr Grammatikübungen,** Activities for Communication, Listening Activities, or **Interaktive Spiele**
- Review test format and provide sample test items for students

Test, Chapter 6 45 min.
- Administer Chapter 6 Test. Select from Testing Program, Alternative Assessment Guide or Test Generator.

Kapitel 6: Medien: stets gut informiert?
Teaching Suggestions, pages 148–175

Before you begin the chapter, you may want to preview the *Video Program* and consult the *Video Guide.* Suggestions for integrating the video into each chapter are given in the *Video Guide.* Activity masters for video selections can be found in the *Video Guide.*

One-Stop Planner CD-ROM

For resource information, see the **One-Stop Planner CD-ROM**, Disc 2.

Advance Organizer

Ask students how they usually get their news information. Do they prefer radio, television, the Internet, or newspapers and magazines? Take a survey of the students' preferences.

PAGES 148–149

CHAPTER OPENER

Pacing Tips

The **Erste Stufe** centers around functions used in a discussion or debate. A presentation of the narrative past (imperfect) occurs on pp. 154–155. The **Zweite Stufe** introduces the function of 'expressing surprise and annoyance.' Students learn to make superlative forms of adjectives on p. 162. Most likely, you will have to spend the same amount of time on both **Stufen.** The **Zum Lesen** reading on pp. 164–166 is "Rumpelstilzchen" by Jakob and Wilhelm Grimm. For Lesson Plans and timing suggestions, see pages 147I–147L.

Meeting the Standards
Communication
- Asking someone to take a position; Asking for reasons; Expressing opinions, p. 153
- Reporting past events, p. 154
- Changing the subject; Interrupting, p. 156
- Expressing surprise or annoyance, p. 161

Cultures
- **Landeskunde,** p. 157
- Teacher Note, p. 147N
- Culture Note, p. 147P

Connections
- Journalism Connection, p. 147M
- Music Connection, p. 147P
- Multicultural Connection, p. 147P

Comparisons
- Language-to-Language, p. 147S
- Language-to-Language, p. 147U

Communities
- Community Link, p. 119C
- Career Path, p. 119S

Connections and Comparisons

Journalism Connection
Ask students about their school's newspaper. What is its name, how often is it published, and what type of information does it provide for the student body?

Thinking Critically
Comparing and Contrasting Have students research several different newspapers and/or news magazines and find an event that was covered by all of them. Have them read each article carefully and find similarities and differences in the coverage in each one. Can students draw conclusions about the way news events are treated in each of the publications? (Vergleicht den Bericht in … mit dem Bericht in … In welcher Hinsicht sind sich die Berichte ähnlich? In welcher Hinsicht sind sie verschieden? In welchem Artikel sind die Tatsachen am sachlichsten dargestellt? Was scheint die Absicht jedes Artikels zu sein?)

LOS GEHT'S!

Teaching Resources
pp. 150–151

PRINT
▸ Lesson Planner, p. 36
▸ Übungsheft, p. 66

MEDIA
▸ One-Stop Planner
▸ Audio Compact Discs, CD6, Tr. 1

> **PAGES 150–151**

Los geht's! Summary

In *Die Macht der Medien,* some students talk about the German media and discuss how they prefer to inform themselves about what is happening in the world. The following learning outcomes listed on p. 149 are modeled in the conversation: asking someone to take a position, asking for reasons, expressing opinions, reporting past events, agreeing or disagreeing, changing the subject, and interrupting.

Preteaching Vocabulary

Guessing Words from Context

Have students skim **Los geht's!** for general meaning, and ask them what the teens are discussing (different types of news media). Then have students scan for cognates that are new to them. After students have a good idea of what **Los geht's!** is about, have them list sentences that are used as connectors or commentary in the conversation, apart from the actual information that is being discussed. Students can then guess the function of the sentences they listed. Then have students use contextual clues to guess the meaning of the phrases. Some of the phrases they might select are: Moment mal, Christof! Lass mich auch mal zu Wort kommen! / Mensch, lass die Nicole mal ausreden! / Komm, Ralf, nicht gleich persönlich werden! / Na, okay. War nur Spaß. Mach weiter! / Wer nimmt mal dazu Stellung? / Kannst du das begründen? / Da ist schon was dran.

Advance Organizer

Take a brief survey in class to find out how many hours per day students spend a) reading newspapers or magazines, b) watching news on TV, and c) listening to news on the radio. (Wie viel Zeit pro Tag verbringt ihr mit a) Zeitung oder Zeitschrift lesen? b) Nachrichten im Fernsehen sehen? c) Nachrichten im Radio hören?)

Cultures and Communities

Language Note

Nicole makes a reference to a particular newspaper using the acronym **SZ.** It stands for *Süddeutsche Zeitung,* which is published in Munich.

Teacher Note

Newspapers like *Bild* and *Bild am Sonntag* are the largest circulating papers in Germany. They are quite sensational. Some of the newspapers that offer extensive coverage of national and international news, business, and the arts are *Die Zeit, Frankfurter Allgemeine Zeitung,* and the *Süddeutsche Zeitung. Der Spiegel* and *Focus* are the leading news magazines. Several **Programmzeitschriften** have information about TV and radio programming, articles about celebrities, and various other features.

Comprehension Check

Cooperative Learning

1 Have students do this activity in cooperative groups. Ask one student to be the recorder and have the rest of the group scan the text to fill in each of the three columns. Call on the reporters of each group to give their findings as you check responses for each of the types of media.

Teaching Suggestion

2 Have pairs of students take turns asking each other the three questions. Then call on students to find out what their partners said.

Visual Learners

If possible, bring in newspapers and magazines from German-speaking countries. Have students work in groups to determine what sections the papers contain and report on one article in a section of their choice.

Career Path

Have students think of reasons why an American journalist might need to know German. (Suggestion: Imagine you are an American employee of an English-language newspaper in Graz, Austria, and need to gather information from local sources.)

Closure

Ask students to review the **Los geht's!** conversation and decide with whose opinion they most identify.

Teaching Resources
pp. 152–157

PRINT
- Lesson Planner, p. 37
- Listening Activities, pp. 43–44, 47–48
- Video Guide, pp. 25–27
- Activities for Communication, pp. 21–22, 76–77, 79–80, 123–124
- Grammatikheft, pp. 46–50
- Grammar Tutor for Students of German, Chapter 6
- Übungsheft, pp. 67–71
- Testing Program, pp. 111–114
- Alternative Assessment Guide, p. 35
- Student Make-Up Assignments, Chapter 6

MEDIA
- One-Stop Planner
- Audio Compact Discs, CD6, Trs. 2–4, 12, 21–23
- Video Program
  Über Kinos und Videos
  Videocassette 1, 49:03–51:40
- Teaching Transparencies
  Situation 6-1
  Mehr Grammatikübungen Answers
  Grammatikheft Answers

PAGE 152

Bell Work
Survey students to find out about their reading habits. Ask them what other things they usually read besides what is required for school. Find out how much time they take to read for pleasure.

Using the Video

Videocassette 1, 49:03–51:40
In the video clip *Über Kinos und Videos,* young people in Würzburg talk about their preferences as to where they like to watch movies—on the big screen in a movie theater or at home, using a rental in their VCR. See *Video Guide,* p. 26, for suggestions.

PRESENTING: Wortschatz

Go over the new vocabulary with students. Then ask them to use at least three of the new words or phrases in sentences of their own.

Communication for All Students

Challenge
Have pairs or small groups of students read "Die TV-Kids" and give several reasons for calling the students in the survey "TV-Kids."

Connections and Comparisons

Thinking Critically
Analyzing Have students look at the six slogans about TV and decide which of them are positive statements and which are negative. Then have small groups of students look more closely at one of the six slogans and discuss possible reasons for the statement. One student should take notes for each group and share the outcome of their discussion with the rest of the class.

Comparing and Contrasting Ask students to find recent statistics on the television viewing habits of young Americans aged 11–13, and then compare their findings with those in the German survey.

Language Note
The word **Glotze** in the **Wortschatz** is a colloquial word referring to the television. An English equivalent to **die Glotze** might be *the tube.*

Teaching Suggestion
Have students group the new vocabulary under headings, such as **Zeitung** or **Fernsehen,** or build "webs" with one of these key words in the center.

PAGE 153

Teaching Suggestions

3 Use these questions to involve all students in a class discussion. One student can read each question to the rest of the class and another can initiate the discussion by giving his or her opinion.

- For part 3 of this activity, have students make their **positiv** and **negativ** list on butcher paper or on the chalkboard.

PRESENTING: So sagt man das!

- Before you introduce these new expressions, review similar expressions students have already learned. Examples:

Wie findest du …?	Ich glaube, …
Wofür bist du?	Ich meine, …
Was hält sie von …?	
Was denkst du über …?	

> **PAGE 154**

- After presenting the new phrases, have students review the **Los geht's!** interview and give the contexts in which the new expressions are used.

Communication for All Students

A Slower Pace

7 Review with students the various types of media that are available to them. Students may then refer to this list during the interview with their partner and for the group interview as well.

PRESENTING: So sagt man das!

Students have seen the narrative past tense in previous reading selections. Have them first read the narrative for general comprehension and then find all the past tense forms.

> **PAGE 155**

PRESENTING: Grammatik

Narrative past Present the three types of verbs to students: weak verbs, strong verbs, and hybrids. Each time, ask students to identify the critical element that makes the verb form a past tense form. Follow with some application exercises. For weak verbs, present other examples to check whether students understand the pattern. For strong verbs, give several additional examples that follow the same pattern to see if students can guess what the past tense will be. Examples:

geben —> gab; sehen —>?; essen —>?
finden —> fand; singen —>?; trinken —>?
fahren —> fuhr; tragen —>?; einladen —>?

Connections and Comparisons

Music Connection

Refer students to the text of the poem *Das Heidenröslein,* Level 1 *Listening Activities,* p. 94, for additional reading. Ask them to circle the narrative past forms they find. You may also want to play the song, Level 1 CD 12, Track 34.

Teaching Suggestions

- Ask students to look back at the text in **So sagt man das!** on p. 154. Have them name all the verbs in the narrative past. Where appropriate, have students give the corresponding forms of the conversational past. This exercise will show students how awkward and cumbersome the conversational past is in comparison to the imperfect for relating past events in a narrative.

9 This activity could be done orally in class and then as a written assignment for homework.

> **PAGE 156**

Cultures and Communities

Culture Note

10 While cable television, VCRs, CD players, and home computers are becoming more widespread in Germany, they are not yet quite as common as they are in the United States. The **Mehrwertsteuer** *(value added tax)* and the smaller German market with less competition are two facts that make these items and services less affordable than comparable products in the United States.

Connections and Comparisons

Multicultural Connection

10 Have students use the format of this survey to interview someone from another country who might be familiar with the use of this equipment. Have them report their findings to the class.

LANDESKUNDE

Building Context

Ask students about their own school newspaper. Do they know students who are involved in producing the paper? Do they read the paper? What do they like or not like about it?

Teaching Suggestion

The **Landeskunde** article has three parts. Although entitled "**Die Schülerzeitung**," it also deals with student government in general and with student government at a specific high school in particular. To begin, read each section to the class and follow up with comprehension questions. Then have students work in pairs or small groups and do the same: read the text aloud, generate some questions, and respond to them. Finally, pairs or groups should answer Questions 1, 2, and 3. Have students share their responses with the class.

Teacher Note

Mention to your students that the **Landeskunde** will also be included in Quiz 6-1B given at the end of the **Erste Stufe**.

Teaching Suggestion

Give students a few moments to think about what they would do with their time if they did not have access to television, VCR, radio, or the Internet for a whole week. (**Wenn du eine Woche lang ohne Fernsehen, Videorekorder, Radio, oder Internet wärst, was würdest du machen?**)

Assess
▶ Testing Program, pp. 111–114
  Quiz 6-1A, Quiz 6-1B
  Audio CD6, Tr. 12

▶ Student Make-Up Assignments
  Chapter 6, Alternative Quiz

▶ Alternative Assessment Guide, p. 35

WEITER GEHT'S!

Teaching Resources
pp. 158–159

PRINT
▶ Lesson Planner, p. 38
▶ Übungsheft, p. 72

MEDIA
▶ One-Stop Planner
▶ Audio Compact Discs, CD6, Trs. 5–7

Weiter geht's! Summary

In *Unsere eigene Zeitung!,* some students talk about their involvement in the school newspaper and present an interview with representatives of the student government. The following learning outcome is modeled in the conversations: expressing surprise or annoyance.

Preteaching Vocabulary

Guessing Words from Context

Have students skim **Weiter geht's!** for general meaning, and ask them what the teens are discussing (their school newspaper). Then have students scan for cognates that are new to them. After students have a good idea of what **Weiter geht's!** is about, have them use contextual clues to find phrases that express surprise, annoyance, or agreement. Some of the phrases they might select are: **Es ist unglaublich … / Da stimm ich dem Guido zu. / Es überrascht mich, … / Was mich stört ist, … / Und ich werde sauer, … / … das ist frustrierend. / Das find ich auch. / Mich hat gestört, …**

Advance Organizer

Briefly discuss the student government in your school. How is it set up? What is the function of the student government? (**Wie funktioniert die Schülervertretung an dieser Schule? Wie kann man Vertreter werden? Wozu gibt es eine Schülervertretung?**)

Cultures and Communities

Background Information

Student government is a tradition in German schools that is supported by faculty and administration, as well as the students, who can participate starting in the 5th grade.

Cultures and Communities

continued from p. 147Q

Each class chooses a **Klassensprecher** and a **Klassensprechervertreter** *(alternate)* who meet regularly with the **Schülervertretung** to discuss questions and problems of the student body. The student government elects an advisor from the faculty who serves as the liaison between faculty, parents, school administration, and student government.

Teaching Suggestion

Play the first part of *Unsere eigene Zeitung!* and have students follow along in the text. Stop at strategic points and ask comprehension questions and clarify new words and expressions using synonyms and paraphrasing. At the end, play the whole conversation again.

Teacher Note

The **Weiter geht's!** text lends itself well to the review of the word order in dependent clauses.

Communication for All Students

A Slower Pace

13 Ask students to work in pairs or groups of three to create a chart with three columns summarizing the statements made by Guido, Rainer, and Natalie. In addition, ask them to elaborate on the function of the **SV** by noting its specific tasks. You may want to collect each group's notes to check for completion or to assign a grade.

A Slower Pace

14 Explain to students that **Redemittel** refers to functional expressions and, on a transparency, give several examples from the text. Ask students to give you the function or purpose of each of the expressions you picked out. Then put students in pairs and have them scan the text for all the other functional expressions used and, in each case, give the purpose for which the speaker uses it.

Closure

Based on what they read in the **Landeskunde** section on p. 157 and the **Weiter geht's!** interview on pp. 158–159, ask students to compare their own school paper and student council to the way they are organized in German schools. (**Vergleicht die Schülerzeitung und die Schülervertretung an unserer Schule mit denen an deutschen Schulen.**)

ZWEITE STUFE

Teaching Resources
pp. 160–163

PRINT
- Lesson Planner, p. 39
- Listening Activities, pp. 45, 49–50
- Activities for Communication, pp. 23–24, 78, 80, 123–124
- Grammatikheft, pp. 51–54
- Grammar Tutor for Students of German, Chapter 6
- Übungsheft, pp. 73–76
- Testing Program, pp. 115–118
- Alternative Assessment Guide, p. 35
- Student Make-Up Assignments, Chapter 6

MEDIA
- One-Stop Planner
- Audio Compact Discs, CD6, Trs. 8–9, 13, 24–26
- Teaching Transparencies Situation 6-2
  Mehr Grammatikübungen Answers
  Grammatikheft Answers

PAGE 160

Bell Work

Ask students about the strengths and weaknesses of their school paper. What would they like eliminated and what are some items they would like to have added? (**Wie findet ihr unsere Schülerzeitung? Was gefällt euch an der Zeitung und was nicht? Was würdet ihr darin gern lesen, was es bis jetzt noch nicht gibt?**)

Communication for All Students

Challenge

After students have read the four letters to the editor, ask them to state the key idea in each in their own words. This can be done orally or in writing.

PRESENTING: Wortschatz

Go over the new vocabulary with your students. Then ask students to think of a situation in which they might overhear a particular phrase or statement from this **Wortschatz**.

Connections and Comparisons

Language-to-Language

You may want to tell your students that the German phrase **Das macht mir nichts aus** is constructed similarly to the French phrase **Ça ne me fait rien.**

PAGE 161

Teaching Suggestion

16 Ask students to go back to **Landeskunde** on p. 157 and review the different tasks involved in publishing a school paper.

PRESENTING: So sagt man das!

Introduce the new expressions. Then provide students with practice by writing the boldface part of each sentence on a transparency or on the board and having students complete the sentences using different contexts.
Examples:
Es ist unglaublich, …
… überrascht mich.
Ich bin überrascht, …

Teaching Suggestion

18 These statements could be used as a basis for brief discussions. Students could react using one of the given phrases and then continue with a thought or two of their own.

PAGE 162

PRESENTING: Grammatik

Superlative forms of adjectives Remind students that adjectives enable them to express various levels of quality and degree. Students learned about the comparative forms of adjectives in Level 2 (Ch. 7). The third and last of these forms is the superlative. To practice and review these adjective forms, ask students questions such as the ones listed below:
Sag mal, was du gern isst!
Was isst du denn noch lieber?
Und was isst du am liebsten?

For Additional Practice

Point out various items in the classroom that lend themselves to comparison and have students compare them. For example, you could show students three pieces of chalk: a short one, a shorter one, and one that is even shorter than the other two and say: **Das Stück Kreide hier ist kurz. Das Stück da ist kürzer. Das Stück dort ist am kürzesten.**

PAGE 163

Teacher Note

20 You might want to point out to students that the form of **dies-** in each sentence signals the gender and number of the noun.

Teaching Suggestion

22 You could prepare a list of topics to help students with this activity.
Examples:

Footballmannschaft	Bücherei
Orchester	Schülerzeitung
Lehrer	Schülervertretung
Cafeteriaessen	

To extend the activity, have students give one reason to support each of their claims.

Total Physical Response

Bring a newspaper to class. If possible, make transparencies of some of the pages, such as the front page or the weather report. Give students commands such as the following:
Zeig mir die Stadt, wo das Wetter am wärmsten/ kältesten ist!
Zeig auf eine Schlagzeile über einen Autounfall!
Zeig auf die letzten Nachrichten aus dem Gebiet Schulsport!

PRESENTING: Wortschatz

Introduce the words of quantity by talking about students in German class in general terms based on what you know about them.
Examples:
Alle Schüler in dieser Klasse lernen Deutsch.
Viele machen nach der Schule Sport.
Einige spielen …

Reteaching: Superlative forms

Ask students to create an original poster illustrating superlative forms of adjectives. For example, they could show three generations of a family to illustrate the three degrees of quality using the adjective **alt.**

Visual Learners

Write a description of a fictitious person with as many positive, comparative, and superlative adjectives as possible. Read the description to the class and have students draw the person. Let them compare their drawings.

Writing Assessment

You may choose to collect the above activity and evaluate the students' written work using the following rubric.

Writing Rubric	Points			
	4	3	2	1
Content (Complete – Incomplete)				
Comprehensibility (Comprehensible – Seldom comprehensible)				
Accuracy (Accurate – Seldom accurate)				
Organization (Well-organized – Poorly organized)				
Effort (Excellent – Minimal)				

18–20: A   16–17: B   14–15: C   12–13: D   Under 12: F

Von der Schule zum Beruf

Before beginning this activity, you might bring several newspapers to class and have students identify and classify the type of information available.

Assess

▶ Testing Program, pp. 115–118
  Quiz 6-2A, Quiz 6-2B
  Audio CD6, Tr. 13

▶ Student Make-Up Assignments
  Chapter 6, Alternative Quiz

▶ Alternative Assessment Guide, p. 35

ZUM LESEN

Teaching Resources
pp. 164–166

PRINT

▶ Lesson Planner, p. 40
▶ Übungsheft, pp. 77–78
▶ Reading Strategies and Skills, Chapter 6
▶ Lies mit mir! 3, Chapter 6

MEDIA

▶ One-Stop Planner
▶ Audio, CD6, Tr.10

Prereading
Building Context

After reading some German short stories and poetry in the original, discussing the following questions may be of interest: Is there any particularly "German" literary form? Or is it more accurate to speak of "literature in the German language?" Is there any particular subject matter that seems to be typically German? How do they suppose the Nazis decided what to accept as "pure German" literature? The reading selection in this chapter has often been identified as being of a type that is "typically German."

Cultures and Communities

Background Information

As early as the 1770s, J. G. Herder had drawn attention to folklore and myth as "primitive poetry" and inspired young German writers (including Goethe) to seek out "Germanic" sources, i.e. those not influenced by Latin or French literary traditions. The brothers Grimm—Jakob (1785–1863) and Wilhelm (1786–1859)—brought to this trend their own background in linguistics, particularly in Indo-European studies, and a conviction that European folk tales were descended from a common Indo-European mythology. Since their methods of gathering folk tales were not what modern anthropologists would consider "scientific," they saw no harm in mixing educated and uneducated sources and then doing a little polishing and ghost-writing of their own in the two-volume *Kinderund Hausmärchen* (1812; 1815).

Connections and Comparisons

Language-to-Language

You may want to tell your students that the German term **Märchen** is a diminutive of the Middle High German **Märe** *(news)*. **Märchen** are characterized by elements of magic or the supernatural. They usually begin with a formula such as *once upon a time.* Their usual theme is the triumph over difficulties, usually by the one person who is the least likely to succeed. The characters are stylized. The hero, however poor and destitute, has easy access to the king and often wins the king's daughter in marriage and inherits the kingdom.

You may want to ask your students to describe stock characters in some of the **Märchen** they know. (Examples: wicked stepmothers, ogres, handsome princes, peasants, artisans)

Reading
Teacher Notes

Rumpelstilzchen is a complex tale that includes at least three separate motifs:

- the impossible task (similar to slaying a dragon or finding a strange and unique item like the golden apples of the Hesperides),

- the lightly-given promise (compare the princess's promises in the "Frog Prince" story), and

- name-guessing, which has a superficial resemblance to the riddle motif in folklore (compare the episode of the Sphinx in the Oedipus story), but derives from an older layer of folklore in which knowledge of someone's name conferred power over that individual.

2 In other literatures, "once upon a time," can be "long, long ago," or "long ago in a faraway place," or "in the days of X."

6 Students will probably guess accurately that the king's demands will come in a sequence of three. They might be interested to know that not all world literatures agree upon 3 as the "magic number." In much Native American lore, the number 4 is crucial.

Thinking Critically

Analyzing This story will probably seem very simple and "artless" to students at first reading, partly because they are so familiar with its general form from their childhood. A closer look at how it is put together, especially the details, may show them that only a very experienced storyteller or talented writer would come up with exactly this version. For example, they should look at the sets of names that the young woman offers near the end of the story. What must have been the source for the first set? What were the three men with those names famous for? (**Kaspar, Melchior,** and **Balzer** are versions of the names of the three kings from the Orient who brought fabulous gifts to the infant Jesus. These are not common names in Germany.) In the second set, what do the compound names actually mean? What kind of person do they suggest? (**Rippenbiest:** *rib-brute,* **Hammelswade:** *mutton-leg,* and **Schnürbein:** *cord-leg,* are ugly and dehumanizing names.) If students know that **Hinz und Kunz** in the third set is the common German expression for "Tom, Dick and Harry" (i.e. any nondescript group of fellows), can they see how the young woman is teasing? Finally, what could **Rumpelstilzchen** mean? (Have students look up **Rumpel:** *rumbling.* **Stilzchen** might be the diminutive of **Stelz,** which means *stilt,* or *peg-leg.*) Does the combination conjure up any mental pictures of this character? (Think again about the scene in which the messenger observes him hopping around the fire.) Is the manner of his demise fitting?

Post-Reading
Teacher Note

Activities 9 and 10 are post-reading tasks that will show whether students can apply what they have learned.

Closure

In contrast to fables, which usually have a moral, or myths, which attempt to explain some aspect of the natural world, **Märchen** use magical elements to exploit some of our most common human fears—of being orphaned, lost, threatened by monsters, and of things that go bump in the night. Aside from the happy ending, which is by no means guaranteed in Grimms' tales, how would students compare *Rumpelstilzchen* with the Kafka short story that they read in Chapter 1? Are the characters any more or less individual? Are the events any more or less unbelievable? Are students any more or less interested in the outcome?

Zum Lesen Answers

Answers to Activity 1
Rumpelstilzchen, der Müller, seine Tochter, der König

Answers to Activity 2
Once upon a time …; fairy tales; as with other Grimm fairy tales, the exact time and place are left undetermined, emphasizing the fantastic quality of the events; however, students could give answers such as in medieval times or in a kingdom somewhere in Germany.

Answers to Activity 3
She must turn a room full of straw into gold by morning. **Rumpelstilzchen** will spin the straw into gold in return for her necklace.

Answers to Activity 4
Answers will vary.

Answers to Activity 5
Answers will vary.

Answers to Activity 6
Time lines should include the three visits from **Rumpelstilzchen** to spin the gold and his three visits to the queen to let her guess his name.

Answers to Activity 7
a. **es traf sich** *es ist passiert;* **die Kammer** *das Zimmer;* **das Männlein** *der kleine Mann;* **die Jungfer** *das Fräulein;* **das Rädchen** *das kleine Spinnrad;* **um das Leben keinen Rat wissen** *nicht wissen, was man tun soll*
b. **Schnurr** is the sound of the spinning wheel. The naming of a thing or action by an imitation of the sound associated with it is called onomatopoeia.

Answers to Activity 8
a. **er:** der Müller; **ihm:** dem König; **ihm:** dem König; **er:** der König; **es:** das Mädchen; **es:** das Männlein (Rumpelstilzchen)
b. **darin** translates as *in it.* It refers back to **die Kammer; davon:** a **da**-compound is used because the object of **von** here is a clause: **wie man Stroh zu Gold spinnen konnte.**

ZUM SCHREIBEN

Teaching Resources
p. 167

PRINT
▸ Lesson Planner, p. 40
▸ Alternative Assessment Guide, p. 21

MEDIA
▸ One-Stop Planner
▸ Test Generator, Chapter 6

Writing Strategy

The targeted strategy in this writing activity is *using an outline.* Students should learn about this strategy before beginning the assignment.

Prewriting
Building Context

Ask students to think of an issue that they recently discussed with their parents, one where the parents disagreed and they had to support their point of view with detailed information. Then ask students how their arguments would have been different had they had to do it in writing.

Teaching Suggestion
A2 If students are unsure about an appropriate subject, brainstorm with the class and make a list of possible topics.

Writing

Communication for All Students

A Slower Pace
B Have students recall the various phrases they have learned to express opinions. Review these phrases and, if necessary, compile a list to which students can refer as they write their essays.

Post-Writing
Teaching Suggestion

C1 If several students in the class write about similar issues from opposite points of view, you might want to assign them to work together so that they can play devil's advocate for each other during the revising phase.

Closure

Have students with opposing essays read them to the class. Afterwards, the other students can debate the subject, deciding with which position they most agree and why.

PAGES 168–171

MEHR GRAMMATIKÜBUNGEN

The **Mehr Grammatikübungen** activities are designed as supplemental activities for the grammatical concepts presented in the chapter. You might use them as additional practice, for review, or for assessment.

For more grammar presentations, review, and practice, refer to the following:
- Grammatikheft
- Grammar Tutor for Students of German
- Grammar Summary on pp. R22–R39
- Übungsheft
- Grammar and Vocabulary quizzes (Testing Program)
- Test Generator
- **Interaktive Spiele** at go.hrw.com

PAGES 172–173

ANWENDUNG

Apply and Assess

Using the Video

Videocassette 1, 51:46–54:20
At this time, you might want to use the authentic advertising footage from German television. See *Video Guide*, p. 26, for suggestions.

Comparing and Contrasting

1 Ask students to compare these suggestions for a school paper with the one published at their own school. Have several copies of a recent issue of the paper in your classroom and ask students to make an outline in German of the different features that are contained in that paper. (**Vergleicht den Aufbau und Inhalt unserer Schülerzeitung mit den Vorschlägen für die deutsche Schülerzeitung! Fehlt etwas in unserer Schülerzeitung? Gibt es etwas, was wir haben, aber was nicht in den Vorschlägen für die deutsche Schülerzeitung erwähnt wurde?**)

Teaching Suggestion

3 This activity could be done orally with a partner in class and then assigned as written homework.

Group Work

5 This project could be shared with other German classes. Students of all levels could contribute features, such as articles, cartoons, jokes, and reviews of books, movies, or TV shows.

Teaching Suggestion

8 Put all the questions on a form labeled "**Umfrage über Medienbenutzung**" with enough space between the questions to record the answers. There should also be a line on the bottom to write in the name of the **Reporter** and the **Befragte(r)**. Give each student an interview form and have them interview one of their classmates. Collect all forms and summarize the results of each question. Give the summary to students and have them discuss the findings in small groups or as a class.

 Portfolio Assessment

8 You might want to suggest this activity as a written and oral portfolio item for your students. See *Alternative Assessment Guide*, p. 21.

PAGE 174

KANN ICH'S WIRKLICH?

This page helps students prepare for the test. It is a brief checklist of the major points covered in the chapter. The students should be reminded that it is only a checklist and not necessarily everything that will appear on the test.

For additional self check options, refer students to the *Grammar Tutor* and the Online self-test for this chapter.

PAGE 175

WORTSCHATZ

Challenge

Ask students to categorize the verbs in the **Wortschatz** under the following headings: Reflexive; Separable Prefix; Stem-Vowel Change; Used with a Preposition. Some verbs will appear under several headings. Have students use each verb in a sentence orally or in writing.

For Additional Practice

Ask students to bring several eye-catching headlines from newspapers to class. Have them use the vocabulary from Chapter 6 to write their own humorous story to fit the headline.

 Circumlocution

Play **Das treffende Wort suchen** to review the **Erste Stufe** vocabulary. Your students have been invited to work as guest editors on a German student newspaper. They discuss the coming edition of the paper with their colleagues, but have forgotten some of the necessary vocabulary and need to describe the terms they want to use. For example, for Drucker, they might say: **Wie heißt die Maschine, die produziert, was ich auf dem Computer geschrieben habe?** See p. 31C for procedures.

Teaching Suggestion

Ask students to explain the difference between the following word pairs:
der Bericht / die Schlagzeile
vermissen / weglassen
Schülervertretung / Schulleitung

 Game

Play the game **Eine unmögliche Geschichte aus dem Schuhkarton** using the vocabulary from this and previous chapters. See p. 147C for the procedure.

Teacher Note

• Give the **Kapitel 6** Chapter Test:
Testing Program, pp. 119–124
Audio CD 6, Trs. 14–16.

• Give the Midterm Exam:
Testing Program, pp. 133–140
Audio CD 6, Trs. 17–20.

6

Medien: stets gut informiert?

Objectives

In this chapter you will learn to

Erste Stufe

- ask someone to take a position
- ask for reasons
- express opinions
- report past events
- agree or disagree
- change the subject
- interrupt

Zweite Stufe

- express surprise or annoyance

internet

go.
hrw
.com

ADRESSE: go.hrw.com
KENNWORT: WK3
WUERZBURG-6

◀ **Wir sind gut informiert. Auch in der Schule.**

Los geht's! · *Die Macht der Medien*

Hier ist ein Ausschnitt aus einer Diskussion von Schülern einer 10. Klasse zum Thema „Medien."

Wie informiert ihr euch? Durch welche Medien erfahrt ihr, was in der Welt passiert?

Sandra: Ja, durch Zeitung, Radio, Fernsehen und Internet.

Christof: Im Radio hört man meistens die Nachrichten; die kommen ja alle halbe Stunden. Und das Radio informiert eben am schnellsten über Neuigkeiten und wichtige Ereignisse.

Frank: Is' doch Quatsch! Solche Informationen bekommst du im Fernsehen oder im Netz genau so schnell!

Christof: Aber nicht, wenn du im Auto unterwegs bist, oder wenn du …

Nicole: Moment mal, Christof! Lass mich auch mal zu Wort kommen!

Christof: Entschuldigung!

Nicole: Also, ich bekomm meine Information meistens aus der Zeitung. Ich blättere alles mal durch, und was mich dann anspricht, das les ich halt.

Frank: Viele Leute lesen nur die Sensationspresse und oft nur die Schlagzeilen.

Nicole: Ja schon, aber wenn man eine seriöse Tageszeitung liest, die Stuttgarter Nachrichten vielleicht oder sogar die SZ, da muss …

Alex: Die liest du doch gar nicht! Das ist …

Christof: Mensch, lass die Nicole mal ausreden!

Subject:

To: Frank@mail.net
From: Christof@email.com
cc:

Lieber Frank:
Erinnerst du dich noch an unsere Debatte über die Macht der
Medien? – Nun, ich bin gerade in den USA angekommen, und was
glaubst du, woher ich meine Info über Deutschland bekomme?
Nicht vom Radio und auch nicht im Fernsehen. Aus dem Internet!
Und stell dir vor, ich kann schon gegen 17 Uhr die deutsche
Presse vom nächsten Tag lesen! Ich lese also doch die Zeitung –
aber im Netz. Schick mir eine E-Mail!

Christof

Nicole: Ja, wo war ich? Ach ja, wenn man so eine Zeitung liest, wie die Süddeutsche Zeitung vielleicht, da muss man sich schon aussuchen, was man lesen will. Da ist einfach zu viel da.

Christof: Eben! Aber ich möcht noch mal auf die anderen Medien zurückkommen, aufs Fernsehen zum Beispiel.

Frank: Richtig! Ich finde nämlich Zeitunglesen langweilig.

Ralf: Ja, weil Zeitunglesen für dich zu anstrengend ist. Du sitzt lieber vor der Glotze!

Martina: Komm, Ralf, nicht gleich persönlich werden!

Ralf: Na, okay. War nur Spaß. Mach weiter!

Frank: Also, ich zum Beispiel bekomm meine Information hauptsächlich durchs Fernsehen. Man kann sich alles viel besser vorstellen als beim Zeitunglesen. Und meiner Meinung nach trägt das Fernsehen am meisten zur Bildung einer eigenen Meinung bei.

Christof: Das ist doch alles Quatsch, was du da sagst! Beim Fernsehen bekommst du kurze, oberflächliche Berichte, und du erfährst nur das, was die Redakteure für wichtig halten. Deine Meinung wird also nur durch die Berichte und Bilder geformt, die gezeigt werden, und durch das, was weggelassen wird.

Frank: Na ja, eine Zeitung beeinflusst die Leser auch.

Christof: Ja, schon. Aber eine Zeitung kann viel mehr bringen; sie kann auch gründlicher berichten. Du bekommst eher das gesamte Bild sozusagen: Tatsachen, Einzelheiten, Hintergrund und auch Kommentare.

Natalie: Jetzt haben wir zwei verschiedene Meinungen gegenüberstehen. Wer nimmt mal dazu Stellung?

Sandra: Ich finde, die Zeitung regt mehr zum Nachdenken an.

Nicole: Meiner Meinung nach eignet sich das Fernsehen am besten zur Unterhaltung und Entspannung. Die Presse, das Radio und das Internet informieren besser.

Frank: Kannst du das begründen?

Nicole: Ja, vielleicht so: Da gab's vor ein paar Jahren mal einen Druckerstreik, und viele Bundesbürger fanden sich nicht richtig informiert. Sie vermissten besonders die Lokalnachrichten und die Annoncen der örtlichen Geschäfte, die ja durchs Fernsehen nicht gesendet werden.

Frank: Da ist schon was dran. Aber andererseits: Möchtest du ohne Fernseher oder Computer sein? Ich nicht.

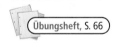

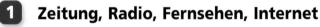

1 **Zeitung, Radio, Fernsehen, Internet**

Schreiben Was haben die Schüler über die verschiedenen Medien gesagt? Mach eine Liste mit vier Spalten: Zeitung, Radio, Fernsehen, Internet! Schreib in Stichworten auf, was die Schüler gesagt haben!

2 **Wie sieht's bei dir aus?**

Sprechen/Schreiben Beantworte die folgenden Fragen.

1. Welche Medien gebrauchst du am meisten? Gib Gründe dafür an!
2. Welche Teile der Tageszeitung interessieren dich am meisten?
3. Welche Radiosender hörst du am meisten? Warum?

Fernsehen verdrängt den Konsum von Büchern, Zeitungen und Zeitschriften.

Fernsehen entspannt.

Das Fernsehen ist ein Fenster zur Welt.

Fernsehen bildet.

FERNSEHEN MACHT BLÖD.

Fernsehen macht Kinder aggressiv.

Die TV-Kids

Das TV-Leben der 6b des Münchner Erasmus-Grasser-Gymnasiums (fünf Mädchen, neunzehn Jungen zwischen elf und dreizehn Jahren): Nur ein Schüler ohne TV-Gerät, sechs mit eigenem Fernseher, sechzehn mit Kabelanschluß. 50 Prozent sahen den Prügelstreifen „Rambo", 40 Prozent kannten den Horrorfilm „Alien". TV-Konsum täglich 30 bis 60 Minuten: 3 Schüler; bis zu 2 Stunden: 3 Schüler; bis 3 Stunden: 15 Schüler; bis 4 Stunden: 3 Schüler.

Zahl des Tages

Von den Deutschen, die Bücher lesen, schaffen 38 Prozent fünf Bände pro Jahr, 26 Prozent lesen sechs bis zehn, 18 Prozent elf bis 20 und gut zehn Prozent 21 bis 50.

(aus FOCUS)

Wortschatz

auf Deutsch erklärt

Ich erfahre es durch das Radio. Ich höre es im Radio.

Romeo vermisst seine Julia. Er ist traurig, dass sie nicht bei ihm ist.

die Glotze der Fernseher

die Neuigkeit etwas Neues

das Ereignis das, was passiert

die Unterhaltung was man zum Spaß macht

die Schlagzeile die großgedruckten Wörter über einem Text

die Tatsache etwas, was geschehen ist

die Einzelheit das Detail

verdrängen den Platz von etwas oder jemandem einnehmen

unterwegs auf dem Weg, nicht zu Hause

gesamt total, alles

der Streik wenn Arbeiter nicht arbeiten

auf Englisch erklärt

Zuviel Fernsehen trägt zur allgemeinen Volksverdummung bei. *Too much TV contributes to the general dumbing down of the people.*

In der Zeitung steht ein Bericht darüber. *There's a report about it in the paper.*

Ich will nur schnell mal die Zeitung durchblättern. *I just want to leaf through the paper real quick.*

Diese Sendung spricht mich an. *This program appeals to me.*

So stelle ich es mir vor. *That's the way I imagine it.*

Die Nachrichten regen mal zum Nachdenken an, mal sind sie oberflächlich. *Sometimes the news stimulates thought, sometimes it's superficial.*

Diese Situation eignet sich gut zu einem Spaß. *This situation is well suited to making a joke.*

p. 147X

Grammatikheft, S. 46, Ü. 1–2

3 **Was sagst du dazu?**

Sprechen Beantworte die folgenden Fragen.

1. Was machen die Deutschen am liebsten in ihrer Freizeit? Was machst du am liebsten? Was steht bei dir ganz oben? Und unten?

2. Was ist ein TV-Kid? Ein Kind, das in seiner Freizeit viel Fernsehen schaut.

3. Welche Aussagen über das Fernsehen auf Seite 152 sind positiv, welche negativ? Stimmst du damit überein? Kannst du noch einige Aussagen hinzufügen?

4 **Wie informieren sie sich?** Script and answers on p. 147G

Zuhören Wer von diesen Leuten informiert sich hauptsächlich durch Zeitunglesen, Fernsehen oder Radiohören? Hör gut zu, und schreib die Information in die entsprechende Spalte!

CD 6 Tr. 2

Schüler	Zeitung	TV	Radio
Kässi			

So sagt man das!

Asking someone to take a position; asking for reasons; expressing opinions 6–1

When having a discussion, you use certain communication strategies. Here are some ways to help you encourage a discussion in German.

To ask someone to take a position on a subject, you could say:

Möchtest du mal dazu Stellung nehmen? *or* **Wer nimmt mal dazu Stellung?**

To ask for reasons you say:

Kannst du das begründen?

To express an opinion you may begin with:

Meiner Meinung nach sollte man Zivi werden.
Ich finde, dass wir zu viel fürs Militär ausgeben.

> Übungsheft, S. 67, Ü. 1–2

> Grammatikheft, S. 47, Ü. 3

5 **Diskussion im Schulhof** Script and answers on p. 147G

Zuhören Im Schulhof wird lebhaft diskutiert. Hör zu und schreib auf, wer von diesen Schülern seine Meinung begründet und wer nicht! Welcher Schüler begründet seine Meinung am besten und warum?

CD 6 Tr. 3

Schüler	Grund	keinen Grund
Markus		
Thomi		

6 **Für mein Notizbuch**

Schreiben Schreib in dein Notizbuch, welches Medium (z.B. Zeitung, Radio, Fernsehen, Internet) du vorziehst! Nimm zu deiner Aussage Stellung, indem du deine Meinung mit mehreren Punkten begründest!

7 Eure Meinung über die Medien, bitte!

Sprechen Bildet Gruppen zu viert! Führt ein Gespräch über die Medien, indem ihr die verschiedenen Fragen unten behandelt! Die Gesprächspartner nehmen dann dazu Stellung.

DU **Meiner Meinung nach trägt die Zeitung am besten zur Bildung einer eigenen Meinung bei.**

PARTNER **Kannst du das mal begründen?**

DU **Ja, man kann die Zeitung in Ruhe lesen, man kann …**

> Tageszeitung   Fernsehen
> Radio

Welches Medium …

berichtet am wahrheitsgetreusten (closest to the truth)?

regt am stärksten zum eigenen Nachdenken an?

berichtet am verständlichsten über (politische) Ereignisse?

informiert über Neuigkeiten und wichtige Ereignisse?

trägt am besten zur Bildung einer eigenen Meinung bei?

bietet den meisten Gesprächsstoff im Freundes– und Bekanntenkreis?

ist am besten zur Unterhaltung und Entspannung geeignet?

8 Nacherzählen

Lesen/Sprechen Lies den folgenden Text, und erzähl ihn einem Partner wieder!

Was würden Sie ohne Fernseher machen?

Vor einiger Zeit führte ein Fernsehsender folgenden Test durch: Zwei Familien erklärten sich bereit, vier Wochen lang ohne Fernsehen zu leben. Und was passierte? In der einen Familie wussten die Leute einfach nicht mehr, was sie ohne Fernseher anfangen sollten! Sie saßen da und starrten sich an. Nichts fiel ihnen ein. Sie hatten vergessen, wie man sich unterhält, wie man sich amüsiert. Sie langweilten sich zu Tode — dann fingen sie sogar an zu streiten. In der anderen Familie fing man an zu reden. Man erzählte sich Witze und Geschichten. Die Familie hörte jetzt Musik, machte Spiele, sie luden wieder Freunde ein. — Nach vier Wochen bekamen beide Familien ihren Fernseher wieder. Das Ergebnis: Die eine Familie sitzt jetzt nach wie vor jeden Abend vor dem Bildschirm, die andere Familie macht jetzt lieber etwas zusammen, anstatt automatisch den Fernseher einzuschalten.

So sagt man das!

Reporting past events

Here is how you might narrate a long sequence of past events:

Vor einiger Zeit **führte** ein Fernsehsender folgenden Test durch: Zwei Familien **erklärten** sich bereit, … Und was **passierte?** Die Leute **wussten** einfach nicht mehr, was sie ohne Fernseher anfangen **sollten.** Sie **saßen** da und **starrten** sich an …

Grammatik

Narrative past (imperfect)

Mehr Grammatikübungen, S. 168–169, Ü. 1–3

Übungsheft, S. 68–69, Ü. 3–6

Grammatikheft, S. 48–49, Ü. 4–5

1. When talking about or relating events that took place in the past, use the following general rules as a guide:
   a. When writing longer sequences, use the narrative past (imperfect).
   b. In conversation, use the conversational past (perfect).
2. Weak verbs and strong verbs form the imperfect as follows:
   a. Weak verbs form the imperfect by adding the past tense marker **-te** to the verb stem.

	hören	führen	erklären
ich	hör**te**	führ**te**	erklär**te**
er, sie, es, man	hör**te**	führ**te**	erklär**te**
wir, sie, Sie	hör**ten**	führ**ten**	erklär**ten**

   b. Strong verbs often have a vowel change in the imperfect: geben — **gab;** finden — **fand.** The imperfect of strong verbs that you had are listed in the Grammar Summary.

	geben	finden
ich	**gab**	**fand**
er, sie, es, man	**gab**	**fand**
wir, sie, Sie	**gaben**	**fanden**

Note: Second-person forms of the imperfect are rarely used and are therefore not given here.

3. There are a number of verbs in German that form the imperfect like weak verbs but also have a vowel change. Here are some you have had so far:

	kennen	nennen	denken	bringen	wissen
ich	**kannte**	**nannte**	**dachte**	**brachte**	**wusste**
er, sie, es, man	**kannte**	**nannte**	**dachte**	**brachte**	**wusste**
wir, sie, Sie	**kannten**	**nannten**	**dachten**	**brachten**	**wussten**

Look at the past tense forms of modals on page 133. How is the past tense formed? What observations can you make when comparing them to weak and strong verbs? How are they similar to the verbs listed above?

9 Grammatik im Kontext

Lesen/Sprechen Erzähle die folgenden Aussagen nach! Verwende dabei das Imperfekt!

a. Ich hab gestern Abend nicht fernsehen können, weil ich keine Zeit gehabt hab. Ich hab gehört, dass der Bericht über die wichtigsten Ereignisse in Südafrika ausgezeichnet gewesen ist. Ich hab nicht gewusst, dass es große Demonstrationen gegeben hat, an denen Tausende teilgenommen haben.

b. Mein Vater hat früher seine Information gewöhnlich aus den Tageszeitungen bekommen. Wie er mir gesagt hat, hat er sich nur seriöse Zeitungen gekauft. Aber er hat ja nicht alles lesen können. Er hat erst alles mal durchgeblättert, und was ihn dann angesprochen hat, hat er gelesen.

„Kannst du mal schön ruhig den ‚Aus'-Knopf drücken?"

lesen — las

bekommen — bekam

ansprechen — sprach an (ansprach)

teilnehmen — nahm teil (teilnahm)

können — konnte

10 Klassenumfrage: Mediennützung

Sprechen Macht in eurer Klasse eine Umfrage! Stellt fest, welche Medien ihr am meisten und welche ihr am wenigsten benutzt! Was könnt ihr noch hinzufügen? Kassetten, CDs hören? Videos sehen? Computer, CD-ROM spielen? Im Internet surfen?

So sagt man das!

Agreeing or disagreeing; changing the subject; interrupting

Here are some more expressions you will find useful when you're having a discussion.

To accept a point someone makes, you can say:

Da ist schon was dran.   Eben!   Richtig!

To reject a point, you might say: (and informally:)

Das stimmt gar nicht!   Das ist alles Quatsch!

To change the subject, use these expressions:

Übrigens, ich wollte etwas anderes sagen.
Ich möchte noch mal (aufs Fernsehen) zurückkommen.

To interrupt someone, you can say:

Lass mich mal zu Wort kommen!
Moment mal! Lass (die Nicole) mal ausreden!

Übungsheft, S. 70, Ü. 7–9
Grammatikheft, S. 50, Ü. 6

---

11 Vor- und Nachteile des Fernsehens Script and answers on p. 147H

Zuhören Im Schulhof unterhalten sich einige Schüler über die Vorteile und Nachteile des Fernsehens. Schreib mindestens drei Vorteile und drei Nachteile auf, die du hörst! Stimmst du auch mit diesen Meinungen überein?

CD 6 Tr. 4

12 Was haltet ihr vom Fernsehen?

Ist Fernsehen nützlich oder schädlich? Diskutiert in der Klasse über diese Frage!

a. Sprechen Lest die Aussagen übers Fernsehen unten und nehmt dazu Stellung! Verwendet dabei die Ausdrücke, die ihr in diesem Kapitel gelernt habt! Nehmt eure Diskussion auf einer Kassette auf!

b. Sprechen Hört euch dann die Diskussion an, und diskutiert über die folgenden Fragen!

1. Wer hat was gesagt?
2. Wer hat seine Aussagen am besten begründet?
3. Welche Ausdrücke habt ihr verwendet? Schreibt diese Ausdrücke in euer Notizheft!

Ist das Fernsehen **nützlich**?
Ja, schon. Denn …
• man erhält eine Fülle von Informationen.
• man hat ein „Fenster zur Welt".
• man wird über viele Probleme informiert und kann dann vielleicht helfen.
• man kann Filme und Theateraufführungen sehen, wozu man sonst keine Gelegenheit hätte.

Ist das Fernsehen **schädlich**?
Fernsehen kann dazu führen, dass man …
• in seiner Freizeit weniger aktiv ist.
• seine künstlerischen Talente vergisst.
• weniger mit anderen Menschen zusammenkommt.
• seine eigenen Ideen und Gefühle weniger ausdrücken kann.
• zu viel isst und zunimmt.

LANDESKUNDE
LANDESKUNDE

Die Schülerzeitung

Übungsheft, S. 71, Ü. 1–4

Für manche Schüler ist die Mitarbeit an der Schülerzeitung nicht nur ein Hobby, sondern auch der Anfang einer Karriere im Journalismus. Wie bei einer Zeitung müssen die Schüler ihre Berichte recherchieren, Photos machen, Grafiken erstellen, Layouts vorbereiten, Platz für Anzeigen an Geschäftsleute verkaufen, den Text säuberlich tippen und für den Drucker vorbereiten — und dann die Zeitung an die Schüler verkaufen.

Eine andere Art, sich für die Schule zu engagieren, ist, in der Schülervertretung mitzuarbeiten. Gewöhnlich werden von jeder Schulklasse zwei Klassensprecher gewählt, die ein Jahr lang ihre Interessen in der SV vertreten. An der Spitze der SV stehen zwei Schulsprecher, die von den Klassensprechern gewählt werden. Schulsprecher dürfen Schulsprecherkonferenzen besuchen, bei denen Schülerprobleme des Bundeslandes diskutiert werden.

Die Schülervertretung am Markgräfler Gymnasium hat sich zum Beispiel sehr verdient gemacht. Sie hat an dem allgemeinen Rauchverbot am Gymnasium mitgearbeitet. Sie hat es durchgesetzt, dass es jetzt eine Graffitiwand an der Schule gibt, und bald sollen auf dem Schulgelände Pingpongtische aus Marmor aufgestellt werden, damit die Schüler auch bei schlechtem Wetter Tischtennis spielen können.

1. Lies den Text durch, und mach dir Notizen! Wovon handelt der Text?

2. Warum interessieren sich die Schüler für die Schülerzeitung und Schülervertretung?

3. Habt ihr auch eine Schülerzeitung und Schülervertretung in eurer Schule? Wie unterscheiden sie sich von den deutschen Schülerorganisationen?

4. Findest du es wichtig, solche Schülerorganisationen zu haben? Was meinst du?

1. **von Schülerinitiativen (Schülerzeitung, Schülervertretung)**
2. Answers will vary. E.g.: **um herauszufinden, wo ihre beruflichen Interessen liegen; um Probleme an der Schule zu lösen; um eigene Ideen an der Schule zu verwirklichen (z.B. Graffitiwand, Pingpongtisch)**

Weiter geht's! · *Unsere eigene Zeitung!*

CD 6 Tr. 5-7

An den meisten Realschulen und Gymnasien gibt es Schülerzeitungen. Da gibt es die „Glatze" am Schwann Gymnasium in Neuss, die „Meinung" am Gymnasium in Starnberg, den „List-Käfer" an der Wirtschafts-Schule in München oder die „Pepo" (People's Post) am Markgräfler Gymnasium in Müllheim, um nur einige Namen zu nennen. — Drei Redaktionsmitglieder unterhalten sich hier über ihre Arbeit mit der „Pepo". CD 6 Tr. 5

Guidl: Es ist unglaublich, wie viel Arbeit wir mit der „Pepo" haben. Und das alles nach der Schule. CD 6 Tr. 6

Rainer: Da stimm ich dem Guido zu. Manchmal frag ich mich, ob sich die viele Arbeit lohnt.

Natalie: Es überrascht mich, dass du das sagst.

Rainer: Die viele Arbeit macht mir nichts aus. Was mich stört ist, dass sich viele Schüler gar nicht für die Zeitung interessieren und die meisten fast gar nichts dazu beitragen. Und ich werde sauer, wenn sie unsere Arbeit bloß kritisieren!

Natalie: Ich kann dich verstehen, das ist frustrierend. Aber trotzdem, ich find die Arbeit anregend.

Guidl: Das ist wahr. Das find ich auch. Übrigens, dein letztes Interview mit der SV war super, bestimmt das beste Interview in der Pepo.

Hier ist Natalies Interview mit der SV, der Schülervertretung. Sprecher: Jürgen und Petra. CD 6 Tr. 7

Natalie: Warum macht ihr bei der SV mit?

Jürgen: Mich hat gestört, dass einige Klassensprecher und viele Schüler am Gymnasium so ganz ohne Interessen waren. Und deshalb wollte ich mich mal selber um Rechte und Pflichten der SV kümmern.

Petra: Es hat mich auch überrascht, als ich gesehen habe, was eine SV so alles erreichen kann!

Natalie: Und was macht die SV?

Petra: Unsere größte Aufgabe ist, schulinterne Dinge zu organisieren, zum Beispiel AGs, Schulfeten, Schüleraustausch, und wir können euch auch mit der Schülerzeitung helfen, wenn ihr mal Probleme mit der Schulleitung habt.

Natalie: Ist das wahr?

Jürgen: Klar. Und ich möchte noch dazu sagen, dass … äh, wir bemühen uns auch um bessere Kontakte zu den Eltern und zu unseren Lehrern.

Natalie: Kannst du mir ein Beispiel geben?

Jürgen: Kann ich. Du erinnerst dich doch, dass einige ältere Schüler und auch mehrere Lehrer mit dem Rauchverbot in der Schule nicht einverstanden waren. Das haben wir jetzt geregelt.

Natalie: Das freut mich für euch. – Übrigens, wie stehen denn die Lehrer zur SV?

Petra: Die Lehrer unterstützen uns; sie informieren uns über unsere Rechte und Pflichten.

Jürgen: Auch helfen sie uns ab und zu mit der Arbeit, wenn die Arbeit zu viel wird und wenn es zu viel Frust gibt.

Übungsheft, S. 72

13 Schülerzeitung und SV

Schreiben/Sprechen Beantworte diese Fragen mit einem Partner!

1. Was sagen die Schüler über ihre Arbeit mit der Schülerzeitung?
2. Was ist die SV? Was macht die SV? 2. Schülervertretung / E.g.: organisiert schulinterne Dinge; löst Probleme mit der Schulleitung; stellt bessere Kontakte zu Eltern und Lehrern her

14 Kannst du die Redemittel erkennen?

Schreiben Schreib die Ausdrücke in dein Notizheft, die die Schüler in ihrer Unterhaltung verwenden! Beachte dabei genau, was diese Redemittel ausdrücken! Welche Ausdrücke sind dir neu, welche sind dir schon bekannt?

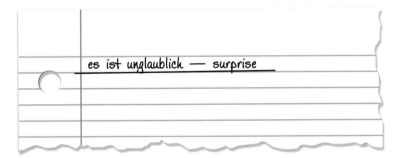

es ist unglaublich — surprise

Leserbriefe an die Redaktion der Pepo

Die Tatsache, dass in der „Meckerecke" auch anonyme Briefe erscheinen, finde ich schwach. Meiner Meinung nach sollte man zu seiner Meinung stehen. Wer Angst hat, was zu schreiben, der sollte es lassen!

Ursel Roth, 9a

Es überrascht mich wirklich, dass die Redaktion der Pepo Tatsachen und Meinungen nicht auseinander halten kann. Tatsache ist, dass wir das letzte Fußballspiel verloren haben. Meinung ist, dass wir nicht Fußball spielen können.

Bernd Rauh, 10b

Ich möchte mehr Berichte und Information über Veranstaltungen in der Schule!

Linda Schuster, 8b

Der Artikel im letzten Heft „Wie man sich in der Klasse gute Notizen macht" war sehr nützlich! Nur möchte ich dazu sagen, dass ich einige Vorschläge etwas unrealistisch fand. Die Lehrer zum Beispiel sprechen nicht immer sehr deutlich, und es ist schwer, ja manchmal unmöglich, alles mitzuschreiben!

Jochen Blick, 11a

Wortschatz

auf Deutsch erklärt

deutlich   klar

sich um jemanden kümmern   wenn man für jemanden alles tut, was man kann

der Schüleraustausch   wenn Schüler von einer anderen Schule zu uns kommen, und Schüler von uns dorthin gehen

unterstützen   einem Menschen helfen und Rat geben

nützlich   man kann es gebrauchen

deshalb   aus diesem Grund

die Schulleitung   die Schuldirektion

anregend   stimulierend

auf Englisch erklärt

Die Schülervertretung (SV) regelt die Veranstaltung.   *The student council takes care of the event.*

Wir haben eine schwere Aufgabe vor uns.   *We have a difficult task in front of us.*

Das macht mir nichts aus.   *That doesn't matter to me.*

Meckere nicht so!   *Don't complain so much!*

Die Redaktion bemüht sich um Klarheit.
The editors strive for clarity.

Du machst ihn sauer, wenn du ihn störst.
He'll get annoyed with you if you disturb him.

Überraschen wir sie mit einer Fete!
Let's surprise her with a party!

Grammatikheft, S. 51, Ü. 7–9

15 Was sagen die Schüler?

Lesen/Sprechen Diskutiert die Leserbriefe auf dieser Seite! Was sagen die Leserbriefe aus? Was ist der Hauptgedanke jedes Briefes? Wer drückt Folgendes aus: Ärger (*annoyance*), Frust (*frustration*), Überraschung (*surprise*)?

16 Die Schülerzeitung Script and answers on p. 147H

Zuhören Ein paar Schüler arbeiten für eine Schülerzeitung und müssen morgen eine neue Ausgabe drucken. Hör ihrem Gespräch gut zu und entscheide, wer diese Arbeit gern macht und wer nicht!

CD 6 Tr. 8

So sagt man das!

Expressing surprise or annoyance

6–2

To express surprise you could say:

Es ist unglaublich, dass die Mannschaft verloren hat.
Das schlechte Spiel **überrascht mich.**
Ich bin überrascht, dass sie so miserabel gespielt haben.

To express annoyance or frustration you could say:

Was mich stört ist, dass wir besser spielen können.
Ich werde sauer, wenn die Spieler so oft meckern.
Es ist frustrierend, dass wir ihnen nicht helfen können.

Übungsheft, S. 73–74, Ü. 1–4

Grammatikheft, S. 52, Ü. 10

17 Überraschung oder Frust? Script and answers on p. 147H

Zuhören Die Mitglieder der Schülerzeitung haben dich zu ihrer Versammlung eingeladen. Hör gut zu, wie einige Schüler Überraschung und Frust ausdrücken! Notiere, wer wie reagiert!

CD 6 Tr. 9

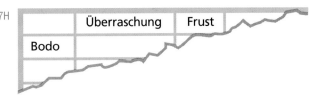

	Überraschung	Frust
Bodo		

18 Bist du überrascht, oder stört es dich?

Sprechen Such dir eine Partnerin! Sie spricht mit dir über einige Probleme an der Schule. Drück deine Überraschung oder deinen Ärger darüber aus! Wechselt einander ab!

1. Wir haben so viel Arbeit mit der Schülerzeitung.
2. Die meisten Schüler interessieren sich nicht einmal für die Zeitung.
3. Die Arbeit ist manchmal sehr frustrierend.
4. Wir haben leider auch keine gute Schülervertretung.
5. Wir haben auch keinen Schüleraustausch mit anderen Schulen.
6. Unsere Eltern haben wenig Kontakt zu den Lehrern.
7. …

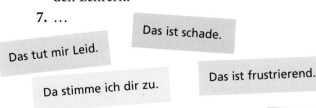

Das tut mir Leid.

Das ist schade.

Da stimme ich dir zu.

Das ist frustrierend.

Ja, das ist eben so.

Das ist aber wahr!

Das stört mich auch!

Da kann man nichts machen.

Grammatik

Superlative forms of adjectives

1. You have been using comparative forms of adjectives in sentences such as:

   Wir haben ein **größeres** Auto (als ihr).   Das ist eine **bessere** Kamera.

2. You have also been making equal and unequal comparisons like these:

   Das Fernsehen informiert **genau so schnell wie** das Radio.
   Das Radio informiert **schneller als** die Zeitung.

3. Superlative forms in German are similar to English superlative forms, for example: fastest, smallest, most expensive, best. The superlative form in German is made by adding **-st** (sometimes **-est**) to the positive form. When used before a noun, the superlative form must have an adjective ending.

4. Most adjectives of one syllable take an umlaut in the comparative and superlative. Here are some examples. For a more complete listing, refer to the Grammar Summary at the end of this textbook.

Positive	Comparative	Superlative	Positive	Comparative	Superlative
alt	älter	ältest-	kurz	kürzer	kürzest-
arm	ärmer	ärmst-	lang	länger	längst-
groß	größer	größt-	oft	öfter	öftest-
hart	härter	härtest-	schwach	schwächer	schwächst-
jung	jünger	jüngst-	stark	stärker	stärkst-
kalt	kälter	kältest-	warm	wärmer	wärmst-

Note that adjectives that end in **-d, -t, -z** add **-est** in the superlative form.

5. Several adjectives have irregular comparative and superlative forms.

Positive	Comparative	Superlative	Positive	Comparative	Superlative
gern	lieber	liebst-	nah	näher	nächst-
gut	besser	best-	viel	mehr	meist-
hoch	höher	höchst-			

6. Superlative forms are often used in the following phrase:

   am *superlative form* + **en**   Was mich **am meisten** stört ist, …

Übungsheft, S. 75, Ü. 5   Grammatikheft, S. 53–54, Ü. 11–13   Mehr Grammatikübungen, S. 170–171, Ü. 4–7

19 Grammatik im Kontext

Sprechen/Schreiben Spiel mit einem Partner die Rollen von zwei Schülern, die für verschiedene Schülerzeitungen mitarbeiten! Ihr denkt natürlich, dass jeder die beste Zeitung hat. Macht Reklame für eure eigene Schülerzeitung, indem ihr nur in Superlativen redet! Was sagt ihr? Was schreibt ihr?

BEISPIEL   **Wir haben die lustigsten Witze!**   *oder*   **Unsere Witze sind am lustigsten!**

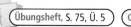

Neuigkeiten   Leserbriefe   Witze
Interviews   Tipps   Geschichten
Anekdoten   Cartoons   Artikel

seriös   spannend   gut   wichtig
witzig   toll   klug   lustig
faszinierend   komisch   schön

20 Grammatik im Kontext

Sprechen/Schreiben Guido hat ganz bestimmte Ansichten, und du, als sein bester Freund, stimmst ihm immer zu! Such dir einen Partner, und spielt zusammen die Rollen von Guido und seinem Freund! Tauscht oft die Rollen aus!

BEISPIEL **GUIDO** Keine Zeitung ist so interessant wie diese.
  DU Da stimm ich dir zu. Es ist die interessanteste Zeitung!

1. Keine Arbeit ist so schwer wie diese.
2. Keine Schüler sind so faul wie diese.
3. Kein Interview ist so langweilig wie dieses.
4. Kein Beispiel ist so blöd wie dieses.
5. Keine Schule ist so gut wie diese.
6. Keine Lehrerin ist so nett wie diese.

21 Grammatik im Kontext

a. **Sprechen** Such dir eine Partnerin, und sprecht einander die Sätze unten vor! Benutzt dabei aber die Superlative statt der Wörter in Klammern!  1. beste; nettesten; tollsten; neusten; wichtigsten

b. **Schreiben** Schreibt dann die neuen Formen dieser Wörter in eure Notizbücher!

1. Der (gut) Radiosender, den wir haben, ist … Dieser Sender hat den (nett) Discjockey, und der spielt die (toll) Hits. Für die (neu) Nachrichten unterbricht er jede Sendung und berichtet die (wichtig) Ereignisse. 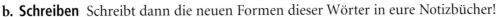 2. älteste; größte; schönsten; lustigsten; beste

2. Die (alt) Zeitung in unserer Stadt ist … Es ist die (groß) Zeitung im ganzen Staat. Die Zeitung hat die (schön) Sportartikel und die (lustig) Comics — ganze zwei Seiten! Meine Mutter sagt, die Zeitung hat auch die (gut) Reklame.

3. Im Sommer haben wir die (langweilig) Fernsehprogramme. Sie zeigen uns die (schlecht) Filme und die (alt) Krimis. Im Herbst haben wir das (gut) Fernsehen. Die (viel) Sendungen sind super, besonders die (neu) Shows.
   3. langweiligsten; schlechtesten; ältesten; beste; meisten; neusten

22 Über Massenmedien

Stellt in der Klasse eine Liste darüber zusammen, welche der drei wichtigen Medien ihr benutzt! Gebraucht die folgenden Hinweise als Hilfe!

1. **Schreiben** Schreibt auf, was ihr am liebsten in der Zeitung lest oder welche Sendungen ihr euch im Radio anhört und im Fernsehen anseht!

2. **Schreiben** Schreibt auf, welche Medien ihr im Unterricht und zu Hause benutzt! Wie oft und wie lange benutzt ihr diese?

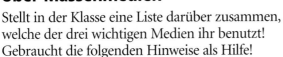

Wortschatz

Words of quantity

Schon bekannt	Neu
wie viele	wenige
keine	einige
ein paar	mehrere
viele	
alle	

Übungsheft, S. 75–76, Ü. 6–9

3. **Sprechen** Stellt diese Fragen euren Eltern, Großeltern, Verwandten und Bekannten! Welche Medieninteressen haben Menschen verschiedenen Alters, Geschlechts und verschiedener Berufe?

4. **Schreiben** Schreib dann einen Bericht über die Ergebnisse dieser Gruppenarbeit!

23 Von der Schule zum Beruf

The marketing director at the newspaper where you work is worried about a decline in readership. He has implemented several strategies meant to increase newspaper sales. Your task is to develop a colorful brochure targeted at the future purchasers of newspapers: teenagers. Try to convince teens that reading the newspaper is an essential step in the path to adulthood. Mention how vital newspapers (especially yours) are to one's social life, studies, and career, and why newspapers are better for getting information than television or the Internet.

Rumpelstilzchen

Gebrüder Grimm

Es war einmal ein Müller, der war arm, aber er hatte eine schöne Tochter. Nun traf es sich, daß er mit dem König zu sprechen kam, und um sich ein Ansehen zu geben, sagte er zu ihm: „Ich habe eine Tochter, die kann Stroh zu Gold spinnen." Der König sprach zum Müller: „Das ist eine Kunst, die mir wohl gefällt; wenn deine Tochter so geschickt ist, wie du sagst, so bring sie morgen in mein Schloß, da will ich sie auf die Probe stellen."

Als nun das Mädchen zu ihm gebracht wurde, führte er es in eine Kammer, die ganz voll Stroh lag, gab ihr Rad und Haspel und sprach: „Jetzt mache dich an die Arbeit, und wenn du diese Nacht durch bis morgen früh dieses Stroh nicht zu Gold versponnen hast, so mußt du sterben!" Darauf schloß er die Kammer selbst zu, und sie blieb darin allein.

Da saß nun die arme Müllerstochter und wußte um ihr Leben keinen Rat; sie verstand gar nichts davon, wie man Stroh zu Gold spinnen konnte, und ihre Angst wurde immer größer, daß sie endlich zu weinen anfing. Da ging auf einmal die Tür auf, und trat ein kleines Männlein herein und sprach: „Guten Abend, Jungfer Müllerin, warum weinst du so sehr?" — „Ach", antwortete das Mädchen, „ich soll Stroh zu Gold spinnen und verstehe das nicht." Sprach das Männchen:

„Was gibst du mir, wenn ich dir's spinne?" — „Mein Halsband", sagte das Mädchen. Das Männchen nahm das Halsband, setzte sich vor das Rädchen, und schnurr, schnurr, schnurr, dreimal gezogen, war die Spule voll. Dann steckte es eine andere auf, und schnurr, schnurr, schnurr, dreimal gezogen, war auch die zweite voll; und so ging's fort bis zum Morgen, da war alles Stroh versponnen, und alle Spulen waren voll Gold.

Bei Sonnenaufgang kam schon der König, und als er das Gold erblickte, staunte er und freute sich. Aber sein Herz ward nur noch goldgieriger. Er ließ die Müllerstochter in eine andere Kammer bringen, die noch viel größer war, und befahl ihr, auch dieses Stroh in einer Nacht zu spinnen, wenn ihr das Leben lieb wäre.

Das Mädchen wußte sich nicht zu helfen und weinte. Da ging abermals die Tür auf, und das kleine Männchen erschien und sprach: „Was gibst du mir, wenn ich dir das Stroh zu Gold spinne?" — „Meinen Ring vom Finger", antwortete das Mädchen. Das Männchen nahm den Ring, fing wieder an zu schnurren mit dem Rade und hatte bis zum Morgen alles Stroh zu glänzendem Gold gesponnen.

Ein Märchen

CD6 Tr. 10

Lesestrategie Predicting outcomes Predicting what will happen in a story is a useful strategy. It helps you read more quickly and easily by focusing your attention on what you expect to happen. Making predictions requires both common sense and imagination.

Getting Started For answers, see p. 147V.

1. Read the title and the first paragraph of the reading selection. What characters are introduced?

2. What is the English equivalent of **Es war einmal ...** ? To which genre of literature does this story belong? When and where does the story take place?

3. Now read the first three paragraphs, paying careful attention to the quotations. Make sure you know who is speaking at each point. What is the daughter's dilemma? How will it be resolved?

4. Before reading further, make some predictions about what might happen next.

Der König freute sich über die Maßen bei dem Anblick, war aber noch immer nicht des Goldes satt, sondern ließ die Müllerstochter in eine noch größere Kammer voll Stroh bringen und sprach: „Die mußt du noch in dieser Nacht verspinnen! Gelingt dir's aber, so sollst du meine Gemahlin werden." — Wenn's auch eine Müllerstochter ist, dachte er, eine reichere Frau finde ich in der ganzen Welt nicht.

Als das Mädchen allein war, kam das Männlein zum drittenmal wieder und sprach: „Was gibst du mir, wenn ich dir noch diesmal das Stroh spinne?" — „Ich habe nichts mehr, das ich geben könnte", antwortete das Mädchen. „So versprich mir, wenn du Königin wirst, dein erstes Kind." — Wer weiß, wie das noch geht, dachte die Müllerstochter und wußte sich auch in der Not nicht anders zu helfen. Sie versprach also dem Männchen, was es verlangte, und das Männchen spann dafür noch einmal das Stroh zu Gold. Und als am Morgen der König kam und alles fand, wie er gewünscht hatte, so hielt er Hochzeit mit ihr, und die schöne Müllerstochter wurde eine Königin.

5. Reread the first three paragraphs and continue reading until the end of the fifth paragraph. Did the predictions you made in Activity 4 prove correct? Continue reading until the end of the story, pausing every few paragraphs to make predictions. Check to see if your predictions were correct.

6. Now create a time line showing the order in which events occur. (Hint: In a European story of this genre, things often occur in sets of three. There are at least two sets of three things happening together in this story. Be sure to include these events in your time line.)

A Closer Look

7. **a.** Identify the following storytelling or antiquated words and phrases in the first three paragraphs and match each with a more common expression.

es traf sich	*der kleine Mann*
die Kammer	*das Fräulein*
das Männlein	*es ist passiert*
die Jungfer	*das kleine Spinnrad*
das Rädchen	*nicht wissen, was*
um das Leben keinen	*man tun soll*
Rat wissen	*das Zimmer*

b. What does the word **schnurr** mean in the third paragraph? What is it the sound of? Explain what the author is doing here.

Über ein Jahr brachte sie ein schönes Kind zur Welt und dachte gar nicht mehr an das Männchen. Da trat es plötzlich in ihre Kammer und sprach: „Nun gib mir, was du versprochen hast!" Die Königin erschrak und bot dem Männchen alle Reichtümer des Königreichs an, wenn es ihr das Kind lassen wollte. Aber das Männchen sprach: „Nein, etwas Lebendiges ist mir lieber als alle Schätze der Welt." Da fing die Königin so an zu jammern und zu weinen, daß das Männchen Mitleid mit ihr hatte. „Drei Tage will ich dir Zeit lassen", sprach es, „wenn du bis dahin meinen Namen weißt, so sollst du dein Kind behalten."

Nun besann sich die Königin die ganze Nacht über auf alle Namen, die sie jemals gehört hatte. Und sie schickte einen Boten über Land, der sollte sich erkundigen weit und breit, was es sonst noch für Namen gäbe. Als am andern Tag das Männchen kam, fing sie an mit Kaspar, Melchior, Balzer und sagte alle Namen, die sie wußte, der Reihe nach her. Aber bei jedem sprach das Männlein: „So heiß' ich nicht."

Den zweiten Tag ließ sie in der Nachbarschaft herumfragen, wie die Leute genannt würden, und sagte dem Männchen die ungewöhnlichsten und seltsamsten Namen vor: „Heißt du vielleicht Rippenbiest oder Hammelswade oder Schnürbein?" Aber es antwortete immer: „So heiß' ich nicht."

Am dritten Tag kam der Bote wieder zurück und erzählte: „Neue Namen habe ich keinen einzigen finden können. Aber wie ich an einem hohen Berge um die Waldecke kam, wo Fuchs und Has' sich gute Nacht sagen, so sah ich da ein kleines Haus, und vor dem Haus brannte ein Feuer, und um das Feuer sprang ein gar zu lächerliches Männchen, hüpfte auf einem Bein und schrie:

,Heute back' ich, morgen brau' ich,
übermorgen hol' ich der Königin ihr Kind;
ach, wie gut, daß niemand weiß,
daß ich Rumpelstilzchen heiß!'"

Da könnt ihr euch denken, wie die Königin froh war, als sie den Namen hörte. Und als bald danach das Männlein hereintrat und fragte: „Nun, Frau Königin, wie heiß' ich?" fragte sie erst: „Heißt du Kunz?" — „Nein." — „Heißt du Hinz?" — „Nein." — „Heißt du etwa Rumpelstilzchen?"

„Das hat dir der Teufel gesagt, das hat dir der Teufel gesagt!" schrie das Männlein und stieß mit dem rechten Fuß vor Zorn so tief in die Erde, daß es bis an den Leib hineinfuhr. Dann packte es in seiner Wut den linken Fuß mit beiden Händen und riß sich selbst mitten entzwei.

Writers use many kinds of cohesive devices (conjunctions, adverbs, and pronouns) to tie the elements of a story together. For example, **aber** lets you know to look for a contrast. Adverbs indicating time are clues to the sequence of events. When you see pronouns, including **da**-compounds, pay attention to the nouns they refer to in order to understand how individual sentences tie together.

8. Read the first three paragraphs again.
   a. Decide which characters the pronouns in the following sentences refer to:
      • Und um sich ein Ansehen zu geben, sagte **er** zu **ihm:** …

   • Als nun das Mädchen zu **ihm** gebracht wurde, führte **er es** in eine Kammer …
   • Dann steckte **es** eine andere auf, …
   b. Identify the **da**-compounds **darin** and **davon** in the second and third paragraphs. What function does each compound serve?

9. Lies die Geschichte noch einmal! Erzähl die Geschichte mit eigenen Worten nach! Verwende dabei ordnende Zeitausdrücke!

10. Übernimm die Rolle von einer der Hauptfiguren, und erzähl die Geschichte aus ihrer Sicht, aber mit deinen eigenen Worten!

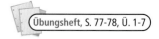
Übungsheft, S. 77-78, Ü. 1-7

Zum Schreiben

When people talk about their opinions, they agree or disagree with one another and ask for clarification and support. When taking a position in writing, another person is not there to disagree or ask for clarification, so you need to state your argument clearly and address possible opposition. In this activity, you will select an issue of importance to you and write an essay about it, clearly stating and supporting your point of view.

Ich nehme dazu Stellung.

Schreib einen Aufsatz von fünf Abschnitten, in dem du Stellung zu einem wichtigen Thema nimmst! Schreib zuerst eine Inhaltsangabe (*outline*), um die Struktur des Aufsatzes im Voraus zu planen!

> **Schreibtipp Using an outline** To write effectively, you need to organize your ideas before you begin. One way to do this is by using an outline. In an outline, you decide what general ideas you want to include, as well as what order you want to discuss them in. Then you group more specific ideas together under your general headings. For a position paper, for example, your outline should include an introduction stating your position, followed by the main reasons for your position. Under each reason you should include supporting details. All of this is followed by a concluding section that ties the whole essay together.

A. Vorbereiten

1. Mach eine Inhaltsangabe für deinen Aufsatz! Schreib die römischen Zahlen I–V auf ein Blatt Papier, und lass viel Platz unter jeder Zahl! Schreib dann jeweils die Buchstaben A, B und C unter II, III und IV!

2. Denk an ein Problem, das dir wichtig ist! Nimm zu diesem Problem Stellung, und drück deine Stellungnahme in einem Satz aus! Schreib diesen Satz neben die Zahl I!

3. Begründe die Stellungnahme mit mindestens drei Punkten! Schreib diese stichwortartig (*in key words*) neben die Zahlen II–IV! Dann unterstütze diese Punkte mit zwei bis drei weiteren Ideen, und schreib diese wieder in Stichworten jeweils neben die Buchstaben A, B und C!

4. Lies dir die Inhaltsangabe durch, und schreib einen Satz, um den ganzen Aufsatz zusammenzufassen! Schreib diesen Satz als Schlusssatz unter die Zahl V!

B. Ausführen

Halte dich an deine Inhaltsangabe, und schreib den Aufsatz! Du musst deine Ideen jetzt nur noch in ganze Sätze umwandeln! Gebrauche auch Nebensätze und Relativsätze, damit die Sprache fließend wirkt!

C. Überarbeiten

1. Such dir jemanden in der Klasse, der eine andere Stellung zu deinem Thema hat! Lies dieser Person deinen Aufsatz vor! Welche Gegenargumente äußert diese Person? Hast du diese Gegenargumente in deinem Aufsatz berücksichtigt? Wie kannst du deine Meinung gegen die Meinung deines Partners verteidigen?

2. Bist du deiner Inhaltsangabe gefolgt? Vergleich den Aufsatz mit dem Entwurf (*draft*)! Hast du etwas vergessen? Hast du überzeugend argumentiert?

3. Lies den Aufsatz noch einmal durch! Hast du alles richtig geschrieben? Gib besonders auf die komparativen und superlativen Adjektive acht!

4. Schreib den korrigierten Aufsatz noch einmal ab!

Mehr Grammatikübungen

Answers

internet
ADRESSE: go.hrw.com
KENNWORT:
WK3 WUERZBURG-6

Erste Stufe

Objectives Asking someone to take a position; asking for reasons; expressing opinions; reporting past events; agreeing or disagreeing; changing the subject; interrupting

1 Schreib die folgende Story ab und schreib dabei die richtige Vergangenheitsform der Verben im Kasten in die Lücken. (**Seite 155**)

brauchen	gehen	fragen
meinen	sagen	wissen
gefallen	sehen	wollen kaufen

Vor einiger Zeit _____ ich auf den Markt, um mir Obst und Gemüse zu kaufen. Das Obst _____ mir so gut, dass ich gleich 1 Kilo Äpfel _____ . Ich _____ für meine Freunde einen Apfelkuchen backen, und ich _____ gar nicht, wie viel Äpfel ich dafür _____ . Die Marktfrau _____ , dass ich genug Äpfel für den Kuchen habe. Sie _____ mich dann, ob ich noch etwas _____ . In diesem Moment _____ ich die schönen Tomaten, und ich _____ sie, woher sie kommen. Sie _____ mir, dass sie aus Italien sind.

ging
gefiel
kaufte, wollte

wusste; brauchte
meinte
fragte
wollte; sah
fragte
sagte

2 Schreib die folgende Story ab und schreib dabei die richtige Vergangenheitsform der Verben im Kasten in die Lücken. (**Seite 155**)

anhalten	vorstellen	sehen	sein	verdienen	aussehen	wollen	fahren
haben	anrufen	machen	holen	können	fragen	lesen	suchen interessieren

Im März letzten Jahres _____ ich meinen 18. Geburtstag. Ich _____ mir im Sommer einen Wagen kaufen, aber wie _____ ich das nur tun? Ich _____ mir eine Zeitung und _____ die Anzeigen. Da _____ ich eine Anzeige, die mich _____ . Die Firma _____ einen jungen Mann. Ich _____ _____ , und schon am nächsten Tag _____ ich mich _____ . Die Arbeit war toll, und ich _____ viel Geld. Nach einem Monat _____ ich den Führerschein, und gleich danach _____ ich mir ein Auto. Es _____ ein gelbes Cabriolet. Ich _____ ganz stolz nach Hause, als mich die Polizei _____ . Ich _____ für die Polizisten zu jung _____ , und sie _____ mich nach meinem Führerschein.

hatte
wollte
konnte; holte
las; sah
interessierte; suchte; rief
an; stellte
vor; verdiente
machte
kaufte; war
fuhr
anhielt; sah; aus
fragten

3 Du schreibst deiner Brieffreundin über verschiedene Sachen, die passiert sind, was du in den Ferien erlebt hast, was du letzten Samstag gemacht hast und über deine Erfahrung mit der Schule und der Bundeswehr. Schreib die folgenden Berichte ab, und schreib dabei die Vergangenheitsform der gegebenen Verben in die Lücken! (**Seite 155**)

1. Letzen Sommer (fahren) _____ ich mit meinen Eltern an die Nordsee. Wir (wohnen) _____ in einem kleinen Dorf. Es (sein) _____ so ruhig! Jeden Tag (schwimmen) _____ wir im Meer und (spielen) _____ Volleyball am Strand. Bei schlechtem Wetter (bleiben) _____ wir in unserer Pension, (lesen) _____ viele Bücher, (hören) _____ Musik, oder wir (faulenzen) _____ einfach. Ja, ich muss sagen, wir (sehen) _____ sehr wenig fern. Jeden Tag (bekommen) _____ wir eine Zeitung, und die (nehmen) _____ wir immer zum Strand mit. Wir (haben) _____ viel Spaß, und die Ferien (gefallen) _____ uns einfach prima!

fuhr

wohnten

war; schwammen

spielten

blieben; lasen

hörten; faulenzten

sahen

bekamen; nahmen

hatten

gefielen

2. Am Samstag (gehen) _____ ich mit meinem Freund auf eine Fete. Ich (vorstellen) _____ ihn meiner Clique _____ , und alle (sein) _____ sehr begeistert von ihm. Mein Freund (aussehen) _____ auch toll _____ . Wir (tanzen) _____ den ganzen Abend und (amüsieren) _____ uns gut. Auf der Fete (geben) _____ es auch tolle Sachen zu essen. Ich (essen) _____ eigentlich nicht sehr viel; ich (sprechen) _____ mit meinen Freunden und (zuhören) _____ , was sie zu erzählen (haben) _____ . Um 11 Uhr (kommen) _____ meine Eltern und (abholen) _____ mich _____ .

ging

stellte; vor; waren

sah

aus; tanzten

amüsierten; gab

aß

sprach; hörte zu

hatten; kamen

holten; ab

3. Also, bei uns an der Schule (geben) _____ es nette Cliquen, und wir (verstehen) _____ uns alle gut. Ich (wegfahren) _____ mit ihnen _____ ; wir (ansehen) _____ uns zusammen Museen _____ und (gehen) _____ in Konzerte und so. Ich (auskommen) _____ eigentlich immer gut mit den Leuten _____ , wir (streiten) _____ uns nie. Als ich siebzehn Jahre alt (sein) _____ , (entscheiden) _____ ich mich für die Bundeswehr; ich (wollen) _____ Offizier werden. Aber das (schaffen) _____ ich leider nicht, denn ich (durchfallen) _____ bei der Musterung _____ . Der Bund (mögen) _____ mich nicht!

gab

verstanden; fuhr; weg

sahen; an; gingen

kam

aus; stritten

war; entschied

wollte; schaffte

fiel; durch

mochte

Zweite Stufe

Objective Expressing surprise or annoyance

4 Vervollständige die folgenden Sätze. Gebrauche dabei den Namen des Artikels in der Abbildung und die richtige Form des Adjektivs in Klammern. (**Seite 162**)

(scharf) **1.** Unsere _____ sind _____ als eure.
2. Es sind die _____ _____ .

Zwiebeln; schärfer
schärfsten Zwiebeln

(süß) **3.** Unser _____ ist _____ als eurer.
4. Es ist der _____ _____ .

Mais; süßer
süßeste Mais

(groß) **5.** Unsere ___ ist ___ als eure.
6. Es ist die ___ ___ .

Wassermelone; größer
größte Wassermelone

(sauer) **7.** Meine ___ ist ___ als deine.
8. Es ist die ___ ___ .

Gurke; saurer
sauerste Gurke

(klein) **9.** Deine ___ sind ___ als meine.
10. Es sind die ___ ___ .

Radieschen; kleiner
kleinsten Radieschen

(lang) **11.** Saras ___ ist ___ als meine.
12. Es ist die ___ ___ .

Gabel; länger
längste Gabel

(gut) **13.** Kurts ___ ist ___ als meiner.
14. Es ist der ___ ___ .

Picknickkorb; besser
beste Picknickkorb

(schön) **15.** Deine ___ ist ___ als meine.
16. Das ist die ___ ___ .

Kühlbox; schöner
schönste Kühlbox

5 Du bist über gewisse Tatsachen (*facts*) überrascht. Schreib die folgenden Sätze ab, und schreib dabei die Superlativform der gegebenen Adjektive in die Lücken! (**Seite 162**)

1. Es ist unglaublich, dass die (gut) _____ Mannschaft verloren hat.   beste
2. Ich bin überrascht, dass unsere Zeitung den (gut) _____ Artikel hatte.   besten
3. Es ist unglaublich, dass unsere Zeitung die (groß) _____ Redaktion hat.   größte
4. Ich bin überrascht, dass unsere Schule die (jung) _____ Schülervertretung hat.   jüngste
5. Es ist unglaublich, dass du den (lang) _____ Bericht geschrieben hast.   längsten
6. Ich bin überrascht, dass du den (alt) _____ Drucker genommen hast.   ältesten
7. Es ist unglaublich, dass du nicht über die (groß) _____ Ereignisse berichtet hast.   größten
8. Ich bin überrascht, dass du die (viel) _____ Zeitungen liest.   meisten
9. Ich bin überrascht, dass du auf den (hoch) _____ Berge gestiegen bist.   höchsten

6 Du bist über bestimmte Tatsachen ganz frustriert. Schreib die folgenden Sätze ab, und schreib dabei die Superlativform der gegebenen Adjektive in die Lücken! (**Seite 162**)

1. Ich bin sauer, dass du die (schnell) _____ Zeit beim Schwimmen hattest.   schnellste
2. Was mich stört ist, dass wir in diesem Jahr den (heiß) _____ Sommer hatten.   heißesten
3. Es ist frustrierend, dass unsere Zeitung die (oberflächlich) _____ Berichte hat.   oberflächlichsten
4. Es ist frustrierend, dass wir diesen Sommer die (kurz) _____ Ferien haben.   kürzesten
5. Was mich stört ist, dass wir im März noch die (kalt) _____ Tage haben.   kältesten
6. Ich bin sauer, dass ich nicht die (gut) _____ Noten bekommen habe.   besten

7 Du drückst deine Meinung in Superlativen aus. Schreib die folgenden Sätze ab, und schreib dabei die Superlativform der gegebenen Adjektive in die Lücken! (**Seite 162**)

1. Diese Leserbriefe sind (schön) am _____ .   schönsten
2. Dieser Bericht hat mir (gut) am _____ gefallen.   besten
3. Dieses Interview hat mich (viel) am _____ interessiert.   meisten
4. Unsere letzte Schwimmveranstaltung hatte ich (gern) am _____ .   liebsten
5. Unser Reporter hat den Bericht (deutlich) am _____ geschrieben.   deutlichsten
6. Ich habe den Hintergrund zu diesem Bericht (nützlich) am _____ gefunden.   nützlichsten

Anwendung

internet

ADRESSE: go.hrw.com
KENNWORT:
WK3 WUERZBURG-6

1 Einige Schüler möchten gern eine Schülerzeitung herausgeben. Mit einem Lehrer zusammen haben sie folgende Gedanken aufgeschrieben. Lies die Aufgaben durch! Welche Aufgaben findest du wichtig, welche nicht so wichtig? Gibt es einige Aufgaben, die du weglassen würdest? Möchtest du etwas hinzufügen? Schreib es auf!

Aufgaben einer Schülerzeitung

A. Anregungen und Information für alle Schüler

1. Gute Schüleraufsätze abdrucken

2. Interessante Bücher und neue Filme besprechen

3. Tipps geben, zum Beispiel, wie man vor einer Arbeit richtig lernt und wie man einen guten Aufsatz schreibt

4. Über Berufe informieren

5. Ratschläge geben über Geldverdienen, Taschengeld, usw.

6. An wichtige Ereignisse und bedeutende Menschen erinnern

7. Geschichten, Witze, Cartoons, lustige Anekdoten bringen

B. Berichte aus dem Schulleben

1. Von Veranstaltungen und Ereignissen in der Schule berichten, zum Beispiel über Konzerte, Theaterspiele, Ausstellungen, Klassenreisen, Sport, usw.

2. Neue Lehrer vorstellen

3. Über allgemeine Schulfragen berichten, wie zum Beispiel die Länge des Schultages, Wahl- und Pflichtfächer, Veränderungen im Schulgebäude oder im Verlauf des Schultages

4. Deutsche und ausländische Schulen vergleichen

C. Sprachrohr der Schüler

1. Fragen an die Schüler richten

2. Meinungen der Schüler veröffentlichen

3. Kritik und Vorschläge diskutieren

4. Stellungnahmen der Lehrer und Schuldirektion bringen

2 Zwei Redaktionsmitglieder einer Schülerzeitung unterhalten sich über Themen, die in der nächsten Ausgabe erscheinen sollen, und danach sprechen sie über einige Arbeiten, die die Schüler noch machen müssen. Hör zu und schreib mindestens drei Themen auf, über die du auch gern in einer Schülerzeitung lesen möchtest! Dann schreib zwei Arbeiten auf, die du gern für deine Schülerzeitung machen möchtest! Script and answers on p. 147I

CD 6 Tr. 11

3 Wenn du an eurer Schule so eine Schülerzeitung hättest, was würde dich am meisten interessieren? Was würdest du regelmäßig lesen? Was interessiert dich nicht? Wenn du die Gelegenheit hättest, an so einer Zeitung mitzuarbeiten, für welche Artikel möchtest du verantwortlich sein?

4 Vergleicht eure Schülerzeitung mit der Liste von Aufgaben, die die Schüler in der ersten Übung aufgestellt haben! Was macht eure Zeitung alles? Was macht sie nicht? Könnt ihr an Hand eurer Zeitung Beispiele geben?

5 Gebt in eurer Deutschklasse eine Schülerzeitung heraus! Stellt zuerst eine Liste mit Aufgaben eurer Zeitung auf! Entscheidet euch, was für Artikel ihr schreiben wollt, und teilt die Arbeit unter den Klassenmitgliedern auf! Jeder bekommt eine Aufgabe.

6 Such dir einen Partner! Macht zusammen eine Umfrage für eure Schülerzeitung! Denkt an die Leute, die ihr in der Schule kennt oder von denen ihr etwas wisst! Seht euch die Kategorien an, und schreibt Sätze wie im Beispiel! Wen wählt ihr für die verschiedenen Kategorien? Vergleicht eure Umfrage mit denen eurer Klassenkameraden!

Kategorien:

sich schick anziehen	gute Noten haben	gescheit sein
tolle Witze erzählen	gut singen	sportlich sein
sich verrückt anziehen	viele Freunde haben	gut aussehen

Umfrage: 1. Wer zieht sich am schicksten an?

2. Wer erzählt die tollsten Witze?

3. Wer ...

7 Nimm Stellung zu folgenden Aussagen, und schreib einen Leserbrief an die Schülerzeitung!

— Muss man immer sagen, was man denkt?
— Darf eine Schülerzeitung Lehrer kritisieren?

8 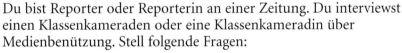 R o l l e n s p i e l

Du bist Reporter oder Reporterin an einer Zeitung. Du interviewst einen Klassenkameraden oder eine Klassenkameradin über Medienbenützung. Stell folgende Fragen:

1. Warum liest du Zeitung?

2. Welche Zeitung(en) liest du?

3. Welche anderen Zeitungen kennst du?

4. Welches sind seriöse Zeitungen und welches Boulevardzeitungen?

5. Welche liest du intensiv? Welche blätterst du nur durch?

6. Welche Programmzeitschriften kennst du?

7. Was hörst du so alles im Radio?

8. Für welche Interessengruppen gibt es besondere Sendungen im Radio?

9. Welche TV-Sendungen sind besonders für Jugendliche geeignet?

10. Welche anderen Medien benützt du?

Can you ask someone to take a position? (p. 153)

1 How would you ask a friend to take a position on an issue or state his or her point of view?   Möchtest du mal dazu Stellung nehmen?

Can you ask for reasons? (p. 153)

2 How would you ask someone for reasons that justify the way he or she feels about something?   Kannst du das begründen?

Can you express opinions? (p. 153)

3 How would you say that in your opinion we're not doing enough to protect the environment?   E.g.: Meiner Meinung nach tun wir nicht genug, um die Umwelt zu schützen.

Can you report past events? (p. 154)

4 How would you rewrite the following anecdote in a more formal style if a newspaper offered you to publish it?   For answers, see below.

Ich bin vier Jahre in der Redaktion der „Pepo" gewesen. Die viele Arbeit hat sich gelohnt, und es hat mir immer viel Spaß gemacht. Was mich ab und zu gestört hat, war, dass sich viele Schüler für die Zeitung nicht interessiert und sie nur kritisiert haben. Ich bin dann auch noch zwei Jahre in der SV gewesen. Wir haben Feten organisiert und unserer Schülerzeitung geholfen, wenn sie Probleme mit der Schulleitung gehabt hat.

Can you agree or disagree? (p. 156)

5 How would you respond if someone said the following things to you?
a. Geld allein macht nicht glücklich. Hauptsache, man ist gesund.   5. a. E.g.: Da ist schon was dran.
b. Was in der Zeitung steht, ist immer richtig.
b. E.g.: Das stimmt gar nicht!

Can you change the subject? (p. 156)

6 How would you tell a friend with whom you're having a conversation that you would like to change the subject and go back to talking about the media?   Ich wollte etwas anderes sagen. Ich möchte nochmal auf die Medien zurückkommen.

Can you interrupt? (p. 156)

7 How would you tell a friend who is talking a lot that you want him or her to let you say something?   E.g.: Lass mich mal zu Wort kommen!

Can you express surprise or annoyance? (p. 161)

8 How would you express your surprise that your school's team didn't win the game?   E.g.: Ich bin überrascht, dass die Schulmannschaft das Spiel nicht gewonnen hat.

9 How would you express your annoyance if someone were constantly criticizing you?   E.g.: Was mich stört ist, dass ich immer kritisiert werde.

4. Ich war vier Jahre in der Redaktion der „Pepo". Die viele Arbeit lohnte sich, und es machte mir immer viel Spaß. Was mich ab und zu störte, war, dass sich viele Schüler nicht für die Zeitung interessierten und sie nur kritisierten. Ich war dann auch noch zwei Jahre in der SV. Wir organisierten Feten und halfen unserer Schülerzeitung, wenn sie Probleme mit der Schulleitung hatte.

Asking someone to take a position

Möchtest du mal dazu Stellung nehmen?	*Would you like to take a position on that?*

Asking for reasons

Kannst du das begründen?	*Can you give a reason for that?*

Expressing opinions

Meiner Meinung nach soll man sich besser informieren.	*In my opinion one should get better informed.*

Agreeing

Da ist schon was dran.	*There's something to that.*
Eben!	*Exactly!*
Richtig!	*Right!*

Disagreeing

Das stimmt gar nicht!	*That's not true at all!*
Das ist alles Quatsch!	*That's all a bunch of baloney!*

Changing the subject

Ich möchte nochmal darauf zurückkommen.	*I would like to get back to that.*

Interrupting

Lass mich mal zu Wort kommen!	*Let me get in a word!*
Moment mal, lass den Berti mal ausreden!	*Hold on there, let Berti finish talking.*

Other useful words

die Bildung	*formation*
der Bericht, -e	*report*
der Drucker, -	*printer*
die Einzelheit, -en	*detail*
das Ereignis, -se	*event*
die Glotze, -n	*television, idiot box*
der Hintergrund, ¨-e	*background*
der Kommentar, -e	*commentary*
die Medien (pl)	*media*
das Nachdenken	*reflection*
die Neuigkeit, -en	*most recent event*
die Redaktion	*editorial staff*
die Schlagzeile, -n	*headline*

der Spaß	*joke*
der Streik, -s	*strike*
die Tatsache, -n	*fact*
die Unterhaltung, -en	*entertainment*
die Veranstaltung, -en	*organized event*
die Wahrheit	*truth*
anregen (sep)	*to encourage, stimulate*
ansprechen (sep)	*to appeal, speak to*
beitragen zu (sep)	*to contribute to*
durchblättern (sep)	*to page through*
s. eignen zu	*to be suited to*
erfahren	*to experience*
verdrängen	*to displace, repress*
vermissen	*to miss*
s. vorstellen (sep)	*to imagine*
weglassen (sep)	*to omit, drop*
oberflächlich	*superficial*
gesamt	*entire*
gründlich	*thorough*
meist-	*most*
unterwegs	*underway*

Zweite Stufe

Expressing surprise

Es ist unglaublich, dass ...	*It's unbelievable that ...*
Das überrascht mich.	*That surprises me.*
Ich bin überrascht, dass ...	*I'm surprised that ...*

Expressing annoyance

Was mich stört, ist ...	*What bothers me is ...*
Ich werde sauer, wenn ...	*I get annoyed when ...*
Es ist frustrierend, wenn ...	*It's frustrating when ...*

Other useful words and expressions

die Aufgabe, -n	*task*
der Schüleraustausch	*student exchange*
die Schülervertretung	*students' representatives*
die Schulleitung	*school administration*
Das macht mir nichts aus.	*That doesn't matter to me.*
Wie stehst du dazu?	*What do you think of that?*
s. bemühen um	*to strive for*
erreichen	*to achieve*

s. kümmern um	*to be concerned about*
meckern	*to complain*
unterstützen	*to support*
ab und zu	*now and then*
anregend	*stimulating*
deshalb	*for this reason*
deutlich	*clearly*
fast immer	*almost always*
nützlich	*useful*
selbst	*oneself*
einige	*some*
mehrere	*several*
wenige	*few*

Frankfurt

Teaching Resources
pp. 176–179

PRINT
- Lesson Planner, pp. 41, 81
- Video Guide, pp. 29–30

MEDIA
- One-Stop Planner
- Video Program
  Frankfurt
  Videocassette 2, 01:38–04:36
- Map Transparency

go.hrw.com

PAGES 176–177

THE PHOTOGRAPH

Background Information

First records refer to the city of Frankfurt in 794 as **Francono Furd** *(ford of the Franks)*. Between 885 and 1792, thirty-six German rulers were elected here. The Golden Bull of 1356 designated Frankfurt as the seat for the election of the Holy Roman emperors. From 1562 on, the Holy Roman emperors were crowned in the **Kaiserdom,** the city's Gothic cathedral. Today this historic cathedral, the fair tower, and numerous bank buildings stand out in the city's skyline. Locals sometimes refer to the city as *Mainhattan* or *Bankfurt.*

Geography Connection

Ask students to refer to the map on p. T76 to find out what river runs through Frankfurt. You may also want to use *Map Transparency* 1. Tell students the name of Germany's largest airport (**Rhein-Main-Flughafen**) and have them give an explanation for its name.

THE ALMANAC AND MAP

The coat of arms of Frankfurt displays a white eagle on a red background. The eagle derives from the heraldic symbol of the medieval Holy Roman Empire. Frankfurt always had a close connection to the Empire, since it was both a Free Imperial City (i.e., not subject to a prince or bishop, but only to the Emperor) and the place where each newly elected emperor was crowned. Even after the end of the Holy Roman Empire in 1806, Frankfurt retained the eagle as its emblem.

Terms in the Almanac

- **Hessen:** The state Hessen covers an area of approximately 21,100 square kilometers (8,145 square miles) with most of its population living in the **Rhein-Main** region.

- **Main:** This river is the main tributary of the Rhine coming from the east. It is 524 kilometers (325.4 miles) long and ends at the city of Mainz. Only parts of it are navigable.

- **Römer:** See Level 2 *Teacher's Edition,* p. 59R and Level 3 *Teacher's Edition,* p. 175B.

- **Goethehaus:** See Level 2 *Teacher's Edition,* p. 59R and Level 3 *Teacher's Edition,* p. 175B.

- **Maria Sybilla Merian:** The Merians were a family of artists involved in engraving, publishing, and painting. Maria was a noted painter of flowers, insects, and animals.

- **J. W. von Goethe:** Goethe, who was born in 1749 in Frankfurt and died in 1832 in Weimar, is regarded as one of the greatest figures in German literary history. He first achieved international fame with his novel *Die Leiden des jungen Werthers* (1774), which describes a sensitive young man suffering because of unrequited love. In 1776, Goethe accepted a high position in the cabinet of the Duke of Sachsen-Weimar. Goethe spent most of his life in Weimar, a town that became the center of German literature. Among Goethe's greatest works are the novel *Wilhelm Meisters Lehrjahre,* volumes of poems such as *Wanderers Nachtlied* and *Der Erlkönig,* and the play *Faust.* Since 1961, the city of Frankfurt has awarded the **Goethepreis** in the amount of 50,000 marks to accomplished authors. Some of the best-known recipients have been Thomas Mann, Hermann Hesse, Max Planck, and Carl Zuckmayer.

- **Otto Hahn:** Hahn was a chemist and physicist whose discovery of the phenomenon of fission in 1938 led to the development of the atomic bomb. He received the Nobel Prize in Chemistry in 1944 for his discovery of the fission of heavy nuclei.

- **Bankwesen:** Frankfurt's connection to banking and finance dates back to the 16th century, when the city was granted permission to mint money. Today the city is home to the **Deutsche Bundesbank** *(central bank of Germany)* as well as 400 other domestic and foreign banks. The **Frankfurter Börse** *(stock exchange)* is the largest in Germany.

- **Buchmesse:** The **Internationale Frankfurter Buchmesse** is one of the major trade fairs that take place in Frankfurt each year.

- **Handkäs mit Musik: Handkäs,** also referred to as **Mainzer** cheese, should be round and well aged. The round cheese is cut into four sections and served with a marinade of vinegar, oil, salt, pepper, and onions. **Handkäs** is served on fresh bread with **Äppelwoi** as the beverage.

- **Äppelwoi:** This is one of the words used for **Apfelwein** in the Hessian dialect. In Level 2, students read about **Äbbewoi,** another word for **Apfelwein.**

Thinking Critically

Comparing and Contrasting Have students list ways in which Frankfurt and New York City are similar. (Examples: located on rivers, noted for their skylines, home of major stock exchanges, important financial centers) Can students tell why Frankfurt has the nicknames *Mainhattan* and *Bankfurt?*

Map Activities

Have students locate Frankfurt on a map. (You may want to use *Map Transparency* 1.) Then ask them to think about how Frankfurt's location has helped make it one of the most important industrial cities in central Europe. (Frankfurt is very centrally located in Europe, and many natural waterways, highways, and railways lead to and away from Frankfurt. The city also has one of the busiest airports in Europe. All of this makes Frankfurt an important crossroad between northern and southern Europe.)

PAGES 178–179

THE PHOTO ESSAY

❶ **Der Römer (Rathaus)** is located in the historic center of the city, the **Römerberg.** It got its name for being the oldest in the set of eleven **Giebelhäuser,** a complex of gabled buildings on the **Römerberg.** Pictured in Photo 1 is a group of three buildings, the **Alt-Limpurg, Zum Römer,** and **Löwenstein.** The upper floor of the **Römer** was used for banquets following the coronation of kings or emperors. Today the **Römer** houses the city government.

❷ The **Dom St. Bartholomäus,** also known as the **Kaiserdom,** was built during the 13th, 14th, and 15th centuries. It is made mostly of sandstone taken from the banks of the Main River.

- **Teaching Suggestion** Ask students to research and make a list of emperors who were crowned in the **Kaiserdom** starting in 1562. This could be done for extra credit.

❸ The lower, rounded building of the **Paulskirche** was originally built as a Protestant church. The building was gutted during World War II and rebuilt through the help of private donations in 1948.

- **Drawing Inferences** Have students read the caption of Photo 3, then ask them to imagine that they are responsible for coordinating events at the **Paulskirche.** For what types of programs might the **Paulskirche** be ideal?

❹ **Das Goethehaus** is the famous writer's birthplace and childhood home. It was destroyed in World War II and rebuilt between 1946 and 1951. It features the workroom where Goethe wrote *Werther, Götz von Berlichingen,* and parts of *Faust.* Today the house is also connected to the **Goethemuseum.**

❺ The restoration of the group of **Fachwerkhäuser** on the east side of the **Römerberg** was completed in the early eighties. For information on **Fachwerk,** see Level 2 *Teacher's Edition,* p. 59R.

LOCATION OPENER

Komm mit nach Frankfurt!

Map of Germany

Bundesland: Hessen

Einwohner: 651 000

Fluss: Main

Sehenswürdigkeiten: Römer, Paulskirche, Dom, Goethehaus

Berühmte Leute:
Maria Sybilla Merian (1647-1717); J.W. von Goethe (1749-1832); Otto Hahn (1879-1968)

Industrie und Handel: Bankwesen, Buchmesse

Bekannte Gerichte: Rippchen mit Kraut, Handkäs mit Musik, Äppelwoi (Apfelwein)

Nordsee · DÄNEMARK · Ostsee · Kiel · Hamburg · NIEDER-LANDE · Berlin · POLEN · BEL. · Hessen Frankfurt · TSCHECHIEN · LUX. · FRANK-REICH · München · ÖSTERREICH · SCHWEIZ

go.
hrw
.com

WK3 FRANKFURT

VIDEO

STANDARDS: 2.2, 3.1

Die Frankfurter Skyline ▶

Frankfurt

Frankfurt feierte 1994 seinen 1200. Geburtstag! Der Ort wurde 794 zum ersten Mal erwähnt als einer der Sitze Karls des Großen, Kaiser des Fränkischen Reiches und seit 800 Kaiser des Heiligen Römischen Reiches Deutscher Nation. Heute ist Frankfurt eine moderne Großstadt, das Finanzzentrum der Bundesrepublik und seit 1998 auch die Finanzmetropole der Europäischen Union.

▼ internet

go.hrw.com
ADRESSE: go.hrw.com
KENNWORT: WK3 FRANKFURT

1 Römer

Der Römer (in der Mitte), das alte Rathaus der Stadt, ist das Wahrzeichen Frankfurts. Im ersten Stock befindet sich der Kaisersaal mit Bildern der deutschen Kaiser, wo glanzvolle Krönungsfeierlichkeiten und Bankette stattfanden. Diese drei Häuser sind im gotischen Stil erbaut.

2 Dom

Der Dom St. Bartholomäus, im 13.-15. Jahrhundert erbaut, ist ein Wahrzeichen Frankfurts. Dieser Dom war von 1356 bis 1792 Wahlkapelle für die deutschen Könige und Kaiser, und seit 1562 fanden hier auch die Kaiserkrönungen statt.

4 **Goethehaus**

Das Goethehaus, Geburtshaus des
großen deutschen Dichters Johann
Wolfgang von Goethe (1749-1832)
ist so eingerichtet, wie es einst war.
Im Arbeitszimmer schrieb Goethe
den „Götz", den „Werther" und
Teile des „Faust". Nebenan ist das
Goethemuseum mit über 100 000
Büchern und Manuskripten.

3 **Paulskirche**

Die Paulskirche (1787-1833) war in den Jahren 1848-1849
Tagungsort der ersten Deutschen Nationalversammlung.
Die Kirche dient heute der Stadt zu repräsentativen Anlässen,
wie zum Beispiel zur Verleihung des Goethepreises oder
des Friedenspreises des Deutschen Buchhandels.

5 **Fachwerk am Römerberg**

Die schönen historischen Fachwerkbauten auf
der Ostseite des Römerbergs gegenüber vom
Römer wurden im Krieg total zerstört und erst
1984 wieder völlig aufgebaut. In zwei dieser
Häuser befinden sich gemütliche
Lokale, wo man im Sommer
auch draußen sitzen und
schmackhafte Frankfurter
Spezialitäten probieren
kann.

Kapitel 7: Ohne Reklame geht es nicht!
Chapter Overview

Los geht's! pp. 182–183	**Werbung—ja oder nein? p. 182**			

	FUNCTIONS	**GRAMMAR**	**VOCABULARY**	**RE-ENTRY**
Erste Stufe pp. 184–189	• Expressing annoyance, p. 185 • Comparing, p. 185	• **Derselbe, der gleiche,** p. 186 • Adjective endings following determiners of quantity, p. 187	• Commercials and advertisements, p. 184	Expressing annoyance, p. 185 (**Kap. 6, III**); the conjunctions **wenn** and **dass**, p. 185 (**Kap. 9, I; 8, II**); comparative and superlative forms of adjectives, p. 185 (**Kap. 7, II; 6, III**); adjective endings, pp. 186, 187 (**Kap. 7/8/11, II**)

Weiter geht's! pp. 190–191	**Image-Werbung, p. 190**			

Zweite Stufe pp. 192–195	• Eliciting agreement and agreeing, p. 192 • Expressing conviction, uncertainty, and what seems to be true, p. 194	• Relative pronouns, p. 193 • Introducing relative clauses with **was** and **wo**, p. 193 • **Irgendein** and **irgendwelche**, p. 195	• Terms useful for judging ads, p. 192 • Words preceded by **irgend**, p. 195	Agreeing, p. 192 (**Kap. 10, II**); relative pronouns, p. 193 (**Kap. 4, III**); word order in dependent clauses, p. 193 (**Kap. 9, I**); expressing conviction, p. 194 (**Kap. 9, II**); expressing uncertainty, p. 194 (**Kap. 5/9, I**); adjective endings, p. 195 (**Kap. 7/8/11, II**)

Zum Lesen pp. 196–198	**Comics lesen**	**Reading Strategy** Using pictures and print type as clues to meaning

Zum Schreiben p. 199	**Es stört mich!**	**Writing Strategy** Using tone and word choice for effect

Mehr Grammatik- übungen	**pp. 200–203** Erste Stufe, pp. 200–201	Zweite Stufe, pp. 202–203

Review pp. 204–207	Anwendung, pp. 204–205	Kann ich's wirklich?, p. 206	Wortschatz, p. 207

CULTURE

• Werbung—pro und contra, p. 184
• **Landeskunde: Warum so wenig Unter- brecherwerbung?** p. 189

• Excerpt from **Frankfurter Allgemeine**, p. 192
• Cartoon, p. 193

Kapitel 7: Ohne Reklame geht es nicht!
Chapter Resources

Lesson Planning

One-Stop Planner

Lesson Planner with Substitute Teacher Lesson Plans, pp. 41–45, 81

Student Make-Up Assignments
- Make-Up Assignment Copying Masters, Chapter 7

Listening and Speaking

Listening Activities
- Student Response Forms for Listening Activities, pp. 51–54
- Additional Listening Activities 7-1 to 7-6, pp. 55–58
- Scripts and Answers, pp. 150–157

Video Guide
- Teaching Suggestions, p. 32
- Activity Masters, pp. 33–34
- Scripts and Answers, pp. 66–67, 75

Activities for Communication
- Communicative Activities, pp. 25–28
- Realia and Teaching Suggestions, pp. 81–85
- Situation Cards, pp. 125–126

Reading and Writing

Reading Strategies and Skills Handbook, Chapter 7

Lies mit mir! 3, Chapter 7

Übungsheft, pp. 79–91

Grammar

Grammatikheft, pp. 55–63

Grammar Tutor for Students of German, Chapter 7

Assessment

Testing Program
- Grammar and Vocabulary Quizzes, **Stufe** Quizzes, and Chapter Test, pp. 147–160
- Score Sheet, Scripts and Answers, pp. 161–167

Alternative Assessment Guide
- Portfolio Assessment, p. 22
- Performance Assessment, p. 36

Student Make-Up Assignments
- Alternative Quizzes, Chapter 7

 Online Activities
- Interaktive Spiele
- Internet Aktivitäten

 Video Program
- Videocassette 2

 Audio Compact Discs
- Textbook Listening Activities, CD 7, Tracks 1–10
- Additional Listening Activities, CD 7, Tracks 15–20
- Assessment Items, CD 7, Tracks 11–14

 Teaching Transparencies
- Situations 7-1 to 7-2
- **Mehr Grammatikübungen** Answers
- **Grammatikheft** Answers

Use the **One-Stop Planner CD-ROM with Test Generator** to aid in lesson planning and pacing.

For each chapter, the **One-Stop Planner** includes:
- Editable lesson plans with direct links to teaching resources
- Printable worksheets from resource books
- Direct launches to the HRW Internet activities
- Video and audio segments
- Test Generator
- Clip Art for vocabulary items

Kapitel 7: Ohne Reklame geht es nicht!

Projects ··

TV Werbung

In this activity students will create their own television commercials. This project can be done individually or in small groups.

> **MATERIALS**
>
> ✂ **Students may need**
> - paper
> - pens
> - pencils
> - props

SUGGESTED SEQUENCE

1. Students brainstorm a list of products they might like to advertise and choose one for their commercial.

2. Students determine the format of their commercials.

3. Students write the script. They can treat their product seriously or make outrageous claims.

4. Students decide what props and sound effects they will need.

5. Students rehearse their commercials several times to make them convincing and easy to understand.

6. Students record their commercials on video or audio tape.

7. Broadcast the commercials in class. The class can judge them on a scale of 1 (lowest) to 5 (highest).

> **GRADING THE PROJECT**
>
> Suggested point distribution (**total = 100 points**)
> Presentation/Dramatization 60
> Originality of idea 20
> Accuracy of language 20

Games ··

Es war einmal …

This game will help students review the vocabulary they have learned thus far.

Preparation Prepare a class set of index cards on which you write words and phrases you would like to review, including one card that says, "**Es war einmal …**".

Procedure As students walk into the classroom, assign each a number from 1 up to the total number of students in your class. Distribute the cards randomly so that each student receives one card. The student with the "**Es war einmal …**" card starts to tell a story, beginning with "**Es war einmal …**" and adding to it. Next, call on the student who was assigned the number 2 to continue the story using the phrase on his or her card. Students with subsequent numbers add to the story until the last student ends the story by incorporating the phrase on his or her card.

NOTE: You may want to record the story and play it back to the class afterwards.

Storytelling

Mini-Geschichte

*This story accompanies Teaching Transparency 7-2. The **Mini-Geschichte** can be told and retold in different formats, acted out, written down, and read aloud to give students additional opportunities to practice all four skills.*

„Du, Otto, schau mal, diese Stadt hat mehr Plakatwände als Häuser!" „Ja, du hast Recht, Erika. Die Stadt ist überflutet mit Werbung. Der Athlet preist irgendeinen Saft an. Da drüben ist eine Reklame für irgendein Shampoo. Welche Ware preisen die Frau und Kinder in den weißen Klamotten an?" „Du, Otto, pass auf! Das Auto vor dir will nach links!" „Ja, ich hab's schon gesehen. Ich kann mir aber gut vorstellen, dass die vielen Plakate öfters Unfälle verursachen. Man schaut auf die Plakate und nicht auf den Verkehr."

Traditions

Die Frankfurter Buchmesse

Kurz nach der Erfindung des Buchdrucks durch Johannes Gutenberg wurde Frankfurt zum wichtigsten Buchplatz Mitteleuropas. Selbst Martin Luther bot hier seine Schriften an. Nach dem Dreißigjährigen Krieg im 17. Jahrhundert verlor Frankfurt die Vorrangstellung an Leipzig. Nach dem Zweiten Weltkrieg verlor Leipzig dann wieder an Bedeutung, denn es lag in der sowjetischen Zone.

Auf der Ersten Frankfurter Buchmesse 1949, die in der Paulskirche stattfand, zeigten über 200 Aussteller 10.000 Titel. Auf der Zweiten Frankfurter Buchmesse 1950 präsentierten 460 Verlage 28.000 Titel und es gab erstmals auch internationale Aussteller.

Die Frankfurter Buchmesse ist heute die größte und bedeutendste Bücherschau der Welt. 6.600 Einzelaussteller und 90 National- und Kollektivaussteller präsentieren jährlich 380.000 Bücher und elektronische Produkte aus 113 Ländern.

Frankfurt am Main

Rezept

Was fehlt?

Fleisch
Geflügel
Fisch
Wurst
Bohnen
Gurken
Karotten
Kartoffeln
Salat
Zwiebel
Eier
Reis
Saft
Kaffee
Kakao
Eier
Mehl
Semmeln
Brot
Kekse
Milch
Sahne
Butter
Joghurt
Käse
Fett
Öl
Eier
Zucker
Honig
Bonbon
Äpfel
Birnen
Bananen
Orangen
Zitronen
Salz
Pfeffer
Paprika
Senf
Ketchup
Reis
Teigwaren
Fleisch
Geflügel
Fisch
Wurst
Bohnen
Gurken
Karotten
Kartoffeln
Salat
Zwiebel
Eier

Handkäs mit Musik

Für 2 Personen

Zutaten

g=Gramm, EL=Esslöffel

1 Handkäs (200 – 250 g)

8 EL Essig

4 EL Öl

4 EL Wasser

3 Zwiebeln

Salz

weißer Pfeffer

Kümmel

Zubereitung

Für die Marinade Essig, Öl und Wasser verrühren und dann mit Salz und Pfeffer kräftig würzen. Die gepellten und klein gewürfelten Zwiebeln und den Kümmel dazugeben. Die Marinade über den Käse verteilen und durchziehen lassen.

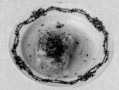

Beilage

Bauernbrot und Butter

Kapitel 7: Ohne Reklame geht es nicht!
Technology

To preview all resources available for this chapter, use the **One-Stop Planner CD-ROM**, Disc 2.

Internet Connection

ADRESSE: go.hrw.com
KENNWORT:
WK3 FRANKFURT-7

*Have students explore the **go.hrw.com** Web site for many online resources covering all chapters. All Chapter 7 resources are available under the keyword **WK3 Frankfurt-7**. Interactive games practice the material and provide students with immediate feedback. You will also find a printable worksheet that provides Internet activities that lead to a comprehensive online research project.*

Interaktive Spiele

You can use the interactive activities in this chapter
- to practice grammar, vocabulary, and chapter functions
- as homework
- as an assessment option
- as a self-test
- to prepare for the Chapter Test

Internet Aktivitäten

Students analyze the language and slogans used in advertisements for cars, perfumes, and watches.

- To prepare students for the **Arbeitsblatt,** have them list adjectives and nouns that they would expect to find in advertisements for cars, perfumes, and watches. Students may include the adjectives provided in Activity 12, p. 188.
- After completing the **Arbeitsblatt,** ask students to compare the language used in ads for small to medium-sized cars with the language used in ads for luxury cars. For example, are ads for a Volkswagen similar to those for a Porsche? Are ads tailored to income, age, or gender of the consumer?

Webprojekt

Have students find ads for toothpaste, shampoo, or soap. Students should report on the language and images used in the ads. Encourage students to exchange useful Web sites with their classmates. Have students document their sources by referencing the names and URLs of all the sites they consulted.

Textbook Listening Activities Scripts

The following scripts are for the listening activities found in the *Pupil's Edition*. For Student Response Forms, see *Listening Activities*, pages 51–54. To provide students with additional listening practice, see *Listening Activities*, pages 55–58.

Erste Stufe

3   p. 185

UDO   Hallo, Brigitte! Hallo, Rudi! Was macht ihr denn gerade?

RUDI   Tag, Udo! Nichts Besonderes. Nur 'ne Kaffeepause.

UDO   Du, Rudi, hast du neue Sportschuhe? Die sind aber schick. Wo hast du die denn her?

RUDI   Tja, die hab ich zum Geburtstag bekommen. Ich wollte diese Schuhe schon seit Monaten haben.

BRIGITTE   Die Schuhe habe ich doch im Fernsehen gesehen, oder? In dieser Werbung mit dem Basketballspieler, der 10 Meter hoch springen kann, also durch die Decke und durch das Dach der Sporthalle oder so was.

UDO   Mensch! Die Werbung geht mir so auf die Nerven! Keiner kann doch so hoch springen!

RUDI   Na ja, Udo, bist du blöd? Das geht doch gar nicht darum, ob es realistisch ist oder nicht! Wichtig ist, dass die Zuschauer von dem Werbespot beeindruckt sind.

UDO   Na ja, aber was mich aufregt, ist, dass die Werbung indirekt behauptet, dass man mit den Sportschuhen irgendwie stärker oder besser wäre. Oder zumindest, dass man gerade mit diesen Schuhen höher springen kann als die anderen Sportler!

BRIGITTE   Genau! Versteckte Mitteilungen nennt man das! Mich regt so was auch auf!

UDO   Ja, es nervt mich halt, dass die Werbemacher versuchen, einen zu manipulieren.

RUDI   Also mir ist das eigentlich egal. Ich lasse mich eben nicht manipulieren. Die Schuhe haben mir auch ohne Reklame gefallen.

BRIGITTE   Na ja, aber ich glaube, dass wir in erster Linie erst durch die Werbung auf ein Produkt aufmerksam gemacht werden.

UDO   Da stimme ich mit Brigitte überein. Mir geht es jedenfalls oft so.

BRIGITTE   Also, ich habe festgestellt, dass ich mir eigentlich ganz gern Werbespots im Fernsehen, Reklamen an Plakatwänden oder in Zeitungsprospekten anschaue. Mir ist es echt egal, ob ich da beeinflusst werde. Ich finde die meisten dieser Werbungen einfach bunt und witzig.

UDO   Du gibst also zu, dass du dich manipulieren lässt?

BRIGITTE   Wenn du es unbedingt so nennen willst! Guckt mal her! Meine Rudolfo-Carmanio-Bluse! Darauf wurde ich durch 'ne ganz bunte Reklame in einer Zeitschrift aufmerksam gemacht. Der Werbespruch war super: „Rudolfo — für die Frau, die sich selbst gefallen möchte!"

RUDI   Und nur wegen des Slogans hast du die Bluse gekauft?

BRIGITTE   Ach Quatsch, Rudi! Die Bluse habe ich gekauft, weil sie mir halt gefallen hat. Aber der Spruch, sag ich euch, der hat mich beeindruckt!

UDO   Mensch, die Rudolfo-Carmanio-Klamotten sind doch aber wahnsinnig teuer, oder?

BRIGITTE   Ja schon! Aber der Preis ist mir egal, wenn die Werbung es geschafft hat, mich für ein Produkt zu interessieren.

UDO   Ja, aber im Grunde genommen bezahlst du für den Namen und für die Werbung mit! Siehst du, das stört mich echt, und deswegen würde ich mir Produkte, für die die Firmen viel Geld für Werbung ausgeben, nicht kaufen!

Answers to Activity 3

Udo: geht es auf die Nerven, wenn eine Werbung unrealistisch ist; regt sich über versteckte Mitteilungen auf; ärgert sich über Manipulation in der Werbung; stört es, wenn man beim Kauf eines Produktes die teuren Werbekosten mitbezahlt

Brigitte: regt sich über versteckte Mitteilungen auf; schaut sich gern Werbung an, und deshalb ist es ihr egal, ob sie beeinflusst wird; ist der Preis eines Produktes egal, wenn die Werbung es geschafft hat, sie für das Produkt zu interessieren

Rudi: sind Manipulationen in der Werbung egal, weil er sich nicht manipulieren lässt

6   p. 185

FRAU W.   Frau Gruber, haben Sie schon das neue Müsli probiert?

FRAU G.   Welches meinen Sie denn, Frau Winter? Das von RITTERMANN mit den extra vielen Rosinen?

FRAU W.   Ja, genau! Ich kaufe es jetzt immer, weil es neben den Rosinen auch noch vier verschiedene Sorten Trockenobst und viele Ballaststoffe hat. Ein richtig gesundes Müsli, sag ich Ihnen!

FRAU G.   Es schmeckt halt viel besser als die anderen Sorten. Meinen Sie nicht auch, Herr Köhler?

HERR K.   Hm … haben Sie schon gesehen, wie viel es kostet? Ich finde, das ist zu teuer für eine Packung Müsli. Da bleibe ich lieber bei meiner alten Marke.

FRAU G.   Übrigens, haben Sie schon gesehen? Orangensaft ist diese Woche im Sonderangebot! Ich nehm mir gleich einen ganzen Kasten mit!

FRAU W.   Welchen meinen Sie denn, Frau Gruber, den aus Orangensaftkonzentrat oder den frisch gepressten?

FRAU G.   Den frisch gepressten, natürlich. Von ORANSINA!

HERR K.   Ja, der ist ausgezeichnet! Davon werde ich mir auch gleich mehrere Flaschen mitnehmen.

FRAU W.   So, ich muss mal auf meine Einkaufsliste schauen! Ach, beinahe hätte ich den Kaffee vergessen!

FRAU G.   Welchen nehmen Sie denn, Frau Winter?

FRAU W.   Also, meine Familie mag nur den koffeinfreien von MOKKAROMA. Der ist am mildesten.

FRAU G.   Ach, dann kaufen Sie also immer nur die eine Sorte?

FRAU W.   Ja genau! Sie denn nicht, Frau Gruber?

FRAU G.   Nein, ich kaufe jedesmal eine andere Marke. Dann haben wir im Geschmack mehr Abwechslung.

HERR K.   Ja, da stimme ich Ihnen zu. Beim Kaffee unterscheidet sich das Aroma sehr zwischen den verschiedenen

Sorten. Ich probiere auch immer wieder andere Marken aus.

FRAU W. So, was brauch ich noch? Ach, fast hätte ich das Waschpulver vergessen. Oh, ÖKOWEISS gibt's jetzt auch als Konzentrat in der Nachfüllpackung! Wie praktisch!

FRAU G. Haben Sie schon mal BLITZWASCH ausprobiert, Frau Winter? Da wird die Wäsche strahlend weiß und duftig! Hier, schauen Sie mal! Ich hab mir gerade die 7,5-Kilo-Packung in den Einkaufswagen gelegt.

FRAU W. Ja, aber leider ist BLITZWASCH nicht biologisch abbaubar! Ich nehme lieber das umweltfreundliche ÖKOWEISS.

FRAU G. Tja, aber leider wäscht es die Flecken nicht so gut raus wie BLITZWASCH. BLITZWASCH hat eben eine stärkere Waschkraft.

FRAU W. Ach du liebe Zeit, es ist ja schon fast halb zwölf. Ich muss schnell heim. Auf Wiedersehen, Herr Köhler! Tschüs, Frau Gruber!

HERR K. Tschüs!

FRAU G. Schönen Tag noch, Frau Winter!

Answers to Activity 6
Frau Winter kauft: Müsli von RITTERMANN, weil es gesund ist; Kaffee von MOKKAROMA, weil er am mildesten ist; ÖKOWEISS-Waschpulver, weil es umweltfreundlich ist.
Frau Gruber kauft: Müsli von RITTERMANN, weil es besser schmeckt; Orangensaft von ORANSINA, weil er im Angebot ist; immer andere Kaffeesorten, um mehr Abwechslung im Geschmack zu haben; BLITZWASCH-Waschpulver, weil es eine stärkere Waschkraft hat.
Herr Köhler kauft: seine alte Müslimarke, weil sie billiger ist; Orangensaft von ORANSINA, weil er im Angebot ist; immer andere Kaffeesorten, um mehr Abwechslung im Geschmack zu haben.

10 p. 187

1. KATZENSCHMAUS, aus reinem Fleisch und hochwertigen Vitaminen! Lässt Ihre Katze garantiert zum Feinschmecker werden!

2. Sehen, was man fühlt: Die einzigartige, neue Pflege von BIOWASCH, damit Ihre neuen Kleidungsstücke auch nach der Wäsche noch wie neu aussehen!

3. Natur pur: Sahnig-fein, cremig-schmelzend! Keine Butter ist besser im Geschmack als DEUTSCHE MARKENBUTTER!

4. Schützen Sie die Zukunft Ihres Haares mit dem Pflegeshampoo von LAREOL! Verwöhnen Sie Ihr Haar mit seidigem Glanz! Erleben Sie die neue Spannkraft in Ihrem Haar! Fühlen Sie die geschmeidige Fülle! Nur mit LAREOL!

5. Für den dynamischen, sportlichen Typ: Der neue AQUARIUS! Ein Wagen, der Sie nie im Stich lässt.

Answers to Activity 10
1. e; 2. b; 3. c; 4. d; 5. a

Zweite Stufe

17 p. 192

ANDREA He, Leute, habt ihr gute Werbespots aus den Zeitungen gesammelt? Okay. Dann lasst mal sehen!

THOMAS Ich habe eine Werbung von einem Fitnessstudio gefunden, die ich ganz super fand. Schaut mal! Eine hübsche, schlanke Frau im Bodysuit und ein

muskulöser Mann daneben. Darunter steht ein Slogan, mit dem das Fitnessstudio die Vorteile eines gut trainierten Körpers anpreist.

UTE Mensch, Thomas, das ist ja ekelhaft! Meint ihr nicht, dass dieses Fitnessstudio ganz einfach versucht, die Leute zu beeinflussen?

ACHIM Na klar, Ute! Das ist doch der Sinn der ganzen Sache! Wenn Leute diese superathletischen Körper in den Zeitungen sehen, dann fühlen sie sich angesprochen und wollen auch so aussehen. Ich finde diese Werbung Klasse!

ANDREA Eben! Achim hat Recht!

UTE Ich mag diese Art von Werbung gar nicht, bei der versucht wird, den Leuten etwas vorzumachen, was eigentlich sehr unrealistisch ist.

ACHIM Ute, selbst wenn die Werbung etwas unrealistisch ist, appelliert sie doch an die Sportmuffel, mal endlich was für ihre Gesundheit zu tun.

UTE Na gut!

ANDREA Ich habe eine Anzeige für ein Blumengeschäft gefunden. Wie findet ihr die?

ACHIM Mensch, Andrea! So was Langweiliges! Wer kauft sich schon Blumen?

THOMAS Viele Leute mögen Blumen.

UTE Ich stimme ganz mit dir überein, Thomas.

ACHIM Wir suchen doch nach einem Werbespot, der die Schüler anspricht, oder?

ANDREA Achim hat Recht. Blumen sind wahrscheinlich nicht so geeignet dafür.

UTE Aber hier ist ein toller Werbespot von einem Fahrradhändler. Der bietet Mountainbikes an.

THOMAS Na ja, Ute. Ich weiß nicht so recht! Heutzutage haben die meisten Schüler doch ein Mofa.

ACHIM Das stimmt doch gar nicht, Thomas! Die meisten Schüler und Studenten besitzen eher ein Fahrrad als ein Mofa.

UTE Das meine ich auch. Es gibt wahnsinnig viele Schüler, die mit dem Fahrrad zur Schule kommen, und deshalb finde ich den Werbespot auch besonders geeignet.

ACHIM Ja, also ich bin dafür, dass wir ihn nehmen.

UTE Hier ist noch eine gute Reklame vom Buchladen am Stadtbad.

ACHIM Ach, diese Werbung eignet sich doch gar nicht für unsere Schülerzeitung! Bücher erinnern die Schüler nur ans Lernen! Wir sollten eine Werbung nehmen, die in erster Linie Spaß suggeriert!

ANDREA Das ist eine gute Idee, Achim! Woran genau denkst du da?

ACHIM Wie wär's denn mit einer Reklame vom neuen Freizeitpark in Hermeskeil?

THOMAS Dafür interessieren sich die Schüler bestimmt!

UTE Das glaub ich auch!

ACHIM Na prima! Dann hätten wir ja genügend Werbespots für die Schülerzeitung.

Answers to Activity 17
Achims Meinungen werden am meisten akzeptiert.

22 p. 194

CHRISTIAN Du, Sebastian, ich finde, dass der Werbespruch: „Weil Ihre Helden ganze Arbeit leisten" ein Versuch ist, die Konsumenten zu beeinflussen!

SEBASTIAN Das mag schon sein. Doch es scheint nicht der Fall zu sein, dass diese Werbung versucht, unsere Gefühle auszunutzen. Was meinst du, Lisa?

LISA	Ich meine, es sieht so aus, als ob in der Cowboywerbung und in diesem Werbespruch viele verborgene Mitteilungen stecken. Erstens will die Werbung sagen, wenn Ihr Kind diese Schokomilch trinkt, wird es sich gesund und kräftig entwickeln. Zweitens zeigt sie den Kindern, dass sie richtige Draufgänger sein können und das nur, wenn sie regelmäßig SCHOKO-SAM trinken. So ganz nach dem Motto: „Wenn ich SCHOKO-SAM trinke, bin ich auch ein Held".
CHRISTIAN	Du meinst also, dass der Werbespruch etwas verspricht, was in Wirklichkeit nicht stimmt.
LISA	Genau!
CHRISTIAN	Das scheint mir auch so!
SEBASTIAN	Und ich finde, dass Mädchen mit dieser Werbung überhaupt nicht angesprochen werden! Hier wird ganz eindeutig nur der kleine Junge als Held gezeigt.
CHRISTIAN	Hm. Da bin ich mir nicht so sicher. Das würde ich nämlich nicht so eng sehen, Sebastian! Meine Schwester, zum Beispiel, mag diese Werbung sehr gern.
LISA	Eben! Ich wäre mir da auch nicht so sicher! Meine kleinen Kusinen imitieren den Cowboy immer, wenn sie diese Werbung im Fernsehen sehen oder wenn sie SCHOKO-SAM trinken.
SEBASTIAN	Aber darum geht es ja gerade! Hier werden doch ganz eindeutig die Gefühle der Eltern ausgenutzt, weil sie das Zeug wirklich für ihre Kinder kaufen. Und die Gefühle der Kinder werden ebenfalls ausgenutzt, weil sie wie Helden sein wollen.
CHRISTIAN	Das mag schon sein, Sebastian. Du kannst aber von Kindern nicht erwarten, dass sie die Werbesprüche im Fernsehen bereits analysieren können.
SEBASTIAN	Ja, aber ich finde, die Eltern lassen sich auch von der Werbung beeinflussen.
LISA	Kann schon sein! Aber ich glaube, dass es genügend Eltern gibt, die sich für ein Produkt aus vernünftigeren Gründen entscheiden, und sich nicht nur an der Werbung orientieren.
SEBASTIAN	Ich finde es außerdem auch unmoralisch, Kinder in der Werbung zu benutzen. Ich bin total dagegen!
CHRISTIAN	Hm. Damit hab ich kein Problem.
LISA	Ja. Mich stört es eigentlich auch nicht, wenn Kinder in Werbespots mitmachen.

Answers to Activity 22
Konsumenten werden beeinflusst: Christian ist überzeugt, dass er Recht hat; Sebastian und Lisa sind nicht sicher.
Gefühle werden ausgenutzt: Christian ist nicht sicher; Sebastian ist überzeugt, dass er Recht hat.
Werbung enthält verborgene Mitteilungen: Christian und Lisa sind überzeugt, dass sie Recht haben.
Mädchen werden mit dieser Werbung nicht angesprochen: Christian und Lisa sind nicht sicher; Sebastian ist überzeugt, dass er Recht hat.
Kinder in Werbung: Sebastian ist dagegen.

Anwendung

2 p. 205

1. POP-TEEN, die moderne Zeitschrift für junge Leute. Immer informiert, immer auf dem neuesten Stand! POP-TEEN hat die heißesten Interviews, die größten Hits und die „coolsten"

One-Stop Planner CD-ROM

For resource information, see the One-Stop Planner CD-ROM, Disc 2.

Tipps zu allem, was Teenager interessiert. Die neueste Ausgabe ist wieder voll gepackt mit Berichten über die größten Stars der Musikszene, mit einer exklusiven Fotoreportage über Madonna und mit der aktuellen Top-Ten Hitliste. Holt sie euch, die neue POP-TEEN.

2. SPORT-AKTIV, das neue Fachgeschäft für Sportbekleidung und Sportausstattung bietet Ihnen eine riesige Auswahl an allem, was das Sportlerherz begehrt. Diese Woche ganz groß im Angebot: Tenniskleidung und Tennisschuhe von führenden Markenherstellern; dazu Stirnbänder mit feschem Design. Kommen Sie, und sehen Sie sich auch unsere enorme Auswahl an Tennisschlägern an! Bei SPORT-AKTIV gibt's garantiert für jeden etwas. Machen Sie auch mit bei unserer Verlosung! Gewinnen Sie eine Reise für zwei Personen nach Wimbledon! Sehen Sie ihre Stars live! Teilnahmebedingung: Kauf einen unserer Tennisartikel im Angebot. Lassen Sie sich diese Chance nicht entgehen! Kommen Sie noch heute zu SPORT-AKTIV!

3. Auch im Alter fit und aktiv mit BIOPUR. Eine spezielle Mischung aus essentiellen Vitalstoffen erhält Ihnen Gesundheit und jugendliche Frische. Konzentrierte, energiespendende Vitamine in BIOPUR helfen Ihnen, den Körper zu regenerieren und das Immunsystem zu stärken. Entdecken Sie die Welt mit neuem Schwung! Werden Sie wieder aktiv! BIOPUR macht einen neuen Menschen aus Ihnen.

4. Treffen Sie die richtige Entscheidung im Leben Ihres Kindes: Kaufen Sie BABYPLUS! Diese einzigartige Baby- und Kleinkindnahrung ist angereichert mit lebenswichtigen Vitaminen und Mineralstoffen, die Ihr Kind für eine gesunde und kräftige Entwicklung braucht. BABYPLUS gibt es in zehn verschiedenen Geschmacksrichtungen. Babys, Mütter und Väter lieben BABYPLUS!

5. Eine große Auswahl an lässiger, moderner Kleidung für junge Leute jetzt bei TOP-MODEN in der Innenstadt. TOP-MODEN hat alles, worauf es ankommt: schicke Hemden und Blusen aus reiner Baumwolle in fetzigen Farben; die neuesten Designerjeans von bester Qualität; modische Lederjacken in den aktuellen Trendfarben, und vieles mehr. Die feschesten Outfits für junge Leute, nur bei TOP-MODEN in der Innenstadt!

Answers to Activity 2
1. b; 2. e; 3. d; 4. a; 5. c

Kapitel 7: Ohne Reklame geht es nicht!
Suggested Lesson Plans *50-Minute Schedule*

Day 1

LOCATION OPENER 15 min.
- Present Location Opener, pp. 176–179
- Background Information, ATE, p. 175A
- The Almanac and Map, ATE, p. 175A
- Show **Frankfurt** Video
- Do Viewing and Post-viewing Activities, Video Guide, pp. 29–30

CHAPTER OPENER 10 min.
- Advance Organizer, ATE, p. 179M
- Culture Notes, ATE, p. 179M

LOS GEHT'S! 20 min.
- Preteaching Vocabulary, ATE, p. 179N
- Building Context, p. 179N
- Thinking Critically, p. 179N
- Play Audio CD for **Los geht's!**
- Have students read **Los geht's!**, pp. 182–183
- Do Activities 1 and 2, p. 183

Wrap-Up 5 min.
- Students respond to questions about their favorite television commercials

Homework Options
Übungsheft, p. 79, Acts. 1–2

Day 2

ERSTE STUFE
Quick Review 10 min.
- Check homework, Übungsheft, p. 79, Acts. 1–2

Reading Selection, p. 184 10 min.
- Group Work, ATE, p. 179O
- Read **Werbung–pro und contra**, p. 184

Wortschatz, p. 184 10 min.
- Presenting **Wortschatz**, ATE, p. 179O
- Do Activities 1–3, pp. 55–56, Grammatikheft

So sagt man das!, p. 185 15 min.
- Presenting **So sagt man das!**, ATE, p. 179P
- Play Audio CD for Activity 3, p. 185
- Do Activities 4 and 5, p. 185

Wrap-Up 5 min.
- Students respond to questions about comparing two advertisements

Homework Options
Grammatikheft, p. 57, Act. 4
Übungsheft, p. 80, Act. 1

Day 3

ERSTE STUFE
Quick Review 15 min.
- Check homework, Grammatikheft, p. 57, Act. 4
- Do Circumlocution Activity, ATE, p. 179X

So sagt man das!, p. 185 15 min.
- Presenting **So sagt man das!**, ATE, p. 179P
- Teaching Transparency 7-1
- Play Audio CD for Activity 6, p. 185
- Do Activity 5, p. 57, Grammatikheft
- Do Activity 2, p. 80, Übungsheft

Grammatik, p. 186 15 min.
- Presenting **Grammatik**, ATE, p. 179P
- Do Activities 7 and 8, p. 186
- Do Activity 3, p. 81, Übungsheft

Wrap-Up 5 min.
- Students respond to questions about types of commercials on German and on American TV

Homework Options
Grammatikheft, p. 58, Acts. 6–7

Day 4

ERSTE STUFE
Quick Review 5 min.
- Check homework, Grammatikheft, p. 58, Acts. 6–7

Grammatik, p. 187 20 min.
- Presenting **Grammatik**, ATE, p. 179Q
- Do Activity 9, p. 187
- Play Audio CD for Activity 10, p. 187
- Do Activity 11, p. 187
- Do Activities 12, 13, and 14, p. 188

LANDESKUNDE 20 min.
- Teaching Suggestions, ATE, p. 179R
- Read **Warum so wenig Unterbrecherwerbung?**, p. 189
- Do Activities 1, 2, and 3, p. 189

Wrap-Up
- Students name determiners of quantity

Homework Options
Pupil's Edition, p. 188, Act. 15
Grammatikheft, p. 59, Act. 8
Übungsheft, pp. 81–83, Acts. 4–9; p. 84, Acts. 1–2

Day 5

ERSTE STUFE
Quick Review 10 min.
- Übungsheft, pp. 81–83, Acts. 4–9; p. 84, Acts. 1–2

Ein großes Angebot (Video) 20 min.
- Teaching Suggestions, Video Guide, p. 32
- Do Pre-viewing, Viewing and Post-viewing Activities, p. 32, Video Guide
- Show **Ein großes Angebot**
- Show **Videoclips: Werbung**
- Do Pre-viewing, Viewing and Post-viewing Activities, pp. 33–34, Video Guide

Quiz Review 20 min.
- **Mehr Grammatikübungen, Erste Stufe**
- Do Additional Listening Activities 7-1 and 7-2, p. 55
- Do Activities for Communication 7-1 or 7-2, pp. 25–26

Homework Options
Activities for Communication, pp. 83 and 85, Realia 7-3; make up words to go in the blank speech bubble
Internet Aktivitäten, see ATE, p. 179E

Day 6

ERSTE STUFE
Quick Review 5 min.
- Check homework, Realia 7-3

Quiz 20 min.
- Quiz 7-1A or 7-1B

WEITER GEHT'S! 20 min.
- Preteaching Vocabulary, ATE, p. 179R
- Play Audio CD for **Weiter geht's!**, pp. 190–191
- Do Activity 16, p. 191

Wrap-Up 5 min.
- Students respond to questions about what they like and dislike about television commercials

Homework Options
Übungsheft, p. 85, Act. 1

For alternative lesson plans by chapter section, to create your own customized plans, or to preview all resources available for this chapter, use the **One-Stop Planner CD-ROM**, Disc 2.

 For additional homework suggestions, see activities accompanied by this symbol throughout the chapter.

Day 7

ZWEITE STUFE

Quick Review 15 min.
- Return and review Quiz 7-1
- Bell Work, ATE, p. 179S
- Check homework, Übungsheft, p. 85, Act. 1

Wortschatz, So sagt man das!, p. 192 15 min.
- Presenting **Wortschatz**, ATE, p. 179S
- Presenting **So sagt man das!**, ATE, p. 179T
- Play Audio CD for Activity 17, p. 192
- Do Activity 18, p. 193

Ein wenig Grammatik, Grammatik, p. 193 15 min.
- Presenting **Ein wenig Grammatik, Grammatik**, ATE, p. 179T
- Do Activities 19, 20, and 21, p. 194

Wrap-Up 5 min.
- Students respond to questions about being surprised or annoyed

Homework Options
Grammatikheft, pp. 60–62, Acts. 9–13

Day 8

ZWEITE STUFE

Quick Review 10 min.
- Check homework, Grammatikheft, pp. 60–62, Acts. 9–13

So sagt man das!, p. 194 10 min.
- Presenting **So sagt man das!**, ATE, p. 179U
- Teaching Transparency 7-2
- Play Audio CD for Activity 22, p. 194

Grammatik, p. 195 10 min.
- Presenting **Grammatik**, ATE, p. 179U
- Do Activity 23, p. 195

Wortschatz , p. 195 15 min.
- Presenting **Wortschatz**, ATE, p. 179U
- Do Activities 24, 25 and 26, p. 195

Wrap-Up 5 min.
- Students respond to questions about what they are sure about, what they are uncertain about and about what seems to be true

Homework Options
Grammatikheft, p. 63, Acts. 14–15
Übungsheft, pp. 86–89, Acts. 1–8

Day 9

ZWEITE STUFE

Quick Review 10 min.
- Check homework, Übungsheft, pp. 86–89, Acts. 1–8

Quiz Review 20 min.
- **Mehr Grammatikübungen, Zweite Stufe**
- Do Communicative Activities 7-3 or 7-4, pp. 27–28
- Do Additional Listening Activities 7-4 and 7-5, pp. 56–57

Quiz 20 min.
- Quiz 7-2A or 7-2B

Homework Options
Activities for Communication, pp. 82, 85, Realia 7-2, list the main points of the ad

Day 10

ZWEITE STUFE

Quick Review 10 min.
- Return and review Quiz 7-2
- Check homework, Realia 7-2

ZUM LESEN 20 min.
- Background Information, ATE, p. 179V
- Teaching Suggestions, ATE, p. 179V
- Present **Lesestrategie**, p. 196
- Do Activities 1–9, pp. 196–198

ZUM SCHREIBEN 15 min.
- Writing Strategy, ATE, p. 179W
- Present **Schreibtipp**, p. 199
- Do Activity A, p. 199

Wrap-Up 5 min.
- Students respond to questions about their favorite advertising slogans

Homework Options
Pupil's Edition, p. 198, Act. 10; p. 199, Act. B
Übungsheft, pp. 90–91, Acts. 1–7

Day 11

ZUM SCHREIBEN

Quick Review 10 min.
- Check homework, Pupil's Edition, p. 198, Act. 10; p. 199, Act. B

ZUM SCHREIBEN 20 min.
- Do Activity C, p. 199
- Present compositions to class

ANWENDUNG 15 min.
- Do Activities 1–4 and 6, pp. 204–205

Wrap-Up 5 min.
- Students respond to questions about expressing conviction and uncertainty

Homework Options
Pupil's Edition, p. 205, Act. 5
Interaktive Spiele, see ATE, p. 179E

Day 12

ANWENDUNG

Quick Review 10 min.
- Check homework, Pupil's Edition, p. 205, Act. 5

Kann ich's wirklich?, p. 206 15 min.
- Do **Kann ich's wirklich?**, Activities 1–6, p. 206

Chapter Review 15 min.
- Review chapter functions, vocabulary, and grammar; choose from **Mehr Grammatikübungen,** Activities for Communication, Listening Activities, or **Interaktive Spiele**
- Review test format and provide sample test items for students

Homework Options
Study for Chapter Test

Assessment

Test, Chapter 7 45 min.
- Administer Chapter 7 Test. Select from Testing Program, Alternative Assessment Guide or Test Generator.

Kapitel 7: Ohne Reklame geht es nicht!
Suggested Lesson Plans 90-Minute Schedule

Block 1

LOCATION OPENER 15 min.
- Present Location Opener, pp. 176–179
- Background Information, ATE, p. 175A
- The Almanac and Map, ATE, p. 175A
- Show **Frankfurt** Video
- Do Viewing and Post-viewing Activities, Video Guide, pp. 29–30

CHAPTER OPENER 10 min.
- Culture Notes, ATE, p. 179M
- Advance Organizer, ATE, p. 179M

LOS GEHT'S! 20 min.
- Preteaching Vocabulary, ATE, p. 179N
- Building Context, p. 179N
- Thinking Critically, p. 179N
- Play Audio CD for **Los geht's!**
- Have students read **Los geht's!**, pp. 182–183
- Do Activities 1 and 2, p. 183

ERSTE STUFE
Reading Selection, p. 184 10 min.
- Group Work, ATE, p. 179O
- Read **Werbung–pro und contra**, p. 184

Wortschatz, p. 184 10 min.
- Presenting **Wortschatz**, ATE, p. 179O
- Do Activities 1–3, pp. 55–56, Grammatikheft

So sagt man das!, p. 185 20 min.
- Presenting **So sagt man das!**, ATE, p. 179P
- Play Audio CD for Activity 3, p. 185
- Do Activities 4 and 5, p. 185
- Do Activity 1, p. 80, Übungsheft

Wrap-Up 5 min.
- Students respond to questions about their favorite television commercials

Homework Options
Grammatikheft, p. 57, Act. 4
Übungsheft, p. 79, Act. 1–2

Block 2

ERSTE STUFE
Quick Review 10 min.
- Check homework, Übungsheft, p. 79, Acts. 1–2

So sagt man das!, p. 185 15 min.
- Presenting **So sagt man das!**, ATE, p. 179P
- Teaching Transparency 7-1
- Play Audio CD for Activity 6, p. 185
- Do Activity 5, p. 57, Grammatikheft
- Do Activity 2, p. 80, Übungsheft

Grammatik, p. 186 15 min.
- Presenting **Grammatik**, ATE, p. 179P
- Do Activities 7 and 8, p. 186
- Do Activity 3, p. 81, Übungsheft

Grammatik, p. 187 25 min.
- Presenting **Grammatik**, ATE, p. 179Q
- Do Activity 9, p. 187
- Play Audio CD for Activity 10, p. 187
- Do Activity 11, p. 187
- Do Activities 12, 13, and 14, p. 188

LANDESKUNDE 20 min.
- Teaching Suggestions, ATE, p. 179R
- Read **Warum so wenig Unterbrecherwerbung?**, p. 189
- Do Activities 1, 2, and 3, p. 189

Wrap-Up 5 min.
- Students respond to questions about types of commercials on German and on American TV

Homework Options
Grammatikheft, p. 58, Acts. 6–7, p. 59, Act. 8
Übungsheft, pp. 81–83, Acts. 4–9; p. 84, Acts. 1–2

Block 3

ERSTE STUFE
Quick Review 10 min.
- Check homework, Grammatikheft, p. 58, Acts. 6–7, p. 59, Act. 8

Ein großes Angebot (Video) 20 min.
- Teaching Suggestions, Video Guide, p. 32
- Do Pre-viewing, Viewing, and Post-viewing Activities, p. 32, Video Guide
- Show **Ein großes Angebot**
- Show **Videoclips: Werbung**
- Do Pre-viewing, Viewing, and Post-viewing Activities, pp. 33–34, Video Guide

Quiz Review 20 min.
- **Mehr Grammatikübungen, Erste Stufe**
- Do Additional Listening Activities 7-1 and 7-2, p. 55
- Do Activities for Communication 7-1 or 7-2, pp. 25–26

Quiz 20 min.
- Quiz 7-1A or 7-1B

WEITER GEHT'S! 20 min.
- Preteaching Vocabulary, ATE, p. 179R
- Play Audio CD for **Weiter geht's!**, pp. 190–191
- Do Activity 16, p. 191

Homework Options
Übungsheft, p. 85, Act. 1

 **One-Stop** Planner CD-ROM

For alternative lesson plans by chapter section, to create your own customized plans, or to preview all resources available for this chapter, use the **One-Stop Planner CD-ROM**, Disc 2.

 For additional homework suggestions, see activities accompanied by this symbol throughout the chapter.

Block 4

ZWEITE STUFE
Quick Review 15 min.
- Return and review Quiz 7-1
- Bell Work, ATE, p. 179S
- Check homework, Übungsheft, p. 85, Act. 1

Wortschatz, So sagt man das!, p. 192 **15 min.**
- Presenting **Wortschatz**, ATE, p. 179S
- Presenting **So sagt man das!**, ATE, p. 179T
- Play Audio CD for Activity 17, p. 192
- Do Activity 18, p. 193

Ein wenig Grammatik, Grammatik, p. 193 **15 min.**
- Presenting **Ein wenig Grammatik, Grammatik**, ATE, p. 179T
- Do Activities 19, 20, and 21, p. 194

So sagt man das!, p. 194 **15 min.**
- Presenting **So sagt man das!**, ATE, p. 179U
- Teaching Transparency 7-2
- Play Audio CD for Activity 22, p. 194

Grammatik, p. 195 **10 min.**
- Presenting **Grammatik**, ATE, p. 179U
- Do Activity 23, p. 195
- Do Activity 14, p. 63, Grammatikheft

Wortschatz, p. 195 **15 min.**
- Presenting **Wortschatz**, ATE, p. 179U
- Do Activities 24, 25, and 26, p. 195

Wrap-Up 5 min.
- Students respond to questions about being suprised or annoyed

Homework Options
Grammatikheft, pp. 60–62, Acts. 9–13; p. 63, Act. 15
Übungsheft, pp. 86–89, Acts. 1–8
Internet Aktivitäten, see ATE, p. 179E

Block 5

ZWEITE STUFE
Quick Review 10 min.
- Übungsheft, pp. 86–89, Acts. 1–8

Quiz Review 15 min.
- **Mehr Grammatikübungen, Zweite Stufe**
- Do Communicative Activities 7-3 and 7-4, pp. 27–28
- Do Additional Listening Activities 7-4 and 7-5, pp. 56–57

Quiz 20 min.
- Quiz 7-2A or 7-2B

ZUM LESEN 20 min.
- Background Information, ATE, p. 179V
- Teaching Suggestions, ATE, p. 179V
- Present **Lesestrategie**, p. 196
- Do Activities 1–9, pp. 196–198

ZUM SCHREIBEN 20 min.
- Writing Strategy, ATE, p. 179W
- Present **Schreibtipp**, p. 199
- Do Activity A, p. 199

Wrap-Up 5 min.
- Students respond to questions about their favorite advertising slogans

Homework Options
Pupil's Edition, p. 198, Act. 10; p. 199, Act. B
Übungsheft, pp. 90–91, Acts. 1–7
Interaktive Spiele, see ATE, p. 179E

Block 6

ZWEITE STUFE
Quick Review 15 min.
- Return and review Quiz 7-2
- Check homework, Pupil's Edition, p. 198, Act. 10; p. 199, Act. B

ZUM SCHREIBEN 20 min.
- Do Activity C, p. 199
- Present compositions to class

ANWENDUNG 30 min.
- Do Activities 1–6, pp. 204–205

Kann ich's wirklich?, p. 206 **20 min.**
- Do Activities 1–6, p. 206

Wrap-Up 5 min.
- Students respond to questions about expressing conviction and uncertainty

Homework Options
Study for Chapter Test

Block 7

ANWENDUNG
Quick Review 15 min.
- Play game, **Es war einmal …**, ATE, p. 179C

Chapter Review 30 min.
- Review chapter functions, vocabulary, and grammar; choose from **Mehr Grammatikübungen,** Activities for Communication, Listening Activities, or **Interaktive Spiele**
- Review test format and provide sample test items for students

Test, Chapter 7 45 min.
- Administer Chapter 7 Test. Select from Testing Program, Alternative Assessment Guide, or Test Generator.

Kapitel 7: Ohne Reklame geht es nicht!
Teaching Suggestions, pages 180–207

PAGES 180–181

CHAPTER OPENER

Pacing Tips

Los geht's! and the Erste Stufe focus on the pros and cons of advertising. The functions introduced are 'expressing annoyance' and 'comparing.' Students also learn when to use derselbe and der gleiche and about adjective endings following determiners of quantity. The topic of Weiter geht's! and the Zweite Stufe is how advertising influences consumers. The functions practiced are 'eliciting agreement and agreeing' and 'expressing conviction, uncertainty, and what seems to be true.' Following the Zweite Stufe is Zum Lesen, which consists of an Asterix und Obelix cartoon. You may want to spend a little extra time on the Erste Stufe since it contains the Landeskunde. The function 'expressing annoyance' also prepares students for Zum Schreiben. For Lesson Plans and timing suggestions, see pages 179I–179L.

Meeting the Standards
Communication
- Expressing annoyance, p. 185
- Comparing, p. 185
- Eliciting agreement, p. 192
- Expressing conviction, uncertainty, and what seems to be true, p. 194

Cultures
- Landeskunde, p. 189
- Culture Notes, p. 179M
- Teacher Note, p. 179Q
- Background Information, p. 179V

Connections
- Language-to-Language, p. 179T
- Music Connection, p. 179T

Comparisons
- Background Information, p. 179R

One-Stop Planner CD-ROM

For resource information, see the **One-Stop Planner CD-ROM**, Disc 2.

Communities
- Community Link, p. 179P

Advance Organizer

Bring in a few ads for products that students in your class may have or even be wearing at the moment, such as sneakers, makeup, or designer clothing. Briefly discuss with your students what they think of the ads and whether they were influenced by them when they bought the specific items. Do they think the ads are informative, or do they just appeal to the eye and emotions?

Cultures and Communities

Culture Notes
- Advertising in Germany is very much influenced by the United States. Slogans for American products sold in Germany are often taken over from the American ads, and many English words are used. Sometimes American ads are used with German texts. The jargon of the advertising profession includes many American expressions.

- Litfaßsäulen are round pillars on which ads and announcements are posted, particularly those for upcoming cultural events. Litfaßsäulen were named after Ernst Litfaß, a printer from Berlin who created this pillar in 1854.

Chapter Sequence

LOS GEHT'S!

Teaching Resources
pp. 182–183

PRINT
▸ Lesson Planner, p. 41
▸ Übungsheft, p. 79

MEDIA
▸ One-Stop Planner
▸ Audio Compact Discs, CD7, Tr. 1

PAGES 182–183

Los geht's! Summary

In *Werbung — ja oder nein?*, two students are interviewed about how they feel they are influenced by advertising. The following learning outcomes listed on p. 181 are modeled in the episode: expressing annoyance and comparing.

Preteaching Vocabulary

Identifying Keywords

Start by asking students to guess the context of Los geht's! (two students being interviewed about the effects of advertising). Then have students use the German they know and the context of the situation to identify key words and phrases that tell what is happening. Students should look for words that seem important or that occur several times. Here are a few of the words they might identify as keywords: **Werbung, Reklame, Konsument, Produkt, nervt, Statussymbole.** List the keywords on the board or on a transparency and separate them according to whether or not they are cognates. Then ask students to guess the meaning of the keywords. Finally, ask students to guess the meaning of **Autoreklame** and **Bildreklame.**

Building Context

Ask individual students to describe their favorite TV commercial to the rest of the class in German. Do other students recognize it? If so, can they add to the description?

Teaching Suggestion

Play the recording of the entire interview and have students follow along in the text. Then divide the text into several sections and play one part at a time.

Follow each section with questions to check for comprehension. Explain new vocabulary, phrases, or constructions in German using actions, synonyms, and paraphrasing. After working through the interview in such a fashion, play the entire conversation again, stopping repeatedly to check students' understanding of the key points. End by playing the interview once again without stopping, and have students listen with their books closed.

Comprehension Check

Auditory Learners

1 After students have jotted down notes, ask them to give a partner a brief oral summary of what Stefan and Constance said. Call on several students to share their synopses with the class. Students may want to record the summary on tape and play it back for self-evaluation. A written summary could be assigned for homework.

Teaching Suggestion

2 Have students give examples of products that are endorsed by high profile athletes in the United States.

Thinking Critically

2 **Analyzing** As students work with the first part of this activity, have them think of words or phrases that indicate information or manipulation. Make a list with students. If possible, use German ads to find examples.

Comparing and Contrasting If possible, bring in ads from a German magazine and an American magazine that advertise the same or similar products. Have students compare the ads.

Career Path

Have students formulate scenarios in which employees of an American advertising company would need to know German. (Suggestion: Imagine that your company has been awarded a lucrative contract to advertise German-made sports equipment.)

Closure

Ask students what type of advertising they pay the most attention to and why. Does it come from television, radio, newspapers, magazines, or the Internet? (**Was für Reklame wirkt am meisten bei euch? Die im Fernsehen, im Radio, in Zeitungen und Zeitschriften oder im Internet?**)

LOS GEHT'S!

ERSTE STUFE

Teaching Resources
pp. 184–189

PRINT

- Lesson Planner, p. 42
- Listening Activities, pp. 51–52, 55–56
- Video Guide, pp. 31–33
- Activities for Communication, pp. 25–26, 83, 85, 125–126
- Grammatikheft, pp. 55–59
- Grammar Tutor for Students of German, Chapter 7
- Übungsheft, pp. 80–84
- Testing Program, pp. 147–150
- Alternative Assessment Guide, p. 36
- Student Make-Up Assignments, Chapter 7

MEDIA

- One-Stop Planner
- Audio Compact Discs, CD7, Trs. 2–4, 11, 15–17
- Video Program
  Ein großes Angebot
  Videocassette 2, 05:10–07:54
- Teaching Transparencies
  Situation 7-1
  Mehr Grammatikübungen Answers

PAGE 184

Bell Work

Visual Learners Record a series of commercials on videocassette, or use some of the **Werbung** clips on the *Video Program* for this chapter, and play them to the class without the sound. Have students think about what the characters or announcer might be saying. Call on volunteers to ad-lib the sound track or voice-over for each commercial.

Group Work

Divide the class into groups of three to four students. Go over the eight statements in *Werbung — pro und contra* and explain in German any unfamiliar phrases or expressions. Write the following questions on the board for students to answer as they reread the eight statements:

1. Von wem könnte diese Aussage stammen? Von der Werbeindustrie oder von Verbrauchern?

2. Welche Aussagen könnte man kombinieren, so dass sie einen Paragraphen bilden? Wenn nötig, fügt ein paar eigene Worte hinzu!

3. Welche Aussagen würden gute widersprechende Argumente abgeben? Schreibt für jedes Argument die beiden Nummern auf, und zwar in der Reihenfolge, wie man sie wiedergeben muss! Dann lest die Argumente laut vor!

Connections and Comparisons

Thinking Critically
Comparing and Contrasting Have students try to arrange the statements in order from the strongest pro-opinion to the strongest con-opinion.

PRESENTING: Wortschatz

- After going over the new vocabulary, ask students to come up with an example using words or phrases in the **auf Deutsch erklärt** column.
  Example:
  (Diesen Wagen kann ich mir nicht leisten.) Ich kann mir diesen Monat keine Zeitschriften mehr leisten. Ich habe nämlich kein Taschengeld mehr.

- For the **auf Englisch erklärt** column, ask students to describe contexts in which these phrases might be heard.
  Example:
  (Lies mal, was auf der Plakatwand steht!) Das sagt ein Freund zu einem anderen, als sie im Bus sitzen und an der Plakatwand vorbeifahren.

PRESENTING: So sagt man das!

- Ask students to review the **Los geht's!** section to find the expressions of annoyance that are used by the German students during the interview. Then have students make up additional expressions that Stefan or Constance could have used, based on what students know about their opinions about advertising.

- Ask students if they can think of other ways to express annoyance using phrases they already know. Make a list together.
Examples:
Ich find es blöd, wenn/dass …
Was mich stört ist, wenn …

Communication for All Students

Visual Learners

4 Provide each group with a large piece of construction paper and a marker. Tell groups to divide the paper into six columns: **Schule, zu Hause, Sport, Fernsehen, Werbung,** and one additional topic of their choice. Group members discuss each topic and then write down three things that annoy them in each column. When all groups have finished, tape each paper on the wall and have the spokesperson for each group go over his or her group's list.

Teaching Suggestion

5 Students will need some data in order to answer Questions 2 and 3. Assign each student one hour of television to watch over the weekend. Each student should record all the products he or she sees advertised during the hour, as well as the slogans used to promote each one.

COMMUNITY LINK

5 Have students get in touch with local television or radio stations to help them gather supporting materials for this activity. They could inquire about the types of advertisements most frequently aired and also find out how time slots determine the types of products being advertised. Have students incorporate their findings in their answers to the three questions.

PRESENTING: So sagt man das!

- Bring items such as youth magazines, different sized sweaters, two different types of sodas, or ads for different types of movies. Show these pairs of items to the class and ask them to compare them using expressions they already know.
Examples:
Dieser Pulli ist länger als der da.
Ich finde Film A besser als Film B.

- To introduce the new phrases, use additional items that would lend themselves for this demonstration.
Example:
Diese Jacke hier von C&A™ hat die gleiche Qualität wie die von Karstadt, aber die Preise sind sehr verschieden. Diese hier kostet …, und diese hier von … kostet …

Communication for All Students

For Additional Practice

6 Ask students about their family members' preferences for certain types of products. How can they explain these preferences?

PRESENTING: Grammatik

Derselbe, der gleiche

Make statements that can be used to demonstrate the uses of **der gleiche** and **derselbe**.
Example:
Sabine und Dieter benutzen das gleiche Deutschbuch.
Meine Schwester und ich sind in demselben Zimmer.

Communication for All Students

A Slower Pace

7 Help students with questions if necessary. Ask students if they and a friend go home the same way, ride the same bus, have the same kind of sneakers, read the same kind of books, or baby-sit for the same people.
Examples:
Habt ihr denselben Weg nach Hause?
Mögt ihr die gleichen Bücher?

ERSTE STUFE

Connections and Comparisons

Thinking Critically

8 **Comparing and Contrasting** Have students think of advertising slogans and give their opinions of them. Which ones do they like better than others? Have them compare ads for soft drinks, sneakers, and other types of products. Do they think one kind of ad is better or more effective than another?

PAGE 187

PRESENTING: Grammatik

Adjective endings following determiners of quantity Give examples of each determiner of quantity, or have students make up examples for each. Compare these and their endings with the normal plural adjective endings following **die, diese,** or **keine.**
Example:
diese ähnlichen Bücher/einige ähnliche Bücher

Communication for All Students

Challenge

9 After students have created sentences that describe their town and its attributes, have them combine the sentences into a cohesive paragraph to persuade an exchange student to visit their town. This could be done in writing or orally, in which case partners could jointly record a convincing message on audiocassette. Remind students to use connectors.

Thinking Critically

10 **Drawing Inferences** Before students listen to the five advertisements, ask them to identify each product. Then have them brainstorm some of the words and phrases they think they will hear when they listen to each sales pitch. Make a list and compare it with the actual recording after listening to it with the class.

Teaching Suggestion

11 Have students decide if the commercial is meant for radio or television. Let students choose one or the other and plan their ad accordingly.

PAGE 188

Teaching Suggestion

12 If students enjoy this activity, bring in ads from magazines and newspapers published in German-speaking countries. Cut out or cover any direct references to the products so that students have to infer what is being advertised. Have students examine the ads and comment on them.

Building on Previous Skills

13 Ask students to think of additional adjectives to describe the four products listed. Which of the consumers' senses are being addressed with the adjectives (**hören, schmecken, sehen, fühlen,** or **riechen**)?

Group Work

14 Students may work in small groups to prepare for the discussion. Have them jot down ideas for each of the statements. Have students refer back to the **So sagt man das!** boxes on p. 185 if they need to.

Using the Video

Videocassette 2, 05:10–07:54
In the video clip *Ein großes Angebot,* consumers in a Berlin grocery store talk about the differences of consumer goods offered before and after German unification. See *Video Guide,* p. 32, for suggestions.

PAGE 189

 **LANDESKUNDE**

Cultures and Communities

Teacher Note

The acronyms ARD, ZDF, and RTL stand for **Arbeitsgemeinschaft der öffentlich-rechtlichen Rundfunkanstalten Deutschlands, Zweites Deutsches Fernsehen,** and **Radio Télévision Luxembourg,** respectively.

Teaching Suggestions

- After students have read the first paragraph, ask them to summarize what was said in one or two sentences. Do the same for the second paragraph. Next have students infer the answers to Questions 1 and 2 with their books closed. Record their answers on a transparency.

- You may need to help students with words and phrases they are not able to guess from the context of the article.
  Examples:
  öffentlich-rechtlicher Sender: *state-regulated station*
  Fernsehgebühren: Geld, das man monatlich für den Fernsehempfang bezahlt
  Einblendung: ein Fernsehprogramm wird von Werbung unterbrochen.
  gesetzlich: vom Staat geregelt; *by law*
  Einnahmequelle: die Möglichkeit, Geld zu erhalten

- After students have worked with the text and can understand it, go back to Questions 1 and 2 and have students reconsider their answers. Were they right? Does anything need to be added?

Connections and Comparisons

Thinking Critically
Comparing and Contrasting Can students compare German networks with their American counterparts based on what they have learned so far?

Background Information
Currently the monthly subscription fee to have TV and radio in a German household is about €16. It costs an extra € 10 to have cable (**Kabel**), and there are varying fees for pay channels, like **Premiere.**

Teacher Note

Mention to your students that the **Landeskunde** will also be included in Quiz 7–1B given at the end of the **Erste Stufe.**

Teaching Suggestion

Act out the following scene with students. In German, ask students to purchase some products that you are fond of, but they are not. Students then try to convince you to switch over to their favorite products. For example, if you tried to convince a student to buy a certain cola by saying: **Diese Cola schmeckt gut!,** he or she might respond with: **Ja schon, aber**

die Cola, die ich trinke, hat weniger Kalorien und ist billiger. Try to get responses from several students for each item you show them, so that all students have a chance to participate.

Assess

▸ Testing Program, pp. 147–150
  Quiz 7-1A, Quiz 7-1B
  Audio CD7, Tr. 11

▸ Student Make-Up Assignments
  Chapter 7, Alternative Quiz

▸ Alternative Assessment Guide, p. 36

WEITER GEHT'S!

Teaching Resources
pp. 190–191

PRINT
▸ Lesson Planner, p. 43
▸ Übungsheft, p. 85

MEDIA
▸ One-Stop Planner
▸ Audio Compact Discs, CD7, Trs. 5–7

> **PAGES 190–191**

Weiter geht's! Summary

In *Image-Werbung,* some German students discuss a particular TV advertisement with their teacher. The following learning outcomes listed on p. 181 are modeled in the conversation: eliciting agreement and agreeing and expressing conviction, uncertainty, and what seems to be true.

Preteaching Vocabulary

Recognizing Cognates
Weiter geht's! contains several words that students will be able to recognize as cognates or borrowed words. Some are compound words in which only part of the word is a cognate. Have students identify these words and describe what is happening in the commercial and then in the discussion. Some cognates are: **Bar, Colt, Saloontür, Cowboy, Sporen, Werbespot, Getränk, kritisch, Image, Firma, Ideen, Zigarettenmarken, Männlichkeit.**

Advance Organizer

Ask students to describe a television commercial they dislike and explain why. Do they think that young people are more or less critical of television ads than adults are? Are adolescents more easily influenced by ads than adults?

Comprehension Check

Auditory Learners

Have students keep their books closed and listen as you read the commercial to them. Can they visualize the sequence of events? What is happening?

Thinking Critically

Drawing Inferences After students have heard or read the text of the commercial, help them to understand the slogan, **Weil Ihre Helden ganze Arbeit leisten!** Point out that **Ihre** is capitalized, that **ganze Arbeit leisten** means *to do a good job*, and that the slogan is only a partial sentence, a dependent clause; the main clause is not expressed but understood. What could the main clause be? Ask students to use the bar scene and the context of the ad to come up with some ideas.
Examples:
Kaufen Sie Schokomilch, …
Schokogetränke sind das beste, …

Teaching Suggestion

16 Have students follow the conversation on pp. 190–191 in their books as they listen to the compact disc. As students listen to the conversation, they should make notes of words or phrases with which they are not familiar. Call on students to find out what parts of the discussion seemed unclear and encourage other students to help out in giving definitions or paraphrasing. Then have students answer questions 1–4.

Closure

Ask students to describe a popular commercial similar in form to the one described on p. 190. They should try not to reveal the product. Have the rest of the class infer what the commercial is advertising.

ZWEITE STUFE

Teaching Resources
pp. 192–195

PRINT
- Lesson Planner, p. 44
- Listening Activities, pp. 52–53, 56–58
- Video Guide, pp. 31–34
- Activities for Communication, pp. 27–28, 81–82, 84–85, 125–126
- Grammatikheft, pp. 60–63
- Grammar Tutor for Students of German, Chapter 7
- Übungsheft, pp. 86–89
- Testing Program, pp. 151–154
- Alternative Assessment Guide, p. 36
- Student Make-Up Assignments, Chapter 7

MEDIA
- One-Stop Planner
- Audio Compact Discs, CD7, Trs. 8–9, 12, 18–20
- Video Program
  Videoclips: Werbung
  Videocassette 2, 08:20–11:56
- Teaching Transparencies
  Situation 7-2
  Mehr Grammatikübungen Answers
  Grammatikheft Answers

> **PAGE 192**

Bell Work
Ask students to name products that are of German origin. Which of these do they see advertised in the United States?

PRESENTING: Wortschatz

Go over the new vocabulary with students. Then incorporate various words and phrases from the **Wortschatz** as you strike up conversations with individual students.
Examples:
Was haltet ihr von Kindern in der Werbung?
Könnt ihr an eine Werbung, denken, die die Gefühle der Leser oder Zuschauer ausnützt?

PRESENTING: So sagt man das!

Ask students to work with a partner to write a statement that would precede or follow each functional expression. Then call on several pairs to role-play their exchanges using the expressions in **So sagt man das!**

Example:
— Werbung für Kriegsspielzeug ist für kleine Kinder schädlich, nicht wahr?
— Ja, damit stimm ich überein.

> **PAGE 193**

Speaking Assessment

18 You may wish to assess speaking performance of individual students using this activity. With you giving the clue, you may choose to evaluate the student's answer using the following rubric.

Speaking Rubric	Points			
	4	3	2	1
Content (Complete – Incomplete)				
Comprehension (Total – Little)				
Comprehensibility (Comprehensible – Incomprehensible)				
Accuracy (Accurate – Seldom accurate)				
Fluency (Fluent – Not fluent)				

18–20: A   16–17: B   14–15: C   12–13: D   Under 12: F

Using the Video

[VIDEO] Videocassette 2, 08:20–11:56
The authentic advertising clips in this section can be analyzed within the context of the chapter: advertising that offers facts (**Informationswerbung**) and advertising that appeals to the senses (**Image-Werbung**). See *Video Guide*, p. 32, for suggestions.

PRESENTING: Ein wenig Grammatik

Relative Clauses You might want to point out to students that in **Ein wenig Grammatik, den** refers to **Werbeslogan.** It is used in the accusative case because of its function in the relative clause.

STANDARDS: 1.2, 3.1, 4.1

PRESENTING: Grammatik

Relative clauses with was and wo Have students compare the use of **was** and **wo** in relative clauses with the way *that, what,* and *where* are used in English relative clauses.

Connections and Comparisons

Language-to-Language

Students might be interested to know that in German, as in French and Spanish, the relative pronoun *that* cannot be omitted as it often can be in English.

Examples:
English: *I've already read the book (that) I bought yesterday.*
German: **Ich habe das Buch, das ich gestern gekauft habe, schon gelesen.**
French: **J'ai déjà lu le livre que j'ai acheté hier.**
Spanish: **Ya leí el libro que compré ayer.**
You may want to ask your students if they can think of clauses in which it would not be possible to omit that in English. (Example: *This book was the first book that dealt with the trial.*)

Music Connection

For additional reading, refer students to Schiller's *An die Freude, Ode to Joy* (music: Beethoven's Ninth Symphony), Level 2 *Listening Activities*, p. 78. Can they find the two relative clauses? (**was die Mode streng geteilt; wo dein sanfter Flügel weilt**) Ask students to give you a rough English translation of the poem. You may also want to play the song, Level 2 CD 10, Tr. 23.

> **PAGE 194**

Communication for All Students

A Slower Pace

19 To prepare students for the partner activity, have them first make up a number of sentences that incorporate the three different introductory clauses and the various ideas for relative clauses. Then, from the list they have created, have students create brief conversations, with student A not only asking questions, but also reacting to what student B says.

Visual Learners

20 Have students bring in ads in which the six comments are being applied. Discuss the ads in class.

Teaching Suggestion

Have students look for relative pronouns in the **Los geht's!** and **Weiter geht's!** conversations. Both episodes contain a variety of uses of relative pronouns. In each case, students need to find the pronoun and its antecedent.
Example:
Ich trag halt gern Sachen, die „in" sind.
(relative pronoun: **die**; antecedent: **Sachen**)

PRESENTING: So sagt man das!

Ask students to list all the expressions of conviction (**Du kannst mir glauben, …; Ich bin sicher, dass …**) and uncertainty (**Ich bin nicht sicher; ich weiß nicht, …**) they have learned so far. Then ask them to study the new expressions in **So sagt man das!**, including those used for stating what seems to be true, and use them to comment on the statements studied in Activity 18 on p. 193. (Example: **Es steht fest, dass Werbung nur Appetit aufs Kaufen macht.**)

> **PAGE 195**

PRESENTING: Grammatik

Irgendein and **irgendwelche** Point out to students that the endings for **irgendein** are the same as for **ein, kein,** and possessives, and those for **irgenwelche** are the same as for **welcher** and the other **der**-words.

Communication for All Students

Challenge

24 When pairs have finished the activity, ask them to look again at the advertisement on p. 190. Have them come up with several other questions that they can pose to the rest of the class. In the responses students should again use the word **irgend-**. (Example: **Mit welchem Western-Star kann man den Jungen vergleichen?**)

PRESENTING: Wortschatz

- Point out that these are some other word combinations using **irgend-**, and tell students that here **irgend-** suggests randomness, or indefiniteness.

- Have students make up statements about themselves using these words. (Example: **Ich habe irgendwie keine Lust mitzukommen.**)

Communication for All Students

A Slower Pace

25 Before beginning the discussion, have students refer back to **So sagt man das!** on pp. 192 and 194 to find some expressions they might use. Instead of discussing all four topics, have students choose one or two.

Challenge

25 Have students think of and write down questions related to each of the statements that they could ask to stimulate and further the discussion.

Reteaching: *Irgendein* and *irgendwelche*

Prepare a list of advertisement slogans on a handout or a transparency. Students make suggestions as to what each slogan could be for, using a form of **irgend-**.
Examples:
… da kauf ich gern ein! (irgendein Kaufhaus oder Geschäft)
… löschen den Durst jedes Mal! (irgendwelche Getränke)

 Game

To review relative clauses with **was**, play the guessing game **Ich sehe was, was du nicht siehst.** One student secretly identifies an object in the classroom and then makes the statement: **Ich sehe was, was ihr nicht seht, und das ist …** (Example: **kaputt**). The rest of the class takes turns at guessing what the object in question could be. The student who guesses correctly starts the next round.

Assess

▶ Testing Program, pp. 151–154
  Quiz 7-2A, Quiz 7-2B
  Audio CD7, Tr. 12

▶ Student Make-Up Assignments
  Chapter 7, Alternative Quiz

▶ Alternative Assessment Guide, p. 36

ZUM LESEN

Teaching Resources
pp. 196–198

PRINT
▸ Lesson Planner, p. 45
▸ Übungsheft, pp. 90–91
▸ Reading Strategies and Skills, Chapter 7
▸ Lies mit mir! 3, Chapter 7

MEDIA
▸ One-Stop Planner

Prereading

Cultures and Communities

Background Information

Asterix is a series created in France, but quite popular in Germany. The clever **Asterix** and his oafish sidekick, **Obelix**, are Gauls, i.e. "proto-Frenchmen," under the not-too-popular administration of the Roman colonial government (their village is the only one remaining that the Romans have not yet subdued). For the inhabitants of Roman Gaul, with its beautifully designed cities, roads, aqueducts, and other civilized features, the tax-levying conquerors were often a lesser evil than the barbarians pushing against the walls. Nevertheless, this comic strip is based on the idea that the Romans were oppressors and that the common folk of the provinces were underdogs to be cheered on in their efforts to make fools of them. The *Asterix* comics also contain many allusions to present-day culture and politics.

Building Context

Have students think of comic strips and books that they enjoy reading. Ask them which ones they think would or would not be popular with German teens. Why? You might want to discuss what types of humor do and do not translate well. For example, puns, word plays, and humor based on "insider" knowledge of a popular culture are quite difficult for non-native speakers to understand in time to laugh.

Teaching Suggestion

1 Have students try to identify the hero(es) of this strip, based only on visual clues. Looking at the cos-

tumes (they are purposely clichéd and will help to identify the Romans and the representatives of the various provinces) might help students make predictions.

Teaching Suggestion

2 Larger type sizes used for emphasis are a familiar comic-strip device and will probably need no explanation. Students may be interested in checking a reference work to see how the artist has suggested "Greek" letters without actually using the Greek alphabet. Perhaps, they have seen **Fraktur** or the so-called "Gothic" letters that were used in German printing until well into this century, and enjoyed a brief resurgence during the Third Reich.

Teacher Note

Activities 1 and 2 are prereading activities.

Reading
Teacher Note

4 Students will probably recognize the "Egyptian pictographs" as clever variants on the international icons used in tourist spots.

Post-Reading
Teacher Note

Activity 10 is a post-reading task that will show whether students can apply what they have learned.

Connections and Comparisons

Thinking Critically

Comparing and Contrasting Ask students how the details in *Asterix* hold the reader's attention. How would they compare this series to the *Flintstones?* In which series is the story line stronger and more important? In which is the humor more dependent on background knowledge and recognition of incongruent detail? (Students may want to look more carefully at the recruits' names and at the settings.) How would they compare *Asterix* to an action-packed series like *Batman* or to a heroic saga like *Prince Valiant?*

Closure

Ask the class to briefly discuss how they would account for the popularity of *Asterix* in Germany. Do they think the series would sell well in the United States? Why or why not? What sort of characters would be the American equivalents of **Asterix** and **Obelix?**

Zum Lesen Answers

Answers to Activity 1
in the Roman Empire; Roman times, approximately the first century, A.D.; expressions of characters indicate conflict; for example, the Roman soldier is yelling.

Answers to Activity 2
denotes tone of voice (e.g. large print indicates someone is yelling), other styles of print used to represent different languages or nationalities of the speakers

Answers to Activity 3
headquarters of the Roman army; time when Roman Empire was conquering other parts of Europe
Asterix: Gaul (France); Obelix: Gaul (France); Militaros: Greece; Eftax: Britain; Mannekenpix: Belgium; **Kriegmichnich:** Goth; **Verkrümeldich:** Goth; **ein Ägypter:** Egypt; **die Römer:** Rome

Answers to Activity 4
for the Egyptian; to caricature his speech

Answers to Activity 5
People from different conquered areas are being inducted into the Roman army; they are registered and then sent to have a physical; no; prisoners; answers will vary.

Answers to Activity 6
interpreter; the character "translates" everything the Egyptian says to the Roman soldier; he can't understand the Egyptian.

Answers to Activity 7
about the facilities; he thinks he's at an inn rather than being inducted into the army.

Answers to Activity 8
to the doctor; to have a physical; get undressed

Answers to Activity 9
skinny; the Goth is very thin.

> **PAGE 199**

ZUM SCHREIBEN

> ### Teaching Resources
> **p. 199**
>
> **PRINT**
> ▸ Lesson Planner, p. 45
> ▸ Alternative Assessment Guide, p. 22
>
> **MEDIA**
> ▸ One-Stop Planner
> ▸ Test Generator, Chapter 7

> ### Writing Strategy
>
> The targeted strategy in this writing activity is *using tone and word choice for effect.* Students should learn about this strategy before beginning the assignment.

Prewriting
Teacher Notes

• This activity is a good opportunity to teach or review the correct form of business letters in German.

• Students may want to write about some of the products for which they created slogans in the chapter.

Building Context

Ask students to think of one product they have bought recently that did not meet their expectations. What did they do about it?

Teaching Suggestion

As students plan their letters, remind them to distinguish between inferior quality of the product and their disappointment in the product. This will help them in their word choice. Remind them also to keep their audience in mind, i.e. the manufacturer of the product. What retribution do they want? A letter of apology? A refund?

Writing
Teaching Suggestion

Encourage students to use as many of the new functions as possible including expressing annoyance, making comparisons with other, similar products, and expressing what they've heard in advertisements. Encourage them to use **der gleiche** and **derselbe** where appropriate.

> ### Communication for All Students
>
> **Challenge**
> If available, have students look for the advertisements of the product with which they are unhappy. Have them pick out specific points in the ad that did not meet their expectations. Students should address these items in their letter.

Post-Writing
Closure

As a follow-up activity, you may want to redistribute the letters and have each student write a response to another student's complaint.

> **PAGES 200–203**

MEHR GRAMMATIKÜBUNGEN

The **Mehr Grammatikübungen** activities are designed as supplemental activities for the grammatical concepts presented in the chapter. You might use them as additional practice, for review, or for assessment.

For more grammar presentations, review, and practice, refer to the following:
- Grammatikheft
- Grammar Tutor for Students of German
- Grammar Summary on pp. R22–R39
- Übungsheft
- Grammar and Vocabulary quizzes (Testing Program)
- Test Generator
- **Interaktive Spiele** at <u>go.hrw.com</u>

▶ **PAGES 204–205**

ANWENDUNG

Teaching Resources
pp. 204–205

PRINT
▶ Lesson Planner, p. 45
▶ Listening Activities, p. 54
▶ Grammar Tutor for Students of German, Chapter 7

MEDIA
▶ One-Stop Planner
▶ Audio Compact Discs, CD7, Tr. 10

Apply and Assess

Teaching Suggestions

1 Ask students to bring American advertisements that intentionally use incorrect language.

1 Ask students to identify the incorrect German in the text. Go over the list and have students first give an English equivalent of the word or phrase and then put each into correct German.

2 Before students listen to the radio ads, let them predict the type of slogans and phrases they expect to hear for each of the five ads based on the pictures (a-e). Make a list of students' ideas so they can later compare their predictions to the actual ads.

📁 Portfolio Assessment

2 You might want to suggest this activity as an oral portfolio item for your students. See *Alternative Assessment Guide*, p. 22.

3 You might want to suggest this activity as a written portfolio item for your students. See *Alternative Assessment Guide*, p. 22.

Apply and Assess

Cooperative Learning

4 Divide the class into groups of three or four students. Each group should have two or three advertisements, which they examine by answering the five questions. Call on the reporters of the groups to discuss their ads. Does the rest of the class agree with the responses?

▶ **PAGE 206**

KANN ICH'S WIRKLICH?

This page helps students prepare for the test. It is a brief checklist of the major points covered in the chapter. The students should be reminded that it is only a checklist and not necessarily everything that will appear on the test.

For additional self-check options, refer students to the *Grammar Tutor* and the Online self-test for this chapter.

▶ **PAGE 207**

WORTSCHATZ

Review and Assess

♟ Game

Play the game **Es war einmal …**, using the vocabulary from this and previous chapters. See p. 179C for the procedure.

Circumlocution

To use the circumlocution game **Das treffende Wort suchen** as a vocabulary review, tell students that they have been hired by a German advertising firm. They realize that they don't remember some German terms and that they need to describe these items.
Example:
Die Plakatwand–Es ist ein Ding, das groß ist. Es steht am Straßenrand und hat viel Reklame darauf. Wie heißt das Ding? Use the vocabulary listed in the **Erste Stufe** for the game. See p. 31C for procedures.

🔊 Teacher Note

Give the **Kapitel 7** Chapter Test:
Testing Program, pp. 155–160
Audio CD 7, Trs. 13–14.

„Und bei welchem brauch ich kein Programmier-Diplom?"

hern Sie uns.

rt

Ohne Reklame geht es nicht!

Objectives

In this chapter you will learn to

Erste Stufe

- express annoyance
- compare

Zweite Stufe

- elicit agreement and agree
- express conviction, uncertainty, and what seems to be true

internet

go. hrw .com	ADRESSE: go.hrw.com
	KENNWORT: WK3
	FRANKFURT-7

◀ **Hier stimmt die Werbung!**

Los geht's! · *Werbung — ja oder nein?*

Constance und ihr Freund Stefan haben mit einem Herrn von einem Meinungsforschungs-Institut gesprochen. Er wollte wissen, ob und wie sie sich von der Werbung beeinflussen lassen.

Interviewer: Wie werden Sie zum Kaufen angeregt, und welche Rolle spielt dabei die Werbung?

Stefan: Ich trag halt gern Sachen, die „in" sind.

Interviewer: Und woher wissen Sie, was „in" ist?

Stefan: Da seh ich ja, was die andern tragen. Und dann les ich auch die Reklame in Zeitschriften und so und an Plakatwänden.

Constance: Ich kann nicht sagen, dass ich von der Werbung beeinflusst werde. Ich seh eben etwas, was mir gefällt — im Fernsehen, in irgendwelchen Zeitschriften — und dann kauf ich es mir eben. Aber zuvor vergleich ich schon die Preise.

Interviewer: Nun, bitte: Sie sagen es ja selbst, dass Sie durch die Werbung zum Kaufen angeregt werden.

Constance: Klar, aber das möchte ich nicht so einfach eingestehen. Es gibt heute so viele Sachen, die alle irgendwie die gleiche Qualität haben oder haben sollen, aber die eben doch verschieden sind. Und hier kann die Reklame informieren, das Produkt beschreiben, den Konsumenten aufklären.

Die Kunst
der leichten Küche. Mit Schwein.

Geniessen auf gut deutsch.

Die Kunst

Stefan: Das meine ich auch, aber ich möchte dazu etwas sagen: Oft beschreibt die Reklame das angepriesene Produkt gar nicht, sondern ... äh ... die Reklame zeigt Leute, die irgendwelche Eigenschaften haben, die der Käufer gern hätte. Er soll also glauben, wenn er dieses Produkt kauft, wird er auch diese Eigenschaften haben. Die Reklame manipuliert also den Käufer. Wer möchte nicht frei und fröhlich sein, nicht wahr? Oder etwas Gutes tun, ja?

Interviewer: Ja, logisch. Und können Sie mir auch ein Beispiel geben?

Stefan: Hm, da muss ich mal überlegen. Ach, ja! Da wird im Werbefunk zum Beispiel irgendein Fertiggericht angepriesen. Da sehen wir die hübsche Mutter in ihrer blitzblanken Küche stehen, im Hintergrund die glücklichen, gut erzogenen Kinder und möglichst noch den gutmütigen Mann, der seine fabelhafte Frau stolz anstrahlt. Man hört überhaupt nichts vom Nährwert des Gerichts, sondern nur solche Werbesprüche wie „Eine weise Hausfrau denkt zuerst an ihre Kinder" oder „aus Liebe zur Familie", und dann kommt der Name des Produktes. Man kauft das Produkt, weil man im Unterbewusstsein glaubt, wenn ich dieses Fertiggericht meiner Familie gebe, wird mein Leben auch so perfekt sein.

Constance:	Ja, das nervt mich auch immer, wenn ich so was höre und sehe — wie zum Beispiel mit der Autoreklame. Da werden immer nur Autos gezeigt in einer schönen Wiese, in den Bergen, wo alles heil ist, aber nie auf einer Straße im Stau. Die versteckte Mitteilung: Mit diesem Auto wirst du nie im Stau sitzen.
Stefan:	Genau! Da hast du ganz Recht.
Constance:	Und was mich noch aufregt ist die Werbung, wo irgendwelche Spitzensportler ein Produkt anpreisen … und dann essen sie es selbst vielleicht überhaupt nicht. Und sie bekommen unheimlich viel Geld für so eine Reklame.
Stefan:	Eben! Und ich kann mir gar nicht leisten, was diese Leute …
Interviewer:	Sie mögen also keine Statussymbole?
Stefan:	Mögen? Klar. Aber ich kann sie mir nicht leisten.
Interviewer:	Wie werden Sie denn auf ein bestimmtes Produkt aufmerksam gemacht?
Constance:	Ach, ich würde sagen, da ist immer zuerst ein Bild, eine Bildreklame, hässlich oder schön … und da schau ich eben hin.
Stefan:	Genau! Oft ist es ein Mädchen, ein Blickfang …
Constance:	Logo, im letzten Jahr zum Beispiel die Quark-Reklame, ein großer, roter Mund …
Stefan:	Ja, daran erinnere ich mich auch. Diese Reklame war schon sehr raffiniert!
Constance:	Was mich dabei nervt ist, dass die Reklame die Frau oft nur als Blickfang benutzt und dass sehr oft das Image der Frau weiterhin in einer traditionellen Rolle gezeigt wird. Es ist immer noch die Frau, die das Bad putzt — und die allwissende, männliche Stimme, die ihr sagt, welche Putzmittel sie dazu gebrauchen soll!
Interviewer:	Na, da ist schon was dran. Und zum Schluss …
Constance:	Ja, zum Schluss möchte ich sagen, dass ich … ja, ich glaube wirklich, dass die Werbung in erster Linie das angepriesene Produkt in einem günstigen Licht zeigt und mit positiven Elementen in Verbindung bringt und weniger die Eigenschaften des Produktes dem Konsumenten beschreibt.
Stefan:	So ist es auch! Damit stimm ich völlig überein!

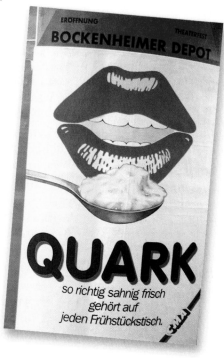

EROFFNUNG
THEATERFEST
BOCKENHEIMER DEPOT

QUARK

so richtig sahnig frisch gehört auf jeden Frühstückstisch.

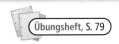
(Übungsheft, S. 79)

1 **Zusammenfassung**

Schreiben Schreib stichwortartig auf, was Stefan und Constance über die Werbung sagen! Schreib dann eine Zusammenfassung (*synopsis*) von dem, was jeder gesagt hat, und lies die Zusammenfassung der Klasse vor!

2 **Was meinst du?**

Sprechen/Schreiben Beantworte die folgenden Fragen.

1. Informiert oder manipuliert Werbung die Konsumenten? Wie tut sie das?
2. Warum machen Spitzensportler Werbung für Produkte? Was soll damit erreicht werden?
3. Welche Werbung beeindruckt dich? Warum? Welche Werbung findest du wirklich blöd?
4. Vergleiche die Werbespots in diesem Kapitel mit denen, die du oft bei dir zu Hause siehst!

Werbung — pro und contra

1 „Werbung weckt verborgene Wünsche, verkauft Träume und macht den Verbraucher kritiklos."

2 „Werbung ist ein Motor der Wirtschaft, sorgt für Absatz und damit auch für Arbeitsplätze."

3 „Ohne Werbung wäre die Welt langweiliger. Werbung macht die Welt bunter."

4 „Werbung muss vielfältig sein. Es liegt allein am Verbraucher, sich von den Appellen an Gefühle nicht beeinflussen zu lassen und nur auf die Informationen zu achten."

5 „Werbung will den Verbraucher dazu verführen, Dinge zu kaufen, die er in Wirklichkeit nicht braucht."

6 „Werbung kostet viel Geld und verteuert dadurch die Waren."

7 „Nur durch Werbung werden Produkte bekannt. Dadurch erfährt der Verbraucher, wie er seine Bedürfnisse befriedigen kann."

8 „Wer Werbung als ‚Verführung' bezeichnet, überschätzt ihre Wirkung maßlos. Die Menschen sind viel zu kritisch: Es hat sich längst herumgesprochen, dass man nicht glücklich wird, nur weil man dieses oder jenes kauft."

Mit welchen Aussagen stimmst du überein? Warum? Mit welchen stimmst du nicht überein? Warum nicht?

Wortschatz

auf Deutsch erklärt
die Reklame Werbung
der Werbespruch ein Slogan für ein Produkt
der Verbraucher der Konsument, Käufer
aufklären informieren
anpreisen mit vielen Worten empfehlen
raffiniert clever
verborgen man kann es nicht sehen
die Wirtschaft die Ökonomie
wahrnehmen man hört oder sieht es
überlegen über etwas nachdenken
glücklich froh
fröhlich gut gelaunt
das Putzmittel ein Produkt, mit dem man etwas sauber macht
Wir stimmen miteinander überein. Wir haben die gleiche Meinung.
Diesen Wagen kann ich mir nicht leisten. Ich habe nicht genug Geld für den Wagen.

auf Englisch erklärt
p. 179X

Lies mal, was auf der Plakatwand steht!
Read what's on the billboard.
Vergleichen wir die Waren! *Let's compare the goods.*
Ich möchte dich auf diese interessante Werbung aufmerksam machen. *I would like to draw your attention to this interesting advertisement.*
Eine typische Eigenschaft von Werbung ist die versteckte Mitteilung. *A typical characteristic of advertising is the hidden message.*
Ich gestehe es ein, dass günstige Preise ein echter Kaufreiz sind. *I admit that favorable prices are a real enticement to buy.*
Wer weiß, was im Unterbewusstsein steckt. *Who knows what lurks in the subconscious.*

Grammatikheft, S. 55–56, Ü. 1–3

So sagt man das!

Expressing annoyance

Here are two useful expressions to help you convey annoyance or irritation:

Was mich aufregt ist, wenn Leute ihre Fehler nie eingestehen.
Es nervt mich, dass Anja sich von allen beeinflussen lässt.

You can use the conjunctions **wenn** and **dass** with both these phrases.
How do you express annoyance in English?

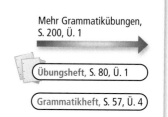

Mehr Grammatikübungen, S. 200, Ü. 1

Übungsheft, S. 80, Ü. 1

Grammatikheft, S. 57, Ü. 4

---

3 **Wie steht ihr zur Werbung?** Script and answers on p. 179G

Zuhören Einige Freunde reden über Werbung, die sie im Fernsehen gesehen haben. Was regt sie auf? Was ist ihnen egal? Hör gut zu und schreib auf, wie diese Schüler reagieren!
CD 7 Tr. 2

4 **Meckerecke**

Sprechen Was nervt euch alles — in der Schule, zu Hause, beim Sport, im Fernsehen, in der Werbung? Bildet eine größere Gruppe und sagt abwechselnd, was euch nervt oder aufregt!

5 **Wie ist die Werbung bei euch?**

Sprechen Besprecht die folgenden Fragen gemeinsam in einer Gruppe!
1. Wo seht ihr die meiste Werbung?
2. Für welche Produkte wird die meiste Werbung gemacht?
3. Welche Werbung und welche Werbeslogans sind am effektivsten? Warum?

So sagt man das!

Comparing

 7–1

Übungsheft, S. 80, Ü. 2

Grammatikheft, S. 57, Ü. 5

When making statements about different things, we often compare them.
You've already learned to make comparisons using the following expressions:

Ich kenne auch **so** einen Spitzensportler **wie** dich.
Diese Werbung ist nicht **so gut wie** diese.
Ich finde diesen Werbeslogan viel **besser als** den da.
Und mir gefällt die Kinoreklame **am besten.**

What are some other comparative adjectives that you often use?
Here are some new ways to talk about comparisons:

Bevor ich mir etwas kaufe, **vergleiche** ich die Preise.
Manche Produkte haben die **gleiche** Qualität, aber die Preise sind oft sehr **verschieden.**
Einige Leute kaufen sich immer **dieselben** Waren.

---

6 **Für welche Produkte entscheiden sich die Leute?** Script and answers on p. 179G

Zuhören Du kaufst in einem deutschen Supermarkt ein und bleibst vor einigen Leuten stehen, die lebhaft einige Produkte vergleichen. Hör ihrem Gespräch gut zu und schreib auf, für welche Produkte sie sich entscheiden und warum!
CD 7 Tr. 3

Grammatik

derselbe, der gleiche

The determiner **derselbe** is a combination of the definite article **der** and the word **selber**, and means *the very same.* The new word changes in form like any other adjective with a preceding definite article.

Ich habe **dieselben** Reklamen gesehen.
Wir haben **denselben** Preis dafür gezahlt.

	Masculine	**Feminine**	**Neuter**	**Plural**
Nominative	derselbe	dieselbe	dasselbe	dieselben
Accusative	denselben	dieselbe	dasselbe	dieselben
Dative	demselben	derselben	demselben	denselben

Der (die, das) gleiche in front of a noun means *the same kind or type* and functions like an adjective. Compare these sentences:

Wir tragen die **gleiche** Jacke und spielen die **gleichen** Kartenspiele.[1]
Mein Freund und ich gehen in **dieselbe** Schule und haben
    denselben Lehrer in Mathe.[2]

Mehr Grammatikübungen, S. 200, Ü. 2

Übungsheft, S. 81, Ü. 3

Grammatikheft, S. 58, Ü. 6–7

Note that **gleiche** can also be used as a noun, as in **das Gleiche**, meaning "the same thing."

---

7 **Grammatik im Kontext**

Sprechen Such dir einen Partner und macht Vergleiche! Hier sind Beispiele.

BEISPIEL   Meine Schwester und ich, wir wohnen in demselben Haus.   *oder*
               Mein Vater und mein Onkel fahren den gleichen Wagen,
                  beide haben einen Opel.   *oder*
               Mein Freund und ich …

8 **Machen wir Vergleiche!**

Sprechen Was meint ihr? Stellt euch gegenseitig die folgenden Fragen, und besprecht sie dann zusammen! Sagt eure Meinungen frei und offen!

1. Welche Werbung ist effektiver, die Radiowerbung oder die Fernsehwerbung? Warum?

2. Welche Jeans sind deiner Meinung nach besser, einfache Jeans oder Designerjeans?

3. Welche Autos sind deiner Meinung nach besser, kleine oder große?

4. Welche Werbeslogans kennst du? Vergleiche sie!

---

1. We wear the same (type of) jacket and play the same (kinds of) card games.
2. My friend and I go to the (very) same school and have the (very) same teacher for math.

Grammatik

Adjective endings following determiners of quantity

Determiners of quantity can be used as determiners before nouns or as pronouns.

1. Adjectives that follow determiners of quantity have the following endings in the nominative and accusative cases. What are the English equivalents of these words?

alle, beide, keine	andere, ein paar, einige, etliche, mehrere, viele, wenige, zwei (drei, vier, usw.)
Nom. alle **-en** Häuser	mehrere **-e** Dörfer
Acc. alle **-en** Häuser	mehrere **-e** Dörfer

2. In the dative case, the determiners of quantity (not the numerals) add the ending **-n,** and any following adjectives have the usual **-en** ending of the dative case.

An einig**en** groß**en** Plakatwände**n** hängen Poster.

 Übungsheft, S. 81–83, Ü. 4–9   Grammatikheft, S. 59, Ü. 8   Mehr Grammatikübungen, S. 201, Ü. 3–4

---

9 Grammatik im Kontext

Sprechen/Schreiben Such dir eine Partnerin! Beschreibt einander eure Stadt oder eine Stadt, die ihr gut kennt! Wie viele Sätze könnt ihr machen?

Es gibt	wenige mehrere ein paar einige etliche viele drei keine	gut schlecht alt neu ausländisch deutsch interessant modern schön	Zeitungen Schulen Kinos Museen Diskotheken Bücherläden Videoläden Restaurants Parks Universitäten Kirchen

10 Grammatik im Kontext

Zuhören Hör jetzt einigen Werbeslogans gut zu! Welcher Werbeslogan, den du hörst, passt zu welchem Produkt unten? Script and answers on p. 179H

CD 7 Tr. 4

a.   b.   c.   d.   e.

11 Schreiben wir auch einen Werbeslogan!

Sprechen/Schreiben Experten in der Werbebranche benutzen viele Adjektive, die weniger das Produkt beschreiben als die Gefühle des Konsumenten ansprechen. Bildet Gruppen von vier Schülern und kreiert drei Werbeslogans für verschiedene Produkte! Dann lest euren besten Werbeslogan der Klasse vor! Diskutiert über eure Slogans und vergleicht sie miteinander! Welche findet ihr gut und welche nicht so gut? Warum?

märchenhaft   erstklassig   sensationell   super   einmalig   neu   modern   fabelhaft   atemberaubend   phantastisch

---

12 Kennst du die Sprache der Werbung?

Sprechen In der Werbung benutzt man sehr viele Adjektive. Manche beschreiben das Produkt und informieren den Konsumenten. Natürlich stellt die Beschreibung das Produkt in ein schönes Licht. Wie beschreibt die Werbung die Produkte unten links? Such dir eine Partnerin, und versucht zusammen, die passenden Adjektive für jedes Produkt zu wählen!

BEISPIEL   **In der Werbung sind Uhren gewöhnlich … und …**

Produkte

Uhren	Kaffee
Autos	Fruchtsaft

Adjektive

rostfrei   wasserdicht   präzis   mild   natürlich

superschnell   geräuscharm   tassenfertig   vitaminreich

13 Werbesprüche

Sprechen/Lesen Wie gut kannst du Werbung und Werbesprüche analysieren? Schau dir die Werbesprüche unten an, und diskutiere über diese Fragen mit einem Partner!

1. Welche Produkte werben mit diesen Werbesprüchen?

2. Versuche, diese vier Texte zu charakterisieren! Welcher Text informiert mehr? Welcher manipuliert mehr? Welcher diskriminiert? Welche Wörter im Text begründen deine Analyse?

3. Was für Konsumenten sollen diese Produkte kaufen? Wie weißt du das vom Text?

14 Zum Überlegen und Diskutieren

Sprechen Diskutiert die folgenden Meinungen in der Klasse! Seid kritisch und gebt Beispiele!

1. Werbung hat die Aufgabe, uns über die Produkte zu informieren.

2. Die Werbung beeinflusst uns, auch wenn wir es nicht immer gleich eingestehen wollen.

3. Die meiste Werbung ist Image-Werbung; sie manipuliert den Käufer nur.

4. Manipulative Werbung sollte verboten werden.

5. Sportler in der Werbung? Nein!

6. Frauen werden in der Werbung oft nur als Blickfang benutzt.

7. Wir brauchen die Werbung überhaupt nicht; wir können auch ohne Werbung leben.

15 Für mein Notizbuch

Schreiben Such dir zwei Themen von Übung 14 aus, und schreib deine eigene Meinung darüber! Gib mindestens drei Gründe für deine Meinung!

LANDESKUNDE · LANDESKUNDE

Warum so wenig Unterbrecherwerbung?

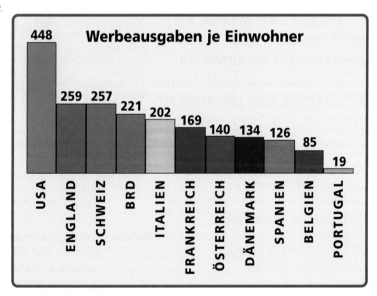

Übungsheft, S. 84, Ü. 1–2

Michael ist seit einer Woche Austauschstudent in Deutschland. Seine Gasteltern sind ausgegangen, und er schaut allein zu Hause Fernsehen. Im ZDF läuft gerade der Film „Raumschiff Enterprise". Michael hat Hunger und möchte sich etwas aus dem Kühlschrank holen, aber er wartet auf einen Werbeblock. Nach zwanzig Minuten gibt es immer noch keine Pause. Wann kommt denn endlich die Reklame, fragt er sich. Er muss bis zum Ende der Sendung warten, bevor er sein Essen holen kann.

Danach schaltet er das Programm auf RTL um. In ein paar Minuten kommt ein Wildwestfilm mit Clint Eastwood. Diesmal holt er sich etwas zu essen, bevor die Sendung anfängt. Aber jetzt fällt ihm etwas auf. In der Mitte der Sendung kommen einige Reklamen. Bis zum Ende des Films gibt es zwei weitere Unterbrechungen (*interruptions*). Er versteht nicht, warum es im ZDF keine Unterbrecherwerbung und im RTL dreimal Unterbrecherwerbung gibt.

1. Warum gibt es bei der Unterbrecherwerbung einen Unterschied zwischen ZDF und RTL? Was meinst du?

2. Welches Programm ist ein Privatsender(*private station*)? Welches ist ein öffentlich-rechtlicher (*public*) Sender? Hast du eine Ahnung (*idea*), wie die Sender finanziert werden?

3. Wie ist die Werbezeit in den USA kontrolliert? Wie oft kommen Werbeblöcke?

For answers, see text below.

Werbeausgaben je Einwohner

Land	Wert
USA	448
ENGLAND	259
SCHWEIZ	257
BRD	221
ITALIEN	202
FRANKREICH	169
ÖSTERREICH	140
DÄNEMARK	134
SPANIEN	126
BELGIEN	85
PORTUGAL	19

Erklärung zu Michaels Situation:

ARD und ZDF sind öffentlich-rechtliche Sender, die vorwiegend aus Fernsehgebühren finanziert werden. Werbeeinblendungen werden daher gesetzlich geregelt. Es dürfen nur 20 Minuten Werbung am Tag gesendet werden, davon dürfen zehn Minuten vor und zehn Minuten nach 20 Uhr laufen. Da RTL ein Privatsender ist, fällt er nicht unter diese Regelung. Für Privatsender, deren wichtigste Einnahmequelle die Werbewirtschaft ist, gelten andere Regeln. Ein Film bis zu 85 Minuten Länge darf nur einmal unterbrochen werden und ein Film von 90 Minuten Länge oder mehr zweimal. Privatsender dürfen täglich 20% ihres Programms mit Werbung füllen.

STANDARDS: 2.1, 2.2, 3.2, 4.2

Weiter geht's! · *Image-Werbung*

CD 7 Trs. 5–7

Im Rahmen des Deutschunterrichts über aktuelle Themen hat Frau Klose ihren Schülern der 11. Klasse folgenden Werbespot gezeigt, der vor einiger Zeit im Werbefernsehen zu sehen war. Danach hat sie mit ihren Schülern über diesen Werbespot gesprochen. CD 7 Tr. 5

CD 7 Tr. 6

SZENE: EINE BAR IM AMERIKANISCHEN „WILDEN" WESTEN. HARTE KERLE STEHEN AM TRESEN, DEN COLT GRIFFBEREIT IM REVOLVERGÜRTEL. DIE SALOONTÜR SCHWINGT AUF. ALLE AUGEN RICHTEN SICH AUF DIE TÜR. EIN COWBOY GEHT LÄSSIG DURCH DEN SALOON AUF DEN TRESEN ZU. ES WIRD MÄUSCHEN-STILL. NUR DAS RHYTHMISCHE KLICKEN DER SPOREN IST ZU HÖREN. DER BARKEEPER SCHIEBT DEM COWBOY ÄNGSTLICH EIN GLAS ZU, DAS BIS AN DEN RAND MIT EINEM KÖSTLICHEN SCHOKO-GETRÄNK GEFÜLLT IST. (HIER ERSCHEINT NATÜRLICH DER NAME DES PRODUKTES.) DER COWBOY LEERT SEIN GLAS — WIE EIN WESTERN-STAR SEINEN WHISKEY IN EINEM ALTEN COWBOYFILM — UND GEHT GENAU SO LÄSSIG, WIE ER KAM. EIN PAAR HARTE BURSCHEN WISCHEN SICH DEN ANGSTSCHWEISS VON DER STIRN. UND NUN KOMMT DER WERBESPRUCH: „WEIL IHRE HELDEN GANZE ARBEIT LEISTEN!" — DEN COWBOY SPIELTE EIN JUNGE, KEINE ZEHN JAHRE ALT.

CD 7 Tr. 7

Lehrerin: Nun, zuerst einmal, wer von euch kann sich noch an diesen Werbespot im Fernsehen erinnern?

Christian: Ich kann mich gut daran erinnern, oder besser gesagt, zu gut!

Gabriele: Logo! Weil dich deine Mutter mit diesem blöden Getränk großgezogen hat. Stimmt's?

Christian: Genau so ist es. Und schau, was aus mir geworden ist! Ich bin groß und kräftig.

Annette: Also, ich muss sagen, ich bin dagegen, dass man Kinder in der Werbung verwendet.

Hans-Jörg: Aber dieser Werbespot richtet sich an Kinder!

Annette: Eben! Aber Kinder wissen noch nicht, was wirklich gut ist für sie. Sie sind noch nicht kritisch genug; sie wollen halt alles, was sie sehen.

Lehrerin: Und was meinst du, Sebastian?

Sebastian: Es scheint, Christians Mutter hat das Getränk gekauft, weil es dem Christian geschmeckt hat.

Kerstin: Was mich eben nervt ist das Image. Wenn Ihr Kind, Ihr Sohn, dieses Getränk trinkt, so wird er einmal ein ganzer Kerl. Er wird ein Mann, der vor keinen anderen Männern Angst hat!

Christian: Du übertreibst, Kerstin.

Kerstin: Überhaupt nicht. Diese Werbung nützt die Gefühle von Eltern und Kindern aus. Und die Firma, die am besten wirbt, die verkauft ja auch leider am meisten, verdient das meiste Geld.

Florian:	Genau! Im österreichischen Fernsehen sollen angeblich Werbespots mit Kindern und für Kinder verboten sein. Nicht wahr, Frau Klose?
Lehrerin:	Es kann sein, aber ich weiß es nicht. Da bin ich überfragt.
Walter:	Mir scheint, die Werbemacher haben's nicht einfach: sie müssen immer neue Ideen haben.
Gabriele:	In der Werbung sieht es so aus, als ob sich jeder alles leisten kann und unbedingt haben muss. Viele Sachen braucht man doch gar nicht!
Annette:	Eben! Ich möchte nur noch mal klarstellen, dass ich nicht gegen Werbung bin, nur gegen übertriebene Image-Werbung. Zigarettenmarken, Rasierwasser, Sportwagen und so passen angeblich zur Männlichkeit, aber die Werbung sagt nicht, wie schädlich zum Beispiel Zigaretten sind.
Hans-Jörg:	Da stimm ich dir zu. Und mit der Werbung für Motorräder, Mode und auch Zigaretten wird uns „Freiheit" versprochen.
Petra:	Da kann ich nur lachen. Und teure Parfüms und die neueste Mode passen nur zu schönen Frauen, was?
Götz:	Na ja, eins steht fest: Wir haben uns an die Werbung gewöhnt.
Uschi:	Das mag schon sein. Was mich aber stört ist, dass ... äh, die Werbung macht uns Appetit aufs Kaufen. Sie zeigt die Welt als ein riesiges Kaufhaus, wo man sich alle Wünsche erfüllen kann.
Götz:	Und warum nicht?
Uschi:	Weil man glaubt, man muss diese Sachen haben, um glücklich, zufrieden und beliebt zu sein. Das Schlimme ist aber, dass es zu viele arme Menschen gibt. Und je weniger Geld man hat, desto mehr sehnt man sich nach einem guten, zufrieden stellenden Leben, nach einem Leben, das die Werbung verspricht, das sich aber die meisten doch nicht leisten können.

„Da haben wir den Salat ... kein Leerdammer im Haus."

Leerdammer. Löcher mit viel Geschmack drumherum.

Reisefieber?
Mit uns fällt Ihr Urlaub nicht ins Wasser!

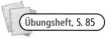

Ihre Apotheke.
Uns können Sie fragen.

Ihre Apotheke hat die richtigen Tips und Produkte, um die Ferien für Sie zu einem ungetrübten Vergnügen zu machen. Bitte fordern Sie Ihre persönliche Urlaubs-Checkliste an unter der Telefon-Nr. 030/19814.

Übungsheft, S. 85

16 Was sagt der Text?

1. **Schreiben** Schreib alle Adjektive und Adverbien, die in der Barszene vorkommen, in dein Notizheft! 1. Adjektive: amerikanisch, hart, rhythmisch, köstlich, alt, ganze / Adverbien: griffbereit, lässig, mäuschenstill, ängstlich

2. **Sprechen** Mach dein Buch zu! Erzähle die Barszene nach, so gut du kannst!

3. **Lesen/Sprechen** Jeder von euch übernimmt die Rolle eines Schülers aus Frau Kloses Klasse. Lest das Klassengespräch dramatisch vor!

4. **Sprechen** Welchen von den Aussagen im Text stimmst du am meisten zu?

Wortschatz

auf Deutsch erklärt

werben Werbung machen

verdienen wenn man Geld für die Arbeit bekommt

klarstellen verständlich machen

Meine Tante hat mich großgezogen. Meine Tante hat mir geholfen, vom Kind zum Erwachsenen zu werden.

Es steht fest. Es ist klar, wahr.

kräftig wenn man starke Muskeln hat

riesig sehr groß

schädlich nicht gut oder ungesund für einen

der Kerl der Mann

Ich bin überfragt. Ich weiß die Antwort nicht.

auf Englisch erklärt

Werbung versucht oft, unsere <u>Gefühle</u> <u>auszunutzen</u>. *Advertising often attempts to take advantage of our feelings.*

Dieser Spot <u>richtet sich an</u> Jugendliche. *This ad is directed at young people.*

<u>Je</u> öfter ich den Namen eines Produktes sehe, <u>desto</u> größer ist die Chance, dass ich es kaufe. *The more I see the name of a product, the greater the chance that I'll buy it.*

Dieser Star spaziert herum, <u>als ob</u> er König wäre. *This star struts around as if he were king.*

<u>Angeblich</u> verdient er sehr viel. *He reportedly earns a lot.*

> Übungsheft, S. 60, Ü. 9–10

So sagt man das!

Eliciting agreement and agreeing

Here are some ways to elicit and express agreement. Which expressions do you know? Which are new?

To elicit agreement, you could say:

> **Die Werbung beeinflusst uns,**
> **nicht?**
> **nicht wahr?**
> **ja?**
> **stimmt's?**
> **oder?**
> **meinst du nicht?**

To agree, you could say:

> **Da hast du ganz Recht.**
> **Damit stimm ich überein.**
> **Das meine ich auch.**
> **Logisch!/Logo!**
> **Genau./Genau so ist es.**
> **Eben!/Klar!/Sicher!**

What similar words or phrases do you use in everyday speech?

> Übungsheft, S. 61, Ü. 11

17 Welche Meinung wird akzeptiert? Script and answers on p. 179H

Zuhören Die Mitarbeiter der Schülerzeitung reden über Werbespots in Zeitungen, die sie gesehen haben. Hör ihrem Gespräch gut zu und entscheide, wessen Meinungen am meisten akzeptiert werden!

CD 7 Tr. 8

18 Einverstanden oder nicht?

Sprechen Constance und Stefan äußern ihre Meinungen über die Werbung. Bist du einverstanden oder nicht mit dem, was sie sagen? Was sagst du dazu? Such dir eine Partnerin und reagiert zusammen auf die Aussagen! Versucht auch, Gründe anzugeben!

CONSTANCE	**Die Werbung versucht nur, den Käufer zu beeinflussen, meinst du nicht?**
DU	**Klar!** *oder* **Das ist nicht ganz wahr. Es gibt Werbung, die auch informiert.**

STEFAN	„Die meisten Reklamen haben Frauen als Blickfang."
CONSTANCE	„Viele Sportler verdienen mit der Werbung zu viel Geld."
STEFAN	„Das Image der Frau wird weiterhin in einer traditionellen Rolle gezeigt."
CONSTANCE	„Es gibt aber auch gute Werbung, die nicht so manipulativ ist."
STEFAN	„Die meisten Werbespots für Kinder find ich sehr blöd."
CONSTANCE	„Die Werbung nutzt oft nur die Gefühle der Kinder aus."
STEFAN	„Die Werbemacher brauchen immer wieder neue Ideen."
CONSTANCE	„Die Werbung macht nur Appetit aufs Kaufen."
STEFAN	„Je weniger Geld man hat, desto mehr sehnt man sich nach einem guten Leben."
CONSTANCE	„Die Werbung verspricht, was sich die meisten nicht leisten können."

Note that **ausnützen** is mostly used in **Süddeutschland**, **Österreich**, and in **die Schweiz**, while in Northern Germany **ausnutzen** is preferred.

Ein wenig Grammatik

Schon bekannt

In **Kapitel 4** you learned about relative clauses. Relative clauses are introduced by relative pronouns, the various forms of **der, die, das.**

> **Das ist ein Werbeslogan, den ich nicht kenne.**

Identify the relative pronoun in this sentence. What does it refer to? What case is it in? Why?

Mehr Grammatikübungen, S. 202, Ü. 5–7

Die bringen in der Werbung immer das, was wir schon haben.

Grammatik

Introducing relative clauses with **was** and **wo**

1. The word **was** introduces a relative clause when it refers back to
   a. indefinite pronouns like **das, alles, etwas, nichts, wenig, viel.**
      Ich sehe **etwas, was** mir gefällt.
   b. the entire idea of the preceding clause.
      Ich kann es mir nicht leisten, was diese Leute anpreisen.
2. The word **wo** is used to refer to places, especially in a broader sense.
      Die Welt ist ein Kaufhaus, **wo** man sich alles kaufen kann.

Relative clauses are dependent clauses. Do you remember what happens to the conjugated verb in dependent clauses?

Mehr Grammatikübungen, S. 203, Ü. 8

Grammatikheft, S. 62, Ü. 12–13

19 Grammatik im Kontext

Sprechen Frag einen Partner, was er möchte! Er antwortet dir, und dann fragt er dich.

1. Was kaufst du dir?   2. Was wünschst du dir?   3. Was gefällt dir?

BEISPIEL   DU   **Was wünschst du dir?**
PARTNER   **Ich wünsche mir nichts, was ich mir nicht leisten kann.**

| das, | wenig, | nichts, |
| etwas, | alles, | viel, |

was

s. (nicht) leisten können

irgendwie Qualität haben

im Fernsehen angepriesen werden

gebrauchen können

(nicht) viel Geld kosten

gefallen

20 Grammatik im Kontext

Sprechen Bist du aufgeregt? Such dir eine Partnerin und sag ihr, was dich alles aufregt! Sie sagt es dir dann auch. Stimmt ihr miteinander überein?

Mich regt Werbung auf, wo …

Werbung verspricht „Freiheit".

Frauen dienen als Blickfang.

Die Gefühle der Leute werden ausgenutzt.

Kinder werben für ein Produkt.

Die Werbesprüche sind besonders blöd.

Die Image-Werbung ist übertrieben.

21 Das Analysieren ist eine Übung, die …

Lesen/Schreiben Suche aus dem Text „Weiter geht's!" alle Relativsätze heraus! Analysiere die Relativpronomen! Was sind ihre Beziehungsworte (*antecedents*)? Sind sie spezifisch oder allgemein?

So sagt man das!

Expressing conviction, uncertainty, and what seems to be true

 7–2

To express conviction, you may say:

Es steht fest, dass Werbung einen großen Einfluss auf uns ausübt.

To express uncertainty, you may say:

Es kann sein, dass …   *oder*   **Das mag schon sein.**

You already know how to express what seems true to you:

Es scheint, dass Sportler immer mehr Geld durch Werbung verdienen.

You also may say:

Es sieht so aus, als ob sie das tun.

Übungsheft, S. 88–89, Ü. 6–8

---

22 Der Werbespruch vom kleinen Cowboy   Script and answers on p. 179H

Zuhören Du hörst jetzt, wie Frau Kloses Schüler über den Werbespruch vom kleinen Cowboy sprechen. Welche Schüler sind überzeugt, dass sie Recht haben? Welche sind nicht sicher oder sogar dagegen? Mach eine Tabelle und füll sie aus!

CD 7 Tr. 9

Grammatik

irgendein and irgendwelche

Mehr Grammatikübungen, S. 203, Ü. 9–10

Irgendein and **irgendwelche** mean *any (at all)*, or *some … or another.*

Grammatikheft, S. 63, Ü. 14

Singular	*Plural*
Da liegt **irgendeine** Zeitung.	Da liegen **irgendwelche** Zeitungen.
Ich suche **irgendeinen** Spruch.	Ich suche **irgendwelche** Sprüche.
Das kommt in **irgendeiner** Werbung.	Das kommt in **irgendwelchen** Werbungen.

What do you notice about these words? What can you say about the endings?

23 Grammatik im Kontext

1. irgendeine; 2. irgendeinen; 3. irgendwelche; 4. irgendein;
5. irgendwelche; 6. irgendeine; 7. irgendeiner; 8. irgendwelchen;
9. Irgendwelche; 10. irgendwelche

Sprechen/Schreiben Welche Form von **irgendein** passt in diese Lücken?

1. Das ist … Reklame für Videos.
2. Er soll … Werbeslogan schreiben.
3. Das sind … Sachen für Kinder.
4. Das ist … Fertiggericht.
5. Das sind … Slogans für Bekleidung.
6. Ich suche … Autoreklame.
7. Das Auto steht auf … Wiese.
8. Die Wiese ist in … Bergen.
9. … Sportler preisen den Wagen an.
10. Ich kann nicht ohne … Statussymbole sein.

24 Grammatik im Kontext

Sprechen/Schreiben Ein Klassenkamerad fragt dich über die Barszene, die Frau Klose in ihrer Klasse gezeigt hat. Du weißt aber sehr wenig darüber. Gebrauche deshalb das Wort „irgend" in deinen Antworten! Tauscht dann die Rollen aus! For answers, see below.

1. Wo spielt sich diese Szene mit dem Jungen ab?
2. Wer sind die Männer, die um den Tresen stehen?
3. Welche Tür schwingt auf?
4. Was für ein Cowboy geht durch den Saloon?
5. Was schiebt der Barkeeper dem Cowboy zu?
6. Wo hast du so einen Cowboy-Star schon gesehen?
7. Durch welche Tür geht dieser Cowboy hinaus?
8. Wann hat man diese Werbung gezeigt?

Wortschatz

Words preceded by **irgend**

irgendetwas	irgendwie
irgendjemand	irgendwo
irgendwann	irgendwohin

Übungsheft, S. 86–88, Ü. 1–5   Grammatikheft, S. 63, Ü. 15

25 Zum Überlegen und Diskutieren

24. 1. In irgendeiner …
2. Irgendwelche …
3. Irgendeine …
4. Irgendein …
5. Irgendein …
6. Irgendwo …
7. Durch irgendeine …
8. Irgendwann …

Sprechen/Schreiben Überlegt euch, was ihr zu folgenden Themen zu sagen habt, und diskutiert in der Gruppe darüber! Schreibt für jedes Thema die Argumente dafür und dagegen auf!

1. Werbespots für Kinder und mit Kindern sollten verboten werden.
2. Die Image-Werbung: dafür oder dagegen?
3. Die Werbung macht uns Appetit aufs Kaufen.
4. Werbung für gesundheitsschädliche Produkte wie Zigaretten und alkoholische Getränke sollte nicht erlaubt sein.

26 Für mein Notizbuch

Schreiben Wähle eins der obigen Themen, und schreib deine Meinung darüber! Gebrauche mindestens sechs Sätze!

Comics lesen

Lesestrategie Using pictures and print type as clues to meaning When reading cartoons and comics, look at the pictures and the way in which words are written before you begin to read. Pictures and print can tell you a lot about what is happening in a story.

Getting Started For answers, see p. 179W.

1. Read the title and then look at the entire sequence of frames. What can you tell about the story just by looking at the pictures? Make some predictions about what you think is happening. For instance, where and when is the story taking place? Is everything going smoothly, or is there some kind of conflict?

2. Before you read the text, notice the different types of print in the bubbles. Looking only at the pictures and print, why do you think the cartoonist uses different types of print?

3. Skim the entire text twice. What is the setting? What is the approximate time period? How many different characters are introduced and where are they from?

A Closer Look

4. Look at the pictures again as you read the story. For which character does the writer use pictures instead of words in the bubbles? Why do you think he does that?

5. What, in general, is happening in the story? Are the characters who come in at the beginning really **Freiwillige**? What are they? Does the text confirm the predictions you made?

Read the comic again more carefully and answer the following questions.

6. Based on the context, what do you think a **Dolmetscher** is? How do you know? Why does the Roman need a **Dolmetscher**?

7. What does the Egyptian want to know? What kind of mix-up has occurred?

8. Where does the Roman soldier take the men after signing them in? Why? What are they supposed to do when they get there?

9. What do you think **mager** means? How do you know?

10. Zeichne jetzt deinen eigenen Comicstrip! Schreib auch die Sprechblasen dazu! Die Handlung darf komisch oder ernst sein, sogar belehrend, wie du willst.

Übungsheft, S. 90–91, Ü. 1-7

Zum Schreiben

Advertisements can be very persuasive. They sometimes portray a product in such a way that you think you can't live without it. But, as we all know from experience, products are not always as good as they seem in the ads. In this activity, you will write a business letter complaining to a manufacturer about a product you have purchased.

Es stört mich!

Wähl ein nicht zufrieden stellendes Produkt, das du benutzt hast, und dessen Werbung du gesehen hast! Schreib einen Brief an den Hersteller, um deinen Ärger als Verbraucher des Produktes auszudrücken!

 Schreibtipp Using tone and word choice for effect
When you write you use words that convey how you feel. It is important to think about and choose words that will create the effect you want. This is exactly what advertisers do to get you to buy their products. Adjectives and adverbs are particularly effective for setting a tone. Different degrees of adjectives and adverbs can be used to intensify the strength of a given statement, such as schlecht vs. schrecklich or gut vs. ausgezeichnet. A person complaining about a product, for example, is likely to use strong adjectives to convey frustration.

A. Vorbereiten

1. Mach zuerst eine Liste von allem, was dich an diesem Produkt stört!

2. Vergleich das Produkt mit anderen, ähnlichen Produkten! Ist es genau so gut? schlechter? teurer? Hat es die gleiche Wirkung? Schreib alles auf!

3. Hat dieses Produkt irgendwelche besonderen Qualitäten? Ist das Produkt so, wie es die Werbung verspricht? Mach dir Notizen!

4. Nimm jetzt deine Notizen zur Hand und suche Adjektive und Adverbien, die deinen Ärger gut ausdrücken!

B. Ausführen

Benutze jetzt deine Notizen, und schreib einen Brief an den Hersteller des Produktes! Vergiss nicht, die Adresse, Anrede und Schlussformulierung dazuzuschreiben!

C. Überarbeiten

1. Lies deinen Brief einem Partner vor und besprecht, ob der Brief den richtigen Ton hat, um deine Beschwerde (complaint) auszudrücken!

2. Besprecht die Adjektive! Was wolltest du mit ihnen ausdrücken? Wirken die Adjektive auf deinen Partner, wie du beabsichtigt hast?

3. Lies deinen Brief noch einmal durch! Hast du den Text in Briefform geschrieben? Hast du eine passende Anrede und eine geeignete Schlussformulierung benutzt? Hast du alles richtig buchstabiert?

4. Schreib den korrigierten Brief noch einmal ab!

internet

go.
hrw
.com

ADRESSE: go.hrw.com
KENNWORT:
    WK3 FRANKFURT-7

Erste Stufe

Objectives Expressing annoyance; comparing

1 Gewisse Reklamen nerven dich. Schreib die folgenden Sätze ab, und schreib dabei die in Klammern gegebene Information als dass-Satz! (**Seite 185**)

1. (Die Werbung beeinflusst uns.)   Es nervt mich, dass _____ .   die Werbung uns beeinflusst
2. (Sie manipuliert den Käufer.)   Es nervt mich, dass _____ .   sie den Käufer manipuliert
3. (Sie preist die Produkte nur an.)   Es nervt mich, dass _____ .   sie die Produkte nur anpreist
4. (Sie zeigt nur eine heile Welt.)   Es nervt mich, dass _____ .   sie nur eine heile Welt zeigt
5. (Sie informiert oft zu wenig.)   Es nervt mich, dass _____ .   sie oft zu wenig informiert
6. (Sie spricht wenig über Qualität.)   Es nervt mich, dass _____ .   sie wenig über Qualität spricht

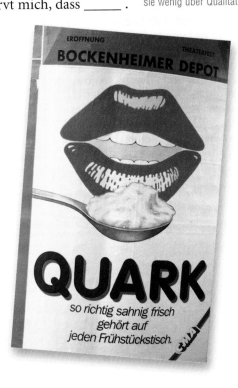

2 Du vergleichst Werbung und Werbeslogans. Schreib die folgenden Sätze ab, und schreib dabei die korrekte Form von **derselbe,** *the same,* in die Lücken! (**Seite 186**)

1. Ich habe _____ Reklame für _____ Wagen im ZDF gesehen.   dieselbe; denselben
2. Ich habe _____ Werbespruch für _____ Putzmittel schon oft gehört.   denselben; dasselbe
3. Ich habe _____ Gericht in _____ Restaurant vor zwei Tagen gegessen.   dasselbe; demselben
4. Ich glaube, dieses Produkt hat _____ Namen und _____ Geschmack.   denselben; denselben
5. Die Reklame für ALA hat _____ Mitteilung und _____ Kaufreiz.   dieselbe; denselben
6. Schau, _____ Werbespruch hängt zweimal an _____ Plakatwand.   derselbe; derselben

3 Schreib die folgenden Sätze ab und schreib dabei das deutsche Wort für den Englischen Ausdruck in die erste Lücke, die richtige Adjektivendung in die zweite Lücke und den passenden Ausdruck aus dem Kasten in die dritte Lücke. Denk daran, dass der letzte Ausdruck ein Dativform ist! (**Seite 187**)

Haarpflegemittel	Butter	Katzenfutter	Waschmittel	Automobile

1. Ich kenne (several) _____ gut_____ Werbungen von _____ .   mehrere; -e; Katzenfutter

2. Ich kenne (many) _____ schön_____ Werbungen von _____ .   viele; -e; Butter

3. Ich kenne (a few) _____ toll_____ Werbungen von _____ .   ein paar; -e; Automobilen

4. Ich kenne (no) _____ neu_____ Werbung von _____ .   keine; -e; Waschmitteln

5. Ich kenne (other) _____ gut_____ Werbungen von _____ .   andere; -e; Haarpflegemitteln

4 Du sprichst über verschiedene Medien. Schreib die folgenden Sätze ab, und schreib dabei die richtigen Endungen in die Lücken! (**Seite 187**)

1. Diese Reklame hat mehrere gut_____ Eigenschaften, aber keine gut_____ Fotos.   e; en

2. Alle deutsch_____ Jungen, aber nur wenige amerikanisch_____ Jungen, kaufen das.   en; e

3. Hier sind alle gut_____ Berichte, aber auch einige schlecht_____ Berichte.   en; e

4. Ich kenne ein paar gut_____ Werbeslogans, aber auch viele schlecht_____ Slogans.   e; e

5. Wir kennen alle gut_____ Putzmittel und auch zwei oder drei schlecht_____ .   en; e

6. An alle_____ groß_____ Plakatwänden und an einige_____ klein_____ hängen Poster.   n; en; n; en

7. Etliche neu_____ Produkte und alle neu_____ Werbesprüche gefallen mir gut.   e; en

8. In viel_____ klein_____ Läden und in alle_____ groß_____ Läden siehst du das Plakat.   en; en; n; en

Zweite Stufe

Objectives Eliciting agreement and agreeing; expressing conviction, uncertainty, and what seems to be true

5 Du sprichst über Werbung und über verschiedene Produkte. Schreib die folgenden Sätze ab, und schreib dabei das korrekte Relativpronomen in die Lücken! (**Seite 193**)

1. Das ist eine Reklame, _____ ich noch nie gesehen habe. die

2. Das ist die Plakatwand, auf _____ ich dieses Reklameposter gesehen habe. der

3. Ich verstehe die Mitteilung nicht, _____ diese Reklame zu machen versucht. die

4. Ich kann die Verbraucher nicht verstehen, _____ so ein Produkt kaufen. die

5. Das Putzmittel, _____ meine Mutter benutzt, siehst du in jeder Werbung. das

6. Die Werbung zeigt natürlich nicht den Stau, _____ wir jeden Abend haben. den

7. Die Leute, mit _____ ich zusammenkomme, kennen dieses Produkt nicht. denen

8. Der Kaufreiz, _____ dieses Produkt hat, ist ganz enorm. den

6 Du sprichst über Werbung und über verschiedene Produkte. Schreib jeweils die zwei gegebenen Sätze als einen Satz, der mit einem Relativpronomen eingeleitet wird! (**Seite 193**)

1. Hier ist eine gute Reklame, die ich kenne.

1. Hier ist eine gute Reklame. Ich kenne sie.

2. Hier ist ein Werbespruch. Ich kenne ihn gut.

3. Hier ist ein Werbespruch. Er ist sehr gut.

3. Hier ist ein Werbespruch, der sehr gut ist.
4. Hier ist ein Putzmittel, das ich gut kenne.

2. Hier ist ein Werbespruch, den ich gut kenne.

4. Hier ist ein Putzmittel. Ich kenne es gut.

5. Hier ist ein toller Wagen. Ich möchte ihn.

6. Hier ist ein Getränk. Ich kaufe es immer.

5. Hier ist ein toller Wagen, den ich möchte.
6. Hier ist ein Getränk, das ich immer kaufe.

7 Schreib Relativsätze und gebrauche dabei die gegebene Illustration in der ersten Lücke und ein Relativpronomen in der zweiten Lücke. (**Seite 193**)

1. Das ist ein _____ , _____ ich gern mal besichtigen möchte.
U-Boot, das

2. Das ist ein _____ , _____ ich gern mal fahren möchte.
Laster, den

3. Das ist ein _____ , _____ ich noch nie gesehen habe.
Panzer; den

4. Das ist ein _____ , _____ ich gern mal ausprobieren möchte.
Shampoo; das

5. Das ist ein _____ , _____ ich mir gern kaufen möchte.
Wagen; den / Auto; das

8 Du sprichst über Werbung und den Kauf von Produkten, für die geworben wird. Schreib die folgenden Sätze ab, und schreib dabei das korrekte Relativpronomen in die Lücken! (**Seite 193**)

1. Ich glaube nicht an das, _____ diese Werbung verspricht. was
2. Ich sehe in dieser Werbung nichts, _____ ich mir kaufen möchte. was
3. Wir kaufen in einem Kaufhaus ein, _____ wir alles finden, _____ wir brauchen. wo; was
4. Es gibt wenig, _____ ich möchte und viel, _____ ich mir nicht leisten kann. was; was
5. Es gibt nichts, für _____ man nicht wirbt und viel, _____ man nicht braucht. was; was
6. Wir leben in einer Stadt, _____ wir alles kaufen können, _____ wir wollen. wo; was

9 Du sprichst über Werbung und drückst dabei eine gewisse Unsicherheit (*uncertainty*) aus. Schreib die folgenden Sätze ab, und schreib dabei die korrekte Form von **irgendein** in die Lücken! (**Seite 195**)

1. Es kann sein, dass das eine Reklame für _____ Film oder _____ Video ist. irgendeinen; irgendein
2. Es scheint, dass das Foto in _____ Zeitung oder in _____ Magazin ist. irgendeiner; irgendeinem
3. Es scheint, dass die Reklame für _____ Putzmittel oder _____ Seife wirbt. irgendein; irgendeine
4. Es kann sein, dass wir uns _____ Buch oder _____ Zeitungen kaufen. irgendein; irgendwelche
5. Es scheint, dass der Wagen _____ Kaufreiz für _____ Leute hat. irgendeinen; irgendwelche
6. Es kann sein, dass _____ Verbraucher _____ Reklame nicht gesehen hat. irgendein; irgendeine

10 Du bereitest mit deinen Freunden ein Picknick vor und du entdeckst, dass ihr noch viele Dinge braucht. Schreib die folgenden Sätze ab und schreib dabei die korrekte Form von **irgendein** in die erste Lücke und den in der Illustration dargestellten Ausdruck in die zweite Lücke. (**Seite 195**)

1. Wir brauchen noch _____ _____ . irgendeinen Picknickkorb

2. Wir brauchen noch _____ _____ . irgendeine Kühlbox

3. Wir brauchen noch _____ _____ . irgendein Schneidebrett

4. Wir brauchen noch _____ _____ . irgendeine Thermosflasche

5. Wir brauchen noch _____ _____ . irgendeinen Becher

Anwendung

1 Lies den folgenden Text, und such dir die Wortkreationen der Werbetexter heraus! Bei allen Ausdrücken handelt es sich um erfundene Wörter. Versuch, diese Ausdrücke in gutes Deutsch zu übertragen! Zum Beispiel „Deutschlands meiste Kreditkarte" bedeutet: „Kreditkarte, die man in Deutschland am meisten benutzt."

unkaputtbar: lässt sich nicht kaputtmachen / BahnCard: Bahnkarte / Geschmackskraft der Natur: hat die Kraft der Natur im Geschmack / Schnupperpreise: Preise, nach denen man sonst suchen muss / Jugend froscht: Jugend forscht / aprilfrisch: so frisch, wie das Wetter im April / tiefenwirksam: eine tiefe, gründliche Wirkung haben / atmungsaktiv: ist lebendig und atmet

Im kreativen Rausch
Zu kühn formuliert: Viele Werbeslogans stoßen bei Sprachexperten auf Kritik

Wenn Katrin M. Frank-Cyrus Schulkindern beim Pausenhof-palaver zuhört, befällt sie leichtes Unbe-hagen. Dann registriert die Geschäfts-führerin der Wiesbadener Gesellschaft für deutsche Sprache (GfdS), dass die Kids gern Slogans aus der Fernsehwer-bung nachplappern — nicht immer, aber immer öfter.

Pädagogen haben Bedenken, denn die Werbetexter gebrauchen in ihrem kreativen Rausch oft inkorrekte For-mulierungen, also Sprache, die gegen die Normen von Grammatik und Semantik verstößt.

Der Sprach-TÜV der Wiesbadener Experten und Expertinnen findet viele Formulierungen einfach zu viel.

Ärgerlich: „Deutschlands meiste Kreditkarte" (Kampagne für Eurocard): absichtlicher Grammatikfehler, um mehr Aufmerksamkeit zu erregen — was auch funktioniert; „unkaputtbar" (Kampagne für Coca-Cola): raffinierte, aber sprachlich völlig unkorrekte Konstruktion; „BahnCard" (Deutsche Bahn): orthographisch (noch) nicht akzeptabel; „Geschmackskraft der Natur" (Food-Werbung): Natur kann weder uns schmecken noch selber schmecken — eine Unsinnsbildung.

Gefällig: „Schnupperpreise" (Kam-pagne für Bekleidung): werbewirksam, sprachlich in Ordnung; „Jugend froscht"[1] (Reiseveranstalter): platter Kalauer, erregt aber Aufmerksamkeit.

Originell: „aprilfrisch", „tiefenwirk-sam", „atmungsaktiv": anschaulich witzig, einprägsam — und korrekt.

> **Rausch:** intoxication; **stoßen:** meet; **Un-behagen:** uneasiness; **nachplappern:** imitieren; **Bedenken:** concerns; **Unsinn:** nonsense; **schnuppern:** to sniff out; **Frosch:** frog; **Kalauer:** dumb joke

1. The slogan „Jugend froscht" alludes to „Jugend forscht", the title of a science contest for young people.

Script and answers on p. 179l

2 Du hörst jetzt einige Werbesendungen im Radio. Schau dir folgende Illustrationen an! Welche Zielgruppe soll mit jeder Werbung erreicht werden?

CD 7 Tr. 10

a.

b.

c.

d.

e.

3 Stellt euch vor, ihr seht die folgenden Reklamen ganz groß auf einer Litfaßsäule! Reagiert darauf! Was findet ihr gut, was nicht? Begründet eure Antworten!

4 Jeder von euch muss eine Werbeanzeige mit in die Klasse bringen. Sprecht darüber, und diskutiert dabei besonders über die folgenden Punkte:

1. Ist das Informationswerbung oder Image-Werbung, oder beides?

2. Mit welchen Worten werden die Produkte angepriesen?

3. Hat die Werbung einen Blickfang? Welchen? Ist er wirkungsvoll?

4. Würdet ihr dieses Produkt kaufen, so wie es beschrieben ist? Warum?

5. Hat diese Werbung eine versteckte Mitteilung? Was für eine?

5 Schreib einen Bericht über „deine" Werbeanzeige! Halte dich dabei an die Diskussionsfragen von Übung 4!

6 **R o l l e n s p i e l**

Gruppen spielen Mitglieder einer Werbeagentur, die einen wichtigen Werbespot fürs Fernsehen entwerfen muss.

Sucht ein Produkt aus, für das ihr werben wollt! Entwerft drei verschiedene Werbesprüche, und schreibt den Werbetext dazu! Einigt euch auf den besten Spruch, und verteilt Rollen an jedes Gruppenmitglied, um der Klasse den Spot vorzuspielen! Wenn möglich, macht auch ein Video davon!

Kann ich's wirklich?

Can you express annoyance? (p. 185)

1 How would you respond if a friend asked you **Was nervt dich alles?**
E.g.: Es nervt mich, dass ich für die Mathearbeit lernen muss.

Can you compare? (p. 185)

2 How would you say Was mich aufregt, ist, wenn Werbungen die Frauen in traditionellen Rollen zeigen.
a. that it annoys you when commercials show women in traditional roles?
b. that it irritates you that commercials always try to manipulate consumers?
Es nervt mich, dass die Werbung immer versucht, die Käufer/Konsumenten zu manipulieren.

3 How would you compare
a. magazine ads and TV ads?   a. E.g.: Werbung in Zeitschriften ist nicht so gut wie Werbung im Fernsehen.
b. your family and your best friend's family?
b. E.g.: Meine Familie wohnt auf der gleichen Straße wie die Familie meines besten Freundes.

4 How would you say that you always compare products, and that you know that product 1 is not as good as product 2? How would you say that you find product 2 to be the best?   Ich vergleiche immer Produkte, und ich weiß, dass (product 1) nicht so gut wie (product 2) ist. / Ich finde (product 2) am besten.

Can you elicit agreement and agree? (p. 192)

5 How would you elicit agreement after making each one of the following statements?
a. Die Werbung manipuliert den Konsumenten.   a. E.g.: …, nicht wahr?; …, stimmt's?
b. Die meisten Werbespots im Fernsehen sind blöd.   b. E.g.: …, oder?; …, ja?
c. Wir haben uns an die Werbung gewöhnt.   c. E.g.: …, meinst du nicht auch?; … nicht?
How would you agree with each of those statements?
E.g.: Da hast du ganz Recht. / Genau. / Eben.

Can you express conviction, uncertainty, and what seems to be true? (p. 194)

6 How would you elaborate on the following statements, indicating that you are convinced, that you are uncertain, or that you feel the statement seems to be true?   a. Es steht fest, dass die Werbung uns Appetit aufs Kaufen macht.
a. Die Werbung macht uns Appetit aufs Kaufen.
b. Kinderwerbung ist unfair.   Es mag schon sein, dass Kinderwerbung unfair ist.
c. Wir kaufen nur das, was wir brauchen.
Es sieht so aus, als ob wir nur das kaufen, was wir brauchen.

Erste Stufe

p. 179X

Expressing annoyance

Was mich aufregt ist, wenn …	What annoys me is when …
Es nervt mich, dass …	It gets on my nerves that …

Comparing

Bevor ich etwas kaufe, vergleiche ich die Preise.	Before I buy something I compare prices.
das Gleiche	the same thing
das gleiche Haus	the same house
derselbe, dieselbe, dasselbe	the same

Other words and useful expressions

aufmerksam machen auf (acc)	to draw attention to
blitzblank	squeaky clean
fröhlich	happy
glücklich	happy

heil	whole, perfect
raffiniert	clever
weise	wise
weiterhin	as before
der Blickfang	eye-catcher
die Eigenschaft, -en	characteristic
der Kaufreiz	temptation to buy
der Konsument, -en	consumer
Linie: in erster Linie	primarily
die Mitteilung, -en	message
die Plakatwand, -̈e	billboard
das Putzmittel, -	cleaning agent
die Reklame, -n	advertisement
Schluss: zum Schluss	finally
der Stau, -s	traffic jam
das Unterbewusstsein	subconscious
der Verbraucher, -	consumer
die Ware, -n	product, ware

der Werbespruch, -̈e	advertising slogan
die Werbung, -en	advertisement
die Wiese, -n	meadow
die Wirtschaft	economy
anpreisen (sep)	to praise
aufklären (sep)	to enlighten
eingestehen (sep)	to admit
s. leisten können	to be able to afford
gebrauchen	to use
überfluten	to flood
überlegen	to consider
verbergen	to hide
verführen	to seduce
vergleichen	to compare
verstecken	to hide
verursachen	to cause
wahrnehmen (sep)	to perceive

Zweite Stufe

Agreeing

Damit stimm ich überein.	I agree with that.
Logisch! Logo!	Of course!
Klar!	Of course!
Genau so ist es.	That's exactly right.

Expressing conviction

Es steht fest, dass …	It's certain that …

Expressing uncertainty

Das mag schon sein.	That may well be.

Expressing what seems to be true

Es sieht so aus, als ob …	It looks as if …
angeblich	ostensibly, reported to be

Other words and useful expressions

je mehr … desto …	the more … the …
kräftig	strong
riesig	huge
schädlich	harmful
überfragt sein	to not know
irgend-	some-
die Freiheit	freedom

das Gefühl, -e	feeling
der Kerl, -e	guy
ausnützen (sep)	to take advantage of
erfüllen	to fulfill
s. gewöhnen an (acc)	to get used to
großziehen (sep)	to raise (a child)
klarstellen (sep)	to make clear
s. richten an (sep)	to be directed at
s. sehnen nach	to long for
verdienen	to earn
verwenden	to use
werben	to advertise

Kapitel 8: Weg mit den Vorurteilen!
Chapter Overview

	FUNCTIONS	**GRAMMAR**	**VOCABULARY**	**RE-ENTRY**
Erste Stufe pp. 212–217	• Expressing surprise, disappointment, and annoyance, p. 213	• The conjunction **als**, p. 215 • Coordinating conjunctions (Summary), p. 216	• Cliché and opinion, p. 212	Expressing surprise, p. 213 **(Kap. 10, II)**; expressing disappointment, p. 213 **(Kap. 3, II)**; **dass**-clauses, p. 213 **(Kap. 9, I)**; conversational past, p. 215 **(Kap. 3, II)**; coordinating conjunctions, p. 216 **(Kap. 1/3/8, I)**

Zweite Stufe pp. 220–223	• Expressing an assumption, p. 221 • Making suggestions and recommendations; giving advice, p. 223	• Verbs with prefixes (Summary), p. 222	• Expressions to describe a person, p. 220	Expressing an assumption p. 221 **(Kap. 10, II)**; Prepositions followed by dative case, p. 222 **(Kap. 9, II)**; Separable-prefix verbs, p. 222 **(Kap 5/7, I)**; Making suggestions, p. 223 **(Kap. 9/11, II)**; Giving advice, p. 223 **(Kap. 3/4, III)**

CULTURE

• Cartoon, p. 214

• Landeskunde: Verständnis für Ausländer? p. 217

• Der sympathische Deutsche, p. 220

Kapitel 8: Weg mit den Vorurteilen!
Chapter Resources

Lesson Planning

One-Stop Planner

Lesson Planner with Substitute Teacher Lesson Plans, pp. 46–50, 82

Student Make-Up Assignments
- Make-Up Assignment Copying Masters, Chapter 8

Listening and Speaking

Listening Activities
- Student Response Forms for Listening Activities, pp. 59–62
- Additional Listening Activities 8-1 to 8-6, pp. 63–66
- Scripts and Answers, pp. 158–166

Video Guide
- Teaching Suggestions, p. 36
- Activity Masters, pp. 37–38
- Scripts and Answers, pp. 67–68, 75

Activities for Communication
- Communicative Activities, pp. 29–32
- Realia and Teaching Suggestions, pp. 86–90
- Situation Cards, pp. 127–128

Reading and Writing

Reading Strategies and Skills Handbook, Chapter 8

Lies mit mir! 3, Chapter 8

Übungsheft, pp. 92–104

Grammar

Grammatikheft, pp. 64–72

Grammar Tutor for Students of German, Chapter 8

Assessment

Testing Program
- Grammar and Vocabulary Quizzes, **Stufe** Quizzes, and Chapter Test, pp. 169–182
- Score Sheet, Scripts and Answers, pp. 183–189

Alternative Assessment Guide
- Portfolio Assessment, p. 23
- Performance Assessment, p. 37

Student Make-Up Assignments
- Alternative Quizzes, Chapter 8

 Online Activities
- Interaktive Spiele
- Internet Aktivitäten

 Video Program
- Videocassette 2

 Audio Compact Discs
- Textbook Listening Activities, CD 8, Tracks 1–12
- Additional Listening Activities, CD 8, Tracks 17–22
- Assessment Items, CD 8, Tracks 13–16

 Teaching Transparencies
- Situations 8-1 to 8-2
- **Mehr Grammatikübungen** Answers
- **Grammatikheft** Answers

 **One-Stop Planner CD-ROM**

Use the **One-Stop Planner CD-ROM with Test Generator** to aid in lesson planning and pacing.

For each chapter, the **One-Stop Planner** includes:
- Editable lesson plans with direct links to teaching resources
- Printable worksheets from resource books
- Direct launches to the HRW Internet activities
- Video and audio segments
- Test Generator
- Clip Art for vocabulary items

Kapitel 8: Weg mit den Vorurteilen!

Projects ····················

Partnerstadt gesucht!

In this activity, the class will work together to prepare a collage and letter representing their town or city to a prospective sister city in Germany. Their objective is to convince the German city to become their sister city.

MATERIALS

✂ **Students may need**

- posterboard
- scissors
- glue
- brochures or photos of their area

SUGGESTED SEQUENCE

1. Students decide which city they would like to have as sister city.

2. Students make an outline of what they will show and tell about their town or city and its people. They should try to view their town or city through the eyes of Germans. The local Chamber of Commerce and Tourism Bureau should be able to provide information and some materials.

3. Students design the layout and arrange the various realia on the posterboard. Each photo or piece of realia should have a caption.

4. For the writing component of this project, students should compose a letter to city officials in which they introduce themselves, briefly describe their town or city, and propose the city partnership program.

5. Before students write the final letter, they should collectively proofread what they have written and make necessary corrections.

6. Students send their collage and letter to the German town that they chose at the beginning of the activity and ask for a response.

GRADING THE PROJECT

Suggested point distribution (**total = 100 points**)

Appearance of collage/Originality........30
Content/Representative examples
    of life in city or town 30
Quality of captions/key descriptors
    used..20
Accurage language usage in captions
    and letter...20

FAMILY LINK

Have students survey family members about their image of Germany. What comes to their minds when they think of the country? What are their associations? Have students share the information with the class and compare with others.

Games ····················

Genau das Gegenteil!

Playing this game will help students review the vocabulary of descriptive adjectives as well as previously learned expressions.

Procedure Divide the class into two teams. A player from Team A forms a sentence describing German or American people. The sentence must include a descriptive adjective such as the ones listed on p. 218. (Example: **Ich finde, dass die Deutschen, die ich kenne, immer sehr höflich sind.**) Then a player from Team B refutes the statement by saying: **Genau das Gegenteil! Ich finde, dass die Deutschen eigentlich ziemlich unhöflich sind.** If the opposing team members use a correct contrasting adjective, they get to come up with a descriptive sentence to which Team A must respond. If an incorrect adjective is used, the team who made the initial statement gets a chance to respond and earn a point. The teacher acts as a monitor and determines the accuracy of statements and awards points accordingly.

Storytelling

*This story accompanies Teaching Transparency 8-2. The **Mini-Geschichte** can be told and retold in different formats, acted out, written down, and read aloud to give students additional opportunities to practice all four skills.*

Liebe Gerlinde:

Ich schau gerade aus meinem Fenster und beobachte die Leute. Als ich hierher kam, hatte ich viele Vorurteile über diese Nachbarschaft. Ich vermutete, dass es hier viel Verkehr und Lärm gibt, aber das waren Klischees. Die Leute hier sind umweltbewusst, friedliebend und hilfreich. Sie sind stolz auf ihre Nachbarschaft und kümmern sich um ihre Nachbarn, insbesondere um die älteren Menschen. Auch war ich äußerst angenehm überrascht, als eine Mechanikerin mein Auto reparierte. Manchmal aber sind die Leute hier zu neugierig. Sie wollen alles über mich wissen!

Traditions

Gref-Völsings Rindswurst

Vor dem Zweiten Weltkrieg hatte Frankfurt eine der größten und einflussreichsten jüdischen Gemeinden Mitteleuropas. Prominente jüdische Familien wie die Oppenheimers, Speyers oder Rothschilds haben lange die kulturelle und wirtschaftliche Entwicklung Frankfurts entscheidend mitbestimmt. Jüdisches Leben war ein wichtiger Wirtschaftsfaktor und viele Geschäfte und Läden spezialisierten sich auf die Wünsche der jüdischen Gemeinde. Als Karl Gref und Wilhelmine Völsing vor über 100 Jahren eine Metzgerei in der Nähe des Judenviertels eröffneten, wollten sie Fleisch- und Wurstwaren anbieten, die auch ihre jüdischen Nachbarn kaufen würden. Und so erfanden sie eine Wurst, die vom Rind und nicht wie die beliebte Frankfurter Wurst vom Schwein kam. Sie machten ihre Wurst aus feinem Bullenfleisch und nannten sie „Gref-Völsings Rindswurst".

Auf den Kochkunstausstellungen in Frankfurt (1905) und Wien (1908) gewann diese einzigartige Wurst eine Goldmedaille. In wenigen Jahren wurde sie auch weit über die Grenzen der Stadt Frankfurt hinaus bekannt. Heute werden täglich 100.000 Gref-Völsings hergestellt und an Metzgereien, Gastwirtschaften und Imbissstuben im Rhein-Main Gebiet verkauft.

Rezept

Rippchen mit Kraut
Für 4 Personen

Zutaten
kg=Kilogramm, l=Liter

1kg	gepökeltes Schweinerippenstück
750 g	Sauerkraut
1	Zwiebel
1	kleiner Apfel
2	Lorbeerblätter
5	Wacholderbeeren
1/8 l	Apfelwein

Zubereitung

Das Fleisch in einen mittelhohen Topf geben. Den Apfel schälen, entkernen und fein schneiden. Die Zwiebel enthäuten und fein würfeln. Das Sauerkraut locker um das Fleisch herumlegen. Die Apfel- und Zwiebelstückchen sowie die Wacholderbeeren und die Lorbeerblätter darunter mischen. Den Apfelwein zugießen, den Deckel schließen und bei mittlerer Hitze zum Dünsten aufheizen. Bei kleiner Hitze ca. 40-45 Minuten garen. Das Rippenstück aus dem Topf nehmen und in Portionsstücke schneiden. Dann mit dem Kraut zusammen servieren.

Beilage
Kartoffelpüree

Technology

One-Stop Planner CD-ROM

To preview all resources available for this chapter, use the **One-Stop Planner CD-ROM**, Disc 2.

Internet Connection .....

internet
ADRESSE: go.hrw.com
KENNWORT: WK3 FRANKFURT-8

*Have students explore the **go.hrw.com** Web site for many online resources covering all chapters. All Chapter 8 resources are available under the keyword **WK3 Frankfurt-8**. Interactive games help students practice the material and provide them with immediate feedback. You will also find a printable worksheet that provides Internet activities that lead to a comprehensive online research project.*

Interaktive Spiele

You can use the interactive activities in this chapter

- to practice grammar, vocabulary, and chapter functions
- as homework
- as an assessment option
- as a self-test
- to prepare for the Chapter Test

Internet Aktivitäten

Students define the term prejudice or racism and visit the sites of German schools that have introduced projects to overcome prejudices.

- To prepare students for the **Arbeitsblatt,** have them discuss in class why they think people have prejudices and suggest ways to overcome prejudices or racism. The information provided in **Landeskunde,** p. 217, may present a good opening for the discussion.

- After completing the **Arbeitsblatt,** ask students to research the history of German immigrants in their hometown or home state. When presenting their research, students should focus especially on events and facts that surprised them.

Webprojekt

Have students find movies depicting contemporary American life that are showing in German movie theaters. Students should give a summary of at least one movie and answer the following questions: 1) Does the movie portray the U.S. and Americans accurately? 2) How could the movie influence the image Germans have of the U.S. and Americans? Encourage students to exchange useful Web sites with their classmates. Have students document their sources by referencing the names and URLs of all the sites they consulted.

Textbook Listening Activities Scripts

The following scripts are for the listening activities found in the *Pupil's Edition*. For Student Response Forms, see *Listening Activities*, pages 59–62. To provide students with additional listening practice, see *Listening Activities*, pages 63–66.

Erste Stufe

2 p. 212

Also, ich bin gerade vor zweieinhalb Wochen aus den Vereinigten Staaten zurückgekommen. Wir haben von der Schule aus ein Austauschprogramm mit einer Schule in der Nähe von Dallas gemacht. Wir waren sechs Monate lang da und haben bei Familien mit Jugendlichen in unserem Alter gewohnt. Ich war vorher noch nie in Amerika, und ich hatte eigentlich keine Ahnung, was mich erwartete. In Deutschland denken viele, dass die Amerikaner alle nur Fastfood essen. Das stimmt eigentlich gar nicht. Das war sogar die eine Sache, die mir in Amerika am besten gefallen hat. Ich war echt erstaunt, aber das Essen dort hat mir phantastisch geschmeckt. Meine Gastmutter hat eigentlich jeden Abend gekocht, und es gab oft mexikanisches Essen, und sogar ein- oder zweimal ein chinesisches Gericht. Wir sind auch öfters zum Essen ausgegangen, und die Gerichte in den Restaurants waren eigentlich immer frisch und sehr lecker. Eine andere Sache, die mir gefallen hat, war, dass die Amerikaner immer sehr hilfreich waren. Sie haben mich gleich akzeptiert und haben mir alles gezeigt. Die Gastfreundschaft der Amerikaner hat mich wirklich begeistert. Auch in der Schule waren alle viel offener als hier in Deutschland. Andererseits muss ich sagen, dass die Amerikaner eigentlich wenig über andere Länder wissen. Im Radio hört man nur selten Nachrichten, und auch die Zeitungen bringen meistens nur Lokalnachrichten. Das fand ich schade. Ich war auch ziemlich enttäuscht, dass es in Amerika viele Probleme mit Rassismus und Vorurteilen gegenüber Minoritäten gibt. Das hat mir dort nicht so gefallen, dass auch die Wohnviertel sehr getrennt sind. Was mir aber absolut super gefallen hat, war das warme, trockene Wetter dort. Seitdem ich wieder in Deutschland bin, regnet es nur. Ich bin aber trotzdem froh, dass ich wieder hier bin. Hier kann ich überall mit dem Fahrrad hinfahren. In Amerika benutzt man eigentlich immer nur das Auto. Die Leute laufen fast nie irgendwo hin, auch wenn es nicht sehr weit ist. Das hat mich irgendwie unheimlich gestört. Außerdem glaube ich, dass wir doch ein wenig vorsichtiger mit unserer Umwelt umgehen. Nicht sehr viele Amerikaner sortieren ihren Müll, und Verpackungen kann man dort auch nicht in den Supermärkten lassen. Außerdem wird viel Plastikgeschirr benutzt, das dann natürlich einfach weggeworfen wird. Da finde ich es schon wesentlich besser, wie wir das hier in Deutschland machen. Insgesamt würde ich sagen, dass jeder Schüler mal einen solchen Austausch machen sollte. Ich habe auf jeden Fall viel dazugelernt.

Answers to Activity 2
Gut: z. B.: Essen hat geschmeckt; Amerikaner sind hilfreich u. gastfreundschaftlich; sind offener in der Schule; warmes Wetter
Nicht gut: z. B.: Amerikaner wissen wenig über andere Länder; Medien bringen meistens Lokalnachrichten; Probleme mit Rassismus u. Vorurteilen; überall mit dem Auto hinfahren; Amerikaner sind nicht so umweltbewusst

5 p. 213

ELKE Ich würde gern auch mal von euch hören, was euch bei dem Austausch in Amerika am meisten gefallen hat, und auch, was euch eigentlich eher gestört hat. Gibt es zum Beispiel auch Sachen, die euch überrascht oder enttäuscht haben?

HEIDI Tja, also Elke, ich war sehr überrascht, wie hilfsbereit und offen die Leute zu mir waren. Ich dachte, dass es bestimmt Vorurteile gegenüber Ausländern dort gibt. Aber die Leute haben mich sofort akzeptiert und waren sehr nett.

FRANZ Ja, da stimme ich dir schon zu, Heidi, aber irgendwie hat es mich gestört, dass die vielen Einladungen, die wir bekommen haben, nicht immer ernst gemeint waren. Freundlich sind die Amerikaner schon, aber es scheint manchmal ein bisschen oberflächlich.

ELKE Meinst du, Franz? Also, ich finde das nicht! Was mich mehr gestört hat, war, dass wir eigentlich nie irgendwo zu Fuß hingegangen sind. Wir sind überall mit dem Auto hingefahren.

HEIDI Ja, ich war auch ein bisschen enttäuscht, dass meine Familie überhaupt kein Interesse am Fahrradfahren oder am Zelten hatte.

FRANZ Also, Heidi, ich muss sagen, da war ich eigentlich überrascht. Meine Familie hat viel draußen gemacht. Wir sind fast jedes Wochenende wandern und angeln gewesen. Das fand ich echt toll.

ELKE Also, ich war überrascht, wie gut das Essen dort war. Meine Vorstellung von Amerika war, dass alle Leute dort nur Fastfood essen. Aber das stimmt überhaupt nicht. Meine Gastmutter hat immer gekocht, und auch in den Restaurants war das Essen lecker.

HEIDI Das stimmt schon, Elke. Aber in den Restaurants hat es mich immer gestört, dass die Portionen viel zu groß waren. Ich konnte immer nur die Hälfte essen, und alles andere wird weggeworfen. Das finde ich wirklich schlimm.

FRANZ Also, am meisten war ich eigentlich enttäuscht, wie wenig manche Amerikaner wirtschaftlich oder politisch über Deutschland informiert sind. Die einzigen Sachen, die sie mit Deutschland in Verbindung bringen, sind Sauerkraut, Autobahnen und das Oktoberfest.

ELKE Das stimmt aber auch nicht immer, Franz. Also, meine Gastfamilie war vor zwei Jahren in Europa im Urlaub, und sie wussten eigentlich viel über Deutschland!

FRANZ Na ja! Ausnahmen gibt es halt immer.

Answers to Activity 5
Elke: Es hat sie gestört, dass man überall mit dem Auto hinfährt und wenig zu Fuß geht. Sie war überrascht, dass es dort gutes Essen gab.
Heidi: Sie war überrascht, dass die Leute hilfsbereit, offen und nett sind. Sie war enttäuscht, dass ihre Familie kein Interesse am Fahrradfahren oder Zelten hatte. Es hat sie gestört, dass die Portionen in den Restaurants zu groß sind.
Franz: Es hat ihn gestört, dass Einladungen oft nicht ernst gemeint sind. Er war überrascht, dass seine Familie viel draußen war zum

Wandern und Angeln. Er war enttäuscht, dass manche Amerikaner zu wenig wirtschaftlich und politisch über Deutschland informiert sind.

Zweite Stufe

19 p. 220

1. Also, bevor ich mit unserem Schüleraustausch nach Deutschland gefahren bin, dachte ich immer, dass die Deutschen nicht sehr freundlich sind und alles sehr genau nehmen. Meine Freundin, die einmal in den Ferien in Deutschland war, hatte mir erzählt, dass die Deutschen Hunde gern haben. Das stimmt wirklich! Meine Gastfamilie hatte zwei Hunde, einen Schäferhund und einen Dackel. Die durften überall mitfahren. Die Deutschen, die ich kennen gelernt habe, sind sehr hundelieb.

2. Ich dachte immer, dass wir hier in Amerika sehr viel sportlicher sind als die Deutschen. Ich hatte mir vorgestellt, dass viele Deutsche sehr unsportlich sind. Jetzt weiß ich, dass das nicht stimmt. Meine Gastfamilie achtet sehr darauf, sich in der Freizeit sportlich zu betätigen. Jeden Sonntag nach dem Mittagessen gehen sie spazieren. Wir sind auch oft Wandern und Bergsteigen gewesen. Meine Gasteltern hatten eine kleine Hütte in den Alpen. Dort sind wir drei- oder viermal hingefahren und haben das Wochenende dort verbracht. Wir haben dann von der Hütte aus Tagestouren gemacht.

3. Also, bevor ich nach Deutschland ging, habe ich eigentlich nie viel über die Umwelt nachgedacht. Das war mir alles so ziemlich egal. Da habe ich in Deutschland viel dazugelernt. Die Deutschen achten sehr auf die Umwelt. In meiner Gastfamilie mussten wir den ganzen Abfall sortieren. Glasflaschen kamen in einen Korb, Plastik in einen andern, und das Papier haben wir gestapelt und zusammengebunden. Einmal in der Woche sind wir dann zu den Recycling-Containern gefahren und haben alles getrennt dort reingeworfen. Mit dem Auto sind wir nur gefahren, wenn wir weit weg mussten. Sonst sind wir meistens mit dem Rad oder mit dem Bus gefahren. Das fand ich echt toll, und ich werde jetzt auch hier in Amerika versuchen, mehr auf die Umwelt zu achten.

4. Ich war echt überrascht, als ich nach Deutschland kam. In meiner Gastfamilie ist es ganz anders als bei mir zu Hause. Meine Eltern haben beide einen Beruf und arbeiten sechzig Stunden in der Woche oder mehr. Ich sehe sie fast nie. Wenn wir zusammen essen, dann gehen wir in ein Restaurant. Sonst hole ich mir einfach etwas aus dem Kühlschrank. Meine Gastmutter in Deutschland hat nur am Vormittag gearbeitet. Jeden Abend haben wir alle zusammen gegessen. Sie hat immer ein sehr leckeres Abendessen gekocht. Am Wochenende gab es auch am Nachmittag Kaffee und selbst gebackenen Kuchen. Wir haben alle zusammen draußen im Garten gesessen und einfach nur geplaudert, manchmal zwei oder drei Stunden lang. Das war wirklich schön. Ich habe viel Deutsch gelernt und die deutsche Gemütlichkeit erlebt.

5. Also, ich bin ein richtiger Fleischfan. Gemüse und Obst, das mag ich nicht so gerne. Ich fand es nicht so gut, dass meine Gastfamilie in Deutschland so viel Gemüse und Obst gegessen hat. Sie waren richtige Fleischmuffel! Ich hatte immer gedacht, dass alle Deutschen jeden Tag Schweinefleisch essen. Das stimmt gar nicht. Einen Braten gab es eigentlich nur am Sonntag. Jeden Morgen gab es Müsli, und dann zum Mittagessen Suppe, Gemüse und Obst. Abends gab es dann belegte Brote und Salat.

Answers to Activity 19
1. d; 2. a; 3. c; 4. b; 5. e

22 p. 221

MANDY Also, ich war noch nie in Deutschland, aber ich stelle mir vor, dass die Deutschen wahnsinnig genau sind und immer nur arbeiten.

JESSE Ja, das kann schon sein, Mandy. Aber ich habe neulich einen Artikel gelesen, wo der Autor sagte, dass das gar nicht stimmt. Ich glaube, dass die Deutschen überhaupt keinen Sinn für Humor haben und immer furchtbar ernst sind. Das sieht man doch auch immer in den Filmen.

HAL Ach komm, Jesse, was du in den Filmen siehst, das stimmt doch gar nicht.

MANDY Mensch, hört doch auf zu streiten, Hal und Jesse! Jeder kann doch seine Meinung haben. Ich, zum Beispiel, vermute, dass viele Deutsche ziemlich dick sind, weil sie immer Schweinefleisch, Wurst und Knödel essen. Das ist doch alles sehr fett.

HAL Ja, da hast du bestimmt Recht, Mandy. Ich nehme an, dass die Deutschen oft in Lederhosen und Dirndln rumlaufen. Das sieht man ja immer auf den Postkarten aus Deutschland.

JESSE Also, ich stelle mir vor, dass die meisten Deutschen sehr arrogant sind.

HAL Ja, genau. Und ich meine auch, dass sie bestimmt unfreundlich sind.

MANDY Also, so schlimm sind sie doch sicherlich nicht. Eigentlich wissen wir doch überhaupt nichts über die Deutschen.

HAL Also, ich glaube schon, dass wir eine Menge über die Deutschen wissen.

MANDY Hm. Da geb ich dir aber nicht Recht, Hal. Ich habe eher den Eindruck, dass dies alles Vorurteile sind.

HAL Hm. Das kann natürlich sein. Eigentlich würde ich ganz gerne mal nach Deutschland, besonders weil die Deutschen alle schnelle Autos fahren. Das muss doch toll sein, mit einem Porsche oder Mercedes auf der Autobahn zu fahren.

MANDY Ja, also ich würde auch gern mal nach Deutschland fliegen. Und du, Jesse?

JESSE Ja, ich auch. Vor allen Dingen möchte ich herausfinden, ob die Deutschen wirklich so viel Bier trinken!

Answers to Activity 22
E.g.: Die Deutschen ...sind genau; arbeiten immer; haben keinen Sinn für Humor; sind ernst; sind dick; essen immer Schweinefleisch, Wurst und Knödel; tragen Lederhosen und Dirndl; sind arrogant; sind unfreundlich; fahren schnelle Autos auf der Autobahn; trinken viel Bier

25 p. 222

CHRISTIAN Hallo, Dorothee! Na, bist du froh, wieder zu Hause zu sein?

DOROTHEE Ja, also eigentlich schon. Es war schön, meine Familie und meinen Hund wieder zu sehen. Und du, Christian? Seit wann bist du denn wieder da?

CHRISTIAN Ach, ich bin schon seit einer Woche aus Berlin zurück. Wie war's denn bei dir?

DOROTHEE Also, ich fand es in Deutschland einfach Spitze. Ich kann nur jedem empfehlen, den Schüleraustausch mitzumachen. Man lernt wirklich so viel über ein Land, wenn man selbst dort hinfährt. Schau mal, da kommt die Lisa, die war letztes Jahr in Deutschland. Hallo, Lisa!

LISA	Hallo, Dorothee! Hallo, Christian! Na, wie geht's euch?
DOROTHEE	Wir haben uns gerade über unseren Austausch unterhalten. Christian war in Berlin und ich in München.
LISA	Ja, also ich finde, es lohnt sich wirklich, ein Semester lang in Deutschland zu verbringen. Man lernt die Sprache viel schneller.
CHRISTIAN	Ja, aber man lernt auch noch andere Sachen!
DOROTHEE	Was meinst du denn?
CHRISTIAN	Na ja, wirf zum Beispiel bloß nicht alles zusammen in den Abfall! Die Deutschen sind wahnsinnig umweltbewusst.
LISA	Ja, das stimmt! Das habe ich auch festgestellt. Meine Familie hat den ganzen Müll sortiert und zum Recycling gebracht.
DOROTHEE	Ach ja, und wisst ihr, wovon ich am meisten überrascht war? Ich dachte immer, dass die Deutschen sehr ausländerfeindlich sind, aber das stimmt gar nicht. Verbreite ja keine Klischees oder Vorurteile! Die meisten Deutschen können das überhaupt nicht leiden.
LISA	Ja, also meine deutschen Freunde fanden das auch immer ganz schlimm.
CHRISTIAN	Habt ihr auch so viel Sport in der Freizeit gemacht wie ich?
LISA	Ja, als ich letztes Jahr dort war, habe ich erst richtig entdeckt, wie viel Spaß Fahrradfahren macht!
CHRISTIAN	Genau! Ich bin in Deutschland auch überall mit dem Fahrrad hingefahren. Egal, was für ein Wetter es gab. Ich kann nur jedem den Tipp geben: bring deine Sportkleidung mit.
DOROTHEE	Nicht nur Sportkleidung, Christian! Es lohnt sich auch, warme Kleidung mitzubringen. Ich war mit der Claudia ein paar Mal wandern, und da war es ziemlich kalt.
CHRISTIAN	Mein Bruder will nächstes Jahr auch beim Austausch mitmachen. Er hat so richtige Klischeevorstellungen von den Deutschen und wollte von mir wissen, ob das alles stimmt.
LISA	Na, also ich würde ihm empfehlen, auf jeden Fall selbst dorthin zu fliegen, damit er sich eine eigene Meinung bilden kann und nicht die Klischees von anderen verbreitet!

Answers to Activity 25
Dorothee: Empfehlung: Schüleraustausch mitmachen / Warnung: keine Vorurteile verbreiten; warme Kleidung mitbringen
Christian: Empfehlung: Sportkleidung mitbringen / Warnung: nicht alles zusammen in den Abfall werfen
Lisa: Empfehlung: ein Semester in Deutschland verbringen; selbst hinfliegen und eigene Meinung bilden

Anwendung

1 p. 232

1. Im Licht der Gastfreundschaft und des gegenseitigen Kennenlernens steht auch diesmal wieder das Austauschprogramm des Marie-Curie-Gymnasiums. Seit Jahren schon bemüht sich dieses Mädchengymnasium um einen regen Austausch mit mehreren Schulen in Chicago,

For resource information, see the **One-Stop Planner CD-ROM**, Disc 2.

Illinois. Die Mädchen, die die Gelegenheit haben, diese Reise anzutreten, wohnen direkt bei den Gastfamilien, die meistens auch Töchter im gleichen Alter haben. Teil des Programms sind außerdem intensive englische Sprachkurse und mehrere Reisen in verschiedene Gegenden der Vereinigten Staaten.

2. Eine erneute Umfrage des städtischen Arbeitsamtes hat auch für Januar wieder ergeben, dass deutsche Frauen im Gegensatz zu ihren männlichen Kollegen immer noch unterbezahlt sind. Das gilt auch, wenn sie die gleiche Arbeit erledigen. Im Durchschnitt erhalten Frauen für die gleiche Arbeit ungefähr 20% weniger Bezahlung als Männer. Außerdem arbeiten die meisten Frauen immer noch in herkömmlichen Frauenberufen, wie zum Beispiel als Krankenschwester, Sekretärin oder Lehrerin. Nur sehr wenige Frauen arbeiten als selbständige Geschäftsführerinnen. Demnach haben wir anscheinend nur wenig Fortschritt gemacht, was die Gleichberechtigung der Frau am Arbeitsplatz betrifft. Die Verteilung am Arbeitsmarkt ist immer noch sehr traditionell.

3. In der Kaserne haben alle Soldaten die Möglichkeit, ihre Wäsche kostenlos zu waschen. Die meisten Soldaten nehmen aber ihre schmutzige Wäsche am Wochenende mit nach Hause und lassen sie dort von der Mutter waschen. Auch die Anschaffung zusätzlicher Wasch- und Trockenautomaten in der Kaserne hat nichts geändert.

4. Immer wieder kann man in den Nachrichten hören und in den Zeitungen lesen, dass die Menschen in der modernen Gesellschaft immer weniger Kontakte zueinander haben. Familien unternehmen nur noch wenig, sondern sitzen jeden Abend vor dem Fernseher. Viele Menschen, die allein in der Großstadt leben, kennen nicht einmal ihre Nachbarn und haben kaum noch Freunde oder Bekannte. Um dieses wachsende Problem zu bekämpfen, gibt es jetzt einen neuen Freundeskreis, der sich mehrmals in der Woche trifft, um Ausflüge zu machen, zu radeln oder einfach miteinander zu reden. Die Menschen, die sich dort zusammenfinden, sagen, dass unsere Gesellschaft wieder partnerschaftlicher werden muss. „Die Menschen müssen wieder mehr miteinander reden. Technischer Fortschritt kann sehr positiv sein, aber er hat uns kontaktarm gemacht", meint ein Mitglied.

5. Im Altenheim Marienbad haben die Besitzer mit einer neuen Idee ihre Bewohner zu einem aktiveren Lebensstil angeregt. Das Altenheim hat in den letzten Monaten damit begonnen, eine Reihe von Sportveranstaltungen anzubieten. Die Bewohner des Hauses Marienbad bilden jetzt mehrmals im Monat Gruppen, um Tennis zu spielen, zu radeln oder Wanderausflüge zu machen. Auch einen Schwimmkurs gibt es inzwischen. Eine begeisterte Seniorin sagt darüber: „Ich finde das einfach toll. Man ist nie zu alt, um irgendeine Art von Sport zu treiben. Seit ich Tennisunterricht nehme, fühle ich mich viel besser, und ich habe auch viele andere Bewohner aus Marienbad näher kennen gelernt."

Answers to Activity 1
Meldung 1: Amerika für junge Mädchen
Meldung 2: Jobs — immer noch nach traditioneller Manier
Meldung 3: Ohne Mutter geht es nicht
Meldung 4: Ein partnerschaftlicheres Leben im Kommen
Meldung 5: Wie alt ist zu alt?

Kapitel 8: Weg mit den Vorurteilen!
Suggested Lesson Plans 50-Minute Schedule

Day 1

CHAPTER OPENER 5 min.
- Teacher Note, ATE, p. 207M
- Advance Organizer, ATE, p. 207M

LOS GEHT'S! 20 min.
- Preteaching Vocabulary, ATE, p. 207N
- Advance Organizer, ATE, p. 207N
- Play Audio CD for Los geht's!
- Have students read Los geht's!, pp. 210–211
- Do Activity 1, p. 211

ERSTE STUFE
Reading Selection, p. 212 10 min.
- Bell Work, p. 207O
- Teaching Suggestion, p. 207O
- Read **Meinung, Vorurteil oder Klischee?**, p. 212

Wortschatz, p. 212 10 min.
- Presenting **Wortschatz**, ATE, p. 207O
- Play Audio CD for Activity 2, p. 212
- Do Activities 3 and 4, pp. 212–213

Wrap-Up 5 min.
- Students respond to questions about prejudices and clichés

Homework Options
Grammatikheft, p. 64, Acts. 1–2
Übungsheft, p. 92, Acts. 1–2

Day 2

ERSTE STUFE
Quick Review 10 min.
- Check homework, Grammatikheft, p. 64, Acts. 1–2

So sagt man das!, p. 213 20 min.
- Presenting **So sagt man das!**, ATE, p. 207O
- Play Audio CD for Activity 5, p. 213
- Do Activities 6, 7, and 8, p. 214

Ein wenig Grammatik, p. 215 15 min.
- Presenting **Ein wenig Grammatik**, ATE, p. 207P
- Do Activities 9, 10, and 11, p. 215

Wrap-Up 5 min.
- Students respond to questions about exchange students' picture of America

Homework Options
Grammatikheft, pp. 65–66, Acts. 3–4
Übungsheft, pp. 93–95, Acts. 1–4

Day 3

ERSTE STUFE
Quick Review 10 min.
- Check homework, Übungsheft, pp. 93–95, Acts. 1–4

Grammatik, p. 216 25 min.
- Presenting **Grammatik**, ATE, p. 207P
- Do Activities 12, 13, 14, and 15, p. 216

Game 10 min.
- Play game, **Genau das Gegenteil!**, ATE, p. 207C

Wrap-Up 5 min.
- Students respond to questions about how they see America

Homework Options
Pupil's Edition, p. 216, Act. 16
Grammatikheft, p. 67, Acts. 5–6
Übungsheft, pp. 95–96, Acts. 5–8

Day 4

ERSTE STUFE
Quick Review 10 min.
- Check homework, Übungsheft, pp. 95–96, Acts. 5-8

LANDESKUNDE 20 min.
- Teaching Suggestion, ATE, p. 207Q
- Community Link, ATE, p. 207Q
- Thinking Critically, ATE, p. 207Q
- Read **Verständnis für Ausländer**, p. 217
- Do Activities 1–4, p. 217

Asylanten in Frankfurt, Ausländer in Berlin (Video) 15 min.
- Teaching Suggestions, Video Guide, p. 36
- Do Pre-viewing, Viewing, and Post-viewing Activities, p. 37, Video Guide
- Show Video, **Ayslanten in Frankfurt, Ausländer in Berlin**

Wrap-Up 5 min.
- Students respond to questions about how they perceive foreigners in America

Homework Options
Übungsheft, p. 97, Acts. 1–2
Mehr Grammatikübungen, Erste Stufe

Day 5

ERSTE STUFE
Quick Review 10 min.
- Check homework, **Mehr Grammatikübungen, Erste Stufe**

Quiz Review 20 min.
- Do Additional Listening Activities 8-1 and 8-2, p. 63
- Do Activities for Communication 8-1 and 8-2, pp. 29–30

Quiz 20 min.
- Quiz 8-1A or 8-1B

Homework Options
Internet Aktivitäten, see ATE, p. 207E

Day 6

ERSTE STUFE
Quick Review 15 min.
- Return and review Quiz 8-1
- Do Realia 8-1, Activities for Communication, pp. 86, 89

WEITER GEHT'S!, 20 min.
- Preteaching Vocabulary, ATE, p. 207R
- Play Audio CD for **Weiter geht's!**, pp. 218–219
- Do Activity 17, p. 219

ZWEITE STUFE
- Bell Work, ATE, p. 207S

Reading Selection, p. 220 10 min.
- Read **Der sympathische Deutsche**, p. 220

Wrap-Up 5 min.
- Students respond to questions about their picture of a typical German

Homework Options
Übungsheft, p. 98, Acts. 1–2

 **One-Stop** Planner CD-ROM

For alternative lesson plans by chapter section, to create your own customized plans, or to preview all resources available for this chapter, use the **One-Stop Planner CD-ROM**, Disc 2.

 For additional homework suggestions, see activities accompanied by this symbol throughout the chapter.

Day 7

ZWEITE STUFE
Quick Review 10 min.
- Check homework, Übungsheft, p. 98, Acts. 1–2

Wortschatz, p. 220 10 min.
- Presenting **Wortschatz**, ATE, p. 207S
- Do Activity 18, p. 220
- Play Audio CD for Activity 19, p. 220
- Do Activities 20 and 21, p. 221

So sagt man das!, p. 221 15 min.
- Presenting **So sagt man das!**, ATE, p. 207S
- Teaching Transparencies 8-1 and 8-2
- Play Audio CD for Activity 22, p. 221
- Do Activities 23 and 24, pp. 221–222

Grammatik, p. 222 10 min.
- Presenting **Grammatik**, ATE, p. 207T
- Play Audio CD for Activity 25, p. 222

Wrap-Up 5 min.
- Students respond to questions about how they get information about current events

Homework Options
Grammatikheft, pp. 68–71, Acts. 7–12
Übungsheft, p. 99, Act. 1

Day 8

ZWEITE STUFE
Quick Review 15 min.
- Check homework, Grammatikheft, pp. 68–71, Acts. 7–12

So sagt man das!, p. 223 15 min.
- Presenting **So sagt man das!**, ATE, p. 207T
- Do Activities 26–30, p. 223

Quiz Review 20 min.
- Do **Mehr Grammatikübungen, Zweite Stufe**
- Do Communicative Activities 8-3 and 8-4, pp. 31–32

Homework Options
Grammatikheft, p. 72, Acts. 13–14
Übungsheft, pp. 100–102, Acts. 2–9

Day 9

ZWEITE STUFE
Quick Review 10 min.
- Check homework, Übungsheft, pp. 100–102, Acts. 2–9

Quiz 20 min.
- Quiz 8-2A or 8-2B

ZUM LESEN 15 min.
- Building Context, ATE, p. 207U
- Teacher Notes, ATE, p. 207U
- Language-to-Language, ATE, p. 207V
- Present **Lesestrategie**, p. 224
- Do Activities 1–4, pp. 224–225

Wrap-Up 5 min.
- Students respond to questions about giving advice to a friend

Homework Options
Pupil's Edition, p. 225, Act. 5
Übungsheft, pp. 103–104, Acts. 1–4

Day 10

ZWEITE STUFE
Quick Review 5 min.
- Check homework, Pupil's Edition, p. 225, Act. 5

ZUM LESEN 20 min.
- Do Activities 6–11, p. 226

ZUM SCHREIBEN 20 min.
- Writing Strategy, ATE, p. 207W
- Present **Schreibtipp**, p. 227
- Do Activity A, p. 227

Wrap-Up 5 min.
- Students name character traits they appreciate in their friends

Homework Options
Pupil's Edition, p. 226, Act. 12; p. 227, Act. B

Day 11

ZUM SCHREIBEN
Quick Review 5 min.
- Check homework, Pupil's Edition, p. 226, Act. 12; p. 227, Act. B

ZUM SCHREIBEN 20 min.
- Do Activity C, p. 227
- Present compositions to class

Wrap-Up 5 min.
- Students respond to questions about expressing assumptions

ANWENDUNG 20 min.
- Do Activities 1–7 and 9, pp. 232–233

Homework Options
Pupil's Edition, p. 233, Act. 8
Interaktive Spiele, see ATE, p. 207E

Day 12

ANWENDUNG
Quick Review 10 min.
- Check homework, Pupil's Edition, p. 233, Act. 8

Kann ich's wirklich?, p. 234 20 min.
- Do **Kann ich's wirklich?**, Activities 1–8, p. 234

Chapter Review 20 min.
- Review chapter functions, vocabulary, and grammar; choose from **Mehr Grammatikübungen**, Activities for Communication, Listening Activities, or **Interaktive Spiele**
- Review test format and provide sample test items for students

Homework Options
Study for Chapter Test

Assessment

Test, Chapter 8 45 min.
- Administer Chapter 8 Test. Select from Testing Program, Alternative Assessment Guide or Test Generator.

Kapitel 8: Weg mit den Vorurteilen!
Suggested Lesson Plans 90-Minute Schedule

Block 1

CHAPTER OPENER 5 min.
- Teacher Note, ATE, p. 207M
- Advance Organizer, ATE, p. 207M

LOS GEHT'S! 20 min.
- Preteaching Vocabulary, ATE, p. 207N
- Advance Organizer, ATE, p. 207N
- Teaching Suggestion, ATE, p. 207N
- Play Audio CD for Los geht's!
- Have students read Los geht's!, pp. 210–211
- Do Activity 1, p. 211

ERSTE STUFE
Reading Selection, p. 212 10 min.
- Teaching Suggestion, p. 207O
- Read **Meinung, Vorurteil oder Klischee?**, p. 212

Wortschatz, p. 212 10 min.
- Presenting **Wortschatz**, ATE, p. 207O
- Play Audio CD for Activity 2, p. 212
- Do Activities 3 and 4, pp. 212–213

So sagt man das!, p. 213 20 min.
- Presenting **So sagt man das!**, ATE, p. 207O
- Play Audio CD for Activity 5, p. 213
- Do Activities 6, 7, and 8, p. 214

Ein wenig Grammatik, p. 215 20 min.
- Presenting **Ein wenig Grammatik,** ATE, p. 207P
- Do Activities 9, 10, and 11, p. 215
- Do Activity 4, p. 66, Grammatikheft

Wrap-Up 5 min.
- Students respond to questions about exchange students' pictures of America

Homework Options
Grammatikheft, p. 64, Acts. 1–2; p. 65, Act. 3
Übungsheft, p. 92, Acts. 1–2; pp. 93–95, Acts. 1–4

Block 2

ERSTE STUFE
Quick Review 10 min.
- Check homework, Übungsheft, p. 92, Acts. 1–2; pp. 93–95, Acts. 1–4

Grammatik, p. 216 30 min.
- Presenting **Grammatik**, ATE, p. 207P
- Do Activities 12, 13, 14, and 15, p. 216
- Do Activities 5 and 6, p. 67, Grammatikheft

Game 10 min.
- Play game, **Genau das Gegenteil!**, ATE, p. 207C

LANDESKUNDE 20 min.
- Teaching Suggestion, ATE, p. 207Q
- Thinking Critically, ATE, p. 207Q
- Read **Verständnis für Ausländer**, p. 217
- Do Activities 1–4, p. 217

Asylanten in Frankfurt, Ausländer in Berlin (Video) 15 min.
- Teaching Suggestions, Video Guide, p. 36
- Do Pre-viewing, Viewing, and Post-viewing Activities, p. 37, Video Guide
- Show Video, **Asylanten in Frankfurt, Ausländer in Berlin**

Wrap-Up 5 min.
- Students respond to questions about how they perceive foreigners in America

Homework Options
Pupil's Edition, p. 216, Act. 16
Übungsheft, pp. 95–96, Acts. 5–8; p. 97, Acts. 1–2

Block 3

ERSTE STUFE
Quick Review 10 min.
- Check homework, Übungsheft, pp. 95–96, Acts. 5–8

Quiz Review 25 min.
- Do Additional Listening Activities 8-1 and 8-2, p. 63
- Do Activities for Communication 8-1 and 8-2, pp. 29–30
- Do **Mehr Grammatikübungen, Erste Stufe**

Quiz 20 min.
- Quiz 8-1A or 8-1B

WEITER GEHT'S! 20 min.
- Preteaching Vocabulary, ATE, p. 207R
- Play Audio CD for **Weiter geht's!**, pp. 218–219
- Do Activity 17, p. 219

ZWEITE STUFE
Reading Selection, p. 220 10 min.
- Teaching Suggestion, ATE, p. 207S
- Read **Der sympathische Deutsche**, p. 220

Wrap-Up 5 min.
- Students respond to questions about how they picture a typical German

Homework Options
Übungsheft, p. 98, Acts. 1–2
Internet Aktivitäten, see ATE, p. 207E

One-Stop Planner CD-ROM

For alternative lesson plans by chapter section, to create your own customized plans, or to preview all resources available for this chapter, use the **One-Stop Planner CD-ROM**, Disc 2.

 For additional homework suggestions, see activities accompanied by this symbol throughout the chapter.

Block 4

ZWEITE STUFE

Quick Review 15 min.
- Return and review Quiz 8-1
- Check homework, Übungsheft, p. 98, Acts. 1–2

Wortschatz, p. 220 10 min.
- Presenting **Wortschatz**, ATE, p. 207S
- Do Activity 18, p. 220
- Play Audio CD for Activity 19, p. 220
- Do Activities 20 and 21, p. 221

So sagt man das!, p. 221 20 min.
- Presenting **So sagt man das!**, ATE, p. 207S
- Teaching Transparencies 8-1 and 8-2
- Play Audio CD for Activity 22, p. 221
- Do Activity 23, p. 221
- Do Activity 24, p. 222
- Do Activity 1, p. 99, Übungsheft

Grammatik, p. 222 10 min.
- Presenting **Grammatik**, ATE, p. 207T
- Play Audio CD for Activity 25, p. 222

So sagt man das!, p. 223 15 min.
- Presenting **So sagt man das!**, ATE, p. 207T
- Do Activities 26–30, p. 223

Quiz Review 20 min.
- Do **Mehr Grammatikübungen, Zweite Stufe**
- Do Communicative Activities 8-3 and 8-4, pp. 31–32

Homework Options
Grammatikheft, pp. 68–71, Acts. 7–12; p. 72, Acts. 13–14
Übungsheft, pp. 100–102, Acts. 2–9
Interaktive Spiele, see ATE, p. 207E

Block 5

ZWEITE STUFE

Quick Review 15 min.
- Check homework, Grammatikheft, pp. 68–71, Acts. 7–12; p. 72, Acts. 13–14

Quiz 20 min.
- Quiz 8-2A or 8-2B

ZUM LESEN 30 min.
- Teacher Notes, ATE, p. 207U
- Language-to-Language, ATE, p. 207V
- Present **Lesestrategie**, p. 224
- Do Activities 1–11, pp. 224–226

ZUM SCHREIBEN 20 min.
- Writing Strategy, ATE, p. 207W
- Present **Schreibtipp**, p. 227
- Do Activity A, p. 227

Wrap-Up 5 min.
- Students respond to questions about giving advice to a friend

Homework Options
Pupil's Edition, p. 226, Act. 12
Übungsheft, pp. 103–104, Acts. 1–4

Block 6

ZWEITE STUFE

Quick Review 15 min.
- Return and review Quiz 8-2
- Check homework, Pupil's Edition, p. 226, Act. 12

ZUM SCHREIBEN 20 min.
- Do Activities B and C, p. 227

ANWENDUNG 30 min.
- Do Activities 1–9, pp. 232–233

Kann ich's wirklich?, p. 234 20 min.
- Do Activities 1–8, p. 234

Wrap-Up 5 min.
- Students respond to questions about expressing assumptions

Homework Options
Study for Chapter Test

Block 7

ANWENDUNG

Quick Review 15 min.
- Do Realia 8-1, Activities for Communication, pp. 86, 89

Chapter Review 30 min.
- Review chapter functions, vocabulary, and grammar; choose from **Mehr Grammatikübungen,** Activities for Communication, Listening Activities, or **Interaktive Spiele**
- Review test format and provide sample test items for students

Test, Chapter 8 45 min.
- Administer Chapter 8 Test. Select from Testing Program, Alternative Assessment Guide or Test Generator.

Kapitel 8: Weg mit den Vorurteilen!
Teaching Suggestions, *pages 208–235*

Using the Video

Before you begin the chapter, you may want to preview the *Video Program* and consult the *Video Guide.* Suggestions for integrating the video into each chapter are given in the *Video Guide* and in the chapter interleaf of the *Teacher's Edition.* Activity masters for video selections can be found in the *Video Guide.*

One-Stop Planner CD-ROM

For resource information, see the **One-Stop Planner CD-ROM**, Disc 2.

PAGES 208–209

CHAPTER OPENER

Pacing Tips

Los geht's! and the **Erste Stufe** focus on the impressions young Germans have after visiting the United States. **Weiter geht's!** and the **Zweite Stufe** center around the impressions young Americans have after visiting Germany. Students learn to express assumptions, make suggestions and recommendations, and give advice. You may want to spend a little more time on the **Erste Stufe** since it contains the **Landeskunde,** where you may want to present the video. For Lesson Plans and timing suggestions, see pages 207I–207L.

Meeting the Standards
Communication
• Expressing surprise, disappointment, and annoyance, p. 213
• Expressing an assumption, p. 221
• Making suggestions and recommendations; giving advice, p. 223

Cultures
• **Landeskunde,** p. 217

Connections
• Music Connection, p. 207P
• Multicultural Connection, p. 207P
• Social Studies Connection, p. 207Q

Comparisons
• Multicultural Connection, p. 207T
• Language-to-Language, p. 207V

Communities
• Family Link, p. 207C
• Community Link, p. 207Q
• Career Path, p. 207Q

Advance Organizer

Ask students to think of a specific incident that led them to falsely stereotype somebody. How and when did they realize that they had formed an opinion prematurely? (Denkt mal an eine bestimmte Situation, in der ihr euch eine falsche Meinung über eine Person gebildet habt. Wie und wann habt ihr aber bemerkt, dass diese Meinung voreilig gemacht wurde?)

Teacher Note

This chapter deals with prejudices, stereotypes, and clichés. The purpose is to help students realize how they view other people and to become critical of stereotypes. They should learn not to assume things just because they have heard them all their lives, but to think, observe, experience, and come to their own conclusions.

Teaching Suggestions

Ask students what the photo makes them think of. Do they think it represents a "typically" German scene? Why or why not? Students may notice the mountainous background that is typical in southern Germany and Austria (where this picture was taken) or Switzerland, but not northern Germany. They may realize, then, that the picture is typical of a specific German-speaking region, but not of Germany in general.

Ask students about the types of events at which they would expect a brass band such as the one in the photo to perform. Would it be at an "authentic" German party for Americans?

Chapter Sequence

LOS GEHT'S!

PAGES 210–211

Los geht's! Summary

In *Wie sehen uns die jungen Deutschen?,* students are introduced to some perceptions young Germans have about the United States. Tanja, Sonja, Michael, and Phillip talk about how their own impressions changed after they visited the United States. The following learning outcomes listed on p. 209 are modeled in the episode: expressing surprise, disappointment, and annoyance.

Preteaching Vocabulary

Guessing Words from Context

Have students skim **Los geht's!** for general meaning, and ask them to identify the topic (what surprised young Germans in the United States). Then have students scan for cognates that are new to them. After students have a good idea of what **Los geht's!** is about, have them use contextual clues to find phrases in the text boxes that express surprise, disappointment, or annoyance. Some of the phrases they might select are: **Ich hatte nicht gewusst, …, / Ich war schon etwas enttäuscht, … / Es hat mich wahnsinnig gestört, … .** Then have students find similar phrases in the conversation among Tanja, Sonja, Michael, and Philipp.

Advance Organizer

Discuss with students the various clichés that they have about German, Russian, French, British, and Chinese people. What do they consider typical of these peoples? How did they form these opinions?

Teaching Suggestion

Before students begin the **Los geht's!** section, bring in the TV section of a German magazine, photocopy a class set, and ask students to scan the guide for all the American TV programs that are featured that day. What types of programs are they? Do those programs reflect an accurate image of the United States?

Comprehension Check

Auditory Learners

With their books closed, have students listen to *Wie sehen uns die jungen Deutschen?* on compact disc. Then have students recall as much as they can remember.

Cooperative Learning

1 After students have listened to the recording and read along in their books once or twice, divide them into groups of three or four. Have students discuss the collage on p. 210, read the opinions of young Germans who visited the United States, and write them out in two columns. Then have the reporter of each group share his or her group's findings with the rest of the class.

Closure

Ask students to complete the following statement:
Nach Meinung dieser deutschen Schüler sind Amerikaner …, weil … .

HOLLYWOOD

ERSTE STUFE

Teaching Resources
pp. 212–217

PRINT
- Lesson Planner, p. 47
- Listening Activities, pp. 59, 63–64
- Video Guide, pp. 35–37
- Activities for Communication, pp. 29–30, 86, 89, 127–128
- Grammatikheft, pp. 64–67
- Grammar Tutor for Students of German, Chapter 8
- Übungsheft, pp. 93–97
- Testing Program, pp. 169–172
- Alternative Assessment Guide, p. 37
- Student Make-Up Assignments, Chapter 8

MEDIA
- One-Stop Planner
- Audio Compact Discs, CD8, Trs. 4–5, 13, 17–19
- Video Program
  Asylanten in Frankfurt
  Videocassette 2, 12:42–16:49
- Teaching Transparencies
  Situation 8-1
  Mehr Grammatikübungen Answers
  Grammatikheft Answers

PAGE 212

Bell Work

Ask students what they would do if they had the opportunity to provide a German exchange student with a representative picture of the United States and its people. Where would they take that exchange student and why? (**Stell dir vor, du hättest die Möglichkeit einem deutschen Austauschschüler ein bisschen von Amerika und seinen Leuten zu zeigen. Was würdest du dem Schüler alles zeigen? Begründe deine Antwort!**)

Communication for All Students

A Slower Pace

Ask students to give examples for each of the following words: **Meinung, Vorurteil,** and **Klischee.**

PRESENTING: Wortschatz

Work with the new vocabulary in three different ways. First, have students find the new word or expression used in the **Los geht's!** text. Then paraphrase the new vocabulary items in oral statements and have students tell you which word or expression you are referring to. Finally, create a cloze exercise by preparing a variety of written statements (in the context of this unit) in which you leave out the new word or phrase. Have students complete each sentence with the appropriate word or phrase.

Teaching Suggestion

3 Students may need help verbalizing their ideas. Help with vocabulary and allow students to work with a dictionary. Encourage them to express their agreement and disagreement with the opinions and suggestions of their classmates. Have them support what they say with examples.

PAGE 213

Thinking Critically

4 **Analyzing** After students have discussed the statements, ask them to examine each one and give possible reasons why Germans could have formed such opinions.

PRESENTING: So sagt man das!

- Ask students to scan the **Los geht's!** section to find as many of the expressions listed in **So sagt man das!** as possible.
- On a transparency, provide a variety of dependent clauses for each function. Ask students to choose an introductory clause from **So sagt man das!** that would be suitable for each one.
  Examples:
  …, dass die Leute so kinderlieb und tierlieb sind.
  …, wenn Leute so dumme Vorurteile haben.
- Have students choose one introductory statement per function (surprise, disappointment, annoyance) and use it in original sentences.

Thinking Critically

5 **Drawing Inferences** Once students have completed the chart, discuss each entry. Have them think about each statement and what it says about the German teenagers' lives.

Teaching Suggestion

6 Remind students as they react to the statements here and throughout the unit how difficult it is to make generalizations about a group of people. Again, ask students how they think foreigners might have gotten these impressions of the United States. If students disagree with the opinions expressed in this activity, have them give reasons why they disagree and support them with examples.

Connections and Comparisons

Language Note

6 The expression used in the third statement, **etwas hat Hand und Fuß**, is equivalent to the English *something is done thoroughly or well.*

Communication for All Students

A Slower Pace

8 Help students brainstorm for additional ideas using their knowledge of problems and issues in American society as a basis. (Examples: too much rich food, not enough exercise, too much crime, people spending more money than they have, not doing enough for the environment)

Building on Previous Skills

9 Have students continue this activity by making additional statements based on what they have previously learned.
Example:
Partner A: In Amerika scheinen weniger Leute zu rauchen.
Partner B: Ich habe nicht gewusst, dass amerikanische Restaurants Raucher- und Nichtraucherecken haben. Das finde ich sehr gut.

PRESENTING: Ein wenig Grammatik

The conjunction als On a transparency write several sentences such as the example below. Have students complete them with subordinate clauses beginning with **als**, using the cues provided.
Example:

_____ [klein sein], war die Luft hier viel sauberer. (Als ich klein war)

Communication for All Students

Challenge

10 After students have combined the sentences, have them write a cohesive letter from Hanno to his parents, incorporating all six sentences. This assignment could be started in class and continued as homework.

Connections and Comparisons

Music Connection

Refer students to the Bavarian folksong *Als wir jüngst in Regensburg waren,* Level 2 *Listening Activities,* p. 14, for additional reading. Why is **als** used instead of **wenn** in the first line? (The author is referring to a single event that took place in the past.) You may also want to play the song, Level 2 CD 2, Tr. 28.

Multicultural Connection

11 Have a group of students prepare a questionnaire, and then interview an exchange student in your school about his or her first experiences and impressions of the United States. Students should report their findings to the class.

PRESENTING: Grammatik

- **Coordinating conjunctions** To help students visualize the different uses of coordinating conjunctions and their effects on word order, compare and contrast them by showing examples on the board or a transparency.
- Let students explain how each conjunction is used, i.e., what type of clause it introduces and how it affects the word order.

Building on Previous Skills

12 In Chapter 7 (p. 192) students learned how to elicit agreement, to agree, and to express conviction, uncertainty, and what seems to be true (p. 194). Help students review the expressions by agreeing or disagreeing with the statements in this activity.
Example:
Ein Schüleraustausch ist ideal.
Damit stimm ich überein. Durch einen Schüleraustausch lernt man das Land und die Leute viel genauer kennen.

ERSTE STUFE

Communication for All Students

Challenge

15 Have each group compose a letter to a German youth magazine in which they address the three questions. The purpose of their letter should be to clarify possible misconceptions Germans might have about Americans.

Teaching Suggestion

16 Before students begin this writing assignment, you may want to review vocabulary and expressions from the **Erste Stufe** that will be helpful to students as they write.

> **PAGE 217**

LANDESKUNDE

Teaching Suggestion

Begin **Landeskunde** by asking students if any of them have ever been or plan to be an exchange student. What did they learn or do they hope to learn through an exchange?

COMMUNITY LINK

Have one or several students contact the local Chamber of Commerce to find out if their town or city has any sister cities. Have them find out when this relationship was established and what type of programs have been developed between the two places. Have students report back to the class. See the project on p. 207C.

Using the Video

Videocassette 2, 12:42–16:49
In the video clip *Asylanten in Frankfurt,* members of a family from Afghanistan talk about why they sought asylum in Germany. See *Video Guide,* p. 36, for suggestions.

Connections and Comparisons

Geography Connection

1 Have students locate Passau, Soltau, and their respective sister cities in an atlas. Then have students compare each American city with its sister city in terms of size and geographic elements.

Social Studies Connection

4 Ask a social studies teacher to come to your class and talk about the number of foreigners residing in the United States.

Teaching Suggestion

4 Put students in groups to answer the last question (**Welche Klischees oder Stereotypen hat man von diesen Gruppen?**). Assign one nationality to each group and have them come up with a list of positive and negative images people have of that group. Have each group present its list of stereotypes to the class.

Thinking Critically

Synthesizing Ask students the following question: If you had the opportunity to be an exchange student in Germany, what kind of questions would you ask your host family to get a more objective view of the German people?

Cultures and Communities

Career Path

Have students think of why it would be useful for an employee of an American computer firm to have a knowledge of German. (Suggestions: Imagine translating a company technical manual into German for use with company products there; imagine using e-mail to communicate with employees of a company affiliate in Germany.)

Assess

▶ Testing Program, pp. 169–172
  Quiz 8-1A, Quiz 8-1B
  Audio CD8, Tr. 13

▶ Student Make-Up Assignments
  Chapter 8, Alternative Quiz

▶ Alternative Assessment Guide, p. 37

WEITER GEHT'S!

Teaching Resources
pp. 218–219

PRINT
▸ Lesson Planner, p. 48
▸ Übungsheft, p. 98

MEDIA
▸ One-Stop Planner
▸ Audio Compact Discs, CD8, Trs. 6–7

PAGES 218–219

Weiter geht's! Summary

In *Wie sehen junge Amerikaner die Deutschen?*, students are introduced to some perceptions young Americans have about Germany. The following learning outcomes listed on p. 209 are modeled in the episode: expressing an assumption, making suggestions and recommendations, and giving advice.

Preteaching Vocabulary

Activating Prior Knowledge

Have students use their prior knowledge to list words on pp. 218-219 that they already know. Students should be able to list at least 20 words. Then have students pick one person on p. 219 and, using the words they already know and the context, guess the meaning of the words they don't already know. Finally, have students identify the two phrases that express an assumption (ich hatte mir vorgestellt / Ich dachte immer).

Advance Organizer

Ask students what impressions they have of Germans and Germany. Discuss briefly with them what comes to their minds and how these impressions were formed.

Thinking Critically

Analyzing Ask students to write down those words from the box on p. 218 that they associate with their image of Germany and its people. Beside each word, ask them to give a reason or explanation for having chosen that characteristic. Discuss these associations briefly with students.

Comprehension Check

Visual Learners

Ask students to study the collage on p. 218. Then have several students take turns interpreting and discussing how Germany and Germans are portrayed here.

Auditory Learners

Ask students to keep their books closed as they listen to the statements. Then ask students to recall as many characteristics as they can remember. Have them listen a second time, but this time let them read along in their books.

Teaching Suggestion

Play the compact disc a third time, stopping after each report and asking some key questions to see if students understand the main points in each one.

Challenge

17 Ask students if they can think of other clichés they could add to this image of the German people.

Closure

Together, come up with a list of clichés about Germans and Germany. Then have students use what they know about the country and the people to refute some of these clichés in German.

ZWEITE STUFE

Teaching Resources
pp. 220–223

PRINT
- Lesson Planner, p. 49
- Listening Activities, pp. 60–61, 65–66
- Video Guide, pp. 35–36, 38
- Activities for Communication, pp. 31–32, 87–88, 89–90, 127–128
- Grammatikheft, pp. 68–72
- Grammar Tutor for Students of German, Chapter 8
- Übungsheft, pp. 99–102
- Testing Program, pp. 173–176
- Alternative Assessment Guide, p. 37
- Student Make-Up Assignments, Chapter 8

MEDIA
- One-Stop Planner
- Audio Compact Discs, CD8, Trs. 8–10, 14, 20–22
- Video Program
  Ausländer in Berlin
  Videocassette 2, 16:53–19:11
- Teaching Transparencies
  Situation 8-2
  Mehr Grammatikübungen Answers
  Grammatikheft Answers

PAGE 220

Bell Work
Tell students that they have to plan a day for German visitors who want to tour their town. What would students want the German visitors to see that is representative of their area and its people?

Teaching Suggestion
After reading *Der sympathische Deutsche,* ask students to scan the text for positive and negative attributes. Make a list on the board.

Thinking Critically
Analyzing Have students determine what information they would need in order to carefully analyze the results of the study. For example, students might want to know which 17 countries were surveyed and what the ages of those surveyed were. Can students think of reasons why this information could be relevant?

PRESENTING: Wortschatz

Ask students to think of a person they know who could be described with one or more of the adjectives listed in **auf Deutsch erklärt.**

Communication for All Students

Challenge
18 Once students have compiled a list, ask them to use some of the characteristics to describe a famous artist, actor, musician, scientist, or political figure. Do all students agree on the same adjectives? If not, why not?

PAGE 221

Communication for All Students

A Slower Pace
20 Students should refer to the **Weiter geht's!** section and to the words listed on p. 218 to help them with this activity. Assist students with any other words they would like to use that are not on the list.

PRESENTING: So sagt man das!

After you introduce the new expressions, have students look back at Activity 21. Ask students to use the new expressions to introduce their impression about the statements they came up with.
Examples:
Ich vermute, dass nicht alle Deutschen schnelle Autos haben.
Ich hatte mir vorgestellt, dass immer viel Bier in deutschen Haushalten getrunken wird.

Communication for All Students

Challenge
23 As students report to their partner about the various ways in which they had to change their opinions about Germans, the partner should react to what he or she hears and ask questions so that the monologue becomes a dialogue.
Example:
A: **Ich habe immer geglaubt, dass die Deutschen nur Lederhosen und Dirndlkleider tragen. Aber das ist nicht wahr. Sie tragen alles, was wir tragen.**

Communication for All Students

(continued from p. 207S)
B: Ja, Jeans sind sehr beliebt, auch T-Shirts und Sweatshirts.
A: Woher weißt du das?
B: Oh, aus Zeitschriften, vom Fernsehen.

Speaking Assessment

23 For assessment, you may want to have student pairs come to your desk to perform their dialogs. The following rubric may aid you in the evaluation.

Speaking Rubric	Points			
	4	3	2	1
Content (Complete – Incomplete)				
Comprehension (Total – Little)				
Comprehensibility (Comprehensible – Incomprehensible)				
Accuracy (Accurate – Seldom accurate)				
Fluency (Fluent – Not fluent)				

18–20: A   16–17: B   14–15: C   12–13: D   Under 12: F

PAGE 222

Thinking Critically

24 Analyzing Ask students to watch for news throughout the week that deals with Germany or Germans. Have students bring the article or share the news with the class. Then ask students to examine the news piece by deciding whether **Tatsachen, Vorurteile,** or **Klischees** are part of the information. What phrases or words helped them decide?

PRESENTING: Grammatik

- **Verbs with prefixes** Point out that separable prefixes are actual words that can stand by themselves. The inseparable verb prefixes, **be-, ver-, ge-, er-, ent-,** cannot stand alone. The past participles of verbs with inseparable prefixes do not add **ge-**. (Examples: **bekommen, enthalten, gewinnen, vergessen,** and **erraten**) Point out also that verbs with inseparable prefixes are stressed on the verb root, not on the prefix (See the following Teacher Note).
- As mentioned in the **Grammatik,** there are certain verbs that look like they have separable prefixes, but actually do not. (Example: **überraschen**)

STANDARDS: 1.1, 1.2, 3.2, 4.2

Teacher Note

One major difference between separable- and inseparable-prefix verbs is the spoken stress. For separable-prefix verbs, the stress falls on the first syllable.

<u>an</u>kommen, <u>an</u>gekommen
<u>ein</u>laden, <u>ein</u>geladen
<u>mit</u>nehmen, <u>mit</u>genommen
<u>über</u>setzen, <u>über</u>gesetzt (what a ferry does with passengers)

For inseparable-prefix verbs, the stress falls on the root verb.

über<u>ra</u>schen, über<u>rascht</u>
wieder<u>ho</u>len, wieder<u>holt</u>
unter<u>stüt</u>zen, unter<u>stützt</u>
über<u>set</u>zen, über<u>setzt</u> (from one language into another)

PAGE 223

PRESENTING: So sagt man das!

- Review some expressions students learned in Level 2 to make suggestions. Here are some expressions students should recognize:
  Ich schlage vor, dass …
  Du solltest …
- Ask students to use the new expressions by making a recommendation for their favorite restaurant, book, or movie. Then have students warn their classmates about a vacation destination, a musician, or a new store in town.

Communication for All Students

A Slower Pace

26 You may need to review the command forms of the verbs listed before doing this activity. Students can also refer to **So sagt man das!** to use the different ways of suggesting, recommending, and warning. Help students find good reasons for doing or not doing the things their partners are trying to convince them to do. List these reasons on a transparency so students can refer to them when speaking with their partners.

Connections and Comparisons

Multicultural Connection

27 Have students interview exchange students or go to other language classes to find out about prejudices that exist in other countries. What are some of these prejudices and at who or what are they directed? Have students report back to the class.

ZWEITE STUFE

Communication for All Students

A Slower Pace
28 Discuss the topic in class first, perhaps making a list on the board of ideas and images students now have about Germany.

 Total Physical Response

Prepare a list of commands using separable- and inseparable-prefix verbs. Following are some suggestions:

Könntet ihr bitte diesen Satz mal übersetzen!
Beginnt jetzt mit euren Hausaufgaben!
Craig, wisch die Tafel ab!
Wiederholt noch einmal eure Hausaufgaben!
Steck diese Papiere in den braunen Umschlag hinein!
Verabschiedet euch von einer Person in der Klasse, bevor es klingelt!
Verlasst diese Klasse ganz leise!

Using the Video

Videocassette 2, 16:53–19:11
In the video clip *Ausländer in Berlin,* young Turkish people talk about their lives in Germany. See *Video Guide,* p. 36, for suggestions.

Assess
▶ Testing Program, pp. 173–176
  Quiz 8-2A, Quiz 8-2B
  Audio CD 8, Tr. 14

▶ Student Make-Up Assignments
  Chapter 8, Alternative Quiz

▶ Alternative Assessment Guide, p. 37

ZUM LESEN

Teaching Resources
pp. 224–226

PRINT
▶ Lesson Planner, p. 50
▶ Übungsheft, pp. 103–104
▶ Reading Strategies and Skills, Chapter 8
▶ Lies mit mir! 3, Chapter 8

MEDIA
▶ One-Stop Planner
▶ Audio Compact Discs, CD8, Tr. 11

Teacher Note
Sabines Eltern is recorded on compact disc. (CD 8, Track 11)

Prereading
Building Context
From the byline at the end of the story, the students can see that the author of this selection has a foreign name. Help them see what possible assumptions can be made based on the author's name: **a.** The author is a foreigner whose work has been translated into German. **b.** The author is bilingual or multilingual and has mastered German well enough to write it for publication. **c.** The author is a native speaker who has foreign relatives and a foreign name. Ask students how the author's choice of subject matter could differ, depending upon whether the case is **a, b,** or **c.** Students can probably use their experiences reading American and world literature as a guide, although it's much more difficult to define a "foreign" name in the United States.

Reading
Teacher Notes
1a Students should easily recognize that the narrative is in the first person, although the character, Ali, is not named until the sixth paragraph.

3 The rhetorical question **Wie ich bin?** following **Sie liebt mich, wie ich bin** is a repetition that introduces Ali's reflection on why it's so important that Sabine loves him as he is.

4 It may not be obvious to the class that, for Ali, having potential in-laws who love him "as their own son" might be as important as having a girlfriend

STANDARDS: 1.2

who loves him for himself. You may want to explain this in terms of Ali's culture and the fact that in much of the world, a marriage is still an alliance between two families and not just the union of two single people.

5 The narrator drops a number of hints, some of them by protesting too much in the fantasy sequence. (Example: "**Sie liebt mich und ich liebe sie. Nur das zählt und nichts anderes.**") He makes Sabine an only child with no threatening brothers. He and the fantasy parents agree to use the euphemism **nicht-einheimisch** and avoid the word **ausländisch.** The parents say they're ashamed at how kind people are to them when they visit Turkey, but that "**Es ist nicht so einfach**" when Ali criticizes German prejudices against foreigners in Germany; the fantasy is played out against the stark background of rejection.

6 Acceptance by Sabine's uncle completes Ali's "adoption" into this circle of kindly Germans. However, the students need to ask themselves why the uncle and aunt find it necessary to say that they "**bewundern sogar meine Freundin, Mut bewiesen zu haben mit mir [Ali.]**" Does this really lead to the conclusion that no one "**hierzulande**" has anything against foreigners?

Connections and Comparisons

Language-to-Language
Students might be interested to know that approximately 1.8 million Turks live in Germany—the largest group of **Arbeitsemigranten** in the country. This group was able to create a new genre in both Turkish and European literature. The thriving and colorful **Migrantenliteratur** (formerly also called **Gastarbeiterliteratur**), written in Turkish or German, comprises films, fiction, poetry, and plays. Ask your students if they can think of other kinds of **Migrantenliteratur.** (Examples: Chicano literature, literature of North Africans in France, Yiddish literature)

You may also want to ask your students if they can think of any Turkish words and/or names that have appeared in *Komm mit!* (Examples: **Güle Güle, Merhaba, Ahmet, Mehmet, Mustafa, Schisch-Kebab**)

Post-Reading
Teacher Note
Activities 11 and 12 are post-reading tasks that will show whether students can apply what they have learned.

Closure
At the close of Paragraph 1, Ali asks: "**Was machen diese alles-Hasser, wenn Europa eins wird?**" What does a story like *Sabines Eltern* say about the European Union? How would the class answer Ali's rhetorical question?

Zum Lesen Answers
Answers to Activity 1
a. Ich-Erzähler; b. die Freundin des Erzählers; c. in Deutschland (Schwaben); 20. Jahrhundert (contemporary Germany)
Answers to Activity 2
The narrator is describing how he feels; he used to be a pessimist, but now he's an optimist (grau, rosarot); he's in love; <u>weil</u> ich eben so glücklich bin. Und <u>warum,</u> will ich auch verraten …
Answers to Activity 3
She loves him for himself; he's not German, but Turkish.
Answers to Activity 4
Sabine's parents; friendly, he's respected; they treat him like a son (Sie lieben mich wie ihren eigenen Sohn.); they like non-Germans.
Answers to Activity 5
Ali has been dreaming; answers will vary.
Answers to Activity 6
That there's no such thing as prejudice or racism; the respect and friendship he receives from Sabine's parents and aunt and uncle
Answers to Activity 7
It casts doubt on his belief that there is no racism; answers will vary.
Answers to Activity 8
It cues the reader that something important is going to happen; the plot will take a new turn. Ali wakes up.
Answers to Activity 9
Answers will vary.
Answers to Activity 10
Answers will vary; the response of Sabine's father: her parents don't know him, but they don't like him because he's Turkish; the parents' feelings toward Ali play a central role in Ali's life; answers will vary.
Answers to Activity 11
Answers will vary.

ZUM SCHREIBEN

Teaching Resources
p. 227

PRINT
▸ Lesson Planner, p. 50
▸ Alternative Assessment Guide, p. 23

MEDIA
▸ One-Stop Planner
▸ Test Generator, Chapter 8

Writing Strategy

The targeted strategy in this writing activity is *selecting a point of view*. Students should learn about this strategy before beginning the assignment.

Prewriting
Teaching Suggestions

A1 Students might benefit from a class discussion to help them get ideas for their short story. Students should think of examples of groups that deal with prejudices or conflict due to a lack of knowledge and communication among a group of people.

• Before students start planning their stories, discuss with them the elements of a good story, such as a quickly developed plot and well-developed characters.

Communication for All Students

Visual Learners

A2 To help students practice describing characters and settings, bring to class several photos of different ethnic groups and their surroundings. Have students focus on details in each photo. Students can use similar details in their own descriptions.
Examples:
Die Frau/Der Mann scheint schüchtern und still zu sein.
Die Schlafstätte dieser Familie sieht ganz gemütlich aus.

Writing
Teaching Suggestions

B Students will still need some guidance during the writing stage. Be available to answer questions and to check students' work informally as they work independently to arrange their notes.

B Remind students that using action verbs and descriptive adjectives can make their story more vivid.

Post-Writing
Teaching Suggestions

C To help students understand the specific strengths and weaknesses of their final story, you may want to use the following grading rubric:

Creativity	25%
Story development	25%
Consistent point of view	25%
Grammar, spelling, and punctuation	25%

• You may want to collect the final copies of students' stories and compile them in a class book to be displayed in the classroom for any student to read.

Closure

Assign one or two of the best stories for all students to read as homework, then have the class discuss the prejudices displayed in the story and the ways in which they were eliminated.

PAGES 228–231

MEHR GRAMMATIKÜBUNGEN

The **Mehr Grammatikübungen** activities are designed as supplemental activities for the grammatical concepts presented in the chapter. You might use them as additional practice, for review, or for assessment.

For more grammar presentations, review, and practice, refer to the following:
• Grammatikheft
• Grammar Tutor for Students of German
• Grammar Summary on pp. R22–R39
• Übungsheft
• Grammar and Vocabulary quizzes (Testing Program)
• Test Generator
• **Interaktive Spiele** at go.hrw.com

ZUM SCHREIBEN

ANWENDUNG

> **Teaching Resources**
> pp. 232–233
>
> PRINT
> ▸ Lesson Planner, p. 50
> ▸ Listening Activities, p. 62
> ▸ Video Guide, pp. 35–36, 38
> ▸ Grammar Tutor for Students of German, Chapter 8
>
> MEDIA
> ▸ One-Stop Planner
> ▸ Video Program
> **Videoclips: Werbung**
> Videocassette 2, 19:18–20:36
> ▸ Audio Compact Discs, CD8, Tr. 12

Apply and Assess

Using the Video

Videocassette 2, 19:18–20:36
At this time, you might want to use the authentic advertising footage from German television. See *Video Guide*, p. 36, for suggestions.

Thinking Critically

3 Drawing Inferences Ask students how they think the stereotypes listed in Activity 2 were formed. Why do these clichéd images of girls and boys persist? What are some "modern" stereotypes of girls and boys, or of women and men?

A Slower Pace

6 Ask students to read the letter again, this time focusing on Julia Bauer. Have them jot down notes that will give a good description of Julia. Then ask students to differentiate between things we know about Julia (**Tatsachen**) and things we might think about her (**Meinungen**).

Portfolio Assessment

6 You might want to suggest this activity as a written and oral portfolio item for your students. See *Alternative Assessment Guide*, p. 23.

Geography Connection

7 Ask students to locate Hagen in an atlas. (Hagen is located in the **Bundesland** North Rhine-Westphalia, northeast of Düsseldorf and south of Dortmund. It has a population of around 214,000.)

KANN ICH'S WIRKLICH?

This page helps students prepare for the test. It is a brief checklist of the major points covered in the chapter. The students should be reminded that it is only a checklist and not necessarily everything that will appear on the test.

For additional self-check options, refer students to the *Grammar Tutor* and the Online self-test for this chapter.

WORTSCHATZ

Review and Assess

Teaching Suggestion
Ask students to list words from the **Wortschatz** that they might use to talk about their **Deutschlandbild**.

Circumlocution

Play **Das treffende Wort suchen** to review the adjectives of the **Wortschatz**. **Durstig, höflich,** and **still** are three adjectives that should be easy to describe. For example, in order to describe **durstig,** one could say **Was ist man, wenn man nichts zu trinken hat?** See p. 31C for procedures.

Challenge
Have students choose three or four incomplete statements from each **Stufe** and ask them to complete them in a meaningful way.
Example:
Es ärgert mich, wenn …
… meine Schwester sich CDs von mir nimmt, ohne mich vorher zu fragen.

Game

Play the game **Genau das Gegenteil!**
See p. 207C for the procedure.

Teacher Note
Give the Kapitel 8 Chapter Test:
Testing Program, pp. 177–182
Audio CD 8, Trs. 15–16.

STANDARDS: 1.1, 3.1

Objectives

In this chapter you will learn to

Erste Stufe

- express surprise, disappointment, and annoyance

Zweite Stufe

- express an assumption
- make suggestions and recommendations
- give advice

 internet

go.hrw.com

ADRESSE: go.hrw.com
KENNWORT: WK3
FRANKFURT-8

◀ **Bergmusik in Tirol**

Los geht's! ▪ *Wie sehen uns die jungen Deutschen?*

CD 8 Trs. 1–3

Was die Deutschen über die Vereinigten Staaten wissen, erfahren sie gewöhnlich durch Presse, Film und Fernsehen, auch durch Reisen in Amerika oder durch Reiseberichte von Freunden und Bekannten. Was sind ihre Eindrücke? CD 8 Tr. 1

Junge Deutsche, die noch nie in den Staaten waren, sehen die USA so:

Junge Deutsche, die in den Staaten waren, sagen: CD 8 Tr. 2

„Ich hatte nicht gewusst, dass das Land so groß ist."

„Ich habe gestaunt, wie gut mir das Essen drüben geschmeckt hat — alles frisch und wenig aus Büchsen."

„Die meisten Amerikaner sind äußerst hilfreich."

„Es ist unwahrscheinlich, wie wenig die Amerikaner lesen. Die Tageszeitung, ja, aber Bücher?"

„Es hat mich furchtbar gestört, dass es dort keine Fahrradwege gibt, jedenfalls nicht dort, wo ich war."

„Ich war schon etwas enttäuscht, dass viele Städte so schmutzig sind."

„Es hat mich wahnsinnig gestört, dass meine Gastfamilie beim Abendessen ferngesehen hat."

„Mir haben die Lehrer gefallen: der Unterricht ist lockerer als bei uns, weniger stressig."

„Ich hatte immer gehört, die Amerikaner haben keinen Geschmack; alles ist aus Plastik, künstliche Blumen und so weiter. Aber das stimmt wirklich nicht."

„Ich war erstaunt, wie wenig die Amerikaner über die Bundesrepublik wissen."

„Ich bedaure, dass die Leute zu wenig für die Umwelt tun."

„Ich fand es unangenehm, wie so viele Leute ihren Kaugummi kauen — ich mein, so richtig kauen!"

„Als ich nach Amerika kam, hatte ich ein ganz anderes Amerikabild. Ich hatte starke Vorurteile gegen die Amerikaner, denn ich kannte sie nur als Touristen in Deutschland — laut angezogen, mit der Kamera um den Hals. Ich hatte angenommen, dass alle Amerikaner so sind."

CD 8 Tr. 3

Vier deutsche Schüler, Tanja, Sonja, Michael und Philipp erzählen, wie sie ihre Vorstellungen von den Vereinigten Staaten nach einem kurzen Besuch ändern mussten.

Sonja: Also, ich war vier Wochen drüben, in der Nähe von Boston, und ich muss sagen, ich war wahnsinnig begeistert von den amerikanischen Jugendlichen. Sie sind viel herzlicher und offener als wir.

Philipp: In diesem Punkt geb ich dir Recht. Aber sie wissen nur viel zu wenig über die Deutschen — sie wissen etwas über das Oktoberfest und unsere Autobahnen …

Michael: Na, komm! Das stimmt aber auch nicht immer. Meine Gastfamilie, und insbesondere mein Gastbruder, wusste eine ganze Menge über Deutschland.

Tanja: Ich hatte vorher überhaupt keinen Bezug zu Amerika. Ich hatte mir immer gedacht, da will ich überhaupt nicht hin, das interessiert mich gar nicht. Aber dadurch, dass ich einige Leute kennen gelernt habe und die so wahnsinnig nett waren, hab ich ein ganz anderes Verhältnis zu dem Land und zu den Leuten.

Michael: Ja, so ein Schüleraustausch ist schon ideal, weil man da mitten in die Familie hineinkommt. Und nur so kann man die Leute richtig kennen lernen, seine eigenen Vorurteile abbauen und seine eigene Meinung bilden.

Philipp: Das möchte ich unterstützen. Man soll sich auf jeden Fall eine eigene Meinung bilden, bevor man eine fremde wiedergibt.

Michael: Ja, genau!

Tanja: Ja, ich würd' auch sagen: nehmt keine Klischeevorstellungen an, und verbreitet auch keine! Fahrt in das Land und schaut euch die Leute an! So hab ich's gemacht und musste sämtliche Meinungen überprüfen, die ich von dem Land und den Leuten hatte.

Sonja: Also, hinfahren, alles gut beobachten, Leute kennen lernen! Nur so kann man sich das beste Urteil über ein Land bilden und nicht von dem, was man von andern hört oder im Fernsehen sieht.

Tanja: Das ist auch meine Meinung.

Übungsheft, S. 92

1 **Hast du alles verstanden?**

Sprechen/Schreiben Beantwortet die folgenden Fragen.

1. Was meinen die Leute, die noch nie in den Staaten waren? Schaut euch die Collage auf Seite 210 an, und sprecht darüber! Welche Vorstellungen sind Klischees, welche nicht?

2. Was meinen die jungen Deutschen, die schon in den Staaten waren?

3. Welche Eindrücke sind positiv, welche negativ? Wieso? Schreib sie in zwei Spalten auf!

Meinung, Vorurteil oder Klischee?

Lesen Lies die folgenden Definitionen!

Was ist eine Meinung?
Eine Meinung ist etwas, was jemand glaubt, für richtig hält, als Tatsache annimmt.
(Meinung = Urteil = Standpunkt)

Was ist ein Vorurteil?
Ein Vorurteil ist eine nicht objektive, meist negative, von Gefühlen bestimmte Meinung, die man sich im Voraus über jemanden oder über etwas gebildet hat.

Was ist eine Klischeevorstellung?
Eine Klischeevorstellung (ein Klischee) ist eine abgedroschene (*trite*) und übermäßig gebrauchte Vorstellung, die unwirksam geworden ist.

Wortschatz

auf Deutsch erklärt	auf Englisch erklärt
das Klischee ein Wort, das man zu oft gebraucht hat; ein Stereotyp	**Deine <u>Vorstellung</u> von Österreich <u>hat</u> wenig <u>Bezug</u> <u>zur</u> Realität!** *Your ideas of Austria have little connection to reality!*
abbauen weniger machen	
locker entspannt, ruhig	**Ich bin <u>erstaunt</u>, was du über das Land weißt.** *I am amazed at what you know about the country.*
herzlich sehr freundlich	
hilfreich wenn man anderen Leuten oft hilft	**Ich muss sagen, dass ich von deinem <u>Urteil</u> <u>äußerst</u> <u>enttäuscht</u> bin.** *I have to say that I'm extremely disappointed in your judgment.*
begeistert wenn man etwas wirklich ganz toll findet	
eine Menge sehr viel	**Manche <u>Klischees</u> sind weit <u>verbreitet</u>, <u>jedenfalls</u> das von dem Deutschen mit der Lederhose.** *Many clichés are widespread, especially the one about the Germans in lederhosen.*
sämtliche alle	
künstlich von Menschenhand gemacht, nicht natürlich	**Ich <u>nehme</u> <u>an</u>, wir wechseln Geld <u>im</u> <u>Voraus</u>.** *I assume we will exchange money in advance.*

p. 207X

Übungsheft, S. 64, Ü. 1–2

2 **Was sagt der Austauschschüler?** Script and answers on p. 207F

Zuhören Ein deutscher Austauschschüler spricht über Amerika und die Amerikaner. Schreib drei Dinge auf, die er gut gefunden hat und drei, die er nicht so gut gefunden hat! Gib Gründe an!

CD 8 Tr. 4

3 **Sprechen wir offen über uns selber!**

1. **Sprechen/Schreiben** Setzt euch zum Brainstorming zusammen! Das Thema heißt: Wie sehen wir uns selbst? Wählt einen Schriftführer, der alle Aussagen aufschreibt! Gebraucht Ausdrücke wie:

   — Wir Amerikaner sind (nicht) …   — Wir glauben, wir …

   — Wir halten uns für …

2. **Lesen/Sprechen** Gruppiert jetzt eure Aussagen in zwei Kategorien: Tatsachen und Meinungen! Gebraucht bei dieser Gruppierung Ausdrücke wie:

   — Ich würd' sagen, das ist eine/keine …   — Ich glaube nicht, dass …

   — … ist eine Tatsache/eine Meinung.   — (John) hat Recht, wenn er sagt, dass …

   — In diesem Punkt geb ich dir Recht.

4 Wie sehen uns die Deutschen?

Lesen/Sprechen Schüler in Deutschland haben folgende Aussagen gemacht. Was ist für dich eine Meinung, was ist ein Vorurteil? Was sagst du zu diesen Aussagen? Diskutiert darüber!

Die Amerikaner ...

sind wahnsinnig naiv

arbeiten furchtbar gern

haben es immer eilig

sehen viel zu viel fern

kochen nicht gern und essen meistens Fertiggerichte oder aus der Büchse

interessieren sich nur für Sport

lernen nicht gern Fremdsprachen

sind kinderlieb

gehen nie zu Fuß, fahren immer nur Auto

tun wenig für die Umwelt

lesen wenig

spielen die Polizisten der Welt

diskutieren selten über Politik

interessieren sich nicht für andere Kulturen

essen zu viel Fastfood

leben im Land der unbegrenzten Möglichkeiten

verdienen zu viel Geld

So sagt man das!

Expressing surprise, disappointment, and annoyance

Comments others make are likely to elicit various feelings. You may feel surprised to hear something, you may be disappointed, or even annoyed or displeased.

To express surprise, you might say:

Ich war überrascht, dass ...
Ich habe gestaunt, ...
Ich habe nicht gewusst, dass ...

Ich hätte nicht gedacht, dass ...
Es ist unwahrscheinlich, dass ...
Ich war erstaunt, ...

To express disappointment, you could begin with:

Ich bedaure, dass ...
Ich finde es schade, dass ...

Ich bin enttäuscht, dass ...

If you are annoyed, you could use one of these expressions:

Es regt mich auf, wenn/dass ...
Es stört mich, wenn/dass ...

Es ärgert mich, wenn/dass ...
Ich finde es unangenehm, wenn/dass

Übungsheft, S. 93–94, Ü. 1–2   Grammatikheft, S. 65, Ü. 3

Mehr Grammatikübungen, S. 228, Ü. 1–2

5 Schüler über Amerika

Script and answers on p. 207G

Zuhören Schüler unterhalten sich über ihre Erfahrungen in Amerika. Worüber sind sie überrascht? Enttäuscht? Was stört sie? Schreib die Tabelle in dein Heft um, und trag die Information in die drei Spalten ein!

CD 8 Tr. 5

Schüler	überrascht	enttäuscht	stört

6 Wie reagierst du darauf?

Sprechen Die Deutschen interessieren sich sehr für Amerika, und jeder Deutsche scheint irgendeine Meinung über Amerika und die Amerikaner zu haben. Stimmen die Meinungen? Was überrascht dich, was enttäuscht dich und worüber regst du dich auf? Sag es deinem Partner!

1. Es gibt zu viele Amerikaner, die Vorurteile gegen andere Menschen haben.

2. Die Leute essen zu viel und haben zu wenig Bewegung.

3. Alles wird nur auf die Schnelle gemacht, nichts hat Hand und Fuß.

4. Die Regierung tut nichts für die Armen.

5. Viele Städte sind alt und sollten renoviert werden.

6. Die meisten Leute werden von der Werbung beeinflusst.

7. Die meisten Leute lesen nur den Sportteil in der Zeitung.

8. Das amerikanische Fernsehen bringt einfach zu viel Reklame!

9. Es gibt kein Familienleben.

— Sind diese Blumen künstlich?
— Natürlich!
— Natürlich?
— Nein, künstlich!

7 Für mein Notizbuch

Schreiben Schreib in dein Notizbuch je drei Sätze über Dinge — in der Schule, zu Hause, auf der Reise — die dich in diesem Jahr überrascht haben, die dich enttäuscht haben und die dich aufgeregt haben! Gib Gründe dafür an!

8 Wie kann man alles beschreiben?

Sprechen Wenn wir Leute oder Dinge beschreiben, können wir die Intensität unserer Beschreibung variieren. Links unten sind einige Wörter, mit denen wir das tun.

a. Such dir eine Partnerin, und füll die Lücke in diesem Satz!
   Die meisten Amerikaner sind …
   hilfreich/naiv.

b. Frag jetzt deine Partnerin, was sie über Amerika sagen würde! Unten rechts stehen ein paar Ideen.

gar nicht	nicht	ziemlich
ein bisschen	so	
sehr	besonders	ganz
	zu	äußerst
furchtbar	wahnsinnig	irre
unheimlich	unwahrscheinlich	

Die meisten Leute sind … arm/reich.

Die meisten Amerikaner sind … nett.

Die meisten Leute lesen … viel/wenig.

Die meisten Leute essen und trinken … viel.

Macht weiter! Was sagt ihr über Amerikaner?

9 **Zwei Austauschschüler unterhalten sich**

Sprechen Zwei deutsche Austauschschüler sprechen über die USA. Spielt die beiden Rollen!

DU **Das Land ist so wahnsinnig groß!**

PARTNER **Das stimmt. Ich hätte …** *oder* **Ich war sehr erstaunt, wie …**

Der Unterricht in der Schule ist sehr locker.

Das Land ist so wahnsinnig groß.

Sie wissen schon eine ganze Menge über Deutschland.

Sie haben wenige Klischeevorstellungen von den Deutschen.

Sie interessieren sich für die Ereignisse in Deutschland.

Mit 16 kann man schon den Führerschein bekommen.

Mein Amerikabild hat sich schnell geändert.

10 **Grammatik im Kontext**

Schreiben Hanno schreibt seinen Eltern in Deutschland von seinem Austauschsemester in den USA. Was sagt er? Hilf ihm mit einem besseren Schreibstil, indem du die Sätze unten verbindest!

1. So ein Schüleraustausch ist ideal. (weil) Man kommt mitten in die Familie hinein.

2. Man lernt die Leute richtig kennen. (wenn) Man wohnt bei ihnen längere Zeit.

3. Meine Gasteltern sind erstaunt. (wie) Das Essen schmeckt mir hier gut.

4. Mir gefällt es so gut. (dass) Ich möchte noch ein Jahr da bleiben.

5. Ich seh mir das Land noch besser an. (bevor) Ich fahre im Juni nach Hause.

6. Ich hatte es mir hier ganz anders vorgestellt. (als) Ich kam nach Amerika.

1. …, weil man mitten in die Familie hineinkommt.
2. …, wenn man bei ihnen längere Zeit wohnt.
3. …, wie gut mir hier das Essen schmeckt. 5. …, bevor ich im Juni nach Hause fahre.
4. …, dass ich noch ein Jahr da bleiben möchte. 6. …, als ich nach Amerika kam.

> ### Ein wenig Grammatik
>
> The subordinating conjunction **als** is generally used with the narrative past (the imperfect) and has the meaning of *when, at the time when.* The **als**-clause can either follow or precede the main clause.
>
> Ich hatte ein ganz anderes Amerikabild, **als** ich nach Amerika **kam.**
> **Als** ich nach Amerika **kam,** hatte ich ein ganz anderes Amerikabild.
>
> What do you observe about the word order in the main clause when it is preceded by a subordinate clause?
>
> Übungsheft, S. 94–95, Ü. 3–4   Mehr Grammatikübungen, S. 229, Ü. 3
> Grammatikheft, S. 66, Ü. 4

11 **Grammatik im Kontext**

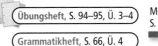

war   aßen   kamen   ging
erkannte schmeckte sah
abholte

Sprechen/Schreiben Zwei Austauschschüler unterhalten sich über ihre Amerikareise. Sie haben die andregleichen Erfahrungen gemacht. Spielt die beiden Rollen, und gebraucht in jeder Wiederholung einen als-Satz!

PARTNER **Ich bin im August nach Amerika gekommen. Es war furchtbar heiß.**

DU **Stimmt. Als ich im August nach Amerika kam, war es auch furchtbar heiß.**

1. Meine Gastfamilie hat mich vom Flughafen abgeholt (*picked up*). Ich habe sie gleich erkannt (*recognized*).

2. Wir sind nach Hause gekommen, und sie wollten mir gleich alles zeigen.

3. Wir haben dann zu Abend gegessen. Es hat mir furchtbar gut geschmeckt.

4. Am nächsten Tag hab ich die Umgebung gesehen. Ich war ganz begeistert.

5. Ich bin mit meinem Gastbruder in die Schule gegangen. Die Schüler waren alle sehr nett und freundlich zu mir.

Coordinating conjunctions (Summary)

The conjunctions **denn, und, oder, aber,** and **sondern** are called coordinating conjunctions because they join two independent clauses.

> Ich hatte Vorurteile, **denn** ich kannte die Amerikaner nur als Touristen.
> Ich möchte meine Vorurteile abbauen, **aber** das ist nicht so einfach!

What do you notice about the word order in clauses introduced by coordinating conjunctions? You have also learned that both **weil** and **denn** can be used to introduce a clause expressing cause or reason, but they are significantly different in the kind of word order that follows each. What is this difference?[1]

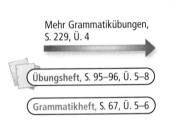

Mehr Grammatikübungen,
S. 229, Ü. 4

Übungsheft, S. 95–96, Ü. 5–8

Grammatikheft, S. 67, Ü. 5–6

12 Grammatik im Kontext

E.g.: 1. ..., weil man da mitten in die Familie hineinkommt.
..., denn da kommt man mitten in die Familie hinein.

Schreiben Verbinde jedes der folgenden Satzpaare einmal mit „weil" und einmal mit „denn"!

1. Ein Schüleraustausch ist ideal. Man kommt da mitten in die Familie hinein.
2. Man kann die eigenen Vorurteile abbauen. Man lernt die Leute richtig kennen.
3. Man kann seine eigene Meinung bilden. Man macht genügend persönliche Erfahrungen.
4. Man sieht die Leute plötzlich ganz anders. Man hat ein anderes Verhältnis zu ihnen.
5. Man nimmt oft Klischeevorstellungen an. Man war selbst noch nie im anderen Land.
6. Der Unterricht in Amerika gefällt mir. Er ist lockerer und weniger stressig.

13 Gruppenprojekt: Wie sehen wir uns selbst?

Lesen/Sprechen Blättert durch eure eigenen Zeitungen und Zeitschriften, und sucht nach Artikeln und Illustrationen, die entweder ein positives oder ein negatives Amerikabild zeigen! Bringt eure Beispiele mit in die Klasse, und macht eine Collage mit diesen Artikeln und Illustrationen! Vielleicht kann einer von euch selbst einige passende Illustrationen machen.

14 Klassendiskussion

Sprechen Diskutiert über eure Collagen! Was für ein Amerikabild stellen sie dar? Gebt Gründe an! Was zeigen sie, und was zeigen sie nicht? Wie könnten sie noch verbessert werden?

15 Was sagst du dazu?

Sprechen Überleg dir folgende Fragen, und sag deiner Gruppe, was du dazu meinst!

1. Was sagst du zu Leuten, die nur Vorurteile über die Vereinigten Staaten haben?
2. Mit welchen Eigenschaften würdest du dich und deine Landsleute beschreiben?
3. Was ist deine eigene Meinung über die Amerikaner? Erwähne Tatsachen, Meinungen, sowie Vorurteile, die du gehört hast, aber an die du selbst nicht glaubst!

16 Für mein Notizbuch

Schreiben Schreib deine Meinung zu dem Thema: „Wie sehe ich die Amerikaner?"! Führe Tatsachen an und begründe sie! Baue Vorurteile ab, die andere Leute haben und die dich stören! Fang so an: Ich glaube, wir Amerikaner sind ...

---

1. As a subordinating conjunction, **weil** requires verb-last position in the clause. As a coordinating conjunction, **denn** requires verb-second position.

Verständnis für Ausländer?

Übungsheft, S. 97, Ü. 1–2

Auch in einer Welt, die durch die Medien und durch Reisen kleiner geworden ist, gibt es noch immer viele Klischeevorstellungen über andere Länder.

Was kann man tun, um solche Klischees abzubauen? Es ist natürlich am besten, selbst in das andere Land zu fahren. Für junge Menschen bestehen viele Möglichkeiten, sich an Ort und Stelle zu informieren. Da gibt es eine Menge Schüleraustauschprogramme, wo junge Deutsche und junge Amerikaner die Lebensgewohnheiten ihrer Austauschpartner kennen lernen können.

Auch gibt es immer mehr Partnerstädte zwischen verschiedenen Ländern. Das Ziel der Städtepartnerschaften ist es, durch gegenseitiges Kennenlernen (z.B. in kulturellen Veranstaltungen, Sportwettkämpfen oder Jugendgruppen) das Verständnis für einander zu fördern (*encourage*) und alte Klischees abzubauen.

1. Schau die Abbildungen an! Mit welchen Städten haben Passau und Soltau eine Partnerschaft? Weißt du, ob die Schulen in deiner Stadt oder deinem Dorf auch ein Austauschprogramm mit ausländischen Schulen haben? Mit welchen Ländern gibt es diese Austauschprogramme?

2. Mit welcher Stadt im Ausland würdest du gern ein Austauschprogramm haben? Was würdest du gern über diese Stadt und die Menschen dieses Landes herausfinden?

3. Was für Folgen (*results*) würde ein Austauschprogramm haben? Was meinst du?

4. In der Bundesrepublik muss man nicht unbedingt ins Ausland reisen, um Ausländer kennen zu lernen. Der Anteil der Ausländer an der Gesamtbevölkerung, der mit knapp neun Prozent zu den höchsten in Europa gehört, bereichert das kulturelle Spektrum. Millionen von Ausländern — Jugoslawen, Spanier, Italiener, Griechen und vor allem Türken — wohnen und arbeiten in Deutschland. Ihre Kinder gehen auf deutsche Schulen und sprechen Deutsch oft besser als ihre Muttersprache. Welche Klischees oder Stereotype hat man von diesen Gruppen?

Weiter geht's!

Wie sehen junge Amerikaner die Deutschen?

CD 8 Trs. 6–7

Junge Amerikaner, die noch nie in Deutschland waren, sehen die Deutschen gewöhnlich so:

Die Deutschen werden oft so charakterisiert. Welche Wörter passen zu deinem Deutschlandbild?   CD 8 Tr. 6

groß   blond   blauäugig   gutmütig   ernst

stur   ordentlich   stark

freundlich   stolz

kameradschaftlich

streng   arrogant

still

reserviert   materialistisch

nett   snobistisch

geduldig   unhöflich   höflich

gemütlich   egoistisch

vorsichtig   gründlich

verwöhnt   pünktlich   athletisch   intolerant

intelligent   fleißig   musikalisch   ehrgeizig

Hier sind einige Aussagen junger Amerikaner, die nach einem kurzen Besuch in den deutschsprachigen Ländern ihre Klischeevorstellungen revidieren (revise) mussten. Diese Aussagen wurden übersetzt, weil die meisten Schüler nur wenig oder gar kein Deutsch sprachen. CD 8 Tr. 7

„Ich weiß nicht warum, aber ich hatte mir vorgestellt, dass die Deutschen in Lederhosen und Dirndlkleidern herumlaufen; aber das stimmt überhaupt nicht; sie sind meistens so angezogen wie wir."

John, 16

„Mir ist aufgefallen, dass die Deutschen die Natur sehr lieben. Überall sieht man Blumen und Pflanzen, drinnen und draußen. Die Deutschen gehen auch viel spazieren. Überall gibt es Spazierwege und Wanderwege!"

Kim, 17

„Ein Klischee ist, dass die Deutschen dick sind, weil sie sehr viel essen, besonders Knödel und Brezeln, auch Bratwurst und Sauerkraut. Ich hab aber gesehen, dass die Leute auch nicht anders essen als wir; viele achten sogar sehr auf ihre schlanke Linie. Meine Gastfamilie isst zum Beispiel sehr viel Obst, Gemüse und Joghurt — eine wirklich ausgewogene Kost."

Jessy, 16

„Es hat mich beeindruckt, dass die Deutschen sehr umweltbewusst sind. Sie bringen leere Flaschen in die Geschäfte zurück oder werfen sie in Container, und sie sammeln Papier."

Cathy, 17

„Ich dachte immer, dass die jungen Deutschen viel Bier trinken. Ich habe aber schnell meine Meinung geändert; sie trinken meistens Spezi, Apfelsaft oder Mineralwasser!"

Rich, 17

„Ich war überrascht, dass die Deutschen so tierlieb sind. Ich hab nie so viele Hunde gesehen wie in Deutschland. Die dürfen sogar mit ins Restaurant gehen, und vor manchen Geschäften hab ich Behälter mit Wasser gesehen für durstige Hunde. Das würde ich auch unseren Geschäftsleuten empfehlen."

Mandy, 15

„Ich war überrascht, wie friedliebend die Deutschen sind. Es gibt bei ihnen Großdemonstrationen gegen Gewaltanwendung, wenn in der Welt ein weiterer Krieg auszubrechen droht. Daran können sich viele ein Beispiel nehmen!"

Eric, 15

 Übungsheft, S. 98

17 Klischees und Tatsachen

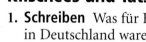

1. **Schreiben** Was für Klischeevorstellungen haben viele junge Amerikaner, die noch nie in Deutschland waren? — Schreib auf, was für Klischeebilder in der Collage auf Seite 218 zu sehen sind.

2. **Sprechen** Wie charakterisieren die jungen Amerikaner, die schon in Deutschland waren, die Deutschen? Stimmst du den Aussagen zu, oder hast du eine andere Meinung? Warum?

3. **Schreiben** Was für Klischeevorstellungen hatten diese jungen Amerikaner und wie mussten sie diese nach ihrem Deutschlandbesuch revidieren? Mach deine eigene Liste!

Name	Klischee oder Vorurteil	„neue" Meinung
John, 16	Lederhosen, Dirndl	so angezogen wie wir
Rich, 17	trinken viel Bier	

Der sympathische Deutsche

1998 hat eine deutsche Zeitschrift eine weltweite Image-Studie gemacht. Mehr als 32 000 Erwachsene in 17 Ländern wurden gefragt, wie sympathisch oder unsympathisch ihnen die Deutschen sind. Das Ergebnis: ein durchweg freundliches Deutschlandbild! „Erfolgreich, fleißig, stark"

lautet das Urteil der 17 befragten Nationen, ein Wirtschaftswunderland und Exportweltmeister. Lange stützte sich das deutsche Image einseitig auf diese industrielle Tatsache. Jetzt rundet sich das Bild: „Friedlich", „modern", „demokratisch" wirken die Deutschen der neunziger

Jahre. Negative Eigenschaften gibt es jedoch auch. Die Deutschen werden auch von vielen als arrogant, humorlos, gefühlslos und intolerant bezeichnet. Resultat der Untersuchung: Die Welt sieht die Deutschen in weit besserem Licht, als die Deutschen selbst bislang geglaubt hatten.

Wortschatz

p. 207X

auf Deutsch erklärt

ehrgeizig wenn man viel plant und erreichen will

stark muskulös, kräftig, kann vieles machen

gutmütig freundlich und hilfsbereit

aufgeschlossen offen, freundlich

friedliebend wenn man keinen Krieg, sondern Frieden will

still ruhig, nicht laut

ordentlich wenn man immer Ordnung macht oder hat

umweltbewusst wenn man etwas zum Schutz der Umwelt tut

auf Englisch erklärt

Es ist uns <u>aufgefallen</u>, wie <u>verwöhnt</u> diese Kinder sind. *We've noticed how spoiled these children are.*

Es <u>beeindruckt</u> mich, wenn Eltern <u>streng</u> aber auch <u>geduldig</u> sind. *It impresses me when parents are both strict and patient.*

Ich bin <u>stolz</u> <u>auf</u> meinen <u>höflichen</u> Sohn. *I am proud of my polite son.*

Du bist so <u>stur</u> wie ein Esel. *You're as stubborn as a mule.*

Grammatikheft, S. 68, Ü. 7–8

---

18 Eigenschaften — gute und schlechte

Schreiben Macht in der Klasse eine Liste von Eigenschaften, guten und schlechten! Ihr könnt die aufschreiben, die auf diesen Seiten erscheinen und auch andere dazufügen.

19 Amerikanische Schüler über Deutschland   Script and answers on p. 207G

Zuhören Was sagen Jugendliche über die Deutschen? Hör gut zu, wie einige amerikanische Schüler ihre Erlebnisse in Deutschland besprechen! Welche Aussage passt zu welchem Bild?

CD 8 Tr. 8

a.

b.

c.

d.

e.

20 Wie sehen wir die Deutschen?

Sprechen/Schreiben Kommt jetzt wieder zu einer Brainstorming-Sitzung zusammen! Das Thema heißt diesmal: Wie sehen wir die Deutschen? Gebt Gründe an! Wählt wieder einen Schriftführer, der alle Aussagen aufschreibt. Verwendet Ausdrücke wie:

Die Deutschen sind …   Ich glaube, dass die Deutschen …

Nicht alle Deutschen sind …   Ich halte die Deutschen für …

Einige/viele Deutsche sind …

21 Tatsachen, Vorurteile, Klischees

Sprechen Seht euch die Aussagen an, die ihr in der letzten Gruppenarbeit erarbeitet habt!

a. Ordnet jetzt diese Aussagen in drei Gruppen: Tatsachen, Vorurteile und Klischees! Die Deutschen haben/sind …

Tatsachen	Vorurteile	Klischees
schnelle Autos	arrogant	tragen Lederhosen, Dirndl

b. Diskutiert jetzt darüber! Äußert eure Meinung und gebraucht dabei Ausdrücke wie:

Das stimmt (nicht). Ich glaube, dass …   (Jessica) hat Recht, wenn sie sagt, dass …

Ich denke, dass …   In diesem Punkt geb ich dir (nicht) Recht.

So sagt man das!

Expressing an assumption   (Übungsheft, S. 99, Ü. 1) (Grammatikheft, S. 69, Ü. 9)   Mehr Grammatikübungen, S. 230, Ü. 5–6

To make an assumption or introduce an impression, you know these phrases:

Ich glaube schon, dass …
Ich meine doch, dass …

Other phrases you can use to make an assumption or introduce an impression are:

Ich nehme an, dass …
Ich vermute, dass …
Ich hatte den Eindruck, dass …
Ich hatte mir vorgestellt, dass …

8–1
8–2

---

22 Wie stellt ihr euch die Deutschen vor?   Script and answers on p. 207H

Zuhören Schüler erzählen, wie sie sich Deutschland und die Deutschen vorstellen. Schreib mindestens fünf Eindrücke auf, die diese Schüler erwähnen!
CD 8 Tr. 9

23 Hast du deine Meinung geändert?

Sprechen Wie hast du dir am Anfang Deutschland und die Deutschen vorgestellt? Sag einem Partner deine Vorstellung! Dann sag ihm, ob du deine Meinung geändert hast! Erkläre ihm auch warum! Tauscht dann die Rollen aus!

BEISPIEL   **Ich hatte mir immer vorgestellt, dass die Deutschen …**
                 Aber das stimmt überhaupt nicht. (Als ich in Deutschland war …)

leben, um zu arbeiten

sind militaristisch

essen viel Fleisch und wenig Gemüse

sind unfreundlich

sind nicht umweltbewusst

tragen nur Lederhosen und Dirndl

haben keinen Humor

trinken immer nur viel Bier

mögen keine Hunde

24 Und du? Woher bekommst du deine Informationen?

Sprechen Such dir eine Partnerin! Überlegt euch, wie man sich ein Bild von anderen Ländern und anderen Leuten macht, während ihr folgende Fragen beantwortet!

1. Woher bekommst du deine Informationen über die deutschsprachigen Länder? Unten sind einige Möglichkeiten aufgelistet.

2. Wie würdest du die Informationen charakterisieren, die du im Fernsehen über Deutschland erhältst?

3. Warum kommt es vor, dass Medien manchmal Vorurteile verstärken oder wenigstens nicht schwächen? Nenne Beispiele!

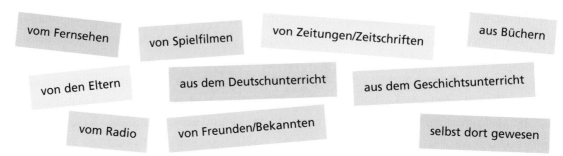

vom Fernsehen

von Spielfilmen

von Zeitungen/Zeitschriften

aus Büchern

von den Eltern

aus dem Deutschunterricht

aus dem Geschichtsunterricht

vom Radio

von Freunden/Bekannten

selbst dort gewesen

Grammatik

Verbs with prefixes (Summary)

1. Some of the most common separable prefixes are: **an, ab, ein, mit, zu, zurück;** also, the words that involve motion, **hin** and **her,** or combinations of these, such as **hinein, heraus, herum.** Compare and contrast the sentences. Explain the differences in the verb forms.

> (**ankommen**) Ich **kam** im August in den Vereinigten Staaten **an.**
> (**einladen**) Meine Gastfamilie **lädt** mich noch immer **ein.**
> (**abbauen**) **Bau** endlich mal deine Vorurteile **ab**!
> (**abholen**) Wer hat dich am Flugplatz **abgeholt**?
> (**mitnehmen**) Wir haben ihn doch auf die Reise **mitgenommen.**
> (**anrufen**) Mein Gastbruder hatte alle Freunde **angerufen.**

2. Of course, when such infinitives are used with **zu,** they get separated by **zu.**

> (**abbauen**) Ich rate dir, deine Vorurteile schnell **abzubauen.**

3. There is another category of verbs with prefixes, called inseparable-prefix verbs. Compare and contrast the sentences. How are the verb forms different?

> (**überraschen**) Das **überrascht** mich überhaupt nicht.
> (**wiederholen**) **Wiederhole** bitte deine Frage!
> (**übersetzen**) Das hast du wirklich prima **übersetzt**!
> (**unterstützen**) Versuch doch mal, mich zu **unterstützen.**

Mehr Grammatikübungen, S. 231, Ü. 7

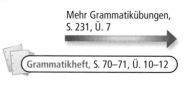

Grammatikheft, S. 70–71, Ü. 10–12

25 Über deutsche Schüler

Script and answers on p. 207I

Zuhören Schüler erzählen von ihren Erfahrungen mit deutschen Jugendlichen in Deutschland. Welches sind Empfehlungen und welches sind Warnungen?

CD 8 Tr. 10

Name	Empfehlung	Warnung
Dorothee		
Christian		

222   *zweihundertzweiundzwanzig*   STANDARDS: 1.1, 4.1   KAPITEL 8   Weg mit den Vorurteilen!

So sagt man das!

Making suggestions and recommendations; giving advice

There are different ways to make suggestions and recommendations, and to give advice. Note how the command forms are used in these examples.

To make a suggestion or a recommendation, you can say:

Ich kann dir einen Tipp geben: fahr nach Deutschland!
Ich empfehl dir, selbst einmal nach Deutschland zu fahren.
Es lohnt sich, einen Schüleraustausch mitzumachen.
Fahr selbst mal hin!　　**Hinfahren!**　　**Leute kennen lernen!**

To give advice, you can say:

Verbreite keine Klischees!
Wiederhole bloß nicht eine fremde Meinung!

Mehr Grammatikübungen,
S. 231, Ü. 8–9

Übungsheft, S. 100–102, Ü. 2–9

Grammatikheft, S. 72, Ü. 13–14

26 Was rätst du deinem Freund?

Sprechen Ein guter Freund von dir will nach Deutschland fahren, aber du findest, dass er viele Vorurteile hat. Unten ist eine Liste mit Dingen, die dein Freund tun soll. Versuche, ihn zu überreden (*convince*), dass er deinem Rat folgt, bevor er wegfliegt!

> Du　**Ich kann dir einen Tipp geben, verbreite keine Klischees!**
> Partner　**Ja, und warum denn (nicht)?**
> Du　**Die Leute werden denken, dass alle Amerikaner Klischees verbreiten!**

keine Klischees verbreiten　　sich eine eigene Meinung bilden　　Vorurteile abbauen/haben

die Leute genau beobachten　　einen Schüleraustausch mitmachen

27 Zum Überlegen und Diskutieren

Sprechen Diskutiert mit euren Klassenkameraden über folgende Fragen!

1. Was für Vorurteile haben manche Deutsche gegen Ausländer und warum?
2. Wisst ihr von ähnlichen Situationen, vielleicht wo du wohnst, wo Vorurteile anderen Menschen gegenüber existieren? Was sind diese Vorurteile?
3. Warum bestehen Vorurteile? Was würdet ihr empfehlen, um Vorurteile abzubauen?

28 Klassenprojekt

Lesen/Sprechen Arbeitet an euerm „Deutschlandbild!" Sammelt Informationen aus Zeitungen und Zeitschriften, und fügt diese zu einer Collage zusammen! Wenn ihr wollt, könnt ihr euer Projekt erweitern und ein Österreichbild und ein Schweizbild erarbeiten.

29 Diskussion

Sprechen Diskutiert über eure Collage, was sie zeigt, was sie nicht zeigt und wie sie noch verbessert werden könnte! Welche Beiträge (*contributions*) informieren, welche verbreiten Klischees?

30 Von der Schule zum Beruf

You work for a company that produces glossy tourism brochures for cities all over the world. Develop an informative cultural brochure for a large American city aimed at German-speaking travelers. Make suggestions and recommendations about what to see and do, give advice and tips concerning the area, and address some of the prejudices or clichés Europeans might have about the region.

Sabines Eltern

CD8 Tr. 11

O Mann, bin ich glücklich! Ich strahle im ganzen Gesicht. Könnte alle Menschen umarmen. Ja, ich würde sogar fliegen, wenn ich es nur könnte. Meine Freude kennt keine Grenzen, seit ein paar Wochen. Plötzlich entdecke ich meine Liebe für Blumen. Ich wußte gar nicht, daß sie so herrlich duften können. Die Welt sieht auf einmal auch ganz anders aus. Sie ist doch nicht grau in grau. Die Welt ist rosarot. Ich bin so unendlich glücklich. Pessimist bin ich nun auch nicht mehr. Seit vier Wochen bin ich ein großer Optimist geworden. Man muß einfach alles positiv sehen. Die Stadt stinkt nicht mehr nach Autoabgasen, und das Ozonloch wird schon wieder werden. Die Wälder, die werden mit Sicherheit wieder gesund — die Umwelthienis malen Bilder, die übertrieben sind. Diese unsere Welt ist noch so gut intakt wie ein Mensch mit 17 Jahren. Wie gesagt, ich sehe alles positiv. Weil ich eben so glücklich bin. Und warum, will ich auch verraten: Ich bin verliebt. Jawohl. Ich habe jetzt eine Freundin, die mich liebt, wie ich bin. Wie ich bin? Eigentlich bin ich ein ganz normaler Mensch. Nur, ich bin kein Inländer. Dafür ist meine Freundin eine Deutsche. Und nicht nur das. Sie ist zudem noch Schwäbin. Durch und durch. Was aber nichts aussagt. Sie liebt mich und ich liebe sie. Nur das zählt und nichts anderes. Wir sehen uns fast jeden Tag. Wenn wir uns auch nur einen einzigen Tag nicht sehen, kommt es mir so vor, als ob ich sie eine kleine Ewigkeit nicht mehr gesehen hätte. Ich liebe sie über alles. So sehr, daß ich den ganzen Tag fast nur an sie denke. Sie ist so wunderschön. Die Mandelaugen schauen mich so an, daß ich beinahe ohnmächtig werde. Und ihre Stupsnase gibt es nur einmal. Diese Nase, diese Nase. Alles an ihr ist einmalig. Auch ihre Eltern! Wie jeder Mensch hat auch meine Freundin Eltern. Aber was für liebe Leute! Sie lieben mich wie ihren eigenen Sohn. Und vielleicht mehr. Wenn ich mit meiner Freundin zu ihren Eltern gehe, stehen sie sogar kurz auf, um mich zu begrüßen. Immer wieder laden sie mich zum Essen ein. Weil sie nur ein Kind haben, sitzen wir zu viert am Tisch. Nach dem Essen spielen wir verschiedene Spiele. Bei einem Pilsbier sprechen wir anschließend über die Probleme der nicht-einheimischen

Stille Grenzen

Lesestrategie Interpreting rhetorical devices When reading a story or essay that seems to be addressed directly to you — the reader — it's helpful to note *rhetorical* questions and exclamations. A question is rhetorical when it has no real answer or if its answer is obvious. Authors sometimes use rhetorical questions and exclamations to make their point more dramatically or to say something about their own doubts or prejudices. Think of these devices as invitations to get involved in the author's thought processes.

Getting Started

1. Read the title and the first paragraph, up to **Wir sehen uns fast jeden Tag.**
   a. In welcher Person wird die Geschichte erzählt?
   b. Schau den Titel an! Was meinst du, wer Sabine ist?
   c. Wann und wo spielt die Handlung? In welchem Land? In welchem Jahrhundert?
2. Read the first part again. What is happening? How has the narrator's view of the world changed in the previous few weeks? (Notice the colors he mentions.) What is the reason for this change? Identify the connecting words that indicate the cause-and-effect relationship.

For answers, see p. 207V.

Leute, um nicht Ausländer zu sagen. Es gibt jedesmal andere Themen. Wen wundert's? Die Eltern meiner Freundin mögen die Nicht-Einheimischen. Natürlich auch mich. Sie waren schon so oft im Ausland. Vor allem in meiner Heimat. In der Türkei. Das gelobte Land der Touristen. Sie erzählen, wie herzlich und freundlich sie empfangen wurden. Jedesmal. Immer wieder. Sie haben sich schämen müssen, sagen sie mir. Ich erwidere aber, daß sie sich nicht zu schämen brauchen. Ich sage, es sollen sich die schämen, die blind alles und jedes hassen, was nicht einheimisch ist. Ausländische Autos, ausländische Waren und auch ausländische Menschen. Es ist nicht so einfach, sagen sie mir. Sie haben recht, denke ich. Was machen diese alles-Hasser, wenn Europa eins wird?

Manchmal kommen Sabine, so heißt übrigens meine Freundin, und ihre Eltern zu uns nach Hause. Meine Eltern mögen sie auch sehr. Meine Mutter kocht türkisch. Das Essen ist für Sabines Eltern nichts Neues. Aber sie essen trotzdem gerne unsere Spezialitäten. Danach trinken sie natürlich Cay, also Tee. Es ist ein Muß. Meine Freundin und ich amüsieren uns unheimlich, wenn unsere Eltern ver-

suchen, miteinander zu sprechen. Es ist ein wenig mühsam, aber zum Schluß verständigen sie sich doch. Ich wünsche mir, daß alle Menschen hier so miteinander leben. Nicht nur unsere Familien.

Wieder einmal bin ich bei ihren Eltern eingeladen. Mit leeren Händen will ich nicht hingehen. Ich kaufe einen schönen großen Strauß. Ich klingle, ihre Mutter macht die Tür auf. Wie immer, werde ich höflich hereingebeten. Wir essen, trinken und danach, auch wie fast immer, spielen wir etwas zusammen. Kaum haben wir angefangen, da klingelt es an der Haustür.

3. What does the narrator mention about the way his girlfriend loves him? Why would this be important?

4. Finish reading the first paragraph. On whom does the narrator focus? What kind of relationship does he have with these people? Support your answer with expressions from the text. What attitude do these people have toward non-Germans?

5. Finish reading the story. What is the unexpected twist? Were you surprised by the ending? If not, did you notice any clues that foreshadowed the ending?

A Closer Look

6. Read the story again more carefully. In the fourth paragraph, of what does Ali become convinced? What has led him to believe this?

7. Now read the fifth paragraph. What is the function of the rhetorical question here? What effect does repeating **nein** have? Are you convinced of what Ali is saying or made more skeptical?

8. What function does the word **plötzlich** serve at the beginning of the sixth paragraph? What happens at this point in the story?

9. Retell the story in your own words. Pay careful attention to how the plot develops. (Look at your answers to questions 2, 6, and 8.)

Herein kommen Sabines Onkel und Tante, väterlicherseits. Als sie mich, zum erstenmal übrigens, sehen, sind sie sehr überrascht. So schauen sie mich jedenfalls an. Ich versuche, höflich zu wirken, stehe auf und grüße sie. Ich bin irgendwie unsicher. Was denken diese Leute über mich? Sind die Nicht-Einheimischen auch ihnen sympathisch? Oder mögen sie sie vielleicht gar nicht? Was wird nun geschehen? Was wird er sagen? »Guten Tag, ich heiße Peter. Wie heißt du?« fragt Sabines Onkel mich lächelnd. Ich bin sehr erleichtert.

»Mein Name ist Ali«, sage ich. »Es freut mich, Sie kennenzulernen«, füge ich hinzu.

Danach sitzen wir, diesmal zu sechst, am Tisch und spielen weiter. Sabines Onkel scheint ein sehr netter Mensch zu sein. Sie bewundern sogar meine Freundin, Mut bewiesen zu haben mit mir. Es ist spät in der Nacht, als sie gehen. Auch sie laden mich zu sich nach Hause ein. Ich freue mich unendlich. Langsam fange ich an zu glauben, daß eigentlich niemand hierzulande etwas gegen Ausländer hat. Sabines Eltern mögen mich, ihr Onkel konnte mich auf Anhieb leiden.

Also was soll das Gerede vom Rassismus? Sowas gibt es doch in meiner zweiten Heimat nicht. Ich lächle und sage immer wieder: nein, sowas gibt es hier nicht. Nein, Antisemitismus gibt es auch nicht. Nein, Herrgott nochmal, das gibt es nicht.

Plötzlich klingelt mein Wecker. Tut, tut, tut. Ich hatte einen schönen Traum. Ich habe von meiner Freundin Sabine geträumt. War irgend etwas passiert? Weil ich abergläubisch bin, rufe ich meine Freundin an. Es ist sieben Uhr morgens. Ihr Vater geht ans Telefon.

»Ich bin's, Ali. Ich möchte bitte mit Sabine sprechen«, sage ich.

Eine unfreundliche Stimme schreit mich an:

»Ich habe Ihnen doch schon einmal gesagt, daß Sie uns nicht anrufen sollen. Lassen Sie uns und meine Tochter in Ruhe.«

Ich habe eine Freundin. Sie heißt Sabine. Ihre Eltern habe ich noch nie gesehen …

Mustafa S.

10. How do you think Ali feels after the telephone call? What causes him to feel this way? Why do you think the story is entitled *Sabines Eltern*? In your opinion, what is the main idea of the story?

11. Ergänze die Geschichte mit einem neuen Schluss, der der Wirklichkeit entspricht! Wo und wie oft treffen sich Ali und Sabine? Wissen ihre Eltern davon? Wie fühlt sich das junge Paar? Wie ist ihr Verhältnis zu der Gesellschaft, in der sie leben?

12. Schreib nach dem folgenden Muster ein Gedicht darüber, wie man sich als Außenseiter fühlt!

a noun	*(the subject of the poem)*
two adjectives	*(describing the subject)*
three verbs	*(actions associated with the subject)*
one sentence	*(expressing an emotion or idea about the subject)*
a noun	*(restating the subject in a different way)*

Übungsheft, S. 103-104, Ü. 1-4

Zum Schreiben

As you have seen in this chapter, prejudices can arise from a lack of knowledge about others. If we could know what others feel and think, we would probably be surprised at how much they are like us, and we would be better able to avoid prejudice. In this activity, you will write a fictional short story about an event that brought people in different groups together and changed their opinions of one another.

Es waren einmal zwei Gruppen ...

Schreib eine fiktive Kurzgeschichte von zwei Gruppen, die eines Tages zusammenkommen und die durch diese Begegnung ein besseres Verständnis zueinander finden! Erzähl was passiert, was die Hauptfiguren denken und wie sie ihre Vorurteile abbauen!

Schreibtipp Selecting a point of view In most of what you have written so far, you have used the first-person point of view, relating feelings and experiences from your personal vantage point. When writing fiction, however, you have more choices, including first person, in which the "I" of the story does not represent you; third person limited, in which the narrator focuses on the thoughts and feelings of one character; and third person omniscient, in which the narrator knows all the thoughts of all the characters. The point of view you choose to use affects the story because it establishes what can be perceived and determines which details can be included. Whichever point of view you select, be sure to remain consistent throughout your story.

A. Vorbereiten

1. Entwickle eine Idee für deine Geschichte! Denke an Gruppen, die traditionelle Vorurteile gegeneinander haben, wie zum Beispiel Männer und Frauen, Ausländer und Einheimische, Cowboys und Indianer, usw.

2. Erfinde Charakterrollen für die Geschichte! Wie heißen die Charaktere? Wie alt sind sie? Wie sehen sie aus? Was denken sie von den anderen? Wie sprechen sie? Stelle auch den Handlungsraum (*setting*) der Geschichte fest!

3. Überleg dir die Handlung und den Konflikt für die Geschichte!

4. Wähle jetzt eine Perspektive, aus der die Geschichte erzählt wird (erste Person oder dritte Person)! Denk an die verschiedenen Charakterrollen und an die Handlung, und entscheide dich, ob du die Gedanken von allen oder nur von einem wiedergeben willst!

B. Ausführen

Benutze deine Notizen, um einen ersten Entwurf der Geschichte abzufassen! Verwende sowohl Dialog als auch Beschreibung, um die Eigenschaften der Hauptfiguren zu entwickeln!

C. Überarbeiten

1. Lies deine Geschichte noch einmal durch! Hat deine Geschichte mehr als eine Perspektive? Streiche alle Sätze durch, die die Erzählperspektive ändern!

2. Denk an die Handlung und die Charakterrollen! Ist die Handlung interessant? Hast du den Konflikt schnell entwickelt und in den Vordergrund gestellt? Bist du mit dem Schluss zufrieden? Passt der Dialog der Hauptfiguren zu ihrer Wesensart?

3. Prüfe jetzt deinen Stil! Hast du die Zeitformen konsequent eingehalten? Wenn du die Vergangenheit gewählt hast, hast du „als" richtig benutzt? Hast du ab und zu Nebensätze verwendet, um den Satzbau zu variieren?

4. Hast du alles richtig buchstabiert? Hast du Kommas richtig gesetzt?

5. Schreib die korrigierte Geschichte noch einmal ab!

Mehr Grammatikübungen

Answers

Erste Stufe

Objectives Expressing surprise, disappointment, and annoyance

1 Ein deutscher Austauschschüler, der gerade in die Vereinigten Staaten gekommen ist, drückt seine Überraschung (*surprise*) aus. Schreib die folgenden Sätze ab, und verwende die Information in Klammern als dass-Satz in den Lücken! (**Seite 213**)

(Meine Gastfamilie hat eine ganze Menge über Deutschland gewusst.)

1. Ich war sehr erstaunt, dass _____ .   meine G. eine ganze Menge über D. gewusst hat

(Die meisten Leute waren so wahnsinnig nett zu mir.)

2. Ich war überrascht, dass _____ .   die meisten Leute so wahnsinnig nett zu mir waren

(Die meisten Leute haben schnell ihre Vorurteile abgebaut.)

3. Ich war erstaunt, wie _____ .   schnell die meisten Leute ihre Vorurteile abgebaut haben

(Viele Leute tun nur sehr wenig für ihre Umwelt.)

4. Es ist unwahrscheinlich, dass _____ .   viele Leute nur sehr wenig für ihre Umwelt tun

(Der Unterricht in den Schulen ist sehr locker.)

5. Ich war überrascht, dass _____ .   der Unterricht in den Schulen sehr locker ist

(Die meisten Jugendlichen sind äußerst hilfreich.)

6. Ich habe gestaunt, dass _____ .   die meisten Jugendlichen äußerst hilfreich sind

2 Ein deutscher Austauschschüler, der gerade in die Vereinigten Staaten gekommen ist, drückt seine Enttäuschung (*disappointment*) aus. Schreib die folgenden Sätze ab, und verwende die Information in Klammern als dass-Satz in den Lücken! (**Seite 213**)

(In vielen Städten gibt es nur wenige Fahrradwege.)

1. Ich finde es schade, dass _____ .   es in vielen Städten nur wenige Fahrradwege gibt

(Viele Leute sehen beim Abendessen fern.)

2. Es stört mich, wenn _____ .   viele Leute beim Abendessen fernsehen

(Viele Jugendliche interessieren sich wenig für andere Kulturen.)

3. Ich bedaure, dass _____ .   sich viele J. wenig für andere Kulturen interessieren

(Die meisten Schüler lernen keine Fremdsprachen.)

4. Es stört mich, dass _____ .   die meisten Schüler keine Fremdsprachen lernen

(Viele Leute fahren nur mit dem Auto und gehen nicht zu Fuß.)

5. Ich finde es schade, dass _____ .   viele L. nur mit dem Auto fahren und nicht zu Fuß gehen

(Viele Schüler sind so naiv und interessieren sich nicht für Politik.)

6. Es stört mich, dass _____ .   viele Sch. so naiv sind und sich nicht für P. interessieren

3 Du berichtest von einem deutschen Austauschschüler, der gerade in die Vereinigten Staaten gekommen ist. Schreib jeden der folgenden Sätze als einen Satz, der mit **als** (*when*) beginnt! (**Seite 215**)

1. Der Austauschschüler kam im Juli nach Amerika. Er war erst 16 Jahre alt. Als der Austauschschüler im Juli nach Amerika kam, war er erst 16 Jahre alt.

2. Ich lernte ihn eine Woche später kennen. Er sprach schon ganz gut Englisch. Als ich ihn eine Woche später kennen lernte, sprach er schon ganz gut Englisch.

3. Er kam dann im August in unsere Klasse. Alle Schüler begrüßten ihn ganz herzlich. Als er dann im August in unsere Klasse kam, begrüßten ihn alle Sch. ganz herzlich.

4. Er bekam in Englisch die zweitbeste Note. Er war ganz begeistert. Als er in Englisch die zweitbeste Note bekam, war er ganz begeistert.

5. Er war ein ganzes Jahr bei uns. Er musste wieder nach Hause fliegen. Als er ein ganzes Jahr bei uns war, musste er wieder nach Hause fliegen.

6. Wir brachten ihn alle zum Flughafen. Wir waren sehr traurig. Als wir ihn alle zum Flughafen brachten, waren wir sehr traurig.

Ein deutscher Schüler berichtet über seinen Besuch in den Staaten. Schreib jedes der folgenden Satzpaare als einen Satz, der mit den Wörtern in den Klammern verbunden ist! (**Seite 216**)

4
1. Ich war ein ganzes Jahr in den Staaten. Ich habe dort viel gesehen. (und) Ich war ein ganzes Jahr in den Staaten, und ich habe dort viel gesehen.

2. Ich hatte am Anfang nicht nur Klischeevorstellungen. Ich hatte auch Vorurteile. (sondern) Ich hatte am Anfang nicht nur Klischeevorstellungen, sondern ich hatte auch Vorurteile.

3. Ich baute allmählich meine Vorurteile ab. Es war nicht so einfach. (aber) Ich baute allmählich meine Vorurteile ab, aber es war nicht so einfach.

4. Ich blieb ein ganzes Jahr dort. Ich wollte Land und Leute richtig kennen lernen. (denn) Ich blieb ein ganzes Jahr dort, denn ich wollte Land und Leute richtig kennen lernen.

5. Kennst du die Vereinigten Staaten gut? Kennst du Deutschland besser? (oder) Kennst du die Vereinigten Staaten gut, oder kennst du Deutschland besser?

Mehr Grammatikübungen

Answers

WK3 FRANKFURT-8

Zweite Stufe

Objectives Expressing an assumption; making suggestions and recommendations; giving advice

5 Du sprichst mit einer Klassenkameradin über ihren Besuch im Ausland, und du machst dabei bestimmte Annahmen (*assumptions*). Schreib die folgenden Sätze ab, und schreib dabei die gegebene Information als dass-Satz in die Lücken! (**Seite 221**)

1. Du hast keine Vorurteile. — Ich nehme an, dass _____ .
   du keine Vorurteile hast

2. Du hattest einen guten Eindruck. — Ich vermute, dass _____ .
   du einen guten Eindruck hattest

3. Es hat dir in Köln gut gefallen. — Ich meine doch, dass _____ .
   es dir in Köln gut gefallen hat

4. Du warst sehr beeindruckt. — Ich glaube schon, dass _____ .
   du sehr beeindruckt warst

5. Du hast doch viel gesehen. — Ich vermute, dass _____ .
   du doch viel gesehen hast

6. Du hast dir deine eigene Meinung gebildet. — Ich glaube, dass _____ .
   du dir deine e. M. gebildet hast

6 Schreib Sätze und gebrauche dabei den Ausdruck in Klammern in der ersten Lücke und ein passendes Verb in der zweiten Lücke. (**Seite 221**)

umweltbewusst sein	wandern	tierliebend sein	im Garten essen	gesund essen

(den Eindruck haben)
1. Ich _____ , dass die Deutschen sehr _____ .
habe den Eindruck / umweltbewusst sind

(annehmen)
2. Mein Bruder _____ , dass die Deutschen gern _____ .
nimmt an / ins Theater gehen

(meinen)
3. Wir _____ , dass die Deutschen sehr _____ .
meinen / tierliebend sind

(glauben)
4. Meine Kusine _____ , dass die Deutschen _____ .
glaubt / gesund essen

(wissen)
5. Ich _____ , dass die Deutschen gern _____ .
weiß / im Garten essen

7 Du sprichst mit einem Freund über seine Vorurteile, und du machst dabei gewisse Annahmen. Schreib die folgenden Sätze ab, und schreib dabei die gegebene Information als dass-Satz in die Lücken! (**Seite 222**)

1. Du baust schnell deine Vorurteile über Deutschland ab.

   — Ich stelle mir vor, dass _____ .   du schnell deine Vorurteile über D. abbaust

2. Deine eigenen Klischeevorstellungen fallen dir gar nicht auf.

   — Ich habe den Eindruck, dass _____ .   dir deine eigenen K. gar nicht auffallen

3. Du nimmst nämlich schon die Klischees von anderen Leuten an.

   — Ich vermute, dass _____ .   du nämlich schon die K. von anderen L. annimmst

4. Du gibst nämlich schon die Meinung anderer Leute wieder.

   — Ich habe den Eindruck, dass _____ .   du nämlich schon die M. anderer L. wiedergibst

5. Du lernst im Ausland schnell viele andere Leute kennen.

   — Ich stelle mir vor, dass _____ .   du im A. schnell viele andere Leute kennen lernst

6. Du machst bestimmt irgendwann mal einen Schüleraustausch mit.

   — Ich vermute, dass _____ .   du bestimmt irgendwann mal einen S. mitmachst

8 Du gibst einem Freund Rat (*advice*) und Empfehlungen (*recommendations*). Schreib die folgenden Sätze ab, und schreib dabei die gegebene Information als dass-Satz in die Lücken! (**Seite 223**)

1. Überprüfe deine Vorurteile! — Ich empfehle dir, deine _____ .   Vorurteile zu überprüfen

2. Bau die Vorurteile ab! — Es lohnt sich, die _____ .   Vorurteile abzubauen

3. Nimm keine Vorurteile an! — Ich rate dir, keine _____ .   Vorurteile anzunehmen

4. Gib keine Klischees wieder! — Ich empfehle dir, keine _____ .   Klischees wiederzugeben

5. Verbreite keine Klischees! — Ich empfehle dir, keine _____ .   Klischees zu verbreiten

6. Mach einen Schüleraustausch mit! Es lohnt sich, einen _____ .   Schüleraustausch mitzumachen

9 Du gibst einem Klassenkameraden guten Rat. Schreib die gegebenen Ratschläge um, indem du jeden Ratschlag als Befehlsform schreibst! (**Seite 223**)

Dein Klassenkamerad soll:

1. erst einmal seine Vorurteile abbauen.   Bau erst einmal deine Vorurteile ab!

2. nie wieder Klischeevorstellungen annehmen.   Nimm nie wieder Klischeevorstellungen an!

3. seine eigene Meinung wiedergeben.   Gib deine eigene Meinung wieder!

4. mal andere Länder und Leute kennen lernen.   Lern mal andere Länder und Leute kennen!

5. mal einen Schüleraustausch mitmachen.   Mach mal einen Schüleraustausch mit!

6. mal einen Jugendlichen im Ausland anrufen.   Ruf mal einen Jugendlichen im Ausland an!

Anwendung

Script and answers on p. 207I

1 Jeden Tag kann man im Radio die Sendung „Kurz notiert" hören. Man liest kurze Meldungen aus Zeitungen und Zeitschriften vor. Hör jetzt gut zu! Welche Schlagzeile unten passt zu welcher Meldung? Schreib einige Notizen für jede Schlagzeile, damit du anschließend über die Meldungen diskutieren kannst. Welche Klischeevorstellungen sind zu erkennen? Diskutier mit deinen Klassenkameraden darüber!

CD 8 Tr. 12

Ohne Mutter geht es nicht   **Amerika für junge Mädchen**

Jobs — immer noch   **Ein partnerschaftlicheres**
nach traditioneller Manier   **Leben im Kommen**

Wie alt ist zu alt?

2 Es gibt viele Vorurteile, wenn es zum Thema Mädchen und Jungen kommt. Diese Wörter sollen zum Nachdenken und Diskutieren anregen. Sieh dir die Wörter im Kasten an, und schreib dann die Eigenschaften in zwei Spalten auf!

Mädchen/Jungen

laut   brav   bescheiden   aggressiv
selbständig   stark   fleißig   eitel
schwach   verschwiegen
ruhig   ängstlich
schüchtern   geschickt
schwatzhaft   ordentlich   mutig
still   zurückhaltend

3 Was ist typisch Mädchen? Was ist typisch Junge? Vergleiche deine Liste mit denen deiner Klassenkameraden! Denkt an andere Eigenschaften, die mit Mädchen und Jungen verbunden werden, und schreibt sie hinzu!

4 Mach eine Umfrage! Du kannst mit einem Partner arbeiten. Frag deine Klassenkameraden und auch Schulkameraden nach ihren Interessen und Hobbys! Schreib deine Ergebnisse in eine ähnliche Tabelle wie in Übung 2, Mädchen und Jungen, aber diesmal mit Tatsachen und nicht nur Stereotypen!

5 Kennst du Leute, die nicht zu den Klischeebildern von Mädchen/Jungen, Frauen/Männern passen? Beschreibe diese Personen!

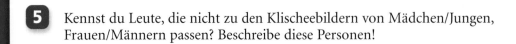

6 Wer als Austauschschüler in ein anderes Land gehen will, muss nicht unbedingt an einem Austauschprogramm teilnehmen. Man kann sich auch an Verwandte oder Bekannte wenden. Anke Weber war im vorigen Jahr als Austauschschülerin in den USA. Von den Webers hat Julia Bauer die Adresse einer amerikanischen Bekannten, die auch Deutsch kann. Lies Julias Brief an Frau Weiß!

> Hagen, den 3. April
>
> Liebe Frau Weiß,
>
> vor ein paar Tagen fragten wir die Webers nach einer amerikanischen Familie, die eventuell ein deutsches Mädchen aufnehmen würde, da wir dachten, dass Anke uns vielleicht weiterhelfen könnte. Herr Weber gab uns dann Ihre Adresse, in der Hoffnung, dass Sie uns helfen könnten. Deshalb wende ich mich jetzt an Sie.
>
> Ich heiße Julia und bin 16 Jahre alt. Da ich hier ziemlich weit von der Stadt entfernt lebe, würde ich es begrüßen, in den USA etwas näher an einer Stadt zu wohnen, wobei die Wohnlage eigentlich das Unwichtigste ist. Die Hauptsache für mich wäre eine nette Familie. Ganz toll fände ich es, wenn die Familie einen Teenager in meinem Alter hätte, damit ich leichten Anschluss zu Gleichaltrigen finden könnte.
>
> Ich möchte entweder für 3 oder 6 Monate in den USA bleiben. Ich wäre sehr an einem Austausch interessiert. Wenn dies nicht möglich ist, würden wir meinen Aufenthalt natürlich bezahlen.
>
> In meiner Freizeit spiele ich sehr gern Tennis. Außerdem mag ich auch Tiere unheimlich gern. Ich wäre sehr glücklich, wenn Sie eine nette Familie für mich ausfindig machen könnten. Im Voraus bedanke ich mich schon recht herzlich bei Ihnen. Hoffentlich sind Sie erfolgreich!
>
> Viele Grüße
> Ihre Julia Bauer

7 Setzt euch in Gruppen zusammen und diskutiert Julias Brief! Kennt ihr eine Familie für Julia? Ist eine von euren Familien geeignet? Warum?

8 Du findest, dass deine Familie für die Julia geeignet ist, oder du kennst eine Familie für sie. Schreib einen Brief an Julia und erzähle davon! (Wenn du keine Familie kennst, erfinde eine!)

9 ## Rollenspiel

Zwei Klassenkameraden spielen die Rollen von deinen Eltern.

1. Du möchtest gern Julia zu euch einladen. Erzähle deinen Eltern davon und versuche, sie zu überzeugen! (*convince*)

2. Du möchtest gern ein Jahr als Austauschschüler in Deutschland verbringen. Du bittest deine Eltern um Erlaubnis. Sie stellen Fragen und du versuchst, sie zu überzeugen.

Kann ich's wirklich?

Can you express surprise, disappointment, and annoyance? (p. 213)

1 How would you express your surprise at hearing that a friend of yours wrote a novel?   E.g.: Ich habe nicht gewusst, dass du einen Roman geschrieben hast.

2 How would you express your disappointment
  a. if your school's team didn't win?   E.g.: Ich bedaure, dass unsere Mannschaft nicht gewonnen hat.
  b. if your teacher said to you **Wir haben keine Austauschschüler aus Deutschland bekommen**?   E.g.: Ich bin enttäuscht, dass wir keine Austauschschüler aus Deutschland bekommen haben.

3 How would you respond if someone annoyed or displeased you by reinforcing stereotypes?   E.g.: Es ärgert mich, dass du denkst, Amerikaner essen nur Fastfood.

Can you express an assumption? (p. 221)

4 How would you express the following assumptions?
  a. Deutsche Wagen sind alle sehr gut.   a. E.g.: Ich vermute, dass deutsche Wagen alle sehr gut sind.
  b. Viele Deutsche haben ihr Amerikabild vom Fernsehen.
  b. Ich nehme an, dass viele Deutsche ihr Amerikabild vom Fernsehen haben.

5 How would you say that before you started studying German, you had the impression all German people drink beer?
Ich hatte mir vorgestellt, dass alle Deutschen Bier trinken.

Can you make suggestions and recommendations? Can you give advice? (p. 223)

6 How would you recommend to someone
  a. that he or she learn German?   a. E.g.: Ich empfehl dir, Deutsch zu lernen.
  b. that he or she visit Germany, Switzerland, and Austria?
  b. E.g.: Es lohnt sich, Deutschland, die Schweiz und Österreich zu besuchen.

7 How would you suggest to someone
  a. to eat a lot of vegetables but little meat?   Ich kann dir einen Tipp geben: iss viel Gemüse aber wenig Fleisch.
  b. to take warm clothes when traveling to Austria?   Ich empfehl dir, warme Kleider mitzunehmen, wenn du nach Österreich reist.
  c. that it is worthwhile to participate in a student exchange program?
  Es lohnt sich, einen Schüleraustausch mitzumachen.

8 How would you advise a friend not to skip class?
E.g.: Schwänz bloß nicht die Schule!

Expressing surprise

Ich hätte nicht gedacht ...	I wouldn't have thought ...
Es ist unwahrscheinlich ...	It's improbable ...
Ich war erstaunt, ...	I was surprised ...
Ich habe gestaunt, ...	I was amazed ...
Ich habe nicht gewusst, ...	I didn't know ...
Ich war überrascht, dass ...	I was surprised that ...

Expressing disappointment

Ich finde es schade, dass ...	I think it's too bad that ...
Ich bin enttäuscht, dass ...	I am disappointed that ...

Expressing annoyance or displeasure

Es regt mich auf, wenn ...	It irritates me when ...
Es stört mich, dass ...	It disturbs me that ...
Es ärgert mich, wenn ...	It annoys me when ...

Ich finde es unangenehm, wenn ...	I think it's unpleasant when ...

Other useful words

die Autobahn, -en	interstate highway
Bezug haben zu	to have a connection to
die Büchse, -n	can
auf jeden Fall	in any case
der, die Jugendliche, -n	teenager
der Kaugummi	chewing gum
das Klischee, -s	cliché
Menge: eine ganze Menge	quite a lot
in der Nähe von	in the vicinity of
in diesem Punkt	in this matter
das Urteil, -e	judgement
die Vorstellung, -en	impression, image
der Weg, -e	path
als (conj)	when, at the time

äußerst	highly
herzlich	heartfelt
hilfreich	helpful
insbesondere	particularly
jedenfalls	in any case
künstlich	artificial
laut	loud
locker	easygoing
nett	nice
offen	open
sämtliche	all
stressig	stressful
begeistert von	enthusiastic about
abbauen (sep): Vorurteile abbauen	to overcome prejudices
annehmen (sep)	to assume
beobachten	to observe
kauen	to chew
überprüfen	to double-check
verbreiten	to spread
wiedergeben (sep)	to repeat
im Voraus	beforehand

Zweite Stufe

Making assumptions

Ich hatte den Eindruck ...	I had the impression ...
Ich hatte mir vorgestellt ...	I had imagined ...
Ich nehme an, dass ...	I assume that ...
Ich vermute, dass ...	I suppose that ...

Making suggestions and recommendations

Ich kann dir einen Tipp geben: ...	I can give you a tip: ...
Ich empfehl dir ...	I recommend ...
Mach das selbst!	Do that yourself!
Es lohnt sich, das zu machen.	It's worth doing.

Other useful words

aufgeschlossen	open, friendly
ausgewogen	well-balanced
dick	fat
durstig	thirsty
ehrgeizig	ambitious
friedliebend	peace-loving
geduldig	patient
gutmütig	good-natured
höflich	polite
kameradschaftlich	friendly
ordentlich	orderly
pünktlich	punctual
stark	strong, robust
still	quiet
stolz sein auf (acc)	to be proud of
streng	strict
stur	stubborn
tierlieb	animal-loving

umweltbewusst	environmentally conscious
der Behälter, -	container
der Container, -	recycling bin
das Dirndl, -	traditional costume for females
die Gewalt	violence
die Pflanze, -n	plant
abholen (sep)	to pick up
auffallen (sep)	to notice
Mir ist aufgefallen ...	I noticed ...
beeindrucken	to impress
empfehlen	to recommend
drohen	to threaten
übersetzen	to translate
verwöhnen	to spoil, pamper

Kapitel 9: Aktiv für die Umwelt!
Chapter Overview

Los geht's! pp. 238–239	*Für eine saubere Umwelt, p. 238*			

	FUNCTIONS	**GRAMMAR**	**VOCABULARY**	**RE-ENTRY**
Erste Stufe pp. 240–243	• Expressing concern, p. 240 • Making accusations, p. 241 • Offering solutions, p. 242 • Making polite requests, p. 243	• Subjunctive forms of **können, müssen, dürfen, sollen**, and **sein**, p. 242	• Products and the environment, p. 240	Adjective endings, p. 240 (**Kap. 7/8/11, II; 7, III**); **dass**-clauses, p. 240 (**Kap. 9, I**); **wenn**-clauses, p. 241 (**Kap. 8, II**); **weil**-clauses, p. 241 (**Kap. 8, I**); **sollen**, p. 242 (**Kap. 8, I**); **könnte**-forms, p. 242 (**Kap. 5, III**); **würde**-forms, p. 243 (**Kap. 11, II**)

Weiter geht's! pp. 244–245	*Die Umwelt-AG diskutiert: Umwelttipps für Schüler, p. 244*			

Zweite Stufe pp. 246–251	• Saying what is being done about a problem, p. 247 • Offering solutions, p. 248 • Hypothesizing, p. 249	• The passive voice, present tense, p. 247 • Use of a conjugated modal verb in the passive, p. 248 • Conditional sentences, p. 249	• Recycling and the environment, p. 246	**Würde**-forms, p. 246 (**Kap. 11, II**); **könnte**-forms, p. 246 (**Kap. 5, III**); **werden**, p. 247 (**Kap. 10, II**); environment vocabulary, p. 248 (**Kap. 7, II**); subjunctive forms, p. 249 (**Kap. 4/5, III**)

Zum Lesen pp. 252–254	Die Welt gehört allen!	**Reading Strategy** Interpreting statistics

Zum Schreiben p. 255	Als Kanzler würde ich alles ändern!	**Writing Strategy** Analyzing your audience

Mehr Grammatik-übungen	**pp. 256–259** Erste Stufe, pp. 256-257	Zweite Stufe, pp. 258–259

Review pp. 260–263	Anwendung, pp. 260–261	Kann ich's wirklich?, p. 262	Wortschatz, p. 263

CULTURE

• Environmental concerns, pp. 240, 241	• Landeskunde: Ein umweltfreundlicher Einkauf, p. 251

Kapitel 9: Aktiv für die Umwelt!
Chapter Resources

Lesson Planning

One-Stop Planner

Lesson Planner with Substitute Teacher Lesson Plans, pp. 51–55, 83

Student Make-Up Assignments
- Make-Up Assignment Copying Masters, Chapter 9

Listening and Speaking

Listening Activities
- Student Response Forms for Listening Activities, pp. 67–70
- Additional Listening Activities 9-1 to 9-6, pp. 71–74
- Scripts and Answers, pp. 167–174

Video Guide
- Teaching Suggestions, p. 40
- Activity Masters, pp. 41–42
- Scripts and Answers, pp. 68–70, 75–76

Activities for Communication
- Communicative Activities, pp. 33–36
- Realia and Teaching Suggestions, pp. 91–95
- Situation Cards, pp. 129–130

Reading and Writing

Reading Strategies and Skills Handbook, Chapter 9

Lies mit mir! 3, Chapter 9

Übungsheft, pp. 105–117

Grammar

Grammatikheft, pp. 73–81

Grammar Tutor for Students of German, Chapter 9

Assessment

Testing Program
- Grammar and Vocabulary Quizzes, **Stufe** Quizzes, and Chapter Test, pp. 191–204
- Score Sheet, Scripts and Answers, pp. 205–211

Alternative Assessment Guide
- Portfolio Assessment, p. 24
- Performance Assessment, p. 38

Student Make-Up Assignments
- Alternative Quizzes, Chapter 9

 Online Activities
- Interaktive Spiele
- Internet Aktivitäten

 Video Program
- Videocassette 2

 Audio Compact Discs
- Textbook Listening Activities, CD 9, Tracks 1–19
- Additional Listening Activities, CD 9, Tracks 24–29
- Assessment Items, CD 9, Tracks 20–23

 Teaching Transparencies
- Situations 9-1 to 9-2
- **Mehr Grammatikübungen** Answers
- **Grammatikheft** Answers

 One-Stop Planner CD-ROM

Use the **One-Stop Planner CD-ROM with Test Generator** to aid in lesson planning and pacing.

For each chapter, the **One-Stop Planner** includes:
- Editable lesson plans with direct links to teaching resources
- Printable worksheets from resource books
- Direct launches to the HRW Internet activities
- Video and audio segments
- Test Generator
- Clip Art for vocabulary items

Kapitel 9: Aktiv für die Umwelt!

Projects

Schule und Umwelt

Students will organize an Adopt-a-Classroom campaign for which they will initiate concrete tasks to help alleviate the environmental concerns with which a typical class might be faced on a daily basis. Students offer ideas through posters, slogans, and practical realia. This project will be done in German but should be designed in such a way that students, that have not taken German, will understand the main idea of this project.

MATERIALS

✂ **Students may need**
- posterboard
- scissors
- markers
- boxes
- glue or tape

SUGGESTED SEQUENCE

1. Students decide to work in pairs or small groups.

2. Each pair or group approaches a teacher or class they would like to adopt. Students could also adopt a common area such as the cafeteria, the library, custodial services, or administrative offices.

3. Students take notes as they examine the problems and needs of the classroom or area on which they plan to work.

4. Students make an outline of the ideas they have for the room.

5. Students then prepare a plan of action which they discuss with the teacher of that class.

6. Students plan and lay out their posters, leaving space for catchy slogans.

7. After all projects are completed, students share and discuss them in class.

8. The final project is then taken to the designated classroom and presented to that teacher and class.

GRADING THE PROJECT

Suggested point distribution (**total = 100 points**)
Appearance of project/Originality 40
Accuracy of language 30
Oral presentation 30

Games

Antworten jagen

*This game, which was first introduced in Level 1 (**Heiß auf der Spur,** p. 331C), can be easily adapted to this chapter and its vocabulary.*

Preparation Compile a list of items or cues that will help students review the vocabulary from this chapter. This list will become the "scavenger list."

Procedure Give a copy of the list to each pair or group of students. Determine a time limit in which students can search for things or answer the questions on their lists. The group that has provided the most correct answers and gathered the most items when time is called wins.

Examples:

Wie viele Mülleimer gibt es in dieser Klasse?

Wo befindet sich der Container für Recyclingpapier auf dieser Etage?

Sucht eine leere Aludose, und bringt sie zur Klasse!

Wo befindet sich der große Abfallcontainer der Schule?

Storytelling

Mini-Geschichte

This story accompanies Teaching Transparency 9-1. The Mini-Geschichte can be told and retold in different formats, acted out, written down, and read aloud to give students additional opportunities to practice all four skills.

Bericht des Raumschiffs Ypsilon über den Planeten Erde:

Wir fliegen in geringer Entfernung über einen Planeten im Sonnensystem. Der Planet hat riesige Ozonlöcher über dem Südpol und auch dem Nordpol, die sich weiterhin vergrößern. Die Ursache sind wahrscheinlich Treibgase. Große Ölteppiche bedecken die Meere. Wir vermuten, dass es in diesen Meeren keine Tiere gibt. Die Atmosphäre ist stark verschmutzt. Die Ursache der Verschmutzung sind wahrscheinlich die Abgase von den vielen Fabriken. Diese Abgase könnten auch das weit verbreitete Waldsterben verursacht haben. Dieser Planet ist stark verschmutzt und scheint äußerst giftig. Kontaktaufnahme wird nicht empfohlen. Ende.

Traditions

Der Osterspaziergang

Tausende von Goethefreunden wanderten am Ostermontag 1999 anlässlich des 250. Geburtstags des Dichters vom Goethehaus zur Gerbermühle.

Dieser Osterspaziergang stellt die Lebensstationen Goethes dar, von seiner Geburt im Goethehaus 1749 bis zu seiner Grablegung 1832 an der Gerbermühle.

Der Osterspaziergang wird jetzt jedes Jahr wiederholt. Das Fest hat den Charakter eines Kunstkarnevals und stellt eine sinnenfrohe Nachahmung eines Kreuzwegs dar. Künstler, Schauspieler, Kabarettisten, und Sänger geben den ganzen Tag lang Aufführungen.

In *Faust I* (1808) beschreibt Goethe einen „Osterspaziergang":

Vom Eise befreit sind Strom und Bäche
Durch des Frühlings holden, belebenden Blick,
Im Tale grünet Hoffnungsglück;
Der alte Winter, in seiner Schwäche,
Zog sich in rauhe Berge zurück.
Von dort her sendet er, fliehend, nur
Ohnmächtige Schauer körnigen Eises
In Streifen über die grünende Flur.

Rezept

Frankfurter Grüne Soße

Zutaten

Frische Küchenkräuter (Schnittlauch, Petersilie, Borretsch, Sauerampfer, Pimpinelle, Zitronenmelisse und Kerbel)

2 mittlere Gewürzgurken

2 Knoblauchzehen

4 Eier (zwei hart gekochte Eier und zwei Eigelbe)

1 Zitrone

Senf

Salz

weißer Pfeffer

Joghurt, saure Sahne und Crème fraîche (zu gleichen Teilen)

Zubereitung

Die zwei hart gekochten Eier fein hacken. Die Kräuter und Zwiebeln fein hacken und die Gewürzgurken fein würfeln. Den Joghurt, die saure Sahne und die Crème fraîche miteinander verrühren. Die zwei Eigelbe dieser Soße unterziehen und die Knoblauchzehen ausgedrückt hinzufügen. Die Soße mit einigen Spritzern Zitronensaft, Senf, Pfeffer und Salz abschmecken. Jetzt die gehackten Eier, Kräuter, Zwiebeln, und Gewürzgurken unterheben.

Beilage

Salzkartoffeln

Kapitel 9: Aktiv für die Umwelt!
Technology

One-Stop Planner CD-ROM

To preview all resources available for this chapter, use the **One-Stop Planner CD-ROM**, Disc 3.

Internet Connection

ADRESSE: go.hrw.com
KENNWORT: WK3 FRANKFURT-9

*Have students explore the __go.hrw.com__ Web site for many online resources covering all chapters. All Chapter 9 resources are available under the keyword **WK3 Frankfurt-9**. Interactive games practice the material and provide students with immediate feedback. You will also find a printable worksheet that provides Internet activities that lead to a comprehensive online research project.*

Interaktive Spiele

You can use the interactive activities in this chapter
- to practice grammar, vocabulary, and chapter functions
- as homework
- as an assessment option
- as a self-test
- to prepare for the Chapter Test

Internet Aktivitäten

Students find the ozone level for Vienna. They analyze environmental laws and read about campaigns in Germany or Austria that aim to reduce air pollution.

- To prepare students for the **Arbeitsblatt,** have them read **Los geht's!** on pp. 238–239 again. Have students look over the list they made in Activity 1 and the notes they took in Activity 2, p. 239.
- After completing the **Arbeitsblatt,** ask students to find out if their community participates in programs to reduce air pollution, e.g., Ozone Action Days. Students should describe the program and provide statistics, if available.

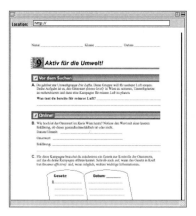

Webprojekt

Have students visit the site of the **Umweltministerium** of a German federal state. Students should report on the history of the department, its function, and at least one of its programs or campaigns. Encourage students to exchange useful Web sites with their classmates. Have students document their sources by referencing the names and URLs of all the sites they consulted.

Textbook Listening Activities Scripts

The following scripts are for the listening activities found in the *Pupil's Edition*. For Student Response Forms, see *Listening Activities*, pages 67–70. To provide students with additional listening practice, see *Listening Activities*, pages 71–74.

Erste Stufe

4   p. 240

JULIA   Also, mir macht am meisten Angst, dass die Müllberge so wahnsinnig wachsen. Manchmal denke ich, dass wir eines Tages in unserem eigenen Müll ersticken! Ich finde es blöd, dass so viele Industrieländer heutzutage in einer Wegwerfgesellschaft leben. Vieles, was man in den Supermärkten kauft, ist zwei- oder dreimal verpackt. Das macht es sehr schwierig, den Müllberg zu verkleinern. Bei uns am Stadtrand gibt es eine riesige Müllkippe. Wenn man sieht, wie viele Lastwagen dort jeden Tag hinfahren, dann bekommt man es schon mit der Angst zu tun. Ich finde, jeder sollte versuchen, in seinem eigenen Haushalt den Müll zu reduzieren. In meiner Familie versuchen alle, möglichst wenig Müll zu produzieren. Wir kaufen nur Pfandflaschen und fast nur Produkte mit dem Grünen Punkt und dem Blauen Engel drauf. Außerdem nehmen wir immer einen Korb und ein paar Stoffbeutel zum Einkaufen mit, damit wir keine Plastiktüten beim Einpacken brauchen. Am Ausgang im Supermarkt schmeißen wir die extra Verpackungen von den Produkten, die wir gekauft haben, in die Tonnen. Dann brauchen wir nämlich den Müll erst gar nicht mit nach Hause zu schleppen. Ich finde das zwar gut, dass die Supermärkte gesetzlich verpflichtet sind, diese überflüssigen Verpackungen zurückzunehmen, aber der Müllberg wird dadurch noch lange nicht reduziert! Ich finde, die Regierung soll noch mehr und vor allem strengere Gesetze machen, damit die Müllberge verkleinert werden.

HELGA   Ich fürchte, dass die Regierungen einfach zu wenig gegen die Umweltverschmutzung unternehmen. Die Industrien in der ganzen Welt tragen wahnsinnig zur Umweltverschmutzung bei, aber es gibt einfach nicht genug Gesetze, um das Problem zu lösen. Also, nehmen wir doch zum Beispiel mal die Produkte mit dem FCKW. Obwohl man wusste, dass sie umweltschädlich sind, hat es einige Jahre gedauert, bis die Produktion mit FCKW verboten wurde. Ich fürchte, dass die Industriekonzerne halt zu mächtig sind und einen zu großen Einfluss auf die Regierung haben. Die FCKW-Produktion wurde auch erst verboten, als die Industrien einen Ersatzstoff gefunden hatten. Da kann man mal sehen, was für eine politische Sache das Ganze ist! Ich fürchte wirklich, dass manchen Regierungen der industrielle Wohlstand wichtiger ist als die Umwelt! Ich habe in letzter Zeit sehr viel über das Ozonloch gelesen. Das wird immer größer. Ich finde, dass nicht nur ein paar Regierungen Gesetze zum Umweltschutz erlassen sollten, sondern es müsste Gesetze zum Umweltschutz geben, die weltweit gültig sind! Alle Regierungen müssten sich daran beteiligen! Ich würde dafür kämpfen, wenn ich Politikerin wäre.

PETER   Ich möchte nach der Schule Forstwirtschaft studieren. Ich interessiere mich sehr für die Natur und gehe viel hier bei uns in Greifswald wandern. Also, mir macht das Waldsterben sehr große Sorgen. Wenn das so weitergeht, dann haben wir bald keine gesunden Bäume mehr in Deutschland! Neulich hat man untersucht, wie groß die Waldschäden in Deutschland sind. Es wurde festgestellt, dass es hier bei uns in Mecklenburg-Vorpommern die größten Waldschäden gibt. 62 Prozent der Bäume sind krank! Das macht mich selbst ganz krank, wenn ich das höre! Der saure Regen und die Luftverschmutzung sind hauptsächlich daran schuld. Wir wohnen ganz in der Nähe von einer Chemiefabrik, und ich könnte mir vorstellen, dass die bestimmt eine ganze Menge Gift in die Luft pumpen. Und das Gift wird von den Bäumen aufgenommen und verdrängt andere Nährstoffe, die lebenswichtig für die Erhaltung der Bäume sind. Eigentlich könnte man viel mehr unternehmen, um die Natur vor der Luftverschmutzung zu schützen. Als Allererstes sollte man weniger Auto fahren und mehr Fahrgemeinschaften bilden. Außerdem sollte die Regierung die öffentlichen Verkehrsmittel viel billiger machen und das Benzin teurer machen.

Answers to Activity 4

Julia: Die wachsenden Müllberge machen ihr Angst. / Sie schlägt vor, dass jeder in seinem eigenen Haushalt den Müll reduzieren sollte und dass die Regierungen mehr Gesetze machen sollen, um die Müllproduktion zu verkleinern.

Helga: Fürchtet, dass die Regierungen zu wenig gegen Umweltverschmutzung tun; fürchtet, dass Industriekonzerne zu mächtig sind und großen Einfluss auf die Regierungen haben; fürchtet, dass manchen Regierungen der industrielle Wohlstand wichtiger ist als die Umwelt. / Schlägt vor, dass es Gesetze zum Umweltschutz geben sollte, die weltweit gültig sind.

Peter: Das Waldsterben macht ihm große Sorgen. / Er schlägt vor, dass man weniger Auto fahren sollte und mehr Fahrgemeinschaften bilden sollte; er schlägt vor, dass die Regierung die öffentlichen Verkehrsmittel billiger machen sollte und das Benzin teurer machen sollte.

8   p. 242

RADIOANSAGER   Fühlen Sie sich öfters müde und schlapp? Merken Sie, wie häufig Sie das Auto nehmen, um zum Einkaufen zu fahren, auch wenn der Supermarkt gleich um die

Ecke ist? In unserer modernen Industrie-gesellschaft treiben die Menschen immer weniger Sport. Es ist bekannt, dass man sich wenig leistungsfähig fühlt, wenn man sich nicht ausreichend körperlich bewegt. Der Deutsche Fahrradclub gibt Ihnen Anregungen, wie Sie sich und unsere

Umwelt gesund erhalten können. Entdecken Sie Ihr Fahrrad wieder! Holen Sie es aus dem Keller, aus der Garage, aus dem Schuppen! Machen Sie mit bei einer der beliebtesten Sportarten der Deutschen: dem Radeln! Radeln Sie allein oder mit einem Freund auf dem Tandem! Radeln Sie im Verein oder mit der Clique! Sparen Sie Benzinkosten! Vermeiden Sie monatliche Gebühren für aerobische Fitnesskurse! Genießen Sie wieder die Natur! Vergessen Sie die ärgerliche Parkplatzsuche! Beteiligen Sie sich nicht an der Umweltverschmutzung, die durch Autoabgase verursacht wird! Tragen Sie zur Erhaltung der sauberen Luft bei! Erledigen Sie Ihre Besorgungen und Besuche im Umkreis mit dem Rad! Sie wer-den sich wundern, wie Sie sich schon nach kurzer Zeit wieder schwungvoll, fit und aktiv fühlen werden! Radeln ist angesagt!

Answers to Activity 8
Possible answers: weil man müde und schlapp ist; weil es eine der beliebtesten Sportarten der Deutschen ist; weil man Benzinkosten sparen kann; weil man keine monatlichen Gebühren für Fitnesskurse ausgeben muss; weil man die Natur genießen kann; weil man keinen Parkplatz suchen muss; weil man sich nicht an der Umweltverschmutzung beteiligt, die durchs Autofahren verursacht wird; weil man zur Erhaltung der sauberen Luft beiträgt; weil man sich wieder schwungvoll, fit und aktiv fühlen wird

Zweite Stufe

17 p. 247

1. Mehr Durst?—Mehr Flaschen!—Mehrwegflaschen!!!
2. Bilden Sie Fahrgemeinschaften! Damit Deutschlands Luft sauber bleibt!
3. Müllberge von heute sind die Zukunft von morgen!
4. Rauf aufs Rad! Rein in die Natur!
5. Haben Sie schon Bekanntschaft mit dem Blauen Engel gemacht?
6. Umweltbewusstsein und Verantwortung durch Recycling!

19 p. 247

MONI Du, Rolf, ich finde, wir haben schon eine ganze Menge in der Umwelt-AG gelernt. Die Beckenbauer macht das wirklich gut!

ROLF Ja, auch mein Interesse an Umweltschutz ist deutlich gestiegen, seit ich in der Umwelt-AG bin, Moni.

ULLA Tja, also ich bin erstaunt, wie viel wir hier in Deutschland schon für den Umweltschutz gemacht haben. Ich wusste gar nicht, dass wir ein Beispiel für andere Länder sind.

MONI Siehst du, Ulla! Und du hattest zuerst keine Lust, bei der Umwelt-AG mitzumachen!

ULLA Na ja, aber ich bin echt geschockt, wie viele andere Länder einfach gar nichts für die Umwelt tun. Man sollte sich echt mal dafür engagieren, dass in diesen Ländern endlich was getan wird!

MONI Ja, Ulla, mich hat es auch geschockt, was wir da in der Umwelt-AG gelernt haben. Aber weißt du, eigentlich bin ich der Meinung, dass man sich zuerst für seine eigene Umgebung einsetzen soll. Ich glaube, es gibt genug, was noch hier zu verbessern wäre.

ROLF Moni hat Recht. Es reicht einfach nicht, nur Glas und Papier zum Container zu bringen.

ULLA Was meinst du, sollten wir noch tun?

ROLF Wir sollten darauf achten, dass wir hauptsächlich Sachen aus Recyclingmaterial kaufen! Hier, schaut mal! Meine Schulhefte zum Beispiel, die sind alle aus wieder verwertetem Altpapier. Viele Leute mögen keine recycelten Sachen, weil sie die Qualität nicht so gut finden. Ich finde, man kann der Umwelt zuliebe ruhig auf einiges verzichten.

ULLA Ja, ich bin deiner Meinung! Ich benutze auch nur Briefpapier, das recycelt ist.

MONI Also, mir ist die Verwendung von Mehrwegflaschen wichtig. Wenn ich unsere Einkäufe für zu Hause erledige, kaufe ich immer Milch in Mehrwegflaschen.

ULLA Ich kaufe immer Joghurt in Glasfläschchen. Ich finde die Plastikbecher verursachen einen zu großen Müllberg.

MONI Ja, und außerdem lassen sich nicht alle Plastiksorten recyceln. Bei Glas ist das kein Problem. Das bringt man einfach zum Container. Glas wird dann verflüssigt und zu neuen Produkten geformt.

ROLF Du musst halt nur Joghurt kaufen, der in Plastikbehältern ist, die man recyceln kann. Die haben doch den Grünen Punkt drauf! Der ist ganz leicht zu erkennen. Zu Hause sammeln wir den Plastikmüll getrennt. Ich find's toll, dass man Plastik einschmelzen kann, um daraus wieder neue Produkte zu machen.

MONI Tja, also warum sprechen wir nicht das nächste Mal in der Umwelt-AG darüber, was wir sonst noch alles außer Recyceln tun könnten?!

ULLA Gute Idee!

Answers to Activity 19
Schulhefte: aus wieder verwertetem Altpapier
Briefpapier: recycelt
Milch: in Mehrwegflaschen
Joghurt: in Glasfläschchen (Glas kann man zum Container zum Recyceln bringen.)
Joghurt: in Plastikbechern mit dem Grünen Punkt (Wieder verwertbares Plastik kann man vom restlichen Müll sortieren, damit es recycelt werden kann.)

23 p. 250

1. ARMIN Wir sortieren den Müll zu Hause und bringen Glas, Plastik und Papier in die Recycling-Container. Ja, und dann gehöre ich einer Umweltschutzgruppe an unserer Schule an. Wir haben uns dafür eingesetzt, dass Aluminium-

und Altpapiercontainer auf dem Schulhof aufgestellt wurden. Außerdem haben wir den Hausmeister erfolgreich davon überzeugt, dass es umweltfreundlicher ist, Getränke in Mehrwegflaschen zu verkaufen und nicht mehr in einzelnen Dosen oder so. Er ist jetzt auch ganz umweltbewusst geworden und hat sogar vorgeschlagen, dass jedes Getränk fünf Cent weniger kostet, wenn die Schüler ihr eigenes Glas oder ihren eigenen Becher mitbringen.

2. MARIA   Es macht mich echt immer traurig, wenn ich vom Waldsterben höre. Diese ganzen Autoabgase sind mit an der Luftverschmutzung schuld! Ich finde, man sollte nicht so viel Auto fahren. Ich hab auch gar keine Lust, mir ein Auto zu kaufen oder den Führerschein zu machen, wenn ich 18 werde! Ich fahre weiterhin mit dem Fahrrad oder gehe zu Fuß. Nur wenn's regnet, dann nehme ich halt den Bus.

3. FELIX   Ich gehöre einer Jugendgruppe an, die sich für den Umweltschutz engagiert. Einmal in der Woche sammeln wir Müll vom Straßenrand und von Kinderspielplätzen auf. Also, ich kaufe sehr viele Sachen aus recyceltem Papier, also Hefte und Schreibblöcke für die Schule, Briefpapier und natürlich auch Toilettenpapier und so.

4. TANJA   Ich kaufe grundsätzlich nur Produkte mit dem Grünen Punkt oder dem Blauen Engel drauf. Außerdem achte ich darauf, dass ich solche Produkte, die einen wahnsinnigen Verpackungsmüll hinterlassen, erst gar nicht kaufe. Und wenn es sich nicht vermeiden lässt, also wenn ich doch mal was brauche, was tausendfach verpackt ist, dann lass ich auf jeden Fall den Müll im Laden zurück.

Answers to Activity 23
1. Armin: sortiert Müll; bringt Glas, Plastik und Papier in Recycling-Container; gehört einer Umweltschutzgruppe an; hat sich mit der Gruppe dafür engagiert, dass der Schulhof Alu- und Altpapier-Container bekommen hat; hat mit der Gruppe den Hausmeister überzeugt, nur noch Mehrwegflaschen beim Getränkeverkauf zu benutzen.
2. Maria: will kein Auto kaufen; fährt mit dem Rad oder geht zu Fuß.
3. Felix: gehört einer Gruppe an, die sich für den Umweltschutz engagiert; sammelt mit der Gruppe Müll vom Straßenrand und von Kinderspielplätzen; kauft Sachen aus recyceltem Papier.
4. Tanja: kauft nur Produkte mit dem Grünen Punkt oder dem Blauen Engel drauf; kauft keine Produkte, die eine große Verpackung haben; lässt Verpackungsmüll im Laden zurück.

Anwendung

2   p. 260

THOMAS   Hallo, alle zusammen! Ich heiße Thomas Burghofer und bin Mitglied der Umwelt-AG hier an der Schule. Wir, das heißt ein Team von fünfzehn Schülern, treffen uns meistens ein- oder zweimal pro Woche, um Aktionen gegen Umweltverschmutzung zu besprechen, zu organisieren und durchzuführen. Manche von euch kennen uns sicherlich schon. Wir waren es, die vor einigen Monaten die Recycling-Container im

One-Stop Planner CD-ROM

For resource information, see the **One-Stop Planner CD-ROM**, Disc 3.

Schulhof aufgestellt haben. Fast jeden Tag sehen wir im Fernsehen Berichte über Naturkatastrophen, verseuchte Landstriche, über das Waldsterben, über die Verschmutzung der Weltmeere und so weiter und so fort. Die Liste kann beliebig lang fortgesetzt werden. Oft fragen wir uns, was wir eigentlich dagegen tun könnten und sind ganz frustriert, wenn wir feststellen, wie wenig Einfluss wir auf den weltweiten Umweltschutz haben. Nun, es mag zwar wahr sein, dass wir nichts gegen solche riesigen Umweltkatastrophen tun können. Aber ihr könnt sicher sein, dass jeder Einzelne, der hier sitzt, einen Beitrag für die Umwelt leisten kann, der unser Umfeld und unsere Umgebung, in der wir leben, entscheidend verbessern kann!

Eins der schlimmsten Probleme ist die Luftverschmutzung durch Abgase von Autos und von der Industrie. Was könnt ihr dagegen tun? Fahrt mit dem Fahrrad oder geht zu Fuß! Öffentliche Verkehrsmittel sind eine andere gute Alternative.

Ein anderes Problem in unserer Gesellschaft ist der wachsende Müllberg. Nehmt Stoffbeutel und Körbe zum Einkaufen mit, und lehnt Plastiktüten an der Kasse ab! Schleppt Verpackungsmüll nicht mit nach Hause, sondern lasst ihn in den Läden! Die Industrie ist gesetzlich dazu verpflichtet, den Müll, den sie mit Verpackungsmaterial produziert, wieder zurückzunehmen.

Jeder von uns produziert Müll. Es ist fast unvermeidbar. Sortiert euren Müll! Bringt Glas, Altpapier, Plastik, Aluminium und Batterien in die entsprechenden Container, damit alles wieder verwertet oder fachgerecht entsorgt werden kann!

Zeigt umweltfreundliches Verhalten bei eurem Pausensnack! Packt eure Pausenbrote nicht jeden Tag in Plastik- oder Aluminiumfolie ein! Nehmt Behälter, die sich auswaschen und wieder verwenden lassen! Kauft eure Getränke in Mehrwegflaschen, nicht in einzelnen Dosen, die weggeschmissen werden!

Vermeidet beim Einkauf umweltschädliche Produkte, die sich nicht im Hausmüll entsorgen lassen! Kauft, zum Beispiel, keine Tintenkiller, die mit gefährlichen Chemikalien getränkt sind!

Answers to Activity 2
Possible answers: mit dem Fahrrad fahren; zu Fuß gehen; öffentliche Verkehrsmittel benutzen; Stoffbeutel und Körbe zum Einkaufen nehmen; Plastiktüten ablehnen; Verpackungsmüll im Laden lassen; Müll sortieren; Müll in Container bringen; Pausensnack in wieder verwendbare Behälter einpacken; Getränke in Mehrwegflaschen kaufen; keine schädlichen Produkte kaufen.

Kapitel 9: Aktiv für die Umwelt!
Suggested Lesson Plans *50-Minute Schedule*

Day 1

CHAPTER OPENER 5 min.
- Teaching Suggestions, ATE, p. 235M

LOS GEHT'S! 20 min.
- Preteaching Vocabulary, ATE, p. 235N
- Advance Organizer, ATE, p. 235N
- Play Audio CD for **Los geht's!**
- Have students read **Los geht's!**, pp. 238–239
- Do Activities 1, 2, and 3, p. 239

ERSTE STUFE

Wortschatz, So sagt man das!, p. 240 10 min.
- Presenting **Wortschatz, So sagt man das!**, ATE, p. 235O
- Play Audio CD for Activity 4, p. 240
- Do Activity 5, p. 241

So sagt man das!, p. 241 10 min.
- Presenting **So sagt man das!**, ATE, p. 235O
- Do Activities 6 and 7, pp. 241–242

Wrap-Up 5 min.
- Students respond to questions about environmental problems

Homework Options
Grammatikheft, pp. 73–75, Acts. 1–5
Übungsheft, pp. 105–107, Acts. 1–3

Day 2

ERSTE STUFE

Quick Review 10 min.
- Check homework, Grammatikheft, pp. 73–75, Acts. 1–5

So sagt man das!, p. 242 10 min.
- Presenting **So sagt man das!**, ATE, p. 235P
- Play Audio CD for Activity 8, p. 242

Grammatik, p. 242 15 min.
- Presenting **Grammatik**, ATE, p. 235P
- Do Activity 9, p. 243

So sagt man das!, p. 243 10 min.
- Presenting **So sagt man das!**, ATE, p. 235P
- Do Activities 10, 11, and 12, p. 243

Wrap-Up 5 min.
- Students respond to questions about what should, could, or must be done for the environment

Homework Options
Grammatikheft, pp. 75–76, Acts. 6–8
Übungsheft, pp. 107–109, Acts. 4–8

Day 3

ERSTE STUFE

Quick Review 10 min.
- Check homework, Übungsheft, pp. 107–109, Acts. 4–8

Umweltprobleme (Video) 15 min.
- Teaching Suggestions, Video Guide, p. 40
- Do Pre-viewing, Viewing, and Post-viewing Activities, p. 40, Video Guide
- Show Video, **Umweltprobleme**

Quiz Review 20 min.
- Do Additional Listening Activities 9-1 and 9-2, p. 71
- Do Activities for Communication 9-1 and 9-2, pp. 33–34
- Do Realia 9-1, Activities for Communication, pp. 91, 94

Wrap-Up 5 min.
- Students respond to questions about environmental problems and solutions for their community

Homework Options
Mehr Grammatikübungen, Erste Stufe

Day 4

ERSTE STUFE

Quick Review 5 min.
- Check homework, **Mehr Grammatikübungen, Erste Stufe**

Quiz 20 min.
- Quiz 9-1A or 9-1B

WEITER GEHT'S! 20 min.
- Preteaching Vocabulary, ATE, p. 235Q
- Play Audio CD for **Weiter geht's!**, pp. 244–245
- Do Activities 13, 14, and 15, p. 245

Wrap-Up 5 min.
- Students respond to questions about environmentally friendly activities in which they could participate at school

Homework Options
Übungsheft, p. 110, Acts. 1–2
Internet Aktivitäten, see ATE, p. 235E

Day 5

ZWEITE STUFE

Quick Review 15 min.
- Return and review Quiz 9-1
- Bell Work, ATE, p. 235R
- Check homework, Übungsheft, p. 110, Acts. 1–2

Wortschatz, p. 246 15 min.
- Presenting **Wortschatz**, ATE, p. 235S
- Do Activity 16, p. 246
- Play Audio CD for Activity 17, p. 247
- Do Activity 18, p. 247

So sagt man das!, Grammatik, p. 247 15 min.
- Presenting **So sagt man das!, Grammatik**, ATE, p. 235S
- Play Audio CD for Activity 19, p. 247
- Do Activity 20, p. 248
- Do Activities 12 and 13, pp. 78–79, Grammatikheft

Wrap-Up 5 min.
- Students respond to questions about what is being done for the environment in their community

Homework Options
Grammatikheft, pp. 77–78, Acts. 9–11
Übungsheft, p. 111, Acts. 1–2

Day 6

ZWEITE STUFE

Quick Review 5 min.
- Check homework, Übungsheft, p. 111, Acts. 1–2

So sagt man das!, p. 248 15 min.
- Presenting **So sagt man das!**, ATE, p. 235S
- Do Activity 21, p. 248
- Do Activity 3, p. 112, Übungsheft

Ein wenig Grammatik, p. 248 20 min.
- Present **Ein wenig Grammatik**, p. 248
- Do Activity 22, p. 248
- Do Activity 14, p. 79, Grammatikheft
- Play game, **Antworten jagen**, ATE, p. 235C

Wrap-Up 5 min.
- Students respond to questions about what can be done to help the environment

Homework Options
Activities for Communication, pp. 93, 95, Realia 9-3; highlight or underline words in different colors indicating different parts of speech

One-Stop Planner CD-ROM

For alternative lesson plans by chapter section, to create your own customized plans, or to preview all resources available for this chapter, use the **One-Stop Planner CD-ROM**, Disc 3.

 For additional homework suggestions, see activities accompanied by this symbol throughout the chapter.

Day 7

ZWEITE STUFE
Quick Review 5 min.
- Check homework, Realia 9-3

So sagt man das!, Grammatik, p. 249
20 min.
- Presenting **So sagt man das!, Grammatik,** ATE, p. 235T
- Teaching Transparency 9-2
- Play Audio CD for Activity 23, p. 250
- Do Activities 24–27, p. 250

LANDESKUNDE 20 min.
- Teaching Suggestions, ATE, p. 235T
- Thinking Critically, ATE, p. 235T
- Multicultural Connection, ATE, p. 235T
- Read **Ein umweltfreundlicher Einkauf,** p. 251
- Do Activities 1–4, p. 251

Wrap-Up 5 min.
- Students respond to questions about which countries they would like to visit if they had the chance

Homework Options
Grammatikheft, pp. 80–81, Acts. 15–17
Übungsheft, pp. 112–114, Acts. 4–9;
p. 115, Acts. 1–3

Day 8

ZWEITE STUFE
Quick Review 10 min.
- Check homework, Grammatikheft, pp. 80–81, Acts. 15–17

Quiz Review 20 min.
- Do **Mehr Grammatikübungen, Zweite Stufe**
- Do Communicative Activities 9-3 or 9-4, pp. 35–36

Quiz 20 min.
- Quiz 9-2A or 9-2B

Homework Options
Interaktive Spiele, see ATE, p. 235E

Day 9

ZWEITE STUFE
Quick Review 15 min.
- Return and review Quiz 9-2

ZUM LESEN 30 min.
- Prereading, Reading, and Post-Reading Notes, ATE, p. 235U
- Present **Lesestrategie,** p. 252
- Do Activities 1–10, pp. 252–254

Wrap-Up 5 min.
- Students answer questions about making hypothetical statements

Homework Options
Übungsheft, pp. 116–117, Acts. 1–4

Day 10

ZWEITE STUFE
Quick Review 10 min.
- Check homework, Übungsheft, pp. 116–117, Acts. 1–4

ZUM SCHREIBEN 35 min.
- Writing Strategy, ATE, p. 235V
- Present **Schreibtipp,** p. 255
- Do Activities A, B, and C, p. 255

Wrap-Up 5 min.
- Students respond to questions about what actions to take to avoid air pollution

Homework Options
Pupil's Edition, p. 255, complete **Zum Schreiben** speech

Day 11

ZUM SCHREIBEN
Quick Review 20 min.
- Read **Zum Schreiben** speeches

ANWENDUNG 25 min.
- Do Activities 1–8, pp. 260–261

Wrap-Up 5 min.
- Students respond to questions about ways to improve the classroom

Homework Options
Interaktive Spiele, see ATE, p. 235E

Day 12

ANWENDUNG
Quick Review 10 min.
- Do Realia 9-2, pp. 92, 94, Activities for Communication

Kann ich's wirklich?, p. 262 20 min.
- Do **Kann ich's wirklich?,** Activities 1–9, p. 262

Chapter Review 20 min.
- Review chapter functions, vocabulary, and grammar; choose from **Mehr Grammatikübungen,** Activities for Communication, Listening Activities, or **Interaktive Spiele**
- Review test format and provide sample test items for students

Homework Options
Study for Chapter Test

Assessment

Test, Chapter 9 45 min.
- Administer Chapter 9 Test. Select from Testing Program, Alternative Assessment Guide or Test Generator.

Kapitel 9: Aktiv für die Umwelt!
Suggested Lesson Plans *90-Minute Schedule*

Block 1

CHAPTER OPENER 5 min.
- Teaching Suggestions, ATE, p. 235M

LOS GEHT'S! 20 min.
- Preteaching Vocabulary, ATE, p. 235N
- Advance Organizer, ATE, p. 235N
- Teaching Suggestion, ATE, p. 235N
- Play Audio CD for **Los geht's!**
- Have students read **Los geht's!**, pp. 238–239
- Do Activities 1, 2 and 3, p. 239

ERSTE STUFE
Wortschatz, So sagt man das!, p. 240 10 min.
- Presenting **Wortschatz, So sagt man das!**, ATE, p. 235O
- Teaching Transparency 9-1
- Play Audio CD for Activity 4, p. 240
- Do Activity 5, p. 241

So sagt man das!, p. 241 10 min.
- Presenting **So sagt man das!**, ATE, p. 235O
- Teaching Transparency 9-1
- Do Activity 6, p. 241
- Do Activity 7, p. 242

So sagt man das!, p. 242 10 min.
- Presenting **So sagt man das!**, ATE, p. 235P
- Play Audio CD for Activity 8, p. 242

Grammatik, p. 242 15 min.
- Presenting **Grammatik**, ATE, p. 235P
- Do Activity 9, p. 243

So sagt man das!, p. 243 15 min.
- Presenting **So sagt man das!**, ATE, p. 235P
- Do Activities 10, 11, and 12, p. 243

Wrap-Up 5 min.
- Students respond to questions about which environmental problems trouble them

Homework Options
Grammatikheft, pp. 73–76, Acts. 1–8
Übungsheft, p. 105, Act. 1 pp. 106–109, Acts. 1–8

Block 2

ERSTE STUFE
Quick Review 10 min.
- Check homework, Grammatikheft, pp. 73–76, Acts. 1–8

Umweltprobleme (Video) 15 min.
- Teaching Suggestions, Video Guide, p. 40
- Do Pre-viewing, Viewing and Post-viewing Activities, p. 41, Video Guide
- Show Video, **Umweltprobleme**

Quiz Review 25 min.
- Do Additional Listening Activities 9-1 and 9-2, p. 71
- Do Activities for Communication, 9-1 and 9-2, pp. 33–34
- Do Realia 9-1, Activities for Communication, pp. 91, 94
- Do **Mehr Grammatikübungen, Erste Stufe**

Quiz 20 min.
- Quiz 9-1A or 9-1B

WEITER GEHT'S! 20 min.
- Presenting **Weiter geht's!**, ATE, p. 235Q
- Play Audio CD for **Weiter geht's!**, pp. 244–245
- Do Activities 13, 14, and 15, p. 245

Homework Options
Übungsheft, p. 110, Acts. 1–2
Internet Aktivitäten, see ATE, p. 235E

Block 3

ZWEITE STUFE
Quick Review 15 min.
- Return and review Quiz 9-1
- Check homework, Übungsheft, p. 110, Acts. 1–2

Wortschatz, p. 246 15 min.
- Presenting **Wortschatz**, ATE, p. 235S
- Do Activity 16, p. 246
- Play Audio CD for Activity 17, p. 247
- Do Activity 18, p. 247

So sagt man das!, Grammatik, p. 247 20 min.
- Presenting **So sagt man das!, Grammatik**, ATE, p. 235S
- Play Audio CD for Activity 19, p. 247
- Do Activity 20, p. 248
- Do Activities 12 and 13, pp. 78–79, Grammatikheft
- Do Activity 2, p. 111, Übungsheft

So sagt man das!, p. 248 15 min.
- Presenting **So sagt man das!**, ATE, p. 235S
- Do Activity 21, p. 248
- Do Activity 3, p. 112, Übungsheft

Ein wenig Grammatik, p. 248 20 min.
- Present **Ein wenig Grammatik**, p. 248
- Do Activity 22, p. 248
- Do Activity 14, p. 79, Grammatikheft
- Play game, **Antworten jagen**, ATE, p. 235C

Wrap-Up 5 min.
- Students respond to questions about what can be done for the environment in their community

Homework Options
Grammatikheft, pp. 77–78, Acts. 9–11
Übungsheft, p. 111, Acts. 1

One-Stop Planner CD-ROM

For alternative lesson plans by chapter section, to create your own customized plans, or to preview all resources available for this chapter, use the **One-Stop Planner CD-ROM**, Disc 3.

 For additional homework suggestions, see activities accompanied by this symbol throughout the chapter.

Block 4

ZWEITE STUFE
Quick Review 10 min.
- Check homework, Grammatikheft, pp. 77–78, Acts. 9–11

So sagt man das!, Grammatik, p. 249 30 min.
- Presenting **So sagt man das!, Grammatik**, ATE, p. 235T
- Play Audio CD for Activity 23, p. 250
- Do Activities 24–27, p. 250
- Do Activities 4–9, pp. 112–114, Übungsheft

LANDESKUNDE 25 min.
- Teaching Suggestions, ATE, p. 235T
- Thinking Critically, ATE, p. 235T
- Multicultural Connection, ATE, p. 235T
- Read **Ein umweltfreundlicher Einkauf**, p. 251
- Do Activities 1–4, p. 251
- Do Activities 1, 2, and 3, p. 115, Übungsheft

Quiz Review 25 min.
- Do **Mehr Grammatikübungen, Zweite Stufe**
- Do Communicative Activities 9-3 and 9-4, pp. 35–36
- Do Realia 9-3, pp. 93 and 95, Activities for Communication

Homework Options
Grammatikheft, pp. 80–81, Acts. 15–17

Block 5

ZWEITE STUFE
Quick Review 10 min.
- Check homework, Grammatikheft, pp. 80–81, Acts. 15–17

Quiz 20 min.
- Quiz 9-2A or 9-2B

ZUM LESEN 35 min.
- Prereading, Reading, and Post-Reading Notes, ATE, p. 235U
- Present **Lesestrategie**, p. 252
- Do Activities 1–10, pp. 252–254

ZUM SCHREIBEN 20 min.
- Writing Strategy, ATE, p. 235V
- Present **Schreibtipp**, p. 255
- Do Activity A, p. 255

Wrap-Up 5 min.
- Students respond to questions about which countries they would like to visit if they had the chance

Homework Options
Pupil's Edition, p. 255, Act. B
Übungsheft, pp. 116–117, Acts. 1–4
Interaktive Spiele, see ATE, p. 235E

Block 6

ZWEITE STUFE
Quick Review 20 min.
- Return and review Quiz 9-2
- Check homework, Pupil's Edition, p. 255, Act. B

ZUM SCHREIBEN 20 min.
- Do Activity C, p. 255
- Present speeches to class

ANWENDUNG 25 min.
- Do Activities 1–8, pp. 260–261

Kann ich's wirklich?, p. 262 20 min.
- Do Activities 1–9, p. 262

Wrap-Up 5 min.
- Students respond to questions about what actions to take to avoid air pollution

Homework Options
Study for Chapter Test

Block 7

ANWENDUNG
Quick Review 15 min.
- Do Realia 9-3, pp. 93 and 95, Activities for Communication

Chapter Review 30 min.
- Review chapter functions, vocabulary, and grammar; choose from **Mehr Grammatikübungen**, Activities for Communication, Listening Activities, or **Interaktive Spiele**
- Review test format and provide sample test items for students

Test, Chapter 9 45 min
- Administer Chapter 9 Test. Select from Testing Program, Alternative Assessment Guide or Test Generator.

Kapitel 9: Aktiv für die Umwelt!
Teaching Suggestions, pages 236–263

Using the Video

Before you begin the chapter, you may want to preview the *Video Program* and consult the *Video Guide.* Suggestions for integrating the video into each chapter are given in the *Video Guide* and in the chapter interleaf of the *Teacher's Edition.* Activity masters for video selections can be found in the *Video Guide.*

PAGES 236–237

CHAPTER OPENER

Pacing Tips

Los geht's! and the **Erste Stufe** center around concerns young people have for the environment. Students learn to express concerns, make accusations, offer solutions, and make polite requests. The subjunctive forms of **können, müssen, dürfen, sollen,** and **sein** are presented on p. 242. **Weiter geht's!** and the **Zweite Stufe** focus on ways to solve environmental problems. Students practice saying what is being done about a problem using the passive voice (p. 247). You might allot a little more time for the **Zweite Stufe** to account for the **Landeskunde.** For Lesson Plans and timing suggestions, see pages 235I–235L.

Meeting the Standards
Communication
- Expressing concern, p. 240
- Making accusations, p. 241
- Offering solutions, p. 242
- Making polite requests, p. 243
- Saying what's being done about a problem, p. 247
- Offering solutions, p. 248
- Hypothesizing, p. 249

Cultures
- **Landeskunde,** p. 251
- Background Information, p. 235Q

Connections
- Multicultural Connection, p. 235Q
- Multicultural Connection, p. 235T
- Speech Connection, p. 235V

Comparisons
- Language-to-Language, p. 235S

One-Stop Planner CD-ROM

For resource information, see the **One-Stop Planner CD-ROM,** Disc 3.

Communities
- Community Link, p. 235M
- Career Path, p. 235P

Advance Organizer

Take a walk with students around school grounds and discuss in German how environmentally friendly the school is. In which areas does the school excel, and which areas could be improved? Have students take notes.

COMMUNITY LINK

Have students find out where the recycling stations are in their area and what materials their neighborhoods recycle.

Teaching Suggestions

Ask students to think of some ways solar energy is or can be used as an energy source. (Examples: sun tea, calculators, hot water, and heating for homes)

Have students describe current environmental issues that concern them. (**Welche derzeitigen Umweltprobleme haltet ihr für wichtig?**)

Chapter Sequence

STANDARDS: 5.2

LOS GEHT'S!

Teaching Resources
pp. 238–239

PRINT
▸ Lesson Planner, p. 51
▸ Übungsheft, p. 105

MEDIA
▸ One-Stop Planner
▸ Audio Compact Discs, CD9, Trs. 1–7

PAGES 238–239

Los geht's! Summary

In *Für eine saubere Umwelt*, adolescents talk about environmental concerns and offer some solutions to the problems. The following learning outcomes listed on p. 237 are modeled in the episode: expressing concern, making accusations, offering solutions, and making polite requests.

Preteaching Vocabulary

Identifying Keywords

Start by asking students to guess the context of **Los geht's!** (students' opinions about the environment). Then have students use the German they know and the context of the situation to identify key words and phrases that are vital to understanding what each German teen thinks. Students should look for words that seem important or that occur several times. Here are a few of the words they might identify as keywords: **Umweltproblem, FCKW, Ozonschicht, Chemikalien, Schadstoffe, Hausmüll, Verschmutzung.** List the keywords on the board or on a transparency and separate them according to whether or not they are cognates. Then ask students to guess the meaning of the keywords. Finally, ask students to identify compound words both among their keywords and in the remainder of the text.

Advance Organizer

Ask students to name one way they and their families help reduce air pollution. (Was tut eure Familie gegen Luftverschmutzung?)

Comprehension Check

Teaching Suggestion

Play the recording of the introduction and then of each report. Have students follow along in the text. Follow each segment with questions to check comprehension. Explain new vocabulary and concepts, including those given in the footnotes, by paraphrasing in German. After working through the four reports, play all of them again. Then ask what they all have in common. Continue with the two long reports on p. 239, again working on one at a time and checking students' understanding of the key points.

Cooperative Learning

Assign small groups of three or four students to do Activities 1 through 3 as a cooperative learning activity within a specified amount of time. Group members should be responsible for one of the three tasks: leader/reader, recorder, and reporter. Upon completion of the assignment, call on the reporters from each group to share their answers and ideas with the rest of the class.

A Slower Pace

To help students get started doing the tasks, ask for volunteers to begin the list for Activities 1 and 2. Put answers on a transparency and discuss them with the class.

Closure

Ask students about ad campaigns that direct their attention toward environmental concerns. What are some of the slogans? (Example: *Don't be a litterbug!*)

STANDARDS: 1.2

ERSTE STUFE

Teaching Resources
pp. 240–243

PRINT
- Lesson Planner, p. 52
- Listening Activities, pp. 67, 71–72
- Video Guide, pp. 39–41
- Activities for Communication, pp. 33–34, 91, 94, 129–130
- Grammatikheft, pp. 73–76
- Grammar Tutor for Students of German, Chapter 9
- Übungsheft, pp. 106-109
- Testing Program, pp. 191–194
- Alternative Assessment Guide, p. 38
- Student Make-Up Assignments, Chapter 9

MEDIA
- One-Stop Planner
- Audio Compact Discs, CD9, Trs. 8–9, 20, 24–26
- Video Program
  Umweltprobleme
  Videocassette 2, 21:16–24:45
- Teaching Transparencies
  Situation 9-1
  Mehr Grammatikübungen Answers
  Grammatikheft Answers

▶ **PAGE 240**

Bell Work

Prepare a **Kreuzworträtsel** for students, using previously learned vocabulary that is related to the environment. Following is a list of words students should know:

Putzmittel *cleaning agent;* **Müll** *garbage;* **wieder verwenden** *to recycle;* **Mehrwegflasche** *refund bottle;* **Altpapier** *recycled paper;* **Lärm** *noise;* **Luft** *air;* **sauber** *clean;* **schmutzig** *dirty;* **Umwelt** *environment*

Using the Video

Videocassette 2, 21:16–24:45
In the video clip *Umweltprobleme,* residents of Würzburg tell what they do for the environment. See *Video Guide,* p. 40, for suggestions.

PRESENTING: Wortschatz

- Present some of the new vocabulary by bringing to class items such as detergent, a plastic bag, and a paper bag. Show these items as you present the words.

- Ask questions in which the new vocabulary is incorporated.
  Examples:
  Kennt ihr Leute, die in einer Fahrgemeinschaft sind?
  Was benutzt deine Familie beim Einkaufen, Papier- oder Plastiktüten?

PRESENTING: So sagt man das!

Have students look over the **Los geht's!** reports on pp. 238–239 and find all phrases that express fear or concern. Then have them make up some additional sentences on their own, reporting what concerns young Germans have.

Communication for All Students

For Additional Practice

4 After students have listened to the conversations and made some notes, ask them if they agree or disagree with each suggestion and if they could offer other suggestions.

▶ **PAGE 241**

Teaching Suggestion

5 Students may need help expressing in complete sentences the reasons given in the **warum?** box. You might first want to practice these with students.
Examples:
Es gibt zu wenige Fahrgemeinschaften.
Leute kaufen zu viele Produkte, die nicht abbaubar sind.

PRESENTING: So sagt man das!

Present the new function to students. Make sure they recognize that the dative case is used in the idiomatic expression **schuld sein an.**

Challenge

6 See if students can come up with more excuses to explain why they don't do more to prevent pollution. Write the additional excuses on a transparency so students can include them in their conversations.
Examples:
Warum soll ich das machen? Andere Leute machen das auch nicht!
Dafür werden Leute bezahlt. Das mache ich nicht umsonst!

▶ PAGE 242

Group Work

7 Divide students into groups of three and have each group chart or diagram the sources of the various environmental problems. Each group should work on a large piece of construction paper and write their ideas with markers. Then have each group share the information with the rest of the class.

Cultures and Communities

Career Path

Ask your students to brainstorm careers in international environmental organizations or aid agencies that would require the knowledge of German. (Suggestions: Imagine you are an environmental engineer studying in Germany; imagine you are a member of an international environment group whose members speak German as their primary language.

PRESENTING: So sagt man das!

- Have students explain why modal verbs are used to express what could or should be done. (They help convey the speaker's feeling or attitude.)

- Remind students that modals have a range of meaning and that the meanings can be quite different from the way the corresponding English modal is used.
Examples:
Wenn wir nur Papierbeutel gebrauchen dürften!
If only we could use paper bags!
Man müsste nur noch Katautos bauen!
They should (would have to) only build cars with catalytic converters!

PRESENTING: Grammatik

- **Subjunctive forms** Remind students that they have already learned the subjunctive forms **hätte** and **würde** in Level 2 (Chapter 11) and the **könnte**-forms in Level 3 (Chapter 5).

- The forms of these modals are the same as the narrative past forms, except that **können, müssen,** and **dürfen** retain the umlaut from the infinitive. **Sein** adds an umlaut to the imperfect form and -e in the first- and third-person singular.

▶ PAGE 243

A Slower Pace

9 Have students respond using simple sentences.
Examples:
Wir müssten Fahrgemeinschaften bilden.
Wir sollten keine Plastiktüten benützen.

PRESENTING: So sagt man das!

Remind students that they already know one way of expressing polite requests by using **möchte.** Explain that this is also a subjunctive form, stemming from **mögen.** On the board or a transparency, make a list of four sentences expressing polite requests. Ask students if they can detect different degrees of politeness or different "registers" of speech. Examples:
Ich möchte bitte einen Papierbeutel.
Könnte ich bitte einen Papierbeutel haben?
Dürfte ich bitte einen Papierbeutel haben?
Würden Sie mir bitte einen Papierbeutel geben?

Kinesthetic Learners

10 Have students role-play this activity. They should use pictures or actual products as props. One student takes on the role of the salesperson, who offers the products listed. Another student plays the customer, who declines the product and requests one that is not harmful to the environment.

Teaching Suggestion

12 In preparation for the journal entry, ask students to complete the statement **Ich wünschte, …,** using a modal verb in the subjunctive. Have them express their environmental concerns.

Examples:
Ich wünschte, man müsste mit dem Fahrrad zur
Schule fahren.
Ich wünschte, die Cafeteria dürfte nur Gläser und
Teller und kein Plastikgeschirr verwenden.

Connections and Comparisons

Multicultural Connection
Have students interview foreign exchange
students or people they know from other countries. They should try to find out about the
environmental problems that other countries
face and the types of solutions that have been
successful.

Assess
▶ Testing Program, pp. 191–194
Quiz 9-1A, Quiz 9-1B
Audio CD9, Tr. 20

▶ Student Make-Up Assignments
Chapter 9, Alternative Quiz

▶ Alternative Assessment Guide, p. 38

WEITER GEHT'S!

Teaching Resources
pp. 244–245

PRINT
▶ Lesson Planner, p. 53
▶ Übungsheft, p. 110

MEDIA
▶ One-Stop Planner
▶ Audio Compact Discs, CD9, Trs. 10–15

 PAGES 244–245

Weiter geht's! Summary

In *Die Umwelt-AG diskutiert: Umwelttipps für
Schüler,* students hold their weekly meeting for their
environmental club. They discuss some articles they
have brought to the meeting. The following learning
outcomes listed on p. 237 are modeled in the
episode: saying what is being done about a problem,
offering solutions, and hypothesizing.

Preteaching Vocabulary

Recognizing Cognates
Weiter geht's! contains many words about the
environment that students will be able to recognize as cognates or borrowed words. Some are
compound words in which only part of the
word is a cognate. Have students identify these
words and describe what is happening in the
article and then in the discussion. Here are just
some of the cognates and borrowed words they
might find: **Energiesparen, Abgase, Abwässer,
Frischwasser, Recyclingpapier, Plastikbecher,
Sonnenkollektor, Tourismus, Skipisten.**

Advance Organizer

Ask students if there are activities in their school in
which students participate to help the environment.
What do they do and what else could be done? (**Wie
könnte man unsere Schule umweltfreundlicher
machen? Könnte noch mehr getan werden?**)

Cultures and Communities

Background Information
• Federal and state agencies, the community, and
the schools in Germany are doing a great deal to
educate people about the environment and
encourage everyone to take part in protecting it.
Students receive instruction, do projects, make
posters, and organize events such as forest and
river cleanups. Students are very conscious of
such things as air and water pollution, damage
to the ozone layer, and the impact of the vanish-
ing rain forests.

• The political party **die Grünen** emerged in 1983
when it won seats in the German **Bundestag** for
the first time. This political party's platform is
based on environmental protection.

Teacher Note

Tintenkiller is a type of pen that students in
Germany use to erase mistakes they make while
writing with a fountain pen. After the **Tintenkiller**
is used to erase a mistake, a special marker, usually
on the other end of the **Tintenkiller**, is used to
correct the mistake.

Connections and Comparisons

Thinking Critically

Comparing and Contrasting Ask students what types of tourist activities could be considered **Sanfter Tourismus**. (Examples: going on a bike tour, visiting a solar-powered resort) What types of activities could not be considered **Sanfter Tourismus**? (Examples: skiing, hunting, driving cross-country)

Comprehension Check

Building on Previous Skills

13 In Level 2, students learned several reading strategies to help them determine the meaning of a text. In this case, the titles of the three articles are very important, in that they give the main idea. Ask students to find supporting details for each title and to write them down. Then put students in pairs or groups of three and have them compare their findings.

Visual Learners

14 Have students use their articles to make a bulletin board display. They could also bring in pictures of various environmentally friendly activities and intersperse the realia with environmental tips, slogans, or titles.
Examples:
Lass die Verpackung da, wo du sie bekommen hast: im Geschäft!
Sei nicht so dumm wie ein Esel, benutz den Drahtesel statt des Autos!

Teaching Suggestion

15 Have students do Activity 15 with a partner. They should make a chart with four columns to write down the suggestions made by the German students. Then call on pairs for their ideas and keep track of them on a transparency or on the board. Ask students to keep their notes as reference for later activities.

Closure

Ask each student to share with the rest of the class one new or interesting fact learned from the **Weiter geht's!** section.

ZWEITE STUFE

Teaching Resources
pp. 246–251

PRINT
▸ Lesson Planner, p. 54
▸ Listening Activities, pp. 68–69, 72–74
▸ Video Guide, pp. 39–41
▸ Activities for Communication, pp. 35–36, 92–93, 94–95, 129–130
▸ Grammatikheft, pp. 77–81
▸ Grammar Tutor for Students of German, Chapter 9
▸ Übungsheft, pp. 111–115
▸ Testing Program, pp. 195–198
▸ Alternative Assessment Guide, p. 38
▸ Student Make-Up Assignments, Chapter 9

MEDIA
▸ One-Stop Planner
▸ Audio Compact Discs, CD9, Trs. 16–18, 21, 27–29
▸ Video Program
  Die Umwelt in der Ex-DDR
  Videocassette 2, 24:47–28:08
▸ Teaching Transparencies
  Situation 9-2
  Mehr Grammatikübungen Answers
  Grammatikheft Answers

> **PAGE 246**

Bell Work
Play the game **Assoziationsfeld** using words from this and previous chapters. See Level 1 (p. 99C) for the procedure. Following are some suggested topics for this **Stufe**: Müll, Luftverschmutzung, Recycling, Umwelt.

Using the Video

Videocassette 2, 24:47–28:08
In the video clip *Die Umwelt in der Ex-DDR*, natives of Dresden talk about environmental problems in the former GDR. See *Video Guide*, p. 40, for suggestions.

PRESENTING: Wortschatz

- Go over the names of the creatures in the **Wortschatz**. Ask students to think of other creatures that are threatened by environmental carelessness.

- Put students in pairs or small groups and have them make sentences with the vocabulary in **auf Deutsch erklärt**.

- When working with the **auf Englisch erklärt** section, ask students to replace one of the words in each sentence but keep the main idea the same.
Example:
Ich müsste ausrechnen, wie viel Benzin ich verbrauche.

Communication for All Students

For Additional Practice

16 Use the art for further practice and review. Students could describe what is happening in each picture and say why it is good or bad. For example, for the first drawing, a student might say: **Die Person wirft die Zeitungen in den Container. Das ist natürlich gut für die Umwelt, denn das Papier wird wieder verwendet.**

PAGE 247

Teaching Suggestion

18 Have students refer to the notes they took for Activity 15. You might also ask some questions such as:
Wie könntest du Energie sparen?
Was könntest du mit alten Batterien tun?

PRESENTING: So sagt man das!

Have students use the new expressions by stating what is currently being done to protect the environment in their home, town, and state.

PRESENTING: Grammatik

- **Passive voice, present tense** Point out to students that in contrast with the active voice, where the subject is the agent, the subject is being acted *upon* in the passive voice. The performer of the action, if stated, is usually indicated by the preposition **von**.

- Have students give the English equivalents for the two examples not translated in the **Grammatik**. (**Das Licht wird ausgemacht.** *The light is being turned off.* **Alte Autos werden wieder verwertet.** *Old cars are (being) recycled.*)

Connections and Comparisons

Language-to-Language

You might want to tell students that in conversational German, the passive voice is used less frequently than in written German. Instead, a number of substitute constructions are often used. For example, the passive sentence "**Das Rad kann nicht mehr repariert werden.**" could be rephrased as:
1. *Man kann* **das Rad nicht mehr reparieren.** (**man** + active verb)
2. **Das Rad** *lässt sich nicht mehr reparieren.* (**sich lassen** + infinitive)
3. **Das Rad** *ist* **nicht mehr** *zu reparieren.* (**sein+zu**+infinitive)

You may want to ask your students about the use of the passive voice in written English. (In general, writers try not to overuse the passive voice because it can make the writing sound weak, awkward, and impersonal. Using the active voice helps make the writing direct and forceful.)

PAGE 248

PRESENTING: So sagt man das!

Ask students to follow the structure of the three examples in **So sagt man das!** as they come up with additional statements using the suggestions from Activity 20.
Example:
Die Wälder müssen geschützt werden.

Communication for All Students

Tactile/Visual Learners

22 Bring to class items or pictures of things to use for this activity. Place them where all students can see them. Have students work with a partner and role-play the functions to be practiced in this activity.
Example: *put out recyclable used items, such as paper, bottles, and batteries*
Student A: **Was soll ich mit diesem Müll hier tun?**
Student B: **Der muss sortiert werden.**
Student A: *sorts items and explains what he or she is doing*

PRESENTING: So sagt man das!

Ask students to compare the two statements in **So sagt man das!** How does the one indicating a realizable condition differ from the one that cannot be realized or fulfilled?

PRESENTING: Grammatik

- **Conditional sentences** Have students observe the word order in the examples. What is the word order in the **wenn**-clauses? What can students observe about the word order in the conclusion when it follows the **wenn**-clause and when it precedes the **wenn**-clause?

- Have students look back at the **Weiter geht's!** section and the statements made by the four students. How many conditional sentences can students find?

Speaking Assessment

25 Have students come to your desk in pairs for assessment of their spoken dialogues. For evaluation, you may wish to use the following rubric.

Speaking Rubric	Points			
	4	3	2	1
Content (Complete – Incomplete)				
Comprehension (Total – Little)				
Comprehensibility (Comprehensible – Incomprehensible)				
Accuracy (Accurate – Seldom accurate)				
Fluency (Fluent – Not fluent)				

18–20: A   16–17: B   14–15: C   12–13: D   Under 12: F

LANDESKUNDE

Teaching Suggestions

- Have students take turns reading the **Landeskunde** text out loud. Stop after each paragraph and clarify new vocabulary by using synonyms or by paraphrasing.

STANDARDS: 1.2, 4.2

- After reading the **Landeskunde** text, ask students what they find interesting or unusual about the way Germans do their grocery shopping. Make a list of students' comments.

- Have students work in groups to answer Questions 1 through 4. Have groups share their answers with the rest of the class.

Connections and Comparisons

Thinking Critically

Comparing and Contrasting Have students reverse the scenario of the **Landeskunde** reading. They should imagine, an exchange student from Germany is staying with an American family. Put students into pairs or groups of three and have each group rewrite the story for the American setting. Have students share their versions with the class.

Multicultural Connection

If possible, have students find out how other countries deal with packing and handling grocery store purchases. Do stores provide bags, help the customer, or accept recyclable packing materials? Have students report their findings to the class.

Teacher Note

Mention to your students that the **Landeskunde** will be also included in Quiz 9-2B given at the end of the **Zweite Stufe**.

(TPR) Total Physical Response

Ask all students to stand up and follow you around the school. On the way, direct commands to individual students, asking them to perform tasks that incorporate some of the functions and vocabulary from the **Erste** and **Zweite Stufen**.
Examples:
Würdest du bitte das Licht in diesem leeren Klassenzimmer ausmachen!
Heb bitte das Butterbrotpapier auf, und wirf es in den Mülleimer!

Assess

▶ Testing Program, pp. 195–198
  Quiz 9-2A, Quiz 9-2B
  Audio CD9, Tr. 21

▶ Student Make-Up Assignments
  Chapter 9, Alternative Quiz

▶ Alternative Assessment Guide, p. 38

ZUM LESEN

Teaching Resources
pp. 252–254

PRINT
▸ Lesson Planner, p. 55
▸ Übungsheft, pp. 116–117
▸ Reading Strategies and Skills, Chapter 9
▸ Lies mit mir! 3, Chapter 9

MEDIA
▸ One-Stop Planner

Prereading
Building Context

Put the following phrase on the board: "Scientific studies show that …" and ask the class to quickly complete it in as many ways they can. (Example: "… brand X toothpaste prevents cavities.") Many of these will probably come from television advertising and be easily recognizable as somewhat extravagant claims. Then ask students to consider the following three completions in terms of what type of claim is expressed and what type of study must have been involved:
a) "… there are more overweight people in the United States now than there were twenty years ago."
b) "… German and Japanese students score much higher in math and science than U.S. students do."
c) "… Rap lyrics are the cause of much juvenile crime." Help students see what groups (or statistics) are being compared in a) and b). Ask them why the third claim seems dubious. Why is it so difficult to prove a cause-and-effect relationship where social trends are concerned?

Teaching Suggestion

Tell students that the article they will read is an interpretation of some studies, and that they should pay careful attention to how the data is being evaluated.

Teacher Note

Activity 1 is a prereading activity.

Reading
Teaching Suggestion

2 Make sure that students notice that the article is divided into two parts. Point out the large-type **O** in the first paragraph and the large-type **W** in Paragraph 5.

Teacher Notes

3 The first part of the essay refers to the second part of the subtitle: *Nevertheless, there is growing ecological awareness and a readiness to make sacrifices for a cleaner environment.* This is implied in the title by "**mehr Bauch**" meaning "*more gut or feeling.*"

4 The second part of the essay contains the assertion that students are still undereducated about environmental issues. This idea is implied in the title by the image of "less **Kopf.**"

Thinking Critically

Evaluation Ask the class what the reader knows about:
a) the researchers who gathered these statistics,
b) the sizes of the samples used (given in Paragraph 1, but not given in Paragraph 8),
c) the actual techniques used to gather/analyze data.
Some discussion questions are:
• Could you make any concrete educational decisions based on the claims made in Paragraph 6? Why or why not?

• Does the Bielefeld study actually show that schools play the most important role in promoting environmental awareness among teens? Does the article include the data needed to prove this implied cause-effect claim?

Post-Reading
Teacher Note

Activities 9 and 10 are post-reading tasks that will show whether students can apply what they have learned.

Teaching Suggestion

10 Before the class designs the group projects, one or more students might want to go to a library and look at a few scientific journals to see how the reporting of statistical findings is handled when the audience is likely to want to replicate the study or base some actions on it. The questionnaires can then be designed to yield more "scientific" results.

Closure

In the final sentence of the article, **DGU-Geschäftsführer** Axel Beyer states that students can influence adults' behavior by serving as good examples, particularly in the area of energy conservation (recycling, etc.). However, the illustrations give a different view of **Schüleraktionen.** Based on this chapter, do students think that the image of dramatic protest or the image of teens working with and encouraging adults in small, everyday actions is more typical of this generation of German youth? How would students compare German and American youth in this respect?

Zum Lesen Answers

Answers to Activity 1
the environment; teens

Answers to Activity 2
a magazine article about a survey; two; **"Opferbereitschaft"**
and **"Ökobewusstsein"**

Answers to Activity 3
(mehr … als, dennoch); Teens know too little about environmental issues, however, environmental awareness and activism are growing; the second part of the main idea

Answers to Activity 4
the first part of the main idea

Answers to Activity 5
The number of students in 1980 and in 1993 who were willing to make monetary sacrifices for the environment; the percentage of students who answered yes to this survey question in 1980 and 1993; **Universität Bielefeld;** A few more teenagers today are willing to make sacrifices for the environment.

Answers to Activity 6
the percentage of students in 1980 and 1993 who took part in various programs to protect the environment (recycling/petitions); teens today are more environmentally active than they were in 1980.

Answers to Activity 7
während, eher, größer, eher, lieber; comparison and contrast

Answers to Activity 8
a. fear for the future
b. The students tested knew very little about current environmental problems.
c. Boys seem to know the facts, but girls tend to be more willing to make sacrifices and take individual action.
d. incorporating environmental education into the curriculum

ZUM SCHREIBEN

> ## Teaching Resources
> ### p. 255
>
> **PRINT**
> ▸ Lesson Planner, p. 55
> ▸ Alternative Assessment Guide, p. 24
>
> **MEDIA**
> ▸ One-Stop Planner
> ▸ Test Generator, Chapter 9

Writing Strategy

The targeted strategy in this writing activity is *analyzing your audience.* Students should learn about this strategy before beginning the assignment.

Prewriting
Building Context

Ask students what they know about campaign speeches. How are they constructed? Make a list of student comments on the board.

Connections and Comparisons

Speech Connection

Ask a student who is taking a speech course to talk about the characteristics of persuasive speech to your class. The next day, model such a speech in German (on a topic other than the environment) that is of interest to students in the school.

Teaching Suggestion

Have students brainstorm German phrases and expressions that could be used to persuade someone of something. Compile a list for students to refer to as they outline their speeches.
Examples:
Wir müssen unbedingt …
Wir sollten …
Glauben Sie mir, wenn ich sage, dass …

Writing

Building on Previous Skills

Students have learned many words and phrases that help organize and shape a text. Remind students to incorporate connectors such as **zuerst, außerdem, erstens, zweitens, zum Schluss, zusammenfassend,** and **weiterhin** in their writing.

Post-Writing

Communication for All Students

Auditory Learners

After students have prepared their speeches, have them record them on audiocassette. Then have students each listen to their own speech, determine the strengths and weaknesses, and make changes before they present their final speech to their audience.

Closure

Let each peer-editing group select the best candidate as in a primary election. Then have the selected candidates give their speeches in front of the class. The class can elect a **Kanzler** based on these speeches. Afterward, have students discuss their reasons for selecting the winner, including the content as well as the style and delivery of the speech.

PAGES 256–259

MEHR GRAMMATIKÜBUNGEN

The **Mehr Grammatikübungen** activities are designed as supplemental activities for the grammatical concepts presented in the chapter. You might use them as additional practice, for review, or for assessment.

For more grammar presentations, review, and practice, refer to the following:
- Grammatikheft
- Grammar Tutor for Students of German
- Grammar Summary on pp. R22–R39
- Übungsheft
- Grammar and Vocabulary quizzes (Testing Program)
- Test Generator
- Interaktive Spiele at go.hrw.com

PAGES 260–261

ANWENDUNG

Teaching Resources
pp. 260–261

PRINT
▸ Lesson Planner, p. 55
▸ Listening Activities, p. 70
▸ Video Guide, pp. 39–40, 42
▸ Grammar Tutor for Students of German, Chapter 9

MEDIA
▸ One-Stop Planner
▸ Video Program
  Videoclips: Werbung
  Videocassette 2, 28:15–33:25
▸ Audio Compact Discs, CD9, Tr. 19

Apply and Assess

 Using the Video
Videocassette 2, 28:15–33:25
At this time, you might want to use the authentic advertising footage from German television. See *Video Guide,* p. 40, for suggestions.

Teaching Suggestion

1 After students have read *Das saubere Klassenzimmer,* ask them to compile a list of the various projects that have been initiated at the **Regino-Gymnasium.** Which of the ideas would students like to try at their school?

Thinking Critically

2 Drawing Inferences After students have listened to the suggestions by the member of the **Umwelt-AG,** ask them which of his suggestions could be adopted by their school. Which ones would not seem necessary or useful? Why?

 Portfolio Assessment

5 You might want to suggest this activity as an oral portfolio item for your students. See *Alternative Assessment Guide,* p. 24.

Teacher Note

5 To analyze the chart, students should know that **Sammelquote** refers to the percentage of each material collected from the total amount that was produced in that year. **Recyclingquote** refers to the percentage of each material recycled from the total amount produced. Students might also want to know that **Verbund** refers to items made up of one or more types of recyclable materials, for example, a paper container with a plastic lining.

Teaching Suggestion

6 After students have compiled their own data (specific information on recycling might be available from the town's recycling center), ask them to compare their data with the German data.

Group Work

7 Divide the class into groups of three or four students and have each group come up with as many examples as possible. Time the activity and see which group comes up with the most ideas.

Portfolio Assessment

7 You might want to suggest this activity as a written portfolio item for your students. See *Alternative Assessment Guide*, p. 24.

▶ **PAGE 262**

KANN ICH'S WIRKLICH?

This page helps students prepare for the test. It is a brief checklist of the major points covered in the chapter. The students should be reminded that it is only a checklist and not necessarily everything that will appear on the test.

For additional self-check options, refer students to the *Grammar Tutor* and the Online self-test for this chapter.

▶ **PAGE 263**

WORTSCHATZ
Thinking Critically

Analyzing Ask students to go over the list of words and determine which of them they consider positive or negative in regard to the environment.

Circumlocution

To review environmental words in both the **Erste Stufe** and the **Zweite Stufe** vocabulary, play **Das treffende Wort suchen**. To set the scene, tell your students that they are discussing various environmental issues with a German **Ökogruppe**. Many of these terms lend themselves to being described by pantomime and sound effects, as well as by using words. For **das Waldsterben**, a combination of verbal clues can be given. For example, for **Wald**, one could say **wo es viele Bäume gibt**, and for **sterben, wenn man das Leben verliert**. See p. 31C for procedures.

Challenge

Ask students to write a story in which they describe an ideal town using as many words from the **Wortschatz** as possible.

Games

Play the game **Antworten jagen**. See p. 235C for the procedure.

Teacher Note

Give the **Kapitel 9** Chapter Test: *Testing Program*, pp. 199–204 Audio CD 9, Trs. 22–23.

REVIEW

9

Aktiv für die Umwelt!

Objectives
In this chapter you will learn to

Erste Stufe

- express concern
- make accusations
- offer solutions
- make polite requests

Zweite Stufe

- say what is being done about a problem
- offer solutions
- hypothesize

 internet

ADRESSE: go.hrw.com
KENNWORT: WK3
FRANKFURT-9

◀ **Ein kleines Auto mit viel Raum**

Los geht's! · *Für eine saubere Umwelt*

Eine saubere Welt und der Umweltschutz sind nach Meinung der meisten Jugendlichen heute ganz besonders wichtig. Manche Jugendliche geben zu, dass sie selbst noch zu wenig für die Umwelt tun; aber die meisten engagieren sich schon aktiv für den Umweltschutz. Was sagen einige Schüler dazu? CD 9 Tr. 1

Das größte Umweltproblem, glaub ich, sind die Abgase. Die verpesten unsere Luft ganz schön. Und hier könnte man einiges tun, wenn nur alle mitmachen würden! Man könnte zum Beispiel Fahrgemeinschaften bilden, damit nicht jeder mit seinem Auto allein fährt. Und man sollte den VV[1] auch billiger machen; dann würden bestimmt mehr Leute mit dem Zug oder mit dem Bus fahren. Und man müsste jetzt nur noch Katautos[2] zulassen — dann könnte unsere Luft bestimmt wieder besser werden.

Mark, 18 CD 9 Tr. 2

Die Luftverschmutzung macht mir große Sorgen und ganz besonders das Ozonloch, das immer größer wird. Ich geh schon gar nicht mehr gern in die Sonne, weil ich vor den UV-Strahlen Angst habe, die Hautkrebs auslösen können. Endlich haben unsere Politiker etwas Positives für die Umwelt getan, das FCKW[3] gesetzlich zu verbieten. FCKW wurde doch als Treibgas in Spraydosen benutzt, und das hat ja wesentlich mit zur Zerstörung der Ozonschicht beigetragen.

Julia, 17 CD 9 Tr. 3

Die Industrie verpestet die Luft immer mehr mit Schmutz. Die Fabriken blasen Schadstoffe und Chemikalien in die Luft, die dann mit dem Regen wieder zurück zur Erde kommen als saurer Regen.

Ulli, 16 CD 9 Tr. 4

Die Abgase von Autos und Lastwagen und die Schadstoffe der Industrie sind am großen Waldsterben schuld — nicht nur hier bei uns in Deutschland, sondern in der ganzen Welt.

Michaela, 17 CD. 9 Tr. 5

---

1. VV ist die Abkürzung für Verkehrsverbund. In den Großstädten der Bundesrepublik darf man innerhalb einer bestimmten Zeit mit einem Fahrschein alle öffentlichen Verkehrsmittel benutzen, die man braucht, um ans Ziel zu gelangen.
2. Katautos sind Autos mit Katalysatoren, die die Luftverschmutzung reduzieren.
3. FCKW ist die Abkürzung für Fluor-Chlor-Kohlenwasserstoff, *chlorofluorocarbons (CFCs)*. Dieses Mittel wurde häufig als Treibgas in Spraydosen benutzt. Solche Spraydosen wurden mehr und mehr durch Pumpzerstäuber ersetzt. Die Verwendung von FCKW in Verbraucherprodukten wurde 1991 gesetzlich verboten. 1995 wurde die gesamte FCKW-Produktion in Deutschland eingestellt.

Wir zu Hause sortieren unseren Hausmüll. Einmal in der Woche bring ich Papier, Flaschen und Aludosen zum Container.[4] Aber ich fürchte, dass viele Leute das nicht tun. Ein grosser Teil des Hausmülls wäre überhaupt vermeidbar. Man müsste Getränke eben ausschließlich in Pfandflaschen kaufen und Einwegflaschen vermeiden. Und man sollte im Geschäft wirklich den Mut haben und sagen: „Dürfte ich bitte einen Papierbeutel haben?", wenn einem ein Plastikbeutel angeboten wird. Plastikbeutel müsste man überhaupt ganz durch Papierbeutel ersetzen.

Stefan, 18
CD 9 Tr. 6

Für mich ist die Verschmutzung des Wassers ein großes Umweltproblem. Durch den sauren Regen gibt es in vielen Seen schon keine Fische mehr, und wenn mal ein riesiger Öltanker irgendwo aufläuft und leck wird, dann verschmutzt das ausgelaufene Öl das Wasser und die Küste kilometerweit. Die Bilder aus Alaska mit den sterbenden Fischen und Vögeln werde ich nie vergessen! Aber ich glaube, jeder muss bei sich selbst anfangen, damit was verändert wird. Man müsste eben wirklich darauf achten, dass man Produkte kauft, die die Umwelt nicht belasten. Wir zu Hause kaufen zum Beispiel umweltfreundliche Wasch- und Spülmittel, die den Blauen Engel[5] draufhaben. Und wir benutzen Naturseife, die zu 99 Prozent biologisch abbaubar ist.

Angie, 18 CD 9 Tr. 7

---

4. In den meisten Dörfern und Städten stehen Container für Papier und Glas. Die Glascontainer sind oft dreigeteilt für Weiß-, Braun- und Grünglas. Auch gibt es heute schon genügend Annahmestellen für verbrauchte Batterien. Batterien gehören nicht in den Hausmüll. Sie enthalten Blei, Cadmium und Quecksilber, alles gefährliche Umweltgifte. Es gibt auch Biotonnen für Küchenabfall und anderen organischen Abfall.

5. Der „Blaue Engel" ist ein Umweltzeichen, das Produkte haben, die umweltfreundlich oder weniger umweltschädlich als andere sind. Es gibt heute schon mehrere tausend Produkte mit diesem Zeichen.

Übungsheft, S. 105

1 Hast du alles verstanden?

Schreiben Mach eine Liste mit Umweltwörtern und Begriffen! Weißt du, wie all diese Ausdrücke auf Englisch heißen? saubere Umwelt, Umweltschutz, Umweltproblem, Abgase, Luft verpesten, Luftverschmutzung, Ozonloch, Sonne, UV-Strahlen, FCKW, Zerstörung der Ozonschicht, Schmutz, Schadstoffe, Chemikalien, saurer Regen, Waldsterben, Hausmüll sortieren, Container, Pfandflaschen, Einwegflaschen

2 Die Umwelt verbessern

Schreiben Die deutschen Schüler nennen in ihren Aussagen Probleme und auch konkrete Vorschläge zur Verbesserung der Umwelt. Schreib diese in Stichwörtern auf! Probleme: Plastikbeutel; Verschmutzung des Wassers, Vorschläge: Papierbeutel; umweltfreundliches Wasch- und Spülmittel, „Blauer Engel", Naturseife, biologisch abbaubar

3 Was läuft bei dir zu Hause?

Sprechen Diskutiert über die einzelnen Vorschläge zur Verbesserung der Umwelt, die die Schüler oben ausgeführt haben! Sind das praktische oder unpraktische Vorschläge? Warum? Wisst ihr, ob einige dieser Vorschläge in den USA schon praktiziert werden? Welche? Wo?

Wortschatz

p. 235X

eine Pfandflasche **eine Plastiktüte** **ein Pumpzerstäuber** **ein Waschmittel**

auf Deutsch erklärt

verschmutzen schmutzig machen

der Schmutz das, was schmutzig ist

der Schadstoff Material, das schädlich ist

verpesten verschmutzen

die Autoabgase Gase, die aus dem Auto kommen und die Luft verschmutzen

eine Fahrgemeinschaft Leute, die gemeinsam mit nur einem Auto zur Arbeit fahren

herstellen produzieren

die Fabrik das Gebäude, wo Produkte hergestellt werden

das Spülmittel damit wäscht man Gläser, Teller und Tassen

auf Englisch erklärt

<u>Giftige</u> <u>Treibgase</u> <u>vergrößern</u> das <u>Ozonloch</u>.
Poisonous gases enlarge the hole in the ozone layer.

Ich <u>fürchte</u>, dass der <u>saure</u> <u>Regen</u> die Umwelt belastet und zum <u>Waldsterben</u> beiträgt. *I'm afraid that acid rain puts a burden on the environment and contributes to the forests dying off.*

Das Gute an <u>Papierbeuteln</u> ist, dass sie <u>biologisch</u> <u>abbaubar</u> sind. *The good thing about paper bags is that they are biodegradable.*

Dem Umweltschutz zuliebe müssten wir <u>Einwegflaschen</u> mit <u>Pfandflaschen</u> <u>ersetzen</u>. *For the sake of environmental protection we should replace non-returnable bottles with returnable ones.*

Übungsheft, S. 106, Ü. 1   Grammatikheft, S. 73–74, Ü. 1–3

So sagt man das!

Expressing concern

 9–1

Many people are concerned about the environment and are apprehensive about the future. To express concern, you may say:

Ich habe Angst, dass das Ozonloch immer größer wird.
Ich fürchte, dass die Leute nicht viel für die Umwelt tun.
Die Luftverschmutzung **macht mir große Sorgen.**

How might you express similar things in English?

Übungsheft, S. 106, Ü. 2

Grammatikheft, S. 74, Ü. 4

4   **Umweltsorgen** Script and answers on p. 235G

 Zuhören Verschiedene Leute drücken ihre Sorge zur Umweltverschmutzung aus. Schreib auf, welche Sorgen jeder hat, und was jeder vorschlägt, um die Umwelt zu verbessern!
CD 9 Tr. 8

5 Was macht dir Sorgen?

Sprechen Wir haben schon viele Umweltprobleme und die Gründe dafür erkannt (*recognized*). Einige sind hier aufgelistet. Sprich mit einem Partner darüber! Sag, was dir Sorgen macht und warum!

BEISPIEL

DU	Wenn du an deine Umwelt denkst, was macht dir da Sorgen?
PARTNER	Das Ozonloch über der Antarktis.
DU	Mir auch. Und ich fürchte, dass die meisten Leute immer noch Spraydosen mit Treibgas benutzen.
PARTNER	Da hast du ganz Recht. *oder* Das glaub ich nicht.

was?

das Ozonloch über der Antarktis
die Autoabgase
die großen Müllberge
die Verschmutzung des Wassers
der saure Regen
die Industrieabgase

warum?

wenige Fahrgemeinschaften
Autos verpesten die Luft
Spraydosen mit Treibgas
Produkte nicht abbaubar
sortieren den Müll nicht
wenig gesetzliche Kontrolle

So sagt man das!

Making accusations

Who is to blame for our environmental problems? To make accusations, you can say:

Du **bist** auch **schuld an** dem Problem, weil du …
Wir Verbraucher **sind schuld daran,** dass … , wenn wir …

An is a two-way preposition, and is used here in an idiomatic phrase. Note which case always follows this phrase!

Mehr Grammatikübungen, S. 256, Ü. 1

Übungsheft, S. 107, Ü. 3

Grammatikheft, S. 74–75, Ü. 5

6 Ihr Umweltverschmutzer!

Sprechen Suse, eine engagierte Umweltschützerin und Mitglied der Umwelt-AG, sagt anderen Klassenkameraden, dass sie auch an der Umweltverschmutzung schuld sind. Aber sie haben viele Ausreden! Spiel die Rolle der Suse, und unterhalte dich mit deinen Klassenkameraden!

BEISPIEL

SUSE	Du bist auch schuld an der Umweltverschmutzung, weil du dich für die Umwelt nicht engagierst.
DU	Ach du, ich habe einfach keine Zeit!
SUSE	Das ist eine schlechte Ausrede. Für die Umwelt solltest du schon Zeit haben.

Vorwürfe *(reproaches):*

den Hausmüll nicht sortieren

sich nicht für die Umwelt engagieren

die Flaschen nicht zum Container bringen

Getränke nur in Einwegflaschen kaufen

Ausreden:

keine Zeit haben

es einfach vergessen

es nicht für nötig halten

nicht daran denken

7 Schuld oder nicht?

Sprechen Du und ein Partner, ihr unterhaltet euch darüber, wer oder was an unserer Umweltverschmutzung schuld ist. Stimmst du deinem Partner zu? Begründe deine Antwort!

BEISPIEL

SUSE Woran sind die Autoabgase schuld?
UWE Am Waldsterben.
SUSE Genau! Denn ... *oder* Das stimmt eigentlich nicht, weil ...

wer oder was?

| der saure Regen? | viele Fabriken? |
| FCKW? | die großen Öltanker? |

schuld an

die Luftverschmutzung
die Wasserverschmutzung
das Ozonloch   das Waldsterben

So sagt man das!

Offering solutions

There are many ways to offer solutions to problems. Here are some ways to say what could or should be done:

Man **könnte** einiges für die Umwelt tun.
Man **müsste** nur noch Katautos bauen.
Man **sollte** den VV billiger machen.
Wenn wir nur Papierbeutel gebrauchen **dürften!**
Ein großer Teil des Mülls **wäre** vermeidbar.

Übungsheft, S. 75, Ü. 6

8 Grammatik im Kontext   Script and answers on p. 235G

Zuhören Der Allgemeine Deutsche Fahrradklub macht Werbung mit einem Bericht im Radio. Hör zu und schreib fünf Gründe auf, warum man öfters Rad fahren sollte!

CD 9 Tr. 9

Grammatik

Subjunctive forms of **können, müssen, dürfen, sollen,** and **sein**

You can use the subjunctive form to express a variety of attitudes. The subjunctive forms of the modals and **sein** can be used to express what could or should be done, or not be done. What similarities and differences can you observe between these forms and the imperfect forms?

	können	**müssen**	**dürfen**	**sollen**	**sein**
ich	könnte	müsste	dürfte	sollte	wäre
du	könntest	müsstest	dürftest	solltest	wärst
er, sie, es, man	könnte	müsste	dürfte	sollte	wäre
wir	könnten	müssten	dürften	sollten	wären
ihr	könntet	müsstet	dürftet	solltet	wärt
sie, Sie	könnten	müssten	dürften	sollten	wären

Übungsheft, S. 107–109, Ü. 4–8   *Grammatikheft, S. 76, Ü. 7*

Mehr Grammatikübungen, S. 256, Ü. 2

9 Grammatik im Kontext

Sprechen/Schreiben Was könnten wir tun, um unsere Umwelt zu verbessern? Unterhaltet euch in der Klasse darüber! Frag deine Mitschüler, was man tun könnte, um verschiedene Umweltprobleme zu verbessern! Ein Mitschüler sagt jemandem, was diese Person nicht mehr machen sollte. Kann man noch etwas dazu sagen? Schreib danach fünf Vorschläge auf!

BEISPIEL   DU   **Was könnten wir denn tun, um (die Luft) zu verbessern?**
PARTNER A   **He, du! Du solltest nicht mehr rauchen!**
PARTNER B   **Das stimmt. (Aber wir müssten auch darauf achten, dass unsere Industrie keine Abgase in die Luft bläst — das trägt zum Waldsterben bei.)**

Vorschläge

nicht rauchen

keine Einwegflaschen kaufen

nur Produkte kaufen, die die Umwelt nicht belasten

Pfandflaschen zurückbringen

Fahrgemeinschaften bilden

keine Plastiktüten annehmen

keine Industrieabgase in die Luft blasen

So sagt man das!

Making polite requests

You can use subjunctive forms to make polite requests:

Könnte ich bitte einen Papierbeutel haben?
Dürfte ich bitte ein umweltfreundliches Waschmittel haben?
Würden Sie bitte den Motor abstellen?

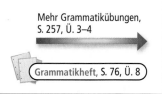

Mehr Grammatikübungen, S. 257, Ü. 3–4

Grammatikheft, S. 76, Ü. 8

10 Ein umweltfreundlicher Mensch   E.g.: Könnte ich bitte einen Solartaschenrechner haben?

Sprechen Du bist in einem Geschäft, und deine Partnerin ist die Verkäuferin. Deine Partnerin bietet dir Produkte an, die du für umweltschädlich hältst. Du bist aber sehr umweltfreundlich, und du sagst der Verkäuferin, was du haben möchtest. Die Verkäuferin gibt dir …

1. einen Taschenrechner mit Batterien.
2. einen Kaffee in einem Plastikbecher.
3. ein Getränk in einer Einwegflasche.
4. ein Waschmittel mit Phosphaten.
5. eine Seife, die die Natur belastet.
6. eine Plastiktüte für deine Einkäufe.

11 Klassenprojekt: Unsere Umwelt

Sprechen Sammelt schriftliche Informationen und Bildinformationen, die Folgendes zeigen:

1. die Belastung unserer Umwelt

2. was wir tun können, um unsere Umwelt zu schützen und zu verbessern

Macht eine Collage am Wandbrett, die Schüler an eurer Schule über Umweltprobleme und Lösungen informiert! Beschreibt die Collage und diskutiert darüber!

12 Für mein Notizbuch

Schreiben Wähl eins der folgenden drei Umweltthemen: Luft, Wasser, Hausmüll! Schreib, warum du besonders an diesem Thema interessiert bist, wie du dich aktiv auf diesem Gebiet engagierst und was noch getan werden sollte, um die Umwelt in diesem Bereich zu verbessern!

Weiter geht's! ▪ *Die Umwelt-AG diskutiert: Umwelttipps für Schüler*

CD 9
Trs. 10–15

Schon seit Jahren ist Umweltschutz ein Bestandteil der Lehrpläne an fast allen Schulen. Die Schüler handeln heute viel umweltbewusster als früher, doch gibt es noch immer eine Menge von Umweltsünden, gegen die man etwas tun könnte. Die Umwelt-AG ist wie immer am Dienstagnachmittag mit ihrem Biolehrer zusammengekommen. Heute haben die Gymnasiasten Artikel aus Zeitungen und Zeitschriften mitgebracht, über die sie diskutieren wollen. CD 9 Tr. 10

CD 9 Tr. 11

Energiesparen: Papier wieder verwenden

Papier wird aus Holz gemacht. Für Papier müssen also Wälder abgeholzt werden. Aber Wälder sind wichtig, weil sie Sauerstoff produzieren und die Luft sauber halten. Zur Herstellung von Papier braucht man Energie (Elektrizität oder Öl), viel Frischwasser und Chemikalien. Außerdem belasten die Abgase und Abwässer der Papierindustrie die Umwelt. Es lohnt sich also, Papier zu sparen, und wieder zu verwerten. Man braucht zur Herstellung von Umweltschutzpapier 98% weniger Frischwasser und 60% weniger Energie!

Vorsicht mit Tintenkillern!

Tintenkiller enthalten das giftige Formaldehyd. Das ist sehr gefährlich! Es ist wichtig, dass man bei der Verwendung von Tintenkillern das Gesicht nicht zu nahe ans Papier bringt, dass man den Stift nicht in den Mund steckt und die Kappe immer sofort aufsteckt. Am besten ist es, solche Stifte nicht zu benutzen.

Die deutsche Industrie sorgt für Sauberkeit!

- Die deutsche Papierindustrie basiert heute schon zu 61% auf Recycling!
- Die Wiederverwertung von Glas liegt heute bei 38%. (Vor fünf Jahren 5,5%)
- Alte Autos werden heute zu etwa 95% wieder verwertet!

Diesem Artikel nach bin ich ein großer Energiesparer. Das Papier und die Hefte, die ich benutze, sind alle aus Recyclingpapier. Aber natürlich könnten wir noch mehr für die Umwelt tun, wenn nur alle Schüler Recyclingpapier benutzen würden und wenn sie ihre Hefte nicht in Plastikumschläge stecken würden. Es wäre auch besser, wenn keiner mehr Kulis, Faserstifte und diese schädlichen Tintenkiller benützen würde! Das sind eben ein paar Vorschläge, die ich persönlich habe.
Sandra, 17 CD 9 Tr. 12

Ihr habt miterlebt, wie viel Müll in einer Woche an unserer Schule zusammenkommt. Freilich könnte dieser Müllberg kleiner werden, wenn jeder seinen Abfall nicht in den Papierkorb, sondern gleich in den Container werfen würde. Und wir alle müssten eben darauf achten, wie wir unsere Pausenbrote verpacken. Alu-Folie, PVC-Folie, Plastikbecher und Dosen müssten eben ganz verschwinden. Meine Mutter könnte mein Pausenbrot genau so gut in Butterbrotpapier einpacken. Ja, und wenn der Hausmeister die Milch in Mehrwegflaschen verkaufen würde, hätten wir viel weniger Abfall.[1]
Gregor, 16 CD 9 Tr. 13

---

1. An vielen deutschen Schulen verkauft oft der Hausmeister Getränke und Esswaren an Schüler.

Ich weiß nicht, wie das bei euch zu Hause ist, aber wir leben schon immer umweltbewusst. Solange ich lebe, höre ich schon immer: „Könntest du bitte das Licht in deinem Zimmer ausschalten!" oder: „Würdest du bitte die Tür schließen?" oder: „Würdest du bitte nicht so lange duschen und nicht so viel Shampoo benutzen?!" Und bei uns wird auch fast nichts weggeworfen, nichts verschwendet. Was zu reparieren ist, wird repariert. Wir haben zum Beispiel auch einen Sonnenkollektor auf unserm Dach. Mein Vater hat sich ausgerechnet, dass sich der Kollektor schon bezahlt gemacht hat.

Oliver, 17   CD 9 Tr. 14

Na ja, so umweltbewusst wie ihr leben wir wohl nicht. Es sieht so aus, als ob wir uns an euch ein Beispiel nehmen könnten. Wir leben mehr naturbewusst, und da tun wir schon einiges für die Umwelt. Meine Mutter liebt Tiere — Vögel, Bienen, Frösche, sogar Ameisen! — und deshalb benutzen wir in unserm Garten keinen Kunstdünger und keine Chemikalien. Und wir radeln viel. Mein Vater würde am liebsten jedes Wochenende nur radeln und lieber das Auto zu Hause lassen. Meine Eltern unterstützen den „sanften Tourismus".[2] Sie sind zum Beispiel letzten Winter mit ihren Freunden nicht zum Skilaufen gefahren. Sie wollten damit gegen den Bau neuer Skipisten protestieren. Und ich wäre so gern mitgefahren!

Viktoria, 17   CD 9 Tr. 15

---

2. Es hat sich gezeigt, dass längere Freizeit und aktiver Urlaub großen Schaden in der Natur angerichtet haben. Immer mehr Leute unterstützen deshalb die Aktion „Sanfter Tourismus", die sich für die Erhaltung der Natur für alle einsetzt.

Übungsheft, S. 110

13 **Hast du alles verstanden?**

Schreiben Lies dir die Zeitungsartikel auf Seite 244 noch einmal durch! Es ist nicht notwendig, dass du jedes einzelne Wort verstehst. Schreib mit eigenen Worten die wichtigsten Punkte jedes Artikels auf!

14 **Vergleiche mit anderen Texten**

Sprechen Such in amerikanischen oder deutschen Zeitungen und Zeitschriften nach einem ähnlichen Artikel wie auf Seite 244! Bring ihn in die Klasse mit und berichte darüber!

15 **Wiederhole die Ansichten!**

Schreiben Schreib auf, was für umweltbewusste Vorschläge Sandra, Gregor, Oliver und Viktoria machen! Was machen die Eltern von Oliver und Viktoria, um Energie zu sparen und die Natur zu erhalten? Sandra: Recyclingpapier benutzen; keine Kulis, Faserstifte, Tintenkiller   Gregor: **keine Alu-Folie, PVC-Folie, Plastikbecher; Butterbrotpapier, Mehrwegflaschen u. Container benutzen**   Oliver: **fast nichts wegwerfen, nichts verschwenden; Sonnenkollektor**   Viktoria: **keinen Kunstdünger u. Chemikalien im Garten benutzen; Rad fahren; „Sanften Tourismus"**

Wortschatz

Was verschwindet, wenn wir zu viel Gift herstellen?

 p. 235X

der Vogel

die Biene

der Frosch

die Ameise

auf Deutsch erklärt

der Abfall   Sachen, die man wegwirft
wieder verwenden   nochmal gebrauchen
wieder verwerten   recyceln
die Mehrwegflasche   eine Flasche, die man zurückbringt und die dann wieder benutzt wird
verzichten auf   wenn man ohne etwas lebt
ausschalten   ausmachen
das Abwasser   schon gebrauchtes Wasser
die Herstellung   die Produktion
der Wald   wo viele Bäume sind
abholzen   wenn man Bäume aus dem Wald nimmt
der Sauerstoff   was wir in die Lungen einnehmen, um zu leben

auf Englisch erklärt

Du musst aufpassen, dass du beim <u>Duschen</u> nicht so viel Wasser <u>verschwendest</u>.
You should take care not to waste so much water when showering.
<u>Außerdem</u> sind <u>Kunstdünger</u> und <u>Tintenkiller</u> <u>giftig</u>.   *Besides that, artificial fertilizer and chemical erasers are poisonous.*
Ich müsste <u>ausrechnen</u>, wie viel <u>Strom</u> ich verbrauche.   *I would have to calculate how much electricity I use.*
Es ist <u>gefährlich</u>, wenn man keine <u>Vorsicht</u> übt.   *It's dangerous when you don't use caution.*

Übungsheft, S. 111, Ü. 1   Grammatikheft, S. 77–78, Ü. 9–11

---

16 ## Würdest du bitte ...

Sprechen Was könnten deine Freunde für die Umwelt tun? Sag es ihnen!

BEISPIEL   Würdet ihr bitte ...
Könntet ihr bitte ...

E.g.: Würdet ihr bitte die Flaschen und die Zeitungen zum Container bringen?

17 **Slogans für Poster**   Script on p. 235H

Zuhören Die Umwelt-AG möchte für jeden Slogan ein Poster entwerfen. Du hörst jetzt die Slogans. Zeichne einfache Skizzen (*sketches*), die die Slogans wiedergeben!
CD 9 Tr. 16

18 **Was für Vorschläge hast du?**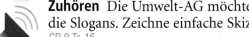

Schreiben Schreib zehn Dinge auf, die du selbst tun könntest oder tun würdest, um deine Umwelt zu schützen!

Ich könnte …   Ich würde …

So sagt man das!

Saying what is being done about a problem

Many things are already being done to protect the environment. Here is how you can express what is being done:

Batterien **werden** jetzt **gesammelt.**
Recyclingpapier **wird benutzt.**
Mehrwegflaschen **werden** schon oft **verkauft.**

How might you express similar intentions in English?

Grammatik

The passive voice, present tense

1. German often uses the passive voice for reporting that something generally is done, without telling who or what does it.

   Papier wird jetzt aus Altpapier gemacht.
   Paper is now made from recycled paper.

2. The present tense of the passive voice is formed by using a present-tense form of **werden** and the past participle of another verb.

	werden	*past participle*
Das Licht	**wird**	**ausgemacht.**
Alte Autos	**werden**	**wieder verwertet.**

3. If necessary, use the preposition **von** to indicate the performer of the action.

   Die Flaschen werden von Schülern zum Container gebracht.
   The bottles are (being) brought by the students to the recycling bin.

4. The passive voice is often used in German to make general statements.

   Heute wird ein Film über Recycling gezeigt.
   A film about recycling is being shown today.

Mehr Grammatikübungen,
S. 258, Ü. 5

Übungsheft,
S. 111, Ü. 2

Grammatikheft,
S. 78–79, Ü. 12–13

19 **Grammatik im Kontext**   Script and answers on p. 235H

Zuhören Schüler unterhalten sich über Umweltfragen. Über welche Produkte sprechen sie, und was erfährst du über diese Produkte? Mach dir Notizen!
CD 9 Tr. 17

20 Grammatik im Kontext

Sprechen/Schreiben Sag verschiedenen Klassenkameraden, was für die Umwelt gemacht wird! Schreib danach auf, was in deiner Gegend für die Umwelt gemacht wird!

E.g.: **Mehrwegflaschen werden in unserer Familie benutzt.**

Dosen mein Sandwich Batterien Recyclingpapier PVC-Folie der Müll Mehrwegflaschen die Wälder Energie Alu-Dosen alte Fahrräder	**wird** **werden**

benutzt   gesammelt   geschützt

gespart   in Butterbrotpapier eingepackt

in den Container geworfen   sortiert

vermieden   repariert

zurückgebracht   wieder verwendet

So sagt man das!

Offering solutions

To express what can, should, or must be done to protect the environment, you can say:

Der Abfall **kann** leicht **sortiert werden.**
Die Flaschen **sollen zurückgebracht werden.**
Alles **muss repariert werden.**

Übungsheft, S. 112, Ü. 3

21 Deine Ideen zur Umweltverbesserung!

Schreiben Schau dir die Bilder und Vorschläge in diesem Kapitel an! Schreib so viele Ideen und Vorschläge zur Umweltverbesserung, wie du kannst!

22 Grammatik im Kontext

Sprechen Du bist bei deinem Freund zu Hause und hilfst ihm beim Aufräumen. Du fragst ihn, was du machen sollst. Stell ihm dann auch ein paar allgemeine Umweltfragen!

DU **Was soll ich mit dem Müll tun? Sortieren?**
FREUND **Ja, der muss sortiert werden.**

1. Was soll ich mit den Flaschen tun? Zurückbringen?
2. Was soll ich mit den Dosen tun? In den Container werfen?
3. Was soll ich mit dem Fahrrad tun? Reparieren?
4. Kann man Kunstdünger überhaupt ersetzen?
5. Kann man überhaupt umweltfreundliche Seife herstellen?
6. Kann man Mehrwegflaschen überhaupt richtig waschen?

Ein wenig Grammatik

When expressing in German what can, should, or must be done about a problem, you use a conjugated modal verb along with a past participle and the infinitive **werden.**

Der Abfall **kann sortiert werden.**
The garbage can be sorted.
Die Umwelt **muss geschützt werden.**
The environment has to be protected.

Grammatikheft, S. 79, Ü. 14

Mehr Grammatikübungen, S. 258, Ü. 6

9–2

Hypothesizing

When making a hypothetical statement, the hypothetical condition can either be fulfilled or not (for example, if it's perhaps too late to do anything about it). If the hypothetical condition can be fulfilled, you say:

Wenn wir die Flaschen zurückbringen würden, hätten wir weniger Müll.
If we returned the bottles, we would have less garbage.

If the condition cannot be fulfilled, you use the past subjunctive:

Wenn wir die Flaschen zurückgebracht hätten, hätten wir weniger Müll gehabt.
If we had returned the bottles, we would have had less garbage.

Grammatik

Conditional sentences

Mehr Grammatikübungen,
S. 259, Ü. 7–8

Conditional sentences can be used to make hypothetical statements.

1. If the hypothesis can be realized or fulfilled, use subjunctive forms such as **hätte, wäre, könnte, dürfte,** or **würde** with the infinitive in both the conditional clause (the **wenn**-clause) and the conclusion.

   Wenn ich Zeit **hätte, würde** ich den Müll **sortieren.**
   If I had time, I would sort the trash.

   Wenn wir klug **wären, würden** wir uns um unsere Umwelt **kümmern.**
   If we were smart, we would be concerned about our environment.

   Wenn ich **könnte, würde** ich das Fenster **schließen.**
   If I could, I would close the window.

   Wenn der Hausmeister die Milch in Mehrwegflaschen **verkaufen würde, hätten** wir weniger Abfall.
   If the custodian sold the milk in recyclable bottles, we would have less garbage.

2. If the hypothesis can no longer be realized or fulfilled, the subjunctive forms are used in the compound tenses; that is, the forms of **hätte** and **wäre,** together with the past participle of the main verb.

   Wenn ich Zeit **gehabt hätte, hätte** ich den Müll **sortiert.**
   If I had had time, I would have sorted the trash.

   Wenn wir klug **gewesen wären, hätten** wir uns um die Umwelt **gekümmert.**
   If we had been clever, we would have taken care of the environment.

   Wenn der Hausmeister die Milch in Mehrwegflaschen **verkauft hätte, hätten** wir weniger Abfall **gehabt.**
   If the custodian had sold the milk in recyclable bottles, we would have had less garbage.

3. Conditional sentences can also start with the conclusion, and then follow with the **wenn**-clause.

   Ich **würde** den Müll **sortieren,** wenn ich Zeit **hätte.**
   Ich **hätte** den Müll **sortiert,** wenn ich Zeit **gehabt hätte.**

Übungsheft, S. 112–114, Ü. 4–9

Grammatikheft, S. 80–81, Ü. 15–17

23 Grammatik im Kontext
Script and answers on p. 235H

Zuhören Du hörst jetzt, was einige Mädchen und Jungen für die Umwelt tun. Schreib ein paar Sachen auf, die sie machen!

CD 9 Tr. 18

24 Grammatik im Kontext

Sprechen/Schreiben Du interviewst deine Klassenkameraden und fragst sie:

Du **Was würdest du für deine Umwelt tun, wenn du wirklich umweltbewusst leben würdest?**

PARTNER **Ich würde (unsern Müll sortieren und selbst zum Container bringen).**

25 Grammatik im Kontext

Sprechen/Schreiben Frag deine Klassenkameraden jetzt, was sie früher für den Umweltschutz getan hätten! Schreib danach acht Dinge auf, die du für die Umwelt getan hättest!

Du **Was hättest du alles für den Umweltschutz getan, wenn du mehr darüber gewusst hättest?**

PARTNER **Ich hätte (nur Mehrwegflaschen gekauft und Einwegflaschen vermieden).**

Recyclingpapier benutzen

Müll sortieren

Pausenbrot in Butterbrotpapier einpacken

Plastikbecher und Dosen sammeln

nicht so viel Wasser verschwenden

nicht so lange duschen

Plastikumschläge vermeiden

Tintenkiller vermeiden

Fenster und Türen schließen

26 Und du? Wie steht's mit dir?

Sprechen Umweltschutz fängt bei jedem einzelnen an. Bilde eine größere Gruppe und beantwortet folgende Fragen!

1. Was tust du für deine Umwelt? Denk daran, dass auch ganz kleine Dinge wichtig sind!
2. Engagierst du dich aktiv in einer Umweltgruppe? Was machst du dort?
3. Was würdest du selbst gern für deine Umwelt tun, wenn du es könntest?
4. Was tut dein Heimatort für den Umweltschutz? Was macht deine Schule?
5. Was für Gesetze gibt es, die für die Erhaltung einer reinen und gesunden Umwelt sind?
6. Wenn du an die Umwelt denkst, siehst du optimistisch oder pessimistisch in die Zukunft?
7. Was wäre für dich eine ideale Umwelt?

 Von der Schule zum Beruf

The large chemical company you work for is in trouble again for polluting the environment. As part of the court decision, the company must produce booklets for schoolchildren warning them about dangers to our environment. Your department is in charge of producing the booklet. Decide on a format (short story, comic book, etc.) and develop a prototype to present at the next meeting. Include illustrations and a list of what kids can do to help the environment.

Ein umweltfreundlicher Einkauf

Übungsheft, S. 115, Ü. 1–3

Chelsea ist Austauschstudentin in Deutschland. Ihr deutscher Freund Martin und sie sind hungrig. Da es nichts Besonderes im Kühlschrank gibt, gehen die beiden einkaufen. Martin nimmt einen Korb und zwei Einkaufstaschen aus Baumwolle mit.

Draußen regnet es, und da Martin schon seinen Führerschein hat, erwartet Chelsea, dass sie mit dem Auto zum Supermarkt fahren. Aber statt dessen gehen die beiden zu Fuß mit Regenschirmen zum Supermarkt. Chelsea denkt, in Amerika würden wir ganz einfach mit dem Auto hinfahren, besonders wenn es regnet.

Im Supermarkt kaufen sie alles ein, was sie brauchen. Als sie an der Kasse stehen, merkt Chelsea, dass die Kassiererin ihnen keine Einkaufstaschen aus Papier oder Plastik gibt, sondern dass Martin die Sachen selber in den Korb und in die Baumwolltaschen einpackt. Bevor sie den Supermarkt verlassen, nimmt Martin das Verpackungsmaterial von verschiedenen Packungen und wirft es in eine große Tonne vor dem Ausgang des Supermarkts. Chelsea fragt sich, warum das Einkaufen hier anders ist. Answers will vary.

1. Chelseas Erlebnis ist ein typischer Einkauf in Deutschland. Was ist beim Einkaufen in den USA anders? Beschreib die Unterschiede!

2. Warum bringt Martin Einkaufstaschen aus Stoff und einen Korb mit? Warum packt er alles an der Kasse selber ein? Warum lässt er das Verpackungsmaterial in der Tonne im Supermarkt?

3. Chelsea und Martin gehen zu Fuß einkaufen, obwohl es regnet. Was würdest du in diesem Fall machen? Warum?

4. Warum ist der Einkauf umweltfreundlich?

In Deutschland ist es üblich, Einkaufstaschen aus Stoff oder Körbe zum Einkaufen mitzubringen. Wenn man keine Taschen bei sich hat, kann man im Supermarkt Plastiktaschen für 10 Cent pro Stück kaufen. Um die zusätzlichen Kosten und den Gebrauch von Plastiktüten zu vermeiden, bringt man gewöhnlich seine eigenen Stofftaschen mit. Natürlich ist es auch umweltfreundlicher. Man darf auch Verpackungsmaterialien im Supermarkt lassen, denn Supermärkte sind gesetzlich verpflichtet, die so genannten „Umverpackungen" zurückzunehmen und zu recyceln. Auch benutzen die Leute gewöhnlich nicht das Auto, um einkaufen zu gehen. In jeder Nachbarschaft gibt es genügend Lebensmittelgeschäfte, die man gut zu Fuß oder mit dem Rad erreichen kann. In der Großstadt ist es außerdem nicht leicht, einen Parkplatz zu finden.

Mit Gasmasken protestieren Berliner Schüler gegen die Luftverschmutzung. In den Greenteams von Greenpeace sind heute rund 10 000 Kinder für die Umwelt aktiv.

Die Welt gehört allen!

Lesestrategie Interpreting statistics When you come across statistics in a text, use the following steps to help make sense of them. Find out 1) what is being compared, 2) what the numbers refer to, and 3) the source of the statistics. Most importantly, once you understand what the statistics represent, you'll want to draw conclusions based on them. Try to put your conclusions in your own words using phrases such as *more than, much less than*, etc., rather than numbers.

Getting Started
For answers, see p. 235V.

Identify the main idea by using the strategies you've learned. Remember that a main idea can be made up of several related ideas.

1. Look at the photo and then read the caption, the title, and subtitle of the reading. What is the topic? What group of people does it focus on?

2. What kind of text is this? Is it a narrative, a news report, or something else? Just by looking at the text, how many sections do you think it has? Can you identify them?

Mehr Bauch als Kopf

Eine Studie belegt: Jugendliche wissen zuwenig über Umweltfragen. Dennoch wachsen Ökobewußtsein und Opferbereitschaft

Ob sie bereit wären, für verbesserten Umweltschutz auch auf einen Teil ihres Taschengeldes zu verzichten, wollten Wissenschaftler der Universität Bielefeld kürzlich von 600 Schülern wissen. Viele sind es. Bei immerhin 30 Prozent macht das Umweltbewußtsein selbst vor dem eigenen Geldbeutel nicht halt. Dieselbe Frage hatten 1980 in einer gleich großen Gruppe noch geringfügig weniger (28 Prozent) bejaht.

Für den Leiter des Forscherteams, Professor Axel Braun, sind solche kleinen Fortschritte »ein Silberstreifen am Horizont«. Aus dem Vergleich der beiden Umfragen im Abstand von 13 Jahren zieht er den Schluß: »Es geht in die richtige Richtung, aber langsam.«

Besonders da, wo die Gesellschaft allgemein dazugelernt hat, ziehen die 15- bis 18-jährigen verstärkt mit. So bringen heute 84 Prozent der Kids nach Partys ihre Flaschen zum Altglascontainer. 1980 machten sich nur 39 Prozent die Mühe. 70 Prozent verschmähen beim Einkaufen die Plastiktüte (1980: 58 Prozent). Die Hälfte schreibt heute »Papier beidseitig voll« (1980: 37 Prozent), und 40 Prozent weisen aufwendig verpackte Ware zurück (1980: 15 Prozent).

Mehr als zwei Drittel sind bereit, für die Umwelt auf die Straße zu gehen, 41 Prozent

---

In **Kapitel 7** you learned that cohesive devices are words or phrases that help tie the individual ideas of a text together. Cohesive devices can be pronouns, including relative pronouns (**die, den, denen**), conjunctions (**aber, ob, wenn**), or adverbs (**dennoch, jetzt, im Vergleich**).

3. Scan the title and subtitle for cohesive devices indicating comparison or contrast. Using these words or phrases as clues, state what you think the main idea of the article is. Now read the first paragraph and decide which part of the main idea the first half of the essay must refer to.

4. Scan the first paragraph of the second part of the article for key words relating to or illustrating the title and subtitle of the article. Decide which part of the main idea this half of the essay refers to.

A Closer Look

Now that you have identified the main idea, look at how the statistics support this point.

5. Look at the statistics given in the first paragraph. What facts are being compared? What do the numbers actually refer to? What is the source for these statistics? Based on the statistics, what conclusion can you draw about differences between teenagers today and those that answered the survey in 1980? Try to state your conclusion in terms that make sense to you.

6. Continue reading the first part of the essay. What do the statistics in the third and fourth paragraphs refer to? What conclusions can you draw from these numbers? How do they fit with your original statement about the main idea of the article?

haben schon an Unterschriften-aktionen teilgenommen, und 38 Prozent beteiligten sich an der Säuberung von Bächen und ähnlichen Einsätzen. Durchweg liegen diese Werte um zehn bis 20 Prozent über denen von 1980.

Was die Jugendlichen bewegt, scheint vor allem Angst zu sein. Ob atomare Strahlung, Wasser-verschmutzung, Klimaveränder-ung, Überbevölkerung oder Müll-Lawine, man sieht die Zukunft schwärzer als früher. Am Fach-wissen mangelt es allerdings nach wie vor. Im Wissenstest erreichten Gymnasiasten nur rund die Hälfte

der möglichen Punkte, Haupt-schüler gut ein Drittel. Braun: »Glatt unbefriedigend.«

Während die Jungen eher sachlich Bescheid wissen, ist bei den Mädchen die persönliche Betroffenheit und die Hand-lungsbereitschaft größer. Jungen lasten die Umweltschäden eher Politik und Wirtschaft an, Mädchen kehren lieber vor der eigenen Haustüre.

Die wichtigste Rolle bei der Förderung des Umweltbewußt-seins spielt nach den Bielefelder Erkenntnissen die Schule. Vor allem, wenn konkrete Probleme

mit anschließenden Aktionen auf dem Stundenplan stehen, »bleibt bei den Schülern deut-lich mehr hängen«.

Nach Umfragen des Kieler Instituts für Pädagogik in den Naturwissenschaften und der Deutschen Gesellschaft für Umwelterziehung (DGU) stieg in den letzten Jahren die Zahl der Schulen, die diesen Grundsatz beherzigen, von 15 auf 40 Prozent. DGU-Geschäftsführer Axel Beyer: »Da wird schon mal durch Schülereinsatz eine vier-spurige Straße auf zwei Spuren verkleinert und Hausmeistern das Energiesparen vorgemacht.«

7. Read the entire second part of the article. In the sixth paragraph, identify cohesive devices and list them. Based on your list, what do you think the writer is showing in this paragraph? A sequence of events? Comparison and contrast? Cause and effect? Or something else?

8. Answer the following questions.

   a. What is the main reason teenagers try to protect the environment?

   b. Why did Herr Braun give the students mentioned in the fifth paragraph the grade **unbefriedigend?**

   c. In what ways do girls and boys differ in their involvement with the environment?

   d. Which single factor has helped most in promoting environmental awareness?

9. Schreib jetzt eine Zusammenfassung des Artikels! Verwende dabei deine Aussage über den Hauptgedanken (Frage 3)! Benutze min-destens drei unterstützende Aussagen von dem Text und einen Schlusssatz!

10. Bildet Gruppen von vier, und haltet jetzt eure eigene Umfrage, indem ihr zwei verschiedene Gruppen (zum Beispiel Mädchen und Jungen oder Schüler und Lehrer) vergleicht. Das Thema heißt Umwelt. Nachdem ihr die Statistiken gesammelt habt, müsst ihr logische Schlüsse daraus ziehen. Schreibt am Ende einen Bericht über die Ergebnisse!

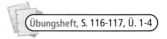
Übungsheft, S. 116-117, Ü. 1-4

Zum Schreiben

As you have discussed in this chapter, you as an individual can do many different things to help protect the environment. Politicians, however, have even more potential to help the environment, since they determine policies for a whole country. In this activity, you will imagine that you are a candidate to become Chancellor of Germany. You will write a campaign speech outlining what you would do for the environment if elected.

Als Kanzler würde ich alles ändern!

Schreib eine Rede als Kanzlerkandidat! Erkläre in der Rede, was du als Kanzler für die Umwelt oder für andere wichtige Probleme der Gesellschaft machen würdest! Kritisiere die alten Politiker! Woran sind sie schuld? Erzähle auch deinem Publikum, was gemacht werden muss und soll!

 Schreibtipp Analyzing your audience Whenever you write, you are writing for someone — your intended audience. Analyzing who that audience is before you begin helps you determine the content as well as the style and tone of what you will write. To analyze your audience, first ask yourself what your intended readers or listeners know and what interests them. If they don't know much about your topic, include background details to inform them; if they already know a lot, focus on particular aspects of the topic that fit their interests. Select a style and tone, too, that are most appropriate to your audience. The more your audience knows, the more in-depth your arguments can be.

A. Vorbereiten

1. Wer wird deine Rede hören? Wofür interessieren sich diese Leute, und was wissen sie schon über das Thema? Entwirf einen Fragebogen in der Klasse, um festzustellen, welche Probleme deinen Klassenkameraden besonders wichtig sind!

2. Wähle die Probleme aus, die du besprechen willst, und schreib sie auf Karteikarten (index cards)! Denk an die Details, die für die Zuschauer interessant wären, und schreib sie auch auf!

3. Wo hältst du die Rede? Wie viel Zeit hast du dazu? Wähle die geeigneten Karten aus, und ordne sie in der gewünschten Reihenfolge an!

4. Denk an die Ausführung der Rede! Willst du Diagramme oder Bilder benutzen?

B. Ausführen

Benutze deine geordneten Karten, um die Rede zu schreiben! Du musst dich während der Rede nicht unbedingt an den geschriebenen Text halten, aber schreibe alles auf, damit du nichts vergisst!

C. Überarbeiten

1. Bildet Gruppen von jeweils vier Schülern und Schülerinnen! Jeder soll der Rede von den anderen zuhören. Hört einander sehr aufmerksam zu, und merkt euch die Fragen, die euch während der Rede einfallen!

2. Besprecht die Wirkung (effect) jeder Rede! Würdet ihr diesen Kandidaten jetzt wählen? Hat er euch mit seinen Gesichtspunkten überzeugt? Hat er seine Stimme und Gesten wirksam eingesetzt?

3. Habt ihr als Zuschauer die Rede interessant gefunden? Habt ihr etwas gelernt, oder habt ihr schon alles gewusst?

4. Lies deine eigene Rede noch einmal! Hast du alles richtig buchstabiert? Beachte besonders die Konjunktivformen der Modalverben! Hast du **konnte** und **könnte** richtig verwendet?

5. Schreib die korrigierte Rede noch einmal ab!

Mehr Grammatikübungen

Answers

↗ internet
ADRESSE: go.hrw.com
KENNWORT:
WK3 FRANKFURT-9

Erste Stufe

Objectives Expressing concern; making accusations; offering solutions; making polite requests

1 Du drückst deine Befürchtungen (*fears*) über die Umwelt aus. Schreib die folgenden Sätze ab, und schreib dabei die gegebene Information als dass-Satz in die Lücken! **(Seite 241)**

1. Das Ozonloch wir immer größer. — Ich habe Angst, dass _____ .   das O. immer größer wird
2. Der saure Regen belastet die Umwelt. — Ich fürchte, dass _____ .   der saure R. die U. belastet
3. Die Abgase verschmutzen die Luft total. — Ich fürchte, dass _____ .   die A. die L. total verschmutzen
4. Der Hausmüll wird immer mehr. — Ich habe Angst, dass _____ .   der H. immer mehr wird
5. Das Waldsterben nimmt zu. — Ich habe Angst, dass _____ .   das Waldsterben zunimmt
6. Die UV-Strahlen lösen Hautkrebs aus. — Ich fürchte, dass _____ .   die UV-Strahlen H. auslösen

2 Du sprichst mit einer Klassenkameradin über mehrere Umweltprobleme, und du sagst, was man verbessern könnte. Schreib die folgenden Sätze ab, und schreib dabei die Konjunktivform (*subjunctive form*) der gegebenen Verben in die Lücken! **(Seite 242)**

1. (können)   Man _____ eine ganze Menge für die Umwelt tun.   könnte
2. (sein)   Ein großer Teil unseres Mülls _____ vermeidbar.   wäre
3. (müssen)   Man _____ mehr Fahrgemeinschaften gründen.   müsste
4. (sollen)   Man _____ Einwegflaschen ganz vermeiden.   sollte
5. (dürfen)   Wir _____ unsere Parks und Straßen sauberer halten.   dürften
6. (müssen)   Du _____ mehr mit dem Rad als mit dem Auto fahren.   müsstest
7. (können)   Du _____ auch viel weniger Putzmittel verwenden.   könntest
8. (sollen)   Du _____ beim Waschen nicht so viel Wasser verbrauchen.   solltest

3 Du sprichst mit verschiedenen Leuten über die Umwelt, und du versuchst dabei, ihre Meinungen zu ändern. Schreib die folgenden Sätze ab, und schreib dabei die Konjunktivform der gegebenen Verben in die Lücken! (**Seite 243**)

1. (dürfen)   _____ ich bitte einen Papierbeutel statt einer Plastiktasche haben?   Dürfte

2. (werden)   _____ Sie mir bitte die Limonade in Pfandflaschen geben?   Würden

3. (können)   Verzeihung, _____ ich bitte ein umweltfreundliches Waschmittel haben?   könnte

4. (dürfen)   _____ ich bitte eine Seife haben, die die Natur nicht so belastet?   Dürfte

5. (werden)   Hallo! _____ du bitte den Motor abstellen, während du hier wartest?   Würdest

6. (können)   _____ du bitte ein Spülmittel kaufen, das den Blauen Engel drauf hat?   Könntest

4 Sei höflich und sag den Leuten, was sie tun sollten. Schreib Sätze und gebrauche dabei eine **würde**-Form in der ersten Lücke und einen passenden Ausdruck aus dem Kasten. (**Seite 243**)

---

beim Aufräumen helfen   nicht so spät nach Hause kommen   die Musik leiser machen

das Zimmer aufräumen   mehr lernen

---

1. _____ du bitte _____ ?   Würdest; das Zimmer aufräumen

2. _____ Sie bitte _____ ?   Würden; die Musik leiser stellen

3. _____ du bitte _____ ?   Würdest; nicht so spät nach Hause kommen

4. _____ du bitte _____ ?   Würdest; beim Aufräumen helfen

5. _____ du bitte _____ ?   Würdest; mehr lernen

Zweite Stufe

Objectives Saying what is being done about a problem; offering solutions; hypothesizing

5 Du sprichst mit Freunden darüber, was bei dir zu Hause für die Umwelt getan wird. Schreib die folgenden Sätze ab, und schreib dabei die Passivform der gegebenen Verben in die Lücken! (**Seite 247**)

1. (sortieren)	Bei uns zu Hause _____ der Müll schon seit Jahren _____ .	wird; sortiert
2. (bringen)	Die leeren Einwegflaschen _____ zum Container _____ .	werden; gebracht
3. (ausschalten)	In leeren Zimmern _____ das Licht immer _____ .	wird; ausgeschaltet
4. (sammeln)	Alte Batterien _____ von meinen Geschwistern _____ .	werden; gesammelt
5. (verschwenden)	Bei uns zu Hause _____ eigentlich wenig Wasser _____ .	wird; verschwendet
6. (sparen)	Wasser _____ im ganzen Haus und im Garten _____ .	wird; gespart
7. (benutzen)	Recyclingpapier _____ bei uns ausschließlich _____ .	wird; benutzt
8. (vermeiden)	Unnötiger Lärm _____ bei uns auch _____ .	wird; vermieden

6 Du sprichst mit deinen Freunden über die Umwelt, und du drückst dabei deine eigene Meinung aus. Schreib die folgenden Sätze ab, und schreib dabei den Infinitiv des Verbs im Passiv (Partizip + **werden**) in die Lücken! (**Seite 248**)

1. (zurückbringen)	Diese Mehrwegflaschen können zum Markt _____ .	zurückgebracht werden
2. (wieder verwerten)	Diese Papierbeutel können doch _____ .	wieder verwertet werden
3. (sortieren)	Unser Abfall muss heute noch _____ .	sortiert werden
4. (werfen)	Die Flaschen können gleich in den Container _____ .	geworfen werden
5. (verschwenden)	Unser Trinkwasser darf nicht so _____ .	verschwendet werden
6. (schützen)	Unsere schönen Wälder müssen _____ .	geschützt werden

7 Was würdest du tun, wenn …? Du sprichst mit deinen Freunden über die Umwelt, und du machst gewisse Vorschläge (*propositions*). Beantworte die folgenden Fragen, indem du sie als wenn-Sätze umschreibst! (**Seite 249**)

1. Was würdest du tun, wenn du mehr Zeit hättest? Den Müll sortieren?
   — Ja, wenn ich _____ . mehr Zeit hätte, würde ich den Müll sortieren

2. Was würdest du tun, wenn du zu Hause wärst? Die Einwegflaschen zum Container bringen? — Ja, wenn ich _____ . zu Hause wäre, würde ich die E. zum C. bringen

3. Was würdest du tun, wenn du etwas für die Umwelt tun könntest? Weniger Wasser verbrauchen? — Ja, wenn ich etwas _____ . für die U. tun könnte, würde ich w. W. verbrauchen

4. Was würdest du tun, wenn du viel Geld hättest? Ein Solarmobil fahren?
   — Ja, wenn ich _____ . viel Geld hätte, würde ich ein Solarmobil fahren

5. Was würdest du tun, wenn du leere Batterien hättest? Sie in den Müll werfen?
   — Nein, wenn ich _____ . leere B. hätte, würde ich sie nicht in den Müll werfen

8 Was hättest du getan, wenn … ? Du denkst an die Vergangenheit (*past*), und du machst gewisse Aussagen (*statements*) darüber, was du getan hättest, wenn … Schreib wenn-Sätze, und gebrauche dabei die gegebene Information! (**Seite 249**)

Was hättest du gemacht, wenn du Zeit gehabt hättest?

1. (den Müll sortieren)   Wenn ich _____ . Zeit gehabt hätte, hätte ich den Müll sortiert
2. (die Batterien wegbringen)   Wenn ich _____ . Zeit gehabt hätte, hätte ich die B. weggebracht
3. (das Licht ausschalten)   Wenn ich _____ . Zeit gehabt hätte, hätte ich das L. ausgeschaltet
4. (Altpapier sammeln)   Wenn ich _____ . Zeit gehabt hätte, hätte ich Altpapier gesammelt
5. (mit dem Rad fahren)   Wenn ich _____ . Zeit gehabt hätte, wäre ich mit dem Rad gefahren
6. (zu Fuß zum Einkaufen gehen)   Wenn ich _____ . Zeit gehabt hätte, wäre ich zu F. zum E. gegangen

1 In vielen Orten und in vielen Schulen gibt es Umweltprojekte. Eine Schule in Prüm, eine kleine Stadt in der Eifel, hat zum Beispiel ein interessantes Projekt durchgeführt. Das Projekt wurde in einer Zeitschrift beschrieben. Lies zuerst den Artikel und versuche danach, dir ein interessantes Umweltprojekt für eure Schule auszudenken!

DAS SAUBERE KLASSENZIMMER

Die Schüler und Schülerinnen einer 11. Klasse am Regino-Gymnasium in Prüm haben sich eine tolle Projektwoche ausgedacht. Während der Projektwoche sollen alle Talente genutzt werden: eine „Müllband" will Instrumente aus Müll bauen und damit ein Konzert geben, Hobby-Köche wollen die Schüler mit Biokost versorgen, Rate-Füchse einen Müllquiz entwickeln, angehende Journalisten wollen Passanten über ihr Müllverhalten befragen, andere Schüler wollen „Kunst aus Müll" herstellen und die Fotogruppe will die Aktionen dokumentieren. Und am

Ende wird's in der Schulturnhalle ein öffentliches Fest geben, bei dem die Ergebnisse präsentiert werden. „Natürlich soll nach einer Woche nicht alles vorbei sein", so die Klassenlehrerin Susanne Faschin, „deshalb möchten wir, daß jede Klasse einen festen Klassenraum erhält, für den sie verantwortlich ist und den sie auch selber reinigen muß. Dann würden viele Jugendliche nicht mehr alles so bedenkenlos wegschmeißen". Außerdem sollen ältere Schüler Patenschaften für jüngere übernehmen, um sie in die Geheimnisse des Müllsparens einzuweihen.

2 Ein Mitglied der Umwelt-AG kommt in die Klasse und erzählt den Schülern, was sie alles für ihre Umwelt machen können. Hör seiner Rede zu und schreib acht Vorschläge auf, die er macht! Script and answers on p. 235l

CD 9 Tr. 19

3 Teilt euch in zwei Gruppen auf! Sucht euch an eurer Schule oder in eurem Ort irgendein Umweltprojekt, an dem ihr aktiv arbeiten könnt. Schreibt eure Erfahrungen auf und macht Fotografien für euren Bericht! Jede Gruppe berichtet dann der anderen Gruppe, was sie gemacht hat und wie umweltbewusst ihre Arbeit war.

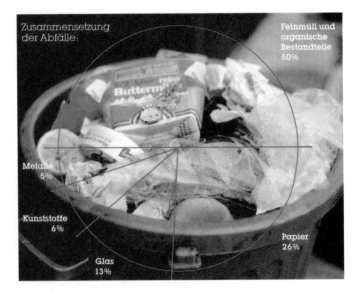

Zusammensetzung der Abfälle:

Feinmüll und organische Bestandteile 50%

Metalle 5%

Kunststoffe 6%

Glas 13%

Papier 26%

4 Du bist aktiv in der Umwelt-AG in deiner Schule. Du musst morgen in eine Grundschulklasse gehen und mit den Kindern über Umweltschutz sprechen. Bereite eine kleine Rede vor, und übe sie mit deinen Klassenkameraden ein! Was halten sie von deiner Rede?

5 Im deutschen Fernsehen gibt es ein Diskussionsprogramm: „Pro und Contra". Eure Klasse wurde dazu eingeladen. Teilt euch in zwei Gruppen auf und bereitet euch vor, für eine von den zwei Ansichten zu argumentieren! Gruppe A ist der Ansicht, dass die Regierung mehr für die Umwelt machen muss; Gruppe B bereitet das Argument vor, dass die Regierung schon genug für die Umwelt macht — es kostet viel Geld und auch Jobs, und das können wir uns nicht leisten. Wählt abwechselnd Schüler von jeder Gruppe und diskutiert darüber!

Abfallvermeidung durch Recycling

Verpackungsstoffe	Sammelquoten (%)		Recyclingquoten (%)	
	1993	1995	1993	2000
Glas	60	80	42	72
Weißblech	40	80	26	72
Aluminium	30	80	18	72
Papier/Pappe	30	80	18	70
Kunststoffe	30	80	9	60
Verbund	20	80	66	4

6 Schau dir die Tabelle an! Welche Daten über Abfallvermeidung in Deutschland werden gezeigt? Welche Verpackungsstoffe werden am meisten gesammelt und wieder verwertet? Mach eine Umfrage in deiner Klasse oder in deiner Schule, und entwirf mit den Ergebnissen eine ähnliche Tabelle!

7 Die Grafik auf Seite 260 zeigt eine Zusammensetzung der gesamten Abfälle. Nenne für jede Kategorie konkrete Beispiele, und überlege dann, wie man diesen Müll wieder verwerten kann, anstatt ihn wegzuwerfen!

8 ## Rollenspiel

Du versuchst, deine Familie umweltbewusster zu machen. Du sprichst mit deinen Eltern und Geschwistern darüber, aber sie haben viele Ausreden. Du gibst dir Mühe, sie zu überzeugen. Deine Klassenkameraden spielen die Rollen von deinen Eltern und Geschwistern.

Kann ich's wirklich?

Can you express concern? (p. 240)

1 How would you express your fear that the hole in the ozone layer is getting larger? 1. Ich habe Angst, dass das Ozonloch immer größer wird.

2 How would you express your concern about air pollution?
2. Die Luftverschmutzung macht mir große Sorgen.

Can you make accusations? (p. 241)

3 How would you blame air pollution on people who always take their cars and never walk or take the bus? 3. Die Autofahrer sind schuld an der Luftverschmutzung, weil sie nie zu Fuß gehen oder den Bus nehmen.

Can you offer solutions? (p. 242)

4 How would you respond if someone asked you **Was könnte man für die Umwelt tun?** 4. E.g.: Man könnte recyceln.

Can you make polite requests? (p. 243)

5 How would you politely ask a salesperson for the following things?

a. a can without CFC? 5. a. E.g.: Könnte ich bitte eine Dose ohne FCKW haben?

b. einen Papierbeutel b. E.g.: Dürfte ich bitte einen Papierbeutel haben?

c. ein Waschmittel ohne Phosphate
c. E.g.: Würden Sie mir bitte ein Waschmittel ohne Phosphate geben?

Can you say what is being done about a problem? (p. 247)
Can you offer solutions? (p. 248)

6 How would you say that in Germany trash is always sorted?
6. In Deutschland wird Müll immer sortiert.

7 How would you respond if someone asked you what can, should, or must be done with the following things?

a. Müll (sortieren) 7. a. Müll kann sortiert werden.

b. Pfandflaschen (zurückbringen) b. Pfandflaschen sollen zurückgebracht werden.

c. alte Fahrräder (reparieren) c. Alte Fahrräder müssen repariert werden.

Can you hypothesize? (p. 249)

8 How would you express the idea that we would have no air pollution if we all left our cars at home and rode bicycles? 8. E.g.: Wenn wir alle unsere Autos zu Hause lassen würden und Fahrrad fahren würden, hätten wir keine Luftverschmutzung.

9 How would you respond if a friend asked you **Was hättest du heute gemacht, wenn du nicht in der Schule gewesen wärst?**
9. E.g.: Wenn ich nicht in der Schule gewesen wäre, hätte ich heute meine Oma besucht.

Erste Stufe

p. 235X

Expressing fear

Ich fürchte, dass ...	I am afraid that ...
Das macht uns große Sorgen.	We are really worried about that.

Saying what you could or should do about a problem

Wenn wir nur Naturprodukte benutzen dürften!	If only we were allowed to use natural products!
Man müsste nur daran denken.	You would only have to think about it.

Other useful words

das Abgas, -e	exhaust
das Treibgas, -e	propulsion gas
die Fabrik, -en	factory
die Fahrgemeinschaft, -en	carpool

das Katauto, -s	car with emission control
das Öl, -e	oil
die Luftverschmutzung	air pollution
das Ozonloch	hole in the ozone layer
der saure Regen	acid rain
der Schadstoff, -e	pollutant
der Schmutz	dirt
das Waldsterben	the dying of the forests
die Aludose, -n	aluminum can
die Einwegflasche, -n	non-returnable bottle
der Papierbeutel, -	paper bag
die Pfandflasche, -n	deposit-only bottle
die Plastiktüte, -n	plastic bag
der Pumpzerstäuber, -	pump spray
das Spülmittel, -	dishwashing liquid
das Waschmittel, -	laundry soap

der Mut	courage
der Teil, -e	part
s. Sorgen machen	to worry
anbieten (sep)	to offer
blasen	to blow
ersetzen	to replace
herstellen (sep)	to produce
leck werden	to spring a leak
sortieren	to sort
vergrößern	to enlarge
verpesten	to poison, pollute
verschmutzen	to pollute
biologisch abbaubar	biodegradable
ausschließlich	exclusively
umweltfreundlich	environmentally safe
vermeidbar	avoidable
giftig	poisonous

Zweite Stufe

Words for talking about the environment

der Umweltschutz	environmental protection
die Ameise, -n	ant
die Biene, -n	bee
der Frosch, -̈e	frog
der Vogel, -̈	bird
der Wald, -̈er	forest
der Sauerstoff	oxygen
der Schaden, -̈	damage
die Skipiste, -n	ski run
die Herstellung, -en	production
die Vorsicht	caution
der Abfall, -̈e	trash, waste
das Abwasser, -̈	wastewater

die Batterie, -n	battery
der Faserstift, -e	felt-tip pen
der Kunstdünger, -	artificial fertilizer
die Mehrwegflasche, -n	reusable bottle
der Strom	electricity
der Tintenkiller, -	chemical eraser
das Gift, -e	poison
das Dach, -̈er	roof
abholzen (sep)	to deforest
ausrechnen (sep)	to calculate
ausschalten (sep)	to switch off
duschen	to shower
miterleben (sep)	to experience

radeln	to bicycle
stecken	to put (into)
verbessern	to improve
verschwenden	to waste
verzichten auf (acc)	to do without
wieder verwenden	to use again
wieder verwerten	to recycle
außerdem	besides that
gefährlich	dangerous
nahe	near
sogar	even

Dresden

LOCATION OPENER

Teaching Resources
pp. 264–267

PRINT
▸ Lesson Planner, p. 56
▸ Video Guide, pp. 43–44

MEDIA
▸ One-Stop Planner
▸ Video Program
   Dresden
   Videocassette 2, 34:18–37:04
▸ Map Transparency

go.hrw.com
WK3 DRESDEN

PAGES 264–265

THE PHOTOGRAPH
Background Information

Dresden got its name from the old Sorbian (altsorbisch) word **drezd'ane** for the *forest people* who first settled the area around 600 (See p. 323D, Traditions, for more information.). Dresden was not documented until 1004 and is believed to have been officially founded around 1216. This view of the city shows several of its famous Baroque buildings which led to its nickname *das Elbflorenz (Florence on the Elbe)*. During World War II, Germans thought that Dresden would be spared from allied attacks because of its architectural and cultural treasures, but it was almost completely destroyed by an Allied air raid in February 1945. Rebuilding of the city started 40 years ago and is still not complete.

Geography Connection

Point out to students the boat landing pier along the river bank. This is called **Anlegestelle der Weißen Flotte** *(moorings of the white fleet)*. It connects the city between spring and fall with Meißen and Bad Schandau. Have students identify the river Elbe, Meißen, and Bad Schandau on a detailed map of Germany.

Home Economics Connection

Have a student ask the home economics teacher about a popular quilting pattern called the "Dresden Plate." Have them find out what it looks like and how it got its name.

THE ALMANAC AND MAP

The coat of arms of Dresden depicts on one side a black lion on a golden background, and on the other side, two black vertical bars on a golden background. While families of the nobility initially developed coats of arms out of military necessity—to distinguish friend from foe in battle—the heraldic symbols of medieval towns and cities generally evolved out of seals used on legal contracts. The first known occurence of the Dresden coat of arms is on a seal from 1309. The lion and the vertical bars refer to the crest of the Margrave of Meißen, who ruled the city at that time. Since then, the coat of arms of Dresden has changed relatively little.

Terms in the Almanac

- **Schloss:** The **Dresdner Schloss** was built in the Renaissance style in the 16th century. The castle was destroyed in 1945, and restoration did not begin until 1985.

- **Kurfürst Friedrich August I.:** Also referred to as **August der Starke,** he was the elector of Saxony from 1694 to 1733. He also become king of Poland after his conversion to Catholicism. He embellished the city of Dresden with ornate Baroque buildings such as the **Zwinger** and the **Frauenkirche.**

- **Kurfürst Friedrich August II.:** He was the son of **August der Starke.**

- **Carl Maria von Weber:** He was a famous composer who wrote both instrumental and vocal music. He is best known for the operas *Euryanthe* (1823), *Oberon* (1826), and his most famous work *Der Freischütz* (1821).

- **Richard Wagner:** This composer was also the conductor of the Dresden symphony. He wrote such famous operas as *Der fliegende Holländer, Tannhäuser, Lohengrin, Tristan und Isolde,* and *Die Walküre.*

- **Genussmittelindustrie:** For many, the production of confection and pastries is synonymous with Dresden. Annual trade fairs for the baking and confectionary trade are held here.

- **Dresdener Stollen:** This traditional sweet Christmas bread is prepared four to six weeks before the holidays and stored in a cool place to develop its flavor. For the complete recipe, see p. 295D.

Teacher Note

Recipes for **Dresdener Stollen** are available in many cookbooks. **Stollen** is also available in many American specialty stores during the holiday season.

Music Connection

Have a student check with a music teacher to learn more about Richard Wagner. Perhaps you can play some excerpts of his works.

Map Activity

Have students locate and trace the path of the Elbe on the map on p. T76. You may also want to use *Map Transparency* 1.

> **PAGES 266–267**

THE PHOTO ESSAY

❶ The **Zwinger** received its name from the original **Zwinger Garten** around which it was built.

❷ **Der Goldene Reiter** is a memorial to **August der Starke.** It is made of gold-plated copper and was put in its present location in 1736. The statue is located at the **Neustädter Markt.**

❸ Originally, in the 16th century, the **Albertinum** was a **Zeughaus** *(arsenal).* It was later converted to a museum to hold the unique collection of the Saxon electors' treasures.

❹ **Die ehemalige Katholische Hofkirche** was commissioned by **Friedrich August II.** and built from 1739 to 1755. Since 1980 it has also been referred to as the **Kathedrale Sanctissimae Trinitatis.** The church houses the largest organ designed by builder Gottfried Silbermann, who died shortly after having tuned this magnificent instrument.

❺ The **Frauenkirche** was commissioned in 1726 and completed in 1738. The church, with its 95-meter (311-foot) dome, was once the best-known landmark of Dresden.

❻ The **Staatsoper** or **Semperoper** has presented the premiere performances of many famous operas, including several by Richard Strauss. The facade is decorated with statues of Shakespeare, Molière, Schiller, and Goethe. In front of the opera stands a statue of **Kurfürst Johann Georg II.** as well as one of composer Carl Maria von Weber.

Thinking Critically

Analyzing Throughout the Location Openers in Levels 1, 2, and 3, students have learned about numerous buildings that were destroyed by war and have been or currently are being restored. Some people do not agree that spending millions on restoration is a good idea, in view of world hunger and other social problems. Why do students think the Germans have invested so much time and money in restoration of historical buildings? Is it worth it? Why or why not?

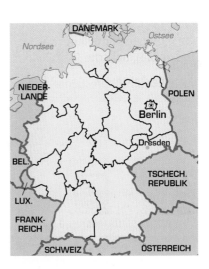

Komm mit nach Dresden!

Bundesland: Sachsen

Einwohner: 500 000

Fluss: Elbe

Sehenswürdigkeiten: Zwinger, Albertinum, Schloss, Semperoper

Berühmte Leute: Kurfürsten Friedrich August I. und II., Carl Maria von Weber (1786-1826), Richard Wagner (1813-1883)

Industrie: Maschinenbau, Elektronik, Arzneimittelproduktion, Genussmittelindustrie (Schokolade), optische Artikel

Bekannte Gerichte: Dresdener Stollen

Map of Germany

Nordsee

Ostsee

DÄNEMARK

NIEDER-LANDE

Berlin

POLEN

BEL.

Dresden

LUX.

TSCHECHIEN

FRANK-REICH

ÖSTERREICH

SCHWEIZ

WK3 DRESDEN

STANDARDS: 2.2, 3.1

Die bekannteste Stadtansicht, Schloss ▶ mit Hofkirche und Semperoper im Hintergrund

Dresden

Dresden, das weltberühmte „Elbflorenz", erlebte seine Glanzzeit unter den prunk-liebenden Kurfürsten Friedrich August I. und seinem Sohn Friedrich August II., beide auch Könige von Polen. In diesem „Augustäischen" Zeitalter (1694-1783) entwickelte sich Dresden zu einer der schönsten barocken deutschen Residenzstädte.

🔼 internet ▬▬▬▬

go.
hrw
.com
ADRESSE: go.hrw.com
KENNWORT: WK3 DRESDEN

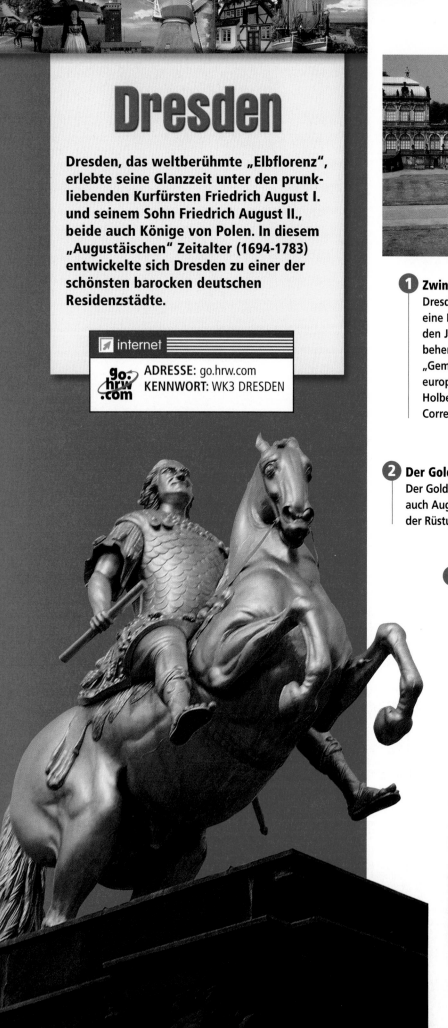

1 Zwinger

Dresdens berühmtestes Baudenkmal ist der Zwinger, eine Perle des Barock von Baumeister Pöppelmann in den Jahren 1711 bis 1732 geschaffen. Der Zwinger beherbergt Dresdens einmalige Kunstsammlung, die „Gemäldegalerie Alte Meister", mit Meisterwerken europäischer Maler wie Rubens, Rembrandt, Dürer, Holbein, Cranach, Velázquez, Raffael, Giorgione, Correggio, Tintoretto und andere Meister.

2 Der Goldene Reiter

Der Goldene Reiter zeigt August I. — auch August der Starke genannt — in der Rüstung eines römischen Cäsaren.

3 Im Albertinum

Das Albertinum enthält die „Gemäldegalerie Neue Meister". Diese Kunstsammlung von Weltruf zeigt Meisterwerke der Romantik, des Biedermeier, des Expressionismus und Impressionismus deutscher und europäischer Meister. Im Albertinum befindet sich auch das „Grüne Gewölbe", eine Kunstsammlung aus der kurfürstlichen Schatzkammer. Ausgestellt sind Gefäße, Schmuck, Waffen und andere Gegenstände, viele aus Gold, Silber und kostbaren Edelsteinen gefertigt.

 Hofkirche

Die ehemalige Katholische Hofkirche, die größte Kirche Sachsens, wurde vom römischen Architekten Gaetano Chiaveri zwischen 1739 und 1755 im Stil des römischen Barock errichtet.

5 Ruine der Frauenkirche

Hier stand einst Deutschlands bedeutendster protestantischer Kirchenbau und das Wahrzeichen Dresdens. Die Kirche, wie auch der größte Teil Dresdens, wurde im Februar 1945 durch Bombenangriffe total zerstört. Die Kirche wird zur Zeit wieder aufgebaut.

6 Semperoper

Die weltberühmte Semperoper, ein Bauwerk von Gottfried Semper im Stil der Hochrenaissance in den Jahren 1871 bis 1878 errichtet, ist Heimat der Dresdner Staatsoper.

Kapitel 10: Die Kunst zu leben
Chapter Overview

Kapitel 10: Die Kunst zu leben
Chapter Resources

Lesson Planning
One-Stop Planner

Lesson Planner with Substitute Teacher Lesson Plans, pp. 56–60, 84

Student Make-Up Assignments
- Make-Up Assignment Copying Masters, Chapter 10

Listening and Speaking
Listening Activities
- Student Response Forms for Listening Activities, pp. 75–78
- Additional Listening Activities 10-1 to 10-6, pp. 79–82
- Scripts and Answers, pp. 175–182

Video Guide
- Teaching Suggestions, p. 46
- Activity Masters, pp. 47–48
- Scripts and Answers, pp. 71, 76

Activities for Communication
- Communicative Activities, pp. 37–40
- Realia and Teaching Suggestions, pp. 96–100
- Situation Cards, pp. 131–132

Reading and Writing
Reading Strategies and Skills Handbook, Chapter 10

Lies mit mir! 3, Chapter 10

Übungsheft, pp. 118–130

Grammar
Grammatikheft, pp. 82–90

Grammar Tutor for Students of German, Chapter 10

Assessment
Testing Program
- Grammar and Vocabulary Quizzes, **Stufe** Quizzes, and Chapter Test, pp. 213–226
- Score Sheet, Scripts and Answers, pp. 227–233

Alternative Assessment Guide
- Portfolio Assessment, p. 25
- Performance Assessment, p. 39

Student Make-Up Assignments
- Alternative Quizzes, Chapter 10

 Online Activities
- Interaktive Spiele
- Internet Aktivitäten

 Video Program
- Videocassette 2

 Audio Compact Discs
- Textbook Listening Activities, CD 10, Tracks 1–9
- Additional Listening Activities, CD 10, Tracks 14–19
- Assessment Items, CD 10, Tracks 10–13

 Teaching Transparencies
- Situations 10-1 to 10-2
- **Mehr Grammatikübungen** Answers
- **Grammatikheft** Answers

 One-Stop Planner CD-ROM

Use the **One-Stop Planner CD-ROM with Test Generator** to aid in lesson planning and pacing.

For each chapter, the **One-Stop Planner** includes:
- Editable lesson plans with direct links to teaching resources
- Printable worksheets from resource books
- Direct launches to the HRW Internet activities
- Video and audio segments
- Test Generator
- Clip Art for vocabulary items

Kapitel 10: Die Kunst zu leben

Projects ·······································

Unser Sommerfest

In this activity, students will plan and coordinate a summer festival for their town. They should work in small groups. Each group should concentrate on one aspect of the festival.

MATERIALS

✂ **Students may need**
- posterboard
- markers
- photos or pictures

SUGGESTED SEQUENCE

1. Ask students to write down their initial ideas of what they would like to include in the summer festival. Then narrow the events/exhibits/performances to a number that can be divided equally among groups of students.

2. Each group brainstorms and compiles information and materials for its part of the festival.

3. The groups work on a poster advertising their event.

4. After students have completed the artistic part of the project (designing and labeling), they must write a paragraph for the local paper advertising their event. The paragraph should describe the type of event and point out its uniqueness to the area, as well as give reasons why it is worth attending.

5. Each group presents its contribution to the festival to the rest of the class. Display the entire program in the classroom.

GRADING THE PROJECT

Suggested point distribution (**total = 100 points**)
- Poster content and appearance.............30
- Oral presentation.................................30
- Written information.............................40

Games ·······································

Künstlerisch begabt

This game will help students review the new vocabulary by sketching a particular word or phrase from an oral description.

Procedure Ask students to choose a word or phrase from the **Wortschatz** on p. 295 which lends itself to being sketched. Each student sketches the word he or she chose, signs the paper, and returns it to the teacher. The teacher mixes up the papers, chooses one at a time, and calls on each student to describe his or her picture without telling what word or phrase it represents. The other students listen carefully and try to draw an identical picture and label it with its corresponding word.

Storytelling

Mini-Geschichte

*This story accompanies Teaching Transparency 10-2. The **Mini-Geschichte** can be told and retold in different formats, acted out, written down, and read aloud to give students additional opportunities to practice all four skills.*

„Was, du hast dir ein Theaterstück angesehen, das einundzwanzig Stunden dauerte?" „Ja, ich habe beide Teile von Goethes *Faust* gesehen. Und die Aufführung war phantastisch! Faust und Mephisto wurden überzeugend dargestellt. Alle technischen Möglichkeiten wurden genutzt (*used*), um dieses Werk in voller Länge aufzuführen. Die Bühne, die Schauspieler, die Handlung — alles war einzigartig. Die Zuschauer haben öfters minutenlang geklatscht. Ich war oft direkt atemlos." „Ich würde bei der Vorstellung einer einundzwanigstündigen Aufführung auch atemlos werden." „Ach, Peter, du bist ein richtiger Kulturmuffel!"

Traditions

Blaues Wunder

Im Jahr 1893 wurde die erste Eisenbahnbrücke ohne Strompfeiler über die Elbe gebaut. Für die damalige Zeit war diese Brücke, die Loschwitz und Blasewitz verbindet, eine technische Spitzenleistung. Claus Köpcke konstruierte die 141 Meter lange und 3500 Tonnen schwere Stahl-Hängekonstruktion. Bei der Fertigstellung wurde ihre Tragfähigkeit getestet: Drei mit Steinen beladene Straßenbahnloren, ein vollbesetzter Straßenbahnwagen, drei Dampfwalzen, sechs Pferdewalzen und vier gefüllte Wassersprengwagen wurden auf die Mitte der Brücke gefahren. Die Brücke bestand den Test! Noch heute trägt sie das Gewicht des täglichen Verkehrs.

Ursprünglich war die Brücke grün gestrichen, aber im Laufe der Zeit wurde sie blau gestrichen. Im Volksmund heißt die deshalb "Blaues Wunder".

Als SS-Leute 1945 Sprengladungen anbrachten, um die Brücke zu sprengen, zerschnitten mutige Dresdner Bürger die Zündkabel der Sprengsätze. So kam es, dass das „Blaue Wunder" die einzige erhaltene Brücke Dresdens blieb.

Was fehlt?

Fleisch
Geflügel
Fisch
Wurst
Bohnen
Gurken
Karotten
Kartoffeln
Salat
Zwiebel
Eier
Reis
Saft
Kaffee
Kakao
Eier
Mehl
Semmeln
Brot
Kekse
Milch
Sahne
Butter
Joghurt
Käse
Fett
Öl
Eier
Zucker
Eier
Reis
Saft
Kaffee
Kakao
Eier
Mehl
Semmeln
Brot
Kekse
Milch
Sahne
Butter
Joghurt
Käse
Fett
Öl
Eier
Zucker
Honig
Bonbon
Äpfel
Birnen
Bananen
Orangen
Zitronen
Salz
Pfeffer
Paprika
Senf
Ketchup
Reis
Teigwaren

Pfefferkuchen

Zutaten

g=Gramm, TL=Teelöffel

4	Eier
500 g	Puderzucker
	abgeriebene Zitronenschale
	Zimt
5 g	Kardamompulver
50 g	Zitronat
50 g	Orangeat
½ TL	gemahlener weißer Pfeffer
500 g	Mehl

Zubereitung

Die Eier und den Zucker in einer Schüssel verrühren, bis sich der Zucker aufgelöst hat. Die Zitronenschale, Zimt und Kardamom einrühren. Zitronat und Orangeat fein würfeln und mit dem Pfeffer untermischen. Dann das Mehl einkneten. Den Teig zu einer Kugel formen, in Plastikfolie wickeln und über Nacht an einem kühlen Ort lagern.

Am nächsten Tag den Teig auf etwas Mehl ausrollen. Aus dem Teig beliebige Formen schneiden. Die Pfefferkuchen auf ein mit Backpapier belegtes Blech legen und bei 175 Grad Celsius ca. 20 Minuten backen.

Kapitel 10: Die Kunst zu leben
Technology

To preview all resources available for this chapter, use the **One-Stop Planner CD-ROM**, Disc 3.

Internet Connection ....

ADRESSE: go.hrw.com
KENNWORT:
WK3 DRESDEN-10

*Have students explore the **go.hrw.com** Web site for many online resources covering all chapters. All Chapter 10 resources are available under the keyword **WK3 Dresden-10**. Interactive games practice the material and provide students with immediate feedback. You will also find a printable worksheet that provides Internet activities that lead to a comprehensive online research project.*

Interaktive Spiele

You can use the interactive activities in this chapter

- to practice grammar, vocabulary, and chapter functions
- as homework
- as an assessment option
- as a self-test
- to prepare for the Chapter Test

Internet Aktivitäten

Students visit the site of a theater, an opera, and a museum and find specific information about a play, a ballet or opera, and an exhibition.

- To prepare students for the **Arbeitsblatt,** have them discuss the cultural events they enjoy most. You may want to ask students to reread **Los geht's!** on pp. 270-271 before starting the discussion.
- After completing the **Arbeitsblatt,** divide the class into small groups and have each group write a short play. After students have had a chance to edit their play, they should perform it for their classmates.

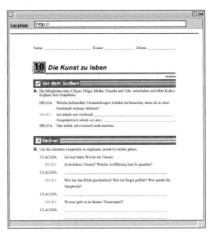

Webprojekt
Have students find a fairy tale by the Brothers Grimm. Students should give a synopsis of the fairy tale and answer the following questions: 1) Does the fairy tale they chose have a moral? 2) Does it have stock characters such as a Prince Charming or a supernatural being? 3) Does it reflect the socioeconomic conditions of the time when it was written? Encourage students to exchange useful Web sites with their classmates. Have students document their sources by referencing the names and URLs of all the sites they consulted.

Kapitel 10: Die Kunst zu leben
Textbook Listening Activities Scripts

The following scripts are for the listening activities found in the *Pupil's Edition*. For Student Response Forms, see *Listening Activities*, pages 75–78. To provide students with additional listening practice, see *Listening Activities*, pages 79–82.

Erste Stufe

4 p. 272

ERWIN   Hallo, Lise, hier ist Erwin! Du, wir wollten doch diese Woche mit der Clique was Kulturelles unternehmen. Hast du schon was aus dem Kulturkalender rausgesucht?

LISE   Hallo, Erwin! Nee, du! Aber warte mal! Ich hole ihn sofort … Also, hier ist er.

ERWIN   Dann lies doch mal vor, was für Veranstaltungen so am Wochenende laufen!

LISE   Also, da gibt es eine historische Ausstellung über das Leben der Juden im Deutschland des 19. Jahrhunderts.

ERWIN   Interessiert dich denn sowas überhaupt?

LISE   Ja, klar! Wir sprechen gerade im Geschichtsunterricht über den Holocaust zur Zeit des NS-Regimes. Da möchte ich schon etwas mehr Hintergrundwissen haben. Und du? Interessierst du dich denn dafür?

ERWIN   Ja, schon! Aber ich würde lieber in ein Konzert gehen. Was läuft denn sonst noch?

LISE   Also, den ganzen Samstag lang gibt's ein Jazzfestival im Stadtpark.

ERWIN   Uii! Klasse! Dazu hätte ich auf jeden Fall Lust! Und du?

LISE   Hmm. Mal sehen. Du, hör mal! Am Samstag gibt es auch eine Kunstausstellung mit Bildern von Andy Warhol … und dann noch ein Konzert des evangelischen Jugendchors in der Sankt-Pius-Kirche.

ERWIN   Hmm … äh …

LISE   Also, mir fällt es echt schwer, mich zu entscheiden. Aber, ich glaub, dass ich am liebsten zur Ausstellung über das Leben der Juden gehen möchte! Tja, und dann würde ich eventuell noch zum Chorkonzert in die Sankt-Pius-Kirche gehen. Und du, Erwin?

ERWIN   Also, wenn ich ehrlich sein soll, würde ich am liebsten tagsüber zum Jazzfestival gehen.

Und dann, am Samstagabend würde ich vielleicht ins Kino gehen.

LISE   Kino??? Ich denke, wir wollten was Kulturelles machen! Und jetzt schlägst du Kino vor!? Das ist ja wohl das Letzte!

ERWIN   Was hast du denn, Lise? Seit wann haben Kinofilme nichts mit Kultur zu tun? Denk doch mal an all die alten Kultfilme mit Humphrey Bogart oder Clark Gable! Das sind echte Klassiker! Kultur pur, sag ich dir!

LISE   Na schön! Und in welchen Kultfilm möchtest du bitte gehen?

ERWIN   Also, am Samstag ist die Premiere von dem neuen Actionthriller mit Arnold Schwarzenegger. Sagenhaft soll der sein!

LISE   Soso, Arnold Schwarzenegger!

ERWIN   Ja, wart's nur ab! In fünfzig Jahren oder so sind seine Filme richtige Klassiker! Das kannst du mir glauben!

LISE   Also, pass mal auf, Erwin! Was hältst du davon, wenn wir zuerst aufs Jazzfestival gehen und abends dann zur historischen Ausstellung über die Juden?

ERWIN   Hm. Okay, einverstanden! Ich ruf die anderen an und sag Bescheid, für welches Programm wir uns entschieden haben.

LISE   Prima! Bis Samstag dann.

Answers to Activity 4
Lise: historische Ausstellung; Chorkonzert
Erwin: Jazzfestival; Kino
Sie entschließen sich, zum Jazzfestival und zur historischen Ausstellung zu gehen.

Zweite Stufe

17 p. 279

SUSI   Hallo, Inge! Wie hat dir unser Klassenausflug gestern Abend gefallen?

INGE   Super! Das Ballett *Giselle* war echt beeindruckend. Außerdem war ich zum ersten Mal in der Staatsoper, du auch, Susi?

SUSI   Ja! Schau mal, da kommen Ömur und Lutz. Ich möchte gern wissen, was sie über das Ballett denken. He, Lutz, Ömur, kommt doch mal hierher! Inge und ich haben uns gerade über die Aufführung gestern in der Staatsoper unterhalten. Was ist eure Meinung dazu?

LUTZ	Also, zu Anfang war ich ja etwas skeptisch. Ich dachte immer, dass Ballett nur was für Mädchen ist.
INGE	Wieso denn das, Lutz?
LUTZ	Ach, das kann ich gar nicht begründen. Ich glaub, das war ein echtes Vorurteil von mir. Aber gestern, im Laufe der Vorstellung, habe ich meine Meinung allerdings geändert.
ÖMUR	Ich war auch zuerst skeptisch. Ich habe nämlich gedacht, dass die Musik mir bestimmt nicht gefällt.
SUSI	Und? Hast du deine Meinung geändert, Ömur?
ÖMUR	Nee, eigentlich nicht! Wisst ihr, ich mag fetzige Musik, und diese Ballettmusik hat einfach zu wenig Power für mich.
INGE	Das ist aber schade, Ömur. Für mich war es echt toll, mal was ganz anderes zu sehen und zu hören. Eben was Besonderes.
ÖMUR	Das mag zwar sein, aber mir hat die Musik nun mal nicht gefallen. Ich kann's auch nicht ändern!
SUSI	Wie fandet ihr denn die Kulissen? Ich glaube, die haben mich am meisten beeindruckt. Die erste Szene mit der Insel im Meer war doch Spitze, meint ihr nicht?
ÖMUR	Ja, das muss ich zugeben; mit den Kulissen haben sie sich echt Mühe gegeben.
INGE	Da stecken wirkliche Künstler dahinter. Ich würde gern mal so eine Aufgabe im Kunstunterricht bei uns in der Schule machen.
LUTZ	Gar keine schlechte Idee. Das würde mir auch Spaß machen. Übrigens war ich sehr begeistert von dem Schiff, das sie da auf der Bühne hatten.
ÖMUR	Da stimme ich euch zu! Aber wisst ihr, was ich ganz toll fand?
INGE	Na sag schon!
ÖMUR	Die Tänzer waren nicht nur gute Balletttänzer, sondern meiner Meinung nach auch hervorragende Schauspieler!
SUSI	Ja, da hast du Recht! Vor allem der bärtige Hilarion, der vor lauter Eifersucht ganz wütend war.
INGE	Der hat mir auch besser gefallen als der junge Maler Albrecht. Der sah zwar toll aus, aber er war gleichzeitig auch ein bisschen langweilig.
LUTZ	Ich fand sie alle gut. Immerhin gab es ja auch noch eine ganze Menge andere Tänzer, die nur in Nebenrollen auftraten, ohne die das Stück aber nicht möglich wäre.
ÖMUR	Na ja, dafür war das Ende des Stückes aber etwas enttäuschend, genau wie die Musik.
LUTZ	Nun hör schon auf mit deinen Beschwerden über die Musik, Ömur! Ich kann eigentlich nicht behaupten, dass ich vom Ende des Stückes enttäuscht war. Meiner Meinung nach muss es nicht immer ein Happyend geben!
SUSI	Hm. Also, ich stimme mit Ömur überein. Ich war auch etwas traurig darüber. Ein Happyend hätte mir viel besser gefallen. Das hätte gut zu der märchenhaften Atmosphäre gepasst.
INGE	Eben! Ach übrigens, was ich noch toll fand, das waren die Kostüme!
SUSI	Ja, stimmt, Susi! Waren die nicht prunkvoll und wunderschön?
INGE	Genau! Also, ich hätte Lust, bald wieder in ein Ballett zu gehen.

Answers to Activity 17
Sie waren im Ballett Giselle.
Inge: gut / fand die Kostüme toll
Susi: gut / fand die Kulissen Spitze
Lutz: gut / hatte zuerst Vorurteile
Ömur: nicht gut / ihm hat die Musik nicht gefallen; war vom Ende enttäuscht

23 p. 280

Guten Tag, sehr verehrte Zuhörer! Ich darf Sie herzlich zu unserem Sonntagskonzert begrüßen. Wir sind heute zu Gast in der Berliner Philharmonie. Das Konzert wird von dem weltberühmten Dirigenten Zubin Mehta dirigiert. Auf dem Programm stehen, wie bereits in unserem Vorspann angekündigt, Werke von Beethoven, Tschaikowski und Bach.

Da wir noch einige Minuten Zeit haben, bevor die Vorstellung beginnt, möchte ich Ihnen kurz beschreiben, was sich im Konzertsaal abspielt. Die Berliner Philharmoniker nahmen bereits vor einer halben Stunde ihre Plätze auf der Bühne ein. Das gesamte Ensemble ist mit den letzten Vorbereitungen beschäftigt. Die Instrumente werden von den Musikern gestimmt. Viele Zuschauer strömen in den Saal und werden zu ihren Sitzplätzen geführt.

Lassen Sie mich, liebe Freunde der klassischen Musik, die Gelegenheit nutzen, ein paar Worte über die Philharmonie einzuschieben. Für alle unsere Zuhörer, die den ungewöhnlichen Bau dieses Gebäudes nicht kennen, hier ein paar Details. Der Konzertsaal der Berliner Philharmonie ist asymmetrisch angelegt und sieht darum wie ein verschobenes Fünfeck aus. Ringsum steigen unregelmäßig angeordnete Logenterrassen an, die allen Zuschauern einen guten Blick auf die Bühne bieten. Die Akustik entfaltet sich dadurch äußerst wirkungsvoll.

Meine sehr verehrten Zuhörer, mittlerweile hat sich der Zuschauerraum fast gefüllt. Die letzten Gäste werden von den Platzanweisern zu ihren Plätzen gebracht. Das muntere Stimmengewirr des Publikums vermischt sich mit den Tönen der Geigen, Posaunen, Harfen und Kontrabässe. Die meisten Musiker sind nun bereit. Sie haben ihre Instrumente abgestellt, um noch ein letztes Mal ihre Noten auf den Notenständern zu überprüfen. Da betritt auch schon der Dirigent die Bühne. Maestro Mehta wird mit lautstarkem Beifall begrüßt. Er steht nun am Podest und erhebt seinen Dirigentenstab. Atemlose Stille füllt den Raum, bevor das Orchester unter Leitung des Maestros das Konzert beginnt. Meine lieben Zuhörer, ich verabschiede mich vorübergehend, damit Sie die harmonischen Klänge dieser wunderbaren Sinfonien genießen können.

Answers to Activity 23
die Musiker; die Zuschauer; den Konzertsaal; die Logen; die Akustik; die Instrumente; den Dirigenten / die Berliner Philharmoniker; Werke von Beethoven, Tschaikowski und Bach (klassische Musik)

Anwendung

 1 p. 292

NICOLE   Hallo, Regina! Komm, setz dich zu uns!

REGINA   Ach, hallo Nicole! Hallo Sascha!

RAINER   Tag! Ich bin der Rainer. Kann ich dir was zu trinken bestellen?

REGINA   Tag, Rainer! Ja, gern. Ich nehm 'nen Cappuccino!

NICOLE   Du, Regina, hättest du nicht Lust, mit Rainer, Sascha und mir am Wochenende was zu unternehmen?

REGINA   Klar! Wofür interessiert ihr euch denn so?

RAINER   Also, wir überlegen gerade, ob wir zum B.B. King Konzert gehen sollen.

REGINA   Gibt es noch Karten?

RAINER   Ja, an der Abendkasse kriegt man immer noch welche! Das Konzert findet am Samstag in Karlsruhe statt. Wisst ihr, dieser Mann ist einfach Spitze. Er ist ja bereits in den Sechzigern, geht aber trotzdem noch regelmäßig auf Tournee. Einfach sagenhaft!

REGINA   Du magst wohl Rhythm 'n Blues, was?

RAINER   Und wie! Du etwa nicht?

REGINA   Doch schon! Aber eigentlich gehe ich nicht so oft in Konzerte. Ich gehe lieber ins Ballett oder in die Oper!

NICOLE   Was? Das wusste ich ja gar nicht, dass du dich für so was interessierst!

REGINA   Doch, leidenschaftlich! Am liebsten mag ich dramatische Opern mit einem tragischen Ende, so wie *La Traviata* zum Beispiel! Und du, Nicole? Was interessiert dich am meisten?

One-Stop Planner CD-ROM

For resource information, see the **One-Stop Planner CD-ROM**, Disc 3.

NICOLE   Tja, also ich bin ein Literaturfan!

SASCHA   Bücherwurm nennt man das!

NICOLE   Ha! Ha! Sehr witzig, Sascha! Ich les halt gern, am liebsten Shakespeare. Und wenn sich die Gelegenheit ergibt, dann sehe ich mir auch gern Stücke im Theater an. Nächste Woche läuft im Landestheater *Andorra* von Max Frisch. Na, Sascha, gehst du mit mir dahin?

SASCHA   Nur wenn du mit mir in die Kunstausstellung im Stadtmuseum gehst!

NICOLE   Was wird denn ausgestellt?

SASCHA   Surrealistische Gemälde von Dali und Magritte. Einfach super! Ich steh total darauf!

REGINA   Hmm. Es sieht so aus, als ob wir alle ziemlich verschiedene Interessen haben.

NICOLE   Willst du damit sagen, dass wir lieber doch nichts zusammen unternehmen sollten?

REGINA   Nein, im Gegenteil! Ich habe einen Vorschlag: warum machen wir nicht alles der Reihe nach? Zuerst gehen wir am Samstag ins B.B. King Konzert. Dann gehen wir nächste Woche ins Theater, dann in die Kunstausstellung und irgendwann auch mal ins Ballett oder in die Oper! Na, wie findet ihr das?

NICOLE   Klasse Idee! Das bringt auf jeden Fall mal etwas Abwechslung in unsere Unternehmungen! Ich bin dabei! Wie sieht's mit euch aus, Jungs?

SASCHA   Klar! Ich mach mit! Und du, Rainer?

RAINER   Ich bin auch dabei!

Answers to Activity 1
Rainer: Konzert; Sascha: Kunstausstellung; Regina: Ballett, Oper; Nicole: Literatur; Theater

Kapitel 10: Die Kunst zu leben
Suggested Lesson Plans *50-Minute Schedule*

Day 1

LOCATION OPENER 15 min.
- Present Location Opener, pp. 264–267
- Background information, ATE, p. 263A
- The Almanac and Map, ATE, p. 263A
- Show **Dresden** Video
- Do Viewing and Post-Viewing Activities, Video Guide, p. 43

CHAPTER OPENER 5 min.
- Drama Connection, ATE, p. 267M
- Teaching Suggestion, ATE, p. 267M

LOS GEHT'S! 25 min.
- Preteaching Vocabulary, ATE, p. 267N
- Advance Organizer, ATE, p. 267N
- Teaching Suggestions, ATE, p. 267N
- Play Audio CD for **Los geht's!**
- Have students read **Los geht's!**, pp. 270–271
- Do Activities 1, 2, and 3, p. 271

Wrap-Up 5 min.
- Students respond to questions about what cultural events German students are interested in

Homework Options
Übungsheft, p. 118, Acts. 1–2

Day 2

ERSTE STUFE
Quick Review 10 min.
- Check homework, Übungsheft, p. 118, Acts. 1–2

Wortschatz, So sagt man das!, p. 272 25 min.
- Presenting **Wortschatz, So sagt man das!**, ATE, p. 267O
- Teaching Transparency 10-1
- Play Audio CD for Activity 4, p. 272
- Do Activities 5, 6, and 7, p. 273

So sagt man das!, p. 273 10 min.
- Presenting **So sagt man das!**, ATE, p. 267P
- Do Activity 8, p. 274

Wrap-Up 5 min.
- Students respond to questions about which cultural events they would attend if they had the time

Homework Options
Grammatikheft, pp. 82–84, Acts. 1–5
Übungsheft, p. 119, Act. 1; p. 120, Act. 4; pp. 121–122, Acts. 5, 7–9

Day 3

ERSTE STUFE
Quick Review 10 min.
- Check homework, Grammatikheft, pp. 82–84, Acts. 1–5

Grammatik, p. 274 35 min.
- Presenting **Grammatik**, ATE, p. 267P
- Do Activities 9 and 10, p. 274
- Do Activities 11–15, p. 275
- Do Activities 2–3, pp. 119–120 and Activity 6, p. 121, Übungsheft

Wrap-Up 5 min.
- Students respond to questions about their cultural interests

Homework Options
Grammatikheft, p. 85, Act. 6

Day 4

ERSTE STUFE
Quick Review 10 min.
- Check homework, Grammatikheft, p. 85, Act. 6

WEITER GEHT'S! 20 min.
- Preteaching Vocabulary, ATE, p. 267Q
- Background Information, ATE, p. 267R
- Teaching Suggestions, ATE, p. 267R
- Career Path, ATE, p. 267R
- Play Audio CD for **Weiter geht's!**, pp. 276–277
- Do Activity 16, p. 277

Game 15 min.
- Play game, **Künstlerisch begabt**, ATE, p. 267C

Wrap-Up 5 min.
- Students name prepositions with the genitive case

Homework Options
Übungsheft, p. 123, Acts. 1–2
Internet Aktivitäten, see ATE, p. 267E

Day 5

ERSTE STUFE
Quick Review 10 min.
- Check homework, Übungsheft, p. 123, Acts. 1–2

Quiz Review 20 min.
- Do Realia 10-2, p. 97, Activities for Communication
- Do Activities for Communication 10-1 and 10-2, pp. 37–38
- Do **Mehr Grammatikübungen, Erste Stufe**

Quiz 20 min.
- Quiz 10-1A or 10-1B

Homework Options
Activities for Communication, p. 98, Realia 10-3; write a letter to a friend about having attended one of the concerts listed

Day 6

ZWEITE STUFE
Quick Review 15 min.
- Return and review Quiz 10-1
- Bell Work, ATE, p. 267S
- Check homework, Activities for Communication, p. 98, Realia 10-3

Wortschatz, So sagt man das!, p. 278 15 min.
- Presenting **Wortschatz, So sagt man das!**, ATE, p. 267S
- Play Audio CD for Activity 17, p. 279
- Do Activity 18, p. 279

Ein wenig Grammatik, p. 279 15 min.
- Presenting **Ein wenig Grammatik**, ATE, p. 267S
- Do Activities 19 and 20, p. 279
- Do Activities 21 and 22, p. 280

Wrap-Up 5 min.
- Students respond to questions concerning what they are happy or sad about

Homework Options
Grammatikheft, pp. 86–87, Acts. 7–9
Übungsheft, p. 124, Acts. 1–2

One-Stop Planner CD-ROM

For alternative lesson plans by chapter section, to create your own customized plans, or to preview all resources available for this chapter, use the **One-Stop Planner CD-ROM**, Disc 3.

 For additional homework suggestions, see activities accompanied by this symbol throughout the chapter.

Day 7

ZWEITE STUFE

Quick Review 10 min.
- Check homework, Grammatikheft, pp. 86–87, Acts. 7–9

So sagt man das!, p. 280 10 min.
- Presenting So sagt man das!, ATE, p. 267T
- Play Audio CD for Activity 23, p. 280
- Do Activity 24, p. 280

Grammatik, p. 281 25 min.
- Presenting **Grammatik**, ATE, p. 267T
- Teaching Suggestion, ATE, p. 267T
- Teaching Transparency 10-2
- Reteaching: Passive Voice, p. 267T
- Do Activities 10, 11, and 12, pp. 88–90, Grammatikheft
- Do Activities 25–28, p. 282

Wrap-Up 5 min.
- Students respond to questions about what is or was being done during a cultural performance

Homework Options
Übungsheft, pp. 125–127, Acts. 3–8

Day 8

ZWEITE STUFE

Quick Review 5 min.
- Check homework Übungsheft, pp. 125–127, Acts. 3–8

LANDESKUNDE 20 min.
- Presenting **Landeskunde**, ATE, p. 267T
- Read **Kultur findet man überall**, p. 283
- Do Activities A and B, p. 283

Geld für Kultur? (Video) 20 min.
- Teaching Suggestions, Video Guide, p. 46
- Do Pre-viewing Activity, Video Guide, p. 47
- Show **Geld für Kultur?** Video
- Do Viewing and Post-viewing Activities, Video Guide, p. 47

Wrap-Up 5 min.
- Students use the passive voice expressing on what cultural venues money is spent

Homework Options
Mehr Grammatikübungen, Zweite Stufe

Day 9

ZWEITE STUFE

Quick Review 10 min.
- Check homework, **Mehr Grammatikübungen, Zweite Stufe**

Quiz Review 20 min.
- Do Additional Listening Activities 10-4 and 10-5, pp. 81–82
- Do Communicative Activities 10-3 and 10-4, pp. 39–40

Quiz 20 min.
- Quiz 10-2A or 10-2B

Homework Options
Interaktive Spiele, see ATE, p. 267E

Day 10

ZWEITE STUFE

Quick Review 10 min.
- Return and review Quiz 10-2

ZUM LESEN 35 min.
- Building Context, ATE, p. 267V
- Teacher Notes, ATE, p. 267V
- Present **Lesestrategie**, p. 284
- Do Activities 1–7, pp. 284–286

Wrap-Up 5 min.
- Students name words they would use when writing a scary story

Homework Options
Übungsheft, pp. 129–130, Acts. 1–7

Day 11

ZWEITE STUFE

Quick Review 5 min.
- Check homework, Übungsheft, pp. 129–130, Acts. 1–7

ZUM SCHREIBEN 40 min.
- Writing Strategy, ATE, p. 267W
- Present **Schreibtipp**, p. 287
- Do Activities A, B, and C, p. 287

Wrap-Up 5 min.
- Students respond to questions about expressing admiration and envy

Homework Options
Pupil's Edition, p. 294, Acts. 1–8, **Kann ich's wirklich?**
Complete **Zum Schreiben** compositions
Interaktive Spiele, see ATE, p. 267E

Day 12

ANWENDUNG

Quick Review 10 min.
- Check homework, Pupil's Edition, p. 294, Acts. 1–8
- Do Activities 1–8, pp. 292–293

Chapter Review 20 min.
- Review chapter functions, vocabulary, and grammar; choose from **Mehr Grammatikübungen,** Activities for Communication, Listening Activities, or **Interaktive Spiele**
- Review test format and provide sample test items for students

Homework Options
Study for Chapter Test

Assessment

Test, Chapter 10 45 min.
- Administer Chapter 10 Test. Select from Testing Program, Alternative Assessment Guide or Test Generator.

Kapitel 10: Die Kunst zu leben
Suggested Lesson Plans *90-Minute Schedule*

Block 1

LOCATION OPENER 15 min.
- Present Location Opener, pp. 264–267
- Background Information, ATE, p. 263A
- The Almanac and Map, ATE, p. 263A
- Show **Dresden** Video
- Do Viewing and Post-viewing Activities, Video Guide, p. 43

CHAPTER OPENER 5 min.
- Drama Connection, ATE, p. 267M
- Teaching Suggestion, ATE, p. 267M

LOS GEHT'S! 25 min.
- Preteaching Vocabulary, ATE, p. 267N
- Advance Organizer, ATE, p. 267N
- Teaching Suggestions, ATE, p. 267N
- Play Audio CD for **Los geht's!**
- Have students read **Los geht's!**, pp. 270–271
- Do Activities 1, 2, and 3, p. 271

ERSTE STUFE
Wortschatz, So sagt man das!, p. 272 25 min.
- Presenting **Wortschatz, So sagt man das!**, ATE, p. 267O
- Teaching Transparency 10-1
- Play Audio CD for Activity 4, p. 272
- Do Activities 5, 6, and 7, p. 273

So sagt man das!, p. 273 15 min.
- Presenting **So sagt man das!**, ATE, p. 267P
- Do Activity 8, p. 274
- Do Activity 4, p. 120, Übungsheft

Wrap-Up 5 min.
- Students respond to questions about which cultural events they would attend if they had the time

Homework Options
Grammatikheft, pp. 82–84, Acts. 1–5
Übungsheft, p. 118, Acts. 1–2, p. 119, Act. 1; pp. 121–122, Acts. 5, 7–9

Block 2

ERSTE STUFE
Quick Review 10 min.
- Check homework, Grammatikheft, pp. 82–84, Acts. 1–5

Grammatik, p. 274 35 min.
- Presenting **Grammatik**, ATE, p. 267P
- Do Activities 9 and 10, p. 274
- Do Activities 11–15, p. 275
- Do Activities 2–3, pp. 119–120 and Activity 6, p. 121, Übungsheft

WEITER GEHT'S! 20 min.
- Preteaching Vocabulary, ATE, p. 267Q
- Background Information, ATE, p. 267R
- Teaching Suggestions, ATE, p. 267R
- Career Path, ATE, p. 267R
- Play Audio CD for **Weiter geht's!**, pp. 276–277
- Do Activity 16, p. 277

Game 20 min.
- Play game, **Künstlerisch begabt**, ATE, p. 267C

Wrap-Up 5 min.
- Students respond to questions about their cultural interests

Homework Options
Grammatikheft, p. 85, Act. 6
Übungsheft, pp. 119–120, Acts. 2–3; p. 121, Act. 6

Block 3

ERSTE STUFE
Quick Review 10 min.
- Check homework, Übungsheft, pp. 119–120, Acts. 2–3; p. 121, Act. 6

Quiz Review 20 min.
- Do Realia 10-2, p. 97, Activities for Communication
- Do Activities for Communication 10-1 and 10-2, pp. 37–38
- Do **Mehr Grammatikübungen, Erste Stufe**

Quiz 20 min.
- Quiz 10-1A or 10-1B

ZWEITE STUFE
Wortschatz, So sagt man das!, p. 278 20 min.
- Presenting **Wortschatz, So sagt man das!**, ATE, p. 267S
- Play Audio CD for Activity 17, p. 279
- Do Activity 18, p. 279
- Do Activity 9, p. 87, Grammatikheft

Ein wenig Grammatik, p. 279 15 min.
- Presenting **Ein wenig Grammatik**, p. 267S
- Do Activities 19 and 20, p. 279
- Do Activities 21 and 22, p. 280

Wrap-Up 5 min.
- Students respond to questions concerning what things they are happy or sad about

Homework Options
Grammatikheft, p. 86, Acts. 7–8
Übungsheft, p. 124, Acts. 1–2

One-Stop Planner CD-ROM

For alternative lesson plans by chapter section, to create your own customized plans, or to preview all resources available for this chapter, use the **One-Stop Planner CD-ROM**, Disc 3.

For additional homework suggestions, see activities accompanied by this symbol throughout the chapter.

Block 4

ZWEITE STUFE
Quick Review 10 min.
- Return and review Quiz 10-1
- Check homework, Übungsheft, p. 124, Acts. 1–2

So sagt man das!, p. 280 10 min.
- Presenting **So sagt man das!**, ATE, p. 267T
- Teaching Transparency 10-2
- Play Audio CD for Activity 23, p. 280
- Do Activity 24, p. 280

Grammatik, p. 281 25 min.
- Presenting **Grammatik**, ATE, p. 267T
- Teaching Suggestion, ATE, p. 267T
- Reteaching: Passive Voice, p. 267T
- Do Activities 10, 11, and 12, pp. 88–90, Grammatikheft
- Do Activities 25–28, p. 282

LANDESKUNDE 20 min.
- Presenting **Landeskunde**, ATE, p. 267T
- Read **Kultur findet man überall**, p. 283
- Do Activities A and B, p. 283

Geld für Kultur? (Video) 20 min.
- Teaching Suggestions, Video Guide, p. 46
- Do Pre-viewing Activity, Video Guide, p. 47
- Show **Geld für Kultur?** Video
- Do Viewing and Post-viewing Activities, Video Guide, p. 47

Wrap-Up 5 min.
- Students respond to questions about what is or was being done during a cultural performance

Homework Options
Übungsheft, pp. 125–127, Acts. 3–8
Mehr Grammatikübungen, Zweite Stufe
Internet Aktivitäten, see ATE, p. 267E

Block 5

ZWEITE STUFE
Quick Review 10 min.
- Check homework, **Mehr Grammatikübungen, Zweite Stufe**

Quiz Review 20 min.
- Do Additional Listening Activities 10-4 and 10-5, pp. 81–82
- Do Communicative Activities 10-3 and 10-4, pp. 39–40

Quiz 20 min.
- Quiz 10-2A or 10-2B

ZUM LESEN 35 min.
- Building Context, ATE, p. 267V
- Teacher Notes, ATE, p. 267V
- Present **Lesestrategie**, p. 284
- Do Activities 1–7, pp. 284–286

Wrap-Up 5 min.
- Students name words they would use when writing a scary story

Homework Options
Übungsheft, pp. 129–130, Acts. 1–7
Interaktive Spiele, see ATE, p. 267E

Block 6

ZWEITE STUFE
Quick Review 10 min.
- Return and review Quiz 10-2
- Check homework, Übungsheft, pp. 129–130, Acts. 1–7

ZUM SCHREIBEN 35 min.
- Writing Strategy, ATE, p. 267W
- Present **Schreibtipp**, p. 287
- Do Activities A, B, and C, p. 287

Kann ich's wirklich?, p. 294 20 min.
- Do **Kann ich's wirklich?** Activities 1–8, p. 294

ANWENDUNG 20 min.
- Do Activities 1–8, pp. 292–293

Wrap-Up 5 min.
- Students respond to questions about expressing admiration and envy

Homework Options
Complete **Zum Schreiben** compositions
Interaktive Spiele, see ATE, p. 267E

Block 7

ANWENDUNG
Quick Review 15 min.
- Check homework, **Zum Schreiben** compositions

Chapter Review 30 min.
- Review chapter functions, vocabulary, and grammar; choose from **Mehr Grammatikübungen**, Activities for Communication, Listening Activities, or **Interaktive Spiele**
- Review test format and provide sample test items for students

Test, Chapter 10 45 min.
- Administer Chapter 10 Test. Select from Testing Program, Alternative Assessment Guide or Test Generator.

Kapitel 10: Die Kunst zu leben
Teaching Suggestions, pages 268–295

Using the Video

Before you begin the chapter, you may want to preview the *Video Program* and consult the *Video Guide.* Suggestions for integrating the video into each chapter are given in the *Video Guide* and in the chapter interleaf of the *Teacher's Edition.* Activity masters for video selections can be found in the *Video Guide.*

PAGES 268–269

CHAPTER OPENER

Pacing Tips

Los geht's! and the **Erste Stufe** focus on art exhibits, plays, and musical performances that German **Gymnasiasten** might attend. Students learn to express preference when given certain possibilities, and to express envy and admiration. Genitive prepositions are presented on p. 274. Quotes from three famous Germans appear on p. 275. **Weiter geht's!** and the **Zweite Stufe** center around a ballet performance. Students practice expressing happiness and sadness and saying that something is or was being done. A complete summary of the passive voice is presented on p. 281. The **Zum Lesen** reading is a horror story called *Die Nacht bei den Wachsfiguren,* which has a surprise ending. The **Wortschatz** on p. 295 is somewhat lengthy. For Lesson Plans and timing suggestions, see pages 267I–267L.

Meeting the Standards
Communication
- Expressing preference, given certain possibilities, p. 272
- Expressing envy and admiration, p. 273
- Expressing happiness and sadness, p. 278
- Saying that something is or was being done, p. 280

Cultures
- Landeskunde, p. 283
- Background Information, p. 267U
- Teacher Notes, p. 267V

Connections
- Drama Connection, p. 267M
- Language Arts Connection, p. 267W

Comparisons
- Language-to-Language, p. 267O

One-Stop Planner CD-ROM

For resource information, see the **One-Stop Planner CD-ROM,** Disc 3.

Communities
- Community Link, p. 267U

Advance Organizer

Ask students about their families' and their own artistic abilities. Do any of them play an instrument or have another artistic talent? (**Ist jemand in eurer Familie musikalisch begabt? Wenn ja, welches Instrument spielt er oder sie? Habt ihr in der Familie jemanden, der noch anders künstlerisch begabt ist?**)

Connections and Comparisons

Drama Connection

Have students find out about the most recent school play. What was the name of the play, and what was it about? Perhaps students can obtain a poster or flyer from a performance and bring it to class.

Teaching Suggestion

Ask students to recall a cultural event they attended in the past. What was it and what did they like or not like about it? (**Berichtet über eine kulturelle Veranstaltung, die ihr besucht habt! Hat euch die Veranstaltung gefallen oder nicht? Erzählt davon, und begründet eure Meinung!**)

Chapter Sequence

LOS GEHT'S!

Teaching Resources
pp. 270–271

PRINT
▸ Lesson Planner, p. 56
▸ Übungsheft, p. 118

MEDIA
▸ One-Stop Planner
▸ Audio Compact Discs, CD10, Trs. 1–2

PAGES 270–271

Los geht's! Summary

In *Was tun für die Kultur?*, Philipp, Michael, Sonja, and Tanja talk about their cultural interests. The following learning outcomes listed on p. 269 are modeled in the episode: expressing preference, given certain possibilities, and expressing envy and admiration.

Preteaching Vocabulary

Recognizing Cognates

Los geht's! contains many words about the arts that students will be able to recognize as cognates or borrowed words. Some are compound words in which only part of the word is a cognate. Have students identify these words and describe what is happening in the article and then in the discussion. Here are just some of the cognates and borrowed words they might find: **Konzertabonnement, Philosophen, Hausmusik, Wunderwerke, grotesk, Volksfest.** In addition to cognates and borrowed words, students should also notice many non-cognate words that they already know.

Advance Organizer

Ask students to name a cultural event they would not want to miss if it came to their area. (**Denkt an eine kulturelle Veranstaltung, die ihr auf keinen Fall verpassen würdet, wenn sie hier in … stattfinden würde!**)

Teaching Suggestion

Divide the conversation into three parts. Play one portion at a time as students follow along in the text. Follow each partial playing with questions to check for comprehension. Explain any new terms, phrases, or constructions in German by paraphrasing or using synonyms. After working through all three segments, play the entire conversation again, stopping repeatedly to check for students' understanding of key points.

Thinking Critically

Drawing Inferences Ask students to think about the possible reasons why students' tickets to cultural events are discounted. Why do state-supported cultural institutions and privately financed institutions do this?

Comprehension Check

Challenge

1 Ask students to work in pairs as they complete the chart with information about the cultural interests of the four German teenagers. Then prepare a blank chart on a transparency and elicit information from students to complete the chart.

Teaching Suggestions

2 This activity could also be used as a game, in which case each group that correctly answers a question from the opposing group receives a point. You can increase the number of questions to eight or ten to extend the game.

3 Expand this project by having one group do music, another art, and a third literature. Each group should take a section of the bulletin board to make a display. Provide a list of representative people from each field, or have students make their own lists. Reports should include examples of these people's work.

3 Refer students to the Almanacs in the four Location Openers where **Berühmte Leute** are mentioned. Many of these people can be included in the groups' projects.

Closure

Ask students how they would describe the interest level of German students in cultural activities. How would they compare it to their own? (**Wie würdest du das Interesse deutscher Schüler an kulturellen Veranstaltungen beschreiben? Vergleich es mit deinem Interesse an kulturellen Veranstaltungen!**)

Teaching Resources
pp. 272–275

PRINT
- Lesson Planner, p. 57
- Listening Activities, pp. 75, 79–80
- Activities for Communication, pp. 37–38, 97–98, 99–100, 131–132
- Grammatikheft, pp. 82–85
- Grammar Tutor for Students of German, Chapter 10
- Übungsheft, pp. 119–122
- Testing Program, pp. 213–216
- Alternative Assessment Guide, p. 39
- Student Make-Up Assignments, Chapter 10

MEDIA
- One-Stop Planner
- Audio Compact Discs, CD10, Trs. 3, 10, 14–16
- Teaching Transparencies Situation 10-1
  Mehr Grammatikübungen Answers
  Grammatikheft Answers

PAGE 272

Bell Work

To play the game **Wer ist das?**, prepare a list of famous Germans. Write the names on separate pieces of paper. Then divide the class in two teams. Teams alternate picking a piece of paper and identifying the individual.
Examples:
Johann Sebastian Bach ——> war ein Komponist.
Wolfgang Borchert ——> war ein Schriftsteller.

PRESENTING: Wortschatz

- After introducing the new words from **auf Deutsch erklärt,** make up sentences in which you arrive at the word using circumlocution. Students have to restate each sentence using the new vocabulary.
- Ask students to use the new vocabulary from the **auf Deutsch erklärt** section in sentences.
- Work with the new vocabulary in the **auf English erklärt** section. Read each sentence aloud and have students do the same. Then ask for variations of each sentence, keeping the structure the same but varying the context.
- Ask students to describe the difference between **Oper** and **Rockkonzert.**

- Have students give several examples of **Grimms Märchen.**

Teacher Note

The **Gebrüder Grimm** published not only numerous fairy tales, but also many reference works on language, such as the first German dictionary, *Deutsches Wörterbuch,* and a book on German grammar, *Deutsche Grammatik.* See also **Lies mit mir! 1,** Ch. 1.

PRESENTING: So sagt man das!

To practice the different phrases for expressing preference given in **So sagt man das!,** tell students to use the information provided in the Location Opener on pp. 264-267 to answer the following question: **Was würdest du gern in Dresden besuchen, wenn du genug Zeit hättest?**

Connections and Comparisons

Language-to-Language

In the recording for Activity 4, Lise tells her friend Erwin about a historical exhibit focusing on the life of Jews in the 19th century. You may want to give your students a brief history of the Yiddish language: Yiddish (meaning "Jewish") is written in Hebrew characters and belongs to the Germanic family of languages. It arose between the 9th and 12th centuries in southwestern Germany as an adaptation of Middle High German dialects to the special needs of Jews. To the original German were added those Hebrew words that pertained to Jewish religious life. Later, when many European Jews moved eastward to Slavic-speaking areas, some Slavic influences were acquired. The vocabulary of the Yiddish spoken in eastern Europe during recent times was approximately 85 percent German, 10 percent Hebrew, and 5 percent Slavic, with traces of Romanian, French, and other elements. Furthermore, many English words and phrases have entered the Yiddish spoken in the United States. Although it is not a national language, Yiddish is spoken by about 4 million Jews all over the world, especially in Argentina, Canada, France, Israel, Mexico, Romania, and the United States.

You may want to ask your students to come up with the German equivalents of the following Yiddish words: **kugel (Kugel), lox (Lachs), mensch (Mensch), shtetl (Städtl=small town), yahrzeit (Jahreszeit), kinder (Kinder), krenk (krank), loch in kop (Loch im Kopf), dreck (Dreck), fress (fressen), gelt (Geld), gesundheit (Gesundheit).** Ask them what they think the Yiddish expressions **folksmensch** and **luftmensch** mean. *(man of the people; an impractical, unrealistic person)*

Teaching Suggestion

5 To prepare students for their partner work, go through all the phrases and elicit both singular and plural versions where appropriate. Students can use these phrases for general statements (plural) and a specific example (singular).
Examples:
sich eine Oper ansehen; sich viele Opern ansehen
in ein Kunstmuseum gehen; in Kunstmuseen gehen

PRESENTING: So sagt man das!

• Point out to students that **der, die, das,** and their forms can be used as emphatic personal pronouns, replacing **er, sie, es,** and their forms.

• To practice the two new expressions, ask students to complete each of the following statements:
Ich beneide …, weil …
Ich bewundere Personen, die …

• Make up some rumors or hearsay about people in the entertainment business and present them to the class. Have students react to what you tell them by telling you why they envy or admire that person.

PRESENTING: Grammatik

Prepositions with the genitive case

• Review with students the forms and uses of the genitive case (see p. 105).

• You may want to let students know that **anstatt** is considered slightly more formal than its short form **statt.**

• Before presenting the prepositional phrases in the **Grammatik,** give students some sentences with prepositions taking the genitive. See if they can identify some of the functions of the prepositions.

Examples:

Während des Sommers habe ich kaum Klavier geübt. Während is used to indicate the duration of an event.

Anstatt klassischer Musik höre ich Rockmusik. Anstatt indicates an alternative or reason.

Communication for All Students

Challenge

10 After students have worked through this activity, have them supply a **weil-**clause instead of a prepositional phrase. Then have them continue their sentence with a phrase using **wegen** or another **weil-**clause.
Examples:
…, weil es mir Spaß macht, nicht wegen …
…, weil ich Musik gern habe, nicht weil, …
…, weil ich Schauspieler werden möchte, nicht wegen …

Communication for All Students

Challenge

12 Have students try to convince the others to attend the event they depicted in their collage. In Chapter 8 (p. 223) students learned to make suggestions and recommendations. Review these expressions with students prior to this activity.

Teaching Suggestions

13 Read the four quotes with students, modeling them first and helping students understand their meaning if necessary. Then ask each group to pick one of the aphorisms to discuss and paraphrase in German.

14 Question 7. asks about tradition. You may want to discuss the concept of tradition with your students. Ask the following questions:

Woran denkt ihr, wenn ihr das Wort Tradition hört?
Hat deine Familie bestimmte Traditionen, oder vielleicht deine Gemeinde oder Stadt?
Hat diese Schule Traditionen? Welche?

ERSTE STUFE

Speaking Assessment

14 Questions 5. and 6. lend themselves for oral assessment. You may choose to have students come to your desk individually and use the following rubric for evaluation.

Speaking Rubric	Points			
	4	3	2	1
Content (Complete – Incomplete)				
Comprehension (Total – Little)				
Comprehensibility (Comprehensible – Incomprehensible)				
Accuracy (Accurate – Seldom accurate)				
Fluency (Fluent – Not fluent)				

18–20: A   16–17: B   14–15: C   12–13: D   Under 12: F

Thinking Critically

Analyzing The German language has a proverb that can be related to artistic abilities: **Es ist noch kein Meister vom Himmel gefallen.** *(Nobody is born a master of his craft.)* Ask students how expressions of admiration go hand in hand with the proverb. (We tend to admire people who have the dedication to develop skills and become masters of their crafts.)

Assess

▸ Testing Program, pp. 213–216
  Quiz 10-1A, Quiz 10-1B
  Audio CD10, Tr. 10

▸ Student Make-Up Assignments
  Chapter 10, Alternative Quiz

▸ Alternative Assessment Guide, p. 39

WEITER GEHT'S!

Teaching Resources
pp. 276–277

PRINT
▸ Lesson Planner, p. 58
▸ Übungsheft, p. 123

MEDIA
▸ One-Stop Planner
▸ Audio Compact Discs, CD10, Trs. 4–5

PAGES 276–277

Weiter geht's! Summary

In *Zeitungsbericht: Schüler besuchen Staatstheater,* students will read an article about a school class that went to the ballet. The following learning outcomes listed on p. 269 are modeled in the episode: expressing happiness and sadness, and saying that something is or was being done.

Preteaching Vocabulary

Guessing Words from Context

Have students skim **Weiter geht's!** for general meaning, and ask them to identify the topic (eighth-graders' impressions of a ballet performance). Then have students scan for cognates that are new to them. After students have a good idea of what **Weiter geht's!** is about, have them use contextual clues to find nouns in the article that have to do with the theater building. Some of the words they might select are: **Rängen, Foyer, Garderobe, Theke, Seitenlogen, Zuschauerraum, Vorhang, Loge, Bühne.**

Advance Organizer

Ask students if they have ever been to the ballet, and if so, what they have seen and where. Read a synopsis of the ballet *Giselle* in English or have students look up the story and report to the class.

Teaching Suggestion

Ask students to read the introductory paragraph. Then have them summarize the purpose of the weekly feature in the *Stuttgarter Zeitung* called "Zeitung in der Schule."

Cultures and Communities

Background Information

The role of Giselle is one that almost all ballerinas want to perform. The story was written by the French poet Théophile Gautier together with Marquis de Saint-Georges. It was inspired by a legend recorded in Heinrich Heine's *Zur Geschichte der neueren schönen Literatur in Deutschland* and set to music by the French composer Adolphe Adam. Adam used leitmotifs, short phrases of music repeated each time a particular character appears. In the ballet, the musical leitmotifs are accompanied by certain dance steps, which here, for example, vary as Giselle changes from a simple village girl to a mad creature and then to a wistful, loving spirit. The subtitle of the ballet, *Les Wilis*, refers to the ghostly spirits of young girls, who, according to the legend, die before their weddings.

Comprehension Check

Teaching Suggestions

Play the recording as students read along in their texts. Stop at short intervals and ask comprehension questions. Explain new vocabulary and difficult constructions in German by using gestures, drawings, and paraphrasing.

Cooperative Learning

16 Divide students into groups of four. Instruct each group to choose a discussion leader, a recorder, a proofreader, and a reporter. Give students a specific amount of time to complete Part 1 of this activity (about 20 minutes). Monitor group work as you walk around, helping students with unfamiliar words or phrases. The recorder of each group can use a transparency or a large sheet of construction paper to write the group's answers. Call on a few group reporters to share their answers to the five questions in Part 1. You may want to do Parts 3 and 4 in the same way on another day.

Teaching Suggestion

16 Put students in pairs or small groups to do Part 2 (read the whole text in the present tense). Before they start, tell them to watch out for the following:
1) past perfect constructions that need to change to present perfect,
2) instances where the past must remain in order to show prior actions (Example: **Die Clowns, die anfangs so heiter und spaßig waren, bleiben ganz ratlos zurück.**),
3) passive voice, when **wurde(n)** needs to be changed to **wird/werden.**

Comprehension Check

Game

After students have changed the text into the present, they can play the following game to check their work. Divide the class into two teams and have a member of Team A start reading the text in the present tense. When a member of Team B thinks the reader has made a mistake in changing the verb form (or changed it when it shouldn't have been changed), the person calls out **Halt!** The reader from Team A must stop, and the member of Team B gives what he or she believes to be the correct form of the verb. If the Team B member is correct, he or she continues reading the text until a member from Team A notices an error and calls out **Halt!** If a reader gets stopped but did not make an error, he or she can continue. The purpose of the game is to see how far students can go without making any errors.

Cultures and Communities

Career Path

Have students work in pairs to brainstorm reasons why an American in the entertainment business might find a knowledge of German helpful. (Suggestions: Imagine you are a concert pianist who just got a contract with the **Wiener Philharmoniker;** imagine you are an American opera singer, classical musician, or jazz pianist who is training with the Vienna School of Music; imagine you are an opera singer performing at the Staatsoper in Vienna; imagine you are in the cast of a musical performing in a Viennese theater.)

Closure

If possible, play a piece of music from the ballet *Giselle* or show students a performance on video. Have students listen or watch for the leitmotifs.

ZWEITE STUFE

Teaching Resources
pp. 278–283

PRINT 📖

▸ Lesson Planner, p. 59
▸ Listening Activities, pp. 77–78, 81–82
▸ Video Guide, pp. 45–47
▸ Activities for Communication, pp. 39–40, 96, 99, 131–132
▸ Grammatikheft, pp. 86–90
▸ Grammar Tutor for Students of German, Chapter 10
▸ Übungsheft, pp. 124–128
▸ Testing Program, pp. 217–220
▸ Alternative Assessment Guide, p. 39
▸ Student Make-Up Assignments, Chapter 10

MEDIA

▸ One-Stop Planner
▸ Audio Compact Discs, CD10, Trs. 6–7, 11, 17–19
▸ Video Program
Geld für Kultur?
Videocassette 2, 37:27–40:20
Teaching Transparencies
Situation 10-2
Mehr Grammatikübungen Answers
Grammatikheft Answers

> **PAGE 278**

Bell Work
Ask students what they would like to see if they were offered a free ticket to any theatrical performance. In which theater would they like to see it, and with whom would they like to go?

PRESENTING: Wortschatz

• Teach the vocabulary in the **auf Deutsch erklärt** section through pantomime, drawing, or by giving examples.

• For the **auf Englisch erklärt** vocabulary, read through the new phrases, and then ask students related questions.
Examples:
Wann bekommst du Herzklopfen?
Wann bekommst du eine Gänsehaut?
Erinnerst du dich an das letzte Mal, an dem du dich bei Freunden oder Eltern über etwas beklagt hast?

PRESENTING: So sagt man das!

• Ask students if they can think of synonyms for **froh** and **traurig**.
Examples:
froh: glücklich, fröhlich, zufrieden, erfreut
traurig: enttäuscht, unglücklich, freudlos
• Ask students to complete the following phrases:
Ich war wirklich froh, dass …
Ich war total traurig, weil …

> **PAGE 279**

Teaching Suggestion

17 After students have completed the listening activity, ask them to recall their most memorable field trip. Have them share their answers while the rest of the class takes notes.

> ## Communication for All Students

A Slower Pace
18 Instead of using a **weil**-clause, have students give two sentences. (Example: **Ich bin froh. Ich habe eine Schülerkarte bekommen.**) After they have practiced this way, they can do the activity using the **weil**-clause. Remind them that the **weil**-clause requires verb-last word order.

Teaching Suggestion

19 You may want to give students a starting point by providing them with a number of topics to discuss using the expressions **froh/traurig sein, dass …**
Examples:
Familie
Freund(in)
Schule

PRESENTING: Ein wenig Grammatik

Da- and wo-compounds

• Students studied **da-** and **wo**-compounds in Chapter 3 (p. 66). If students need to review these materials, you may want to refer them to that page.
• Remind students that these two types of compounds are used only when reference is made to things and not to people.

PRESENTING: So sagt man das!

- Have students point out and explain how the two sets of sentences differ. Can students think of English equivalents for each of the four sentences?

- Have students go back to **Weiter geht's!** and point out all the sentences that tell what was being done.

Communication for All Students

Tactile Learners

23 Let students listen to the description a second time with a pencil and paper in front of them. Have them imagine the concert hall and draw what they visualize. After students have completed their drawings, have them share their work with the rest of the class.

PRESENTING: Grammatik

The passive voice

- To review the difference between active and passive voice, ask students to change the sentences in the **Grammatik** to the active voice.

- Perform several activities around the classroom, tell students what you are doing, and let them say what is or was being done. (Example: clean the chalkboard and say **Ich wische die Tafel ab.** Students might say **Die Tafel wird/wurde abgewischt.**)

- Have students imagine they are planning a big party at their house this weekend. They must tell what needs to be done. When finished, have students share their ideas with the rest of the class.

Teaching Suggestion

26 Encourage students to work this activity like a puzzle and to do the easier parts first, working up to the more difficult sentences with the past participles that are left.

Communication for All Students

Challenge

26 Ask students to find different participles than those given for as many sentences as they can.
Examples:
Dann wurden wir auf unsere Plätze gebracht.
In der Pause wurde etwas zu essen gekauft.

Teaching Suggestion

28 To help students with the changes from active to passive, ask them first to find the object of each of the active sentences. Remind students that the object of the active sentence will become the subject of the passive sentence. Remind them also that the tense must remain the same. Have students work on one movie critique at a time. Then check their transformation into the passive.

Reteaching: Passive Voice

Ask students to help you describe in detail how to plan a costume party for a large group of friends. Make a list on the board.
Examples:
Zuerst wird das Datum festgelegt.
Dann wird eine Gästeliste gemacht.
Challenge students to be as detailed as possible.

LANDESKUNDE

Building on Previous Skills

Throughout their German studies, students have learned about famous German-speaking people who contributed to the arts, literature, and music. Let students brainstorm a list of famous German-speaking people and have them name at least one significant thing each person did. If students cannot come up with something specific a person has done, they should indicate the type of work the person is known for. (Examples: **Dirigent, Dichter, Künstler, Komponist, Bildhauer**)

Teaching Suggestions

- Ask students how they were exposed to culture as children. Did they do special activities with their families? If so, what were they? How about now? How much of an interest in and exposure to cultural activities do they have now? Have students share their experiences with the class.

- Read the **Landeskunde** text out loud to students. Pause after each paragraph and have students summarize its content orally in English.

B Assign Activity B as an individual writing activity. Ask students for a paragraph of at least eight connected sentences.

COMMUNITY LINK

Have some students find out from the local Chamber of Commerce or Tourism Bureau what types of cultural activities are planned for their community this year. Students should make a list of the various programs and activities and report the information in class.

Cultures and Communities

Background Information

In Germany, there is much state support for the arts. Federal, state, and local monies subsidize artists, musicians, and writers, as well as theater and ballet companies, orchestras, and various academies and professional schools for the arts. Reduced price tickets are available for students in order to make cultural experiences accessible to young people. In recent years, efforts have been made to increase museum attendance and make museums more attractive to the general public and young people in particular. A number of innovative ideas have come from museums in the United States. Most museums now have a cafeteria, evening hours, free tours, and some even have special children's sections.

Connections and Comparisons

Thinking Critically

Comparing and Contrasting Have students find out how many museums, theaters, symphonies, libraries, galleries, and special exhibits are located in their town or city.

Teacher Note

Mention to your students that the **Landeskunde** will be also included in Quiz 10-2B given at the end of the **Zweite Stufe.**

Using the Video

Videocassette 2, 37:27–40:20
In the video clip *Geld für Kultur?*, residents of East Berlin talk about whether public funds should be used for public housing or the restoration of monuments. See *Video Guide*, p. 46, for suggestions.

Group Work

Provide each group with a list of words and phrases. Students sit in a circle with the list in front of them and ask each other questions using the words from the list. (Examples: **die Eintrittskarte, die Aufführung, die Bühne, das Ballett, die Oper, das Theaterstück, die Abendvorstellung, das Instrument, atemlos, applaudieren**)
Example:
Weißt du, wie viel gute Eintrittskarten zu einem Theaterstück kosten?

Assess
▶ Testing Program, pp. 217–220
  Quiz 10-2A, Quiz 10-2B
  Audio CD10 Tr. 11

▶ Student Make-Up Assignments
  Chapter 10, Alternative Quiz

▶ Alternative Assessment Guide, p. 39

ZUM LESEN

Teaching Resources
pp. 284–286

PRINT
▸ Lesson Planner, p. 60
▸ Übungsheft, pp. 129–130
▸ Reading Strategies and Skills, Chapter 10
▸ Lies mit mir! 3, Chapter 10

MEDIA
▸ One-Stop Planner
▸ Audio, CD10, Tr. 8

Prereading
Building Context

Ask students whether any of them have ever visited a wax museum. What kind of figures are usually depicted in a wax museum—characters from fairy tales, plays, movies, or real figures from history? Probably all the students will have an idea that wax museums are associated with "scary" figures in some way. Ask them what kind of pleasure people get from visiting such exhibits. How would they compare it to going to an art museum? Or to a historical museum? Tell them to think about this as they answer Questions 1 and 2.

Reading

Cultures and Communities

Teacher Notes
6 Deveroux, einer von Wallensteins Mördern, would have both historical and literary associations for most Germans. The historical Albrecht von Wallenstein played a questionable role in the Thirty Years' War, first pushing his way up to the office of General of the Imperial (mercenary) Army, then entering into secret negotiations with the other side—the Protestant Swedes and Saxonians as well as with the French. He was finally relieved of his command, and assassinated in February 1634, by order of the Irish Colonel Buttler. Wallenstein's story inspired a 3-part epic drama by Schiller. Since its premiere in 1799, it has been standard fare in German theaters, and is required reading in schools.

Cultures and Communities

In Europe, game poachers were historically viewed as desperate outlaws and depicted in much the same way as American western movies depict gangs of horse thieves or train robbers. Someone masquerading as a **Wilderer** would attempt to appear rough and threatening.

Post-Reading
Teacher Note

Activity 7 is a post-reading task that will show whether students can apply what they have learned.

Closure

Ask students the following questions: What kind of "horror" story is this? What do you think is the effect of finding out that it was just a nightmare? If someone wanted to film this story for American television, what kind of audience would it be suitable for? What time slots would be best? Would students make any changes in the story? What exactly would they change and why?

Zum Lesen Answers
Answers to Activity 1
Answers will vary; horror
Answers to Activity 2
a. in der Nacht; b. ein Junge; c. in einem Wachsmuseum;
d. die Hauptfigur schaut die Figuren an und wird müde; im dritten Stock setzt er sich hin.
Answers to Activity 3
Stock(werk) *floor;* gähnte *yawned;* dämmerig *dim;* Aufseher *guard;* anstrengend *exhausting;* Säle *rooms*
Answers to Activity 4
weil er müde ist; predictions will vary.
Answers to Activity 5
a. Hein; b. er schläft ein; c. irgendjemand hat ihm auf die Schulter getippt; d. eine Wachsfigur; e. aus dem Museum; f. unbehaglich
Answers to Activity 6
a. ängstlich; er befürchtet, dass er im Museum eingesperrt ist.
b. ein Mörder
c. dass ihm jemand einen Streich spielt; nein
d. den Wilderer, dessen Kopf mit einem Messer auseinander gespalten ist; fast ohnmächtig vor Angst
e. Hein erwacht aus seinem Traum.

ZUM SCHREIBEN

Teaching Resources
p. 287

PRINT
▶ Lesson Planner, p. 60
▶ Alternative Assessment Guide, p. 25

MEDIA
▶ One-Stop Planner
▶ Test Generator, Chapter 10

Writing Strategy

The targeted strategy in this writing activity is *using figurative language and sound devices*. Students should learn about this strategy before beginning the assignment.

Prewriting
Building Context

Ask students about the last time they wrote or tried to write a poem. Can they recall any of the lines or why they wrote it?

Teaching Suggestion

To help students with the initial step into creative writing, show them a picture that lends itself to imaginative expression. (Examples: an idyllic landscape, the Berlin Wall coming down, a portrait or still life) Ask students to express their immediate thoughts and ideas about the picture(s).

Communication for All Students

Challenge

A Once students have chosen a topic, encourage them to make a list of antonyms and synonyms to increase the range of material for their poem.

Connections and Comparisons

Language Arts Connection

Have students find examples of forms for similes, metaphors, personification, and concrete imagery.

Writing
Teaching Suggestions

B Using the figurative expressions they have gathered and the plan they have devised, students should write their poem from beginning to end. They should not worry too much about rhyme, and they should not translate poetic images directly from English. Once they have the thoughts and feelings on paper, they can go back and rearrange phrases for more effective visual or sound impressions.

B Encourage students to say their lines out loud as they write them and to listen to the melody of the language.

Post-Writing

Communication for All Students

Auditory Learners

When students have completed their assignment, suggest that they record themselves on audio-cassette. Then tell them to listen to their work and self-edit and evaluate it.

Teaching Suggestion

Have students put their poems on a transparency. Each student then delivers his or her poem or song orally.

Closure

Ask students to recall at least two issues that made a lasting impression on them about a particular poem that was read in class. (**Ihr habt jetzt viele Gedichte gehört. Könnt ihr zwei Themen nennen, die einen besonderen Eindruck auf euch gemacht haben?**)

▶ *PAGES 288–291*

MEHR GRAMMATIKÜBUNGEN

The **Mehr Grammatikübungen** activities are designed as supplemental activities for the grammatical concepts presented in the chapter. You might use them as additional practice, for review, or for assessment.

For more grammar presentations, review, and practice, refer to the following:
• Grammatikheft
• Grammar Tutor for Students of German
• Grammar Summary on pp. R22–R39
• Übungsheft
• Grammar and Vocabulary quizzes (Testing Program)
• Test Generator
• **Interaktive Spiele** at <u>go.hrw.com</u>

ANWENDUNG

Teaching Resources
pp. 292–293

PRINT
▸ Lesson Planner, p. 60
▸ Listening Activities, p. 78
▸ Video Guide, pp. 45–46, 48
▸ Grammar Tutor for Students of German, Chapter 10

MEDIA
▸ One-Stop Planner
▸ Video Program
  Videoclips: Werbung
  Videocassette 2, 40:27–41:37
▸ Audio Compact Discs, CD10, Tr. 9

Apply and Assess

Using the Video
Videocassette 2, 40:27–41:37
At this time, you might want to use the authentic advertising footage from German television. See *Video Guide,* p. 46, for suggestions.

A Slower Pace
1 Let students take notes as they listen for key words that indicate certain cultural interests.

Music Connection
2 If possible, play a recording by Nigel Kennedy in class after students have read the critique.

Portfolio Assessment
3 You might want to suggest this activity as a written portfolio item for your students. See *Alternative Assessment Guide,* p. 25.

Visual Learners
4 Suggest that students use posterboard and visuals such as brochures, flyers, and ads from the entertainment section of the local paper to illustrate their arts and entertainment calendar. The visuals should be accompanied by brief descriptions of the featured events.

Portfolio Assessment
6 You might want to suggest this activity as an oral portfolio item for your students. See *Alternative Assessment Guide,* p. 25.

KANN ICH'S WIRKLICH?

This page helps students prepare for the test. It is a brief checklist of the major points covered in the chapter. The students should be reminded that it is only a checklist and not necessarily everything that will appear on the test.

For additional self-check options, refer students to the *Grammar Tutor* and the Online self-test for this chapter.

WORTSCHATZ

Review and Assess

Teaching Suggestions
• Have students list the words that are related to music or a musical performance. Which words refer to a theater production? Which words are related to museums? Some words may appear on more than one of the lists.

• Tell students to identify all the cognates from the **Wortschatz** and list them with their English equivalents.

Circumlocution
Circumlocution can be used to review the various entertainment and cultural activity words in the **Wortschatz.** These words lend themselves well to circumlocution. Although there are many other ways in which to describe it, **die Hausmusik** might be humorously described as **viel Lärm zu Hause. Die Geige** could be easily pantomimed, as could **der Dirigent,** although both words can be verbally described as well. See p. 31C for procedures.

Game
Play the game **Künstlerisch begabt** using the vocabulary from this chapter. See p. 267C for the procedure.

Teacher Note

Give the **Kapitel 10** Chapter Test: Testing Program, pp. 221–226
Audio CD 10, Trs. 12–13.

10
Die Kunst zu leben

Objectives

In this chapter you will learn to

Erste Stufe

- express preference, given certain possibilities
- express envy and admiration

Zweite Stufe

- express happiness and sadness
- say something is or was being done

 internet

ADRESSE: go.hrw.com
KENNWORT: WK3
DRESDEN-10

◀ **Auf der Landshuter Hochzeit**

Los geht's! · *Was tun für die Kultur?*

CD 10 Tr. 1

Wie sieht es mit dem kulturellen Leben bei deutschen Gymnasiasten aus? Interessieren sie sich für Kunst? Besuchen sie Theateraufführungen? Gehen sie in Konzerte? Hier unterhalten sich vier Gymnasiasten über ihre kulturellen Interessen außerhalb der Schule.

CD 10 Tr. 2

Frage: Was sind eure kulturellen Interessen außerhalb der Schule?

Philipp: Also, ich würd' sagen, hauptsächlich Theater, eventuell mal ein klassisches Konzert. Meine Eltern haben ein Konzertabonnement, und da kaufen sie ab und zu mal eine Karte für mich und nehmen mich mit. Aber sonst? Ich les zum Beispiel ausgesprochen wenig. Ich hab kaum Zeit dazu. Für den Deutschunterricht, ja da lesen wir Goethe, Schiller und wie sie alle heißen.[1] Das langt.

Michael: Bei mir ist es genau dasselbe. Ich konzentrier mich so auf wissenschaftliche Werke, Informationen und so, aber Bücher … so Philosophen lesen wie Nietzsche,[2] ja, ich beneide alle, die so was lesen können. Aber ich hätt' nicht die Geduld dazu. Mich interessiert also mehr das Wissenschaftliche als das Literarische.

Anne-Sophie Mutter

Sonja: Also ich muss sagen, dass ich sehr viel lese und dass ich lieber lese als — meinetwegen — Hausaufgaben mache. Ich les wahnsinnig gern Romane, historische Romane.

Tanja: Musik ist mein Hobby. Ich könnte mir ein Leben ohne Musik nicht vorstellen. Also, ich selbst spiele Geige, schon zwölf Jahre lang, und hab zweimal in der Woche Unterricht. Ich spiel ganz gut; bin zwar keine Anne-Sophie Mutter und werde auch kaum in der Jungen Deutschen Philharmonie[3] spielen. Aber ich hab viel Spaß daran. Ich mach oft mit Freunden Hausmusik,[4] klassische Musik von Bach, Beethoven und so. Aber ich mag auch Jazz, besonders New Orleans Jazz. Den find ich stark, den find ich Spitze!

Frage: Geht ihr in Museen und Ausstellungen?

Michael: Wenn ich in ein Museum gehe, dann nur ins Deutsche Museum. Das ist ein technisch-wissenschaftliches Museum und äh … aber so Kunstausstellungen, nö.

---

1. An deutschen Gymnasien bestehen für alle Fächer feste Lehrpläne. Für den Deutschunterricht in allen Klassen gibt es Listen von Autoren und ihren Werken, aus denen die Deutschlehrer geeignetes Material für den Unterricht aussuchen können.
2. Friedrich Nietzsche (1844–1900), der als Philosoph und Kulturbeobachter großen Ruhm erlangt hat, zeichnete sich auch durch seinen gehobenen Schreibstil aus.
3. Die Junge Deutsche Philharmonie ist ein Orchester, das aus zirka 150 begabten Musikstudenten und -studentinnen zwischen 18 und 28 besteht. Zweimal im Jahr übt das Orchester mit berühmten Dirigenten zwei Wochen lang. Dann geht das Orchester auf Tournee und spielt in bekannten Konzerthallen der Welt.
4. Hausmusik ist beliebt. Rund eine Million Bundesbürger, so schätzt man, spielen zu Hause oder im Freundeskreis ein Instrument.

Tanja: Bei mir ist es gerade umgekehrt. Irgendwelche technisch-wissenschaftlichen Ausstellungen interessieren mich überhaupt nicht. Wenn, dann geh ich eben in Galerien, Bilderausstellungen.

Michael: Im technischen Museum blüh ich auf! Wenn ich die Wunderwerke der Technik sehe und wenn man da so alles verstehen kann, aber nicht, wenn ich da so vor einem Bild stehe.

Philipp: Aber ich glaub, die meisten Museumsbesuche gehen doch von der Schule aus, dass man an irgendwelchen Schulausflugstagen eben in ein Museum geht.

Sonja: Für die Schüler wird schon wahnsinnig viel getan. Wenn man da mit seinem Schülerausweis an die Abendkasse geht, kann man sich für sechs Euro eine Oper oder ein schönes Theaterstück anschauen. Was da alles für die Schüler geboten wird! Man nützt es einfach zu wenig aus.

Tanja: Ist doch grotesk der Unterschied: wenn man in ein Café geht und sich etwas bestellt, da sind gleich so zehn Euro weg. Wenn man ins Theater oder ins Konzert geht, da kostet eine Karte nur sechs Euro, und man hat bestimmt mehr davon.

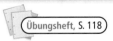

Frage: Wie sieht's bei euch mit dem Wort „Tradition" aus?

Philipp: Von Tradition ist wenig vorhanden bei uns.

Frage: Kennt ihr überhaupt noch Sagen und Märchen?

Tanja: Natürlich. Märchen haben mir unheimlich gut gefallen.

Michael: Mir auch. Meine Mutter hat mir immer Märchen vorgelesen, als ich klein war ... ja, „Hänsel und Gretel" oder ...

Sonja: Teilweise hat man Märchen später auch selber gelesen. Ich, zum Beispiel, hab's getan.

Frage: Besucht ihr während des Jahres mal ein Volksfest?

Philipp: Schon, aber nur zum Vergnügen, nicht unbedingt wegen der Tradition.[5]

---

5. In den deutschsprachigen Ländern besteht eine große, regionale Tradition. Es gibt z. B. viele Theaterstücke bekannter Autoren, die im Dialekt geschrieben und auch im Dialekt aufgeführt werden. Auch gibt es Gesangsvereine und Volksfeste in jeder Region. Das größte und bekannteste Volksfest ist das Oktoberfest in München.

Übungsheft, S. 118

1 ## Was sind ihre Interessen?

Lesen/Schreiben Lies dir den Text noch einmal durch! Dann mach eine Tabelle mit vier Spalten! Schreib auf, was für Interessen jeder der vier Gymnasiasten hat!

2 ## Kannst du das beantworten?

Sprechen Bildet zwei Gruppen! Jede Gruppe überlegt sich fünf Fragen zu dem Text, die die andere Gruppe beantworten muss. Zum Beispiel: Was ist ein Konzertabonnement? Warum spricht Tanja über die Violinistin Anne-Sophie Mutter?

3 ## Kennst du diese Personen?

Sprechen Sammelt in kleinen Gruppen Informationen über die berühmten Personen, die im Text erwähnt werden! Berichtet der Klasse darüber!

Wortschatz

auf Deutsch erklärt

das Vergnügen etwas, was viel Spaß macht

vorlesen lesen, so dass es alle hören können

die Hausmusik Musik, die man zu Hause macht

die Geige die Violine

die Abendkasse wo man Karten für die Abendvorstellung verkauft

eventuell vielleicht

teilweise zum Teil

unheimlich sehr groß, sehr viel

auf Englisch erklärt   p. 267X

Meinetwegen brauchen wir nicht in die **Oper** zu gehen, ich gehe lieber ins Rockkonzert. *As far as I'm concerned, we don't need to go to the opera; I'd rather go to a rock concert.*

Es gibt **Unterschiede** zwischen den **Märchen** der Gebrüder Grimm. *There are differences between the Grimms' fairy tales.*

Man braucht viel **Geduld**, wenn man die **wissenschaftlichen Werke** der Gebrüder Grimm **durchlesen** will. *You need a lot of patience if you want to read through the research of the Grimm Brothers.*

Die Picasso **Ausstellung** wird **möglicherweise verlängert**. *The Picasso exhibit will possibly be extended.*

Übungsheft, S. 119, Ü. 1   Grammatikheft, S. 82, Ü. 1–3

So sagt man das!

Expressing preference, given certain possibilities

10–1

You have learned several ways to express preference. Here is another way to express general preference. If someone asks you:

> **Welche kulturellen Veranstaltungen würdest du besuchen, wenn du genug Zeit hättest?**

You might say:

> **Ich würde mir hauptsächlich** ausländische Filme ansehen.

Mehr Grammatikübungen
S. 288–289, Ü. 1–2

You could continue the thought by expressing specific possibility:

> **Und ich würde** — eventuell / vielleicht / möglicherweise — auch mal in ein Konzert gehen.

Übungsheft, S. 120, Ü. 4

Grammatikheft, S. 83, Ü. 4

---

4 **Kultur am Wochenende**   Script and answers on p. 267G

CD 10
Tr. 3

Zuhören Erwin hat Lust, mit einigen Klassenkameraden an diesem Wochenende irgendeine kulturelle Veranstaltung zu besuchen. Er ruft seine Klassenkameradin Lise an und bittet sie, ihm aus ihrem Kulturkalender vorzulesen. Hör gut zu, wie sie die Veranstaltungen besprechen! Welche kulturellen Interessen haben die beiden? Zu welchen Veranstaltungen entschließen sie sich? Mach dir Notizen, und vergleiche sie mit denen einer Klassenkameradin!

5 Und ihr? Wenn ihr viel Zeit hättet?

Sprechen/Schreiben Was würdest du tun, wenn du viel Zeit für kulturelle Interessen hättest? Sag einem Partner, was du hauptsächlich — also generell — und was du möglicherweise — also spezifisch — tun würdest! Du kannst das auch aufschreiben.

DU **Ich würd' hauptsächlich Comics lesen, eventuell auch mal ein Märchen.**
PARTNER **Ich würd' …**

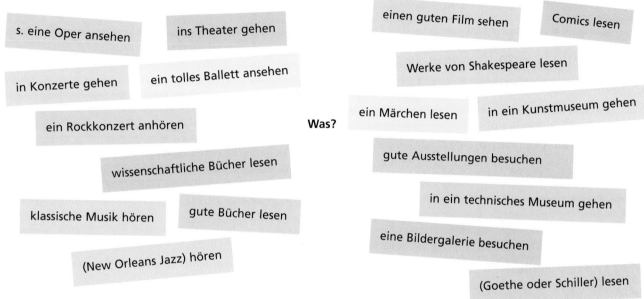

s. eine Oper ansehen

ins Theater gehen

einen guten Film sehen

Comics lesen

in Konzerte gehen

ein tolles Ballett ansehen

Werke von Shakespeare lesen

ein Rockkonzert anhören

Was?

ein Märchen lesen

in ein Kunstmuseum gehen

wissenschaftliche Bücher lesen

gute Ausstellungen besuchen

klassische Musik hören

gute Bücher lesen

in ein technisches Museum gehen

(New Orleans Jazz) hören

eine Bildergalerie besuchen

(Goethe oder Schiller) lesen

6 Was ist für euch wichtig?

Sprechen Sagt jetzt einander, was für euch wichtig ist und was weniger wichtig ist!

PARTNER **Es ist für mich wichtig, ab und zu mal in ein Museum zu gehen.**
DU **In ein Museum zu gehen, ist für mich weniger wichtig. Wichtig ist für mich, am Wochenende einen guten Film zu sehen.**

7 Was könntet ihr euch nicht vorstellen?

Sprechen Was möchtet ihr im Leben nicht vermissen? Ohne welche kulturellen Möglichkeiten könntet ihr euch das Leben nicht vorstellen?

DU **Also, ich könnte mir ein Leben ohne klassische Musik nicht vorstellen.**
PARTNER **Tja, ich …**

| Sport | Bücher | Kunst | Filme |
| Fernsehen | Musik | Reisen | |

So sagt man das!

Expressing envy and admiration

You can use the verb **beneiden** to express envy:

Ich beneide meinen Freund. Der kann jeden Monat ins Theater gehen.

and the verb **bewundern** to express admiration:

Ich bewundere alle, die sich für Philosophie interessieren.

Übungsheft,
S. 121–122, Ü. 5, 7–9

Grammatikheft,
S. 84, Ü. 5

8 Wen beneidest du? Wen bewunderst du?

Sprechen Sag deinem Partner, wen du beneidest und wen du bewunderst und warum! Denk auch an berühmte Leute!

DU **Ich beneide meine Schwester! Die fährt im Sommer nach England.**

PARTNER **Ich bewundere meinen Freund! Er übt sehr viel und spielt gut Klavier.**

Grammatik

Prepositions with the genitive case

Certain prepositions are always followed by the genitive case.

anstatt eines Konzerts	*instead of a concert*
außerhalb der Schule	*outside of school*
innerhalb des Hauses	*inside the house*
während des Jahres	*during the year*
wegen der Tradition	*because of tradition*

Mehr Grammatikübungen,
S. 289, Ü. 3 →

Übungsheft, S. 119–121; Ü. 2–3; 6

Grammatikheft, S. 85, Ü. 6

9 Grammatik im Kontext

Lesen/Schreiben Lies den folgenden Absatz, den der Realschüler Jörg über seine kulturellen Interessen für die Schule schreiben musste! Da es leider auf sein Papier geregnet hat, fehlen jetzt einige Wörter. Setz die Wörter aus dem Kasten in die Lücken, damit er eine gute Note bekommt! Vergiss die richtigen Artikel nicht! Sag dann einem Partner, ob du ähnliche Interessen hast!

	des Jahrhunderts	der Meister
des Komponisten		
	der Wissenschaft	
des Lyrikers		
	eines Konzerts	des Winters

Meine kulturellen Interessen? Nun, ich mache oft während ~~des Winters~~ Hausmusik, besonders Musik ~~des~~ großen ~~Komponisten~~ Beethoven, und ich gehe auch gern in Konzerte. Wenn das Wetter schlecht ist, besuche ich anstatt ~~eines Konzerts~~ ein Museum, besonders das Museum ~~der Wissenschaft~~ und Technik. In Kunstmuseen gehe ich weniger gern. Die meisten Gemälde ~~der~~ alten ~~Meister~~ langweilen mich. Moderne Kunst ist schon besser. Ja, außerdem lese ich ziemlich viel. Im Moment ist es Literatur ~~des~~ neunzehnten ~~Jahrhunderts~~, besonders Eichendorff und Keller, auch Werke ~~des Lyrikers~~ Heinrich Heine.

10 Was besuchst du?

Sprechen Sag einer Partnerin, was du besuchst und warum!

DU **Besuchst du Volksfeste?**

PARTNER **Ja, schon. Aber nur zum Vergnügen, nicht wegen der Tradition.**

was?	wozu/warum?	(nicht) wegen
Konzerte	zum Vergnügen	Tradition
Museen	zum Spaß	Musiker
Ausstellungen	zur Abwechslung	Schauspieler
Theateraufführungen	zum Zeitvertreib	Wissenschaft
Galerien	für die Schule	Gemälde
Volksfeste	für meine Eltern	Kunst

11 Klassenprojekt: Eine Collage machen

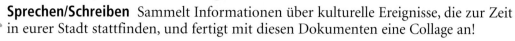

Sprechen/Schreiben Sammelt Informationen über kulturelle Ereignisse, die zur Zeit in eurer Stadt stattfinden, und fertigt mit diesen Dokumenten eine Collage an!

12 Zeig mal deine Collage her!

Sprechen Seht euch eure Collagen an und sprecht darüber! Wofür interessiert ihr euch? Welche Veranstaltungen würdet ihr gern besuchen? Welche habt ihr schon gesehen? Welche Aufführungen sind mehr für Erwachsene, welche mehr für Jugendliche oder Kinder geeignet?

13 Aphorismen

Lesen/Sprechen In der Schule müssen Schüler die Werke berühmter Autoren lesen. Dazu gehören auch Aphorismen und Sprüche. Lest die folgenden Zitate (*quotes*) und diskutiert darüber!

> „Zwei Dinge sollen Kinder von ihren Eltern bekommen: Wurzeln und Flügel."
> **Johann Wolfgang von Goethe**
> **(1749–1832)**

> „Es ist nicht genug zu wissen; man muß es auch anwenden; es ist nicht genug zu wollen; man muß es auch tun."
> **Goethe**

> „Was der Frühling nicht säte, kann der Sommer nicht reifen, der Herbst nicht ernten und der Winter nicht genießen."
> **Johann Gottfried Herder**
> **(1744–1803)**

> „Kenntnisse kann jedermann haben, aber die Kunst zu denken ist das seltsamste Geschenk der Natur."
> **Friedrich der Große**
> **(1712–1786)**

14 Und du?

Sprechen/Schreiben Was sind deine kulturellen Interessen? Überleg dir folgende Fragen und beantworte sie! Mach dir dabei stichwortartige Notizen!

1. Welche kulturellen Interessen hast du? Berichte deiner Gruppe darüber!
2. Welche Schriftsteller oder Dichter kennst du, und welche Werke von ihnen hast du schon gelesen?
3. Wie sieht es bei dir mit Musik aus? Bist du auch an klassischer Musik interessiert? Welche Werke bekannter Komponisten kennst du?
4. Spielst du ein Instrument und, wenn ja, was für Musik spielst du? Spielst du in einer Gruppe? In welcher? Hast du auch andere musikalische Interessen?
5. Welche Museen hast du schon besucht? Welche Ausstellungen? Was hat dir besonders gut gefallen? Warum?
6. An welchen kulturellen Ereignissen würdest du gern mal teilnehmen, und warum hast du das bisher nicht getan?
7. Wie sieht es bei dir in der Familie mit „Tradition" aus?
8. Wer oder was trägt zu deiner kulturellen Erziehung am meisten bei? Erzähle darüber!

15 Für mein Notizbuch

Schreiben Schreib einen Absatz darüber, welche kulturellen Interessen für dich wichtig sind! Hörst du lieber klassische Musik oder Pop und Rock? Welchen kulturellen Zeitvertreib (*pastime*) würdest du als dein Hobby bezeichnen?

Weiter geht's! ▪ *Zeitungsbericht: Schüler besuchen Staatstheater*

CD 10
Trs. 4–5

Die Stuttgarter Zeitung druckt einmal in der Woche eine Seite
„Zeitung in der Schule", die nur von Schülern für Schüler geschrieben wird.
Hier haben junge Menschen die Möglichkeit, eine große Tageszeitung als
Forum für ihre Ideen und Erfahrungen zu benutzen. CD 10 Tr. 4

CD 10 Tr. 5

Ein <u>kulturelles</u> Erlebnis für die Schüler

Die 8b der Friedensschule beim
„Musikunterricht" im Staatstheater

Für einen Ballettabend in das <u>prächtige</u> Reich der Wilis

Immer wieder mal zieht unser Klassenlehrer aus dem Schulhaus hinaus, und wir sind natürlich dabei! Diesmal verlegte er seinen Musikunterricht in die Staatsoper. Nach vielen <u>vergeblichen</u> Versuchen hatten wir endlich Glück: Schülerkarten für das Ballett „Giselle".[1] Das war schon etwas Besonderes! Die Buben waren <u>skeptisch</u>. Ballett, Theater, Großes Haus — das kannten die meisten kaum. Im Kino und auf dem Sportplatz waren sie eher zu Hause. Da es sich um eine <u>richtige</u> Abendvorstellung handelte, mußte auch die Kleiderfrage geklärt werden. Unser Lehrer erzählte uns einiges über Handlung, Musik und Tanz. Er sprach auch übers Große Haus mit seinen drei Rängen, übers Foyer, über Garderobe und Theke. Langsam wurden wir <u>neugierig</u>.

Am Tag der Aufführung wurden die Eintrittskarten verteilt, und irgendwie war der Nachmittag <u>anders</u> als sonst. Dauernd schaute ich auf die Uhr. Gegen Abend erwischte ich mich immer wieder vor dem Spiegel. Die meisten waren viel zu früh vor dem Theater. Die einen wurden zum <u>zweiten</u> Range hinaufbegleitet, andere hatten ihre Plätze in den Seitenlogen. Da öffneten sich die Türen des Zuschauerraums. Was für eine Pracht! <u>Super</u>, <u>riesig</u>, echt <u>nobel</u>, <u>prunkvoll</u>, <u>großartig</u> — so hörten wir uns sagen. Wir sahen uns in aller Ruhe um. Die meisten Zuschauer waren recht <u>schick</u> gekleidet, gut, daß wir unsere <u>besten</u> Klamotten angezogen hatten. Unten stimmten die Musiker ihre Instrumente, die Bläser, die Streicher; nur Michael sah sie kaum, auch nicht die Pauken oder die Harfe, er saß nämlich genau hinter der <u>großen</u> Krone über der Königsloge.

Die Kronleuchter wurden hochgezogen, das <u>letzte</u> Klingelzeichen ertönte, einige Spätkommer suchten noch ihre Plätze. Das Licht ging ganz langsam aus, <u>atemlose</u> Stille! Vor lauter Spannung bekam Snjezana eine Gänsehaut, und ihre Nebensitzerin hatte sogar Herzklopfen vor lauter Aufregung.

Der Dirigent wurde mit Klatschen begrüßt. Nach einem kurzen Vorspiel der Instrumente ging der Vorhang auf: Eine Insel im Meer. Wir kamen aus dem Staunen nicht mehr heraus, denn dort landeten laufend neue Gäste mit einem Schiff. Im bunten Treiben auf dem Jahrmarkt erkannten wir die verträumte Giselle, die von zwei Männern geliebt wird. Der junge Maler Albrecht sah ganz toll aus, der bärtige Hilarion, wütend vor Eifersucht, gefiel uns besser. Sie alle tanzten und stellten ihre Pantomimen so gut dar, daß wir verstanden, um was es ging, obwohl weder gesprochen noch gesungen wurde. Das war besonders auch für die vielen ausländischen Schüler unserer Klasse leichter. Nur Serken beklagte sich über die Musik, sie hatte für ihn zu wenig Power. Dafür freute er sich auf die Pause. Hier schauten wir uns, nun schon sicherer geworden, überall um. Erdal aus der Türkei zeigte uns seine Loge. Ihm blieb beinahe die Spucke weg, als er erfuhr, daß sein Platz normalerweise 49 Euro gekostet hätte. Leider war der zweite Akt gar nicht mehr so lustig. Im romantischen Reich der Königin der Wilis mit ihren wunderschönen Kostümen war wohl alles recht märchenhaft, doch die meisten von uns waren traurig, weil es kein Happy-End gab. Die Clowns, die anfangs heiter und spaßig waren, blieben ganz ratlos zurück. Wir aber waren glücklich, weil wir einen so schönen Abend erlebt hatten. Alle fanden es toll; wir klatschten, bis uns die Hände weh taten, besonders, als die Blumensträuße für die Tänzer auf die Bühne flogen.

Der nächste Morgen — wieder im Schulalltag: Die einen träumten noch vom Balletterlebnis, andere diskutierten darüber. Wann gehen wir wieder ins Theater?
Sandra, Ralf, Manuela, Indir und die 8b der Friedensschule Stuttgart-West

1. a. **in die Staatsoper**   b. **Weil die meisten Ballett, Theater und Oper nicht kannten.**   c. **Er hat der Klasse einiges über die Oper erzählt.**   d. **Snjezana: bekam eine Gänsehaut; Snjezanas Platznachbarin: hatte Herzklopfen; Erdal: „blieb die Spucke weg"** (i.e. **vor Staunen sprachlos sein**)   e. **Sie klatschten, bis ihnen die Hände wehtaten.**

1. „Giselle" (auch „Les Wilis" genannt) ist das Symbol des romantischen Balletts. Es beruht auf einem Gedicht von Heinrich Heine (1797–1856). Das Ballett wurde 1841 zum ersten Mal in Paris aufgeführt, wo Heine seit 1831 lebte.

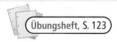
Übungsheft, S. 123

16 Arbeiten mit dem Text For answers see above.

1. **Sprechen** Beantworte mit deinen Klassenkameraden folgende Fragen!

   a. Wohin hat der Lehrer den Musikunterricht verlegt?

   b. Warum sind besonders die Jungen skeptisch über den Besuch?

   c. Wie hat der Lehrer seine Klasse auf den Ballettbesuch vorbereitet?

   d. Für welche Schüler war der Besuch im Staatstheater ein besonderes Erlebnis? Wie zeigt sich das?

   e. Wie zeigt es sich, dass den Schülern die Aufführung gut gefallen hat?

2. **Lesen** Lest den Bericht euren Partnern vor, diesmal in der Gegenwart!

3. **Schreiben** Schreib aus dem Text die Stellen heraus, die Enthusiasmus, Skepsis, Erwartung (*expectation*) und Bewunderung zeigen!

4. **Schreiben** Schreib eine Liste mit Adjektiven und Adverbien, die in diesem Text erscheinen! 4. For answer see underlined words in text.

Wortschatz

Was findet man im Theater oder in der Oper?

einen Vorhang

eine Bühne

einen Rang

einen Dirigenten

auf Deutsch erklärt

begrüßen   jemanden grüßen, willkommen heißen
begleiten   mit jemandem mitgehen
Zuschauer   Besucher einer Veranstaltung, bei der es etwas zu sehen gibt
die Aufführung   die Show
Handlung   was passiert
aufführen   im Theater etwas präsentieren
klatschen   applaudieren
heiter   gut gelaunt, froh
Bube   (süddeutsch) Junge

auf Englisch erklärt

Unser <u>Versuch</u>, Karten zu bekommen, war zuerst <u>vergeblich</u>. *Our attempt to get tickets was futile at first.*

Es <u>handelte</u> <u>sich</u> <u>um</u> eine Vorstellung, die <u>weder</u> ich <u>noch</u> mein Freund kannte. *It was about a performance that neither I nor my friend knew.*

Die Kleiderfrage <u>war</u> <u>geklärt</u> <u>worden</u>. *The issue of what to wear had been resolved.*

Ich war <u>atemlos</u> vor <u>lauter</u> Aufregung, bekam <u>Herzklopfen</u> und sogar eine <u>Gänsehaut</u>. *I was breathless from sheer excitement, my heart started pounding, and I even got goose bumps.*

Die Musiker <u>stimmten</u> ihre Instrumente. *The musicians tuned their instruments.*

Serken <u>beklagte</u> <u>sich</u> darüber. *Serken complained about that.*

Ich <u>erkannte</u> Giselle. *I recognized Giselle.*

Die Pantomimen der Tänzer waren so gut, dass wir verstanden, wor<u>um</u> <u>es</u> <u>ging</u>. *The pantomimes of the dancers were so good that we understood what it was all about.*

Übungsheft, S. 86, Ü. 7–8

So sagt man das!

Expressing happiness and sadness

Here is one way to use **froh** for expressing happiness:

    (**Erdal**) **war froh, dass** er einen billigen Platz hatte.

And here is a way to express sadness using **traurig**:

    (**Sie**) **waren traurig, weil** es kein Happyend gab.

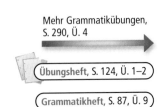

Mehr Grammatikübungen, S. 290, Ü. 4

Übungsheft, S. 124, Ü. 1–2

Grammatikheft, S. 87, Ü. 9

17 Der Klassenausflug
Script and answers on p. 267G

Zuhören Du hörst jetzt einen Bericht über einen Klassenausflug. Was haben die Freunde gemacht? Wie hat es ihnen gefallen? Schreib die wichtigsten Dinge auf, die sie sagen!
CD 10 Tr. 6

18 Froh oder traurig?

Sprechen Worüber sind die Schüler, die das Ballett besucht haben, froh, und worüber sind sie traurig? Du und deine Klassenkameraden übernehmen die Rollen der verschiedenen Schüler.

PARTNER **Ja, ich bin die Sandra, und ich bin froh, dass …**
DU **Gut, ich bin der Serken, und ich bin traurig, weil …**

Gründe

Schülerkarten bekommen

der Vorhang endlich aufgehen

in die Oper gehen können

eine Abendvorstellung sein

die Pause so lange dauern

der 2. Akt nicht so lustig sein

die besten Klamotten anziehen können

(k)einen guten Platz haben

kein Happyend geben

einen schönen Abend erleben

wieder in die Schule müssen

die Handlung (nicht) kennen

19 Grammatik im Kontext

Sprechen Sag einer Partnerin, worüber du jetzt froh oder traurig bist und warum! Sie sagt es dir dann auch.

20 Grammatik im Kontext

Sprechen/Schreiben Sag einem Partner, wofür du dich interessierst und warum! Dein Partner kann dir dann sagen oder schreiben, ob er sich auch dafür interessiert oder nicht.

DU **Ich interessiere mich für Musik, weil ich selbst ein Instrument spiele.**
PARTNER **Ich interessiere mich auch dafür, aber ich kann nur das Radio spielen.**
DU **Na prima!**

Musik — Instrument spielen

Oper — gern singen

Ballett — gern tanzen

Bücher — gern lesen

Gemälde — gern malen

Theater — Theater spielen

Ein wenig Grammatik

Schon bekannt

Do you remember how to form **da-** and **wo-**compounds? If someone said the following to you, but you didn't hear the last word well, how would you form a question to get the desired information?

Es handelt sich um eine Abendvorstellung.

DU **… handelt es sich?**[1]

If someone said something to you and you basically agreed with the statement, how might you restate it without being too redundant?

Ein Schüler beklagt sich über die Musik.

DU **Ich möchte mich auch …**[2]

———————
1. **Worum** 2. **darüber beklagen.**

21 **Verben mit Präpositionen**

Lesen/Schreiben Lies dir die Texte **Los geht's!** and **Weiter geht's!** noch einmal durch und schreib alle Verben mit Präpositionen auf: teilnehmen an, sich unterhalten über, usw.! Schreib dann eine Frage mit jedem Verb, indem du ein Interrogativ mit „wo" gebrauchst!

22 **Für mein Notizbuch**

Schreiben Wie ist es bei dir? Schreib deine Antworten in dein Notizbuch, und erkläre sie dann auch!

1. Worauf freust du dich?
2. Wofür interessierst du dich am meisten?
3. Wozu hast du keine Geduld?
4. Woran möchtest du auch gern mal teilnehmen?
5. Wovon träumst du manchmal?
6. Worüber beklagst du dich am meisten?

So sagt man das!

Saying that something is or was being done

10–2

In speaking, we often turn the sentence around to focus on the thing being done, for example:

Die Instrumente werden vor der Aufführung gestimmt.
Die Musiker werden vom Dirigenten geleitet.

Of course, you can also express something that was being done, i.e., in the past.

Die Schüler wurden auf ihre Plätze geführt.
Das Ballett ist gestern nicht aufgeführt worden.

---

23 **Das Konzert** Script and answers on p. 267H

CD 10
Tr. 7

Zuhören Du setzt dich in einen bequemen Sessel, um an einem ruhigen Sonntagnachmittag etwas Musik im Radio zu hören. Du hörst, wie der Ansager die Konzerthalle und die Vorbereitungen der Musiker auf das Konzert beschreibt. Was beschreibt er genau? Wer spielt, und was für Musik wird gespielt? Mach dir Notizen!

24 **Was passiert hier?** Hier werden Fotos entwickelt. Hier wird Schnitzel angeboten. Hier werden Aprikosen verkauft. Hier wird Basketball gespielt.

Sprechen Sieh dir die Illustrationen und die Verbformen im Kasten an! Sag dann deinem Partner, was hier passiert! Wechselt einander ab!

BEISPIEL Hier wird/werden …

angeboten
entwickelt
gespielt
verkauft

The passive voice (Summary)

1. You have been using the passive voice in sentences to express that something is being done:

Der Tisch wird (eben/jetzt) gedeckt.

that something was being done:

Der Dirigent wurde mit Klatschen begrüßt.

or that something must still get done:

Der Wagen muss (noch) gewaschen werden.

2. The passive construction is very similar in English and in German. One construction, the impersonal passive, is different. It uses **es** as the subject:

Es wurde nicht **gesungen.**   *There was no singing.*
Es wird viel **geklatscht.**   *There is a lot of applause.*

When **es** is not used at the beginning of the sentence, it is omitted:

Nach der Aufführung **wurde** lange **geklatscht.**
…, obwohl weder **gesprochen** noch **gesungen wurde.**

3. The following is a summary of the tenses in the passive voice:

Present	Die Schülerkarten **werden verteilt.**
	The student tickets are being distributed.
Imperfect	Der Dirigent **wurde** vom Publikum **begrüßt.**
	The conductor was greeted by the audience.
Perfect	Ein Ballett **ist aufgeführt worden.**
	A ballet has been performed.
Past Perfect	Eine Oper **war** am Abend vorher **gezeigt worden.**
	An opera had been performed on the previous evening.
Future	Ein Film **wird** von unserem Lehrer **gezeigt werden.**
	A movie will be shown by our teacher.

with modals:

Present	Dieses Museum **muss** von den Schülern **besucht werden.**
	This museum must be visited by the students.
Past	Die Kleiderfrage **konnte geklärt werden.**
	The question of what to wear could be cleared up.

with subjunctive forms:

Die Karten { **könnten abgeholt werden.** / **müssten abgeholt werden.** / **sollten abgeholt werden.** }   The tickets { *could be picked up.* / *should be picked up.* / *ought to be picked up.* }

Note:

a. The past participle is used in all tenses: even in the present!

b. In the perfect tenses, forms of **sein** are used with **worden** (which comes from **geworden**, the past participle of **werden**).

c. To also say who performed the action, you use **von** and the dative case.

Übungsheft, S. 125–127, Ü. 3–8   Grammatikheft, S. 88–90, Ü. 10–12   Mehr Grammatikübungen, S. 290–291, Ü. 5–9

25 **Grammatik im Kontext**

Lesen/Schreiben Lies dir den Text auf Seite 276-77 noch mal durch! Achte beim Lesen besonders darauf, wie diese Schüler ihren Ballettbesuch in der Staatsoper beschrieben haben! Mach dann eine Liste von den Verbformen, die das Imperfekt und das Passiv zeigen!

Imperfekt	Passiv
er verlegte, wir hatten Glück,	geklärt werden, werden verteilt, …

26 **Grammatik im Kontext**

Sprechen/Schreiben Erzähle einem Partner, was alles am Ballettabend passiert ist! Benutze dabei das Passiv! Schreib danach auf, was du gesagt hast.   1. wurden/verteilt   2. wurden/geführt   3. wurden/gestimmt   4. wurde/ausgemacht/hochgezogen   5. wurde/begrüßt   6. wurde/gespielt/wurde/getanzt/gesprochen/gesungen   7. wurde/gegessen/getrunken   8. wurde/geklatscht

1. Zuerst … die Eintrittskarten …
2. Dann … wir auf unsere Plätze …
3. Die Instrumente … noch …
4. Dann … das Licht …, und der Kronleuchter …
5. Der Dirigent … mit Klatschen …
6. Dann … Musik …, und es … nur …, nicht … und nicht …
7. In der Pause … etwas … und …
8. Am Ende der Aufführung … laut …

ausgemacht   begrüßt   gegessen

geführt   geklatscht   gesungen

gesprochen   hochgezogen   gestimmt

getanzt   verteilt   gespielt   getrunken

27 **Spielen wir Dramaturgen!**

Sprechen/Schreiben Entwickelt eine Idee für ein Theaterstück! Schreibt dazu in Stichwörtern Folgendes auf: Zeit, Ort, Personen, Handlung und das Ende! Das Stück soll nicht in der Gegenwart spielen, und es soll in einem anderen Land stattfinden und auch ein Happyend haben. Denkt euch dann einen Titel aus! Vergleicht, was sich jede Gruppe ausgedacht hat!

28 **Rezensionen** *(critiques)* **in Schlagzeilen**

Schreiben Unten stehen Schlagzeilen über den Film „Der mit dem Wolf tanzt", den du vielleicht gesehen hast. Schreib mit Hilfe einer Partnerin diese Schlagzeilen ins Passiv um, soweit es geht!

„Costner stellt die Indianer einmal anders dar: als Menschen mit Gefühl. Endlich!"
Friesen Nachrichten

„Ich kann diesen Film nur jedem empfehlen. Ein Genie hat ein Meisterwerk geschaffen."
Frank Huebner

„Man hat den Film mit sieben Oscars ausgezeichnet! Sagenhaft!"
Süddeutsche Zeitung

„Hollywood glaubte nicht, daß man heutzutage einen Western mit Indianern vermarkten kann. Costner hat das Gegenteil bewiesen."
Angelika Wertheimer

Die Indianer werden von Costner einmal anders dargestellt: …
Der Film wurde mit sieben Oscars ausgezeichnet! …

… Ein Meisterwerk wurde von einem Genie geschaffen.
… Das Gegenteil wurde von Costner bewiesen.

LANDESKUNDE ◀ ▶ LANDESKUNDE

Kultur findet man überall!

Übungsheft, S. 128, Ü. 1–4

Die deutschsprachige Jugend hat sehr viele Möglichkeiten, am kulturellen Leben ihrer Stadt teilzunehmen. Sie brauchen diese Möglichkeiten nur zu nutzen. Wenn Kinder noch klein sind, lesen ihnen ihre Eltern die Sagen, Märchen und Geschichten vor, die schon seit Generationen erzählt werden.

Ein gutes Buch ist noch immer ein passendes Geschenk zu Weihnachten oder zum Geburtstag. Viele Eltern nehmen ihre Kinder zu kulturellen Veranstaltungen mit, in Konzerte, in die Oper, in Museen und zu Sonderausstellungen. In Deutschland gibt es heute rund 4000 Museen, 150 Theater, über 180 Orchester, 800 Musikschulen und mehr als 25 000 Bibliotheken.

Das Interesse der Jugendlichen an Musik ist groß. Die meisten Jugendlichen hören sich „ihre" Musik an, aber viele zeigen auch Interesse an klassischer Musik. Viele Jugendliche spielen selbst ein Instrument; sie spielen in irgendwelchen Gruppen in der Schule oder in der Gemeinde, oder sie machen Hausmusik mit Freunden und Bekannten. In der Schule selbst werden die Schüler mit Literatur, Philosophie, Musik und den bildenden Künsten vertraut gemacht. Die Unterrichtspläne für die verschiedenen Klassen beinhalten Museumsbesuche und Besuche zu anderen kulturellen Veranstaltungen. Für freiwillige Besuche zu kulturellen Veranstaltungen werden oft eine Anzahl von Freikarten für Schüler bereitgestellt, und die Schüler selbst können mit ihrem Schülerausweis die meisten kulturellen Veranstaltungen zu verbilligten Preisen besuchen.

A. 1. Wovon handelt der Text? Welche kulturellen Möglichkeiten werden genannt, an denen die Jugend teilnehmen kann? Mach eine Liste!

2. Warum interessiert man sich für solche kulturellen Veranstaltungen? Was meinst du?

3. Macht deine Klasse auch oft Besuche zu kulturellen Veranstaltungen? Zu welchen?

4. Findest du, dass es wichtig ist, solche Veranstaltungen zu besuchen oder daran teilzunehmen? Warum oder warum nicht?

B. Was ist Kultur für dich? Zum Beispiel, erlebt man Kultur nur, wenn man in die Oper, ins Theater oder ins Museum geht? Oder meinst du, dass man Kultur auch auf eine andere Art definieren kann? Gehören zum Beispiel Rockkonzerte und Kultfilme auch dazu?

A. 1. **vom kulturellen Angebot / Bücher lesen; kulturelle Veranstaltungen besuchen (Konzerte, Opern, Museen, Sonderausstellungen, Theater); Instrument in einer organisierten Gruppe spielen; Hausmusik machen; kultureller Unterricht in der Schule (z. B. Museumsbesuche)**

STANDARDS: 2.1, 2.2, 3.2, 4.2

Die Nacht bei den Wachsfiguren

Eine Gruselgeschichte

Getting Started For answers, see p. 267V.

1. Read the title of the story. What do you think the story might be about? What genre does it probably belong to?

2. Look at the title again and read the first paragraph. Try to answer the following questions.

   a. Wann spielt die Handlung?

   b. Wer ist die Hauptfigur?

   c. Wo findet die Handlung statt?

   d. Was passiert im ersten Absatz?

Als er das erste Stockwerk durchlaufen hatte, gähnte er lange und ausgiebig. Im zweiten Stock mußte er sich schon dreimal fünf Minuten auf einen der rotgepolsterten, leicht angestaubten Plüschsessel setzen. In der nächsten Etage aber drückte er sich in eine der dämmerigen Ecken, wo ihn kein Aufseher beobachten konnte, streckte genießerisch die Beine von sich und stellte zum soundsovielenmal fest, daß es doch sehr anstrengend war, durch ein Museum zu gehen — auch wenn seine einzelnen Säle mit den interessantesten Wachsfiguren angefüllt waren, die man sich denken konnte: Kaiser, Wilderer und Mörder, Erfinder und Schwindler, Gauner und berühmte Künstler.

Hein fühlte, wie ihn der Schlaf überkam. Er stützte den rechten Ellenbogen aufs Knie und legte den schweren Kopf in die rechte Hand. So schlief er ein.

Er konnte noch nicht lange geschlafen haben — oder täuschte er sich? — da schreckte er zusammen. Irgend jemand hatte ihm auf die Schulter getippt.

Hein guckte sich um. Hinter ihm stand eine Wachsfigur in Lebensgröße; sie hielt die rechte Hand weit von sich gestreckt, und in dieser Hand trug sie — man sah ihn deutlich glänzen — einen Dolch. „Deveroux, einer von Wallensteins Mördern", entzifferte Hein auf dem Messingschildchen am Boden. Der Junge beugte sich hinter die Figur, ob sich vielleicht dort jemand versteckt hielt. Niemand! Auch hinter den anderen Wachsplastiken niemand.

„Aber irgend jemand hat mich doch angestupst!" murmelte Hein und schritt auf den Zehenspitzen quer durch den Saal. Er wollte zum Ausgang zurück. Es bedrückte ihn, keinem Menschen zu begegnen. Und mit jedem Schritt wuchs dieses dumme Gefühl des Unbehagens noch mehr an.

Auch im nächsten Saal war Hein der einzige Besucher.

Im übernächsten wagte er leise „Hallo?" zu rufen. Doch niemand gab Antwort. Nur weiter vorne schien sich etwas bewegt zu haben: aber als Hein näher kam, war auch dort alles leblos und still.

Jetzt bekam es der Junge mit der Angst zu tun. „Ich werde doch nicht so lange geschlafen haben, daß das Museum inzwischen geschlossen worden ist?" stammelte er. „Das war — ja — nicht — auszudenken!" Halt! Waren das nicht Schritte gewesen? Hein erstarrte, als sei er selber aus Wachs.

Da kam doch wer? Ein Wärter vielleicht, der nochmals einen Rundgang machte? Hein hätte jubeln mögen — aber die Lippen blieben ihm geschlossen, als seien sie aufeinandergeklebt. Der da vorne um die Ecke bog, war doch — war

Weißt du noch? When using context to guess the meaning of unfamiliar words, it's helpful to look at grammatical and lexical clues. For example, ask yourself if the word is a noun, verb, adjective, conjunction, and so on. Then decide to which category the word belongs. For example, does the word represent a location, person, or object? If it is an object, to which class of objects does it belong?

3. Skim the first paragraph again, locating the following words: **Stock(werk)**, **gähnte**, **dämmerig**, **Aufseher**, **anstrengend**, and **Säle**. Using context, decide what these words might mean.

4. Reread the first paragraph and adjust your original answers to question 2, if necessary.

Now answer the following question: **Warum setzt sich die Hauptfigur hin?** Before reading further, use what you know about stories of this genre to make predictions about what might happen.

A Closer Look

5. Lies die nächsten fünf Absätze, und beantworte die folgenden Fragen!
   a. Wer ist „er"?
   b. Was tut er im dritten Stock?
   c. Was weckt ihn plötzlich?
   d. Was oder wen sieht er?
   e. Wohin will er zunächst gehen?
   f. Wie fühlt er sich dabei?

doch — ja ganz gewiß: war niemand anders als Deveroux! Hein erkannte ihn an dem dreieckigen Spitzhut und an der ausgestreckten Hand, die den Dolch hielt.

Dem Jungen setzte das Herz einen Schlag lang aus. Was war denn hier los? Ging denn das noch mit rechten Dingen zu? Plötzlich überfiel Hein ein Zittern. „Wenn mich der Wallenstein-Mörder nur nicht entdeckt!" flüsterte er. Und ohne sich recht bewußt zu werden, was er tat, drängte sich Hein unter die neben ihm stehende Gruppe. Wilderer stellten diese Wachsfiguren dar; sie trugen schwarze Bärte, dicke Rucksäcke und lange Flinten. Und als Hein sich jetzt in ihre Mitte schob, wichen — wichen — wichen sie ein paar Schritte zur Seite und machten dem Jungen bereitwillig Platz!

Der Junge wagte kaum zu atmen, als jetzt — wenige Meter von ihm entfernt — Wallensteins Mörder in einen anderen Raum hinüberschritt. Er ging, ohne den Kopf zu wenden, mit steifen Knien und hatte die Hand mit dem Dolch weit nach rechts ausgestreckt. Ganz deutlich hörte man es, wenn er die Füße aufsetzte. Tapp — tapp — tapp — tapp. Langsam ebbte das Geräusch ab und verwehte nun völlig. „Nur jetzt nicht schlappmachen", redete er sich ein, „sonst bin ich unter diesen unheimlichen Gesellen unweigerlich verloren!"

Am liebsten hätte er schnell einmal die Wilderer studiert, die neben ihm standen und ihm vorhin Platz gemacht hatten. Aber er traute sich nicht einmal die Pupillen zu bewegen; obgleich er fühlte, daß ihn jemand starr ansah. Endlich faßte er sich ein Herz und hob unmerklich den Blick. Und — sah einem der Wilderer direkt ins Gesicht.

War das wirklich noch eine Wachsfigur? Eine tote, zusammengebastelte Wachsfigur? Der Kerl lebte doch! Auch wenn er sich Mühe gab, geradeaus zu schauen! Freilich, man sah doch, wie seine Lippen ganz leicht bebten!

Hatten sich hier vielleicht ein paar übermütige Kerle maskiert, um Hein einen Schrecken einzujagen? Schon wollte Hein hell hinauslachen, um denen zu zeigen, daß er ihr Spiel durchschaut hatte, da sah er es.

Er sah es, und er dachte nur noch: Mensch, ich werde verrückt!

Er sah nämlich, daß eben diesem Wilderer der Hut mitsamt dem ganzen Kopf von einem furchtbaren Messerhieb auseinandergespalten war.

Hein fühlte, daß er jetzt gleich zusammensinken würde; da packte ihn der Wilderer vorne an der Jacke und schrie: „He, junger Mann! Aufwachen! Das Museum wird in zehn Minuten geschlossen!"

nach Thomas Burger

6. Lies die Erzählung zu Ende und versuche, die Ereignisse jedes Absatzes in Stichwörtern zusammenzufassen! Dann beantworte die folgenden Fragen!

   a. Wie fühlt sich Hein, als er keine Besucher im Museum findet? Was befürchtet Hein?

   b. Wer war Deveroux?

   c. Im vierten Absatz vor dem Ende, was meint Hein, was passiert? Stimmt das?

   d. Was sieht er plötzlich? Wie fühlt er sich?

   e. Wie wird der Konflikt gelöst?

7. Bildet Gruppen zu dritt, und schreibt jetzt eure eigene Gruselgeschichte! Ein Schüler leitet die Gruppe, der zweite schreibt die Geschichte auf und der dritte liest sie nachher der Klasse vor. Einer fängt mit einem Satz an, der Nächste ergänzt die Geschichte, indem er einen neuen Satz hinzufügt, usw. Macht weiter, bis ihr drei oder vier Absätze geschrieben habt! Versucht auch, eurer Gruselgeschichte eine überraschende Wende (*turn*) zu geben wie in „Die Nacht bei den Wachsfiguren"!

Übungsheft, S. 129–130, Ü. 1–7

Zum Schreiben

In this chapter you have learned new ways to express feelings of fear, happiness, and sadness. The expression of feelings is central to some of the cultural activities you have discussed, as well as such works of art, poetry, and song. In this activity, you will write a poem or a song to express your feelings about a place, a memory, a person, or an image that had a strong impact on you.

Ein Gedicht — ein Bild mit Wörtern gemalt

Schreib ein Gedicht oder ein Lied über etwas (ein Erlebnis, einen Ort, eine Person, oder ein Bild), was dich tief beeindruckt hat! Drück in dem Gedicht ein bestimmtes Gefühl wie Furcht, Freude oder Traurigkeit in malerischer Sprache aus!

 Schreibtipp Using figurative language and sound devices Different types of writing are distinguished in large part by the type of language used in them. Newspaper articles, critical reviews, and business letters are composed of matter-of-fact writing for the purpose of conveying information efficiently and clearly. But creative writing, especially poetry and song, is often composed of figurative language and sound devices. Use figurative language such as metaphors, similes, personification, and concrete imagery to evoke sensory images and to create an appropriate mood for the emotion you want to convey. Use sound devices such as rhyme, rhythm, assonance and alliteration to play with the musical sounds of language itself.

A. Vorbereiten

1. Such eine Idee für dein Gedicht oder Lied! Sieh dir alte Fotos an, und lies alte Tagebücher und Briefe, die du einmal geschrieben hast! Wähl einen Moment in deiner Vergangenheit, wo du ein starkes Gefühl erlebt hast!

2. Such ein Wort für das Gefühl, das du in dem Gedicht ausdrücken willst! Stell dir den Moment vor, und denk an die verschiedenen Empfindungen und Gefühle, die du mit dem Moment verbindest!

3. Schreib malerische Ausdrücke auf, die zu diesem Gefühl passen! Wähle Metaphern, Gleichnisse und Personifizierungen, um die Details zu beschreiben! Denk auch an den Klang der Sprache!

4. Mach einen Plan für das Gedicht oder Lied! Wie lang soll es sein? Wie viele Strophen soll es haben? Soll es einen bestimmten Rhythmus oder Reim haben?

B. Ausführen

Benutze deinen Plan und die Ausdrücke, die du aufgelistet hast, und schreibe das Gedicht oder das Lied! Wenn du ein Lied schreibst, achte auf die Melodie und den Rhythmus der Musik, damit die Musik und die Wörter gut zusammenpassen!

C. Überarbeiten

1. Lies dein Gedicht oder Lied einem Partner vor! Kann sich der Partner die Gefühle vorstellen, die du ausdrückst? Rufen deine Wörter die richtige Wirkung hervor?

2. Lies das Gedicht noch einmal laut vor, und pass diesmal auf den Klang der Wörter auf! Verwende Stabreim und Assonanz, um die Sprache musikalischer zu machen!

3. Hör jetzt auf den Rhythmus der Wörter! Nimm Silben heraus oder setze Wörter ein, um den Rhythmus zu verbessern!

4. Hast du alles richtig buchstabiert? Hast du Präpositionen mit dem Akkusativ und Dativ richtig verwendet?

5. Schreib das verbesserte Gedicht oder Lied noch einmal ab!

Mehr Grammatikübungen

Answers

internet

go.hrw.com

ADRESSE: go.hrw.com
KENNWORT:
WK3 DRESDEN-10

Erste Stufe

Objectives Expressing preference, given certain possibilities; expressing envy and admiration

1 Beantworte jede Frage und gebrauche dabei eine würde-Form und Wörter wie zum Beispiel „eventuell" oder „vielleicht" und die Information, die in den Illustrationen gezeigt werden. (**Seite 272**)

1. Welche Stadt würdest du vielleicht einmal besuchen?

2. Ich _____ _____ die Stadt _____ besuchen, die deutsche _____ von Coldwater, Michigan.
würde; vielleicht; Soltau; Partnerstadt

3. Was für eine Schule würde Mark eventuell besuchen, um den Führerschein zu machen?

4. Mark _____ _____ eine _____ besuchen, um _____ .
würde; eventuell; Fahrschule; den Führerschein zu machen

5. Was für Früchte würdet ihr hauptsächlich essen, um gesund zu bleiben?

6. Wir _____ _____ die _____ , Orangen und _____ essen, um gesund zu bleiben.
würden; hauptsächlich; Vitamin-C-reichsten Früchte; Zitronen

7. Was würdest du möglicherweise tun, um dir Geld zu sparen?

8. Ich _____ mir _____ meine Klamotten selber _____ , um _____ . würde; möglicherweise; nähen; Geld zu sparen

2 Du drückst aus, was du unter gewissen Bedingungen (*conditions*) tun würdest. Schreib die folgenden Sätze ab, und schreib dabei die gegebenen Informationen als wenn-Sätze! (**Seite 272**)

Was würdest du tun, wenn du genug Zeit hättest?

1. (zum Volksfest gehen)   Wenn ich _____ .   genug Zeit hätte, würde ich zum V. gehen
2. (eine Bildergalerie besuchen)   Wenn ich _____ .   genug Zeit hätte, würde ich eine B. besuchen
3. (in ein Kunstmuseum gehen)   Wenn ich _____ .   genug Zeit hätte, würde ich in ein K. gehen
4. (viel mehr Literatur lesen)   Wenn ich _____ .   genug Zeit hätte, würde ich viel mehr L. lesen
5. (s. mit Musik beschäftigen)   Wenn ich _____ .   genug Z. hätte, würde ich mich mit M. besch.
6. (s. alle CDs von Mozart anhören) Wenn ich _____ .   genug Z. hätte, würde ich mir alle C. v. M. anhören

3 Du sprichst mit einer Freundin über deine kulturellen Aktivitäten. Schreib die folgenden Sätze ab, und schreib dabei die Genitivform der gegebenen Information in die Lücken! (**Seite 274**)

1. (die Ferien)   Während _____ haben wir viele Veranstaltungen besucht.   der Ferien
2. (die Vorstellung)   Die Leute klatschten während _____ .   der Vorstellung
3. (das Jahr)   Während _____ gehen wir bestimmt in drei Opern.   des Jahres
4. (die Woche)   Ich kann während _____ kaum in ein Konzert gehen.   der Woche
5. (die Schule)   Was macht ihr so außerhalb _____ ?   der Schule
6. (das Konzert)   Wegen _____ kann ich nicht Fußball spielen.   des Konzerts
7. (ein Jahr)   Innerhalb _____ habe ich vier Ausstellungen gesehen.   eines Jahres
8. (die Tradition)   Meine Eltern gehen wegen _____ ins Theater.   der Tradition

Mehr Grammatikübungen

Zweite Stufe

Objectives Expressing happiness and sadness; saying that something is or was being done

4 Du sprichst mit deinen Klassenkameraden über deinen Ballettbesuch. Du warst froh, aber auch traurig über gewisse Dinge. Schreib die folgenden Sätze ab, und schreib dabei die gegebene Information als dass-Satz! (**Seite 278**)

1. (Wir bekamen Theaterkarten.)   Wir waren froh, dass _____ .   *wir Theaterkarten bekamen*
2. (Die Karten waren für „Giselle".)   Wir waren froh, dass _____ .   *die Karten für „Giselle" waren*
3. (Wir waren schick gekleidet.)   Wir waren froh, dass _____ .   *wir schick gekleidet waren*
4. (Erdal saß allein in der Loge.)   Wir waren traurig, dass _____ .   *Erdal allein in der Loge saß*
5. (Es gab kein Happyend.)   Wir waren traurig, dass _____ .   *es kein Happyend gab*
6. (Wir mussten heimfahren.)   Wir waren traurig, dass _____ .   *wir heimfahren mussten*

5 Was passiert, bevor du ins Ballett gehen kannst? Schreib die folgenden Sätze ab, und schreib dabei die Passivform der gegebenen Verben in die Lücken! (**Seite 281**)

1. (bestellen)   Zuerst _____ die Karten telefonisch _____ .   *werden; bestellt*
2. (kaufen)   Wenn es Karten gibt, _____ sie sofort _____ .   *werden; gekauft*
3. (abholen)   Dann _____ die Karten vom Musiklehrer _____ .   *werden; abgeholt*
4. (verteilen)   Danach _____ sie an die Schüler _____ .   *werden; verteilt*
5. (besprechen)   Oft _____ das Stück vorher in der Klasse _____ .   *wird; besprochen*
6. (zeigen)   Manchmal _____ auch Dias _____ .   *werden; gezeigt*
7. (vorbereiten)   Die Schüler _____ also sehr gut auf das Stück _____ .   *werden; vorbereitet*

6 Du berichtest darüber, was geschehen ist, bevor die Vorstellung angefangen hat. Schreib die folgenden Sätze ab, und schreib dabei die Passivform der gegebenen Verben in die Lücken! Gebrauche dabei die Vergangenheitsform (*past tense form*)! (**Seite 281**)

1. (begleiten)   Die Schüler _____ auf ihre Plätze _____ .   *wurden; begleitet*
2. (stimmen)   Dann _____ die Instrumente _____ .   *wurden; gestimmt*
3. (hochziehen)   Etwas später _____ die Kronleuchter _____ .   *wurden; hochgezogen*
4. (ausmachen)   Und bald danach _____ das Licht _____ .   *wurde; ausgemacht*
5. (begrüßen)   Dann _____ der Dirigent mit lautem Klatschen _____ .   *wurde; begrüßt*
6. (sprechen)   Jetzt _____ nicht mehr _____ . Das Ballett begann.   *wurde; gesprochen*

7 Du berichtest über die Vorstellung, die du besucht hast. Schreib die folgenden Sätze ab, und schreib dabei die Passivform der gegebenen Verben in die Lücken! Gebrauche jetzt dabei das Perfekt! (**Seite 281**)

1. (zeigen)   Das Stück _____ schon dreimal _____ _____ .   ist; gezeigt; worden
2. (aufführen)   Das Spiel _____ letztes Jahr _____ _____ .   ist; aufgeführt; worden
3. (erwarten)   Die Schauspieler _____ mit Spannung _____ _____ .   sind; erwartet; worden
4. (darstellen)   Die Giselle _____ ausgezeichnet _____ _____ .   ist; dargestellt; worden
5. (applaudieren) Es _____ kräftig _____ _____ .   ist; applaudiert; worden
6. (begleiten)   Das Orchester _____ von einem Solisten _____ _____ . ist; begleitet; worden

8 Du berichtest jetzt darüber, was alles getan werden muss, bevor die Vorstellung beginnen kann. Schreib Sätze mit einer Form von **müssen** und der Infinitivform des Passivs (past participle + **werden**) der gegebenen Verben! (**Seite 281**)

1. (bestellen)   Die Karten _____ _____ _____ .   müssen; bestellt; werden
2. (kaufen)   Die Karten _____ _____ _____ .   müssen; gekauft; werden
3. (verteilen)   Die Karten _____ _____ _____ .   müssen; verteilt; werden
4. (besprechen)   Das Stück _____ _____ _____ .   muss; besprochen; werden
5. (erklären)   Es _____ den Schülern _____ _____ .   muss; erklärt; werden
6. (klären)   Ja, und die Kleiderfrage _____ _____ _____ . muss; geklärt; werden

9 Du sagst jetzt, was man im Allgemeinen (*in general*) nicht tun darf. Schreib Sätze und benütz dabei die Befehlsform (*command form*) und das Partizip der Vergangenheit (*past participle*) der gegebenen Verben! (**Seite 281**)

1. (singen)   Hier _____ nicht _____ !   wird; gesungen
2. (tanzen)   Hier _____ nicht _____ !   wird; getanzt
3. (essen)   Hier _____ nicht _____ !   wird; gegessen
4. (trinken)   Hier _____ nicht _____ !   wird; getrunken
5. (schlafen) In der Schule _____ nicht _____ !   wird; geschlafen
6. (streiten) In meiner Klasse _____ nicht _____ !   wird; gestritten
7. (faulenzen) In der Deutschstunde _____ nicht _____ !   wird; gefaulenzt
8. (sprechen) Hier _____ nicht Englisch _____ !   wird; gesprochen

Script and answers on p. 267I

1 Du hörst jetzt einige junge Leute über kulturelle Interessen sprechen. Schreib auf, wovon jeder spricht: von Literatur, von Kunst, von einem Konzert, von einer Oper oder von einem Ballett!
CD 10 Tr. 9

2 Der folgende Artikel ist eine typische Rezension eines Musikabends mit dem berühmten englischen Geiger Nigel Kennedy. Lies diese Rezension, und diskutier darüber mit deinen Klassenkameraden! Hast du Nigel Kennedy schon gesehen oder gehört? Was hältst du von ihm?

Super-Geiger im Punk-Look

Die Presse hatte die Musikfanatiker schon genügend auf den jungen Super-Geiger vorbereitet. Trotzdem

schienen anfangs einige Musiklieb-haber „schockiert". Er trug nämlich keinen schwarzen Frack. Die Haare hatte er punkig hochgekämmt. So präsentierte sich der junge englische Geiger Nigel Kennedy dem Frankfurter Musikpublikum. Ein Kulturschock? Überhaupt nicht! Der junge Geiger ist ein netter Kerl, der auf dem Klavier modernen Jazz genau so perfekt spielt wie klassische Musik auf seiner Guarnerius-Geige. Nigel Kennedy spielt nämlich in Stephane Grappellis Jazzgruppe mit — das ist lustig, aber noch kein Grund zur Panik. Kennedy ist auch ein Fußballfreak — so aber auch der berühmte Tenor Placido Domingo.

Die Freunde der ernsten Musik hörten gestern abend einen Musiker von großer Energie. Bachs a-Moll-Konzert wurde kraftvoll perfekt gespielt. Danach kamen Vivaldis „Vier Jahreszeiten" — exakt gegeigt, nicht besonders unorthodox oder sogar aufsässig, nein — nur etwas rigoros vielleicht. Der junge Geiger machte außerdem ein paar witzige Bemerkungen am Mikrofon, und das Publikum fand das prima. Demnächst will Kennedy in München spielen. Seine Fans in der bayrischen Hauptstadt warten schon eifrig auf ihn!

3 Schreib eine Rezension über ein Konzert, eine Theateraufführung oder einen Film, den du erlebt hast!

4 Entwerft in der Klasse einen kulturellen Veranstaltungskalender für diesen Monat! Was für Konzerte, Theateraufführungen, Kunstausstellungen werden angeboten? Wann finden sie statt, oder wann fanden sie statt? Welche Veranstaltungen habt ihr schon besucht? Was könnt ihr darüber berichten?

 5 Schau dir den Veranstaltungskalender an, den du mit deinen Klassenkameraden entworfen hast! Wähle eine Veranstaltung, die du noch nicht kennst! Besuche sie, schreib eine Rezension darüber, und lies sie der Klasse vor!

 6 Stellt mit Hilfe eures Lehrers oder eurer Lehrerin eine Liste zusammen mit Namen von berühmten Deutschen auf den Gebieten der Kunst, der Musik, der Literatur und der Philosophie! Teilt euch in vier Gruppen auf! Jede Gruppe ist für ein Gebiet verantwortlich und macht für dieses Gebiet eine Ausstellung. Die Ausstellung soll aus schriftlichen Berichten und visuellen Materialien bestehen. Die Mitglieder jeder Gruppe sollen dann ihre Ausstellung der Klasse zeigen und beschreiben.

 7 Macht jetzt ein „Kulturspiel"! Schreibt die Namen aus der Liste mit berühmten deutschen Frauen und Männern auf Zettel! Teilt euch in zwei Teams auf! Team A bekommt einen Zettel und muss die Person identifizieren: Maler, Komponisten, Sänger, Philosophen, Schriftsteller, Dichter, usw. Dann kommt Team B dran. Welches Team hat die meisten Personen richtig identifiziert?

8 ## Rollenspiel

Bereite eins von den beiden Rollenspielen mit drei anderen Schülern vor!

a. Stellt euch vor, ihr geht ins Theater zu einer Vorstellung von „Giselle". Ihr seid gerade am Theater angekommen und wollt nun eure Karten abholen. Alle sind gespannt auf die Vorstellung und reden darüber. Euer Dialog endet, wenn das Licht ausgeht und der Vorhang aufgeht.

b. Lest die Gruselgeschichte „Die Nacht bei den Wachsfiguren" noch einmal. Nun stellt euch vor, ihr erlebt eine ähnliche gruselige Situation. Denkt euch eine gespenstische Geschichte aus. Sie kann zum Beispiel auf einer einsamen Straße oder in einem leeren Theater spielen. Schreibt dann einen Dialog dafür.

Kann ich's wirklich?

Can you express preference, given certain possibilities? (p. 272)

1 How would you ask a friend what book he or she would read if he or she were on vacation? How would your friend respond if he or she wanted to read *It* by Stephen King?

Welches Buch würdest du lesen, wenn du Ferien hättest? — Ich würde „It" von Stephen King lesen.

2 How would you respond if someone asked you **Welche kulturellen Veranstaltungen würdest du besuchen, wenn du genug Zeit hättest?** How would you then express specific possibility?

Ich würde in ein Konzert gehen. / Ich würde eventuell/vielleicht/möglicherweise in ein Rockkonzert gehen.

Can you express envy and admiration? (p. 273)

3 How would you express envy if your friend told you

a. that he or she got a new car as a birthday present?

Eg. Ich beneide dich. Du hast ein neues Auto zum Geburtstag bekommen.

b. that he or she won a trip to Hawaii?

Eg. Ich beneide dich. Du hast eine Reise nach Hawaii gewonnen!

c. that he or she got an A in French?

Eg. Ich beneide dich. Du hast eine Eins in Französisch bekommen.

4 How would you express your admiration if your friend told you

a. that he or she speaks several languages?

Eg. Ich bewundere dich. Du sprichst mehrere Sprachen.

b. that he or she has read the books of the German philosopher Nietzsche in German?

Eg. Ich bewundere dich, weil du die Bücher des deutschen Philosophen Nietzsche auf Deutsch gelesen hast.

c. that he or she has seen the Seven Wonders of the World?

Eg. Ich bewundere dich, weil du die sieben Weltwunder gesehen hast.

Can you express happiness and sadness? (p. 278)

5 How would you say that you are happy about the following things?

a. **Ich darf ins Theater gehen.** Ich bin froh, dass ich ins Theater gehen darf.

b. **Die Plätze sind sehr gut.** Ich bin froh, dass die Plätze sehr gut sind.

6 How would you say that you are sad about the following things?

a. **Die Karten fürs Ballett waren ausverkauft.**

b. **Unsere Schulklasse darf keinen Ausflug machen.**

6. a. Ich bin traurig, dass die Karten fürs Ballett ausverkauft waren.
b. Ich bin traurig, dass unsere Schulklasse keinen Ausflug machen darf.

Can you say that something is or was being done? (p. 280)

7 How would you say that you and your classmates are taught (**unterrichtet**) by very good teachers?

7. Meine Klassenkameraden und ich werden von sehr guten Lehrern unterrichtet.

8 How would you say that *Cats* was performed in your town last year?

8. Voriges Jahr wurde „Cats" in unserer Stadt aufgeführt.

Erste Stufe

 p. 267X

Expressing preference, given certain possibilities

Ich höre mir hauptsächlich Jazz an.	I listen mainly to jazz.
Ich würde mir möglicherweise auch klassische Musik anhören.	I would possibly also listen to classical music.
Und eventuell noch Country-Western.	And perhaps also country western.

Expressing envy and admiration

Wir beneiden unseren Freund, weil …	We envy our friend because …
Ich bewundere Steffi Graf, da …	I admire Steffi Graf since …

Other useful words

die Abendkasse, -n	ticket window
die Ausstellung, -en	exhibition
das Abonnement, -s	subscription
die Geige, -n	violin
die Hausmusik	house music
die Sage, -n	legend
das Märchen, -	fairy tale
der Philosoph, -en	philosopher
das Wunder, -	wonder, miracle
das Volksfest, -e	regional festival
die Geduld	patience
das Vergnügen, -	pleasure
der Unterschied, -e	difference
das Werk, -e	(literary) work, achievement
aufblühen (sep)	to blossom, thrive
ausgehen von (sep)	to be initiated by

vorhanden sein	to exist
vorlesen (sep)	to read aloud
verlängern	to extend
grotesk	grotesque
unheimlich (gut)	really (well)
historisch	historical
wissenschaftlich	scientific
meinetwegen	as far as I'm concerned
zwar	indeed
teilweise	partly

Prepositions with the genitive case

während	during
wegen	because of
anstatt	instead of
innerhalb	inside of

Zweite Stufe

Telling that something is or was being done

Die Instrumente werden vor der Aufführung gestimmt.	The instruments are being tuned before the performance.
Es ist kräftig applaudiert worden.	There was strong applause.

Other useful words

die Aufführung, -en	performance
die Bühne, -n	stage
der Dirigent, -en	conductor
die Handlung, -en	plot
der Rang, ¨e	(theater) balcony
der Vorhang, ¨e	curtain
der Zuschauer, -	spectator
der Tänzer, -	dancer

die Aufregung, -en	excitement;
vor lauter Aufregung	from sheer excitement
die Eifersucht	jealousy
die Gänsehaut	goose bumps
das Herzklopfen	pounding heart
die Spannung, -en	tension, excitement
der Bube, -n	(southern German) boy
die Königin, -nen	queen
die Pracht	splendor
der Spiegel, -	mirror
der Versuch, -e	attempt
aufführen (sep)	to perform
begleiten	to accompany
begrüßen	to greet
s. beklagen über (acc)	to complain about

darstellen (sep)	to play (act)
erkennen	to recognize
erleben	to experience
es geht um	it is about
s. handeln um	to be about
klären	to clear up
klatschen	to applaud
stimmen	to tune (an instrument)
träumen	to dream
s. umsehen (sep)	to look around
verteilen	to distribute
atemlos	breathless
bärtig	bearded
heiter	cheerful
vergeblich	futile
weder … noch	neither … nor

Kapitel 11: Deine Welt ist deine Sache!
Chapter Overview

CULTURE

- **Ein wenig Landeskunde:** German universities, p. 302   • **Umfragen und Tests,** p. 308
- **Landeskunde: Wie findet man eine Arbeitsstelle in Deutschland?** p. 305

Kapitel 11: Deine Welt ist deine Sache!
Chapter Resources

Lesson Planning

⚡ **One-Stop Planner**

Lesson Planner with Substitute Teacher Lesson Plans, pp. 61–65, 85

Student Make-Up Assignments
- Make-Up Assignment Copying Masters, Chapter 11

Listening and Speaking

Listening Activities
- Student Response Forms for Listening Activities, pp. 83–86
- Additional Listening Activities 11-1 to 11-6, pp. 87–90
- Scripts and Answers, pp. 183–191

Video Guide
- Teaching Suggestions, p. 50
- Activity Masters, pp. 51–52
- Scripts and Answers, pp. 71–72, 76

Activities for Communication
- Communicative Activities, pp. 41–44
- Realia and Teaching Suggestions, pp. 101–105
- Situation Cards, pp. 133–134

Reading and Writing

Reading Strategies and Skills Handbook, Chapter 11

Lies mit mir! 3, Chapter 11

Übungsheft, pp. 131–143

Grammar

Grammatikheft, pp. 91–99

Grammar Tutor for Students of German, Chapter 11

Assessment

Testing Program
- Grammar and Vocabulary Quizzes, **Stufe** Quizzes, and Chapter Test, pp. 235–248
- Score Sheet, Scripts and Answers, pp. 249–255

Alternative Assessment Guide
- Portfolio Assessment, p. 26
- Performance Assessment, p. 40

Student Make-Up Assignments
- Alternative Quizzes, Chapter 11

 Online Activities
- Interaktive Spiele
- Internet Aktivitäten

 Video Program
- Videocassette 2

 Audio Compact Discs
- Textbook Listening Activities, CD 11, Tracks 1–17
- Additional Listening Activities, CD 11, Tracks 22–27
- Assessment Items, CD 11, Tracks 18–21

 Teaching Transparencies
- Situations 11-1 to 11-2
- **Mehr Grammatikübungen** Answers
- **Grammatikheft** Answers

Use the **One-Stop Planner CD-ROM** with **Test Generator** to aid in lesson planning and pacing.

For each chapter, the **One-Stop Planner** includes:
- Editable lesson plans with direct links to teaching resources
- Printable worksheets from resource books
- Direct launches to the HRW Internet activities
- Video and audio segments
- Test Generator
- Clip Art for vocabulary items

Kapitel 11: Deine Welt ist deine Sache!

Projects

Karrieren mit Fremdsprachen

*In this activity, students will create an extensive collage called **Karrieren mit Fremdsprachen**. The project should be completed in German by individuals or pairs of students. Final projects should be presented and then displayed in the foreign language area.*

MATERIALS

✂ Students will need

- posterboard
- paper
- dictionaries
- pencils
- magazine cutouts
- materials from the counseling office

SUGGESTED SEQUENCE

1. Have students make a list of professions that require a foreign language or are enhanced by one. Have them find information at the high school's career center, the local library, and in ads in newspapers such as the *Wall Street Journal*. You might also want to show them again the Career Path features that appear throughout all three levels of the *Komm mit! Teacher's Editions*.

2. From this list, students choose one profession they plan to research in detail.

3. Students make an outline of the information they plan to include in their presentation.

4. Students collect visual materials and design the layout of their collage.

5. For the written component, students should incorporate some of the new phrases and expressions they have learned in this chapter, particularly in the chart next to Activity 11 on p. 302.

6. The final product should include visuals, accompanied by a job description and describe the advantages of such a career.

7. Students present their collage to the rest of the class.

GRADING THE PROJECT

Suggested point distribution (**total = 100 points**)

Accurate descriptions and
correct language usage 50
Appearance 25
Oral presentation...................................25

FAMILY LINK

Have students interview their family members about their first jobs. How did they find out about the job? What did they have to do to apply? What work did they have to do, and how much did the job pay?

Games

Erratet den Beruf!

This game tests students' knowledge of German professions and the skills necessary for these jobs.

Procedure Make a list of all the professions that students have learned thus far. Then divide the class into two teams. The first player on team A comes up to the front. You point to the first word on the list, and the student has to describe what this person does at his or her job without using the job title. The team that guesses the correct profession wins a point. Teams alternate giving job descriptions. The team with the most points at the end of the game wins.

Examples:

Er kümmert sich um Patienten, aber er ist kein Arzt. (Krankenpfleger)

Sie hackt und verkauft Fleisch. (Metzgerin)

Storytelling

Mini-Geschichte

*This story accompanies Teaching Transparency 11-2. The **Mini-Geschichte** can be told and retold in different formats, acted out, written down, and read aloud to give students additional opportunities to practice all four skills.*

Mein Traumjob

Geregelte Arbeitszeiten sind wichtig. Ich will auf keinen Fall Überstunden machen oder am Wochenende arbeiten. Der Job darf nicht langweilig sein, sonst vergeht die Zeit zu langsam. Er muss auch meinen Horizont erweitern. Ich will eine Arbeit, die die Welt entweder sozial oder gesundheitlich verbessert. Aber vor allem muss mein idealer Job viel bezahlen, denn ich will bald ein Jahr lang Urlaub machen. Mit fünfundzwanzig möchte ich eine Weltreise gemacht haben. Glaubst du, es gibt so einen Job?

Traditions

Der Dresdner Striezelmarkt

Der Dresdner Striezelmarkt ist einer der ältesten und traditions-reichsten Weihnachtsmärkte Deutschlands. Als städtischer Markt wurde er bereits 1434 urkundlich erwähnt. Der Name des Marktes kommt von jenem Backwerk, das heute als Dresdner Christstollen weltbekannt ist. Striezel nannte man im Mittelhochdeutschen ein Hefegebäck in länglicher Form. Zur Eröffnung des Striezelmarktes wird jedes Jahr ein Riesenstollen gebacken, dessen Länge (in cm) der Jahreszahl entspricht. Im Jahre 2000, zum Beispiel, war der Stollen 2000 Zentimeter oder 20 Meter lang.

Zum Striezelmarkt gehört aber nicht nur der Stollen, sondern auch die Pflaumentoffel. Diese Männchen aus Backpflaumen sind den Schlotfegerjungen nachgebildet. Diese oft erst sieben Jahre alten Jungen mussten in die Kamine klettern, um sie von innen zu reinigen. Viele arme Familien bastelten die Pflaumentoffel zu Hause und schickten dann ihre Kinder, um diese Männchen zwischen den Buden des Striezelmarktes zu verkaufen. 1910 wurde der Verkauf durch Kinder untersagt. Heute werden die Pflaumentoffel in Serienproduktion hergestellt und als Glücksbringer verkauft.

Rezept

Dresdner Stollen
Für 2 Stollen

Zutaten
g=Gramm, ml=Milliliter, TL=Teelöffel, EL=Esslöffel

Teig

540 g	Weizenmehl	500 g	Rosinen
85 g	Hefe	3	Tropfen
90 g	Zucker		Zitronenaroma
85 g	Butterschmalz	¼ TL	Vanillemark
250 g	Butter	¼ TL	Macisblüte
50 g	Zitronat		
50 g	Orangeat	*Glasur*	
120 g	geriebene Mandeln	100 g	
30 g	Marzipanrohmasse		Butterschmalz
140 ml	Milch	100 g	Zucker
1 TL	Salz	125 g	Puderzucker

Zubereitung

Am Abend vorher alle Zutaten (außer der Milch und Hefe) abwiegen und bei Zimmertemperatur stehen lassen.

Am nächsten Tag einen Teil der Milch erwärmen und mit der zerbröckelten Hefe und einer Prise Zucker vermischen, etwas Mehl dazugeben und ca. 20 Minuten gehen lassen. Das restliche Mehl, Zucker, Milch, Salz, Butterschmalz, Butter und Marzipanrohmasse dazugeben und zu einem Teig verkneten. Zum Schluss die restlichen Zutaten unterarbeiten. Den Teig zugedeckt eine Stunde gehen lassen, dann kurz durchkneten und in zwei Stücke teilen. Jeweils einen Laib formen, mit der Kuchenrolle in der Mitte längs eindrücken und nach einer Seite flach rollen. Das ausgerollte Teigstück nach oben klappen und festdrücken. In der Zwischenzeit den Backofen auf 220 Grad Celsius vorheizen. Die beiden Stollen auf ein Blech setzen. Anfangs bei 220 Grad Celsius und zum Schluss bei 200 Grad Celsius 50 - 60 Minuten backen. Die ausgekühlten Stollen mit flüssigem Butterschmalz begießen und zuckern.

One-Stop Planner CD-ROM

To preview all resources available for this chapter, use the **One-Stop Planner CD-ROM**, Disc 3.

Internet Connection ....

internet

ADRESSE: go.hrw.com
KENNWORT:
WK3 DRESDEN-11

*Have students explore the **go.hrw.com** Web site for many online resources covering all chapters. All Chapter 11 resources are available under the keyword **WK3 Dresden-11**. Interactive games practice the material and provide students with immediate feedback. You will also find a printable worksheet that provides Internet activities that lead to a comprehensive online research project.*

Interaktive Spiele

Use the interactive activities in this chapter

- to practice grammar, vocabulary, and chapter functions
- as homework
- as an assessment option
- as a self-test
- to prepare for the Chapter Test

Internet Aktivitäten

Students investigate the career choices German youths have after finishing high school. They visit an online employment office and find a job for a biologist or a physicist.

- To prepare students for the **Arbeitsblatt,** have them reread **Los geht's!,** p. 298, and analyze the results of the **Umfrage,** Activity 3, p. 299.
- After completing the **Arbeitsblatt,** have students contact a career counselor at their school or at the nearest college or university and get information on the profession(s) in which they are interested. They should report on the requirements, length of study or training, and job prospects.

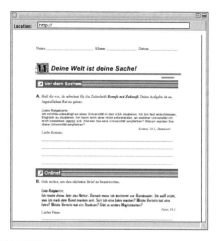

Webprojekt

Have students research the life and accomplishments of their idol or a famous person they admire. Alternatively, you may want to have students do research on a person who is listed in the box on p. 308. In addition to presenting a brief biography, students should explain why they chose a certain person. Encourage students to exchange useful Web sites with their classmates. Have students document their sources by referencing the names and URLs of all the sites they consulted.

Kapitel 11: Deine Welt ist deine Sache!
Textbook Listening Activities Scripts

The following scripts are for the listening activities found in the *Pupil's Edition*. For Student Response Forms, see *Listening Activities*, pages 83–86. To provide students with additional listening practice, see *Listening Activities*, pages 87–90.

Erste Stufe

4 p. 301

GERD Hallo, Ulla! Hallo, Ralf! Stör ich?

RALF Ach was, natürlich nicht! Wir haben uns gerade über unsere Pläne nach dem Schulabschluss unterhalten. Hast du schon darüber nachgedacht, was du nach der Schule machen willst, Gerd?

GERD Na klar! Ich weiß schon ziemlich genau, was ich machen werde.

ULLA Beneidenswert! Ich hab mich noch nicht entschieden, ob ich studieren oder einen Beruf erlernen soll.

RALF Das klingt aber sehr allgemein. Weißt du denn wenigstens, was du studieren würdest, oder in welchem Beruf du später einmal arbeiten möchtest?

ULLA In den letzten Wochen habe ich mir darüber sehr viele Gedanken gemacht. Ich habe mich entschlossen, einen medizinischen Beruf zu erlernen. Aber ich weiß noch nicht, ob ich mir ein so schwieriges Studium zutraue. Ich könnte auch eine Ausbildung als Krankenschwester machen. Das dauert nur drei Jahre.

RALF Vielleicht solltest du dich mal mit einem Arzt oder einer Krankenschwester über diese Berufe unterhalten. Ich könnte mir vorstellen, dass es dir helfen würde, die richtige Entscheidung zu treffen.

ULLA Gute Idee! Daran habe ich noch gar nicht gedacht. Du, Gerd! Du hast gesagt, dass du schon ganz genau weißt, was du nach dem Abi machen wirst. Lass mal hören!

GERD Also, zuerst muss ich ja meinen Wehrdienst leisten. Danach fange ich ein Studium an. Ich habe mich entschieden, Englisch und Spanisch zu studieren.

ULLA Kein Wunder! Du hast ja auch immer Supernoten in den beiden Fächern.

GERD Ich hoffe, dass ich einen Studienplatz bekomme. Ich möchte Simultandolmetscher werden.

RALF Mensch, ich beneide dich, Gerd. Das stelle ich mir wahnsinnig schwierig vor.

GERD Ist es auch! Deshalb wird es auch nicht einfach sein, einen Studienplatz hier in Deutschland zu bekommen. Im Notfall werde ich eben ins Ausland gehen, wie zum Beispiel nach London oder auch nach New York. Ich muss mir das noch überlegen.

ULLA Klasse! Und wer finanziert deine Auslandspläne? Deine Eltern? Das muss doch ziemlich teuer sein.

GERD Wahrscheinlich würden sie mich schon finanziell unterstützen, aber eigentlich hoffe ich darauf, ein Stipendium zu bekommen.

RALF Ich bin echt beeindruckt, Gerd. Du hast wirklich an alles gedacht. Ich selbst hab beschlossen, Maschinenbau zu studieren. Als Diplomingenieur kann ich mich später entweder selbständig machen, oder ich kann in die Industrie gehen.

ULLA Wo willst du denn Maschinenbau studieren?

RALF Ich weiß noch nicht, ob ich nach Braunschweig oder nach Kaiserslautern gehen soll. Beide Unis sollen ein ausgezeichnetes Studienprogramm für Maschinenbau haben. Wenn das Studium gut läuft, bin ich fest entschlossen, ein Jahr in den USA oder in Kanada einzuschieben. Aber das kommt erst später.

GERD Na ja, es scheint, als ob wir alle ziemlich genau wissen, was wir nach der Schule anfangen. Mensch, wenn doch bloß der Stress mit dem Abi schon vorbei wäre!

RALF He, Leute! Da fällt mir gerade was ein. Ich hab gehört, dass der Geßner, der Klassenlehrer von der 13b, in zwei Wochen eine Party für alle gestressten Abiturienten macht. Geht ihr hin?

ULLA Das kommt ja wie gerufen! Eine Party haben wir uns schon lange verdient. Find ich toll, dass der Geßner uns alle einlädt. Also, ich muss jetzt los. Tschüs, ihr beiden!

GERD Tschüs, Ulla!

RALF Ciao!

Answers to Activity 4
feste Pläne: Gerd, Ralf
noch nicht sicher: Ulla

12 p. 303

HORST He, Steffi! Na, wie geht's?

STEFFI Hallo, Horst! Ich hab dich gar nicht gesehen. Ist ja wieder mal ziemlich voll im Café Goethe.

HORST Sag mal, Steffi, hast du dir schon überlegt, was du nach dem Abitur anfangen willst?

STEFFI Ja, hab ich! Ich bin nicht besonders interessiert daran zu studieren. Das steht auf jeden Fall fest.

HORST Wieso nicht? Was stört dich denn so sehr an einem Studium?

STEFFI Weißt du, ich lege einfach keinen großen Wert darauf, die nächsten fünf, sechs Jahre weiterhin nur lernen zu müssen.

HORST Das müsstest du doch auch, wenn du einen Beruf erlernen willst.

STEFFI Da gibt es aber einen großen Unterschied. Für mich ist es am wichtigsten, dass ich endlich mal etwas Praktisches tun werde. Ich habe es satt, ständig nur über den Büchern zu sitzen.

HORST Woran hast du denn gedacht?

STEFFI Am liebsten würde ich an einem Projekt von UNICEF arbeiten. Ich lege großen Wert darauf, dass den Menschen in den Entwicklungsländern und vor allem den Kindern dort geholfen wird. Mir ist weniger wichtig, dass ich gut verdiene. Menschen in Not zu helfen, ist mir mehr wert als eigener Luxus.

HORST   Ich wusste gar nicht, dass du auf diesem Gebiet so engagiert bist.

STEFFI   Ja, als mir klar wurde, wie wichtig diese Ziele für mich sind, habe ich mich entschieden, diesen Weg zu wählen. Aber wir reden ja die ganze Zeit nur von meinen Zukunftsplänen. Erzähl doch mal, was du so vorhast!

HORST   Ich werde wahrscheinlich erst einmal meinen Zivildienst machen.

STEFFI   Zivildienst statt Wehrdienst?

HORST   Ausschlaggebend für mich ist, dass ich beim Zivildienst nicht mit Waffen umgehen muss. Lieber arbeite ich als Sozialarbeiter, Altenpfleger oder sonst etwas in der Richtung. Nach dem Zivildienst möchte ich am liebsten Jura studieren.

STEFFI   Jura! Da wirst du ewig an der Uni sein.

HORST   Es ist nicht entscheidend für mich, dass das Studium lang und hart ist. Ich finde es wichtig, dass das Gesetz vertreten wird.

STEFFI   Hast du dir schon überlegt, in welche Richtung du später einmal gehen möchtest?

HORST   Vielleicht Grundstücksrecht.

STEFFI   Wie kommst du denn ausgerechnet auf Grundstücke?

HORST   Tja, also ich glaube, dass die Spezialisierung auf Grundstücksrecht Zukunft hat. Nimm zum Beispiel mal die ganzen Grundstücke in der ehemaligen DDR. Die Rechtsfrage wird auch in den nächsten fünf bis zehn Jahren noch nicht geklärt sein.

STEFFI   Hm. Das mag schon sein. Ich wünsch dir auf jeden Fall viel Spaß mit deinen Zukunftsplänen. Also, ich muss wieder los. Tschüs, Horst!

HORST   Tschüs, Steffi!

Answers to Activity 12
Wichtig für Steffi: etwas Praktisches tun; Menschen in Entwicklungsländern helfen / Wichtig für Horst: nicht mit Waffen umgehen zu müssen; dass das Gesetz vertreten wird / z.B.: Es macht Horst nichts aus, weiter zu studieren, aber Steffi will lieber etwas Praktisches tun; Steffi möchte sich mit Problemen in Entwicklungsländern beschäftigen, und Horst interessiert sich für Rechtsfragen in Deutschland.

Zweite Stufe

20   p. 309

MEIKE   Hallo, Conny! Toll, dass du kommen konntest. Felix und Harry sind schon da.

CONNY   Das war übrigens eine gute Idee von dir, Meike, zusammen für die nächste Englischarbeit zu lernen. Hallo, Felix! Hallo, Harry! Na, lernt ihr schon fleißig?

FELIX   Hi, Conny! Eigentlich haben wir uns gerade darüber unterhalten, was wir uns im Leben mal wünschen.

MEIKE   Interessant! Erzähl doch mal! Was wünschst du dir denn als Erstes nach dem Schulabschluss, Felix?

FELIX   Also, am liebsten wäre mir, wenn es keine Wehrpflicht gäbe. Das ist doch alles bloß eine riesige Zeitverschwendung. Mit physischer Gewalt stimme ich sowieso nicht überein. Was meinst du, Harry?

HARRY   Du kannst ja auch verweigern und statt dessen Zivildienst machen.

FELIX   Dazu brauche ich aber auch mindestens eineinhalb Jahre. Gleich nach der Schule mit dem Studium anzufangen, wäre mir viel wichtiger.

CONNY   Das kann ich gut verstehen, Felix. Mir wäre es auch lästig, wenn ich so eine Verpflichtung hätte. Mein Wunschtraum wäre, genug Geld zu haben, um ein ganzes Jahr in der Welt herumzureisen.

MEIKE   Klingt super, Conny! Da würde ich garantiert mitkommen. Es gibt so viele interessante Sachen auf der ganzen Welt zu sehen. Es wäre nur schön, wenn es keine Umweltkatastrophen mehr gäbe.

HARRY   Da hast du Recht, Meike. Bei all den Erdbeben und Wirbelstürmen, die die Welt in letzter Zeit erlebt hat, kann ich deinen Wunsch verstehen. Ich muss allerdings eingestehen, dass ich bei meinen Wünschen etwas egoistischer bin. Ein toller Beruf, der viel Geld, aber auch viel Freizeit bringt, wäre mir sehr wichtig.

FELIX   Nicht schlecht, Harry. Mir wäre außerdem noch wichtig, dass ich mal ein tolles Haus habe.

MEIKE   Ihr habt wirklich sehr materialistische Wünsche. Mir ist es ganz gleichgültig, ob ich mal reich werde oder ein tolles Haus habe. Viel wichtiger wären mir echte Freunde, denen man ein ganzes Leben lang vertrauen kann.

HARRY   Jeder wünscht sich eben etwas anderes, und das ist auch gut so, sonst wäre die Welt unheimlich langweilig.

MEIKE   He, es ist ja schon bald halb fünf! Jetzt müssen wir uns aber ganz schön beeilen, wenn wir überhaupt noch was für die Englischarbeit lernen wollen. Immerhin müssen wir erst einmal die Schule hinter uns bringen, sonst bleiben alle unsere Wünsche nur Träume!

Answers to Activity 20
Felix: keine Wehrpflicht; gleich nach der Schule mit dem Studium anfangen zu können; tolles Haus
Conny: genug Geld zu haben, um zu reisen
Meike: keine Umweltkatastrophen; echte Freunde
Harry: tollen Beruf mit viel Geld und viel Freizeit
Answers will vary.

26   p. 310

DANIEL   He, Jürgen! Was liest du denn so Spannendes? Du hast uns gar nicht kommen hören.

JÜRGEN   Hallo, Daniel! Ach, da kommen ja auch Sylvia und Sophie.

SYLVIA   Du bist ja ziemlich in dein Buch vertieft. Zeig doch mal, was du da liest, Jürgen!

JÜRGEN   Es ist eine Biographie über John F. Kennedy. Habt ihr überhaupt eine Ahnung, was der alles in seinem Leben erreicht hat? Schon als junger Mann hatte der was drauf, sag ich euch. Mit 29 Jahren war er bereits Abgeordneter im Repräsentantenhaus in der amerikanischen Regierung. Ich möchte unbedingt auch eine politische Karriere begonnen haben, wenn ich dreißig bin.

DANIEL   In die Politik willst du?

JÜRGEN   Ja, ich möchte mich auch mal so für mein Land und das Volk engagieren, wie Kennedy das für sein Land getan hat.

SYLVIA   Du hast ja große Pläne, Jürgen.

JÜRGEN   Ach, komm, Sylvia! So wie ich dich kenne, hast du doch bestimmt große Ambitionen, oder?

SYLVIA   Ja, stimmt! Mit dreißig möchte ich in einer Karriere als Börsenmaklerin etabliert sein und bereits eine Menge Geld gespart haben. Für mich sind komfortable finanzielle Verhältnisse sehr wichtig. In zehn Jahren will ich mir jedenfalls keine Gedanken mehr um Geld machen müssen.

DANIEL   Ihr wisst schon so genau, wie ihr euch euer Leben in zehn Jahren vorstellt, Jürgen und Sylvia. Ich weiß noch gar nicht, was ich einmal machen werde, wenn ich dreißig bin. Ziemlich sicher bin ich mir jedoch, dass ich irgendwann mal heiraten und eine Familie haben will. Vielleicht werde ich bis dahin ja meine Traumfrau gefunden haben.

SYLVIA   Daniel, das finde ich toll. Wir haben alle nur an die berufliche Seite gedacht. Sophie, du hast noch gar nichts gesagt. Wie stellst du dir dein Leben mit dreißig vor?

SOPHIE   Ich würde gern Schauspielerin werden, aber alle machen sich immer über meinen Berufswunsch lustig.

JÜRGEN   Du musst zugeben, dass die Chancen in dem Beruf nicht gerade rosig sind, weil es so viele Menschen gibt, die diesen Wunschtraum haben.

SOPHIE   Trotzdem glaube ich, dass ich eine gute Schauspielerin wäre. Bis ich dreißig bin, will ich es geschafft haben, im Deutschen Theater oder im Berliner Schauspielhaus gespielt zu haben. Ich glaube jedenfalls an mein Talent und an meine Chancen.

JÜRGEN   Ich wünsche dir viel Glück dabei. Wir sollten uns alle in zwölf Jahren wieder treffen, meint ihr nicht? Ich möchte wirklich mal sehen, ob wir unsere Träume verwirklichen können!

Answers to Activity 26
Jürgen: will sich politisch engagieren
Sylvia: will Karriere machen und viel Geld haben
Daniel: will heiraten und eine Familie haben
Sophie: will Schauspielerin werden
Answers will vary.

Anwendung

1 p. 320

CARMEN   Martin, Simone, so ein Zufall, dass ich euch hier treffe!

SIMONE   Hallo, Carmen! So ein Zufall ist das nun auch wieder nicht. Wir sind oft in diesem Eiscafé. Die haben hier das beste Eis in der ganzen Stadt.

MARTIN   Stimmt! Setz dich doch, Simone! Wir haben uns gerade über unsere Berufswünsche unterhalten.

CARMEN   Was möchtest du denn mal machen, Martin?

MARTIN   Ich möchte gern Journalismus studieren. Am liebsten würde ich später mal als Journalist für eine große Zeitung oder für ein politisches Magazin arbeiten.

SIMONE   Das ist sicher wahnsinnig interessant. Du kommst mit vielen wichtigen Leuten zusammen und wirst auf jeden Fall ein paar Politiker kennen lernen.

MARTIN   Ja, Simone, das denke ich auch, und darauf freue ich mich ganz besonders.

CARMEN   Wird deine Arbeitszeit aber nicht sehr unregelmäßig sein? Ich kann mir vorstellen, dass du zum Beispiel an einer heißen Story rund um die Uhr dranbleiben musst.

MARTIN   Na ja, Carmen, solche Fälle gibt es sicher auch hin und wieder, aber bestimmt nicht jeden Tag. Mir macht Journalismus einfach Spaß, und das ist es, worauf es mir ankommt. Was für eine Karriere hast du denn geplant, Carmen?

CARMEN   Ich möchte gern Erzieherin werden.

One-Stop Planner CD-ROM

For resource information, see the **One-Stop Planner CD-ROM**, Disc 3.

SIMONE   Du magst Kinder, nicht wahr? Wird es dir denn nicht zu viel werden, Tag für Tag mit kleinen Kindern umgehen zu müssen? Das ist doch sehr anstrengend.

CARMEN   So sehe ich das eben nicht. Für mich gibt es viele positive Seiten an diesem Beruf. Ich mag Kinder sehr gern. Ich finde es faszinierend, mit so vielen kleinen Menschen umzugehen und zu sehen, wie sie sich kreativ entfalten. Außerdem macht es mir Spaß, bei der Erziehung der Kinder mitzuwirken.

MARTIN   Mensch, Carmen, mir wäre diese Verantwortung viel zu groß. Die Kinder sind doch alle verschieden in ihren Charaktereigenschaften.

CARMEN   Darin besteht eben die Herausforderung an mich. Ich muss einerseits Leitfigur sein, muss mich andererseits aber auch in die Kinder hineinversetzen können. Ich freue mich schon darauf.

MARTIN   Viel Glück wünsche ich dir, Carmen. Sag mal, Simone, welchen Berufswunsch hast du eigentlich?

SIMONE   Ich habe beschlossen, Zahnärztin zu werden.

CARMEN   Zahnmedizin ist aber ein langes und hartes Studium. Außerdem kenne ich keinen, der sich darauf freut, zum Zahnarzt zu gehen. Meinst du, das wird dir auf Dauer Spaß machen?

SIMONE   Mit dem Studium hast du Recht, Carmen. Ich glaube allerdings, dass ich das schon schaffen werde. Und übrigens finde ich, dass die Angst vorm Zahnarzt ein Klischee ist. Nicht jeder macht schlechte Erfahrungen. Zum Teil hängt es ja auch von der mehr oder weniger guten Zahnpflege der Patienten ab, ob sie sich vorm Zahnarzt fürchten oder nicht.

MARTIN   Ich kann mir vorstellen, dass du dich mal bemühen wirst, dieses Klischee aus der Welt zu räumen, Simone. Du wirst bestimmt mal eine gute Zahnärztin.

CARMEN   Zahnärzte verdienen doch auch ganz gut, oder?

SIMONE   Ja, das stimmt. Geldprobleme werde ich wohl keine haben, aber das ist nicht entscheidend für mich.

MARTIN   Wenn du dich selbständig machst, kannst du dir auch deine Arbeitszeit einteilen, wie du willst.

SIMONE   Richtig, Martin. Ich werde als Zahnärztin viel Urlaub machen können, ganz gut verdienen, und ich werde vor allem einen Beruf haben, der mir Spaß macht.

CARMEN   Das freut mich für dich, Simone.

MARTIN   Ich glaube, wir bestellen jetzt endlich unser Eis. Hallo, Bedienung! Wir möchten gern bestellen!

Answers to Activity 1
Martin: Journalist / interessanter Beruf; man lernt wichtige Leute kennen / unregelmäßige Arbeitszeit
Carmen: Erzieherin / macht Spaß, bei der Erziehung der Kinder mitzuwirken / anstrengender Beruf; große Verantwortung
Simone: Zahnärztin / langes, hartes Studium; viele Leute gehen nicht gern zum Zahnarzt / guter Verdienst; man kann sich selbständig machen; man kann sich die Arbeitszeit einteilen.

Kapitel 11: Deine Welt ist deine Sache!
Suggested Lesson Plans *50-Minute Schedule*

Day 1

CHAPTER OPENER 5 min.
- Background Information, ATE, p. 295M
- Culture Note, ATE, p. 295M

LOS GEHT'S! 20 min.
- Preteaching Vocabulary, ATE, p. 295N
- Building on Previous Skills, ATE, p. 295N
- Play Audio CD for **Los geht's!**
- Have students read **Los geht's!**, pp. 298–299
- Do Activities 1, 2, and 3, p. 299

ERSTE STUFE
Wortschatz, So sagt man das!, p. 300 20 min.
- Presenting **Wortschatz, So sagt man das!**, ATE, p. 295O
- Teaching Transparency 11-1
- Play Audio CD for Activity 4, p. 301
- Do Activities 5, 6, and 7, p. 301

Wrap-Up 5 min.
- Students respond to questions about their decisions for the future

Homework Options
Grammatikheft, pp. 91–93, Acts. 1–5
Übungsheft, p. 131, Acts. 1–2; p. 132, Acts. 1–2; p. 135, Acts. 8–9

Day 2

ERSTE STUFE
Quick Review 10 min.
- Check homework, Grammatikheft, pp. 91–92, Acts. 1–3

Ein wenig Landeskunde, p. 302 20 min.
- Presenting, **Ein wenig Landeskunde**, ATE, p. 295P
- Do Activities 8, 9, 10 and 11, p. 302

So sagt man das!, p. 303 15 min.
- Presenting **So sagt man das!**, ATE, p. 295P
- Play Audio CD for Activity 12, p. 303
- Do Activity 13, p. 303

Wrap-Up 5 min.
- Students respond to questions about what will be important to them in the future

Homework Options
Grammatikheft, p. 94, Act. 6
Übungsheft, pp. 133–135, Acts. 3–7

Day 3

ERSTE STUFE
Quick Review 15 min.
- Check homework, Übungsheft, pp. 133–135, Acts. 3–7

Ein wenig Grammatik, p. 303 15 min.
- Present **Ein wenig Grammatik**, p. 303
- Do Activity 14, p. 304

Wortschatz, p. 304 15 min.
- Presenting **Wortschatz**, ATE, p. 295Q
- Do Activities 15 and 16, p. 304

Wrap-Up 5 min.
- Students respond to questions about what profession they would like to consider for the future

Homework Options
Grammatikheft, p. 94, Act. 7

Day 4

ERSTE STUFE
Quick Review 10 min.
- Check homework, Grammatikheft, p. 94, Act. 7

Neue Lehrpläne (Video) 15 min.
- Teaching Suggestions, Video Guide, p. 50
- Do Pre-viewing, Viewing and Post-viewing Activities, p. 50, Video Guide
- Show **Neue Lehrpläne** Video

LANDESKUNDE 20 min.
- Presenting **Landeskunde**, ATE, p. 295Q
- Teaching Suggestion, ATE, p. 295Q
- Multicultural Connection, ATE, p. 295Q
- Read **Wie findet man eine Arbeitsstelle in Deutschland?**, p. 305
- Do Activities A and B, p. 305

Wrap-Up 5 min.
- Students respond to questions about how one applies for a job in the United States and in Germany

Homework Options
Übungsheft, p. 136, Acts. 1–2
Internet Aktivitäten, see ATE, p. 295E

Day 5

ERSTE STUFE
Quick Review 10 min.
- Check homework, Übungsheft, p. 136, Acts. 1–2

Quiz Review 20 min.
- Do Additional Listening Activities 11-1 and 11-2, p. 87
- Do Activities for Communication 11-1 and 11-2, pp. 41–42
- Do **Mehr Grammatikübungen, Erste Stufe**

Quiz 20 min.
- Quiz 11-1A or 11-1B

Homework Options
Activities for Communication, p. 102, Realia 11-2; Read lists, check attributes important to you

Day 6

ERSTE STUFE
Quick Review 10 min.
- Return and review Quiz 11-1
- Check homework, Realia 11-2

WEITER GEHT'S! 20 min.
- Preteaching Vocabulary, ATE, p. 295R
- Play Audio CD for **Weiter geht's!**, pp. 306–307
- Do Activities 17 and 18, p. 307

Azubis in Dresden (Video) 15 min.
- Teaching Suggestions, Video Guide, p. 50
- Do Pre-viewing, Viewing and Post-viewing Activities, p. 50, Video Guide
- Show **Azubis in Dresden** Video

Wrap-Up 5 min.
- Students respond to questions about what plans young Germans have for the future

Homework Options
Übungsheft, p. 137, Acts. 1–2

One-Stop Planner CD-ROM

For alternative lesson plans by chapter section, to create your own customized plans, or to preview all resources available for this chapter, use the **One-Stop Planner CD-ROM**, Disc 3.

 For additional homework suggestions, see activities accompanied by this symbol throughout the chapter.

Day 7

ZWEITE STUFE

Quick Review 10 min.
- Check homework, Übungsheft, p. 137, Acts. 1–2
- Reading Selection, p. 308
- Present charts, **Wie sieht die Jugend ihre Zukunft?**, p. 308

Wortschatz, p. 308 10 min.
- Presenting **Wortschatz**, ATE, p. 295S
- Do Activity 19, p. 309

So sagt man das!, p. 309 10 min.
- Presenting **So sagt man das!**, ATE, p. 295S
- Play Audio CD for Activity 20, p. 309
- Do Activity 21, p. 309

So sagt man das!, p. 309 10 min.
- Presenting **So sagt man das!**, ATE, p. 295T
- Teaching Transparency 11-2
- Do Activities 22, 23, and 24, p. 310

Wrap-Up 5 min.
- Students respond to questions about what they wish or hope for in the future

Homework Options
Grammatikheft, pp. 95–97, Acts. 8–14

Day 8

ZWEITE STUFE

Quick Review 10 min.
- Check homework, Grammatikheft, pp. 95–97, Acts. 8–14

Ein wenig Grammatik, So sagt man das!, p. 310 15 min.
- Present **Ein wenig Grammatik, So sagt man das!**, ATE, p. 295T
- Do Activity 25, p. 310
- Play Audio CD for Activity 26, p. 310

Grammatik, p. 311 10 min.
- Presenting **Grammatik**, ATE, p. 295T
- Do Activities 27 and 28, p. 311

So sagt man das!, p. 311 10 min.
- Presenting **So sagt man das!**, ATE, p. 295T
- Do Activities 29, 30, and 31, p. 311

Wrap-Up 5 min.
- Students respond to questions about what they would like to have done in 20 years

Homework Options
Grammatikheft, pp. 98–99, Acts. 15–18
Übungsheft, pp. 138–141, Acts. 1–8
Interaktive Spiele, see ATE, p. 295E

Day 9

ZWEITE STUFE

Quick Review 10 min.
- Check homework, Übungsheft, pp. 138–141, Acts. 1–8

Quiz Review 20 min.
- Do **Mehr Grammatikübungen, Zweite Stufe**
- Do Communicative Activities 11-3 and 11-4, pp. 43–44

Quiz 20 min.
- Quiz 11-2A or 11-2B

Homework Options
Activities for Communication, p. 103, Realia 11-3; Underline cognates and adopted English words

Day 10

ZWEITE STUFE

Quick Review 10 min.
- Return and review Quiz 11-2
- Check homework, Realia 11-3

ZUM LESEN 35 min.
- Background Information, ATE, p. 295U
- Present **Lesestrategie**, p. 312
- Do Activities 1–10, pp. 312–314

Wrap-Up 5 min.
- Students name expressions that refuse or accept with certainty

Homework Options
Übungsheft, pp. 142–143, Acts. 1–5

Day 11

ZWEITE STUFE

Quick Review 10 min.
- Check homework, Übungsheft, pp. 142–143, Acts. 1–5

ZUM SCHREIBEN 35 min.
- Building Context, ATE, p. 295W
- Present **Schreibtipp**, p. 315
- Do Activities A, B, and C, p. 315

Wrap-Up 5 min.
- Students express certainty

Homework Options
Pupil's Edition, p. 322, **Kann ich's wirklich?**
Interaktive Spiele, see ATE, p. 295E

Day 12

ANWENDUNG

Quick Review 10 min.
- Check homework, Pupil's Edition, p. 322, **Kann ich's wirklich?**

ANWENDUNG 20 min.
- Do Activities 1–9, pp. 320–321

Chapter Review 20 min.
- Review chapter functions, vocabulary, and grammar; choose from **Mehr Grammatikübungen,** Activities for Communication, Listening Activities, or **Interaktive Spiele**
- Review test format and provide sample test items for students

Homework Options
Study for Chapter Test

Assessment

Test, Chapter 11 45 min.
- Administer Chapter 11 Test. Select from Testing Program, Alternative Assessment Guide or Test Generator.

Kapitel 11: Deine Welt ist deine Sache!
Suggested Lesson Plans *90-Minute Schedule*

Block 1

CHAPTER OPENER 5 min.
- Background Information, ATE, p. 295M
- Culture Note, ATE, p. 295M

LOS GEHT'S! 20 min.
- Preteaching Vocabulary, ATE, p. 295N
- Building on Previous Skills, ATE, p. 295N
- Play Audio CD for **Los geht's!**
- Have students read **Los geht's!**, pp. 298–299
- Do Activities 1, 2, and 3, p. 299

ERSTE STUFE
Wortschatz, So sagt man das!, So sagt man das!, p. 300 20 min.
- Presenting **Wortschatz, So sagt man das!**, ATE, p. 295O
- Teaching Transparency 11-1
- Play Audio CD for Activity 4, p. 301
- Do Activities 5, 6, and 7, p. 301

Ein wenig Landeskunde, p. 302 20 min.
- Presenting **Ein wenig Landeskunde**, ATE, p. 295P
- Do Activities 8, 9, 10, and 11, p. 302

So sagt man das!, p. 303 20 min.
- Presenting **So sagt man das!**, ATE, p. 295P
- Play Audio CD for Activity 12, p. 303
- Do Activity 13, p. 303
- Do Activity 6, p. 94, Grammatikheft

Wrap-Up 5 min.
- Students respond to questions about what will be important to them in the future

Homework Options
Grammatikheft, pp. 91–93, Acts. 1–5
Übungsheft, p. 131, Acts. 1–2; p. 132, Acts. 1–2; pp. 133–135, Acts. 3–9

Block 2

ERSTE STUFE
Quick Review 10 min.
- Check homework, **Grammatikheft**, pp. 91–93, Acts. 1–5

Ein wenig Grammatik, p. 303 15 min.
- Present **Ein wenig Grammatik**, p. 303
- Do Activity 14, p. 304

Wortschatz, p. 304 15 min.
- Presenting **Wortschatz**, ATE, p. 295Q
- Do Activities 15 and 16, p. 304

Neue Lehrpläne (Video) 15 min.
- Teaching Suggestions, Video Guide, p. 50
- Do Pre-viewing, Viewing and Post-viewing Activities, p. 50, Video Guide
- Show **Neue Lehrpläne** Video

LANDESKUNDE 30 min.
- Presenting **Landeskunde**, ATE, p. 295Q
- Teaching Suggestion, ATE, p. 295Q
- Multicultural Connection, ATE, p. 295Q
- Read **Wie findet man eine Arbeitsstelle in Deutschland?**, p. 305
- Do Activities A and B, p. 305
- Do Activities 1 and 2, p. 136, Übungsheft

Wrap-Up 5 min.
- Students respond to questions about how one applies for a job in the United States and in Germany

Homework Options
Grammatikheft, p. 94, Act. 7
Internet Aktivitäten, see ATE, p. 295E

Block 3

ERSTE STUFE
Quick Review 10 min.
- Check homework, Grammatikheft, p. 94, Act. 7

Quiz Review 20 min.
- Do Additional Listening Activities 11-1 and 11-2, p. 87
- Do Activities for Communication 11-1 and 11-2, pp. 41–42
- Do **Mehr Grammatikübungen, Erste Stufe**

Quiz 20 min.
- Quiz 11-1A or 11-1B

WEITER GEHT'S! 20 min.
- Preteaching Vocabulary, ATE, p. 295R
- Play Audio CD for **Weiter geht's!**, pp. 306–307
- Do Activities 17 and 18, p. 307

Azubis in Dresden (Video) 15 min.
- Teaching Suggestions, Video Guide, p. 50
- Do Pre-viewing, Viewing and Post-viewing Activities, p. 50, Video Guide
- Show **Azubis in Dresden** Video

Wrap-Up 5 min.
- Students respond to questions about what plans young Germans have for the future

Homework Options
Übungsheft, p. 137, Acts. 1–2

One-Stop Planner CD-ROM

For alternative lesson plans by chapter section, to create your own customized plans, or to preview all resources available for this chapter, use the **One-Stop Planner CD-ROM**, Disc 3.

For additional homework suggestions, see activities accompanied by this symbol throughout the chapter.

Block 4

ZWEITE STUFE
Quick Review 10 min.
- Check homework, Übungsheft, p. 137, Acts. 1–2
- Reading Selection, p. 308
- Present charts, **Wie sieht die Jugend ihre Zukunft?**, p. 308

Wortschatz, p. 308 10 min.
- Presenting **Wortschatz**, ATE, p. 295S
- Do Activity 19, p. 309

So sagt man das!, p. 309 10 min.
- Presenting **So sagt man das!**, ATE, p. 295S
- Play Audio CD for Activity 20, p. 309
- Do Activity 21, p. 309

So sagt man das!, p. 309 10 min.
- Presenting **So sagt man das!**, ATE, p. 295T
- Teaching Transparency 11-2
- Do Activities 22, 23, and 24, p. 310

Ein wenig Grammatik, So sagt man das!, p. 310 20 min.
- Present **Ein wenig Grammatik, So sagt man das!**, ATE, p. 295T
- Do Activity 25, p. 310
- Play Audio CD for Activity 26, p. 310
- Do Activity 1, p. 138, Übungsheft

Grammatik, p. 311 10 min.
- Presenting **Grammatik**, ATE, p. 295T
- Do Activities 27 and 28, p. 311

So sagt man das!, p. 311 10 min.
- Presenting **So sagt man das!**, ATE, p. 295T
- Do Activities 29, 30, and 31, p. 311

Wrap-Up 5 min.
- Students respond to questions about what they would like to have done in 20 years

Homework Options
Grammatikheft, pp. 95–99, Acts. 8–18
Übungsheft, pp. 138–141, Acts. 2–8
Internet Aktivitäten, see ATE, p. 295E

Block 5

ZWEITE STUFE
Quick Review 10 min.
- Check homework, Übungsheft, pp. 138–141, Acts. 2–8

Quiz Review 20 min.
- Do **Mehr Grammatikübungen, Zweite Stufe**
- Do Communicative Activities 11-3 and 11-4, pp. 43–44

Quiz 20 min.
- Quiz 11-2A or 11-2B

ZUM LESEN 35 min.
- Background Information, ATE, p. 295U
- Present **Lesestrategie**, p. 312
- Do Activities 1–10, pp. 312–314

Wrap-Up 5 min.
- Students name expressions that accept or refuse with certainty

Homework Options
Übungsheft, pp. 142–143, Acts. 1–5

Block 6

ZWEITE STUFE
Quick Review 10 min.
- Return and review Quiz 11-2
- Check homework, Übungsheft, pp. 142–143, Acts. 1–5

ZUM SCHREIBEN 35 min.
- Building Context, ATE, p. 295W
- Present **Schreibtipp**, p. 315
- Do Activities A, B, and C, p. 315

ANWENDUNG 20 min.
- Do Activities 1–9, pp. 320–321

Kann ich's wirklich? 20 min.
- Do Activities 1–10, p. 322

Wrap-Up 5 min.
- Students express certainty

Homework Options
Interaktive Spiele, see ATE, p. 295E

Block 7

ANWENDUNG
Quick Review 15 min.
- Play game, **Erratet den Beruf!**, ATE, p. 295C

Chapter Review 30 min.
- Review chapter functions, vocabulary, and grammar; choose from **Mehr Grammatikübungen**, Activities for Communication, Listening Activities, or **Interaktive Spiele**
- Review test format and provide sample test items for students

Test, Chapter 11 45 min.
- Administer Chapter Test. Select from Testing Program, Alternative Assessment Guide or Test Generator.

Kapitel 11: Deine Welt ist deine Sache!
Teaching Suggestions, pages 296–323

Using the Video

Before you begin the chapter, you may want to preview the *Video Program* and consult the *Video Guide.* Suggestions for integrating the video into each chapter are given in the *Video Guide* and in the chapter interleaf of the *Teacher's Edition.* Activity masters for video selections can be found in the *Video Guide.*

 One-Stop Planner CD-ROM

For resource information, see the **One-Stop Planner CD-ROM,** Disc 3.

Advance Organizer

Ask students these questions: Wer von euch hat schon mal eine Arbeit gehabt? Wann war das, was für Arbeit habt ihr gemacht?

Cultures and Communities

Background Information

After finishing school, students often go to the **Arbeitsamt.** The German **Arbeitsamt** can be compared to an employment office in the United States. Its functions include job placement, vocational guidance, and promotion of vocational training. Furthermore, it provides financial assistance for retraining to people who need to adapt their skills to the changing demands of the labor market.

Culture Note

The type of high school from which students graduate determines which diplomas they can earn. At the **Hauptschule,** the diploma is called **Hauptschulabschluss.** At the **Mittelschule** or **Realschule,** it is called **Mittlere Reife** or **Realschulabschluss.** At the **Gymnasium** or **Oberschule,** students graduate with the **Abitur** or **Reifeprüfung** referred to as **Matura** in Austria and Switzerland. The career path of a graduating student depends to a large degree on the type of secondary school he or she attended. For additional information, see p. 31R of the Level 2 *Teacher's Edition.*

PAGES 296–297

CHAPTER OPENER

Pacing Tips

Los geht's! and the **Erste Stufe** focus on what young Germans do after graduation. Students learn to express determination or indecision. **Weiter geht's!** and the **Zweite Stufe** center around what German teenagers see themselves doing at age 30. The **Erste Stufe** might take a bit longer to teach than the **Zweite Stufe.** For Lesson Plans and timing suggestions, see pages 295I–295L.

Meeting the Standards

Communication
- Expressing determination, p. 300
- Talking about whether something is important or not important, p. 303
- Expressing wishes, p. 309
- Expressing certainty and refusing or accepting with certainty, p. 309
- Talking about goals for the future, p. 310
- Expressing relief, p. 311

Cultures
- **Ein wenig Landeskunde,** p. 302
- **Landeskunde,** p. 305
- Background Information, p. 295M
- Culture Note, p. 295M
- Background Information, p. 295U

Connections
- Multicultural Connection, p. 295Q
- History Connection, p. 295U
- Theater Connection, p. 295W

Comparisons
- Language-to-Language, p. 295V

Communities
- Family Link, p. 295C

Chapter Sequence

LOS GEHT'S!

Teaching Resources
pp. 298–299

PRINT
▶ Lesson Planner, p. 61
▶ Übungsheft, p. 131

MEDIA
▶ One-Stop Planner
▶ Audio Compact Discs, CD11, Trs. 1–5

> **PAGES 298–299**

Los geht's! Summary

In *Was kommt nach der Schule?,* four students from a **Gymnasium** talk about what they plan to do after graduation. The following learning outcomes are modeled in the episode: expressing determination or indecision, and talking about whether something is important or not important.

Preteaching Vocabulary

Guessing Words from Context

First, have students scan **Los geht's!** for cognates and get a good idea of what the selection is about (what German students plan to do after graduation). Then ask students what types of functions they would expect in a discussion of what to do after graduation, and list these functions on the board or on a transparency. Be sure that the functions emphasized in the **Erste Stufe,** *expressing determination or indecision* and *talking about whether something is important or not important,* are among the functions listed. Students should then read through **Los geht's!** for German phrases that match the functions they mentioned. List these phrases next to their functions.

Advance Organizer

Ask students what they plan to do immediately after graduation. Many older students will have definite plans. Younger students will probably be less definite, but should be able to speculate. (**Was werdet ihr machen, wenn ihr mit der High School fertig seid?**)

Building on Previous Skills

Have students read the introductory paragraph. Based on what students know from previous learning, can they give examples of the kinds of careers these four students can prepare for, knowing that they will

graduate with the **Abitur?** Make a list of students' ideas. (**Auf welche Berufe können sich diese Gymnasiasten vorbereiten?**)

Comprehension Check

Teaching Suggestion

1 Let students listen to the recorded statements as they read along in their textbooks. Stop the compact disc after each report and ask questions to check for understanding. Explain any new terms or phrases in German by paraphrasing or using synonymous expressions. Let students read Activity 1a. Have them read and listen to the statements again, one at a time, taking notes as they go along. This can be done individually or with a partner. Discuss students' findings with the entire class.

A Slower Pace

1b Taking one of the four reports as an example, work with the whole class to summarize the report in students' own words. Put students into three groups, and have each group cover one of the three German students not discussed before.

A Slower Pace

2 Help students verbalize the statistics in **Nach dem Abi?** (Examples: **51% der jungen Männer machen nach dem Abi den Wehr- oder den Zivildienst. 30% der jungen Frauen machen ein Studium.**) This is an excellent way to recycle the genitive case.

Teaching Suggestions

2c On the day before starting Activity 2c, take a quick written survey of all students in your German classes. Ask them to write down their main interests, listing them in order of priority from 1 to 5. Summarize the survey in percentages for each of the main interest areas mentioned. Put the results on a transparency and use them to compare with the findings in **Information für junge Leute.**

3 If you do this as a class project, the questions should be asked in German. (Examples: **Was wirst du wahrscheinlich ein halbes Jahr nach deinem Schulabschluss machen? Wirst du studieren? Arbeiten? Eine Ausbildung machen? Zum Militär gehen?**) If you decide to do this activity as a school-wide project, the questions will be asked in English, but the results translated into German.

Closure

Ask students about their impressions of young German people's ideas about their future.

Teaching Resources
pp. 300–305

PRINT 📖
- Lesson Planner, p. 62
- Listening Activities, pp. 83–84, 87–88
- Video Guide, pp. 49–51
- Activities for Communication, pp. 41–42, 101, 103, 104–105, 133–134
- Grammatikheft, pp. 91–94
- Grammar Tutor for Students of German, Chapter 11
- Übungsheft, pp. 132–136
- Testing Program, pp. 235–238
- Alternative Assessment Guide, p. 40
- Student Make-Up Assignments, Chapter 11

MEDIA 💿📹🖥
- One-Stop Planner
- Audio Compact Discs, CD11, Trs. 6–7, 18, 22–24
- Video Program
  Neue Lehrpläne
  Videocassette 2, 42:22–44:42
- Teaching Transparencies
  Situation 11-1
  Mehr Grammatikübungen Answers
  Grammatikheft Answers

PAGE 300

Bell Work

Play charades to help kinesthetic learners review the vocabulary of professions. Prepare a set of index cards with a profession in German written on each. (Examples: **Dirigent, Komponist, Lehrer, Verkäufer, Arzt, Metzger, Bäcker**) Then divide the class into two teams. A member of Team A comes to the front and draws a card from the stack of index cards. This student must then try to act out the job to his or her own team within a set time. Members of Team A may ask yes/no questions as they try to guess the profession. If Team A is not able to guess the profession within the set time, Team B gets a chance to win the point. Teams alternate sending members to the front.

PRESENTING: Wortschatz

Introduce the new vocabulary in the **auf Deutsch erklärt** section. Make up sentences using the definitions and ask students to restate your sentences using the new words.
Examples:
Hast du dich übers Wochenende gut entspannt?
Hast du dich übers Wochenende ausgeruht?
Ask students to use the new vocabulary in the **auf Deutsch erklärt** section in sentences of their own. Then work with the new vocabulary in the **auf Englisch erklärt** section. Model each sentence and have students repeat. Ask for variations of the sentences, keeping essentially the same context.
Example:
Auf alle Fälle gibt es gute Gründe, Beamter zu werden.
Bestimmt hast du viele gute Gründe, Beamter zu werden.

PRESENTING: So sagt man das!

After you have introduced the new expressions, call on individual students to personalize each statement by completing it.
Example:
Ich hab beschlossen, heute ins Kino zu gehen.
Ich kann noch nicht sagen, ob ich dieses Wochenende Zeit habe.

PAGE 301

Teaching Suggestion

5 Before starting the activity, have students do two things. First, practice the section **Wünsche und Pläne** giving infinitive phrases with **zu**. Write on a transparency or on the chalkboard **Ich bin entschlossen, …** and **Ich hab mich entschieden, …** and have students complete the sentence. Then brainstorm for additional reasons why your students would make certain choices for the future. Have students write these ideas in their notebooks.
Examples:
studieren: ein Stipendium haben; (Ärztin) werden wollen
arbeiten: Geld brauchen; etwas Praktisches machen wollen
ins Ausland gehen: Freunde (Verwandte) dort haben; eine andere Kultur kennen lernen wollen

Communication for All Students

A Slower Pace
5 Do two to three questions together with the whole class and practice giving reasons. Once students feel comfortable with the format, they should continue the activity with a partner. Remind students that the dependent clauses in the expressions of indecision require verb-last word order.

Teaching Suggestions
6 Do this activity as a chain around the room. Each student says something he or she has decided to do, expressing the decision in a different way than the preceding person. To help students out, put all starting phrases on a transparency or on the chalkboard:

Ich hab mich entschieden, …
Ich bin entschlossen, …
Ich hab beschlossen, …
Ich weiß, dass …
Ich werde bestimmt …

7 The reflexive makes constructing these sentences a little harder. Do two to three sentences orally with the class, including one in which the cue contains a **man**-construction that needs to be changed to **ich**. Then let students work in pairs, doing this activity orally and in writing. Call on pairs to read their roles.

> **PAGE 302**

PRESENTING: Ein wenig Landeskunde
Ask students why they think the fields of study listed in the chart are popular. They might answer, for example: **Jura ist ein interessantes Studium, und man verdient später viel Geld** or **Gestaltung** (design) **ist auch ein interessantes Studium, und man kann sich künstlerisch entfalten.**

You might also have students research some of the universities in Germany, Switzerland, and Austria to find out how old they are.

Using the Video
 Videocassette 2, 42:22–44:42
In the video clip *Neue Lehrpläne,* students talk about how their lives and especially their educational system have changed since unification. See *Video Guide,* p. 50, for suggestions.

Communication for All Students

Challenge
8 As students work in pairs, they should make notes about their partner's responses. Then call on several students and ask them how their partner responded to a certain question.
Example:
Emily sagte, dass sie noch nicht so genau weiß, ob sie studieren möchte.

A Slower Pace
11 Be sure students understand what the terms in the chart mean. Explain difficult terms in German.
Example:
Einkommenshöhe: wie viel Geld man pro Monat oder pro Jahr verdient

> **PAGE 303**

PRESENTING: So sagt man das!
Model the phrases in **So sagt man das!**, adding a short **dass**-clause after each. Have students repeat. Then have them express these phrases in English. To practice the expressions, ask students to answer your questions.
Example:
Was ist für dich am wichtigsten?
Für mich ist es am wichtigsten, dass ich gesund und fit bin.

Thinking Critically
12 **Analyzing** Have students take notes while they listen to Steffi and Horst, and then have them compare their responses to the survey on p. 299 (**Nach dem Abi?**). Are these statements representative of the results of the survey?

PRESENTING: Wortschatz/Und dann noch …

To introduce the new vocabulary, model the words and have students repeat. (Although most of them are cognates, there is a shift in stress from the English.) Then have students give a brief description of the professions by saying what people do or where they work.

Teaching Suggestion

15 Let students know that the suggested phrases are ideas to get them started. Encourage them to think of other reasons and give more detail.

Communication for All Students

Challenge

16 Have students write down their responses to each of the seven questions. Then tell students to arrange their notes into an outline and finally into a cohesive paragraph. They should refer back to the writing skills they have learned in the **Zum Schreiben** sections of the previous chapters.

Reteaching: Vocabulary

Ask students to assume the role of an interviewer who is making an outline of questions for a potential employee. Using the vocabulary of the **Erste Stufe**, ask students to make a list of at least ten questions they plan to ask. Allow students to work in pairs or small groups.

LANDESKUNDE

Teaching Suggestion

Survey students about their previous or current work experience. How did they find out about the job, and how did they apply for it? (**Von denjenigen von euch, die schon mal berufstätig waren oder immer noch sind, möchte ich gern wissen, wie ihr über den Job gehört habt. Und wie habt ihr euch um den Job beworben?**)

Teaching Suggestion

Introduce some additional vocabulary to increase students' comprehension of the text.

sich bewerben/Bewerbung: eine Arbeit suchen

das Stellenangebot: die Stellenofferte

die Samstagsausgabe: die Zeitung, die am Samstag verkauft wird

der Sonderteil: ein Teil, den man nicht immer in der Zeitung findet

tabellarisch: in Form einer Tabelle

der Lebenslauf: die schriftliche Beschreibung des Lebens einer Person

der Absolvent: jemand, der seine Ausbildung beendet hat

gut dotierte Führungsposition: Managerstellung, in der man viel verdient

verfügen über: etwas tun können / eine Eigenschaft besitzen

gute Umgangsformen: gute Manieren / gutes Benehmen

eigenverantwortliche Führung: kann selbständig/allein arbeiten

die Einarbeitung: die ersten Wochen in der neuen Stelle

Cooperative Learning

A/B Divide the class into groups of three or four students. Each group should have a writer, a discussion leader, a proofreader, and a reporter. Allow 45 min. for this activity. Before groups read the text, you will need to introduce the additional vocabulary. Then ask students to work through the text (article and ad) and answer the questions. When students have finished, ask groups to share their responses to questions A and B with the rest of the class.

Connections and Comparisons

Multicultural Connection

Ask students to interview foreign exchange students, other foreign language teachers, or anyone else they know from a different country about seeking employment. What are the procedures in that particular country? Ask students to share their answers with the rest of the class.

Cultures and Communities

Career Path

Have students work in small groups to think of reasons why an architect might need a working knowledge of German. (Suggestion: Imagine you are an architect working in a firm that specializes in **Jugendstil**; imagine you are a volunteer for Habitat for Humanity International in Germany.)

Thinking Critically

Drawing Inferences Ask students about their plans for their future. How are their parents involved in their decision making? What type of training and education will they need for their career choice? (**Inwiefern haben eure Eltern mit der Wahl eurer Zukunftspläne zu tun? Diskutiert ihr darüber in der Familie? Welche Ausbildung braucht ihr, um euer Berufsziel zu erreichen?**)

Assess

▸ Testing Program, pp. 235–238
  Quiz 11-1A, Quiz 11-1B
  Audio CD11, Tr. 18

▸ Student Make-Up Assignments
  Chapter 11, Alternative Quiz

▸ Alternative Assessment Guide, p. 40

WEITER GEHT'S!

Teaching Resources
pp. 306–307

PRINT
▸ Lesson Planner, p. 63
▸ Übungsheft, p. 137

MEDIA
▸ One-Stop Planner
▸ Audio Compact Discs, CD11, Trs. 8–13

PAGES 306–307

Weiter geht's! Summary

In *Wenn ich mal dreißig bin, …,* five teenagers talk about their plans for the future and the goals they want to have achieved by the age of thirty. The following learning outcomes listed on p. 297 are modeled in

the episode: expressing wishes, expressing certainty and refusing or accepting with certainty, talking about goals for the future, and expressing relief.

Preteaching Vocabulary

Identifying Keywords

Start by asking students to guess the context of **Weiter geht's!** (what German teenagers think they will have accomplished by the age of 30). Then have students use the German they know and the context of the situation to identify key words and phrases that are vital to understanding what each German teen thinks. Students should look for words that seem important or that occur several times. Here are a few of the words they might identify as keywords: **Zukunft, Osten, Beruf, Angst, Sorgen, verheiratet.** List the keywords on the board or on a transparency and separate them according to whether or not they are cognates. Then ask students to guess the meaning of the keywords.

Advance Organizer

Ask students to picture their lives at age 30. What will they be doing? (**Wie stellt ihr euch das Leben vor, wenn ihr dreißig seid? Was werdet ihr dann tun?**)

Teaching Suggestion

17 With their books open, let students listen to the five interviews. Pause after each interview, ask questions to check for understanding, and explain any difficult words or passages in German. Ask students to take notes of key points made by each interviewee. Play the interviews at least twice.

Closure

Ask students to write a **Stellenangebot** for a job they would like to have. What would it have to offer? Have students share their job ad with a small group and have group members help each other with suggestions for improving wording and layout. Make a display of final **Stellenangebote.**

Teaching Resources
pp. 308–311

PRINT
▸ Lesson Planner, p. 64
▸ Listening Activities, pp. 84–85, 88–90
▸ Video Guide, pp. 49–50, 52
▸ Activities for Communication, pp. 43–44, 102, 104–105, 133–134
▸ Grammatikheft, pp. 95–99
▸ Grammar Tutor for Students of German, Chapter 11
▸ Übungsheft, pp. 138–141
▸ Testing Program, pp. 239–242
▸ Alternative Assessment Guide, p. 40
▸ Student Make-Up Assignments, Chapter 11

MEDIA
▸ One-Stop Planner
▸ Audio Compact Discs, CD11, Trs. 14–15, 19, 25–27
▸ Video Program
   Azubis in Dresden
   Videocassette 2, 44:44–47:42
   Teaching Transparencies
   Situation 11-2
   Mehr Grammatikübungen Answers
   Grammatikheft Answers

PAGE 308

Bell Work
Brainstorm with students about surveys typically conducted of young people. What kinds of questions are asked by newspapers or magazines? Have students think of questions other than those already discussed. (Example: **wichtige Bedingungen am Arbeitsplatz**) Make a list of topics or questions in German.

Using the Video

Videocassette 2, 44:44–47:42
In the video clip *Azubis in Dresden,* young apprentices in Dresden talk about the apprenticeship program that is preparing them to become industrial mechanics. See *Video Guide,* p. 50, for suggestions.

Teaching Suggestion
Help students verbalize the statistics in the four charts.
Examples:
63% der Jugendlichen halten es für sehr wichtig, den richtigen Beruf zu wählen.
Für Jungen steht ein gesundes Leben an erster Stelle.

PRESENTING: Wortschatz
• Present the new vocabulary in its original context. From the five reports in the **Weiter geht's!** section, write those sentences that contain the new vocabulary on a transparency. For each new word or phrase, provide as much context as necessary to help students derive its meaning and to paraphrase it.

• Use the new words and phrases in statements of your own, to which students have to react.
Examples:
Es ist gut, dass wir in der Schule geregelte Verhältnisse haben.
Weißt du schon, was auf dich zukommt, wenn du mit der High School fertig bist?

PAGE 309

Thinking Critically
19 Drawing Inferences Before students discuss Question 3, ask them to define a **Vorbild.** Does it have to be a known personality? Make a list of typical characteristics and attributes a **Vorbild** has to have. (Wie charakterisiert ihr ein Vorbild?)

PRESENTING: So sagt man das!
• Refer students back to *Der Panther* in the Chapter 2 **Zum Lesen** section to see how the subjunctive is used.

• Ask students to complete the second sentence in **So sagt man das!** expressing their own wishes: **In meiner idealen Welt …**

Communication for All Students

Tactile Learners

21 Have students use the suggestions in the box to illustrate their ideal world in a picture or a collage. This can be done in class or as a homework assignment.

PRESENTING: So sagt man das!

- Present students with a situation in the form of a question or statement to which they must react with certainty.
Examples:
Weißt du schon, ob du einmal heiratest?
Du wirst aufs College gehen, nicht wahr?

- Present situations to which students react with any phrase from the second set of expressions (refusing/accepting).
Examples:
Du musst deine Autoversicherung selbst bezahlen?
Du wirst sicher zu Hause wohnen, wenn du auf die Uni gehst.

- Ask students to think of other ways to express the phrases.

> **PAGE 310**

Teaching Suggestions

22 Do this activity as a chain. Each student should ask a classmate about his or her future. That student answers and then asks another classmate a question, and so forth. To facilitate the conversations, write some other topics on the board from which students can choose. (Examples: **Schule, Familie, Umwelt, Politik, Beziehung zu Eltern und Freunden**) Help students formulate some sample statements and questions that bring about refusal or acceptance.

24 Prepare a list of phrases that can be used to give a reason (see Chapter 3, p. 75) Let students refer to this list as they justify the ranking of things on their list.

PRESENTING: Ein wenig Grammatik

Expressing future

- Review the forms of the verb **werden** with the class.

- Have students compare the two sentences in **Ein wenig Grammatik** and review the two ways of expressing future time (with present or future tense). Discuss with them the questions in the box.

PRESENTING: So sagt man das!

Present to students several sets of sentences that contrast the present or future with the perfect infinitive. Example:
Ich möchte eine politische Karriere beginnen.
Ich möchte eine politische Karriere begonnen haben.
In English, ask students to explain how the different tenses affect the meaning of the sentences. Which sentence in each set expresses speculation that an action projected into the future will have been completed at a certain time?

Teaching Suggestion

25 On a transparency or on the chalkboard, give students additional phrases for building sentences in the future tense.
Examples:
sehr gesund leben
eine gute Universität wählen
(Elektrotechnik) studieren
viel Geld verdienen
einen tollen Beruf ausüben
(meine) Lebensweise selbst bestimmen
in einem Vorort (in der Stadt, auf dem Land) wohnen
im Ausland leben

> **PAGE 311**

PRESENTING: Grammatik

The perfect infinitive with modals and werden

To practice the verb forms in the **Grammatik,** have students predict the outcome of the following:
a) a family member having found a new job,
b) additions/alterations made to the school building,
c) an election (school, local, state, or federal) won or lost,
d) a sport event won or lost.

Teaching Suggestion

27 Before writing complete sentences, ask students to supply the perfect infinitive for each verb listed.

PRESENTING: So sagt man das!

Ask students how they would express relief in English. Then present the expressions in **So sagt man das!** to students.

Writing Assessment

28 You might want to assign this activity as written homework and then assess it using the following rubric.

Writing Rubric	Points			
	4	3	2	1
Content (Complete – Incomplete)				
Comprehensibility (Comprehensible – Seldom comprehensible)				
Accuracy (Accurate – Seldom accurate)				
Organization (Well-organized – Poorly organized)				
Effort (Excellent – Minimal)				

18–20: A   16–17: B   14–15: C   12–13: D   Under 12: F

Connections and Comparisons

History Connection

29 Ask students to use the format of the activity to express relief about either a historical event they have studied, or a current social or political event.

Reteaching: Perfect infinitive with modals and *werden*

Ask students to compile a list of at least five goals they will have accomplished by the year 2020. (**Macht eine Liste von mindestens fünf Zielen, von denen ihr glaubt, dass ihr sie im Jahr 2020 erreicht haben werdet.**)

Von der Schule zum Beruf

31

Encourage students to collect as much input as possible from adult relatives and friends to complete this assignment.

Assess

> Testing Program, pp. 239–242
> Quiz 11-2A, Quiz 11-2B
> Audio CD11, Tr. 19

> Student Make-Up Assignments
> Chapter 11, Alternative Quiz

> Alternative Assessment Guide, p. 40

ZUM LESEN

Teaching Resources
pp. 312–314

PRINT
> Lesson Planner, p. 65
> Übungsheft, pp. 142–143
> Reading Strategies and Skills Handbook, Chapter 11
> Lies mit mir! 3, Chapter 11

MEDIA
> One-Stop Planner
> Audio, CD11, Tr. 16

Prereading

Cultures and Communities

Background Information

• Generally, literary theory makes a distinction between **Volksmärchen** and **Kunstmärchen**: respectively, folk tales that were passed down orally and tales intended for publication. Nineteenth-century German writers, particularly those of the Romantic school, consciously revived the **Märchen** in order to use the elements of fantasy and wonder in various ways, often playfully or ironically. Any contemporary writer can count on the reading public's familiarity with this tradition. Fairy tale and folk motifs and familiar symbols can thus be used to carry an implicit message, especially when they are combined with realistic settings or situations from contemporary everyday life.

• Wolf Biermann was born in Hamburg in 1936. His father, a stables foreman who was active in the Communist resistance movement, died at Auschwitz in 1943. Following his own political leanings, Biermann moved to the GDR in 1953, where he studied political economy, philosophy, and mathematics at Humboldt University in East Berlin. Since then, he has written numerous poems, protest songs, ballads, chansons, narrative texts, and a play. As of 1965, he was no longer allowed to publish or perform his works in the GDR. During a concert tour in the West in November of 1975, he was suddenly expatriated from the GDR. Today, Biermann lives in Hamburg.

Building Context

After presenting the background information to the class, ask the students to predict whether Biermann's **Märchen** is likely to be a children's story or a fable for adults. Explain that a fable differs from other kinds of tales in that it usually has a moral or a message that can be applied to everyday life. It doesn't matter whether the students predict correctly or not, since they will be reading to check their predictions and have plenty of opportunities to change their minds.

Reading

Teacher Notes

6 Citizens of the former DDR were required to carry a **Personalausweis** to identify themselves at all times, even when they left their homes for a short walk (note that Moritz' I.D. case was worn out).

8 In answering this question, students can keep from going too far afield by asking themselves how the symbols they choose would fit into the motif of transformation, as it traditionally occurs in folklore. For example, the growth and wilting of the flowers, the change in the people's moods, and **Herr Moritz**' hair loss are all part of that motif.

Thinking Critically

Analyzing One of the interesting features of this type of writing is that, while the story has a message of some kind, it is implicit rather than explicit. The students are probably familiar with other works, particularly science fiction and fantasy, in which the story carries a strong social or political message. Some examples might include *Brave New World, 1984,* and *Slaughterhouse-Five.* After the class has decided what the main ideas of Biermann's **Märchen** are, they may be interested in discussing how and why this form of presentation is more effective than writing an editorial about the same ideas. How does the literary form help make the ideas seem more current and present to readers in different countries and different eras?

Connections and Comparisons

Language-to-Language

You may want to tell your students that languages import not only words from other languages, but entire literary genres. For example, H.J. von Grimmelshausen's *Simplicissimus* (1669) is a picaresque novel, a genre that originated in Spain with *Lazarillo de Tormes* (1554; author unknown). A picaresque novel deals with the adventures of a heroic protagonist who is a footloose rascal. Mark Twain's *Huckleberry Finn* is an example of an American picaresque novel.

Connections and Comparisons

Previous Knowledge

Ask your students if they know of literary genres that have originated in the United States and name some of its works and authors. [Example: the western genre; authors and some of their works include James Fenimore Cooper's *The Prairie* (1827), Owen Wister's *The Virginian* (1902), Zane Grey's *Riders of the Purple Sage* (1912), Larry McMurtry's *Lonesome Dove* (1985).]

Post-Reading

Teacher Note

Activity 10 is a post-reading task that will show whether students can apply what they have learned.

Closure

In many places and at many different times, literature has been used as a vehicle for criticizing repressive regimes and disseminating "subversive" ideas. The students may already realize that if the censors catch on, the work may not get printed or performed, or the book may be seized and burned, or the play closed. Therefore, authors frequently try to avoid censorship by writing works that claim to be "pure fantasy." (Much pre-glasnost Russian science fiction is actually political protest literature.) Ask the students to decide whether Biermann's **Märchen** could be printed in countries such as North Korea, Singapore, or the People's Republic of China.

Zum Lesen Answers
Answers to Activity 1
Märchen; Answers will vary. Possible answers: characters with magical powers, fantastic events; a. **Herr Moritz**; b. **klein, große Schuhe, schwarzer Mantel, trägt Regenschirm**; c. **im Winter in der Großstadt Berlin**
Answers to Activity 2
The people of the city are very surly because of the long winter; supporting details: paragraphs 2 to 7 are all specific examples of how the long winter is making people angry.
Answers to Activity 3
Answers will vary. Possible answers: **Ein Mann will die Leute glücklich machen, indem er Blumen wachsen lässt. Ein Polizist aber macht ihm Angst, so dass die Blumen verschwinden und er seine Haare verliert.**
Answers to Activity 4
1st paragraph: **Eines Tages … ,** 8th paragraph: **An einem solchen kalten Schneetag … ;** the first phrase introduces the general setting of the story, and the second phrase begins the actual narration of events.
Answers to Activity 5
a. **dass die Leute alle böse sind; Blumen wachsen aus seinem Kopf; Sie freuen sich;** b. **den Ausweis von Herrn Moritz; die Blumen schrumpfen zusammen und verschwinden;** c. **Er bekommt eine Glatze.**

Answers to Activity 6
Answers will vary. Possible answers: because **Herr Moritz** is doing something out of the ordinary, stands out, and is different: this attracts the policeman's attention; **Herr Moritz** becomes frightened, and the negative feelings make him unable to use his energy for the flowers and for making people happy.

Answers to Activity 7
Answers will vary. Possible answers: **Herr Moritz** is essentially powerless; the average citizen; the police state, the repressive powers, the bureaucracy

Answers to Activity 8
Answers will vary.

Answers to Activity 9
Answers will vary. Possible answers: **Individualität wird manchmal in einer Gesellschaft unterdrückt. Die Gesellschaft erwartet von ihren Mitgliedern Anpassung und Beachtung der gesellschaftlichen Regeln.**

▶ **PAGE 315**

ZUM SCHREIBEN

> ### Teaching Resources
> #### p. 315
>
> **PRINT**
> ▸ Lesson Planner, p. 65
> ▸ Alternative Assessment Guide, p. 26
>
> **MEDIA**
> ▸ One-Stop Planner
> ▸ Test Generator, Chapter 11

Writing Strategy

The targeted strategy in this writing activity is *writing drafts and revising.* Students should learn about this strategy before beginning the assignment.

Prewriting
Building Context

Ask students to think of TV shows or dramas that address typical situations of today's teenagers. Which of these shows are especially popular and why?

Connections and Comparisons

Theater Connection

Have students check with the drama teacher to see if they can look at samples of scripts and how they are laid out. They should take notes of essential elements that are part of a script.

Writing

Communication for All Students

A Slower Pace

B Remind students to refer to the expressions in **So sagt man das!** on pp. 300, 303, 309, and 310 as they write.

Post-Writing
Teaching Suggestion

Reread the **Schreibtipp** with students and point out to them that when they make changes to improve their writing, they can use four basic revision techniques: adding, cutting, replacing, and reordering (**hinzufügen, auslassen, ersetzen, umgestalten**). These steps are important to help clean up a piece of writing.

Closure

Ask students to name the main topic or concern from each scene. In addition, students should be able to recall how at least two of the problems were resolved.

▶ **PAGES 316–319**

MEHR GRAMMATIKÜBUNGEN

The **Mehr Grammatikübungen** activities are designed as supplemental activities for the grammatical concepts presented in the chapter. You might use them as additional practice, for review, or for assessment.

For more grammar presentations, review, and practice, refer to the following:
• Grammatikheft
• Grammar Tutor for Students of German
• Grammar Summary on pp. R22-R39
• Übungsheft
• Grammar and Vocabulary quizzes (Testing Program)
• Test Generator
• Interaktive Spiele at go.hrw.com

ANWENDUNG

Teaching Resources
pp. 320–321

PRINT
▸ Lesson Planner, p. 65
▸ Listening Activities, p. 86
▸ Video Guide, pp. 49–50, 52
▸ Grammar Tutor for Students of German, Chapter 11

MEDIA
▸ One-Stop Planner
▸ Video Program
  Videoclips: Werbung
  Videocassette 2, 47:49–48:36
▸ Audio Compact Discs, CD11, Tr. 17

Apply and Assess

Using the Video
Videocassette 2, 47:49–48:36
At this time, you might want to use the authentic advertising footage from German television. See *Video Guide*, p. 50, for suggestions.

Teaching Suggestions
1 Have students review their notes from this listening activity. Do they agree with the **Vorteile** and **Nachteile?** Can they add at least two more **Vorteile** and **Nachteile** to each **Berufswunsch?**

2 Have students give examples of jobs which would correspond to the lists they have prepared. Help students with names for professions they might not know in German.
Examples:
Mit vielen Leuten zusammenkommen:
    Reiseführer(in), Flugpersonal, Verkäufer(in), Lehrer(in)
Anderen Menschen helfen: Krankenschwester/ Krankenpfleger, Arzt/Ärztin

5 Have students answer all ten questions individually in writing as a basis for the discussion and tabulation that follow in Activity 6.

6 Start the comparison of results and the discussion in small groups. Encourage students to ask each other why-questions and to give reasons for their own answers. Then complete a chart of responses to each question with the whole class. Have students discuss the findings.

Apply and Assess

Portfolio Assessment
7 You might want to suggest this activity as a written portfolio item for your students. See *Alternative Assessment Guide*, p. 26.

9 You might want to suggest this activity as an oral portfolio item for your students. See *Alternative Assessment Guide*, p. 26.

KANN ICH'S WIRKLICH?

This page helps students prepare for the test. It is a brief checklist of the major points covered in the chapter. The students should be reminded that it is only a checklist and not necessarily everything that will appear on the test.

For additional self-check options, refer students to the *Grammar Tutor* and the Online self-test for this chapter.

WORTSCHATZ

Review and Assess

Game
Play the game **Erratet den Beruf!** to review the vocabulary of this chapter. See p. 295C for the procedure.

Circumlocution
To use the circumlocution game **Das treffende Wort suchen** as a vocabulary review, ask students to describe each of the professions and nouns related to future plans in the **Wortschatz.** The student could begin by saying **Ich habe mich noch nicht entschieden, was ich machen will, aber vielleicht werde ich …** and then go on to describe the profession into which he or she would like to enter, or the type of study he or she would like to undertake. See p. 31C for procedures.

Teacher Note
Give the **Kapitel 11** Chapter Test:
Testing Program, pp. 243–248
Audio CD 11, Trs. 20–21

11
Deine Welt ist deine Sache!

Objectives

In this chapter you will learn to

Erste Stufe

- express determination or indecision
- talk about whether something is important or not important

Zweite Stufe

- express wishes
- express certainty and to refuse or accept with certainty
- talk about goals for the future
- express relief

 internet

 ADRESSE: go.hrw.com
KENNWORT: WK3
DRESDEN-11

◀ **Hast du dich schon für einen Beruf entschieden?**

Los geht's! ▪ *Was kommt nach der Schule?*

CD 11
Trs. 1–5

Ein Schulabschluss ist wichtig für alle jungen Leute. Mit einem guten Schulabschluss haben sie eine bessere Möglichkeit, sich auf einen richtigen Beruf vorbereiten zu können. Hier unterhalten sich vier Gymnasiasten über ihre Wünsche und Vorstellungen für die Zukunft. CD 11 Tr. 1

Ich will auf alle Fälle studieren; ich weiß nicht, warum. Ich kann dafür keinen konkreten Grund angeben. Ich wüsste gar nicht, was ich anderes machen sollte. Wir haben ja hier 13 Jahre nichts anderes getan als gelernt. — Was ich studieren möchte? Nun, ich kann mich noch nicht entscheiden. Wirtschaftswissenschaften vielleicht oder Jura. Ich muss mir das mal überlegen. Für mich spielt die größere Rolle, dass ich nach dem Studium wirklich etwas anfangen kann. Es kommt eben darauf an, ob es dann einen Job in meinem Fach gibt, wenn ich fertig bin. Ich muss mal zum Arbeitsamt gehen und mich erkundigen, wie es in fünf bis sechs Jahren aussehen wird. Aber erst mal mach ich Ferien, ruh mich von der Schule aus. Ich hab's nötig.

Sonja CD 11 Tr. 2

Ich lege großen Wert darauf, an einer guten Universität zu studieren. Ich würde gern in den USA studieren, ja, weil die USA halt … ja, erst mal wegen der Sprache. Ich mein, Englisch oder Amerikanisch ist nun mal Wissenschaftssprache, und zweitens: ich war in Amerika, und mir hat die Mentalität der Leute so wahnsinnig gut gefallen, und drittens, weil es eins der führenden Länder auf dem technologischen und wissenschaftlichen Sektor ist. Ja, für mich ist es am wichtigsten, dass ich wirklich etwas lerne und mich auf eine gute Karriere vorbereiten kann.

Michael CD 11 Tr. 3

Ja, ich wollte mal studieren, aber jetzt bin ich nicht mehr besonders daran interessiert. Ich wüsste gar nicht, was ich studieren sollte. An der Uni beruht alles auf freiwilliger Basis, und ich bin zu undiszipliniert, ich würde das gar nicht schaffen. Entscheidend für mich ist, dass ich mal einen Beruf ausüben kann, der mir Spaß macht. Ich werd also wahrscheinlich auf die Modehochschule gehen, weil ich an Mode besonders interessiert bin.

Tanja CD 11 Tr. 4

Also, besonders vorbereiten tu ich mich eigentlich nur durch die Schule, also dadurch, dass ich jetzt eben in der Schule die Kurse gewählt hab, die für mich im Studium am wichtigsten sein können. Ich mach jetzt zum Beispiel einen Physik-Leistungskurs mit, denn Physik braucht man, wenn man Medizin studieren will. Ausschlaggebend ist für mich erst mal ein gutes Abi, denn nur so kann man überhaupt Medizin studieren. Zuerst aber werd ich wohl zum Bund müssen. Ich werd mal sehen, dass ich zum Sanitätskorps komme. Das ist eine gute, praktische Erfahrung für meinen späteren Beruf.

Philipp CD 11 Tr. 5

Nach dem Abi?

Von je 100 Schulabgängern machen ein halbes Jahr nach dem Abitur	
junge Männer	**junge Frauen**
51% Wehrdienst/Zivildienst	30% ein Studium
21% ein Studium	29% eine Lehre
15% eine Lehre	13% eine Fachschule
3% eine Berufstätigkeit	9% ein Praktikum
2% eine Beamtenausbildung	4% eine Beamtenausbildung
1% ein Praktikum	2% eine Berufstätigkeit
5% Jobben, Ferien, usw.	13% Jobben, Ferien, usw.

Information für junge Leute

*** 71 Prozent aller Mädchen interessieren sich für Umweltschutz, danach folgen Mode (35%), dann Politik (26%), Religion (17%) und Wirtschaft (16%) *** Ein Drittel aller Abiturienten entscheidet sich für eine Lehre vor dem Studium *** Sechs Prozent aller Jugendlichen unter 18 sind auf Sozialhilfe angewiesen ***

Übungsheft, S. 131

1 Hast du alles verstanden?

a. Schreiben Mach eine Liste und schreib auf, was für Wünsche und Ziele diese vier jungen Leute haben!

b. Sprechen Such dir einen von diesen vier Schülern aus, und berichte an Hand deiner Notizen über ihn oder über sie in der Klasse!

1. a. **Sonja:** Studium; Ferien / **Michael:** Studium in den USA; Karriere / **Tanja:** Beruf, der Spaß macht / **Philipp:** gutes Abi; Medizinstudium; Bundeswehr; Beruf

2 Genauer lesen

Sprechen Schaut euch die beiden Grafiken an und sprecht darüber!

a. Welche Fakten stehen hinter folgenden Zahlen: 51%, 30%, 15%, 29%?

b. Was machen die jungen Leute ein halbes Jahr nach dem Abitur? Diskutiert über die Unterschiede zwischen jungen Männern und jungen Frauen!

c. Was für allgemeine Interessen haben deutsche Mädchen? Vergleicht diese mit euren eigenen Interessen!

2. a. Wehrdienst/Zivildienst (junge Männer); Studium (junge Frauen); Lehre (junge Männer); Lehre (junge Frauen)
2. c. Umweltschutz; Mode; Politik; Religion; Wirtschaft

3 Umfrage

Sprechen Macht in eurer Klasse eine ähnliche Umfrage um festzustellen, was ihr ein halbes Jahr nach eurem Schulabschluss wahrscheinlich machen werdet! Vergleicht das Ergebnis mit dem Ergebnis der deutschen Umfrage! Diskutiert über die Unterschiede!

Wortschatz

auf Deutsch erklärt

Schulabschluss das Ende der Schulzeit, wenn man die Schule erfolgreich beendet
fertig wenn man zu Ende gekommen ist
Zukunft zeitlich nicht jetzt, sondern alles das, was noch kommen wird
anfangen beginnen
Beruf der hauptberufliche Job
jobben arbeiten, aber nicht hauptberuflich
Arbeitsamt von der Stadt organisierte Stelle, wo man Arbeit suchen kann
s. ausruhen s. entspannen
nötig haben wenn man etwas sehr braucht
beschließen s. entscheiden
entschlossen man hat sich entschieden
auf etwas Wert legen wenn man etwas für wichtig hält

auf Englisch erklärt

Ich möchte <u>mich nach</u> der <u>Möglichkeit</u> erkundigen, eine <u>Lehre</u> als Schreiner anzufangen. *I would like to get information on the possibility of beginning an apprenticeship as a carpenter.*
Andreas muss <u>sich auf</u> das Studium der <u>Naturwissenschaft</u> vorbereiten. *Andreas has to prepare himself for his studies in the natural sciences.*
<u>Auf</u> <u>alle</u> <u>Fälle</u> gibt es gute <u>Gründe</u>, Beamter zu werden. *In any case, there are good reasons to become a civil servant.*
Wenn man die <u>Sprache</u> eines Landes nicht kann, <u>ist</u> man <u>auf</u> Handbewegungen <u>angewiesen</u>. *When you can't speak the language of a country, you have to rely on gestures.*

> Übungsheft, S. 132, Ü. 1–2

> Grammatikheft, S. 91–92, Ü. 1–3

So sagt man das!

Expressing determination or indecision

11–1

Sometimes, when you have made a firm decision, you'll want to express your determination. You can say:

> **Ich hab beschlossen,** Jura zu studieren.
> **Ich hab mich entschieden,** einen Beruf zu erlernen.
> **Ich bin fest entschlossen,** in den USA zu studieren.
> **Ich weiß jetzt, dass** …

Of course, you may not be quite sure about something. This is the way you might express indecision:

> **Ich weiß nicht, ob** ich Musik studieren soll.
> **Ich hab mich noch nicht entschieden, was/ob** …
> **Ich kann (das) noch nicht sagen, was/ob** …
> **Ich muss mir das überlegen.**
> **Es kommt darauf an, was/ob** …
> **(Ich werde) mal sehen, ob** …

Mehr Grammatikübungen, S. 316–317, Ü. 1–3

> Übungsheft, S. 135, Ü. 8–9

> Grammatikheft, S. 93, Ü. 4–5

4 Schon feste Pläne? Script and answers on p. 295G

Zuhören Drei Schüler machen bald ihren Schulabschluss. Hör ihrem Gespräch gut zu und entscheide dich, wer schon feste Pläne hat und wer sich über seine Zukunft noch nicht so sicher ist!

CD 11 Tr. 6

5 Wie sieht's bei dir aus?

Sprechen Sprich mit einer Partnerin über deine Pläne für die Zukunft! Wofür habt ihr euch entschieden? Was ist noch ungewiss? Was sind die Gründe?

> PARTNER **Weißt du schon, ob oder was du studieren willst?**
> DU **Ich bin fest entschlossen, Jura zu studieren. Rechtsanwalt ist ein Beruf mit Zukunft.**

Wünsche und Pläne

zuerst studieren
eine Lehre machen
einen Job suchen
nach der Schule nichts machen
im Ausland studieren
im Ausland arbeiten
auf die (Musikhochschule) gehen
Wehrdienst oder Zivildienst machen

Gründe

ein Beruf mit Zukunft sein
mit dem Studium etwas
   anfangen können
einen besseren Job nach
   dem Studium haben
erst einmal Ferien machen
wegen der Sprache
sich auf eine Karriere vorbereiten

6 Und du? Was möchtest du alles?

Sprechen/Schreiben Sag oder schreib einer Partnerin, was du alles machen möchtest, nachdem du deinen Schulabschluss hast!

> DU **Ich möchte …** *oder*
> **Ich hab mich entschieden, …** *oder*
> **Ich hab beschlossen, …**

Was?

die Universität besuchen

(Jura) studieren

einen Beruf erlernen

einen tollen Beruf ausüben

eine gute Allgemeinbildung haben

in (Deutschland) studieren

erst mal Ferien machen

7 Du machst dasselbe

Sprechen Dein Partner sagt dir, was er macht. Sag ihm, dass du beschlossen hast, dasselbe zu tun!

> PARTNER **Ich bereite mich auf eine gute Karriere vor.**
> DU **Ich hab auch beschlossen, mich auf eine gute Karriere vorzubereiten.**

s. auf eine gute Karriere vorbereiten

s. beim Arbeitsamt erkundigen, wie der Arbeitsmarkt aussieht

s. zuerst mal umsehen, was man alles machen kann

s. um ein Studium in Deutschland bewerben

s. gut überlegen, was man werden will

Ein wenig Landeskunde

Im Jahre 1386 wurde die älteste deutsche Hochschule, die Universität Heidelberg, gegründet. In Deutschland gibt es viele alte Universitäten und auch ganz junge. Seit 1960 sind mehr als zwanzig Universitäten gegründet worden. Immer mehr junge Deutsche wollen heute studieren. 1960 begannen nur fünf Prozent eines Altersjahrgangs ein Studium. Heute bewirbt sich fast jeder dritte Jugendliche um einen Studienplatz. Im Wintersemester 2000/2001 studierten fast 1,8 Millionen in Deutschland. Davon waren rund 122 000 Ausländer. Der Anteil der Frauen liegt bei 47%. Der Staat fördert nämlich das Studium von Ausländern an deutschen Hochschulen als Beitrag zur internationalen Verständigung.

Studienwünsche männlicher Abiturienten		Studienwünsche von Abiturientinnen	
Fach	Anteil (%)	Fach	Anteil (%)
Wirtschaft	14	Wirtschaft	11
Maschinenbau	13	Jura	7
Elektrotechnik	11	Sozialwesen	6
Jura	5	Medizin	6
Informatik	5	Architektur	5
Bauingenieurwesen	4	Gestaltung	4
Architektur	4	Erziehungswissenschaft	4
Medizin	3	Germanistik	3
Physik	3	Biologie	3
Chemie	3	Psychologie	3

8 Fragen an dich

Sprechen Sag einer Partnerin, wie du dich zu den folgenden Fragen stellst! Hast du zu diesen Fragen schon eine feste Meinung, oder kannst du dich noch nicht entscheiden? — Gebrauch in deiner Antwort die Ausdrücke, die auf Seite 300 aufgelistet sind!

1. Hast du schon feste Vorstellungen von deiner Zukunft?
2. Weißt du schon, was du nach der Schule machen willst?
3. Möchtest du studieren? — Wenn ja, was?
4. Welchen Beruf würdest du gern einmal ausüben?
5. Wirst du zum Arbeitsamt gehen, um dich nach Job-Möglichkeiten zu erkundigen?
6. Was machst du erst mal ganz bestimmt, wenn du mit der Schule fertig bist?
7. Würdest du gern in Deutschland oder anderswo im Ausland studieren oder arbeiten?
8. Möchtest du gleich nach der Schule heiraten und eine Familie gründen?

9 Für mein Notizbuch

Schreiben Mach eine Liste mit fünf Plänen, für die du dich schon entschieden hast, und mit fünf Ideen, die du dir noch überlegen musst!

10 Klassendiskussion

1. **Lesen/Sprechen** Vergleicht eure Listen in der Klasse und diskutiert über die Unterschiede in euren Wünschen und Zielen für die Zukunft!
2. **Schreiben** Macht eine Klassenliste, die euch zeigt, wofür sich die meisten schon entschieden haben, und was sich die meisten von euch noch überlegen müssen!

11 Was ist am Arbeitsplatz wichtig?

Sprechen Es gibt viele Gesichtspunkte, nach denen man einen Arbeitsplatz beurteilen kann. Hier ist das Ergebnis einer Umfrage. Es zeigt, was den Deutschen am wichtigsten ist und was ihnen weniger wichtig ist. (Die Nummern zeigen, wievielmal die einzelnen Gesichtspunkte erwähnt wurden.) Diskutiert über das Ergebnis der Umfrage! Was würde bei euch ganz oben stehen? Ganz unten? — Schreibt eure eigene Liste von Prioritäten am Arbeitsplatz!

Einkommenshöhe 53
Bedingungen am Arbeitsplatz 45
Inhalt der Arbeit 34
Kontakte mit Kollegen 34
Aufstiegschancen 23
Sicherheit vor Entlassung 22
Arbeitszeit 19
Verhältnis zum Boss 17
Sicherheit am Arbeitsplatz 15
Mitbestimmung im Betrieb 13
Angenehmes Arbeitstempo 9
Zugang zu Informationen 3

Talking about whether something is important or not important

To say what is important, you can use the following phrases:

> Ich lege großen Wert darauf, dass …
> Ich bin interessiert daran, dass …
> Für mich spielt die größte Rolle, dass …
> Mir ist wichtig, dass …
> Entscheidend für mich ist, dass …
> Für mich ist es am wichtigsten, dass …
> Ausschlaggebend ist für mich, dass …

To say that something is not important, you can say:

> Ich lege keinen großen Wert darauf, dass …
> Ich bin nicht besonders interessiert daran, dass …
> Es ist nicht entscheidend für mich, dass …
> Mir ist weniger wichtig, dass …

Übungsheft, S. 133–135, Ü. 3–7

Grammatikheft, S. 94, Ü. 6

---

12 **Über die Zukunft sprechen** Script and answers on p. 295G

Zuhören Hör Steffi und Horst gut zu, wie sie über ihre Wünsche und Pläne für die Zukunft sprechen! Was für Dinge sind Steffi wichtig? Und Horst? Wie unterscheiden sich die zwei?
CD 11 Tr. 7

13 **Grammatk im Kontext**

Sprechen/Schreiben Wenn ihr an die Zukunft denkt, worauf legt ihr da großen Wert? — Drückt eure Meinungen auf verschiedene Arten aus! Jeder in der Gruppe kommt einmal dran. Ihr könnt eure Meinungen auch schreiben.

FRAGE **Worauf legst du großen Wert?**
SCHÜLER 1 **Ich lege großen Wert auf eine gute Universität.**
SCHÜLER 2 **Entscheidend ist für mich, dass ich eine gute Universität besuche.**

nette Mitarbeiter haben

viel Freizeit haben

gute Universität besuchen

vernünftige Arbeitszeit haben

Sicherheit am Arbeitsplatz haben

Zugang zu Information haben

gutes Gehalt bekommen

Aufstiegschancen haben

angenehmes Arbeitstempo haben

große Karriere vorbereiten

interessanten Beruf erlernen

Ein wenig Grammatik

Schon bekannt

Do you remember how to use **wo**-compounds to ask a question? If someone said **Wir interessieren uns für Politik** and you didn't hear the end of their sentence, how would you ask for clarification?[1]
Look at the following sentence:

> **Es kommt darauf an, ob ich einen guten Job finde.**

What does **darauf** anticipate?[2]

Mehr Grammatikübungen, S. 317, Ü. 4

---
1. **Wofür interessiert ihr euch?**
2. It anticipates the entire clause that follows.

14 **Und du? Wie steht's mit dir?**

Sprechen/Schreiben Denk an deine Wünsche und Ziele für die Zukunft, und beantworte die folgenden Fragen!

1. Woran denkst du schon mit (16) Jahren?
2. Worauf bereitest du dich vor?
3. Woran bist du am meisten interessiert?

4. Wofür wirst du dich entscheiden?
5. Worauf kommt es dir am meisten an?
6. Worauf legst du den größten Wert?

Wortschatz

Berufe

Tierärztin

Musiker

Biologe

Kauffrau

Und dann noch...

Apotheker(in)
Architekt(in)
Biologe/Biologin
Computerspezialist(in)
Diplomat(in)
Ingenieur(in)
Journalist(in)
Kaufmann, -frau
Krankenschwester, -pfleger
Musiker(in)
Physiker(in)
Politiker(in)
Professor(in)
Rechtsanwalt, -anwältin
Reporter(in)
Sekretär(in)
Soldat(in)
Tierarzt, -ärztin

p. 295X

Grammatikheft, S. 94, Ü. 7

15 **Was möchtest du mal werden?**

Sprechen Sag, was du mal werden möchtest und warum! Frag deine Klassenkameraden, was sie werden möchten! Jeder muss einen Grund angeben.

(Kinder) gern haben

gut sein in ...

Talent dazu haben

ein Beruf mit Zukunft

mein Vater/meine Mutter ist auch ...

interessante Arbeit

viel reisen können

16 **Für mein Notizbuch**

Schreiben Schreib über deine eigenen Zukunftswünsche und Pläne! Folgende Fragen können dir dabei helfen.

1. Was möchtest du machen, wenn du mit der High School fertig bist?
2. Was für einen Beruf möchtest du einmal ausüben?
3. Was ist dir wichtig, wenn du an einen späteren Beruf denkst? Was ist dir weniger wichtig?
4. Mit wem besprichst du deine Zukunftspläne? Wer hilft dir bei deinen Entscheidungen?
5. Der zukünftige Beruf ist natürlich wichtig, aber was für andere Wünsche und Pläne hast du? Möchtest du zum Beispiel viel reisen oder eine Zeit lang im Ausland leben?
6. Möchtest du einmal heiraten und eine Familie gründen?
7. Wo möchtest du einmal wohnen?

Wie findet man eine Arbeitsstelle in Deutschland?

Übungsheft, S. 136, Ü. 1–2

Wie bewirbt man sich um einen Job oder um eine Arbeitsstelle in Deutschland, wenn man mit der Schule fertig ist? Wer eine Arbeitsstelle sucht, sollte hauptsächlich die Stellenangebote in der Zeitung lesen. Alle Tageszeitungen in Deutschland haben in der Samstagsausgabe einen Sonderteil für Stellenangebote, den „Stellenmarkt". Hat man eine Anzeige gefunden, für die man sich interessiert, fertigt man eine schriftliche Bewerbung an. Zu den vollständigen Bewerbungsunterlagen gehören ein tabellarischer Lebenslauf, getippt oder handgeschrieben, ein Foto und Kopien von Schul- und Arbeitszeugnissen. Außerdem schreibt man einen Brief, in welchem man kurz erwähnt, warum man sich für diese Stelle interessiert.

Hier siehst du ein typisches Stellenangebot aus einer deutschen Tageszeitung.

A. 1. Lies zuerst den Text oben! Wie findet man eine Arbeitsstelle in Deutschland? Welche Unterlagen (*documents*) schickt man an die Firma?

2. Lies jetzt das Stellenangebot (*job offer*)! Wer würde sich für diese Anzeige interessieren? Welche Ausbildung ist für die angebotene Position nötig? Welche persönlichen Eigenschaften soll der Bewerber (*applicant*) haben? Was bietet die Firma dem Bewerber?

B. 1. Wie bewirbt man sich bei einer Firma in den USA? Was schickt man gewöhnlich an die Firma?

2. Wie unterscheidet sich das Bewerbungsverfahren in Deutschland von dem amerikanischen? Was schickt man in Deutschland, aber nicht hier? Welches Verfahren findest du besser? Warum?

3. Welche Fähigkeiten (*skills*) hast du, die eine Firma von einem Bewerber erwartet? Welche Leistungen (*benefits*) soll dir die Firma bieten?

WERTMARKT

Ihr steiler Weg nach oben

Wir suchen

Absolventen von Hoch- und Fachhochschulen der Studienrichtung Betriebswirtschaft

(mit Berufserfahrung)

SIE: suchen eine gut dotierte Führungsposition; sind bereit, Verantwortung zu tragen und selbständig Entscheidungen zu treffen; bringen die Fähigkeit mit, Mitarbeiter zu führen und zu motivieren; verfügen über gute Umgangsformen und ein gepflegtes Erscheinungsbild.

WIR: bieten Ihnen die eigenverantwortliche Führung eines Filialbereiches für eines der führenden Lebensmittel–Filialunternehmen in Deutschland als leitender Angestellter und Vorgesetzter; zahlen ein übertarifliches Gehalt bereits während der Einarbeitung; stellen Ihnen einen neutralen PKW zur Verfügung, den Sie auch privat nutzen können.

Ihre Bewerbung mit den üblichen Unterlagen wie handgeschriebenem Lebenslauf, Lichtbild, Zeugniskopien und Gehaltswunsch richten Sie bitte an:

WERTMARKT Lebensmittelfilialbetrieb GmbH z. Hd. Herrn Reinke Kaiserstraße 10 97070 Würzburg

A. 1. hauptsächlich durch Stellenangebote in der Zeitung / tabellarischen Lebenslauf; Foto; Kopien von Schul- und Arbeitszeugnissen; Brief

A. 2. jemand, der eine Führungsposition in einer Lebensmittelfirma sucht; der ein Studium der Betriebswirtschaft absolviert hat und Berufserfahrung hat / Studium der Betriebswirtschaft / soll bereit sein, Verantwortung zu tragen und selbständig Entscheidungen zu treffen; soll die Fähigkeit haben, Mitarbeiter zu führen und zu motivieren; soll gute Umgangsformen und ein gepflegtes Erscheinungsbild haben / eigenverantwortliche Führung eines Filialbereiches; übertarifliches Gehalt; PKW

STANDARDS: 1.2, 2.1, 2.2, 3.2, 4.2

Fünf Jugendliche sprechen darüber, wie sie ihre Zukunft sehen und was sie mit dreißig Jahren erreicht haben möchten. CD 11 Tr. 8

Bis vor kurzem hab ich meine Zukunft ziemlich pessimistisch gesehen. Manchmal hatte ich richtige Angst, dass unsere Welt kaputtgeht an der Umweltverschmutzung und vor allem am Ost-West Konflikt: Panzer, Raketen, Krieg — vor einem Atomkrieg hab ich mir große Sorgen gemacht. Gott sei Dank hab ich diese Angst jetzt nicht mehr. Gut, dass der Osten vernünftig geworden ist. Was sich jetzt im Osten tut, gibt mir große Hoffnung für meine Zukunft. Jetzt will ich wirklich einen guten Schulabschluss machen, einen Beruf erlernen, Geld verdienen und reisen, in die ehemaligen Ostblockländer, vielleicht sogar dort arbeiten. Wer weiß?

Sandra, 16 CD 11 Tr. 9

Mit dreißig möchte ich eine politische Karriere begonnen haben. Mein Vater ist Politiker, und ich steh auch auf Politik. Und was gerade in dieser Zeit auf uns zukommt, ist unbeschreiblich! Die Demokratisierung des Ostens und ein großes, vereintes Europa — da möchte ich auf jeden Fall einmal dabei sein. Ich bin froh, dass ich in der Schule gut bin, und ich werde das Abi ganz bestimmt schaffen. Nun, es steht fest, dass ich Politik und Sprachen studieren werde. Wer nämlich eine, zwei oder sogar mehrere Sprachen kann, der hat bessere Chancen im Beruf und im Leben überhaupt. Und ich mit dreißig? Vielleicht werd ich bis dahin einen Traumjob gefunden haben oder im Bundestag sein, oder vielleicht werd ich irgendwo in der Welt herumreisen oder sogar schon verheiratet sein und Kinder haben. Wer weiß? Es ist jedenfalls interessant, so viele Möglichkeiten vor sich zu haben.

Uta, 17 CD 11 Tr. 10

Wenn ich dreißig bin, möchte ich einen tollen Beruf ausüben — Raumfahrttechniker vielleicht, weil das ein Beruf mit Zukunft ist. Auf alle Fälle möchte ich keine materiellen Sorgen haben und ganz bestimmt viel reisen. Eine Familie haben? Kommt nicht in Frage! Nicht mit dreißig, vielleicht mit vierzig Jahren. Ich möchte ganz bestimmt erst mal viel mehr von der Welt sehen, einen weiteren Horizont kriegen.

Alexander, 17 CD 11 Tr. 11

Ich freu mich direkt auf meine Zukunft. Mit dreißig möchte ich schon viel Geld verdienen, eine schöne Wohnung oder ein Haus haben, ich möchte verheiratet sein und Kinder haben, ja, natürlich auch ein tolles Auto fahren. Nun, das klingt wohl alles ziemlich materialistisch. Aber man muss Ziele im Leben haben und Sachen, an denen man sich freuen kann. Zum Glück bin ich gesund, und ich bin bereit, hart zu arbeiten, um das alles möglich zu machen.

Oliver, 16 CD 11 Tr. 12

Ich hab noch keine großen Pläne für die Zukunft. Im Sommer werd ich mit dem Realgymnasium fertig, und dann werde ich bei einer Bank oder bei einer Versicherung eine Lehre anfangen. Bis ich mal Bankkaufmann bin, vergeht noch eine Weile. Ich werde weiterhin bei meinen Eltern wohnen; ausziehen kommt für mich nicht in Frage. Ich liebe geregelte Verhältnisse. Ich komm mit meinen Eltern prima aus, und ich möchte weiterhin so leben wie jetzt und auch noch eine Weile so bleiben, wie ich bin. Angst vor der Zukunft hab ich nicht.

Christian, 17 CD 11 Tr. 13

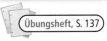
Übungsheft, S. 137

17 **Was sagen die Jugendlichen?**

Schreiben Mach eine Liste und schreib auf, was für Wünsche und Ziele diese fünf Jugendlichen für ihre Zukunft haben!

Sandra: guter Schulabschluss; Beruf; Geld; Reisen / Uta: politische Karriere; Studium; Reisen; Heirat; Kinder / Alexander: toller Beruf; keine materiellen Sorgen haben; viel reisen; Familie später / Oliver: Geld; Wohnung oder Haus; Heirat; Kinder; Auto

18 **Brainstorming**

Sprechen/Schreiben Unterhaltet euch in der Klasse über eure Wünsche und Ziele für die Zukunft! Macht eine Liste, und schreibt sie in euer Notizheft!

Zweite Stufe

Objectives Expressing wishes; expressing certainty and refusing or accepting with certainty; talking about goals for the future; expressing relief

go.
hrw
.com

WK3 DRESDEN-11

Wie sieht die Jugend ihre Zukunft?

Lesen In Zeitschriften findet man oft Umfragen und Tests. Hier sind einige Beispiele.

Die Jugendlichen: Was ist ihnen wichtig?

	sehr wichtig	ziemlich wichtig	kaum wichtig	nicht wichtig
den richtigen Beruf wählen	63%	33%	2,5%	1,5%
keine materiellen Sorgen haben	48%	47%	4%	1%
schöne Wohnung / schönes Haus haben	32%	52%	15%	1%
die Lebensweise selbst bestimmen	34%	50%	15%	1%
heiraten und Kinder haben	31%	34%	27%	8%

Wer sind deine Vorbilder? Welche Männer und Frauen bewunderst du besonders?

Albert Schweitzer
Mutter Theresa
Martin Luther King
Sandra Day O'Connor
Tiger Woods
Mia Hamm
andere Personen

Wenn du an deine Zukunft denkst, welche Ziele hast du da? Rangliste

	Mädchen	Jungen
sicheren Arbeitsplatz	2	2
gutes Einkommen	1	5
gesund leben	5	1
Partnerschaft	4	3
anderen Menschen helfen	6	4
schönes Haus haben	3	7
politisch aktiv sein	7	6

Möchtest du später mal heiraten?

	Jugendliche insgesamt	Mädchen	Jungen
Ja	48%	40%	55%
Nein	22%	25%	20%
Unentschieden	30%	35%	25%

Wortschatz

auf Deutsch erklärt

der Atomkrieg Krieg mit Nuklearwaffen geführt
das kommt nicht in Frage daran wird überhaupt nicht gedacht
die Hoffnung was man hat, wenn man auf etwas hofft
die Raumfahrt was die Astronauten machen
dabei sein mitmachen
vereint zusammen als eins
der Bundestag das deutsche Parlament
geregelt ordentlich
Ich stehe auf Politik. Ich bin von Politik begeistert.
vor allem besonders
auf jeden Fall ganz bestimmt
jedenfalls sicher, gewiss
ehemalig- früher-

auf Englisch erklärt

Ich liebe geregelte Verhältnisse. Ich werde eine Lehre bei einer Versicherung anfangen. *I like orderly conditions. I will become an apprentice with an insurance company.*
Es vergeht noch eine Weile, bis ich Bankkaufmann bin. *It is going to take a while for me to become a banker.*
Bis dahin weiß ich, was auf mich zukommt. *By then, I'll know what's in store for me.*
Auf alle Fälle muss man ein Ziel haben. *In any case, one must have a goal.*

Grammatikheft, S. 95–96, Ü. 8–11

KAPITEL 11   Deine Welt ist deine Sache!

19 Was sagt ihr dazu?

1. **Sprechen** Überlegt euch mal, was ihr zu den Umfragen auf Seite 308 sagen würdet!
2. **Sprechen** Was würdet ihr an diesen Umfragen ändern? Hinzufügen? Weglassen? Diskutiert mit euren Klassenkameraden darüber!
3. **Schreiben** Stellt eine Liste mit Leuten auf, die für euch Vorbilder sind!
4. **Sprechen** Macht die Umfragen in der Klasse, und diskutiert die Ergebnisse!

So sagt man das!

Expressing wishes

When discussing the future, you often talk about how you wish or hope it might be.

Viel Geld wäre mir nicht wichtig.
In meiner idealen Welt gäbe es keinen Krieg.

Note that **gäbe** is a subjunctive form like **wäre**.

Mehr Grammatikübungen,
S. 318, Ü. 5

Grammatikheft, S. 96, Ü. 12

20 Wünsche der Schüler   Script and answers on p. 295H

Zuhören Hör zu und schreib auf, was sich diese Schüler wünschen! Wer hat mehr realistische Wünsche und wer mehr ideale? Mit welchem Schüler kannst du dich am besten identifizieren?

CD 11 Tr. 14

21 Was gäbe es in deiner idealen Welt?

Sprechen Sag einem Partner, was es in deiner idealen Welt gäbe und was nicht!

Es gäbe viel ...   Es gäbe wenig ...   Es gäbe kein ...

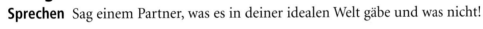

Geld	Musik	Theater	Kunst	Sport	Freunde	ein guter Job	Reisen

Hunger   Armut   Krieg   Konflikt   Krankheit   Tiere   Hobbys   Bücher

Umweltverschmutzung   Blumen   Kinder   ein schönes Haus   eine glückliche Ehe

So sagt man das!

Expressing certainty and refusing or accepting with certainty

11–2

If you are certain about something, you can say:

Es steht fest, dass ...   *or*   **Es ist sicher, dass ...**
Ich möchte unbedingt ...

If someone asks you if you'd like to do something, here is how you might say that you absolutely refuse:

Nein, tut mir Leid.
Kommt nicht in Frage!
Auf keinen Fall!

or certainly accept:

Ja, natürlich! *or* **Ganz bestimmt.**
Auf jeden Fall. *or* **Auf alle Fälle.**

Grammatikheft,
S. 97, Ü. 13–14

22 Wie steht's mit euch?

Sprechen Sagt, was bei euch feststeht, und was bei euch nicht in Frage kommt! Benutzt in euren Fragen und Antworten die Liste, die ihr in Übung 18 erstellt habt!

PARTNER 1 **Hast du Angst vor der Zukunft?**
DU **Ganz bestimmt. Ich weiß gar nicht, was kommt!** *oder* **Auf keinen Fall.**
DU **Möchtest du in der Welt herumreisen?**
PARTNER 2 **Ja! Ich möchte unbedingt einen Beruf erlernen, wo ich viel reisen kann.**
oder **Kommt nicht in Frage, ich reise gar nicht gern.**

23 Für mein Notizbuch

Schreiben Schreib zehn Sachen auf eine Liste, die dir für deine Zukunft sehr wichtig sind! Das Wichtigste muss oben stehen.

24 Vergleicht eure Pläne!

Sprechen Vergleicht jetzt eure Listen miteinander und sprecht über die Unterschiede, die ihr entdeckt! Denkt daran, dass ihr Gründe für eure Rangordnung angeben müsst!

25 Grammatik im Kontext

Sprechen/Schreiben Was wirst du in der Zukunft machen? Was werden deine Freunde machen? Deine Geschwister? Deine Klassenkameraden? Bilde Sätze mit „werden"!

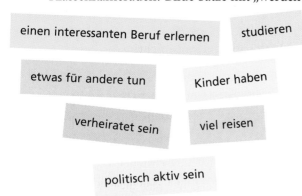

einen interessanten Beruf erlernen

studieren

etwas für andere tun

Kinder haben

verheiratet sein

viel reisen

politisch aktiv sein

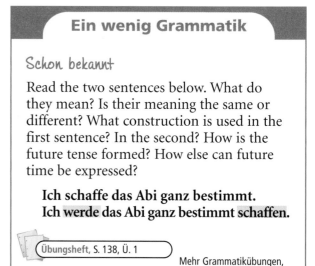

Ein wenig Grammatik

Schon bekannt

Read the two sentences below. What do they mean? Is their meaning the same or different? What construction is used in the first sentence? In the second? How is the future tense formed? How else can future time be expressed?

Ich schaffe das Abi ganz bestimmt.
Ich werde das Abi ganz bestimmt schaffen.

Übungsheft, S. 138, Ü. 1

Grammatikheft, S. 98, Ü. 15–16

Mehr Grammatikübungen, S. 318, Ü. 6

So sagt man das!

Talking about goals for the future

When thinking about the future, you often speculate on what you would like to have accomplished by a certain time in your life. You could say:

Mit dreißig **möchte ich** eine politische Karriere **begonnen haben.**
Vielleicht **werde ich** bis dahin einen Traumjob **gefunden haben.**

Übungsheft, S. 138, Ü. 2

26 Große Pläne   Script and answers on p. 295H

Zuhören Schreib auf, was diese Jugendlichen mit dreißig Jahren erreicht haben möchten! Wer von ihnen hat große Pläne?
CD 11 Tr. 15

Grammatik

The perfect infinitive with modals and **werden**

1. To express that something will have happened or have been completed in the future, you can use the perfect infinitive with a modal or with **werden**.

   Ich **möchte** eine politische Karriere **begonnen haben**.
   Ich **werde** einen Traumjob **gefunden haben**.

2. The perfect infinitive consists of the infinitives **haben** or **sein** (when the main verb requires **sein**), and the past participle of the main verb.

   Ich werde fertig **studiert haben**.   *or*   Wir werden weit **gereist sein**.

Mehr Grammatikübungen, S. 318–319, Ü. 7–9

Übungsheft, S. 139, Ü. 3–4

Grammatikheft, S. 99, Ü. 17–18

27 Grammatik im Kontext

Sprechen Sagt euren Klassenkameraden, was ihr mit dreißig alles getan haben werdet, wenn es nach euren Wünschen geht!

> Du   **Mit dreißig werd ich viel von der Welt gesehen haben.**
> Partner   **Mit dreißig …**

Was?

viel von der Welt sehen

viel erleben

überallhin reisen

ein Haus kaufen

schon heiraten

das Studium abschließen

schon viel Geld verdienen

28 Was werde ich alles erreicht haben?

Schreiben Schreib auf, was du mit 20 und mit 25 Jahren erreicht haben wirst, wenn alles so kommt, wie du es dir vorstellst!

So sagt man das!

Expressing relief Übungsheft, S. 140–141, Ü. 5–8

These are some ways of saying that you are relieved about something:

Gut, dass …   **Gott sei Dank, dass …**
Ein Glück, dass …   **Zum Glück habe ich …**
Ich bin froh, dass …

29 Worüber seid ihr froh?

Sprechen Jeder in der Klasse sagt, worüber er oder sie froh ist. Jeder muss der Reihe nach etwas anderes sagen!

> Du   **Gut, dass ich meine Zukunft nicht so pessimistisch sehe.**
> Partner 1 **Gott sei Dank, dass es keinen Ost-West Konflikt mehr gibt!**
> Partner 2 **Zum Glück habe ich …**

30 Für mein Notizbuch

Schreiben Eine Bewerbung fürs College oder für die Universität verlangt häufig einen Aufsatz, in dem man sich vorstellt. Schreib einen solchen Aufsatz in dein Notizheft! Erwähne in deinem Aufsatz Folgendes:

1. Was sind deine Wünsche und Ziele?
2. Wie bereitest du dich darauf vor?
3. Was willst du mit 30 erreicht haben?
4. Was würde dir Zufriedenheit geben?

31 **Von der Schule zum Beruf**

You have recently taken over a business. As part of your long-term planning, get with a committee to develop a mission statement for your company. Then write a Five-Year Plan and a Ten-Year Plan. Include goals and wishes for the future, and also express what is important or not important for the company. Then sum up your plans in a letter or booklet to be sent to the company's investors and shareholders.

CD 11 Tr. 16

Das Märchen vom kleinen Herr Moritz

von Wolf Biermann

Eines Tages geht ein kleiner älterer Herr spazieren. Er heißt Herr Moritz und hat sehr große Schuhe und einen schwarzen Mantel dazu und einen langen schwarzen Regenschirmstock, und damit geht er oft spazieren. Dann kommt nun der lange Winter, der längste Winter auf der Welt in Berlin, da werden die Menschen allmählich böse:

Die Autofahrer schimpfen, weil die Straßen so glatt sind, daß die Autos ausrutschen.

Die Verkehrspolizisten schimpfen, weil sie immer auf der kalten Straße rumstehen müssen.

Literatur der Ex-DDR

Lesestrategie Interpreting symbols In works of fiction authors often use objects and characters as symbols that stand for something greater than themselves, usually something abstract. For example, objects and characters may symbolize emotions, ideas, or abstract concepts, such as good and evil; characters may represent particular groups of people or different aspects of society. A character's name is often a key to understanding what that character symbolizes.

Getting Started

1. Read the title and the first paragraph of the reading selection. To what genre of literature does this story belong? What elements are usually included in a **Märchen?** Answer the following questions:

   a. Wer ist die Hauptfigur?

   b. Wie sieht er aus?

   c. Wann und wo findet die Handlung statt?

2. Reread the first paragraph and continue reading to **An einem solchen …** What is the main idea of that part of the story? Which statements support the main idea?

For answers, see p. 295W.

Die Verkäuferinnen schimpfen, weil ihre Verkaufsläden so kalt sind.

Die Männer von der Müllabfuhr schimpfen, weil der Schnee gar nicht alle wird.

Der Milchmann schimpft, weil ihm die Milch in den Milchkannen zu Eis friert.

Die Kinder schimpfen, weil ihnen die Ohren ganz rot gefroren sind, und die Hunde bellen vor Wut über die Kälte schon gar nicht mehr, sondern zittern nur noch und klappern mit den Zähnen vor Kälte, und das sieht auch sehr böse aus.

An einem solchen kalten Schneetag geht Herr Moritz mit seinem blauen Hut spazieren, und er denkt: „Wie böse die Menschen alle sind, es wird höchste Zeit, daß es wieder Sommer wird und die Blumen wachsen." Und als er so durch die schimpfenden Leute in der Markthalle geht, wachsen ganz schnell und ganz viele Krokusse, Tulpen, Maiglöckchen, Rosen und Nelken, auch Löwenzahn und Margeriten auf seinem Kopf. Er merkt es aber erst gar nicht, und dabei ist schon längst sein Hut vom Kopf hoch gegangen, weil die Blumen immer mehr werden und auch immer länger.

Da bleibt vor ihm eine Frau stehen und sagt: „O, Ihnen wachsen aber schöne Blumen auf dem Kopf!"

„Mir Blumen auf dem Kopf?" sagt Herr Moritz, „so was gibt es gar nicht!"

„Doch! Schauen Sie hier in das Schaufenster, Sie können sich darin spiegeln. Darf ich eine Blume abpflücken?"

Und Herr Moritz sieht im Schaufensterspiegelbild, daß wirklich Blumen auf seinem Kopf wachsen, bunte und große, und er sagt: „Aber bitte, wenn Sie eine wollen …"

„Ich möchte gerne eine kleine Rose", sagt die Frau und pflückt sich eine.

„Und ich eine Nelke für meinen Bruder", sagt ein kleines Mädchen und Herr Moritz bückt sich, damit das Mädchen ihm auf den Kopf langen kann. Er braucht sich aber nicht so sehr tief zu bücken, denn er ist etwas kleiner als andere Männer. Viele Leute kommen und brechen sich Blumen vom Kopf des kleinen Herr Moritz, und es tut ihm nicht weh, und die Blumen wachsen immer gleich nach, und es kribbelt so schön am Kopf, als ob ihn jemand freundlich streichelte. Herr Moritz ist froh, daß er den Leuten mitten im kalten Winter Blumen geben kann. Immer mehr Menschen kommen zusammen und lachen und wundern sich und brechen sich Blumen vom Kopf des kleinen Herrn Moritz. Keiner, der eine Blume erwischt, sagt an diesem Tag noch ein böses Wort.

Aber da kommt auf einmal auch der Polizist Max Kunkel. Max Kunkel ist schon seit zehn Jahren in der Markthalle als Markthallenpolizist tätig, aber so was hat er nocht nicht gesehen! Mann mit Blumen auf dem Kopf! Er drängelt sich durch die vielen lauten Menschen, und als er vor dem kleinen Herrn Moritz steht, schreit er: „Wo gibt's denn so was! Blumen auf dem Kopf, mein Herr. Zeigen Sie doch bitte mal sofort Ihren Personalausweis!"

---

3. Lies die ganze Geschichte einmal! Schreib in zwei bis drei Sätzen, worum es in dieser Geschichte geht!

A Closer Look

4. Scan the first eight paragraphs to identify those that begin with sequencing expressions. Read the sentences or paragraphs that are introduced by those expressions. What different purposes do those expressions serve?

5. Lies die Geschichte noch einmal, und beantworte die folgenden Fragen!

   a. Woran denkt Herr Moritz, als er durch die Markthalle geht? Was passiert ihm dort? Wie reagieren die Leute darauf?

   b. Was will der Polizist sehen? Was geschieht, als Herr Moritz danach sucht?

   c. Was passiert dem Herrn Moritz am Ende der Geschichte?

Read the story again and discuss the following questions with a partner. Share your ideas with the rest of the class.

6. Why does the policeman want to see Herr Moritz's identification card? Why do you think the flowers wilt as Herr Moritz searches for his card?

7. Why do you think Herr Moritz is described as **klein?** What does the word **klein** suggest to you? Whom or what might Herr Moritz represent? Think about his name, his appearance, and what you know about his

Und der kleine Herr Moritz sucht und sucht und sagt verzweifelt: „Ich habe ihn doch immer bei mir, ich habe ihn doch in der Tasche!" Und je mehr er sucht, um so mehr verschwinden die Blumen auf seinem Kopf.

„Aha", sagt der Polizist Max Kunkel, „Blumen auf dem Kopf haben Sie, aber keinen Ausweis in der Tasche!!"

Und Herr Moritz sucht immer ängstlicher seinen Ausweis und ist ganz rot vor Verlegenheit, und je mehr er sucht — auch im Jackenfutter — um so mehr schrumpfen die Blumen zusammen, und der Hut geht allmählich wieder herunter auf den Kopf! In seiner Verzweiflung nimmt Herr Moritz seinen Hut ab, und siehe da, unter dem Hut liegt in der abgegriffenen Gummihülle der Personalausweis. Aber was noch!? Die Haare sind alle weg! Kein Haar mehr auf dem Kopf hat der kleine Herr Moritz. Er streicht sich verlegen über den kahlen Kopf und setzt dann schnell den Hut darauf.

„Na, da ist ja der Ausweis", sagt der Polizist Max Kunkel freundlich, „und Blumen haben Sie wohl auch nicht mehr auf dem Kopf, wie?!"

„Nein", sagt Herr Moritz und steckt schnell seinen Ausweis ein und läuft, so schnell wie man auf den glatten Straßen laufen kann, nach Hause. Dort steht er lange vor dem Spiegel und sagt zu sich: „Jetzt hast du eine Glatze, Herr Moritz!"

character from his actions in the story. What might the policeman represent?

8. There are many objects in this fairy tale that could be thought of as symbols, for example, the flowers or even the long, cold winter. What other symbols can you find in the story? What might they represent? Do your answers help to make the story more meaningful?

9. Was meinst du, was der Hauptgedanke der Geschichte ist? Schreib deine Idee in einem Satz auf!

10. Wähle zusammen mit einem Partner eine der folgenden Situationen, und entwickle ein passendes Gespräch dazu! Führ danach die Szene der Klasse vor!

a. Einige Reporter haben von den Ereignissen in der Markthalle gehört. Du bist ein Augenzeuge der Ereignisse. Mit deinem Partner übernimm die Rollen von Reporter und Zeuge! Erzähl dem Reporter alles, was passiert ist, damit er einen Bericht darüber schreiben kann!

b. Du bist Herr Moritz und triffst dich mit einem guten Freund einen Tag nach den Ereignissen in der Markthalle. Er will wissen, warum du ganz plötzlich eine Glatze hast. Erzähl ihm, was dir gestern alles passiert ist! Erzähl auch, wie du dich jetzt fühlst!

Übungsheft, S. 142-143, Ü. 1-5

Zum Schreiben

You have been reading about teenagers in Germany making career decisions that can be major turning points in their lives. Such pivotal moments are often the subject of TV shows and dramas. Imagine a show in which the characters must make a difficult decision that might result in arguments with parents or cause shifts in their relationships with others. In this activity you and your classmates will write a scene, as from a TV show or a movie, about such a turning point.

Von einem Wendepunkt erzählen

Bildet Gruppen von zwei bis vier Schülern, und schreibt zusammen eine Szene, in der jeder von euch eine Rolle hat! Die Szene soll von einer wichtigen Entscheidung und einem dadurch entstandenen Wendepunkt handeln.

 Schreibtipp **Writing drafts and revising** When you first sit down to write, the task can seem overwhelming, so don't try to make your writing perfect the first time through. Instead, write several drafts following your outlines and plans, yet allowing yourself the freedom to be creative and add any new ideas that come to you. Between drafts, share your writing with friends to get constructive criticism. They can tell you what they don't understand so you'll know where you need to clarify your ideas. You may also want to wait a little while between drafts so that you can gain an objective perspective on what you have already written and improve upon it.

A. Vorbereiten

1. Bildet eine Gruppe und besprecht eure Szene! Wer übernimmt welche Rolle? Was ist die wichtige Entscheidung? Was ist der Wendepunkt? Wo und wann spielt sich die Szene ab?

2. Jeder wählt eine Rolle und entwickelt seine Persönlichkeit. Was sind die Gefühle, Hoffnungen, Ziele und Erwartungen, die in dieser Rolle ausgearbeitet werden müssen?

3. Kommt zusammen und spielt eine Szene spontan vor! Schreibt alle guten Ideen auf, die während der Improvisation vorkommen! Denkt auch an die körperlichen Bewegungen, die die einzelnen Darsteller auf der Bühne ausführen sollen!

B. Ausführen

Verwendet eure Ideen von der Improvisation und den ausgearbeiteten Rollen, und schreibt zusammen die Szene! Achtet darauf, dass die Rollen glaubhaft sind! Sie sollen schon in der geschriebenen Form einen lebendigen Charakter erhalten.

C. Überarbeiten

1. Spielt eure Szene als Gruppe unter euch vor! Denkt an die Rollen der anderen, und gebt einander konstruktive Kritik!

2. Tauscht eure Rollen aus, damit ihr eine andere Perspektive gewinnt! Versteht ihr die Rollen der anderen? Müsst ihr irgendwelche Regie- oder Bühnenanweisungen hinzufügen, damit die anderen die Rollen überzeugend spielen können?

3. Verbessert die Szene, indem ihr eine neue Version schreibt! Spielt sie danach vor, und verbessert sie noch einmal, bis ihr alle damit zufrieden seid!

4. Lest eure Szene zusammen laut vor! Habt ihr alles richtig geschrieben?

5. Schreibt die endgültige Version der Szene auf!

Mehr Grammatikübungen

Answers

Erste Stufe

Objectives Expressing determination or indecision; talking about whether something is important or not important

1 Du fragst verschiedene Freunde nach ihren Zukunftsplänen, und sie sagen dir, was sie beschlossen haben. Ergänze (*complete*) die folgenden Sätze mit der Information, die in den Fragen gegeben ist! Gebrauche Infinitivsätze! (**Seite 300**)

1. Was hast du beschlossen? Willst du an der Universität von Hamburg studieren? — Ja, ich _____ .   *hab beschlossen, an der U. von H. zu studieren*

2. Wozu hast du dich entschieden? Willst du eine Lehre machen? — Ja, ich _____ .   *hab mich entschieden, eine Lehre zu machen*

3. Was hast du beschlossen? Willst du dir zuerst einen Job suchen? — Ja, ich _____ .   *hab beschlossen, mir zuerst einen Job zu suchen*

4. Wozu hast du dich entschieden? Willst du erst einmal Ferien machen? — Ja, ich _____ .   *hab mich entschieden, erst einmal F. zu machen*

5. Was hast du beschlossen? Willst du den Wehrdienst machen? — Ja, ich _____ .   *hab beschlossen, den Wehrdienst zu machen*

6. Wozu hast du dich entschieden? Willst du mit dem Studium anfangen? — Ja, ich _____ .   *hab mich entschieden, mit dem S. anzufangen*

7. Was hast du beschlossen? Willst du dich auf eine Karriere vorbereiten? — Ja, ich _____ .   *hab beschlossen, mich auf eine K. vorzubereiten*

2 Du hast dich noch nicht entschieden, was du machen willst. Deshalb kannst du deinen Freunden noch keine Antworten auf ihre Fragen geben. Schreib die folgenden Sätze ab, und schreib dabei die direkte Frage als indirekte Frage! (**Seite 300**)

1. Was wirst du studieren?   Ich kann noch nicht sagen, _____ .   *was ich studieren werde*

2. Wo wirst du studieren?   Ich weiß noch nicht, _____ .   *wo ich studieren werde*

3. Wofür hast du Interesse?   Ich muss mir überlegen, _____ .   *wofür ich Interesse habe*

4. Wirst du im Ausland studieren?   Ich kann noch nicht sagen, _____ .   *ob ich im A. studieren werde*

5. Musst du im Herbst anfangen?   Ich weiß noch nicht, _____ .   *ob ich im H. anfangen muss*

6. Kannst du im Ausland arbeiten?   Ich weiß nicht, _____ .   *ob ich im A. arbeiten kann*

3 Rosalyn hat Pläne für die Zukunft. Schreib die folgenden Sätze ab und schreib dabei den richtigen Ausdruck aus dem Kasten in die Lücken. (**Seite 300**)

kommt	entschlossen	überlegen
entscheidend	beschlossen	entschieden

1. Ich hab _____ , einen guten Schulabschluss zu haben.   beschlossen
2. Ich hab mich _____ , zuerst einmal einen Computerkurs mitzumachen.   entschieden
3. Ich bin auch fest _____ , im nächsten Jahr auf die Uni zu gehen.   entschlossen
4. Ich muss mir aber zuerst _____ , was für ein Fach ich studieren sollte.   überlegen
5. Es _____ aber auch sehr darauf an, wie viel Geld das Studium kostet.   kommt
6. Also, _____ für mich ist, dass ich einmal einen guten Job finde.   entscheidend

4 Du sprichst darüber, was dir im Leben wichtig ist. Vervollständige die folgenden Sätze, indem du in die erste Lücke ein "**da**-compound" schreibst, und in die zweite Lücke einen Infinitivsatz! Verwende dabei die Information in Klammern! (**Seite 303**)

1. Ich lege großen Wert auf ein gutes Abitur. (ein gutes Abitur machen) — Ich lege großen Wert _____ , _____ .   darauf; ein gutes Abitur zu machen
2. Ich bin an einem guten Job interessiert. (einen guten Job haben) — Ich bin interessiert _____ , _____ .   daran; einen guten Job zu haben
3. Ich lege großen Wert auf einen guten Schulabschluss. (einen guten Schulabschluss haben) — Ich lege großen Wert _____ , _____ .   darauf; einen guten Schulabschluss zu haben
4. Ich bin an einer guten Karriere interessiert. (eine gute Karriere zu machen) — Ich bin interessiert _____ , _____ .   daran; eine gute Karriere zu machen
5. Ich lege großen Wert auf einen sicheren Arbeitsplatz. (eine sicheren Arbeitsplatz haben) — Ich lege großen Wert _____ , _____ .   darauf; einen sicheren Arbeitsplatz zu haben
6. Ich bin am Zivildienst interessiert. (den Zivildienst machen) — Ich bin interessiert _____ , _____ .   daran; den Zivildienst zu machen

Mehr Grammatikübungen

Answers

WK3 DRESDEN-11

Zweite Stufe

Objectives Expressing wishes; expressing certainty and refusing or accepting with certainty; talking about goals for the future; expressing relief

5 Du drückst deine Wünsche für eine ideale Welt aus. Ergänze die folgenden Sätze, indem du in den Lücken die Konjunktivform von **es gibt** und die Information in Klammern verwendest! (**Seite 309**)

1. (kein Krieg)   In meiner idealen Welt _____ .   gäbe es keinen Krieg
2. (kein Hunger)   In meiner idealen Welt _____ .   gäbe es keinen Hunger
3. (keine Konflikte)   In meiner idealen Welt _____ .   gäbe es keine Konflikte
4. (keine Armut)   In meiner idealen Welt _____ .   gäbe es keine Armut
5. (kein Streit)   In meiner idealen Welt _____ .   gäbe es keinen Streit
6. (keine Angst vor der Zukunft)   In meiner idealen Welt _____ .   gäbe es keine A. v. d. Z.

6 Du drückst deine Wünsche für die Zukunft aus, und ein Freund versichert (*assures*) dir, dass deine Ziele in Erfüllung gehen werden. Schreib die folgenden Sätze ab, und schreib dabei die Zukunftsform (*future*) der gegebenen Verben in die Lücken! (**Seite 310**)

1. Hoffentlich schaffe ich das Abitur. — Ja, du _____ das Abitur bestimmt _____ .   wirst; schaffen
2. Hoffentlich bekomme ich einen Job. — Du _____ bestimmt einen Job _____ .   wirst; bekommen
3. Hoffentlich kann ich studieren. — Ja, du _____ bestimmt _____ _____ .   wirst; studieren; können
4. Hoffentlich habe ich eine Familie. — Ja, du _____ bestimmt eine Familie _____ .   wirst; haben
5. Hoffentlich kann ich viel reisen. — Du _____ bestimmt viel _____ _____ .   wirst; reisen; können
6. Hoffentlich habe ich kein Pech. — Du _____ bestimmt kein Pech _____ .   wirst; haben

7 Was für Wünsche hast du? Sie dir die Rangliste an und schreib sechs Sätze, die deine Hoffnung für die Zukunft ausdrücken. Fang jeden Satz mit „Ich möchte einmal" an. (**Seite 311**)

BEISPIEL   **Ich möchte einmal einen sicheren Arbeitsplatz haben.**

Wenn du an deine Zukunft denkst, welche Ziele hast du da? Rangliste		
	Mädchen	Jungen
sicheren Arbeitsplatz	2	2
gutes Einkommen	1	5
gesund leben	5	1
Partnerschaft	4	3
anderen Menschen helfen	6	4
schönes Haus haben	3	7
politisch aktiv sein	7	6

1. _____ .   ein gutes Einkommen haben
2. _____ .   gesund leben
3. _____ .   eine gute Partnerschaft haben
4. _____ .   anderen Menschen helfen
5. _____ .   ein schönes Haus haben
6. _____ .   politisch aktiv sein

318 *dreihundertachtzehn*   KAPITEL 11   **Deine Welt ist deine Sache!**

8 Du sprichst über deine Zukunft, und du sagst, was du mit dreißig Jahren alles getan haben wirst. Schreib die folgenden Sätze ab, und schreib dabei eine Form von **werden** und den Infinitiv des Perfekts der gegebenen Verben in die Lücken! (**Seite 311**)

1. (mein Studium abschließen)   Mit dreißig _____ .   werde ich mein S. abgeschlossen haben
2. (einen guten Job finden)   Mit dreißig _____ .   werde ich einen guten Job gefunden haben
3. (schon viel Geld verdienen)   Mit dreißig _____ .   werde ich schon viel Geld verdient haben
4. (schon um die Welt reisen)   Mit dreißig _____ .   werde ich schon um die Welt gereist sein
5. (viel von der Welt sehen)   Mit dreißig _____ .   werde ich schon viel von der W. gesehen haben
6. (schon viel erleben)   Mit dreißig _____ .   werde ich schon viel erlebt haben

9 Du drückst deine Erleichterung (*relief*) aus. Du sagst, dass du froh bist, schon viele Ziele in deinem Leben erreicht zu haben. Schreib die folgenden Sätze ab, und schreib dabei das Perfekt der gegebenen Information in die Lücken! (**Seite 311**)

1. (das Studium beginnen)   Ich bin froh, dass _____ .   ich das Studium begonnen habe
2. (sich ein Auto kaufen)   Ein Glück, dass _____ .   ich mir ein Auto gekauft habe
3. (eine Fachschule besuchen)   Gott sei Dank, dass _____ .   ich eine Fachschule besucht habe
4. (eine Fremdsprache lernen)   Ich bin froh, dass _____ .   ich eine Fremdsprache gelernt habe
5. (schon sehr viel reisen)   Ein Glück, dass _____ .   ich schon sehr viel gereist bin
6. (sich vor der Prüfung ausruhen)   Ich bin froh, dass _____ .   ich mich vor der P. ausgeruht habe

Anwendung

1 Hör zu, wie einige Schüler sich über ihre Berufswünsche unterhalten! Was möchte jeder werden? Welche Vorteile und welche Nachteile erwähnen die Schüler? Mach dir Notizen!
CD 11 Tr. 17

Script and answers on p. 295l

2 Wenn man einen Beruf wählt, muss man sich die Vorteile und die Nachteile überlegen. Was für den einen ein Vorteil ist, kann für den anderen ein Nachteil sein. Wie würdest du Folgendes einschätzen? Ist das für dich ein Vorteil oder ein Nachteil? Mach zwei Listen, und besprich diese mit deinen Klassenkameraden!

es ist nicht monoton

interessant

harte Arbeit

ein sicherer Arbeitsplatz

man ist draußen in der Natur

vielseitige Arbeit

wenig Geld

viel Urlaub

man kommt mit vielen Leuten zusammen

man muss viele Jahre studieren

schmutzige Arbeit

schwer, eine Stelle zu finden

man arbeitet abends und am Wochenende

ein Beruf mit Zukunft

man lernt viel in diesem Beruf

wenig Urlaub

anderen Menschen helfen

viel reisen

3 Was sind die Berufswünsche der Klassenkameraden? Stellt eine Liste auf! Wer will was werden? Wie viele von euch haben denselben Berufswunsch? Besprecht die Gründe für eure Berufswahl!

4 Klassenprojekt: Eure Schule hat vielleicht ein „Career Center". Dort findet ihr Information über die Ausbildung für alle Berufe. Jeder von euch wählt einen Beruf und sammelt darüber Informationen im „Career Center". Dann berichtet jeder der Klasse darüber — auf Deutsch, natürlich! Ihr müsst Antworten auf Fragen haben, wie: Wie lange dauert die Ausbildung? Wie teuer ist sie? Welche Schulfächer braucht man für diesen Beruf? Hat dieser Beruf eine Zukunft? Wie viel kann man verdienen?

5 Ab und zu wird in einer Zeitung oder Zeitschrift die Frage gestellt: Hat die Familie als soziale Institution eine Zukunft? Was meinst du? Lies den folgenden Fragebogen! Überleg dir die Fragen, bevor du sie beantwortest!

Fragebogen

1. Möchtest du einmal heiraten?

2. Wie viele Kinder möchtest du haben?

3. Wo möchtest du leben?

4. Welchen Beruf möchtest du am liebsten haben?

5. Werden beide Eltern den Beruf ausüben, wenn Kinder kommen?

6. Sollten beide Ehepartner sich die tägliche Hausarbeit teilen?

7. Was findest du in deiner Familie gut? Weniger gut?

8. Findest du, dass deine Eltern Fehler in deiner Erziehung gemacht haben? Welche?

9. Was würdest du als Vater oder Mutter anders machen?

10. Möchtest du später einmal so leben wie deine Eltern?

6 Diskutier über die ausgefüllten Fragebögen mit deinen Klassenkameraden! —Wie sieht es aus? Stellt gemeinsam eine Tabelle auf, und füllt die Ergebnisse der Klassenumfrage ein! Sprecht dann über die Ergebnisse!

7 Nehmen wir an, du willst einmal heiraten! Welche Charakteristika soll dein idealer Lebenspartner haben? Hier sind zwei Listen von Qualifikationen, die dich zu eigenen Wünschen und Vorstellungen anregen sollen. Wie wichtig sind dir zum Beispiel Geld und Statussymbole? — Was wäre für dich bei der Wahl eines Partners ausschlaggebend, und worauf legst du weniger Wert?

attraktiv	humorvoll
sportlich	reich
musikalisch	intelligent
unkompliziert	verständnisvoll
treu	fröhlich
tierlieb	kinderlieb
großzügig	witzig
zuverlässig	phantasievoll

gern reisen   gern lesen   gern kochen

gern tanzen   gern zu Hause bleiben

gern Karten spielen

gern ausgehen   gern ins Kino gehen

8 Schreib einen kurzen Brief an einen Briefpartner oder an eine Briefpartnerin! Berichte zuerst etwas über dich selbst, worauf du im Leben Wert legst und was für dich nicht so wichtig ist, und schreib dann, was du von deinem Lebenspartner erwartest!

9  **R o l l e n s p i e l**

Du bist Personalchef in einer Firma, und du interviewst einen Bewerber für einen Job.

Sucht euch ein Stellenangebot aus der Zeitung heraus, und bereitet euch auf das Interview vor, indem du einige Fragen dafür schreibst und dein Partner sich einige Dinge ausdenkt, die man bei so einer Situation vielleicht sagen müsste! Spielt dann das Interview!

Kann ich's wirklich?

WK3 DRESDEN-11

Can you express determination or indecision? (p. 300)

1 How would you tell someone that you are determined to
  a. study at a university?   a. E.g.: Ich hab beschlossen, an einer Universität zu studieren.
  b. have an interesting profession?   b. E.g.: Ich bin fest entschlossen, einen interessanten Beruf zu haben.

2 How would you say that you're undecided about the following things you might do after graduation?
  a. E.g. Ich weiß nicht, ob ich nach dem Schulabschluss erst einmal Ferien machen soll.
  a. **erst einmal Ferien machen**
  b. **im Ausland studieren**   b. Ich hab mich noch nicht entschieden, ob ich nach dem Schulabschluss im Ausland studieren soll.

Can you talk about whether something is important or not important? (p. 303)

3 How would you respond if a friend asked you what is important to you?
E.g.: Ich lege großen Wert darauf, dass ich einen guten Schulabschluss mache.

4 How would you express that something is of no importance to you?
E.g.: Es ist nicht entscheidend für mich, dass ich modische Klamotten habe.

Can you express wishes? (p. 309)

5 How would you respond if someone asked you what your ideal world would be like?   E.g.: In meiner idealen Welt gäbe es keine Umweltverschmutzung.

Can you express certainty and refuse or accept with certainty? (p. 309)

6 How would you mention two things you are certain about?
E.g.: Es steht fest, dass ich nächsten Monat meinen Führerschein mache. Es ist sicher, dass ich einen Studienplatz in Boston bekomme.

7 How would you tell someone that you absolutely refuse to take drugs (**Drogen**)?   E.g.: Ich nehme auf keinen Fall Drogen!

8 How would you tell a friend that you certainly accept his or her invitation to see a movie?   E.g.: Ja, natürlich!; Ganz bestimmt!

Can you talk about goals for the future? (p. 310)

9 How would you respond if someone asked you what your plans for the future are, and how you envision your life at age 30?
E.g.: In der Zukunft werde ich eine Weltreise machen. Mit dreißig möchte ich eine eigene Firma haben.

Can you express relief? (p. 311)

10 How would you tell a friend you're relieved about the following things?
  a. **Es gibt keinen Ost-West Konflikt.**
  b. **Wir haben heute in Mathe keine Klassenarbeit.**
  a. E.g.: Gut, dass es keinen Ost-West Konflikt gibt.
  b. E.g.: Ein Glück, dass wir heute in Mathe keine Klassenarbeit haben.

KAPITEL 11   Deine Welt ist deine Sache!

Expressing determination

Ich hab beschlossen, …	I've decided …
Ich hab mich entschieden, …	I have decided …
Ich bin fest entschlossen, …	I am determined …

Expressing indecision

Ich hab mich noch nicht entschieden, was/ob …	I haven't decided yet what/ whether …
Ich muss mir das überlegen.	I have to consider that.

Talking about whether something is important

Ich lege großen Wert darauf, …	I place great emphasis on …
Ich bin interessiert daran, …	I am interested in …
Für mich spielt die größte Rolle, dass …	What counts most for me is …
Mir ist wichtig, dass …	Important to me is that …

Entscheidend für mich ist, …	Decisive for me is …
Für mich ist es auch am wichtigsten, …	For me it's also most important …
Ausschlaggebend ist für mich, dass …	The determining factor for me is that …

Professions

der Beruf, -e	profession
Biologe/Biologin, -n/nen	biologist
die Kauffrau, -en	businesswoman
Musiker(in), -/nen	musician
Tierarzt, -ärztin	veterinarian

Other words

die Fachschule, -n	vocational school
die Lehre, -n	apprenticeship
das Arbeitsamt, ¨er	employment office
die Erfahrung, -en	experience
die Tätigkeit, -en	occupation
die Karriere, -n	career

die Zukunft	future
Jura	(study of) law
die Wissenschaft, -en	science
die Mentalität	mentality
die Möglichkeit, -en	possibility
der Grund, ¨e	reason
die Sprache, -n	language
der Schulabschluss, ¨e	diploma
anfangen (sep)	to begin
angeben (sep)	to indicate
s. ausruhen (sep)	to rest
ausüben (sep)	to practice (a profession)
beruhen auf (sep)	to be based on
s. erkundigen nach	to inquire about
jobben	to have a job
nötig haben	to require
s. vorbereiten (sep) auf (acc)	to prepare for
angewiesen sein auf (acc)	to be dependent on
fertig	finished

Zweite Stufe

Expressing wishes

Viele Freunde haben, wäre mir wichtig.	To have many friends would be important to me.
In meiner idealen Welt gäbe es nur Frieden.	In my ideal world there would only be peace.

Refusing or accepting with certainty

Kommt nicht in Frage!	It's out of the question!
Auf keinen Fall!	No chance!
Auf jeden Fall.	In any case.
Auf alle Fälle.	By all means.
Ganz bestimmt.	Certainly.

Expressing certainty

Es steht fest, …	It's definite …
Ich möchte unbedingt …	I certainly would like …

Talking about goals for the future

Mit dreißig möchte ich … gemacht haben.	At thirty I would like to have done …

Expressing relief

Gott sei Dank, …	Thank God!
Ein Glück, dass …	Lucky that …
Zum Glück …	Luckily …

Other words

die Versicherung, -en	insurance company
der Bankkaufmann, –leute	banker
der Bundestag	German Federal Parliament
der Ostblock	Eastern Bloc
der Osten	east
der Atomkrieg, -e	nuclear war
die Hoffnung, -en	hope

der Horizont	horizon
die Raumfahrt	space travel
der Traum, ¨e	dream
das Verhältnis, -se	situation
die Weile	while
die Welt, -en	world
das Ziel, -e	goal
klingen	to sound
stehen auf (acc)	to like
vergehen	to pass (time)
zukommen (sep) auf (acc)	to be in store for
dabei sein	to take part
bis (acc)	until
bis dahin	by, until then
vor allem	most of all
geregelt	orderly
vereint	unified
ehemalig-	former

Kapitel 12: Die Zukunft liegt in deiner Hand! *Review Chapter*

Chapter Overview

Los geht's! pp. 326–327	**Mitgehört, p. 326**

	FUNCTIONS	GRAMMAR	VOCABULARY	RE-ENTRY
Erste Stufe pp. 328–333	• Reporting past events, p. 328 • Expressing surprise and disappointment, p. 329 • Agreeing; agreeing, with reservations; giving advice, p. 329 • Giving advice and giving reasons, p. 331	• Narrative past, p. 328 • The **würde**-forms, p. 329 • Infinitive forms of verbs, p. 331	• Occupations, p. 330	• Chapter 12 is a global review of Chapters 1–11, Level 3.

Weiter geht's! pp. 334–335	**Pläne für die Zukunft, p. 334**

	FUNCTIONS	GRAMMAR	VOCABULARY	RE-ENTRY
Zweite Stufe pp. 336–340	• Expressing determination or indecision, p. 337 • Talking about what is important or not important, p. 338 • Hypothesizing, p. 338	• Direct and indirect object pronouns, p. 338 • Subjunctive, p. 338	• Modern professions, p. 337	• Chapter 12 is a global review of Chapters 1–11, Level 3.

Zum Schreiben p. 341	Eine Selbstbiographie schreiben	**Writing Strategy** Evaluating your writing
Zum Lesen pp. 342–345	Zeitgenössische Literatur	**Reading Strategy** Applying strategies on your own
Mehr Grammatik-übungen	**pp. 346–349** **Erste Stufe**, pp. 346–348	**Zweite Stufe**, pp. 348–349
Review pp. 350–351	**Kann ich's wirklich?**, p. 350	**Wortschatz**, p. 351

CULTURE

- **Kummerkasten**, p. 332
- **Landeskunde: Pauken allein reicht nicht**, p. 333
- **Claudias Pläne für die Zukunft**, p. 336
- **Textbilder**, p. 340

Chapter Resources

PRINT

Lesson Planning
One-Stop Planner
Lesson Planner with Substitute Teacher Lesson Plans, pp. 66–70, 86
Student Make-Up Assignments
- Make-Up Assignment Copying Masters, Chapter 12

Listening and Speaking
Listening Activities
- Student Response Forms for Listening Activities, pp. 91–94
- Additional Listening Activities 12-1 to 12-6, pp. 95–98
- Scripts and Answers, pp. 192–199

Video Guide
- Teaching Suggestions, p. 54
- Activity Masters, pp. 55–56
- Scripts and Answers, pp. 72–73, 76

Activities for Communication
- Communicative Activities, pp. 45–48
- Realia and Teaching Suggestions, pp. 106–110
- Situation Cards, pp. 135–136

Reading and Writing
Reading Strategies and Skills Handbook, Chapter 12
Lies mit mir! 3, Chapter 12
Übungsheft, pp. 144–156

Grammar
Grammatikheft, pp. 100–108
Grammar Tutor for Students of German, Chapter 12

Assessment
Testing Program
- Grammar and Vocabulary Quizzes, **Stufe** Quizzes, and Chapter Test, pp. 257–270
- Score Sheet, Scripts and Answers, pp. 271–277
- Final Exam, pp. 279–286
- Final Exam Score Sheets, Scripts and Answers, pp. 287–292

Alternative Assessment Guide
- Portfolio Assessment, p. 27
- Performance Assessment, p. 41

Student Make-Up Assignments
- Alternative Quizzes, Chapter 12

MEDIA

Online Activities
- **Interaktive Spiele**
- **Internet Aktivitäten**

Video Program
- Videocassette 2

Audio Compact Discs
- Textbook Listening Activities, CD 12, Tracks 1–21
- Additional Listening Activities, CD 12, Tracks 29–34
- Assessment Items, CD 12, Tracks 22–28

Teaching Transparencies
- Situations 12-1 to 12-2
- **Mehr Grammatikübungen** Answers
- **Grammatikheft** Answers

One-Stop Planner CD-ROM

Use the **One-Stop Planner CD-ROM with Test Generator** to aid in lesson planning and pacing.
For each chapter, the **One-Stop Planner** includes:
- Editable lesson plans with direct links to teaching resources
- Printable worksheets from resource books
- Direct launches to the HRW Internet activities
- Video and audio segments
- Test Generator
- Clip Art for vocabulary items

Projects

Unsere Sprache

Students will design and describe their own original games to review specific German language-related concepts.

> **MATERIALS**
> ✄ **Students may need**
> - posterboard
> - scissors
> - their textbooks, or dictionaries
> - glue or masking tape
> - markers

OUTLINE

This project should be started as soon as you begin Chapter 12. Students can work in pairs or individually.

The game should include:
- a title,
- simple procedure written in German, and
- a sample of what the game looks like.

SUGGESTED SEQUENCE

1. Before students begin working on an original game, have them look through their German book(s) to identify a theme. (Examples: vocabulary, grammar point)

2. Once students have decided on what they plan to address in their game, they should think of a creative way to review these materials.

3. Once the game has been designed, students should write directions, including an answer key if necessary.

4. Students test their game by explaining it to their classmates and then playing it in class.

> **GRADING THE PROJECT**
> Suggested point distribution (**total = 100 points**)
> Originality of the game.........................25
> Completion of assignment
>   requirements....................................25
> Correct language usage in directions ...25
> Oral presentation of the game.............25

Games

Zeichenspiel

Play this game to review the profession vocabulary from this chapter.

Preparation Make a list of the vocabulary you would like to review.

Procedure Divide the class into two teams and set up an overhead projector in front of the class. Have a member from Team A come to the overhead projector. Point to one of the professions on your list and give the signal to the student to make a drawing that represents the profession. While the student is sketching on the transparency, both teams try to guess the name of the profession. The first team that correctly identifies the profession gets a point. Teams alternate drawing on the transparency. The team with the most points wins.

Storytelling

Mini-Geschichte

*This story accompanies Teaching Transparency 12-2. The **Mini-Geschichte** can be told and retold in different formats, acted out, written down, and read aloud to give students additional opportunities to practice all four skills.*

Guter Rat ist teuer

Ich möchte gern PR-Beraterin werden. Ich möchte Sängerinnen und Schauspielerinnen über ihr Image beraten. Ich würde ihnen sagen, wann und wie eine Ehe oder Scheidung ihren beruflichen Erfolg beeinflusst. Ich würde ihnen erklären, wie sie um die Gunst der Leute werben (*to woo*) müssen. Ich würde ihnen sagen, welche Kleider sie anziehen sollen, damit sie gut aussehen. Ich würde dann für eine Arbeit bezahlt werden, die ich jetzt ohne Bezahlung mache, denn meine Freundinnen fragen mich ständig, was sie zu dieser oder jener Fete anziehen sollen oder was sie in Herzensangelegenheiten machen sollen.

Traditions ·······························

Dresden, Stadt an der Elbe

Es gibt in Deutschland etwa 100.000 Sorben (Serby, Serba). Dieser elbslawische Volksstamm, der hauptsächlich in den Bezirken Cottbus und Dresden lebt, hat über 1000 Jahre seine nationale Eigenheit und Kultur erhalten. Die Sorben haben auch ihre eigene westslawische Sprache. „Dresden" kommt von dem altsorbischen Wort „dresd'ane" (*forest people*). Um 1700 entwickelten die Sorben sogar ihre eigene Schriftsprache.

Die Sorben wurden von ihren deutschen Nachbarn immer wieder bedrängt ihre Identität aufzugeben. Von den Nationalsozialisten wurden sie brutal unter-drückt und durften ihre Sprache nicht mehr sprechen. Die Kulturpolitik der DDR beschützte die Sorben mit dem sogenannten Sorbengesetz. Heute wird an über 50 Schulen die sorbische Muttersprache gelehrt.

Vor allem die katholischen Sorben haben viele alte Bräuche lebendig gehalten. Tausende von Besuchern kommen jährlich, um die Osterreiter zu sehen, die auf kostbar geschmückten Pferden betend über die Felder reiten.

Dresdner Eierschecke

Zutaten

g=Mehl l=Milch, EL=Esslöffel

Teig		*Eieraufguss*	
500 g	Mehl	125 g	Butter
1	Packet Trockenhefe	6-8	Eier
80 g	Zucker	125 g	Zucker
1/4 l	Buttermilch	125 g	Rosinen
100 g	Butter	1 El	Mehl

Füllung	
1500 g	Quark
3	Eier
100 g	Zucker
Zitronensaft	

Zubereitung

Das Mehl mit der Trockenhefe mischen und die Butter schmelzen. Zu dem geschmolzenen Fett die Buttermilch und den Zucker geben. Die Mischung darf nur lauwarm sein. Unter ständigem Rühren langsam das Gemisch dem Mehl zugeben und den Teig kneten, bis er sich vom Rand der Schüssel löst. Den Teig etwa 30 Minuten warm stellen und gehen lassen, bis er sich verdoppelt hat. Danach den Teig ca. 2-3 Minuten kräftig durchkneten, auf einem gefetteten Backblech gleichmäßig ausrollen und noch einmal etwa 15 Minuten gehen lassen.

Für die Füllung den Quark mit den Eiern und dem Zucker schaumig rühren, mit etwas Zitronensaft abschmecken und diese Masse gleichmäßig dick auf den Hefeteig streichen.

Für den Eierguss die Eier trennen, die Butter mit dem Eigelb und dem Zucker gut schaumig rühren und das Eiweiß mit einer Prise Salz zu steifem Schnee schlagen. Den Eischnee mit dem Mehl unter die Butter-Eier Mischung heben und diese Masse wiederum gleichmässig auf die Quarkmasse verteilen. Die Eierschecke mit den Rosinen bestreuen und bei etwa 175 Grad Celsius etwa 40-50 Minuten im Backofen goldgelb backen.

Technology

One-Stop Planner CD-ROM

To preview all resources available for this chapter, use the **One-Stop Planner CD-ROM**, Disc 3.

Internet Connection

ADRESSE: go.hrw.com
KENNWORT: WK3 DRESDEN-12

*Have students explore the **go.hrw.com** Web site for many online resources covering all chapters. All Chapter 12 resources are available under the keyword **WK3 Dresden-12.** Interactive games help students practice the material and provide them with immediate feedback. You will also find a printable worksheet that provides Internet activities that lead to a comprehensive online research project.*

Interaktive Spiele

You can use the interactive activities in this chapter

- to practice grammar, vocabulary, and chapter functions
- as homework
- as an assessment option
- as a self-test
- to prepare for the Chapter Test

Internet Aktivitäten

Students describe three professions and write a newspaper ad seeking an apprenticeship.

- To prepare students for the **Arbeitsblatt,** have them study **So sagt man das!, Hypothesizing,** p. 338, and do Activity 24, p. 339.
- After completing the **Arbeitsblatt,** have students write a job announcement (at least 50 words) for one of the professions listed in **Aktivität B.**

Webprojekt

Have students research the likes and dislikes of youths in a German-speaking country. (You may want to direct students to the site of the **Shell-Studie 2000** or the **Deutsche Jugendinstitut.**) Students should report on their research and support their findings with graphs, tables, or diagrams. Encourage students to exchange useful Web sites with their classmates. Have students document their sources by referencing the names and URLs of all the sites they consulted.

Textbook Listening Activities Scripts

The following scripts are for the listening activities found in the *Pupil's Edition*. For Student Response Forms, see *Listening Activities*, pages 91–94. To provide students with additional listening practice, see *Listening Activities*, pages 95–98.

Erste Stufe

3 p. 328

ARTHUR	Hallo, Sabine! Ich habe dich ja schon lange nicht mehr gesehen. Wo hast du denn gesteckt?
SABINE	Du, Arthur, ich bin erst vor kurzem aus Frankreich zurückgekommen.
ARTHUR	Hast du Urlaub gemacht?
SABINE	Nein, ich habe an einem Austauschprogramm teilgenommen. Ich war sechs Monate lang an der Sorbonne in Paris.
ARTHUR	Mensch, Sabine! Das hört sich ja toll an. Erzähl doch mal!
SABINE	Na ja, es war schon super. Ich habe 'ne Menge gelernt. Und mein Französisch hat sich enorm verbessert, sag ich dir! Vor einem halben Jahr hatte ich noch richtige Hemmungen, Französisch zu sprechen. Aber du hättest mich mal in Paris hören sollen!
ARTHUR	Das glaub ich dir gern. Hast du auch nette Leute kennen gelernt?
SABINE	Ja, und stell dir vor, verliebt hab ich mich auch in einen Franzosen. Jean-Luc heißt er. Ich bin richtig traurig, dass ich wieder hier bin. Ich war so glücklich in Frankreich.
ARTHUR	Ja, das kann ich verstehen. Schau mal! Da kommt Markus. Aber … was ist denn bloß mit ihm los? Er geht auf Krücken … hallo, Markus!
MARKUS	Ach, hallo, ihr beiden!
SABINE	Was ist denn mit deinem Bein los, Markus?
MARKUS	Tja, ich hatte vor einem halben Jahr einen Autounfall und bin ziemlich schwer verletzt worden. Drei Monate lang war ich im Krankenhaus.
ARTHUR	Und wie geht's dir jetzt? Wird dein Bein wieder ganz gesund?
MARKUS	Tja, das wissen die Ärzte noch nicht so genau. Ich mache nun schon seit drei Monaten Krankengymnastik, aber das Bein ist immer noch nicht ganz beweglich.
SABINE	Ach, das tut mir Leid, Markus. Ich hoffe, dass du bald Erfolg mit deiner Therapie hast.
MARKUS	Ja, das hoffe ich auch. Und was ist bei euch so los? Seit unserer Abiturfeier haben wir uns ja gar nicht mehr gesehen.
ARTHUR	Tja, ich hab direkt nach dem Abitur angefangen zu jobben. Ich wollte mir so schnell wie möglich ein

Motorrad kaufen und hatte auch schon die Hälfte des Geldes fürs Motorrad gespart.

MARKUS	Und, was ist dir dazwischengekommen?
ARTHUR	Tja, leider ist mir der Bund dazwischengekommen. Ich musste den Job aufgeben. Das Motorrad kann ich erst mal vergessen. Seit einem halben Jahr bin ich nun schon beim Bund. Echt langweilig, sag ich euch! Hoffentlich bekomme ich nach meiner Dienstzeit den Superjob in der Computerfirma wieder, den ich aufgeben musste.

Answers to Activity 3
Sabine: hat ein Austauschprogramm in Frankreich gemacht; hat sich in Französisch verbessert; hat sich in einen Franzosen verliebt; ist traurig, wieder in Deutschland zu sein.
Markus: hatte einen Autounfall; kann sein Bein kaum bewegen.
Arthur: hat gejobbt, um sich ein Motorrad kaufen zu können; musste den Job aufgeben, weil er zur Bundeswehr musste.
Answers will vary.

8 p. 329

SANDRA	Gregor, du siehst richtig deprimiert aus. Was ist denn los?
GREGOR	Ach, nichts, womit ihr mir helfen könntet.
BIRGIT	Na, komm schon! Wozu sind denn Freunde da?
SANDRA	Genau! Birgit hat Recht. Komm, erzähl schon!
MARKUS	Also, gut! Wenn ihr's unbedingt wissen wollt! Claudia und ich, wir hatten Streit. Ich glaub, es ist aus zwischen uns!
SANDRA	Ach, ich hätte nicht geglaubt, dass ihr euch streitet. Claudia ist doch so nett. Was war denn los?
GREGOR	Also, ich glaube, dass sie die Leute aus meiner Clique nicht mag. Sie hat sich beklagt, dass ich zu viel Zeit mit der Clique verbringe. Ich war wirklich überrascht, dass sie so etwas gesagt hat. Ich habe gedacht, dass sie gern mit den Leuten aus meiner Clique zusammen ist.
SANDRA	Ach, Gregor! Ich glaube nicht, dass sie deine Freunde nicht leiden kann. Sie will bestimmt, daß du mehr Zeit mit ihr verbringst. Vielleicht kannst du mal etwas mehr Zeit mit ihr und ihrer Clique verbringen. Du wirst sehen, dann gibt es keinen Streit mehr zwischen euch.
GREGOR	Hmm, ich weiß nicht. Also, ich bin enttäuscht von Claudia. Ich glaube nicht, dass wir uns so schnell wieder vertragen.
BIRGIT	Ach, Gregor! Nun lass den Kopf nicht hängen! Andere Leute haben auch Probleme. Da bist du nicht der Einzige!
SANDRA	So? Hast du etwa auch Streit mit jemandem, Birgit?
BIRGIT	Nein, eigentlich nicht. Ich habe Probleme mit Frau Wagner, meiner Deutschlehrerin. Sie mag meine Kommentare im Unterricht nicht. Ich glaube, sie findet, dass ich zu kritisch bin.
SANDRA	Zu kritisch? Das gibt's doch gar nicht. Ich find's gut, wenn jemand mal eine andere Meinung äußert und nicht immer alles akzeptiert, was so gesagt wird.
BIRGIT	Tja, sag das mal Frau Wagner! Ich finde es schade, dass sie nicht versteht, dass ich ihren Unterricht

eigentlich ganz toll finde, mich aber kritisch mit der Thematik auseinandersetze. Ich befürchte, dass ich dieses Jahr eine schlechte Note in Deutsch bekomme.

GREGOR Hast du schon mal mit Frau Wagner darüber gesprochen?

BIRGIT Nein, eigentlich nicht! Ich habe einfach nur das Gefühl, dass sie meine Art nicht mag.

GREGOR Hm. Also, ich würde sagen, du gehst mal nach dem Unterricht zu ihr hin und redest mit ihr. Wenn du ihr ehrlich sagst, dass du ihren Unterricht magst und es toll findest, dass die Schüler im Unterricht offen ihre Meinung sagen dürfen, dann wird sie sich bestimmt nicht mehr durch deine kritischen Kommentare gestört fühlen.

BIRGIT Ja, vielleicht sollte ich wirklich mal mit ihr reden. Danke für deinen Rat, Gregor.

Answers to Activity 8
Gregor: hat Streit mit seiner Freundin / soll mehr Zeit mit ihr verbringen
Birgit: hat Probleme mit ihrer Deutschlehrerin / soll mit der Lehrerin darüber sprechen

11   p. 331

HANNES He, Stefan und Nicole, habt ihr Lust, mit zum Imbissstand zu kommen? Ich will mir was zu essen holen.

STEFAN Nee du, ich hab keinen Hunger.

NICOLE Ach, komm doch, Stefan! Wir holen uns 'ne Kleinigkeit.

HANNES Ja, genau! Was ist denn mit dir los? Sonst hast du doch immer so einen Bärenhunger in der großen Pause.

STEFAN Tja, weißt du, Hannes, ich will ein bisschen abnehmen. Ich fühle mich in letzter Zeit so schlapp und ohne Energie. Ich glaube, ich esse zu viele ungesunde Sachen.

HANNES Hm. Ja, also wenn du wirklich mit Erfolg abnehmen willst, dann solltest du auf jeden Fall Sport machen. An deiner Stelle würde ich jeden Tag joggen gehen. Du wirst dich bestimmt dann auch viel fitter fühlen.

STEFAN Sport … also, ich weiß nicht. Ich versuche lieber, weniger zu essen.

NICOLE Mensch, pass mal auf, Stefan! Damit erreichst du gar nichts! Du bekommst nur schlechte Laune, wenn du ständig Hungergefühle hast. Ich finde, du solltest lieber deine Ernährung ändern als weniger zu essen.

STEFAN Und was soll ich deiner Meinung nach tun?

NICOLE Also, du solltest viel Obst und Gemüse essen, viel Wasser trinken und zwischendurch nur fettreduzierte oder fettfreie Snacks zu dir nehmen. Einen Joghurt, zum Beispiel.

STEFAN Okay! Ich probiere es gleich aus. Also, kommt, lasst uns zum Imbissstand gehen! Ich hole mir einen gemischten Salat.

HANNES Das ist vernünftig! Wenn du was im Bauch hast, kannst du dich auch gleich viel besser auf die Mathearbeit konzentrieren und denkst nicht immer nur ans Essen.

NICOLE Apropos Mathearbeit! Ich hab in der letzten Arbeit wieder nur 'ne Vier bekommen. Dabei hatte ich alle Formeln auswendig gelernt. Ich weiß einfach nicht

mehr, was ich machen soll. In der Arbeit, die wir gleich schreiben, bekomme ich bestimmt auch wieder eine schlechte Note. Ich bewundere dich wirklich, Hannes. Du bist so ein Mathegenie!

HANNES Ach, nun übertreib mal nicht, Nicole! Mathe macht mir einfach Spaß. Weißt du, ich glaube es bringt nichts, wenn man die Matheformeln einfach nur auswendig lernt. Du musst sie auch anwenden können. Versuch doch mal, die Formeln ganz systematisch in einer Aufgabe anzuwenden. Du wirst schon sehen, es ist alles total logisch!

NICOLE Tja. Das sagst du so einfach. Ich versteh die Aufgaben aber nun mal nicht so schnell wie du.

STEFAN An deiner Stelle würde ich Nachhilfeunterricht nehmen. Du musst jemanden finden, der dir die Aufgaben in aller Ruhe erklärt. Du wirst sehen, das hilft bestimmt.

NICOLE Ja, vielleicht hast du Recht, Stefan. Ich häng gleich nach der Pause einen Zettel ans Schwarze Brett.

Answers to Activity 11
Hannes rät Stefan, dass er Sport machen soll, um abzunehmen, damit er sich fitter fühlt.
Nicole rät Stefan, dass er lieber seine Ernährung ändern soll, anstatt gar nichts zu essen, damit er keine Hungergefühle hat.
Hannes rät Nicole, dass sie die Matheformeln systematisch anwenden soll, damit sie die Logik der Aufgaben versteht.
Stefan rät Nicole, dass sie Nachhilfeunterricht nehmen soll, damit sie die Matheaufgaben in Ruhe erklärt bekommt.

Zweite Stufe

20   p. 337

PETRA Du, Katja! Stell dir vor, ich weiß jetzt endlich, was ich studieren werde!

KATJA Na, sag's schon!

PETRA Also, ich hab mich entschieden, Kunst zu studieren. Kunst ist schon immer in der Schule mein Lieblingsfach gewesen.

KATJA Hm. Klingt gut! Du hast ja auch immer gute Noten im Kunstunterricht bekommen. Und was willst du nach dem Studium machen?

PETRA Tja, eigentlich reicht mir das Kunststudium nicht aus. Ich muss mir überlegen, ob ich danach noch zusätzlich eine Ausbildung als graphische Designerin machen soll. Ich glaube, wenn man praktische Erfahrung hat, hat man bessere Chancen auf einen guten Job. Aber ich bin mir noch nicht sicher. Wie sehen denn deine Zukunftspläne aus?

KATJA Ach, weißt du, Petra, ich weiß noch gar nicht so genau, was ich mal machen will. Meine Eltern haben ein Schuhgeschäft in der Innenstadt und möchten, dass ich eine Ausbildung als Schuhverkäuferin mache. Wahrscheinlich wollen sie, dass ich später mal das Geschäft übernehme.

PETRA Hm. Es hört sich so an, als ob du gar nicht so begeistert bist von der Idee.

KATJA Ja, das kann man wohl sagen. Mich interessiert das Schuhgeschäft eben nicht so richtig. Ich bin mir nicht sicher, ob ich wirklich dort arbeiten will. Ach, schau mal! Da kommt Mario.

MARIO Hallo! Was habe ich da gehört? Du interessierst dich nicht fürs Schuhgeschäft? Mensch, wäre ich froh,

wenn meine Eltern ein Geschäft hätten, wo ich ein-
steigen könnte.

KATJA   Was willst du denn nach der Schule machen?

MARIO   Ach, ich will erst mal ein paar Monate bei meinen
Großeltern in Sizilien verbringen.

PETRA   Soso, einfach nur faulenzen willst du!

MARIO   Stimmt nicht! Ich hab da schon eine Idee! Ich hab
nämlich beschlossen, mich in Italien nach
Geschäftskontakten zu erkundigen.

PETRA   Das hört sich ja enorm wichtig an. Was hast du vor?

MARIO   Tja, ich will mir so schnell wie möglich hier ein
kleines eigenes Unternehmen aufbauen. Mir ist es
wichtig, selbständig und unabhängig zu sein.

KATJA   Hm. Was für Geschäftskontakte willst du denn
knüpfen?

MARIO   Tja, ich will italienische Lebensmittel nach
Deutschland importieren, also Pasta, Parma-
schinken, Olivenöl und so. Ich muss in Italien nur
gute Einkaufsquellen finden. Kunden in
Deutschland zu finden, ist kein Problem.

PETRA   Klasse! Ich wünsch dir viel Erfolg mit deiner Idee!

KATJA   Ja, ich dir auch! Wenigstens weißt du schon genau,
wie deine Zukunftspläne aussehen. Ich hab noch
keine Idee!

MARIO   He, Katja! Du kannst meine Geschäftspartnerin
werden!

KATJA   Nee, danke! Da kann ich ja gleich im Schuhgeschäft
meiner Eltern anfangen. Mich interessiert Einkauf
und Verkauf nun mal nicht.

MARIO   Na siehst du! Dann weißt du ja wenigstens, was du
NICHT willst!

Answers to Activity 20
Petra: ist sich sicher, dass sie Kunst studieren will; es ist ihr
Lieblingsfach / ist sich nicht sicher, ob sie eine zusätzliche
Ausbildung machen soll; man hat bessere Jobchancen, wenn man
praktische Erfahrung hat.
Katja: ist sich nicht sicher, ob sie eine Ausbildung als
Schuhverkäuferin machen soll; interessiert sich nicht richtig dafür.
Mario: ist sich sicher, dass er ein eigenes Unternehmen haben will;
will selbständig und unabhängig sein.

23   p. 338

ANDREAS   He, schaut mal! Hier in der Pop-Rocky gibt's ein
Preisausschreiben. Man kann eine Reise nach
Griechenland gewinnen!

HARTMUT   Und was soll man einsenden, Andreas?

ANDREAS   Ganz einfach: Pläne und Wünsche für die Zukunft.
Wer den besten Wunsch oder Plan hat, gewinnt.
Los, kommt, da machen wir mit! Also, Hartmut, du
fängst an!

HARTMUT   Hm. Ich möchte mal gern wissen, wie die entscheiden wollen, welches der beste Wunsch oder Plan ist.

ANDREAS   Ach, ist doch egal! Es macht doch einfach nur Spaß,
überhaupt mitzumachen.

HARTMUT   Also gut! Ich wünsche mir, dass ich mal ein
weltberühmter Opernsänger an der Scala von
Mailand werde. Ich will so berühmt werden wie
Plácido Domingo oder Luciano Pavarotti!

VANESSA   Mensch, Hartmut. Du hast wirklich eine tolle
Stimme. Du solltest mal irgendwo vorsingen, damit
du entdeckt wirst!

HARTMUT   Tja, wenn meine Eltern nicht so dagegen wären,
würde ich wirklich gern eine Gesangsausbildung

One-Stop Planner CD-ROM

For resource information, see the **One-Stop
Planner CD-ROM**, Disc 3.

machen. Aber leider meinen sie, ich sollte lieber was
„Vernünftiges" lernen.

ANDREAS   Tja, typisch Eltern! Was sind denn deine
Zukunftspläne, Vanessa?

VANESSA   Also, ich wünsche mir, eines Tages in Afrika zu
leben. Ich möchte gern dort Entwicklungshilfe leisten. Wenn ich viel Geld hätte, würde ich ein
Kinderhilfswerk gründen. Mir ist wichtig, Leuten,
besonders Kindern, zu helfen. Ich lege keinen Wert
auf ein großes Haus, ein teures Auto, schicke
Klamotten und Schmuck oder so was.

ANDREAS   He, Vanessa, dieser Wunsch passt wirklich sehr gut
zu dir. Du bist fast die Einzige aus unserer Clique,
die sich immer überall freiwillig für eine gute Sache
engagiert. Ich find's toll, dass du so was in deiner
Zukunft machen willst. Hoffentlich geht dein
Wunsch in Erfüllung.

VANESSA   Martina, hast du dir schon einen Zukunftswunsch
überlegt?

MARTINA   Mein Zukunftswunsch ist ganz einfach, dass ich
einen der heiß umkämpften Studienplätze für
Medizin bekomme. Wenn ich in Biologie und
Mathe eine Eins bekommen würde, hätte ich ziemlich gute Chancen.

ANDREAS   Ach, Martina! Dieser Wunsch ist aber nicht sehr
originell! Damit wirst du bestimmt nicht den Preis
nach Griechenland gewinnen.

MARTINA   Ach, weißt du, Andreas, der Preis ist mir eigentlich
ziemlich egal. Für meine Zukunft ist mir wirklich
am wichtigsten, einen Studienplatz in Medizin zu
bekommen, damit ich meinen Traumberuf als
Ärztin verwirklichen kann.

HARTMUT   Jetzt bin ich aber mal gespannt, was dein
Zukunftswunsch ist, Andreas. Lass mal hören!

ANDREAS   Also, ich möchte gern eine große Familie haben.

MARTINA   Waaas? Das ist dein Zukunftswunsch? Eine große
Familie mit vielen Kindern?

ANDREAS   Ja, aber das ist noch nicht alles. Ich möchte am liebsten Kinder adoptieren, für die es so gut wie keine
Zukunft gibt. Zum Beispiel Kinder aus
Krisengebieten wie Bosnien, deren Eltern im Krieg
gestorben sind. Mein Zukunftswunsch ist es, wenigstens ein paar Kindern ein schönes Leben zu
ermöglichen, damit diese Kinder selber mal Pläne
für die Zukunft schmieden können.

Answers to Activity 23
Hartmut: will ein weltberühmter Opernsänger werden.
Vanessa: will in Afrika leben und in der Entwicklungshilfe arbeiten.
Martina: will einen Studienplatz in Medizin bekommen, um Ärztin
zu werden.
Andreas: will eine große Familie haben und Kinder aus
Krisengebieten adoptieren.

Kapitel 12: Die Zukunft liegt in deiner Hand! *Review Chapter*

Suggested Lesson Plans 50-Minute Schedule

Day 1

CHAPTER OPENER 5 min.
- Advance Organizer, ATE, p. 323M
- Teaching Suggestions, ATE, p. 323M

LOS GEHT'S! 20 min.
- Preteaching Vocabulary, ATE, p. 323N
- Teaching Suggestions, ATE, p. 323N
- Play Audio CD for Los geht's!
- Have students read Los geht's!, pp. 326–327
- Do Activities 1 and 2, p. 327

ERSTE STUFE
So sagt man das!, p. 328 20 min.
- Presenting So sagt man das!, ATE, p. 323O
- Play Audio CD for Activity 3, p. 328
- Do Activity 4, p. 328

Wrap-Up 5 min.
- Students respond to questions about what they were doing 6 months ago

Homework Options
Grammatikheft, p. 100, Act. 1
Übungsheft, p. 144, Acts. 1–2

Day 2

ERSTE STUFE
Quick Review 10 min.
- Check homework, Grammatikheft, p. 100, Act. 1

Ein wenig Grammatik, p. 328 20 min.
- Present Ein wenig Grammatik, p. 328
- Do Activity 5, p. 328

So sagt man das!, p. 329 15 min.
- Presenting So sagt man das!, ATE, p. 323O
- Do Activities 6 and 7, p. 329
- Play Audio CD for Activity 8, p. 329
- Do Activity 9, p. 330

Wrap-Up 5 min.
- Students respond to questions eliciting surprise, disappointment, agreement, or disagreement

Homework Options
Grammatikheft, p. 101, Act. 2
Übungsheft, pp. 145–146, Acts. 1–4

Day 3

ERSTE STUFE
Quick Review 10 min.
- Check homework, Grammatikheft, p. 101, Act. 2

Wortschatz, p. 330 10 min.
- Presenting Wortschatz, ATE, p. 323P
- Teaching Transparency 12-1
- Do Activity 10, p. 331
- Play Audio CD for Activity 11, p. 331

So sagt man das!, p. 331 10 min.
- Present So sagt man das!, p. 331
- Do Activity 12, p. 331

Ein wenig Grammatik, p. 331 15 min.
- Present Ein wenig Grammatik, p. 331
- Do Activities 13 and 14, p. 332

Wrap-Up 5 min.
- Students respond to questions about giving advice

Homework Options
Grammatikheft, pp. 103–104, Acts. 4–7
Übungsheft, pp. 147–148, Acts. 5–8

Day 4

ERSTE STUFE
Quick Review 10 min.
- Check homework, Übungsheft, pp. 147–148, Acts. 5–8

LANDESKUNDE 15 min.
- Presenting Landeskunde, ATE, p. 323Q
- Teacher Note, ATE, p. 323Q
- Read Pauken allein reicht nicht, p. 333
- Do Activities A and B, p. 333

WEITER GEHT'S! 15 min.
- Preteaching Vocabulary, ATE, p. 323Q
- Play Audio CD for Weiter geht's!, pp. 334–335
- Do Activities 15 and 16, p. 335

Wrap-Up 5 min.
- Students name professions that interest them

Homework Options
Übungsheft, p. 149, Acts. 1–4; p. 150, Act. 1

Day 5

ERSTE STUFE
Quick Review 10 min.
- Check homework, Übungsheft, p. 149, Acts. 1–4; p. 150, Act. 1

Quiz Review 20 min.
- Do Additional Listening Activities 12-1 and 12-2, pp. 95–96
- Do Activities for Communication 12-1 and 12-2, pp. 45–46
- Do Mehr Grammatikübungen, Erste Stufe

Quiz 20 min.
- Quiz 12-1A or 12-1B

Homework Options
Internet Aktivitäten, see ATE, p. 323E

Day 6

ZWEITE STUFE
Quick Review 10 min.
- Return and review Quiz 12-1
- Bell Work, ATE, p. 323R

Reading Selection, p. 336 20 min.
- Read Claudias Pläne, p. 336
- Do Activity 17, p. 336
- Do Activities 18 and 19, p. 337
- Play Audio CD for Activity 20, p. 337

So sagt man das!, Wortschatz, p. 337 15 min.
- Presenting So sagt man das!, Wortschatz, ATE, p. 323S
- Do Activity 21, p. 337
- Do Activities 1 and 2, p. 151, Übungsheft

Wrap-Up 5 min.
- Students respond to questions about their plans for the future

Homework Options
Grammatikheft, p. 105, Acts. 8–9

One-Stop Planner CD-ROM

For alternative lesson plans by chapter section, to create your own customized plans, or to preview all resources available for this chapter, use the **One-Stop Planner CD-ROM**, Disc 3.

 For additional homework suggestions, see activities accompanied by this symbol throughout the chapter.

Day 7

ZWEITE STUFE

Quick Review 10 min.
- Check homework, Grammatikheft, p. 105, Acts. 8–9

So sagt man das!, p. 338 15 min.
- Presenting **So sagt man das!**, ATE, p. 323S
- Teaching Transparency 12-2
- Do Activity 22, p. 338
- Play Audio CD for Activity 23, p. 338

So sagt man das!, Ein wenig Grammatik, p. 338 20 min.
- Presenting **So sagt man das!**, ATE, p. 323S
- Present **Ein wenig Grammatik,** p. 338
- Do Activities 24–29, p. 339

Wrap-Up 5 min.
- Students respond to questions about what is important and what is not important in their future

Homework Options
Grammatikheft, pp. 106–108, Acts. 10–14
Übungsheft, pp. 152–154, Acts. 3–8

Day 8

ZWEITE STUFE

Quick Review 10 min.
- Check homework, Übungsheft, pp. 152–154, Acts. 3–8

Wohnungsnot der Studenten (Video) 20 min.
- Teaching Suggestions, Video Guide, p. 54
- Do Pre-viewing, Viewing and Post-viewing Activities, p. 55, Video Guide
- Show **Wohnungsnot der Studenten** Video

Quiz Review 15 min.
- Do Communicative Activities 12-3 and 12-4, pp. 47–48
- Do Additional Listening Activities 12-4, 12-5, and 12-6, pp. 97–98

Wrap-Up 5 min.
- Students respond to questions about the video

Homework Options
Mehr Grammatikübungen, Zweite Stufe
Interaktive Spiele, see ATE, p. 323E

Day 9

ZWEITE STUFE

Quick Review 5 min.
- Check homework, **Mehr Grammatikübungen, Zweite Stufe**

Quiz 20 min.
- Quiz 12-2A or 12-2B

ZUM SCHREIBEN 20 min.
- Presenting **Zum Schreiben,** ATE, p. 323U
- Present **Schreibtipp,** p. 341
- Do Activity A, p. 341

Wrap-Up 5 min.
- Students name modern professions

Homework Options
Pupil's Edition, p. 341, Act. B
Activities for Communication, p. 108, Realia 12-3; List claims for this profession that are facts

Day 10

ZWEITE STUFE

Quick Review 10 min.
- Return and review Quiz 12-2
- Check homework, Realia 12-3

ZUM SCHREIBEN 15 min.
- Do Activity C, p. 341

ZUM LESEN 15 min.
- Background Information, ATE, p. 323V
- Present **Lesestrategie,** p. 342
- Do Activities 1–4, pp. 342–343
- Read **Der hellgraue Frühjahrsmantel,** pp. 342–345

Wrap-Up 5 min.
- Students answer questions about the reading selection

Homework Options
Pupil's Edition, pp. 343–344, Acts. 5–11

Day 11

ZWEITE STUFE

Quick Review 10 min.
- Check homework, Pupil's Edition, pp. 343–344, Acts. 5–11

ZUM LESEN 20 min.
- Do Activities 12–14, pp. 344–345

Game 20 min.
- Play game, **Zeichenspiel,** ATE, p. 323C

Wrap-Up 5 min.
- Students respond to questions about advantages and disadvantages of professions guessed in the **Zeichenspiel**

Homework Options
Übungsheft, pp. 155–156, Acts. 1–6
Interaktive Spiele, see ATE, p. 323E

Day 12

REVIEW

Quick Review 10 min.
- Check homework, Übungsheft, pp. 155–156, Acts. 1–6

Kann ich's wirklich?, p. 350 20 min.
- Do Activities 1–10, p. 350

Chapter Review 20 min.
- Review chapter functions, vocabulary, and grammar; choose from **Mehr Grammatikübungen,** Activities for Communication, Listening Activities, or **Interaktive Spiele**
- Review test format and provide sample test items for students

Homework Options
Study for Chapter Test

Assessment

Test, Chapter 12 45 min.
- Administer Chapter 12 Test. Select from Testing Program, Alternative Assessment Guide or Test Generator.

Kapitel 12: Die Zukunft liegt in deiner Hand! *Review Chapter*

Suggested Lesson Plans *90-Minute Schedule*

Block 1

CHAPTER OPENER 5 min.
- Advance Organizer, ATE, p. 323M
- Teaching Suggestion, ATE, p. 323M

LOS GEHT'S! 20 min.
- Preteaching Vocabulary, ATE, p. 323N
- Teaching Suggestions, ATE, p. 323N
- Play Audio CD for Los geht's!
- Have students read Los geht's!, pp. 326–327
- Do Activities 1 and 2, p. 327

ERSTE STUFE
So sagt man das!, p. 328 20 min.
- Presenting So sagt man das!, ATE, p. 323O
- Play Audio CD for Activity 3, p. 328
- Do Activity 4, p. 328

Ein wenig Grammatik, p. 328 20 min.
- Present Ein wenig Grammatik, p. 328
- Do Activity 5, p. 328

So sagt man das!, p. 329 20 min.
- Presenting So sagt man das!, ATE, p. 323O
- Do Activities 6 and 7, p. 329
- Play Audio CD for Activity 8, p. 329
- Do Activity 9, p. 330
- Do Activity 3, p. 102, Grammatikheft

Wrap-Up 5 min.
- Students respond to questions eliciting surprise, disappointment, agreement, or disagreement

Homework Options
Grammatikheft, pp. 100–101, Acts. 1–2
Übungsheft, p. 144, Acts. 1–2; pp. 145–146, Acts. 1–4

Block 2

ERSTE STUFE
Quick Review 10 min.
- Check homework, Grammatikheft, pp. 100–101, Acts. 1–2

Wortschatz, p. 330 10 min.
- Presenting Wortschatz, ATE, p. 323P
- Teaching Transparency 12-1
- Do Activity 10, p. 331
- Play Audio CD for Activity 11, p. 331

So sagt man das!, p. 331 10 min.
- Present So sagt man das!, p. 331
- Do Activity 12, p. 331

Ein wenig Grammatik, p. 331 15 min.
- Present Ein wenig Grammatik, p. 331
- Do Activities 13 and 14, p. 332

LANDESKUNDE 20 min.
- Presenting Landeskunde, ATE, p. 323Q
- Teacher Note, ATE, p. 323Q
- Read Pauken allein reicht nicht, p. 333
- Do Activities A and B, p. 333

WEITER GEHT'S! 20 min.
- Preteaching Vocabulary, ATE, p. 323Q
- Play Audio CD for Weiter geht's!, pp. 334–335
- Do Activities 15 and 16, p. 335

Wrap-Up 5 min.
- Students respond to questions about giving advice

Homework Options
Grammatikheft, pp. 103–104, Acts. 4–7
Übungsheft, pp. 147–148, Acts. 5–8; p. 149, Acts. 1–4; p. 150, Act. 1

Block 3

ERSTE STUFE
Quick Review 10 min.
- Check homework, Grammatikheft, pp. 103–104, Acts. 4–7

Quiz Review 20 min.
- Do Additional Listening Activities 12-1 and 12-2, pp. 95–96
- Do Activities for Communication 12-1 and 12-2, pp. 45–46
- Do Mehr Grammatikübungen, Erste Stufe

Quiz 20 min.
- Quiz 12-1A or 12-1B

ZWEITE STUFE
Reading Selection, p. 336 20 min.
- Read Claudias Pläne, p. 336
- Do Activity 17, p. 336
- Do Activities 18 and 19, p. 337
- Play Audio CD for Activity 20, p. 337

So sagt man das!, Wortschatz, p. 337 15 min.
- Presenting So sagt man das!, Wortschatz, ATE, p. 323S
- Do Activity 21, p. 337
- Do Activities 1 and 2, p. 151, Übungsheft

Wrap-Up 5 min.
- Students respond to questions about their plans for the future

Homework Options
Grammatikheft, p. 105, Acts. 8–9
Internet Aktivitäten, see ATE, p. 323E

One-Stop Planner CD-ROM

For alternative lesson plans by chapter section, to create your own customized plans, or to preview all resources available for this chapter, use the **One-Stop Planner CD-ROM**, Disc 3.

 For additional homework suggestions, see activities accompanied by this symbol throughout the chapter.

Block 4

ZWEITE STUFE
Quick Review 10 min.
- Return and review Quiz 12-1
- Bell Work, ATE, p. 323R
- Check homework, Grammatikheft, p. 105, Acts. 8–9

So sagt man das!, p. 338 20 min.
- Presenting **So sagt man das!**, ATE, p. 323S
- Teaching Transparency 12-2
- Do Activity 22, p. 338
- Play Audio CD for Activity 23, p. 338
- Do Activities 3–4, p. 152, Übungsheft

So sagt man das!, Ein wenig Grammatik, p. 338 20 min.
- Presenting **So sagt man das!**, ATE, p. 323S
- Present **Ein wenig Grammatik**, p. 338
- Do Activities 24–29, p. 339

Wohnungsnot der Studenten (Video) 20 min.
- Teaching Suggestions, Video Guide, p. 54
- Do Pre-viewing, Viewing and Post-viewing Activities, p. 55, Video Guide
- Show **Wohnungsnot der Studenten** Video

Quiz Review 15 min.
- Do Communicative Activities 12-3 and 12-4, pp. 47–48
- Do Additional Listening Activities 12-4, 12-5, and 12-6, pp. 97–98

Homework Options
Grammatikheft, pp. 106–108, Acts. 10–14
Übungsheft, pp. 152–154, Acts. 3–8
Mehr Grammatikübungen, Zweite Stufe
Interaktive Spiele, see ATE, p. 323E

Block 5

ZWEITE STUFE
Quick Review 5 min.
- Check homework, **Mehr Grammatikübungen**

Quiz 20 min.
- Quiz 12-2A or 12-2B

ZUM SCHREIBEN 40 min.
- Teaching Suggestion, ATE, p. 323U
- Present **Schreibtipp**, p. 341
- Do Activities A, B, and C, p. 341

Game 20 min.
- Play game, **Zeichenspiel**, ATE, p. 323C

Wrap-Up 5 min.
- Students respond to questions about advantages and disadvantages of professions guessed in the **Zeichenspiel**

Homework Options
Complete **Zum Schreiben** compositions
Pupil's Edition, pp. 343–345, prepare reading selection
Interaktive Spiele, see ATE, p. 323E

Block 6

ZWEITE STUFE
Quick Review 20 min.
- Return and review Quiz 12-2
- Check homework, **Zum Schreiben** compositions

ZUM LESEN 45 min.
- Background Information, ATE, p. 323V
- Present **Lesestrategie**, p. 342
- Do Activities 1–4, pp. 342–343
- Read **Der hellgraue Frühjahrsmantel**, pp. 342–345
- Do Activities 5–14, pp. 343–345

REVIEW
Kann ich's wirklich?, p. 350 20 min.
- Do **Kann ich's wirklich?** Activities 1–10, p. 26

Wrap-Up 5 min.
- Students respond to questions about the reading selection

Homework Options
Übungsheft, pp. 155–156, Acts. 1–6

Block 7

REVIEW
Quick Review 15 min.
- Check homework, Übungsheft, pp. 155–156, Acts. 1–6

Chapter Review 30 min.
- Review chapter functions, vocabulary, and grammar; choose from **Mehr Grammatikübungen,** Activities for Communication, Listening Activities, or **Interaktive Spiele**
- Review test format and provide sample test items for students

Test, Chapter 12 45 min.
- Administer Chapter 12 Test. Select from Testing Program, Alternative Assessment Guide or Test Generator.

Using the Video

Before you begin the chapter, you may want to preview the *Video Program* and consult the *Video Guide.* Suggestions for integrating the video into each chapter are given in the *Video Guide* and in the chapter interleaf of the *Teacher's Edition.* Activity masters for video selections can be found in the *Video Guide.*

One-Stop Planner CD-ROM

For resource information, see the **One-Stop Planner CD-ROM**, Disc 3.

PAGES 324–325

CHAPTER OPENER

🕐 Pacing Tips

Chapter 12 is a review chapter. **Los geht's!** and the **Erste Stufe** include an extensive review of different topics and functions that are important to young people. A few **Buchstaben-Spiele** appear on p. 331. **Weiter geht's!** and the **Zweite Stufe** center around plans that German teenagers have for the future. Students again review several functions and grammatical concepts. Some examples of **Textbilder** occur on p. 340. The **Zum Lesen** selection is *Der hellgraue Frühjahrsmantel,* which is discussed on p. 323V. The **Zum Schreiben** topic is **Eine Selbstbiographie schreiben.** Because this is a review chapter, there is no **Anwendung,** and the **Wortschatz** is rather short. For Lesson Plans and timing suggestions, see pages 323I–323L.

Meeting the Standards

Communication
- Reporting past events, p. 328
- Expressing surprise and disappointment, p. 329
- Agreeing; agreeing, with reservations, p. 329
- Giving advice and giving reasons, p. 331

Cultures
- Ein wenig Landeskunde, p. 302
- Landeskunde, p. 333

Connections
- History Connection, p. 323T

Comparisons
- Language-to-Language, p. 323U

Communities
- Career Path, p. 323O
- Community Link, p. 323P

Advance Organizer

Ask students what they might be thinking about as they get ready for graduation. (**Worüber macht ihr euch Gedanken, wie ihr euch dem Schulabschluss nähert?**)

Teaching Suggestions

- Ask students if they have any concrete plans for the future. (**Habt ihr schon feste Pläne für eure Zukunft?**)

- Have students think about where they would like to live if they had the choice. (**Wenn ihr die Wahl hättet, wo würdet ihr am liebsten leben? Warum da?**)

Chapter Sequence

LOS GEHT'S!

> **PAGES 326–327**

Los geht's! Summary

In *Mitgehört,* we hear excerpts from conversations of different students discussing a variety of topics. The following learning outcomes listed on p. 325 are modeled in the episode: reporting past events, expressing surprise and disappointment, agreeing, agreeing with reservations, giving advice, and giving reasons.

Preteaching Vocabulary

Activating Prior Knowledge

Have students use their prior knowledge as they read through the text to recall what the words mean. Students should keep a list of words they see that they do not know, and try to guess the meaning of those words through context. After that, have students share any words remaining on their lists, and have the entire class together try to guess the meaning of those words.

Advance Organizer

Ask students to talk about issues that they are most concerned about at this point in their lives. Have them write these down for comparison later. (**Worüber sorgt ihr euch zur Zeit am meisten?**)

Comprehension Check

Teaching Suggestions

- Ask students about resolutions they have made for themselves this past year. Which of these have they accomplished, and which ones did they need to reevaluate? (**Welche Vorsätze habt ihr im letzten Jahr gefasst? Welche davon habt ihr ausgeführt und welche musstet ihr ändern?**)

- Ask students how they would dress for a job interview. (**Was würdet ihr zu einem Jobinterview anziehen?**)

- Ask students to look around the classroom and point out materials that can or should be recycled.

Analyzing

Ask students to discuss the advantages and disadvantages of mandatory military service in Germany. (**Welche Vor- oder Nachteile hat eurer Meinung nach der obligatorische Wehrdienst?**)

Thinking Critically

1 **Comparing and Contrasting** After students have read the statements and made a list of topics, have them compare these with their own concerns that they wrote down in the Motivating Activity. Are their concerns similar to or different from those of the German teenagers?

Auditory Learners

2 Put students in pairs and ask them to role-play two or three of the situations. One student reads the statement from the **Los geht's!** section, and the other responds to it. Have students share their exchanges with the class.

Closure

Ask students to write down German phrases or words from the eight statements that correspond to some of the functions listed.

ERSTE STUFE

Teaching Resources
pp. 328–333

PRINT
- Lesson Planner, p. 67
- Listening Activities, pp. 91–92, 95–97
- Activities for Communication, pp. 45–46, 106–107, 109–110, 135–136
- Grammatikheft, pp. 100–104
- Grammar Tutor for Students of German, Chapter 12
- Übungsheft, pp. 145–149
- Testing Program, pp. 257–260
- Alternative Assessment Guide, p. 41
- Student Make-Up Assignments, Chapter 12

MEDIA
- One-Stop Planner
- Audio Compact Discs, CD12, Trs. 10–12, 22, 29–31
- Teaching Transparencies Situation 12-1
- **Mehr Grammatikübungen** Answers
- Grammatikheft Answers

> **PAGE 328**

Bell Work
Ask students how they would react if they found out that they were accepted by the college of their choice. How would they react if they were turned down?

Communication for All Students

Challenge
4 After the **Unzufriedenheiten** have been written on pieces of paper, put all the pieces into a hat. Let students pull out a piece of paper and read the **Unzufriedenheit** to the class. The rest of the students will try to give advice about how to overcome it.

PRESENTING: So sagt man das!
Read the text with students, and then have them identify all the verbs in the text. Have students continue the text with a few more statements in the narrative past.

Teaching Suggestion
5 Remind students to use the narrative past as they complete Elke's journal entry.

> **PAGE 329**

PRESENTING: So sagt man das!
After reviewing the expressions in **So sagt man das!**, ask students to talk about something that surprises or disappoints them. You may want to list some topics such as friends, politics, or TV shows.

Communication for All Students

Challenge
6 In addition, have partners talk about what they would do if they were Elke. Ask students to share their ideas and suggestions for Elke with the rest of the class.

For Additional Practice
8 Have students add a piece of advice for each person in the listening activity.
Example:
Außerdem würde ich ihm/ihr noch vorschlagen, dass …

PRESENTING: So sagt man das!
In order for students to review the functions *agreeing and giving advice,* set up different situations to which students have to react.
Examples:
Ich finde, Zahnarzt ist ein langweiliger Beruf!
Ich brauche eine neue Kamera, aber ich habe nicht viel Geld!

Cultures and Communities

Career Path
Have students brainstorm reasons why it would be advantageous for an American lawyer to speak German. (Suggestions: Imagine that you represent a client who is suing a German company for copyright violations; imagine that your client is being sued by a German company for non-delivery of a large shipment of cotton fabric.)

Communication for All Students

A Slower Pace

9 Instead of assigning the four scenes to pairs right away, first engage the whole class. Dramatize each statement and ask students to react to you. Follow up each student response with a reply of your own. Try to get several reactions to each statement so that all three functions can be modeled.

PRESENTING: Wortschatz

- Have students give the female or male counterpart of each occupation illustrated (pay attention to the irregular change in **die Friseuse**).
- Put the class into two teams of boys and girls. Have the boys give the name of a profession and challenge the girls to quickly give the female counterpart. Reverse roles.
- Have students group the professions listed here in the Wortschatz and others they already know into four categories: **praktische Berufe, technische Berufe, soziale Berufe,** and **medizinisch-wissenschaftliche Berufe.**
- Have students identify the **Schulabschluss** that is required for each of the jobs listed. (Example: **Ein Friseur muss einen Hauptschulabschluss haben.**)
- Have students pick out at least three professions from the list and recommend a person of that profession to the rest of the class. (Example: **Ich kenne einen tollen Friseur. Der hat sein Geschäft in der …straße, und der heißt …**)

Teaching Suggestion

10 Before students begin Activity 10, practice several genitive constructions. (Example: **Mich interessiert der Beruf eines Zahnarztes.**) Allow students to also express which occupations they are not interested in and give reasons. (Example: **Der Beruf eines Steuerberaters interessiert mich nicht, weil ich nicht gut in Mathe bin.**)

PRESENTING: So sagt man das!

Review the expressions in **So sagt man das!** and then ask students to whom they have given advice recently. What were the circumstances and what kind of advice did they give?
Example:
Mein Bruder hilft nie zu Hause. Ich habe ihm gesagt: „Du solltest wirklich mithelfen: abwaschen, abtrocknen, den Tisch decken." Die Mutter wäre sehr froh.

COMMUNITY LINK

10 Have students contact an employment office to find out about current job trends. What fields and professions are a lot of people entering now and why?

Communication for All Students

13 A Slower Pace

To help students get started, prepare a list on the board of suggested topics for giving advice. Solicit ideas from students.
Examples:
Schularbeit
Sport
Freundschaften
Umwelt
Zukunftspläne

Group Work

14 Divide the class into four groups and assign each group one letter from the **Kummerkasten** to which they respond in writing. After groups have outlined, revised, edited, and written a final draft of their responses, have them read their letters to the rest of the class.

Portfolio Assessment

14 You might want to suggest this activity as an oral portfolio item for your students. See *Alternative Assessment Guide,* p. 27

ERSTE STUFE

LANDESKUNDE

Teaching Suggestion

Ask students to think of ways their community encourages involvement to improve social conditions in their area.

Communication for All Students

A Slower Pace

A1 Do this activity with the whole class and use a transparency or the chalkboard to gather and record students' findings.

Teaching Suggestions

A3 Have students ask this question of other students in the school and share their findings with the rest of the class.

B Before students discuss changes, have them name (possibly research) the various organizations involved in social projects. Where would they go to find out about such organizations, and what would they have to do to get involved?

Teacher Note

Mention to your students that the **Landeskunde** will also be included in Quiz 12–1B given at the end of the **Erste Stufe.**

Teaching Suggestion

Have students think of one piece of advice they would give to a person they are close to and then share it with the class.

Assess

▸ Testing Program, pp. 257–260
   Quiz 12-1A, Quiz 12-1B
   Audio CD12, Tr. 22

▸ Student Make-Up Assignments
   Chapter 12, Alternative Quiz

▸ Alternative Assessment Guide, p. 41

WEITER GEHT'S!

Teaching Resources
pp. 334–335

PRINT
▸ Lesson Planner, p. 68
▸ Übungsheft, p. 150

MEDIA
▸ One-Stop Planner
▸ Audio Compact Discs, CD12, Trs. 13–18

Weiter geht's! Summary

In *Pläne für die Zukunft,* students talk about their plans for the future. The following learning outcomes are modeled in the episode: expressing determination or indecision, talking about what is important or not important, and hypothesizing.

Preteaching Vocabulary

Activating Prior Knowledge

Have students scan the text in order to get a general idea of what the discussion is about (plans that German tenth-graders have for the future). Then have students read each sentence and identify the tense of the verb and whether it is in the active or passive voice. Make a list of the types of constructions on the board or on a transparency, and keep a tally of how many of each type there are. Remind students to be on the lookout for subjunctive forms.

Advance Organizer

Have students recall the first time they thought about plans for their future. This can date back to their preschool or elementary school years. How have their plans and expectations changed over the years? What are their plans now?

Thinking Critically

Analyzing The interviews in this section were conducted with students in the tenth grade at a **Gymnasium.** Their average age is 15 to 16, and they are three years from graduation. Can students think of reasons why students would be so serious and concerned about their future plans at that early a point in their lives?

Comprehension Check

Auditory Learners

Ask students to keep their books closed as they listen to the interviews on compact disc. Pause after each interview and check students' comprehension by having them recall ideas, facts, and phrases from what they have heard.

Thinking Critically

Analyzing Have students read the individual interviews as they listen to the recording. Stop after each interview and have students give the key points made in each. (**Was sind die wichtigsten Punkte in dem [ersten] Interview?**)

Teaching Suggestions

15 Go over the four activities with students orally in class and discuss them. Students take notes for each of the activities. Then have them respond to the questions in writing. This can be assigned for homework. Students refer to their notes to complete the task.

16 Have students include several questions in their letter that they would like to ask the German student.

Closure

Ask students what tenth-graders at their school are typically concerned about. Are their views similar to those of the German students in the interviews? What seems to be important to American tenth-graders today?

Besichtigung der Kirche und Turmbesteigung →

Teaching Resources
pp. 336–340

PRINT 📖
- Lesson Planner, p. 69
- Listening Activities, pp. 93–94, 97–98
- Video Guide, pp. 53–55
- Activities for Communication, pp. 47–48, 108, 110, 135–136
- Grammatikheft, pp. 105–108
- Grammar Tutor for Students of German, Chapter 12
- Übungsheft, pp. 151–154
- Testing Program, pp. 261–264
- Alternative Assessment Guide, p. 41
- Student Make-Up Assignments, Chapter 12

MEDIA
- One-Stop Planner
- Audio Compact Discs, CD12, Trs. 19–20, 23, 32–34
- Video Program
  Wohnungsnot der Studenten
  Videocassette 2, 49:12–51:29
- Teaching Transparencies
  Situation 12-2
  Mehr Grammatikübungen Answers
  Grammatikheft Answers

PAGE 336

((• Bell Work

The proverb **Die Glücklichen sind reich, die Reichen nicht immer glücklich** (similar to *Money can't buy you happiness*) often becomes an issue when making plans for the future. Ask students how important money is to them as they plan for the future. Discuss the underlying message of this proverb with your students.

17 Cooperative Learning

Divide students into cooperative learning groups. Have them assume the roles of reader, recorder, and reporter as they complete the tasks in Activity 17.

Communication for All Students

For Additional Practice

18 In addition to questioning Claudia's plans, have the partner think of at least three suggestions he or she would have for Claudia. At the end, call on students to find out what type of advice was offered.

A Slower Pace

19 Before students begin the writing activity, you may want to review the functions of making recommendations (Chapter 8) and talking about goals for the future (Chapter 11).

 Portfolio Assessment

19 You might want to suggest this activity as a written portfolio item for your students. See *Alternative Assessment Guide,* p. 27.

PRESENTING: So sagt man das!

- After reviewing the expressions, ask students how various people could incorporate the phrases in a speech or discussion. (Examples: a politician giving a speech, an employment agent interviewing a prospective employee, a principal reprimanding a student, parents discussing a new curfew for their child)

- Ask students to look at the reports in the **Weiter geht's!** section. Have them restate what those five students said using expressions of determination or indecision, depending on how sure they are about their plans for the future.

PRESENTING: Wortschatz

- Introduce the new vocabulary by describing what the individual jobs entail.

- For additional vocabulary, look through the classified ads of a recent German paper.

- Have students write out the names of other modern professions.

PRESENTING: So sagt man das!

Review the expressions by asking students questions to which they respond by completing the statements or varying those given in the box.
Examples:
Sag mal, was ist für dich wichtig?
Worauf legst du keinen großen Wert?

Teaching Suggestion

22 Expand the list in the word box by brainstorming with students other positive attributes a person can have. Students should then use ideas from this list to create a detailed profile of their ideal partner. Remind students to use connectors in their descriptions.

Communication for All Students

Auditory Learners

23 Plan to have a tape recorder on hand for this activity. Without much notice, ask students to use the same format as they talk about their future. Walk around the class and record these spontaneous interviews. Once you have completed the interviews, play them back to the entire class.

PRESENTING: So sagt man das!

- To review and practice subjunctive forms, play **Kettenspiel** by having students complete the following phrase:
Wenn ich reich wäre, würde ich …
Each student adds his or her own statement after repeating the ones previously mentioned.

- Have students look back at the Dresden Location Opener on pp. 264–267 and talk about the things they would do and see in Dresden if they had a chance to visit the city. (**Wenn du Dresden besuchen könntest, was würdest du da alles besichtigen? Welche kulturellen Veranstaltungen würdest du besuchen?**)

ZWEITE STUFE

Connections and Comparisons

History Connection

27 Have students continue working with their partner. One of the students assumes the role of a historical figure who is discussing his or her future with a friend. Let students role-play this situation as they imagine what worries, concerns, and goals that person might have had.

Von der Schule zum Beruf

28

Encourage students to discuss this topic with other youths or adult relatives and friends.

Speaking Assessment

29 As a final opportunity for speaking assessment, have the class form groups, each with one counselor, one student, and a parent. Have each group prepare their own skit. For evaluation, you may use the following rubric.

Speaking Rubric	Points			
	4	3	2	1
Content (Complete – Incomplete)				
Comprehension (Total – Little)				
Comprehensibility (Comprehensible – Incomprehensible)				
Accuracy (Accurate – Seldom accurate)				
Fluency (Fluent – Not fluent)				

18–20: A   16–17: B   14–15: C   12–13: D   Under 12: F

Teaching Suggestion

30 Encourage students to invent their own text pictures. Make it a competition with the whole class voting on the designs. Give out ribbons for **erster Platz**, **zweiter Platz**, and so on. Display the finished products for other German classes to enjoy. You might want to publish winning designs in the school newspaper.

STANDARDS: 1.3, 3.1

Reteaching: Vocabulary for *moderne Berufe*

Have students write a brief newspaper ad advertising a position for one of the **moderne Berufe** listed in the **Wortschatz** on p. 337.

Using the Video

Videocassette 2, 49:12–51:29
In the video clip *Wohnungsnot der Studenten,* students talk about their problems finding adequate housing at reasonable prices. See *Video Guide,* p. 54, for suggestions.

Teaching Suggestion

To review the vocabulary and expressions presented in the **Zweite Stufe,** design (or have students design) a crossword puzzle that contains words needed to complete some expressions. Here are a few examples:

Sie untersucht die Nahrungsmittel, die in Supermärkten verkauft werden. (die Lebensmittelkontrolleurin)
Steffi Graf hat viel _____ in ihrer sportlichen Karriere. (Erfolg)
Wenn man etwas zu tun versucht, muss man _____. (sich anstrengen)

Assess

▸ Testing Program, pp. 261–264
Quiz 12-2A, Quiz 12-2B
Audio CD12, Tr. 23

▸ Student Make-Up Assignments
Chapter 12, Alternative Quiz

▸ Alternative Assessment Guide, p. 41

ZWEITE STUFE

ZUM SCHREIBEN

Teaching Resources
p. 341

PRINT
▸ Lesson Planner, p. 70
▸ Alternative Assessment Guide, p. 27

MEDIA
▸ One-Stop Planner
▸ Test Generator, Chapter 12

Writing Strategy

The targeted strategy in this writing activity is *evaluating your writing*. Students should learn about this strategy before beginning the assignment.

Prewriting
Building Context

Have students review all eleven **Zum Schreiben** assignments they have completed in Level 3. Which was their favorite piece of writing and why?

Teaching Suggestion

You may want to model *evaluating* by having a student volunteer one of his or her previous assignments. Copy the piece of writing onto a transparency, or make copies for all students. Show students how to analyze the writing, using specific examples to help them understand how certain parts can be improved. Encourage objective class input.

Building on Previous Skills

A Remind students to analyze their audience, as they did in the **Zum Schreiben** activity for Chapter 9 (p. 255). Their autobiography should be adapted to a specific audience as well. They should ask themselves the following questions:
Was weiß der Leser bereits über mich?
Was würde den Leser interessieren?
Was sollte ich genauer erklären?
Welchen Ton soll ich benutzen?

Writing

Communication for All Students

Visual Learners
B Encourage students to accompany their writing with visuals. Remind students that the visuals should help organize their ideas and support their writing.

Post-Writing
Teaching Suggestion

Have students post their autobiographies throughout the classroom on bulletin boards. If some students have home movies or slides they would like to show, they could present them in class along with their biographies.

Closure

Have students look back over evidence of the writing process for this piece. What parts of it were difficult to write about and why?

Connections and Comparisons

Language-to-Language
Although there are some scattered examples of autobiographical literature in antiquity and the Middle Ages, autobiography began, generally speaking, with the Renaissance in the 15th century. There are four kinds of autobiography: thematic, like Simone de Beauvoir's *Mémoires d'une jeune fille rangée (Memoirs of a Dutiful Daughter)* and Christopher Reeve's *Still Me*; religious, like St. Augustine's *Confessions*; intellectual, like John Stuart Mill's *Autobiography* and Henry Adams' *The Education of Henry Adams*; and fictional, like George Santayana's *The Last Puritan*. You may want to ask your students if they have read any autobiographies, and if so, what kind.

ZUM LESEN

Teaching Resources
pp. 342–345

PRINT
▸ Lesson Planner, p. 70
▸ Übungsheft, pp. 155–156
▸ Reading Strategies and Skills Handbook, Chapter 12
▸ Lies mit mir! 3, Chapter 12

MEDIA
▸ One-Stop Planner
▸ Audio CD12, Tr. 21

Prereading
Background Information

Wolfgang Hildesheimer was born in Hamburg in 1916. He lived in Palestine, in England, and in Germany (Nürnberg) before moving to Switzerland in the fifties. He has published three novels, a collection of short stories, two collections of dramas, a biography of Mozart, and a fictitious "biography" called *Marbot.* He is also recognized as a painter and has had his work exhibited in Darmstadt, Bonn, Munich, Zurich, and Urbino.

Building Context

After reading a number of contemporary authors, students may have noticed a trend in which the writer avoids explaining the psychological states or motivations of the characters and concentrates on simply describing their actions in concrete detail. The short story is an ideal vehicle for this kind of cool, terse style that leaves the interpretation of events up to the reader. As the students read Hildesheimer's story, they should be aware of how he maintains an objective distance from his characters—even from the first-person narrator. If a comparison is helpful, they could ask themselves while reading: How is this style different from the style of *Sabines Eltern*? Ask the class to watch for and flag instances in which characters act—or perhaps fail to react—in unexplained ways. Further, ask them to watch for moments at which there seems to be some kind of failure of language or communication breakdown going on within the world of the story.

Teacher Note

Activities 1-4 are prereading activities.

Reading
Teaching Suggestion

2 If students have trouble getting started, ask them which of the other texts in Levels 2 and 3 they think this story resembles. They can think about the strategies they used with those texts. Make sure they have noticed the fact that, besides the narrative look of the first paragraph, this text includes quotation marks—and therefore dialogue—and three personal letters given in full.

Teacher Notes

4 The class may want to refer to previous chapters in Level 3 and perhaps to reread some of the **Lesestrategie** boxes to see how to apply various strategies that have been suggested by class members.

7 In addition to noting that Kolhaas is given cousin Eduard's coat as a replacement, students should notice that he doesn't complain or even seem very surprised at the loss of his own coat.

Teaching Suggestion

10 Help students recognize the **indirekte Rede** of Eduard's reply. You can restate "Er habe nämlich in dem Mantel ..." to "Aber Blockflöten seien in Australien nicht erhältlich." in direct quote form in order to facilitate their comprehension.

Teacher Note

13 The students might need help recognizing what is odd about paragraph 3—that the wife is putting a heating coil in the flower vase in order to boil eggs—or the end of the story, where she's taking the coffee grinder apart. They might also need help recognizing why it's comically in character for the wife to say that she wouldn't have been interested in seeing *Tannhäuser* anyway, but not to ask why the tickets are 12 years old.

Thinking Critically

Analyzing At first glance, this short story might seem like it would be much easier to film than the Kafka story the class read at the beginning of Level 3. Ask the students to use their answers to Questions 5 through 11 to make some story boards for a film of *Der hellgraue Frühjahrsmantel.* Next, ask them to consider how they would handle the letters in a film, and how they would handle such essentials as the narrator's description of his wife's character. Are there places where they would have to write their own material—dialogue lines or even whole scenes—in order to make the film coherent? How would they preserve the understated quality of the humor in a film version?

Post-Reading

Teacher Note

Activity 14 is a post-reading task that will show whether students can apply what they have learned.

Closure

Have students write a review of the story as if for a newspaper or magazine.

Zum Lesen Answers

Answers to Activity 5
Eduard ist vor zwölf Jahren nach Australien ausgewandert; Eduard hat neulich geschrieben; Eduard will seinen hellgrauen Frühjahrsmantel.

Answers to Activity 6
den Mantel von Herrn Kolhaas; der Erzähler hat den Mantel mit dem Mantel seines Cousins (Vetters) verwechselt.

Answers to Activity 7
Er bekommt den Mantel des Cousins.

Answers to Activity 8
Pilze; Herr Kolhaas will sich für das Buch für Pilzsammler bedanken.

Answers to Activity 9
Herr Kolhaas findet einen Brief; Der Brief war für einen Freund vom Cousin bestimmt; Der Cousin hatte vergessen, den Brief abzuschicken.

Answers to Activity 10
Der Mantel ist länger geworden; eine Tenorblockflöte

Answers to Activity 11
Sie reagiert ganz sachlich darauf.

> **PAGES 346–349**

MEHR GRAMMATIKÜBUNGEN

The **Mehr Grammatikübungen** activities are designed as supplemental activities for the grammatical concepts presented in the chapter. You might use them as additional practice, for review, or for assessment.

For more grammar presentations, review, and practice, refer to the following:
- Grammatikheft
- Grammar Tutor for Students of German
- Grammar Summary on pp. R22–R39
- Übungsheft
- Grammar and Vocabulary quizzes (Testing Program)
- Test Generator
- Interaktive Spiele at go.hrw.com

KANN ICH'S WIRKLICH?

This page helps students prepare for the test. It is a brief checklist of the major points covered in the chapter. The students should be reminded that it is only a checklist and not necessarily everything that will appear on the test.

For additional self-check options, refer students to the *Grammar Tutor* and the Online self-test for this chapter.

WORTSCHATZ

Review and Assess

Circumlocution

Play **Das treffende Wort suchen** with the professions discussed in this chapter. Have the students describe each occupation and tell what kind of person might be interested in the occupation. For instance, for **Steuerberater(in)**, one could say **eine Person, die anderen Rat über Geld gibt** (damit man am 15. April nicht so viel Geld zahlen muss.) To talk about what kind of person might be interested in this occupation, one might say **Eine Person, die sich für Mathe interessiert, könnte in diesem Beruf glücklich werden.** See p. 31C for procedures.

Challenge

Ask students to choose one of the professions from the **Wortschatz** page. Tell them to imagine they are going to be interviewed about their field of work. They should be able to describe a typical day on the job and include some background information such as job requirements, training, and advantages of that particular job.

Review and Assess

Game

 Play the game **Zeichenspiel.** See p. 323C for the procedure.

Tactile Learners

Give students each a 3 x 5 index card and ask them to make their own business card for one of the professions listed on the **Wortschatz** page. The business card should include their name, title, address of business, a catchy phrase, and the logo of their business.

Career Path

Ask students to identify all professions on the **Wortschatz** page for which a foreign language would be useful. Students should also explain why they think foreign languages would be helpful for each of the professions they identify.

Total Physical Response

Divide students into groups of three or four and have them develop their own TPR activities. They should use the vocabulary and functions from this chapter as the basis for their commands. Allow enough time for each group to try out their commands on their classmates.

Using the Video

 Videocassette 2, 51:34–53:28
At this time, you might want to use the authentic advertising footage from German television. See *Video Guide,* p. 54, for suggestions.

Teacher Note

• Give the **Kapitel 12** Chapter Test:
Testing Program, pp. 265–270
Audio CD 12, Trs. 24–25.

• Give the Final Exam:
Testing Program, pp. 279–286
Audio CD 12, Trs. 26–28.

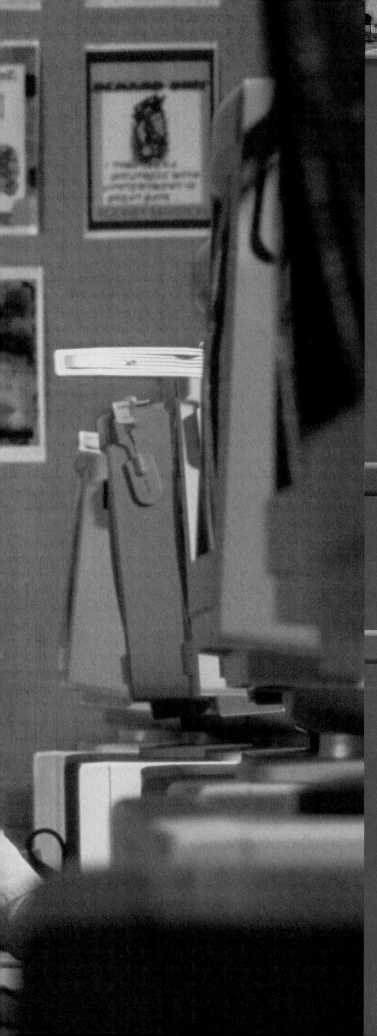

12

Die Zukunft liegt in deiner Hand!

Objectives

In this chapter you will learn to

Erste Stufe

- report past events
- express surprise and disappointment
- agree
- agree with reservations
- give advice
- give advice and give reasons

Zweite Stufe

- express determination or indecision
- talk about what is important or not important
- hypothesize

 internet

go.hrw.com

ADRESSE: go.hrw.com
KENNWORT: WK3
DRESDEN-12

◀ Keinen Job ohne Computerkenntnisse!

Los geht's! ▪ *Mitgehört*

CD 12
Trs. 1–9

Diese Gesprächsfetzen stammen aus diversen Gesprächen mit Schülern aus verschiedenen Realschulen und Gymnasien. Wovon handeln diese Aussagen? CD 12 Tr. 1

„Für mich steht fest, dass ich nach dem Abitur erst einmal den Zivildienst mache, bevor ich studiere. Wenn ich mich nicht irre, dauert der Zivildienst ja nur 12 Monate."

Uwe CD 12 Tr. 2   He is incorrect. See **Ein wenig Landeskunde**, p. 132.

„Es ist wichtig, dass die Verbraucher ihre Getränke nur in Mehrwegflaschen kaufen; Einwegflaschen und vor allem Aludosen müssten eigentlich verboten werden."

CD 12 Tr. 3 **Veronika**

„Ich lege keinen großen Wert darauf, wie ich mich kleide, wie ich aussehe, und darüber bin ich sehr glücklich."

Hannes CD 12 Tr. 4

„Ich weiß noch nicht, ob ich Kunst oder Sprachen studieren soll, denn ich bin gut in beiden Fächern. Fest steht jedoch, dass ich nicht Physik studiere, denn in diesem Fach bin ich eine absolute Niete."

CD 12 Tr. 5 **Brigitte**

„Ich habe beschlossen, meine Diät zu ändern und ein gesundes Leben zu führen. Und ich empfehle euch, dasselbe zu tun."

CD 12 Tr. 6 **Jens**

„Dein Husten macht mir aber langsam Sorgen, und ich bin wirklich sehr erstaunt, dass du noch nicht zum Arzt gegangen bist."

Katja CD 12 Tr. 7

„Meiner Meinung nach solltest du mal diese Uhr reparieren lassen. Was mich stört ist, dass du alles immer gleich wegwerfen willst und dir was Neues kaufst."

CD 12 Tr. 8 **Markus**

„Ich geb Ihnen Recht, das Theaterstück war super. Als der Vorhang aufging und ich die bunten Kostüme der Schauspieler sah, bekam ich eine Gänsehaut."

Claudia CD 12 Tr. 9

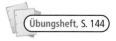

Übungsheft, S. 144

1 Hast du alles verstanden?

a. Schreiben Über welche Themen sprechen diese Schüler? Mach eine Liste!

b. Sprechen Was drückt jede dieser Aussagen aus? Diskutier darüber mit einem Partner!

a. Zivildienst; Umwelt; Aussehen; Studium; Ernährung; Gesundheit; Umweltbewusstsein; Kultur

2 Und du?

Schreiben Was würdest du diesen Schülern antworten, wenn sie diese Aussagen dir gegenüber gemacht hätten? Schreib zwei Antworten auf, und lies sie der Klasse vor!

Erste Stufe

Objectives Reporting past events; expressing surprise and disappointment; agreeing; agreeing, with reservations; giving advice; giving advice and giving reasons

WK3 DRESDEN-12

3 Was hat sich geändert? Script and answers on p. 323G

Zuhören Junge Leute erzählen, wie ihr Leben vor nur einem halben Jahr war, wie es jetzt ist und warum es sich geändert hat. Schreib die wichtigsten Tatsachen auf! Wer hat die größten Änderungen erlebt?

CD 12 Tr. 10

4 Unzufrieden? Worüber denn?

Sprechen/Schreiben Setzt euch in kleinen Gruppen zusammen, und erzählt euch gegenseitig, worüber jeder von euch schon mal im Leben unzufrieden war und warum! Einer von euch muss dabei die einzelnen „Unzufriedenheiten" auf einen Zettel schreiben.

So sagt man das!

Reporting past events

Schon bekannt

What do you observe about the following text?

> **Vor drei Wochen hatte ich eine schwere Erkältung. Ich fühlte mich gar nicht wohl und konnte nicht in die Schule gehen. Als es mir nach zwei Tagen noch immer nicht besser ging, rief meine Mutter unseren Hausarzt an. Der sagte, …**

What verb forms are used here? Why?

Grammatikheft, S. 100, Ü. 1

5 Worüber war Elke unzufrieden?

Schreiben Elke war gerade dabei, etwas über sich selbst in ihr Tagebuch zu schreiben, als sie ans Telefon gerufen wurde. Schreib für sie die Eintragung fertig! Ein paar Ideen dafür stehen rechts unten. Lest danach eure Texte einander vor!

Ein wenig Grammatik

Schon bekannt

For the forms of the narrative past (imperfect), used to report past events, see the Grammar Summary.

Mehr Grammatikübungen, S. 346, Ü. 1

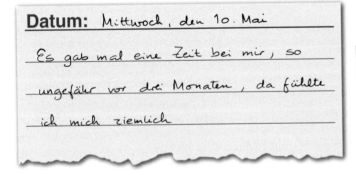

Datum: Mittwoch, den 10. Mai

Es gab mal eine Zeit bei mir, so ungefähr vor drei Monaten, da fühlte ich mich ziemlich

sich nicht wohl fühlen

schlechte Noten haben

es gibt zu viel Schmutz und Lärm

keine tollen Klamotten haben

kein Geld für Konzertkarten haben

keine Zukunft sehen

mit jemandem Streit haben

So sagt man das!

Expressing surprise and disappointment

Schon bekannt

When expressing surprise, you may begin your statement by saying:

Ich bin/war überrascht, dass Elke Streit mit ihrem Freund hat/hatte.
Ich war erstaunt, dass sie so schlechte Noten hatte.
Ich hätte nicht geglaubt, dass sie überhaupt Probleme hat.

When expressing disappointment, you may begin your statement by saying:

Ich bin enttäuscht, dass Elke mir nichts gesagt hat.
Ich bedaure, dass sie sich keine neuen Klamotten leisten kann.
Ich finde es schade, dass wir ihr nicht helfen können.

What would you tell a beginning German student about the position of the conjugated verb in **dass**-clauses?

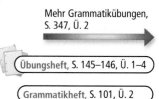

Mehr Grammatikübungen, S. 347, Ü. 2

Übungsheft, S. 145–146, Ü. 1–4

Grammatikheft, S. 101, Ü. 2

---

6 Arme Elke!

Sprechen Such dir eine Partnerin, und schaut euch Übung 5 noch mal an! Sprecht über Elkes Probleme der letzten drei Monate, und drückt dabei eure Überraschung und Enttäuschung aus!

7 Für mein Notizbuch

Schreiben Womit warst du in der letzten Zeit nicht zufrieden? Schreib einen kurzen Bericht darüber!

8 Wer hat Probleme? Script and answers on p. 323G

CD 12
Tr. 11

Zuhören Junge Leute unterhalten sich über verschiedene Probleme. Hör gut zu und schreib auf, was die einzelnen Probleme sind und welcher Rat gegeben wird, wie man das Problem vielleicht lösen könnte!

wer?	Problem?	was tun?

So sagt man das!

Agreeing; agreeing, with reservations; giving advice

Schon bekannt

When agreeing, you may say:

Da geb ich dir Recht, … *or* **Bei uns ist es auch so; wir …**

When agreeing, but with reservations, you may say:

Das stimmt zwar, aber … *or* **Es kommt darauf an, ob …**

When giving advice, you may say:

Vielleicht kannst du … *or*
Es ist wichtig, dass … *or*
Ich würde sagen, du gehst …

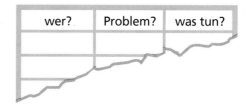

Ein wenig Grammatik

Schon bekannt
For the **würde**-forms, see the Grammar Summary.

Mehr Grammatikübungen, S. 347, Ü. 3

---

9 **Was meinst du?**

Sprechen Such dir eine Partnerin! — Die Aufgabe ist, über jede der folgenden Aussagen zu diskutieren. Deine Partnerin liest zuerst eine der aufgelisteten Aussagen vor, als ob diese von ihr wäre. Du nimmst dazu Stellung: du gibst ihr Recht und sagst warum, oder du hast Vorbehalte (*have reservations*). Darauf rät dir deine Partnerin, was du tun sollst.

BEISPIEL   PARTNERIN   **Also, ich stehe auf Country Western: die Musik ist immer super, und die Texte sind immer aktuell.**

              DU   **Da geb ich dir Recht. Ich …**   *oder*
                       Na ja, aber es kommt doch darauf an, wer oder welche Gruppe singt, denn …

     PARTNERIN   **Ich würde sagen, dass du dir mal die (…) anhören solltest, denn die sind wirklich fetzig.**

1. „Also, ich stehe auf Country Western: die Musik ist immer super, und die Texte sind immer aktuell."

2. „Es hat keinen Sinn für mich, Kunst zu studieren, weil ich später damit wenig anfangen kann — davon kann ich nicht leben."

3. „Ich weiß nicht, ob ich als zweite Fremdsprache Italienisch oder Spanisch lernen soll. Meine Freunde meinen, ich soll Japanisch lernen."

4. „Meiner Meinung nach tun wir bei uns zu Hause noch nicht genug für die Umwelt. Wir sortieren oft unseren Müll nicht, und wir benutzen meistens nur Einwegflaschen."

Wortschatz

Welche Berufe interessieren dich? Vielleicht der …

p. 323X   12–1

eines Schornsteinfegers

eines Steuerberaters

einer Rundfunkmoderatorin

einer Toningenieurin

eines Friseurs

einer Schweißerin

eines Schreiners

einer Glasbläserin

Und dann noch…

Anästhesist(in)	technische(r)
Elektroinstallateur(in)	Zeichner(in)
Fotograf(in)	Winzer(in)
Koch/Köchin	Zahnarzt/Zahnärztin
Optiker(in)	Zimmermann
Schuhmacher(in)	

 Grammatikheft, S. 103, Ü. 4–5

10 Was willst du werden?

Sprechen Sag einigen Klassenkameraden, welche von den auf Seite 330 aufgelisteten Berufen dich interessieren und warum! Kennst du auch Leute, die diese Berufe ausüben?

 11 Guter Rat ist teuer! Script and answers on p. 323H

Zuhören Schüler unterhalten sich. Was raten einige Schüler ihren Klassenkameraden, und welche Gründe geben sie dafür an? Mach dir Notizen! Welcher Rat, findest du, passt am besten zu welchem Schüler?

CD 12 Tr. 12

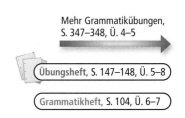

wer?	welcher Rat?	warum?

So sagt man das!

Giving advice and giving reasons   *Schon bekannt*

When giving advice, you may say:

> **Versuch doch mal,** etwas gesünder zu leben!
> **An deiner Stelle würde ich** nicht rauchen.
> **Und du solltest** wirklich auch mehr schlafen.

When giving reasons for others to do something, you may say:

> Du solltest mehr Fisch als Fleisch essen, **weil Fisch gesünder ist.**
> Du solltest mehr Sport treiben, **damit du dich besser fühlst.**

When giving your own reasons for doing something, you may say:

> Ich treibe viel Sport, **um wirklich fit zu bleiben.**

What words are used to introduce the clauses stating the reasons? How do they differ in meaning?

Mehr Grammatikübungen, S. 347–348, Ü. 4–5

Übungsheft, S. 147–148, Ü. 5–8

Grammatikheft, S. 104, Ü. 6–7

 12 Was ich alles tun sollte und warum!

Schreiben Denk an fünf verschiedene Dinge, die du für dich selbst tun sollst, und schreib sie auf! Schreib auch einen Grund daneben!

Ein wenig Grammatik

Schon bekannt

For infinitive forms of verbs, see the Grammar Summary.

13 Rat geben

Sprechen Such dir eine Partnerin! — Sag ihr drei Dinge, die du tun solltest, und nenne einen Grund dafür! Sie gibt dir Rat und begründet ihren Rat.

BEISPIEL   DU   Ich sollte erst mal mehr Zeit für Deutsch verwenden, um eine bessere Note zu bekommen. Und zweitens …

         PARTNERIN   An deiner Stelle würde ich versuchen, alle Noten zu verbessern, damit du einen guten Schulabschluss machst und …

14 Leserbriefe beantworten

Schreiben Lies die Leserbriefe im Kummerkasten! — Als Jugendpsychologe der Kummerkasten-Seite eines Jugendmagazin hast du die Aufgabe, solche Briefe zu beantworten. Such dir einen der vier Briefe aus und beantworte ihn! Drück in deiner Antwort Verständnis für die Probleme aus, und gib den Leuten einen guten Rat, den sie auch befolgen können! Lies dann deine Antwort einem Partner vor!

KUMMERKASTEN

Meine Eltern fahren dieses Wochenende weg, und ich muss auf das Haus achten. Ich würde in dieser Zeit gern meine Clique einladen zum Musikhören oder Videoschauen. Ich weiß aber, dass meine Eltern dagegen wären. Soll ich meine Freunde trotzdem einladen?

Haussitter Tobias

Ich habe vier Wochen „Hausarrest", weil ich letzten Samstag erst um Mitternacht nach Hause gekommen bin anstatt, wie fest versprochen, um 22.30 Uhr. Ich darf jetzt in den nächsten vier Wochen das Haus nach 19.00 Uhr nicht mehr verlassen. In zwei Wochen hat nun mein bester Freund eine Fete, zu der ich eingeladen bin. Die Fete geht bis 23.00 Uhr, und ich möchte gern dabei sein, kann es aber nicht. Was soll ich tun?

„Arrestant" Michael

Ich habe Probleme in der Schule, und meine Eltern werden deshalb bestimmt bald einen blauen Brief[1] erhal-

ten. Soll ich meine Eltern darauf vorbereiten? In zwei Wochen wird es sich entscheiden. Meine einzige Chance ist, eine gute Lateinarbeit zu schreiben, aber dafür müsste ich jetzt jeden Tag 3-4 Stunden und noch länger lernen. Ich habe aber wenig Lust, so viel Zeit mit Latein zu verbringen.

Antje, ein Lateinmuffel

Ich war mit meiner besten Freundin beim Einkaufen. In einem großen Bekleidungsgeschäft hat sie ein Halstuch gesehen, das ihr so gut gefallen hat. Sie hat es sich umgebunden, wir haben noch andere Sachen angeschaut — und plötzlich waren wir draußen auf der Straße. Ich habe meiner Freundin geraten, zurückzugehen und das Halstuch zu bezahlen. Aber das wollte sie nicht. Sie hatte Angst, dass man denkt, sie wollte es stehlen. Jetzt will ich mit meiner Freundin nie wieder einkaufen gehen!

Monika

---

1. Ein blauer Brief ist ein Mahnschreiben der Schule an die Eltern, wenn die Versetzung des Schülers in die nächste Klasse gefährdet ist.

Übungsheft,
S. 149, Ü. 1–4

Pauken allein reicht nicht

Für den Schulabschluss braucht man
gute Noten und muss sehr fleißig lernen.
Doch wo bleibt das soziale Lernen? Wer
engagiert sich für seine Mitmenschen?
Wie engagiert man sich? Zwei Schüler
haben dazu Stellung genommen. Lies,
auf welche Arten sie sich sozial
engagieren!

„Man muss sich einmischen", meint Judith. Die Abiturientin hat oft
nach diesem Motto gehandelt. Als Schulsprecherin versuchte sie immer „in
Erfahrung zu bringen, was die Mitschülerinnen bedrückte". Sie vermittelte
bei Konflikten und organisierte Feten und Konzerte für die Schulgemeinde.
Der Schulkiosk verkauft dank ihrer Initiative statt „Süßkram" jetzt
Biobrötchen. Judith setzte eine Mülltrennaktion an der Schule durch und
engagierte sich für eine Kroatienhilfe. „Wenn ich mich über etwas aufrege,
werde ich aktiv", erklärt die Schülerin, die am liebsten im Team arbeitet.
Ihrer Meinung nach erzieht das Gymnasium heute zu viele „Einzelkämpfer": „Später im Beruf arbeitet man doch meistens in Gruppen."

Judith

„Man kann etwas verändern", weiß Ingo. Das hat der Abiturient eines
Wirtschaftsgymnasiums selbst erfahren. Mit einem Freund sammelte er
Kleidung und Nahrung für Menschen im ehemaligen Jugoslawien. Der
Erfolg war groß. „Die anderen Schüler konnten sehen, dass sich
Engagement lohnt", sagt Ingo heute. Etwas Besonderes haben sich Ingo
und seine Mitschüler zum Abitur einfallen lassen: Es gibt Zeugnisse für
Lehrer. Bewertet werden zum Beispiel Unterrichtsgestaltung, Toleranz,
Charisma, Stärken und Schwächen. Besonders viel Lob hat Ingo für
seinen Deutschlehrer: „Ein echter Pädagoge, wie es ihn nur selten gibt. Er
hat Zeit für die Probleme der Heranwachsenden, nimmt uns als Schüler
ernst und stellt dafür auch mal den Unterrichtsstoff zurück."

Ingo

A. 1. Mach dir Notizen darüber, was jeder Schüler für seine Mitmenschen macht! Wie
unterscheiden sich die Schüler voneinander?

2. Welche Gründe geben die Schüler an, sich für andere zu engagieren?

3. Glaubst du, dass man die Verantwortung hat, sich für seine Mitmenschen zu engagieren?
Was meinst du dazu?

4. Wie engagiert sich deine Klasse oder Schule auf sozialer Ebene? Habt ihr schon mal was
verändert oder verbessert?

B. Welche Veränderungen könnte man erreichen (*achieve*), wenn man an sozialen Projekten
teilnimmt? Wie würde die Welt deiner Meinung nach dann aussehen?

A. 1. Judith: vermittelte bei Konflikten; organisierte Feten und Konzerte; hat durch ihre Initiative bewirkt, dass es Biobrötchen am
Pausenstand gibt; setzte eine Mülltrennaktion an der Schule durch; engagierte sich für Kroatienhilfe. Ingo: sammelt Kleidung und
Nahrung für Menschen im ehemaligen Jugoslawien; stellte Zeugnisse für Lehrer aus. Unterschiede zwischen beiden Schülern: Judith en-
gagiert sich hauptsächlich für ihre Umgebung; ihr ist es wichtig, dass ihre Mitschüler sich gesund ernähren und umweltbewusst sind.
Ingo ist es wichtig, welchen Eindruck Lehrer auf Schüler ausüben.

STANDARDS: 2.1, 2.2, 3.2, 4.2

Weiter geht's! · *Pläne für die Zukunft*
CD 12 Tr. 13

Gymnasiasten einer 10. Klasse erzählen von ihren Zukunftsplänen.

1. Ich möchte Jura studieren und Strafverteidigerin werden. Erst dann möchte ich heiraten und eine Familie gründen, denn ich möchte immer unabhängig von meinem Mann sein (finanziell) im Fall einer Scheidung, damit ich meine Kinder auch alleine ernähren kann. Trotzdem wünsche ich mir ein Haus, eine gute und glückliche Ehe, zwei bis drei Kinder und Erfolg im Beruf.
   CD 12 Tr. 14

2. Ich möchte später Zahntechniker werden, gut verdienen und eine Familie mit zwei Kindern haben. Und ein Haus wäre nicht schlecht. Ich würde vielleicht gern im Ausland arbeiten, weil man dort besser verdienen kann und die Menschen vielleicht nicht so kalt sind wie hier.
   CD 12 Tr. 15

3. Wenn ich 35 bin, möchte ich einen Mann haben und vielleicht auch schon ein Kind — und gesund und glücklich sein. Natürlich einen guten Job und viel Geld. Ich möchte in Deutschland leben bleiben, weil ich es hier ganz schön finde. In anderen Ländern, mit anderen Glauben, gibt es nur Konflikte und oft auch Kriege; das wäre nichts für mich. Aber nach Frankreich oder England zu ziehen, könnte ich mir schon vorstellen. In anderen Ländern werden Frauen immer noch zu stark unterdrückt. CD 12 Tr. 16

4. Nach meinem Schulabschluss habe ich mir schon mal leise überlegt, ob ich nicht vielleicht Jura studieren sollte. Durch das Jurastudium habe ich natürlich auch gute Chancen auf einen guten Beruf, viel Geld und ein Häuschen. Ich würde gerne heiraten und auch ein oder mehrere Kinder haben.
CD 12 Tr. 17

5. Sicherlich möchte ich später einmal einen guten Job und viel Geld haben. Ich weiß aber auch, dass ich mich sehr anstrengen muss, denn wie auch in Amerika ist es hier schwer, eine Arbeit zu finden, die einem wirklich gefällt. Ich glaube nicht, dass ich heiraten werde, denn ich habe es gern, unabhängig zu sein und machen zu können, was ich will. Durch meine Arbeit und andere Pflichten werde ich sowieso schon genug eingeengt sein. CD 12 Tr. 18

(Übungsheft, S. 150)

15 Was sagst du zu diesen Aussagen?

Sprechen Beantworte die folgenden Fragen.

1. Welche von diesen Aussagen stammen von einem Jungen und welche von einem Mädchen? Welche können von beiden sein? Wie weißt du das? 1. Mädchen; 2. Junge; 3. Mädchen; 4. beide; 5. beide
2. Welche Aussagen haben etwas gemeinsam (*in common*), und welche sind verschieden? Begründe deine Antwort!
3. Wer von diesen Gymnasiasten hat sich deiner Meinung nach die meisten Gedanken über die Zukunft gemacht? Warum meinst du das?
4. Was für einen allgemeinen Eindruck hast du von diesen Aussagen?

16 Eine Antwort

Schreiben Mit welchem von diesen Gymnasiasten kannst du dich am besten identifizieren? — Schreib ihm oder ihr einen kurzen Brief, und berichte von deinen eigenen Plänen für die Zukunft!

In einer Zeit, in der es für Jugendliche nicht so einfach ist, Pläne für die Zukunft zu machen, hat die 16-jährige Claudia aus Hamburg jedoch feste Pläne für ihre Zukunft. Lies, was sie geschrieben hat!

> ### Pläne für die Zukunft
>
> Nachdem ich die Schule mit einem Abi-Durchschnitt von 2,5 oder besser beendet habe, studiere ich Betriebswirtschaftslehre.
>
> Nach meinem Studium werde ich eine Lehre in einem großen, berühmten Hotel machen.
>
> Dann möchte ich für einige Zeit im Ausland arbeiten, am liebsten in Frankreich oder in den USA.
>
> Wenn ich so zwischen 25 und 30 Jahre alt bin, ziehe ich nach Frankreich, um dort ein eigenes Hotel zu bauen, oder ein anderes, gutlaufendes Hotel zu übernehmen.
>
> Dort werde ich meinen zukünftigen Mann kennenlernen und ihn heiraten. In den Flitterwochen fahren wir nach Hawaii.
>
> Dann möchte ich 2 Kinder haben. Es sollen Zwillinge sein (ein Mädchen und ein Junge).
>
> Wenn die beiden etwas älter sind, so etwa 14/15/16, sollen sie im Hotel mithelfen, soweit die Schule es ermöglicht.
>
> Claudia Müller (16)

by Claudia Müller, student in Herr Boelicke's class at Johann-Rist-Gymnasium in Wedel, Germany

17 Claudias Pläne

Sprechen Beantworte die folgenden Fragen.

1. Wie viele konkrete Pläne hat Claudia erwähnt? Liste sie auf!
2. Welche Ausdrücke gebraucht Claudia, wenn sie über ihre Pläne spricht? Was drückt sie damit aus?
3. Was ist dein Eindruck von Claudia? Begründe deine Meinung!

18 Bist du so sicher, Claudia?

Sprechen Such dir eine Partnerin! Sie übernimmt die Rolle von Claudia. Versuche nun, die einzelnen Pläne in Claudias Brief in Frage zu stellen! Claudia muss ihre Pläne verteidigen oder eine andere Möglichkeit erwähnen.

 19 Eine Antwort an Claudia

Schreiben Schreib Claudia einen Brief! Schreib ihr, was du von ihren Plänen hältst und was für Pläne du für deine Zukunft hast!

 20 Zukunftspläne Script and answers on p. 323H

Zuhören Schüler sprechen über ihre Zukunftspläne. Einige von ihnen haben schon feste Pläne, andere wissen noch nicht genau, was sie machen wollen. Schreib auf, was jeder vorhat, und schreib auch die Gründe auf, die jeder für seine Entscheidung angibt!

CD 12
Tr. 19

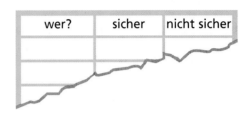

wer?	sicher	nicht sicher

So sagt man das!

Expressing determination or indecision

Schon bekannt

When expressing determination, you may say:

Ich weiß jetzt, dass ich Jura studieren werde.
Ich hab beschlossen, Strafverteidigerin zu werden.
Ich hab mich entschieden, finanziell unabhängig zu sein.

When expressing indecision, you may say:

Ich weiß nicht, ob ich studieren soll.
Ich kann noch nicht sagen, wann ich nach England ziehe.
Ich muss mir überlegen, wo ich einmal arbeiten werde.

Mehr Grammatikübungen,
S. 348, Ü. 6–7

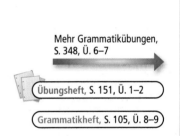

Übungsheft, S. 151, Ü. 1–2

Grammatikheft, S. 105, Ü. 8–9

 21 Deine Pläne

Sprechen Frag eine Partnerin, was für Pläne sie für die Zukunft hat, und ob sie sich schon für etwas fest entschieden hat oder noch nicht ganz sicher ist! Frag sie auch nach den Gründen! — Erzähl ihr danach von deinen eigenen Plänen!

Wortschatz

Moderne Berufe

Gesundheitswissenschaftler(in)
Sportökonom(in)
Umweltökonom(in)
Mediaplaner(in)
Kommunikationselektroniker(in)
Industriedesigner(in)
PR-Berater(in)
Touristikfachwirt(in)
Lebensmittelkontrolleur(in)

einige Gründe:

unabhängig sein

viel Geld verdienen

Familie

Haus

guter Job

im Ausland arbeiten

nicht eingeengt sein

So sagt man das!

Talking about what is important or not important

Schon bekannt 12–2

To talk about what is important to you, you may say:

> **Ich lege großen Wert darauf, dass …**
> **Mir ist wichtig, dass …**
> **Entscheidend für mich ist, dass …**

To talk about what is not important to you, you may say:

> **Ich lege keinen großen Wert auf** ein großes Haus.
> **Ich lege keinen Wert darauf, dass** das Haus einen Pool hat.
> Ein großer Wagen **ist mir überhaupt nicht wichtig.**

Mehr Grammatikübungen,
S. 349, Ü. 8–9

Übungsheft, S. 152, Ü. 3–4

Grammatikheft, S. 106, Ü. 10–11

---

22 ## Partner für die Zukunft

Was wäre für dich bei der Wahl eines Partners sehr wichtig, und worauf legst du keinen Wert?

a. Schreiben Mach zuerst eine Liste mit Qualifikationen, die dein Partner oder deine Partnerin haben sollte!

b. Sprechen Diskutier dann mit einem Klassenkameraden über deine Vorstellungen von einem idealen Partner! Im Kasten rechts stehen ein paar Ideen.

> humorvoll
> kinderlieb
> Nichtraucher
> s. für Musik interessieren
> sportlich
> gern reisen

---

23 ## Wünsche für die Zukunft!

Zuhören Hör diesen Leuten zu, wie sie über ihre Zukunft reden! Welche Wünsche drücken sie aus? Was würden sie gern tun? Mach dir Notizen! Script and answers on p. 323l

CD 12 Tr. 20

So sagt man das!

Hypothesizing Übungsheft, S. 153–154, Ü. 5–8 Grammatikheft, S. 107–108, Ü. 12–14 *Schon bekannt*

When making hypotheses, you can say:

Mehr Grammatikübungen,
S. 349, Ü. 10

> **Wenn ich** in Deutsch fleißiger **wäre, würde ich** eine Eins **bekommen.**
> **Wenn ich** mehr Geld **hätte, würde ich** nach Deutschland **ziehen.**
> **Wenn ich könnte, würde ich** gern Jura **studieren.**

What do these sentences mean?
What does each one express?

Ein wenig Grammatik

Schon bekannt

Identify the verb forms in these sentences. When can you use such forms? For subjunctive forms, see the Grammar Summary.

---

24 Wenn das Wörtchen wenn nicht wär', ...

Sprechen/Schreiben Ein deutsches Sprichwort heißt: „Wenn das Wörtchen wenn nicht wär', wär' mein Vater Millionär." — Nun, setzt euch alle zusammen, und sucht so viele Möglichkeiten wie ihr könnt, um folgende Sätze zu ergänzen! Wenn möglich, gebt auch einen Grund für eure Antworten an!

BEISPIEL Also, wenn ich gut fotografieren könnte, würde ich Werbefotograf werden, weil man dann viel Geld verdient.

1. Also, wenn ich viel Geld hätte, …
2. Wenn ich mehr Zeit hätte, …
3. Wenn ich in (Mathe) eine Eins hätte, …
4. Wenn ich zwei Fremdsprachen könnte, …
5. Wenn ich einen guten Beruf hätte, …
6. Wenn ich nicht so müde wäre, …
7. Wenn ich jetzt nicht so schlampig angezogen wäre, …
8. …

25 Wenn ich ...

Sprechen Welche Vorteile und welche Nachteile hättest du deiner Meinung nach, wenn du:

a. studieren würdest?
b. schon sehr jung heiraten würdest?
c. in ein anderes Land ziehen würdest?

Denk über diese Fragen nach, und mach dir Notizen! Such dir dann einen Partner, und diskutiert darüber, was jeder von euch aufgeschrieben hat! (Ihr dürft euch auch andere Themen aussuchen.)

26 Für mein Notizbuch

Schreiben Mach dir kurze Notizen über deine Zukunft! Was hast du schon beschlossen, und was weißt du noch nicht? Worauf legst du großen Wert und worauf weniger oder keinen Wert? Was würdest du gern tun, wenn du deine Zukunft so einrichten könntest, wie du möchtest?

27 Über Pläne diskutieren

Sprechen Such dir einen Partner! Diskutiert über eure Pläne für die Zukunft, und gebraucht dabei die Notizen, die ihr in eure Notizbücher geschrieben habt!

28 Von der Schule zum Beruf

As a financial planner, you often use this exercise to help new clients discover why money is so important to them. First, ask your client what is so important to him about money. Then ask why that thing is important, and repeat until he can't go any further (you may need to coach him along). The results represent what money means to him. Example: "Money is important to me because I can pay off my debts. Then I won't worry about losing my home or car. Then I can save money and . . ." Write down the client's statements on a special form for his file. Explain that the idea of the exercise is to motivate him to save more money.

29 Rollenspiel

Die Klasse soll sich in vier Gruppen teilen. Eine Gruppe spielt Berater an eurer Schule, die zweite Gruppe spielt Studenten im ersten Jahr (*freshmen*), die dritte Gruppe spielt Eltern, und der Rest spielt Schüler, die bald ihren Schulabschluss machen. Die Schüler sollen Fragen über ihre Zukunft vorbereiten, die anderen sollen sich typische Ratschläge ausdenken, die sie den Schülern geben können. Jeder Schüler geht dann zu einer Person in jeder der drei Gruppen und holt sich Rat. Wie unterscheiden sich die Ratschläge?

30 **Textbilder**

Lesen/Schreiben Seht euch diese Textbilder an! Experimentiert danach mit Buchstaben, und entwerft eure eigenen Textbilder!

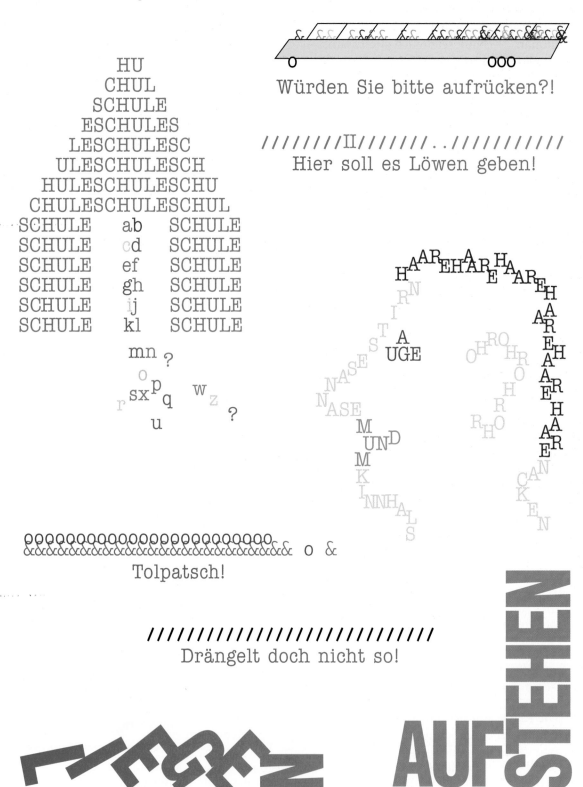

```
             HU
           CHUL
          SCHULE
        ESCHULES
      LESCHULESC
    ULESCHULESCH
   HULESCHULESCHU
 CHULESCHULESCHUL
SCHULE   ab   SCHULE
SCHULE   cd   SCHULE
SCHULE   ef   SCHULE
SCHULE   gh   SCHULE
SCHULE   ij   SCHULE
SCHULE   kl   SCHULE

         mn ?
        o
      r sx p  w
           q   z  ?
          u
```

Würden Sie bitte aufrücken?!

////////II///////..///////////
Hier soll es Löwen geben!

```
ооооооооооооооооооооооооооооо& o &
       Tolpatsch!
```

/////////////////////////////
Drängelt doch nicht so!

LIEGEN

AUFSTEHEN

Zum Schreiben

Throughout this book you have been learning how to express yourself in German in more and more sophisticated and personal ways. You have also learned how to write in many different styles, including journals, short stories, poems and songs, letters, speeches, and many others. In this activity, you will write a short autobiographical piece expressing something important about yourself.

Eine Selbstbiographie schreiben

Wähle einen Stil, den du gern hast, und schreib etwas Selbstbiographisches. Denk an etwas (an ein Ereignis, eine bestimmte Zeit, eine Person, ein Ding), was irgendwie in deinem Leben wichtig ist! Versuche, nicht nur Daten und Fakten aus deinem Leben aufzulisten, sondern beschreib auch deine Gefühle, Reaktionen, usw.!

 Schreibtipp Evaluating your writing After you have conceived a plan and written several drafts, you should evaluate your writing by asking yourself questions that address many of the points you have learned throughout this book. Ask yourself, for example, whether the writing achieves a clear purpose, whether you have arranged your ideas in a coherent and effective way, and whether the tone and the choice of words is appropriate for your purpose and your audience. Don't worry about mechanical aspects of writing such as spelling, grammar, and punctuation until you are satisfied with the content and structure of your writing. When you do finally proofread, focus carefully on each line and use reference guides to check your work.

A. Vorbereiten

1. Wähle einen Stil, der am besten zu deiner Persönlichkeit passt!

2. Denk an dein Leben! Sieh dir alte Fotos, Dias, Tagebücher, persönliche Dokumente und Videos an! Welche wichtigen Ereignisse und Personen haben in deinem Leben eine bedeutende Rolle bei deiner persönlichen Entwicklung gespielt?

3. Mach eine Stichwortsammlung für deine Selbstbiographie, zum Beispiel in Form einer Inhaltsangabe oder einer Skizze! Wähle ein Organisationsprinzip! Willst du deine Biographie chronologisch oder thematisch organisieren?

B. Ausführen

Benutze die Stichwortsammlung, die Fotos und deine Erinnerungen, und schreib jetzt deine Selbstbiographie! Vergiss nicht, dass du nicht nur persönliche Daten und Ereignisse wiedergeben sollst, sondern auch ein Porträt deiner Persönlichkeit vermitteln sollst. Beschreib dich, damit dich Unbekannte erkennen oder verstehen können!

C. Überarbeiten

1. Tausch deine Selbstbiographie mit der Biographie eines Klassenkameraden aus, ohne deinen Namen auf das Papier zu schreiben! Kann der Klassenkamerad dich in deiner Selbstbiographie erkennen? Kannst du ihn erkennen? Hast du dich treffend beschrieben?

2. Besprich deine Selbstbiographie mit einigen Klassenkameraden! Glauben sie, dass du einen passenden Stil gewählt hast?

3. Stell dir die folgenden Fragen: Hast du ein zentrales Thema deines Lebens dargestellt? Hast du die Ideen gut organisiert und einen geeigneten Ton gefunden? Ist die Sprache auf dem richtigen Niveau?

4. Wenn du mit dem Inhalt zufrieden bist, überprüfe Rechtschreibung und Grammatik!

5. Schreib deine korrigierte Selbstbiographie noch einmal auf ein Blatt Papier! Füge Fotos oder sonstige Illustrationen hinzu, die zu deiner Selbstbiographie passen!

CD 12 Tr. 21

Der hellgraue Frühjahrsmantel
von Wolfgang Hildesheimer

Vor zwei Monaten — wir saßen gerade beim Frühstück — kam ein Brief von meinem Vetter Eduard. Mein Vetter Eduard hatte an einem Frühlingsabend vor zwölf Jahren das Haus verlassen, um, wie er behauptete, einen Brief in den Kasten zu stecken, und war nicht zurückgekehrt. Seitdem hatte niemand etwas von ihm gehört. Der Brief kam aus Sydney in Australien. Ich öffnete ihn und las:

Lieber Paul!

Könntest Du mir meinen hellgrauen Frühjahrsmantel nachschicken? Ich kann ihn nämlich brauchen, da es hier oft empfindlich kalt ist, vor allem nachts. In der linken Tasche ist ein „Taschenbuch für Pilzsammler." Das kannst Du herausnehmen und behalten. Eßbare Pilze gibt es hier nämlich nicht. Im voraus vielen Dank.

Herzlichst Dein Eduard

Ich sagte zu meiner Frau: „Ich habe einen Brief von meinem Vetter Eduard aus Australien bekommen." Sie war gerade dabei, den Tauchsieder in die Blumenvase zu stecken, um Eier darin zu kochen, und fragte: „So? Was schreibt er?"

Daß er seinen hellgrauen Mantel braucht und daß es in Australien keine eßbaren Pilze gibt. — „Dann soll er doch etwas anderes essen", sagte sie. — „Da hast du recht", sagte ich.

Später kam der Klavierstimmer. Er war ein etwas schüchterner und zerstreuter Mann, ein wenig weltfremd sogar, aber er war sehr nett, und natürlich sehr musikalisch. Er stimmte nicht nur Klaviere, sondern reparierte auch Saiteninstrumente und erteilte Blockflötenunterricht. Er hieß Kolhaas. Als ich vom Tisch aufstand, hörte ich ihn schon im Nebenzimmer Akkorde anschlagen.

Zeitgenössische Literatur

Lesestrategie Applying strategies on your own When reading German on your own, you'll want to continue to use the reading strategies you've learned. Most likely you will use a combination of strategies, and your choice will depend on what you're reading and why. Are you looking in the newspaper to find out when a movie starts? Are you reading a short story for enjoyment? Or reading information that you'll need for a test? Which strategies would you use?

1. Take a moment to look at the reading selection. Scan the passage to determine what type of text it is.

2. Choose your own combination of reading strategies for working with this selection. In making your choice, be aware of 1) the type of text you're working with, and 2) the purpose for which you're reading.

For answers, see p. 323W.

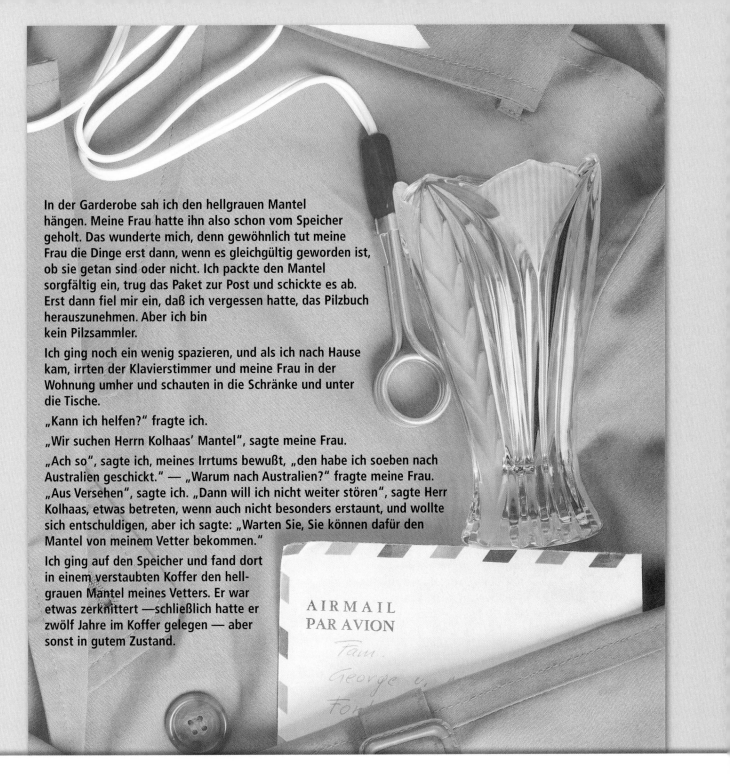

In der Garderobe sah ich den hellgrauen Mantel hängen. Meine Frau hatte ihn also schon vom Speicher geholt. Das wunderte mich, denn gewöhnlich tut meine Frau die Dinge erst dann, wenn es gleichgültig geworden ist, ob sie getan sind oder nicht. Ich packte den Mantel sorgfältig ein, trug das Paket zur Post und schickte es ab. Erst dann fiel mir ein, daß ich vergessen hatte, das Pilzbuch herauszunehmen. Aber ich bin kein Pilzsammler.

Ich ging noch ein wenig spazieren, und als ich nach Hause kam, irrten der Klavierstimmer und meine Frau in der Wohnung umher und schauten in die Schränke und unter die Tische.

„Kann ich helfen?" fragte ich.

„Wir suchen Herrn Kolhaas' Mantel", sagte meine Frau.

„Ach so", sagte ich, meines Irrtums bewußt, „den habe ich soeben nach Australien geschickt." — „Warum nach Australien?" fragte meine Frau. „Aus Versehen", sagte ich. „Dann will ich nicht weiter stören", sagte Herr Kolhaas, etwas betreten, wenn auch nicht besonders erstaunt, und wollte sich entschuldigen, aber ich sagte: „Warten Sie, Sie können dafür den Mantel von meinem Vetter bekommen."

Ich ging auf den Speicher und fand dort in einem verstaubten Koffer den hellgrauen Mantel meines Vetters. Er war etwas zerknittert —schließlich hatte er zwölf Jahre im Koffer gelegen — aber sonst in gutem Zustand.

AIRMAIL PAR AVION

3. Before you make your final choice of strategies, discuss some of your ideas with your classmates and find out which strategies they find useful.

4. Before reading, make sure you understand how to apply the strategies you've chosen and what kind of information you will gain from each.

A Closer Look

After you have worked with the story, check your comprehension by answering the following questions.

5. Was hat Eduard vor zwölf Jahren getan? Warum erwähnt der Erzähler ihn überhaupt? Was will Eduard?

6. Was schickt der Erzähler nach Australien und warum?

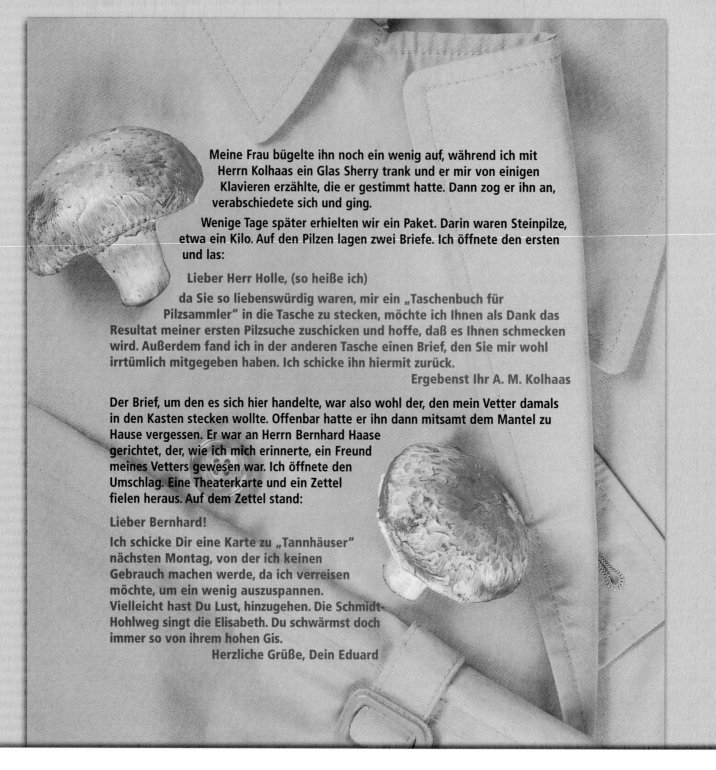

Meine Frau bügelte ihn noch ein wenig auf, während ich mit Herrn Kolhaas ein Glas Sherry trank und er mir von einigen Klavieren erzählte, die er gestimmt hatte. Dann zog er ihn an, verabschiedete sich und ging.

Wenige Tage später erhielten wir ein Paket. Darin waren Steinpilze, etwa ein Kilo. Auf den Pilzen lagen zwei Briefe. Ich öffnete den ersten und las:

Lieber Herr Holle, (so heiße ich)

da Sie so liebenswürdig waren, mir ein „Taschenbuch für Pilzsammler" in die Tasche zu stecken, möchte ich Ihnen als Dank das Resultat meiner ersten Pilzsuche zuschicken und hoffe, daß es Ihnen schmecken wird. Außerdem fand ich in der anderen Tasche einen Brief, den Sie mir wohl irrtümlich mitgegeben haben. Ich schicke ihn hiermit zurück.

Ergebenst Ihr A. M. Kolhaas

Der Brief, um den es sich hier handelte, war also wohl der, den mein Vetter damals in den Kasten stecken wollte. Offenbar hatte er ihn dann mitsamt dem Mantel zu Hause vergessen. Er war an Herrn Bernhard Haase gerichtet, der, wie ich mich erinnerte, ein Freund meines Vetters gewesen war. Ich öffnete den Umschlag. Eine Theaterkarte und ein Zettel fielen heraus. Auf dem Zettel stand:

Lieber Bernhard!

Ich schicke Dir eine Karte zu „Tannhäuser" nächsten Montag, von der ich keinen Gebrauch machen werde, da ich verreisen möchte, um ein wenig auszuspannen. Vielleicht hast Du Lust, hinzugehen. Die Schmidt-Hohlweg singt die Elisabeth. Du schwärmst doch immer so von ihrem hohen Gis.

Herzliche Grüße, Dein Eduard

7. Was bekommt Herr Kolhaas?

8. Was schickt Herr Kolhaas dem Erzähler und seiner Frau? Warum?

9. Was findet Herr Kolhaas noch im Mantel? Für wen war das bestimmt? Warum war es noch im Mantel?

10. Was fällt Eduard am Mantel auf? Worum bittet er seinen Cousin?

11. Wie reagiert die Frau des Erzählers auf die Briefe?

12. Discuss the story with your classmates. Find out what they thought it was about. Which strategies did they find useful? Which strategies allowed each of you to enjoy the story most and get the most out of it?

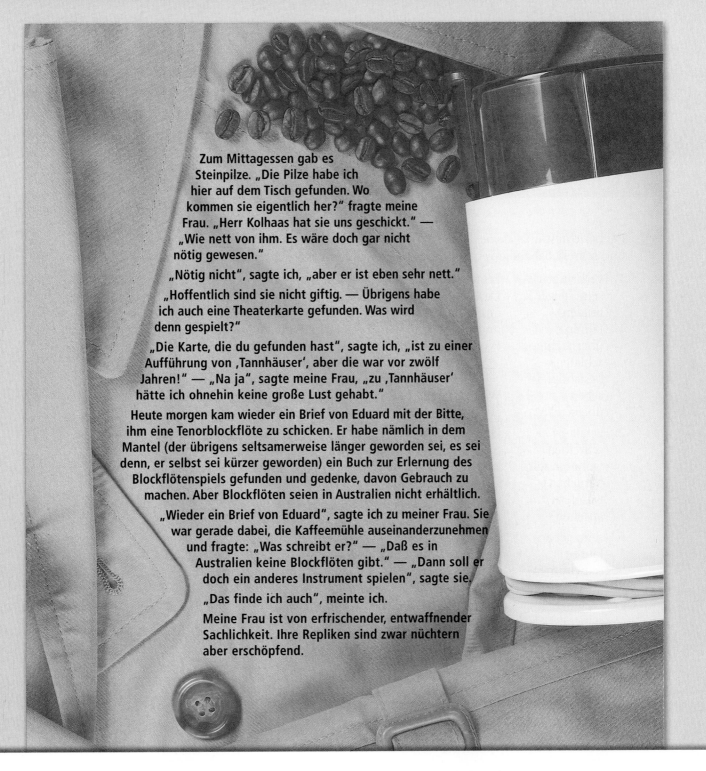

Zum Mittagessen gab es Steinpilze. „Die Pilze habe ich hier auf dem Tisch gefunden. Wo kommen sie eigentlich her?" fragte meine Frau. „Herr Kolhaas hat sie uns geschickt." — „Wie nett von ihm. Es wäre doch gar nicht nötig gewesen."

„Nötig nicht", sagte ich, „aber er ist eben sehr nett."

„Hoffentlich sind sie nicht giftig. — Übrigens habe ich auch eine Theaterkarte gefunden. Was wird denn gespielt?"

„Die Karte, die du gefunden hast", sagte ich, „ist zu einer Aufführung von ‚Tannhäuser', aber die war vor zwölf Jahren!" — „Na ja", sagte meine Frau, „zu ‚Tannhäuser' hätte ich ohnehin keine große Lust gehabt."

Heute morgen kam wieder ein Brief von Eduard mit der Bitte, ihm eine Tenorblockflöte zu schicken. Er habe nämlich in dem Mantel (der übrigens seltsamerweise länger geworden sei, es sei denn, er selbst sei kürzer geworden) ein Buch zur Erlernung des Blockflötenspiels gefunden und gedenke, davon Gebrauch zu machen. Aber Blockflöten seien in Australien nicht erhältlich.

„Wieder ein Brief von Eduard", sagte ich zu meiner Frau. Sie war gerade dabei, die Kaffeemühle auseinanderzunehmen und fragte: „Was schreibt er?" — „Daß es in Australien keine Blockflöten gibt." — „Dann soll er doch ein anderes Instrument spielen", sagte sie.

„Das finde ich auch", meinte ich.

Meine Frau ist von erfrischender, entwaffnender Sachlichkeit. Ihre Repliken sind zwar nüchtern aber erschöpfend.

13. Reread the story with the following question in mind: Which actions or dialogues deviate from what you would consider to be "normal" reactions or responses? For example, what do you expect to be in the first letter from the cousin? Are your expectations met? How do these instances make the story humorous?

14. Erzähl die Geschichte zusammen mit deinen Klassenkameraden nach! Fang die Geschichte mit einem Satz an, und eine Klassenkameradin erzählt weiter, indem sie einen neuen Satz hinzufügt. Jeder kommt einmal dran, bis die Geschichte zu Ende ist. Verwende ordnende Zeitausdrücke (zuerst, dann usw.) in der Nacherzählung!

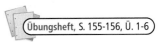

Übungsheft, S. 155-156, Ü. 1-6

Mehr Grammatikübungen

Erste Stufe

Objectives Reporting past events; expressing surprise and disappointment; agreeing; agreeing, with reservations; giving advice; giving advice and giving reasons

1 Du berichtest über deine letzten Ferien in Deutschland. Schreib die folgenden drei Berichte ab, und schreib dabei die Vergangenheitsform der gegebenen Verben in die Lücken! (**Seite 328**)

1. (verbringen) Letzten Sommer _____ wir unsere Ferien in Deutschland.   verbrachten
(sein; fliegen) Das _____ absolute Spitze! Nun, wir _____ von Chicago   war; flogen
(mieten) direkt nach Frankfurt. Dort _____ wir uns einen Wagen,   mieteten
(fahren) und wir _____ die nächsten vier Wochen überall umher.   fuhren
(übernachten) Wir _____ gewöhnlich in einfachen Hotels, aber einmal   übernachteten
(schlafen) _____ wir im berühmten Wartburg Hotel! Echt super! Wir   schliefen
(besichtigen) _____ die Wartburg, die hoch oben auf einem Berg steht.   besichtigten
(sehen) Wir _____ das berühmte Luther Zimmer, wo Martin Luther   sahen
(übersetzen) das Neue Testament vom Griechischen ins Deutsche _____ .   übersetzte

2. (gefallen) Die Goethestadt Weimar _____ uns besonders gut. Hier   gefiel
(schreiben) _____ der große Dichter viele seiner Werke. Viele Jahre   schrieb
(wohnen; sein) lang _____ auch Schiller in Weimar, und die beiden _____   wohnte; waren
(besuchen) gut befreundet. Wir _____ natürlich das Goethemuseum,   besuchten
(wandern) und wir _____ an einem schönen Nachmittag durch den   wanderten
(ansehen) Park an der Ilm, wo wir uns Goethes Gartenhaus _____ .   ansahen

3. (sein; geben) Berlin _____ der Höhepunkt unserer Reise. Hier _____ es   war; gab
(fahren) so viel zu sehen und so viel zu tun. Wir _____ hinaus an   fuhren
(schwimmen) den Tegeler See und _____ in klarem Seewasser. Wir   schwammen
(gehen; hören) _____ in einige Museen und _____ zwei ganz tolle Konzerte.   gingen; hörten
(machen) Wir _____ auch eine Stadtrundfahrt mit einem Ausflugs-   machten
(sein) schiff — kann ich empfehlen — und wir _____ auf dem   waren
(anschauen) Olympiaturm, wo wir uns Berlin von oben _____ .   anschauten

Wartburg

Schloss in Weimar

2 Du bist überrascht und auch enttäuscht von Entscheidungen (*decisions*), die ein Freund von dir getroffen hat, und du sagst ihm das auch. Schreib die folgenden Sätze ab, und schreib dabei die gegebene Information in die Lücken! Gebrauche dabei das Präsens! (**Seite 329**)

1. (Sprachen studieren wollen)   Ich bin überrascht, dass du nicht _____ .   Sprachen studieren willst
2. (auf die Uni gehen können)   Ich bin enttäuscht, dass du nicht _____ .   auf die Uni gehen kannst
3. (so schlechte Noten haben)   Ich bin enttäuscht, dass du _____ .   so schlechte Noten hast
4. (ein gesundes Leben führen)   Ich bin überrascht, dass du _____ .   ein gesundes Leben führst
5. (s. für Mode interessieren)   Ich bin überrascht, dass du _____ .   dich für Mode interessierst
6. (keine gute Musik hören)   Ich bin enttäuscht, dass du _____ .   keine gute Musik hörst

3 Du fragst eine Klassenkameradin, welchen Rat verschiedene Leute geben würden. Schreib die folgenden Sätze ab, und schreib dabei in die erste Lücke eine Form von **würde** und in die zweite Lücke eine Befehlsform der in Klammern gegebenen Information! (**Seite 329**)

1. Was würde dein Lehrer sagen, wenn du eine schlechte Note bekommst? (fleißig lernen) Mein Lehrer _____ sagen: _____ !   würde; Lern fleißig
2. Was würdest du sagen, wenn ich eine schlechte Note bekomme? (nicht so faul sein) Also, ich _____ sagen: _____ !   würde; Sei nicht so faul
3. Was würden deine Eltern sagen, wenn du nicht mehr zu Hause wohnen wolltest? (ausziehen) — Meine Eltern _____ sagen: _____ !   würden; Zieh aus
4. Was würde dein Cousin sagen, wenn du mit seinem Rad fahren möchtest? (dein eigenes Rad nehmen) — Mein Cousin _____ sagen : _____ !   würde; Nimm dein eigenes Rad
5. Rat mal, was ich sagen würde, wenn du Geld von mir möchtest. (dein eigenes Geld verdienen) — Ja, du _____ sagen: _____ !   würdest; Verdien dein eigenes Geld

4 Du rätst einer Freundin, wie sie gesünder leben könnte. Schreib die folgenden Sätze ab, und schreib dabei die gegebene Information in einen Infinitivsatz um! (**Seite 331**)

1. (ein gesundes Leben führen)   Versuch doch mal, _____ !   ein gesundes Leben zu führen
2. (deine Diät ändern)   Versuch doch mal, _____ !   deine Diät zu ändern
3. (weniger Fleisch essen)   Versuch doch mal, _____ !   weniger Fleisch zu essen
4. (die Sonne vermeiden)   Versuch doch mal, _____ !   die Sonne zu vermeiden
5. (mehr Sport machen)   Versuch doch mal, _____ !   mehr Sport zu machen
6. (deine Fehler zugeben)   Versuch doch mal, _____ !   deine Fehler zuzugeben
7. (weniger auffallen)   Versuch doch mal, _____ !   weniger aufzufallen
8. (ein neues Leben anfangen)   Versuch doch mal, _____ !   ein neues Leben anzufangen

Mehr Grammatikübungen

5 Du sagst, was du versuchst, um ein besseres Leben zu führen. Schreib die folgenden Sätze ab, und schreib dabei die gegebene Information in einen Infinitivsatz um! **(Seite 331)**

1. (ein gesundes Leben führen)   Ich versuche alles, um _____ .   ein gesundes L. zu führen
2. (sich fit halten)   Ich versuche alles, um _____ .   mich fit zu halten
3. (die Umwelt verbessern)   Ich versuche alles, um _____ .   die Umwelt zu verbessern
4. (besser aussehen)   Ich versuche alles, um _____ .   besser auszusehen
5. (mit der Mode mitmachen)   Ich versuche alles, um _____ .   mit der Mode mitzumachen
6. (keine Vorurteile annehmen)   Ich versuche alles, um _____ .   keine Vorurteile anzunehmen

Zweite Stufe

Objectives Expressing determination or indecision; talking about what is important or not important; hypothesizing

6 Du hast dich entschieden, viele Ziele in deinem Leben zu verwirklichen, und du berichtest einer Klassenkameradin darüber. Schreib die folgenden Sätze ab, und schreib dabei die gegebene Information als Infinitivsatz in die Lücken! **(Seite 337)**

1. (einen guten Abschluss machen)   Ich hab beschlossen, _____ .   einen guten A. zu machen
2. (Fremdsprachen studieren)   Ich hab mich entschieden, _____ .   Fremdsprachen zu studieren
3. (Mediaplanerin werden)   Ich hab beschlossen, _____ .   Mediaplanerin zu werden
4. (im Ausland arbeiten)   Ich hab mich entschieden, _____ .   im Ausland zu arbeiten
5. (sich mehr anstrengen)   Ich hab beschlossen, _____ .   mich mehr anzustrengen
6. (großen Erfolg haben)   Ich hab mich entschieden, _____ .   großen Erfolg zu haben
7. (eine sichere Stellung annehmen)   Ich hab beschlossen, _____ .   eine sichere S. anzunehmen

7 Ein Freund stellt dir viele Fragen über deine Zukunft. Du hast dich über viele Dinge noch nicht entschieden, und du sagst ihm das. Schreib die folgenden Sätze ab, und schreib dabei die Fragen deines Freundes als indirekte Fragen in die Lücken! **(Seite 337)**

1. Sag mal, Uwe, was wirst du später einmal machen? — Ich kann noch nicht sagen, _____ .   was ich später einmal machen werde
2. Was wirst du einmal studieren? — Ich muss mir noch überlegen, _____ .   was ich einmal studieren werde
3. Wo wirst du studieren? — Ich weiß nicht, _____ .   wo ich studieren werde
4. Wie lange wird das Studium dauern? — Ich kann noch nicht sagen, _____ .   wie lange das Studium dauern wird
5. Warum möchtest du nicht im Ausland studieren? — Ich weiß nicht, _____ .   warum ich nicht im Ausland studieren möchte
6. Wie viel Geld wird dein Studium kosten? — Ich kann noch nicht sagen, _____ .   wie viel Geld mein Studium kosten wird

8 Was ist dir wichtig, und was ist dir nicht wichtig? Schreib die folgenden Sätze ab, und schreib dabei in die erste Lücke ein „**da**-compound" und in die zweite die gegebene Information als Infinitivsatz! (**Seite 338**)

1. (einen guten Abschluss machen) Worauf legst du großen Wert? — Ich lege großen Wert _____ , _____ .   darauf; einen guten Abschluss zu machen

2. (im Ausland Jura studieren) Worauf legst du keinen großen Wert? — Ich lege keinen großen Wert _____ , _____ .   darauf; im Ausland Jura zu studieren

3. (finanziell unabhängig sein) Worauf legst du großen Wert? — Ich lege großen Wert _____ , _____ .   darauf; finanziell unabhängig zu sein

4. (ein großes Haus mit Pool haben) Worauf legst du keinen großen Wert? — Ich lege keinen großen Wert _____ , _____ .   darauf; ein großes Haus mit Pool zu haben

5. (andern Menschen helfen können) Worauf legst du großen Wert? — Ich lege großen Wert _____ , _____ .   darauf; andern Menschen helfen zu können

6. (Strafverteidigerin werden) Worauf legst du keinen großen Wert? — Ich lege keinen großen Wert _____ , _____ .   darauf; Strafverteidigerin zu werden

9 Was ist anderen Leuten wichtig? Sie sagen es dir. Schreib die folgenden Sätze ab, und schreib dabei in die erste Lücke das richtige Personalpronomen und in die zweite Lücke die gegebene Information als dass-Satz! (**Seite 338**)

1. Was ist deinem Bruder wichtig? Ein gutes Abitur zu machen?
   — Ja, _____ ist wichtig, dass _____ .   ihm; er ein gutes Abitur macht

2. Was ist für dich entscheidend? Jura in München studieren zu können?
   — Ja, entscheidend für _____ ist, dass _____ .   mich; ich in München Jura studieren kann

3. Was ist deiner Kusine wichtig? In den Vereinigten Staaten Sport zu studieren?
   — Ja, _____ ist wichtig, dass _____ .   ihr; sie in den V.S. Sport studiert

4. Was ist für euch entscheidend, Uwe und Anna? Sofort einen guten Job zu finden?
   — Ja, entscheidend für _____ ist, dass _____ .   uns; wir sofort einen guten Job finden

5. Was ist deinen Geschwistern wichtig? Ein eigenes Zimmer zu haben?
   — Ja, _____ ist wichtig, dass _____ .   ihnen; sie ein eigenes Zimmer haben

6. Was ist für Sie entscheidend, Herr Meier? Jeden Sommer nach Deutschland zu fliegen?
   — Ja, entscheidend für _____ ist, dass _____ .   mich; ich jeden Sommer nach D. fliege

10 Was würdest du tun, wenn . . . ? Schreib die folgenden Sätze ab, und schreib dabei die korrekten Konjunktivformen der Verben **haben, sein,** oder **werden** in die Lücken! (**Seite 338**)

1. Wenn ich mehr Geld _____ , _____ ich mir ein neues Auto kaufen.   hätte; würde

2. Was _____ du dir kaufen, wenn du mehr Geld _____ ? Auch ein Auto?   würdest; hättest

3. Wenn wir mit dem Studium fertig _____ , _____ wir eine Reise machen.   wären; würden

4. Was _____ ihr machen, wenn ihr mit dem Studium fertig _____ ?   würdet; wärt

5. Was _____ du machen, wenn du in New York _____ ?   würdest; wärst

6. Wenn ich in New York _____ , _____ ich viel unternehmen.   wäre; würde

Kann ich's wirklich?

Can you report past events? (p. 328)

1 How would you respond if someone said to you **Erzähl mir alles, was du in den letzten Ferien gemacht hast!**? E.g.: In meinen letzten Ferien hatte ich einen Ferienjob im Supermarkt.

Can you express surprise? (p. 329)

2 How would you respond to the following statements, made by a friend of yours? E.g. Ich bin überrascht, dass sie dir so viel Geld geschenkt hat.

a. Meine Tante Klara hat mir 20 000 Euro zum Geburtstag geschenkt.

b. Ich fliege morgen in die Vereinigten Staaten, um dort zu studieren. E.g. Ich bin erstaunt, dass du schon morgen dorthin fliegst!

Can you express disappointment? (p. 329)

3 How would you respond if you heard

a. that one of your best friends takes drugs (**Drogen**)? E. g.: Ich finde es schade, dass er Drogen nimmt.

b. that your best friend is moving to Australia? E.g.: Ich bin enttäuscht, dass sie nach Australien zieht.

Can you agree? (p. 329)

4 How would you agree with someone who said **Wir schauen zu viel Fernsehen, anstatt zu lesen**? E.g.: Bei uns ist es auch so.

Can you agree with reservations? (p. 329)

5 How would you agree, but with reservations, if someone said **Wer Geld hat, hat auch Freunde**? E.g.: Es kommt darauf an. Manchen Freunden ist Geld egal.

Can you give advice? (p. 329)

6 How would you respond if a friend said to you **Ich weiß nicht mehr, was ich machen soll; ich bekomme immer schlechte Noten**? E.g.: Vielleicht kannst du etwas mehr lernen.

Can you give advice and give reasons? (p. 331)

7 How would you tell someone that he or she should exercise and why? How would you give your own reason for exercising regularly? E.g.: Du solltest mehr Sport treiben, weil er dich fit hält.; Ich treibe viel Sport, um wirklich fit zu bleiben.

Can you express determination or indecision? (p. 337)

8 How would you say

a. what you're determined to do after high school? a. E.g.: Ich hab mich entschieden, nach der Schule Biologie zu studieren.

b. that you're not yet sure what you'll do? b. E.g.: Ich weiß noch nicht, was ich nach der Schule machen soll.

Can you talk about what is important or not important? (p. 338)

9 How would you tell a friend

a. what is important to you? E.g.: Mir ist wichtig, gesund zu essen.

b. what is not important? E.g.: Ich lege keinen großen Wert auf modische Klamotten.

Can you hypothesize? (p. 338)

10 How would you respond if someone asked you **Was würdest du tun, wenn du Millionär wärst?** E.g.: Wenn ich Millionär wäre, würde ich eine Weltreise machen.

Erste Stufe

p. 279T

Professions

Schornsteinfeger(in), -/nen	chimney sweep
Steuerberater(in), -/nen	tax consultant
Rundfunk- moderator(in), -en/nen	radio moderator
Toningenieur(in), -e/nen	sound engineer
Friseur/Friseuse, -e/n	hairstylist
Schweißer(in), -/nen	welder
Schreiner(in), -/nen	cabinet maker
Glasbläser(in), -/nen	glass blower

Anästhesist(in), -en/nen	anesthesiologist
Elektroinstallateur(in), -e/nen	electrician
Fotograf(in), -en/nen	photographer
Koch (Köchin), ¨e/nen	chef
Optiker(in), -/nen	optician
Schuhmacher(in), -/nen	shoemaker
technische(r) Zeichner(in), -/nen	technical designer
Winzer(in), -/nen	vintner
der Zahnarzt, ¨e	dentist

die Zahnärztin, -nen	(female) dentist
der Zimmermann, -leute	carpenter

Other useful words

die Niete, -n	failure (in a subject)
die Diät, -en	diet
das Kostüm, -e	costume
führen	to lead

Zweite Stufe

Modern professions

Zahntechniker(in), -/nen	dental technician
Strafverteidiger(in), -/nen	lawyer for the defense
Gesundheitswissen- schaftler(in), -/nen	nutritional scientist
Sportökonom(in), -en/nen	sports scientist
Umweltökonom(in), -en/nen	environmental scientist
Mediaplaner(in), -/nen	media planner
Kommunikations- elektroniker (in), -/nen	communications engineer
Industriedesigner(in), -/nen	industrial designer
PR-Berater(in), -/nen	PR-consultant
Touristikfachwirt(in), -e/nen	tourism special- ist
Lebensmittelkon- trolleur(in), -e/nen	health inspector

Other useful words

die Ehe, -n	marriage
die Scheidung, -en	divorce
der Erfolg, -e	success
der Konflikt, -e	conflict
die Chance, -n	chance
ziehen	to move (residence)
unterdrücken	to oppress
gründen	to found
s. anstrengen (sep)	to make an effort
einengen (sep)	to confine
finanziell	financially
im Fall	in the case (of)
sicherlich	certainly

Reference Section

Summary of Functions

Functions are probably best defined as the ways in which you use a language for specific purposes. When you find yourself in specific situations, such as in a restaurant, in a grocery store, or at school, you will want to communicate with those around you. In order to do that, you have to "function" in the language so that you can be understood: you place an order, make a purchase, or talk about your class schedule.

Such functions form the core of this book. They are easily identified by the boxes in each chapter that are labeled SO SAGT MAN DAS! These functions are the building blocks you need to become a speaker of German. All the other features in the chapter—the grammar, the vocabulary, even the culture notes—are there to support the functions you are learning.

Here is a list of the functions from Levels 1, 2, and 3 accompanied by the German expressions you will need in order to communicate in a wide range of situations. The level of the book is indicated by a Roman numeral I, II, or III. The chapter and page on which the expressions were introduced is also indicated.

You have learned to communicate in a variety of situations. Using these expressions, you will be able to communicate in many other situations as well.

Socializing

Saying hello
I, Ch. 1, p. 21
Guten Morgen!
Guten Tag!
Morgen! ⎱
Tag! ⎰ *shortened forms*
Hallo! ⎱
Grüß dich! ⎰ *informal*

Saying goodbye
I, Ch. 1, p. 21
Auf Wiedersehen!
Wiedersehen! *shortened form*
Tschüs! ⎱
Tschau! ⎰ *informal*
Bis dann! ⎰

Offering something to eat and drink
I, Ch. 3, p. 74
Was möchtest du trinken?
Was möchte *(name)* trinken?
Was möchtet ihr essen?

Responding to an offer
I, Ch. 3, p. 74
Ich möchte *(beverage)* trinken.
Er/Sie möchte im Moment gar nichts.
Wir möchten *(food/beverage)*, bitte.

Saying please
I, Ch. 3, p. 76
Bitte!

Saying thank you **I, Ch. 3, p. 76**
Danke!
Danke schön!
Danke sehr!

Saying you're welcome **I, Ch. 3, p. 76**
Bitte!
Bitte schön!
Bitte sehr!

Giving compliments **I, Ch. 5, p. 139**
Der/Die/Das *(thing)* sieht *(adjective)* aus!
Der/Die/Das *(thing)* gefällt mir.

II, Ch. 8, p. 222
Dein/Deine *(clothing item)* sieht echt fetzig aus.
Sie/Er/Es passt dir auch echt gut.
Und dieser/diese/dieses *(clothing item)*
   passt dir prima!
Sie/Er/Es passt gut zu deiner/deinem
   (clothing item).

Responding to compliments
I, Ch. 5, p. 139
Ehrlich?
Wirklich?
Nicht zu *(adjective)*?
Meinst du?

II, Ch. 8, p. 222
Meinst du wirklich?
Ist er/sie/es mir nicht zu *(adjective)*?
Das ist auch mein/meine Lieblings
   (clothing item).
Echt?

Starting a conversation
I, Ch. 6, p. 161

Wie geht's?
Wie geht's denn? } *Asking how someone is doing*

Sehr gut!
Prima!
Danke, gut!
Gut!
Danke, es geht.
So lala.
Nicht schlecht.
Nicht so gut.
Schlecht.
Sehr schlecht.
Miserabel. } *Responding to* **Wie geht's?**

Making plans
I, Ch. 6, p. 166

Was willst du machen?   Ich will *(activity)*.
Wohin will *(person)*   Er/Sie will in/ins
gehen?   *(place)* gehen.

Ordering food and beverages
I, Ch. 6, p. 170

Was bekommen Sie?   Ich bekomme *(food/ beverage)*.

Ja, bitte?
Was essen Sie?   Einen/Eine/Ein *(food)*, bitte.

Was möchten Sie?   Ich möchte *(food/ beverage)*, bitte.

Was trinken Sie?   Ich trinke *(beverage)*.
Was nimmst du?   Ich nehme *(food/ beverage)*.

Was isst du?   Ich esse *(food)*.

II, Ch. 11, p. 314

Haben Sie schon   Ja, bringen Sie mir
gewählt?   bitte den/die/das *(menu item)*.

Und was hätten   Ich hätte gern den/die/
Sie gern?   das *(menu item)*.

Talking about how something tastes
I, Ch. 6, p. 172

Wie schmeckt's?   Gut!
                      Prima!
                      Sagenhaft!
                      Der/Die/Das *(food/ beverage)* schmeckt lecker!
                      Der/Die/Das *(food/ beverage)* schmeckt nicht.
Schmeckt's?   Ja, gut!
                      Nein, nicht so gut.
                      Nicht besonders.

Paying the check
I, Ch. 6, p. 172

Hallo! Ich will/   Das macht (zusammen)
möchte zahlen.   *(total)*.
Stimmt schon!

Extending an invitation
I, Ch. 7, p. 194; Ch. 11, p. 313

Willst du *(activity)*?
Wir wollen *(activity)*. Komm doch mit!
Möchtest du mitkommen?
Ich habe am *(day/date)* eine Party. Ich lade dich ein. Kannst du kommen?

Responding to an invitation
I, Ch. 7, p. 194; Ch. 11, p. 313

Ja, gern!
Toll!
Ich komme gern mit.
Aber sicher!
Natürlich! } *accepting*

Das geht nicht.
Ich kann leider nicht. } *declining*

Accepting with certainty
III, Ch. 11, p. 309

Ja, natürlich!
Ganz bestimmt.
Auf jeden Fall.
Auf alle Fälle.

Refusing with certainty
III, Ch. 11, p. 309

Nein, tut mir Leid.
Kommt nicht in Frage!
Auf keinen Fall.

Expressing obligations
I, Ch. 7, p. 194

Ich habe keine Zeit. Ich muss *(activity)*.

Offering help
I, Ch. 7, p. 199

Was kann ich für dich tun?
Kann ich etwas für dich tun? } *asking*
Brauchst du Hilfe?
Gut! Mach ich!   *agreeing*

Asking what you should do
I, Ch. 8, p. 222

Was soll ich für   Du kannst für mich
dich tun?   *(chore)*.
Wo soll ich *(thing/*   Beim (Metzger/Bäcker).
things) kaufen?   In der/Im *(store)*.
Soll ich *(thing/*   Nein, das kannst du
things) in der/im   besser in der/im *(store)*
(store) kaufen?   kaufen.

Getting someone's attention
I, Ch. 9, p. 250
Verzeihung!
Entschuldigung!

Offering more
I, Ch. 9, p. 258
Möchtest du noch etwas?
Möchtest du noch einen/eine/ein
(food/beverage)?
Noch einen/eine/ein (food/beverage)?

Saying you want more
I, Ch. 9, p. 258
Ja, bitte. Ich nehme noch einen/eine/ein
(food/beverage).
Ja, bitte. Noch einen/eine/ein (food/beverage).
Ja, gern.

Saying you don't want more
I, Ch. 9, p. 258
Nein, danke! Ich habe keinen Hunger mehr.
Nein, danke! Ich habe genug.
Danke, nichts mehr für mich.
Nein, danke, keinen/keine/kein (food/beverage)
mehr.

Using the telephone
I, Ch. 11, p. 310
Hier (name).
Hier ist (name).
Ich möchte bitte
(name) sprechen.
Kann ich bitte
(name) sprechen?
Tag! Hier ist (name). } starting a conversation
Wiederhören!
Auf Wiederhören!
Tschüs! } ending a conversation

Talking about birthdays
I, Ch. 11, p. 314
Wann hast du   Ich habe am (date)
Geburtstag?   Geburtstag.
                  Am (date).

Expressing good wishes
I, Ch. 11, p. 314
Alles Gute zum/zur (occasion)!
Herzlichen Glückwunsch zum/zur (occasion)!

II, Ch. 11, p. 315
Zum Wohl!
Prost!
Auf dein/euer/Ihr Wohl!
Guten Appetit!
Mahlzeit!

Changing the subject
III, Ch. 6, p. 156
Ich möchte noch mal auf (topic)
zurückkommen.
Übrigens, ich wollte etwas anderes sagen.

Interrupting
III, Ch. 6, p. 156
Lass mich mal zu Wort kommen!
Moment mal! Lass (person) mal ausreden!

Making polite requests
III, Ch. 9, p. 243
Könnte ich bitte ...?
Dürfte ich bitte ...?
Würden Sie bitte ...?

Exchanging Information

Asking someone his or her name and giving yours
I, Ch. 1, p. 22
Wie heißt du?   Ich heiße (name).
Heißt du (name)?   Ja, ich heiße (name).

Asking and giving someone else's name
I, Ch. 1, p. 22
Wie heißt der Junge? Der Junge heißt (name).
Heißt der Junge   Ja, er heißt (name).
(name)?
Wie heißt das   Das Mädchen heißt (name).
Mädchen?
Heißt das Mädchen   Nein, sie heißt (name).
(name)?

Asking and telling who someone is
I, Ch. 1, p. 23
Wer ist das?   Das ist der/die (name).

Asking someone his or her age and giving yours
I, Ch. 1, p. 25
Wie alt bist du?   Ich bin (number) Jahre alt.
                      Ich bin (number).
                      (Number).
Bist du schon   Nein, ich bin (number).
(number)?

Asking and giving someone else's age
I, Ch. 1, p. 25
Wie alt ist der Peter? Er ist (number).
Und die Monika? Ist   Ja, sie ist auch (number).
sie auch (number)?

R4

Asking someone where he or she is from and telling where you are from I, Ch. 1, p. 28

Woher kommst du?	Ich komme aus (place).
Woher bist du?	Ich bin aus (place).
Bist du aus (place)?	Nein, ich bin aus (place).

Asking and telling where someone else is from I, Ch. 1, p. 28

Woher ist (person)?	Er/Sie ist aus (place).
Kommt (person) aus (place)?	Nein, sie kommt aus (place).

Talking about how someone gets to school I, Ch. 1, p. 30

Wie kommst du zur Schule?	Ich komme mit der/dem (mode of transportation).
Kommt Ahmet zu Fuß zur Schule?	Nein, er kommt auch mit der/dem (mode of transportation).
Wie kommt Ayla zur Schule?	Sie kommt mit der/dem (mode of transportation).

Talking about interests I, Ch. 2, p. 48

Was machst du in deiner Freizeit?	Ich (activity).
Spielst du (sport/ instrument/game)?	Ja, ich spiele (sport/ instrument/game).
	Nein, (sport/instrument/ game) spiele ich nicht.
Was macht (name)?	Er/Sie spielt (sport/ instrument/game).

Asking about interests II, Ch. 8, p. 221; Ch. 10, p. 276

Interessierst du dich für (thing)?
Wofür interessierst du dich?
Was für Interessen hast du?

Expressing interest II, Ch. 8, p. 221; Ch. 10, p. 276

Ja, (thing) interessiert mich.
Ich interessiere mich für (thing).

Expressing disinterest II, Ch. 8, p. 221

(Thing) interessiert mich nicht.
Ich hab kein Interesse an (thing).

Expressing indifference II, Ch. 8, p. 221

(Thing) ist mir egal.

Saying when you do various activities I, Ch. 2, p. 55

Was machst du nach der Schule?	Am Nachmittag (activity). Am Abend (activity).
Und am Wochenende?	Am Wochenende (activity).
Was machst du im Sommer?	Im Sommer (activity).

Talking about where you and others live I, Ch. 3, p. 73

Wo wohnst du?	Ich wohne in (place). In (place).
Wo wohnt der/die (name)?	Er/Sie wohnt in (place). In (place).

Describing a room I, Ch. 3, p. 79

Der/Die/Das (thing) ist alt.
Der/Die/Das (thing) ist kaputt.
Der/Die/Das (thing) ist klein, aber ganz bequem.
Ist (thing) neu? Ja, er/sie/es ist neu.

Talking about family members I, Ch. 3, p. 82

Ist das dein/deine (family member)?	Ja, das ist mein/ meine (family member).
Und dein/deine (family member)? Wie heißt er/sie?	Er/Sie heißt (name).
Wo wohnen deine (family members)?	In (place).

Describing people I, Ch. 3, p. 84

Wie sieht (person) aus?	Er/Sie hat (color) Haare und (color) Augen.

Talking about class schedules I, Ch. 4, p. 106

Welche Fächer hast du?	Ich habe (classes).
Was hast du am (day)?	(Classes).
Was hat die Katja am (day)?	Sie hat (classes).
Welche Fächer habt ihr?	Wir haben (classes).
Was habt ihr nach der Pause?	Wir haben (classes).
Und was habt ihr am Samstag?	Wir haben frei!

Using a schedule to talk about time I, Ch. 4, p. 107

Wann hast du (class)?	Um (hour) Uhr (minutes).
Was hast du um (hour) Uhr?	(Class).
Was hast du von (time) bis (time)?	Ich habe (class).

Sequencing events I, Ch. 4, p. 109

Welche Fächer hast du am (day)?	Zuerst hab ich (class), dann (class), danach (class), und zuletzt (class).

Summary of Functions

Talking about prices
I, Ch. 4, p. 115

Was kostet *(thing)*?	Er/Sie kostet nur *(price)*.
Was kosten *(things)*?	Sie kosten *(price)*.
Das ist *(ziemlich)* teuer!	
Das ist *(sehr)* billig!	
Das ist *(sehr)* preiswert!	

Pointing things out
I, Ch. 4, p. 116

Wo sind die *(things)*?	Schauen Sie!
	Dort!
	Sie sind dort drüben!
	Sie sind da hinten.
	Sie sind da vorn.

Expressing wishes when shopping
I, Ch. 5, p. 134

Was möchten Sie?	Ich möchte einen/eine/ein *(thing)* sehen, bitte.
	Ich brauche einen/eine/ein *(thing)*.
Was bekommen Sie?	Einen/Eine/Ein *(thing)*, bitte.
Haben Sie einen Wunsch?	Ich suche einen/eine/ein *(thing)*.

Describing how clothes fit
I, Ch. 5, p. 137

Es passt prima.
Es passt nicht.

Talking about trying on clothes
I, Ch. 5, p. 143

Ich probiere den/die/das (item of clothing) an.
Ich ziehe den/die/das (item of clothing) an.

If you buy it:	*If you don't:*
Ich nehme es.	Ich nehme es nicht.
Ich kaufe es.	Ich kaufe es nicht.

Telling time
I, Ch. 6, p. 162

Wie spät ist es jetzt?	Es ist *(time)*.
Wie viel Uhr ist es?	Es ist *(time)*.

Talking about when you do things
I, Ch. 6, p. 162

Wann gehst du *(activity)*?	Um *(time)*.
Um wie viel Uhr *(action)* du?	Um *(time)*.
Und du? Wann *(action)* du?	Um *(time)*.

Talking about how often you do things
I, Ch. 7, p. 198

Wie oft *(action)* du?	(Einmal) in der Woche.
Und wie oft musst du *(action)*?	Jeden Tag.
	Ungefähr (zweimal) im Monat.

Explaining what to do
I, Ch. 7, p. 199

Du kannst für mich *(action)*.

Talking about the weather
I, Ch. 7, p. 203

Wie ist das Wetter heute?	Heute regnet es. Wolkig und kühl.
Wie ist das Wetter morgen?	Sonnig, aber kalt.
Regnet es heute?	Ich glaube schon.
Schneit es am Abend?	Nein, es schneit nicht.
Wie viel Grad haben wir heute?	Ungefähr 10 Grad.

Talking about quantities
I, Ch. 8, p. 226

Wie viel *(food item)* bekommen Sie?	500 Gramm *(food item)*. 100 Gramm, bitte.

Asking if someone wants anything else
I, Ch. 8, p. 227

Sonst noch etwas?
Was bekommen Sie noch?
Haben Sie noch einen Wunsch?

Saying you want something else
I, Ch. 8, p. 227

Ich brauche noch einen/eine/ein *(food/beverage/thing)*.
Ich bekomme noch einen/eine/ein *(food/beverage/thing)*.

Telling someone you don't need anything else
I, Ch. 8, p. 227

Nein, danke.
Danke, das ist alles.

Giving a reason
I, Ch. 8, p. 230

Jetzt kann ich nicht, weil ...
Es geht nicht, denn ...

III, Ch. 3, p. 75

..., weil ich ...
..., damit ...
..., um ... zu ...

Saying where you were I, Ch. 8, p. 231

| Wo warst du heute Morgen? | Ich war in/im/an/am (place). |
| Wo warst du gestern? | Ich war in/im/an/am (place). |

Saying what you bought
I, Ch. 8, p. 231

Was hast du gekauft? Ich habe (thing) gekauft.

Talking about where something is located
I, Ch. 9, p. 250

Verzeihung, wissen Sie, wo der/die/das (place) ist?	In der Innenstadt. Am (place name). In der (street name).
Wo ist der/die/das (place)?	Es tut mir Leid. Das weiß ich nicht.
Entschuldigung! Weißt du, wo der/die/das (place) ist?	Keine Ahnung! Ich bin nicht von hier.

Asking for directions
I, Ch. 9, p. 254

Wie komme ich zum/zur (place)?
Wie kommt man zum/zur (place)?

II, Ch. 9, p. 254

Entschuldigung! Wo ist bitte (place).
Verzeihung! Wissen Sie vielleicht, wie ich zum/zur (place) komme?

Giving directions
I, Ch. 9, p. 254

Gehen Sie geradeaus bis zum/zur (place).
Nach rechts/links.
Hier rechts/links.

II, Ch. 9, p. 254

Sie biegen hier (direction) in die (streetname) ein.
Dann kommen Sie zum/zur (place).
Das ist hier (direction) um die Ecke.
Ich weiß es leider nicht. Ich bin nicht von hier.

Talking about what there is to eat and drink
I, Ch. 9, p. 257

| Was gibt es hier zu essen? | Es gibt (foods). |
| Und zu trinken | Es gibt (beverage) und auch (beverage). |

Talking about what you did in your free time
I, Ch. 10, p. 258

| Was hast du (time phrase) gemacht? | Ich habe ... (person/thing) gesehen. (book, magazine, etc.) gelesen. mit (person) über (subject) gesprochen. |

Discussing gift ideas
I, Ch. 11, p. 318

Schenkst du (person) einen/eine/ein (thing) zum/zur (occasion)?	Nein, ich schenke ihm/ihr einen/eine/ein (thing).
Was schenkst du (person) zum/zur (occasion)?	Ich weiß noch nicht. Hast du eine Idee?
Wem schenkst du den/die/das (thing)?	Ich schenke (person) den/die/das (thing).

Asking about past events
II, Ch. 3, p. 65; Ch. 3, p. 71

Was hast du (time phrase) gemacht?
Was hat (person) (time phrase) gemacht?

Asking what someone did
II, Ch. 3, p. 65

Was hast du (time phrase) gemacht?
Was hat (person) (time phrase) gemacht?

Telling what someone did
II, Ch. 3, p. 65

Ich habe (activity + past participle).
Er/Sie hat (activity + past participle).

Asking where someone was II, Ch. 3, p. 71

Wo bist du gewesen?
Und wo warst du?

Telling where you were II, Ch. 3, p. 71

Ich bin in/im/an/am (place) gewesen.
Ich war in/im/an/am (place).
Ich war mit (person) in/im/an/am (place).

Asking for information
II, Ch. 4, p. 107; Ch. 10, p. 284

Ich habe eine Frage: ...?
Sag mal, ...?
Wie steht's mit (thing)?
Darf ich dich etwas fragen? ...?
Wissen Sie, ob ...?
Können Sie mir sagen, ob ...?

Stating information
II, Ch. 10, p. 284

Ich glaube schon, dass ...
Ich meine doch, dass ...

Responding emphatically II, Ch. 4, p. 107

Ja, natürlich!
Na klar!
Aber sicher!

Agreeing, with reservations
II. Ch. 4, p. 107

Ja, das kann sein, aber ...
Das stimmt, aber ...
Eigentlich schon, aber ...

Asking what someone may or may not do
II, Ch. 4, p. 110
> Was darfst du (nicht) tun?
> Was darfst du (nicht) essen/trinken?
> Darfst du (activity)?

Telling what you may or may not do
II, Ch. 4, p. 110
> Ich darf (nicht) (activity).
> Ich darf (food/drink) (nicht) essen/trinken.

Expressing skepticism
II, Ch. 5, p. 130
> Was soll denn das sein, dieser/diese/dieses (thing)?

Making certain
II, Ch. 5, p. 130
> Du isst nur vegetarisch, was?   Ja/Nein.
> Du isst wohl viel Fleisch, ja?   Nicht unbedingt!
> Du magst Joghurt, oder?   Na klar!
> Du magst doch Quark, nicht wahr?   Sicher!

Calling someone's attention to something and responding
II, Ch. 5, p. 134
> Schau mal!   Ja, was denn?
> Guck mal!   Ja, was bitte?
> Sieh mal!   Was ist denn los?
> Hör mal!   Was ist?
> Hör mal zu!   Was gibt's?

Asking for specific information
II, Ch. 5, p. 123
> Welchen/Welche/Welches (thing) magst du?   Ich mag (thing).
> Welchen/Welche/Welches (thing) willst du?   Diesen/Diese/Dieses (thing), bitte!

Inquiring about someone's health
II, Ch. 6, p. 157
> Wie fühlst du dich?
> Wie geht es dir?
> Ist dir nicht gut?
> Ist was mit dir?
> Was fehlt dir?

Responding to questions about your health
II, Ch. 6, p. 157
> Ich fühl mich wohl!
> Es geht mir (nicht) gut!
> Mir ist schlecht
> Mir ist nicht gut.

Responding to statements about someone's health
II, Ch. 6, p. 157
> Ach schade!
> Gute Besserung!
> Hoffentlich geht es dir bald besser!

Asking about pain
II, Ch. 6, p. 163
> Tut's weh?
> Was tut dir weh?
> Tut dir was weh?
> Tut dir (body part) weh?

Expressing pain II, Ch. 6, p. 163
> Au!
> Aua!
> Es tut weh!
> Der/Die/Das (body part) tut mir weh.
> Ja, ich hab (body part)schmerzen.

Expressing wishes
II, Ch. 7, p. 192
> Was möchtest du gern mal haben?   Ich möchte gern mal einen/eine/ein (thing)!
> Was wünschst du dir mal?   Ich wünsche mir mal ...
> Und was wünscht ihr euch?   Wir wünschen uns ...

III, Ch. 11, p. 309
> (Thing) wäre mir (nicht) wichtig.
> In meiner idealen Welt gäbe es (kein/en/e) (thing).

Talking about plans
II, Ch. 10, p. 288
> Ich werde (activity).
> (Time phrase) werde ich (activity).

Expressing hearsay
II, Ch. 11, p. 310
> Ich habe gehört, dass ...
> Man hat mir gesagt, dass ...
> (Thing) soll (adjective) sein.

Admitting something
III, Ch. 3, p. 76
> Ich geb's zu.
> Ich geb's zu, dass ich ...
> Ich muss zugeben, dass ...

Reporting past events
III, Ch. 5, p. 132; Ch. 6, p. 154
> Wir haben letzten Monat einen Bundeswehroffizier eingeladen. Die Diskussion war sehr interessant, und wir konnten uns gut informieren. Wir wollten noch mehr hören, aber wir mussten zum Unterricht gehen.

Vor einiger Zeit führte eine Fernsehstation folgenden Test durch: Zwei Familien erklärten sich bereit, ... Und was passierte? Die Leute wussten einfach nicht mehr, was sie ohne Fernseher anfangen sollten. Sie saßen da und starrten sich an ...

Saying that something is going on right now
III, Ch. 5, p. 131

Wir *(action)* gerade.
Wir sind dabei, *(person/place/thing)* zu *(action)*.
Wir sind am (beim) *(action)*.

Comparing
III, Ch. 7, p. 185

Ich kenne auch so einen/eine *(type of person)* wie dich.
Dieser/Diese/Dieses *(thing)* ist nicht so gut wie dieser/diese/dieses.
Ich finde diesen/diese/dieses *(thing)* viel besser als den/die/das da.
Und mir gefällt der/die/das *(thing)* am besten.

Saying what is being done about a problem
III, Ch. 9, p. 247

(Things) werden jetzt *(past participle)*.
(Thing) wird *(past participle)*.
(Things) werden schon oft *(past participle)*.

Saying that something is being done
III, Ch. 10, p. 280

Die *(people/places/things)* werden *(past participle)*.
Die *(people/places/things)* werden vom *(person)* *(past participle)*.

Saying that something was being done
III, Ch. 10, p. 280

Die *(people/places/things)* wurden *(past participle)*.
Der/Die/Das *(person/place/thing)*ist (nicht) *(past participle)* worden.

Talking about goals for the future
III, Ch. 11, p. 310

Mit dreißig möchte ich ...
Vielleicht werde ich bis dahin ...

Expressing Attitudes and Opinions

Asking for an opinion
I, Ch. 2, p. 57; Ch. 9, p. 260

Wie findest du *(thing/activity/place)*?

III, Ch. 3, p. 65

Was hältst du von *(person/place/thing)*?
Was würdest du dazu sagen?

Expressing your opinion
I, Ch. 2, p. 57; Ch. 9, p. 260

Ich finde *(thing/activity/place)* langweilig.
(Thing/Activity/Place) ist Spitze!
(Activity) macht Spaß!
Ich finde es toll, dass ...
Ich glaube, dass ...

III, Ch. 3, p. 65; Ch 6, p. 153

Ich halte viel/wenig davon.
Ich halte nichts davon.
Ich würde sagen, dass ...
Meiner Meinung nach ...
Ich finde, dass ...

Asking for reasons III, Ch. 6, p. 153

Kannst du das begründen?

Eliciting agreement
III, Ch. 7, p. 192

..., nicht?
..., nicht wahr?
..., ja?
..., stimmt's?
..., oder?
..., meinst du nicht?

Agreeing I, Ch. 2, p. 58

Ich auch!
Das finde ich auch!
Stimmt!

II, Ch. 10, p. 287

Da stimm ich dir zu!
Da hast du (bestimmt) Recht!
Einverstanden!

III, Ch. 4, p. 97; Ch. 6, p. 155; Ch. 7, p. 192

Da geb ich dir Recht.
Ganz meine Meinung.
Bei mir ist es auch so.
Da ist schon was dran.
Eben!
Richtig!
Da hast du ganz Recht.
Damit stimm ich überein.
Das meine ich auch.
Logisch! Logo!
Genau. Genau so ist es.
Eben!
Klar!
Sicher!

Disagreeing I, Ch. 2, p. 58

Ich nicht!
Das finde ich nicht!
Stimmt nicht!

II, Ch. 10, p. 287
Das stimmt (überhaupt) nicht!

III, Ch. 6, p. 156
Das stimmt gar nicht!
Das ist alles Quatsch!

Agreeing with reservations
II, Ch. 7, p. 199
Ja, schon, aber ...
Ja, aber ...
Eigentlich schon, aber ...
Ja, ich stimme dir zwar zu, aber ...

Commenting on clothes
I, Ch. 5, p. 137
Wie findest du den/die/das *(clothing item)*?   Ich finde ihn/sie/es *(adjective)*. Er/Sie/Es gefällt mir (nicht).

Expressing uncertainty
I, Ch. 5, p. 137; Ch. 9, p. 250
Ich bin nicht sicher.
Ich weiß nicht.
Keine Ahnung!

III, Ch. 7, p. 194
Es kann sein, dass ...
Das mag schon sein.

Expressing what seems to be true
III, Ch. 7, p. 194
Es scheint, dass ...
Es sieht so aus, als ob ...

Expressing certainty
III, Ch. 11, p. 309
Es steht fest, dass ...
Es ist sicher, dass ...
Ich möchte unbedingt ...

Expressing regret **I, Ch. 9, p. 250**
Es tut mir Leid.

II, Ch. 5, p. 129
Ich bedaure, ...
Was für ein Pech, ...
Leider, ...

III, Ch. 3. p. 78
Leider!
Ich bedaure, dass ...
Ich bedaure es wirklich, dass ...

Downplaying **II, Ch. 5, p. 129**
Das macht nichts!
Schon gut!
Nicht so schlimm!
Dann *(action)* ich eben *(alternative)*.
Dann *(action)* ich halt *(alternative)*.

Asking how someone liked something
II, Ch. 3, p. 76
Wie war's?
Wie hat dir Dresden gefallen?
Wie hat es dir gefallen?
Hat es dir gefallen?

Responding enthusiastically
II, Ch. 3, p. 76
Na, prima!
Ja, Spitze!
Das freut mich!

Responding sympathetically
II, Ch. 3, p. 76
Schade!
Tut mir Leid!
Das tut mir aber Leid!

Expressing enthusiasm
II, Ch. 3, p. 76
Phantastisch!
Es war echt super!
Es hat mir gut gefallen.
Wahnsinnig gut!

Expressing sympathy
III, Ch. 3, p. 73
Es tut mir Leid! Wirklich!
Das ist ja schlimm!
Das muss schlimm sein!
Wie schrecklich!
So ein Pech!

Expressing disappointment
II, Ch. 3, p. 76
Na ja, soso!
Nicht besonders.
Es hat mir nicht gefallen.
Es war furchtbar!

III, Ch. 8, p. 213
Ich bedaure, dass ...
Ich finde es schade, dass ...
Ich bin enttäuscht, dass ...

Expressing approval
II, Ch. 4, p. 100
Es ist prima, dass ...
Ich finde es toll, dass ...
Ich freue mich, dass ...
Ich bin froh, dass ...

Expressing disapproval
II, Ch. 4, p. 100
Es ist schade, dass ...
Ich finde es nicht gut, dass ...

Expressing indecision
II, Ch. 9, p. 245
> Was machen wir jetzt?
> Was sollen wir bloß machen?

Expressing an assumption
II, Ch. 10, p. 284
> Ich glaube schon, dass ...
> Ich meine doch, dass ...

III, Ch. 8, p. 221
> Ich nehme an, dass ...
> Ich vermute, dass ...
> Ich hatte den Eindruck, dass ...
> Ich hatte mir vorgestellt, dass ...

Introducing another point of view
III, Ch. 4, p. 103
> Das mag schon sein, aber ...
> Es kommt darauf an, ob ...
> Aber denk doch mal daran, dass ...
> Du darfst nicht vergessen, dass ...

Hypothesizing
III, Ch. 4, p. 104; Ch. 9, p. 249
> Wenn du ... wärest, dann würdest ...
> Wenn sie ... hätte, dann würde sie ...
> Wenn wir (activity) würden, hätten wir ...
> Wenn wir (activity + past participle) hätten,
>   hätten wir ...

Talking about what is possible
III, Ch. 5, p. 125
> Ich könnte (action).
> Du könntest (action).

Saying what you would have liked to do
III, Ch. 5, p. 126
> Ich hätte gern (activity + past participle).
> Ich wäre gern (activity + past participle).

Asking someone to take a position
III, Ch. 6, p. 153
> Möchtest du mal dazu Stellung nehmen?
> Wer nimmt mal dazu Stellung?

Talking about whether something is important
III, Ch. 11, p. 303
> Ich lege großen Wert darauf, dass ...
> Ich bin interessiert daran, dass ...
> Für mich spielt die größte Rolle, dass ...
> Mir ist wichtig, dass ...
> Entscheidend für mich ist, dass ...
> Für mich ist es am wichtigsten, dass ...
> Ausschlaggebend ist für mich, dass ...

Saying something is not important
III, Ch. 11, p. 303
> Ich lege keinen großen Wert darauf, dass ...
> Ich bin nicht besonders interessiert daran, dass ...
> Es ist nicht entscheidend für mich, dass ...
> Mir ist weniger wichtig, dass ...

Expressing Feelings and Emotions

Asking about likes and dislikes
I, Ch. 2, p. 50; Ch. 4, p. 110; Ch. 10, p. 282
> Was (action) du gern?
> (Action) du gern?
> Magst du (things/activities)?
> Was für (things/activities) magst du?

Expressing likes
I, Ch. 2, p. 50; Ch. 4, p. 110; Ch. 10, p. 282
> Ich (action) gern.
> Ich mag (things/activities).
> (Thing/Activities) mag ich (sehr/furchtbar) gern.

Expressing dislikes
I, Ch. 2, p. 50; I, Ch. 10, p. 282
> Ich (action) nicht so gern.
> Ich mag (things/action) (überhaupt) nicht.

Talking about favorites
I, Ch. 4, p. 110
> Was ist dein   Mein Lieblings(category)
>   Lieblings(category)?   ist (thing).

Responding to good news
I, Ch. 4, p. 121
> Toll!
> Das ist prima!
> Nicht schlecht.

Responding to bad news
I, Ch. 4, p. 112
> Schade!
> So ein Pech!
> So ein Mist!
> Das ist sehr schlecht!

Expressing familiarity
I, Ch. 10, p. 284
> Kennst du (person/   Ja, sicher!
>   place/thing)?   Ja, klar! or
>   Nein, den/die/das kenne
>   ich nicht.
>   Nein, überhaupt nicht.

Expressing preferences
I, Ch. 10, p. 285

(Siehst) du gern ...?	Ja, aber ... (sehe) ich lieber. Und am liebsten (sehe) ich ...
(Siehst) du lieber ... oder ...?	Lieber ...

II, Ch. 5, p. 139; Ch. 7, p. 189

Welche *(thing)* magst du lieber? *(Thing)* oder *(thing)*?	*(Thing)* mag ich lieber.
Welchen/Welche/Welches *(food item)* schmeckt dir besser? *(Food item)* oder *(food item)*?	*(Food item)* schmeckt mir besser.
Mir gefällt *(person/place/ thing)* besser als *(person/place/thing)*.	
Ich finde die *(person/place/ thing)* schöner.	
Ich ziehe *(person/place/ thing)* vor.	

Expressing strong preference and favorites
I, Ch. 10, p, 285

Was (siehst) du am liebsten?	Am liebsten (sehe) ich ...

II, Ch, 5, p. 139

Welches *(thing)* magst du am liebsten?	Am liebsten mag ich *(thing)*.
Welche *(food item)* schmeckt dir am besten?	*(Food item)* schmeckt mir am besten.

Expressing preference given certain possibilities
III, Ch. 10, p. 272

Ich würde (hauptsächlich) *(activity)*.
... eventuell mal ...
... vielleicht ...
... möglicherweise ...

***Expressing hope* II, Ch. 6, p. 168**

Ich hoffe, ...
Wir hoffen, ...
Hoffentlich ...

Expressing doubt
II, Ch. 9, p. 249

Ich weiß nicht, ob ...
Ich bezweifle, dass ...
Ich bin nicht sicher, ob ...

Expressing resignation
II, Ch. 9, p. 249

Da kann man nichts machen.
Das ist leider so.

III, Ch. 3, p. 73; Ch. 5, p. 134

Was kann ich schon tun?
Es ist halt so.
Ich habe eben eine Pechsträhne.
Ach, was soll's! Das ist leider so.

***Expressing conviction* II, Ch. 9, p. 249**

Du kannst mir glauben: ...
Ich bin sicher, dass ...

III, Ch. 7, p. 194

Es steht fest, dass ...

***Expressing determination* III, Ch. 11, p. 300**

Ich habe beschlossen, ...
Ich habe mich entschieden, ...
Ich bin fest entschlossen, ...

***Expressing indecision* III, Ch. 11, p. 300**

Ich weiß nicht, ob ich ...
Ich habe mich noch nicht entschieden, was/ob ...
Ich kann noch nicht sagen, ob ...
Ich muss mir das überlegen.
Es kommt darauf an, was/ob ...
Ich werde mal sehen, ob ...

***Expressing surprise* II, Ch. 10, p. 287**

Das ist ja unglaublich!
(Das ist) nicht möglich!
Das gibt's doch nicht!

III, Ch. 5, p. 134; Ch. 6, p. 161; Ch. 8, p. 213

Das ist mir (völlig) neu!
Es ist unglaublich, dass ...
... überrascht mich.
Ich bin überrascht, dass ...
Ich war überrascht, dass ...
Ich habe gestaunt, ...
Ich habe nicht gewusst, dass ...
Ich hätte nicht gedacht, dass ....
Es ist unwahrscheinlich, dass ...
Ich war erstaunt, ...

***Expressing relief* III, Ch. 5, p. 134**

Ich bin (sehr) froh, dass ...

Expressing annoyance
III, Ch. 6, p. 161; Ch. 7, p. 185; Ch. 8, p. 213

Was mich stört ist, dass ...
Ich werde sauer, wenn ...
Es ist frustrierend, dass ...
Was mich aufregt ist, wenn ...
Es nervt mich, dass ...
Es regt mich auf, wenn/dass ...
Es stört mich, wenn/dass ...
Es ärgert mich, wenn/dass ...
Ich finde es unangenehm, wenn/dass ...

Expressing concern III, Ch. 9, p. 240
Ich habe Angst, ...
Ich fürchte, dass ...
... macht mir große Sorgen.

Expressing envy III, Ch. 10, p. 273
Ich beneide *(people)*.

Expressing admiration III, Ch. 10, p. 273
Ich bewundere ...

Expressing happiness III, Ch. 10, p. 278
(Person) war froh, dass ...

Expressing sadness III, Ch. 10, p. 278
(People) waren traurig, weil ...

Expressing relief III, Ch. 11, p. 311
Gut, dass ...
Gott sei Dank, dass ...
Ein Glück, dass ...
Zum Glück habe ich ...
Ich bin froh, dass ...

PERSUADING

Telling someone what to do
I, Ch. 8, p. 223
Geh bitte *(action)!*
(Thing/Things) holen, bitte!

Asking for suggestions
II, Ch. 9, p. 245; Ch. 11, p. 306
Hast du eine Idee?
Was schlägst du vor?
Was sollen wir machen?
Wofür bist du?

Making suggestions
II, Ch. 6, p. 158; Ch. 9, p. 245; Ch. 11, p. 306
Möchtest du *(activity)?*
Willst du *(activity)?*
Du kannst für mich *(activity).*
(Activity) wir mal!
Sollen wir mal *(activity)?*
Wir können mal *(activity).*
Ich schlage vor, ...
Ich schlage vor, dass ...
Ich bin dafür, dass ...
Wie wär's mit *(activity/place)?*

III, Ch. 8, p. 223
Ich kann dir einen Tip geben: ...!
Ich empfehl dir, ...
Es lohnt sich, ..

Responding to suggestions II, Ch. 11, p. 306
Das wäre nicht schlecht.

Asking for advice II, Ch. 6, p. 167
Was soll ich machen?
Was soll ich bloß tun?

Giving advice II, Ch. 6, p. 167
Am besten ...
Du musst unbedingt ...

III, Ch. 3, p. 74; Ch. 4, p. 103; Ch. 8, p. 223
Warum machst du nicht ... ?
Versuch doch mal ... !
Du solltest mal ...
An deiner Stelle würde ich versuchen, ...
Lass dir doch ... !
Vielleicht kannst du ...
Es ist wichtig, dass ...
Ich würde ...

Persuading someone to buy or wear something
II, Ch. 8, p. 226
Warum kaufst du dir keinen/keine/kein *(thing)?*
Kauf dir doch diesen/diese/dieses *(thing)!*
Trag doch mal etwas *(adjective)!*

Persuading someone not to buy something
II, Ch. 8, p. 226
Kauf dir ja keinen/keine/kein *(thing)!*
Trag ja nichts aus *(material)!*

Asking for permission II, Ch. 10, p. 283
Darf ich (bitte) *(activity)?*
Kann ich bitte mal *(activity)?*
He, du! Lass mich mal *(activity)!*

Giving permission
II, Ch. 10, p. 283
Ja, natürlich!
Bitte schön!
Bitte!
Gern!

Making accusations
III, Ch. 9, p. 241
Du bist auch schuld an dem Problem, weil du ...
Wir Verbraucher sind schuld daran, dass ...,
wenn wir ...

Offering solutions
III, Ch. 9, p. 242; Ch. 9, p. 248
Man könnte *(action).*
Man müsste *(action).*
Man sollte *(action).*
Wenn wir nur *(action)* dürften!
(Thing) kann leicht *(past participle)* werden.
(Things) sollen *(past participle)* werden.
Alles muss *(past participle)* werden.

Additional Vocabulary

This list includes additional vocabulary that you may want to use to personalize activities. If you can't find the words you need here, try the German–English and English–German vocabulary sections beginning on page R42.

SPORT UND INTERESSEN
(Sports and hobbies)

Aerobic machen	to do aerobics
amerikanischen Fußball spielen	to play football
Baseball spielen	to play baseball
bergsteigen	to go mountain climbing
Bodybuilding machen	to lift weights
Handball spielen	to play handball
Kajak fahren	to go kayaking
Kanu fahren	to go canoeing
malen	to paint
Münzen sammeln	to collect coins
nähen	to sew
reiten	to ride (a horse)
Rollschuh laufen	to roller-skate
rudern	to row
schnorcheln	to snorkle
Skateboard fahren	to skateboard
Ski laufen	to (snow) ski
sticken	to embroider
stricken	to knit
Tischtennis spielen	to play table tennis
Videospiele spielen	to play video games
zelten	to go camping

FAMILIE (Family)

der Enkel, -	grandson
die Enkelin, -nen	granddaughter
der Halbbruder, ̈	half-brother
die Halbschwester, -n	half-sister
der Neffe, -n	nephew
die Nichte, -n	niece
der Schwager, ̈	brother-in-law
die Schwägerin, -nen	sister-in-law
die Schwiegermutter, ̈	mother-in-law
der Schwiegervater, ̈	father-in-law
der Stiefbruder, ̈	stepbrother
die Stiefmutter, ̈	stepmother
die Stiefschwester, -n	stepsister
der Stiefvater, ̈	stepfather
die Urgroßmutter, ̈	great-grandmother
der Urgroßvater, ̈	great-grandfather

ZUM DISKUTIEREN (Topics to Discuss)

der Präsident	president
die Reklame	advertising
das Verbrechen	crime
der Wehrdienst	military service
der Zivildienst	community service
die Drogen	drugs
Gewalt im Fernsehen	violence on TV

TIERE (Animals)

der Affe, -n	monkey
der Bär, -en	bear
der Büffel, -	buffalo
der Bulle, -n	bull
die Eidechse, -n	lizard
die Ente, -n	duck
der Frosch, ̈e	frog
der Fuchs, ̈e	fox
die Gans, ̈e	goose
die Giraffe, -n	giraffe
der Hahn, ̈e	rooster
der Hamster, -	hamster
der Hase, -n	hare
die Henne, -n	hen
das Huhn, ̈er	chicken
der Kanarienvogel, ̈	canary

das Kaninchen, -	rabbit	die Erdbeere, -n	strawberry
die Klapperschlange, -n	rattlesnake	die Erdnussbutter	peanut butter
die Kuh, ⁻e	cow	das Gebäck	baked goods
der Löwe, -n	lion	das Gulasch	goulash
die Maus, ⁻e	mouse	der Hamburger, -	hamburger
das Meerschweinchen, -	guinea pig	die Himbeere, -n	raspberry
das Nashorn, ⁻er	rhinoceros	die Karotte, -n	carrot
das Nilpferd, -e	hippopotamus	der Ketchup	ketchup
der Ochse, -n	ox	die Magermilch	low-fat milk
der Papagei, -en	parrot	die Mayonnaise	mayonnaise
das Pferd, -e	horse	die Melone, -n	melon
die Robbe, -n	seal	die Nuss, ⁻e,	nut
der Seelöwe, -n	sea lion	die Orange, -n	orange
das Schaf, -e	sheep	das Plätzchen, -	cookie
die Schildkröte, -n	turtle	der Pudding, -s or -e	pudding
die Schlange, -n	snake	die Sahne	cream
der Schmetterling, -e	butterfly	die Vollmilch	whole milk

das Schwein, -e	pig
der Stier, -e	steer
der Tiger, -	tiger
der Truthahn, ⁻e	turkey
der Vogel, ⁻	bird
der Wal, -e	whale
das Walross, -e	walrus
der Waschbär, -en	racoon
der Wolf, ⁻e	wolf
die Ziege, -n	goat

FARBEN (Colors)

beige	beige
golden	gold
lila	purple
orange	orange
rosa	pink
silbern	silver
türkis	turquoise

GETRÄNKE (Beverages)

der Grapefruitsaft	grapefruit juice
der Kakao	cocoa
der Kirschsaft	cherry juice
der Kräutertee	herbal tea
das Leitungswasser	tap water
das Malzbier	(sweet, non-alcoholic beverage)
der Milkshake	milkshake
der Tomatensaft	tomato juice

KLEIDUNGSSTÜCKE (Clothing)

der Badeanzug, ⁻e	swimsuit
das Halstuch, ⁻er	scarf
der Handschuh, -e	glove
der Mantel, ⁻	coat
der Minirock, ⁻e	miniskirt
der Parka, -s	parka
der Rollkragenpullover, -	turtleneck sweater
die Sandalen (pl)	sandals
die Strumpfhose, -n	panty hose
die Weste, -n	vest

SPEISEN (Foods)

die Ananas, -	pineapple
der Apfelstrudel, -	apple strudel
der Chip, -s	potato chip
der Eintopf	stew

STOFFE (Materials)

Acryl	acrylic
Kaschmir	cashmere

ADDITIONAL VOCABULARY

Kunstfasern	synthetic fibers
Kunstseide	rayon
Nylon	nylon
Polyacryl	acrylic
Polyester	polyester

FÄCHER (School Subjects)

Algebra	algebra
Chemie	chemistry
Chor	choir
Französisch	French
Hauswirtschaft	home economics
Informatik	computer science
Italienisch	Italian
Literatur	literature
Orchester	orchestra
Philosophie	philosophy
Physik	physics
Politik	political science
Russisch	Russian
Spanisch	Spanish
Sozialkunde	social studies
Werken	shop
Wirtschaftslehre	economics

KÖRPERTEILE (Parts of the Body)

die Augenbraue, -n	eyebrow
das Augenlid, -er	eyelid
die Faust, ¨e	fist
die Ferse, -n	heel
das Gesicht, -er	face
die Handfläche, -n	palm of the hand
das Handgelenk, -e	wrist
die Hüfte, -n	hip
der Kiefer, -	jaw
das Kinn	chin
die Lippe, -n	lip
der Magen	stomach
der Nacken, -	neck
die Nase, -n	nose
das Ohr, -en	ear
der Schenkel, -	thigh

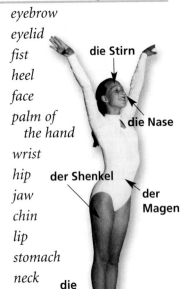

die Stirn
die Nase
der Shenkel
der Magen
die Ferse

das Schienbein, -e	shin
die Stirn	forehead
die Wade, -n	calf
die Wange, -n	cheek
die Wimper, -n	eyelash
der Zahn, ¨e	tooth
der Zeh, -en	toe
der Zeigefinger, -	index finger
die Zunge, -n	tongue

INSTRUMENTE (Musical Instruments)

die Blockflöte, -n	recorder
die Bratsche, -n	viola
das Cello (Violoncello), -s	cello
die elektrische Gitarre, -n	electric guitar
die Flöte, -n	flute
die Geige, -n	violin
die Harfe, -n	harp
das Horn, ¨er	French ho
die Klarinette, -n	clarinet
der Kontrabass, ¨e	double bass
die Mandoline, -n	mandolin
die Mundharmonika, -s	harmonica
die Oboe, -n	oboe
die Posaune, -n	trombone
das Saxophon, -e	saxophon
das Schlagzeug, -e	drums
die Trompete, -n	trumpet
die Tuba, (pl) Tuben	tuba

HAUSARBEIT (Housework)

den Fußboden kehren	to sweep the floor
sauber machen	to clean
die Wäsche aufhängen	to hang clothes up
die Wäsche einräumen	to put clothes away
die Wäsche zusammenlegen	to fold clothes

MÖBEL (Furniture)

das Bild, -er	picture
der Kleiderschrank, ¨e	wardrobe
die Kommode, -n	chest of drawers

| der Nachttisch, -e | night stand |
| der Vorhang, ⁻e | curtain |

COMPUTERS

abbrechen	to close
abrufen (die E-Mail abrufen) (sep)	to check the e-mail
anklicken	to click
Anzeige, die	prompt
Bedienungsfeld, das	control panel
bei (auch at)	at (@)
Benutzer, der	user
Bild ↓ (Bild runter)	page down
Bild ↑ (Bild rauf)	page up
Bildschirm, der	screen

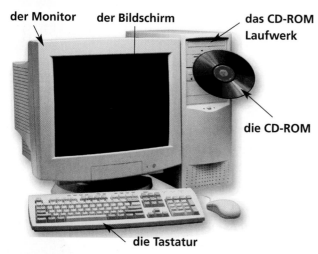

der Monitor   der Bildschirm   das CD-ROM Laufwerk

die CD-ROM

die Tastatur

blättern	to scroll
Browser, der	browser
CD-ROM	CD-ROM
CD-ROM, die	CD-ROM disc
CD-ROM Laufwerk, das	CD-ROM drive
Computer, der	computer
Crash, der	crash
Datei, die	file; data (file)
Diskette, die	diskette, floppy disc
drucken	to print
drücken auf	to press
E-Mail, die	e-mail
E-Mailadresse, die	e-mail address
einfügen	to insert
der Cursor	cursor
Eingabetaste, die	return key

einladen (sep)	to upload
einloggen (sep)	to log on
entfernen	to delete
Entferntaste, die	delete key
erstellen	to create
Feedback, das	feedback
Festplatte, die	hard drive
Feststelltaste, die	caps lock
formatieren	to format
herunterladen (sep)	to download
Homepage, die	home page
Internet, das	Internet
Internet-Adresse, die	internet address
Kennwort, das	password
kopieren	to copy
Laufwerk, das	disk drive
Lesezeichen, das	bookmark
Link, der	link
löschen	to cancel
Maus, die	mouse
Mausklick, der	click
Modem, das	modem
Monitor, der	monitor
Netz, das (das Internet)	Internet
Netzwerk, das	network
neustarten	to reboot, restart
öffnen	to open
online	online
Pfeiltaste, die	arrow tab
Rückstelltaste, die	return
Schlüsselwort, das	keyword
Schnittstelle, die	interface
senden	to send
Server, der	server
Software, die	software
Speicher, der	memory
speichern	to save
Steuerung, die	control
suchen	to search
Suchmaschine, die	search engine
surfen (im Internet surfen)	to surf (the Net)
Tabulator, der	tab
Tastatur, die	keyboard

Textverarbeitung, die	*word processing*
Umschalttaste, die	*shift*
versenden	*to post*
Verzeichnis, das	*directory*
Webpage, die	*Web site*
Zeichen, das	*icon*
Zentraleinheit, die	*CPU (central processing unit)*
ziehen (auf Symbole)	*to drag (to icons)*

IN DER STADT   (Places around Town)

die Brücke, -n	*bridge*
die Bücherei, -en	*library*
der Flughafen, (pl) Flughäfen	*airport*
das Fremdenverkehrs-amt, (pl) Fremden-verkehrsämter	*tourist office*
der Frisiersalon, -s	*beauty shop*
das Krankenhaus, (pl) Krankenhäuser	*hospital*
der Kreis, -e	*district, county*
die Minigolfanlage	*mini-golf course*
die Polizei	*police*
das Stadion, (pl) Stadien	*stadium*
der Stadtrand	*outskirts*
der Stadtteil, -e	*urban district*
das Stadtzentrum, (pl) Stadtzentren	*downtown*

AUF DEM LAND   (In the Country)

auf dem Land wohnen	*to live in the country*
Tiere haben/züchten/ füttern	*to have/raise/feed animals*
pflügen	*to plow*
der Bauernhof, ¨e	*the farm*
das Feld, -er	*field*
das Korn/Getreide	*grains*
die Landschaft, -en	*countryside*
der Mais	*corn*
die Scheune, -n	*barn*
die Sojabohnen (pl)	*soybeans*
der Weizen	*wheat*
die Wiese, -n	*meadow*

KULTURELLE VERANSTALTUNGEN (Cultural Events)

die Ausstellung, -en	*exhibit*
das Chorkonzert, -e	*choir concert*
das Kabarett	*cabaret*
das Symphoniekonzert, -e	*symphony*
der Vorverkauf, ¨e	*advance ticket sales*
der Zirkus, -se	*circus*

GESCHENKIDEEN   (Gift Ideas)

das Bild, -er	*picture*
die Kette, -n	*chain, necklace*
die Puppe, -n	*doll*
das Puppenhaus, ¨er	*doll house*
das Spielzeug, -e	*toy*

AUTO (Automobiles)

die Alarmanlage, -n	*alarm system*
die Alufelge, -n	*aluminum rim, mag wheel*
der Aufkleber, -	*(bumper) sticker*
die Automatik, -en	*automatic transmission*
das 5-Gang-Getriebe	*five speed (standard) transmission*
das Kabriolett, -s	*convertible*
der Kassettenspieler, -	*cassette player*
der Kombiwagen, -	*station wagon*
die Lautsprecherbox, -en	*speaker*
der Rallyestreifen, -	*racing stripe*
die Servolenkung	*power steering*
die Servobremsen (pl)	*power brakes*
der Sitzschoner, -	*seat cover*
das Stereo-Radio, -s	*stereo*
die Zentralverriegelung, -en	*power locks*

IM HAUSHALT   (Household Utensils)

die Bratpfanne, -n	*frying pan*
die Butterdose, -n	*butter dish*
der Deckel, -	*lid*
der Herd, -e	*stove*
die Kaffeekanne, -n	*coffee pot*

ADDITIONAL VOCABULARY

der Kamin	*fireplace*
der Kaffeelöffel, -	*coffee spoon*
der Kochtopf, ⸚e	*large pot*
der Korkenzieher, -	*corkscrew*
die Kuchenplatte, -n	*cake plate*
die Lampe, -n	*lamp*
die Müslischüssel, -n	*cereal bowl*
das Salatbesteck, -e	*salad server*
die Schöpfkelle, -n	*ladle*
die Schüssel, -n	*serving dish*
der Spiegel, -	*mirror*
das Spülbecken, -	*sink*
die Tasse, -n	*cup*
der Teekessel, -	*tea kettle*
das Tischtuch, ⸚er	*table cloth*
der Topf, ⸚e	*pot*
die Untertasse, -n	*saucer*
die Zuckerdose, -n	*sugar dish*

AUSSEHEN (Appearance)

zum Friseur gehen	*to go to a barber shop/ hairdresser*
zur Friseuse gehen	*to go to a hairdresser*
der Haarschnitt/die Frisur	*haircut*
sich die Haare schneiden lassen	*to get a haircut*
die Dauerwelle, -n	*permanent wave*
sich eine Dauer- welle machen lassen	*to get a perm*
sich maniküren lassen	*to get a manicure*
die Nagelschere, -n	*manicure scissors*
die Wimperntusche	*mascara*
der Lippenstift, -e	*lipstick*
der Augenbrauenstift, -e	*eyebrow pencil*
der Fön	*blow dryer*
sich das Haar fönen	*to blow-dry one's hair*
der Handspiegel , -	*hand mirror*
die Haarbürste, -n	*hairbrush*
der Rasierapparat	*electric razor*
der Lockenstab, ⸚e	*curling iron*
die Lockenwickler (pl)	*curlers*
das Deodorant	*deodorant*

FESTE (Holidays)

Advent	*Advent (the four Sundays before Christmas)*
Allerheiligen	*All Saint's Day (Nov. 1)*
Chanukka	*Hanukkah*
Christi Himmelfahrt	*Ascension*
Erntedankfest	*Thanksgiving*
Heiligabend	*Christmas Eve*
Karneval	*Carnival, Mardi Gras*
Karfreitag	*Good Friday*
Martinstag	*St. Martin's Day (Nov. 11)*
Muttertag	*Mothers' Day*
Neujahr	*New Year*
Nikolaus	*St. Nicholas' Day (Dec. 6)*
Ostern	*Easter*
Silvester	*New Year's Eve*
Tag der Arbeit/ Maifeiertag	*May Day (Labor Day)*
Tag der Deutschen Einheit	*Day of German Unity*
Vatertag	*Fathers' Day*
Weihnachten	*Christmas*

DAS WETTER (Weather)

bedeckt	*cloudy*
feucht	*wet*
gewittrig	*stormy*
halbbedeckt	*partially overcast*
heiter	*sunny*
neblig	*foggy*
trüb	*hazy*
schwül	*humid*
windig	*windy*
es blitzt	*there is lightning*
es donnert	*it is thundering*
es nieselt	*it is drizzling*
es regnet	*it is raining*
es schneit	*it is snowing*
der Blitz, -e	*lightning*
der Donner	*thunder*
der Regen	*rain*
der Schnee	*snow*

BERUFE *(Careers)*

Anästhesist(in), -en/innen	*anesthesiologist*
Apotheker(in), -/innen	*pharmacist*
Architekt(in), -en/innen	*architect*
Beamte/Beamtin, -n/innen	*civil servant*
Computerspezialist(in), -en/innen	*computer specialist*
Diplomat(in), -en/innen	*diplomat*
Elektroinstallateur(in), -/innen	*electrician*
Fotograf(in), -en/innen	*photographer*
Friseur/Friseuse, -e/n	*hair stylist*
Gesundheitswissen-schaftler(in), -/innen	*nutritional scientist*
Industriedesigner(in), -/innen	*industrial designer*
Ingenieur(in), -e/innen	*engineer*
Kaufmann/Kauffrau, -leute	*merchant*
Koch/Köchin, ̈e/innen	*chef*
Kommunikations-elektroniker(in), -/innen	*communications engineer*
Krankenschwester, -n	*nurse*
Krankenpfleger, -	*(male) nurse*
Mediaplaner(in), -/innen	*media planner*
Lebensmittelkontrolleur(in), -e/innen	*health inspector*
Lehrer(in), -/innen	*teacher*
Optiker(in), -/innen	*optician*
Physiker(in), -/innen	*physicist*
Politiker(in), -/innen	*politician*
PR-Berater(in), -/innen	*PR consultant*
Professor(in), -en/innen	*professor*
Rechtsanwalt/Rechtsanwältin, ̈e/innen	*lawyer*
Reporter(in), -/innen	*reporter*
Rundfunksprecher(in), -/innen	*radio announcer*
Schreiner(in), -/innen	*cabinet maker*
Schweißer(in), -/innen	*welder*
Steuerberater(in), -/innen	*tax consultant*

Sekretär(in), -e/innen	*secretary*
Soldat(in), -en/innen	*soldier*
Sportökonom(in), -en/innen	*sports scientist*
Strafverteidiger(in), -/innen	*lawyer for the defense*
technischer Zeichner, -	*(male) drafter*
technische Zeichnerin, -nen	*(female) drafter*
Toningenieur(in), -e/innen	*sound engineer*
Touristikfachwirt(in), -e/innen	*tourism specialist*
Unternehmer(in), -/innen	*entrepreneur*
Winzer(in), -/innen	*vintner*
Zahnarzt(̈in), ̈e/innen	*dentist*
Zahntechniker(in), -/innen	*dental technician*
Zimmermann, -leute	*carpenter*

ERDKUNDE *(GEOGRAPHY)*

Here are some terms you will find on German-language maps:

LÄNDER *(States)*

Most of the states in the United States (**die Vereinigten Staaten**) have the same spelling in German that they have in English. Listed below are those states that have a different spelling.

Kalifornien	*California*
Neumexiko	*New Mexico*
Nordkarolina	*North Carolina*
Südkarolina	*South Carolina*
Süddakota	*South Dakota*

KONTINENTE *(Continents)*

Afrika	*Africa*
die Antarktis	*Antarctica*
Asien	*Asia*
Europa	*Europe*
Nordamerika	*North America*
Südamerika	*South America*

MEERE (Bodies of Water)

der Atlantik	the Atlantic
der Golf von Mexiko	the Gulf of Mexico
der Indische Ozean	the Indian Ocean
das Mittelmeer	the Mediterranean
der Pazifik	the Pacific
das Rote Meer	the Red Sea
das Schwarze Meer	the Black Sea

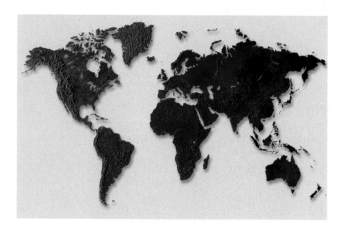

Geographische Begriffe (Geographical Terms)

der Breitengrad	latitude
die Ebene, -n	plain
der Fluss, ⸚e	river
das … Gebirge	… mountains
die Grenze, -n	border
die Hauptstadt, ⸚e	capital
der Kontinent, -e	continent
das Land, ⸚er	state or country
der Längengrad	longitude
das Meer, -e	ocean, sea
der Nordpol	the North Pole
der See, -n	lake
der Staat, -en	country or state
der Südpol	the South Pole
das Tal, ⸚er	valley

LAND UND LEUTE

Staat		Adjektiv	Bewohner	Währung
Argentinien	Argentina	argentinisch	Argentinier	Peso
Australien	Australia	australisch	Australier	Dollar
Brasilien	Brazil	brasilianisch	Brasilianer	Cruzeiro
Haiti	Haiti	haitianisch	Haitianer	Gourde
Indien	India	indisch	Inder	Rupie
Indonesien	Indonesia	indonesisch	Indonesen	Rupie
Israel	Israel	israelisch	Israeli	Schekel
Jamaika	Jamaica	jamaikanisch	Jamaikaner	Dollar
Kolumbien	Columbia	kolumbisch	Kolumbianer	Peso
Korea	Korea	koreanisch	Koreaner	Won
Kuba	Cuba	kubanisch	Kubaner	Peso
Mexiko	Mexico	mexikanisch	Mexikaner	Peso
Neuseeland	New Zealand	neuseeländisch	Neuseeländer	Dollar
Norwegen	Norway	norwegisch	Norweger	Krone
Panama	Panama	panamaisch	Panamaer	Balboa
Philippinen	Phillipines	philippinisch	Philippiner	Peso
Puerto Rico	Puerto Rico	puertoricanisch	Puertoricaner	Dollar
Schweden	Sweden	schwedisch	Schweden	Krone
Südafrika	South Africa	südafrikanisch	Südafrikaner	Rand
Vietnam	Vietnam	vietnamesisch	Vietnamesen	Dong

Grammar Summary

NOUNS AND THEIR MODIFIERS

In German, nouns (words that name a person, place, or thing) are grouped into three classes or genders: masculine, feminine, and neuter. All nouns, both persons and objects, fall into one of these groups. There are words used with nouns that signal the class of the noun. One of these is the definite article. In English there is one definite article: *the*. In German, there are three, one for each class: **der, die,** and **das**.

THE DEFINITE ARTICLE

SUMMARY OF DEFINITE ARTICLES

	Nominative	Accusative	Dative	Genitive
Masculine	der	den	dem	des
Feminine	die	die	der	der
Neuter	das	das	dem	des
Plural	die	die	den	der

When the definite article is combined with a noun, a noun phrase is formed. Noun phrases that are used as subjects are in the nominative case. Nouns that are used as direct objects or the objects of certain prepositions (such as **für**) are in the accusative case. Nouns that are indirect objects, the objects of certain prepositions (such as **mit, bei**), or the objects of special verbs (see page R33) are in the dative case. Below is a summary of the definite articles combined with nouns to form noun phrases.

SUMMARY OF NOUN PHRASES

	Nominative	Accusative	Dative	Genitive
Masculine	der Vater der Ball	den Vater den Ball	dem Vater dem Ball	des Vaters des Balls
Feminine	die Mutter die Kassette	die Mutter die Kassette	der Mutter der Kassette	der Mutter der Kassette
Neuter	das Mädchen das Haus	das Mädchen das Haus	dem Mädchen dem Haus	der Mädchens der Hauses
Plural	die Kassetten die Häuser	die Kassetten die Häuser	den Kassetten den Häusern	der Kassetten der Häuser

GRAMMAR SUMMARY

DIESER-WORDS

The determiners **dieser, jeder, welcher,** and **alle** are called **dieser**-words. Their endings are similar to those of the definite articles.

SUMMARY OF DIESER-WORDS

dieser	*this, that, these*	welcher	*which, that*
jeder	*each, every*	mancher	*many, many a*
alle	*all*	solcher	*such, such a*

	Nominative		Accusative		Dative		Genitive	
Masculine	dieser	jeder	diesen	jeden	diesem	jedem	dieses	jedes
Feminine	diese	jede	diese	jede	dieser	jeder	dieser	jeder
Neuter	dieses	jedes	dieses	jedes	diesem	jedem	dieses	jedes
Plural	diese	alle	diese	alle	diesen	allen	dieser	aller

DERSELBE

	Nominative	Accusative	Dative	Genitive
Masculine	derselbe	denselben	demselben	desselben
Feminine	derselbe	dieselbe	derselben	derselben
Neuter	dasselbe	dasselbe	demselben	desselben
Plural	dieselben	dieselben	denselben	derselben

THE INDEFINITE ARTICLE

Another type of word that is used with nouns is the *indefinite article:* **ein, eine, ein** in German, *a, an* in English. There is no plural form of **ein.**

SUMMARY OF INDEFINATE ARTICLES

	Nominative	Accusative	Dative	Genitive
Masculine	ein	einen	einem	eines
Feminine	eine	eine	einer	einer
Neuter	ein	ein	einem	eines
Plural	—	—	—	—

THE NEGATING WORD **KEIN**

The word **kein** is also used with nouns and means *no, not,* or *not any.* Unlike the **ein, kein** has a plural form.

	Nominative	Accusative	Dative	Genitive
Masculine	kein	keinen	keinem	keines
Feminine	keine	keine	keiner	keiner
Neuter	kein	kein	keinem	keines
Plural	keine	keine	keinen	keiner

THE POSSESSIVES

These words also modify nouns and tell you *whose* object or person is being referred to (*my* car, *his* book, *her* mother). These words have the same endings as **kein**.

SUMMARY OF POSSESSIVES

	Before Masculine Nouns				Before Feminine Nouns		
	Nom	**Acc**	**Dat**	**Gen**	**Nom & Acc**	**Dat**	**Gen**
my	mein	meinen	meinem	meines	meine	meiner	meiner
your	dein	deinen	deinem	deines	deine	deiner	deiner
his	sein	seinen	seinem	seines	seine	seiner	seiner
her	ihr	ihren	ihrem	ihres	ihre	ihrer	ihrer
our	unser	unseren	unserem	unseres	unsere	unserer	unserer
your	euer	eueren	euerem	eueres	euere	euerer	euerer
their	ihr	ihren	ihrem	ihres	ihre	ihrer	ihrer
your	Ihr	Ihren	Ihrem	Ihres	Ihre	Ihrer	Ihrer

	Before Neuter Nouns			Before Plural Nouns		
	Nom & Acc	**Dat**	**Gen**	**Nom & Acc**	**Dat**	**Gen**
my	mein	meinem	meines	meine	meinen	meiner
your	dein	deinem	deines	deine	deinen	deiner
his	sein	seinem	seines	seine	seinen	seiner
her	ihr	ihrem	ihres	ihre	ihren	ihrer
our	unser	unserem	unseres	unsere	unseren	unserer
your	euer	euerem	eueres	euere	eueren	euerer
their	ihr	ihrem	ihres	ihre	ihren	ihrer
your	Ihr	Ihrem	Ihres	Ihre	Ihren	Ihrer

Commonly used short forms for unseren: unsren *or* unsern   *for* unsere: unsre
eueren: euren *or* euern   euere: eure
for unserem: unsrem *or* unserm   *for* unserer: unsrer
euerem: eurem *or* euerm   euerer: eurer
for unseres: unsres
eures: eures

DETERMINERS OF QUANITITY

alle	*all*	**manche**	*some*
andere	*other*	**mehrere**	*several*
beide	*both*	**solche**	*such*
ein paar	*a few*	**viele**	*many*
einige	*a few, some*	**wenige**	*few*

NOUN PLURALS

Noun class and plural forms are not always predictable. Therefore, you must learn each noun together with its article (**der, die, das**) and with its plural form. As you learn more nouns, however, you will discover certain patterns. Although there are always exceptions to these patterns, you may find them helpful in remembering the plural forms of many nouns.

Most German nouns form their plurals in one of two ways: some nouns add endings in the plural; some add endings and/or change the sound of the stem vowel in the plural, indicating the sound change with the umlaut (¨). Only the vowels **a, o, u,** and the diphthong **au** can take the umlaut. If a noun has an umlaut in the singular, it keeps the umlaut in the plural. Most German nouns fit into one of the following five plural groups.

1. Nouns that do not have any ending in the plural. Sometimes they take an umlaut.
   NOTE: There are only two feminine nouns in this group: **die Mutter** and **die Tochter**.

der Bruder, die Brüder	der Schüler, die Schüler	das Fräulein, die Fräulein
der Lehrer, die Lehrer	der Vater, die Väter	das Mädchen, die Mädchen
der Onkel, die Onkel	die Mutter, die Mütter	das Poster, die Poster
der Mantel, die Mäntel	die Tochter, die Töchter	das Zimmer, die Zimmer

2. Nouns that add the ending **-e** in the plural. Sometimes they also take an umlaut.
   NOTE: There are many one-syllable words in this group.

der Bleistift, die Bleistifte	der Sohn, die Söhne	das Jahr, die Jahre
der Freund, die Freunde	die Stadt, die Städte	das Spiel, die Spiele

3. Nouns that add the ending **-er** in the plural. Whenever possible, they take an umlaut, i.e., when the noun contains the vowels **a, o,** or **u,** or the diphthong **au. NOTE:** There are no feminine nouns in this group. There are many one-syllable words in this group.

das Buch, die Bücher	das Haus, die Häuser
das Fach, die Fächer	das Land, die Länder

4. Nouns that add the ending **-en** or **-n** in the plural. These nouns never add an umlaut.
   NOTE: There are many feminine nouns in this group.

der Herr, die Herren	die Frau, die Frauen	die Küche, die Küchen
der Junge, die Jungen	die Klasse, die Klassen	die Schwester, die Schwestern
die Briefmarke, die Briefmarken	die Karte, die Karten	die Tante, die Tanten
die Familie, die Familien	der Name, die Namen	die Wohnung, die Wohnungen
die Farbe, die Farben	der Vetter, die Vettern	die Zahl, die Zahlen

   Feminine nouns ending in **-in** add the ending **-nen** in the plural.

die Freundin, die Freundinnen	die Verkäuferin, die Verkäuferinnen

5. Nouns that add the ending **-s** in the plural. These nouns never add an umlaut.
   NOTE: There are many words of foreign origin in this group.

der Kuli, die Kulis	das Auto, die Autos
die Kamera, die Kameras	das Hobby, die Hobbys

SUMMARY OF PLURAL ENDINGS

Group	1	2	3	4	5
Ending:	-	-e	-er	-(e)n	-s
Umlaut:	sometimes	sometimes	always	never	never

MASCULINE NOUNS WITH THE ENDINGS -N OR -EN IN THE SINGULAR

	Nominative	Accusative	Dative	Genitive
Singular	der Name der Polizist	den Namen den Polizisten	dem Namen dem Poizisten	des Namen des Polizisten

Some other nouns that add **-n**: der Achtzehnjahrige, der Auszubildene, der Bekannte, der Deutsche, der Erwachsene, der Gedanke, der Herr, der Junge, der Nachbar, der Reisende, der Verwandte, der Vorfahre

Some other nouns that add **en**: der Astronaut, der Dirigent, der Gymnasiast, der Held, der Klassenkamerad, der Konsument, der Mensch, der Philosoph, der Planet, der Tourist

PRONOUNS

PERSONAL   **REFLEXIVE**

	Nominative	Accusative	Dative	Accusative	Dative
Singular					
1st person	ich	mich	mir	mich	mir
2nd person	du	dich	dir	dich	dir
3rd person *m.*	er	ihn	ihm		
f.	sie	sie	ihr	sich	sich
n.	es	es	ihm		
Plural					
1st person	wir	uns	uns	uns	uns
2nd person	ihr	euch	euch	euch	euch
3rd person	sie	sie	ihnen	sich	sich
you (formal, sing. & pl.)	Sie	Sie	Ihnen	sich	sich

DEFINITE ARTICLES AS DEMONSTRATIVE PRONOUNS

The definite articles can be used as demonstrative pronouns, giving more emphasis to the sentences than the personal pronouns **er, sie, es.** Note that these demonstrative pronouns have the same forms as the definite articles, with the exception of the dative plural form, which is **denen**.

Wer bekommt *den* Cappuccino? *Der* ist für mich.
Wer sagt es *den* Schülern? *Denen* sag ich es nicht.

	Nominative	Accusative	Dative
Masculine	der	den	dem
Feminine	die	die	der
Neuter	das	das	dem
Plural	die	die	denen

DEFINITE ARTICLES AS RELATIVE PRONOUNS

The definite articles can be used as relative pronouns. Relative pronouns introduce relative clauses. Note that **was** is used as a relative pronoun after **alles, das, etwas, nichts, viel, wenig,** and when referring to a whole clause. **Wo** is used as a relative pronoun to refer to places, literally or in a broader sense.

	Nominative	Accusative	Dative
Masculine	der	den	dem
Feminine	die	die	der
Neuter	das	das	dem
Plural	die	die	denen

INTERROGATIVES

INTERROGATIVE PRONOUNS

	People		Things	
Nominative	**wer?**	*who?*	**was?**	*what?*
Accusative	**wen?**	*whom?*	**was?**	*what?*
Dative	**wem?**	*to, for whom?*		

OTHER INTERROGATIVES

wann? *when?*	**wie viele?** *how many?*	**welche-?** *which?*	
warum? *why?*	**wo?** *where?*	**was für (ein)?** *what kind of (a)?*	
wie? *how?*	**woher?** *from where?*		
wie viel? *how much? how many?*	**wohin?** *to where?*		

WAS FÜR (EIN)?

	Nominative	Accusative	Dative
Masculine	**Was für ein** Lehrer ist er?	**Was für einen** Lehrer hast du?	**Mit was für einem** Lehrer?
Feminine	**Was für eine** Uhr ist das?	**Was für eine** Uhr kaufst du?	**Mit was für einer** Uhr?
Neuter	**Was für ein** Buch ist das?	**Was für ein** Buch liest du?	**Mit was für einem** Buch?
Plural	**Was für Bücher** sind das?	**Was für** Bücher hast du?	**Mit was für** Büchern?

PREPOSITIONS

Accusative	durch, für, gegen, ohne, um
Dative	aus, bei, mit, nach, seit, von, zu, gegenüber
Two-Way: *Dative-**wo?*** *Accusative-**wohin?***	an, auf, hinter, in, neben, über, unter, vor, zwischen
Genitive	(an)statt, außerhalb, innerhalb, trotz, während, wegen

CONJUNCTIONS

COORDINATING CONJUNCTIONS

Coordinating conjunctions join independent or main clauses — clauses that can stand alone as complete sentences. When independent clauses are joined together by a coordinating conjunction, both clauses maintain verb-second word order.

aber	*but, (however)*	**oder**	*or*	**und**	*and*
denn	*because, for*	**sondern**	*but (on the contrary)*		

SUBORDINATING CONJUNCTIONS

Subordinating conjunctions introduce dependents or subordinating clauses — clauses that cannot stand alone because they do not make complete sense without the main clause. Dependent clauses may either follow or precede the main clause, but they always require verb-last position.

als	*(at the time) when*	**dass**	*that*	**seit(dem)**	*since (that time)*
als ob	*as if*	**bevor**	*before*	**während**	*while*
bis	*until*	**indem**	*while, as, by*	**weil**	*because*
damit	*in order (so) that*	**ob**	*whether*	**wenn**	*if, when, whenever*

WORD ORDER

POSITION OF VERBS IN A SENTENCE

The conjugated verb is in ***first*** *position in:*	yes/no *questions (questions that do not begin with an interrogative)* **Trinkst du Kaffee?** **Spielst du Tennis?** **Möchtest du ins Konzert gehen?** *both formal and informal commands* **Kommen Sie bitte um 2 Uhr!** **Geh doch mit ins Kino!**
The conjugated verb is in ***second*** *position in:*	*statements with normal word order* **Wir spielen heute Volleyball.** *statements with inverted word order* **Heute spielen wir Volleyball.** *questions that begin with an interrogative* **Wohin gehst du?** **Woher kommst du?** **Was macht er?** *sentences connected by* **und, oder, aber, denn** **Ich komme nicht, denn ich habe keine Zeit.**
The conjugated verb is in ***second*** *position and the infinitive or past participle is* ***final*** *in:*	*statements with modals* **Ich möchte heute ins Kino gehen.** *statements in conversational past* **Ich habe das Buch gelesen.** *statements with* **werde** *and* **würde** **Ich werde im Mai nach Berlin fliegen.** **Die Oma würde gern ins Theatre gehen.**
The conjugated verb is in ***final*** *position in:*	*clauses that begin with interrogatives (***wo, wann, warum***, etc.)* **Ich weiß, wo das Hotel ist.** **Ich weiß nicht, wer heute Morgen angerufen hat.** *clauses that begin with* **weil, dass,** *or* **ob** **Ich gehe nicht ins Kino, weil ich kein Geld habe.** **Ich glaube, dass er Rockmusik gern hört.** **Ich komme morgen nicht, weil ich zu Hause helfen muss.** **Ich weiß nicht, ob er den Film schon gesehen hat.**

POSITION OF **NICHT** IN A SENTENCE

To negate the entire sentence, as close to end of sentence as possible:	**Er fragt seinen Vater**		**nicht.**
Before a separable prefix:	**Ich rufe ihn**	**nicht**	**an.**
Before any part of a sentence you want to negate, contrast, or emphasize:	**Er kommt**	**nicht**	**heute.** **(Er kommt morgen.)**
Before part of a sentence that answers the question **wo?**	**Ich wohne**	**nicht**	**in Berlin.**

ADJECTIVES

ENDINGS OF ADJECTIVES AFTER DER- AND DIESER-WORDS

	Nominative			Accusative			Dative			Genitive		
Masculine	der	-e	Vorort	den	-en	Vorort	dem	-en	Vorort	des	-en	Vororts
Feminine	die	-e	Stadt	die	-e	Stadt	der	-en	Stadt	der	-en	Stadt
Neuter	das	-e	Dorf	das	-e	Dorf	dem	-en	Dorf	des	-en	Dorfes
Plural	die	-en	Vororte	die	-en	Vororte	den	-en	Vororten	der	-en	Vororte

NOTE: 1. Names of cities used as adjectives always have the ending -er: **der Frankfurter Zoo, das Münchner Oktoberfest**

2. Adjectives such as **super, klasse, spitze**, and **rosa, lila, beige**, and **orange** never take endings.
   Das ist ein klasse Wagen. Möchtest du auch so einen klasse Wagen?
   Ich möchte auch so ein schönes rosa Hemd.

ENDINGS OF ADJECTIVES AFTER EIN AND KEIN

	Nominative			Accusative			Dative			Genitive		
Masculine	ein	-er	Vorort	einen	-en	Vorort	einem	-en	Vorort	eines	-en	Vororts
Feminine	eine	-e	Stadt	eine	-e	Stadt	einer	-en	Stadt	einer	-en	Stadt
Neuter	ein	-es	Dorf	ein	-es	Dorf	einem	-en	Dorf	eines	-en	Dorfes
Plural	keine	-en	Vororte	keine	-en	Vororte	keinen	-en	Vororten	keiner	-en	Vororte

ENDINGS OF ADJECTIVES AFTER THE POSSESSIVES

	Nominative			Accusative			Dative			Genitive		
Masculine	mein	-er	Vorort	meinen	-en	Vorort	meinem	-en	Vorort	meines	-en	Vororts
Feminine	meine	-e	Stadt	meine	-e	Stadt	meiner	-en	Stadt	meiner	-en	Stadt
Neuter	mein	-es	Dorf	mein	-es	Dorf	meinem	-en	Dorf	meines	-en	Dorfes
Plural	meine	-en	Vororte	meine	-en	Vororte	meinen	-en	Vororten	meiner	-en	Vororte

ENDINGS OF UNPRECEDED ADJECTIVES

	Nominative		Accusative		Dative	
Masculine	-er	Salat	-en	Salat	-em	Salat
Feminine	-e	Suppe	-e	Suppe	-en	Suppe
Neuter	-es	Eis	-es	Eis	-em	Eis
Plural	-e	Getränke	-e	Getränke	-en	Getränken

ENDINGS OF ADJECTIVES AFTER DETERMINERS OF QUANTITY

	Nominative	Accusative	Dative
alle, beide solche, manche	alle **-en** Haüser	alle **-en** Haüser	alle **-en** Haüsern
andere, ein paar, einige, mehrere, viele, wenige, etc.	mehrere **-e Dörfer**	mehrere **-e** Dörfer	mehreren **-en** Dörfern

MAKING COMPARISONS

	Positive	*Comparative*	*Superlative*
1. *All comparative forms end in* **-er.**	schnell	schneller	am schnellsten
2. *Most one-syllable forms have an umlaut.*	alt	älter	am ältesten
3. *Exceptions must be learned as they appear.*	dunkel gut	dunkler besser	am dunkelsten am besten

Equal Comparisons:	Er spielt **so gut wie** ich (spiele). *He plays as well as I (do).*	
Unequal Comparisons:	Sie spielt **besser als** ich (spiele). *She plays better than I (do).*	
Comparative and superlative adjectives before nouns:	der **bessere** Wagen ein **schöneres** Auto	der **beste** Wagen mein **schönstes** Kleid.

NOTE: Comparative adjectives before nouns have the same endings as descriptive adjectives (see page R30).

ORDINAL NUMBERS

1. Ordinal numbers are formed by adding **-t** or **-st** to the cardinal numbers. They are used to express a place in a series. Irregular ordinal numbers are printed in boldface below.

eins	der, die, das **erst-**	sieben	der, die, das **siebt-**
zwei	zweit-	acht	acht-
drei	**dritt-**	neun	neunt-
vier	viert-	zehn	zehnt-
fünf	fünft-	zwanzig	zwanzigst-
sechs	sechst-	dreißig	dreißigst-

2. Ordinal numbers are most often used as adjectives. They take regular adjective endings.

> Heute ist der erst**e** Mai.
> Tu das nicht ein zweit**es** Mal!
> In der dritt**en** Stunde haben wir Deutsch.
> Ostern ist dieses Jahr am fünft**en** April.
> Wann hat Heinrich der Acht**e** gelebt?

VERBS

PRESENT TENSE VERB FORMS

		Regular	-eln Verbs	Stem Ending with t/d	Stem Ending with s/ß
INFINITIVES		spiel -en	bastel -n	find -en	heiß -en
PRONOUNS		stem + ending	stem + ending	stem + ending	stem + ending
I	ich	spiel -e	bastl -e	find -e	heiß -e
you	du	spiel -st	bastel -st	find -est	heiß -t
he she it*	er sie es	spiel -t	bastel -t	find -et	heiß -t
we	wir	spiel -en	bastel -n	find -en	heiß -en
you (plural)	ihr	spiel -t	bastel -t	find -et	heiß -t
they	sie	spiel -en	bastel -n	find -en	heiß -en
you (formal)	Sie	spiel -en	bastel -n	find -en	heiß -en

NOTE: There are important differences between the verbs in the above chart:

1. Verbs ending in **-eln** (**basteln, segeln**) drop the **e** of the ending **-eln** in the **ich**-form: **ich bastle, ich segle** and add only **-n** in the **wir-, sie-,** and **Sie**-forms. These forms are always identical to the infinitive: **basteln, wir basteln, sie basteln, Sie basteln.** Verbs ending in **-ern** (**wandern**) sometimes drop the **e** of the ending **-ern** in the **ich**-form: **ich wandre** and add only **-n** in the **wir-, sie-,** and **Sie**-forms. These forms are always identical to the infinitive: **wandern.**

2. Verbs with a stem ending in **d** or **t**, such as **finden**, add an **e** before the ending in the **du**-form (**du findest**) and the **er**- and **ihr**-forms (**er findet, ihr findet**).

3. All verbs with stems ending in an **s**-sound (**heißen**) add only **-t** in the **du**-form: **du heißt.**

VERBS WITH A STEM-VOWEL CHANGE

There are a number of verbs in German that change their stem vowel in the **du**- and **er/sie**-forms. A few verbs, such as **nehmen** (*to take*), have a change in the consonant as well. You cannot predict these verbs, so it is best to learn each one individually. They are usually irregular only in the **du**- and **er/sie**-forms.

	e → i			e → ie		a → ä	
	essen	geben	nehmen	lesen	sehen	fahren	einladen
ich	esse	gebe	nehme	lese	sehe	fahre	lade ein
du	isst	gibst	nimmst	liest	siehst	fährst	lädst ein
er, sie	isst	gibt	nimmt	liest	sieht	fährt	lädt ein
wir	essen	geben	nehmen	lesen	sehen	fahren	laden ein
ihr	esst	gebt	nehmt	lest	seht	fahrt	ladet ein
sie	essen	geben	nehmen	lesen	sehen	fahren	laden ein
Sie	essen	geben	nehmen	lesen	sehen	fahren	laden ein

SOME IMPORTANT IRREGULAR VERBS: HABEN, SEIN, WISSEN, AND WERDEN

	haben	sein	wissen	werden
ich	habe	bin	weiß	werde
du	hast	bist	weißt	wirst
er, sie	hat	ist	weiß	wird
wir	haben	sind	wissen	werden
ihr	habt	seid	wisst	werdet
sie	haben	sind	wissen	werden
Sie	haben	sind	wissen	werden

VERBS FOLLOWED BY AN OBJECT IN THE DATIVE CASE

antworten, *to answer*	**gratulieren,** *to congratulate*
danken, *to thank*	**helfen,** *to help*
gefallen, *to like*	**passen,** *to fit*
glauben, *to believe*	

Es geht (mir) gut.	**Es steht (dir) gut.**
Es schmeckt (mir) nicht.	**Es macht (mir) Spaß.**
Es tut (mir) Leid.	**Es tut (mir) weh.**
Was fehlt (dir)?	

MODAL (AUXILIARY) VERBS

The verbs **dürfen, können, müssen, sollen, wollen, mögen** (and the **möchte**-forms) are usually used with an infinitive at the end of the sentence. If the meaning of that infinitive is clear, it can be left out: **Du musst sofort nach Hause!** (**Gehen** is understood and omitted.)

	dürfen	können	müssen	sollen	wollen	mögen	möchte
ich	darf	kann	muss	soll	will	mag	möchte
du	darfst	kannst	musst	sollst	willst	magst	möchtest
er, sie	darf	kann	muss	soll	will	mag	möchte
wir	dürfen	können	müssen	sollen	wollen	mögen	möchten
ihr	dürft	könnt	müsst	sollt	wollt	mögt	möchtet
sie	dürfen	können	müssen	sollen	wollen	mögen	möchten
Sie	dürfen	können	müssen	sollen	wollen	mögen	möchten

VERBS WITH SEPARABLE PREFIXES

Some verbs have separable prefixes: prefixes that separate from the conjugated verbs and are moved to the end of the sentence.

Present:	
einladen	Meine Gastfamilie **lädt** mich immer noch **ein**.
abbauen	**Bau** endlich mal deine Vorurteile **ab**!
Narrative Past (Imperfect):	
ankommen	Ich **kam** im August in den Vereinigten Staaten **an**.
hingehen	Er **ging** sofort **hin** und **holte** sein Gepäck **ab**.
abholen	Wir **holten** die Kinder am Flugplatz **ab**.
Conversational Past:	
abholen	Wer **hat** dich am Flughafen **abgeholt**?
Past Perfect:	
mitnehmen	Mein Vater **hatte** alle Kinder **mitgenommen**.
Infinitives used with zu:	
anrufen	Ich hatte vor, unsern Biolehrer **anzurufen**.
Certain prefixes are never separated from the verb:	
überraschen	Das **überrascht** mich überhaupt nicht.
wiederholen	**Wiederhole** bitte deine Frage!
übersetzen	Das hast du wirklich prima **übersetzt**.

COMMAND FORMS

Regular Verbs	gehen	spielen
with **du** (singular)	Geh!	Spiel!
with **ihr** (pl)	Geht!	Spielt!
with **Sie** (sing & pl)	Gehen Sie!	Spielen Sie!
"let's" form	Gehen wir!	Spielen wir!

Separable-prefix Verbs	mitkommen	anrufen	aufräumen	anziehen	ausgehen
	Komm mit!	Ruf an!	Räum auf!	Zieh an!	Geh aus!
	Kommt mit!	Ruft an!	Räum auf!	Zieht an!	Geht aus!
	Kommen Sie mit!	Rufen Sie an!	Räumen Sie auf!	Ziehen Sie an!	Gehen Sie aus!
	Kommen wir mit!	Rufen wir an!	Räumen wir auf!	Ziehen wir an!	Gehen wir aus!

Stem-changing Verbs	essen	nehmen	geben	sehen	fahren
	Iss!	Nimm!	Gib!	Sieh!	Fahr!
	Esst!	Nehmt!	Gebt!	Seht!	Fahrt!
	Essen Sie!	Nehmen Sie!	Geben Sie!	Sehen Sie!	Fahren Sie!
	Essen wir!	Nehmen wir!	Geben wir!	Sehen wir!	Fahren wir!

NOTE: The vowel changes **e → i** and **e → ie** are maintained in the **du**-form of the command. The vowel change **a → ä** does not occur in the command form.

EXPRESSING FUTURE TIME

In German, there are three ways to express future time:

1. present tense verb forms	Ich **kaufe** eine Jeans. Ich **finde** bestimmt etwas.	*I'm going to buy a pair of jeans.* *I will surely find something.*
2. present tense verb forms with words like *morgen, später*	Er kommt **morgen**. Elke ruft **später** an.	*He's coming tomorrow.* *Elke will call later.*
3. **werden**, *will*, plus infinitive	Ich **werde** ein Hemd **kaufen**. Er **wird** bald **gehen**.	*I'll buy a shirt.* *He'll go soon.*

To express that something will have happened or be completed in the future, you can use the perfect infinitive with a modal or with **werden:**

Ich möchte eine politische Karriere begonnen haben.
Ich werde einen Traumjob gefunden haben.

THE CONVERSATIONAL PAST

German verbs are divided into two groups: weak verbs and strong verbs. Weak verbs usually follow a regular pattern, such as the English verb forms *play — played — has played*. Strong verbs usually have irregularities, like the English verb forms *run — ran — has run* or *go — went — has gone*.

The conversational past tense of weak and strong verbs consists of the present tense of **haben** or **sein** and a form called the past participle, which is usually in last position in the clause or sentence.

Die Schüler Sabine	**haben** **ist**	ihre Hausaufgaben schon gestern zu Hause	**gemacht.** **geblieben.**

FORMATION OF PAST PARTICIPLES				

Weak Verbs
  with inseparable prefixes
  with separable prefixes
	spielen
	besuchen
	aufräumen
		(er) spielt
		(er) besucht
		(er) räumt auf
			gespielt
			besucht
			aufgeräumt
				Er hat gespielt.
				Er hat ihn besucht.
				Er hat aufgeräumt.

Strong Verbs
  with inseparable prefixes
  with separable prefixes
	kommen
	bekommen
	mitkommen
		(er) kommt
		(er) bekommt
		(er) kommt mit
			gekommen
			bekommen
			mitgekommen
				Er ist gekommen
				Er hat es bekommen.
				Er ist mitgekommen.

NOTE: For past participles of strong verbs and irregular verbs, see pages R38–R39.

WEAK VERBS FORMING THE PAST PARTICIPLE WITH **SEIN**

bummeln, *to stroll*	ist gebummelt	**surfen,** *to surf*	ist gesurft
reisen, *to travel*	ist gereist	**wandern,** *to hike*	ist gewandert

THE NARRATIVE PAST (IMPERFECT)

When relating a longer sequence that took place in the past, the narrative past is generally used.
NOTE: The **du-** and **ihr**-forms are rarely used in the narrative past.

Weak verbs add the past tense marker **-te** to the verb stem:

	hören	führen	sagen
ich	hörte	führte	sagte
du	hörtest	führtest	sagtest
er, sie	hörte	führte	sagte
wir	hörten	führten	sagten
ihr	hörtet	führtet	sagtet
sie, Sie	hörten	führten	sagten

Strong verbs often have a vowel change in the imperfect:

	haben	sein	werden	geben	finden
ich	hatte	war	wurde	gab	fand
du	hattest	warst	wurdest	gabst	fandest
er, sie, es	hatte	war	wurde	gab	fand
wir	hatten	waren	wurden	gaben	fanden
ihr	hattet	wart	wurdet	gabt	fandet
sie, Sie	hatten	waren	wurden	gaben	fanden

The modals in the imperfect do not have the umlaut of the infinitive:

	dürfen	können	mögen	müssen	sollen	wollen
ich	durfte	konnte	mochte	musste	sollte	wollte
du	durftest	konntest	mochtest	musstest	solltest	wolltest
er, sie	durfte	konnte	mochte	musste	sollte	wollte
wir	durften	konnten	mochten	mussten	sollten	wollten
ihr	durftet	konntet	mochtet	musstet	solltet	wolltet
sie, Sie	durften	konnten	mochten	mussten	sollten	wollten

There are some verbs in German that form the imperfect like weak verbs but also have a stem vowel change:

	kennen	nennen	denken	bringen	wissen
ich	kannte	nannte	dachte	brachte	wusste
du	kanntest	nanntest	dachtest	brachtest	wusstest
er, sie	kannte	nannte	dachte	brachte	wusste
wir	kannten	nannten	dachten	brachten	wussten
ihr	kanntet	nanntet	dachtet	brachtet	wusstet
sie, Sie	kannten	nannten	dachten	brachten	wussten

THE SUBJUNCTIVE FORMS

	haben	sein	werden	wissen
ich	hätte	wär	würde	wüsste
du	hättest	wärst	würdest	wüsstest
er, sie, es	hätte	wär	würde	wüsste
wir	hätten	wären	würden	wüssten
ihr	hättet	wärt	würdet	wüsstet
sie, Sie	hätten	wären	würden	wüssten

	können	müssen	dürfen	sollen	wollen
ich	könnte	müsste	dürfte	sollte	wollte
du	könntest	müsstest	dürftest	solltest	wolltest
er, sie, es	könnte	müsste	dürfte	sollte	wollte
wir	könnten	müssten	dürften	sollten	wollten
ihr	könntet	müsstet	dürftet	solltet	wolltet
sie, Sie	könnten	müssten	dürften	sollten	wollten

CONDITIONAL SENTENCES

Conditional sentences can be used to make hypothetical statements.

fulfillable	Wenn ich Zeit **hätte, würde** ich den Müll **sortieren.** Wenn wir **könnten, würden** wir dir **helfen.** Sie **würde kommen,** wenn sie nicht so viel zu **tun hätte.**
unfulfillable	Wenn ich Zeit **gehabt hätte, hätte** ich den Müll **sortiert.** Wenn du **gekommen wärst, hättest** du auch Spaß **gehabt.** Ich **wäre gekommen,** wenn du mich **eingeladen hättest.**

PASSIVE VOICE

The passive voice is used to express that something is being done or that something has to be done. It can also describe customary occurrence. The following is a summary:

Present *Imperfect* *Perfect* *Past Perfect* *Future*	Die Karten **werden verteilt.** Der Dirigent **wurde begrüßt.** Ein Ballett **ist aufgeführt worden.** Eine Oper **war gezeigt worden.** Ein Film **wird gezeigt werden.**	*The tickets are being distributed.* *The conductor was greeted.* *A ballet has been performed.* *An opera had been shown.* *A movie will be shown.*
with modals: *Present* *Past*	Dieses Museum **muss renoviert werden.** Die Kleiderfrage **konnte geklärt werden.**	*This museum must be renovated.* *The question of what to wear was able to be cleared up.*
with subjunctive forms up.	Die Karten { **könnten abgeholt werden.** **müssten abgeholt werden.** **sollten abgeholt werden.**	The tickets { *could be picked up.* *should be picked up.* *ought to be picked up.*

PRINCIPAL PARTS OF VERBS

This list includes the strong verbs listed in the **Wortschatz** sections of Level 1, Level 2, and Level 3. Weak verbs with stem vowel changes and other irregularites are also listed. Past participles formed with **sein** are indicated. All other past participles on the list are formed with **haben.** Usually, only one English meaning of the verb is given. Other meanings may be found in the German-English Vocabulary.

INFINITIVE	PRESENT	IMPERFECT	PAST PARTICIPLE	MEANING
abnehmen	nimmt ab	nahm ab	abgenommen	*to lose weight*
anbieten	bietet an	bot an	angeboten	*to offer*
anfangen	fängt an	fing an	angefangen	*to begin*
angeben	gibt an	gab an	angegeben	*to indicate*
anpreisen	preist an	pries an	angepriesen	*to praise*
abheben	hebt ab	hob ab	abgehoben	*to lift*
annehmen	nimmt an	nahm an	angenommen	*to assume*
anrufen	ruft an	rief an	angerufen	*to call up*
ansprechen	spricht an	sprach an	angesprochen	*to address, speak to*
anziehen	zieht an	zog an	angezogen	*to put on (clothes)*
auffallen	fällt auf	fiel auf	aufgefallen	*to be conspicuous*
aushalten	hält aus	hielt aus	ausgehalten	*to endure*
ausleihen	leiht aus	lieh aus	ausgeliehen	*to borrow, lend*
aussehen	sieht aus	sah aus	ausgesehen	*to look, appear*
beitragen	trägt bei	trug bei	beigetragen	*to contribute*
bekommen	bekommt	bekam	bekommen	*to get, receive*
beschreiben	beschreibt	beschrieb	beschrieben	*to describe*
bestreichen	bestreicht	bestrich	bestrichen	*to spread, to butter*
blasen	bläst	blies	geblasen	*to blow*
bleiben	bleibt	blieb	(ist) geblieben	*to stay*
brechen	bricht	brach	gebrochen	*to break*
denken	denkt	dachte	gedacht	*to think*
eingestehen	gesteht ein	gestand ein	eingestanden	*to admit*
einladen	lädt ein	lud ein	eingeladen	*to invite*
einziehen	zieht ein	zog ein	eingezogen	*to draft*
erfahren	erfährt	erfuhr	erfahren	*to experience*
erkennen	erkennt	erkannte	erkannt	*to recognize*
essen	isst	aß	gegessen	*to eat*
fahren	fährt	fuhr	(ist) gefahren	*to drive, ride*
fernsehen	sieht fern	sah fern	ferngesehen	*to watch TV*
finden	findet	fand	gefunden	*to find*
geben	gibt	gab	gegeben	*to give*
gefallen	gefällt	gefiel	gefallen	*to like, be pleasing to*
gehen	geht	ging	(ist) gegangen	*to go*
gießen	gießt	goss	gegossen	*to pour, to water*
großziehen	zieht groß	zog groß	großgezogen	*to raise (a child)*
haben	hat	hatte	gehabt	*to have*
halten	hält	hielt	gehalten	*to keep*
heben	hebt	hob	gehoben	*to lift*
heißen	heißt	hieß	geheißen	*to be called*
helfen	hilft	half	geholfen	*to help*
herausnehmen	nimmt heraus	nahm heraus	herausgenommen	*to take out*
kennen	kennt	kannte	gekannt	*to know*
klingen	klingt	klang	geklungen	*to sound*
kommen	kommt	kam	(ist) gekommen	*to come*

INFINITIVE	PRESENT	IMPERFECT	PAST PARTICIPLE	MEANING
lassen	lässt	ließ	gelassen	to let
laufen	läuft	lief	(ist) gelaufen	to run
lesen	liest	las	gelesen	to read
messen	misst	maß	gemessen	to measure
nachsehen	sieht nach	sah nach	nachgesehen	to check
nehmen	nimmt	nahm	genommen	to take
Rad fahren	fährt Rad	fuhr Rad	(ist) Rad gefahren	to bicycle
scheinen	scheint	schien	geschienen	to shine
schief gehen	geht schief	ging schief	(ist) schief gegangen	to go badly
schießen	schießt	schoss	geschossen	to shoot
schlafen	schläft	schlief	geschlafen	to sleep
schlagen	schlägt	schlug	geschlagen	to hit; to slam
schreiben	schreibt	schrieb	geschrieben	to write
schwimmen	schwimmt	schwamm	(ist) geschwommen	to swim
sehen	sieht	sah	gesehen	to see
sein	ist	war	(ist) gewesen	to be
sprechen	spricht	sprach	gesprochen	to speak
stehen	steht	stand	gestanden	to stand
streiten	streitet	stritt	gestritten	to quarrel
tragen	trägt	trug	getragen	to wear; to carry
trinken	trinkt	trank	getrunken	to drink
tun	tut	tat	getan	to do
übertreiben	übertreibt	übertrieb	übertrieben	to exaggerate
s. umsehen	sieh s. um	sah s. um	umgesehen	to look around
umziehen	zieht um	zog um	(ist) umgezogen	to move (residence)
unterbrechen	unterbricht	unterbrach	unterbrochen	to interrupt
s. unterhalten	unterhält s.	unterhielt s.	unterhalten	to discuss
unternehmen	unternimmt	unternahm	unternommen	to undertake
unterschreiben	unterschreibt	unterschrieb	unterschrieben	to sign
verbergen	verbirgt	verbarg	verborgen	to hide
verbieten	verbietet	verbot	verboten	to forbid
s. verbrennen	verbrennt s.	verbrannte s.	verbrannt	to burn oneself
vergehen	vergeht	verging	(ist) vergangen	to pass (time)
vergleichen	vergleicht	verglich	verglichen	to compare
s. verlassen	verlässt s.	verließ s.	verlassen	to count on
verlieren	verliert	verlor	verloren	to lose
vermeiden	vermeidet	vermied	vermieden	to avoid
vorlesen	liest vor	las vor	vorgelesen	to read aloud
vorschlagen	schlägt vor	schlug vor	vorgeschlagen	to suggest
versprechen	verspricht	versprach	versprochen	to promise
vorhaben	hat vor	hatte vor	vorgehabt	to plan
vorziehen	zieht vor	zog vor	vorgezogen	to prefer
wahrnehmen	nimmt wahr	nahm wahr	wahrgenommen	to perceive
waschen	wäscht	wusch	gewaschen	to wash
weggeben	gibt weg	gab weg	weggegeben	to give away
weglassen	lässt weg	ließ weg	weggelassen	to omit, to drop
wegtragen	trägt weg	trug weg	weggetragen	to take away
wegwerfen	wirft weg	warf weg	weggeworfen	to throw away
werben	wirbt	warb	geworben	to advertise
wiedergeben	gibt wieder	gab wieder	wiedergegeben	to repeat
wissen	weiß	wusste	gewusst	to know
zugeben	gibt zu	gab zu	zugegeben	to admit
zukommen	kommt zu	kam zu	(ist) zugekommen	to be in store for
zunehmen	nimmt zu	nahm zu	zugenommen	to gain weight
zurückbringen	bringt zurück	brachte zurück	zurückgebracht	to bring back

German-English Vocabulary

German-English Vocabulary

This vocabulary includes almost all the German words in the textbook, both active (for production) and passive (for recognition only). Active words and phrases, indicated by bold-faced type, are practiced in the chapter and are listed in the Wortschatz section at the end of each chapter. You are expected to know and be able to use active vocabulary. All other words are for recognition only and can often be understood from the context.

With some exceptions, the following are not included: proper nouns, verb conjugations, and forms of determiners. You will find irregular forms of past participles and the narrative past.

Nouns are listed with definite article and plural form, where applicable. The numbers after the entries refer to the level and chapter where the word or phrase first appears or where it becomes an active vocabulary word. Vocabulary from the location openers is followed by a "Loc" and the chapter number directly following the location spread.

The following abbreviations are used in this list: acc (accusative case), adj (adjective), coll (colloquial), conj (conjunction), dat (dative case), gen (genitive case), pl (plural), poss adj (possessive adjective), prep (preposition), s. (*sich*, or reflexive), sep (separable-prefix verb), and sing (singular).

ab (dat prep) *down, off*, III 1
ab und zu *now and then*, III6
abbaubar *degradable*, III9
abbauen (sep): **Vorurteile abbauen** *to overcome prejudices*, III8
abbilden (sep) *to depict, draw*, III1
die Abbildung, -en *drawing, picture*, III8
abbrechen (sep) *to break off*, III4
abdrucken (sep) *to print, reprint*, III6
der Abend, -e *evening*, I; **am Abend** *in the evening*, I
das Abendessen, - *dinner, evening meal*, II
die Abendkasse, -n *ticket booth*, III10
das Abendkleid, -er *evening gown*, II
abends *evenings*, III4
die Abendvorstellung, -en *evening performance*, III10
der Abenteuerfilm, -e *adventure film*, I
abenteuerlich *adventurous*, III3
aber (conj) *but*, I; **aber sicher!** *but of course!*, II
abergläubisch *superstitious*, III8
abermals *over and over again*, III6
der Abfall, ¨e *trash, waste*, III9
die Abfalltüte, -n *trash bag*, III2
das Abgas, -e *exhaust*, III9
abgedroschen *trite, hackneyed*, III5
abgefahren (slang) *worn out*, III3
abgegriffen *well-worn, shabby*, III11
abgeschlossen *finished*, III11

abgeschnitten *cut-off*, II
abgeworben *enticed away*, III2
abhängen von (sep) *to be dependent on*, III12
abhauen (sep) (coll) *to leave*, III4
abheben (sep) *to pick up*, I; **den Hörer abheben** *to pick up the receiver*, I
s. abheben von (sep, dat) *to contrast with*, III3
abholen (sep) *to pick up*, III8
abholzen (sep) *to deforest*, III9
das Abi=Abitur, III3
das Abitur (*final exam and diploma from a German high school*), III4
Abiturient(in), -en/nen *student studying for the Abitur*, III5
die Abkürzung, -en *abbreviation*, III9
das Ablagefach, ¨er *storage shelf*, II
ablehnen (sep) *to turn down, reject*, III3
s. **ablenken mit** (sep) *to divert oneself with*, III3
abnehmen (sep) *to lose weight*, III3
das Abonnement, -s *subscription*, III10
abpflücken (sep) *to pick (from a plant)*, III11
abräumen (sep) *to clean up, clear off*, I
die Abrechnung, -en *deduction, settlement of an account*, III5
der Absatz, ¨e *paragraph*, III3; *sales*, III7; *shoe heel*, II
abschließen (sep) *to lock up*, III1; *finish* III 2
der Abschluss, ¨e *end, conclusion; diploma*, III11

der Abschnitt, -e *paragraph*, III6
der Absender, - *sender*, III4
abschreiben (sep) *to copy*, III4
absichtlich *on purpose*, III4
absolut *absolute(ly), unconditional(ly)*, III3
der Absolvent, -en *graduate*, III11
s. **absondern von** (sep) *to separate oneself from*, III4
der Abstand: im Abstand von *at an interval of*, III9
abstellen (sep) *to switch off*, II
abstreiten (sep) *to dispute, contest*, III5
die Abteilung, -en *division, department*, III4
die Abteilungsleiterin, -nen *head of a department*, III4
abwarten (sep) *to wait and see*, III2
das Abwasser, ¨ *wastewater*, III9
abwechselnd *alternating, one after the other*, III1
die Abwechslung, -en *variety*, III10
abwechslungsreich *varied, diversified*, II
Ach *Oh!*, I; **Ach ja!** *Oh yeah!*, I
Ach schade! *That's too bad.*, II
achten auf (acc) *to pay attention to*, III3
ächzend *groaning*, III2
der Actionfilm, -e *action movie*, I
das Adjectiv, -e *adjective*, III2
die Adresse, -n *address*, III2
das Adverb, (pl) Adverbien *adverb*, III1
aggressiv *aggressive*, III8
ägyptisch (adj) *Egyptian*, II

ahnen *to suspect, surmise,* III1
ähnlich *similar,* III1
die Ahnung, -en *idea, notion,* III4;
  Keine Ahnung! *I have no idea!,* I
der Akkord, -e *agreement,* III12
der Akt, -e *act, action,* III10
die Aktion, -en *activity, initiative,* III9
  aktiv *active,* III1
  aktuell *current, contemporary,* III7
  akzeptabel *acceptable,* III7
  akzeptieren *to accept,* III4
der **Alkohol, -e** *alcohol,* II
  all- *all,* II
  alle werden *run out,* III11
  allein *alone,* III5
  allerdings *certainly, by all means,*
    III3
die Allergie, -n *allergy,* III1
  allergisch (gegen) *allergic (to),* II
  allerkleinst- *the littlest,* III2
  allernötigst- *indispensible,* III3
  alles *everything,* II
  allgemein *general,* III5
die Allgemeinbildung *all-round
    education, general knowledge,* III11
  allmählich *gradually,* III11
der Alltag, -e *weekday, workday
    routine,* III1
die Alltäglichkeit, -en *everyday
    occurence,* III4
  alltäglich *daily, ordinary,* III1
  allwissend *omniscient,* III7
  als *than,* II; **als** (conj) *when, at the
    time,* III8
  als ob (conj) *as if, as though,* III7
  also (part) *well, okay,* III2
  alt *old,* I
das Altenheim, -e *home for the elderly,*
    III5
  älter *older,* II
die Altersgruppe, -n *age group,* III5
der Altersjahrgang, ⁻e *year of birth,*
    III11
das Altpapier *recyclable paper,* III9
das Alu=Aluminium *aluminum,* III9
die **Aludose, -n** *aluminum can,* III9
  am=an dem *at the,* I; **am Abend**
    in the evening, I; **am ersten (Juli)**
    on the first (of July), I; **am letzten
    Tag** *on the last day,* II; **am
    liebsten** *most of all,* I; **am Tag**
    during the day, II
die **Ameise, -n** *ant,* III9
das Amerikabild *impression of
    America,* III8
die **Ampel, -n** *traffic light,* I; **bis zur
    Ampel** *until you get to the traffic
    light,* I
  s. amüsieren *to have a good time,* III6
  an (acc, dat prep) *to; at,* II; **an der
    Schule** *at school,* II
  an: Was an dir gut ist, ist ... *What I
    like about you is ...,* III4
die Analyse, -n *analysis,* III7
  analysieren *to analyze,* III7
  Anästhesist(in), -en/nen
    anesthesiologist, III12

anbieten (sep) *to offer,* III9
der Anblick, -e *view, sight, look,* III6
  ander- *other,* I; **ein(-) ander-**
    another (a different) one, II
  andererseits *on the other hand,* III5
  s. **ändern** *to change oneself,* III5
  anders *different,* III4
  anderswo *elsewhere,* III11
die Änderung, -en *change,* III12
die Anekdote, -n *anecdote,* III6
  anerkennen (sep) *to recognize,
    acknowledge,* III5
der Anfang, ⁻e *beginning,* III1
  anfangen (sep) *to begin,* III11
der **Anfänger, -** *beginner,* II
  anfangs *in the beginning,* III10
  anfüllen (sep) *to fill up,* III10
  angeben (sep) *to indicate, state,*
    III11
  angeblich *ostensibly, reported to be,*
    III7
das **Angebot, -e** *offer,* I; **Angebot der
    Woche** *weekly special,* I
  angeboten *offered,* III2
  angehören (sep, dat) *to belong to,*
    III4
  angehend- *would-be, future,* III9
  angeht: was (das) angeht *as far as
    (that) goes,* III3
der Angeklagte, -n *the accused,* III5
  angeln *to fish,* II
  angenehm *comfortable, pleasant,*
    III5
  angenommen *accepted, assumed,*
    III8
  angepriesen *praised,* III7
  angespannt *tense,* III2
  angesprochen *spoken to,* III6
  angestaubt *old, dusty,* III10
der Angestellte, -n *employee,* III2
  angewiesen sein auf (acc) *to be
    dependent on,* III11
  angezogen *dressed,* III3
  Angst haben vor (dat) *to be afraid
    of,* III2
  ängstlich *anxious,* III7
der Angstschweiß *cold sweat,* III7
  anhaben (sep) *to have on,* III3
der Anhaltspunkt, -e *guiding principle,
    deciding factor,* III7
  anhand *based on,* III3
  Anhieb: jemanden auf Anhieb
    leiden können *to take an instant
    liking to someone,* III8
  anhören (sep) *to listen to,* III1
  ankommen (sep) *to arrive,* III1; **Es
    kommt darauf an, ob ...** *It
    depends on whether ...,* III4;
  ankommen bei (sep) *to be
    accepted by,* III3
  ankreuzen (sep) *to cross, mark off,*
    III3
die **Anlage, -n** *grounds, site,* II; *system,
    installation,* II
  anlaufen: rot anlaufen *to blush,* III4
der Anlass, ⁻e *occasion,* III5
  anlasten (sep) *to blame,* III9

die Anleitung, -en *direction,
    introduction,* III3
  anlocken (sep) *to lure,* III2
die Annahmestelle, -n *receiving area,*
    III9
  annehmen (sep) *to assume,* III8
die Annonce, -n *ad, announcement,*
    III6
  anonym *anonymous,* III6
der **Anorak, -s** *parka,* II
  s. **anpassen** (sep) *to conform to,* III3
  anpreisen (sep) *to praise,* III7
  anprobieren (sep) *to try on,* I
die Anrede, -n *speech, address,* III7
  anregen (sep) *to encourage,
    stimulate,* III6
  anregend *stimulating, exciting,* III6
die Anregung, -en *stimulation,
    incitement,* III2
die Anreise, -n *arrival,* III2
  anrichten (sep) *to produce, cause,
    prepare,* III9
  anrufen (sep) *to call (on the
    phone),* I
der Ansager, - *announcer,* III10
  ansah (*imperfect of* ansehen), III10
  anschauen (sep) *to look at,* III4
  anschaulich *clear, vivid,* III7
der **Anschlag, ⁻e** *announcement,* II
  anschlagen (sep) *to strike; to post,*
    III12
  anschließend *following, adjacent,*
    III1
das Ansehen: Ansehen geben *to hold in
    high esteem,* III6
  s. ansehen (sep) *to have a look at,* III2
die Ansicht, -en *view, point of view,* III9
  ansprechen (sep) *to talk to,* to
    appeal to, III6
  anstatt (gen prep) *instead of,* III10
  anstrahlen (sep) *to shine on; to
    smile at,* III7
  s. **anstrengen** (sep) *to make an effort,*
    III12
  anstrengend *strenuous,* III5
  anstupsen (sep) *to nudge,* III10
der Anteil, -e *portion, share,* III8
der Antisemitismus *antisemitism,* III8
  antreten *to start*
die Antwort, -en *answer,* III2
  antworten (dat) *to answer,* III1
  anvertrauen (sep, dat) *to entrust to,*
    III5
der Anwalt, ⁻e *lawyer,* III11
die Anwältin, -nen *lawyer,* III11
die Anweisung, -en *order, instruction,*
    III5
  anwenden (sep) *to make use of,*
    III10
die Anwendung, -en *application, use,*
    III3
die Anzahl *number, quantity,* III10
die Anzeige, -n *ad,* III6
  anziehen (sep) *to put on, wear,* I
der Anziehungspunkt, -e *center of
    attraction,* III1
  der **Anzug, ⁻e** *suit,* II

der Apfel, ⸚ *apple*, I
der Apfelkuchen, - *apple cake*, I
der Apfelsaft, ⸚e *apple juice*, I; **ein Glas Apfelsaft** *a glass of apple juice*, I
der Aphorismus, Aphorismen *aphorism*, III10
der Apostel - *apostle*, Loc4
die Apotheke, -n *pharmacy*, II
der Apotheker, - *pharmacist*, III5
der Apothekerin, -nen *pharmacist (female)*
der Apparat, -e *telephone*, I
der Appell, -e *appeal*, III7
der Appetit: Guten Appetit! *Bon appétit!*, II
applaudieren *to applaud*, III10
die Aprikose, -n *apricot*, II
der April *April*, I
die Arbeit, -en *work*, III1
arbeiten *to work*, II
der Arbeiter, - *worker*, III6
das Arbeitsamt, ⸚er *employment office*, III11
der Arbeitsmarkt, ⸚e *job market*, III11
der Arbeitsplatz, ⸚e *job*, III5
die Arbeitsstelle, -n *job position*, III11
das Arbeitstempo, -s *work rate*, III11
der Arbeitsvertrag, ⸚e *work contract*, III5
die Arbeitszeit, -en *working hours*, III5
das Arbeitszeugnis, -se *work performance review*, III11
der Architekt, -en *architect*, III11
die Architektur *architecture*, III11
der Ärger *irritation, annoyance*, III6
ärgerlich *annoying*, III1
s. ärgern *to get annoyed*, III8
argumentieren *to argue*, III2
der Arm, -e *arm*, II
das Armband, ⸚er *bracelet*, II
die Armbanduhr, -en *wristwatch*, I
die Armee, -n *army*, II
der Armeelaster, - *army truck*, III5
ärmellos *sleeveless*, II
die Armen (pl) *poor*, III8
die Armut *poverty*, II
der Arrestant, -en *prisoner*, III12
die Art, -en *kind, sort*, III11; auf ihre Art *in their own way*, III3
der Artikel, - *article, commodity*, III3
die Arzneimittelproduktion *pharmaceutical production*, Loc10
der Arzt, ⸚e *doctor*, II
die Ärztin, -nen *doctor (female)*
die Assonanz *assonance*, III10
aßen (*imperfect of* essen), III8
atemberaubend *breathtaking*, III7
atemlos *breathless*, III10
athletisch *athletic*, III8
atmen *to breathe*, III10
atomar *nuclear*, III9
der Atomkrieg, -e *nuclear war*, III11
attraktiv *attractive*, III11
Au!, Aua! *Ouch!*, II
auch *also*, I; **Ich auch.** *Me too.*, I; **auch noch** *also*, II; **auch schon** *also*, II

auf (acc, dat prep) *on, onto, to*, II; **Auf dein/Ihr/euer Wohl!** *To your health!*, II; **auf dem Land** *in the country*, I; **Auf Wiederhören!** *Goodbye!*, I; **auf einer Fete** *at a party*, II
aufbauen (sep) *to construct*, Loc7
aufbewahren (sep) *to preserve, store*, III1
aufblühen (sep) *to blossom*, III10
aufeinander kleben (sep) *to stick, glue together*, III10
der Aufenthaltsraum, ⸚e *waiting room*, III2
auffallen (sep) *to be conspicuous*, III8
aufführen (sep) *to perform*, III10
die Aufführung, -en *performance*, III10
die Aufgabe, -n *assignment*, III6
aufgehen (sep) *to rise, expand*, III10
aufgeschlossen *open, friendly*, III8
aufgeschrieben *written down*, III1
aufging (*imperfect of* aufgehen), III12
aufkeimend *budding, dawning*, III5
aufklären (sep) *to enlighten*, III7
auflaufen (sep) *to run aground*, III9
auflegen (sep) *to hang up (the telephone)*, I
auflisten (sep) *to list*, III8
auflösen (sep) *to solve*, III3
aufmerksam *attentive*, III9
aufmerksam machen auf (acc) *to draw attention to*, III7
die Aufmerksamkeit, -en *attention*, III7
aufnehmen (sep) *to take, pick up*, III4
aufpassen (sep) *to pay attention*, III3
aufräumen (sep) *to clean up*, I
der Aufräumetag, -e *clean-up day*, III1
aufregen (sep) *to excite, to annoy*, III7
die Aufregung, -en *excitement*, III10
aufrücken *to move up*, III12
aufsässig *rebellious*, III4
der Aufsatz, ⸚e *essay*, III3
aufschieben (sep) *to push open*, III2
aufschneiden (sep) *to cut open*, III1
der Aufschnitt *cold cuts*, I
aufschreiben (sep) *to write down*, III2
der Aufseher, - *supervisor*, III10
aufsetzen (sep) *to put or place on*, III10
aufstand (*imperfect of* aufstehen), III12
aufstecken (sep) *to put up*, III9
aufstehen (sep) *to get up*, III5
die Aufstiegschance, -n *chance for promotion*, III11
die Aufstiegsmöglichkeit, -en *possibility for promotion*, III5
aufwachen (sep) *to wake up*, III10

aufwachsen (sep) *to grow up*, III4
aufwendig: aufwendig verpackt *elaborately wrapped*, III9
aufzeigen (sep) *to show, exhibit*, III10
das Auge, -n *eye*, I
der Augenblick, -e *moment*, III1
der August *August*, I
aus (dat prep) *from, out of*, II; **aus Baumwolle** *made of cotton*, I; **aus dem (16.) Jahrhundert** *from the (16th) century*, II
ausarbeiten (sep) *to work out in detail*, III11
ausbilden (sep) *to educate*, III4
die Ausbildung, -en *education*, II
der Ausbildungsvertrag, ⸚e *apprenticeship contract*, III5
ausbleiben (sep) *to stay out*, III1
ausbrechen (sep) *to break out*, III8
die Ausdauer *perseverance, endurance*, III3
ausdenken (sep) *to think, work out*, III10
der Ausdruck, ⸚e *expression*, III2
ausdrücken (sep) *to express*, III3
auseinander *from each other*, III3
auseinander halten *to hold, keep apart*, III6
auseinander nehmen *to take apart*, III12
auseinander spalten *to split apart*, III10
ausfindig machen *to find*, III8
der Ausflug, ⸚e *excursion*, II
das Ausführen *developing, development*, III1
ausführlich *detailed*, III1
die Ausführung, -en *execution, delivery*, III9
ausfüllen (sep) *to fill out*, III11
die Ausgabe, -n *edition*, III6
der Ausgangspunkt, -e *point of departure*, III1
ausgeben (sep) *to give out; to spend (money)*, III3
ausgebildet *trained*
ausgedacht *thought up*, III10
ausgefallen *unusual*, III3
ausgeflippt (slang) *flipped-out*, III3
ausgegangen *gone out*, III7
ausgehen (sep) *to go out*, III4
ausgehen von (sep) *to be initiated by*, III10
ausgelassen *omitted*, III1
ausgeliehen *borrowed, checked out*, III1
ausgerechnet (you) *of all (people)*, III9
ausgesprochen *particularly*, III5
ausgewogen *well-balanced*, III8
ausgezeichnet *excellent, outstanding*, II; (past participle of auszeichnen) *put a price tag on*, III1

ausgezogen *moved out*, III4
ausgiebig *extensive, exhaustive*, III10
aushalten (sep) *to endure, stand something*, III3
auskommen: Wir kommen gut mit ihm aus. *We get along well with him.*, III4
die Auskunft, ⁻e *information*, III3
auslachen (sep) *to laugh (at someone)*, III2
das Ausland *foreign country*, III8
Ausländer(in), -/nen *foreigner*, III4
ausländisch *foreign*, II
ausleihen (sep) *to borrow, lend*, III1
auslösen (sep) *to trigger, cause*, III9
die Auslösung, -en *cause*, III5
s. **ausmachen** (sep) *to make up, constitute*, III9; **Das macht mir nichts aus.** *That doesn't matter to me.*, III6
ausnutzen (sep) *to take advantage of*, III7
ausquetschen (sep) *to squeeze out*, III5
ausrechnen (sep) *to calculate*, III9
die Ausrede, -n *excuse*, III9
ausreden (sep) *to finish speaking*, III6
s. **ausruhen** (sep) *to relax, rest*, III11
ausrutschen (sep) *to slip*, III1
die Aussage, -n *statement*, III1
aussagen: Das sagt etwas über mich aus. *That says something about me.*, III3
ausschalten (sep) *to switch off*, III9
ausschlaggebend *decisive*, III11
ausschließlich *exclusively*, III9
der Ausschluss, ⁻e *exclusion*, III5
der Ausschnitt, -e *excerpt*, III6
aussehen (sep) *to look like, to appear*, I; **der Rock sieht ... aus.** *The skirt looks...*, I; **Wie sieht er aus?** *What does he look like?*, I
das Außengelände *surroundings*, III2
außerdem *besides that*, III9
außerhalb (gen prep) *outside of*, III4
äußern *to express*, III3
äußerst *highly*, III8
die Äußerung, -en *comment, remark*, III3
ausspannen (sep) *to spread, stretch out*, III12
ausstatten (sep) *to equip*, III2
die Ausstattung, -en *equipment, furnishing*, III2
aussteigen (sep) *to get off (a train)*, III1
ausstellen (sep) *to exhibit, display*, Loc10
die **Ausstellung, -en** *exhibition*, III10

ausstrecken (sep) *to stick out*, III10
s. **aussuchen** (sep) *to pick out, select*, III1
der Austausch, -e *exchange*, III4
austauschen (sep) *to exchange*, III4
der Austauschschüler, - *exchange student*, III1
der Austauschstudent, -en *exchange student*, III7
die **Auster, -n** *oyster*, II
Austria *Österreich*, I
ausüben (sep) *to practice, pursue*, III11
auswählen (sep) *to choose from*, III2
der **Ausweis, -e** *identification*, III2
auswendig *by heart, rote*, III5
auswickeln (sep) *to unwrap, undo*, III10
ausziehen (sep) *to move out, away*, III4; *to undress*, III7
der Auszug, ⁻e *excerpt*, III5
das **Auto, -s** *car*, I; **mit dem Auto** *by car*, I
die Autobahn, -en *interstate highway*, III8
der Autofahrer, - *driver*, III11
automatisch *automatic*, III6
Autor(in), -en/nen *author*, III10
der Autounfall, ⁻e *car accident*, III1
die Autoversicherung, -en *car insurance*, III5
Azubi(=Auszubildende), -s *trainee, apprentice*, III4

backen *to bake*, III6
der **Bäcker, -** *baker*, I
die **Bäckerei, -en** *bakery*, I
die Backsteingotik *gothic architecture style with red brick*, III1
baden *to swim*, I; **baden gehen** *to go swimming*, I
der Badeort, -e *swimming resort*, III1
das **Badezimmer, -** *bathroom*, II
die **Bahn, -en** *train*, II
der **Bahnhof, ⁻e** *train station*, I
bald *soon*, I
das **Ballett, -e** *ballet*, II
die **Banane, -n** *banana*, II
bang *anxious*, III2
die **Bank, -en** *bank*, III1
Bankangestellte, -n *bank employee*, III1
das Bankett, -e *banquet*, Loc7
die Bankkauffrau, -en *banker*, III11
der **Bankkaufmann, -leute** *banker*, III11
der Bankschalter, - *bank window*, III5
das Bankwesen *banking*, Loc7

das Barock *baroque style*, Loc4
barock *baroque*, Loc10
bärtig *bearded*, III10
basieren auf (acc) *to establish, base on*, III9
die Basilika, (pl) Basiliken *basilica*, Loc 1
die Basis, Basen *basis*, III11
Basketball *basketball*, I
die Bassschläge (pl) *bass beats*, III3
basteln *to do crafts*, I
die **Batterie, -n** *battery*, III9
der Bau *construction*, III8
der **Bauch, ⁻e** *stomach*, II
die **Bauchschmerzen** (pl) *stomachache*, II
der Baudenabend, -e *folkloristic evening entertainment at a cabin*, III2
das **Baudenkmal, ⁻er** *monument*, II
bauen *to build*, III8
der Bauhelm, -e *hardhat*, III3
der **Baum, ⁻e** *tree*, II
der Baumeister, - *architect*, Loc10
die **Baumwolle** *cotton*, I
das Bauwerk, -e *structure, building*, Loc10
beabsichtigen *to intend*, III7
beachten *to notice, heed, regard*, III6
der Beamte, -n *offical, civil servant*, III11
die Beamtin, -nen *offical, civil servant*, III11
beantworten *to answer*, III1
bearbeiten *to work at, process*, III2
beben *to shake, tremble*, III10
der **Becher, -** *mug*, III2
bedauern *to be sorry about*, II
die Bedenken (pl) *misgivings*, III7
bedeuten *to mean*, III1
bedeutend *important*, Loc 1
die Bedeutung, -en *meaning*, III4
bedienen: die Kamera bedienen *to operate the camera*, II
die Bedingung, -en *condition*, III11
bedrücken *to depress*, III10
das Bedürfnis, -se *need*, III3
beeindrucken *to impress*, III8
beeinflussen *to influence*, III3
beenden *to end*, III3
befahl (*imperfect of* befehlen), III6
befallen *to befall*, III7
befehlen *to command*, III6
s. befinden *to find oneself, to be*, Loc1
befolgen *to obey, follow*, III12
befragen *to ask questions*, III8
befriedigen *to satisfy*, III7
befürchten *to fear, suspect*, III10
begabt *gifted*, III10
begann (*imperfect of* beginnen), III3
begegnen (dat) *to run into, meet*, III10
die Begegnung, -en *meeting, encounter*, III2
begeistert sein von *to be enthusiastic about*, III8

der Beginn *beginning*, III5
beginnen *to begin*, III11
begleiten *to accompany*, III10
begonnen *begun*, Loc7
der Begriff, -e *concept, idea*, III3
begründen *to found; to give a reason for*, III6
der Begründer, - *founder*, III5
die Begründung, -en *reason; foundation*, III2
begrüßen *to greet*, III10
behalten *to keep*, III6
der Behälter, - *container*, III8
behandeln *to handle, treat*, III4
behaupten *to claim, assert*, III12
beherbergen *to shelter*, Loc4
beherrschen *to rule*, III7
beherzigen *to take to heart*, III9
behindertenfreundlich *accessible to the physically challenged*, III2
bei (dat prep) *by, near, at*, II; **beim Bäcker** *at the baker's*, I; **Bei mir ist es auch so.** *That's the way it is with me, too.*, III4
beide *both*, III2
beidseitig *on both sides, mutual*, III9
die Beilage, -n *side dish*, II
das Bein, -e *leg*, II
beinahe *almost*, III8
beinhalten *to contain*, III10
das Beispiel, -e *example*, III1
beitreten *to join*, III1
der Beitrag, ⸚e *contribution*, III11
beitragen zu (sep) *to contribute to*, III6
bejahen *to concur, agree*, III9
bekam (*imperfect of* **bekommen**), III6
der Bekannte, -n *acquaintance*, III4
bekannt *known*, III1
der Bekanntenkreis, -e *circle of acquaintances*, III6
s. beklagen über (acc) *to complain about*, III10
die Bekleidung, -en *clothes*, III7
das Bekleidungsgeschäft, -e *clothing store*, III12
bekommen *to get, receive*, I
bekömmlich *wholesome, beneficial*, III10
belasten *to weigh on, burden*, III5
die Belastung, -en *burden*, III9
belegen *to cover; to register for*, III1; *to verify*, III9
belehrend *didactic*, III7
beliebt *popular*, II
bellen *to bark, howl*, III11
die Bemerkung, -en *comment, remark*, III1
s. bemühen um *to strive for*, III6
s. benehmen *to behave*, III4
beneiden *to envy*, III10
benötigen *to need*, III5
benutzen *to use*, II
beobachten *to observe*, III8
die Beobachtung, -en *observation*, III4

bequem *comfortable*, I
beraten *to advise*, III2
der Berater, - *advisor*, III12
der Bereich, -e *area, field, region*, III9
bereichern *to enrich*, III8
bereit *willing, prepared*, III3
bereits *already*, III11
bereitstellen (sep) *to make ready*, III10
bereitwillig *willing*, III10
der Berg, -e *mountain*, II
bergen *to hide*, III2
das Bergsteigen *mountain climbing*, II
die Bergtour, -en *tour or trip in the mountains*, III1
der Bericht, -e *report*, III6
berichten *to report*, III3
berücksichtigen *to take into consideration*, III5
der Beruf, -e *profession*, III11
beruflich *professional(ly)*, III5
die Berufsarmee, -n *professional army*, II
die Berufserfahrung, -en *professional experience, work experience*, III11
die Berufstätigkeit, -en *occupation*, III11
die Berufswahl, -en *choice of profession*, III11
beruhen auf (acc) *to be founded on*, III11
berühmt *famous*, III2
besann (*imperfect of* besinnen), III6
s. beschäftigen mit *to keep busy with*, III3
die Bescheidenheit, -en *modesty*, III5
bescheiden *modest*, III8
bescheuert *dumb*, III3
beschleunigen *to accelerate*, III4
beschließen *to decide*, III11
beschlossen *decided*, III11
beschränken *to limit*, III1
beschreiben *to describe*, II
die Beschreibung, -en *description*, III2
beschrieben *described*, III1
die Beschwerde, -n *trouble, complaint*, III7
beschwören *to implore*, III5
die Beseitigung, -en *removal, elimination*, III5
besetzt *busy (on the telephone)*, I
besichtigen *to sightsee, visit a place*, II
die Besichtigung, -en *sightseeing, visit*, III2
besiegt *defeated*, III1
besinnen *to think about, consider*, III6
besonders *especially*, I
besorgen *to provide*, III1
die Besorgung, -en *errand*, III5
besprechen *to discuss*, III5
besser *better*, I
die Besserung, -en *improvement*, II; **Gute Besserung!** *Get well soon!*, II
der Bestandteil, -e *part, component*, III9

das Besteck *silverware*, III2
bestehen aus *to consist of*, III5
bestellen *to order*, II
besten: am besten *the best*, II
bestimmen *to determine*, III2
bestimmt *certainly, definitely*, I
bestreichen *to spread, to butter*, III1
der Besuch, -e *visit*, III4
besuchen *to visit*, I
betäuben *to stun, anesthetize*, III2
s. beteiligen an (dat) *to take part in*, III9
betrachten *to observe*, III11
der Betrag, ⸚e *amount*, III1
betreten *to step on; to enter*, III12
betreuen *to take care of*, III5
der Betrieb, -e *business, firm*, Loc 10
die Betriebswirtschaft *business administration*, III11
die Betroffenheit, -en *dismay*, III9
betrogen *deceived, defrauded*, III5
das Bett, -en *bed*, I
betten *to make one's bed*, III12
beugen *to bend*, III10
beurteilen nach *to judge according to*, III3
der Beutel, - *bag, pouch, sack*, III9
die Bevölkerung *population, inhabitants*, III5
bevor (conj) *before*, III5
bewachen *to guard*, III5
s. bewähren *to prove oneself*, III5
bewegen *to move*, III10
die Bewegung, -en *movement, motion*, III8
beweisen *to prove*, III10
s. bewerben *to apply*, III11
der Bewerber, - *applicant*, III2
die Bewerbung, -en *application*, III11
die Bewerbungsunterlage, -n *application material*, III11
das Bewerbungsverfahren *application process*, III11
bewerten *to assess*, III12
bewiesen *proven*, III10
bewundern *to admire*, III10
die Bewunderung *astonishment, marvel*, III10
bewusst *conscious(ly)*, III3
bezahlen *to pay*, III1
bezeichnen *to indicate*, III2
die Bezeichnung, -en *indication, description*, III4
s. beziehen auf (acc) *to refer to*, III3
die Beziehung, -en *relationship*, III3
das Beziehungswort, ⸚er *antecedent*, III7
Bezug haben zu *to have a connection to*, III8
bezweifeln *to doubt*, II
die Bibliothek, -en *library*, III10
bieder *upright, bourgeois*, III5
biegen *to bend, curve, turn*, II; **einbiegen** (sep): **Biegen Sie hier ein!** *Turn here!*, II

die **Biene, -n** *bee*, III9
bieten *to offer*, III1
das **Bild, -er** *picture*, III2
bilden *to form, construct*, III1
bildend: die bildenden Künste *the visual arts*, III10
die **Bilderausstellung, -en** *picture exhibit*, III10
die **Bildergalerie, -n** *picture gallery*, III10
der **Bildhauer, -** *sculptor*, Loc1
bildreich *rich in imagery*, III10
der **Bildschirm, -e** *display screen*, III6
die **Bildung, -en** *formulation*, III6
der **Bildungsweg, -e** *educational path*, III4
das **Bildungswesen** *education*, III4
billig *cheap*, I
die **Biokost** *organic food*, III3
Biologe/Biologin -n/nen, *biologist*, III11
die **Biologie=Bio** *biology*, I
die **Biologielehrerin, -nen** *biology teacher*, I
biologisch abbaubar *biodegradable*, III9
birgst du *are you hiding*, III2
die **Birne, -n** *pear*, II
bis (acc prep) *until*, III11; **Bis dann!** *Till then! See you later!*, I; **bis dahin** *until then*, III11
der **Bischof, -̈e** *bishop*, Loc4
bisher *up to now*, III10
bislang *up to now*, III8
das **Bistum, -̈er** *episcopate, diocese*, Loc4
bitte *please*, I; **Bitte (sehr/schön)!** *You're (very) welcome!*, I; **Bitte! Hier!** *Here you go!*, II
bitten *to request*, III1
bitter *bitter*, II
bisschen: ein bisschen *a little*, I
blasen *to blow*, III9
der **Bläser, -** *wind instrument player*, III10
die **Blaskapelle, -n** *brass-band*, III8
das **Blatt, -̈er** *leaf*, III1
blättern *leaf through*, III6
blau *blue*, I
die **Blaubeere, -n** *blueberry*, II
der **Blazer, -** *blazer*, II
das **Blei** *lead*, III9
bleiben *to stay, remain*, II
der **Bleistift, -e** *pencil*, I
der **Blick, -e** *glance, view*, III2
der **Blickfang** *eye-catcher*, III7
der **Blickpunkt, -e** *point of view*, III2
blieb (*imperfect of* **bleiben**), III4
blitzblank *squeaky clean*, III7
die **Blockflöte, -n** *recorder (flute)*, III12
blöd *dumb*, I
blond *blonde*, I
der **Blouson, -s** *bomber jacket*, II
bloß *only*, I; **Was soll ich bloß machen?** *Well, what am I supposed to do?*, II
blühen *to flower, blossom*, III10

die **Blume, -n** *flower*, I
der **Blumenkohl** *cauliflower*, II
der **Blumenstrauß, -̈e** *flower bouquet*, I
die **Bluse, -n** *blouse*, II
das **Blut** *blood*, III5
der **Boden** *floor, ground*, III10
das **Bogenschießen** *archery*, II
die **Bohne, -n** *bean*, II
der **Bombenangriff, -e** *bomb attack*, Loc10
der **Bomber, -** *bomber*, III5
das **Boot, -e** *boat*, II; **Boot fahren** *to go for a boat ride*, II
böse *angry, evil*, III4
der **Bote, -n** *messenger*, III6
der **Botengang, -̈e** *errand*, III1
die **Boulevardzeitung, -en** *tabloid newspaper*, III6
brachte (*imperfect of* bringen), III6
der **Brandanschlag, -̈e** *arson*, III5
brannte (*imperfect of* brennen), III7
der **Braten** *roast*, II
die **Bratkartoffeln** (pl) *fried potatoes*, II
brauchbar *useful*, III5
brauchen *to need*, I
brauen *to brew*, III6
braun *brown*, I
brav *well-behaved*, III8
s. **brechen (etwas)** *to break (something)*, II; **er/sie bricht sich etwas** *he/she breaks (a bone)*, II
die **Brechung, -en** *breaking*, III5
breit *large, wide*, III7
die **Bremse, -n** *brake*, II
brennen *to burn*, III3
das **Brettspiel, -e** *board game*, I; **ein Brettspiel spielen** *to play a board game*, I
die **Brezel, -n** *pretzel*, I
der **Brief, -e** *letter*, III10
die **Briefmarke, -n** *postage stamp*, I
der **Briefpartner, -** *pen pal*, III2
die **Brille, -n** *a pair of glasses*, I
bringen *to bring*, I
der **Brokkoli** *broccoli*, II
die **Bronzeskulptur, -en** *bronze sculpture*, Loc1
das **Brot, -e** *bread*, I
das **Brötchen, -** *breakfast roll*, III1
der **Bruder, -̈** *brother*, I
der **Brunnen, -** *fountain*, II
brutal *brutal, violent*, I
der **Bube, -n** *(southern German) boy*, III10
das **Buch, -̈er** *book*, I
die **Bücherei, -en** *lending library*, III1
der **Bücherladen, -̈** *bookstore*, III7
der **Buchhandel** *book trade*, Loc1
der **Buchladen, -̈** *bookstore*, III1
die **Buchmesse, -n** *book trade fair*, Loc7
die **Büchse, -n** *can*, III8
der **Buchstabe, -n** *letter (of the alphabet)*, III6
buchstabieren *to spell*, III7
die **Bucht, -en** *bay*, II
s. **bücken** *to bend*, III11

bügeln *to iron*, II
die **Bühne, -n** *stage*, III10
die **Bühnenanweisung, -en** *stage instruction*, III11
der **Bummel** *stroll*, III1
der **Bund=Bundeswehr**, III5
der **Bundesadler** *federal eagle*, III1
der **Bundesbürger, -** *citizen of the Federal Republic*, III6
der **Bundesgrenzschutz** *Federal Border Patrol*, III5
das **Bundesland, -̈er** *(German or Austrian) federal state*, I
der **Bundesrat** *House of Representatives*, III5
der **Bundestag** *German Federal Parliament*, III11
Bundestagsabgeordnete, -n *parliamentarian*, III5
die **Bundeswehr** *German Federal Defense Force*, III5
bunt *colorful*, II
die **Burg, -en** *castle*, III2
der **Bürger, -** *citizen*, III2
bürgerlich *civic, civil*, II; **gutbürgerliche Küche** *good home-cooked food*, II
der **Bursche, -n** *young man*, III7
der **Bus, -se** *bus*, I
die **Busfahrt, -en** *bus trip*, III2
die **Butter** *butter*, I
das **Butterbrotpapier** *waxed paper*, III9
das **Butterschmalz** *shortening*, I
bzw.=beziehungsweise *respectively*, III5

das **Café, -s** *café*, I
der **Camembert Käse** *Camembert cheese*, II
der **Cäsar, -en** *Caesar*, Loc10
der **Cent,-** *Cent*, III1
der **Cent, -** *cent*, (smallest unit of the euro; 1/100th of a euro), I
Ćevapčići *(Serbocroat: rolled spicy ground meat)*, II
die **CD, -s** *compact disc*, I
die **Chance, -n** *chance*, III12
Chanukka *Hanukkah*, I; **Frohes Chanukka-Fest!** *Happy Hanukkah!*, I
der **Charakter** *character, personality, quality*, III10
charakterisieren *to characterize*, III7
die **Charakteristik, -en** *characteristic*, III11
der **Chef, -s** *boss*, III4
der **Chefkoch, -̈e** *head chef*, II
die **Chemie** *chemistry*, I
die **Chemikalie, -n** *chemical*, III9
chic *smart* (looking), I

chinesisch (adj) *Chinese*, II
das Chlor *chlorine*, III9
die Chronologie, -n *chronology*, III7
  chronologisch *chronological*, III12
die Clique, -n *clique*, II
das Cola, -s *cola (also:* **die Cola***)*, I
die Collage, -n *collage*, III8
die Comics (pl) *comic books*, I
der Computer, - *computer*, I
  Computerspezialist(in), -en/nen
    computer specialist, III11
der Container, - *recycling bin*, III8
  cool (adj) *cool*, II
die Couch, -en *couch*, I
der Court, -s *(tennis) court*, II
der Couscous=Kuskus *couscous*, II
der Cousin, -s *cousin (male)*, I
die Creme, -s *cream*, II
die Crêpes (pl) *crepes*, II

da *there*, II; **Da hast du (bestimmt)
  Recht!** *You're right about that!*, II;
  da hinten *there in the back*, I; **da
  vorn** *there in the front*, I; **Da
  stimm ich dir zu!** *I agree with
  you about that!*, II
da (conj) *since*, (part) *there*, III1
  da gewesen *been there*, III3
dabei sein *to take part*, III11
  dabeihaben (sep) *to bring along*,
    III2
das Dach, ¨er *roof*, III9
  dachte (*imperfect of* **denken**), III4
dafür *for it*, II; **Ich bin dafür,
  dass ...** *I am for doing...*, II
  daher (conj) *for this reason*, III2
  dahin gehend *in that respect*
  dalli *schnell*, III7
damals *at that time*, III2
damit (conj) *so that, in order to*,
    III3
  dämmerig *dim, shadowy, vague*,
    III10
danach *after that*, I
Danke (sehr/schön)! *Thank you
  (very much)!*, I; **Danke! Dir/Ihnen
  auch!** *Thank you! Same to you!*,
  II; **Danke gleichfalls!** *Thank you
  and the same to you!*, II
  danken (dat) *to thank*, III3
dann *then*, II; **Dann nehm ich
  eben ...** *In that case I'll take...*, II;
  Dann trink ich halt ... *I'll drink
  instead...*, II
Darf ich (bitte) ...? *May I
  (please)...?*, II
darstellen (sep) *to play (act)*, III10
der Darsteller, - *actor*, III11
die Darstellung, -en *depiction,
    performance*, III5

darüber *over it*, II
darunter *under it, underneath*, II
dass (conj) *that*, I
dauern *to last*, III5
dauernd *continually*, III1
der Daumen, - *thumb*, III1
  dazu *in addition*, III4
  dazufügen (sep) *to add to*, III8
die DDR (Deutsche Demokratische
    Republik) *former East Germany*,
    Loc 1
die Decke, -n *blanket*, III2
  decken *to cover*, II; **den Tisch
    decken** *to set the table*, I
  definieren *to define*, III4
die Definition, -en *definition*, III8
  deftig *robust*, II
  dein (poss adj) *your*, I
die Delikatesse, -n *delicacy*, II
  demnach *accordingly*, III4
  demnächst *before long*, III10
die Demokratie, -n *democracy*, III5
  demokratisch *democratic*, III8
die Demokratisierung, -en
    democratization, III11
die Demonstration, -en
    demonstration, III6
  denken an (acc) *to think of or
    about*, III2; **Aber denk doch mal
    daran, dass ...** *But just consider
    that ...*, III4
der Denker, - *intellectual*, III2
das Denkmal, ¨er: ein Denkmal
    setzen, *to put up a monument for
    someone*, Loc1
  denn (conj) *because, for*, I; **denn**
    (particle), I
  dennoch *however*, III9
  deprimierend *depressing*, III5
  derselbe *the same*, III7
  deshalb *therefore*, III6
  dessen *of him, it; of whose*, III4
  desto: je mehr ... desto ... *the
    more ... the ...*, III7
  deutlich *clear*, III6
das Deutsch *German* (language), I;
    (school subject), I
  Deutschland *Germany*, I
der Deutschlehrer, - *German teacher*, I
die Deutschlehrerin, -nen *German
    teacher*, I
  deutschsprachig *German-speaking*,
    III8
der Deutschunterricht, -e *German
    instruction*, III2
der Dezember *December*, I
das Dia, -s *slide*, II
der Dialekt, -e *dialect*, III10
der Dialog, -e *dialogue*, III3
die Diät, -en *diet*, III12
der Dichter, - *writer, poet*, Loc1
  dick (adj) *fat*, III8; **dick machen**
    to be fattening, II
  dienen (dat) *to serve*, III5
der Dienst, -e *service*, III5
der Dienstag *Tuesday*, I
  dienstags *Tuesdays*, II

die Dienstzeit, -en *term of service*, III5
  dies- *this*, II
  diesmal *this time*, III1
der Dilettant, -en *dilettante, amateur*,
    III5
das Ding, -e *thing*, II; vor allen Dingen
    especially, III1
der Dinosaurier, - *dinosaur*, III3
der Diplomat, -en *diplomat*, III11
  dir *to you*, II
  direkt *direct*, III10
der Dirigent, -en *conductor*, III10
das Dirndl, - *traditional costume for
    females*, III8
die Disko, -s *disco*, I; **in eine Disko
    gehen** *to go to a disco*, I
die Diskothek, -en *discothek*, II
  diskriminieren *to discriminate*, III7
die Diskussion, -en *discussion*, II
das Diskuswerfen *discus throw*, II
  diskutieren *to discuss*, III2
  diszipliniert *disciplined*, III11
  divers *sundry, diverse*, III12
  DM=Deutsche Mark *German
    mark (former monetary unit)*, I
  doch (particle) *yes, it is!*, I; **Ich
    meine doch, dass ...,** *I really
    think that...*, II
das Dokument, -e *document*, III2
der Dolch, -e *dagger*, III10
der Dolmetscher, - *interpreter*, III7
der Dom, -e *cathedral*, II
der Donnerstag *Thursday*, I
  donnerstags *Thursdays*, II
  doof *dumb*, I
das Dorf, ¨er *village*, II
  dort *there*, I; **dort drüben** *over
    there*, I
  dorthin *to there*, III2
die Dose, -n *can*, III9
  dotiert: gut dotiert, *well-funded*,
    III11
  dramatisch *dramatic*, III7
der Dramaturg, -en *theatrical
    producer*, III10
  dran=daran, III10
  s. drängeln *to jostle, shove*, III11
  drängen *to push, crowd*, III10
  draußen *outside*, III8
  drehen *to turn*, III2
  dreieckig *triangular*, III10
  dreigeteilt *three-part*, III9
  dreischiffig *with three naves*, Loc1
  drin=darin, III1
  drinnen *inside*, III3
  dritt- *third*, III4
das Drittel: ein Drittel *one third*, III11
  drittens *thirdly*, III3
die Droge, -n *drug*, III12
die Drogerie, -n *drugstore*, II
  drohen (dat) *to threaten*, III8
die Drohmittel (pl) *threatening
    measures*, III5
  dröhnen *to roar, boom*, III3
  drüben *over there*, III4
  drücken *to press, squeeze*, III1
der Drucker, - *printer*, III6

der Druckerstreik, -s *print workers' strike*, III6

der Druckknopf, ⁻e *snap*, II

duften *to be fragrant, smell sweet*, III8

dumm *dumb, stupid*, I

die Dummheit, -en *stupidity*, III10

dunkel *dark*, II

dünn *thin*, III4

durch (acc prep) *through*, II

durchaus *thoroughly*, III5

durchblättern (sep) *to page through*, III6

durchfallen (sep) *to fail*, III5

die Durchgangsstation, -en *intermediate station*, III3

durchlaufen (sep) *to run through*, III10

durchlesen (sep) *to read through*, III10

durchschauen (sep) *to see through*, III10

der Durchschnitt *average*, III12

durchsetzen (sep) *to achieve*, III6

durchstreichen (sep) *to cross out*, III4

durchweg *throughout*, III8

dürfen *to be allowed to*, II; **er/sie/es darf** *he/she/it is allowed to*, II

dürfte: Wenn wir nur Naturprodukte benutzen dürften! *If we were allowed to use only natural products!*, III9

dürr *barren, dry*, III2

der Durst *thirst*, II; **Durst haben** *to be thirsty*, II

durstig *thirsty*, III8

duschen *to shower*, III9

düster *dark, sinister*, III2

ebben *to subside*, III10

eben (gerade) *just now*, III2; **eben** (particle), II; **Dann nehm ich eben ...** *In that case I'll take...*, II; **eben nicht** *actually not*, II

die Ebene, -n *level*, III12

ebenfalls *likewise*, III3

echt *real(ly)*, II; *genuine*, II

die Ecke, -n *corner*, II

eckig *with corners*, I

der Edelstein, -e *precious stone*, Loc10

effektiv *effective*, III3

egal *alike, equal*, II; **egal sein: Mode ist mir egal.** *I don't care about fashion.*, II

egoistisch *egoistic*, III8

die Ehe, -n *marriage*, III12

ehemalig *former*, III11

der Ehepartner, - *spouse*, III11

eher *sooner; rather*, III3

die Ehre, -n *honor*, III5

ehrgeizig *ambitious*, III8

ehrlich *honest(ly)*, III3

das Ei, -er *egg*, I

das Eichenlaub *oak leaves*, III1

die Eifersucht *jealousy*, III10

eifrig *eager*, III10

eigen *(one's) own*, II

die Eigenschaft, -en *characteristic*, III7

eigentlich *actual(ly)*, III1; **Eigentlich schon, aber ...** *Well yes, but...*, II

eigenverantwortlich *solely responsible*, III11

s. eignen zu *to be suited to*, III6

eilen *to hurry*, III1

eilig *quick, hurried*, III1

ein(-) ander- *another (a different) one*, II

einander *one another*, III3

die Einarbeitung, -en *familiarization*, III11

einbiegen (sep) *to turn*, II

einbeziehen *to include*, III2

der Eindruck, ⁻e *impression*, III8

einengen (sep) *to confine*, III12

einerlei *the same (to me, him)*, III5

einfach *simple, simply*, III1

Einfach! *That's easy!*, I

einfallen (dat, sep) *to occur to*, III12

der Einfluss, ⁻e *influence*, III7

eingebettet *embedded*, III2

eingeführt *introduced*, III1

eingestehen (sep) *to admit*, III7

eingestellt sein auf (acc) *to be set up for*, III2

eingeweiht *dedicated*, Loc1

eingezeichnet *written in, indicated*, III1

einheimisch *local, native*, III8

die Einheit, -en *unity, unit*, III5

einholen (sep) *to catch up with*, III5

einige *some*, III6

s. einigen auf (acc) *to agree*, III1

einjagen: ihm einen Schrecken einjagen (sep) *to scare him*, III10

der Einkauf, ⁻e *purchase*, III9

einkaufen (sep) *to shop*, I; **einkaufen gehen** *to go shopping*, I

die Einkaufstasche, -n *shopping bag*, III9

der Einkaufsweg *shopping route*, III2

der Einkaufszettel, - *shopping list*, III2

das Einkommen, - *income*, II

die Einkommenshöhe *earnings, income level*, III11

einladen (sep) *to invite*, I; **er/sie lädt ... ein** *he/she invites*, I

die Einladung, -en *invitation*, III2

der Einlass *admission*, III3

einlegen (sep): **ein Video einlegen** *to insert a video*, II

einmal *once*, I; **einmal am Tag** *once a day*, II

einmalig *unique*, III7

s. einmischen (sep) *to get involved*, III12

die Einnahmequelle, -n *source of income*, III7

einnehmen (sep) *to take*, III6

einpacken (sep) *to pack up*, III9

einparken *park*, III5

einprägen (sep) *to memorize*, III4

einprägsam *easily remembered, impressive*, III7

einrichten (sep) *to furnish, arrange*, III2

die Einrichtung, -en *arrangement*, III2

einsam *lonely*, III3

einsame Spitze! *simply fantastic!*, III1

der Einsatz, ⁻e *effort*, III9

einschalten (sep) *to switch on*, III6

einschätzen (sep) *to estimate*, III11

die Einschränkung, -en *limitation*, III1

einschreiben (sep) *to enroll*, III7

einseitig *one-sided*, III8

einsetzen (sep) *to put, fill in*, III9

einst *once, formerly*, III1

einstellen (sep) *to hire*, III5

einstig *former, one-time*, III1

eintauschen (sep) *to exchange*, III1

eintragen (sep) *to enter*, III1

s. eintragen lassen *to register*, III7

die Eintragung, -en *entry*, III1

eintreten (sep) *to enter*, III5

eintritt (*imperfect of* eintreten), III5

die Eintrittskarte, -n *admission ticket*, III10

Einverstanden! *Agreed!*, II

der Einwand, ⁻e *objection*, III12

die Einwegdose, -n *non-returnable can*, III9

die Einwegflasche, -n *non-returnable bottle*, III9

einweihen in (sep, acc), - *to initiate into*, III9

der Einwohner, - *resident*, III7

die Einzelheit, -en *detail*, III6

der Einzelkämpfer, - *lone fighter*, III3

einzeln *single, individual*, III2

Einzelreisende, -n *lone traveler*, III2

einziehen (sep) *to move in*, III5

einzig *only; unique*, III3

einzigartig *unique*, Loc4

das Eis *ice cream*, I

der Eisbecher, - *a dish of ice cream*, I

die Eisenbahnstrecke, -n *train route*, III2

eiskalt *ice cold*, III2

eitel *vain*, III8

der Ekel *loathing, nausea*, III5

elegant *elegant*, II

die Elektrizität *electricity*, III9

Elektroinstallateur(in), -e/nen *electrician*, III12

die Elektronik *electronic industry*, Loc4

die Elektrotechnik *electrical engineering*, III11

das Element, -en *element*, III7

der Ellbogen, - *elbow*, III1

Ellenbogen=Ellbogen, III3

die **Eltern** (pl) *parents*, I
die **Emaille** *here: nail polish*, III3
der **Empfang**, ⸚e *reception*, III7
  empfangen *to greet, receive*, III8
  empfehlen *to recommend*, III8
die **Empfehlung, -en** *recommendation*, III8
  empfindlich *sensitive*, III12
die **Empfindung, -en** *sensation, feeling*, III10
das **Ende, -n** *end*, III1
  enden *to end*, III2
  endgültig *final(ly), last(ly)*, III1
  endlich *at last*, III7
die **Energie, -n** *energy*, III9
das **Energiesparen**, *energy saving*, III9
  eng *tight*, I
das **Engagement, -s** *commitment*, III12
  s. engagieren *to be active in*, III5
der **Engel, -** *angel*, III9
das **Englisch** *English* (school subject), I; (language), I
  entdecken *to discover*, III8
  entfernt *away, at a distance*, III2
  enthalten *to contain*, III2
  enthalten sein *to be included*, III2
der **Enthusiasmus** *enthusiasm*, III10
  entlang *along*, III1
  entlarven *to uncover*, III3
die **Entlassung, -en** *dismissal*, III11
  s. entscheiden *to decide*, III5
  entscheidend *crucial*, III11
die **Entscheidung, -en** *decision*, III5
  entschieden *decided*, III1
  s. entschließen *to decide*, III11
  entschlossen *decided*, III11
  entschuldigen *to excuse*, III12
die **Entschuldigung, -en** *excuse*, III1
  Entschuldigung! *Excuse me!*, I
  s. entspannen *to relax*, III3
die **Entspannung, -en** *relaxation*, III6
  entsprechen (dat) *to correspond to, to agree with*, III1
  entstanden *originated*, III11
  enttäuschen *to disappoint*, III8
die **Enttäuschung, -en** *disappointment*, III12
  entwaffnen *to disarm*, III12
  entweder: entweder ... oder *either ... or*, III8
  entwerfen *to draw up, design*, III7
  entwickeln *to develop*, III3
die **Entwicklung, -en** *development*, Loc4
  entworfen *sketched, outlined*, III10
der **Entwurf**, ⸚e *sketch, outline*, III6
  entziffern *to decipher*, III10
  entzwei *in two pieces*, III6
die **Epoche, -n** *epoch*, Loc1
  er *he*, I; *it*, I
  erarbeiten *to gain by working for*, III8
  erbärmlich *pitiful*, III5
  erbaut *built, constructed*, Loc7
  erblicken *to catch sight of*, III6
die **Erbse, -n** *pea*, II
die **Erdbeere, -n** *strawberry*, II

die **Erde, -n** *earth*, III5
die **Erdkunde** *geography*, I
die **Erdnussbutter** *peanut butter*, III1
  erdulden *to suffer, endure*, III5
das **Ereignis, -se** *event*, III1
  erfahren *to experience*, III6
  Erfahrene, -n *experienced (person)*, II
die **Erfahrung, -en** *experience*, III11
  erfinden *to invent*, III1
der **Erfinder, -** *inventor*, III10
der **Erfolg, -e** *success*, III12
  erfolgreich *successful*, III8
  erfordern *to demand, require*, III1
  erfrischen *to refresh, revive*, III12
  erfuhr (*imperfect of* erfahren), III10
  erfüllen *to fulfill*, III7
die **Erfüllung: in Erfüllung gehen**, *come true, be fulfilled*, III5
  erfunden *invented*, III7
  ergänzen *to add to, complete*, III10
  ergebenst *respectfully*, III12
das **Ergebnis, -se** *result*, III6
  erglänzen *to shine*, Loc1
  ergreifen *to seize, take*, III5
  erhalten *to get, receive*, III5; **gut erhalten** *well maintained*, II
  erhalten bleiben *to survive*, Loc 1
  erhältlich *obtainable*, III12
die **Erhaltung** *preservation*, III9
  erheben *to raise, edify*, III5
  erhielt (*imperfect of* erhalten), III12
  erhob (*imperfect of* erheben), Loc4
  s. erinnern an (acc) *to remember*, III2
die **Erkältung, -en** *cold (illness)*, II
  erkannte (*imperfect of* erkennen), III10
  erkennen *to recognize*, III10
die **Erkenntnis, -se** *realization*, III5
  erklären *to explain*, III1
die **Erklärung, -en** *explanation*, III3
  s. erkundigen nach *to inquire about*, III11
  erlangen *to attain*, III10
  s. erlauben (dat) *to permit*, III5
  erleben *to experience*, III10
das **Erlebnis, -se** *experience*, III1
  erledigen *to take care of*, III1
die **Erleichterung** *relief*, III5
  erleiden *to suffer*, III1
  erlernen *to learn*, III11
die **Erlernung** *learning*, III12
der **Erlkönig** *elf-king*, III2
  ermöglichen *to make possible*, III12
  ermüdet *exhausted*, III1
  s. ernähren *to feed, nourish*, II
die **Ernährung** *food*, III3
  ernst *serious*, III5
  ernten *to harvest*, III10
  erregen *to excite*, III7
  erreichen *to reach*, III6
  errichten *to construct*, Loc4
der **Ersatzdienst** *alternative service to military service*, III5
  erscheinen *to appear*, III6

das **Erscheinungsbild, -er** *appearance*, III11
  erschien (*imperfect of* erscheinen), III6
  erschöpfend *exhausting*, III12
  erschrak (*imperfect of* erschrecken), III6
  erschrecken *to be frightened*, III7
  erschüttert *shaken*, III5
  ersetzen *to replace*, III9
  erst- *first*, III4
  erstarren *to freeze up*, III10
  erstaunt sein *to be astonished*, III8
  erstellen *to make available*, III6
  ersten: am ersten *on the first*, I
  erstens *in the first place*, III3
  ersticken *to suffocate*, III5
  erstklassig *first-class*, III7
  erstmal *first of all*, III12
  erteilen (dat) *to give, grant*, III12
  ertönen *to make a sound*, III10
  erwachsen sein *to be grown up*, III4
  Erwachsene, -n *adult*, III3
  erwähnen *to mention*, III1
  erwarten *to expect*, III5
die **Erwartung, -en** *expectation*, III10
  erwecken *to waken*, III10
  erweitern *to expand*, III8
  erwerben *to obtain*, III5
  erwidern *to reply*, III8
  erwischen *to catch*, III10
  erwünscht *desirable*, III3
  erzählen *to tell*, III1
  Erzähler(in), -/nen *story-teller, writer*, III12
die **Erzählung, -en** s*tory*, III10
  erziehen *to raise*, III12
die **Erziehung** *upbringing, education*, III10
  erzogen: gut erzogen, *well-behaved*, III7
der **Esel, -** *donkey*, III8
  essbar *edible*, III12
  essen *to eat*, I; **er/sie isst** *he/she eats*, I
die **Essgewohnheit, -en** *eating habit*, III1
der **Esstisch, -e** *dining table*, I
die **Esswaren** (pl) *food*, III9
das **Esszimmer, -** *dining room*, II
die **Etage, -n** *floor, story*, III10
das **Etikett, -e** *label*, III3
  etlich- *some, a certain*, III7
  etwa *about, more or less*, III7
  etwas *something*, I; **Noch etwas?** *Anything else?*, I
  euch (pl, acc case) *you*, I; (pl, dat case) *to you*, II; (reflexive) *yourselves*, II
  euer (poss adj) *your*, II
der **Euro,-** *euro* (the national currency of most European countries), I
  eventuell *possibly*, III10
  ewig *eternal*, III3
die **Ewigkeit, -en** *eternity*, III8
  existieren *to exist*, III8

die Exkursion, -en *excursion,* III2
experimentieren *to experiment,* III12

fabelhaft *fabulous, amazing,* III7
die Fabrik, -en *factory,* III9
das Fach, ̈er *school subject,* I
das Fachabitur *vocational degree,* III4
die Fachhochschule, -n *vocational college,* III11
die Fachoberschule, -n *vocational school,* III4
die Fachoberschulreife *(degree from a vocational school),* III4
die Fachschule, -n *vocational school,* III11
die Fachschulreife *(degree from a vocational school),* III4
das Fachwerkhaus, ̈er *cross-timbered house,* II
das Fachwissen *expertise,* III9
die Fähigkeit, -en *ability,* III11
der Fahranfänger, - *beginning driver,* III5
fahren *to go, ride, drive,* I; **er/sie fährt** *he/she drives,* I; **Fahren wir mal nach ... !** *Let's go to... !,* II
die Fahrerlaubnis, -se *permission to drive,* III5
die Fahrgemeinschaft, -en *carpool,* III9
der Fährhafen, ̈ *ferry port,* III1
das Fahrrad, ̈er *bicycle,* II
das Fahrrad-Depot, -s *bicycle racks,* II
der Fahrradweg, -e *bike trail,* III8
der Fahrschein, -e *ticket,* III9
das Fahrzeug, -e *vehicle,* III7
der Fakt, -en *fact,* III11
der Falke, -n *falcon,* Loc4
der Fall, ̈e *fall,* Loc1; *case,* III1; **im Fall in the case (of);** III12; **auf alle Fälle** *by all means,* III11; **auf jeden Fall** *in any case,* III8; **Auf keinen Fall!** *No chance!,* III11
fallen *to fall,* III5
falsch *false, wrong,* III3
der Faltenrock, ̈e *pleated skirt,* II
die Familie, -n *family,* I
das Familienleben *family life,* III8
fand *(imperfect of* **finden**), III4
der Fantasyroman, -e *fantasy novel,* I
das Farbbild, -er *color photograph,* II
die Farbe, -n *color,* I
färben *to color, paint,* III3
das Farbfernsehgerät, -e *color TV set,* II
die Faser, -n *thread, material,* II
der Faserstift, -e *felt-tip pen,* III9
fasste: s. ein Herz fassen *to gather courage,* III10
fast *almost,* III6

faszinierend *fascinating,* III6
faul *lazy,* II
faulenzen *to be lazy,* II
die Faust, ̈e *fist,* III3
das Fax, - *fax,* III2
der Februar *February,* I
fechten *to fence,* II
fehlen *to be missing,* III5; **Was fehlt dir?** *What's wrong with you?,* II
der Fehler, - *mistake,* III1
feiern *to celebrate,* III1
der Feiertag, -e *holiday,* I
fein *fine, exquisite,* II
das Fenster, - *window,* I
die Ferien (pl) *vacation* (from school), II
die Ferienlektüre, -n *vacation reading,* III1
der Ferienort, -e *vacation spot,* III1
die Ferienreise, -n *vacation trip,* III1
die Ferienwoche, -n *week of vacation,* III2
die Fernbedienung, -en *remote control,* II
die Ferne *distance,* III1
ferner *further,* III5
Fernseh gucken (colloquial) *to watch TV,* II
der Fernseh- und Videowagen *TV and video cart,* II
das Fernsehen *the medium of television,* III3
fernsehen (sep) *to watch TV,* II
Fernsehen schauen *to watch TV,* I
der Fernseher, - *television set,* II
die Fernsehgebühren *television fees,* III7
das Fernsehgerät, -e *television set,* II
der Fernsehraum, ̈e *TV room,* II
der Fernsehsender, - *television station,* III6
die Ferse, -n *heel,* III1
fertig *finished,* III11
fertigen *to finish,* Loc10
das Fertiggericht, -e *frozen food,* III7
fesch *stylish, smart,* I
fest *firm,* III3
das Festland *mainland,* III1
festlich *festive,* III3
feststehen (sep) *to be certain,* III7; **Es steht fest, dass ...** *It's certain that ...,* III7
feststellen (sep) *to determine,* III3
die Festung, -en *fortress,* Loc4
die Fete, -n *party,* III4
fetenmäßig *partywise,* III3
fett *fat, greasy,* II
das Fett: hat zu viel Fett *has too much fat,* II
die Fettucine (pl) *fettucine,* II
fetzig *really sharp (looking),* II
das Feuer, - *fire,* III6
das Fieber, - *fever,* II
fiel *(imperfect of* fallen), III4
fies *awful,* III5

die Figur, -en *figure, character,* III10
fiktiv *fictitious,* III8
der Filialbereich, -e *subsidiary region,* III11
das Filialunternehmen, - *subsidiary operation,* III11
der Film, -e *movie,* I; *roll of film,* II
filmen *to film, videotape,* II
finanziell *financially,* III12
finanzieren *to finance,* III7
die Finanzmetropole, -n *financial center,* Loc7
das Finanzzentrum, die Finanzzentren *financial center,* III7
finden *to think about,* I; **Das finde ich auch.** *I think so, too.,* I; **Ich finde es gut/schlecht, dass ...** *I think it's good/bad that ...,* I; **Ich finde den Pulli stark!** *The sweater is awesome!,* I
fing an *(imperfect of* **anfangen**), III3
der Fingernagel, ̈ *finger nail,* III1
die Firma, (pl) Firmen *firm, business,* III5
der Fisch, -e *fish,* I
der Fischerhafen, ̈e *fishing harbor,* III1
das Fischstäbchen, - *fish stick,* II
s. fit halten *to stay fit,* II
die Fitness *fitness,* III3
der Fitnessraum, ̈e *training and weight room,* II
flach *flat,* II
die Fläche, -n *flat area, surface,* Loc1
flammen *to burn,* III5
die Flasche, -n *bottle,* III1
der Flaschenöffner, - *bottle opener,* III2
das Fleisch *meat,* I
fleißig *hard-working,* II
die Fliege, -n *bow tie,* II
fliegen *to fly,* III5
fließend *running (water),* III3; *flowing,* III4
die Flinte, -n *shot-gun, musket,* III10
die Flitterwochen, (pl) *honeymoon,* III12
flogen *(imperfect of* fliegen), III10
der Flug, ̈e *flight,* II
das Flugblatt, ̈er *pamphlet, flyer,* III2
der Flügel, - *wing,* III10
der Flughafen, ̈ *airport,* III8
der Flugplatz, ̈e *municipal airport,* III8
das Flugzeug, -e *airplane,* II
flüstern *to whisper,* III10
der Fluss, ̈e *river,* II
Föhn: Mama kriegt 'nen Föhn. *Mom's going crazy.,* III3
die Folge, -n *consequence,* III5
folgen (dat) *to follow,* III4
folgend- *following,* III1
die Folie, -n *foil,* III9
fördern *to encourage,* III2
die Förderung *promotion,* III9
die Forelle, -n *trout,* II
formen *to form,* III4
formulieren *to formulate,* III4
die Formulierung, -en *formulation,* III3

forschen *to research*, III7
der Forscher, - *researcher*, III9
die Forschung *research*, III7
fortgehen (sep) *to leave*, III1
Fortgeschrittene, -n *advanced (person)*, II
der Fortschritt *progress*, III9
das Foto, -s *photo*, III11
das Fotoalbum, -alben *photo album*, III4
Fotograf(in), -en/nen *photographer*, III12
fotografieren *to photograph*, II
das Foyer, -s *lobby*, III10
der Frack, ¨e *tux with tails*, III10
die Frage, -n *question*, II; **Das kommt nicht in Frage!** *It's out of the question!*, III11
der Fragebogen, ¨ *questionnaire*, III9
fragen *to ask*, II
französisch (adj) *French*, II
die Frau, -en *woman; Ms.*, I
frech *fresh, insolent*, III5
frei *free*, III1; **Wir haben frei.** *We have off (from school).*, I
die Freiheit *freedom*, III7
die Freikarte, -n *free ticket*, III4
freilich *to be sure, quite so*, III9
der Freitag *Friday*, I
freitags *Fridays*, II
freiwillig *voluntary*, III5
die Freizeit *free time, leisure time*, I
die Freizeitbeschäftigung, -en *freetime activity*, II
die Freizeiteinrichtung, -en *leisure area*, III2
die Freizeitgestaltung *leisure planning*, III2
das Freizeitheim, -e *leisure center*, III4
fremd *foreign; other; strange*, III4
das Fremdenverkehrsamt, ¨er *tourist information*, Loc4
die Fremdsprache, -n *foreign language*, III8
das Freskogemälde, - *fresco painting*, Loc4
die Freude *happiness*, III4
s. freuen über (acc) *to be happy about*, II; **Ich freue mich, dass ...** *I am happy that...*, II; **s. freuen auf** (acc) *to look forward to*, II
der Freund, -e *friend*, I
die Freundesgruppe, -n *group of friends*, III4
der Freundeskreis, -e *circle of friends*, III4
freundlich *friendly*, II
die Freundlichkeit *friendliness*, III4
die Freundschaft, -en *friendship*, III4
der Frieden *peace*, III5
der Friedenspreis *Medal of Freedom*, Loc7
friedlich *peaceful*, II
friedliebend *peace-loving*, III8
frieren *to freeze*, III4
frisch *fresh*, III2

das Frischwasser *fresh water*, III9
Friseur/Friseuse, -e/n *hair stylist*, III12
die Frisur, -en *hair style*, III3
froh *happy*, II
fröhlich *happy*, III7
die Front *front, battle line*
fror (*imperfect of* frieren), III4
der Frosch, ¨e *frog*, III9
die Frucht, ¨e *fruit*, III3
fruchtbar *productive*, III5
früh *early*, III1
früher *earlier*, III5
der Frühjahrsmantel, ¨ *light coat*, III12
der Frühling *spring* (season), I
das Frühstück, -e *breakfast*, II
der Frust *frustration*, III6
frustrierend *frustrating*, III6
der Fuchs, ¨e *fox*, III6
s. fühlen *to feel*, II; **Ich fühle mich wohl!** *I feel great!*, II
fuhr (*imperfect of* fahren), III10
führen *to lead*, III12
der Führer, - *leader*, III5
der Führerschein, -e *driver's license*, II
die Führung *leadership*, III5
die Führungsposition, -en *position of leadership*, III11
die Fülle *abundance*, III6
füllen *to fill*, III4
funktionieren *to function*, III7
für (acc prep) *for*, I
die Furcht *fear, terror*, III10
furchtbar *terrible, awful*, I; **furchtbar gern haben** *to like a lot*, I
fürchten *to fear*, III9
fürs=für das, II
der Fürstbischof, ¨e *prince bishop*, Loc4
das Fürstentum, ¨er *principality*, III2
der Fuß, ¨e *foot*, II
Fußball *soccer*, I
das Fußballspiel, -e *soccer game*, III1
die Fußbremse, -n *foot brake*, II
der Fußgänger, - *pedestrian*, III4
die Fußgängerzone, -n *pedestrian zone*, III1
fußkrank sein *too lazy to walk*, III2
füttern *to feed*, I
futtern *to stuff oneself*, III2

gab (*imperfect of* geben), III6
gäbe=würde geben, III7
die Gabel, - *fork*, III2
gähnen *to yawn*, III10
die Galerie, -n *gallery*, III10
die Gänsehaut *goose bumps*, III10
ganz *all, whole*, III1; **Ganz klar!** *Of course!*, I; **ganz wohl** *extremely well*, II; **Ganz meine**

Meinung. *I completely agree.*, III4; **Ganz bestimmt.** *Certainly*, III11
gar nicht gern haben *not to like at all*, I
die Garage, -n *garage*, II; **die Garage aufräumen** *to clean the garage*, II
die Garderobe, -n *coat check-room*, III10
gären *to ferment*, III5
der Garten, ¨ *garden, yard*, II
das Gartenhaus, ¨er *garden house*, III2
die Gärtnerei, -n *gardening, nursery*, III4
das Gas, -e *gas*, III9
die Gasmaske, -n *gas mask*, III9
die Gasse, -n *alley*, III1
der Gast, ¨e *guest*, III2
das Gästehaus, ¨er *hotel*, III2
die Gasteltern *host parents*, III1
der Gasthof, ¨e *restaurant, inn*, II
der Gastschüler, - *visiting student*, III1
der Gauner, - *cheat, rogue*, III10
das Gebäude, - *building*, III9
geändert, *changed*
geben *to give*, I; **er/sie gibt** *he/she gives*, I; **es gibt** *there is/are*, I; **Das gibt's doch nicht!** *There's just no way!*, II
gebeten *asked*, II
das Gebiet, -e *area*, III4
gebildet *educated*, III4
das Gebirge, - *mountains*, III8
geblieben *remained, stayed*, II
geblümt *flowery*, II
geboren *born*, III4
geboten *offered*, III10
gebracht *brought*, III1
gebraten *fried*, II
der Gebrauch, ¨e *custom*, III4; Gebrauch machen *to use*, III12
gebrauchen *to use*, III7
gebrochen *broken*, II
die Gebrüder (pl) *brothers*, III10
die Gebühr, -en *fee*, III7
gebunden an (acc) *connected with*, III2
das Geburtsdatum, -daten *birthdate*, III2
der Geburtstag, -e *birthday*, I; **Alles Gute zum Geburtstag!** *Best wishes on your birthday!*, I; **Herzlichen Glückwunsch zum Geburtstag!** *Best wishes on your birthday!*, I; **Ich habe am ... Geburtstag.** *My birthday is on...*, I
gedacht *thought*, III8
der Gedanke, -n *thought, idea*, III1
s. Gedanken machen über (acc) *to think about*, III3
gedehnt *extended*, III3
gedenken *to consider*, III12
die Gedenkstätte, -n *monument*, III2
das Gedicht, -e *poem*, III10
die Geduld *patience*, III10
geduldig *patient*, III8

geeignet *suitable*, III7

gefährdet *endangered*, III12

gefährlich *dangerous*, III9

gefallen *to like*; **Wie hat es dir gefallen?** *How did you like it?*, II

gefällig *agreeable*, III7

gefangen *captured*, III4

das Gefäß, -e *container (for liquid)*, Loc10

gefiel (*imperfect of* **gefallen**), III4

gefroren *frozen*, III11

das Gefühl, -e *feeling*, III7

gefühlslos *insensitive, without feelings*, III8

gefüllt: das gefüllte Ei, -er *deviled egg*, II

gefunden *found, discovered*, III1

gefüttert *padded*, II

gegangen *gone*, II

gegen (acc prep) *against*, III1

die Gegend, -en *area*, III2

gegenseitig *mutual(ly)*, III1

der Gegenstand, -̈e *object*, Loc10

das Gegenteil, -e *opposite*, III5

gegenüber (dat prep) *across from*, II

gegenüberstehen (dat, sep) *to stand across from, oppose*, III6

die Gegenwart *present*, III10

gegenwärtig *current*, III3

gegessen *eaten*, II

gegrillt *grilled*, II

das Gehalt, -̈er *salary*, III11

der Gehaltswunsch, -̈e *desired income*, III11

geheim *secret*, III5

die Geheimkonferenz, -en *secret conference*, III5

das Geheimnis, -se *secret*, III9

der Geheimtip, -s *secret tip*, II

gehen *to go*, I; **Das geht nicht.** *That won't work*, I; **Es geht.** *It's okay*, I; **Wie geht's (denn)?** *How are you?*, I; **Gehen wir mal auf den Golfplatz!** *Let's go to the golf course!*, II; gut gehen *to go well*, III3

gehoben *elevated*, III10

geholfen *helped*, II

gehören (dat) *to belong to*, III1

die Geige, -n *violin*, III10

geigen *to play the violin*, III10

Geigenbaumeister(in), -/nen *master violin maker*, III10

der Geiger, - *violinist*, III10

geil *great*, III3

geistern *to wander*, III3

die Geistesfreiheit *freedom of ideas*, III5

die Geistesgeschichte *history of thought*, III2

gekauft *bought*, I

gekleidet *dressed*, II

gelangen *to acquire*, III9

gelaunt: gut gelaunt *in a good mood*, II

gelb *yellow*, I

das Geld *money*, I

der Geldbeutel *wallet*, III9

der Geldschein, -e *bill*, III1

gelegen *appropriate*, III12

die Gelegenheit, -en *opportunity*, III6

gelesen (pp) *read*, I

gelingen (dat) *to succeed*, III6

gelten *to mean, count*, III7

gemacht *done*, I; **Was hast du am Wochenende gemacht?** *What did you do on the weekend?*, I

die Gemahlin *wife*, III6

das Gemälde, - *painting*, II

die Gemäldegalerie, -n *picture gallery*, Loc10

gemein *mean*, III9

die Gemeinde, -n *community*, III8

gemeinsam *in common; joint, together*, III2

die Gemeinsamkeit, -en *common interest*, III5

das Gemüse *vegetables*, I; **im Obst- und Gemüseladen** *at the produce store*, I

der Gemüseladen, -̈ *produce store*, I

gemütlich *comfortable*, II

genannt *named*, III7

genau *exact(ly)*, III1

genau: Genau so ist es. *That's exactly right.*, III7

genauso *just so*, III3

der General, -̈e *general*, III5

die Generation, -en *generation*, III3

generell *generally*, III7

genial *ingenious*, III5

das Genie, -s *genius*, III10

genießen *to enjoy*, III10

die Genitivform, -en *genitive form*, III4

genommen *taken*, III4

der Genosse, -n *comrade*, III5

genug *enough*, I

genügen *to be enough*, III2

genügend *enough*, II; **genügend schlafen** *to get enough sleep*, II

der Genuss, -̈e *pleasure*, III1

die Genussmittelindustrie *industry producing luxury articles*, Loc10

die Geografie *geography*, III2

gepflegt *well cared-for, well-groomed*, III11

gepunktet *polka-dotted*, II

gerade *just*, III1; *straight*, II; **Das ist gerade passiert.** *It just happened.*, II

geradeaus *straight ahead*, III10

geradezu *outright*, III1

das Gerät, -e *appliance*, III6

geraten *to get into*, Loc1

geräuchert *smoked*, II

das Geräusch, -e *sound*, III10

geräuscharm *low-noise*, III7

das Gerede *talk*, III8

geregelt *ordered, fixed*, III11; *regulated*, III5

das Gericht, -e *meal, entrée*, III1

geringfügig *negligible, trivial*, III9

die Germanistik (sing) *German studies*, III11

gern (machen) *to like (to do)*, I; **gern haben** *to like*, I; **Gern geschehen!** *My pleasure!*, I; **besonders gern** *especially like*, I; **Gern! Hier ist es!** *Here! I insist!*, II

gesamt *entire, whole*, III6

die Gesamtbevölkerung *total population*, III8

der Gesangsverein, -e *choral society*, III10

die Gesäßtasche, -n *back pocket*, II

das Geschäft, -e *store; business*, I

der Geschäftsabschluss, -̈e *business deal*, III1

die Geschäftsführerin, -nen *manager*, III7

geschehen *to happen*, III6

gescheit *smart, clever*, III4

das Geschenk, -e *gift*, I

die Geschenkidee, -n *gift idea*, I

die Geschichte *history*, I;

die Geschichte, -n *story*, III3

geschichtlich *historical*, III1

geschickt *skillful*, III6

das Geschirr *dishes*, I; **Geschirr spülen** *to wash the dishes*, I

das Geschlecht, -er *gender*, III2

geschlossen *closed*, III10

der Geschmack *taste*, III3

die Geschmackskraft *power of taste*, III7

geschmeidig *smooth*, III2

geschrieben *written*, II

die Geschwister (pl) *brothers and sisters*, I

geschwommen *swum*, II

gesehen (pp) *seen*, III1

der Geselle, -n *fellow*, III10

die Gesellschaft, -en *social group; society*, III3

das Gesetz, -e *law, by law*, III1

gesetzlich *legal*, III7

das Gesicht, -er *face*, III3

der Gesichtspunkt, -e *point of view*, II9

gespart *saved*, III1

gesponnen *spun*, III7

das Gespräch, -e *conversation*, III1

der Gesprächspartner, - *conversation partner*, III6

die Gesprächsfetzen (pl) *scraps of conversation*, III2

der Gesprächsstoff *topic, subject of conversation*, III6

gesprochen *spoken*, I; **Worüber habt ihr gesprochen?** *What did you talk about?*, I

die Gestalt, -en *figure, form*, III2

gestalten *to form, arrange*, III4

die Gestaltung *arrangement, formation*, III11

gestern *yesterday*, I; **gestern Abend** *yesterday evening*, I

gestiegen *climbed*, II

die Gestik *gestures*, III1

gestreift *striped*, II

gesund *healthy*, II

die **Gesundheit** *health*, II
gesundheitsschädlich *injurious to health*, III7
Gesundheitswissenschaftler(in), **-/nen** *nutritional scientist*, III12
gesungen *sung*, III10
gesunken *sunk*, III5
getan *done*, III1
das **Getränk, -e** *drink*, II
der **Getränkemarkt, ̈e** *beverage shop*, III1
getroffen *met*, III1
getrunken *drunk*, III10
die **Gewalt** *violence*, III8
die **Gewaltanwendung** *use of force*, III5
das **Gewand, ̈er** *robe*, III2
das **Gewehr, -e** *gun, rifle*, III5
gewesen *been*, II
gewinnen *to win*, III5
gewiss *certain(ly)*, III4
das **Gewitter, -** *storm*, I
s. **gewöhnen an** (acc) *to get used to*, III7
die **Gewohnheit, -en** *habit*, III2
gewöhnlich *usually*, II
das **Gewölbe, -** *archway, vault*, Loc10
geworden *became*, II
geworfen *thrown*, III9
gewusst *known*, III1
gezogen *pulled*, III7
gichtig *arthritic*, III3
der **Giebel, -** *gable*, III1
gießen *to water*, I
das **Gift, -e** *poison*, III9
giftig *poisonous*, III9
gigantisch *gigantic*, III3
ging (*imperfect of* **gehen**), III4
Gis *g-sharp*, III12
die **Gitarre, -n** *guitar*, I
glänzen *to shine*, III10
glänzend *sparkling*, III6
glanzvoll *magnificent, glorious*, Loc7
die **Glanzzeit** *golden age*, Loc10
das **Glas, ̈er** *glass*, I; **ein Glas Apfelsaft** *a glass of apple juice*, I
Glasbläser(in), -/nen *glas blower*, III12
glatt *slick*, III9
die **Glatze, -n** *bald head*, I
der **Glaube** *religion*, III12
glauben *to believe*, I; **Ich glaube nicht, dass ...** *I don't think that...*, II
glaubhaft *believable*, III5
gleich *immediately*, III4; *same*, III7
gleichaltrig *of the same age*, III4
die **Gleichberechtigung** *equality (of rights)*, III5
gleichen (dat) *to be equal to, be alike*, III3
gleichfalls: Danke, gleichfalls! *Thank you and the same to you!*, II
gleichgültig *no matter*, III5; **es ist gleichgültig geworden** *it no longer matters*, III12
das **Gleichnis, -se** *simile*, III10

gleichzeitig *at the same time*, III3
das **Glied, -er** *limb*, III2
die **Gliederung, -en** *organizaton*, III4
die **Glotze, -n** *television, idiot box*, III6
das **Glück** *luck*, I; **So ein Glück!** *What luck!*, I; **Ein Glück, dass ...** *Lucky that ...*, III11; **Zum Glück habe ich ...** *Luckily I have ...*, III11
glücklich *happy*, III7
das **Goethehaus** *(Goethe's birthplace)*, II
das **Gold** *gold*, III6
goldgierig *lusting for gold*, III6
der **Goldschmuck** *gold jewelry*, III1
Golf *golf*, I
der **Golfplatz, ̈e** *golf course*, II
gotisch *Gothic*, Loc 1
der **Gott, ̈er** *God*, III11; **Gott sei Dank, dass ...** *Thank God that ...*, III11
der **Graben, ̈** *ditch*, III2
das **Grabmal, ̈er** *tomb*, Loc4
der **Grad** *degree(s)*, I; **zwei Grad** *two degrees*, I; **Wie viel Grad haben wir?** *What's the temperature?*, I
der **Graf, -en** *count*, III10
die **Grafik, -en** *illustration*, grid, III4
der **Grafiker, -** *graphic artist*, Loc1
das **Gramm** *gram*, I
der **Grammatikfehler, -** *grammar mistake*, III7
grau *gray*, I; **in Grau** *in gray*, I
grausam *cruel*, I
die **Grenze, -n** *border*, Loc1
griechisch (adj) *Greek*, II
griffbereit *handy*, III7
groß *big*, I
großartig *wonderful*, II
die **Größe, -n** *size*, I
die **Großeltern** (pl) *grandparents*, I
größer *bigger*, II
großgedruckt *in capital letters*, III6
großgezogen *raised (a child)*, III7
die **Großmutter, ̈** *grandmother*, I
die **Großschachanlage, -n** *open-air chessboard with giant-sized pieces*, III2
die **Großstadt, ̈e** *big city*, II
der **Großvater, ̈** *grandfather*, I
großziehen (sep) *to raise (a child)*, III7
großzügig *generous*, III11
grotesk *grotesque*, III10
grün *green*, I; **in Grün** *in green*, I
der **Grund, ̈e** *reason*, III11
gründen *to found*, III12
das **Grundgesetz** *basic law, constitution*, III5
gründlich *thorough(ly)*, III6
der **Grundsatz, ̈e** *principle*, III9
die **Grundschule, -n** *grade school*, III4
der **Grundstein, -e** *corner stone*, Loc1
der **Grundwehrdienst** *basic military training*, III5
die **Gruppe, -n** *group*, I
gruppieren *to group*, III8
die **Gruppierung, -en** *grouping*, III8

die **Gruselgeschichte, -n** *horror story*, III10
der **Gruselroman, -e** *horror novel*, I
der **Gruß, ̈e** *greeting*, III12
grüßen *to greet* III4; **Grüß dich! Hi!**, I
gucken *to look*, II; **Guck mal! Look!**, II; **Fernseh gucken** *to watch TV* (colloquial), II
gülden (poetic) *golden*, III2
der **Gummihandschuh, -e** *rubber glove*, III3
die **Gummihülle, -n** *rubber covering*, III11
günstig *favorable*, III2
die **Gurke, -n** *cucumber*, II; **die saure Gurke** *pickle*, III1
der **Gürtel, -** *belt*, I
gut *good*, I; **gut gelaunt** *good-tempered*, II; **Gut! Mach ich!** *Okay, I'll do that!*, I; **gut sein: Ist dir nicht gut?** *Are you not feeling well?*, II
gutmütig *good-natured*, III8
Gymnasiast(in), -en/nen *student in Gymnasium*, III3
das **Gymnasium, (pl) Gymnasien** *(German academic) high school*, III6
die **Gymnastik** *exercise, calisthenics*, II; **Gymnastik machen** *to exercise*, II
das **Gyros** *gyros*, I

das **Haar, -e** *hair*, I
das **Haarwachs** *hair wax*, III3
haben *to have*, I; **er/sie hat** *he/she has*, I; **Haben Sie das auch in Rot?** *Do you also have that in red?*, I
das **Hackfleisch** *ground meat*, I
der **Hafen, ̈** *harbor*, III1
das **Hähnchen, -** *chicken*, I
halb *half*, I; **halb (eins, zwei, usw.)** *half past (twelve, one, etc.)*, I
halblang: **Macht halblang!** *Don't exaggerate!*, III1
die **Hälfte, -n** *half*, III1
die **Halle, -n** *hall*, II
das **Hallenbad, ̈er** *indoor pool*, II
Hallo! Hi! Hello!, I
der **Hals, ̈e** *throat*, II
das **Halsband, ̈er** *necklace*, III7
die **Halskette, -n** *necklace*, II
die **Halsschmerzen** (pl) *sore throat*, II
das **Halstuch, ̈er** *kerchief*, III12
halt (particle), I; **Die Kleinstadt gefällt mir gut, weil es da halt ruhiger ist.** *I like a small town because it's just quieter there.*, II

Halt machen (sep) to stop, III9
halten to stop, hold, III1; **halten für** to consider as, III5; **s. fit halten** to keep fit, II; **halten von** to think of, III3
die Haltestelle, -n (bus) stop, III2
die Hand, ⸚e hand, II
die Handbewegung, -en hand movement, III11
die Handbremse, -n emergency brake, II
die Handcreme hand cream, II
s.handeln um to be about, III10
handeln von to deal with, be about, III5
das Handgelenk, -e wrist, III1
handgeschrieben handwritten, III11
die Handlung, -en plot, III10
die Handlungsbereitschaft readiness to act, III9
der Handlungsraum ⸚e setting, III8
die Handtasche, -n handbag, II
das Handy, -s cell phone, I
hängen to hang, III4
die Hansestadt, ⸚e Hanseatic city, III1
die Harfe, -n harp, III10
harmlos harmless, III3
hart hard, tough, III7
der Hase, -n rabbit, III6
das Hasenfleisch rabbit meat, III1
die Haspel, -n reel, III7
hassen to hate, III5
hässlich ugly, I
hätte: Ich hätte gern ... I would like..., II
häufig frequent(ly), III9
hauptberuflich as a main profession, III11
die Hauptfigur, -en main character, III8
der Hauptgedanke, -n main idea, III3
das Hauptgericht, -e main dish, II
das Hauptmerkmal, -e main characteristic, III4
der Hauptpunkt, -e main point, III3
hauptsächlich mainly, III3
der Hauptschulabschluss degree (from a Hauptschule), III4
die Hauptstadt, ⸚e capital, I
die Hauptstraße, -n main street, II
das Hauptthema, -themen main theme, III1
das Hauptziel, -e main objective, III9
das Haus, ⸚er house, II; **zu Hause bleiben** to stay at home, II
die Hausarbeit, -en housework, III11
der Hausarrest house arrest, III12
die Hausaufgaben (pl) homework, I; **Hausaufgaben machen** to do homework, I
das Häuschen, - small house, III12
hauseigen belonging to the house, in-house, III2
der Haushalt, -e household, III3
der Hausmeister, - janitor, III9
der Hausmüll garbage, III9

die Hausmusik house music, III10
das Haustier, -e pet, I
das Haustor, -e gate, III1
die Haut, ⸚e skin, II
der Hautkrebs skin cancer, III9
hautnah very close, III2
heben to lift, III3
das Heer army
das Heft, -e notebook, I
heil whole, perfect, III7
der Heilbutt halibut, II
heilig holy, Loc7
heim home, III3
die Heimat home, Loc1; homeland, III5
der Heimatort, -e native place, III1
heiraten to marry, III5
heiter cheerful, III10
heiß hot, I
heißen to be called, I; **er heißt** his name is, I
der Held, -en hero, III7
helfen (dat) to help, I
hell bright, II
hellgrau light gray, III12
das Hemd, -en shirt, I
der Hemdknopf, ⸚e shirt button, III4
der Hemdkragen, - shirt collar, III4
heranwachsen (sep) to grow up, III12
heraus out, III1
herausbringen (sep) to publish, III6
herausfinden (sep) to find out, III8
herausgeben (sep) to publish, III6
herauskommen to come out, III5
herausnehmen (sep) to take out, II
heraussuchen (sep) to pick out, select, III1
die Herberge, -n hostel, III2
herbfrisch tangy fresh, III7
der Herbst fall (season), I; **im Herbst** in the fall, I
der Herd, -e stove, I
hereingebeten asked in, III8
hereintrat (imperfect of hereintreten), III7
hereintreten (sep) to enter, III7
hergehen: hin- und hergehen to go back and forth, III3
der Herr Mr., I
der Herrgott God, III8
herrlich fantastic, III5
herstellen (sep) to produce, III9
der Hersteller, - manufacturer, III7
die Herstellung, -en production, III9
herum around; about, III3
herumblättern (sep) to leaf through (a newspaper), III3
herumirren to wander around, III12
herumlaufen (sep) to run around, III4
herumreisen (sep) to travel around, III11
s. herumsprechen to get around, III7
herunter down, III11
hervor out of, III10

hervorrufen give rise to, III5
das Herz, -en heart, III7
herzhaft hearty, II
das Herzklopfen pounding heart, III10
herzlich heartfelt, III8; **Herzlichen Glückwunsch zum Geburtstag!** Best wishes on your birthday!, I
der Herzog, ⸚e duke, Loc4
hetzen to chase, harass, III5
heute today, I; **heute Morgen** this morning, I; **heute Nachmittag** this afternoon, I; **heute Abend** tonight, this evening, I
heutig of today, today's, III3
heutzutage nowadays, III5
hielt (imperfect of halten), III7
hier here, I; **Hier bei ...** The ... residence., I; **Hier ist ...** This is..., I
hiermit with this, herewith, III12
hieß (imperfect of **heißen**), III3
hierzulande around here, III8
die Hilfe, -n help, III5
hilfreich helpful, III8
der Hilfsarbeiter, - unskilled worker, III4
hilfsbereit helpful, cooperative, III8
die Himbeermarmelade, -n raspberry marmalade, II
hin to, III2
hinaufbegleiten (sep) to take up, upstairs, III10
hinaus out, III10
hinauslachen (sep) to laugh at, III10
hingefallen fallen, III1
hingehen (sep) to go to, III4
s. hinlegen (sep) to lie down, III3
hinrichten (sep) to execute, III5
s. hinsetzen (sep) to sit down, III4
Hinsicht: in dieser Hinsicht as far as that goes, III5
hinten at the back, II; **da hinten** there in the back, I
der Hintergrund, ⸚e background, III6
hinterlassen to leave behind, III9
hinüberschreiten (sep) to walk across, III10
hinüberschritt (imperfect of hinüberschreiten), III10
hinunterstampfen (sep) to stomp downstairs, III1
hinwegströmen (sep) to flow away, III5
hinzufügen (sep) to add to, III6
historisch historical, III10
hob (imperfect of **heben**), III4
das Hobby, -s hobby, II
hoch high, III4
hochgezogen pulled up, III10
hochhinaufragend reaching high up, III1
hochkämmen (sep) to comb up, III10
die Hochschule, -n university, III3
höchst highest, greatest, III8
die Hochzeit, -en wedding, III6
hoffen to hope, II

Hoffentlich ... *Hopefully...*, II; **Hoffentlich geht es dir bald besser!** *I hope you'll get better soon.*, II
die **Hoffnung, -en** *hope*, III11
die **Hofkirche, -n** *church of the royal court*, Loc10
höflich *polite*, III8
hoh- *high*, III1
die Höhenzüge (pl) *hills*, III2
der Höhepunkt, -e *climax, peak*, III5
hohl *hollow, empty*, III3
holen *to get, fetch*, I
Holland *Holland*, III1
das **Holz** *wood*, I; **aus Holz** *out of wood*, I
homogen *homogenous*, III4
der Honig *honey*, III1
hören: Hör mal zu! *Listen to this!*, II; **Hör mal!** *Listen!*, II; **Musik hören** *to listen to music*, I; **Hör gut zu!** *Listen carefully.*, I
der **Hörer, -** *listener; receiver;* **den Hörer abheben** *to pick up the receiver*, I; **den Hörer auflegen** *to hang up (the telephone)*, I
der Höreranruf, -e *call from a listener*, III3
der Hörfunk *radio*, III6
der **Horizont** *horizon*, III11
der **Horrorfilm, -e** *horror movie*, I
der Hörsturz *hearing failure*, III3
die **Hose, -n** *pants*, I
das **Hotel, -s** *hotel*, II
hübsch *pretty, handsome*, III3
die **Hüfte, -n** *hip*, II
das **Huhn, ¨er** *chicken*, II
das Hühnerfleisch *chicken meat*, III3
der **Hummer, -** *lobster*, II
humorlos *humorless*, III8
humorvoll *humorous*, III11
der **Hund, -e** *dog*, I
der Hundertmarkschein *hundred mark bill*, III1
der **Hunger** *hunger*, I; **Ich habe Hunger.** *I am hungry*, II
das Hungergefühl, -e *hungry feeling*, III1
hungrig *hungry*, III9
hupen *to honk the horn*, II
hüpfen *to hop, jump*, III7
der **Hürdenlauf, ¨e** *hurdling*, II
der **Husten** *cough*, II
der **Hut, ¨e** *hat*, II

ich *I*, I; **Ich auch.** *Me too.*, I; **Ich nicht.** *I don't.*, I
ideal *ideal*, III4
die **Idee, -n** *idea*, II; **Gute Idee!** *Good idea!*, II; **Hast du eine Idee?** *Do you have an idea?*, II

der Ideenbaum *tree of ideas*, III3
identifizieren *to identify*, III1
die Ideologie, -n *ideology*, III3
ihm *to, for him*, I
ihn *it, him*, I
ihnen *to them*, II
Ihnen (formal) *to you*, II
ihr (poss adj) *her, their*, I; *to, for her*, I; (pl) *you*, I
Ihr (poss adj, formal, pl, sing) *your*, II
die Illustration, -en *illustration*, III1
illustrieren *to illustrate*, III2
im=in dem; im Frühling *in the spring*, I; **im Januar** *in January*, I; **(einmal) im Monat** *(once) a month*, I
die Image-Werbung, -en *image advertisement*, III7
die **Imbissstube, -n** *snack bar*, II
imitieren *to imitate*, III7
immer *always*, I
immerhin *nevertheless, at least*, III5
die Improvisation *improvisation*, III11
in (acc, dat prep) *into, in*, II; **in Blau** *in blue*, I; **in der (Basketball) Mannschaft** *on the (basketball) team*, II; **in die Apotheke gehen** *to go to the pharmacy*, II
indem (conj) *in that*, III8
indisch (adj) *(Asian) Indian*, II
die Industrie, -n *industry*, III9
die Industrieabgase *industrial emissios*, III9
Industriedesigner(in), -/nen *industrial designer*, III12
die Informatik *computer science*, III11
die **Informatik** *computer science*, I
die Information, -en *information*, III2
informativ *informative*, III7
s. **informieren** *to inform oneself*, III2
Ingenieur(in), -e/nen *engineer*, III11
das Ingenieurwesen *engineering*, III11
der Inhalt *content*, III11
die Inhaltsangabe, -n *table of contents* III6
die Initiative, -n *initiative*, III12
inkorrekt *incorrect*, III7
der Inländer, - *native* III8
die **Innenstadt, ¨e** *downtown*, II
inner *interior*, III2
die **Innereien** (pl) *innards*, III1
innerhalb (gen prep) *within, on the inside*, III10
innerlich *on the inside*, III3
insbesondere *particularly*, III8
die **Insel, -n** *island*, II
insgesamt *altogether*, III11
das Institut, -e *institute* III7
die Institution, -en *institution*, III1
das **Instrument, -e** *instrument*, I
intakt *intact*, III8
intelligent *intelligent*, II
die Intensität *intensity*, III8
interessant *interesting*, III1

das **Interesse, -n** *interest*, I; **Hast du andere Interessen?** *Do you have any other interests?*, I; **Ich habe kein Interesse an Mode.** *I am not interested in fashion.*, II
s. **interessieren für** *to be interested in*, II; **Interessierst du dich für Mode?** *Are you interested in fashion?*, II
interessiert sein an (dat) *to be interested in*, III11
international *international*, III2
das **Internet** *internet*, I
der Internist, en *internist*, III3
das Interrogativ *interrogative*, III10
interviewen *to interview*, III4
inzwischen *in the meantime*, III10
irgend- *some-*, III7
ironisch *ironic*, III2
s. **irren** *to be mistaken*, III5
der Irrtum, ¨er *error, misunderstanding*, III12
irrtümlich *erroneous(ly), mistaken(ly)*, III12
isoliert *isolated*, III4
ist: sie ist aus ... *she's from...*, I; **Ist was mit dir?** *Is something wrong?*, II
italienisch (adj) *Italian*, II

ja *yes*, I; **Ja klar!** *Of course!*, I; **Das ist ja unglaublich!** *That's really unbelievable!*, II; **Ja, kann sein, aber ...** *Yes, maybe, but...*, II; **Ja, natürlich!** *Certainly!*, II; *Yes, of course!*, II; **Ja, schon, aber ...** *Well yes, but...*, II; **Ja? Was denn?** *Okay, what is it?*, II
die **Jacke, -n** *jacket*, I
das Jackenfutter *jacket lining*, III11
das **Jahr, -e** *year*, I; **Ich bin ... Jahre alt.** *I am... years old.*, I
jahrelang *for years*, Loc1
jähren: das jährt sich *it's been a year (ago) since*, III2
die Jahreszeit, -en *season*, III10
das **Jahrhundert, -e** *century*, II; **aus dem 17. Jahrhundert** *from the 17th century*, II
jahrhundertealt *centuries old*, III1
jährig *year-old*, III3
jährlich *yearly, annual*, Loc4
der Jahrmarkt, ¨e *annual fair* III10
jammern *to mourn, lament*, III7
der **Januar** *January*, I; **im Januar** *in January*, I
Japanisch (das) *Japanese*, III12
die Jazzgruppe, -n *jazz group*, III10
je *each, every*, III1; **je ... desto** *the more ... the*, III7

die **Jeans** (mostly sing) *jeans,* I
die **Jeansweste, -n** *jeans vest,* II
    jed- *every,* II; **jede Woche** *every week,* II; **jeden Tag** *every day,* I
    jedenfalls *in any case,* III8
    jedermann *everyone,* III10
    jedoch *however, nevertheless,* III1
    jemals *ever,* III7
    jemand *someone, somebody,* III3
    jener *that one,* III5
    jetzig *present, current,* III8
    jetzt *at present, now,* I
    jeweils *in each case, respectively,* III2
der **Job, -s** *job,* II
    jobben *to have a job,* III11
    joggen *to jog,* I
der **Jogging-Anzug, ⸚e** *jogging suit,* I
das **Joghurt, -s** (or **der**) *yogurt,* II
der Journalismus *journalism,* III6
    Journalist(in) -en/nen *journalist,* III11
    jubeln *to rejoice,* III10
die Jugend *youth,* III3
das Jugendgästehaus, ⸚er *youth hostel* III2
das Jugendheim *youth center,* III4
die **Jugendherberge, -n** *youth hostel,* II
der Jugendherbergsausweis, -e *youth hostel I.D.,* III2
    Jugendliche, -n *teenager,* III8
der Jugendpsychologe, -n *psychologist for young people,* III12
die Jugendsprache *youth language,* III3
die Jugendzeitschrift, -en *teen magazine,* III1
der **Juli** *July,* I
    jung *young,* II
der **Junge, -n** *boy,* I
    jünger *younger,* II
die Jungfer, -n *maiden* III7
der **Juni** *June,* I
der Junker, - *(young) nobleman, Junker,* Loc 1
    Jura *law,* III11
das Jurastudium *study of law,* III12

der Kabelanschluss, ⸚e *cable connection,* III6
der Käfer, - *bug, beetle,* III6
der **Kaffee** *coffee,* I
die Kaffeemühle, -n *coffee grinder,* III12
    kahl *bald,* III11
die Kaiserkrönung, -en *coronation of an emperor,* Loc7
der Kaisersaal *imperial banquet hall,* Loc4
der **Kakao** *chocolate milk,* II
der Kalauer *dumb joke,* III7
der **Kalender, -** *calendar,* I

die Kalkleisten (pl) *(ironic) parents,* III3
    kalt (adj) *cold,* I
die Kälte, -n *cold, coldness,* III11
    kam (*imperfect of* **kommen**), III4
die **Kamera, -s** *camera,* II
die Kameradschaft *comradeship,* III5
    kameradschaftlich *friendly,* III8
der Kaminabend. -e *evening by the fireplace,* III2
der **Kaminraum, ⸚e** *room with open fireplace,* III2
    s. kämmen *to comb one's hair,* II
die Kammer, -n *chamber,* III7
die Kampagne, -n *campaign,* III7
der **Kampf, ⸚e** *struggle, battle* III5
    kämpfen *to fight,* III5
der Kampfpanzer, - *battle tank,* III5
der Kandidat, -en *candidate,* III5
    kannten (*imperfect of* **kennen**), III10
der Kantor, -en *choirmaster, organist,* Loc1
der Kanzler, - *chancellor,* III9
das Kapitel, - *chapter,* III1
die Kappe, -n *cap,* III9
das **Käppi, -s** *(baseball) cap,* II
    kaputt *ruined, broken,* I
    kaputtgehen (sep) *to go to pieces,* III11
die **Kapuze, -n** *hood,* II
    kariert *checked,* II
das **Karo, -s** *(pattern) check, diamond,* II
der **Karpfen, -** *carp,* II
die **Karriere, -n** *career,* III11
die **Karte, -n** *card; ticket,* I
die Karteikarte, -n *index cards,* III9
die **Kartoffel, -n** *potato,* I
der **Käse, -** *cheese,* I
das **Käsebrot, -e** *cheese sandwich,* I
die Kaserne, -n *barracks,* III5
die Kasse, -n *cash register,* III9
die **Kassette, -n** *cassette,* I
die Kassiererin, -nen *cashier,* III9
der Kasten, ⸚ *box,* III2
der Katalysator, -en *catalytic converter,* III9
das **Katauto, -s** *car with emission control,* III9
die Kategorie, -n *category,* III1
die **Katze, -n** *cat,* I
    kauen *to chew,* III8
der Kauf, ⸚e *purchase,* III5
    kaufen *to buy,* I
der Käufer, - *buyer,* III7
die **Kauffrau, -en** *saleswoman,* III11
das Kaufhaus, ⸚er *department store,* III4
der **Kaufmann,** (pl) **Kaufleute** *salesman,* III11
das Kaufmannshaus, ⸚er *commercial building,* III1
der **Kaufreiz** *temptation to buy,* III7
der **Kaugummi** *chewing gum,* III8
    kaum *barely, hardly,* II
    kein *no, none, not any,* I; **Ich habe keine Zeit.** *I don't have time.,* I;

    Ich habe keinen Hunger mehr. *I'm not hungry any more.,* I; **Keine Ahnung!** *I have no idea!,* I
der **Keks, -e** *cookie,* I
der **Keller, -** *cellar,* III2
der **Kellner, -** *waiter,* III2
    keltisch *celtic,* Loc4
    kennen *to know, be familiar or acquainted with,* I
    kennen lernen *to get to know,* III2
die Kenntnis, -se *knowledge,* III10
der **Kerl, -e** *fellow,* III7
die Kette, -n *chain,* III11
der Kiefer, - *jaw,* III1
das **Kilo=Kilogramm, -** *kilogram,* I
    kilometerweit *for kilometers,* III9
das **Kind, -er** *child,* II
    kinderlieb *fond of children,* III8
das Kinderlied, -er *children's song,* III2
das **Kino, -s** *cinema,* I; **ins Kino gehen** *to go to the movies,* I
die **Kirche, -n** *church,* I
die **Kirsche, -n** *cherry,* II
    klagen *to lament,* III3
die Klammer, -n *parenthesis,* III6
die **Klamotten** (pl) *(casual term for) clothes,* I
der **Klang, ⸚e** *sound, ring,* III10
    klappen: *es klappt it works,* III4
    klappern *to rattle, clatter,* III11
    Klar! *Of course!,* III7
    klar werden *to become clear,* III9
    klären *to clarify,* III10
die Klarheit *clarity,* III6
    klarstellen (sep) *to make clear,* III7
    Klasse! *Great!; Terrific!,* I
die **Klasse, -n** *grade level,* I; *class,* II
der Klassenausflug, ⸚e *class trip,* III10
    Klassenkamerad(in), -en/nen *classmate,* III1
der Klassenlehrer, - *teacher,* III10
die Klassenliste, -n *class roster,* III11
die Klassenreise, -n *school trip,* III2
der Klassensprecher, - *class representative,* III6
die Klassenumfrage, -n *class survey,* III6
das Klassenzimmer, - *classroom,* III9
die Klassik *classical period,* III2
die Klassikermetropole *capital of the classicists,* III2
    klassisch *classic(al),* I
    klatschen *to applaud,* III10
das **Klavier, -e** *piano,* I; **Ich spiele Klavier.** *I play the piano.,* I
der Klavierstimmer, - *piano tuner,* III12
    kleben *to glue, stick,* III2
das **Kleid, -er** *dress,* I
    s. kleiden *to dress, get dressed,* III3
die **Kleider** (pl) *clothes,* III3
die Kleiderfrage, -n *question of what to wear,* III10
die **Kleidung** *clothing,* III3
    klein *small,* I
die **Kleinstadt, ⸚e** *town,* II

die **Klimaanlage, -n** *air conditioning*, II
die **Klimaveränderung** *climatic change*, III9
klingeln *to ring*, III4
das **Klingelzeichen, -** *reminder bell*, III10
klingen *to sound*, III11
die **Klinik, -en** *clinic*, III1
die **Klinke, -n** *door handle*, III1
die **Klippe, -n** *cliff*, II
das **Klischee, -s** *cliché*, III8
das **Klischeebild, -er** *clichéd image*, III8
die **Klischeevorstellung, -en** *clichéd image, impression*, III8
klopfen *to knock, pound*, III2
die **Klosteranlage, -n** *monastery grounds*, III1
der **Kloß, -̈e** *dumpling*, II
klug *intelligent*, III6
der **Knabe, -n** *(small) boy*, III2
knapp *scarce(ly)*, III1
die **Knebelung** *gagging*, III5
kneten *to knead*, III3
das **Knie, -** *knee*, II
die **Kniescheibe, -n** *knee cap*, III1
knistern *to rustle, crackle*, III10
der **Knoblauch** *garlic*, II
der **Knöchel, -** *ankle*, II
der **Knödel, -** *dumpling*, III8
der **Knopf, -̈e** *button*, II
Koch/Köchin, -̈e/nen *chef*, III12
kochen *to cook*, II
der **Koffer, -** *suitcase*, III12
der **Kofferraumdeckel, -** *trunk lid*, II
der **Kohlenwasserstoff** *hydrocarbon*, III9
der **Koks** *degassified coal, coke*, III2
die **Kollegstufe** *(last three years at a Gymnasium)*, III4
der **Kollektor, -en** *collector*, III9
die **Kombination, -en** *combination*, III3
kombinieren *to combine*, III7
komisch *funny; strange*, III6
kommandieren *to command*, III5
kommen *to come*, I; **er kommt aus** *he's from*, I; **Komm doch mit!** *Why don't you come along?*, I; **Wie komme ich zum (zur) ... ?** *How do I get to...?*, I
der **Kommentar, -e** *commentary*, III6
kommerziell *commercial*, III2
der **Kommilitone, -n** *fellow-student (university)*, III5
die **Kommilitonin, -nen** *fellow-student (university)*, III5
Kommunikationselektroniker(in), -/nen *communications engineer*, III12
die **Komödie, -n** *comedy*, I
der **Komponist, -en** *composer*, Loc1
der **Konflikt, -e** *conflict*, III12
der **König, -e** *king*, III6
die **Königin, -nen** *queen*, III10
das **Königreich, -e** *kingdom*, III6
die **Königsloge** *royal box (theater)*, III10

die **Konjunktion, -en** *conjunction*, III4
konkret *concrete*, III9
die **Konkurrenz** *competition*, III1
können *to be able to*, I; **Kann ich bitte Andrea sprechen?** *Could I please speak with Andrea?*, I
könnte *could*, III5
konservativ *conservative*, II
der **Konsum** *consumption*, III6
der **Konsument, -en** *consumer*, III7
der **Kontakt, -e** *contact*, III4
die **Kontaktlinse, -n** *contact lense*, III5
die **Kontrolle, -n** *control*, III9
kontrollieren *to control, check*, III7
die **Konzentrationsfähigkeit** *ability to concentrate*, III3
konzentrieren *to concentrate*, III10
das **Konzert, -e** *concert*, I; **ins Konzert gehen** *to go to a concert*, I
das **Konzertabonnement, -s** *concert subscription*, III10
die **Konzerthalle, -n** *concert hall*, III10
der **Kopf, -̈e** *head*, II; **den Kopf in den Sand stecken** *to hide one's head in the sand*, III12
der **Kopfhörer, -** *headphones*, II
der **Kopfhöreranschluss, -̈e** *headphone outlet*, II
die **Kopfschmerzen** (pl) *headache*, II
das **Kopftuch, -̈er** *head scarf*, III4
das **Kopfweh** *headache*, III1
die **Kopie, -n** *copy*, III11
der **Korb, -̈e** *basket*, III9
körperlich *physical(ly)*, III1
der **Körperteil, -e** *part of the body*, III1
korrekt *correct, proper*, III3
die **Korrektur, -en** *correction*, III3
korrigieren *to correct*, III1
kostbar *precious, valuable*, III5
die **Kosten** (pl) *costs*, III9
kosten *to cost*, I; *to taste*, II
köstlich *delicious, charming*, III7
die **Köstlichkeit, -en** *delicacy*, II
das **Kostüm, -e** *costume*, III12
kotzen *to vomit*, III2
die **Krabbe, -n** *crab*, II
der **Krach** *quarrel*, III4
kräftig *strong*, III7
Kraft: in Kraft treten *to become effective*
das **Krafttraining** *weight lifting*, III3
kraftvoll *powerful, vigorous*, III10
krank *sick*, II
das **Krankenhaus, -̈er** *hospital*, III4
der **Krankenpfleger, -** *male nurse*, III4
die **Krankenschwester, -n** *female nurse*, III11
die **Krankheit, -en** *illness, disease*, III11
die **Krawatte, -n** *tie*, II
kreativ *creative*, III7
der **Kredit, -e** *credit*, III5
kreieren *to create*, III7
der **Kreis, -e** *circle; district*, III2
das **Kreuz, -e** *lower back*, III5
die **Kreuzung, -en** *crossing, junction*, III4

kribbeln *to tickle*, III11
der **Krieg, -e** *war*, II
kriegen *to get, receive*, III3
der **Kriegsfilm, -e** *war movie*, I
der **Krimi, -s** *detective movie*, I; *detective novel*, I
die **Kritik, -en** *criticism, critique*, III6
kritiklos *uncritical*, III7
kritisch *critical*, III3
kritisieren *to criticize*, III3
die **Kroatienhilfe** *support for Croatia*, III12
die **Kroketten** (pl) *potato croquettes*, II
der **Krokus, -se** *crocus*, III11
die **Krone, -n** *crown*, III1
der **Kronleuchter, -** *chandelier*, III10
die **Krönungsfeierlichkeit, -en** *coronation festivity*, Loc7
die **Küche, -n** *kitchen*, I; *cuisine*, II
der **Kuchen, -** *cake*, I
das **Küchenfenster, -** *kitchen window*, III1
das **Kugelstoßen** *shot put*, II
kühl *cool*, I
die **Kühlbox, -en** *cooler*, III2
der **Kühlschrank, -̈e** *refrigerator*, I
kühn *bold, brave*, III7
der **Kuli, -s** *ballpoint pen*, I
der **Kultfilm, -e** *cult film*, III10
die **Kultur, -en** *culture*, Loc1
kulturbedingt *having to do with the culture*, III4
der **Kulturbeobachter, -** *observer of the cultural scene*, III10
kulturell *cultural*, III2
der **Kulturkalender, -** *calendar of cultural events*, III10
der **Kulturmuffel** *a person who ignores cultural events*, III2
der **Kulturschock** *culture shock*, III10
das **Kulturspiel, -e** *cultural event*, III10
die **Kulturstadt, -̈e** *city of great cultural significance*, III2
die **Kulturstätte, -n** *cultural sight*, Loc1
die **Kulturszene** *culture scene, art scene*, III2
der **Kummerbund, -e** *cummerbund*, II
der **Kummerkasten** *grief column (in a newspaper)*, III12
s. kümmern um *to be concerned about*, III6
der **Kumpel, -** *buddy*, III4
künden *to tell (of), herald*, III1
künftig *future, next*, III5
die **Kunst, -̈e** *art*, I
die **Kunstausstellung, -en** *art exhibition*, Loc1
der **Kunstdünger, -** *artificial fertilizer*, III9
Künstler(in), -/nen *artist*, III10
künstlerisch *artistic*, III6
künstlich *artificial*, III8
die **Kunstsammlung, -en** *art collection*, Loc10
der **Kunststoff, -e: aus Kunststoff** *made of plastic*, I

der Kurfürst, -en *elector (of a king)*, Loc10

kurios *strange*, III5

der Kurs, -e *course*, III11

die Kurve, -n *curve*, II

kurz *short*, I

der Kurzbericht, -e *brief report*, III3

kurzfristig *on short notice*, III5

kürzlich *recently*, III9

die Kusine, -n *cousin (female)*, I

die Küste, -n *coast*, II

lächeln *to smile*, III4

lachen *to laugh*, III2

lächerlich *ridiculous*, III6

der Lachs, -e *salmon*, II

der Lackschuh, -e *patent leather shoe*, II

der Laden, ¨ *store*, I

lag (*imperfect of* liegen), Loc1

die Lage, -n *setting, place*, III2

das Lammfleisch *lamb*, II

die Lampe, -n *lamp*, I

das Land, ¨er *country*, I; **auf dem Land** *in the country*, I

landen *to land*, III10

die Landkarte, -n *map of the country*, III1

die Landschaft, -en *countryside*, III1

die Landschaftsmalerei *landscape painting*, III1

die Landsleute (pl) *compatriots*, III8

lang *long*, I

die Länge, -n *length*, III7

langen *to reach*, III11; **es langt** *that's enough*, III2

langsam *slow(ly)*, II

längst *long ago, since*, III4

der Langstreckenlauf, ¨e *long distance run*, II

langt: das langt *that's enough*, III2

s. langweilen *to be bored*, II

langweilig *boring*, I

der Lappen, - (coll) *money*, III3

der Lärm *noise*, II

las (*imperfect of* lesen), III6

lassen *to let, allow*, II; **er/sie lässt** *he/she lets*, II; **Lass mich mal ...** *Let me...*, II

lässig *casual*, I

der Laster, - *truck*, III5

der Lastkraftwagen (Lkw), - *truck*, II

der Lastwagen, - *truck*, III9

Latein *Latin*, I

der Lateinmuffel, - *a person who does not like Latin*, III12

die Latzhose, -n *bib pants*, III3

der Lauf, ¨e *run*, II; **der 100-Meter-Lauf** *the 100-meter dash*, II

laufen *to run*, II; **er/sie läuft** *he/she runs*, II; **Was läuft im Fernsehen?** *What's on TV?*, II

die Laune *mood*, III3

laut *loud*, III8

lauten *to sound, read*, III3

läuten *to ring*, III4

lauter: vor lauter ... *because of pure...*, III5

lautlos *soundless, silent*, III2

der Lautstärkeregler, - *volume control*, II

das Leben *life*, II

lebendig *lively*, III7

die Lebensaufgabe, -n *life-work*, III1

die Lebensfreude *joy of living*, III3

die Lebensgewohnheit, -en *lifelong habit*, III8

die Lebensgröße *life-size, actual-size*, III10

das Lebensjahr, -e *age*, III5

der Lebenslauf, ¨e *curriculum vitae*, III11

die Lebensmittel (pl) *groceries*, I

der Lebensmittelfilialbetrieb, -e *grocery store branch*, III11

das Lebensmittelgeschäft, -e *grocery store*, III9

Lebensmittelkontrolleur(in), -e/nen *health inspector*, III12

der Lebenspartner, - *partner (to share one's life with)*, III11

der Lebensraum *living space*, III5

die Lebensweise *way of life*, III11

die Lebenswelt *world one lives in*, III10

die Leber *liver*, III1

der Leberkäs (*a Bavarian specialty*), I

die Leberwurst *liverwurst*, III2

lebhaft *lively*, III6

leblos *lifeless, inanimate*, III10

leck werden *to spring a leak*, III9

lecker *tasty, delicious*, I

das Leder *leather*, I

die Lederhose, -n *leather pants*, III8

die Lederjacke, -n *leather jacket*, II

leer *empty*, III1

leeren *to empty*, III7

legen *to lay*, Loc1; **Wert legen auf** (acc) *to consider important*, III11

legendär *legendary*, Loc 1

die Lehre *apprenticeship*, III4; *instruction*, III11

Lehrer(in), -/nen *teacher*, I

der Lehrplan, ¨e *teaching curriculum*, III9

die Lehrstelle, -n *apprenticeship*, III4

der Leib, -er *body*, III7

leicht *easy, simple*, II; *light*, II

die Leichtathletik *track and field*, II

das Leid *harm, injury*, III2; **Es tut mir Leid.** *I'm sorry.*, I

leiden: Das kann ich nicht leiden! *I can't stand that!*, III4

leider *unfortunately*, I; **Ich kann leider nicht.** *Sorry, I can't.*, I; **Das ist leider so.** *That's the way it is unfortunately.*, II; **Ich hab leider nur ...** *I only have...*, II

das Leinen, - *linen*, II

leise *soft, lightly*, III2

leisten: s. leisten *to afford*, III7; ganze Arbeit leisten *to do a complete job*, III7

s. leisten können *to be able to afford*, III7

die Leistung, -en *service, effort*, III2; *benefit*, III11

die Leistungsfähigkeit *efficiency*, III3

der Leistungskurs, -e *special course (at a Gymnasium)*, III11

leiten *to guide, lead*, III10

der Leiter, - *leader*, III9

die Leitung, -en *direction*, Loc4

die Lektion, -en *lesson*, III4

die Lektüre, -n *reading*, III1

lenken *to steer*, III3

lernen *to learn, study*, III3; kennen lernen *to get to know*, III2

lesen *to read*, I; **er/sie liest** *he/she reads*, I

Leser(in), -/nen *reader*, III2

der Leserbrief, -e *letter (to the editor)*, III1

letzt- *last*, I; **letztes Wochenende** *last weekend*, I

die Leute (pl) *people*, I

das Licht, -er *light, lamp*, III8

das Lichtbild, -er *photograph*, III11

der Lichtschutzfaktor, -en *sun protection factor*, II

lieb *dear*, III2

lieben *to love*, III3

liebenswürdig *charming, kind*, III7

lieber: lieber mögen *to prefer*, I

der Liebesfilm, -e *romance*, I

der Liebesroman, -e *romance novel*, I

Lieblings- *favorite*, I

liebst: Ich würde am liebsten ... *I would rather...*, II

das Lied, -er *song*, I

liegen *to lie (on)*, III1

liegen an (dat) *to depend on*, III1

die Liegewiese, -n *lawn for relaxing and sunning*, II

die Limo, -s (Limonade, -n) *lemon drink*, I

die Linie, -n *line*, III2; **Linie: in erster Linie** *primarily*, III7

link-, *left*, III2

die Lippe, -n *lip*, III10

die Liste, -n *list*, III1

der Liter, - *liter*, I

literarisch *literary*, III10

die Literatur *literature*, III10

die Litfaßsäule, -n *advertising column*, III7

der Lkw=Lastkraftwagen, - *truck*, II

loben *to praise*, III8

das Loch, ¨er *hole*, I

locken *to lure, tempt*, III3

locker *easygoing*, III8

der Löffel, - *spoon*, III2

die Loge, -n *(theater) box*, III10

Logisch! (Logo!) *Of course!*, III7
s. lohnen *to be worth it*, III5; **Es lohnt sich, das zu machen.** *It's worth doing.*, III8
das Lokal, -e *small restaurant*, II
los *detached*, III1; **Was ist los?** *What's going on?*, III3
lösen *to solve*, III4
loslegen (sep) *to get going*, III3
die Lösung, -en *solution*, III3
der Löwe, -n *lion*, III12
der Löwenzahn *dandelion*, III11
die Lücke, -n *blank*, III7
die Luft *air*, II
der Luftsprung, ¨e *jump*, III2
die Luftverschmutzung *air pollution*, III9
die Luftwaffe, -n *air force*, III5
die Lunge, -n *lung*, III9
Lust haben *to want to, to feel like*, III2
lustig *funny*, I
Lyriker(in), -/nen *lyricist*, III10

machen *to do*, I; **Das macht (zusammen) ...** *That comes to...*, I; **Gut! Mach ich!** *Okay, I'll do that!*, I; **Machst du Sport?** *Do you play sports?*, I; **Hausaufgaben machen** *to do homework*, I; **macht dick** *is fattening*, II; **Macht nichts!** *That's all right*, II
der Machtinstinkt, -e *instinct to seize power*, III5
das Mädchen, - *girl*, I
mager *meager, scrawny*, III6
magisch *magic(al)*, III1
mähen *to mow*, I; **den Rasen mähen** *to cut the grass*, III1
die Mahlzeit *meal, mealtime*, III10; **Mahlzeit!** *Bon appétit*, II
das Mahnschreiben, -n *reminder notice*, III12
der Mai *May*, I; **im Mai** *in May*, I
das Maiglöckchen, - *lily of the valley*, III11
der Mais *corn*, III1
mal (particle), I
das Mal, -e *time*, III1
malen *to paint*, III8
der Maler, - *painter*, III2
malerisch *picturesque*, III2
man *one, you* (in general), *people*, I; **Man hat mir gesagt, dass ...** *Someone told me that...*, II
manch- *some*, II
manchmal *sometimes*, I
die Mandelaugen (pl) *almond-shaped eyes*, III8

mangeln: es mangelt an *there is a lack of*, III9
die Manier, -en *style*, III8
manipulativ *manipulative*, III7
manipulieren *to manipulate*, III7
der Mann, ¨er *man*, I; *husband*, III12
das Männchen, - *little man*, III7
das Männlein, - *little man*, III7
männlich *male*, III7
die Männlichkeit *masculinity*, III7
die Mannschaft, -en *team*, II
das Manöver, - *maneuver*, III5
das Märchen, - *fairy tale*, III10
märchenhaft *legendary, fairy-tale like*, III7
die Margarine *margarine*, II
die Margeriten (pl) *daisies*, III11
die Marine *navy*
mariniert *marinated*, II
die Mark, - *mark* (German monetary unit), I
die Marke, -n *emblem*, III7
der Markt, ¨e *market*, III1
die Markthalle, -n *indoor market*, III11
der Marktplatz, ¨e *market square*, I
die Marmelade *marmalade*, II
der Marmor *marble*, III6
der März *March*, I
der Maschinenbau *mechanical engineering*, Loc10
das Maschinengewehr, -e *machine gun*, III5
maskieren *to mask*, III10
die Masse, -n *mass* (of people), III3
maßlos *boundless(ly)*, III7
die Mastente, -n *fattened duck*, II
die Materialien (pl) *materials*, III10
materialistisch *materialistic*, III8
materiell (adj) *material*, III11
die Mathematik=Mathe *math*, I
die Mauer, -n *wall*, Loc1
maulfaul *reserved, tight-lipped*, III3
mäuschenstill *very quiet*, III7
die Meckerecke, -n *complaint column* (newspaper), III7
meckern *to complain, nag*, III6
Mediaplaner(in), -/nen *media planner*, III12
die Medien (pl) *media*, III6
die Mediennützung *use of media*, III6
mediterran *Mediterranean*, II
die Medizin *medicine*, III11
das Meer, -e *ocean*, III1
der Meeresduft, ¨e *fragrance of the sea*, III7
das Mehl *flour*, I
mehr *more*, I; **Ich habe keinen Hunger mehr.** *I'm not hungry anymore.*, I
mehrere *several*, III6
die Mehrheit *majority*
die Mehrwegflasche, -n *reusable bottle*, III9
mein (poss adj) *my*, I
meinen: Meinst du? *Do you think so?*, I

meinetwegen *as far as I'm concerned*, III10
die Meinung, -en *opinion*, III4; **Meiner Meinung nach ...** *In my opinion...*, III6
die Meinungsäußerung, -en *expression of opinion*, III5
die Meinungsforschung, -en *opinion research*, III7
meist- *most*, III6
meistens *most of the time*, II
der Meister, - *master, champion*, III1
das Meisterwerk, -e *masterpiece*, III10
die Meldung, -en *announcement, report*, III8
die Melodie, -n *melody*, III3
die Menge, -n *a lot*, III8; **eine ganze Menge** *quite a lot*, III8
der Mensch, -en *human, person*, III3
das Menschenprodukt *human product*, III1
die Mentalität *mentality*, III11
merken *to notice, pay attention to*, III1
messen: Fieber messen *to take someone's temperature*, II; **er/sie misst** *he/she measures*, II
das Messer, - *knife*, III2
der Messerhieb, -e *knife blow*, III10
das Messingschildchen, - *brass tag*, III10
die Metapher, -n *metaphor*, III10
die Methode, -n *method*, III5
der Metzger, - *butcher*, I
die Metzgerei, -en *butcher shop*, I
mexikanisch (adj) *Mexican*, II
mich *me, myself*, I
mickrig *lousy*, III3
mieten *to rent*, III5
das Mikrofon, -e *microphone*, III10
die Milch *milk*, I
die Milchkanne, -n *milk jug*, III11
der Milchmann, ¨er *milkman*, III11
mild *mild*, II
das Militär *military, armed forces*, III5
die Militärakademie, -n *military academy*, III5
der Militärdienst *military service*, III5
militaristisch *militaristic*, III8
die Million, -en *million*, III11
der Millionär, -e *millionaire*, III12
die Mimik *mime*, III1
die Minderwertigkeit *inferiority*, III5
die Minderwertigkeitsempfindung, -en *feeling of inferiority*, III5
mindestens *at least*, III1
die Mineralien (pl) *minerals*, III3
das Mineralwasser *mineral water*, I
das Minikleid, -er *mini-dress*, III3
die Minute, -n *minute*, III6
mir *to, for me*, II; **Mir gefällt ...** *I like...*, II
mischen *to mix*, III3
miserabel *miserable*, I
Mist: So ein Mist! *Darn it!*, I
mit (dat prep) *with, by*, I; **mit dem Auto** *by car*, I

die Mitarbeit *cooperation*, III6
mitarbeiten (sep) *to cooperate*, III6
der Mitarbeiter, - *co-worker, colleague*, III2
die Mitbestimmung *co-determination*, III11
mitbringen (sep) *to bring along*, III1
miteinander *with one another*, III1
miterleben (sep) *to experience*, III9
mitfahren (sep) *to go along, come along*, III2
mitgeben (sep) *to give (to)*, III12
mitgebracht *brought along*, III1
mitgehen (sep) *to go along*, III10
mitgehört *overheard*, III12
das Mitglied, -er *member*, III5
die Mithilfe *cooperation*, III2
mitkommen (sep) *to come along*, I
das Mitleid *pity*, III3
mitmachen mit (sep) *to go along with*, III3
die Mitmenschen (pl) *fellow-men, neighbors*, III12
mitnehmen (sep) *to take along*, III2
mitsamt *including*, III10
mitschreiben (sep) *to write down*, III6
Mitschüler(in), -/nen *schoolmate*, III1
mitspielen (sep) *to play along, take part in*, III3
mittag: heute Mittag *this noon*, III1
das Mittagessen *lunch*, II
mittags *at noon*, III3
die Mitte *middle*, III2
die Mitteilung, -en *message*, III7
das Mittel, - *means, method*, III9
das Mittelalter *the Middle Ages*, Loc1
mittelalterlich *medieval*, III1
der Mittelpunkt *center*, III2
die Mitternacht *midnight*, III12
der Mittwoch *Wednesday*, I; **am Mittwoch** *on Wednesday*, I
mittwochs *Wednesdays*, II
mitziehen (sep) *to pull along*, III9
die Möbel (pl) *furniture*, I
möchten *would like to*, I; **Ich möchte noch ein ...** *I'd like another...*, I; **Ich möchte kein ... mehr.** *I don't want another...*, I
die Mode, -n *fashion*, I
die Modehochschule *fashion school*, III11
das Modell, -e *model*, III7
modern *modern*, I
die Modezeitschrift, -en *fashion magazine*, III3
modisch *fashionable*, II
das Mofa, -s *moped*, III4
mögen *to like, care for*, I; **Ich mag kein ...** *I don't like...*, II; **Das mag schon sein, aber ...** *That may well be, but...*, III4
möglich *possible*, II
möglicherweise *possibly*, III10
die Möglichkeit, -en *possibility*, III4

die Möhre, -n *carrot*, II
Moll (musical key) *minor*, III10
der Moment, -e *moment*, I; **Einen Moment, bitte!** *Just a minute, please.*, I; **im Moment gar nichts** *nothing at the moment*, I
der Monat, -e *month*, I; **einmal im Monat** *once a month*, I
monatlich *monthly*, III1
monoton *monotonous*, III11
der Montag *Monday*, I; **am Montag** *on Monday*, I
montags *Mondays*, II
das Moped, -s *moped*, I
der Mörder, - *murderer*, III10
morgen *tomorrow*, I
der Morgen, - *morning*, I; **Guten Morgen!** *Good morning!*, I; morgens *in the mornings*, III1
motivieren *to motivate*, III11
der Motor, -en *motor*, II
das Motorrad, ̈-er *motorcycle*, II
das Motto, -s *motto*, III12
die Moussaka *moussaka*, II
müde *tired*, II
die Mühe *trouble, pains*, III2
mühsam *with difficulty*, III8
der Müll *trash*, I; **den Müll sortieren** *to sort the trash*, I
die Müllabfuhr *garbage collection*, III11
der Müllberg, -e *mountain of trash*, III9
der Müller, - *miller*, III6
die Müll-Lawine *avalanche of garbage*, III9
die Mülltrennaktion *separation of garbage campaign*, III12
das Müllverhalten *attitude toward garbage*, III9
der Mund, ̈-er *mouth*, III2
der Mundschutz *mouth protection*, III3
die Münze, -n *coin*, I; **Münzen einstecken** *to insert coins*, I
murmeln *to murmer, mutter*, III10
das Museum, (pl) Museen *museum*, II
das Musical, -s *musical*, II
die Musik *music*, I; **klassische Musik** *classical music*, I
musikalisch *musical(ly)*, III8
Musiker(in), -/nen *musician*, III11
der Musikfanatiker, - *music fanatic*, III10
die Musikhochschule, -n *music conservatory*, III11
der Musikladen, ̈- *music store*, III1
der Musikliebhaber, - *music fan*, III10
das Musikpublikum *music audience*, III10
der Musikunterricht *music instruction*, III10
der Muskel, -n *muscle*, III7
muskulös *muscular*, III8
müssen *to have to*, I; **ich muss** *I have to*, I
müsste: Man müsste nur daran denken. *You would only have to think about it.*, III9

das Muster, - *pattern*, II
die Musterung, -en *recruitment physical*, III5
der Mut *courage*, III9
mutig *brave*, III8
die Mutter, ̈ *mother*, I
die Muttersprache, -n *native language*, III4
der Muttertag *Mother's Day*, I; **Alles Gute zum Muttertag!** *Happy Mother's Day!*, I
die Mütze, -n *cap*, II

Na ja, soso. *Oh, all right.*, II
Na klar! *Of course!*, II
nach (dat prep) *after*, I; **nach der Schule** *after school*, I; **nach links (rechts)** *to the left (right)*, I; **nach Hause gehen** *to go home*, I; **nach dem Mittagessen** *after lunch*, II
nachäffen (sep) *to imitate, ape*, III3
der Nachbar, -n *neighbor*, III4
die Nachbarschaft *neighborhood*, III4
nachdem (conj) *after*, III11
das Nachdenken *reflection, thinking over*, III6
nacherzählen (sep) *to retell*, III6
die Nacherzählung, -en *retelling*, III1
nachher *afterwards*, II
der Nachmittag, -e *afternoon*, I
nachmittags *in the afternoon*, III4
nachplappern (sep) *to parrot, imitate*, III7
die Nachricht, -en *message*, III2
die Nachrichten (pl) *the news*, II10
nachschicken (sep) *to send on, forward*, III12
nachsehen (sep) *to check on*, III3
die Nachspeise, -n *dessert*, II
nächst- *next*, II; **die nächste Straße** *the next street*, I; **die nächste Woche** *next week*, I
die Nacht, ̈-e *night*, III2
der Nachteil, -e *disadvantage*, II
der Nachtisch, -e *dessert*, II
nächtlich *nocturnal*, III2
nachts *nights, at night*, III12
nahe *near*, III9
Nähe: in der Nähe von *near to*, III8
nähen *to sew*, III3
nahm (*imperfect of* **nehmen**), III4
der Nährstoff, -e *nutrient*, III3
die Nahrung *nutrition*, III1
der Nährwert *nutritional value*, III3
naiv *naive*, III8
der Name, -n *name*, III2
nämlich *namely*, III2
nannte (*imperfect of* nennen), III4
narkotisieren *to drug*, III5
die Nase, -n *nose*, III8

nass *wet*, I
die Nation, -en *nation*, III8
der Nationalpark, -s *national park*, III1
die Nationalversammlung *National Assembly*, Loc7
die Natur *nature*, III2
naturbewusst *nature conscious*, III9
Natürlich! *Certainly!*, I; **natürlich** *natural*, II8
die Naturseife, -n *soap with natural ingredients*, III9
die Natursendung, -en *nature program*, II
der Nebel *fog*, III5
der Nebelstreif *streak of mist*, III2
neben (acc, dat prep) *next to*, II
nebenan *close by*, Loc7
der Nebensatz, ¨e *dependent clause*, III4
Nebensitzer(in), -/nen *neighbor*, III10
nebenstehend *accompanying*, III3
die Nebenumstände (pl) *minor details*, III1
das Nebenzimmer, - *adjoining room*, III12
negativ *negative*, III1
nehmen *to take*, I; **er/sie nimmt** *he/she takes*, I; **Ich nehme ...** *I'll take...*, I
nein *no*, I
die Nelke, -n *carnation*, III11
nennen *to name*, III1
nerven: Es nervt mich, dass ... *It gets on my nerves that...*, III7
nett *nice*, III8
neu *new*, I
neugierig *curious*, II
die Neuigkeit, -en *most recent event*, III6
neulich *the other day*, III1
nicht *not*, I; **Nicht besonders.** *Not really (especially).*, I; **nicht gern haben** *to dislike*, I; **Ich nicht.** *I don't.*, I
nicht nur ... sondern auch *not only... but also*, III4
Nichtraucher(in), -/nen *nonsmoker*, II
nichts *nothing*, I; **Nichts mehr, danke!** *Nothing else, thanks!*, I
nicken *to nod*, III4
nie *never*, I
nieder *down*, III5
nieder (adj) *low, base*, III5
die Niederlande *the Netherlands*, III1
niemand *no one*, III10
die Niete, -n *failure* (in a subject), III12
nikotinarm *low in nicotine*, III7
nimmermehr *by no means, never again*, III5
das Niveau, -s *level*, III12
nobel *noble*, III10
noch *yet, still*, I; **Haben Sie noch einen Wunsch?** *Would you like anything else?*, I; **Ich brauche noch ...** *I also need...*, I; **Möchtest du noch etwas?** *Would you like something else?*, I; **Noch einen Saft?** *Another glass of juice?*, I; **noch höher** *still higher*, II; **noch nie** *not yet, never*, II
nochmal *again*, III3
nochmals *once more, a second time*, III10
der Norden *north*, III2
die Norm, -en *norm, standards*, III7
normalerweise *normally, usually*, II
die Note, -n *grade*, I
notieren *to note, jot down*, III1
nötig *necessary*, III2
nötig haben *to need, require*, III11
die Notiz, -en *note*, III4
das Notizbuch, ¨er *notebook*, III1
notwendig *necessary*, III5
der November *November*, I
nüchtern *sober*, III12
die Nudel, -n *noodle*, III1
die Nudelsuppe, -n *noodle soup*, I
die Nuklearwaffen (pl) *nuclear weapons*, III11
null *zero*, I
die Nummer, -n *number*, III11
nur *only*, II
nützen *to make use of, use*, III5
nützlich *useful*, III6
die Nützung *utilization*, III6

die Oase, -n *oasis*, II
ob (conj) *whether*, II
oben *above*, III1
ober- *upper*, III4
der Oberbürgermeister, - *Lord Mayor*, III2
oberflächlich *superficial*, III6
obgleich *although*, III10
obig *above (-mentioned)*, III7
das Obst *fruit*, I
der Obst- und Gemüseladen, ¨ *fresh produce store*, I
obwohl (conj) *although*, III1
oder (conj) *or*, I
der Ofen, ¨ *oven*, I
offen *open*, III8; **offen stehen** *to be open*, III2
offenbar *obviously*, III12
die Offensive, -n *offensive*, III5
öffentlich *public*, III2
öffentliche Verkehrsmittel (pl) *public transportation*, II
offiziell *official*, III5
der Offizier, -e *officer*, III5
öffnen *to open*, III2
oft *often*, I
öfters *quite often*, III4
ohne (acc prep) *without*, III3; **ohne weiteres** *easily, readily*, III3;

ohne ... zu machen *without doing ...*, III3
ohnehin *in any case*, III12
ohnmächtig *passed out*, III1
das Ohr, -en *ear*, III11
die Ohrenschmerzen (pl) *earache*, II
der Ohrring, -e *earring*, II
das Ökobewusstsein *environmental consciousness*, III9
die Ökonomie *economy*, III7
der Oktober *October*, I
das Öl, -e *oil*, III9
die Olive, -n *olive*, III2
der Öltanker, - *oil tanker*, III9
der Olympiasieger, - *olympic champion*, II
die Oma, -s *grandmother*, I
der Onkel, - *uncle*, I
der Opa, -s *grandfather*, I
die Oper, -n *opera*, I
die Operette, -n *operetta*, II
die Opferbereitschaft *readiness for sacrifice*, III9
opfern *to sacrifice*, III5
Optiker(in), -/nen *optician*, III12
optimistisch *optimistic*, III9
optisch *optical*, Loc10
die Orange, -n *orange*, III3
das Orchester, - *orchestra*, III10
ordentlich *orderly*, III8
ordnen *to put into sequence, order*, III1
die Ordnung *order*, III1
das Organisationsprinzip *organizational principle*, III3
organisieren *to organize*, III2
die Orientierungsstufe *(beginning years of the Gymnasium)*, III4
originell *original*, III7
der Ort, -e *place; location*, III1; an Ort und Stelle *there and then*, III8
orthographisch *orthographic*, III7
örtlich *local*, III6
der Ortsname, -n *place name*, III2
der Ostblock *Eastern Bloc*, III11
der Osten *east*, III11
das Ostern *Easter*, I; **Frohe Ostern!** *Happy Easter*, I
das Ozonloch *hole in the ozone layer*, III9
die Ozonschicht *ozone layer*, III9

paar: ein paar, *a few*, I; ein paar Mal *a few times*, III1
packen *to pack, grab*, III1
die Packung *packaging*, III9
der Pädagoge *teacher*, III3
die Paella, -s *paella*, II
das Paket, -e *package*, III12
die Panik *panic*, III10

der Pantomime, -n *mimic*, III10
der Panzer, - *tank*, III5
das Papier, -e *paper*, III2
der Papierbeutel, - *paper bag*, III9
der Papierkorb, ̈e *paper basket, waste basket*, III9
die Paprika *bell pepper*, III1
das Parfüm, -e *perfume*, I
parfümiert *perfumed*, II
der Park, -s *park*, I; **in den Park gehen** *to go to the park*, I
die Parkanlage, -n *park*, III2
der Parkplatz, ̈e *parking spot, lot*, II
die Parkuhr, -en *parking meter*, III3
das Parlament, -e *parliament*, III11
die Parole, -n *slogan*, III5
die Partei, -en *(political) party*, III5
Partner(in), -/nen *partner*, I
die Partnerschaft -en *partnership*, III8; *sponsorship*, III9
partnerschaftlich *fair*, III8
die Party, -s *party*, I
passen *to fit*, I; **Der Rock passt prima!** *The skirt fits great!*, I
passend *fitting*, III7
passieren *to occur*, III1; **Das ist gerade passiert.** *It just happened.*, II
Passt auf! *Pay attention!*, I
die Patenschaft, -en *sponsorship*, III9
pauken (coll) *to study*, III10
die Pause, -n *break*, I
das Pausenbrot, -e *sandwich* (a school snack), II
das Pausenhofpalaver *schoolyard chatting*, III7
das Pech *bad luck*, I; **So ein Pech!** *Bad luck!*, I; **Was für ein Pech!** *That's too bad!*, II
die Pechsträhne, -n *streak of bad luck*, III3
die Peking Ente, -n *Peking duck*, II
die Pension, -en *inn, bed and breakfast*, II
perfekt *perfect*, III3
die Perle, -n *pearl*, III2
die Person, -en *person*, III1
der Personalausweis, -e *identity card*, III11
der Personalchef, -s *director of personnel*, III11
die Personifizierung, -en *personification*, III10
persönlich *personal(ly)*, III2
die Persönlichkeit, -en *personality*, III11
die Perspektive, -n *perspective*, III5
pessimistisch *pessimistic*, III9
die Pfandflasche, -n *deposit-only bottle*, III9
das Pfannengericht, -e *pan-cooked entrée*, II
das Pfd.=Pfund *pound*, I
der Pfefferstreuer, - *pepper shaker*, III2
der Pfennig, - (smallest unit of former German currency; 1/100 of a mark), I

pfiff rein (*imperfect of* reinpfeifen), III3
der Pfirsich, -e *peach*, II
die Pflanze, -n *plant*, III1
das Pflanzenprodukt, -e *vegetable produce*, III1
das Pflanzenschutzmittel, - *herbicide*, III1
der Pflegedienst *nursing*
der Pflegedienst *nursing service*, III5
die Pflicht, -en *obligation*, III5
das Pflichtfach, ̈er *obligatory subject*, III6
pflücken *to pick* (fruit), III11
das Pfund, - (Pfd.) *pound*, I
phantasievoll *imaginative*, I
Phantastisch! *Fantastic!*, II
die Philharmonie *philharmonic orchestra*, III10
Philosoph(in), -en/nen *philosopher*, III10
das Phosphat, -e *phosphate*, III9
die Phrase, -n *expression*, III5
die Physik *physics*, I
Physiker(in), -/nen *physicist*, III11
das Picknick, -s *picnic*, III2
picknicken *to picnic*, III2
der Picknickkorb, ̈e *picnic basket*, III2
die Pilotin, -nen *pilot*, III5
die Pilotin, -nen *pilot (female)*
der Pilz, -e *mushroom*, II
der Pilzsammler, - *mushroom gatherer*, III12
die Pizza, -s *pizza*, I
der Pkw, -s *car*, II
plädieren *to plea*, III5
die Plakatwand, ̈e *billboard*, III7
der Plan, ̈e *plan*, III2
planen *to plan*, III2
die Plastik *plastic*, III8
der Plastikbecher, - *plastic mug*, III9
der Plastikbeutel, - *plastic bag*, III9
der Plastiksack, ̈e *plastic bag*, III3
die Plastiktüte, -n *plastic bag*, III9
der Plastikumschlag, ̈e *plastic envelope*, III9
der Platz, ̈e *place, site*, II
plötzlich *sudden(ly)*, III4
der Plüschsessel, - *club chair*, III10
das Plüschtier, -e *stuffed animal*, III3
polieren *to polish*, II
die Politik (sing) *politics*, I
Politiker(in), -/nen *politician*, III11
politisch *political*, III5
der Polizist, -en *policeman*, III8
die Pommes (frites) (pl) *French fries*, II
der Pool, -s *swimming pool*, II
das Porträt, -s *portrait*, III12
positiv *positive*, III3
die Post *post office*, I; *mail*, III1
das Poster, - *poster*, I
PR-Berater(in), -/nen *PR-consultant*, III12
die Pracht *splendor*, III10
prächtig *splendid*, III1
prägen *to leave a mark*, III4
das Praktikum *apprenticeship, in-*

service training, III11
praktisch *practical(ly)*, III11
praktizieren *to practice*, III9
die Praline, -n *fancy chocolate*, I
die Präposition, -en *preposition*, III1
präsentieren *to present*, III10
präzis *precise*, III7
der Preis, -e *price*, III2
preisen *to praise*, III7
preisgünstig *cheap*, III7
das Preisschild, -er *price tag*, III1
preiswert *reasonably priced*, I; **Das ist preiswert.** *That's a bargain.*, I
die Presse (news) *press*, III6
Prima! *Great!* I
der Prinz, -en *prince*, III1
die Prinzessin, -nen *princess*, III4
die Priorität, -en *priority*, III11
privat *private*, III11
der Privatsender, - *private television station*, III7
das Privathaus, ̈er *private home*, II
die Probe: auf Probe *on a trial basis*, III5; auf die Probe stellen: *to put to the test*, III6
probieren *to try*, I
das Problem, -e *problem*, III3
problematisch *problematic*, III4
das Produkt, -e *product*, III1
die Produktion, -en *production*, III9
produktiv *productive*, III4
produzieren *to produce*, II
der Profanbau, -ten *secular building*, Loc4
Professor(in), -en/nen *professor*, III11
das Programm, -e *schedule of shows*, II
das Projekt, -e *project*, III12
propagandistisch *propagandist*, III5
der Prospekt, -e *brochure, pamphlet*, III1
Prost! *Cheers!*, II
protestantisch (adj) *Protestant*, III1
protestieren *to protest*, III9
der Proviant *provisions, food*, III2
provozieren *to provoke*, III3
das Prozent *percent*, III4
der Prozess, -e *trial*, III5
die Prüfung, -en *exam*, III5
der Prügelstreifen, - *brutal flick*, III6
prunkliebend *loving splendor*, Loc10
prunkvoll *stately, grand*, III1
der Psychologe, -n *psychologist*, III3
die Psychologie *psychology*, III4
das Publikum *public; audience*, III10
der Pulli, -s *pullover, sweater*, I
der Pullover, - *sweater*, I
der Pumpzerstäuber, - *pump spray*, III9
der Punker, - *punker*, III3
punkig *punk-like*, III10
Punkt: in diesem Punkt *in this matter*, III8
pünktlich *punctual*, III8
die Pupille, -n (eye) *pupil*, III2

putzen *to clean, shine,* I; **Fenster putzen** *to wash the windows,* I
das Putzmittel, - *cleaning agent,* III7

die Qualifikation, -en *qualification,* III12
die Qualität *quality,* III7
der Quark (a soft cheese similar to ricotta or cream cheese), II
Quatsch! *Baloney!,* III6
das Quecksilber *quicksilver, mercury,* III9
quer *across,* III10

das Rad, ̈er *bike; wheel,* II; **mit dem Rad** *by bike,* I; **Rad fahren** (sep) *to ride a bike,* II
das Rädchen, - *little wheel,* III7
radeln *to bicycle,* III9
der Radiergummi, -s *eraser,* I
das Radieschen, - *radish,* III1
radikal *radical,* III11
das Radio, -s *radio,* II
der Radwechsel, - *tire change,* III2
raffiniert *clever,* III7
der Rahmen: im Rahmen *in the scope of,* III7
die Rakete, -n *rocket,* III11
die Randgruppe, -n *fringe group,* III4
der Rang, ̈e (theater) *balcony,* III10
die Rangliste, -n *ranking list,* III11
die Rangordnung *pecking order,* III11
der Rasen, - *lawn,* I; **den Rasen mähen** *to mow the lawn,* I
das Rasierwasser, - *shaving lotion,* III7
die Rasse, -n *race,* III5
der Rassismus *racism,* III8
der Rat *advice,* III3; **Komm, ich geb dir mal einen guten Rat!** *Okay, let me give you some good advice.,* III3
raten (dat) *to guess* III1; *to give advice,* III4
die Ratesendung, -en *quiz show,* II
der Ratgeber, - *advisor, advice column,* III4
das Rathaus, ̈er *city hall,* I
ratlos *perplexed,* III10
der Ratschlag, ̈e *piece of advice,* III3
rauchen *to smoke,* II
das Rauchverbot *no-smoking regulation,* III6
rauh *tough,* III5

die Raumfahrt *space travel,* III11
der Raumfahrttechniker, - *space technician,* III11
das Raumschiff, -e *spaceship,* III7
raus=heraus *out, away,* III2
der Rausch, ̈e *intoxication,* III7
reagieren auf (acc) *to react to,* III1
die Reaktion, -en *reaction,* III2
das Realgymnasium, -gymnasien (type of a German high school), III11
realistisch *realistic,* III11
die Realität *reality,* III8
rebellieren *to rebell,* III3
recherchieren *to do research, collect facts,* III6
rechnen *to tabulate, calculate,* III2; rechnen mit *to reckon with,* III2
die Rechnung, -en *bill, invoice,* III1
das Recht -e *law, right,* III5; **Recht haben** *to be right,* II; **Recht geben: Da geb ich dir Recht.** *I agree with you about that.,* III4
recht- *right, right-hand,* I; **nach rechts** *to the right,* I
rechtlich *lawful,* III7
Rechtsanwalt(-anwältin), ̈e/nen *lawyer,* III11
die Rechtschreibung *spelling,* III12
recyceln *to recycle,* III9
der Redakteur, -e *editor,* III6
die Redaktion, -en *editorial office,* III6
die Rede, -n *speech,* III5
das Redemittel, - *(communicative) expression,* III4
reden *to speak,* III4
reduzieren *to reduce,* III9
das Reformhaus, ̈er *health food shop,* III3
das Regal, -e *bookcase,* I
die Regel, -n *rule,* III2
regelmäßig *regularly,* III3
regeln *to arrange,* III6
regelrecht *regular, regularly,* III2
die Regelung, -en *ruling,* III7
der Regen *rain,* I
der Regenschirm, -e *umbrella,* III9
der Regenschirmstock, ̈e *walking umbrella,* III11
die Regieanweisung, -en *artistic direction,* III11
regieren *to rule,* III5
der Regierende, -n *ruler,* III5
die Regierung, -en *government,* III5
regional *regional,* III10
registrieren *to register,* III7
regnen *to rain,* III1; **Es regnet.** *It's raining.,* I
das Rehfleisch *venison, deer meat,* III1
reich *rich,* III3
reicht: Es reicht. *That's enough.,* III12
der Reichtum, ̈er *wealth,* III1
Reife: die Mittlere Reife (name of a high school diploma), III4

reifen *to ripen, become mature,* III10
Reih: in Reih und Glied *in rank and file,* III7
die Reihe, -n *row; line,* III7
die Reihenfolge, -n *sequence,* III9
der Reihn (*poetic for* Reigen) *circle dance,* III2
der Reim, -e *rhyme,* III10
rein *pure, clean,* III3
die Reinigung, -en *cleaners,* II
s. reinpfeifen (sep) *to toss down,* III3
der Reis *rice,* II
die Reise, -n *trip, voyage,* III1
das Reisebüro, -s *travel office,* III2
der Reisemuffel, - *person who does not like to travel,* III2
reisen *to travel, take a trip,* III1
das Reiseziel, -e *travel destination,* III2
reißen *to tear,* III6
der Reißverschluss, ̈e *zipper,* II
reiten *to ride a horse,* III2
der Reiz, -e *charm,* III1
reizen *to entice, charm,* III2
die Reklame, -n *advertisement, advertising,* III7
der Rekrut, -en *recruit,* III5
relativ *relative(ly),* III2
das Relativpronomen *relative pronoun,* III4
relaxen *to relax,* III3
die Religion, -en *religion* (school subject), I
Rennen: das Rennen machen *to compete,* III2
renovieren *to renovate,* III8
reparieren *to repair,* III5
die Replike, -n *answer, reply,* III12
Reporter(in), -/nen *reporter,* III3
die Republik, -en *republic,* III1
reservieren *to reserve,* III8
die Residenz, -en *prince's residence,* Loc4
resigniert *resigned to, depressed,* III2
respektieren *to respect,* III5
der Rest, -e *remainder,* I12
das Restaurant, -s *restaurant,* II
restaurieren *to restore,* Loc 1
restlich *remaining,* III4
das Resultat, -e *result,* III8
revidieren *to revise,* III8
revolutionieren *to revolutionize,* III5
der Revolvergürtel, - *gun belt,* III7
die Rezension, -en *critique,* III10
das Rezept, -e *recipe,* III1
rhythmisch *rhythmic,* III7
der Rhythmus *rhythm,* III3
richten *to direct,* III12
s.richten an (acc) *to be directed at,* III7
richten: Wir richten uns nach euch. *We'll do whatever you want to do.,* III4
der Richter, - *judge,* III5
richtig *correct, proper(ly),* II
die Richtung, -en *direction,* III9

riechen *to smell*, III1
rief an (*imperfect of* **anrufen**), III4
riesig *huge*, III7
rigoros *rigorous*, III10
das **Rindersteak** (*beef*) *steak*, II
das **Rindfleisch** *beef*, II; **Rind schmeckt mir besser.** *Beef tastes better to me.*, II
der **Ring, -e** *ring*, II
der **Ringel, -** *ringlet*, II
die **Rippchen** (pl) *ribs*, III1
die **Rippe, -n** *rib* III1
riss (*imperfect of* reißen), III6
robust *robust*, III7
der **Rock, ⸚e** *skirt*, I; *jacket*, III4
rodeln *to sled*, II
roh *raw*, II
die Rolle, -n *role*, III1
der Rollstuhlfahrer, - *person in a wheelchair*, III2
der **Roman, -e** *novel*, I
romanisch *Romanic*, Loc4
die Romantik *Romantic period*, III1
romantisch *romantic*, III1
der Römer (*name of the city hall in Frankfurt*), I
römisch *Roman*, III6
rosarot *rose-colored*, III8
der **Rosenkohl** *Brussels sprouts*, III1
die **Rosine, -n** *raisin*, III1
rostfrei *free of rust*, III7
rot *red*, I; **in Rot** *in red*, I; rot gepolstert *upholstered in red*, III10
Rote Grütze (*red berry dessert*), II
der **Rotkohl** *red cabbage*, II
der Rotmarmor *red marble*, Loc4
die Route, -n *route*, III1
rüber=herüber *from there to here*, III1
die Rubrik, -en *column* III1
der **Rücken, -** *back*, II
der Rucksack, ⸚e *knapsack, backpack*, III3
die Rückseite, -n *reverse side* III1
rücksichtslos *ruthless*, III5
rufen *to call*, III12
die Ruhe *calm, quiet*, III4
die Ruhestätte, -n *place of rest*, Loc1
ruhig *calm(ly)*, II
der Ruhm, III10
rühmen *to praise*, III1
die Ruine, -n *ruin*, Loc10
rumstehen=herumstehen (sep) *to stand around*, III11
rund *round*, I
runden *to round (out)*, III8
Rundfunkmoderator(in), -en/nen *moderator on the radio*, III12
Rundfunksprecher(in), -/nen *radio announcer*, III12
der Rundgang, ⸚e *tour, walk*, III10
runzelig *wrinkled*, III4
russisch (adj) *Russian*, II
die Rüstung, -en *armor*, III5
das Rüstungspotential *armament capacity*, III5

S

der Saal, (pl) Säle *(large) room*, III10
das **Sachbuch, ⸚er** *non-fiction book*, I
die **Sache, -n** *thing*, III3
die Sachlichkeit *factuality*, III12
säen *to sow*, III10
der **Saft, ⸚e** *juice*, I
saftig *juicy*, III2
die **Sage, -n** *legend*, III10
sagen *to say*, I; **Sag mal ...** *Tell me...*, II; **Was sagt der Wetterbericht?** *What does the weather report say?*, I
sagenhaft *great*, I
sah (*imperfect of* **sehen**), III4
die Sahne, -n *cream*, III1
das Saiteninstrument, -e *string instrument*, III12
der **Sakko, -s** *business jacket*, II
der **Salat, -e** *lettuce; salad*, I
das Salatblatt, ⸚er *lettuce leaf*, III1
die Säle (pl) *(large) rooms*, III10
salopp *casual*, II
das **Salz** *salt*, I
salzig *salty*, II
der **Salzstreuer, -** *salt shaker*, III2
der Sammelbehälter, - *container*, III9
sammeln *to collect*, I
der **Samstag** *Saturday*, I
samstags *Saturdays*, II
die Samstagsausgabe *Saturday edition*, III11
sämtlich *all*, III8
der **Sandstrand, ⸚e** *sand beach*, II
sanft *soft*, III3
Sänger(in), -/nen *singer*, I
der Sängerwettstreit *contest of the minstrels*, Loc1
das Sanitätskorps *medical unit*, III11
saß (*imperfect of* sitzen), III4
satt *full*, III7
der Satz, ⸚e *sentence*, III1
der Satzanfang, ⸚e *beginning of a sentence*, III2
die Satzlücke, -n *blank*, III4
der Satzteil, -e *part of a sentence*, III4
sauber *clean*, II; sauber halten *to keep clean*, III9
die Sauberkeit *cleanliness*, III9
säuberlich *neat(ly)*, III6
die Säuberung *cleaning*, III9
sauer werden *to get annoyed*, III6
das **Sauerkraut** *sauerkraut*, II
der **Sauerstoff** *oxygen*, III9
saugen: Staub saugen *to vacuum*, I
die **Sauna, -s** *sauna*, II
die **saure Gurke, -n** *pickle*, III1
der **saure Regen** *acid rain*, III9
säuseln *to rustle*, III2
das **Schach** *chess*, I
schade sein um *to be a shame, waste*, III5
Schade! *Too bad!*, I
der **Schaden, ⸚** *damage*, III9

schädlich *harmful*, III7
der **Schadstoff, -e** *pollutant*, III9
schaffen *to accomplish, do, create*, III5
der **Schafskäse** *goat cheese*, III2
der **Schal, -s** *scarf*, II
s. **schämen** *to be ashamed of*, III8
scharf *sharp*, II; *spicy, hot*, II
der **Schatz, ⸚e** *treasure*, Loc1
schätzen *to estimate*, III10
die **Schatzkammer, -n** *royal treasury*, Loc10
schauen *to look*, I; **Schau mal!** *Look!*, II
das Schaufenster, - *display window*, III11
das Schaufensterspiegelbild, -er *image in the display window*, III11
das **Schauspiel, -e** *play*, II
Schauspieler(in), -/nen *actor*, I
die **Scheibe, -n** *slice*, III1
der **Scheibenwischer, -** *windshield wiper*, II
die **Scheidung, -en** *divorce*, III12
der **Schein, -e** *(money) bill*, III1
scheinen *to seem*, III5; *to shine*, I; **Die Sonne scheint.** *The sun is shining.*, I
der **Scheinwerfer, -** *headlight*, II
schematisch *schematic*, III4
schenken *to give (a gift)*, I; **Was schenkst du deiner Mutter?** *What are you giving your mother?*, I
scheußlich *hideous*, I
schick *smart (looking)*, I
schicken *to send*, III11
das **Schicksal** *fate*, III5
das **Schiebedach, ⸚er** *sun roof*, II
schief *suspicious*, III5; **schief gegangen** *went wrong*, III3; **schief gehen** *to go wrong*, III3
schien (*imperfect of* **scheinen**), III10
schießen *to shoot*, III5
das **Schiff, -e** *ship*, II
schildern *to tell, report, describe*, III2
schimpfen mit *to scold*, III4
der **Schinken, -** *ham*, II
das **Schisch-Kebab** *shish kebab*, II
der **Schlaf** *sleep*, III2
schlafen *to sleep*, II
schlaff *slack, lax*, III3
das **Schlafzimmer, -** *bedroom*, II
der **Schlag, ⸚e** *blow, knock*, III4
schlagen *to strike*, III5
das **Schlagwort, ⸚er** *key-word*, III2
die **Schlagzeile, -n** *headline*, III6
schlampig *sloppy*, III3
die **Schlange, -n** *line*, III5
schlank *slim*, II
schlappmachen (sep) *to quit, lose it*, III10
schlau *smart*, III12
die **Schlaufe, -n** *belt loop*, II
schlecht *bad(ly)*, I; **schlecht gelaunt** *in a bad mood*, II; **Mir ist schlecht.** *I feel sick.*, II

GERMAN-ENGLISH VOCABULARY **R65**

die **Schleife, -n** *loop, bow,* II
schlief (*imperfect of* **schlafen**), III10
schließen *to close,* III2
schließlich *at the end, after all,* III12
die **Schließung** *closing,* III5
schlimm *bad,* II
Schlittschuh laufen *to ice skate,* I
das **Schloss,** ¨er *castle,* III2
die **Schlucht, -en** *ravine,* III1
schlucken *to swallow,* II; **Ich kann kaum schlucken.** *I can barely swallow.,* II
schlug (*imperfect of* schlagen), III4
der **Schluss** *end,* III1; **zum Schluss** *finally,* III7; **Schluss machen** *to end one's life,* III1; **den Schluss ziehen** *to draw the conclusion,* III9
der **Schlüssel, -** *key,* III4
das **Schlüsselbein** *collarbone,* III1
die **Schlussformulierung, -en** *complimentary closing,* III7
der **Schlusssatz,** ¨e *final, crowning sentence,* III3
schmackhaft *tasty,* Loc7
schmalzig *corny, mushy,* I
schmecken *to taste,* III12; **Schmeckt's?** *Does it taste good?,* I; **Wie schmeckt's?** *How does it taste?,* I; **schmeckt mir nicht** *doesn't taste good,* II; **schmeckt mir am besten** *tastes best to me,* II
der **Schmerz, -en** *pain,* II
schmerzen *to hurt,* III4
s. schminken *to put on makeup,* III3
der **Schmuck** *jewelry,* I
der **Schmutz** *dirt,* III9
schmutzig *dirty,* II
der **Schnee** *snow,* I
das **Schneidebrett, -er** *cutting board,* III2
schneiden: s. die Haare schneiden lassen *to get your hair cut,* III3
schneien: Es schneit. *It's snowing.,* I
schnell *fast,* II
die **Schnelle: etwas auf die Schnelle machen,** *to do something in a hurry,* III8
die **Schnelligkeit** *speed,* III1
Schnitt: im Schnitt *on average,* III5
der **Schnittlauch** (sing) *chives,* II
das **Schnitzel, -** *cutlet* (pork or veal), II
der **Schnupfen** *runny nose,* II
schnuppern *to sniff, detect,* III7
Schnupperpreise *prices to attract shoppers,* III7
schnurren *to whir,* III7
schob (*imperfect of* schieben) *pushed* III10
schockiert *shocked,* III10
die **Schokolade, -n** *chocolate,* II
schon *already,* I; **Schon gut!** *It's okay!,* II; **schon oft** *a lot, often,* II; **Ich glaube schon, dass ...** *I do believe that...,* II
schön *pretty, beautiful,* I

die **Schöpfung** *creation,* III3
Schornsteinfeger(in), -/nen *chimney sweep,* III12
der **Schrank,** ¨e *cabinet,* I
der **Schrebergarten,** ¨ *community garden,* III1
schrecken *to scare,* III5
schrecklich: Wie schrecklich! *How terrible!,* III3
Schrei: der letzte Schrei *the latest fashion,* III3
schreiben *to write,* I
der **Schreibfehler, -** *spelling mistake,* III2
die **Schreibhilfe, -n** *writing aid,* III3
der **Schreibstil** *writing style,* III10
der **Schreibtisch, -e** *desk,* I
die **Schreibübung, -en** *writing activity,* III10
schreien *to scream,* III1
Schreiner(in), -/nen *cabinet maker,* III12
schreiten *to step,* III10
schrie (*imperfect of* schreien), III4
schrieb (*imperfect of* **schreiben**), III2
der **Schriftführer, -** *recorder, note-taker,* III1
schriftlich *written,* III9
die **Schriftsprache, -n** *written language,* Loc1
Schriftsteller(in), -/nen *author,* III4
schritt (*imperfect of* schreiten), III10
der **Schritt, -e** *step,* III2
schrumpfen *to shrink,* III11
schüchtern *shy,* III12
der **Schuh, -e** *shoe,* II
Schuhmacher(in), -/nen *shoemaker,* III12
der **Schulabschluss** *degree, diploma from school,* III4
der **Schulalltag** *daily school routine,* III10
der **Schulausflug,** ¨e *school trip,* III10
die **Schulbildung** *school education,* III11
schuld sein an (dat) *to be at fault,* III4
die **Schule, -n** *school,* I
Schüler(in), -/nen *student, pupil,* III1
der **Schüleraustausch** *student exchange program,* III6
der **Schülerausweis, -e** *student I.D.,* III10
der **Schülereinsatz** *student effort,* III9
die **Schülerkarte, -n** *student pass, ticket,* III10
die **Schülervertretung, -en** *student representation,* III6
die **Schülerzeitung, -en** *student newpaper,* III6
das **Schulfach,** ¨er *school subject,* III5
die **Schulfete, -n** *school party,* III6
der **Schulfreund, -e** *friend from school,* III1
das **Schulgebäude, -** *school building,* III6
das **Schulgelände** *school property,* III6

die **Schulgemeinde** *school community,* III12
der **Schulhof,** ¨e *schoolyard,* III6
schulintern *in-school,* III6
der **Schulkiosk, -e** *kiosk, snack stand,* III12
die **Schulleitung** *school administration,* III6
die **Schulsachen** (pl) *school supplies,* I
Schulsprecher(in), -/nen *student representative,* III6
die **Schultasche, -n** *schoolbag,* I
die **Schulter, -n** *shoulder,* II
das **Schulterblatt,** ¨er *shoulder blade,* III1
die **Schulung** *schooling,* III5
die **Schuluniform, -en** *school uniform,* III3
der **Schutz** *protection,* III9
schützen *to protect,* III9
der **Schutzfaktor, -en** *protection factor,* II
der **Schutzheilige, -n** *patron saint,* Loc4
die **Schwäbin, -nen** *Swabian,* III8
schwach *weak,* III6
die **Schwäche, -n** *weakness,* III12
schwächen *weaken,* III8
schwänzen *to cut class,* III5
schwärmen *to rave,* III12
schwarz *black,* I
schwatzhaft *talkative,* III8
schwebend *suspended,* Loc1
der **Schweif** *tail, train,* III2
schweigen *to be silent,* III2
das **Schwein, -e** *pig, pork,* III1
das **Schweinefleisch** *pork,* III1
das **Schweinekotelett, -s** *pork chop,* II
das **Schweinerückensteak, -s** *pork loin steak,* II
der **Schweiß** *sweat,* III7
Schweißer(in), -/nen *welder,* III12
der **Schweizer Käse** *Swiss cheese,* II
schwer *heavy; difficult,* III3
das **Schwermetall, -e** *heavy metal,* III1
die **Schwester, -n** *sister,* I
schwieg (*imperfect of* schweigen), III2
die **Schwierigkeit, -en** *difficulty,* III4
das **Schwimmbad,** ¨er *swimming pool,* I
schwimmen *to swim,* I
der **Schwimmverein, -e** *swim club,* III4
der **Schwindler, -** *cheater,* III10
schwingen *to swing,* III7
der **Sciencefictionfilm, -e** *science fiction movie,* I
der **Sciencefictionroman, -e** *science fiction novel,* I
der **See, -n** *lake,* II
die **See, -n** *ocean, sea,* II
segeln *to sail,* II
sehen *to see,* I; **er/sie sieht** *he/she sees,* I
sehenswert *worth seeing,* Loc1
die **Sehenswürdigkeit, -en** *place of interest,* III2
s. sehnen nach *to long for,* III7

die Sehnenzerrung *pulled tendon*, III1
sehr *very*, I; **Sehr gut!** *Very well!*, I;
   sehr gesund leben *to live in a*
   very healthy way, II
   seid: ihr seid *you* (pl) *are*, I
die Seide, -n *silk*, I
das Seidenhemd, -en *silk shirt*, II
die Seife, -n *soap*, II
   sein *to be*, I; **er ist** *he is*, I
   sein (poss adj) *his*, I
   seit (dat prep) *since*, II
   seitdem *(ever) since*, III4
die Seite, -n *page*, III1
die Seitenloge, -n *side balcony*, III10
   Sekretär(in), -e/nen *secretary*, III11
der Sektor, -en *sector*, III11
die Sekunde, -n *second*, III12
   selber *self*, III4
   selbst *self*, III6
   selbständig *independent*, III8
die Selbstbedienung *self-service*, III2
die Selbstbiographie, -n
   autobiography, III12
das Selbstdenken *independent*
   thinking, III5
das Selbstporträt, -s *self-portrait*, III1
das Selbstvertrauen *self-confidence*,
   III3
   selten *seldom*, II
   seltsam *strange*, III10
   seltsamerweise *strangely*, III12
die Semantik *semantics*, III7
die Semmel, -n *roll*, I
   senden *to send*, III7
der Sender, - *station, transmitter,*
   channel, II
die Sendung, -en *show, program*, II
der Senf *mustard*, I
   sensationell *sensational*, I
die Sensationspresse *tabloid press*, III6
der September *September*, I
   seriös *sound, reliable*, III6
   servierfähig *ready to be served*, III7
die Serviette, -n *napkin*, III2
der Sessel, - *armchair*, I
   setzen *to put*, Loc1
das Shampoo, -s *shampoo*, II
die Shorts (sing or pl) *pair of shorts*, I
   sich *herself, himself, itself, yourself,*
   themselves, yourselves, II
   sicher *secure*, II
   Sicher! *Certainly!*, I; **Ich bin nicht**
   sicher. *I'm not sure.*, I; **Aber si-**
   cher! *But of course!*, II; **Ich bin**
   sicher, dass ... *I'm certain that...*, II
die Sicherheit *security, safety*, III8
   sicherlich *certainly*, III12
die Sicht *visibility*, III7
   sie *she; it; they; them*, I
   Sie *you* (formal), I
der Sieg, -e *victory*, III5
   siegend *victorious*, III5
der Sieger, - *victor*, III5
die Silbe, -n *syllable*, III10
das Silber *silver*, II; **aus Silber** *made*
   of silver, II
der Silberstreifen, - *silver lining*, III9

sind: sie sind *they are*, I; **Sie**
   (formal) **sind** *you are*, I; **wir sind**
   we are, I
   singen *to sing*, III2
der Sinn *sense*, III12
   sinnlos *senseless*, III5
   sinnvoll *sensible*, III3
die Sitten und Gebräuche (pl) *customs*
   and habits, III4
   sittlich *moral, ethical*, III5
die Situation, -en *situation*, III11
der Sitz, -e *seat*, Loc7
   sitzen *to be sitting*, III2
die Sitzung, -en *meeting*, III8
der Skandal, -e *scandal*, III1
die Skepsis *scepticism, doubt*, III10
   skeptisch *skeptical*, III10
   Ski laufen (sep) *to ski*, III9
die Skipiste, -n *ski run*, III9
die Skizze, -n *sketch*, III1
die Skulptur, -en *sculpture*, Loc 1
der Smoking, -s *tuxedo*, II
   snobistisch *snobbish*, III8
   so *so, well, then*, I; **so lala** *so so*, I;
   So sagt man das! *Here's how to say*
   it!, I; **so genannt** *so-called*,
   III5
   so was *the like; like that*, III4
   so ... wie *as ... as*, II
   sobald *as soon as*, III3
die Socke, -n *sock*, II
   soeben *right now*, III12
das Sofa, -s *sofa*, I
   sofort *immediately*, III1
   sogar *even*, III9
der Sohn, ⸚e *son*, II
die Sojasprossen (pl) *bean sprouts*, II
   solange *as long as*, III9
   solch- *such*, III3
   Soldat(in), -en/nen *soldier*, III5
   sollen *should, to be supposed to*, I
   sollte *should*, III3
der Sommer, - *summer*, I
die Sommerferien *summer vacation*,
   III1
die Sonderausstellung, -en *special*
   exhibition, III10
   sondern *but*, III8
der Sonderteil, -e *special part*, III11
die Sonne *sun*, II
der Sonnenaufgang, ⸚e *sunrise*, III6
die Sonnenbrille, -n *sunglasses*, III3
die Sonnencreme *sun tan lotion*, II
die Sonnenmilch *sun tan lotion*, II
der Sonnenstich, -e *sunstroke*, II
   sonnig *sunny*, I
der Sonntag, -e *Sunday*, I
   sonntags *Sundays*, II
   sonst *otherwise*, III4; **Sonst noch**
   etwas? *Anything else?*, II
die Sorge, -n *worry*, III3
   sorgen für *to make sure that*, III9
  s. Sorgen machen *to worry*, III9
   sorgfältig *careful(ly)*, III1
   sortieren *to sort*, III9
   soundsovieltenmal: (zum-) *for the*
   umpteenth time, III10

der Souverän *king*, III7
   soviel *as much*, III10
   soweit *as far as*, III10
   sowie *and*, III2
   sowieso *in any case, anyhow*, III12
   sowohl ... als auch ... *...as well as...*,
   III1
   sozial *social*, III11
die Sozialarbeit *social work*, III1
die Sozialhilfe *welfare*, III11
das Sozialwesen *social system*, III11
   sozusagen *so to speak*, III6
die Spalte, -n *column*, III2
   spanisch (adj) *Spanish*, II
   spann (*imperfect of* spinnen), III7
   spannend *exciting, thrilling*, I
die Spannkraft *vitality*, III3
die Spannung, -en *tension, excitement*,
   III10
   sparen *to save money*, III3
der Spargel, - *asparagus*, III1
   sparsam *frugal*, III1
der Spaß, ⸚e *joke*, III6; *fun*, I; **(Tennis)**
   macht keinen Spaß *(Tennis) is no*
   fun, I
   spaßig *funny*, III10
   spät *late*, III2
   später *later*, III11
der Spätkommer, - *latecomer*, III10
   spazieren *to walk, stroll*, II;
   spazieren gehen *to go for a walk*,
   III3
der Spaziergang, ⸚e *stroll*, III4
der Speck *bacon*, III1
das Speerwerfen *javelin throw*, II
der Speicher, - *attic*, III12
die Speise, -n *food*, II
das Spektrum *spectrum*, III8
   spekulativ *speculative*, III4
   spekulieren *to speculate*, III4
die Spezialität, -en *specialty*, I
   spezifisch *specific*, III7
der Spiegel, - *mirror*, III10
   spiegeln *to mirror*, III11
das Spiel, -e *game*, I
   spielen *to play*, I
die Spielshow, -s *game show*, II
der Spinat *spinach*, I
   spinnen *to spin*, III7
das Spinnrad, ⸚er *spinning wheel*, III7
   Spitze! *Super!*, I
die Spitze, -n *top*, III6
der Spitzensportler, - *top athlete*, III7
der Spitzhut *pointed hat*, III10
   spontan *spontaneous*, III1
die Spore, -n *spur*, III7
der Sport *sports*, I; *physical education*, I
die Sportanlage, -n *sport facility*, II
die Sportart, -en *type of sport*, III2
das Sportgeschäft, -e *sports store*, III1
   sportlich *sporty*, II
die Sportmannschaft, -en *sport team*,
   III5
   Sportökonom(in), -en/nen *sports*
   scientist, III12
der Sportplatz, ⸚e *sports field*, III10
der Sportteil, -e *sports section*, III8

die Sportübertragung, -en *sports telecast*, II

der Sportverein, -e *sports club*, III4

der Sportwettkampf, ⸚e *sports competition*, III8

sprach (*imperfect of* **sprechen**), III3

die Sprache, -n *language*, III11

der Sprachexperte, -n *linguist*, III7

der Sprachforscher, - *linguist*, III3

der Sprachführer, - *dictionary, phrase book*, III3

sprachlich *linguistic*, III7

sprachlos *speechless*, III3

das Sprachrohr *mouthpiece*, III6

die Sprachschule, -n *language school*, III11

die Spraydose, -n *spray can*, III9

die Sprechblase, -n *speech bubble*, III3

sprechen *to speak*, II; **er/sie spricht über** *he/she talks about, discusses*, I; **Kann ich bitte Andrea sprechen?** *Could I please speak with Andrea?*, I

das Sprichwort, ⸚er *saying*, III12

der Spruch, ⸚e *saying, proverb*, III3

Spucke: Ihm blieb die Spucke weg. *He was dumbfounded.*, III10

das Spülbecken, - *sink*, I

die Spule, -n *spool*, III6

spülen *to wash*, I

das Spülmittel, - *dishwashing liquid*, III9

die Spur, -en *track, trail*, III1

der Staat, -en *country, state*, III5

das Staatswesen *political system*, III5

der Stab, ⸚e *bar*, III2

der Stabhochsprung *pole vault*, II

der Stabreim, -e *alliteration*, III10

der Stacheldraht, ⸚e *barbed wire*, Loc1

die Stadt, ⸚e *city*, I; **in der Stadt** *in the city*, I; **in die Stadt gehen** *to go downtown*, I

die Stadtansicht, -en *view of the city*, Loc10

die Stadtführung, -en *guided city tour*, III2

die Stadtmauer, -n *city wall*, III1

der Stadtplan, ⸚e *city map*, III1

der Stadtplaner, - *city planner*, III2

die Stadtrundfahrt, -en *city sightseeing tour*, II

das Stadttor, -e *city gate*, II

der Stahlhelm, -e *steel helmet*, III5

der Stamm, ⸚e *trunk, stem*, III3

stammeln *to stammer*, III10

stammen *to stem (from)*, III12

stand (*imperfect of* **stehen**), III10

ständig *constant(ly)*, Loc1

der Standpunkt, -e *standpoint*, III8

starb (*imperfect of* sterben), III1

stark *strong, robust*, I

die Stärke, -n *strength*, III12

stärken *to strengthen*, III3

starr *staring*, III10

starren *to stare*, III6

die Statistik (sing) *statistics*, III4

statt (gen prep) *instead of*, III10

stattdessen *in place of which*, III9

die Stätte, -n *place, sight*, III2

stattfand (*imperfect of* stattfinden), Loc7

stattfinden (sep) *to take place*, III1

stattgefunden *taken place*, Loc1

das Statussymbol, -e *status symbol*, III7

der Stau, -s *traffic jam*, III7

der Staub *dust*, I; **Staub saugen** *to vacuum*, I; **Staub wischen** *to dust*, II

der Staubsauger, - *vacuum cleaner*, III3

staunen *to marvel (at)*, III8

das Steak, -s *steak*, II

stecken *to put (into)*, III9

die Steghose, -n *stirrup pants*, II

stehen *to stand, be*, III2; **Das steht dir prima!** *That looks great on you!*, II; **Wie steht's mit ...** *So what about...?*, II; **stehen auf** (acc) *to like*, III11; **Wie stehst du dazu?** *What do you think of that?*, III6; **Wie steht's?** *How's it going?*, III3

stehlen *to steal*, III12

steif *stiff*, III10

steigen *to climb*, II

steil *steep*, III11

der Steinpilz, -e *cèpe*, III12

die Stelle, -n *position; job*, III1; **an deiner Stelle** *if I were you*, III3

stellen *to put*, III1; Stell deinem Partner Fragen! *Ask your partner questions.*, III1

das Stellenangebot, -e *job offer*, III11

der Stellenmarkt *job market*, III11

die Stellung, -en *position*, III12; **Stellung nehmen** *to take a position*, III6

die Stellungnahme *point of view*, III6

sterben *to die*, III7

das Stereo-Farbfernsehgerät, -e *color stereo television set*, II

die Stereoanlage, -n *stereo*, I

das Stereotyp, -e *stereotype*, III8

stets *always*, III6

das Steuer *steering wheel*, III5

Steuerberater(in), -/nen *tax consultant*, III12

das Stichwort, ⸚er *key word*, III3

stichwortartig *using key words*, III6

die Stichwortsammlung, -en *collection of notes*, III12

der Stiefel, - *boot*, I

stieg (*imperfect of* **steigen**), III4

stieß (*imperfect of* stoßen), III6

der Stift, -e *pencil*, III9

der Stil, -e *style*, II

still *quiet*, III8

die Stille *quietness*, III2

die Stimme, -n *vote; voice*, III4

stimmen *to be correct*, II; **Stimmt (schon)!** *Keep the change.*, I; **Stimmt!** *That's right! True!*, I; **Stimmt (überhaupt) nicht!** *That's not right (at all)!*, II; **Stimmt, aber ...** *That's true, but...*, II

stimmen *to tune* (an instrument), III10

stimulierend *stimulating*, III6

stinken *to stink*, III8

die Stirn, -en *forehead*, III7

das Stirnband, ⸚er *head band*, II

das Stockwerk, -e *floor*, III10

der Stoff, -e *material*, III9

stöhnen *to moan, groan*, III3

stolpern *to stumble, trip*, III1

stolz sein auf (acc) *to be proud of*, III8

stören *to bother*, III6

stoßen *to push, shove*, III6

Strafverteidiger(in), -/nen *lawyer for the defense*, III12

der Strahl, -en *ray*, III9

strahlen *to beam*, III8

die Strahlung *radiation*, III9

strähnig *in strands*, III3

der Strand, ⸚e *beach*, II

die Straße, -n *street*, I; **bis zur ...straße** *until you get to ... Street*, I; **in ...straße** *on ... Street*, I

der Straßenhang *(street) shoulder*, III2

der Straßenverkehr *street traffic*, III5

die Strategie, -n *strategy*, III5

der Strauch, ⸚er *bush*, II

der Strauß, ⸚e *bouquet*, I

strecken *to stretch*, III10

streicheln *to pet*, III11

streichen *to paint; to cross out*, III11

der Streicher, - *stringed instrument player*, III10

der Streifen, - *stripe*, II

der Streik, -s *strike*, III6

der Streit *quarrel, argument*, III4

streiten *to quarrel*, III2

die Streitigkeit, -en *quarrel*, III4

die Streitkräfte (pl) *armed forces*, III5

der Streitpunkt, -e *point of controversy*, III4

streng *strict*, III8

stressig *stressful*, III8

das Stroh *straw*, III6

der Strom *electricity*, III9

die Strophe, -n *stanza*, III10

die Struktur *structure*, III5

der Strumpf, ⸚e *stocking*, II

das Stück, -e *piece*, I; **ein Stück Kuchen** *a piece of cake*, I

Student(in), -en/nen *(college) student*, III5

die Studie *study, essay*, III8

der Studienplatz, ⸚e *enrollment slot*, III11

die Studienrichtung *course of study*, III11

studieren *to study, to attend a university*, III4

das Studium *college education, program of studies*, III5

die Stufe, -n *step*, III1

der Stuhl, ⸚e *chair*, I

stumm *silent*, III3

die Stunde, -n *hour*, III1

der Stundenplan, ⸚e *class schedule*, I

die Stupsnase, -n *snub-nose*, III8
stur *stubborn*, III8
stützen auf (acc) *to prop up* (one's arms), III4
suchen *to look for, search for*, I
Südafrika (das) *South Africa*, III6
der Süden *south*, III2
südlich *southern*, III2
super *super*, I
der Superlativ, -e *superlative*, III6
der Supermarkt, -̈e *supermarket*, I
supertoll *really great*, II
die surfen *to surf*, I
Suppe, -n *soup*, II
süß *sweet*, II
die Süßigkeiten (pl) *sweets*, III3
der Süßkram *sweet junk food*, III12
die Süßwaren (pl) *sweets*, III10
das Symbol, -e *symbol*, III1
sympathisch *nice, pleasant*, II
die Synagoge, -n *synagogue*, II
die Szene, -n *scene*, III7

das T-Shirt, -s *T-shirt*, I
tabellarisch *in tabular form*, III11
die Tabelle, -n *table, grid*, III1
die Tacos *tacos*, II
der Tag, -e *day*, I; **eines Tages** *one day*, I
das Tagebuch, -̈er *diary*, III1
die Tagebucheintragung, -en *diary entry*, III1
der Tagesablauf *daily routine*, III2
die Tageszeitung, -en *daily (newspaper)*, III6
täglich *daily*, III1
der Tagungsort, -e *meeting place*, Loc7
das Tal, -̈er *valley*, III1
das Talent, -e *talent*, III6
die Talkshow, -s *talk show*, II
die Tante, -n *aunt*, I
der Tanz, -̈e *dance*, III2
tanzen *to dance*, I; **tanzen gehen** *to go dancing*, I
Tänzer(in), -/nen *dancer*, III10
die Tasche, -n *bag; pocket*, II
das Taschenbuch, -̈er *pocket book*, III12
das Taschengeld *allowance*, III3
der Taschenrechner, - *pocket calculator*, I
das Taschentuch, -̈er *handkerchief*, III1
die Tasse, -n *cup*, III1
tassenfertig *ready to be served in a cup*, III7
tat (*imperfect of* **tun**), III10
tätig sein *to be busy, employed*, III11
die Tätigkeit, -en *activity*, III11
die Tatsache, -n *fact*, III6
tauchen *to dive*, II

der Tauchsieder, - *immersion heater*, III12
tausend *thousand*, III2
die Technik *technology*, III3
technisch *technical*, III10
technische(r) Zeichner(in), -/nen *technical artist*, III12
technologisch *technological*, III11
der Tee *tea*, I; **ein Glas Tee** *a glass of tea*, I
der Teer *tar*, III1
die Teigwaren (pl) *pasta*, III1
der Teil, -e *part*, III9
teilen *to divide, share*, III5
teilgenommen *taken part*, III6
teilnahm (*imperfect of* teilnehmen), III6
teilnehmen an (sep, dat) *to participate in*, III6
der Teilnehmer, - *participant*, III2
der Teilnehmerpreis *price for each participant*, III2
teilweise *partly*, III10
das Telefon, -e *telephone*, I
telefonieren *to call*, I
die Telefonkarte -n *phone card*, I
die Telefonnummer, -n *telephone number*, I
die Telefonzelle, -n *telephone booth*, I
der Teller, - *plate*, III2
das Tellergericht *meal*, III10
die Temperatur, -en *temperature*, II
Tennis *tennis*, I
der Tennisplatz, -̈e *tennis court*, II
der Tennisschläger, - *tennis racket*, II
die Tenorblockflöte, -n *recorder*, III12
der Teppich, -e *carpet*, I
die Terrasse, -n *terrace, porch*, II
teuer *expensive*, I
der Teufel, - *devil*, III6
der Text, -e *text*, III1
das Theater, - *theater*, I; **ins Theater gehen** *to go to the theater*, I
die Theateraufführung, -en *theatrical performance*, III10
die Theaterkarte, -n *theater ticket*, III12
das Theaterstück, -e *play*, II
die Theke, -n *counter, bar*, III10
das Thema, (pl) Themen *subject, topic*, III5
die Thermosflasche, -n *thermos bottle*, III2
der Thunfischsalat *tuna fish salad*, III1
ticken *tick*, III4
tief *deep*, III7
das Tier, -e *animal*, III9
Tierarzt(-ärztin) -̈e/nen *veterinarian*, III11
tierlieb *animal-loving*, III8
das Tierprodukt, -e *animal product*, III1
die Tiersendung, -en *animal documentary*, II
der Tilsiter Käse *Tilsiter cheese*, II
der Tintenkiller, - *chemical eraser*, III9
der Tip, -s *tip*, III8

tippen *to type*, III6
der Tisch, -e *table*, I
die Tischplatte, -n *table top*, III4
der Titel, - *title*, III2
Tja ... *Well...*, I
die Tochter, -̈ *daughter*, II
der Tod *death*, III2
der Todfeind, -e *arch enemy*, III5
der Tofu *tofu*, II
die Toilette, -n *bathroom, toilet*, II
tolerant *tolerant*, III4
die Toleranz *tolerance*, III4
toll *great, terrific*, I
der Tolpatsch, -e *clumsy oaf*, III12
die Tomate, -n *tomato*, I
Toningenieur(in), -e/nen *sound engineer*, III12
die Tonkassette, -n *audio cassette*, III4
die Tonne, -n *drum, container*, III9
das Tor, -e *gate*, III1
die Torte, -n *layer cake*, I
Tote, -n *dead person*, III5
der Tourismus *tourism*, III9
der Tourist, -en *tourist*, III2
Touristikfachwirt(in), -e/nen *tourism specialist*, III12
die Tournee: auf Tournee gehen *to tour*, III10
die Tradition, -en *tradition*, III10
traditionell *traditional*, III7
traf (*imperfect of* **treffen**), III7
tragen *to wear; to carry*, II; **er/sie trägt zu** *he/she wears with*, II
der Träger, - *strap*, II
das Trägerhemd, -en *camisole*, II
der Trainingsanzug, -̈e *track suit*, III3
trank (*imperfect of* **trinken**), III12
das Transportflugzeug, -e *transport plane*, III5
trat auf *came on stage*, III2
die Traube, -n *grape*, I
trauen (dat) *to trust*, III10
der Traum, -̈e *dream*, III11
träumen *to dream*, III10
der Traumjob, -s *dream job*, III11
traurig *sad*, I
die Traurigkeit *sadness*, III10
treffen *to meet*, III3
treffend *apt(ly)*, III12
das Treiben *activity*, III10
treiben: Sport treiben *to do sports*, III3
das Treibgas, -e *propulsion gas*, III9
der Trend, -s *trend*, III3
die Treppe, -n *staircase*, III1
das Treppenhaus, -̈er *well of a staircase*, Loc4
der Tresen, - *counter, bar*, III7
treu *faithful*, III11
die Trillerpfeife, -n *whistle*, III3
trinken *to drink*, I
trocken *dry*, I
das Trommelfell *ear drum*, III3
trommeln *to drum*, III4
trotz (gen prep) *in spite of, despite*, III1
trotzdem *in spite of that*, III1

trotzen *to be obstinate*, III2
trug (*imperfect of* **tragen**), III2
trutzig *defiant*, III1
Tschau! *Bye! So long!*, I
Tschüs! *Bye! So long!*, I
das Tuch, ¨er *towel, rag*, III1
die Tulpe, -n *tulip*, III11
tun *to do*, I; **Leid tun: Es tut mir Leid.** *I'm sorry.*, I; **Tut mir Leid. Ich bin nicht von hier.** *I'm sorry. I'm not from here.*, II; **wehtun: Tut dir was weh?** *Does something hurt?*, II; **Tut's weh?** *Does it hurt?*, II
die Tür, -en *door*, III10
türkisch (adj) *Turkish*, II
der **Turnschuh, -e** *sneaker, athletic shoe*, I
der TÜV=Technischer Überwachungsverein *motor vehicle inspection agency*, III7
typisch *typical*, III10

die **U-Bahn=Untergrundbahn, -en** *subway*, I
die **U-Bahnstation, -en** *subway station*, I
das **U-Boot, -e** *submarine*, III5
übel *evil, bad*, III5
üben *to practice*, III4
über (acc, dat prep) *over; about; above*, III1
überall *everywhere; all over*, III1
überallhin *everywhere, in all directions*, III11
das Überarbeiten *revising*, III1
die Überbevölkerung *overpopulation*, III9
überdurchschnittlich *above-average, outstanding*, III4
übereinstimmen (sep) *to agree*, III7
überfallen *to overcome*, III10
überfiel (*imperfect of* überfallen), III10
überflüssig *superfluous*, III9
überfluten *to flood*, III7
überfragt sein *to not know*, III7
überfüllt *overcrowded*, III2
überhaupt *generally; absolutely, at all*, III1; **überhaupt nicht** *not at all*, I; **überhaupt nicht gern haben** *to strongly dislike*, I; **überhaupt nicht wohl** *not well at all*, II
überkam (*imperfect of* überkommen), III10
überkommen *to come over*, III4
überlegen *to consider*, III7
übermäßig *excessive*, III8
übermorgen *the day after tomorrow*, III7

übermütig *playful*, III10
übernächst- *the (one) after*, III10
übernachten *to spend the night*, II
der Übernachtungspreis *room rate*, III2
übernehmen *to take over*, III2
überprüfen *to reexamine*, III8
überraschen *to surprise*, III6
die Überraschung, -en *surprise*, III5
überreden *to persuade*, III8
überschätzen *to overestimate*, III7
überschreiten *to cross over*, Loc1
übersetzen *to translate*, III8
übertariflich: übertarifliches Gehalt *salary in excess of the agreed scale*, III11
übertragen *to transfer*, III1
die Übertragung, -en *telecast, transmission*, II
übertreiben *to exaggerate*, III3
übertrieben *exaggerated*, III7
übertrumpfen *to surpass*, III5
überzeugen *to convince*, III2
üblich *usual*, III9
übrig sein *to be left over*, III5
übrigens *by the way*, III1
die Übung, -en *exercise*, III1
die **Uhr, -en** *watch, clock*, III2; **um ein Uhr** *at one o'clock*, I; **Wie viel Uhr ist es?** *What time is it?*, I; **Um wie viel Uhr?** *At what time?*, I
um (acc prep) *at; around*, II
um ... zu machen *in order to do ...*, III3
umarmen *to embrace*, III8
umbenannt *renamed*, III4
die Umfrage, -n *survey, poll*, III3
die Umgangsform, -en *manners*, III11
umgebunden *tied around*, III12
die Umgebung, -en *surrounding area*, II
umgekehrt *vice-versa*, III5
umher *around, on all sides*, III12
umschalten (sep) *to switch over*, III7
der Umschlag, ¨e *envelope*, III12
umschreiben (sep) *to rewrite, rework*, III3
s. **umsehen** (sep) *to look around*, III10
umso: umso besser *the better*, III7
umstellen (sep) *to transpose*, III3
umtauschen (sep) *to exchange*, III1
die Umverpackung *outer wrappings*, III9
umwandeln (sep) *to change*, III6
umwechseln (sep) *to change (money)*, III1
die **Umwelt** *environment*, II
umweltbewusst *environmentally conscious*, III8
das Umweltbewusstsein *environmental consciousness*, III9
umweltfreundlich *environmentally safe*, III9
das Umweltgift *environmental poisoning*, III9

der Umweltheini, -s *environmental fanatic*, III8
Umweltökonom(in), -en/nen *environmental scientist*, III12
der Umweltschaden, ¨ *environmental damage*, III9
umweltschädlich *harmful to the environment*, III9
der **Umweltschutz** *environmental protection*, III9
die Umweltsünde, -n *sin against the environment*, III9
der Umweltverschmutzer, - *polluter*, III9
die Umweltverschmutzung *pollution*, III9
das Umweltzeichen *environmental logo*, III9
unabhängig sein *to be independent*, III5
unangenehm *unpleasant*, III1
unbedingt *absolutely, by all means*, III1; **Nicht unbedingt!** *Not entirely! Not necessarily!*, II
unbefriedigend *unsatisfactory*, III9
unbegrenzt *unlimited*, III8
das Unbehagen *discomfort*, III7
Unbekannte, -n *unknown person*, III12
unbeliebt *unpopular*, III4
unbequem *uncomfortable*, I
unberechtigt *unjustified*, III3
unbeschreiblich *indescribable*, III11
und (conj) *and*, I
undeutlich *unclear*, III1
undiszipliniert *undisciplined*, III11
unendlich *infinite*, III8
unentschieden *undecided*, III11
unfähig *incapable*, III1
der **Unfall, ¨e** *accident*, III1
die Unfallquote, -n *accident rate*, III5
unfreundlich *unfriendly*, II
die Ungeduld *impatience*, III2
ungefähr *about, approximately*, I
ungekocht *unboiled*, II
ungenügend *insufficient*, III3
die Ungerechtigkeit, -en *injustice*, III5
ungewiss *uncertain*, III11
ungewöhnlich *unusual*, III6
unglaublich *unbelievable*, II
unglücklich *unhappy*, III4
unheimlich *weird, creepy*, III10
die Uni, -s=Universität *university*, III11
die Universität, -en *university*, III4
unkompliziert *uncomplicated*, III11
Unmenge: eine Unmenge *quite a lot*, III1
unmerklich *unnoticable*, III10
unmöglich *impossible*, Loc 1
uns *us*, I; *ourselves*, II; *to us*, II
unser (poss adj) *our*, II
der Unsinn *nonsense*, III7
die Unsinnsbildung, -en *nonsense word*, III7
unsympathisch *unfriendly, unpleasant*, II

unten *underneath, below*, III1
unter (acc, dat prep) *under*, III1
unter sich bleiben *to keep to oneselves*, III4
das **Unterbewusstsein** *subconscious*, III7
unterbrechen *to interrupt*, III5
die Unterbrecherwerbung *commercial interrupting a TV program*, III7
die Unterbrechung *interruption*, III7
unterbrochen *interrupted*, III7
unterdrücken *to oppress*, III12
untereinander *among one another*, III4
der Untergang *decline, ruin*, III5
untergebracht *quartered, housed*, III2
s. **unterhalten über** (acc) *to talk about*, III5
die **Unterhaltung, -en** *conversation; entertainment*, III6
unterhielt (imperfect of **unterhalten**), III4
die **Unterkunft,** ⸚e *accomodations*, III2
die Unterlage, -n *document*, III11
unternehmen *to undertake*, III2
der **Unterricht** *class, lesson*, III5
unterrichten *to teach*, III10
die Unterrichtsgestaltung *way of teaching*, III12
der Unterrichtsplan, ⸚e *lesson plan*, III10
der Unterrichtsstoff *subject matter*, III12
unterscheiden *to distinguish*, III4
der **Unterschied, -e** *difference*, III10
unterschiedlich *distinct, different*, III2
unterschreiben *to sign*, III5
die Unterschriftenaktion *collecting of signatures*, III9
unterstreichen *to underscore*, III1
unterstrichen *underscored*, III1
unterstützen *to support*, III6
die Untersuchung, -en *inspection, examination*, III8
unterwegs *on the way, underway*, III6
unterzeichnen *to sign*, III5
unumgänglich *unavoidable*, III7
unverdorben *unspoiled*, III2
unvergesslich *unforgettable*, III1
unverständlich *incomprehensible*, III1
unwahrscheinlich *incredible*, III1
unweigerlich *without fail, inevitable*, III10
unwirksam *ineffective*, III8
unzufrieden *dissatisfied*, III12
die Unzufriedenheit *dissatisfaction*, III12
der **Urlaub, -e** *vacation* (time off from work), II
das **Urteil, -e** *judgement*, III8
usw.=und so weiter *et cetera, and so on*, III1
die UV-Strahlen *UV-rays*, III9

die **Vanillemilch** *vanilla-flavored milk*, II
variabel *variable*, III2
variieren *to vary*, III8
der **Vater,** ⸚ *father*, I
väterlicherseits *on the father's side*, III8
der **Vatertag** *Father's Day*, I; **Alles Gute zum Vatertag!** *Happy Father's Day!*, I
der Veganer, - *complete vegetarian*, III1
der Vegetarier, - *vegetarian*, III1
vegetarisch (adj) *vegetarian*, III1
verabscheuungswürdig *detestable*, III5
s. verabschieden *to say goodbye*, III12
verächtlich *scornful*, III5
verändern *to modify, change*, III2
die Veränderung, -en *change*, III3
der Veranstalter, - *organizer*, III7
die **Veranstaltung, -en** *performance, show*, III6
verantwortlich *responsible*, III6
die Verantwortung, -en *responsibility*, III5
verantwortungslos *irresponsible*, III5
verbergen *to hide*, III7
verbessern *to improve*, III3
die Verbesserung, -en *improvement*, III9
verbieten (dat) *to forbid*, III4
verbilligen *to make cheaper*, III10
verbinden *to connect*, III1
die Verbindung, -en *connection*, III7
verborgen *hidden*, III7
verstoßen (gegen) *to infringe (upon)*, III7
verboten *forbidden*, III5
verbracht *spent*, III1
verbrannt *burned*, III2
verbrauchen *to consume, use up*, III9
der **Verbraucher, -** *consumer*, III7
das Verbraucherprodukt, -e *consumer product*, III9
verbreiten *to spread*, III8
s. **verbrennen** *to burn oneself*, III1
verbringen *to spend (time)*, I
der Verbund *composite*, III9
der Verdacht *suspicion*, III2
verdanken (dat) *to owe, be indebted*, III2
verderben *to spoil*, III5
verdienen *to earn*, III7
s. verdient machen *to prove one's worth*, III6
verdrängen *to displace, repress*, III6
verdrehen *to twist*, III5
der **Verein, -e** *association, club*, III5
vereinigen *to unite*, III8

vereint *unified*, III11
das Verfahren, - *method, procedure*, III11
verfolgen *to persecute, haunt*, III5
verfügen über (acc) *to have something at one's disposal*, III11
die Verfügung, -en *decree*, III11
verführen *to seduce*, III7
die Verführung, -en *temptation, enticement*, III7
vergangen- *past*, III5
die Vergangenheit *past*, III10
vergaß (imperfect of **vergessen**), III4
vergeblich *futile*, III10
vergehen *(time) passes*, III11
vergessen *to forget*, III4
vergleichen *to compare*, III7
verglichen *compared*, III5
das **Vergnügen, -** *pleasure, fun*, III10
vergrößern *to enlarge*, III9
das Verhalten, - *behavior*, III1
das **Verhältnis, -se** *relationship*, III4; *situation*, III11
verheiratet sein *to be married*, III4
verkaufen *to sell*, III6
Verkäufer(in), -/nen *salesperson*, III1
der Verkaufsladen, ⸚ *store*, III11
der **Verkehr** *traffic*, II
das **Verkehrsmittel, -** *means of transportation*, II
der Verkehrspolizist, -en *traffic policeman*, III11
der Verkehrsverbund *local transportation organisation*, III9
die Verkleidung *disguise*, III3
verkleinern *to make smaller*, III9
verkrampfen: die Hände verkrampfen *to clench one's hands*, III4
verkrampft *tense, rigid*, III4
verlangen *to demand*, III7
verlängern *to lengthen*, III10
verlassen *to leave*, III12
s. **verlassen auf** (acc) *to count on*, III5
der Verlauf *course*, III6
verlegen *to move to*, III10; *embarrassed, self-conscious*, III11
die Verlegenheit *embarrassment*, III11
verlegte *moved*, III10
die Verleihung, -en *bestowal, award*, Loc7
s. **verletzen** *to injure (oneself)*, II
die Verletzung, -en *injury*, III1
verliebt *in love*, III8
verlieren *to lose*, III2
verließ (imperfect of verlassen), III4
verloren *lost*, III2
vermarkten *to market*, III10
vermeidbar *avoidable*, III9
vermeiden *to avoid*, II
vermiesen *to spoil, ruin*, III1
vermissen *to miss*, III6
vermitteln *to mediate*, III12
vermögen *to be able to*, III1
vermuten *to suppose*, III8

vernünftig *reasonable, sensible,* III1; **vernünftig essen** *to eat sensibly,* II

veröffentlichen *to publish,* III6

verpacken *to wrap,* III9

die Verpackung, -en *wrapping,* III9

das Verpackungsmaterial *packaging material,* III9

verpesten *to poison, pollute,* III9

verpflichten *to enlist,* III5

verquer *against the grain,* III3

verraten *to disclose, betray,* III8

verreisen *to leave on a trip,* III1

verringern *to diminish,* III5

verrückt *crazy,* III3

versagen *to fail,* III4

die Versammlung, -en *assembly, meeting,* III6

verschieden *different,* I

verschmähen *to scorn,* III9

verschmutzen *to pollute,* III9

die **Verschmutzung** *pollution,* III9

verschwenden *to waste,* III9

verschwiegen *kept secret,* III2

verschwinden *to disappear,* III1

das Versehen *mistake,* III12

die Versetzung *promotion,* III12

die **Versicherung, -en** *insurance company,* III11

versorgen mit *to supply with,* III9

versperren *to block,* III5

verspielen *to lose,* III2

verspinnen *to use up by spinning,* III7

versponnen *spun,* III7

versprach (*imperfect of* versprechen), III7

versprechen *to promise,* III1

versprochen *promised,* III1

verstand (*imperfect of* verstehen), III7

verstanden *understood,* III1

verständigen *to communicate,* III8

die Verständigung *communication,* III11

verständlich *understandable,* III6

das Verständnis, -se *comprehension; sympathy,* III8

verständnisvoll *understanding, sympathetic,* III11

verstärken *to reinforce,* III8

verstaubt *dusty,* III12

s. **verstauchen** *to sprain,* II

verstecken *to hide,* III7

verstehen *to understand,* III3; **Ich verstehe mich super mit ihr.** *She and I really get along.,* III4

verstorben *late, deceased,* III2

verstoßen *to give offense,* III7

verstoßen (gegen) *to infringe (upon),* III7

der **Versuch, -e** *attempt,* III10

versuchen *to attempt, try;* **Versuch doch mal, etwas zu machen!** *Why don't you try to do something?,* III3

verteidigen *to defend,* III3

verteilen *to distribute,* III10

verteuern *to raise the price,* III7

der **Vertrag, -̈e** *contract, agreement,* III5; **einen Vertrag abschließen,** *to sign a contract,* III5

Vertrauen *trust,* III4

vertrauen (dat) *to trust,* III3

verträumt *dreamy, sleepy,* III10

vertraut *familiar, intimate,* III10

vertreten *to represent,* III6

verursachen *to cause,* III7

verurteilen *to condemn,* III5

die Verwaltung *administration*

Verwandte, -n *relative,* III1

verwehen *to die out,* III10

verwehren *to deny, prevent,* III10

das Verweilen *staying, lingering,* III2

verweilen *to stay,* III2

verwenden *to use,* III7

die Verwendung, -en *use, application,* III9

verwirklicht *realized,* III2

die Verwirrung, -en *confusion,* III1

verwöhnen *to spoil, pamper,* III8

das **Verzeichnis, -se** *listing,* III2

Verzeihung! *Excuse me!,* I; *Pardon me!,* II

verzichten auf (acc) *to do without,* III9

verzweifeln *to despair,* III4

die Verzweiflung *despair,* III11

der Vetter, -n *male cousin,* III12

das **Video, -s** *video film,* I

die **Videocassette, -n** *video cassette,* II

die **Videokamera, -s** *camcorder,* II

der Videoladen, -̈ *video store,* III7

der **Videorecorder, -** *video cassette recorder,* II

der **Videowagen, -** *VCR cart,* II

viel *a lot,* I; **viel zu** *much too,* I; **viel Obst essen** *to eat lots of fruit,* II

viele *many,* I; **Vielen Dank!** *Thank you very much!,* I

vielfältig *various,* III2

vielleicht *maybe, perhaps,* I

vielseitig *versatile,* III11

vierspurig *four-lane,* III9

das **Viertel: Viertel nach** *a quarter after,* I; **Viertel vor** *a quarter till,* I

die Villenanlage, -n *area of expensive homes,* III2

die Violine, -n *violin,* III10

Violinist(in), -en/nen *violinist,* III10

visuell *visual,* III10

das Vitamin, -e *vitamine,* III3

vitaminreich *rich in vitamins,* III7

der **Vogel, -̈** *bird,* III9

das Vogelgezwitscher *bird chirping,* III4

das Volk, -̈er *people,* III3

das **Volksfest, -e** *festival,* III10

die Volkshochschule, -n *adult education program,* III3

die Volksverdummung *brainwashing (of the public),* III6

voll *full,* III1

vollenden *to complete,* III2

Volleyball *volleyball,* I

vollführen *to carry out,* III2

völlig *completely,* III1

volljährig *of age,* III5

die Volljährigkeit *majority, full age,* III5

das Vollkornbrötchen, - *whole-wheat roll,* III1

die **Vollkornsemmel, -n** *whole wheat roll,* I

vollständig *complete,* III11

die Vollverpflegung *all meals included,* III2

vollwertig *nutritious,* III3

von (dat prep) *from, of,* II; **von 8 Uhr bis 8 Uhr 45** *from 8:00 until 8:45,* I; **von hinten** *from behind,* II

vor (acc, dat prep) *before, in front of,* II; **zehn vor ...** *ten till...,* I; **vor allem** *most of all,* III11; **vor kurzem** *recently,* III1

Voraus: im Voraus *beforehand,* III8

voraussichtlich *probable, probably,* III1

der Vorbehalt: Vorbehalte haben *to have reservations,* III12

vorbei *along, by, past,* III1

das Vorbereiten *preparing,* III1

s. **vorbereiten auf** (sep, acc) *to prepare for,* III11

die Vorbereitung, -en *preparation,* III10

die Vorbesprechung, -en *preliminary discussion,* III1

das Vorbild, -er *model, idol,* III11

der Vorfall, -̈e *incident, event,* III1

vorführen (sep) *to present, show,* III1

Vorgesetzte, -n *boss,* III11

vorgestern *day before yesterday,* I

vorhaben (sep) *to plan,* III3

vorhanden sein *to exist,* III10

der **Vorhang, -̈e** *curtain,* III10

vorher *before, beforehand,* III1

vorhin *before, a short time ago,* III10

vorig- *last,* III5

vorkommen (sep) *to happen,* III7

vorlesen (sep) *to read aloud,* III0

vorliegen *to be submitted*

vormachen (sep) *to present, model,* III9

der Vormittag, -e *morning,* III5

vorne: von vorne *from the beginning,* III5

der **Vorort, -e** *suburb,* I

der Vorsatz, -̈e *intention,* III3

der **Vorschlag, -̈e** *suggestion, proposition, proposal,* II; **Das ist ein guter Vorschlag.** *That's a good suggestion.,* II

vorschlagen (sep) *to suggest,* II

die **Vorsicht** *caution,* III9

vorsichtig *careful(ly),* III1

die **Vorspeise, -n** *appetizer,* II

das **Vorspiel, -e** *prelude, overture,* III10

vorspielen (sep) *to act out,* III7

der Vorsprung *lead, advantage,* III5

s. **vorstellen** (sep) *to present, introduce; to imagine,* III6

die **Vorstellung, -en** *impression, image*, III8; *performance*, III10; *idea, vision*, III11
der **Vortag** *the day before*, III1
der **Vorteil, -e** *advantage*, II
der **Vortrag, ⸚e** *lecture, presentation*, III2
 vorübergehen (sep) *to pass by, go past*, III2
das **Vorurteil, -e** *prejudice*, III4
 vorwiegend *primarily, prevailing*, III7
der **Vorwurf, ⸚e** *reproach*, III9
 vorziehen (sep) *to prefer*, II

das Wachs *wax*, III10
 wachsen *to grow*, III9
die Wachsfigur, -en *wax statue*, III10
die Wachsplastik, -en *wax sculpture*, III10
die **Wade, -n** *calf*, III1
die **Waffe, -n** *weapon*, III5
 wagen *to risk*, III10
der **Wagen, -** *car, truck, wagon*, II
die Wahl, -en *election*, III5
 wählbar *electable*, III5
 wahlberechtigt *entitled to vote*, III5
 wählen *to choose; elect*, II
die Wahlkapelle, -n *chapel where the emperors were elected*, Loc7
 wahnsinnig *insanely, extremely*, III5; **Wahnsinnig gut!** *Extremely well!*, II
 wahr *true*, III1
 während (gen prep) *during*, III10
die **Wahrheit, -en** *truth*, III6
 wahrheitsgetreu *faithful, true*, III6
 wahrnehmen (sep) *to perceive*, III7
 wahrscheinlich *probably*, I
die Währung, -en *currency*, III1
die Währungsunion *monetary union*, III1
das Wahrzeichen, - *landmark, symbol*, Loc7
der **Wald, ⸚er** *forest*, III9
die Waldecke, -n *edge of the wood*, III6
das **Waldsterben** *the dying of the forests*, III9
das Wandbrett, -er *poster board*, III9
 wandern *to hike*, I
die Wanderung, -en *hike*, III1
der Wanderweg, -e *hiking trail*, III2
 wann? *when?*, I
die Wanne, -n *bathtub*, III12
 war: ich war *I was*, I
 ward=wurde, III7
 wäre: Das wäre toll! *That would be great!*, II; **Das wär' nicht schlecht.** *That wouldn't be bad.*, II; **Viele Freunde haben, wäre mir wichtig.**

 To have many friends would be important to me., III11
die **Ware, -n** *product, ware*, III7
 warm *warm*, I
die Warnung, -en *warning*, III8
 warten auf (acc) *to wait for*, III1
der **Wärter, -** *attendant, guard*, III10
 warum? *why?*, I
 was für? *what kind of?*, I; **Was für ein Pech!** *That's too bad!*, II
 was=etwas *something*, II; **Ist was mit dir?** *Is something wrong?*, II
 was? *what?*, I; **Was noch?** *What else?*, I; **Was gibt's?** *What is it?*, II; **Was ist?** *What is it?*, II
die **Wäsche** *laundry, clothes*, II
 waschen *to wash*, II
 s. **waschen** *to wash oneself*, II
das **Waschmittel, -** *laundry soap*, III9
der **Waschtag, -e** *laundry day*, III1
das **Wasser** *water*, I
 wasserdicht *waterproof*, III7
die **Wassermelone, -n** *watermelon*, III1
der Wechselkurs *exchange rate*, III1
 wechseln *to exchange*, III1
 wecken *to awaken*, III7
der **Wecker, -** *alarm clock*, II
 weder ... noch *neither ... nor*, III10
der **Weg, -e** *path*, III8
 wegbleiben (sep) *to stay away*, III4
 wegen (gen prep) *because of*, III10
 wegfahren (sep) *to go, drive away*, III2
der Weggang *departure*, III1
 weggebracht *taken away, removed*, III1
 weggehen (sep) *to go away*, III4
 weggeworfen *thrown away*, III9
 weglassen (sep) *to omit, drop*, III6
 wegschmeißen (sep) *to throw away*, III9
der **Wehrdienst** *armed service*, III5
die **Wehrmacht** (sing) *armed forces*, III5
die **Wehrpflicht** *compulsory military service*, III5
 wehrpflichtig *liable to military service*, III5
die **Wehrübung, -en** *military maneuver*, III5
 wehtun (sep) *to hurt*, II
 weich *soft*, II
 weichen (dat) *to give way, recede*, III10
die Weide, -n *willow tree*, III2
 Weihnachten *Christmas*, I; **Fröhliche Weihnachten!** *Merry Christmas!*, I
 weil (conj) *because*, I
die **Weile** *while*, III11
der Weinbau *wine growing*, Loc4
 weinen *to cry*, III2
 weise *wise*, III7
 weiß *white*, I
das Weißblech *metal*, III9
die **Weißwurst, ⸚e** *(southern German sausage specialty)*, I

 weit *far; wide*, I; **weit von hier** *far from here*, I
 weiter *further*, III1
 weitergehen (sep) *to continue on*, III2
 weiterhin *as before*, III7
 weitgehend *extensive, largely*, III5
der **Weitsprung** *long jump*, II
 welch-? *which?*, I; **Welche Fächer hast du?** *Which subjects do you have?*, I
die Welle, -n *wave*, III5
die **Welt, -en** *world*, III11
 weltanschaulich *ideological*, III5
die Weltanschauung, -en *world view*, III2
der Weltbegriff *understanding of the world*, III5
 weltberühmt *world famous*, Loc10
 weltfremd *innocent, starry-eyed*, III12
der Weltkrieg, -e *world war*, III5
der Weltkriegsgefreite *private first-class in a world war*, III5
der Weltruf *international reputation*, Loc10
 weltweit *worldwide, global*, Loc1
 wem? *whom?, to whom?, for whom?*, I
 wen? *whom?*, I
die Wende, -n *turning point*, III10
 wenden *to turn*, III5
der Wendepunkt, -e *turning point*, III11
 wenige *few*, III6
 wenigstens *at least*, III1
 wenn (conj) *whenever*, II
 wer? *who?*, I; **Wer ist das?** *Who is that?*, I
die Werbeagentur, -en *advertising agency*, III7
die Werbeanzeige, -n *advertisement*, III7
die Werbeausgaben (pl) *advertising expenditures*, III7
der Werbeblock, ⸚e *block of advertising*, III7
die Werbebranche, -n *advertising industry*, III7
die Werbeeinblendung, -en *advertisement fade-in*, III7
der Werbefotograf, -en *commercial photographer*, III12
der Werbefunk *radio commercials*, III7
der Werbemacher, - *advertisement creator*, III7
 werben *to advertise*, III7
die **Werbesendung, -en** *commercial*, II
der Werbeslogan, -s *advertising slogan*, III7
der Werbespot, -s *commercial spot*, III7
der **Werbespruch, ⸚e** *advertising slogan*, III7
der Werbetexter, - *advertisement writer*, III7
 werbewirksam *effective advertising*, III7

die Werbewirtschaft *advertising industry*, III7
die **Werbung** *advertising*, III7
werden *will*, II; **er/sie wird** *he/she will*, II; **Ich werde mir ... kaufen.** *I'll buy myself...*, II
werfen *to throw*, III8
das **Werk, -e** *literary work*, III10; *factory*, Loc1
Werkzeugmacher(in), -/nen *tool maker*, III12
der Wert, -e *value*, III9
Wert: Ich leg viel Wert darauf. *That's real important to me.*, III11
wert sein *to be worth*, III1
die Wesensart *nature*, III8
wesentlich *substantial(ly)*, III9
weshalb? *for what reason?*, III4
wessen *whose*, III7
der **Westen** *the west*, III7
der **Western, -** *western (movie)*, I
das **Wetter** *weather*, I
der **Wetterbericht, -e** *weather report*, II
die **Wetterjacke, -n** *rain jacket*, II
der **Wettkampf, ⁻e** *contest, competition*, III8
der **Whirlpool, -s** *whirlpool*, II
wichen (*imperfect of* weichen), III10
wichtig *important*, III1
widerspiegeln *to reflect*, Loc 1
widersprechen *to contradict, oppose*, III5
die Widerstandsbewegung, -en *resistance movement*, III5
wie lange *how long*, II
wie? *how?*, I; **wie oft?** *how often?*, I; **Wie spät ist es?** *What time is it?*, I; **Wie steht's mit ...?** *So what about...?*, II; **Wie wär's mit ...?** *How would... be?*, II; **Wie war's?** *How was it?*, II; **wie viel?** *how much?*, I; **Wie viel Grad haben wir?** *What's the temperature?*, I; **Wie viel Uhr ist es?** *What time is it?*, I
wieder *again*, I; **wieder verwenden** *to use again*, III9; **wieder verwerten** *to recycle*, III9
wiedergeben (sep) *to repeat*, III8
wiederholen *to repeat*, III1
die Wiederholung, -en *repetition*, III8
Wiederhören *Bye!* (on the telephone), I; **Auf Wiederhören!** *Goodbye!* (on the telephone), I
Wiedersehen! *Bye!*, I; **Auf Wiedersehen!** *Goodbye!*, I
die Wiederverwertung, -en *recycling*, III9
wiegen *to weigh*, I
das **Wiener Schnitzel, -** *breaded veal cutlet*, II
die **Wiese, -n** *meadow*, III7
wieso? *why?; how?*, III8
der Wilderer, - *poacher*, III10
die **Wildlederjacke, -n** *suede jacket*, II
der **Wildwestfilm, -e** *wild west film*, II
der Wille *will, volition*, III2

willig *willing*, III2
willkommen *welcome*, III2
die **Windjacke, -n** *windbreaker*, II
windsurfen *to wind surf*, II
winselnd *whimpering*, III1
der **Winter** *winter*, I
das Wintersemester. - *winter semester*, III11
Winzer(in), -/nen *vintner*, III12
wippen *to rock*, III4
wir *we*, I
wirken *to cause, effect*, III6
wirklich *really*, I
die Wirklichkeit, -en *reality*, III7
wirksam *effective*, III7
die Wirkung, -en *effect, consequence*, III2
wirkungsvoll *effective*, III3
die **Wirtschaft** *economy*, III7
die Wirtschaftswissenschaft *applied study of business*, III11
das Wirtschaftswunderland, *country with an economic miracle*, III8
wischen *to wipe*, III7
wissen *to know* (a fact, information, etc.), I; **Das weiß ich nicht.** *That I don't know.*, I; **Ich weiß nicht, ob ...** *I don't know whether...*, II
die **Wissenschaft, -en** *science*, III11
Wissenschaftler(in) -/nen *scientist*, III9
wissenschaftlich *scientific*, III10
die Wissenschaftssprache, -n *scientific language*, III11
der Witz, -e *joke*, III6
witzig *fun, witty*, II
wo? *where?*, I
woandershin *to somewhere else*, III2
wobei *whereby*, III1
die **Woche, -n** *week*, I; **(einmal) in der Woche** *(once) a week*, I
das **Wochenende, -n** *weekend*, I
wofür? *for what?*, III1; **Wofür interessierst du dich?** *What are you interested in?*, II
woher? *from where?*, I; **Woher bist du?** *Where are you from?*, I; **Woher kommst du?** *Where are you from?*, I
wohin? *where (to)?*, I; **Wohin fahren wir?** *Where are we going?*, II
wohl *well*, III1; **Ich fühle mich wohl.** *I feel great.*, II
das Wohlbefinden *good health, well-being*, III3
wohnen *to live*, I
das **Wohnhaus, ⁻er** *residence*, II
die Wohnlage, -n *(residential) area*, III8
der Wohnsitz, -e *place of residence*, III5
die **Wohnung, -en** *apartment*, II
das **Wohnzimmer, -** *living room*, II
wolkig *cloudy*, I
die **Wolle** *wool*, II
wollen *to want (to)*, I

das **Wollhemd, -en** *wool shirt*, II
das **Wort, ⁻er** *word*, III4
das **Wörtchen, -** *short word*, III12
das **Wörterbuch, ⁻er** *dictionary*, I
wortlos *speechless*, III3
der Wortschatz *vocabulary*, III1
die Wortstellung *word order, syntax*, III1
worum: Worum geht es? *What's it about?*, III4
wozu? *why?; to what purpose?*, III3
wuchs (*imperfect of* wachsen), III10
das **Wunder, -** *wonder, miracle*, III10
wunderbar *wonderful*, III10
s. **wundern** *to be amazed*, III8
wunderschön *incredibly beautiful*, III2
das Wunderwerk, -e *miracle work*, III10
der **Wunsch, ⁻e** *wish*, I; **Haben Sie einen Wunsch?** *May I help you?*, I; **Haben Sie noch einen Wunsch?** *Would you like anything else?*, I
s. **wünschen** *to wish*, II; **Ich wünsche mir ...** *I wish for...*, II
würde *would*, II; **Würdest du gern mal ...?** *Wouldn't you like to...?*, II
würgen *to choke*, III3
die **Wurst, ⁻e** *sausage*, I
das **Wurstbrot, -e** *bologna sandwich*, I
die Wurzel, -n *root*, III10
würzig *spicy*, II
die Wut *rage*, III4
wütend *furious*, III1

Z

die Zahl, -en *number*, III6
zahlen (dat) *to pay*, III3; **Ich möchte/will zahlen!** *The check please!*, I
zahlreich *countless*, II
das Zahlungsmittel, - *means of payment*, III1
der **Zahn, ⁻e** *tooth*, II
Zahnarzt(⁻in), ⁻e/nen *dentist*, III12
die **Zahnpasta** *toothpaste*, II
die **Zahnschmerzen** (pl) *toothache*, II
Zahntechniker(in), -/nen *dental technician*, III12
die **Zehe, -n** *toe*, III1
die Zehenspitze, -n *tip-toe*, III10
der **Zehnkämpfer, -** *decathlete*, II
das Zeichen, - *sign*, III9
zeichnen *to draw*, I
Zeichner: technische(r) Zeichner(in), -/nen *technical artist*, III12
die Zeichnung, -en *drawing*, III3
zeigen *to show*, III1; es zeigt sich, dass ... *it appears that...*, III1

die **Zeit** *time*, I; **zur Zeit** *right now*, II
das Zeitalter *age, era*, Loc10
die Zeitausdrücke (pl) *time expressions*, III12
die Zeitform *grammatical tense*, III1
zeitgenössisch *contemporary*, I II12
Zeitlang: eine Zeitlang *for a while*, III4
zeitlich *temporal, time*, III11
die **Zeitschrift, -en** *magazine*, I
die **Zeitung, -en** *newspaper*, I
der Zeitungsbericht, -e *newspaper report*, III10
der Zeitvertreib *diversion, amusement*, III10
zelten *to camp out*, III2
das Zentrum, (pl) Zentren *center*, Loc1
der Zerfall *ruin, decay*, Loc1
zerknittert *wrinkled, crumpled*, III12
zerreissen *to tear apart*, III3
zerstört *destroyed*, Loc1
die Zerstörung, -en *destruction*, III9
zerstreut *absentminded*, III12
der Zettel, - *note*, III1
der Zeuge, -n *witness*, III11
das **Zeugnis, -se** *report card*, I
die Zeugniskopie, -n *copy of report card*, III11
ziehen *to move* (residence), III12; den Schluss ziehen *to draw the conclusion*, III9
das **Ziel, -e** *goal*, III11
die Zielgruppe, -n *target group*, III7
ziemlich *rather*, I
das **Zimmer, -** *room*, I; **mein Zimmer aufräumen** *to clean my room*, I
die **Zimmerantenne, -n** *indoor antenna*, II
der **Zimmermann, -leute** *carpenter*, III12
der **Zimt** *cinnamon*, I
zirka *approximately*, III2
das Zitat, -e *quotation*, III10
die **Zitrone, -n** *lemon*, I

zittern *to tremble*, III10
der **Zivildienst** *community service*, III5
der Zivilschutzverband *national guard*, III5
zog (*imperfect of* **ziehen**), III4
der **Zoo, -s** *zoo*, I
der Zorn *anger*, III6
zu *too; to*, I; **zu Fuß** *on foot*, I; **zu Hause helfen** *to help at home*, I; **zu bitter** *too bitter*, II; **zu viel** *too much*, II; **zu viele** *too many*, II; zu wenig *too little*, III9
der **Zucker** *sugar*, I
zuerst *first*, I
zufrieden *satisfied*, III2; zufrieden stellend *satisfactory*, III7
die Zufriedenheit, -en *satisfaction*, III11
der Zug, ⸚e *train*, III1
der Zugang *access*, III11
zugeben (sep) *to admit*, III3
zuhören (sep) *to listen to*, II; **Hör gut zu!** *Listen carefully!*, I
zukam (*imperfect of* **zukommen**), III11
zukneifen (sep) *to squeeze shut*, III4
zukniff (*imperfect of* zukneifen), III4
zukommen auf (sep, acc) *to be in store for*, III11
die **Zukunft** *future*, III11
zukünftig *(in) future*, III11
zulassen (sep) *to admit, approve*, III9
zuletzt *last of all*, I
zuliebe: der Umwelt zuliebe *for the love of the environment*, III9
zum=zu dem: zum Abendessen *for dinner*, II; **Zum Wohl!** *To your health!*, II 1
zunächst *for the time being*, III10
zunehmen (sep) *to gain weight*, III3
zunicken (sep) *to nod to*, III4
zurück *back*, III5
zurückbringen (sep) *to bring back, return*, III1
zurückgebracht *brought back*, III1
zurückhalten (sep) *to hold back, retain*, III5

zurückkehren (sep) *to return*, III12
zurückkommen auf (sep, acc) *to get back to*, III6
zurückweisen (sep) *to reject*, III9
zusammen *together*, III1
zusammenbasteln (sep) *to rig together*, III10
zusammenfassen (sep) *to summarize*, III6
die Zusammenfassung, -en *synopsis*, III3
zusammenhängen (sep) *to be connected*, III1
zusammenkommen (sep) *to come together*, III2
zusammenpassen (sep) *to go together, match*, III3
die Zusammensetzung, -en *composition*, III9
zusammensinken (sep) *to collapse*, III10
zusammenstellen (sep) *to compile, to plan*, III1
zusätzlich *additional(ly)*, III2
der **Zuschauer, -** *spectator*, III10
zuschicken (sep) *to send to*, III12
zuschlagen (sep) *to slam*, II
zuschließen (sep) *to close*, III6
der Zustand, ⸚e *state, condition*, III12
zustimmen (sep, dat) *to agree*, II
die Zustimmung, -en *consent, agreement*, III3
zutreffend *correct, applicable*, III2
zuverlässig *dependable*, III11
zuvor *before*, III7
zwar *indeed*, III10
der **Zweck, -e** *purpose, object*, III6
der Zweig, -e *branch*, III3
zweimal *twice*, I
zweit- *second*, III4
zweitens *secondly*, III11
die **Zwetschge, -n** *plum*, II
die **Zwiebel, -n** *onion*, I
der **Zwilling, -e** *twin*, II
zwischen (acc, dat prep) *between*, II

English-German Vocabulary

English-German Vocabulary

This vocabulary includes all of the words in the **Wortschatz** sections of the chapters. These words are considered active—you are expected to know them and be able to use them.

Idioms are listed under the English word you would be most likely to look up. German nouns are listed with the definite article and plural ending, when applicable. The numbers after each German word or phrase refer to the level and chapter in which it becomes active vocabulary. To be sure you are using the German words and phrases in the correct context, refer to the book and chapter in which they appear.

The following abbreviations are used in the vocabulary: acc (accusative), adj (adjective), dat (dative), gen (genitive), masc (masculine), pl (plural), poss adj (possessive adjective), sep (separable–prefix verb), and sing (singular).

a few *wenige*, III6
a, an *ein(e)*, I
able: to be able to *können*, I
about *ungefähr*, I
accept: to be accepted by *ankommen bei* (sep), III3
accessible to the physically challenged *behindertenfreundlich*, III2
accident *der Unfall, ¨-e*, III1
accomodations *die Unterkunft, ¨-e*, III2
accompany *begleiten*, III10
achieve *erreichen*, III6; *schaffen*, III5
achievement *das Werk, -e*, III10
acid rain *der saure Regen*, III9
across from *gegenüber*, II
action movie *der Actionfilm, -e*, I
active: to be active in *s. engagieren für*, III5
actor *der Schauspieler, -*, I
actress *die Schauspielerin, -nen*, I
address *ansprechen* (sep), III6
administration: school administration *die Schulleitung*, III 6
admire *bewundern*, III10
admit *eingestehen* (sep), III7; *zugeben* (sep), III3
advanced: to be advanced (person) *der Fortgeschrittene, -n*, II
advantage *der Vorteil, -e*, II; **to take advantage of** *ausnützen* (sep), III7
advertise *werben*, III7
advertisement *die Reklame, -n*, III7; *die Werbung, -en*, III7
advertising slogan *der Werbespruch, ¨-e*, III7
advice *der Rat*, III3; **to give advice** *raten* (dat), III4

afford: to be able to afford *s. leisten können*, III7
afraid: to be afraid *Angst haben*, III2; *fürchten*, III9
after *nach*, I; **after that** *danach*, I
afternoon *der Nachmittag, -e*, I; **in the afternoon** *am Nachmittag*, I
afterward *nachher*, II
again *wieder*, I
agree: to agree with *übereinstimmen mit* (sep), III7; *Recht geben* (dat), III4; **I agree with you on that!** *Da stimm ich dir zu!*, II; **Yes, I do agree with you, but ...** *Ja, ich stimme dir zwar zu, aber ...*, II
Agreed! *Einverstanden!*, II
air *die Luft*, II; **air conditioning** *die Klimaanlage, -n*, II; **air pollution** *die Luftverschmutzung*, III9
airplane *das Flugzeug, -e*, III
alarm clock *der Wecker, -*, II
alcohol: to not drink alcohol *keinen Alkohol trinken*, II
all *all-*, II; *sämtlich-*, III8
all right: Oh, (I'm) all right. *Na ja, soso!*, II
allergic: I am allergic to... *Ich bin allergisch gegen ...*, II
allowed: to be allowed to *dürfen*, II
almost always *fast immer*, III6
along: Why don't you come along! *Komm doch mit!*, I
aloud: to read aloud *vorlesen* (sep), III10
already *schon*, I
also *auch*, I; *auch schon*, II; **I also need ...** *Ich brauche noch ...*, I
alternate: alternate service *der Zivildienst*, III5
aluminum can *die Aludose*, III9
always *immer*, I
amaze: to be amazed *staunen*, III8

ambitious *ehrgeizig*, III8
among one another *untereinander*, III4
and *und*, I
anesthesiologist *Anästhesist(in), -en/nen*, III12
animal product *das Tierprodukt, -e*, III1
animal-loving *tierlieb*, III8
ankle *der Knöchel, -*, II
announcement *der Anschlag, ¨-e*, II
annoy: to get annoyed *s. ärgern*, III8; *s. aufregen* (sep), III7; *sauer werden*, III6
another *noch ein*, I; **I don't want any more ...** *Ich möchte kein(e)(en) ... mehr.*, I; **I'd like another ...** *Ich möchte noch ein(e)(en) ...,*, I
another (a different) one *ein(-) ander-*, II
ant *die Ameise, -n*, III9
antenna: indoor antenna *die Zimmerantenne, -n*, II
anything: Anything else? *Sonst noch etwas?*, I, II
apartment *die Wohnung, -en*, II
appear *aussehen* (sep), I
appetizer *die Vorspeise, -n*, II
applaud *klatschen*, III10
apple *der Apfel, ¨-*, I
apple cake *der Apfelkuchen, -*, I
apple juice *der Apfelsaft, ¨-e*, I
apprenticeship *die Lehre, -n*, III11
approximately *ungefähr*, I
apricot *die Aprikose, -n*, II
April *der April*, I
archery *das Bogenschießen*, II
area *die Gegend, -en*, III2
argue against *abstreiten* (sep), III5
argument *der Streit*, III4
arm *der Arm, -e*, II
armchair *der Sessel, -*, I

armed: armed service *der Wehrdienst,* III5; **armed services** *die Streitkräfte* (pl), III5
around *um,* II
art *die Kunst,* I
artificial *künstlich,* III8
artificial fertilizer *der Kunstdünger, -,* III9
as … as *so … wie,* II
as: as if *als ob,* III7
asparagus *der Spargel, -,* III1
assume *annehmen* (sep), III8
at *an, in,* II
at: at 8 o'clock *um 8 Uhr,* I; **at one o'clock** *um ein Uhr,* I; **at the baker's** *beim Bäcker,* I; **At what time?** *Um wie viel Uhr?,* I
athletic *sportlich,* II
attempt *der Versuch, -e,* III10; **to attempt, try** *versuchen,* III3
attention: to draw attention to *aufmerksam machen auf* (acc), III7; **to pay attention** *aufpassen* (sep), III3; **to pay attention to** *achten auf* (acc), III3
August *der August,* I
aunt *die Tante -n,* I
Austria *Österreich,* I
avoid *vermeiden,* II
avoidable *vermeidbar,* III9
away, at a distance *entfernt,* III2
awesome *stark,* I; **The sweater is awesome!** *Ich finde den Pulli stark!,* I
awful *fies,* III5; *furchtbar,* I

back *der Rücken, -,* II
background *der Hintergrund, ⸚e,* III6
bacon *der Speck,* III1
bad *schlecht,* I; **badly** *schlecht,* I; **Bad luck!** *So ein Pech!,* I; **It's too bad that …** *Es ist schade, dass …,* II; **That's not so bad.** *Nicht so schlimm!,* II; **That's too bad!** *Was für ein Pech!,* II; *Ach schade!,* II
bad: a streak of bad luck *die Pechsträhne,* III3
badly: to go badly *schief gehen,* III3
bag: paper bag *der Papierbeutel, -,* III9; **plastic bag** *die Plastiktüte, -n,* III9
baker *der Bäcker, -,* I; **at the baker's** *beim Bäcker,* I
bakery *die Bäckerei, -en,* I
balanced: well-balanced *ausgewogen,* III8
bald: to be bald *eine Glatze haben,* I
ballet *das Ballett, -e,* I
ballpoint pen *der Kuli, -s,* I
banana *die Banane, -n,* II
bank *die Bank, -en,* I

banker *der Bankkaufmann, -leute,* III11
bargain: That's a bargain. *Das ist preiswert.,* I
base: to be based on *beruhen auf* (acc), III11
basket: picnic basket *der Picknickkorb, ⸚e,* III2
basketball *Basketball,* I
bathroom *das Badezimmer, -,* II; **toilet** *die Toilette, -n,* II
battery *die Batterie, -n,* III9
battle *der Kampf, ⸚e,* III5
bay *die Bucht, -en,* II
be *sein,* I
be: to be, stand *stehen,* III2; **to be about** *s. handeln um,* III10
beach *der Strand, ⸚e,* II; **sand beach** *der Sandstrand, ⸚e,* II
bean (green) *die (grüne) Bohne, -n,* II
bearded *bärtig,* III10
beautiful *schön,* I
because *denn, weil,* I
because of *wegen,* III10
become *werden,* II
bed *das Bett, -en,* I
bed and breakfast *die Pension, -en,* II
bedroom *das Schlafzimmer, -,* II
bee *die Biene, -n,* III9
beef *das Rindfleisch,* II
before *bevor* (conj), III5
before: as before *weiterhin,* III7
beforehand *im Voraus,* III8
begin *anfangen* (sep), III11
beginner *der Anfänger, -,* II
behind: from behind *von hinten,* II
believe *glauben,* I; **You can believe me on that!** *Das kannst du mir glauben!,* II; **I do believe that …** *Ich glaube schon, dass …,* II
bell pepper *die Paprika,* III1
belong to *angehören* (sep, dat), III4
belt *der Gürtel, -,* I; **belt loop** *die Schlaufe, -n,* II
besides that *außerdem,* III9
best: Best wishes on your birthday! *Herzlichen Glückwunsch zum Geburtstag!,* I
better *besser,* I
between *zwischen,* II
beverage shop *der Getränkemarkt, ⸚e,* III1
bicycle *radeln,* III9; *Rad fahren* (sep), II; *das Fahrrad, ⸚er,* I; **by bike** *mit dem Rad,* I
bicycle racks *das Fahrrad-Depot, -s,* II
big *groß,* I; *weit,* II
bigger *größer,* II
bill, invoice *die Rechnung, -en,* III1
billboard *die Plakatwand, ⸚e,* III7
biodegradable *biologisch abbaubar,* III9
biologist *Biologe/Biologin, -n/nen,* III11
biology *Bio (die Biologie),* I
biology teacher *die Biologielehrerin, -nen,* I
bird *der Vogel, ⸚,* III9

birthday *der Geburtstag, -e,* I; **Best wishes on your birthday!** *Herzlichen Glückwunsch zum Geburtstag!,* I; **Happy Birthday!** *Alles Gute zum Geburtstag!,* I; **My birthday is on …** *Ich habe am … Geburtstag.,* I; **When is your birthday?** *Wann hast du Geburtstag?,* I
bitter: too bitter *zu bitter,* II
black *schwarz,* I
blanket *die Decke, -n,* III2
blazer *der Blazer, -,* II
blossom *aufblühen* (sep), III10
blouse *die Bluse, -n,* I
blow *blasen,* III9
blower: glass blower *Glasbläser(in), -/nen,* III12
blue *blau,* I; **blue eyes** *blaue Augen,* I; **in blue** *in Blau,* I
blueberry *die Blaubeere, -n,* II
board game *das Brettspiel, -e,* I
board: cutting board *das Schneidebrett, -er,* III2
boat *das Boot, -e,* II; **to go for a boat ride** *Boot fahren,* II
bologna sandwich *das Wurstbrot, -e,* I
bomber *der Bomber, -,* III5
bomber jacket *der Blouson, -s,* II
Bon appétit *Mahlzeit!,* II; *Guten Appetit!,* II
book *das Buch, ⸚er,* I
bookcase *das Regal, -e,* I
boot *der Stiefel, -,* I
bored: to be bored *sich langweilen,* II
boring *langweilig,* I
born *geboren,* III4
borrow, lend *ausleihen* (sep), III1
both *beide,* III2
bother, disturb *stören,* III6
bottle *die Flasche, -n,* III1; **deposit-only bottle** *die Pfandflasche, -n,* III9; **non-returnable bottle** *die Einwegflasche, -n,* III9
bottle opener *der Flaschenöffner, -,* III2
bought *gekauft,* I
bouquet of flowers *der Blumenstrauß, ⸚e,* I
bow *die Schleife, -n,* II
bow tie *die Fliege, -n,* II
boy *der Junge, -n,* I; *(southern German) der Bube, -n,* III10
bracelet *das Armband, ⸚er,* II
brake: (foot, hand) brake *die (Fuß-, Hand-,)bremse, -n,* II
bread *das Brot, -e,* I
break *die Pause, -n,* I; **after the break** *nach der Pause,* I; **to break something** *sich etwas brechen,* II
breakfast *das Frühstück,* II; **For breakfast I eat …** *Zum Frühstück ess ich …,* II
breathless *atemlos,* III10
bright *hell,* II
bring: Please bring me … *Bringen Sie mir bitte …,* II

bring back *zurückbringen* (sep), III1
broad *weit*, II
broccoli *der Brokkoli, -*, II
brochure *der Prospekt, -e*, III1
broken *kaputt*, I
brother *der Bruder, ¨*, I; **brothers and sisters** *die Geschwister* (pl), I
brown *braun*, I; **in brown** *in Braun*, I
brush one's teeth *sich die Zähne putzen*, II
Brussels sprouts *der Rosenkohl*, III1
brutal *brutal*, I
buddy *der Kumpel, -*, III4
bumps: goose bumps *die Gänsehaut*, III10
burden *belasten*, III5
burn oneself *s. verbrennen*, III1
bus *der Bus, -se*, I; **by bus** *mit dem Bus*, I
bush *der Strauch, ¨er*, II
business *das Geschäft, -e*, I
businesswoman *die Kauffrau, -en*, III11
busy (telephone) *besetzt*, I
busy: to keep busy with *s. beschäftigen mit*, III3
but *aber*, I; **not only … but also** *nicht nur … sondern auch*, III4
butcher *der Metzger, -*, I
butcher shop *die Metzgerei, -en*, I; **at the butcher's** *beim Metzger*, I
butter *die Butter*, I
button *der Knopf, ¨e*, II
buy *kaufen*, I; **Why don't you just buy …** *Kauf dir doch …!*, I, II
buy: temptation to buy *der Kaufreiz*, III7
by *bei*, II; **by bike** *mit dem Rad*, I; **by bus** *mit dem Bus*, I; **by car** *mit dem Auto*, I; **by moped** *mit dem Moped*, I; **by subway** *mit der U-Bahn*, I
by the way *übrigens*, III1
Bye! *Wiedersehen! Tschau! Tschüs!*, I; (on the telephone) *Wiederhören!*, I

C

cabinet *der Schrank, ¨e*, I
cabinet: cabinet maker *Schreiner(in), -/nen*, III12
café *das Café, -s*, I; **to the café** *ins Café*, I
cake *der Kuchen, -*, I; **a piece of cake** *ein Stück Kuchen*, I
calculate *ausrechnen* (sep), III9
calendar *der Kalender, -*, I
calf *die Wade, -n*, III1
call *anrufen* (sep), *telefonieren*, I
called: be called *heißen*, I
calm *ruhig*, II
calories: has too many calories *hat zu viele Kalorien*, II

camcorder *die Videokamera, -s*, II
Camembert cheese *der Camembert Käse*, II
camera *die Kamera, -s*, II
can *die Büchse, -n*, III8; **aluminum can** *die Aludose, -n*, III9
can *können*, I; **Can I please …?** *Kann ich bitte …?*, II; **Can I ask (you) something?** *Kann ich (euch) etwas fragen?*, II; **Can you tell me whether …?** *Können Sie mir sagen, ob …?*, II
cap *die Mütze, -n*, II; (baseball) **cap** *das Käppi, -s*, II
capital *die Hauptstadt, ¨e*, I
car *das Auto, -s*, I; *der Wagen, -*, II; **by car** *mit dem Auto*, I; **He's slamming the car door (the trunk)!** *Er schlägt die Autotür (den Kofferraumdeckel) zu!*, II; **to polish the car** *das Auto polieren*, II
card *die Karte, -n*, I
care for *mögen*, I; *betreuen*, III5
care: I don't care about fashion. *Mode ist mir egal.*, II
career *die Karriere, -n*, III11
careful *vorsichtig*, III1
carp *der Karpfen, -*, II
carpenter *der Zimmermann, -leute*, III12
carpet *der Teppich, -e*, I
carpool *die Fahrgemeinschaft, -en*, III9
carrot *die Möhre, -n*, II
case: in any case *auf jeden Fall*, III8; *jedenfalls*, III8; **in the case (of)** *im Fall*, III12
cassette *die Kassette, -n*, I
castle *die Burg, -en*, III2
casual *lässig*, I; *salopp*, II
cat *die Katze, -n*, I; **to feed the cat** *die Katze füttern*, I
cathedral *der Dom, -e*, II
cauliflower *der Blumenkohl*, II
cause *verursachen*, III7
caution *die Vorsicht*, III9
cellar *der Keller, -*, II
cell phone *das Handy, -s*, I
cent *der Cent, -*, I
century *das Jahrhundert, -s*, I
certain: I am certain that … *Ich bin sicher, dass …*, II; **It's certain.** *Es steht fest.*, III7
Certainly! *Natürlich!*, I; *Sicher!*, I; *Ja, natürlich!*, II; *Ganz bestimmt.*, III11; *sicherlich*, III12
chair *der Stuhl, ¨e*, I
challenged: accessible to the physically challenged *behindertenfreundlich*, III2
chance *die Chance, -n*, III12; **No chance!** *Auf keinen Fall!*, III11
change (money) *umwechseln* (sep), III1; **to change oneself** *s. ändern*, III5

change: Keep the change! *Stimmt (schon)!*, I
channel *der Sender, -*; *das Programm, -e*, II
characteristic *die Eigenschaft, -en*, III7
cheap *billig*, I
check on *nachsehen* (sep), III2
check: The check please! *Ich möchte/will zahlen!*, I
checked *kariert*, II
cheerful *heiter*, III10
Cheers! *Prost!*, II
cheese *der Käse, -*, I; **Swiss cheese** *der Schweizer Käse*, II; **cheese sandwich** *das Käsebrot, -e*, I
chef *Koch/Köchin, ¨e/nen*, III12
chemical eraser *der Tintenkiller, -*, III9
chemistry *(die) Chemie*, I
cherry *die Kirsche, -n*, II
chess *Schach*, I
chessboard (open-air, with giant-sized pieces) *die Großschachanlage, -n*, III2
chew *kauen*, III8
chicken *das Hähnchen, -*, I; *das Huhn, ¨er*, II
child *das Kind, -er*, II
chimney sweep *Schornsteinfeger(in), -/nen*, III12
Chinese *chinesisch* (adj), II
chives *der Schnittlauch*, II
chocolate *die Schokolade*, II; **chocolate milk** *der Kakao*, II; **fancy chocolate** *die Praline, -n*, I
choose *wählen*, II; *s. aussuchen* (sep), III1
Christmas *das Weihnachten, -*, I; **Merry Christmas!** *Fröhliche Weihnachten!*, I
church *die Kirche, -n*, I
cinema *das Kino, -s*, I
cinnamon *der Zimt*, I
circle of friends *der Freundeskreis, -e*, III4
city *die Stadt, ¨e*, I; **in the city** *in der Stadt*, I; **city gate** *das Stadttor, -e*, II; **in a big city** *in einer Großstadt*, II
city hall *das Rathaus, ¨er*, I
class *die Klasse, -n*; **in class** *in der Klasse*, II; **class, school** *der Unterricht*, III5
class schedule *der Stundenplan, ¨e*, I
classical *klassisch*, I
classical music *klassische Musik*, I
clean *(sich) putzen*, II; *sauber* (adj), II; **squeaky clean** *blitzblank*, III7
cleaner: cleaning agent *das Putzmittel, -*, III7
clear: to clear the table *den Tisch abräumen* (sep), I; **to clear up** *klären*, III10; **to make clear** *klarstellen* (sep), III7
clearly *deutlich*, III6
clever *raffiniert*, III7; **clever(ly)** *witzig*, II

cliché das Klischee, -s, III8
cliff die Klippe, -n, II
climb steigen, II
clique die Clique, II
clothes Kleider (pl), III3; (casual term
  for) die Klamotten (pl), I; **to pick
  up my clothes** meine Klamotten
  aufräumen (sep), I
clothing die Kleidung, III3
cloudy wolkig, I
club der Verein, -e, III5
coast die Küste, -n, II
coffee der Kaffee, I; **a cup of coffee**
  eine Tasse Kaffee, I
coin die Münze, -n, I
cold kalt, I
cold cuts der Aufschnitt, I
collect sammeln, I
color die Farbe, -n, I
colorful bunt, II
comb (sich) kämmen, II
come kommen, I; **That comes to …**
  Das macht (zusammen) …, I; **to
  come along** mitkommen (sep), I
comedy die Komödie, -n, I
comfortable bequem, I; gemütlich, II
comics die Comics, I
command kommandieren, III5
commentary der Kommentar, -e, III6
communications engineer Kommuni-
  kationselektroniker(in), -/nen, III12
compact disc die CD, -s, I
compare vergleichen, III7
complain meckern, III6; **to complain
  about** s. beklagen über (acc),
  III10
compulsory military service die
  Wehrpflicht, III5
computer der Computer, -, I
computer science die Informatik, I
concern: to be concerned about s.
  kümmern um, III6; **as far as I'm
  concerned** meinetwegen, III10
concert das Konzert, -e, I; **to go to a
  concert** ins Konzert gehen, I
conductor der Dirigent, -en, III10
confine einengen (sep), III12
conflict der Konflikt, -e, III12
conform to s. richten nach, III4; s.
  anpassen (sep, dat), III3
connection: to have a connection to
  Bezug haben zu , III8
conscious: environmentally conscious
  umweltbewusst, III8
conservative konservativ, II
consider überlegen, III7; **to consider
  something as** halten für, III5
conspicuous: to be conspicuous
  auffallen (sep), III8
constitution: basic law (constitution)
  das Grundgesetz, III5
consultant: PR-consultant PR-
  Berater(in), -/nen, III12; **tax
  consultant** Steuerberater(in),
  -/nen, III12
consumer der Konsument, -en, III7; der
  Verbraucher, -, III7

container der Behälter, -, III8
contention: point of contention der
  Streitpunkt, -e, III4
continually dauernd, III1
contract der Vertrag, ⁓e, III5
contribute: to contribute to zu etwas
  beitragen (sep), III6
cook kochen, II
cookie der Keks, -e, I; **a few cookies**
  ein paar Kekse, I
cool kühl, I, II
cooler die Kühlbox, -en, III2
corn der Mais, III1
corner die Ecke, -n, II; **That's right
  around the corner.** Das ist hier
  um die Ecke., II; **with corners**
  eckig, I
corny schmalzig, I
cost kosten, I; **How much does … cost?**
  Was kostet …?, I
costume das Kostüm, -e, III12
cotton die Baumwolle, I; **made of
  cotton** aus Baumwolle, I
couch die Couch, -en, I
cough der Husten, II
could könnte, III5
count on s. verlassen auf (acc), III5
countless zahlreich, II
country das Land, ⁓er, I; **in the
  country** auf dem Land, I
courage der Mut, III9
course: of course klar, III7; logisch,
  III7; logo, III7
court der Court, -s, II
cousin (female) die Kusine, -n, I;
  cousin (male) der Cousin,
  -s, I
cozy gemütlich, II
crab die Krabbe, -n, II
crafts: do crafts basteln, I
crazy verrückt, III3
cream: hand cream die Handcreme, II
crime drama der Krimi, -s, I
cross-timbered house das
  Fachwerkhaus, ⁓er, II
cruel grausam, I
cucumber die Gurke, -n, II
culture: for cultural reasons
  kulturbedingt, III4
cummerbund der Kummerbund, -e, II
curious neugierig, II
curtain der Vorhang, ⁓e, III10
curve: You're taking the curve too fast!
  Du fährst zu schnell in die
  Kurve!, II
customs and habits die Sitten und
  Gebräuche (pl), III4
cut: cutting board das Schneidebrett,
  -er, III2
cut class chwänzen, III5
cut-off abgeschnitten, II
cutlet das Schnitzel, -, II

D

damage der Schaden, ⁓, III9
dance tanzen, I; **to go dancing** tanzen
  gehen, I
dancer Tänzer(in), -/nen, III10
dancing das Tanzen, I
dangerous gefährlich, III9
dark dunkel, II
dark blue dunkelblau, I; **in dark blue**
  in Dunkelblau, I
Darn it! So ein Mist!, I
dash: 100-meter dash der 100-Meter-
  Lauf, II
daughter die Tochter, ⁓, II
day der Tag, -e, I; **day before yesterday**
  vorgestern, I; **every day** jeden Tag,
  I; **on the last day** am letzten Tag,
  II; **the other day** neulich, III1
decathlete der Zehnkämpfer, -, II
December der Dezember, I
decide beschließen, III11; s.
  entschließen, III11; **to decide on** s.
  entscheiden für, III5
decision die Entscheidung, -en, III5
defense: German Federal Defense
  Force die Bundeswehr, III5
definite: It's definite. Es steht fest., III11
definitely bestimmt, I
deforest abholzen (sep), III9
degree der Grad, -, I
delicacy die Delikatesse, -n, II; die
  Köstlichkeit, -en, II
Delicious! Lecker!, I
democracy die Demokratie, -n, III5
dental technician Zahntechniker(in),
  -/nen, III12
dentist Zahnarzt, ⁓e, Zahnärztin,
  -nen, III12
depend on auf etwas ankommen
  (sep, acc), III4
dependent: to be dependent on
  angewiesen sein auf (acc), III11
describe beschreiben, II
designer: industrial designer
  Industriedesigner(in), -/nen, III12
desk der Schreibtisch, -e, I
dessert die Nachspeise, -n, II
detail die Einzelheit, -en, III6
detective movie der Krimi, -s, I
detective novel der Krimi, -s, I
determining: to be the determining
  factor ausschlaggebend sein, III11
develop entwickeln, III3
dial wählen, I; **to dial the number** die
  Nummer wählen, I
diamonds: check, diamond (pattern)
  das Karo, -s, II
dictionary das Wörterbuch, ⁓er, I
diet die Diät, -en, III12
difference der Unterschied, -e, III10
different anders, III4; verschieden, I
difficulty die Schwierigkeit, -en, III4

dining room *das Esszimmer, -,* II
dining table *der Esstisch, -e,* I
dinner *das Abendessen,* II; **For dinner we are having …** *Zum Abendessen haben wir …,* II
diploma *der Abschluss, ̈e* III11
direct: to be directed at *s. richten an* (acc), III7
directly *direkt,* I
dirt *der Schmutz,* III9
dirty *schmutzig,* II
disadvantage *der Nachteil, -e,* II
disagree: I disagree. *Das finde ich nicht.,* I
disappoint: to be disappointed *enttäuscht sein,* III8
disco *die Disko, -s,* I; **to go to a disco** *in eine Disko gehen,* I
discothek *die Diskothek, -en,* II
discus throw *das Diskuswerfen,* II
discuss *s. unterhalten über* (acc), III5
discussion *die Diskussion, -en,* II
dish: main dish *das Hauptgericht, -e,* II
dishes *das Geschirr,* I; **to wash the dishes** *das Geschirr spülen,* I
dishwashing liquid *das Spülmittel, -,* III9
dislike *nicht gern haben,* I; **strongly dislike** *überhaupt nicht gern haben,* I
displace, repress *verdrängen,* III6
distance: away, at a distance *entfernt,* III2
distribute *verteilen,* III10
disturb, bother *stören,* III6
dive *tauchen,* II
diverse *abwechslungsreich,* II
divert oneself *s. ablenken* (sep), III3
divorce *die Scheidung, -en,* III12
do *machen,* I; *tun,* I; **to do crafts** *basteln,* I
doctor *der Arzt, ̈e,* II
documentary: animal documentary *die Tiersendung, -en,* II
dog *der Hund, -e,* I
don't you: You like quark, don't you? *Du magst doch Quark, nicht wahr?,* II; **You like yogurt, don't you?** *Du magst Joghurt, oder?,* II
done *gemacht* (pp), I
doubt: I doubt that … *Ich bezweifle, dass …,* II
downtown *die Innenstadt, ̈e,* I, II; **to go downtown** *in die Stadt gehen,* I
draft *einziehen* (sep), III5
draw *zeichnen,* I
dream *der Traum, ̈e,* III11; *träumen,* III10
dress *das Kleid, -er,* I
dressed *gekleidet,* II12
drink *trinken,* I; *das Getränk, -e,* II
drive *fahren,* I
drop, omit *weglassen,* III6
drugstore *die Drogerie, -n,* II
dry *trocken,* I

dry clothes *die Wäsche trocknen,* II
duck: fattened duck *die Mastente, -n,* II; **Peking duck** *die Peking Ente, -n,* II
dumb *blöd,* I; *doof, dumm,* I
dumpling *der Kloß, ̈e,* II
during *während,* III10
dust *Staub wischen,* II
duty *die Pflicht, -en,* III5

E

each, every *jed-,* II
earache *die Ohrenschmerzen* (pl), II
earlier *früher,* III5
earn *verdienen,* III7
earring *der Ohrring, -e,* II; **a pair of earrings** *ein Paar Ohrringe,* II
easily, readily *ohne weiteres,* III3
east *der Osten,* III11; **Eastern Bloc** *der Ostblock,* III11
Easter *das Ostern, -,* I; **Happy Easter!** *Frohe Ostern!,* I
easy *einfach,* I; **That's easy!** *Also, einfach!,* I
easygoing *locker,* III8
eat *essen,* I; **to eat sensibly** *vernünftig essen,* II; **eat and drink** *sich ernähren,* II
emissions: car with emission control *das Katauto, -s,* III9
emphasis: to place emphasis on *Wert legen auf* (acc), III11
employment office *das Arbeitsamt, ̈er,* III11
empty *leer,* III1
encourage *anregen* (sep), III6
endure *aushalten* (sep), III3
engineer: communications engineer *Kommunikationselektroniker(in), -/nen,* III12; **sound engineer** *Toningenieur(in), -e/nen,* III12
enlarge *vergrößern,* III9
enlighten *aufklären* (sep), III7
enough *genug,* I; **that's enough** *es langt,* III2; **to be enough** *genügen,* III2
entertainment *die Unterhaltung,* III6
entire *gesamt,* III6
entranceway *der Flur, -e,* II
enthusiastic *begeistert,* III8
environment *die Umwelt,* I; **environmental scientist** *Umweltökonom(in), -en/nen,* III12; **environmentally conscious** *umweltbewusst,* III8; **environmentally safe** *umweltfreundlich,* III9
envy *beneiden,* III10
equality *die Gleichberechtigung,* III5
eraser *der Radiergummi, -s,* I; **chemical eraser** *der Tintenkiller, -,* III9

especially *besonders,* I; **to especially like** *besonders gern haben,* I; **Not especially.** *Nicht besonders.,* II
euro *der Euro, -,* I
even *sogar,* III9
evening *der Abend, -e,* I; **in the evening** *am Abend,* I
event *das Ereignis, -se,* III6; **organized event** *die Veranstaltung, -en,* III6
every day *jeden Tag,* I
everything *alles,* II4
exactly *eben,* III6
exaggerate *übertreiben,* III3
excellent *ausgezeichnet,* II
exchange *umtauschen* (sep), III1
excitement *die Aufregung, -en,* III10; *die Spannung, -en,* III10
exciting *spannend,* I
exclusively *ausschließlich,* III9
excursion *der Ausflug, ̈e,* II
Excuse me! *Entschuldigung!, Verzeihung!,* I, II
exercise *Gymnastik machen,* II
exhaust *das Abgas, -e,* III9
exhibition *die Ausstellung, -en,* III10
exist *vorhanden sein,* III10
expensive *teuer,* I
experience *die Erfahrung, -en,* III11; *erfahren,* III6; *erleben,* III10; *miterleben* (sep), III9
experienced (person) *der, die Erfahrene, -n,* II
express *ausdrücken* (sep), III3
exquisite *fein,* II
extend *verlängern,* III10
eye *das Auge, -n,* I; **blue eyes** *blaue Augen,* I
eye-catcher *der Blickfang,* III7

F

fact *die Tatsache, -n,* III6
factory *die Fabrik, -en,* III9
failure (in a subject) *die Niete, -n,* III12
fairy tale *das Märchen, -,* III10
fall *der Herbst,* I; **in the fall** *im Herbst,* I
family *die Familie, -n,* I
famous *berühmt,* III2
fancy chocolate *die Praline, -n,* I
Fantastic! *Phantastisch!,* II
fantasy novel *der Fantasyroman, -e,* I
far *weit,* I; **far from here** *weit von hier,* I; **as far as (that) goes** *was (das) angeht,* III3; **as far as this goes** *in dieser Hinsicht,* III5
fashion *die Mode,* I; **the latest fashion** *der letzte Schrei,* III3
fashionable *modisch,* II
fast *schnell,* II
fat *dick,* III8; **has too much fat** *hat zu viel Fett,* II; **It is fattening.** *Es macht dick.,* II

father *der Vater, ⸚,* I; **Father's Day** *der Vatertag,* I; **Happy Father's Day!** *Alles Gute zum Vatertag!,* I
fault: to be at fault *schuld sein an etwas (dat),* III4
favorite *Lieblings-,* I; **Which vegetable is your favorite?** *Welches Gemüse magst du am liebsten?,* II
February *der Februar,* I
feed *füttern,* I
feel *sich fühlen,* II; **How do you feel?** *Wie fühlst du dich?,* II; **I feel great!** *Ich fühle mich wohl!,* II; **Are you not feeling well?** *Ist dir nicht gut?,* II
feeling *das Gefühl, -e,* III7
felt-tip pen *der Faserstift, -e,* III9
fence *fechten,* II
fertilizer: artificial fertilizer *der Kunstdünger, -,* III9
festival: regional festival *das Volksfest, -e,* III10
fetch *holen,* I
fettucine *die Fettucine (pl),* II
fever *das Fieber,* II; **to take one's temperature** *Fieber messen,* II
few: a few *ein paar,* I; **a few cookies** *ein paar Kekse,* I
fibers: made from natural fibers *aus Naturfasern,* II
film, videotape *filmen,* II; **adventure film** *der Abenteuerfilm, -e,* II
finally *zum Schluss,* III7
financially *finanziell,* III12
fine *fein,* II
fingernail *der Fingernagel, ⸚,* III1
finished *fertig,* III11
first *erst-,* I; **first of all** *zuerst,* I; **on the first of July** *am ersten Juli,* I
fish *angeln,* II; **fish stick** *das Fischstäbchen, -,* II
fit *passen,* I; **The skirt fits great!** *Der Rock passt prima!,* I; **to keep fit** *sich fit halten,* II
flats *Schuhe mit flachen Absätzen,* II
flight *der Flug, ⸚e,* II12
flood *überfluten,* III7
flower *die Blume, -n,* I
flowery *geblümt,* II
food *die Speise, -n,* II
foods: to only eat light foods *nur leichte Speisen essen,* II
foot: to walk on foot *zu Fuß gehen,* I
for *für,* I; *denn (conj),* I; **I am for doing …** *Ich bin dafür, dass …,* II; **for whom?** *für wen?,* II
forbid *verbieten (dat),* III4
foreign *ausländisch,* II
foreigner *Ausländer(in), -/nen,* III4
forest *der Wald, ⸚er,* III9; **the dying of the forests** *das Waldsterben,* III9
forget *vergessen,* III4
fork *die Gabel, -n,* III2
former *ehemalig,* III11
formulation *die Bildung,* III6

found *gründen,* III12
fountain *der Brunnen, -,* II
free time *die Freizeit,* I
freedom *die Freiheit,* III7
French *französisch (adj),* II
fresh *frisch,* I
fresh produce store *der Obst- und Gemüseladen, ⸚,* I
Friday *der Freitag,* I; **Fridays** *freitags,* II
fried *gebraten,* II; **fried potatoes** *die Bratkartoffeln (pl),* II
friend (male) *der Freund, -e,* I; (female) *die Freundin, -nen,* I; **to visit friends** *Freunde besuchen,* I; **circle of friends** *der Freundeskreis, -e,* III4
friendliness *die Freundlichkeit,* III4
friendly *freundlich,* II; *kameradschaftlich, aufgeschlossen,* III8
fries: french fries *die Pommes frites (pl),* II
fringe group *die Randgruppe, -n,* III4
frog *der Frosch, ⸚e,* III9
from *aus,* I; *von,* I; **from 8 until 8:45** *von 8 Uhr bis 8 Uhr 45,* I; **from the fifteenth century** *aus dem fünf-zehnten Jahrhundert,* II
from where? *woher?,* I; **I'm from …** *ich bin (komme) aus …,* I; **Where are you from?** *Woher bist (kommst) du?,* I
front: in front of *vor,* II; **there in the front** *da vorn,* I
frugal *sparsam,* III1
fruit *das Obst,* I, II; **a piece of fruit** *ein Stück Obst,* I; **to eat lots of fruit** *viel Obst essen,* II
frustrating *frustrierend,* III6
fulfill *erfüllen,* III7
fun *der Spaß,* I; **(Tennis) is fun.** *(Tennis) macht Spaß.,* I; **(Tennis) is no fun.** *(Tennis) macht keinen Spaß.,* I
funny *lustig,* I, II
furniture *die Möbel (pl),* I
futile *vergeblich,* III10
future *die Zukunft,* III11

G

gain weight *zunehmen (sep),* III3
garage *die Garage, -n,* II
garbage *der Müll,* II
garden *der Garten, ⸚,* I
garlic *der Knoblauch,* II
gas: propulsion gas *das Treibgas, -e,* III9
geography *die Erdkunde,* I
German teacher (male) *der Deutschlehrer, -,* I; (female) *die Deutschlehrerin, -nen,* I
Germany *Deutschland,* I

get *bekommen,* I; *holen,* I; **Get well soon!** *Gute Besserung!,* II
get along *auskommen (sep),* III4; *s. verstehen mit,* III4
gift *das Geschenk, -e,* I
gift idea *die Geschenkidee, -n,* I
girl *das Mädchen, -,* I
give *geben,* I; **he/she gives** *er/sie gibt,* I
give (a gift) *schenken,* I
glad: I'm really glad! *Das freut mich!,* II
glass *das Glas, ⸚er,* I; **a glass of tea** *ein Glas Tee,* I
glasses: a pair of glasses *eine Brille, -n,* I
go *gehen,* I; **to go home** *nach Hause gehen,* I; **goes with: The pretty blouse goes (really) well with the blue skirt.** *Die schöne Bluse passt (toll) zu dem blauen Rock.,* II
go: to go along with *mitmachen mit (sep),* III3
goal *das Ziel, -e,* III11
God: Thank God! *Gott sei Dank!,* III11
Goethe's birthplace *das Goethehaus,* II
gold: made of gold *aus Gold,* II
golf *Golf,* I; **golf course** *der Golfplatz, ⸚e,* II
good *gut,* I; **Good!** *Gut!,* I; **good: what's good about someone** *was an jemandem gut ist,* III4
Good morning! *Guten Morgen!, Morgen!,* I
Goodbye! *Auf Wiedersehen!,* I; (on the telephone) *Auf Wiederhören!,* I
goose bumps *die Gänsehaut,* III10
gown: evening gown *das Abendkleid, -er,* III
grade *die Note, -n,* I
grade level *die Klasse, -n,* I
grades: a 1, 2, 3, 4, 5, 6 *eine Eins, Zwei, Drei, Vier, Fünf, Sechs,* I
gram *das Gramm, -,* I
grandfather *der Großvater ⸚,* I; *Opa, -s,* I
grandmother *die Großmutter, ⸚,* I; *Oma, -s,* I
grandparents *die Großeltern (pl),* I
grape *die Traube, -n,* I, II
gray *grau,* I; **in gray** *in Grau,* I
great: It's great that … *Es ist prima, dass …,* II; **really great** *supertoll,* II; *Echt super!,* II; **Great!** *Prima!,* I; *Sagenhaft!,* I; *Klasse!, Toll!,* I

H

hair: hair stylist *Friseur/Friseuse, -e/n,* III12; **to get your hair cut** *s. die Haare schneiden lassen,* III3

half *halb*, I; **half past (twelve, one, etc.)** *halb (eins, zwei, usw.)*, I
halibut *der Heilbutt*, II
hall *die Halle, -n*, II
hallway *der Flur, -e*, II
ham *der Schinken, -*, II
hand cream *die Handcreme*, II
handbag *die Handtasche, -n*, II
hang up (the telephone) *auflegen (sep)*, I
Hanukkah *Chanukka*, I; **Happy Hanukkah!** *Frohes Chanukka Fest!*, I
happy *fröhlich*, III7; *glücklich*, III7; **I am happy that …** *Ich freue mich, dass …*, II; *Ich bin froh, dass …*, II
hard-working *fleißig*, II
harmful *schädlich*, III7
hat *der Hut, ̈-e*, II
have *haben*, I; **I have no classes on Saturday.** *Am Samstag habe ich frei.*, I; **I'll have …** *Ich bekomme …*, I
have to *müssen*, I
he *er*, I; **he is** *er ist*, I; **he's from** *er ist (kommt) aus*, I
head *der Kopf, ̈-e*, II; **headband** *das Stirnband, ̈-er*, II; **headache** *die Kopfschmerzen (pl)*, II
headlight *der Scheinwerfer, -*, II
headline *die Schlagzeile, -n*, III6
headphones (stereo) *der (Stereo) Kopfhörer, -*, II
health: To your health! *Auf dein/Ihr/ euer Wohl!*, *Zum Wohl!*, II; **to do a lot for your health** *viel für die Gesundheit tun*, II; **health inspector** *Lebensmittelkontrolleur (in) -e/nen*, III12
hear *hören*, I
heard: I heard that … *Ich habe gehört, dass …*, II
heart: pounding heart *das Herzklopfen*, III10
heartfelt *herzlich*, III8
hearty *herzhaft, deftig*, II
heel *die Ferse, -n*, III1
heel (shoe) *der Absatz, ̈-e*, II; **flats** *Schuhe mit flachen Absätzen*, II; **high heel shoe** *Schuh mit hohen Absätzen*, II
Hello! *Guten Tag!*, *Tag!*, *Hallo!*, *Grüß dich!*, I
help *helfen*, I
helpful *hilfreich*, III8
Here you go! *Bitte! Hier!*, II; **Here! I insist!** *Gern! Hier ist es!*, II
herself *sich*, II
hide *verbergen*, III7; *verstecken*, III7
hideous *scheußlich*, I
highly *äußerst*, III8
highway: interstate highway *die Autobahn, -en*, III8
hike *wandern*, I
him *ihn*, I
himself *sich*, II

hip *die Hüfte, -n*, II
hire *einstellen (sep)*, III5
historical *historisch*, III10
history *die Geschichte*, I
hobby *das Hobby, -s*, II
hobby book *das Hobbybuch, ̈-er*, I
hole *das Loch, ̈-er*, II
holiday *der Feiertag, -e*, I
home: good home cooked food *gutbürgerliche Küche, -n*, II; **private home** *das Privathaus, ̈-er*, II; **to stay at home** *zu Hause bleiben*, II
homework *die Hausaufgabe, -n*, I
honestly *ehrlich*, I
honk (the horn) *hupen*, II
hood *die Kapuze, -n*, II
hope *die Hoffnung, -en*, III11
hope: I hope that … *Ich hoffe, dass …*, II; **I hope you'll get better soon.** *Hoffentlich geht es dir bald besser!*, II
hopefully *hoffentlich*, II
horizon *der Horizont*, III11
horror movie *der Horrorfilm, -e*, I
horror novel *der Gruselroman, -e*, I
hostel: youth hostel *die Jugendherberge, -n*, III2
hot *heiß*, I; **hot (spicy)** *scharf*, II
hotel *das Hotel, -s*, I
house *das Haus, ̈-er*, II
how? *wie?*, I; **How are you?** *Wie geht es dir?*, I, II; **How do I get to …?** *Wie komme ich zum (zur) …?*, I; **How does it taste?** *Wie schmeckt's?*, I; **How's the weather?** *Wie ist das Wetter?*, I; **How was it?** *Wie war's?*, II; **How about …?** *Wie wär's mit …?*, II
how much? *wie viel?*, I; **How much does … cost?** *Was kostet …?*, I
how often? *wie oft?*, I
huge *riesig*, III7
hunger *der Hunger*, I
hungry: I'm hungry. *Ich habe Hunger.*, I; **I'm not hungry any more.** *Ich habe keinen Hunger mehr.*, I
hurdling *der Hürdenlauf*, II
hurt: Does it hurt? *Tut's weh?*, II; **Does your … hurt?** *Tut dir … weh?*, II; **It hurts!** *Es tut weh!*, II; **My … hurts.** *… tut mir weh.*, II; **What hurts?** *Was tut dir weh?*, II

I *ich*, I; **I don't.** *Ich nicht.*, I
ice cream *das Eis*, I; **a dish of ice cream** *ein Eisbecher*, I
ice skate *Schlittschuh laufen*, I
idea: I have no idea! *Keine Ahnung!*, I;

Do you have an idea? *Hast du eine Idee?*, II; **Good idea!** *Gute Idee!*, II
identification *der Ausweis, -e*, III2
if I were you *an deiner Stelle*, III3
image *die Vorstellung, -en*, III8
imaginative *phantasievoll*, I
imagine: to imagine something *s. etwas vorstellen (sep)*, III6
immediately *gleich*, III4
impossible: (That's) impossible! *(Das ist) nicht möglich!*, II
impress *beeindrucken*, III8
impression *der Eindruck*, III8; *die Vorstellung, -en*, III8
improve *verbessern*, III9
in *in*, I; **in the afternoon** *am Nachmittag*, I; **in the city** *in der Stadt*, I; **in the country** *auf dem Land*, I; **in the evening** *am Abend*, I; **in the fall** *im Herbst*, I; **in the kitchen** *in der Küche*, I
in spite of that *trotzdem*, III1
income *das Einkommen*, II
indeed *zwar*, III10
independent: to be independent *unabhängig sein*, III5
Indian: (Asian) Indian *indisch (adj)*, II
indicate *angeben (sep)*, III11
industry: industrial designer *Industriedesigner(in), -/nen*, III12
influence *beeinflussen*, III3
inform: to inform oneself *s. informieren*, III2
initiate: to be initiated by *ausgehen von (sep)*, III10
injure (oneself) *sich verletzen*, II
inn *die Pension, -en*, II
innards *die Innereien (pl)*, III1
inquire: to inquire about *s. erkundigen nach*, III11
insert *einstecken (sep)*, I; **to insert coins** *Münzen einstecken*, I
inspector: health inspector *Lebensmittelkontrolleur(in), -e/nen*, III12
instead: I'll drink … instead *Dann trink ich halt …*, II
instead of *anstatt (gen)*, III10
instrument *das Instrument, -e*, I; **Do you play an instrument?** *Spielst du ein Instrument?*, I
insurance company *die Versicherung, -en*, III11
intelligent *intelligent*, II
interest *das Interesse, -n*, I; **Do you have any other interests?** *Hast du andere Interessen?*, I; **I'm not interested in fashion.** *Ich hab kein Interesse an Mode.*, II; **to be interested in** *s. interessieren für*; **Fashion doesn't interest me.** *Mode interessiert mich nicht.*, II; **Are you interested in fashion?** *Interessierst du dich für Mode?*, II; **What are you interested in?** *Wofür interessierst du dich?*, II; **to be interested in** *interessiert sein an (dat)*, III11

interesting *interessant*, I
Internet *das Internet*, I
interrupt *unterbrechen*, III5
into *in*, II
invite *einladen (sep)*, I
island *die Insel, -n*, II
Italian *italienisch (adj)*, II

J

jacket *die Jacke, -n*, I; **bomber jacket**
der Blouson, -s, II; **business jacket**
der Sakko, -s, II; **leather jacket** *die
Lederjacke, -n*, II
jam: traffic jam *der Stau, -s*, III7
January *der Januar*, I; **in January** *im
Januar*, I
javelin throw *das Speerwerfen*, II
jealousy *die Eifersucht*, III10
jeans *die Jeans, -*, I
jewelry *der Schmuck*, I
job *der Job, -s*, II; **to have a job** *jobben*,
III11
jog *joggen*, I, II
jogging suit *der Jogging-Anzug, ⸚e*, I
joke *der Spaß*, III6
judge: to judge according to *beurteilen
nach*, III3
judgement *das Urteil, -e*, III8
juice *der Saft, ⸚e*, I
July *der Juli*, I
jump: long jump *der Weitsprung*, II
June *der Juni*, I
just *gerade*, III1; **Just a minute, please.**
Einen Moment, bitte!, I; **Just don't
buy …** *Kauf dir ja kein …!*, II;
That just happened. *Das ist
gerade passiert.*, II

K

Keep the change! *Stimmt (schon)!*, I
keep to oneselves *unter sich bleiben*,
III4
kilogram *das Kilo, -*, I
king *der König, -e*, III7
kitchen *die Küche, -n*, I; **in the kitchen**
in der Küche, I; **to help in the
kitchen** *in der Küche helfen*, II
knee *das Knie, -*, II
knee cap *die Kniescheibe, -n*, III1
knife *das Messer, -*, III2
know (a fact, information, etc.)
wissen, I; **Do you know whether
…?** *Weißt du, ob …?*, II
know (be familiar or acquainted with)
kennen, I
know: to not know *überfragt sein*, III7

L

lake *der See, -n*, II
lamb *das Lammfleisch*, II
lamp *die Lampe, -n*, I
language *die Sprache. -n*, III11
last *dauern*, III5
last *letzt-*, I; *vorig-*, III5; **last of all**
zuletzt, I; **last week** *letzte Woche*, I
latest: the latest fashion *der letzte
Schrei*, III3
Latin *Latein*, I
laundry *die Wäsche*, II
laundry soap *das Waschmittel, -*, III9
law: (study of) law *Jura*, III11
lawn *der Rasen, -*, I; **to mow the lawn**
den Rasen mähen, I; **lawn for
relaxing and sunning** *die
Liegewiese, -n*, II
lawyer for the defense
Strafverteidiger(in), -/nen, III12
layer cake *die Torte, -n*, I
lazy *faul*, II; **to be lazy** *faulenzen*, II;
(ironic) to be too lazy to walk
fußkrank sein, III2
lead *führen*, III12
leaf *das Blatt, ⸚er*, III1
leak: to spring a leak *leck werden*, III9
leather *das Leder*, I
left: to the left *nach links*, I
leg *das Bein, -e*, I
legend *die Sage, -n*, III10
lemon *die Zitrone, -n*, I
lemon drink *die Limo, -s*, I
let, allow *lassen*, II; **Let me …** *Lass
mich mal …*, II; **Let's go to the
golf course!** *Gehen wir mal
auf den Golfplatz!*, II; **Let's go
to …!** *Fahren wir mal
nach …!*, II
lettuce *der Salat, -e*, I
library: lending library *die Bücherei,
-en*, III1
license: driver's license *der
Führerschein, -e*, II
life *das Leben*, II
lift *heben*, III3
light blue *hellblau*, I
like *gefallen, mögen, gern haben*, I, II;
like *stehen auf (acc)*, III11; **I like
it.** *Er/Sie/Es gefällt mir.*, I; **I like
them.** *Sie gefallen mir.*, I; **Did you
like it?** *Hat es dir gefallen?*, II; **to
like an awful lot** *furchtbar gern
haben*, I; **to not like at all** *gar
nicht gern haben*, I; **to not like very
much** *nicht so gern haben*, I; **I
don't like …** *Ich mag kein …*, II; **I
like to go to the ocean.** *Ich fahre
gern ans Meer.*, II; **I would like …**
Ich hätte gern …, II; **like (to do)**
gern (machen), I; **to not like (to
do)** *nicht gern (machen)*, I

linen *das Leinen*, II
listen (to) *hören*, I; *zuhören, (sep)*, I;
Listen! *Hör mal!*, II; **Listen to
this!** *Hör mal zu!*, II
listing *das Verzeichnis, -se*, III2
liter *der Liter, -*, I
little *klein*, I; **a little** *ein bisschen*, I
live *wohnen*, I; *leben*, II
liver *die Leber*, III1
living room *das Wohnzimmer, -*, II; **in
the living room** *im Wohnzimmer*, I
lobster *der Hummer, -*, II
long *lang*, I
long for *s. sehnen nach*, III7
look *schauen*, I; **Look!** *Schauen Sie!*, I;
Guck mal!, Schau mal!, Sieh mal!,
II; **That looks great on you!** *Das
steht dir prima!*, II; **look for**
suchen, I; **look like** *aussehen
(sep)*, I; **look around** *s. umsehen
(sep)*, III10
look forward to *s. freuen auf (acc)*, II10
lose *verlieren*, III2
lose weight *abnehmen (sep)*, III3
lot: quite a lot *eine ganze Menge*, III8; **a
lot** *viel*, I
loud *laut*, III8
lousy *mickrig*, III3
luck: Bad luck! *So ein Pech!*, I; **What
luck!** *So ein Glück!*, I; **Luckily**
Zum Glück, III11; **Lucky that …**
Ein Glück, dass …, III11
lunch *das Mittagessen*; **For lunch there
is …** *Zum Mittagessen gibt
es …*, II

M

made: made of cotton *aus Baumwolle*, I
magazine *die Zeitschrift; -en*, I
mail *die Post*, III1
mainly *hauptsächlich*, III3
make *machen*, I; **make, achieve**
schaffen, III5
makeup: to put on makeup *s.
schminken*, III3
man *der Mann, ⸚er*, I
many *viele*, I
March *der März*, I
margarine *die Margarine*, II
marinated *mariniert*, II
market square *der Marktplatz, ⸚e*, I
marmalade *die Marmelade, -n*, II
marriage *die Ehe, -n*, III12
marry *heiraten*, III5
math *Mathe (die Mathematik)*, I
matter: in this matter *in diesem Punkt*,
III8; **to not matter** *s. nichts
ausmachen (sep)*, III6
May *der Mai*, I
may: May I help you? *Haben Sie einen
Wunsch?*, I; **May I (please) …?**

Darf ich (bitte) …?, II; **That may well be.** *Das mag schon sein.*, III4
maybe *vielleicht*, I; **Yes, maybe, but …** *Ja, das kann sein, aber …*, II
me *mich, mir*, I; **Me too!** *Ich auch!*, I
meadow *die Wiese, -n*, III7
means: By all means. *Auf alle Fälle.*, III11
measure *messen*, II; **he/she measures** *er/sie misst*, II
meat *das Fleisch*, I; **You eat a lot of meat, right?** *Du isst wohl viel Fleisch, ja?*, II
media planner *Mediaplaner(in), -/nen*, III12
meet *treffen*, III3
member *das Mitglied, -er*, III5
mentality *die Mentalität*, III11
mention *erwähnen*, III1
mess: What a mess! *So ein Mist!*, I
message *die Mitteilung, -en*, III7
miracle, wonder *das Wunder, -*, III10
mirror *der Spiegel, -*, III10
miss *vermissen*, III6
missing: to be missing *fehlen*, III5
mood *die Laune*, III3
moped *das Moped, -s*, I
more *mehr*, I; **the more … the** *je mehr … desto*, III7
morning *der Morgen*, I; **Morning!** *Morgen!*, I
most *meist-*, III6; **most of all** *am liebsten*, I; *vor allem*, III11; **most of the time** *meistens*, II
mother *die Mutter, ¨*, I; **Mother's Day** *der Muttertag*, I; **Happy Mother's Day!** *Alles Gute zum Muttertag!*, I
motor *der Motor, -en*, II
motorcycle *das Motorrad, ¨er*, II
mountain *der Berg, -e*, II; **in the mountains** *in den Bergen*, II
moussaka *die Moussaka*, II
mouth *der Mund, ¨er*, III2
move (residence) *ziehen*, III12
movie *der Film, -e*, I; **movie theater** *das Kino, -s*, I; **to go to the movies** *ins Kino gehen*, I
mow *mähen*, I; **to mow the lawn** *den Rasen mähen*, I
Mr. *Herr*, I
Ms. *Frau*, I
much *viel*, I; **much too** *viel zu*, I
mug *der Becher, -*, III2
museum *das Museum, (pl) Museen*, I
mushroom *der Pilz, -e*, II
music *die Musik*, I; **house music** *die Hausmusik*, III10; **to listen to music** *Musik hören*, I
music store *der Musikladen, ¨*, III1
musical *das Musical, -s*, II
musician *Musiker(in), -/nen*, III11
mustard *der Senf*, I
my *mein (poss adj)*, I; **my name is** *ich heiße*, I
myself *mich*, II

name *der Name, -n*, I; **her name is** *sie heißt*, I; **What's the boy's name?** *Wie heißt der Junge?*, I
namely *nämlich*, III2
napkin *die Serviette, -n*, III2
native language *die Muttersprache, -n*, III4
nature *die Natur*, III2
nature: good-natured *gutmütig*, III8
nauseated: I'm nauseated. *Mir ist schlecht.*, II
near *nahe*, III9
near to *in der Nähe von*, III8
nearby *in der Nähe*, I
necklace *die Halskette, -n*, II
need *brauchen*, I
neither … nor *weder … noch*, III10
nerves: to get on the nerves *nerven*, III7
never *nie*, I; **not yet** *noch nie*, II
new *neu*, I
news: the news *die Nachrichten (pl)*, II
newspaper *die Zeitung, -en*, I
next: next week *nächste Woche*, I; **the next street** *die nächste Straße*, I
next to *neben*, II
nice *nett*, III8
night *die Nacht, ¨e*, III2
night: to spend the night *übernachten*, II
no *kein*, I; **No more, thanks!** *Nichts mehr, danke!*, I
no way: There's just no way! *Das gibt's doch nicht!*, II
noise *der Lärm*, II
non-fiction book *das Sachbuch, ¨er*, I
none *kein*, I
nonsense, baloney *Quatsch*, III6
noodle soup *die Nudelsuppe, -n*, I
nor: neither … nor *weder … noch*, III10
normally *normalerweise*, II
North: the North Sea *die Nordsee*, II
nose: runny nose *der Schnupfen*, II
not *nicht*, I; **not at all** *überhaupt nicht*, I; **to not like at all** *gar nicht gern haben*, I; **Not really.** *Nicht besonders.*, I; **not any** *kein*, I; **Not entirely! / Not necessarily!** *Nicht unbedingt!*, II; **actually not** *eben nicht*, II
notebook *das Notizbuch, ¨er*, I; *das Heft, -e*, I
nothing *nichts*, I; **nothing at the moment** *im Moment gar nichts*, I; **Nothing, thank you!** *Nichts, danke!*, I; **There's nothing you can do.** *Da kann man nichts machen.*, II
notice: on short notice *kurzfristig*, III5
novel *der Roman, -e*, I
November *der November*, I

now *jetzt*, I; **just now** *eben, gerade*, III2; **now and then** *ab und zu*, III6
nuclear war *der Atomkrieg, -e*, III11
number *die (Telefon)nummer*, I; **to dial the number** *die Nummer wählen*, I
nutritional scientist *Gesundheitswissenschaftler(in), -/nen*, III12
nutritious *vollwertig*, III3

O

o'clock: at 1 o'clock *um 1 Uhr*, I
oasis *die Oase, -n*, II
observe *beobachten*, III8
occupation *die Tätigkeit, -en*, III11
ocean *das Meer, -e; die See, -n*, II
October *der Oktober*, I
of *von*, II; **made of wool** *aus Wolle*, II
Of course! *Ja klar!*, I; *Ganz klar!*, I; *Na klar!*, II; **Yes, of course!** *Ja, natürlich!*, II
offer *anbieten (sep)*, III9; *das Angebot, -e*, I
office: employment office *das Arbeitsamt, ¨er*, III11
officer *der Offizier, -e*, III5
often *oft*, I; *schon oft*, II
Oh! *Ach!*, I; **Oh yeah!** *Ach ja!*, I
oil *das Öl, -e*, I
Okay! I'll do that! *Gut! Mach ich!*, I; **It's okay.** *Es geht.*, I; *Schon gut!*, II; **well, okay** *also (part)*, III2
old *alt*, I; **How old are you?** *Wie alt bist du?*, I; **older** *älter*, II
olympic champion *der Olympiasieger, -*, II
omit, drop *weglassen (sep)*, III6
on: on … Square *am …platz*, I; **on … Street** *in der …straße*, I; **to walk on foot** *zu Fuß gehen*, I; **on Monday** *am Montag*, I; **on the first of July** *am ersten Juli*, I; **on a lake** *an einem See*, II; **on a river** *an einem Fluss*, II
once *einmal*, I; **once a month** *einmal im Monat*, I; **once a week** *einmal in der Woche*, I; **once a day** *einmal am Tag*, II
oneself *selbst*, III6
onion *die Zwiebel, -n*, I
only *bloß*, I; *nur*, II
onto *auf*, II
open *offen*, III8
opener: bottle opener *der Flaschenöffner, -*, III2
opera *die Oper, -n*, I; **opera house** *die Oper, -n*, II
operetta *die Operette, -n*, II
opinion: in my opinion *meiner Meinung nach*, III6

oppress *unterdrücken*, III12
optician *Optiker(in), -/nen*, III12
or *oder*, I
orange juice *der Orangensaft, ⸚e*, I
order *bestellen*, II; **in order to do …** *um … zu machen*, III3
orderly *geregelt*, III11; *ordentlich*, III8
organic food *die Biokost*, III3
ostensibly *angeblich*, III7
other *andere*, I; **the other day** *neulich*, III1
Ouch! *Au!, Aua!*, II
ourselves *uns*, II
out of *aus* (dat), II
outside of *außerhalb* (gen), III4
outstanding *ausgezeichnet*, II
oven *der Ofen, ⸚*, I
over it *darüber*, II
over there *dort drüben*, I; **over there in the back** *da hinten*, I
overcast *trüb*, I
own: (one's) own *eigen-* (adj), II
oxygen *der Sauerstoff*, III9
oyster *die Auster, -n*, II
ozone: hole in the ozone layer *das Ozonloch*, III9

padded *gefüttert*, II
paella *die Paella, -s*, II
page through *durchblättern* (sep), III6
pain *der Schmerz, -en*, II
painting *das Gemälde, -*, II
pair *das Paar, -e*, II
pan dish *das Pfannengericht, -e*, II
pants *die Hose, -n*, I
Pardon me! *Verzeihung!*, II
parents *die Eltern* (pl), I
park *der Park, -s*, I, II; **to go to the park** *in den Park gehen*, I
parka *der Anorak, -s*, II
parking place/lot *der Parkplatz, ⸚e*, II
parliament: German Federal Parliament *der Bundestag*, III11
part *der Teil, -e*, III9
part: to take part *dabei sein*, III11
particularly *ausgesprochen*, III5; *insbesondere*, III8
partly *teilweise*, III10
party *die Party, -s*, I; *die Fete, -n*, III4
pass: time passes *vergehen*, III11
past *vergangen-*, III5
pasta *die Teigwaren* (pl), III1
path *der Weg, -e*, III8
patience *die Geduld*, III10
patient *geduldig*, III8
pattern *das Muster, -*, II
pay *bezahlen*, III1
pea *die Erbse, -n*, II
peace *der Frieden*, III5

peace-loving *friedliebend*, III8
peaceful *friedlich*, 7
peach *der Pfirsich, -e*, II
peanut butter *die Erdnussbutter*, III1
pear *die Birne, -n*, II5
pencil *der Bleistift, -e*, I
people *die Leute* (pl), I
pepper shaker *der Pfefferstreuer, -*, III2
perceive *wahrnehmen* (sep), III7
perch: filet of perch *das Seebarschfilet, -s*, II
perfect, whole *heil*, III7
perform *aufführen* (sep), III10
performance *die Aufführung, -en*, III10
perfume *das Parfüm, -e or -s*, I
perfumed *parfümiert*, II
perhaps *vielleicht*, I; *eventuell*, III10
permit oneself *s. erlauben*, III5
pet *das Haustier, -e*, I
pharmacy *die Apotheke, -n*, II
philosopher *der Philosoph, -en*, III10
phone card *die Telefonkarte, -n*, I
photograph *fotografieren*, II; **color photograph** *das Farbbild, -er*, II
photographer *Fotograf(in), -en/nen*, III12
physical education *der Sport*, I
physically: accessible to the physically challenged *behindertenfreundlich*, III2
physics *(die) Physik*, I
piano *das Klavier, -e*, I; **I play the piano.** *Ich spiele Klavier.*, I
pick out *s. aussuchen* (sep), III1
pick up *aufräumen* (sep), I; *abholen* (sep), III8; **to pick up the telephone** *den Hörer abheben* (sep), I
pickle *die saure Gurke, -n*, III1
picnic *das Picknick, -s*, III2
picnic basket *der Picknickkorb, ⸚e*, III2
piece *das Stück, -e*, I; **a piece of cake** *ein Stück Kuchen*, I
pity, sympathy *das Mitleid*, III3
pizza *die Pizza, -s*, I
place *der Platz, ⸚e*, II
plan *der Plan, ⸚e*, II; *vorhaben* (sep), III3
plant *die Pflanze, -n*, III1
plastic *der Kunststoff, -e*, I; **made of plastic** *aus Kunststoff*, I
plate *der Teller, -*, III2
play *spielen*, I; **to play a board game** *ein Brettspiel spielen*, I; *das Schauspiel, -e*, II; *das Theaterstück, -e*, II
play (act) *darstellen* (sep), III10
pleasant *angenehm*, III5; *sympathisch*, II
please *bitte*, I
pleasure *das Vergnügen, -*, III10; **My pleasure!** *Gern geschehen!*, I
plot *die Handlung, -en*, III10

plum *die Zwetschge, -n*, II
pocket *die Tasche, -n*, II; **back pocket** *die Gesäßtasche, -n*, II
pocket calculator *der Taschenrechner, -*, I
poison *das Gift, -e*, III9; **to poison, pollute** *verpesten*, III9
poisonous *giftig*, III9
pole vault *der Stabhochsprung*, II
polite *höflich*, III8
political discussion *eine Diskussion über Politik*, II
politics *die Politik* (sing), I
polka-dotted *gepunktet*, I
pollutant *der Schadstoff, -e*, III9
pollute *verschmutzen*, III9
pollution: air pollution *die Luftverschmutzung*, III9
pool *der Pool, -s*, II; **indoor pool** *das Hallenbad, ⸚er*, II
popular *beliebt*, II9
porch *die Terrasse, -n*, II
pork *das Schweinefleisch*, III1
pork chop *das Schweinekotelett, -s*, II; **pork loin steak** *das Schweinerückensteak, -s*, II
position: to take a position *Stellung nehmen*, III6
possibility *die Möglichkeit, -en*, III4
possible *möglich*, II
possibly *möglicherweise*, III10
post office *die Post*, I
poster *das Poster, -*, I
potato *die Kartoffel, -n*, I; **fried potatoes** *die Bratkartoffeln* (pl), II; **potato croquettes** *die Kroketten* (pl), II
pound *das Pfund, -*, I
pounding heart *das Herzklopfen*, III10
poverty *die Armut*, II
practice (a profession) *ausüben* (sep), III11
praise *anpreisen* (sep), III7
prefer *lieber (mögen)*, I; *vorziehen* (sep), II; **I prefer …** *Ich ziehe … vor*, II; **I prefer noodle soup.** *Nudelsuppe mag ich lieber.*, II; **I prefer that …** *Ich bin dafür, dass …*, II
prejudice *das Vorurteil, -e*, III4
prepare for *s. vorbereiten* (sep) *auf* (acc), III11
pretty *hübsch*, I; *schön*, I
pretzel *die Brezel, -n*, I
primarily *in erster Linie*, III7
printer *der Drucker, -*, III6
probably *wahrscheinlich*, I
produce *herstellen* (sep), III9; *produzieren*, II
produce store *der Obst- und Gemüseladen, ⸚*, II
product *das Produkt, -e*, III1; **product, ware** *die Ware, -n*, III7
production *die Herstellung, -en*, III9
profession *der Beruf, -e*, III11

program (TV) *die Sendung, -en*, II;
  family program *die Familien-
  sendung, -en*, II; **nature program**
  die Natursendung, -en, II
promise *versprechen*, III1
proper(ly) *richtig*, II4
protection: environmental protection
  der Umweltschutz, III9
proud: to be proud of *stolz sein auf*
  (acc), III8
pullover *der Pulli, -s*, I
pump spray *der Pumpzerstäuber,
  -*, III9
punctual *pünktlich*, III8
purpose: on purpose *absichtlich*,
  III4
put (into) *stecken*, III9
put on *anziehen* (sep), I

qualify, make less absolute
  relativieren, III8
quark *der Quark*, II
quarrel *der Krach*, III4; *die Streitigkeit,
  -en*, III4; *streiten*, III2; **argument**
  der Streit, III4
quarter: a quarter after *Viertel nach*, I;
  a quarter to *Viertel vor*, I
queen *die Königin, -nen*, III10
question *die Frage, -n*, II; **It's out of
  the question!** *Kommt nicht in
  Frage!*, III11
quiet *still*, III8
quiz show *die Ratesendung,
  -en*, II

rabbit meat *das Hasenfleisch*, III1
radio *das Radio, -s*, II
radio announcer *Rundfunksprecher
  (in), -/nen*, III12
radish *das Radieschen, -*, III1
railroad station *der Bahnhof, ̈-e*, I
rain *der Regen*, I; **It's raining.** *Es
  regnet.*, I
rain: acid rain *der saure Regen*, III9
rainy *regnerisch*, I
raise (a child) *großziehen* (sep), III7
raisin *die Rosine, -n*, III1
raspberry marmalade *die
  Himbeermarmelade, -n*, II
rather *ziemlich*, I
raw *roh*, II
read *lesen*, I
read aloud *vorlesen* (sep), III10

reading *die Lektüre, -n*, III1
really *ganz*, I; *wirklich*, I; *echt*, II; **Not
  really.** *Nicht besonders.*, I
really (well) *unheimlich (gut)*, III10
reason *der Grund, ̈-e*, III11; **for this
  reason** *deshalb*, III6; **to give a
  reason** *begründen*, III6
rebellious *aufsässig*, III4
receive *bekommen*, I
receiver *der Hörer, -*, I
recent: most recent event *die
  Neuigkeit, -en*, III6
recently *vor kurzem*, III1
recognize *erkennen*, III10
recommend *empfehlen*, III8
recycle *wieder verwerten*, III9
recycling bin *der Container, -*, III8
red *rot*, I; **in red** *in Rot*, I
red berry dessert *Rote Grütze*, II
red cabbage *der Rotkohl*, II
reduce *abbauen* (sep), III8
reexamine *überprüfen*, III8
refrigerator *der Kühlschrank, ̈-e*, I
regularly *regelmäßig*, III3
relationship *das Verhältnis*, III4
relax *s. entspannen*, III3
religion *die Religion, -en*, I
remember *s. erinnern an* (acc),
  III2
remote control *die Fernbedienung,
  -en*, II
repeat *wiedergeben* (sep), III8
replace *ersetzen*, III9
report *der Bericht, -e*, III6
report card *das Zeugnis*, I
reported to be *angeblich*, III7
require *nötig haben*, III11
residence *das Wohnhaus, ̈-er*, II; **the …
  residence** *Hier bei … ,* I
rest *s. ausruhen* (sep), III11
restaurant *das Restaurant, -s*, II; *der
  Gasthof, ̈-e*, II; **small restaurant**
  das Lokal, -e, II
return: to come back to (a topic)
  zurückkommen auf (sep, acc),
  III6
returnable: non-returnable bottle *die
  Einwegflasche, -n*, III9
reusable bottle *die Mehrwegflasche,
  -n*, III9
ribs *die Rippchen* (pl), III1
rice *der Reis*, II
right *das Recht, -e*, III5
right: That's all right. *Macht nichts!*, II;
  That's not right (at all)! *Das
  stimmt (überhaupt) nicht!*, II;
  You're right about that! *Da hast
  du Recht!*, II
right: to the right *nach rechts*, I
ring *der Ring, -e*, II
ringlet *der Ringel, -*, II
river *der Fluss, ̈-e*, II; **on a river** *an
  einem Fluss*, II
roast *der Braten*, II
robust, strong *stark*, III8
role *die Rolle, -n*, III11
roll *die Semmel, -n*, I

roll of film *der Film, -e*, II
romance *der Liebesfilm, -e*, I; **romance
  novel** *der Liebesroman, -e*, I
roof *das Dach, ̈-er*, III9
room *das Zimmer, -*, I; **to clean up my
  room** *mein Zimmer aufräumen*
  (sep), I
room with open fireplace *der
  Kaminraum, ̈-e*, III2
round *rund*, I
ruined *kaputt*, I, II
run *laufen*, II; **long distance run** *der
  Langstreckenlauf*, II
run: ski run *die Skipiste, -n*, III9
runny nose *der Schnupfen*, II
Russian *russisch* (adj), II

S

sad *traurig*, I
safe: environmentally safe
  umweltfreundlich, III9
sail *segeln*, II
salad *der Salat, -e*, I
salmon *der Lachs, -e*, II
salt *das Salz*, I
salt shaker *der Salzstreuer, -*, III2
salty: too salty *zu salzig*, II
same *gleich*, III7; *derselbe*, III7
sandwich *das Sandwich, -es*, II; **What
  do you have on your sandwich?**
  Was hast du denn auf dem Brot?, II
Saturday *der Samstag*, I; **Saturdays**
  samstags, II
sauerkraut *das Sauerkraut*, II
sauna *die Sauna, -s*, II
sausage *die Wurst, ̈-e*, I
save money *sparen*, III3
say *agen*, I; **Say!** *Sag mal!*, I **to say
  something about** *aussagen über*
  (sep), III3
scan (a newspaper) *herumblättern*
  (sep), III3
scarf *der Schal, -s*, II
schedule of shows *das Programm, -e*, II
school *die Schule, -n*, I; **after school**
  nach der Schule, I; **How do you get
  to school?** *Wie kommst du zur
  Schule?*, I; **at school** *an der
  Schule*, II
school administration *die
  Schulleitung*, III6
school subject *das Fach, ̈-er*, I
school supplies *die Schulsachen* (pl), I
school, class *der Unterricht*, III5
schoolbag *die Schultasche, -n*, I
science *die Wissenschaft, -en*, III11
science fiction movie *der Sciencefictionfilm, -e*, I
science fiction novel *der
  Sciencefictionroman, -e*, I
scientific *wissenschaftlich*, III10

scold *schimpfen,* III4
sea *die See, -n; das Meer, -e,* II
search (for) *suchen,* I
second *zweit-,* I; **the second street** *die zweite Straße,* I
secret tip *der Geheimtip, -s,* II
secure *sicher,* II
seduce *verführen,* III7
see *sehen,* I; **See you later!** *Bis dann!,* I; **to see a movie** *einen Film sehen,* I
seem *scheinen,* III5
seldom *selten,* II
sensational *sensationell,* I
senseless *sinnlos,* III5
separate oneself from *s. absondern von* (sep), III4
September *der September,* I
seriously *im Ernst,* III5
service *die Leistung, -en,* III2
services: armed services *die Streitkräfte,* III5
set the table *den Tisch decken,* I
several *mehrere,* III6
sew *nähen,* III3
shaker: salt and pepper shaker *der Salz- und Pfefferstreuer,* III2
shame: to be a shame about something *schade um etwas sein,* III5
shampoo *das Shampoo, -s,* II
sharp (clothing) *scharf,* II; **really sharp** *fetzig,* II
shine: the sun is shining *die Sonne scheint,* I
ship *das Schiff, -e,* II
shirt *das Hemd, -en,* I
shish kebab *das Schisch Kebab,* 11
shoe *der Schuh, -e,* II; **patent leather shoe** *der Lackschuh, -e,* II
shoemaker *Schuhmacher(in), -/nen,* III12
shoot *schießen,* III5
shop *einkaufen* (sep), I; **to go shopping** *einkaufen gehen,* I
short *kurz,* I; **on short notice** *kurzfristig,* III5
shortening *das Butterschmalz,* I
shorts: pair of shorts *die Shorts, -,* I
shot put *das Kugelstoßen,* II
should *sollen,* I
shoulder *die Schulter, -n,* II
show *die Sendung, -en,* II
shower *duschen,* III9
sick *krank,* II6
side dish *die Beilage, -n,* II
sightsee *etwas besichtigen,* II
sign *unterschreiben,* III5
silk *die Seide,* I; **made of silk** *aus Seide,* I; **silk shirt** *das Seidenhemd, -en,* II; **real silk** *echte Seide,* II
silly, strange *grotesk,* III10
silver: made of silver *aus Silber,* II
silverware *das Besteck,* III2
since *seit,* III9
singer (female) *die Sängerin, -nen,* I; **singer** (male) *der Sänger, -,* I

sink *das Spülbecken, -,* I
sister *die Schwester, -n,* I; **brothers and sisters** *die Geschwister* (pl), I
site *die Anlage, -n,* II
situation *das Verhältnis, -se,* III11
size *die Größe, -n,* I
ski run *die Skipiste, -n,* III9
skin *die Haut,* II
skirt *der Rock, ̈e,* I; **pleated skirt** *der Faltenrock, ̈e,* II
sledding *rodeln,* II
sleep: to get enough sleep *genügend schlafen,* II
sleeveless *ärmellos,* II
sleeves: with long sleeves *mit langen Ärmeln,* II; **with short sleeves** *mit kurzen Ärmeln,* II
slender *schlank,* II
slice *die Scheibe, -n,* III1
slide *das Dia, -s,* II
slip *ausrutschen* (sep), III1
slogan: advertising slogan *der Werbespruch, ̈e,* III7
sloppy *schlampig,* III3
slow(ly) *langsam,* II
small *klein,* I
smart (looking) *fesch, schick, chic,* I
smoke *rauchen,* II
smoked *geräuchert,* II
snack bar, stand *die Imbissstube, -n,* I
snap *der Druckknopf, ̈e,* II
sneaker *der Turnschuh, -e,* I
snow *der Schnee,* I; **It's snowing.** *Es schneit.,* I
so *so,* I; **So long!** *Tschau! / Tschüs!,* I; **so so** *so lala,* I
so that, in order to *damit* (conj), III3
soap *die Seife, -n,* II; **laundry soap** *das Waschmittel, -,* III9
soccer *Fußball,* I
sock *die Socke, -n,* I
soda: lemon-flavored soda *die Limo, -s (die Limonade, -n),* I; **cola and lemon soda** *das Spezi, -s,* II
sofa *das Sofa, -s,* I
soft *weich,* II
some *einige,* III6; **some-** *irgend-,* III7
Someone told me that … *Man hat mir gesagt, dass …,* II
something *etwas,* I
sometimes *manchmal,* I
son *der Sohn, ̈e,* II
song *das Lied, ̈er,* I
soon *bald,* I
sorry: to be sorry *bedauern,* II; *Leid tun,* II; **I'm sorry.** *Es tut mir Leid.,* I; **Sorry, I can't.** *Ich kann leider nicht.,* I; **Sorry, but unfortunately we're all out of couscous.** *Tut mir Leid, aber der Couscous ist leider schon alle.,* II; **I'm so sorry.** *Das tut mir aber Leid!,* II
sort *sortieren,* I
sound *klingen,* III11
sound engineer *Toningenieur(in), -e/nen,* III12
soup *die Suppe, -n,* II

space travel *die Raumfahrt,* III11
Spanish *spanisch* (adj), II
speak *reden,* III4; **to finish speaking** *ausreden* (sep), III6
specialist: tourism specialist *Touristikfachwirt(in), -e/nen,* III12
specialty *die Spezialität, -en,* III11
spectator *der Zuschauer, -,* III10
spend (time) *verbringen,* I; **spend (the night)** *übernachten,* II
spicy *würzig,* II; **spicy, hot** *scharf,* II
spinach *der Spinat,* II
splendor *die Pracht,* III10
spoil, pamper *verwöhnen,* III8
spoon *der Löffel, -,* III2
sport(s) *der Sport,* I; **sport facility** *die Sportanlage, -n,* II; **sports telecast** *die Sportübertragung, -en,* II; **Do you play sports?** *Machst du Sport?,* I
sports scientist *Sportökonom(in), -en/nen,* III12
sporty *sportlich,* II
sprain (something) *sich (etwas) verstauchen,* II
spray: pump spray *der Pumpzerstäuber, -,* III9
spread *verbreiten,* III8; **spread, to butter** *bestreichen,* III1
spring *der Frühling,* I; **in the spring** *im Frühling,* I
spring a leak *leck werden,* III9
sprouts (bean) *die Sojasprossen,* II
square *der Platz, ̈e,* I; **on … Square** *am …platz,* I
stage *die Bühne, -n,* III10
stamp *die Briefmarke, -n,* I; **to collect stamps** *Briefmarken sammeln,* I
stand, to be *stehen,* III2; **to not be able to stand something** *etwas nicht leiden können,* III4
state: German federal state *das Bundesland, ̈er,* I
station *der Sender, -,* II
stay, remain *bleiben,* II
steak *das Steak, -s,* II
steak (beef) *das Rindersteak, -s,* II
stereo *die Stereoanlage, -n,* I
stimulate, encourage *anregen* (sep), III6
stimulating *anregend,* III6
stinks: That stinks! *So ein Mist!,* I
stirrup pants *die Steghose, -n,* II
stocking *der Strumpf, ̈e,* II
stomach *der Bauch, ̈e,* II; **stomachache** *die Bauchschmerzen* (pl), II
storage shelf *das Ablagefach, ̈er,* II
store *der Laden, ̈,* I; *das Geschäft, -e,* I
store: to be in store for *zukommen auf* (sep, acc), III11
storm *das Gewitter, -,* I
stove *der Herd, -e,* I
straight ahead *geradeaus,* I
strange, silly *grotesk,* III10
strawberry *die Erdbeere, -n,* II; **strawberry marmalade** *die Erdbeermarmelade,* II

street *die Straße, -n*, I; **on … Street** *in der …straße*, I; **main street** *die Hauptstraße, -n*, II
stressful *anstrengend*, III5; *stressig*, III8
strict *streng*, III8
strike *der Streik, -s*, III6
stripe *der Streifen, -*, II
striped *gestreift*, I
stroll *spazieren*, II
strong *stark*, I; *kräftig*, III7
struggle, battle *der Kampf, ⁐e*, III5
stubborn *stur*, III8
student exchange *der Schüleraustausch*, III6
students' representatives *die Schülervertretung*, III6
studies: university studies *das Studium*, III5
study *lernen*, III3
stuff oneself *futtern*, III2
stupid *blöd*, I
style *der Stil, -e*, II
stylist: hair stylist *Friseur/Friseuse, -e/n*, III12
subconscious *das Unterbewusstsein*, III7
subject (school) *das Fach, ⁐er*, I
submarine *das U-Boot, -e*, III5
subscription *das Abonnement, -s*, III10
suburb *der Vorort, -e*, I; **in a suburb** *in einem Vorort*, II
subway *die U-Bahn*, I; **by subway** *mit der U-Bahn*, I
subway station *die U-Bahnstation, -en*, I
success *der Erfolg, -e*, III12
suede jacket *die Wildlederjacke, -n*, II
sugar *der Zucker*, I
suggest *vorschlagen*, II; **I suggest that …** *Ich schlage vor, dass …*, II
suggestion *der Vorschlag, ⁐e*, II
suit *der Anzug, ⁐e*, II
suit: to be suited to *s. eignen zu*, III6
summer *der Sommer*, I; **in the summer** *im Sommer*, I
sun *die Sonne*, I
sun protection factor *der Lichtschutzfaktor, -en*, II
sun tan lotion *die Sonnenmilch*, II; *die Sonnencreme*, II
Sunday *der Sonntag*, I; **Sundays** *sonntags*, II
sunny *sonnig*, I
sunroof *das Schiebedach, ⁐er*, II
sunstroke *der Sonnenstich, -e*, II
Super! *Spitze!, Super!*, I
superficial *oberflächlich*, III6
supermarket *der Supermarkt, ⁐e*, I; **at the supermarket** *im Supermarkt*, I
support *unterstützen*, III6
suppose *vermuten*, III8; **I suppose so, but …** *Eigentlich schon, aber …*, II
supposed to *sollen*, I; **The fish is supposed to be great.** *Der Fisch soll prima sein.*, II; **Well, what**

am I supposed to do? *Was soll ich bloß machen?*, II; **What's that supposed to be?** *Was soll denn das sein?*, II
Sure! *Aber sicher!, Ja, gern!*, I
sure: I'm not sure. *Ich bin nicht sicher.*, I
surf *surfen*, I
surprise *überraschen*, III6; **to be surprised** *erstaunt sein*, III8
surrounding area *die Umgebung, -en*, II
swallow: I can hardly swallow. *Ich kann kaum schlucken.*, II
sweater *der Pulli, -s*, I
sweet *süß*, II
swim *schwimmen*, I; **to go swimming** *baden gehen*, I
swimming pool *das Schwimmbad, ⁐er*, I; *der Pool, -s*, II; **to go to the (swimming) pool** *ins Schwimmbad gehen*, I
switch off *abstellen* (sep), II; *ausschalten* (sep), III9
sympathy, pity *das Mitleid*, III3
synagogue *die Synagoge, -n*, II

T-shirt *das T-Shirt, -s*, I
table *der Tisch, -e*, I; **to clear the table** *den Tisch abräumen* (sep), I
tacos *die Tacos*, II
take *nehmen*, I
take care of *erledigen*, III1
take part *dabei sein*, III11
talk about *sprechen über*, I; **What did you (pl) talk about?** *Worüber habt ihr gesprochen?*, I
tank *der Panzer, -*, III5
task *die Aufgabe, -n*, III6
taste *der Geschmack*, III3; *schmecken*, I; **Does it taste good?** *Schmeckt's?*, I; **How does it taste?** *Wie schmeckt's?*, I; **doesn't taste good** *schmeckt mir nicht*, II; **Beef tastes better to me.** *Rind schmeckt mir besser.*, II; **Which soup tastes best to you?** *Welche Suppe schmeckt dir am besten?*, II
Tasty! *Lecker!*, I
tax consultant *Steuerberater(in), -/nen*, III12
tea *der Tee*, I; **a glass of tea** *ein Glas Tee*, I
teacher (male) *der Lehrer, -*, I; (female) *die Lehrerin, -nen*, I
team *die Mannschaft, -en*, II; **on the (basketball) team** *in der (Basketball) mannschaft*, II
technical designer *technische(r) Zeichner(in), -/nen*, III12

teenager *der, die Jugendliche, -n*, III8
telecast, transmission *die Übertragung, -en*, II
telephone *das Telefon, -e, der Apparat, -e*, I; **to pick up the telephone** *den Hörer abheben* (sep), I
telephone booth *die Telefonzelle, -n*, I
telephone number *die Telefonnummer, -n*, I
television (medium of) *das Fernsehen*, I; **TV set** *der Fernseher, -*, II; **idiot box** *die Glotze, -n*, III6; **to watch TV** *Fernsehen schauen*, I; *fernsehen* (sep), *Fernseh gucken*, II; **color stereo television set** *das Stereo-Farbfernsehgerät, -e*, II; **TV and video cart** *der Fernseh- und Videowagen, -*, II; **What's on TV?** *Was läuft im Fernsehen?*, II
tell *erzählen*, III1
temptation to buy *der Kaufreiz*, III7
tension *die Spannung, -en*, III10
terrible *schrecklich*, III3
test *die Prüfung, -en*, III5
Thank you (very much)! *Danke (sehr-/schön)!*, I; *Vielen Dank!*, I; **Thank you and the same to you!** *Danke gleichfalls!*, II; *Danke! Dir/Ihnen auch!*, II
that *dass* (conj), I; **That's all.** *Das ist alles.*, I; **That's …** *Das ist …*, I
theater *das Theater, -*, I; (theater) **balcony** *der Rang, ⁐e*, III10
theme *das Thema, Themen*, III5
then *dann*, I
there *dort*, I
There is/are … *Es gibt…*, I
there: to be there, take part *dabei sein* (sep), III5
thermos bottle *die Thermosflasche, -n*, III2
thing *die Sache, -n*, III3
think *denken*, I
think: Do you think so? *Meinst du?*, I; **I think** *ich glaube*, I; **I think (tennis) is …** *Ich finde (Tennis) …*, I; **I think so too.** *Das finde ich auch.*, I; **I don't think that …** *Ich glaube nicht, dass …*, II; **I really think that …** *Ich meine doch, dass …*, II; **I think I'm sick.** *Ich glaube, ich bin krank.*, II; **I think it's great that …** *Ich finde es toll, dass …*, II
think a lot of *viel halten von*, III3; **to think about** *s. Gedanken machen über* (acc), III3; **to think of or about** *denken an* (acc), III2; **thinking over** *das Nachdenken*, III6
think: What do you think of that? *Wie stehst du dazu?*, III6
third *dritt-*, I
thirst *der Durst*, II2; **to be thirsty** *Durst haben*, II2

thirsty *durstig*, III8
this *dies-*, II; **this afternoon** *heute Nachmittag*, I; **This is …** (on the telephone) *Hier ist …*, I; **this morning** *heute Morgen*, I
thorough *gründlich*, III6
threaten *drohen* (dat), III8
three times *dreimal*, I
thrilling *spannend*, I
thrive *aufblühen* (sep), III10
throat *der Hals, ¨-e*, II; **sore throat** *die Halsschmerzen* (pl), II
through *durch*, II
thumb *der Daumen, -*, III1
Thursday *der Donnerstag*, I; **Thursdays** *donnerstags*, II
ticket window *die Abendkasse, -n*, III10
tie *die Krawatte, -n*, II; **bow tie** *die Fliege*, I; **It's too tight on you.** *Es ist dir zu eng.*, II
tight *eng*, I; **It's too tight on you.** *Es ist dir zu eng.*, II
till: ten till two *zehn vor zwei*, I
Tilsiter cheese *der Tilsiter Käse*, II
time *die Zeit*, I; **At what time?** *Um wie viel Uhr?*, I; **I don't have time.** *Ich habe keine Zeit.*, I; **What time is it?** *Wie spät ist es?, Wie viel Uhr ist es?*, I; **(time) passes** *vergehen*, III11; **at that time** *damals*, III2
tip *der Tip, -s*, III8
tire: wide tire *der Breitreifen, -*, II
tired *müde*, II
to *an, auf, nach*, II; **Let's drive to the ocean.** *Fahren wir ans Meer!*; **Are you going to the golf course?** *Gehst du auf den Golfplatz?*; **We're going to Austria.** *Wir fahren nach Österreich.*, II
today *heute*, I
toe *die Zehe, -n*, III1
tofu *der Tofu*, II
together: to go together (clothing) *zusammenpassen* (sep), III3
toilet *die Toilette, -n*, II
tolerance *die Toleranz*, III4
tomato *die Tomate, -n*, I
tomorrow *morgen*, I
tonight *heute Abend*, I
too *zu*, I; **Too bad!** *Schade!*, I
toothache *die Zahnschmerzen* (pl), II
toothpaste *die Zahnpasta*, II
tour *besichtigen*, I; **to tour the city** *die Stadt besichtigen*, I; **city tour** *die Stadrundfahrt, -en*, II
tourism specialist *Touristikfachwirt(in), -e/nen*, III12
toward *nach*, II
town *die Kleinstadt, ¨-e*, II; **in a town** *in einer Kleinstadt*, II
traffic *der Verkehr*, II
traffic jam *der Stau, -s*, III7
train *die Bahn, -en*, II
train station *der Bahnhof, ¨-e*, I
training and weight room *der Fitnessraum, ¨-e*, II
translate *übersetzen*, III8
transmitter *der Sender, -*, II

transport plane *das Transportflugzeug, -e*, III5
transportation *das Verkehrsmittel, -*, II; **public transportation** *öffentliche Verkehrsmittel* (pl), II
trash *der Müll*, I; **trash, waste** *der Abfall, ¨-e*, III9
trash bag *die Abfalltüte, -n*, III2
tree *der Baum, ¨-e*, II
trout *die Forelle, -n*, II
truck *der Laster, -*, III5; *der Lastkraftwagen, -, (LKW, -s)*, II
true: Not true! *Stimmt nicht!*, I; **That's right!** *Stimmt!*, I; **That's true, but …** *Das stimmt, aber …*, II
truth *die Wahrheit*, III6
try *probieren*, I
try hard *s. bemühen um*, III6
try on *anprobieren* (sep), I
Tuesday *der Dienstag*, I; **Tuesdays** *dienstags*, II
tuna fish salad *der Thunfischsalat*, III1
tune (an instrument) *stimmen*, III10
Turkish *türkisch* (adj), II
turn *einbiegen* (sep); **Turn in here!** *Biegen Sie hier ein!*, II
tuxedo *der Smoking, -s*, II
twice *zweimal*, I
twin *der Zwilling, -e*, II
type *der Typ, -en*, II

ugly *hässlich*, I
unbelievable *unglaublich*; **That's really unbelievable!** *Das ist ja unglaublich!*, II
unboiled *ungekocht*, II12
uncle *der Onkel, -*, I
uncomfortable *unbequem*, I
under it, underneath *darunter*, II
undertake *unternehmen*, III2
underway *unterwegs*, III6
unfortunately *leider*, I; **Unfortunately I can't.** *Leider kann ich nicht.*, I; **That's the way it is, unfortunately.** *Das ist leider so.*, II
unfriendly *unsympathisch*, II
unhealthy *ungesund*, II; *nicht gut für die Gesundheit*, II
unified *vereint*, III11
university studies *das Studium*, III5
unpleasant *unsympathisch*, II
unpopular *unbeliebt*, III4
until *bis* (acc), III11; **from 8 until 8:45** *von 8 Uhr bis 8 Uhr 45*, I; **until you get to … Square** *bis zum …platz*, I; **until you get to … Street** *bis zur … straße*, I; **until you get to the traffic light** *bis zur Ampel*, I; **until then** *bis dahin*, III11

unusual *ausgefallen*, III3
use *benutzen*, II6; *gebrauchen*, III7; *verwenden*, III7; **use again** *wieder verwenden*, III9
used: to get used to *s. gewöhnen an* (acc), III7
useful *nützlich*, III6
usually *gewöhnlich*, II

vacation (from school) *die Ferien* (pl), II; **vacation** (from work) *der Urlaub, -e*, II; **What did you do on your vacation?** *Was hast du in den Ferien gemacht?*, II
vacuum *Staub saugen*, I
vanilla-flavored milk *die Vanillemilch*, II
varied *abwechslungsreich*, II
vegetable produce *das Pflanzenprodukt, -e*, III1
vegetables *das Gemüse*, I
vegetarian *vegetarisch*; **You're vegetarian, right?** *Du isst wohl vegetarisch, was?*, II
venison *das Rehfleisch*, III1
very *sehr*, I; **Very well!** *Sehr gut!*, I
vest: jeans vest *die Jeansweste, -n*, II
veterinarian *Tierarzt, -ärztin*, III11
vice-versa *umgekehrt*, III5
video: use a video camera/a camera *die Videokamera/die Kamera bedienen*, II
video cassette *das Video, -s*, I; *die Videocassette, -n*, II; **insert a video cassette** *ein Video einlegen* (sep), II; **take out the video cassette** *das Video herausnehmen* (sep), II
village *das Dorf, ¨-er*, II; **in a village** *in einem Dorf*, II
vintner *Winzer(in), -/nen*, III12
violence *die Gewalt*, III8
violent *brutal*, I
violin *die Geige, -n*, III10
visit *besuchen*, I
visit (a place) *besuchen, besichtigen*, II; **I visited (the cathedral).** *Ich habe (den Dom) besichtigt.*, II
vocational school *die Fachschule, -n*, III11
volleyball *Volleyball*, I
volume control *der Lautstärkeregler*, II
voluntary *freiwillig*, III5
vote for *wählen*, III5

wait and see *abwarten* (sep), III2
walk *spazieren*, II
want (to) *wollen*, I; *Lust haben*, III2; **What do you want to do?** *Was willst du machen?*, II
war *der Krieg, -e*, II; **war movie** *der Kriegsfilm, -e*, I
warm *warm*, I
wash *spülen*, I; **to wash the dishes** *das Geschirr spülen*, I; **to wash** *(sich) waschen*, II; **to wash clothes** *die Wäsche waschen*, II
waste *verschwenden*, III9
wastewater *das Abwasser, ̈-*, III9
watch *schauen*, I; **to watch TV** *Fernsehen schauen*, I; **fernsehen** (sep), II; (colloquial) *Fernsehen gucken*, II
water *das Wasser*, I; **a glass of (mineral) water** *ein Glas (Mineral-) Wasser*, I
water the flowers *die Blumen gießen*, I
watermelon *die Wassermelone, -n*, III1
weapon *die Waffe, -n*, III5
wear *anziehen* (sep), I; *tragen*, II; **Don't wear anything made of …** *Trag ja nichts aus …!*, II; **Go ahead and wear …** *Trag doch mal …!*, II
weather *das Wetter*, I; **How's the weather?** *Wie ist das Wetter?*, I
weather report *der Wetterbericht, -e*, II
Wednesday *der Mittwoch*, I; **Wednesdays** *mittwochs*, II
week *die Woche, -n*, I; **every week** *jede Woche*, II
weekend *das Wochenende, -n*, I; **on the weekend** *am Wochenende*, I
weekly special *das Angebot der Woche*, I
weigh *wiegen*, I
weigh on, burden *belasten*, III5
weight lifting *das Krafttraining*, III3
welder *Schweißer(in), -/nen*, III12
well, okay *also* (part), III2
well: Well yes, but … *Eigentlich schon, aber …*, II; *Ja, schon, aber …*, II; **extremely well** *ganz wohl*, II; **Get well soon!** *Gute Besserung!*, II; **I'm (not) doing well.** *Es geht mir (nicht) gut!*, II; *Mir ist (nicht) gut.*, II; **not well at all** *überhaupt nicht wohl*, II

were: Where were you? *Wo bist du gewesen?*, I
western (movie) *der Western, -*, I
wet *nass*, I
what *was*; **What are we going to do now?** *Was machen wir jetzt?*, II; **What is it?** *Was gibt's?*, II; *Was ist?*, II; **Okay, what is it?** *Ja? Was denn?*, II; **So what about …?** *Wie steht's mit …?*, II; **Yes, what?** *Ja, was bitte?*, II; **What can I do for you?** *Was kann ich für dich tun?*, I; **What else?** *Noch etwas?*, I
what kind of? *was für?*, I; **What kinds of music do you like?** *Was für Musik hörst du gern?*, I
What's it about? *Worum geht es?*, III4
What's there to eat *Was gibt's zu essen?*, I
when, at the time *als* (conj), III8
when? *wann?*, I
whenever *wenn* (conj), II
where (from)? *woher?*, I
where (to)? *wohin?*, I; **Where are we going?** *Wohin fahren wir?*, II
where? *wo?*, I
whether *ob* (conj), II
which *welch-*, I
while *die Weile*, III11
whirlpool *der Whirlpool, -s*, II
white *weiß*, I; **in white** *in Weiß*, I
who? *wer?*, I
whole wheat roll *die Vollkornsemmel, -n*, I
whole, perfect *heil*, III7
whom? *wen?*, I; **to, for whom?** *wem?*, I
why? *warum?*, I; **Why don't you come along!** *Komm doch mit!*, I
wide *weit*, I
will *werden*, II
windsurf *windsurfen*, II
windbreaker *die Wind-, Wetterjacke, -n*, II
window *das Fenster, -*, I; **to clean the windows** *die Fenster putzen*, I
windshield wiper *der Scheibenwischer, -*, II
winter *der Winter*, I; **in the winter** *im Winter*, I
wise *weise*, III7
wish *sich wünschen*; **I wish for …** *Ich wünsche mir …*, II; **What would you wish for?** *Was wünschst du dir (mal)?*, II
with *mit*, I; **with corners** *eckig*, I
without *ohne* (acc), III3; **without doing …** *ohne … zu machen*,

III3; **to do without** *verzichten auf* (acc), III9
witty *witzig*, II
woman *die Frau, -en*, I
wonder, miracle *das Wunder, -*, III10
wonderful *großartig*, II
wood: made of wood *aus Holz*, I
wool *die Wolle*, II
wool shirt *das Wollhemd, -en*, II
work *arbeiten*, II; **That won't work.** *Das geht nicht.*, I; **work, achievement** *das Werk, -e*, III10
world *die Welt, -en*, III11
worry *s. Sorgen machen*, III9
worse than *schlechter als*, II
worth: to be worth it *s. lohnen*, III5
would have (been) *wäre*, III5
would have (had) *hätte*, III5
wrist *das Handgelenk, -e*, III1
wrong: to be wrong *s. irren*, III5

yard *der Garten, ̈-*, II
year *das Jahr, -e*, I; **I am … years old.** *Ich bin … Jahre alt.*, I
yellow *gelb*, I; **in yellow** *in Gelb*, I
yes *ja*, I; **Yes?** *Bitte?*, I; **Yes, I do!** *Doch!*, II
yesterday *gestern*, I; **yesterday evening** *gestern Abend*, I; **the day before yesterday** *vorgestern*, I
yogurt *der Joghurt, -*, II
you're (very) welcome! *Bitte (sehr/schön)!*, I
younger *jünger*, II
youth hostel *die Jugendherberge, -n*, III2

zero *null*, I
zipper *der Reißverschluss, ̈-e*, II
zoo *der Zoo, -s*, I; **to go to the zoo** *in den Zoo gehen*, I

Page numbers in boldface type refer to **Grammatik** and **Ein wenig Grammatik** presentations. Other page numbers refer to grammar structure presented in **So sagt man das!, Sprachtipp, Lerntrick, Wortschatz,** and **Landeskunde** sections. Page numbers beginning with R refer to the Grammar Summary in this Reference Section.

A

aber: I: 79; *see also* conjunctions; R28

accusative case: definite article I: **135;** noun phrase in I: **135;** indefinite article I: **135, 171, 258;** third person pronoun singular I: **140;** third person pronoun singular and plural I: **200;** first and second person pronoun singular and plural I: **200;** the interrogative pronoun **wen** I: **200;** following **für** I: 199, **200;** following **es gibt** I: **257;** of reflexive pronouns II: 102; of **jeder** II: 106; of **kein,** I: 258, **259,** II: 110; of possessives II: 136; adjective following **der-** and **dieser**-words II: 217; following **durch** and **um** II: 254; relative pronouns III: 99; following **in, auf, an,** to express going somewhere II: 246, 250; *see also* direct object

adjectives: comparative forms of II: 190; endings following **ein**-words II: 194; endings of comparatives II: 200; endings following **der-** and **dieser**-words II: 217; endings of unpreceded adjectives II: 311; use of numbers as III: 98; superlative forms of III: 162; following determiners of quantity III: 187; **irgendein** and **irgendwelche** III: 195; *see also* R30

adjective endings: *see* adjectives

als: in comparison II: 190; with narrative past III: 215

am: contraction of **an dem** II: 73

am liebsten: I: 285; use of, with **würde** II: 307

an: followed by dative (location) II: 73; followed by accusative (direction) II: 246

anprobieren: present tense forms of I: **143;** R34; *see also* separable-prefix verbs

ans: contraction of **an das** II: 246

anstatt: followed by genitive III: 274

anziehen: present tense forms of I: 143; R34; *see also* separable-prefix verbs

article: *see* definite article, indefinite article

auf: followed by dative (location) II: 135; followed by accusative (direction) II: 246; use of, with **s. freuen** II: 277; use of, with **warten** III: 66

aufs: contraction of **auf das** II: 246

aus: followed by dative II: 254; R28

aussehen: present tense forms of I: 144

außerhalb: followed by genitive III: 274

auxiliary: *see* modal auxiliary verbs

B

bei: followed by dative II: 254; R330

beim: contraction of **bei dem** II: 254

s. brechen: present tense of II: 165

C

case: I: **135, 319;** R22-R31; *see also* nominative case, accusative case, dative case;

class: definition of I: 24

clauses: I: 230, 250; R29; *see also* dependent clauses

command forms: du-commands I: 223, **224, 337; ihr**-commands I: 223, **224,** 255, 337; **Sie**-commands I: 254, **255;** inclusive commands II: 159; *see also* R336

comparatives: I: 285; R34; *see also* adjectives

conditional: III: 249, R37; *see also* subjunctive forms

conjugations: *see* present tense; present perfect

conjunctions: **denn** and **weil** I: **230;** II: 39; **dass** I: **260; wenn** II: 227; **ob** II: 250; coordinating conjunctions, **denn, und, oder, aber,** and **sondern** III: 216; *see also* R28

connecting words: *see* conjunctions

contractions: of **in dem, im** II: 65; of **an dem, am** I: 162, 165; II: 73; of **zu dem, zum** I: 254; II: 141; of **zu der, zur** I: 30, 254; II: 141; of **an das, ans** II: 246; of **auf das, aufs** II: 246; of **in das, ins** II: 246; of **bei dem, beim** II: 254; of **von dem, vom** II: 254

conversational past: II: 66-67; R35; *see also* past participle, perfect

coordinating conjunctions: *see* conjunctions

D

da-compounds: II: 277; III: 66, 279

dass-clauses: I: **260;** verb in final position II: 101; with reflexive verbs II: 102; *see also* R29; conjunctions

dative case: introduction to I: **319;** following **mit** I: **319;** following **in** and **an** when expressing location II: 73; with **gefallen** II: 77; of **ein**-words II: 79; following **auf** when expressing location II: 135; of possessives II: 136; verbs used with dative forms, **gefallen, schmecken** II:

verb endings
verb-final position: in **weil**-clauses I: **230**; II: 189; in clauses
following **wissen** I: **250**; in **dass**-clauses I: **260**; II: 101; in
wenn-clauses II:227; in **ob**-clauses II: 250; with **werden**
in clauses beginning with **dass, ob, wenn, weil** II: 289; in
relative clauses III: 99 *see also* R29
verb-second position I: **56, 167**; R29
vom: contraction of **von dem** II: 254
von: followed by dative II: 254; use of in passive voice III: 246,
281
vor: followed by accusative (direction) or dative (location) II:
255

wäre; III: 104; further uses of III: 116, R37
während: followed by genitive III: 274
was: as interrogative I: 50; relative clauses introduced with III:
193; *see also* R27
waschen: present tense of II: 165; R39
wegen: followed by genitive III: 274
wehtun: as a separable prefix verb II: 163; use of dative with II:
163
weil: I: 230; R28; *see also* conjunctions
weil-clauses: verb in final position II: 189; R29
welcher: forms of II: 140; R23; *see also* **dieser**
wenn: see conjunctions
wenn-clauses: verb in final position II: 227, R29; in
conditional sentences III: 249
werden: use of, to express future, forms of II: 289; use of, in
passive voice III: 247, 299; use of with a conjugated
modal III: 248; *see also* R35

wissen: present tense forms of I: 250, 339; R39
wo: questions beginning with II: 73; location questions II: 250
wo-compounds: II: 277; III: 303
wollen: present tense forms of I: **166;** R33; past tense of III:
133, R36; subjunctive of R37; *see also* modal auxiliary
verbs
word order: questions beginning with a verb I: 23; questions
beginning with a question word I: **23;** verb in second
position I: **56, 167, 399;** with modals I: **166;** in **denn** and
weil-clauses I: **230;** verb final in clauses following **wissen**
I: **250;** verb-final in **dass**-clauses I: **260;** with dative case
I: **320;** in **weil**-clauses II: 165; in **wenn**-clauses II: 227; in
ob-clauses II: 250; with **werden** in clauses beginning
with **dass, ob, wenn, weil** II: 289; in relative clauses III:
99; in main clause preceded by subordinate clause III:
215; see also infinitive; questions; separable prefixes; *see
also* R29
worüber: I: 291
s. wünschen: with dative reflexive pronoun II: 192
würde: forms of II: 307; R37

zu: II: 141; preposition followed by dative II: 223; in infinitive
phrases III: 75
zum: contraction of **zu dem** II: 141
zur: contraction of **zu der** II: 141
zwischen: followed by accusative (direction) or dative
(location) II: 255

Credits

ACKNOWLEDGMENTS (continued from page ii)

Heinrich Bauer Verlag, SZV, Germany: "Unsere heutige Jugend und ihre Sprüche" by Emily Reuter from *bella: für die Moderne Frau,* no. 43, October 21, 1993. Copyright © 1993 by Heinrich Bauer Verlag.

Bayerisches Staatsministerium für Landesentwicklung und Umweltfragen, Rosenkavalierplatz 2, 81925 München, Germany: Graph, "Zusammensetzung der Abfälle" from *Der Abfall: Umweltschutz in Bayern.*

Bunte/Burda Publications: "Liebe," "Lisa, 15," "Raver," and "Sprache" from *Bunte,* no. 22, May 26, 1994, pp. 39 & 42. Copyright © 1994 by Burda Publications.

Deutsche Bank: Table, "USA: Devisen Kurse," published by Deutsche Bank.

Deutsches Jugendherbergswerk, Hauptverband für Jugendwandern und Jugendherbergen e.V.: From "Willkommen!" from *DJH Willkommen.* From "Jugendgästehaus Weimar: Pauschalprogramm" from *Klassen Mobil: Schulfahrten und Schullandheim-aufenthalte in Jugendherbergen 92/93: Region Ost.*

Reinhard Döhl: "Apfel" by Reinhard Döhl from *An Anthology of Concrete Poetry,* edited by Emmett Williams. Copyright © 1965, 1966 by Reinhard Döhl. Published by Something Else Press, New York, Villefranche, Frankfurt and Edition Hansjörg Mayer, Stuttgart. "menschenskind" by Reinhard Döhl from *Poem Structures in the Looking Glass* by Klaus Burkhardt and Reinhard Döhl. Copyright © 1969 by Reinhard Döhl.

Focus Magazin Verlag GmbH: Text from "Verführt von dummen, mörderischen Sprüchen" from *Focus: das moderne Nachrichtenmagazin,* no. 20, May 16, 1994. Copyright © 1994 by Focus Magazin Verlag GmbH.

Hamburgische Staatsoper Hamburg: Cover of brochure, *Hamburg Oper: Spielplan-Vorschau,* April 1993.

Harenberg Lexikon-Verlag: Table, "Abfallvermeidung durch Recycling" from *Harenberg Lexikon der Gegenwart, Aktuell '94,* p. 416. Copyright © 1993 by Harenberg Lexikon-Verlag in Harenberg Kommunikation Verlags und Mediengesellschaft mbH & Co. KG, Dortmund.

Luchterhand Literaturverlag GmbH, München: "ottos mops" from *Der künstliche Baum* by Ernst Jandl. Copyright © 1974 by Hermann Luchterhand Verlag GmbH & Co. KG, Darmstadt und Neuwied.

Prälat Berthold Lutz: "Die Nacht bei den Wachsfiguren" by Thomas Burger from *Das Gespenstergespenst.*

Claudia Müller: "Pläne für die Zukunft" by Claudia Müller.

MVG Medien Verlags GmbH & Co.: From "Je schlampiger, umso schöner! ..." from *Mädchen,* No. 13, June 2, 1993, p. 11. Copyright © 1993 by MVG Medien Verlagsgesellschaft GmbH & Co.

Sanacorp eG Pharmazeutische Großhandlung, D-82152 Planegg: Advertisement, "Reisefieber?" from *stern,* no. 22, May 26, 1994, p. 179.

Schocken Books, distributed by Pantheon Books, a division of Random House, Inc.: "Eine alltägliche Verwirrung" from *Franz Kafka: The Complete Stories* by Franz Kafka. Copyright © 1946, 1947, 1948, 1949, 1954, 1958, 1971 by Schocken Books, Inc.

Steidl Verlag: "Kinderlied" by Günter Grass from *Gedichte und Kurzprosa (Studienausgabe Band II).* Copyright © 1994 by Steidl Verlag, Göttingen.

STERN Magazine, Hamburg: "Mehr Bauch als Kopf" by Georg Wedemeyer from *stern,* no. 22, May 26, 1994, p. 96. Copyright © 1994 by Gruner & Jahr AG & Co.

Stuttgarter Zeitung: "Für einen Ballettabend in das prächtige Reich der Wilis" by the students of class 8b of "Musikunterricht im Staatstheater" from *Stuttgarter Zeitung,* Saturday, November 25, 1989, no. 272, p. 34. Copyright © 1989 by Stuttgarter Zeitung.

Suhrkamp Verlag: "Der hellgraue Frühjahrsmantel" by Wolfgang Hildesheimer from *Lieblose Legenden.* Copyright © 1962 by Suhrkamp Verlag, Frankfurt am Main. "Der Radwechsel" by Bertolt Brecht from *Gesammelte Werke.* Copyright © 1967 by Suhrkamp Verlag, Frankfurt am Main. "Ein Tisch ist ein Tisch" from *Kindergeschichten* by Peter Bichsel. Copyright © 1969 by Luchterhand Literaturverlag. All rights administered through Suhrkamp Verlag Frankfurt am Main.

Thames and Hudson Ltd: Map of the Roman World by John Woodcock from *The Birth of Western Civilization: Greece and Rome* by George Huxley et al. Copyright © 1964 by Thames and Hudson Ltd.

Tiefdruck Schwann-Bagel GmbH: From "Tekkno-Fieber" from *JUMA: das Jugendmagazin,* 2/93, April 1993, p. 4. From "Judith," and "Pauken allein reicht nicht" from *JUMA: das Jugendmagazin,* 3/94, pp. 23, 24, 26.

Tourismusverband Rügen e.V.: Text from Rügen: eine Liebeserklärung: Urlauberkatalog '93 by Gunter Reymann. Copyright © 1993 by Fremdenverkehrsverband Rügen e.V.

Verlag Kiepenheuer & Witsch GmbH, Köln: "Das Märchen vom kleinen Herrn Moritz" by Wolf Biermann.

Verlag Moritz Diesterweg GmbH & Co., Frankfurt am Main: From pp. 102-103 from "Wortspiele" from *Texte und Fragen,* edited by Siegfried Buck and Wenzel Wolff. Copyright © 1977 by Verlag Moritz Diesterweg GmbH & Co., Frankfurt am Main. All rights reserved.

Verlag Neues Leben GmbH Berlin: Cover of *Schiller: Hundert Gedichte,* illustrated by Jörn Hennig. Copyright © 1987 by Verlag Neues Leben, Berlin.

PHOTOGRAPHY CREDITS

Front cover (bkgd), Morton Beebe/Corbis; (c), Steve Ewert/HRW Photo; Back cover (c), Hans Wolf/The Image Bank; (c), ©2003 Image Farm, Inc.; Title page (c), Steve Ewert/HRW Photo.

All photos by George Winkler/Holt, Rinehart and Winston, Inc. except:

Border fabric: Victoria Smith/HRW

All Euro currency photos: ©European Communities

All Globe photos: Mountain High Maps ® copyright 1997 Digital Wisdom, Inc.

All Theater mask photos: ©PhotoSpin, Inc.

TABLE OF CONTENTS: Page ix (t), Beryl Goldberg; x (t), © Digital Vision; xi (b), Beryl Goldberg; xiv (b), David Peevers; xvi (t), Beryl Goldberg; xvii (b), Geopress/H. Armstrong Roberts; xviii (t), © Image 100 Ltd.; xix (b), CORBIS/Michael Pole

UNIT ONE:

3 (bc, br, cr), Courtesy of Dom zu Güstrow

Chapter One: 6 (tr, br), Thomas Kanzler/Viesti Associates; 7 (tr), Thomas Kanzler/Viesti Collection, Inc.; 14 (tr, bl, br), Thomas Kanzler/Viesti Collection, Inc.; 15 (tr, cr), Thomas Kanzler/Viesti Collection, Inc.; 24 (tr), CORBIS/ Bettman.

Chapter Two: 33-34 (all), Beryl Goldberg; 34 (tr, cr, br, bc), Michelle Bridwell/Frontera Fotos; 35 (tr), Michelle Bridwell/Frontera Fotos; 36 (tr), Courtesy of DJH; 42 (tr, cl, br), Michelle Bridwell/Frontera Fotos; 43 (tl), Michelle Bridwell/Frontera Fotos; 49 (tl), Courtesy Tourist Office of Weimer; 54 (bl), Michelle Bridwell/Frontera Fotos; 56 (bl), Michelle Bridwell/Frontera Fotos.

Chapter Three: 60-61 (all), © Digital Vision; 62 (tr, cl, bl), Kevin Galvin/HRW Photo; 68 (tl), *JUMA,* April, 1993 Edition; 68 (bl), Arno Al Doori/*Mädchen Magazine;* 68 (r), Frank Lange/*JUMA,* February, 1992 Edition; 69 (tl), *Bunte* Magazine, May 26, 1994 Edition; 69 (tr), *Bunte* Magazine, May 26, 1994 Edition; 69 (bl), Volker Wenzlawski/*JUMA,*

April, 1994 Edition; 70 (tr), Kevin Galvin/HRW Photo; 72 (tr, bl), Kevin Galvin/HRW Photo; 78 (tl), Heinrich Bauer Verlag.

UNIT TWO:

88-89 (all), SuperStock; 90 (tr), Foto Marburg; 91 (b), Steve Vidler/Superstock; 91 (t), Joachim Messerschmidt/Bruce Coleman, Inc.

Chapter Four: 92-93 (all), Beryl Goldberg; 94 (t, c), Kevin Galvin/HRW Photo; 95 (tr), Kevin Galvin/HRW Photo; 100 (tr), Ed Kashi; 101 (tr), Thomas Mayer/Fotoarchiv/ Black Star; 102 (bl), AP/Wide World Photos; 102 (bcr), Harald Thiessen/Bavaria Bildagentur; 102 (br), Lisa Davis/ HRW Photo; 109 (cr), Gscheidle/HRW Photo; 111 (cl), Russell Dian/HRW Photo; 113 (bl, br), Kevin Galvin/ HRW Photo; 115 (cl), AP/Wide World Photos; 115 (cr), Harald Thiessen/Bavaria Bildagentur.

Chapter Five: 122 (tr, cl, br), Kevin Galvin/HRW Photo; 123 (tl), Kevin Galvin/HRW Photo; 129 (tr), Thomas Stephen/Fotoarchiv/Black Star; 129 (cl), Fritz Lang/ Bavaria Bildagentur GmbH; 130 (tr), Herman Kokojan/ Black Star; 136-138 (bkgd), AP/Wide World Photos, Heinrich Hoffman, Ullstein Bilderdienst, Pierre Zucca (background and border photos); 137 (tc), Archiv Interfoto; 144 (b), AKG Photo, London.

Chapter Six: 150 (tr), Thomas Stephen/HRW Photo; 150 (br), Digital imagery® copyright 2003 PhotoDisc, Inc.; 151 (tl), Thomas Stephen/HRW Photo; 157 (tr, bl), Thomas Stephen/HRW Photo; 158 (tl, br), Thomas Stephen/HRW Photo; 159 (t), Thomas Stephen/HRW Photo; 164-165 (bkgd), From *Rumpelstiltskin* by Paul O. Zelinsky. ©1986 by Paul O. Zelinsky. Used by permission of Dutton Children's Books, a division of Penguin Books, USA, Inc.

UNIT THREE:

Chapter Seven: 180-181 (all), David Peevers; 196-198 (bkgd), © 1994 Les Editions Albert Rene/Goscinny-Uderzo.

Chapter Eight: 210 (tl), Lance Shriner/HRW Photo; 210 (collage), Stock Editions/HRW Photo; 210 (lc), Courtesy U.S. Air Force; 210 (bc), Claude Poulet/HRW Photo; 210 (r), Russell Dian/HRW Photo; 210 (tr), Courtesy of Monsanto; 210 (br), Courtesy of the Architect of the Capitol; 218 (c, b), Digital imagery® copyright 2003 PhotoDisc, Inc.; 225 (tr), Sam Dudgeon/HRW 229 (collage), HRW Photo; 231 (bl, br), Digital imagery® copyright 2003 PhotoDisc, Inc.

Chapter Nine: 237-238 (all), Beryl Goldberg; 239 (cr, tl), Kevin Galvin/HRW Photo; 251 (br), Sam Dudgeon/HRW; 252-254 (bkgd), Mark Antman/HRW Photo; 252 (t), Peter Herbster/Greenpeace Germany; 256 (b), Beryl Goldberg; 260 (br), Staatsministerium fur Landesentwicklung und Umweltfragen, München.

UNIT FOUR:

264-265 (all), Joachim Messerschmidt/Bruce Coleman, Inc.; 266 (br), Wolfgang Staiger/Visum.

Chapter Ten: 268-269 (all), Geopress/H. Armstrong Roberts; 270 (tr), Kevin Galvin/HRW Photo; 270 (cl), Courtesy of http://www.anne-sophie-mutter.de; 271 (c), Kevin Galvin/HRW Photo; 276 (br), Otto/Bavaria Bildgagentur GmbH; 277 (tr), J. Alexandre/Bavaria Bildgagentur; 283 (r), © Beryl Goldberg Photography; 284-285 (t), Sam Dudgeon/Courtesy Molly & George Winkler/HRW Photo; 289 (b), J. Alexandre/Bavaria Bildgagentur; 291 (b), Otto/Bavaria Bildgagentur GmbH; 292 (l), Tim Hall/Redferns/Retna.

Chapter Eleven: 296-297 (all), ©Image 100 Ltd; 298 (tl, br), Kevin Galvin/HRW Photo; 299 (tl), Sam Dudgeon/HRW; 306 (br), Sam Dudgeon/HRW; 307 (tr), Lufthansa Bildarchiv; 307 (br), C. von der Goltz/HRW Photo; 316 (b), Kevin Galvin/HRW Photo; 317 (c), Kevin Galvin/HRW Photo; 319 (cr), Lufthansa Bildarchiv.

Chapter Twelve: 324-325 (all), CORBIS/Michael Pole; 342-345 (bkgd), Sam Dudgeon/HRW; 346 (br), Courtesy of Dom zu Güstrtow.

Reference Section: R14 (baseball & bat, bird, paintbrushes), Digital imagery® copyright 2003 PhotoDisc, Inc.; R14 (skis), ©1997 Radlund & Associates for Artville; R15 (goat), Digital imagery® copyright 2003 PhotoDisc, Inc.; R15 (swimsuit), ©Stockbyte; R15 (orange, cow), Digital imagery® copyright 2003 PhotoDisc, Inc.; R15 (tea), Victoria Smith/HRW Photo; R15 (hamburger), Corbis Images; R16 (fabric), Digital imagery® copyright 2003 PhotoDisc, Inc.; R16 (drums), EyeWire, Inc., Image Club Graphics ©1998 Adobe Systems, Inc.; R16 (gymnast), Digital imagery® copyright 2003 PhotoDisc, Inc.; R16 (flute), Digital imagery® copyright 2003 PhotoDisc, Inc.; R16 (violin), EyeWire, Inc., Image Club Graphics ©1998 Adobe Systems, Inc.; R17 (all), Digital imagery® copyright 2003 PhotoDisc, Inc.; R18 (house), ©Stockbyte; R18 (car), Digital imagery® copyright 2003 PhotoDisc, Inc.; R18 (tr), Courtesy of http://www.anne-sophie-mutter.de; R18 (cl), Digital imagery® copyright 2003 PhotoDisc, Inc.; R18 (corn), Corbis Images; R19 (tr), Digital imagery® copyright 2003 PhotoDisc, Inc.; R19 (sink), Digital imagery® copyright 2003 PhotoDisc, Inc.; R19 (bl), HRW Photo; R19 (bc, cr), Corbis Images; R20 (cl, bl), Digital imagery® copyright 2003 PhotoDisc, Inc.; R20 (tr), Corbis Images; R21 (c), © Digital Vision.

TEACHER'S EDITION PHOTO CREDITS
(continued from page T6)

91H (br), Scott Van Osdol/HRW Photo. Chapter Five: 119D (cl), Superstock, (cr), Victoria Smith/HRW Photo; 119N (br), Scott Van Osdol/HRW Photo. Chapter Seven: 179C (b), Scott Van Osdol/HRW; 179D (bl), Sam Dudgeon/HRW; 179O (br), Scott Van Osdol/HRW. Chapter Eight: 207D (cl), Victoria Smith/HRW. Chapter Nine: 235D (cr), Konnie Brown/HRW. Chapter Ten: 267C (br), Courtesy of http://www.anne-sophie-mutter.de/; 267D (cr), Victoria Smith/HRW; 267P (br), Scott Van Osdol/HRW Photo; 267R (br), Scott Van Osdol/HRW; 267T (bl), Scott Van Osdol/HRW Photo. Chapter Eleven: 295D (cl, cr), Victoria Smith/HRW. Chapter Twelve: 323U (br), Scott Van Osdol/HRW Photo; 323X (br), Scott Van Osdol/HRW Photo.

ART CREDITS

Abbreviated as follows: (t) top, (b) bottom, (l) left, (r) right, (c) center.

All art, unless otherwise noted, by Holt, Rinehart & Winston.

Chapter 1: Page 1, MapQuest.com; 10, Tom Rummonds; 16 (b), Giorgio Mizzi; 17 (l), Jutta Tillmann; 17 (r), Maria Lyle; 18, Antonia Enthoven; 19 (t), Biruta Schöol; 19 (b), Michael Krone; 20, Giorgio Mizzi; 21, Eduard Böhm; 22, MapQuest.com; 27, Tom Rummonds; 28, Antonia Enthoven. Chapter 2: Page 37, Michael Krone; 41 (t), George McLeod; 41 (b), Aletha Reppel; 47, Antonia Enthoven; 57, Antonia Enthoven. Chapter 3: Page 64, Meryl Henderson; 73, Eduard Böhm; 74, Giorgio Mizzi; 81, Meryl Henderson; 82, Eduard Böhm; 83 (t), Eduard Böhm; 83 (c), George McLeod; 84, Frank Rosenzweig.

Chapter 4: Page 88, MapQuest.com; 96, Giorgio Mizzi; 112, Giorgio Mizzi. Chapter 5: Page 124, Eduard Böhm; 125, Frank Rosenzweig; 127, Michael Krone; 131, Peter Pichler; 132, Giorgio Mizzi; 138, Jocelyne Bouchard; 140, Frank Rosenzweig; 141, Aletha Reppel; 142, Giorgio Mizzi; 143, Frank Rosenzweig. Chapter 6: Page 153, Jon Sayer; 155, Frank Rosenzweig; 161, Jon Sayer; 168, Eduard Böhm; 170, Jutta Tillmann.

Chapter 7: Page 176, MapQuest.com; 187, Holly Cooper; 190, Michael Krone; 193, Jon Sayer; 201, Holly Cooper; 202, Holly Cooper; 203, Antonia Enthoven; 205 (t), Meryl Henderson; 205 (bl), Peter Pichler; 205 (bc), Giorgio Mizzi; 205 (br), Jutta Tillmann. Chapter 8: Page 214, Jon Sayer; 220, Peter Pichler; 230, Peter Pichler. Chapter 9: Page 240, Antonia Enthoven; 246 (t), Jutta Tillmann; 246 (b), Peter Pichler; 257, Giorgio Mizzi; 259, Peter Pichler.

Chapter 10: Page 264, MapQuest.com; 278, Jutta Tillmann; 288, Frank Rosenzweig; 290, Jutta Tillmann. Chapter 11: Page 304, Giorgio Mizzi; 312, Michael Krone; 314, Michael Krone. Chapter 12: Page 330, Meryl Henderson; 347, Antonia Enthoven; 348, Meryl Henderson.